DETROIT TIGERS

DETROIT TIGERS

The Complete Record of Detroit Tigers Baseball

Historical Text by
George Sullivan
and
David Cataneo

Tigers Graphics by
John Warner Davenport

COLLIER BOOKS
MACMILLAN PUBLISHING COMPANY
New York

COLLIER MACMILLAN PUBLISHERS
London

Macmillan Publishing Company
866 Third Avenue, New York, N.Y. 10022
Collier Macmillan Canada, Inc.

Library of Congress Cataloging in Publication Data
Sullivan, George, 1927-
The Detroit Tigers.
1. Detroit Tigers (Baseball team)—Statistics.
2. Baseball—United States—Records. I. Cantaneo, David.
II. Title.
GV875.D6S84   1985   796.357′64′0977434   85-4177
ISBN 0-02-028390-3

Macmillan books are available at special discounts for bulk pur-
chases for sales promotions, premiums, fund-raising, or educational
use. Special editions or book excerpts can also be created to specifi-
cation. For details, contact:

Special Sales Director
Macmillan Publishing Company
866 Third Avenue
New York, New York 10022

10 9 8 7 6 5 4 3 2

Printed in the United States of America

Contents

The All-Time Tigers Leaders

This section provides information on individual all-time single season and lifetime Tigers leaders. Included for all the various categories are leaders in batting, base running, fielding, and pitching. All the information is self-explanatory with the possible exception of Home Run Percengage, which is the number of home runs per 100 times at bat.

LIFETIME LEADERS

Batting. The top ten men are shown in batting and base-running categories. For averages, a minimum of 1500 at bats is necessary to qualify, except for pinch-hit batting average where 45 pinch-hit at bats is the minimum necessary to qualify. If required by ties, 11 players are shown. If ties would require more than 11 men to be shown, none of the last tied group is included.

Pitching. The top ten pitchers are shown in various categories. For averages, a minimum of 750 innings pitched is necessary to qualify. If required by ties, 11 players are shown. If ties would require more than 11 men to be shown, none of the last tied group is included. For relief pitching categories, the top five are shown.

Fielding. The top five in each fielding category are shown for each position. For averages, the minimum for qualification at each position except pitcher is 350 games played. For pitchers, 750 innings pitched are necessary. If required by ties, six players are shown. If ties would require more than six men to be shown, none of the last tied group is shown.

ALL-TIME SINGLE SEASON LEADERS

Batting. The top ten men are shown in batting and base-running categories. For averages, a player must have a total of at least 3.1 plate appearances for every scheduled game to qualify, except for pinch-hit batting average where 30 pinch-hit at bats are the minimum necessary to qualify. If required by ties, 11 players are shown. If ties would require more than 11 men to be shown, none of the last tied group is included.

Pitching. The top ten pitchers are shown in various categories. For averages, innings pitched must equal or exceed the number of scheduled games in order for a pitcher to qualify. If required by ties, 11 players are shown. If ties would require more than 11 men to be shown, none of the last tied group is included.

Fielding. The top five in each fielding category are shown for each position. For averages, the minimum for qualification at first base, second base, shortstop, third base, and catcher is 100 games played. For outfield, games played must equal or exceed two-thirds of the number of scheduled games. For pitchers, innings pitched must equal or exceed the number of scheduled games. If required by ties, 6 players are shown. If ties would require more than 6 men to be shown, none of the last tied group is shown.

BATTING AVERAGE

1. Ty Cobb, 1911	.420
2. Ty Cobb, 1912	.410
3. Harry Heilmann, 1923	.403
4. Ty Cobb, 1922	.401
5. Harry Heilmann, 1927	.398
6. Harry Heilmann, 1921	.394
7. Harry Heilmann, 1925	.393
8. Ty Cobb, 1913	.390
9. Ty Cobb, 1921	.389
0. Ty Cobb, 1910	.385

SLUGGING AVERAGE

1. Hank Greenberg, 1938	.683
2. Hank Greenberg, 1940	.670
3. Hank Greenberg, 1937	.668
4. Norm Cash, 1961	.662
5. Rudy York, 1937	.651
6. Harry Heilmann, 1923	.632
7. Hank Greenberg, 1935	.628
8. Hank Greenberg, 1939	.622
9. Ty Cobb, 1911	.621
10. Harry Heilmann, 1927	.616

HITS

1. Ty Cobb, 1911	248
2. Harry Heilmann, 1921	237
3. Ty Cobb, 1912	227
3. Charlie Gehringer, 1936	227
5. Harry Heilmann, 1925	225
5. Ty Cobb, 1917	225
7. George Kell, 1950	218
8. Sam Crawford, 1911	217
9. Ty Cobb, 1909	216
10. Dale Alexander, 1929	215
10. Charlie Gehringer, 1929	215

DOUBLES

1. Hank Greenberg, 1934	63
2. Charlie Gehringer, 1936	60
3. George Kell, 1950	56
4. Gee Walker, 1936	55
5. Harry Heilmann, 1927	50
5. Hank Greenberg, 1940	50
5. Charlie Gehringer, 1934	50
8. Hank Greenberg, 1937	49
9. Dale Alexander, 1931	47
9. Ty Cobb, 1911	47
9. Charlie Gehringer, 1930	47

TRIPLES

1. Sam Crawford, 1914	26
2. Sam Crawford, 1903	25
3. Ty Cobb, 1911	24
4. Ty Cobb, 1912	23
4. Ty Cobb, 1917	23
4. Sam Crawford, 1913	23
7. Sam Crawford, 1912	21
8. Ty Cobb, 1908	20

HOME RUNS

1. Hank Greenberg, 1938	58
2. Rocky Colavito, 1961	45
3. Hank Greenberg, 1946	44
4. Norm Cash, 1961	41
4. Hank Greenberg, 1940	41
6. Hank Greenberg, 1937	40
7. Norm Cash, 1962	39
8. Rocky Colavito, 1962	37
9. Willie Horton, 1968	36
9. Hank Greenberg, 1935	36

RUNS

1. Ty Cobb, 1911	147
2. Hank Greenberg, 1938	144
2. Ty Cobb, 1915	144
2. Charlie Gehringer, 1930	144
2. Charlie Gehringer, 1936	144
6. Hank Greenberg, 1937	137
7. Charlie Gehringer, 1934	134
8. Charlie Gehringer, 1937	133
8. Charlie Gehringer, 1938	133
0. Lu Blue, 1922	131
0. Charlie Gehringer, 1929	131

RUNS BATTED IN

1. Hank Greenberg, 1937	183
2. Hank Greenberg, 1935	170
3. Hank Greenberg, 1940	150
4. Hank Greenberg, 1938	146
5. Ty Cobb, 1911	144
6. Rocky Colavito, 1961	140
7. Hank Greenberg, 1934	139
7. Harry Heilmann, 1921	139
9. Dale Alexander, 1929	137
10. Dale Alexander, 1930	135

STOLEN BASES

1. Ty Cobb, 1915	96
2. Ty Cobb, 1911	83
3. Ron LeFlore, 1979	78
4. Ty Cobb, 1909	76
5. Ty Cobb, 1916	68
5. Ron LeFlore, 1978	68
7. Ty Cobb, 1910	65
8. Ty Cobb, 1912	61
9. Ron LeFlore, 1976	58
10. Ty Cobb, 1917	55

RUNS PER GAME

1. Ty Cobb, 1911	1.01
2. Ty Cobb, 1921	.97
3. Charlie Gehringer, 1936	.94
3. Charlie Gehringer, 1930	.94
5. Hank Greenberg, 1938	.93
6. Charlie Gehringer, 1937	.92
7. Ty Cobb, 1915	.92
8. Lu Blue, 1922	.90
9. Hank Greenberg, 1937	.89
0. Pete Fox, 1935	.89

RUNS BATTED IN PER GAME

1. Hank Greenberg, 1937	1.19
2. Hank Greenberg, 1935	1.12
3. Hank Greenberg, 1940	1.01
4. Rudy York, 1937	.99
5. Ty Cobb, 1911	.99
6. Harry Heilmann, 1929	.96
7. Hank Greenberg, 1938	.94
8. Rudy York, 1938	.94
9. Harry Heilmann, 1921	.93
10. Hank Greenberg, 1934	.91

HOME RUN PERCENTAGE

1. Hank Greenberg, 1938	10.4
2. Rudy York, 1937	9.3
3. Hank Greenberg, 1946	8.4
4. Rocky Colavito, 1961	7.7
5. Norm Cash, 1962	7.7
6. Norm Cash, 1961	7.7
7. Hank Greenberg, 1940	7.2
8. Rudy York, 1938	7.1
9. Norm Cash, 1971	7.1
10. Willie Horton, 1968	7.0

AT BATS

1. Harvey Kuenn, 1953 679
2. Ron LeFlore, 1978 666
3. Jake Wood, 1961 663
4. Harvey Kuenn, 1954 656
5. Ron LeFlore, 1977 652
6. Lou Whitaker, 1983 643
7. Rusty Staub, 1978 642
8. Charlie Gehringer, 1936 641
8. George Kell, 1950 641
10. Roy Johnson, 1929 640

EXTRA BASE HITS

1. Hank Greenberg, 1937 103
2. Hank Greenberg, 1940 99
3. Hank Greenberg, 1935 98
4. Hank Greenberg, 1934 96
5. Charlie Gehringer, 1936 87
6. Hank Greenberg, 1938 85
6. Rudy York, 1940 85
8. Dale Alexander, 1929 83
9. Hank Greenberg, 1939 82
10. Ty Cobb, 1911 79

TOTAL BASES

1. Hank Greenberg, 1937 ....
2. Hank Greenberg, 1935 ......
3. Hank Greenberg, 1940 ......
4. Hank Greenberg, 1938 ......
5. Ty Cobb, 1911 ....
6. Harry Heilmann, 1921 ......
7. Dale Alexander, 1929 ....
8. Hank Greenberg, 1934 ....
8. Charlie Gehringer, 1936 ....
10. Norm Cash, 1961 ....

BASES ON BALLS

1. Roy Cullenbine, 1947 137
2. Eddie Yost, 1959 135
3. Eddie Yost, 1960 125
4. Norm Cash, 1961 124
5. Eddie Lake, 1947 120
6. Hank Greenberg, 1938 119
7. Donie Bush, 1915 118
7. Ty Cobb, 1915 118
9. Donie Bush, 1912 117
10. Rocky Colavito, 1961 113

STRIKEOUTS

1. Jake Wood, 1961 141
2. Ron LeFlore, 1975 139
3. Ron LeFlore, 1977 121
4. Lance Parrish, 1984 120
5. Dick McAuliffe, 1967 118
6. Ron LeFlore, 1976 111
7. Willie Horton, 1968 110
8. Lance Parrish, 1980 109
8. Willie Horton, 1975 109
10. Lance Parrish, 1983 106

HIGHEST STRIKEOUT AVERAGE

1. Ron LeFlore, 1975 ....
2. Willie Horton, 1968 ....
3. Lance Parrish, 1979 .. ..
4. Jake Wood, 1961 ....
5. Dick McAuliffe, 1967 .. .
6. Lance Parrish, 1984 ..
7. Norm Cash, 1967 ..
8. Ron LeFlore, 1976 .. ..
9. Lance Parrish, 1982 ...
10. Willie Horton, 1965 .. ..

BB AVERAGE

1. Roy Cullenbine, 1947 .... .228
2. Eddie Yost, 1959 ... ... .206
3. Eddie Yost, 1960 ... ... .201
4. Mickey Cochrane, 1935. .189
5. Norm Cash, 1961 .... .188
6. Donie Bush, 1912 .... .186
7. Charlie Gehringer, 1941 .179
8. Johnny Bassler, 1925. .. .177
9. Hank Greenberg, 1938 .. .176
10. Donie Bush, 1915 .... .174

PINCH HITS

1. Bob Fothergill, 1929 19
2. Gates Brown, 1968 18
3. Sammy Hale, 1920 17
3. Vic Wertz, 1962 17
5. Gates Brown, 1974 16
6. Gus Zernial, 1958 15
7. Billy Rhiel, 1932 13
7. Gates Brown, 1966 13
7. Dalton Jones, 1971 13
7. Pat Mullin, 1953 13

PINCH HIT AT BATS

1. Pat Mullin, 1953 ....
2. Gates Brown, 1974 ....
2. Vic Wertz, 1962 ....
2. Bob Fothergill, 1929 ....
5. Sammy Hale, 1920 ......
6. Charlie Maxwell, 1961 ....
6. Dalton Jones, 1971 ....
8. Sandy Amoros, 1960 ....
8. Rip Radcliff, 1943 ....
8. Neil Chrisley, 1960 ....

PINCH HIT BATTING AVERAGE

1. Gates Brown, 1968 .... .462
2. Johnny Pesky, 1953 .. .. .400
3. Gus Zernial, 1958 ... ... .395
4. Bob Fothergill, 1929 .. ... .358
5. Jo-Jo White, 1936 ... ... .333
6. Sammy Hale, 1920 .... .327
7. Gates Brown, 1966 .... .325
8. Vic Wertz, 1962 .... .321
9. Earl Averill, 1940 .... .316
10. Tim Corcoran, 1977 .. .. .313

GAMES

1. Willie Hernandez, 1984	80
2. Aurelio Lopez, 1984	71
3. Fred Scherman, 1971.	69
4. Aurelio Lopez, 1980	67
5. John Hiller, 1973	65
6. Aurelio Lopez, 1979	61
6. Chuck Seelbach, 1972.	61
6. Tom Timmerman, 1970	61
9. John Hiller, 1974	59
10. Aurelio Lopez, 1983	57
10. Fred Scherman, 1972.	57

WINS

1. Denny McLain, 1968.	31
2. George Mullin, 1909	29
2. Hal Newhouser, 1944.	29
4. Dizzy Trout, 1944.	27
5. Hal Newhouser, 1946.	26
6. Wild Bill Donovan, 1907	25
6. Hal Newhouser, 1945.	25
6. Ed Killian, 1907.	25
6. Mickey Lolich, 1971	25

LOSSES

1. George Mullin, 1904.	23
2. Hooks Dauss, 1920.	21
2. Mickey Lolich, 1974	21
2. George Mullin, 1907	21
5. Art Houtteman, 1952.	20
5. Bobo Newsom, 1941.	20
5. Ed Killian, 1904.	20
5. George Mullin, 1907.	20

COMPLETE GAMES

1. George Mullin, 1904.	42
2. Roscoe Miller, 1901.	35
2. George Mullin, 1906.	35
2. George Mullin, 1905.	35
2. George Mullin, 1907.	35
6. Wild Bill Donovan, 1903	34
7. Ed Killian, 1905.	33
7. Dizzy Trout, 1944.	33
9. Ed Killian, 1904.	32
10. George Mullin, 1903. . . .	31

WINNING PERCENTAGE

1. Wild Bill Donovan, 1907	.862
2. Schoolboy Rowe, 1940. .	.842
3. Denny McLain, 1968. . .	.838
4. Bobo Newsom, 1940. . .	.808
5. George Mullin, 1909. . .	.784
6. Hal Newhouser, 1944. . .	.763
7. Schoolboy Rowe, 1934.	.750
8. Hal Newhouser, 1946. . .	.743
9. Hal Newhouser, 1945. . .	.735
10. Denny McLain, 1969. . .	.727
10. Denny McLain, 1965. . .	.727

EARNED RUN AVERAGE

1. Ed Summers, 1908	1.64
2. Ed Killian, 1909.	1.71
3. Ed Killian, 1907.	1.78
4. Hal Newhouser, 1945. . .	1.81
5. Ed Siever, 1902.	1.91
6. Hal Newhouser, 1946. . . .	1.94
7. Denny McLain, 1968. . . .	1.96
8. Harry Coveleski, 1916 . .	1.97
9. Al Benton, 1945	2.02
10. Wild Bill Donovan, 1908 . .	2.08

INNINGS PITCHED

1. George Mullin, 1904.	382
2. Mickey Lolich, 1971	376
3. George Mullin, 1907.	357
4. Dizzy Trout, 1944.	352
5. George Mullin, 1905.	348
6. Denny McLain, 1968.	336
7. Roscoe Miller, 1901.	332
8. Ed Killian, 1904.	332
9. George Mullin, 1906.	330
10. Mickey Lolich, 1972	327

STRIKEOUTS

1. Mickey Lolich, 1971	308
2. Denny McLain, 1968.	280
3. Hal Newhouser, 1946.	275
4. Mickey Lolich, 1969	271
5. Mickey Lolich, 1972	250
6. Joe Coleman, 1971	236
7. Jack Morris, 1983	232
8. Mickey Lolich, 1970	230
9. Mickey Lolich, 1965	226
10. Joe Coleman, 1972.	222

BASES ON BALLS

1. Joe Coleman, 1974.	158
2. Paul Foytack, 1956.	142
3. George Mullin, 1905.	138
4. Hal Newhouser, 1941.	137
5. George Mullin, 1904.	131
6. Howard Ehmke, 1920.	124
6. Virgil Trucks, 1949.	124
8. Mickey Lolich, 1969	122
9. Tommy Bridges, 1932.	119
10. Bobo Newsom, 1941.	118
10. Earl Whitehill, 1931.	118

HITS PER 9 INNINGS

1. Denny McLain, 1968 . . . . . . 6.46
2. Hal Newhouser, 1946 . . . . 6.62
3. Hal Newhouser, 1942 . . . . 6.71
4. Hank Aguirre, 1962 . . . . . 6.75
5. Virgil Trucks, 1949 . . . . . 6.84
6. Mickey Lolich, 1969 . . . . . 6.86
7. Hal Newhouser, 1945 . . . . 6.86
8. Earl Wilson, 1966 . . . . . . 6.94
9. Joe Coleman, 1972 . . . . . . 6.95
10. Jack Morris, 1981 . . . . 6.95

STRIKEOUTS PER 9 INNINGS

1. Mickey Lolich, 1969 . . . . . 8.69
2. Hal Newhouser, 1946 . . . . 8.47
3. Mickey Lolich, 1965 . . . . . 8.35
4. Mickey Lolich, 1968 . . . . . 8.06
5. Denny McLain, 1965 . . . . . 7.84
6. Les Cain, 1970 . . . . 7.76
7. Mickey Lolich, 1967 . . . . . 7.68
8. Mickey Lolich, 1966 . . . . . 7.64
9. Mickey Lolich, 1970 . . . . . 7.58
10. Denny McLain, 1968 . . . . . 7.50

BASES ON BALLS PER 9 INNINGS

1. Fred Hutchinson, 1951 . . . 1.
2. Frank Kitson, 1903 . . . . . . 1.
3. Dave Rozema, 1977 . . . . . 1.
4. Ed Siever, 1902 . . . . 1.
5. Ed Summers, 1908 . . . . . 1.
6. Ed Summers, 1909 . . . . . 1.
7. Denny McLain, 1968 . . . . 1.
8. Ed Siever, 1907 . . . . 1.
9. Frank Kitson, 1904 . . . . . 1.
10. John Cronin, 1901 . . . . . . 1.

SHUTOUTS

1. Denny McLain, 1969 9
2. Hal Newhouser, 1945 8
2. Ed Killian, 1905 8
4. Billy Hoeft, 1955 7
4. Dizzy Trout, 1944 7
4. George Mullin, 1904 7

RELIEF GAMES

1. Willie Hernandez, 1984 80
2. Aurelio Lopez, 1984 71
3. Fred Scherman, 1971 68
4. Aurelio Lopez, 1980 66
5. John Hiller, 1973 65

RELIEF WINS

1. John Hiller, 1974 . . . .
2. Aurelio Lopez, 1980 . . . .
3. Hooks Dauss, 1926 . . . .
3. John Hiller, 1976 . . . .

SAVES

1. John Hiller, 1973 38
2. Willie Hernandez, 1984 32
3. Tom Timmerman, 1970 . . . 27
4. Aurelio Lopez, 1979 21
4. Aurelio Lopez, 1980 21

RELIEF WINS PLUS SAVES

1. John Hiller, 1973 48
2. Willie Hernandez, 1984 41
3. Aurelio Lopez, 1980 34
4. Tom Timmerman, 1970 33
5. Aurelio Lopez, 1979 31

RELIEF WINNING PERCENTAGE

1. Aurelio Lopez, 1984 90
2. Ken Holloway, 1924 81
3. Willie Hernandez, 1984 75
4. Hooks Dauss, 1926 73
5. Aurelio Lopez, 1980 72

PUTOUTS		ASSISTS		FIELDING AVERAGE	
B					
1. Jason Thompson, 1977	1599	1. Rudy York, 1943	149	1. Norm Cash, 1964	.997
2. George Burns, 1914	1576	2. Rudy York, 1942	146	2. Norm Cash, 1967	.995
3. Lu Blue, 1922	1506	3. Roy Cullenbine, 1947	139	3. Norm Cash, 1963	.994
4. Jason Thompson, 1978	1503	4. Walt Dropo, 1953	127	4. Jack Burns, 1936	.994
5. Hank Greenberg, 1938	1484	4. Norm Cash, 1961	127	5. Norm Cash, 1969	.994
B					
1. Gerry Priddy, 1950	440	1. Charlie Gehringer, 1933	542	1. Lou Whitaker, 1982	.988
2. Gerry Priddy, 1951	437	1. Gerry Priddy, 1950	542	2. Dick McAuliffe, 1971	.987
3. Ralph Young, 1920	405	3. Charlie Gehringer, 1936	524	3. Frank Bolling, 1959	.987
4. Charlie Gehringer, 1929	404	4. Charlie Gehringer, 1934	516	4. Lou Whitaker, 1979	.986
5. Germany Schaefer, 1905	403	5. Charlie Gehringer, 1928	507	5. Dick McAuliffe, 1968	.986
B					
1. Ossie Vitt, 1916	208	1. Aurelio Rodriguez, 1974	389	1. Aurelio Rodriguez, 1978	.987
2. Marty McManus, 1929	206	2. Ossie Vitt, 1916	385	2. George Kell, 1946	.984
3. Marv Owen, 1934	202	3. Aurelio Rodriguez, 1975	375	3. George Kell, 1950	.982
4. Bob Jones, 1921	194	4. Aurelio Rodriguez, 1972	348	4. Aurelio Rodriguez, 1976	.978
5. Ossie Vitt, 1915	191	5. Aurelio Rodriguez, 1971	341	5. Don Wert, 1967	.978
S					
1. Donie Bush, 1914	425	1. Donie Bush, 1909	567	1. Ed Brinkman, 1972	.990
2. Donie Bush, 1911	372	2. Donie Bush, 1911	556	2. Alan Trammell, 1981	.983
3. Charley O'Leary, 1905	358	3. Donie Bush, 1912	547	3. Ed Brinkman, 1971	.980
4. Charley O'Leary, 1907	353	4. Donie Bush, 1914	544	4. Alan Trammell, 1984	.980
5. Donie Bush, 1915	340	5. Billy Rogell, 1933	526	5. Alan Trammell, 1980	.980
F					
1. Bill Tuttle, 1955	442	1. Jimmy Barrett, 1901	31	1. Mickey Stanley, 1970	1.000
2. Ron LeFlore, 1978	440	1. Harry Heilmann, 1924	31	1. Mickey Stanley, 1968	1.000
3. Barney McCosky, 1939	428	3. Ty Cobb, 1907	30	1. Al Kaline, 1971	1.000
4. Chet Lemon, 1984	427	4. Jimmy Barrett, 1904	29	4. Hoot Evers, 1950	.997
5. Mickey Stanley, 1973	420	5. Ty Cobb, 1921	27	5. Charlie Maxwell, 1957	.997
		5. Ty Cobb, 1917	27		
1. Bill Freehan, 1968	971	1. Oscar Stanage, 1911	212	1. Gus Triandos, 1963	.998
2. Bill Freehan, 1967	950	2. Oscar Stanage, 1914	190	2. Bill Freehan, 1970	.997
3. Bill Freehan, 1964	923	3. Boss Schmidt, 1908	184	3. Frank House, 1957	.997
4. Bill Freehan, 1971	912	4. Oscar Stanage, 1912	168	4. Bill Freehan, 1971	.996
5. Bill Freehan, 1966	898	5. Oscar Stanage, 1910	148	5. Bill Freehan, 1966	.996
1. Dan Petry, 1984	38	1. George Mullin, 1904	163		
1. George Mullin, 1903	38	2. Hooks Dauss, 1915	137		
3. Denny McLain, 1968	36	3. George Mullin, 1905	134		
4. Frank Lary, 1961	32	4. George Mullin, 1907	133		
5. Jack Morris, 1980	31	5. Harry Coveleski, 1914	123		

TOTAL CHANCES	TOTAL CHANCES PER GAME	DOUBLE PLAYS
1B		
1. Jason Thompson, 1977 1712	1. George Burns, 1914 ... ... 12.3	1. Rudy York, 1944 ......
2. George Burns, 1914 1685	2. George Burns, 1915 ... ... 11.8	2. Jason Thompson, 1978 ....
3. Hank Greenberg, 1938 1618	3. Del Gainor, 1913 .... 11.6	3. Hank Greenberg, 1938 ......
4. Jason Thompson, 1978 1606	4. George Burns, 1916 ... ... 11.5	4. Hank Greenberg, 1935 ......
5. Lu Blue, 1925 1600	5. George Burns, 1917 ... ... 11.5	4. Rudy York, 1945 ....
2B		
1. Gerry Priddy, 1950 1001	1. Gerry Priddy, 1950 ... . 6.4	1. Gerry Priddy, 1950 ......
2. Charlie Gehringer, 1936 946	2. Charlie Gehringer, 1927 .. 6.4	2. Eddie Mayo, 1944 ....
3. Charlie Gehringer, 1929 . . 928	3. Kid Gleason, 1901 .... 6.3	3. Lou Whitaker, 1982 ......
4. Charlie Gehringer, 1932 .. 921	4. Germany Schaefer, 1906 . 6.3	4. Gerry Priddy, 1951 ......
5. Charlie Gehringer, 1930 .. 919	5. Charlie Gehringer, 1936 . 6.1	5. Charlie Gehringer, 1936 ..
5. Charlie Gehringer, 1928 .. 919		
3B		
1. Ossie Vitt, 1916 615	1. Ossie Vitt, 1916 .... 4.1	1. Aurelio Rodriguez, 1974 ..
2. Bob Jones, 1921 545	2. Doc Casey, 1901 .... 4.1	2. Jack Warner, 1927 .....
3. Aurelio Rodriguez, 1974 542	3. Doc Casey, 1902 .... 4.0	2. George Kell, 1951 ....
4. Aurelio Rodriguez, 1975 . 536	4. Bob Jones, 1921 .... 3.9	
5. Doc Casey, 1902 534	5. George Moriarty, 1910 ... 3.8	
5. Ossie Vitt, 1915 534		
SS		
1. Donie Bush, 1914 1027	1. Kid Elberfeld, 1901 ... . 6.8	1. Johnny Lipon, 1950 ....
2. Donie Bush, 1911 1003	2. Donie Bush, 1911 .... 6.7	2. Billy Rogell, 1933 ....
3. Donie Bush, 1909 946	3. Kid Elberfeld, 1902 ... ... 6.6	3. Billy Rogell, 1935 ....
4. Donie Bush, 1912 930	4. Donie Bush, 1914 .... 6.5	4. Billy Rogell, 1937 ....
5. Billy Rogell, 1933 903	5. Donie Bush, 1912 .... 6.5	5. Joe Hoover, 1944 ....
OF		
1. Bill Tuttle, 1955 461	1. Chet Lemon, 1984 .... 3.1	1. Ty Cobb, 1907 ....
2. Ron LeFlore, 1978 460	2. Ron LeFlore, 1976 ... . 3.1	2. Ty Cobb, 1911 ....
3. Barney McCosky, 1939 441	3. Barney McCosky, 1939 ... 3.0	3. Ty Cobb, 1916 ....
4. Chet Lemon, 1984 435	4. Hoot Evers, 1947 .... 3.0	3. Ty Cobb, 1917 ....
4. Ty Cobb, 1924 435	5. Bill Tuttle, 1955 .... 3.0	
C		
1. Bill Freehan, 1968 1050	1. Bill Freehan, 1968 .... 7.6	1. Bill Freehan, 1968 ......
2. Bill Freehan, 1967 1021	2. Bill Freehan, 1969 .... 7.3	2. Boss Schmidt, 1907 .....
3. Bill Freehan, 1964 991	3. Bill Freehan, 1966 .... 7.3	2. Johnny Bassler, 1925 ....
4. Bill Freehan, 1971 966	4. Bill Freehan, 1965 ... . 7.2	2. Oscar Stanage, 1912 ......
5. Bill Freehan, 1966 958	5. Bill Freehan, 1964 ... . 7.0	2. Ray Hayworth, 1933 ....
P		
1. George Mullin, 1904 204	1. George Mullin, 1904 ... ... 4.5	1. George Gill, 1938 ....
2. George Mullin, 1905 160	2. George Mullin, 1903 ... ... 3.8	1. Dan Petry, 1983 ....
3. George Mullin, 1903 156	3. George Mullin, 1905 ... . 3.6	3. Dizzy Trout, 1945 ......
4. George Mullin, 1907 154	4. Joe Yeager, 1902 .... 3.6	4. Don Mossi, 1961 ....
5. Hooks Dauss, 1915 153	5. Jean Dubuc, 1913 .... 3.6	4. Ed Summers, 1909 ......
		4. Dizzy Trout, 1944 ......

PUTOUTS PER GAME		ASSISTS PER GAME	
B			
1. George Burns, 1914	11.5	1. Roy Cullenbine, 1947	1.0
2. George Burns, 1915	11.1	2. Rudy York, 1943	1.0
3. Del Gainor, 1913	11.0	3. Rudy York, 1942	1.0
4. George Burns, 1916	10.9	4. Walt Dropo, 1953	.8
5. George Burns, 1917	10.8	5. Charlie Carr, 1903	.8
B			
1. Germany Schaefer, 1906	3.1	1. Charlie Gehringer, 1927	3.6
2. Gerry Priddy, 1951	2.8	2. Charlie Gehringer, 1933	3.5
3. Gerry Priddy, 1950	2.8	3. Gerry Priddy, 1950	3.5
4. Frank Bolling, 1960	2.7	4. Charlie Gehringer, 1937	3.4
5. Kid Gleason, 1902	2.7	5. Charlie Gehringer, 1936	3.4
B			
1. Ossie Vitt, 1916	1.4	1. Doc Casey, 1901	2.6
2. Bob Jones, 1921	1.4	2. Ossie Vitt, 1916	2.5
3. Marty McManus, 1929	1.4	3. Aurelio Rodriguez, 1975	2.5
4. Bob Jones, 1922	1.4	4. George Moriarty, 1914	2.5
5. Doc Casey, 1902	1.3	5. Aurelio Rodriguez, 1974	2.4
S			
1. Kid Elberfeld, 1901	2.7	1. Donie Bush, 1912	3.8
2. Donie Bush, 1914	2.7	2. Donie Bush, 1911	3.7
3. Charley O'Leary, 1906	2.6	3. Donie Bush, 1909	3.6
4. Charley O'Leary, 1907	2.6	4. Kid Elberfeld, 1902	3.5
5. Kid Elberfeld, 1902	2.5	5. Donie Bush, 1914	3.5
F			
1. Chet Lemon, 1984	3.1	1. Jimmy Barrett, 1901	.2
2. Barney McCosky, 1939	3.0	2. Ty Cobb, 1921	.2
3. Ron LeFlore, 1976	2.9	3. Harry Heilmann, 1924	.2
4. Hoot Evers, 1947	2.9	4. Ty Cobb, 1907	.2
5. Bill Tuttle, 1955	2.9	5. Matty McIntyre, 1906	.2
1. Bill Freehan, 1968	7.0	1. Oscar Stanage, 1910	1.8
2. Bill Freehan, 1969	6.8	2. Oscar Stanage, 1914	1.6
3. Bill Freehan, 1966	6.8	3. Boss Schmidt, 1908	1.5
4. Bill Freehan, 1965	6.7	4. Oscar Stanage, 1911	1.5
5. Bill Freehan, 1964	6.5	5. Oscar Stanage, 1912	1.4
1. Dan Petry, 1984	1.1	1. George Mullin, 1904	3.6
2. Earl Wilson, 1966	1.0	2. Jean Dubuc, 1913	3.1
3. George Mullin, 1903	.9	3. Ed Willett, 1912	3.1
4. Frank Lary, 1961	.9	3. Ed Willett, 1910	3.1
5. Denny McLain, 1968	.9	5. George Mullin, 1905	3.0

GAMES

1. Al Kaline......... 2834
2. Ty Cobb......... 2805
3. Charlie Gehringer......... 2323
4. Sam Crawford......... 2114
5. Norm Cash......... 2018
6. Harry Heilmann......... 1989
7. Donie Bush......... 1872
8. Bill Freehan......... 1774
9. Dick McAuliffe......... 1656
10. Bobby Veach......... 1605

DOUBLES

1. Ty Cobb......... 665
2. Charlie Gehringer......... 574
3. Al Kaline......... 498
4. Harry Heilmann......... 497
5. Sam Crawford......... 403
6. Hank Greenberg......... 366
7. Bobby Veach......... 345
8. Harvey Kuenn......... 244
9. Bill Freehan......... 241
9. Norm Cash......... 241

BATTING AVERAGE

1. Ty Cobb......... .3
2. Harry Heilmann......... .3
3. Bob Fothergill......... .3
4. Dale Alexander......... .3
5. George Kell......... .3
6. Heinie Manush......... .3
7. Charlie Gehringer......... .3
8. Hank Greenberg......... .3
9. Gee Walker......... .3
10. Harvey Kuenn......... .3

AT BATS

1. Ty Cobb......... 10586
2. Al Kaline......... 10116
3. Charlie Gehringer......... 8860
4. Sam Crawford......... 7994
5. Harry Heilmann......... 7297
6. Donie Bush......... 6966
7. Norm Cash......... 6593
8. Bill Freehan......... 6073
9. Bobby Veach......... 5982
10. Dick McAuliffe......... 5898

TRIPLES

1. Ty Cobb......... 286
2. Sam Crawford......... 250
3. Charlie Gehringer......... 146
4. Harry Heilmann......... 145
5. Bobby Veach......... 136
6. Al Kaline......... 75
7. Donie Bush......... 73
8. Dick McAuliffe......... 70
9. Hank Greenberg......... 69
10. Lu Blue......... 66

SLUGGING AVERAGE

1. Hank Greenberg......... .6
2. Harry Heilmann......... .5
3. Ty Cobb......... .5
4. Dale Alexander......... .5
5. Rudy York......... .5
6. Rocky Colavito......... .5
7. Norm Cash......... .4
8. Ray Boone......... .4
9. Bob Fothergill......... .4
10. Charlie Gehringer......... .4

HITS

1. Ty Cobb......... 3902
2. Al Kaline......... 3007
3. Charlie Gehringer......... 2839
4. Harry Heilmann......... 2499
5. Sam Crawford......... 2466
6. Bobby Veach......... 1860
7. Norm Cash......... 1793
8. Donie Bush......... 1744
9. Bill Freehan......... 1591
10. Hank Greenberg......... 1528

HOME RUNS

1. Al Kaline......... 399
2. Norm Cash......... 373
3. Hank Greenberg......... 306
4. Willie Horton......... 262
5. Rudy York......... 239
6. Bill Freehan......... 200
7. Dick McAuliffe......... 192
8. Charlie Gehringer......... 184
9. Harry Heilmann......... 164
10. Lance Parrish......... 162

HOME RUN PERCENTAGE

1. Hank Greenberg
2. Rocky Colavito
3. Norm Cash
4. Rudy York
5. Charlie Maxwell
6. Willie Horton
7. Lance Parrish
8. Jason Thompson
9. John Wockenfuss
10. Ray Boone

EXTRA BASE HITS

1. Ty Cobb......... 1063
2. Al Kaline......... 972
3. Charlie Gehringer......... 904
4. Harry Heilmann......... 806
5. Hank Greenberg......... 741
6. Sam Crawford......... 723
7. Norm Cash......... 654
8. Bobby Veach......... 540
9. Rudy York......... 517
10. Willie Horton......... 504

TOTAL BASES

1. Ty Cobb......... 5475
2. Al Kaline......... 4852
3. Charlie Gehringer......... 4257
4. Harry Heilmann......... 3778
5. Sam Crawford......... 3579
6. Norm Cash......... 3233
7. Hank Greenberg......... 2950
8. Bobby Veach......... 2654
9. Willie Horton......... 2549
10. Bill Freehan......... 2502

STOLEN BASES

1. Ty Cobb......... 8
2. Donie Bush......... 4
3. Sam Crawford......... 3
4. Ron LeFlore......... 2
5. George Moriarty......... 1
6. Bobby Veach......... 1
7. Charlie Gehringer......... 1
8. Davy Jones......... 1
9. Al Kaline......... 1
10. Gee Walker......... 1

RUNS

1. Ty Cobb 2087
2. Charlie Gehringer 1774
3. Al Kaline 1622
4. Donie Bush 1242
5. Harry Heilmann 1209
6. Sam Crawford 1115
7. Norm Cash 1028
8. Hank Greenberg 980
9. Bobby Veach 859
10. Dick McAuliffe 856

RUNS BATTED IN PER GAME

1. Hank Greenberg .... .95
2. Rudy York .... .74
3. Harry Heilmann .... .73
4. Goose Goslin .... .70
5. Rocky Colavito .... .68
6. Ray Boone .... .67
7. Rusty Staub .... .65
8. Ty Cobb .... .65
9. Bobby Veach .... .65
10. Vic Wertz .... .64

STRIKEOUTS

1. Norm Cash 1081
2. Al Kaline 1020
3. Willie Horton 945
4. Dick McAuliffe 932
5. Hank Greenberg 771
6. Bill Freehan 753
7. Lance Parrish 674
8. Rudy York 672
9. Ron LeFlore 628
10. Jim Northrup 603

RUNS BATTED IN

1. Ty Cobb 1828
2. Al Kaline 1583
3. Harry Heilmann 1454
4. Charlie Gehringer 1427
5. Sam Crawford 1264
6. Hank Greenberg 1202
7. Norm Cash 1087
8. Bobby Veach 1042
9. Rudy York 936
10. Willie Horton 886

BASES ON BALLS

1. Al Kaline 1277
2. Charlie Gehringer 1185
3. Ty Cobb 1148
4. Donie Bush 1125
5. Norm Cash 1025
6. Dick McAuliffe 842
7. Harry Heilmann 792
8. Hank Greenberg 748
9. Sam Crawford 646
10. Rudy York 640

HIGHEST STRIKEOUT AVERAGE

1. Kirk Gibson .... .207
2. Lance Parrish .... .198
3. Jake Wood .... .193
4. Ron LeFlore .... .192
5. Willie Horton .... .175
6. Jason Thompson .... .170
7. Norm Cash .... .164
8. Hank Greenberg .... .161
9. Charlie Maxwell .... .160
10. Dick McAuliffe .... .158

RUNS PER GAME

1. Hank Greenberg .... .77
2. Charlie Gehringer .... .76
3. Ty Cobb .... .74
4. Lu Blue .... .72
5. Barney McCosky .... .69
6. Ron LeFlore .... .68
7. Pete Fox .... .67
8. Donie Bush .... .66
9. Goose Goslin .... .66
10. Jimmy Barrett .... .65

BB AVERAGE

1. Roy Cullenbine .... .192
2. Eddie Lake .... .173
3. Johnny Bassler .... .159
4. Lu Blue .... .148
5. Dick Wakefield .... .144
6. Donie Bush .... .139
7. Hank Greenberg .... .135
8. Norm Cash .... .135
9. Jo-Jo White .... .132
10. Steve Kemp .... .130

LOWEST STRIKEOUT AVERAGE

1. Doc Cramer .... .032
2. George Kell .... .032
3. Johnny Bassler .... .033
4. Ossie Vitt .... .039
5. Charlie Gehringer .... .042
6. Sam Crawford .... .047
7. Harvey Kuenn .... .047
8. Ty Cobb .... .049
9. Eddie Mayo .... .050
10. Johnny Lipon .... .051

PINCH HITS

1. Gates Brown 107
2. Bob Fothergill 47
3. Jo-Jo White 40
3. Pat Mullin 40
5. Al Kaline 37
6. Charlie Maxwell 33
7. Vic Wertz 31
8. Johnny Neun 29
8. John Wockenfuss 29
8. Norm Cash 29

PH BATTING AVERAGE

1. Al Kaline .... .322
2. Bob Fothergill .... .311
3. Jo-Jo White .... .310
4. Dalton Jones .... .296
5. Johnny Neun .... .282
6. Mickey Stanley .... .273
7. Charlie Maxwell .... .270
8. Vic Wertz .... .263
9. Gates Brown .... .258
10. John Wockenfuss .... .257

GAMES

1. John Hiller............ 545
2. Hooks Dauss........ 538
3. Mickey Lolich........ 508
4. Dizzy Trout........ 493
5. Hal Newhouser........ 460
6. George Mullin 435
7. Tommy Bridges 424
8. Hank Aguirre........ 334
9. Earl Whitehill 325
10. Virgil Trucks........ 316

COMPLETE GAMES

1. George Mullin 336
2. Hooks Dauss......... 245
3. Wild Bill Donovan....... 213
4. Hal Newhouser........ 212
5. Tommy Bridges 207
6. Mickey Lolich........ 190
7. Dizzy Trout........ 156
8. Earl Whitehill 148
9. Ed Killian........ 142
10. Ed Willett........ 127

INNINGS PITCHED

1. George Mullin 33
2. Hooks Dauss 33
3. Mickey Lolich........ 33
4. Hal Newhouser........ 29
5. Tommy Bridges 28
6. Dizzy Trout........ 25
7. Earl Whitehill 21
8. Wild Bill Donovan........ ... 21
9. Frank Lary........ 20
10. Jim Bunning........ 18

WINS

1. Hooks Dauss........ 221
2. George Mullin 209
3. Mickey Lolich........ 207
4. Hal Newhouser........ 200
5. Tommy Bridges 194
6. Dizzy Trout........ 161
7. Wild Bill Donovan........ 141
8. Earl Whitehill 133
9. Frank Lary........ 123
10. Jim Bunning........ 118

WINNING PERCENTAGE

1. Denny McLain .... .654
2. Schoolboy Rowe.... ..... .629
3. Harry Coveleski .... .616
4. Dan Petry .... .605
5. Ed Summers .... .602
6. Eldon Auker .... .597
7. Wild Bill Donovan.... ..... .595
8. Bobo Newsom .... .588
9. Jack Morris........ ..... .588
10. Earl Wilson .... .587

STRIKEOUTS

1. Mickey Lolich........ 26
2. Hal Newhouser........ 17
3. Tommy Bridges 16
4. Jim Bunning........ 14
5. George Mullin 13
6. Hooks Dauss........ 12
7. Dizzy Trout........ 11
8. Denny McLain 11
9. Wild Bill Donovan........ ... 10
10. Virgil Trucks........ 10

LOSSES

1. Hooks Dauss........ 183
2. George Mullin 179
3. Mickey Lolich........ 175
4. Dizzy Trout........ 153
5. Hal Newhouser........ 148
6. Tommy Bridges 138
7. Earl Whitehill 119
8. Frank Lary........ 110
9. Vic Sorrell........ 101
10. Wild Bill Donovan........ 96
10. Virgil Trucks........ 96

EARNED RUN AVERAGE

1. Harry Coveleski 2.34
2. Ed Killian........ .... 2.38
3. Ed Summers 2.42
4. Wild Bill Donovan.... ..... 2.49
5. Ed Siever........ .... 2.61
6. George Mullin 2.76
7. John Hiller........ .... 2.83
8. Ed Willett........ .... 3.05
9. Jean Dubuc........ ..... 3.06
10. Hal Newhouser........ ..... 3.07

BASES ON BALLS

1. Hal Newhouser........ 12
2. Tommy Bridges 11
3. George Mullin 11
4. Hooks Dauss........ 10
5. Mickey Lolich........ 10
6. Dizzy Trout........ 9
7. Earl Whitehill 8
8. Virgil Trucks........ 7
9. Vic Sorrell........ 7
10. Wild Bill Donovan........ 68

HITS PER 9 INNINGS

1.	Denny McLain	7.46
2.	John Hiller	7.54
3.	Bernie Boland	7.75
4.	Earl Wilson	7.76
5.	Harry Coveleski	7.80
6.	Wild Bill Donovan	7.83
7.	Hank Aguirre	7.87
8.	Joe Sparma	7.97
9.	Jean Dubuc	8.06
10.	Hal Newhouser	8.07

SHUTOUTS

1.	Mickey Lolich	39
2.	George Mullin	34
3.	Tommy Bridges	33
3.	Hal Newhouser	33
5.	Wild Bill Donovan	29
6.	Dizzy Trout	28
7.	Denny McLain	26
8.	Virgil Trucks	22
8.	Hooks Dauss	22
10.	Frank Lary	20

SAVES

1.	John Hiller	125
2.	Aurelio Lopez	80
3.	Terry Fox	55
4.	Al Benton	45
5.	Hooks Dauss	40

STRIKEOUTS PER 9 INNINGS

1.	John Hiller	7.51
2.	Mickey Lolich	7.17
3.	Jim Bunning	6.78
4.	Earl Wilson	6.63
5.	Denny McLain	6.50
6.	Joe Coleman	6.39
7.	Joe Sparma	6.07
8.	Bobo Newsom	5.95
9.	Hank Aguirre	5.76
10.	Ted Gray	5.48

RELIEF GAMES

1.	John Hiller	502
2.	Aurelio Lopez	300
3.	Fred Gladding	216
4.	Fred Scherman	208
5.	Terry Fox	207

WINS PLUS SAVES

1.	John Hiller	197
2.	Aurelio Lopez	128
3.	Terry Fox	81
4.	Hooks Dauss	80
5.	Al Benton	62

BASES ON BALLS PER 9 INNINGS

1.	Don Mossi	1.75
2.	Ed Siever	1.80
3.	Ed Summers	1.99
4.	Dave Rozema	2.08
5.	Harry Coveleski	2.37
6.	Fred Hutchinson	2.39
7.	George Uhle	2.43
8.	Schoolboy Rowe	2.51
9.	Stubby Overmire	2.54
10.	Denny McLain	2.54

RELIEF WINS

1.	John Hiller	72
2.	Aurelio Lopez	48
3.	Hooks Dauss	40
4.	Terry Fox	26
4.	Fred Gladding	26

RELIEF WINNING PERCENTAGE

1.	Schoolboy Rowe	.750
2.	Fred Gladding	.703
3.	Fred Hutchinson	.696
4.	Ken Holloway	.692
5.	Aurelio Lopez	.686

	GAMES			CHANCES PER GAME			FIELDING AVERAGE	

1B

GAMES		CHANCES PER GAME		FIELDING AVERAGE	
1. Norm Cash	1915	1. George Burns	11.8	1. Jason Thompson	.9
2. Hank Greenberg	1019	2. Claude Rossman	11.2	2. Norm Cash	.9
3. Rudy York	943	3. Lu Blue	10.9	3. Walt Dropo	.9
4. Lu Blue	894	4. Harry Heilmann	10.6	4. Hank Greenberg	.9
5. Jason Thompson	604	5. Jason Thompson	10.3	5. Rudy York	.9

2B

GAMES		CHANCES PER GAME		FIELDING AVERAGE	
1. Charlie Gehringer	2206	1. Gerry Priddy	6.0	1. Jerry Lumpe	.9
2. Lou Whitaker	973	2. Charlie Gehringer	5.8	2. Lou Whitaker	.9
3. Dick McAuliffe	918	3. Germany Schaefer	5.6	3. Frank Bolling	.9
4. Ralph Young	874	4. Ralph Young	5.6	4. Gerry Priddy	.9
5. Frank Bolling	779	5. Eddie Mayo	5.4	5. Eddie Mayo	.9

3B

GAMES		CHANCES PER GAME		FIELDING AVERAGE	
1. Aurelio Rodriguez	1236	1. Ossie Vitt	3.7	1. George Kell	.9
2. Don Wert	1036	2. George Moriarty	3.6	2. Don Wert	.9
3. Pinky Higgins	842	3. Bob Jones	3.4	3. Aurelio Rodriguez	.9
4. George Kell	826	4. Ray Boone	3.4	4. Marty McManus	.9
5. Bob Jones	774	5. Marty McManus	3.3	5. Ray Boone	.9

SS

GAMES		CHANCES PER GAME		FIELDING AVERAGE	
1. Donie Bush	1846	1. Charley O'Leary	5.9	1. Ed Brinkman	.97
2. Billy Rogell	1148	2. Donie Bush	5.8	2. Alan Trammell	.97
3. Alan Trammell	960	3. Billy Rogell	5.4	3. Ray Oyler	.96
4. Harvey Kuenn	747	4. Jackie Tavener	5.3	4. Harvey Kuenn	.96
5. Dick McAuliffe	663	5. Johnny Lipon	5.2	5. Tom Veryzer	.96

OF

GAMES		CHANCES PER GAME		FIELDING AVERAGE	
1. Ty Cobb	2722	1. Bill Tuttle	2.8	1. Mickey Stanley	.99
2. Al Kaline	2488	2. Ron LeFlore	2.8	2. Jim Delsing	.99
3. Sam Crawford	1906	3. Chet Lemon	2.7	3. Chet Lemon	.99
4. Bobby Veach	1567	4. Barney McCosky	2.7	4. Charlie Maxwell	.98
5. Harry Heilmann	1481	5. Hoot Evers	2.7	5. Bill Bruton	.98

C

GAMES		CHANCES PER GAME		FIELDING AVERAGE	
1. Bill Freehan	1581	1. Bill Freehan	6.8	1. Bill Freehan	.99
2. Oscar Stanage	1073	2. Boss Schmidt	5.7	2. Lance Parrish	.99
3. Lance Parrish	834	3. Lance Parrish	5.6	3. Red Wilson	.99
4. Johnny Bassler	731	4. Red Wilson	5.5	4. Frank House	.98
5. Ray Hayworth	642	5. Oscar Stanage	5.5	5. Bob Swift	.98

P

GAMES		CHANCES PER GAME	
1. John Hiller	545	1. Win Mercer	3.5
2. Hooks Dauss	538	2. Joe Yeager	3.5
3. Mickey Lolich	508	3. Roscoe Miller	3.4
4. Dizzy Trout	493	4. George Mullin	3.4
5. Hal Newhouser	460	5. Red Donahue	3.1

PUTOUTS		PUTOUTS PER GAME		ASSISTS	
B					
1. Norm Cash	14926	1. George Burns	11.1	1. Norm Cash	1303
2. Hank Greenberg	9581	2. Claude Rossman	10.4	2. Rudy York	733
3. Lu Blue	9082	3. Lu Blue	10.2	3. Hank Greenberg	645
4. Rudy York	8617	4. Harry Heilmann	9.8	4. Lu Blue	563
5. Jason Thompson	5763	5. Jason Thompson	9.5	5. Jason Thompson	398
B					
1. Charlie Gehringer	5369	1. Gerry Priddy	2.8	1. Charlie Gehringer	7068
2. Lou Whitaker	2085	2. Germany Schaefer	2.6	2. Lou Whitaker	2949
3. Ralph Young	2065	3. Eddie Mayo	2.5	3. Ralph Young	2603
4. Dick McAuliffe	2032	4. Charlie Gehringer	2.4	4. Dick McAuliffe	2184
5. Frank Bolling	1863	5. Frank Bolling	2.4	5. Frank Bolling	2055
B					
1. Aurelio Rodriguez	1011	1. Ossie Vitt	1.3	1. Aurelio Rodriguez	2729
2. George Kell	933	2. Marty McManus	1.2	2. Don Wert	1980
3. Bob Jones	917	3. Bob Jones	1.2	3. George Kell	1663
4. Don Wert	912	4. George Moriarty	1.2	4. Pinky Higgins	1616
5. Pinky Higgins	874	5. Marv Owen	1.1	5. Bob Jones	1566
>					
1. Donie Bush	4004	1. Charley O'Leary	2.4	1. Donie Bush	6057
2. Billy Rogell	2245	2. Donie Bush	2.2	2. Billy Rogell	3700
3. Alan Trammell	1580	3. Jackie Tavener	2.0	3. Alan Trammell	2742
4. Charley O'Leary	1516	4. Billy Rogell	2.0	4. Harvey Kuenn	2114
5. Harvey Kuenn	1343	5. Johnny Lipon	1.9	5. Ed Brinkman	1981
=					
1. Ty Cobb	5964	1. Chet Lemon	2.6	1. Ty Cobb	376
2. Al Kaline	5035	2. Bill Tuttle	2.6	2. Sam Crawford	197
3. Bobby Veach	3431	3. Ron LeFlore	2.6	3. Bobby Veach	190
4. Sam Crawford	2916	4. Barney McCosky	2.6	4. Al Kaline	170
5. Mickey Stanley	2819	5. Hoot Evers	2.5	5. Harry Heilmann	167
1. Bill Freehan	9941	1. Bill Freehan	6.3	1. Oscar Stanage	1379
2. Oscar Stanage	4270	2. Red Wilson	5.0	2. Bill Freehan	721
3. Lance Parrish	4142	3. Lance Parrish	5.0	3. Johnny Bassler	666
4. Birdie Tebbetts	2823	4. Frank House	4.6	4. Boss Schmidt	617
5. Johnny Bassler	2507	5. Birdie Tebbetts	4.6	5. Lance Parrish	446
1. George Mullin	217	1. Dan Petry	.8	1. George Mullin	1172
2. Dizzy Trout	184	2. Jack Morris	.7	2. Hooks Dauss	1128
3. Frank Lary	157	3. Joe Yeager	.7	3. Dizzy Trout	617
4. Jack Morris	152	4. Mark Fidrych	.6	4. Hal Newhouser	604
5. Tommy Bridges	144	5. Roscoe Miller	.6	5. Ed Willett	603

ASSISTS PER GAME		DOUBLE PLAYS		CHANCES	
1B					
1. Rudy York	.8	1. Norm Cash	1328	1. Norm Cash	163
2. Walt Dropo	.7	2. Hank Greenberg	888	2. Hank Greenberg	103
3. Norm Cash	.7	3. Rudy York	757	3. Lu Blue	97
4. Jason Thompson	.7	4. Lu Blue	637	4. Rudy York	94
5. Hank Greenberg	.6	5. Jason Thompson	560	5. Jason Thompson	62
2B					
1. Charlie Gehringer	3.2	1. Charlie Gehringer	1444	1. Charlie Gehringer	127
2. Gerry Priddy	3.1	2. Lou Whitaker	665	2. Lou Whitaker	51
3. Lou Whitaker	3.0	3. Frank Bolling	521	3. Ralph Young	48
4. Ralph Young	3.0	4. Dick McAuliffe	519	4. Dick McAuliffe	43
5. Eddie Mayo	2.9	5. Eddie Mayo	367	5. Frank Bolling	39
3B					
1. George Moriarty	2.2	1. Aurelio Rodriguez	252	1. Aurelio Rodriguez	38
2. Ossie Vitt	2.2	2. Don Wert	172	2. Don Wert	29
3. Aurelio Rodriguez	2.2	3. George Kell	156	3. George Kell	26
4. Ray Boone	2.1	4. Marv Owen	125	4. Pinky Higgins	26
5. Bob Jones	2.0	5. Pinky Higgins	121	5. Bob Jones	26
SS					
1. Donie Bush	3.3	1. Billy Rogell	772	1. Donie Bush	107
2. Billy Rogell	3.2	2. Alan Trammell	592	2. Billy Rogell	62
3. Ed Brinkman	3.2	3. Donie Bush	574	3. Alan Trammell	44
4. Charley O'Leary	3.1	4. Harvey Kuenn	430	4. Charley O'Leary	37
5. Jackie Tavener	3.0	5. Johnny Lipon	402	5. Harvey Kuenn	35
OF					
1. Jimmy Barrett	.2	1. Ty Cobb	105	1. Ty Cobb	65
2. Roy Johnson	.1	2. Sam Crawford	44	2. Al Kaline	52
3. Ty Cobb	.1	3. Bobby Veach	39	3. Bobby Veach	37
4. Matty McIntyre	.1	4. Harry Heilmann	32	4. Sam Crawford	32
5. Davy Jones	.1	5. Al Kaline	29	5. Mickey Stanley	29
C					
1. Boss Schmidt	1.4	1. Oscar Stanage	107	1. Bill Freehan	107
2. Oscar Stanage	1.3	2. Bill Freehan	98	2. Oscar Stanage	58
3. Johnny Bassler	.9	3. Johnny Bassler	66	3. Lance Parrish	46
4. Birdie Tebbetts	.7	4. Lance Parrish	56	4. Birdie Tebbetts	33
5. Larry Woodall	.6	5. Birdie Tebbetts	54	5. Johnny Bassler	32
P					
1. Win Mercer	2.9	1. Dizzy Trout	61	1. George Mullin	14
2. George Mullin	2.7	2. Hal Newhouser	40	2. Hooks Dauss	12
3. Rube Kisinger	2.7	3. Dan Petry	27	3. Dizzy Trout	8
4. Roscoe Miller	2.6	3. George Mullin	27	4. Hal Newhouser	7
5. Joe Yeager	2.6	5. Hooks Dauss	25	5. Ed Willett	7

The Tigers and Their Players
Year-by-Year

This section is a chronological listing of every Tigers season through 1984. All format information and abbreviations are explained below.

ROSTER INFORMATION

POS	Fielding Position		R	Runs
B	Bats B(oth), L(eft), or		RBI	Runs Batted In
	R(ight)		BB	Bases on Balls
G	Games		SO	Strikeouts
AB	At Bats		SB	Stolen Bases
H	Hits			
2B	Doubles		*Pinch-Hit*	
3B	Triples		AB	Pinch-Hit At Bats
HR	Home Runs		H	Pinch Hits
HR%	Home Run Percentage			
	(the number of home		BA	Batting Average
	runs per 100 times at		SA	Slugging Average
	bat)			

Regulars. The men who appear first on the team roster are considered the regulars for that team at the positions indicated. There are several factors for determining regulars of which "most games played at a position" and "most fielding chances at a position," are the two prime considerations.

Substitutes. Appearing directly beneath the regulars are the substitutes for the team. Substitutes are listed by position: first infielders, then outfielders, then catchers. Within these areas, substitutes are listed in order of most at bats, and can be someone who played most of the team's games as a regular, but not at one position. The rules for determining the listed positions of substitutes are as follows:

One Position Substitutes. If a man played at least 70% of his games in the field at one position, then he is listed only at that position, except for outfielders, where all three outfield positions are included under one category.

Two Position Substitutes. If a man did not play at least 70% of his games in the field at one position, but did play more than 90% of his total games at two positions, then he is shown with a combination fielding position. For example, if a player has an "S2" shown in his position column, it would mean that he played at least 90% of his games at shortstop and second base. These combinations are always indicated by the first letter or number of the position. The position listed first is where the most games were played.

Utility Players. If a player has a "UT" shown in his position column, it means that he did not meet the above 70% or 90% requirement and is listed as a utility player.

Pinch Hitters. Men who played no games in the field are considered pinch hitters and are listed as "PH."

Individual League Leaders. (Applies to batting, fielding, and pitching.) Statistics that appear in bold-faced print indicate the player led or tied for the league lead in the particular statistical category.

Traded League Leaders. (Applies to batting, fielding, and pitching.) An asterisk (*) next to a particular figure indicates that the player led the league that year in the particular statistical category, but since he played for more than one team, the figure does not necessarily represent his league-leading total or average.

Meaningless Averages. Indicated by use of a dash (-). In batting, the dash may appear in averages. This means that the player had no official at bats even though he played in at least one game. A batting average of .000 would mean he had at least one at bat with no hits. In pitching, the dash may appear in winning percentage. This means that the pitcher never had a decision even though he pitched in at least one game. A percentage of .000 would mean that he had at least one loss.

Anytime the symbol "infinity" (∞) is shown for a pitching average, it means that the pitcher allowed at least one earned run, hit, or base on balls without retiring a batter.

INDIVIDUAL FIELDING INFORMATION

T	Throws L(eft) or R(ight)		E	Errors
	(blank if not available)		DP	Double Plays
G	Games		TC/G	Total Chances per
PO	Putouts			Game
A	Assists		FA	Fielding Average

Each man's fielding record is shown for each position he played during the year. Fielding information for pitchers is not included.

TEAM AND LEAGUE INFORMATION

W	Wins		*Fielding*	
L	Losses		E	Errors
PCT	Winning Percentage		DP	Double Plays
GB	Games Behind the		FA	Fielding Average
	League Leader			
R	Runs Scored			
OR	Opponents' Runs		*Pitching*	
	(Runs Scored Against)		CG	Complete Games
			BB	Bases on Balls
Batting			SO	Strikeouts
			ShO	Shutouts
2B	Doubles		SV	Saves
3B	Triples		ERA	Earned Run Average
HR	Home Runs			
BA	Batting Average			
SA	Slugging Average			
SB	Stolen Bases			

Team League Leaders. Statistics that appear in bold-faced print indicate the team led or tied for the league lead in the particular statistical category. When teams are tied for league lead, the figures for all teams who tied are shown in boldface.

INDIVIDUAL PITCHING INFORMATION

T	Throws R(ight) or L(eft)		BB	Bases on Balls Allowed
W	Wins		SO	Strikeouts
L	Losses		R	Runs Allowed
PCT	Winning Percentage		ER	Earned Runs Allowed
ERA	Earned Run Average		ShO	Shutouts
SV	Saves		H/9	Hits Allowed Per 9
G	Games Pitched			Innings Pitched
GS	Games Started		BB/9	Bases on Balls Allowed
CG	Complete Games			Per 9 Innings Pitched
IP	Innings Pitched		SO/9	Strikeouts Per 9
H	Hits Allowed			Innings Pitched

The abbreviations for the teams appear as listed below.

BAL	Baltimore	MIN	Minnesota
BOS	Boston	NY	New York
CAL	California	OAK	Oakland
CHI	Chicago	PHI	Philadelphia
CLE	Cleveland	SEA	Seattle
DET	Detroit	STL	St. Louis
KC	Kansas City	TEX	Texas
LA	Los Angeles	TOR	Toronto
MIL	Milwaukee	WAS	Washington

BEFORE THE BEGINNING

George Tweedy Stallings, retained to manage the Western League's Detroit franchise in 1896, immediately decided to make changes. The alteration with greatest long-range impact appeared on his team's uniforms. "I put striped stockings on them, black and sort of yellowish brown," Stallings said. "I didn't think of their resemblance to a tiger's stripes at the time." Others did. A *Detroit Free Press* editor had first used the nickname on April 16, 1895. Before they had been called the Detroits, the Wolverines, and the Creams. But this time the nickname stuck. Now they would be known as the Tigers.

Detroit, hardly a bustling city prior to the internal combustion engine, played in the National League from 1881 to 1888. In 1882 Detroit authored its first season over .500 at 42–41. In 1886 the team won 87 and lost 36 to finish second, two-and-a-half games behind Chicago. And in 1887 they won the pennant to meet St. Louis of the American Association in the 15-game forerunner of the World Series (played as a cross-country tour). By Game 12—played in less-than-balmy Detroit on October 24—the Detroits had clinched the series eight games to three. But the remaining three went on as scheduled. A feast for both teams and a parade preceded Game 14, during which appreciative fans presented catcher Charley Bennett (after whom they'd name Bennett Park) a wheelbarrow of silver dollars. After the series ended a few days later in St. Louis, Detroit team president Frederick Stearns received a cable from Cincinnati's American Association team president A. S. Stern:

"Inasmuch as the Cincinnati club was the only team in the American Association to win the year's series from the St. Louis Browns, and your team has just defeated the Browns in the recent series, I now challenge you to one game in Cincinnati for the championship."

Stearns's reply was terse: "Your challenge is rejected."

Baseball fever didn't last. After a mediocre 1888 season, Stearns and co-owner Charles W. Smith found themselves saddled with one of the largest payrolls in the league. So the team that had been paraded through Detroit's streets the year before was auctioned; the players were sold piecemeal for $45,000 and the franchise was removed from the National League.

The next year Detroit dropped into the minor leagues, eventually surfacing in Ban Johnson's revived Western League in 1894. In 1900 the Western League changed its name to the American League, but was still a minor circuit. Stallings, who had left to manage Philadelphia for two seasons, returned to Detroit and tapped some of his old National League connections, recruiting shortstop Kid Elberfeld, outfielders Ducky Holmes and Dick Cooley, catchers Lew McAllister and Jack Ryan, and third baseman Doc Casey. The following winter Johnson declared war on the National League, raiding it for stars like Nap Lajoie, Joe McGinnity, Jesse Burkett, Jimmy Collins, Cy Young, Wilbert Robinson, and Roger Bresnahan. Stallings picked up second baseman Kid Gleason, pitcher Frank Owen, and German-born catcher Fred Buelow. And in 1901, the American League declared itself major. Detroit—along with Chicago, Boston, Philadelphia, Baltimore, Washington, Cleveland, and Milwaukee—was back in the bigs.

MANAGER	W	L	PCT
George Stallings	74	61	.548

POS	Player	B	G	AB	H	2B	3B	HR	HR %	R	RBI	BB	SO	SB	Pinch Hit AB	Pinch Hit H	BA	SA
REGULARS																		
1B	Pop Dillon	L	74	281	81	14	6	1	0.4	40	42	15		14	0	0	.288	.391
2B	Kid Gleason	L	135	547	150	16	12	3	0.5	82	75	41		32	0	0	.274	.364
SS	Kid Elberfeld	R	122	436	135	21	11	3	0.7	76	76	57		24	0	0	.310	.429
3B	Doc Casey	L	128	540	153	16	9	2	0.4	105	46	32		34	1	0	.283	.357
RF	Ducky Holmes	L	131	537	158	28	10	4	0.7	90	62	37		35	0	0	.294	.406
CF	Jimmy Barrett	L	135	542	159	16	9	4	0.7	110	65	76		26	0	0	.293	.378
LF	Doc Nance	R	132	461	129	24	5	3	0.7	72	66	51		9	0	0	.280	.373
C	Fritz Buelow	R	70	231	52	5	5	2	0.9	28	29	11		2	1	0	.225	.316
SUBSTITUTES																		
PS	Joe Yeager		41	125	37	7	1	2	1.6	18	17	4		3	2	0	.296	.416
1B	Davey Crockett		28	102	29	2	2	0	0.0	10	14	6		1	1	0	.284	.343
SS	Harry Lochhead		1	4	2	0	0	0	0.0	2	0	0		0	0	0	.500	.500
UT	Sport McAllister	B	90	306	92	9	4	3	1.0	45	57	15		17	4	2	.301	.386
C1	Al Shaw	R	55	171	46	7	0	1	0.6	20	23	10		2	4	0	.269	.327
PITCHERS																		
P	Roscoe Miller		38	130	27	5	4	0	0.0	14	14	9		2	0	0	.208	.308
P	Ed Siever	L	38	107	18	3	0	0	0.0	12	7	6		1	0	0	.168	.196
P	John Cronin	R	31	85	21	3	2	0	0.0	7	10	4		2	0	0	.247	.329
P	Emil Frisk	L	20	48	15	3	0	1	2.1	10	7	3		0	6	2	.313	.438
P	Frank Owen		9	20	1	1	0	0	0.0	1	1	1		0	0	0	.050	.100
P	Ed High		4	7	0	0	0	0	0.0	0	0	2		1	0	0	.000	.000
	TEAM TOTAL			4680	1305	180	80	29	0.6	742	611	380	0	205	19	4	.279	.370

INDIVIDUAL FIELDING

POS	Player	T	G	PO	A	E	DP	TC/G	FA	POS	Player	T	G	PO	A	E	DP	TC/G	FA
1B	P. Dillon	R	74	777	44	18	57	11.3	.979	OF	J. Barrett	L	135	300	31	21	7	2.6	.940
	D. Crockett		27	317	15	11	20	12.7	.968		D. Nance	R	132	240	20	19	6	2.1	.932
	McAllister	R	28	261	10	16	16	10.3	.944		D. Holmes	R	131	217	18	24	5	2.0	.907
	A. Shaw	R	9	83	3	5	7	10.1	.945		McAllister	R	11	13	0	5	0	1.6	.722
2B	K. Gleason	R	135	334	457	64	67	6.3	.925		E. Frisk	R	2	3	0	1	0	2.0	.750
	J. Yeager	R	1	2	1	0	0	3.0	1.000		J. Cronin	R	1	2	0	0	0	2.0	1.000
SS	K. Elberfeld	R	121	332	411	76	62	6.8	.907		F. Owen	R	1	0	0	1	0	1.0	.000
	A. Shaw	R	1	0	0	0	0	0.0	.000										
	J. Yeager	R	12	18	37	6	8	5.1	.902	C	F. Buelow	R	69	213	84	10	4	4.4	.967
	McAllister	R	3	5	10	2	1	5.7	.882		A. Shaw	R	42	134	46	12	5	4.6	.938
	H. Lochhead	R	1	2	4	1	0	7.0	.857		McAllister	R	35	95	37	15	1	4.2	.898
3B	D. Casey	R	127	133	324	58	25	4.1	.887										
	McAllister	R	10	7	9	4	1	2.0	.800										
	A. Shaw	R	2	0	1	0	0	0.5	1.000										

Detroit joyously celebrated its big-league return. On April 25, the city's long-suffering baseball enthusiasts filled Bennett Park to see their heroes end a 13-year absence from the majors, against Hugh Duffy's Milwaukee Brewers. The 6,000-person capacity stands overflowed; with standees, paid attendance ballooned to 10,023. And many unpaid spectators crashed the coming-out party, eluding Detroit policemen to climb over or sramble under wooden fences. They were nearly disappointed. After falling behind, 7–0, and committing seven errors in the first eight innings, Detroit came to bat in the ninth behind, 13–4. The fans restlessly goaded the players. But the Tigers rallied for 10 runs, and the fans grew more frenzied with each score. They exploded past the restraining ropes when Pop Dillon doubled home Kid Gleason and Doc Casey for the tying and winning runs, then danced on the field for an hour to celebrate the triumphant 14–13 debut.

Little more than a week later in Chicago, the Tigers entered the ninth trailing 5–2, and conjured another last-minute flurry to gain a 7–5 lead. But as the early spring dusk engulfed the South Side Grounds, White Sox manager-pitcher Clark Griffith stalled and hoped the game would be called. Fed up with Griffith's dallying, the umpire awarded the new league's first forfeit to Detroit, 9–0. The White Sox initiated a heated argument, but wisely diverted their energies to help quiet the potentially violent Chicago crowd, some of whom suggested lynching the umpire.

Overall the Tigers finished third, eight-and-a-half games behind the champion White Sox. It was an inaugural year that saw one Detroit regular hit .300 (Kid Elberfeld, .310), one pitcher top 20 victories (Roscoe "Rubberlegs" Miller, 23–13), and the Tigers on the final afternoon of the season edge Connie Mack's Athletics for third place by a half game.

TEAM   STATISTICS

	W	L	PCT	GB	R	OR	Batting 2B	3B	HR	BA	SA	SB	Fielding E	DP	FA	CG	BB	Pitching SO	ShO	SV	ERA
HI	83	53	.610		819	632	173	89	32	.276	.370	280	345	100	.941	110	312	394	11	2	2.98
OS	79	57	.581	4	759	608	183	104	37	.279	.382	157	337	104	.943	123	294	396	7	1	3.04
ET	74	61	.548	8.5	742	696	180	80	29	.279	.370	205	410	127	.930	118	313	307	9	2	3.30
HI	74	62	.544	9	805	760	239	86	35	.288	.394	173	337	93	.942	124	374	350	6	1	4.00
AL	68	65	.511	13.5	761	750	179	111	24	.293	.396	207	401	76	.926	115	344	271	4	3	3.73
AS	61	73	.455	21	683	771	191	83	34	.269	.365	127	323	97	.943	118	284	308	8	1	4.09
LE	55	82	.401	28.5	666	831	197	68	12	.271	.348	125	329	99	.942	122	464	334	7	4	4.12
IL	48	89	.350	35.5	641	828	192	66	26	.261	.345	176	393	106	.934	107	395	376	3	4	4.06
EAGUE TOTAL					5876	5876	1534	687	229	.277	.371	1450	2875	802	.938	937	2780	2736	55	18	3.66

INDIVIDUAL   PITCHING

ITCHER	T	W	L	PCT	ERA	SV	G	GS	CG	IP	H	BB	SO	R	ER	ShO	H/9	BB/9	SO/9
oscoe Miller		23	13	.639	2.95	1	38	36	35	332	339	98	79	168	109	3	9.19	2.66	2.14
d Siever	L	18	15	.545	3.24	0	38	33	30	288.2	334	65	85	166	104	2	10.41	2.03	2.65
ohn Cronin	R	13	15	.464	3.89	0	30	28	21	219.2	261	42	62	145	95	1	10.69	1.72	2.54
e Yeager	R	12	11	.522	2.61	1	26	25	22	199.2	209	46	38	105	58	3	9.42	2.07	1.71
mil Frisk	R	5	4	.556	4.34	0	11	7	6	74.2	94	26	22	60	36	0	11.33	3.13	2.65
ank Owen	R	1	3	.250	4.34	0	8	5	3	56	70	30	17	43	27	0	11.25	4.82	2.73
d High	L	1	0	1.000	3.50	0	4	1	1	18	21	6	4	9	7	0	10.50	3.00	2.00
EAM TOTAL		73	61	.545	3.30	2	155	135	118	1188.2	1328	313	307	696	436	9	10.05	2.37	2.32

MANAGER	W	L	PCT
Frank Dwyer	52	83	.385

POS	Player	B	G	AB	H	2B	3B	HR	HR %	R	RBI	BB	SO	SB	Pinch Hit AB	Pinch Hit H	BA	SA
REGULARS																		
1B	Pop Dillon	L	66	243	50	6	3	0	0.0	21	22	16		2	0	0	.206	.255
2B	Kid Gleason	L	118	441	109	11	4	1	0.2	42	38	25		17	0	0	.247	.297
SS	Kid Elberfeld	R	130	488	127	17	6	1	0.2	70	64	55		19	0	0	.260	.326
3B	Doc Casey	L	132	520	142	18	7	3	0.6	69	55	44		22	0	0	.273	.352
RF	Ducky Holmes	L	92	362	93	15	4	2	0.6	50	33	28		16	0	0	.257	.337
CF	Jimmy Barrett	L	136	509	154	19	6	4	0.8	93	44	74		24	0	0	.303	.387
LF	Dick Harley	L	125	491	138	9	8	2	0.4	59	44	36		20	0	0	.281	.344
C	Deacon McGuire	R	73	229	52	14	1	2	0.9	27	23	24		0	2	0	.227	.323
SUBSTITUTES																		
UT	Sport McAllister	B	66	229	48	5	2	1	0.4	19	32	5		1	5	0	.210	.262
1B	Erve Beck	R	41	162	48	4	0	2	1.2	23	22	4		3	0	0	.296	.358
21	John O'Connell		8	22	4	0	0	0	0.0	1	0	3		0	0	0	.182	.182
UT	Joe Yeager		50	161	39	6	5	1	0.6	17	23	5		0	1	0	.242	.360
O1	Pete LePine	L	30	96	20	3	2	1	1.0	8	19	8		1	2	0	.208	.313
OF	Harry Arndt		10	34	5	0	1	0	0.0	4	7	6		0	0	0	.147	.206
OF	E. Post		3	12	1	0	0	0	0.0	2	2	0		0	0	0	.083	.083
OF	Lou Schiappacasse	R	2	5	0	0	0	0	0.0	0	1	1		0	0	0	.000	.000
C	Fritz Buelow	R	66	224	50	5	2	2	0.9	23	29	9		3	0	0	.223	.290
PITCHERS																		
P	George Mullin	R	40	120	39	4	3	0	0.0	20	11	8		1	2	0	.325	.408
P	Win Mercer		35	100	18	2	0	0	0.0	8	6	6		1	0	0	.180	.200
P	Ed Siever	L	25	66	10	1	0	0	0.0	3	6	1		0	0	0	.152	.167
P	Roscoe Miller		20	60	11	1	1	0	0.0	2	6	0		0	0	0	.183	.233
P	Arch McCarthy		10	28	2	0	0	0	0.0	2	1	1		0	0	0	.071	.071
P	Rube Kisinger	R	5	19	3	1	0	0	0.0	1	0	0		0	0	0	.158	.211
P	Wish Egan	R	3	8	2	0	0	0	0.0	1	0	0		0	0	0	.250	.250
P	John Cronin	R	4	7	0	0	0	0	0.0	0	0	0		0	0	0	.000	.000
P	Sam McMackin		1	4	2	0	0	0	0.0	1	0	0		0	0	0	.500	.500
P	John Terry		1	2	0	0	0	0	0.0	0	0	0		0	0	0	.000	.000
P	Ed Fisher	R	1	2	0	0	0	0	0.0	0	0	0	0	0	0	0	.000	.000
	TEAM TOTAL			4644	1167	141	55	22	0.5	566	488	359	0	130	12	0	.251	.320

INDIVIDUAL FIELDING

POS	Player	T	G	PO	A	E	DP	TC/G	FA
1B	P. Dillon	R	66	709	52	19	45	11.8	.976
	E. Beck	R	36	343	26	11	24	10.6	.971
	McAllister	R	26	237	14	2	13	9.7	.992
	P. LePine	L	8	59	7	3	5	8.6	.957
	J. O'Connell		2	23	0	0	1	11.5	1.000
	F. Buelow	R	2	16	0	0	2	8.0	1.000
	H. Arndt	R	1	1	1	0	0	2.0	1.000
2B	K. Gleason	R	118	320	349	42	66	6.0	.941
	J. Yeager	R	12	16	30	2	1	4.0	.958
	J. O'Connell		6	14	20	3	2	6.2	.919
	McAllister	R	3	3	7	3	1	4.3	.769
SS	K. Elberfeld	R	130	326	459	67	63	6.6	.921
	McAllister	R	6	14	19	5	2	6.3	.868
	J. Yeager	R	3	4	10	2	1	5.3	.875
3B	D. Casey	R	132	174	309	51	17	4.0	.904
	McAllister	R	6	1	14	2	1	2.8	.882
	J. Yeager	R	1	2	1	1	0	4.0	.750

POS	Player	T	G	PO	A	E	DP	TC/G	FA
OF	J. Barrett	L	136	**326**	22	14	6	2.7	.961
	D. Harley	R	125	238	15	19	1	2.2	.930
	D. Holmes	R	92	155	16	9	5	2.0	.950
	P. LePine	L	19	18	2	0	1	1.1	1.000
	J. Yeager	R	13	23	1	1	0	1.9	.960
	H. Arndt	R	10	23	0	1	0	2.4	.958
	McAllister	R	12	21	1	0	1	1.8	1.000
	E. Beck	R	5	5	1	1	0	1.4	.857
	E. Post		3	4	0	1	0	1.7	.800
	G. Mullin	R	4	4	0	0	0	1.0	1.000
	Schiappacasse	R	2	0	0	1	0	0.5	.000
C	D. McGuire	R	70	210	65	14	6	4.1	.952
	F. Buelow	R	63	174	81	**20**	5	4.4	.927
	McAllister	R	9	25	12	2	1	4.3	.949

While the rest of the American League continued to raid the senior circuit for players, the Tigers dipped into the National League talent pool and came up with an umpire for their new manager. Detroit in its second season acquired a new field leader in Frank Dwyer and a new owner in Samuel Angus, and plummeted to seventh place, 30 1/2 games out of first, just 3 1/2 out of last.

Dwyer arrived touted as a pitching expert. But no one on his Tiger staff won more than they lost. And only Ed Siever, with a league-best 1.91 ERA (which still only helped him to an 8–11 record) and "Wabash George" Mullin (13–16) distinguished themselves. Mullin, who signed on with the Tigers over the winter, would prove a worthy acquisition, going on to win 20 games five times for Detroit, including a record of 29–8 in 1909.

The hitting, or lack of it, didn't help. Only outfielder Jimmy Barrett hit .300 (.303) while first baseman Pop Dillon's average plunged 82 points, shortstop Kid Elberfeld's 48 points, and outfielder Ducky Holmes's 37 points from the previous year. By mid-season the Tigers began to vent their frustrations upon umpires. One July weekend against Washington, Dillon was ejected on Friday, Elberfeld on Saturday, and outfielder Dick Harley on Sunday.

After the season mercifully ended, Dwyer was fired. But even in the off-season, the Tigers weren't crisis-free. The team that had slipped in the standings nearly slipped out of town. Winter rumors of a Tigers move to Pittsburgh stayed strong until provisions of the January 1903 AL-NL peace treaty mandated that the American League stay out of the Steel City.

TEAM STATISTICS

	W	L	PCT	GB	R	OR	Batting					SB	Fielding			CG	BB	Pitching			
							2B	3B	HR	BA	SA		E	DP	FA			SO	ShO	SV	ERA
PHI	83	53	.610		775	636	235	67	38	.287	.389	201	270	75	.953	114	368	455	5	2	3.29
TL	78	58	.574	5	619	607	208	61	29	.265	.353	137	274	122	.953	120	343	348	8	2	3.34
OS	77	60	.562	6.5	664	600	195	95	42	.278	.383	132	263	101	.955	123	326	431	6	1	3.02
HI	74	60	.552	8	675	602	170	50	14	.268	.335	265	257	125	.955	130	312	300	2	1	3.41
LE	69	67	.507	14	686	667	248	68	33	.289	.389	140	287	96	.950	116	411	361	16	3	3.28
AS	61	75	.449	22	709	790	261	66	48	.283	.396	121	316	70	.945	116	331	346	11	0	4.36
ET	52	83	.385	30.5	566	657	141	55	22	.251	.320	130	332	111	.943	116	370	245	9	3	3.56
AL	50	88	.362	34	715	850	202	107	33	.277	.385	189	357	109	.938	119	354	258	3	1	4.33
EAGUE TOTAL					5409	5409	1660	569	259	.275	.369	1315	2356	809	.949	954	2815	2744	60	13	3.57

INDIVIDUAL PITCHING

PITCHER	T	W	L	PCT	ERA	SV	G	GS	CG	IP	H	BB	SO	R	ER	ShO	H/9	BB/9	SO/9
in Mercer	R	15	18	.455	3.04	1	35	33	28	281.2	282	80	40	129	95	4	9.01	2.56	1.28
George Mullin	R	13	16	.448	3.67	0	35	30	25	260	282	95	78	155	106	0	9.76	3.29	2.70
d Siever	L	8	11	.421	1.91	1	25	23	17	188.1	166	32	36	73	40	4	7.93	1.53	1.72
oscoe Miller		6	12	.333	3.69	1	20	18	15	148.2	158	57	39	85	61	1	9.57	3.45	2.36
oe Yeager	R	6	12	.333	4.82	0	19	15	14	140	171	41	28	90	75	0	10.99	2.64	1.80
rch McCarthy		2	7	.222	6.13	0	10	8	8	72	90	31	10	57	49	0	11.25	3.88	1.25
ube Kisinger	R	2	3	.400	3.12	0	5	5	5	43.1	48	14	7	20	15	0	9.97	2.91	1.45
ish Egan	R	0	2	.000	2.86	0	3	3	2	22	23	6	0	12	7	0	9.41	2.45	0.00
ohn Cronin	R	0	0	—	9.35	0	4	0	0	17.1	26	8	5	23	18	0	13.50	4.15	2.60
am McMackin		0	1	.000	3.24	0	1	1	1	8.1	9	4	2	5	3	0	9.72	4.32	2.16
ohn Terry		0	1	.000	3.60	0	1	1	1	5	8	1	0	3	2	0	14.40	1.80	0.00
d Fisher	R	0	0	—	0.00	0	1	0	0	4	4	1	0	0	0	0	9.00	2.25	0.00
EAM TOTAL		52	83	.385	3.56	3	159	137	116	1190.2	1267	370	245	652	471	9	9.58	2.80	1.85

MANAGER	W	L	PCT
Ed Barrow	65	71	.478

POS	Player	B	G	AB	H	2B	3B	HR	HR %	R	RBI	BB	SO	SB	Pinch Hit AB	Pinch Hit H	BA	SA
REGULARS																		
1B	Charlie Carr	R	135	548	154	23	11	2	0.4	59	79	10		10	0	0	.281	.374
2B	Heinie Smith	R	93	336	75	11	3	1	0.3	36	22	19		12	0	0	.223	.283
SS	Sport McAllister	B	78	265	69	8	2	0	0.0	31	22	10		5	5	1	.260	.306
3B	Joe Yeager		109	402	103	15	6	0	0.0	36	43	18		9	0	0	.256	.323
RF	Sam Crawford	L	137	550	184	23	25	4	0.7	88	89	25		18	0	0	.335	.489
CF	Jimmy Barrett	L	136	517	163	13	10	2	0.4	95	31	74		27	0	0	.315	.391
LF	Billy Lush	B	119	423	116	18	14	1	0.2	71	33	70		14	1	0	.274	.390
C	Deacon McGuire	R	72	248	62	12	1	0	0.0	15	21	19		3	2	0	.250	.306
SUBSTITUTES																		
S2	Herman Long	L	69	239	53	12	0	0	0.0	21	23	10		11	1	1	.222	.272
SS	Kid Elberfeld	R	35	132	45	5	3	0	0.0	29	19	11		6	0	0	.341	.424
3S	Ernie Courtney	L	23	74	17	0	0	0	0.0	7	6	5		1	1	0	.230	.230
2B	John Burns	R	11	37	10	0	0	0	0.0	2	3	1		0	0	0	.270	.270
SS	Soldier Boy Murphy		5	22	4	1	0	0	0.0	1	1	0		0	0	0	.182	.227
SS	Simon Nicholls	L	2	8	3	0	0	0	0.0	0	0	0		0	0	0	.375	.375
3B	Willie Greene		1	3	0	0	0	0	0.0	0	0	0		0	0	0	.000	.000
OF	Doc Gessler	L	29	105	25	5	4	0	0.0	9	12	3		1	1	0	.238	.362
C	Fritz Buelow	R	63	192	41	3	6	1	0.5	24	13	6		4	0	0	.214	.307
PITCHERS																		
P	George Mullin	R	46	126	35	9	1	1	0.8	11	12	2		1	4	1	.278	.389
P	Wild Bill Donovan	R	40	124	30	3	2	0	0.0	11	12	4		3	2	0	.242	.298
P	Frank Kitson	L	36	116	21	0	2	0	0.0	12	4	2		2	0	0	.181	.216
P	Rube Kisinger	R	16	47	6	0	0	0	0.0	4	1	1		1	0	0	.128	.128
P	John Deering		10	24	8	1	1	0	0.0	4	3	0		0	0	0	.333	.458
P	Mal Eason		7	20	2	0	0	0	0.0*	0	0	0		0	0	0	.100	.100
P	John Skopec	L	6	13	2	0	0	0	0.0	0	1	1		0	0	0	.154	.154
P	Harry Kane	L	3	7	1	0	0	0	0.0	0	1	1		0	0	0	.143	.143
P	Alex Jones		2	4	0	0	0	0	0.0	1	0	0		0	0	0	.000	.000
	TEAM TOTAL			4582	1229	162	91	12	0.3	567	451	292	0	128	17	3	.268	.351

INDIVIDUAL FIELDING

POS	Player	T	G	PO	A	E	DP	TC/G	FA	POS	Player	T	G	PO	A	E	DP	TC/G	FA
1B	C. Carr	R	135	1276	111	25	60	10.5	.982	OF	J. Barrett	L	136	303	19	15	7	2.5	.955
	F. Buelow	R	2	24	1	0	1	12.5	1.000		B. Lush	R	101	227	17	8	4	2.5	.968
	McAllister	R	1	3	0	0	0	3.0	1.000		S. Crawford	L	137	225	16	10	3	1.8	.960
	D. McGuire	R	1	1	0	1	0	2.0	.500		D. Gessler	R	28	36	1	1	1	1.4	.974
											G. Mullin	R	1	0	0	0	0	0.0	.000
2B	H. Smith	R	93	200	267	36	30	5.4	.928		F. Kitson	R	5	6	0	0	0	1.2	1.000
	H. Long	R	31	71	91	5	6	5.4	.970		W. Donovan	R	1	1	2	0	0	3.0	1.000
	J. Burns	R	11	19	33	1	5	4.8	.981		McAllister	R	5	2	0	1	0	0.6	.667
	B. Lush	R	3	9	3	2	1	4.7	.857										
	W. Donovan	R	1	0	1	0	0	1.0	1.000	C	D. McGuire	R	69	330	73	17	9	6.1	.960
											F. Buelow	R	60	254	66	13	6	5.6	.961
SS	McAllister	R	46	77	129	26	12	5.0	.888		McAllister	R	18	85	32	3	2	6.7	.975
	H. Long	R	38	90	107	27	12	5.9	.879										
	K. Elberfeld	R	34	73	119	14	11	6.1*	.932										
	E. Courtney	R	9	11	30	3	1	4.9	.932										
	S. Murphy		5	7	16	4	1	5.4	.852										
	B. Lush	R	3	6	6	3	1	5.0	.800										
	S. Nicholls	R	2	3	3	4	0	5.0	.600										
	J. Yeager	R	1	1	7	1	1	9.0	.889										
	W. Donovan	R	2	0	3	2	1	2.5	.600										
3B	J. Yeager	R	107	126	176	26	9	3.1	.921										
	B. Lush	R	12	15	17	2	0	2.8	.941										
	E. Courtney	R	13	17	13	2	1	2.5	.938										
	McAllister	R	4	3	8	3	0	3.5	.786										
	W. Greene		1	3	0	1	0	4.0	.750										
	K. Elberfeld	R	1	1	0	0	0	1.0	1.000										

The year started with an eerie twist. Pitcher Win Mercer was promoted to player-manager, but killed himself before the start of spring training. His suicide in a San Francisco hotel was ascribed to women or gambling or both, not an aversion to piloting the '03 Tigers. The job then went to Ed Barrow, future builder of the New York Yankee empire. He was then 35, feisty and apt to challenge recalcitrant players to clubhouse fistfights. Barrow took over a team with seven new regulars and forged a season of modest improvement.

The Tigers began strongly, were in first place May 1, and a close second on May 26. Two of Barrow's top performers were defectors from the National League: pitcher Wild Bill Donovan, who jumped from Brooklyn, and power-hitting rightfielder Sam Crawford, who abandoned Cincinnati to become a Detroit fixture for 15 seasons en route to the Hall of Fame. Donovan compiled a 17–16, 2.29 year; George Mullin finished 19–15, 2.25; and Crawford hit a then-team record .335. But the Tigers nevertheless lapsed into a June swoon, falling to sixth place. The nosedive commenced when Kid Elberfeld was traded to the Highlanders for the over-the-hill shortstop Herman Long and mediocre third baseman Ernie Courtney—a deal engineered by league president Ban Johnson to strengthen New York. "I was furious," said Barrow. "With Elberfeld out, we started to skid before the month was out."

A minor resurgence followed the skid, the Tigers moving up to fourth. But they finished fifth, six games below .500, 25 games out of first.

TEAM STATISTICS

	W	L	PCT	GB	R	OR	2B	3B	HR	BA	SA	SB	E	DP	FA	CG	BB	SO	ShO	SV	ERA
								Batting						**Fielding**				**Pitching**			
OS	91	47	.659		707	505	222	113	48	.272	.392	141	239	86	.959	123	269	579	20	4	2.57
HI	75	60	.556	14.5	597	519	228	68	31	.264	.362	157	217	66	.960	112	315	728	10	1	2.97
LE	77	63	.550	15	639	578	230	95	31	.270	.378	176	322	99	.946	125	271	521	20	1	2.66
NY	72	62	.537	17	579	573	193	62	18	.250	.331	160	264	87	.953	111	245	463	8	2	3.08
DET	65	71	.478	25	567	539	162	91	12	.268	.351	128	281	82	.950	123	336	554	15	2	2.75
STL	65	74	.468	26.5	500	525	166	78	12	.242	.319	101	268	94	.953	124	237	511	12	4	2.77
CHI	60	77	.438	30.5	516	613	176	49	14	.247	.314	180	297	85	.949	114	287	391	9	4	3.02
WAS	43	94	.314	47.5	438	691	172	72	18	.231	.311	131	260	86	.954	122	306	452	6	2	3.82
LEAGUE TOTAL					4543	4543	1549	628	184	.256	.345	1174	2148	685	.953	954	2266	4199	100	20	2.95

INDIVIDUAL PITCHING

PITCHER	T	W	L	PCT	ERA	SV	G	GS	CG	IP	H	BB	SO	R	ER	ShO	H/9	BB/9	SO/9
George Mullin	R	19	15	.559	2.25	2	41	36	31	320.2	284	106	170	128	80	6	7.97	2.98	4.77
Wild Bill Donovan	R	17	16	.515	2.29	0	35	34	34	307	247	95	187	104	78	4	7.24	2.79	5.48
Frank Kitson	R	15	16	.484	2.58	0	31	28	28	257.2	277	38	102	112	74	2	9.68	1.33	3.56
Rube Kisinger	R	7	9	.438	2.96	0	16	14	13	118.2	118	27	33	58	39	2	8.95	2.05	2.50
John Deering	R	3	4	.429	3.86	0	10	8	5	60.2	77	24	14	38	26	0	11.42	3.56	2.08
Mal Eason	R	2	5	.286	3.36	0	7	6	6	56.1	60	19	21	33	21	1	9.59	3.04	3.36
John Skopec	L	2	2	.500	3.43	0	6	5	3	39.1	46	13	14	22	15	0	10.53	2.97	3.20
Harry Kane	L	0	2	.000	8.50	0	3	3	2	18	26	8	10	22	17	0	13.00	4.00	5.00
Joe Yeager	R	0	1	.000	4.00	0	1	1	1	9	15	0	1	7	4	0	15.00	0.00	1.00
Alex Jones	L	0	1	.000	12.46	0	2	2	0	8.2	19	6	2	15	12	0	19.73	6.23	2.08
TEAM TOTAL		65	71	.478	2.75	2	152	137	123	1196	1169	336	554	539	366	15	8.80	2.53	4.17

MANAGER	W	L	PCT
Ed Barrow	32	46	.410
Bobby Lowe	30	44	.405

POS	Player	B	G	AB	H	2B	3B	HR	HR %	R	RBI	BB	SO	SB	Pinch Hit AB	Pinch Hit H	BA	SA
REGULARS																		
1B	Charlie Carr	R	92	360	77	13	3	0	0.0	29	40	14		6	0	0	.214	.267
2B	Bobby Lowe	R	140	506	105	14	6	0	0.0	47	40	17		15	0	0	.208	.259
SS	Charley O'Leary	R	135	456	97	10	3	1	0.2	39	16	21		9	0	0	.213	.254
3B	Ed Gremminger	R	83	309	66	13	3	1	0.3	18	28	14		3	0	0	.214	.285
RF	Sam Crawford	L	150	571	143	21	17	2	0.4	49	73	44		20	0	0	.250	.357
CF	Jimmy Barrett	L	162	624	167	10	5	0	0.0	83	31	79		15	0	0	.268	.300
LF	Matty McIntyre	L	152	578	146	11	10	2	0.3	74	46	44		11	0	0	.253	.317
C	Lew Drill	R	51	160	39	6	1	0	0.0	7	13	20		2	0	0	.244	.294
SUBSTITUTES																		
UT	Rabbit Robinson	R	101	320	77	13	6	0	0.0	30	37	29		14	5	1	.241	.319
3B	Bill Coughlin	R	56	206	47	6	0	0	0.0	22	17	5		1	0	0	.228	.257
1B	Piano Legs Hickman	R	42	144	35	6	6	2	1.4	18	22	11		3	1	1	.243	.410
P1	Wild Bill Donovan	R	46	140	38	2	1	1	0.7	12	6	3		2	2	1	.271	.321
2B	John Burns	R	4	16	2	0	0	0	0.0	3	1	1		1	0	0	.125	.125
OF	Frank Huelsman	R	4	18	6	1	0	0	0.0	1	4	1		1	0	0	.333	.389
C	Bob Wood	R	49	175	43	6	2	1	0.6	15	17	5		1	2	0	.246	.320
C1	Monte Beville	L	54	174	36	5	1	0	0.0	14	13	8		2	2	0	.207	.247
C	Fritz Buelow	R	42	136	15	1	1	0	0.0	6	5	8		2	0	0	.110	.132
C	Frank McManus		1	0	0	0	0	0	—	0	0	0		0	0	0	—	—
PITCHERS																		
P	George Mullin	R	53	151	45	11	2	0	0.0	14	8	10		1	6	2	.298	.397
P	Ed Killian	L	40	126	18	4	2	0	0.0	8	6	5		1	0	0	.143	.206
P	Frank Kitson	L	27	72	15	0	0	1	1.4	9	4	1		0	1	0	.208	.250
P	Jesse Stovall	L	25	56	11	0	1	0	0.0	5	2	3		2	0	0	.196	.232
P	Charlie Jaeger		8	17	1	0	0	0	0.0	0	0	1		0	0	0	.059	.059
P	Cy Ferry	R	3	6	2	1	0	0	0.0	2	2	0		0	0	0	.333	.500
P	Bugs Raymond	R	5	5	0	0	0	0	0.0	0	0	0		0	0	0	.000	.000
TEAM TOTAL				5326	1231	154	70	11	0.2	505	431	344	0	112	19	5	.231	.293

INDIVIDUAL FIELDING

POS	Player	T	G	PO	A	E	DP	TC/G	FA
1B	C. Carr	R	92	901	99*	17	46	11.1	.983
	P. Hickman	R	39	396	23	13	18	11.1	.970
	M. Beville	R	24	225	14	9	9	10.3	.964
	W. Donovan	R	8	52	0	1	1	6.6	.981
	L. Drill	R	2	14	0	0	1	7.0	1.000
	J. Stovall	R	3	7	1	2	0	3.3	.800
2B	B. Lowe	R	140	328	402	27	44	5.4	.964
	R. Robinson	R	19	43	68	1	6	5.9	.991
	J. Burns	R	4	11	9	1	1	5.3	.952
SS	C. O'Leary	R	135	308	439	54	48	5.9	.933
	R. Robinson	R	30	54	94	12	7	5.3	.925
3B	E. Gremminger	R	83	103	123	12	3	2.9	.950
	B. Coughlin	R	56	53	104	12	2	3.0	.929
	R. Robinson	R	26	23	51	9	4	3.2	.892

POS	Player	T	G	PO	A	E	DP	TC/G	FA
OF	J. Barrett	L	162	339	29	11	6	2.3	.971
	M. McIntyre	L	152	334	16	15	4	2.4	.959
	S. Crawford	L	150	230	18	7	8	1.7	.973
	R. Robinson	R	20	31	3	0	0	1.7	1.000
	G. Mullin	R	2	0	0	0	0	0.0	.000
	F. Huelsman	R	4	5	0	0	0	1.3	1.000
	W. Donovan	R	1	0	0	2	0	2.0	.000
C	B. Wood	R	47	232	69	8	5	6.6	.974
	L. Drill	R	49	195	51	13*	6*	5.3	.950
	F. Buelow	R	42	179	52	6	1	5.6	.975
	M. Beville	R	30	129	27	7	2	5.4	.957
	F. McManus	R	1	0	0	0	0	0.0	.000

The winter again brought changes. William H. Yawkey bought out Sam Angus for $60,000. Frank Navin, a poker-faced bookkeeper who would later serve 28 years as team president, joined the franchise as business manager. Navin held Yawkey's ear and helped block a number of deals engineered by Barrow. Barrow nevertheless worked to build the coming pennant winners by securing Charley O'Leary at shortstop, Matty McIntyre in left field, and Rowdy Bill Coughlin at third. He also arranged for second baseman Herman "Germany" Schaefer to join the team in 1905.

O'Leary, who with second-base partner Schaefer would later make an unsuccessful foray into vaudeville, played shortstop with exceptional fervor. Against the White Sox one afternoon, he tagged out Chicago player-manager Fielder Jones in a close play at second. Jones protested, claiming O'Leary never touched him. On an almost identical play later, O'Leary knocked Jones cold, then commented to the umpire, "I guess this time there's no doubt I tagged him."

That was a rare instance of Tiger slugging that season. Centerfielder Jimmy Barrett led the team at .268 as Sam Crawford's average dived 85 points to .250. No wonder three Tiger pitchers compiled ERAs near 2.50 but still suffered 59 losses among them. George Mullin's 2.40 ERA earned him just a 17–23 mark (the 23 losses are still a Tiger record, as are his 382.1 innings and 42 complete games).

Navin's meddling increasingly annoyed Barrow, who finally quit in August. The club was in seventh place and stayed there under player-manager Bobby Lowe, finishing 32 games behind the defending champion Red Sox. In all it was a year during which Detroit's most notable on-field accomplishment came from its participation in a major-league record 10 ties.

TEAM STATISTICS

	W	L	PCT	GB	R	OR	Batting 2B	3B	HR	BA	SA	SB	Fielding E	DP	FA	CG	BB	Pitching SO	ShO	SV	ERA
BOS	95	59	.617		608	466	194	105	26	.247	.340	101	242	83	.962	148	233	612	21	1	2.12
NY	92	59	.609	1.5	598	526	195	91	27	.259	.347	163	275	90	.958	123	311	684	15	1	2.57
CHI	89	65	.578	6	600	482	193	68	14	.242	.316	216	238	95	.964	134	303	550	26	3	2.30
CLE	86	65	.570	7.5	647	482	225	90	26	.262	.356	189	255	86	.959	141	285	627	20	0	2.22
PHI	81	70	.536	12.5	557	503	197	77	31	.249	.336	137	250	67	.959	137	366	887	26	0	2.35
STL	65	87	.428	29	481	604	153	53	10	.239	.293	150	267	78	.960	135	333	577	13	1	2.83
DET	62	90	.408	32	505	627	154	70	11	.231	.293	112	273	92	.959	143	433	556	15	2	2.77
WAS	38	113	.252	55.5	437	743	171	57	10	.227	.288	150	314	97	.951	137	347	533	8	4	3.62
LEAGUE TOTAL					4433	4433	1482	611	155	.245	.321	1218	2114	688	.959	1098	2611	5026	144	12	2.60

INDIVIDUAL PITCHING

PITCHER	T	W	L	PCT	ERA	SV	G	GS	CG	IP	H	BB	SO	R	ER	ShO	H/9	BB/9	SO/9
George Mullin	R	17	23	.425	2.40	0	45	44	42	382.1	345	131	161	154	102	7	8.12	3.08	3.79
Ed Killian	L	14	20	.412	2.44	1	40	34	32	331.2	293	93	124	118	90	4	7.95	2.52	3.36
Wild Bill Donovan	R	17	16	.515	2.46	0	34	34	30	293	251	94	137	111	80	3	7.71	2.89	4.21
Frank Kitson	R	8	13	.381	3.07	1	26	24	19	199.2	211	38	69	100	68	0	9.51	1.71	3.11
Jesse Stovall	R	3	13	.188	4.42	0	22	17	13	146.2	170	45	41	97	72	1	10.43	2.76	2.52
Charlie Jaeger		3	3	.500	2.57	0	8	6	5	49	49	15	13	29	14	0	9.00	2.76	2.39
Bugs Raymond	R	0	1	.000	3.07	0	5	2	1	14.2	14	6	7	9	5	0	8.59	3.68	4.30
Cy Ferry	R	0	1	.000	6.23	0	3	1	1	13	12	11	4	9	9	0	8.31	7.62	2.77
TEAM TOTAL		62	90	.408	2.77	2	183	162	143	1430	1345	433	556	627	440	15	8.47	2.73	3.50

MANAGER	W	L	PCT
Bill Armour	79	74	.516

POS	Player	B	G	AB	H	2B	3B	HR	HR %	R	RBI	BB	SO	SB	Pinch Hit AB	H	BA	SA
REGULARS																		
1B	Pinky Lindsay		88	329	88	14	1	0	0.0	38	31	18		10	0	0	.267	.316
2B	Germany Schaefer	R	153	554	135	17	9	2	0.4	64	47	45		19	0	0	.244	.318
SS	Charley O'Leary	R	148	512	109	13	1	1	0.2	47	33	29		13	0	0	.213	.248
3B	Bill Coughlin	R	138	489	123	20	6	0	0.0	48	44	34		16	1	0	.252	.317
RF	Sam Crawford	L	154	575	171	40	10	6	1.0	73	75	50		22	0	0	.297	.433
CF	Duff Cooley	L	99	377	93	11	9	1	0.3	25	32	26		7	1	1	.247	.332
LF	Matty McIntyre	L	131	495	130	21	5	0	0.0	59	30	48		9	0	0	.263	.325
C	Lew Drill	R	71	211	55	9	0	0	0.0	17	24	32		7	1	0	.261	.303
SUBSTITUTES																		
P1	John Eubank	L	6	11	4	0	1	0	0.0	1	1	0		0	0	0	.364	.545
O1	Piano Legs Hickman	R	59	213	47	12	3	2	0.9	21	20	12		3	0	0	.221	.333
UT	Bobby Lowe	R	60	181	35	7	2	0	0.0	17	9	13		3	2	0	.193	.254
OF	Ty Cobb	L	41	150	36	6	0	1	0.7	19	15	10		2	0	0	.240	.300
PO	Wild Bill Donovan	R	46	130	25	4	0	0	0.0	16	5	12		8	0	0	.192	.223
OF	Jimmy Barrett	L	20	67	17	1	0	0	0.0	2	3	6		0	2	0	.254	.269
C	Jack Warner	L	36	119	24	2	3	0	0.0	12	7	8		2	0	0	.202	.269
C	Tom Doran		34	94	15	3	0	0	0.0	8	4	8		2	2	1	.160	.191
C	John Sullivan		12	31	5	0	0	0	0.0	4	4	4		0	0	0	.161	.161
C	Bob Wood	R	8	24	2	1	0	0	0.0	1	0	1		0	1	0	.083	.125
C	Nig Clarke	B	3	7	3	0	0	1	14.3	1	1	0		0	1	0	.429	.857
PITCHERS																		
P	George Mullin	R	47	135	35	4	0	0	0.0	15	12	12		4	2	0	.259	.289
P	Ed Killian	L	39	118	32	3	4	0	0.0	12	19	2		2	0	0	.271	.364
P	Frank Kitson	L	33	87	16	2	0	0	0.0	8	4	3		0	0	0	.184	.207
P	George Disch		8	19	2	0	0	0	0.0	0	0	0		0	0	0	.105	.105
P	Jimmy Wiggs	B	7	15	2	0	0	0	0.0	1	1	0		0	0	0	.133	.133
P	Gene Ford	R	7	10	0	0	0	0	0.0	0	0	2		0	0	0	.000	.000
P	Eddie Cicotte	B	3	7	3	0	0	0	0.0	1	0	0		0	0	0	.429	.429
P	Charlie Jackson		2	4	1	0	0	0	0.0	1	0	0		0	0	0	.250	.250
P	Frosty Thomas	R	2	2	0	0	0	0	0.0	0	0	0		0	0	0	.000	.000
P	Andy Bruckmiller	R	1	1	0	0	0	0	0.0	0	0	0		0	0	0	.000	.000
P	Walt Justis	R	1	0	0	0	0	0	–	0	0	0		0	0	0	–	–
TEAM TOTAL				4967	1208	190	54	14	0.3	511	421	375	0	129	13	2	.243	.312

INDIVIDUAL FIELDING

POS	Player	T	G	PO	A	E	DP	TC/G	FA		POS	Player	T	G	PO	A	E	DP	TC/G	FA
1B	P. Lindsay		88	761	57	18	40	9.5	.978		OF	M. McIntyre	L	131	286	18	10	6	2.4	.968
	S. Crawford	L	51	478	41	11	22	10.4	.979			D. Cooley	R	97	223	12	10	5	2.5	.959
	P. Hickman	R	12	103	8	5	4	9.7	.957			S. Crawford	L	103	152	18	2	3	1.7	**.988**
	B. Lowe	R	1	9	0	0	0	9.0	1.000			T. Cobb	R	41	85	6	4	1	2.3	.958
	J. Eubank	R	1	2	1	0	0	3.0	1.000			P. Hickman	R	47	72	7	5	3	1.8	.940
												B. Lowe	R	25	42	5	1	0	1.9	.979
2B	G. Schaefer	R	151	**403**	389	37	35	5.5	.955			J. Barrett	L	18	29	0	0	0	1.6	1.000
	B. Lowe	R	6	17	8	1	0	4.3	.962			W. Donovan	R	8	10	4	0	0	1.8	1.000
	W. Donovan	R	2	2	2	1	0	2.5	.800		C	L. Drill	R	70	345	73	13	10	6.2	.970
SS	C. O'Leary	R	148	358	411	55	40	5.6	.933			J. Warner	R	36	185	40	6	2	6.4	.974
	B. Lowe	R	4	9	5	1	0	3.8	.933			T. Doran	L	32	123	33	6	0	5.1	.963
	G. Schaefer	R	3	7	5	0	0	4.0	1.000			J. Sullivan	R	12	56	21	2	0	6.6	.975
3B	B. Coughlin	R	137	137	255	37	12	3.1	.914			B. Wood	R	7	26	13	5	0	6.3	.886
	B. Lowe	R	22	16	36	1	1	2.4	.981			N. Clarke	R	2	11	3	0	0	7.0	1.000

The year brought to Detroit yet another new manager, an improved ballclub, and an 18-year-old outfielder eventually known as the Player of the Century.

Former Cleveland manager Bill Armour became the Tigers' fifth manager in five seasons and led the club over the .500 mark (79–74) to a third-place finish, 15 1/2 games out. Detroit was in the first division virtually throughout the year. There was more good news: outfielder Sam Crawford hit .297, and the pitching staff for the the the first time produced two 20-game winners—Ed Killian at 23–14 and George Mullin at 21–21. But the best came in August.

That spring the Tigers had trained in Augusta, Georgia. To compensate the local minor league club for use of its facilities, the Tigers gave them young Detroit-born pitcher Ed Cicotte, later a central figure in the Black Sox scandal. In return the Tigers were granted first pick among Augusta players later in the season. Detroit cashed in on that when Armour, his team suffering injuries in the outfield, returned to Georgia in midsummer to look at "that crazy kid we saw last spring." The crazy kid was out with a spiked thumb, but on the advice of scout Heinie Youngman, Armour still purchased the lefthand-hitting outfielder for $750.

The newest Tiger debuted on August 30 against New York at Detroit's Bennett Field. He drove in two runs in the first inning when he cracked one of Jack Chesbro's spitballs for a double. His average was an unremarkable .240, but his baseball philosophy had already fully blossomed. "Baseball is a red-blooded game for red-blooded men," the rookie declared. "Baseball is like war. It's no pink tea. Mollycoddles had better stay out. It's a struggle for supremacy. A survival of the fittest."

Thus was Ty Cobb a Tiger.

TEAM STATISTICS

	W	L	PCT	GB	R	OR	2B	3B	HR	BA	SA	SB	E	DP	FA	CG	BB	SO	ShO	SV	ERA
HI	92	56	.622		**617**	486	**256**	51	24	.255	**.339**	189	264	64	.958	117	409	**895**	**20**	0	2.19
HI	92	60	.605	2	613	**443**	200	55	11	.237	.304	194	**217**	**95**	**.968**	131	329	613	17	0	**1.99**
ET	79	74	.516	15.5	511	608	190	54	14	.243	.312	129	265	80	.957	124	474	578	17	1	2.83
OS	78	74	.513	16	583	557	165	69	**29**	.234	.311	131	294	75	.953	125	**292**	652	15	1	2.84
LE	76	78	.494	19	559	582	211	**72**	18	**.255**	.335	188	229	84	.963	**139**	334	555	16	0	2.85
Y	71	78	.477	21.5	587	644	163	61	23	.248	.319	**200**	293	88	.952	88	396	642	19	**7**	2.93
AS	64	87	.424	29.5	560	613	193	68	22	.223	.302	169	318	76	.951	118	385	539	11	3	2.87
TL	54	99	.353	40.5	509	606	153	49	16	.232	.289	130	295	78	.955	133	389	633	11	2	2.74
AGUE TOTAL					4539	4539	1531	479	157	.241	.314	1330	2175	640	.957	975	3008	5107	126	14	2.65

INDIVIDUAL PITCHING

PITCHER	T	W	L	PCT	ERA	SV	G	GS	CG	IP	H	BB	SO	R	ER	ShO	H/9	BB/9	SO/9
eorge Mullin	R	21	21	.500	2.51	0	44	41	35	**347.2**	303	**138**	168	149	97	1	7.84	3.57	4.35
d Killian	L	23	14	.622	2.27	0	39	37	33	313.1	263	102	110	108	79	8	7.55	2.93	3.16
ild Bill Donovan	R	18	15	.545	2.60	0	34	32	27	280.2	236	101	135	111	81	5	7.57	3.24	4.33
ank Kitson	R	12	14	.462	3.47	1	33	27	21	225.2	230	57	78	120	87	3	9.17	2.27	3.11
eorge Disch		0	2	.000	2.64	0	8	3	1	47.2	43	8	14	19	14	0	8.12	1.51	2.64
mmy Wiggs	R	3	3	.500	3.27	0	7	7	4	41.1	30	29	37	25	15	0	6.53	6.31	8.06
ene Ford	R	0	1	.000	5.66	0	7	1	1	35	51	14	20	30	22	0	13.11	3.60	5.14
ddie Cicotte	R	1	1	.500	3.50	0	3	1	1	18	25	5	6	8	7	0	12.50	2.50	3.00
hn Eubank	R	1	0	1.000	2.08	0	3	2	0	17.1	13	3	1	12	4	0	6.75	1.56	0.52
arlie Jackson		0	2	.000	5.73	0	2	2	1	11	14	7	3	12	7	0	11.45	5.73	2.45
osty Thomas	R	0	1	.000	7.50	0	2	1	0	6	10	3	5	8	5	0	15.00	4.50	7.50
alt Justis	R	0	0	–	8.10	0	2	0	0	3.1	4	6	0	3	3	0	10.80	16.20	0.00
ndy Bruckmiller	R	0	0	–	27.00	0	1	0	0	1	4	1	1	3	3	0	36.00	9.00	9.00
EAM TOTAL		79	74	.516	2.83	1	185	154	124	1348	1226	474	578	608	424	17	8.19	3.16	3.86

MANAGER	W	L	PCT
Bill Armour	71	78	.477

POS	Player	B	G	AB	H	2B	3B	HR	HR %	R	RBI	BB	SO	SB	Pinch Hit AB	Pinch Hit H	BA	SA
REGULARS																		
1B	Pinky Lindsay		141	499	112	16	2	0	0.0	59	33	45		18	2	0	.224	.265
2B	Germany Schaefer	R	124	446	106	14	3	2	0.4	48	42	32		31	2	1	.238	.296
SS	Charley O'Leary	R	128	443	97	13	2	2	0.5	34	34	17		8	1	1	.219	.271
3B	Bill Coughlin	R	147	498	117	15	5	2	0.4	54	60	36		31	0	0	.235	.297
RF	Sam Crawford	L	145	563	166	25	16	2	0.4	65	72	38		24	0	0	.295	.407
CF	Ty Cobb	L	98	350	112	13	7	1	0.3	45	41	19		23	1	0	.320	.406
LF	Matty McIntyre	L	133	493	128	19	11	0	0.0	63	39	56		29	0	0	.260	.343
C	Boss Schmidt	B	68	216	47	4	3	0	0.0	13	10	6		1	1	0	.218	.264
SUBSTITUTES																		
UT	Bobby Lowe	R	41	145	30	3	0	1	0.7	11	12	4		3	2	0	.207	.248
2B	Frank Scheibeck	R	3	10	1	0	0	0	0.0	1	0	2		0	0	0	.100	.100
3B	Gus Hetling	R	2	7	1	0	0	0	0.0	0	0	0		0	0	0	.143	.143
OF	Davy Jones	L	84	323	84	12	2	0	0.0	41	24	41		21	0	0	.260	.310
OF	Sam Thompson	L	8	31	7	0	1	0	0.0	4	3	1		0	0	0	.226	.290
CO	Fred Payne	R	72	222	60	5	5	0	0.0	23	20	13		4	7	3	.270	.338
C	Jack Warner	L	50	153	37	4	2	0	0.0	15	10	12		4	1	0	.242	.294
PITCHERS																		
P	George Mullin	R	50	142	32	6	4	0	0.0	13	6	4		2	8	3	.225	.324
P	Wild Bill Donovan	R	28	91	11	0	1	0	0.0	5	0	1		6	0	0	.121	.143
P	Red Donahue	R	29	81	10	2	1	0	0.0	2	1	3		0	0	0	.123	.173
P	Ed Siever	L	30	77	12	0	0	0	0.0	5	3	1		0	0	0	.156	.156
P	John Eubank	L	26	60	12	1	1	0	0.0	8	1	0		1	1	0	.200	.250
P	Ed Killian	L	21	53	9	2	0	0	0.0	7	0	2		0	0	0	.170	.208
P	Ed Willett	R	3	9	0	0	0	0	0.0	0	0	0		0	0	0	.000	.000
P	Jack Rowan	R	1	4	1	0	0	0	0.0	1	0	0		0	0	0	.250	.250
P	Jimmy Wiggs	B	4	3	1	0	0	0	0.0	0	0	0		0	0	0	.333	.333
	TEAM TOTAL			4919	1193	154	66	10	0.2	517	411	333	0	206	26	8	.243	.307

INDIVIDUAL FIELDING

POS	Player	T	G	PO	A	E	DP	TC/G	FA
1B	P. Lindsay		122	1122	66	28	55	10.0	.977
	S. Crawford	L	32	287	17	2	10	9.6	.993
2B	G. Schaefer	R	114	348	328	37	42	6.3	.948
	B. Lowe	R	17	56	60	5	2	7.1	.959
	P. Lindsay		17	40	38	8	4	5.1	.907
	F. Scheibeck	R	3	8	8	2	2	6.0	.889
	W. Donovan	R	3	5	3	1	0	3.0	.889
	J. Eubank	R	1	0	1	0	0	1.0	1.000
SS	C. O'Leary	R	127	**326**	398	**58**	37	**6.2**	.926
	B. Lowe	R	19	40	71	11	1	6.4	.910
	G. Schaefer	R	7	20	24	6	3	7.1	.880
3B	B. Coughlin	R	147	**188**	265	29	**16**	3.3	.940
	P. Lindsay		1	0	0	0	0	0.0	.000
	B. Lowe	R	5	3	5	0	0	1.6	1.000
	G. Hetling	R	2	3	2	0	0	2.5	1.000

POS	Player	T	G	PO	A	E	DP	TC/G	FA
OF	M. McIntyre	L	133	254	25	5	8	2.1	.982
	T. Cobb	R	96	208	14	9	4	2.4	.961
	D. Jones	R	84	193	10	4	3	2.5	.981
	S. Crawford	L	116	171	19	3	2	1.7	.984
	F. Payne	R	17	36	5	1	3	2.5	.976
	S. Thompson		8	14	0	0	0	1.8	1.000
	J. Eubank	R	2	5	0	0	0	2.5	1.000
	W. Donovan	R	1	1	0	1	0	2.0	.500
	R. Donahue	R	1	0	0	1	0	1.0	.000
C	B. Schmidt	R	67	257	104	16	4	5.6	.958
	J. Warner	R	49	193	79*	6	3	5.7	.978
	F. Payne	R	47	177	49	8	3	5.0	.966

Ty Cobb and the Tigers didn't immediately combine for glory. The team tumbled out of the first division into sixth place, 21 games out. Cobb hit .320 part-time as manager Bill Armour chose to shuffle his young outfielder in and out of the lineup.

Cobb also failed to catch on with his teammates, who resented the rookie's brashness and southern roots. To welcome him, they knotted his clothing, banished him at batting practice, and sawed his bats in half. Cobb characteristically responded in force, fighting his tormentors and tormenting victims of his own. He gleefully tortured Boss Schmidt, a burly workhorse catcher who for amusement punched railroad spikes into the clubhouse floor with his fist. The pranks included kicking Schmidt's suitcase out of his hand and off train platforms and pouring toothpicks into his soup.

The switchhitting backstop, who eventually gave in to temptation and throttled Cobb twice that season, usually restrained himself partly because of Cobb's value to the team. No other Tiger hit .300, and only Sam Crawford came close (.295). Matty McIntyre (.260) was the only other regular to top .238. Whatever the Tigers got they usually stole. Six swiped 20 or more bases; two—Wild Bill Donovan and third baseman Bill Coughlin —stole their way around the bases, a feat accomplished by only two others in team history (Cobb six times and Jackie Tavener twice).

The high point of the season, and an indicator of good things to come, occurred in September. The Tigers beat New York three straight to knock the Highlanders out of the pennant race. But that wasn't enough to save Armour. He was fired, a move he long resented in light of the impending pennant years. "The plums were ripe," he said, "and ready to fall."

TEAM STATISTICS

	W	L	PCT	GB	R	OR	2B	3B	HR	BA	SA	SB	E	DP	FA	CG	BB	SO	ShO	SV	ERA
HI	93	58	.616		570	460	152	52	7	.230	.286	214	243	80	.963	117	**255**	543	**32**	5	2.13
Y	90	61	.596	3	643	544	166	**77**	17	.266	.339	192	272	69	.957	99	351	605	18	4	2.78
LE	89	64	.582	5	**663**	482	**240**	73	11	**.279**	**.357**	203	**216**	**111**	**.967**	**133**	365	530	27	4	**2.09**
HI	78	67	.538	12	561	536	213	49	**32**	.247	.330	166	267	86	.956	107	425	**749**	19	4	2.60
TL	76	73	.510	16	565	501	145	60	20	.247	.312	221	290	80	.954	**133**	314	558	17	5	2.23
ET	71	78	.477	21	518	596	154	66	10	.242	.306	206	260	86	.959	128	389	469	7	4	3.06
AS	55	95	.367	37.5	518	670	144	65	26	.238	.309	**233**	279	78	.955	115	451	558	12	1	3.25
OS	49	105	.318	45.5	**462**	711	160	75	13	.239	.306	99	335	84	.949	124	285	549	6	**6**	3.41
AGUE TOTAL					4500	4500	1374	517	136	.249	.319	1534	2162	674	.958	956	2835	4561	138	33	2.69

INDIVIDUAL PITCHING

TCHER	T	W	L	PCT	ERA	SV	G	GS	CG	IP	H	BB	SO	R	ER	ShO	H/9	BB/9	SO/9
eorge Mullin	R	21	18	.538	2.78	0	40	40	35	330	315	**108**	123	**139**	102	2	8.59	2.95	3.35
ed Donahue	R	13	14	.481	2.73	0	28	28	26	241	260	54	82	96	73	3	9.71	2.02	3.06
d Siever	L	14	11	.560	2.71	0	30	25	20	222.2	240	45	71	95	67	1	9.70	1.82	2.87
ild Bill Donovan	R	9	15	.375	3.15	0	25	25	22	211.2	221	72	85	92	74	0	9.40	3.06	3.61
d Killian	L	10	6	.625	3.43	2	21	16	14	149.2	165	54	47	71	57	0	9.92	3.25	2.83
hn Eubank	R	4	10	.286	3.53	2	24	12	7	135	147	35	38	69	53	1	9.80	2.33	2.53
d Willett	R	0	3	.000	3.96	0	3	3	3	25	24	8	16	12	11	0	8.64	2.88	5.76
mmy Wiggs	R	0	0	–	5.23	0	4	1	0	10.1	11	7	7	9	6	0	9.58	6.10	6.10
ck Rowan	R	0	1	.000	11.00	0	1	1	1	9	15	6	0	13	11	0	15.00	6.00	0.00
AM TOTAL		71	78	.477	3.06	4	176	151	128	1334.1	1398	389	469	596	454	7	9.43	2.62	3.16

MANAGER	W	L	PCT
Hughie Jennings	92	58	.613

POS	Player	B	G	AB	H	2B	3B	HR	HR %	R	RBI	BB	SO	SB	Pinch Hit AB	H	BA	SA
REGULARS																		
1B	Claude Rossman	L	153	571	158	21	8	0	0.0	60	69	33		20	0	0	.277	.342
2B	Red Downs	R	105	374	82	13	5	1	0.3	28	42	13		3	4	1	.219	.289
SS	Charley O'Leary	R	139	465	112	19	1	0	0.0	61	34	32		11	1	0	.241	.286
3B	Bill Coughlin	R	134	519	126	10	2	0	0.0	80	46	35		15	0	0	.243	.270
RF	Ty Cobb	L	150	605	**212**	29	15	5	0.8	97	**116**	24		**49**	0	0	**.350**	**.473**
CF	Sam Crawford	L	144	582	188	34	17	4	0.7	**102**	81	37		18	0	0	.323	.460
LF	Davy Jones	L	126	491	134	10	6	0	0.0	101	27	60		30	0	0	.273	.318
C	Boss Schmidt	B	104	349	85	6	6	0	0.0	32	23	5		8	1	0	.244	.295
SUBSTITUTES																		
UT	Germany Schaefer	R	109	372	96	12	3	1	0.3	45	32	30		21	2	0	.258	.315
UT	Bobby Lowe	R	17	37	9	2	0	0	0.0	2	5	4		0	2	0	.243	.297
S2	Hughie Jennings	R	1	4	1	1	0	0	0.0	0	0	0		0	0	0	.250	.500
OF	Matty McIntyre	L	20	81	23	1	1	0	0.0	6	9	7		3	0	0	.284	.321
OF	Red Killefer	R	1	4	0	0	0	0	0.0	0	0	0		0	0	0	.000	.000
C	Fred Payne	R	53	169	28	2	2	0	0.0	17	14	7		4	1	0	.166	.201
C	Jimmy Archer	R	18	42	5	0	0	0	0.0	6	0	4		0	0	0	.119	.119
C	Tex Erwin	L	4	5	1	0	0	0	0.0	0	1	1		0	0	0	.200	.200
PITCHERS																		
P	George Mullin	R	70	157	34	5	3	0	0.0	16	13	12		2	20	5	.217	.287
P	Ed Killian	L	46	122	39	5	3	0	0.0	16	11	4		3	1	0	.320	.410
P	Wild Bill Donovan	R	37	109	29	7	2	0	0.0	20	19	6		4	4	0	.266	.367
P	Ed Siever	L	39	91	14	2	1	0	0.0	5	4	0		1	0	0	.154	.198
P	John Eubank	L	15	31	4	0	1	0	0.0	1	1	0		0	0	0	.129	.194
P	Ed Willett	R	10	13	1	0	0	0	0.0	1	1	1		0	0	0	.077	.077
P	Elijah Jones	R	4	4	0	0	0	0	0.0	0	0	0		0	0	0	.000	.000
P	Herm Malloy		1	4	0	0	0	0	0.0	0	0	0		0	0	0	.000	.000
TEAM TOTAL				5201	1381	179	76	11	0.2	696	548	315	0	192	36	6	.266	.336

INDIVIDUAL FIELDING

POS	Player	T	G	PO	A	E	DP	TC/G	FA		POS	Player	T	G	PO	A	E	DP	TC/G	FA
1B	C. Rossman	L	153	1478	62	30	57	10.3	.981		OF	S. Crawford	L	144	311	22	12	2	2.4	.965
	E. Killian	L	1	1	3	0	0	4.0	1.000			D. Jones	R	126	282	15	9	2	2.4	.971
	S. Crawford	L	2	2	0	0	0	1.0	1.000			T. Cobb	R	150	238	30	11	**12**	1.9	.961
2B	G. Schaefer	R	74	188	206	16	23	5.5	.961			M. McIntyre	L	20	43	3	0	1	2.3	1.000
	R. Downs	R	80	149	207	27	10	4.8	.930			R. Downs	R	20	39	3	3	1	2.3	.933
	J. Archer	R	1	2	4	1	0	7.0	.857			G. Schaefer	R	1	0	0	0	0	0.0	.000
	H. Jennings	R	1	1	2	1	0	4.0	.750			F. Payne	R	5	8	1	0	1	1.8	1.000
SS	C. O'Leary	R	138	**353**	448	44	35	6.1	.948			E. Killian	L	2	5	0	0	0	2.5	1.000
	G. Schaefer	R	18	30	48	4	0	4.6	.951			R. Killefer	R	1	2	0	0	0	2.0	1.000
	R. Downs	R	1	0	0	0	0	0.0	.000			B. Lowe	R	4	1	0	0	0	0.3	1.000
	H. Jennings	R	1	1	1	2	0	4.0	.500		C	B. Schmidt	R	104	446	132	**34**	**14**	5.9	.944
	B. Lowe	R	2	2	1	0	0	1.5	1.000			F. Payne	R	46	205	55	5	4	5.8	.981
3B	B. Coughlin	R	133	163	236	30	9	3.2	.930			J. Archer	R	17	62	16	2	0	4.7	.975
	R. Downs	R	1	0	0	0	0	0.0	.000			T. Erwin	R	4	7	3	1	0	2.8	.909
	G. Schaefer	R	14	21	32	3	0	4.0	.946											
	B. Lowe	R	10	4	16	3	0	2.3	.870											

Hughie Jennings, the former National League star shortstop who liked to pull fistfuls of grass from the third-base coach's box and bray "Ee-Yah!" like a mule while dancing on one leg, assumed command and led the Tigers to their first American League pennant. He won it with virtually the same lineup he had inherited from Bill Armour. Ty Cobb, not yet 21, won his first batting title at .350 (with a league-leading 116 RBI). Sam Crawford finished second in the league at .323. Wild Bill Donovan was 25–4, Twilight Ed Killian 25–13, and George Mullin 20–20, his third straight 20-victory season.

They carried the Tigers into the September stretch amid a three-way race with Philadelphia and Chicago. By the last weekend of the month the Tigers had whittled away the front-running Athletics' lead to three percentage points before entering a three-game series at Philadelphia. The Tigers won the first game to take a thin lead. The second game was a wild 17-inning, 9–9 tie that would prove the pennant-winner for Detroit. Cobb tied it on a ninth-inning home run. Then in the 14th the game erupted. The Athletics' Harry Davis hit a long fly. Crawford gave chase, but a Philadelphia policeman on duty in the outfield got in the way. The umpire called Davis out because of interference, sparking a predictable brawl among cops, Athletics, and Tigers. (One officer started to arrest Donovan but, after being informed that Wild Bill was a Philadelphia native, arrested first baseman Claude Rossman instead.) The umpire's decision stood. The next batter, Danny Murphy, followed with a long single that would have scored Davis. And Connie Mack forever maintained he'd been robbed of the pennant, which Detroit captured a week later by six percentage points.

The World Series proved far less dramatic. In Game 1 at Chicago, Boss Schmidt—in a Mickey Owen–like gaffe—failed to hold a game-winning third strike in the ninth inning, which allowed the Cubs to tie. The game was eventually called at 3–3 in the 12th because of darkness. The Cubs went on to sweep the next four straight. The Tigers spent the winter with blemished reputations.

TEAM STATISTICS

	W	L	PCT	GB	R	OR	Batting 2B	3B	HR	BA	SA	SB	Fielding E	DP	FA	CG	BB	Pitching SO	ShO	SV	ERA
ET	92	58	.613		696	519	180	76	11	.266	.336	192	260	79	.959	120	380	512	15	7	2.33
HI	88	57	.607	1.5	582	509	220	45	22	.255	.330	138	263	67	.958	106	378	789	27	6	2.35
HI	87	64	.576	5.5	584	475	148	34	6	.237	.283	175	233	101	.966	112	305	604	17	9	2.22
LE	85	67	.559	8	528	523	182	68	11	.241	.310	193	264	137	.960	127	362	513	20	5	2.26
Y	70	78	.473	21	604	671	150	67	14	.249	.314	206	334	79	.947	93	428	511	9	5	3.03
TL	69	83	.454	24	538	560	154	63	9	.253	.312	144	266	97	.959	129	352	463	15	9	2.61
OS	59	90	.396	32.5	466	556	155	48	18	.234	.292	124	274	103	.959	100	337	517	17	6	2.45
AS	49	102	.325	43.5	505	690	137	57	12	.243	.300	223	311	69	.952	106	341	569	11	5	3.11
EAGUE TOTAL					4503	4503	1326	458	103	.247	.310	1395	2205	732	.958	893	2883	4478	131	52	2.54

INDIVIDUAL PITCHING

PITCHER	T	W	L	PCT	ERA	SV	G	GS	CG	IP	H	BB	SO	R	ER	ShO	H/9	BB/9	SO/9
eorge Mullin	R	20	20	.500	2.59	3	46	42	35	357.1	346	106	146	153	103	5	8.71	2.67	3.68
d Killian	L	25	13	.658	1.78	1	41	34	29	314	286	91	96	103	62	3	8.20	2.61	2.75
d Siever	L	18	11	.621	2.16	1	39	33	22	274.2	256	52	88	89	66	3	8.39	1.70	2.88
ild Bill Donovan	R	25	4	.862	2.19	1	32	28	27	271	222	82	123	96	66	3	7.37	2.72	4.08
hn Eubank	R	3	3	.500	2.67	0	15	8	4	81	88	20	17	40	24	1	9.78	2.22	1.89
d Willett	R	1	5	.167	3.70	0	10	6	1	48.2	47	20	27	31	20	0	8.69	3.70	4.99
ijah Jones	R	0	1	.000	5.06	1	4	1	1	16	23	4	9	15	9	0	12.94	2.25	5.06
erm Malloy		0	1	.000	5.63	0	1	1	1	8	13	5	6	10	5	0	14.63	5.63	6.75
EAM TOTAL		92	58	.613	2.33	7	188	153	120	1370.2	1281	380	512	537	355	15	8.41	2.50	3.36

MANAGER	W	L	PCT
Hughie Jennings	90	63	.588

POS	Player	B	G	AB	H	2B	3B	HR	HR %	R	RBI	BB	SO	SB	Pinch Hit AB	Pinch Hit H	BA	SA
REGULARS																		
1B	Claude Rossman	L	138	524	154	33	13	2	0.4	45	71	27		8	0	0	.294	.418
2B	Red Downs	R	84	289	64	10	3	1	0.3	29	35	5		2	1	0	.221	.287
SS	Germany Schaefer	R	153	584	151	20	10	3	0.5	96	52	37		40	0	0	.259	.342
3B	Bill Coughlin	R	119	405	87	5	1	0	0.0	32	23	23		10	0	0	.215	.232
RF	Ty Cobb	L	150	581	**188**	**36**	**20**	4	0.7	88	**108**	34		39	0	0	**.324**	**.475**
CF	Sam Crawford	L	152	**591**	184	33	16	**7**	1.2	102	80	37		15	1	0	.311	.457
LF	Matty McIntyre	L	151	569	168	24	13	0	0.0	**105**	28	83		20	0	0	.295	.383
C	Boss Schmidt	B	122	419	111	14	3	1	0.2	45	38	16		5	1	1	.265	.320
SUBSTITUTES																		
SS	Charley O'Leary	R	65	211	53	9	3	0	0.0	21	17	9		4	0	0	.251	.322
UT	Red Killefer	R	28	75	16	1	0	0	0.0	9	11	3		4	0	0	.213	.227
SS	Donie Bush	B	20	68	20	1	1	0	0.0	13	4	7		2	0	0	.294	.338
3B	Clay Perry	R	5	11	2	0	0	0	0.0	0	0	0		0	0	0	.182	.182
OF	Davy Jones	L	56	121	25	2	1	0	0.0	17	10	13		11	21	3	.207	.240
C	Ira Thomas	R	40	101	31	1	0	0	0.0	6	8	5		0	11	4	.307	.317
C	Fred Payne	R	20	45	3	0	0	0	0.0	3	2	3		1	2	0	.067	.067
PITCHERS																		
P	George Mullin	R	55	125	32	2	2	1	0.8	13	8	7		2	14	3	.256	.328
P	Ed Summers	B	40	113	14	2	0	0	0.0	6	5	0		0	0	0	.124	.142
P	Wild Bill Donovan	R	30	82	13	1	0	0	0.0	5	2	10		2	0	0	.159	.171
P	Ed Killian	L	28	73	10	3	0	0	0.0	5	6	0		0	1	0	.137	.178
P	Ed Willett	R	30	67	11	1	0	0	0.0	4	8	0		0	0	0	.164	.179
P	Ed Siever	L	11	18	3	0	0	0	0.0	0	2	0		0	0	0	.167	.167
P	George Winter		7	18	2	0	0	0	0.0	0	0	0		0	0	0	.111	.111
P	George Suggs	R	6	10	2	1	0	0	0.0	1	1	1		0	0	0	.200	.300
P	Herm Malloy		3	9	3	0	0	0	0.0	0	1	0		0	0	0	.333	.333
TEAM TOTAL				5109	1347	199	86	19	0.4	645	520	320	0	165	52	11	.264	.347

INDIVIDUAL FIELDING

POS	Player	T	G	PO	A	E	DP	TC/G	FA
1B	C. Rossman	L	138	1429	**102**	29	70	11.3	.981
	S. Crawford	L	17	176	13	6	12	11.5	.969
2B	R. Downs	R	82	180	265	36	24	5.9	.925
	G. Schaefer	R	58	122	160	15	22	5.1	.949
	R. Killefer	R	16	30	35	3	7	4.3	.956
	C. O'Leary	R	1	1	0	0	0	1.0	1.000
SS	G. Schaefer	R	68	162	254	37	35	6.7	.918
	C. O'Leary	R	64	130	179	27	15	5.3	.920
	D. Bush	R	20	42	63	7	9	5.6	.938
	R. Killefer	R	7	17	13	5	1	5.0	.857
3B	B. Coughlin	R	119	129	214	21	12	3.1	.942
	G. Schaefer	R	29	35	65	5	1	3.6	.952
	C. Perry	R	5	4	7	1	1	2.4	.917
	R. Killefer	R	4	1	6	4	1	2.8	.636
	R. Downs	R	1	1	1	0	1	2.0	1.000
OF	M. McIntyre	L	151	**329**	17	8	4	2.3	.977
	S. Crawford	L	134	252	9	8	2	2.0	.970
	T. Cobb	R	150	212	**23**	14	5	1.7	.944
	D. Jones	R	32	67	5	3	2	2.3	.960
	F. Payne	R	2	2	0	0	0	1.0	1.000
C	B. Schmidt	R	121	541	**184**	37	12	6.3	.951
	I. Thomas	R	29	124	15	4	3	4.9	.972
	F. Payne	R	16	52	10	3	1	4.1	.954

During an evening of libation over the previous winter, Bill Yawkey and Frank Navin had reportedly flipped a coin for complete ownership of the club. Navin won, and in the ensuing season so did the Tigers. But not without a tight race.

After a spring of horrendous weather, the Tigers struggled through an awful start, plummeting to sixth place by the middle of May. But by month's end they were tied with New York for first. And by the Fourth of July, the eastern clubs stepped back and let the season develop into a battle among Chicago, Cleveland, St. Louis, and Detroit.

Cobb (.324, good for his second straight batting title) and Sam Crawford (.311) again teamed as the league's best one-two punch, finishing first and second in average and RBIs. Wild Bill Donovan (18–7) and George Mullin (17–13) contributed solid seasons. But Hughie Jennings's staff was carried by right-handed knuckleballer Ed "Kickapoo" Summers, a 23-year-old rookie who finished 24–12 with a 1.64 ERA—the only Tiger to win 20 that season.

The Tigers would need every drop of help. As late as September 27, just 23 percentage points separated the four contenders. The issue wasn't decided until the last game of the season: the Tigers versus the White Sox at Chicago. The winner would take the pennant; the loser would drop to third behind Cleveland.

Detroit won the one-game battle with ease. Donovan helped Chicago's Hitless Wonders live up to their nickname, limiting the White Sox to two hits while Cobb and Crawford led a 7–0 victory for the Tigers' second straight pennant.

The World Series against the Cubs provided a painful replay for Detroit disciples. The Tigers won Game 3 after dropping the first two, but from there on managed just seven hits and zero runs. "Don't feel too badly about it," Jennings consoled his troops afterward. "We were beaten again by a great team."

National League enthusiasts weren't quite as gracious. After winning their second straight World Series with ease, they started calling Ban Johnson's circuit "just a good minor league."

TEAM STATISTICS

	W	L	PCT	GB	R	OR	Batting 2B	3B	HR	BA	SA	SB	Fielding E	DP	FA	CG	BB	Pitching SO	ShO	SV	ERA
DET	90	63	.588		645	552	199	86	19	.264	.347	165	305	95	.953	120	318	553	15	5	2.40
CLE	90	64	.584	0.5	570	471	188	58	18	.239	.309	169	257	95	.962	108	328	548	18	5	2.02
CHI	88	64	.579	1.5	535	480	145	41	3	.224	.271	209	232	82	.966	107	284	623	23	10	2.22
STL	83	69	.546	6.5	543	478	173	56	21	.245	.312	126	237	97	.964	107	387	607	16	5	2.15
BOS	75	79	.487	15.5	563	515	116	88	14	.246	.312	168	297	71	.955	102	366	624	12	7	2.27
PHI	68	85	.444	22	487	554	183	49	21	.223	.291	116	272	68	.957	102	409	740	23	4	2.57
WAS	67	85	.441	22.5	479	530	131	74	8	.235	.295	170	275	89	.958	105	348	649	14	7	2.34
NY	51	103	.331	39.5	458	700	142	51	12	.236	.291	230	337	78	.947	91	457	584	11	3	3.16
LEAGUE TOTAL					4280	4280	1277	503	116	.239	.304	1353	2212	675	.958	842	2897	4928	132	46	2.39

INDIVIDUAL PITCHING

PITCHER	T	W	L	PCT	ERA	SV	G	GS	CG	IP	H	BB	SO	R	ER	ShO	H/9	BB/9	SO/9
Ed Summers	R	24	12	.667	1.64	1	40	32	24	301	271	55	103	112	55	5	8.10	1.64	3.08
George Mullin	R	17	13	.567	3.10	0	39	30	26	290.2	301	71	121	142	100	1	9.32	2.20	3.75
Wild Bill Donovan	R	18	7	.720	2.08	0	29	28	25	242.2	210	53	141	78	56	6	7.79	1.97	5.23
Ed Willett	R	15	8	.652	2.28	1	30	22	18	197.1	186	60	77	67	50	2	8.48	2.74	3.51
Ed Killian	L	12	9	.571	2.99	1	27	23	15	180.2	170	53	47	78	60	0	8.47	2.64	2.34
Ed Siever	L	2	6	.250	3.50	0	11	9	4	61.2	74	13	23	37	24	1	10.80	1.90	3.36
George Winter	R	1	5	.167	1.60	1	7	6	5	56.1	49	7	25	19	10	0	7.83	1.12	3.99
George Suggs	R	1	1	.500	1.67	1	6	1	1	27	32	2	8	8	5	0	10.67	0.67	2.67
Term Malloy		0	2	.000	3.71	0	3	2	2	17	20	4	8	11	7	0	10.59	2.12	4.24
TEAM TOTAL		90	63	.588	2.40	5	192	153	120	1374.1	1313	318	553	552	367	15	8.60	2.08	3.62

MANAGER	W	L	PCT
Hughie Jennings	98	54	.645

POS	Player	B	G	AB	H	2B	3B	HR	HR %	R	RBI	BB	SO	SB	Pinch Hit AB	H	BA	SA
REGULARS																		
1B	Claude Rossman	L	82	287	75	8	3	0	0.0	16	39	13		10	5	0	.261	.310
2B	Germany Schaefer	R	87	280	70	12	0	0	0.0	26	22	14		12	1	0	.250	.293
SS	Donie Bush	B	157	532	145	18	2	0	0.0	114	33	**88**		53	0	0	.273	.314
3B	George Moriarty	R	133	473	129	20	4	1	0.2	43	39	24		34	3	1	.273	.338
RF	Ty Cobb	L	156	573	**216**	33	10	9	1.6	116	107	48		76	0	0	**.377**	**.517**
CF	Sam Crawford	L	156	589	185	**35**	14	6	1.0	83	97	47		30	0	0	.314	.452
LF	Matty McIntyre	L	125	476	116	18	9	1	0.2	65	34	54		13	2	0	.244	.326
C	Boss Schmidt	B	84	253	53	8	2	1	0.4	21	28	7		7	2	1	.209	.269
SUBSTITUTES																		
32	Charley O'Leary	R	76	261	53	10	0	0	0.0	29	13	6		9	0	0	.203	.241
1B	Tom Jones	R	44	153	43	9	0	0	0.0	13	18	5		9	0	0	.281	.340
2B	Jim Delahanty	R	46	150	38	10	1	0	0.0	29	20	17		9	0	0	.253	.333
2B	Red Killefer	R	23	61	17	2	2	1	1.6	6	4	3		2	4	1	.279	.426
1B	Del Gainor	R	2	5	1	0	0	0	0.0	0	0	0		0	0	0	.200	.200
1B	Hughie Jennings	R	2	4	2	0	0	0	0.0	1	2	0		0	0	0	.500	.500
OF	Davy Jones	L	69	204	57	2	2	0	0.0	44	10	28		12	10	1	.279	.309
C	Oscar Stanage	R	77	252	66	8	6	0	0.0	17	21	11		2	0	0	.262	.341
C	Heinie Beckendorf	R	15	27	7	1	0	0	0.0	1	1	2		0	0	0	.259	.296
C	Joe Casey	R	3	5	0	0	0	0	0.0	1	0	1		0	0	0	.000	.000
PITCHERS																		
P	George Mullin	R	53	126	27	7	0	0	0.0	13	17	13		2	10	1	.214	.270
P	Ed Willett	R	42	112	22	5	3	0	0.0	10	10	3		0	0	0	.196	.295
P	Ed Summers	B	35	94	10	1	0	0	0.0	4	3	4		0	0	0	.106	.117
P	Ed Killian	L	25	62	10	0	0	0	0.0	4	0	2		0	0	0	.161	.161
P	Wild Bill Donovan	R	22	45	9	0	0	0	0.0	6	1	2		0	0	0	.200	.200
P	Kid Speer	L	13	25	3	1	0	0	0.0	1	2	2		0	0	0	.120	.160
P	Ralph Works	L	16	17	1	0	0	0	0.0	2	0	0		0	0	0	.059	.059
P	George Suggs	R	9	15	1	1	0	0	0.0	0	0	1		0	0	0	.067	.133
P	Bill Lelivelt	R	4	6	2	0	0	0	0.0	0	0	2		0	0	0	.333	.333
P	Elijah Jones	R	2	4	1	0	0	0	0.0	1	0	0		0	0	0	.250	.250
P	Ed Lafitte	R	3	4	1	0	0	0	0.0	0	0	0		0	0	0	.250	.250
TEAM TOTAL				5095	1360	209	58	19	0.4	666	521	397	0	280	37	5	.267	.342

INDIVIDUAL FIELDING

POS	Player	T	G	PO	A	E	DP	TC/G	FA
1B	C. Rossman	L	75	913	36	18	30	12.9	.981
	T. Jones	R	44	446	28	8	20	11.0	.983
	G. Moriarty	R	24	283	12	3	12	12.4	.990
	S. Crawford	L	17	189	10	6	2	12.1	.971
	D. Gainor	R	2	12	1	1	0	7.0	.929
	H. Jennings	R	2	9	1	0	2	5.0	1.000
2B	G. Schaefer	R	86	180	273	16	26	5.5	.966
	J. Delahanty	R	46	88	127	13*	13	5.0	.943
	R. Killefer	R	17	28	55	8	3	5.4	.912
	C. O'Leary	R	15	36	35	1	3	4.8	.986
SS	D. Bush	R	157	308	**567**	71	38	6.0	.925
	C. O'Leary	R	4	6	9	2	1	4.3	.882
3B	G. Moriarty	R	106	117	253	24	11	3.7	**.939**
	C. O'Leary	R	54	59	118	15	4	3.6	.922

POS	Player	T	G	PO	A	E	DP	TC/G	FA
OF	S. Crawford	L	139	297	7	11	2	2.3	.965
	T. Cobb	R	156	222	24	14	7	1.7	.946
	M. McIntyre	L	122	217	14	6	1	1.9	.975
	D. Jones	R	57	103	4	2	1	1.9	.982
	R. Killefer	R	1	0	0	0	0	0.0	.000
	B. Schmidt	R	1	0	0	0	0	0.0	.000
	C. O'Leary	R	2	3	0	0	0	1.5	1.000
	E. Willett	R	1	2	0	0	0	2.0	1.000
	G. Schaefer	R	1	1	0	0	0	1.0	1.000
	G. Mullin	R	2	1	0	0	0	0.5	1.000
C	B. Schmidt	R	81	315	107	**20**	7	5.5	.955
	O. Stanage	R	77	324	80	15	12	5.4	.964
	H. Beckendorf	R	15	36	9	2	4	3.1	.957
	J. Casey	R	3	9	5	0	1	4.7	1.000

Aiming at an unprecedented third straight American League flag, Detroit exploded to a fast start, holding first place for all but one day from April 26 through August and at one point winning 14 straight (a team record equaled in 1934). Ty Cobb was capturing the only Triple Crown in team history at .377 with 107 RBI and nine home runs; he also had 76 stolen bases (and further managed to fuel the already simmering anti-Cobb sentiment when he spiked Athletics third baseman Frank "Home Run" Baker). George Mullin would lead the majors at 29–8, followed by Ed Willett at 21–10, and Ed Summers at 19–9.

Still, the Tigers slumped while the Athletics, flexing the muscles that would soon bring them four pennants in five years, surged. Jennings raced to Navin for help. So the Tigers gave their infield a late-summer overhaul. Germany Schaefer went to Washington for second baseman Jim Delahanty, and Claude Rossman to the Browns for sure-fielding first baseman Tom Jones. The deals worked. Philadelphia visited Bennett Park in first place for a three-game series in late August, lost all three, and never held first again. Detroit finished three-and-a-half games ahead.

This time the World Series pitted Detroit against Pittsburgh—and Cobb against Honus Wagner. Wagner won the batting battle, .333 to Cobb's .231, and the Pirates won the war, four games to three in the first seven game Series. The teams alternated victories in Games 1 through 6 until unheralded rookie Babe Adams blanked the Tigers in Game 7 at Detroit. It marked Adams's third win of the Series—and the Tigers' third failure in three tries at the World Series championship. "We do all right in the World Series," seethed American League president Ban Johnson, "except when that damn National Leaguer Jennings gets into it."

TEAM STATISTICS

	W	L	PCT	GB	R	OR	Batting 2B	3B	HR	BA	SA	SB	Fielding E	DP	FA	CG	BB	Pitching SO	ShO	SV	ERA
DET	98	54	.645		666	493	209	58	19	.267	.342	280	276	87	.959	117	359	528	17	12	2.26
PHI	95	58	.621	3.5	600	414	186	89	20	.257	.343	205	245	92	.961	111	386	728	27	3	1.92
BOS	88	63	.583	9.5	590	561	151	69	20	.263	.333	215	292	95	.955	75	384	555	11	15	2.60
CHI	78	74	.513	20	494	465	145	56	4	.221	.275	211	246	101	.964	112	341	671	26	4	2.04
NY	74	77	.490	23.5	591	580	143	61	16	.248	.311	187	329	94	.948	94	422	597	18	7	2.68
CLE	71	82	.464	27.5	519	543	173	81	10	.241	.313	174	275	110	.957	110	349	569	15	2	2.39
STL	61	89	.407	36	443	574	116	45	11	.232	.280	136	267	107	.958	105	383	620	21	4	2.88
WAS	42	110	.276	56	382	655	148	41	9	.223	.275	136	280	100	.957	99	424	653	11	2	3.04
LEAGUE TOTAL					4285	4285	1271	500	109	.244	.309	1544	2210	786	.957	823	3048	4921	146	49	2.47

INDIVIDUAL PITCHING

PITCHER	T	W	L	PCT	ERA	SV	G	GS	CG	IP	H	BB	SO	R	ER	ShO	H/9	BB/9	SO/9
George Mullin	R	29	8	.784	2.22	1	40	35	29	303.2	258	78	124	96	75	3	7.65	2.31	3.68
Ed Willett	R	21	10	.677	2.34	1	41	34	25	292.2	239	76	89	112	76	3	7.35	2.34	2.74
Ed Summers	R	19	9	.679	2.24	1	35	32	24	281.2	243	52	107	91	70	3	7.76	1.66	3.42
Ed Killian	L	11	9	.550	1.71	1	25	19	14	173.1	150	49	54	45	33	3	7.79	2.54	2.80
Wild Bill Donovan	R	8	7	.533	2.31	2	21	17	13	140.1	121	60	76	50	36	4	7.76	3.85	4.87
Kid Speer	L	4	4	.500	2.83	1	12	8	4	76.1	88	13	12	39	24	0	10.38	1.53	1.41
Ralph Works	R	4	1	.800	1.97	2	16	4	4	64	62	17	31	19	14	0	8.72	2.39	4.36
George Suggs	R	1	3	.250	2.03	1	9	4	2	44.1	34	10	18	12	10	0	6.90	2.03	3.65
Bill Lelivelt	R	0	1	.000	4.50	1	4	2	1	20	27	2	4	12	10	0	12.15	0.90	1.80
Ed Lafitte	R	0	1	.000	3.86	1	3	1	1	14	22	2	11	14	6	0	14.14	1.29	7.07
Elijah Jones	R	1	1	.500	2.70	0	2	2	0	10	10	0	2	3	3	0	9.00	0.00	1.80
TEAM TOTAL		98	54	.645	2.26	12	208	158	117	1420.1	1254	359	528	493	357	16	7.95	2.27	3.35

MANAGER	W	L	PCT
Hughie Jennings	86	68	.558

POS	Player	B	G	AB	H	2B	3B	HR	HR %	R	RBI	BB	SO	SB	Pinch Hit AB	Pinch Hit H	BA	SA
REGULARS																		
1B	Tom Jones	R	135	432	110	13	4	0	0.0	32	45	35		22	0	0	.255	.303
2B	Jim Delahanty	R	106	378	111	16	3	2	0.5	67	45	43		15	0	0	.294	.368
SS	Donie Bush	B	142	496	130	13	4	3	0.6	90	34	78		49	0	0	.262	.323
3B	George Moriarty	R	136	490	123	24	3	2	0.4	53	60	33		33	1	0	.251	.324
RF	Sam Crawford	L	154	588	170	26	19	5	0.9	83	120	37		20	0	0	.289	.423
CF	Ty Cobb	L	140	509	196	36	13	8	1.6	106	91	64		65	3	1	.385	.554
LF	Davy Jones	L	113	377	100	6	6	0	0.0	77	24	51		25	9	0	.265	.313
C	Oscar Stanage	R	88	275	57	7	4	2	0.7	24	25	20		1	4	0	.207	.284
SUBSTITUTES																		
2S	Charley O'Leary	R	65	211	51	7	1	0	0.0	23	9	9		7	2	0	.242	.284
13	Hack Simmons	R	42	110	25	3	1	0	0.0	12	9	10		1	10	3	.227	.273
UT	Chick Lathers	L	41	82	19	2	0	0	0.0	4	3	8		0	14	3	.232	.256
2B	Jay Kirke	L	8	25	5	1	0	0	0.0	3	3	1		1	0	0	.200	.240
OF	Matty McIntyre	L	83	305	72	15	5	0	0.0	40	25	39		4	6	1	.236	.318
C	Boss Schmidt	B	71	197	51	7	7	1	0.5	22	23	2		2	5	2	.259	.381
C	Joe Casey	R	23	62	12	3	0	0	0.0	3	2	2		1	0	0	.194	.242
C	Heinie Beckendorf	R	3	13	3	0	0	0	0.0	0	2	1		0	1	1	.231	.231
PITCHERS																		
P	George Mullin	R	50	129	33	6	2	1	0.8	15	11	8		1	9	0	.256	.357
P	Ed Willett	R	38	83	11	3	1	0	0.0	5	4	2		0	0	0	.133	.193
P	Ed Summers	B	30	76	14	1	0	2	2.6	4	7	1		1	0	0	.184	.276
P	Wild Bill Donovan	R	26	69	10	1	0	0	0.0	6	2	5		0	0	0	.145	.159
P	Sailor Stroud	R	28	39	1	0	0	0	0.0	2	1	4		0	0	0	.026	.026
P	Ralph Works	L	18	30	8	2	0	0	0.0	3	1	0		0	0	0	.267	.333
P	Ed Killian	L	11	27	4	0	0	0	0.0	1	1	1		0	0	0	.148	.148
P	Hub Pernoll	R	11	16	1	0	0	0	0.0	3	0	0		1	0	0	.063	.063
P	Frank Browning	R	11	14	0	0	0	0	0.0	0	0	1		0	0	0	.000	.000
P	Art Loudell	R	5	7	1	0	0	0	0.0	1	1	1		0	0	0	.143	.143
P	Marv Peasley	L	2	3	0	0	0	0	0.0	0	0	2		0	0	0	.000	.000
P	Dave Skeels	L	1	3	0	0	0	0	0.0	0	0	0		0	0	0	.000	.000
P	Bill Lelivelt	R	1	2	1	0	0	0	0.0	0	0	1		0	0	0	.500	.500
TEAM TOTAL				5048	1319	192	73	26	0.5	679	548	459	0	249	64	11	.261	.344

INDIVIDUAL FIELDING

POS	Player	T	G	PO	A	E	DP	TC/G	FA
1B	T. Jones	R	135	1405	67	23	50	11.1	.985
	H. Simmons	R	22	229	13	4	10	11.2	.984
	S. Crawford	L	1	11	1	0	0	12.0	1.000
2B	J. Delahanty	R	106	246	267	33	36	5.2	.940
	C. O'Leary	R	38	81	93	12	10	4.9	.935
	C. Lathers	R	7	15	20	3	0	5.4	.921
	J. Kirke	R	7	16	17	3	1	5.1	.917
SS	D. Bush	R	141	310	487	51	31	6.0	.940
	C. O'Leary	R	16	35	60	4	2	6.2	.960
	C. Lathers	R	4	0	5	3	2	2.0	.625
3B	G. Moriarty	R	134	165	302	37	17	3.8	.927
	C. Lathers	R	13	15	35	4	3	4.2	.926
	H. Simmons	R	7	9	15	2	0	3.7	.923
	C. O'Leary	R	6	5	14	0	3	3.2	1.000
	D. Bush	R	1	0	2	0	0	2.0	1.000

POS	Player	T	G	PO	A	E	DP	TC/G	FA
OF	T. Cobb	R	137	305	18	14	4	2.5	.958
	S. Crawford	L	153	223	10	9	2	1.6	.963
	D. Jones	R	101	181	13	9	2	2.0	.956
	M. McIntyre	L	77	147	12	9	2	2.2	.946
	J. Kirke	R	1	0	0	0	0	0.0	.000
	E. Willett	R	1	0	0	0	0	0.0	.000
	G. Mullin	R	2	2	0	1	0	1.5	.667
	H. Simmons	R	2	2	0	0	0	1.0	1.000
C	O. Stanage	R	84	344	148	25	6	6.2	.952
	B. Schmidt	R	66	239	80	9	1	5.0	.973
	J. Casey	R	22	101	33	5	2	6.3	.964
	H. Beckendorf	R	2	8	2	1	1	5.5	.909

The Tigers not only failed to win a fourth straight pennant, but didn't even come close, finishing third, 18 games behind the first-place Athletics. Detroit didn't challenge for many reasons. George Mullin won 21, and Wild Bill Donovan won 17, but the overall pitching was inadequate. Sam Crawford won his first of three RBI crowns, but tumbled below .300. Injuries sidelined second baseman George Moriarty and first baseman Tom Jones. And Cobb provided frequent distractions, including a row with a black waiter in Cleveland that attracted much front-page notoriety.

Meanwhile, Frank Navin introduced Sunday baseball to Detroit, an experiment that nearly ended early when one Sabbath game against the Red Sox erupted into a riot. It started when Moriarty slid across home to win the game in the bottom of the ninth. Frustrated Sox catcher Bill Carrigan squirted tobacco juice in his eye, and Moriarty answered with a right to the jaw. The irate crowd spilled onto the field, the players fought each other into the clubhouse, and Navin stood atop the dugout trying to restore order.

Detroit fans were still treated to one magnificent late-season race: Ty Cobb versus Cleveland second baseman Nap Lajoie for the batting title and the Chalmers automobile that went with it. Their battle stayed close entering the final weekend of the season. Trailing by eight points, Lajoie hit eight-for-eight in a final Sunday doubleheader—a feat that stirred skepticism since it was well known that nearly everyone in the league, including many Tigers, rooted against Cobb, and since six of the less-than-speedy Lajoie's eight hits were bunts. But Cobb beat Lajoie anyway for his fourth straight batting title by a point at .385, close enough for Chalmers to award each a car.

TEAM STATISTICS

	W	L	PCT	GB	R	OR	Batting 2B	3B	HR	BA	SA	SB	Fielding E	DP	FA	CG	BB	Pitching SO	ShO	SV	ERA
PHI	102	48	.680		672	439	194	106	19	.266	.356	207	230	117	.965	123	450	789	24	5	1.79
NY	88	63	.583	14.5	629	502	163	75	20	.248	.322	288	284	95	.956	110	364	654	14	8	2.59
DET	86	68	.558	18	679	580	192	73	26	.261	.344	249	288	79	.956	108	460	532	17	5	3.00
BOS	81	72	.529	22.5	637	564	175	87	43	.259	.351	194	309	80	.954	100	414	670	13	6	2.46
CLE	71	81	.467	32	539	654	185	63	9	.244	.308	189	247	112	.964	92	487	614	13	5	2.89
CHI	68	85	.444	35.5	456	495	115	58	7	.211	.261	183	314	100	.954	103	381	785	23	7	2.01
WAS	66	85	.437	36.5	498	552	145	46	9	.236	.289	192	264	99	.959	119	374	675	19	3	2.46
STL	47	107	.305	57	454	778	131	60	12	.220	.276	169	377	113	.944	100	532	557	9	3	3.09
LEAGUE TOTAL					4564	4564	1300	568	145	.243	.314	1671	2313	795	.956	855	3462	5276	132	42	2.53

INDIVIDUAL PITCHING

PITCHER	T	W	L	PCT	ERA	SV	G	GS	CG	IP	H	BB	SO	R	ER	ShO	H/9	BB/9	SO/9
George Mullin	R	21	12	.636	2.87	0	38	32	27	289	260	102	98	125	92	5	8.10	3.18	3.05
d Summers	R	13	12	.520	2.53	0	30	25	18	220.1	211	60	82	83	62	1	8.62	2.45	3.35
Wild Bill Donovan	R	17	7	.708	2.42	0	26	23	20	208.2	184	61	107	74	56	3	7.94	2.63	4.62
d Willett	R	16	11	.593	3.60	0	37	25	18	147.1	175	74	65	85	59	4	10.69	4.52	3.97
Sailor Stroud	R	5	9	.357	3.25	1	28	15	7	130.1	123	41	63	54	47	3	8.49	2.83	4.35
Ralph Works	R	3	6	.333	3.57	1	18	10	5	85.2	73	39	36	47	34	0	7.67	4.10	3.78
d Killian	L	4	3	.571	3.04	0	11	9	5	74	75	27	20	38	25	1	9.12	3.28	2.43
Hub Pernoll	L	4	3	.571	2.96	0	11	5	4	54.2	54	14	25	20	18	0	8.89	2.30	4.12
Frank Browning	R	2	2	.500	3.00	3	11	6	2	42	51	10	16	17	14	0	10.93	2.14	3.43
Art Loudell	R	1	1	.500	3.38	0	5	2	1	21.1	23	14	12	13	8	0	9.70	5.91	5.06
Marv Peasley	L	0	1	.000	8.10	0	2	1	0	10	13	14	4	14	9	0	11.70	9.90	3.60
Bill Lelivelt	R	0	1	.000	1.00	0	1	1	1	9	6	3	2	4	1	0	6.00	3.00	2.00
Dave Skeels	R	0	0	--	12.00	0	1	1	0	6	9	4	2	8	8	0	13.50	6.00	3.00
TEAM TOTAL		86	68	.558	3.00	5	219	155	108	1298.1	1257	460	532	582	433	17	8.71	3.19	3.69

MANAGER	W	L	PCT
Hughie Jennings	89	65	.578

POS	Player	B	G	AB	H	2B	3B	HR	HR %	R	RBI	BB	SO	SB	Pinch Hit AB	Pinch Hit H	BA	SA
REGULARS																		
1B	Jim Delahanty	R	144	542	184	30	14	3	0.6	83	94	56		15	1	0	.339	.463
2B	Charley O'Leary	R	74	256	68	8	2	0	0.0	29	25	21		10	0	0	.266	.313
SS	Donie Bush	B	150	561	130	18	5	1	0.2	126	36	98		40	0	0	.232	.287
3B	George Moriarty	R	130	478	116	20	4	1	0.2	51	60	27		28	0	0	.243	.308
RF	Sam Crawford	L	146	574	217	36	14	7	1.2	109	115	61		37	0	0	.378	.526
CF	Ty Cobb	L	146	591	248	47	24	8	1.4	147	144	44		83	0	0	**.420**	**.621**
LF	Davy Jones	L	98	341	93	10	0	0	0.0	78	19	41		25	4	1	.273	.302
C	Oscar Stanage	R	141	503	133	13	7	3	0.6	45	51	20		3	0	0	.264	.336
SUBSTITUTES																		
1B	Del Gainor	R	70	248	75	11	4	2	0.8	32	25	20		10	0	0	.302	.403
2B	Paddy Baumann	R	26	94	24	2	4	0	0.0	8	11	6		1	0	0	.255	.362
UT	Chick Lathers	L	29	45	10	1	0	0	0.0	5	4	5		0	4	2	.222	.244
1B	Jack Ness	R	12	39	6	0	0	0	0.0	6	2	2		0	0	0	.154	.154
2O	Guy Tutwiler	L	13	32	6	2	0	0	0.0	3	3	2		0	3	0	.188	.250
OF	Delos Drake	R	91	315	88	9	9	1	0.3	37	36	17		20	9	3	.279	.375
OF	Biff Schaller	L	40	60	8	0	1	1	1.7	8	7	4		1	17	6	.133	.217
C	Boss Schmidt	B	28	46	13	2	1	0	0.0	4	2	0		0	17	6	.283	.370
C	Joe Casey	R	15	33	5	0	0	0	0.0	2	3	3		0	0	0	.152	.152
C	Squanto Wilson	B	5	16	3	0	0	0	0.0	2	0	2		0	0	0	.188	.188
PITCHERS																		
P	George Mullin	R	40	98	28	7	2	0	0.0	4	5	10		1	8	2	.286	.398
P	Ed Willett	R	39	82	22	4	3	1	1.2	15	7	8		1	0	0	.268	.427
P	Ed Lafitte	R	31	70	11	2	0	1	1.4	6	6	1		0	0	0	.157	.229
P	Ed Summers	B	30	63	16	2	0	0	0.0	4	3	3		0	0	0	.254	.286
P	Ralph Works	L	31	61	9	1	0	0	0.0	2	3	2		0	0	0	.148	.164
P	Wild Bill Donovan	R	24	60	12	3	1	1	1.7	11	6	11		1	1	1	.200	.333
P	Jack Lively	L	20	43	11	2	1	0	0.0	6	4	4		0	2	1	.256	.349
P	Tex Covington	L	17	32	6	0	0	0	0.0	6	3	2		0	0	0	.188	.188
P	Wiley Taylor	R	3	6	0	0	0	0	0.0	0	0	0		0	0	0	.000	.000
P	Clarence Mitchell	L	5	4	2	0	0	0	0.0	2	0	1		0	0	0	.500	.500
P	Pug Cavet	L	1	1	0	0	0	0	0.0	0	0	0		0	0	0	.000	.000
TEAM TOTAL				5294	1544	230	96	30	0.6	831	674	471	0	276	66	22	.292	.388

INDIVIDUAL FIELDING

POS	Player	T	G	PO	A	E	DP	TC/G	FA	POS	Player	T	G	PO	A	E	DP	TC/G	FA
1B	J. Delahanty	R	72	744	21	17	17	10.9	.978	OF	T. Cobb	R	146	**376**	24	18	**10**	**2.9**	.957
	D. Gainor	R	69	671	38	18	36	10.5	.975		S. Crawford	L	146	181	16	5	3	1.4	.975
	J. Ness	R	12	119	9	3	4	10.9	.977		D. Jones	R	92	156	15	9	3	2.0	.950
	D. Drake	L	2	14	1	2	0	8.5	.882		D. Drake	L	83	141	4	9	1	1.9	.942
	G. Moriarty	R	1	5	1	0	0	6.0	1.000		B. Schaller	R	16	26	1	0	1	1.7	1.000
	C. Lathers	R	3	6	0	0	0	2.0	1.000		B. Schmidt	R	1	0	0	0	0	0.0	.000
	B. Schaller	R	1	1	1	0	0	2.0	1.000		P. Baumann	R	3	10	0	0	0	3.3	1.000
											G. Tutwiler	R	3	4	0	0	0	1.3	1.000
2B	C. O'Leary	R	67	169	201	13	19	5.7	.966		E. Lafitte	R	2	3	0	0	0	1.5	1.000
	J. Delahanty	R	59	158	182	19	19	6.1	.947		J. Casey	R	3	2	0	1	0	1.0	.667
	P. Baumann	R	23	58	71	6	6	5.9	.956	C	O. Stanage	R	141	**599**	**212**	41	13	6.0	.952
	G. Tutwiler	R	6	10	11	6	0	4.5	.778		J. Casey	R	12	33	10	2	1	3.8	.956
	C. Lathers	R	9	4	9	2	1	1.7	.867		B. Schmidt	R	9	29	10	0	0	4.3	1.000
SS	D. Bush	R	150	**372**	**556**	75	42	**6.7**	.925		S. Wilson	R	5	20	7	3	0	6.0	.900
	C. Lathers	R	4	7	8	2	1	4.3	.882										
3B	G. Moriarty	R	129	157	273	33	11	3.6	.929										
	J. Delahanty	R	12	15	22	12	5	4.1	.755										
	C. O'Leary	R	6	9	11	1	3	3.5	.952										
	C. Lathers	R	8	4	16	1	0	2.6	.952										

"The Tigers can't lose and the rest of them might as well quit the race," a Detroit newspaper declared as the hometown team won 21 of its first 23 to leap to a dizzying early-season lead. But it was the Tigers who quit. The team that owned a .408 edge over its nearest competitors on May 8—and stayed in first all but one day through August 4—unraveled and struggled in the stretch to stagger home a poor second, 13 1/2 games behind Connie Mack's Athletics.

Ty Cobb, inspired by his rivalry with Cleveland's Shoeless Joe Jackson, authored the best season of his distinguished career. Cobb won his fifth straight batting title at .420, still the highest in Tiger history. He also totaled 248 hits, scored 147 runs, and strung together a 40-game hitting streak—all still team records. He also led the league with 144 RBIs and 83 steals. And new first baseman Del Gainor (.302) had Detroit fans in the spring talking about him in the same sentence with Cobb.

But these two also featured in the nosedive. Cobb, late and overweight for spring training, came into his own as a prima donna. Sam Crawford and Donie Bush, who resented Cobb's special privileges, didn't speak to him. And Gainor was lost during the team's first trip to Philadelphia when his wrist was broken by a pitch.

Still the Tigers, particularly Cobb, had Detroit enraptured. Frank Navin had added bleachers and grandstand seats to Bennett Field to swell capacity to 14,000. That still proved inadequate. So that winter the old wooden stands would come down, a new concrete single deck would go up, and the field would be moved around. Navin Field—grandfather to Tiger Stadium—was about to be born.

TEAM STATISTICS

	W	L	PCT	GB	R	OR	2B	3B	Batting HR	BA	SA	SB	E	Fielding DP	FA	CG	BB	Pitching SO	ShO	SV	ERA
PHI	101	50	.669		861	601	235	93	35	.296	.397	226	225	100	.965	97	487	739	13	13	3.01
DET	89	65	.578	13.5	831	777	230	96	30	.292	.388	276	318	78	.951	108	460	538	8	3	3.73
CLE	80	73	.523	22	691	709	238	81	20	.282	.369	209	302	108	.954	93	550	673	6	6	3.37
CHI	77	74	.510	24	717	627	179	92	20	.269	.350	201	252	98	.961	87	384	752	16	11	3.01
BOS	78	75	.510	24	680	647	203	66	35	.274	.362	190	323	93	.949	87	475	713	10	8	2.73
NY	76	76	.500	25.5	686	726	190	96	26	.272	.363	270	328	99	.949	91	406	667	5	3	3.54
WAS	64	90	.416	38.5	624	760	159	53	16	.258	.320	215	305	90	.953	106	410	628	13	3	3.52
STL	45	107	.296	56.5	567	810	187	63	17	.239	.312	125	358	104	.945	92	463	383	8	1	3.83
LEAGUE TOTAL					5657	5657	1621	640	199	.273	.358	1712	2411	770	.953	761	3635	5093	79	48	3.34

INDIVIDUAL PITCHING

PITCHER	T	W	L	PCT	ERA	SV	G	GS	CG	IP	H	BB	SO	R	ER	ShO	H/9	BB/9	SO/9
George Mullin	R	18	10	.643	3.07	0	30	29	25	234.1	245	61	87	99	80	2	9.41	2.34	3.34
Ed Willett	R	13	14	.481	3.66	1	38	27	15	231.1	261	80	86	136	94	2	10.15	3.11	3.35
Ed Summers	R	11	11	.500	3.66	1	30	20	13	179.1	189	51	65	108	73	0	9.49	2.56	3.26
Ed Lafitte	R	11	8	.579	3.92	1	29	20	15	172.1	205	52	63	113	75	0	10.71	2.72	3.29
Wild Bill Donovan	R	10	9	.526	3.31	0	20	19	15	168.1	160	64	81	83	62	1	8.55	3.42	4.33
Ralph Works	R	11	5	.688	3.87	1	30	15	9	167.1	173	67	68	93	72	3	9.30	3.60	3.66
Jack Lively	R	7	5	.583	4.59	0	18	14	10	113.2	143	34	45	73	58	0	11.32	2.69	3.56
Tex Covington	R	7	1	.875	4.09	0	17	6	5	83.2	94	33	29	43	38	0	10.11	3.55	3.12
Wiley Taylor	R	0	2	.000	3.79	0	3	2	1	19	18	10	9	11	8	0	8.53	4.74	4.26
Clarence Mitchell	L	1	0	1.000	8.16	0	5	1	0	14.1	20	7	4	13	13	0	12.56	4.40	2.51
Pug Cavet	L	0	0	—	4.50	0	1	1	0	4	6	1	1	5	2	0	13.50	2.25	2.25
TEAM TOTAL		89	65	.578	3.73	4	221	154	108	1387.2	1514	460	538	777	575	8	9.82	2.98	3.49

MANAGER	W	L	PCT
Hughie Jennings	69	84	.451

POS	Player	B	G	AB	H	2B	3B	HR	HR%	R	RBI	BB	SO	SB	Pinch Hit AB	Pinch Hit H	BA	SA
REGULARS																		
1B	George Moriarty	R	105	375	93	23	1	0	0.0	38	54	26		27	1	1	.248	.315
2B	Baldy Louden	R	121	403	97	12	4	1	0.2	57	36	58		28	2	1	.241	.298
SS	Donie Bush	B	144	511	118	14	8	2	0.4	107	38	117		35	0	0	.231	.301
3B	Charlie Deal	R	41	142	32	4	2	0	0.0	13	11	9		4	0	0	.225	.282
RF	Sam Crawford	L	149	581	189	30	21	4	0.7	81	109	42		41	0	0	.325	.470
CF	Ty Cobb	L	140	553	**227**	30	23	7	1.3	119	90	43		61	0	0	**.410**	**.586**
LF	Davy Jones	L	97	316	93	5	2	0	0.0	54	24	38		16	15	4	.294	.323
C	Oscar Stanage	R	119	394	103	9	4	0	0.0	35	41	34		3	0	0	.261	.305
SUBSTITUTES																		
2O	Jim Delahanty	R	78	266	76	14	1	0	0.0	34	41	42		9	1	0	.286	.346
1B	Del Gainor	R	51	179	43	5	6	0	0.0	28	20	18		14	0	0	.240	.335
32	Red Corriden	R	38	138	28	6	0	0	0.0	22	5	15		4	3	0	.203	.246
1B	Eddie Onslow	L	35	128	29	1	2	1	0.8	11	13	3		3	0	0	.227	.289
32	Paddy Baumann	R	13	42	11	1	0	0	0.0	3	7	6		4	1	0	.262	.286
2B	Charley O'Leary	R	3	10	2	0	0	0	0.0	1	1	0		0	0	0	.200	.200
2B	Jim McGarr	R	1	4	0	0	0	0	0.0	0	0	0		0	0	0	.000	.000
SS	Ollie O'Mara	R	1	4	0	0	0	0	0.0	0	0	0		0	0	0	.000	.000
1B	Joe Sugden	B	1	4	1	0	0	0	0.0	1	0	0		0	0	0	.250	.250
3B	Ed Irvin		1	3	2	0	2	0	0.0	0	0	0		0	0	0	.667	2.000
SS	Pat Meaney		1	2	0	0	0	0	0.0	0	0	0		0	1	0	.000	.000
3B	Billy Maharg	R	1	1	0	0	0	0	0.0	0	0	0		0	0	0	.000	.000
3B	Jack Smith		1	0	0	0	0	0	-	0	0	0	0	0	0	0	-	-
UT	Ossie Vitt	R	73	273	67	4	4	0	0.0	39	19	18		17	7	1	.245	.289
OF	Bobby Veach	L	23	79	27	5	1	0	0.0	8	15	5		2	1	0	.342	.430
OF	Hank Perry	L	13	36	6	1	0	0	0.0	3	0	3		0	6	3	.167	.194
OF	Red McDermott	R	5	15	4	1	0	0	0.0	2	0	0		1	0	0	.267	.333
UT	Wild Bill Donovan	R	6	13	1	0	0	0	0.0	3	0	1		0	0	0	.077	.077
OF	Al Bashang	B	5	12	1	0	0	0	0.0	3	0	3		0	0	0	.083	.083
OF	Bill Leinhauser	R	1	4	0	0	0	0	0.0	0	0	0		0	0	0	.000	.000
OF	Dan McGarvey		1	3	0	0	0	0	0.0	0	0	0		1	0	0	.000	.000
OF	Hap Ward		1	2	0	0	0	0	0.0	0	0	0		0	0	0	.000	.000
C	Jack Onslow	R	31	69	11	1	0	0	0.0	7	4	10		1	0	0	.159	.174
C	Brad Kocher	R	24	63	13	3	1	0	0.0	5	9	2		0	1	0	.206	.286
C	Deacon McGuire	R	1	2	1	0	0	0	0.0	0	0	1		0	0	0	.500	.500
PH	Hughie Jennings	R	1	1	0	0	0	0	0.0	0	0	0		0	1	0	.000	.000
PITCHERS																		
P	Ed Willett	R	38	115	19	4	1	2	1.7	6	10	4		0	1	1	.165	.270
P	Jean Dubuc	R	40	108	29	6	2	1	0.9	16	9	3		0	1	0	.269	.389
P	George Mullin	R	38	90	25	5	1	0	0.0	13	12	17		0	8	1	.278	.356
P	Joe Lake	R	26	60	8	0	0	1	1.7	4	4	1		0	0	0	.133	.183
P	Ralph Works	L	27	56	8	1	0	0	0.0	3	4	1		0	0	0	.143	.161
P	Tex Covington	L	14	15	2	1	0	0	0.0	1	0	3		0	0	0	.133	.200
P	Bill Burns	B	6	13	3	2	0	0	0.0	0	0	3		0	0	0	.231	.385
P	Charlie Wheatley	R	5	12	0	0	0	0	0.0	0	0	0		0	0	0	.000	.000
P	Bill Jensen	L	4	11	0	0	0	0	0.0	0	0	0		0	0	0	.000	.000
P	George Boehler	R	4	10	1	0	0	0	0.0	0	0	1		0	0	0	.100	.100
P	Ed Summers	B	3	6	3	0	0	0	0.0	0	0	0		0	0	0	.500	.500
P	Harry Moran	L	5	5	1	0	0	0	0.0	1	0	0		0	0	0	.200	.200
P	Hooks Dauss	R	2	4	1	1	0	0	0.0	0	0	0		1	0	0	.250	.500
P	Hub Pernoll	R	3	3	0	0	0	0	0.0	0	0	0		0	0	0	.000	.000
P	Allan Travers	R	1	3	0	0	0	0	0.0	0	0	0		0	0	0	.000	.000
P	Bun Troy	R	1	2	0	0	0	0	0.0	0	0	0		0	0	0	.000	.000
P	Ed Lafitte	R	1	0	0	0	0	0	-	0	0	0		0	0	0	-	-
P	Pat McGehee	L	1	0	0	0	0	0	-	0	0	0		0	0	0	-	-
P	Alex Remneas	R	1	0	0	0	0	0	-	0	0	1		0	0	0	-	-
TEAM TOTAL				5141	1375	189	86	19	0.4	720	576	530	0	270	49	12	.267	.349

INDIVIDUAL FIELDING

POS	Player	T	G	PO	A	E	DP	TC/G	FA
1B	G. Moriarty	R	71	800	27	11	19	11.8	.987
	D. Gainor	R	50	547	22	8	25	11.5	.986
	E. Onslow	L	35	408	15	12	19	12.4	.972
	J. Sugden	R	1	13	3	1	0	17.0	.941
	W. Donovan	R	2	5	0	1	0	3.0	.833
2B	B. Louden	R	86	200	288	25	25	6.0	.951
	J. Delahanty	R	44	95	117	16	19	5.2	.930
	O. Vitt	R	15	29	42	4	3	5.0	.947
	R. Corriden	R	7	16	21	5	0	6.0	.881
	P. Baumann	R	5	16	15	6	1	7.4	.838
	C. O'Leary	R	3	5	11	0	0	5.3	1.000
	J. McGarr	R	1	1	3	1	0	5.0	.800
SS	D. Bush	R	144	317	**547**	66	45	**6.5**	.929
	B. Louden	R	5	10	21	3	0	6.8	.912
	R. Corriden	R	3	6	10	3	0	6.3	.842
	O. O'Mara	R	1	2	4	1	0	7.0	.857
	P. Meaney	R	1	3	2	1	1	6.0	.833
3B	C. Deal	R	41	48	113	10	3	4.2	.942
	G. Moriarty	R	33	42	70	8	6	3.6	.933
	B. Louden	R	26	32	61	11	0	4.0	.894
	O. Vitt	R	24	30	55	3	4	3.7	.966
	R. Corriden	R	25	28	50	6	5	3.4	.929
	P. Baumann	R	6	3	8	3	0	2.3	.786
	J. Smith	R	1	2	1	0	1	3.0	1.000
	E. Irvin	R	1	0	1	1	0	2.0	.500
	B. Maharg	R	1	0	2	0	0	2.0	1.000

POS	Player	T	G	PO	A	E	DP	TC/G	FA
OF	T. Cobb	R	140	324	21	22	5	2.6	.940
	S. Crawford	L	149	169	16	3	5	1.3	.984
	D. Jones	L	81	141	13	6	4	2.0	.963
	J. Delahanty	R	33	53	3	7	0	1.9	.889
	O. Vitt	R	27	50	2	4	1	2.1	.929
	B. Veach	R	22	46	5	4	0	2.5	.927
	P. Baumann	R	1	0	0	0	0	0.0	.000
	W. Donovan	R	2	0	0	0	0	0.0	.000
	H. Perry	R	7	20	2	0	0	3.1	1.000
	R. McDermott	R	5	7	1	0	0	1.6	1.000
	A. Bashang	R	5	6	0	0	0	1.2	1.000
	D. McGarvey		1	1	1	1	0	3.0	.667
	H. Ward		1	2	0	0	0	2.0	1.000
	J. Dubuc	R	2	1	1	0	0	1.0	1.000
	B. Leinhauser	R	1	0	1	0	0	1.0	1.000
C	O. Stanage	R	119	440	**168**	32	**14**	5.4	.950
	J. Onslow	R	31	109	38	8	4	5.0	.948
	B. Kocher	R	23	68	26	10	3	4.5	.904
	E. Irvin	R	0	0	0	0	0	0.0	.000
	D. McGuire	R	1	2	3	2	0	7.0	.714

Navin Field opened on April 20, two days late because of rain and wet grounds—an ominous start for Detroit's dour season. Despite the acquisition of several promising rookies including outfielder Bobby Veach and pitcher Jean Dubuc, the Tigers fell out of the first division into sixth place, 36 1/2 games behind the eventual World Champion Red Sox. Detroit never rose above fourth and struggled to stay ahead of the seventh-place Browns. The only on-the-field highlights were George Mullin's Fourth of July no-hitter (the first ever by a Tiger) over St. Louis, and Ty Cobb's second straight .400-plus season, giving him his sixth straight title.

Cobb's off-field slugging was just as notable. At New York's Hilltop Park in May, Cobb, fed up by a fan's incessant baiting, jumped into the stands to batter the heckler. "He hit me in the face with his fist, knocked me down, jumped on me, kicked me, spiked me, and booted me behind the ear," the fan claimed. Responded Cobb: "I'm pleased I didn't overlook any important punitive measures.' The umpires threw Cobb out of the game and Ban Johnson suspended him indefinitely. The Tigers were furious, voting not to take the field four days later against the Athletics in Philadelphia. Jennings and his coaches (who themselves would have to play) scrambled to field a team. They recruited local semipros and college players including pitcher Al Travers, who would become a priest. The curious collection of Tigers drew 20,000, who watched the Athletics fatten their batting averages, 24–2 (the Athletics did not help themselves into heaven, hammering the future priest for 26 hits).

A fuming Johnson caught a train to Philadelphia and threatened to drum the strikers out of baseball; he eventually fined them $100 each. Cobb was fined $50 and given a 10-day suspension.

TEAM STATISTICS

	W	L	PCT	GB	R	OR	2B	3B	Batting HR	BA	SA	SB	E	Fielding DP	FA	CG	BB	Pitching SO	ShO	SV	ERA
OS	105	47	.691		800	544	269	84	29	.277	.380	185	267	88	.957	108	385	712	18	6	2.76
AS	91	61	.599	14	698	581	202	86	20	.256	.341	274	297	92	.954	98	525	828	11	6	2.69
HI	90	62	.592	15	780	656	204	108	22	.282	.377	258	263	115	.959	100	518	601	11	9	3.32
HI	78	76	.506	28	640	647	174	80	17	.255	.329	205	291	102	.956	85	426	697	14	16	3.06
LE	75	78	.490	30.5	680	681	218	77	10	.273	.352	194	287	124	.954	94	523	622	7	7	3.30
ET	69	84	.451	36.5	720	768	189	86	19	.267	.349	270	338	91	.950	107	517	506	7	5	3.78
TL	53	101	.344	53	556	790	166	71	19	.249	.320	176	341	127	.947	85	442	547	8	5	3.71
Y	50	102	.329	55	632	839	168	79	18	.259	.334	247	382	77	.940	105	436	637	4	3	4.13
EAGUE TOTAL					5506	5506	1590	671	154	.265	.348	1809	2466	816	.952	782	3772	5150	80	57	3.34

INDIVIDUAL PITCHING

ITCHER	T	W	L	PCT	ERA	SV	G	GS	CG	IP	H	BB	SO	R	ER	ShO	H/9	BB/9	SO/9
d Willett	R	17	15	.531	3.29	0	37	31	28	284.1	281	84	89	144	104	1	8.89	2.66	2.82
ean Dubuc	R	17	10	.630	2.77	3	37	26	23	250	217	109	97	106	77	2	7.81	3.92	3.49
eorge Mullin	R	12	17	.414	3.54	0	30	29	22	226	214	92	88	112	89	2	8.52	3.66	3.50
oe Lake	R	9	11	.450	3.10	1	26	14	12	162.2	190	39	86	94	56	0	10.51	2.16	4.76
alph Works	R	5	10	.333	4.24	1	27	17	9	157	185	66	64	101	74	1	10.61	3.78	3.67
ex Covington	R	3	4	.429	4.12	0	14	9	2	63.1	58	30	19	33	29	1	8.24	4.26	2.70
ill Burns	L	1	4	.200	5.35	0	6	5	2	38.2	52	9	6	29	23	0	12.10	2.09	1.40
harlie Wheatley	R	1	4	.200	6.17	0	5	5	2	35	45	17	14	31	24	0	11.57	4.37	3.60
eorge Boehler	R	0	2	.000	6.68	0	4	4	2	31	49	14	13	31	23	0	14.23	4.06	3.77
ill Jensen	R	1	2	.333	5.40	0	4	3	1	25	30	14	4	19	15	0	10.80	5.04	1.44
ooks Dauss	R	1	1	.500	3.18	0	2	2	2	17	11	9	7	7	6	0	5.82	4.76	3.71
d Summers	R	1	1	.500	4.86	0	3	3	1	16.2	16	3	5	11	9	0	8.64	1.62	2.70
arry Moran	L	0	1	.000	4.91	0	5	2	1	14.2	19	12	3	14	8	0	11.66	7.36	1.84
ild Bill Donovan	R	1	0	1.000	0.90	0	3	1	0	10	5	2	6	2	1	0	4.50	1.80	5.40
ub Pernoll	L	0	0	–	6.00	0	3	0	0	9	9	4	3	6	6	0	9.00	4.00	3.00
llan Travers	R	0	1	.000	15.75	0	1	1	1	8	26	7	1	24	14	0	29.25	7.88	1.13
un Troy	R	0	1	.000	5.40	0	1	1	0	6.2	9	3	1	4	4	0	12.15	4.05	1.35
d Lafitte	R	0	0	–	16.20	0	1	0	0	1.2	2	2	0	4	3	0	10.80	10.80	0.00
lex Remneas	R	0	0	–	27.00	0	1	0	0	1.2	5	0	0	5	5	0	27.00	0.00	0.00
at McGehee	R	0	0	–	0.00	0	1	1	0		1	1	0	1	0	0	∞	∞	–
EAM TOTAL		69	84	.451	3.78	5	211	154	108	1358.1	1424	517	506	777	570	7	9.44	3.43	3.35

MANAGER	W	L	PCT
Hughie Jennings	66	87	.431

POS	Player	B	G	AB	H	2B	3B	HR	HR %	R	RBI	BB	SO	SB	Pinch Hit AB	Pinch Hit H	BA	SA
REGULARS																		
1B	Del Gainor	R	104	363	97	16	8	2	0.6	47	25	30	45	10	2	1	.267	.372
2B	Ossie Vitt	R	99	359	86	11	3	2	0.6	45	33	31	18	5	2	0	.240	.304
SS	Donie Bush	B	153	593	149	19	10	1	0.2	98	40	80	32	44	0	0	.251	.322
3B	George Moriarty	R	102	347	83	5	2	0	0.0	29	30	24	25	33	0	0	.239	.265
RF	Sam Crawford	L	153	610	193	32	23	9	1.5	78	83	52	28	13	0	0	.316	.489
CF	Ty Cobb	L	122	428	167	18	16	4	0.9	70	67	58	31	52	0	0	**.390**	.535
LF	Bobby Veach	L	138	494	133	22	10	0	0.0	54	64	53	31	22	1	0	.269	.354
C	Oscar Stanage	R	80	241	54	13	2	0	0.0	19	21	21	35	5	2	2	.224	.295
SUBSTITUTES																		
2B	Paddy Baumann	R	49	191	57	7	4	1	0.5	31	22	16	18	4	0	0	.298	.393
UT	Baldy Louden	R	72	191	46	4	5	0	0.0	28	23	24	22	6	2	0	.241	.314
1B	Eddie Onslow	L	17	55	14	1	0	0	0.0	7	8	5	9	1	0	0	.255	.273
3B	Charlie Deal	R	16	50	11	0	2	0	0.0	3	3	1	7	2	1	0	.220	.300
1B	Guy Tutwiler	L	14	47	10	0	1	0	0.0	4	7	4	12	2	0	0	.213	.255
1B	Wally Pipp	L	12	31	5	0	3	0	0.0	3	5	2	6	0	2	0	.161	.355
2B	Les Hennessy	R	12	22	3	0	0	0	0.0	2	0	3	6	2	2	0	.136	.136
3B	Pepper Peploski	R	2	4	2	0	0	0	0.0	1	0	0	0	0	0	0	.500	.500
3B	Steve Partenheimer	R	1	2	0	0	0	0	0.0	0	0	0	0	0	0	0	.000	.000
OF	Hugh High	L	80	183	42	6	1	0	0.0	18	16	28	24	6	19	5	.230	.273
OF	Al Platte	L	7	18	2	1	0	0	0.0	1	0	1	1	0	2	0	.111	.167
OF	Joe Burns	L	4	13	5	0	0	0	0.0	0	1	2	4	0	0	0	.385	.385
OF	Ray Powell	L	2	0	0	0	0	0	—	0	0	0	0	0	0	0	—	—
C	Red McKee	L	67	187	53	3	4	1	0.5	18	20	21	21	7	6	0	.283	.358
C1	Henri Rondeau	R	35	70	13	2	0	0	0.0	5	5	14	16	1	13	2	.186	.214
C	Frank Gibson	B	20	57	8	1	0	0	0.0	8	2	3	9	2	0	0	.140	.158
PITCHERS																		
P	Jean Dubuc	R	68	135	36	5	3	2	1.5	17	11	2	17	1	28	3	.267	.393
P	Ed Willett	R	35	92	26	4	1	1	1.1	8	13	3	23	0	1	0	.283	.380
P	Hooks Dauss	R	35	79	14	3	2	0	0.0	15	7	9	14	0	0	0	.177	.266
P	Marc Hall	R	30	45	4	1	0	0	0.0	2	3	1	9	0	0	0	.089	.111
P	Joe Lake	R	28	45	12	3	1	1	2.2	4	4	1	10	1	0	0	.267	.444
P	Ralph Comstock	R	10	22	5	2	0	0	0.0	2	3	0	7	0	0	0	.227	.318
P	Carl Zamloch	R	17	22	4	0	0	0	0.0	3	0	0	5	0	0	0	.182	.182
P	George Mullin	R	12	20	7	0	0	0	0.0	1	1	4	1	0	3	1	.350	.350
P	Al Klawitter	R	8	11	0	0	0	0	0.0	0	0	0	0	0	0	0	.000	.000
P	Fred House	R	19	10	0	0	0	0	0.0	0	1	1	7	0	0	0	.000	.000
P	Lefty Williams	R	5	10	1	0	0	0	0.0	1	0	1	5	0	0	0	.100	.100
P	Al Clauss	L	5	4	0	0	0	0	0.0	0	0	0	3	0	0	0	.000	.000
P	George Boehler	R	1	3	1	1	0	0	0.0	0	0	0	0	0	0	0	.333	.667
P	Charlie Grover	L	2	3	0	0	0	0	0.0	0	0	1	0	0	0	0	.000	.000
P	Lefty Lorenzen	L	1	2	1	0	0	0	0.0	1	1	0	0	0	0	0	.500	.500
P	Lou North	R	1	2	0	0	0	0	0.0	0	0	0	0	0	0	0	.000	.000
P	Erwin Renfer	R	1	2	0	0	0	0	0.0	0	0	0	0	0	0	0	.000	.000
P	Heinie Elder	L	1	1	0	0	0	0	0.0	0	0	0	0	0	0	0	.000	.000
P	Charlie Harding	R	1	0	0	0	0	0	—	0	0	0	0	0	0	0	—	—
TEAM TOTAL				5064	1344	180	101	24	0.5	624	519	496	501	219	88	14	.265	.355

INDIVIDUAL FIELDING

POS	Player	T	G	PO	A	E	DP	TC/G	FA	POS	Player	T	G	PO	A	E	DP	TC/G	FA
1B	D. Gainor	R	102	1118	50	14	55	**11.6**	.988	OF	T. Cobb	R	118	262	22	16	8	2.5	.947
	E. Onslow	L	17	191	7	2	9	11.8	.990		B. Veach	R	137	250	16	24	3	2.1	.917
	S. Crawford	L	13	156	7	6	6	13.0	.964		S. Crawford	L	140	201	14	8	5	1.6	.964
	G. Tutwiler	R	14	140	10	2	10	10.9	.987		H. High	L	50	104	8	2	0	2.3	.982
	W. Pipp	L	10	80	4	2	6	8.6	.977		R. Powell	R	1	0	0	0	0	0.0	.000
	H. Rondeau	R	6	54	4	4	1	10.3	.935		G. Moriarty	R	7	14	0	1	0	2.1	.933
2B	O. Vitt	R	78	151	234	16	24	5.1	.960		A. Platte	L	5	8	0	2	0	2.0	.800
	P. Baumann	R	49	97	136	14	15	5.0	.943		J. Burns	L	4	7	0	0	0	1.8	1.000
	B. Louden	R	32	43	72	12	6	4.0	.906		B. Louden	R	5	5	1	0	0	1.2	1.000
	L. Hennessy	R	9	8	14	3	0	2.8	.880		O. Vitt	R	2	4	0	0	0	2.0	1.000
SS	D. Bush	R	153	331	510	56	61	5.9	.938		J. Dubuc	R	3	1	0	1	0	0.7	.500
	B. Louden	R	6	5	14	0	1	3.2	1.000		F. Gibson	R	1	0	0	1	0	1.0	.000
3B	G. Moriarty	R	93	122	183	20	9	3.5	.938	C	O. Stanage	R	77	277	106	16	6	5.2	.960
	B. Louden	R	26	23	59	5	4	3.3	.943		R. McKee	R	61	237	84	17	5	5.5	.950
	O. Vitt	R	17	19	49	7	1	4.4	.907		F. Gibson	R	19	57	17	7	1	4.3	.914
	C. Deal	R	15	14	35	9	3	3.9	.845		H. Rondeau	R	14	46	22	0	1	4.9	1.000
	Partenheimer	R	1	0	3	1	0	4.0	.750										
	P. Peploski	R	2	0	1	0	0	0.5	1.000										

From start to finish, it was not a good year. The weather was foul in the spring, the Tigers foul all season. Detroit finished sixth for the second straight year, 30 games behind the Athletics.

Before the season, Ty Cobb had conducted his by-then annual holdout, jousting with Frank Navin for a $2000 raise to $12,000. "Cobb is becoming a real threat," said the tight-fisted owner. "He may or may not belong on our team. But does he want to wind up owning it?" Cobb, who would finish his baseball days salaried at more than $40,000 per season, said, in effect, Pay me or trade me. "I want security," he argued. "I don't know when I'm going to get hurt and be forced out of the game. I want to give my best to the game. But I want all the money I can get in return." Navin whined that $12,000 would bankrupt him. Georgia Senator Hoke Smith then began to question whether baseball violated federal antitrust laws. Navin gave the Georgia Peach his raise.

Cobb responded by capturing his seventh straight batting crown at .390. And although Sam Crawford slowed down in the outfield, he hit .316 and led the league in total bases with 298. But no other Tiger hit close to .300.

Hugh Jennings in turn tried to experiment, occasionally using outfielder Ossie Vitt at second and third. He also picked up pitcher Charley "Sea Lion" Hall, diminutive outfielder Hughie High, and catcher Henri Rondeau. Nothing helped. The pitching staff particularly hurt. Wild Bill Donovan and Charley O'Leary had departed the previous season. The other leftover from the three-time pennant winners, George Mullin, won one and lost six with his fading fastball before getting shipped to Washington. Ed Willett finished 13–14. And while three Tigers hurlers (Jean Dubuc, Hooks Dauss, and Joe Lake) topped .500, each did it by a single victory.

TEAM STATISTICS

	W	L	PCT	GB	R	OR	Batting 2B	3B	HR	BA	SA	SB	Fielding E	DP	FA	CG	BB	Pitching SO	ShO	SV	ERA
HI	96	57	.627		794	593	223	80	33	.280	.376	221	212	108	.966	69	532	630	17	22	3.19
AS	90	64	.584	6.5	596	566	156	80	20	.252	.327	287	261	122	.960	78	465	757	23	20	2.72
LE	86	66	.566	9.5	631	529	205	74	16	.268	.348	191	242	124	.962	95	502	689	18	5	2.52
OS	79	71	.527	15.5	630	607	221	101	17	.269	.364	189	237	84	.961	87	442	710	11	11	2.93
HI	78	74	.513	17.5	486	492	157	66	23	.236	.310	156	255	104	.960	86	438	602	17	8	2.33
ET	66	87	.431	30	624	720	180	101	24	.265	.355	219	300	105	.954	90	504	468	4	7	3.41
Y	57	94	.377	38	529	669	154	45	9	.237	.293	203	293	94	.954	75	455	530	8	7	3.27
TL	57	96	.373	39	528	642	179	73	18	.237	.312	209	301	125	.954	104	454	476	14	5	3.06
AGUE TOTAL					4818	4818	1475	620	160	.256	.336	1675	2101	866	.959	684	3792	4862	112	85	2.93

INDIVIDUAL PITCHING

TCHER	T	W	L	PCT	ERA	SV	G	GS	CG	IP	H	BB	SO	R	ER	ShO	H/9	BB/9	SO/9
ean Dubuc	R	15	14	.517	2.89	2	36	28	22	242.2	228	91	73	111	78	1	8.46	3.38	2.71
d Willett	R	13	14	.481	3.09	0	34	30	19	242	237	89	59	117	83	0	8.81	3.31	2.19
ooks Dauss	R	13	12	.520	2.68	1	33	29	22	225	188	82	107	101	67	2	7.52	3.28	4.28
arc Hall	R	10	12	.455	3.27	0	30	21	8	165	154	79	69	79	60	1	8.40	4.31	3.76
e Lake	R	8	7	.533	3.28	1	28	12	6	137	149	24	35	65	50	0	9.79	1.58	2.30
rl Zamloch	R	1	6	.143	2.45	1	17	5	3	69.2	66	23	28	31	19	0	8.53	2.97	3.62
alph Comstock	R	2	5	.286	5.37	1	10	7	1	60.1	90	16	37	55	36	0	13.43	2.39	5.52
ed House	R	1	2	.333	5.20	0	19	2	0	53.2	64	17	16	40	31	0	10.73	2.85	2.68
eorge Mullin	R	1	6	.143	2.75	0	7	7	4	52.1	53	18	16	28	16	0	9.11	3.10	2.75
Klawitter	R	1	2	.333	5.91	0	8	3	1	32	39	15	10	25	21	0	10.97	4.22	2.81
fty Williams	L	1	3	.250	4.97	1	5	4	3	29	34	4	9	18	16	0	10.55	1.24	2.79
Clauss	L	0	1	.000	4.73	0	5	1	0	13.1	11	12	1	9	7	0	7.43	8.10	0.68
narlie Grover	R	0	0	—	3.38	0	2	1	0	10.2	9	7	2	4	4	0	7.59	5.91	1.69
eorge Boehler	R	0	1	.000	6.75	0	1	1	1	8	11	6	2	9	6	0	12.38	6.75	2.25
u North	R	0	1	.000	6.00	0	1	1	0	6	10	9	3	11	10	0	15.00	13.50	4.50
win Renfer	R	0	1	.000	6.00	0	1	1	0	6	5	3	1	5	4	0	7.50	4.50	1.50
einie Elder	L	0	0	—	8.10	0	1	0	0	3.1	4	5	0	3	3	0	10.80	13.50	0.00
narlie Harding	R	0	0	—	4.50	0	1	0	0	2	3	1	0	1	1	0	13.50	4.50	0.00
fty Lorenzen	L	0	0	—	18.00	0	1	0	0	2	4	3	0	4	4	0	18.00	13.50	0.00
AM TOTAL		66	87	.431	3.41	7	240	153	90	1360	1359	504	468	716	516	4	8.99	3.34	3.10

MANAGER	W	L	PCT
Hughie Jennings	80	73	.523

POS	Player	B	G	AB	H	2B	3B	HR	HR %	R	RBI	BB	SO	SB	Pinch Hit AB	Pinch Hit H	BA	SA
REGULARS																		
1B	George Burns	R	137	478	139	22	5	5	1.0	55	57	32	56	23	0	0	.291	.389
2B	Marty Kavanagh	R	127	439	109	21	6	4	0.9	60	35	41	42	16	8	1	.248	.351
SS	Donie Bush	B	157	596	150	18	4	0	0.0	97	32	112	54	35	0	0	.252	.295
3B	George Moriarty	R	130	465	118	19	5	1	0.2	56	40	39	27	34	0	0	.254	.323
RF	Sam Crawford	L	157	582	183	22	26	8	1.4	74	104	69	31	25	0	0	.314	.483
CF	Ty Cobb	L	97	345	127	22	11	2	0.6	69	57	57	22	35	0	0	.368	.513
LF	Bobby Veach	L	149	531	146	19	14	1	0.2	56	72	50	29	20	3	3	.275	.369
C	Oscar Stanage	R	122	400	77	8	4	0	0.0	16	25	24	58	2	0	0	.193	.233
SUBSTITUTES																		
23	Ossie Vitt	R	66	195	49	7	0	0	0.0	35	8	31	8	10	8	0	.251	.287
3B	Billy Purtell	R	26	76	13	4	0	0	0.0	4	3	2	7	0	8	1	.171	.224
2B	Paddy Baumann	R	3	11	0	0	0	0	0.0	1	0	2	1	0	0	0	.000	.000
SS	Fred McMullin	R	1	1	0	0	0	0	0.0	0	0	0	1	0	0	0	.000	.000
1B	Del Gainor	R	1	0	0	0	0	0	–	0	0	0	0	0	0	0	–	–
OF	Hugh High	L	80	184	49	5	3	0	0.0	25	17	26	21	7	19	3	.266	.326
UT	Harry Heilmann	R	67	182	41	8	1	2	1.1	25	22	22	29	1	11	3	.225	.313
C	Del Baker	R	43	70	15	2	1	0	0.0	4	1	6	9	0	3	0	.214	.271
C	Red McKee	L	32	64	12	1	1	0	0.0	7	8	14	16	1	5	1	.188	.234
PH	Ray Demmitt	L	1	0	0	0	0	0	–	0	0	0	0	0	0	0	–	–
PITCHERS																		
P	Jean Dubuc	R	70	124	28	8	1	1	0.8	9	11	7	11	1	32	6	.226	.331
P	Hooks Dauss	R	45	97	21	4	0	1	1.0	8	7	11	24	0	0	0	.216	.289
P	Harry Coveleski	B	44	95	23	2	1	0	0.0	6	12	6	28	0	0	0	.242	.284
P	Pug Cavet	L	31	47	5	1	0	0	0.0	3	2	2	22	0	0	0	.106	.128
P	Alex Main	L	32	40	4	0	0	0	0.0	1	0	3	15	0	0	0	.100	.100
P	Marc Hall	R	25	23	1	0	0	0	0.0	0	0	0	7	0	0	0	.043	.043
P	Ross Reynolds	R	26	21	1	0	0	0	0.0	1	0	0	8	0	0	0	.048	.048
P	George Boehler	R	18	17	3	0	1	0	0.0	2	3	1	4	1	0	0	.176	.294
P	Red Oldham	L	9	15	4	2	0	0	0.0	1	1	0	6	0	0	0	.267	.400
P	Johnny Williams	R	4	3	0	0	0	0	0.0	0	0	0	1	0	0	0	.000	.000
P	Ed McCreery	R	3	1	0	0	0	0	0.0	0	0	0	0	0	0	0	.000	.000
P	Lefty Williams	R	1	0	0	0	0	0	–	0	0	0	0	0	0	0	–	–
	TEAM TOTAL			5102	1318	195	84	25	0.5	615	517	557	537	211	97	18	.258	.344

INDIVIDUAL FIELDING

POS	Player	T	G	PO	A	E	DP	TC/G	FA		POS	Player	T	G	PO	A	E	DP	TC/G	FA
1B	G. Burns	R	137	1576	79	30	72	12.3	.982		OF	B. Veach	R	145	282	22	11	6	2.2	.965
	H. Heilmann	R	16	165	12	4	9	11.3	.978			S. Crawford	L	157	193	18	5	4	1.4	.977
	M. Kavanagh	R	4	36	1	2	0	9.8	.949			T. Cobb	R	96	177	8	10	0	2.0	.949
	G. Moriarty	R	3	26	1	0	0	9.0	1.000			H. High	L	53	92	2	4	1	1.8	.959
	D. Gainor	R	1	4	0	0	0	4.0	1.000			H. Heilmann	R	29	35	5	6	1	1.6	.870
												O. Vitt	R	2	5	0	0	0	2.5	1.000
2B	M. Kavanagh	R	115	228	333	43	30	5.3	.929											
	O. Vitt	R	36	48	112	6	9	4.6	.964		C	O. Stanage	R	122	532	190	30	11	6.2	.960
	H. Heilmann	R	6	9	14	1	1	4.0	.958			D. Baker	R	38	79	25	9	3	3.0	.920
	P. Baumann	R	3	5	8	0	1	4.3	1.000			R. McKee	R	27	87	20	4	2	4.1	.964
	B. Purtell	R	1	1	2	0	0	3.0	1.000											
SS	D. Bush	R	157	425	544	58	64	6.5	.944											
	F. McMullin	R	1	1	1	1	0	3.0	.667											
	B. Purtell	R	1	1	0	1	0	2.0	.500											
	O. Vitt	R	1	0	1	0	0	1.0	1.000											
3B	G. Moriarty	R	126	125	312	20	16	3.6	.956											
	O. Vitt	R	16	15	42	3	4	3.8	.950											
	B. Purtell	R	16	19	34	3	2	3.5	.946											

The year a shooting war exploded in Europe, a bidding war erupted in baseball, as the newly formed Federal League wooed players from the American and National. The Tigers lost only pitcher Ed Willett and part-time third baeman Baldy Louden—and lots of cash. With the Federals offering to double their salaries, Ty Cobb and Sam Crawford held out through spring training. Cobb was finally signed for more than $20,000. Crawford, at age 35, got a four-year pact. The one-two punch rejoined the Tigers just before the team started north.

At first, team president Frank Navin got his money's worth. The Tigers raced to a fast start. By May 21 they sat in first place at 19–9. The Athletics caught them by Memorial Day, but as late as July 22 the Tigers held second, just a game behind Philadelphia.

Then injuries struck, including a pair to Cobb: a broken rib, then a broken thumb incurred during a brawl with a Detroit butcher boy. Several players fell into batting slumps. And Detroit fell into fourth place, where it finished—seven games over .500, 19 1/2 games out. Cobb, despite the injuries and appearing in only 97 games, won his eighth straight batting crown at .368. Crawford led the league in RBIs and triples.

Hughie Jennings acquired a gem for his pitching staff. Harry Coveleski, a former National Leaguer who joined the Tigers from Chattanooga, became Detroit's first 20-game winner in four years at 22–12, for the lefthander's first of three straight 20-win seasons.

It was also the summer of rookie outfielder–first baseman Harry Heilmann's arrival. Heilmann hit just .225 in 67 games, and he'd be optioned to San Francisco in 1915. But lifetime he'd hit .342, second only to Cobb among Tigers, and spend 15 summers in Detroit en route to Cooperstown.

TEAM STATISTICS

	W	L	PCT	GB	R	OR	2B	3B	HR	BA	SA	SB	E	DP	FA	CG	BB	SO	ShO	SV	ERA
									Batting				Fielding			Pitching					
HI	99	53	.651		749	520	165	80	29	.272	.352	231	213	116	.966	89	521	720	24	17	2.78
OS	91	62	.595	8.5	588	511	226	85	18	.250	.338	177	242	99	.963	88	397	605	24	8	2.35
AS	81	73	.526	19	572	519	176	81	18	.244	.320	220	254	116	.961	75	520	784	25	20	2.54
ET	80	73	.523	19.5	615	618	195	84	25	.258	.344	211	286	101	.958	81	498	567	14	12	2.86
TL	71	82	.464	28.5	523	614	185	75	17	.243	.319	233	317	114	.952	81	540	553	15	11	2.85
HI	70	84	.455	30	487	568	161	71	19	.243	.311	167	299	90	.955	74	401	660	17	11	2.48
Y	70	84	.455	30	536	550	149	52	12	.229	.287	251	238	93	.963	98	390	563	9	5	2.81
LE	51	102	.333	48.5	538	708	178	70	10	.245	.312	167	300	119	.953	69	666	688	10	3	3.21
AGUE TOTAL					4608	4608	1435	598	148	.248	.323	1657	2149	848	.959	655	3933	5140	138	87	2.73

INDIVIDUAL PITCHING

TCHER	T	W	L	PCT	ERA	SV	G	GS	CG	IP	H	BB	SO	R	ER	ShO	H/9	BB/9	SO/9
arry Coveleski	L	22	12	.647	2.49	2	44	36	23	303.1	251	100	124	109	84	5	7.45	2.97	3.68
ooks Dauss	R	18	15	.545	2.86	4	45	35	22	302	286	87	150	126	96	3	8.52	2.59	4.47
an Dubuc	R	13	14	.481	3.46	1	36	27	15	224	216	76	70	124	86	2	8.68	3.05	2.81
ug Cavet	L	7	7	.500	2.44	2	31	14	6	151.1	129	44	51	61	41	1	7.67	2.62	3.03
ex Main	R	6	6	.500	2.67	3	32	12	5	138.1	131	59	55	51	41	1	8.52	3.84	3.58
arc Hall	R	4	6	.400	2.69	0	25	8	1	90.1	88	27	18	38	27	0	8.77	2.69	1.79
oss Reynolds	R	5	3	.625	2.08	0	26	7	3	78	62	39	31	26	18	1	7.15	4.50	3.58
eorge Boehler	R	2	3	.400	3.57	0	18	6	2	63	54	48	37	39	25	0	7.71	6.86	5.29
ed Oldham	L	2	4	.333	3.38	0	9	7	3	45.1	42	8	23	22	17	0	8.34	1.59	4.57
ohnny Williams	R	0	2	.000	6.35	0	4	3	1	11.1	17	5	4	12	8	0	13.50	3.97	3.18
d McCreery	R	1	0	1.000	11.25	0	3	1	0	4	6	3	4	5	5	0	13.50	6.75	9.00
efty Williams	L	0	1	.000	0.00	0	1	1	0	1	3	2	0	5	0	0	27.00	18.00	0.00
EAM TOTAL		80	73	.523	2.86	12	274	157	81	1412	1285	498	567	618	448	13	8.19	3.17	3.61

MANAGER	W	L	PCT
Hughie Jennings	100	54	.649

POS	Player	B	G	AB	H	2B	3B	HR	HR %	R	RBI	BB	SO	SB	Pinch Hit AB	Pinch Hit H	BA	SA
REGULARS																		
1B	George Burns	R	105	392	99	18	3	5	1.3	49	50	22	51	9	1	0	.253	.352
2B	Ralph Young	B	123	378	92	6	5	0	0.0	44	31	53	31	12	0	0	.243	.286
SS	Donie Bush	B	155	561	128	12	8	1	0.2	99	44	118	44	35	0	0	.228	.283
3B	Ossie Vitt	R	152	560	140	18	13	1	0.2	116	48	80	22	26	0	0	.250	.334
RF	Sam Crawford	L	156	612	183	31	19	4	0.7	81	112	66	29	24	0	0	.299	.431
CF	Ty Cobb	L	156	563	208	31	13	3	0.5	144	99	118	43	96	0	0	.369	.487
LF	Bobby Veach	L	152	569	178	40	10	3	0.5	81	112	68	43	16	0	0	.313	.434
C	Oscar Stanage	R	100	300	67	9	2	1	0.3	27	31	20	41	5	0	0	.223	.277
SUBSTITUTES																		
12	Marty Kavanagh	R	113	332	98	14	13	4	1.2	55	49	42	44	8	20	10	.295	.452
1O	Baby Doll Jacobson	R	37	65	14	6	2	0	0.0	5	4	5	14	0	20	5	.215	.369
3B	George Moriarty	R	31	38	8	1	0	0	0.0	2	0	5	7	1	10	2	.211	.237
2B	Frank Fuller	B	14	32	5	0	0	0	0.0	6	2	9	7	2	2	1	.156	.156
C	Del Baker	R	68	134	33	3	3	0	0.0	16	15	15	15	3	3	0	.246	.313
C	Red McKee	L	55	106	29	5	0	1	0.9	10	17	13	16	1	15	2	.274	.349
C	John Peters	R	1	3	0	0	0	0	0.0	0	0	0	1	0	0	0	.000	.000
PITCHERS																		
P	Jean Dubuc	R	60	112	23	2	1	0	0.0	7	14	8	15	0	17	5	.205	.241
P	Harry Coveleski	B	50	103	18	2	0	0	0.0	9	6	7	29	0	0	0	.175	.194
P	Hooks Dauss	R	46	103	15	2	2	0	0.0	9	6	16	26	2	0	0	.146	.204
P	Bernie Boland	R	47	63	11	1	0	0	0.0	5	1	7	14	0	0	0	.175	.190
P	Bill Steen	R	20	28	5	0	0	0	0.0	2	2	1	6	0	0	0	.179	.179
P	Pug Cavet	L	17	24	6	3	0	0	0.0	3	1	2	12	1	0	0	.250	.375
P	Bill James	B	11	21	6	1	0	0	0.0	4	2	3	6	0	0	0	.286	.333
P	Red Oldham	L	17	14	2	1	0	0	0.0	2	0	2	8	0	0	0	.143	.214
P	Grover Lowdermilk	R	7	8	1	0	0	0	0.0	0	0	1	1	0	0	0	.125	.125
P	George Boehler	R	9	4	3	1	0	0	0.0	2	1	0	0	0	0	0	.750	1.000
P	Ross Reynolds	R	4	3	0	0	0	0	0.0	0	0	0	2	0	0	0	.000	.000
P	Razor Ledbetter	R	1	0	0	0	0	0	—	0	0	0	0	0	0	0	—	—
TEAM TOTAL				5128	1372	207	94	23	0.4	778	647	681	527	241	88	25	.268	.358

INDIVIDUAL FIELDING

POS	Player	T	G	PO	A	E	DP	TC/G	FA	POS	Player	T	G	PO	A	E	DP	TC/G	FA
1B	G. Burns	R	104	1155	57	17	65	11.8	.986	OF	T. Cobb	R	156	328	22	18	7	2.4	.951
	M. Kavanagh	R	44	500	24	7	16	12.1	.987		B. Veach	R	152	297	19	8	4	2.1	.975
	B. Jacobson	R	10	114	4	2	5	12.0	.983		S. Crawford	L	156	219	8	6	1	1.5	.974
	G. Moriarty	R	1	3	0	0	0	3.0	1.000		B. Jacobson	R	7	8	1	0	0	1.3	1.000
2B	R. Young	R	119	233	371	32	44	5.3	.950		M. Kavanagh	R	2	4	0	0	0	2.0	1.000
	M. Kavanagh	R	42	59	95	12	7	4.0	.928		G. Moriarty	R	1	1	0	0	0	1.0	1.000
	G. Moriarty	R	1	0	0	0	0	0.0	.000	C	O. Stanage	R	100	395	111	19	0	5.3	.964
	F. Fuller	R	9	7	18	1	1	2.9	.962		D. Baker	R	61	184	53	15	8	4.1	.940
	O. Vitt	R	2	0	1	0	0	0.5	1.000		R. McKee	R	35	116	30	7	4	4.4	.954
SS	D. Bush	R	155	340	504	57	61	5.8	.937		J. Peters	R	1	6	3	0	0	9.0	1.000
	F. Fuller	R	1	1	2	1	0	4.0	.750										
	M. Kavanagh	R	2	0	2	0	1	1.0	1.000										
3B	O. Vitt	R	151	191	324	19	19	3.5	.964										
	G. Moriarty	R	12	7	14	3	1	2.0	.875										

The Tigers won 100 games for the first time. They also became the first American League team (one of six in major league history) ever to win 100 and not win the pennant: Detroit finished second at 100–54, two-and-a-half games behind the soon-to-be World Champion Red Sox. "It was a great disappointment," said Ty Cobb. "I was little more than a youngster in my three Series. By this time I had matured and I think I could have shown those National Leaguers something."

Cobb could hardly blame himself. He won his ninth straight batting title at .369 and stole a career-high 96 bases (he was also caught 38 times, both all-time Tiger highs). And he formed a formidable outfield with Sam Crawford (.299, league-leading 112 RBIs) in right and Bobby Veach (.313, also with 112 RBIs) in left. Leading the pitching staff was Hooks Dauss at 24–13 and Harry Coveleski at 22–13.

So the Tigers started splendidly, owning first place most of the first month. For the remainder of the season they held a close second. But they never again held first because they couldn't beat the Red Sox, who took the season series, 14–8. That included the pennant-showdown at Fenway Park in mid-September, labeled "the little World Series" by newspapers that incited their readers with reminders of both teams' rough reputations: the Red Sox for beanballs, the Tigers for high spikes.

Cobb immediately imprinted his mark on the duel. In the Thursday opener, submariner Carl Mays threw a brushback pitch at Cobb, who in turn threw his bat at Mays. That riled Boston fans—never enamored with Cobb—enough to necessitate a squad of police to escort the Detroit star when he left the field. Dauss helped the Tigers win that first game, 6–1, but the Sox swept the next three, helped by the performance of a rookie lefthander named Babe Ruth. That gave the Red Sox a cushion the Tigers couldn't deflate during the final two weeks of the season. Hugh Jennings called it his biggest disappointment in Detroit.

TEAM STATISTICS

	W	L	PCT	GB	R	OR	Batting 2B	3B	HR	BA	SA	SB	Fielding E	DP	FA	Pitching CG	BB	SO	ShO	SV	ERA
OS	101	50	.669		668	499	202	76	14	.260	.339	118	226	95	.964	82	446	634	19	15	2.39
ET	100	54	.649	2.5	778	573	207	94	23	.268	.358	241	258	107	.961	86	489	550	9	19	2.86
HI	93	61	.604	9.5	717	509	163	102	25	.258	.348	233	222	95	.965	92	350	635	17	9	2.43
AS	85	68	.556	17	571	492	152	79	12	.244	.312	186	230	101	.964	87	455	715	21	13	2.31
Y	69	83	.454	32.5	583	596	167	50	31	.233	.305	198	217	118	.966	101	517	559	12	2	3.09
L	63	91	.409	39.5	521	693	166	65	19	.246	.315	202	335	144	.949	76	612	566	6	7	3.07
E	57	95	.375	44.5	539	670	169	79	20	.241	.317	138	280	82	.957	62	518	610	11	10	3.13
HI	43	109	.283	58.5	545	890	183	72	16	.237	.311	127	338	118	.947	78	827	588	6	2	4.33
AGUE TOTAL					4922	4922	1409	617	160	.248	.326	1443	2106	860	.959	664	4214	4857	101	77	2.94

INDIVIDUAL PITCHING

TCHER	T	W	L	PCT	ERA	SV	G	GS	CG	IP	H	BB	SO	R	ER	ShO	H/9	BB/9	SO/9
arry Coveleski	L	22	13	.629	2.45	4	50	38	20	312.2	271	87	150	123	85	1	7.80	2.50	4.32
ooks Dauss	R	24	13	.649	2.50	2	46	35	27	309.2	261	112	132	115	86	1	7.59	3.26	3.84
an Dubuc	R	17	12	.586	3.21	2	39	33	22	258	231	88	74	116	92	5	8.06	3.07	2.58
rnie Boland	R	13	7	.650	3.11	2	45	18	8	202.2	167	75	72	86	70	1	7.42	3.33	3.20
l Steen	R	5	1	.833	2.72	4	20	7	3	79.1	83	22	28	35	24	0	9.42	2.50	3.18
g Cavet	L	4	2	.667	4.06	1	17	7	2	71	83	22	26	39	32	0	10.52	2.79	3.30
l James	R	7	3	.700	2.42	0	11	9	3	67	57	33	24	26	18	1	7.66	4.43	3.22
d Oldham	L	3	0	1.000	2.81	4	17	2	1	57.2	52	17	17	22	18	0	8.12	2.65	2.65
over Lowdermilk	R	4	1	.800	4.18	0	7	5	0	28	17	24	18	16	13	0	5.46	7.71	5.79
orge Boehler	R	1	1	.500	1.80	0	8	0	0	15	19	4	7	10	3	0	11.40	2.40	4.20
ss Reynolds	R	0	1	.000	6.35	0	4	2	0	11.1	17	5	2	9	8	0	13.50	3.97	1.59
zor Ledbetter	R	0	0	—	0.00	0	1	0	0	1	1	0	0	0	0	0	9.00	0.00	0.00
AM TOTAL		100	54	.649	2.86	19	265	156	86	1413.1	1259	489	550	597	449	9	8.02	3.11	3.50

MANAGER	W	L	PCT
Hughie Jennings	87	67	.565

POS	Player	B	G	AB	H	2B	3B	HR	HR %	R	RBI	BB	SO	SB	Pinch Hit AB	Pinch Hit H	BA	SA
REGULARS																		
1B	George Burns	R	135	479	137	22	6	4	0.8	60	73	22	30	12	11	3	.286	.382
2B	Ralph Young	B	153	528	139	16	6	1	0.2	60	45	62	43	20	0	0	.263	.322
SS	Donie Bush	B	145	550	124	5	9	0	0.0	73	34	75	42	19	0	0	.225	.267
3B	Ossie Vitt	R	153	597	135	17	12	0	0.0	88	42	75	28	18	0	0	.226	.295
RF	Harry Heilmann	R	136	451	127	30	11	2	0.4	57	76	42	40	9	16	5	.282	.410
CF	Ty Cobb	L	145	542	201	31	10	5	0.9	113	68	78	39	68	0	0	.371	.493
LF	Bobby Veach	L	150	566	173	33	15	3	0.5	92	91	52	41	24	0	0	.306	.433
C	Oscar Stanage	R	94	291	69	17	3	0	0.0	16	30	17	48	3	0	0	.237	.316
SUBSTITUTES																		
SS	Ben Dyer	R	4	14	4	1	0	0	0.0	4	1	1	1	0	0	0	.286	.357
2B	Frank Fuller	B	20	10	1	0	0	0	0.0	2	1	1	4	3	1	0	.100	.100
3B	Babe Ellison	R	2	7	1	0	0	0	0.0	0	1	0	1	0	0	0	.143	.143
3B	George Maisel	R	7	5	0	0	0	0	0.0	2	0	0	2	0	0	0	.000	.000
OF	Sam Crawford	L	100	322	92	11	13	0	0.0	41	42	37	10	10	15	8	.286	.401
UT	Marty Kavanagh	R	58	78	11	4	0	0	0.0	6	5	9	15	0	39*	6	.141	.192
OF	George Harper	L	44	56	9	1	0	0	0.0	4	3	5	8	0	24	4	.161	.179
OF	Jack Dalton	R	8	11	2	0	0	0	0.0	1	0	0	5	0	2	1	.182	.182
C	Del Baker	R	61	98	15	4	0	0	0.0	7	6	11	8	2	1	0	.153	.194
C	Red McKee	L	32	76	16	1	2	0	0.0	3	4	6	11	0	6	2	.211	.276
C	Tubby Spencer	R	19	54	20	1	1	1	1.9	7	10	6	6	2	0	0	.370	.481
C	Billy Sullivan	R	1	0	0	0	0	0	-	0	0	0	0	0	0	0	-	-
PITCHERS																		
P	Harry Coveleski	B	44	118	25	3	2	0	0.0	7	7	0	38	0	0	0	.212	.271
P	Jean Dubuc	R	52	78	20	0	2	0	0.0	3	7	7	12	0	12	2	.256	.308
P	Hooks Dauss	R	39	72	16	3	2	1	1.4	8	5	15	30	0	0	0	.222	.361
P	Bill James	B	30	44	3	0	0	0	0.0	3	1	3	24	0	0	0	.068	.068
P	George Cunningham	R	35	41	11	2	2	0	0.0	7	3	8	12	0	0	0	.268	.415
P	Willie Mitchell	R	23	36	9	0	0	0	0.0	3	3	5	6	0	0	0	.250	.250
P	Bernie Boland	R	49	32	8	0	0	0	0.0	4	2	5	12	0	0	0	.250	.250
P	Howard Ehmke	R	5	14	2	0	0	0	0.0	1	1	0	5	0	0	0	.143	.143
P	Earl Hamilton	L	5	13	1	0	0	0	0.0	0	2	1	6	0	0	0	.077	.077
P	Eric Erickson	R	8	4	0	0	0	0	0.0	0	0	0	2	0	0	0	.000	.000
P	George Boehler	R	5	3	0	0	0	0	0.0	1	0	2	0	0	0	0	.000	.000
P	Deacon Jones	R	1	2	0	0	0	0	0.0	0	0	0	0	0	0	0	.000	.000
P	Bill McTigue	L	3	1	0	0	0	0	0.0	0	0	0	0	0	0	0	.000	.000
P	Grover Lowdermilk	R	1	0	0	0	0	0	-	0	0	0	0	0	0	0	-	-
TEAM TOTAL				5193	1371	202	96	17	0.3	673	563	545	529	190	127	31	.264	.350

INDIVIDUAL FIELDING

POS	Player	T	G	PO	A	E	DP	TC/G	FA	POS	Player	T	G	PO	A	E	DP	TC/G	FA
1B	G. Burns	R	124	1355	54	22	71	11.5	.985	OF	B. Veach	R	150	342	14	12	4	2.5	.967
	H. Heilmann	R	30	316	17	3	16	11.2	.991		T. Cobb	R	143	325	18	17	9	2.5	.953
	S. Crawford	L	2	19	0	0	1	9.5	1.000		H. Heilmann	R	77	110	10	6	0	1.6	.952
	T. Cobb	R	1	10	0	0	0	10.0	1.000		S. Crawford	L	79	85	6	2	2	1.2	.978
											M. Kavanagh	R	11	19	1	0	0	1.8	1.000
2B	R. Young	R	146	352	417	27	55	5.5	.966		G. Harper	R	14	15	3	2	0	1.4	.900
	H. Heilmann	R	9	7	20	4	0	3.4	.871		J. Dalton	R	4	3	0	0	0	0.8	1.000
	F. Fuller	R	8	4	7	2	2	1.6	.846										
	M. Kavanagh	R	2	0	1	0	0	0.5	1.000	C	O. Stanage	R	94	387	108	15	11	5.4	.971
											D. Baker	R	59	164	29	5	4	3.4	.975
SS	D. Bush	R	144	278	435	34	41	5.2	.954		R. McKee	R	26	76	31	5	3	4.3	.955
	F. Fuller	R	1	0	0	0	0	0.0	.000		T. Spencer	R	19	58	21	1	1	4.2	.988
	R. Young	R	6	26	18	2	1	7.7	.957		B. Sullivan	R	1	0	0	0	0	0.0	.000
	B. Dyer	R	4	4	7	0	0	2.8	1.000										
	O. Vitt	R	2	2	4	0	0	3.0	1.000										
3B	O. Vitt	R	151	208	385	22	32	4.1	.964										
	G. Maisel	R	3	1	5	1	1	2.3	.857										
	B. Ellison	R	2	4	1	0	0	2.5	1.000										
	R. Young	R	1	2	1	0	0	3.0	1.000										
	M. Kavanagh	R	2	1	0	0	1	0.5	1.000										

The high point of the season came on August 25, when Detroit—in second place behind Boston for weeks—leaped into first, prompting the Tigers to adopt a "From here on, watch our smoke" battle slogan. But the smoke quickly cleared. The Tigers held first for two days, faded to second, then settled into third in the September stretch. They stayed there, finishing four games behind first-place Boston and two behind second-place Chicago. That was one failure. Another came from Ty Cobb, whose string of nine straight batting titles was snapped by Tris Speaker. The Cleveland centerfielder, and closest of Cobb's few ballplayer friends, hit .386 to Cobb's .371.

Cobb may have lost the crown, but Detroit gained a future batting champion in Harry Heilmann, who joined the team full-time and hit .282 while playing first, second, and the outfield. But Heilmann's glory years were years ahead. For the present, only Cobb and Bobby Veach (.306) topped .300. Indicative of the Tigers' less-than-powerful attack: the most memorable offensive feat of the year came on May 9, when the Tigers drew a still-standing major-league record 18 walks against the Athletics.

Among pitchers, only Harry Coveleski reached 20 victories at 21–11, followed by Hooks Dauss at 19–12. No other Tiger won more than 10. At third, Ossie Vitt with 593 chances set a major-league fielding record that would stand for 21 years. Vitt considered the record momentous enough to hold out the following spring. Third place notwithstanding, Tiger attendance for the first time exceeded a half-million at 616,772.

TEAM STATISTICS

W	L	PCT	GB	R	OR	2B	3B	Batting HR	BA	SA	SB	Fielding E	DP	FA	CG	BB	Pitching SO	ShO	SV	ERA
)S	91	63	.591		548	480	196	56	14	.248	.318	129	183	108	.972	76	463	584	24	16	2.48
·I	89	65	.578	2	601	500	194	100	17	.251	.339	197	203	134	.968	73	405	644	20	15	2.36
.T	87	67	.565	4	673	573	202	96	17	.264	.350	190	211	110	.968	81	578	531	8	13	2.97
Y	80	74	.519	11	575	561	194	59	35	.246	.326	179	219	119	.967	84	476	616	12	17	2.77
·L	79	75	.513	12	591	545	181	50	13	.245	.307	234	248	120	.963	72	478	505	9	13	2.58
E	77	77	.500	14	630	621	233	66	16	.250	.331	160	232	130	.965	65	467	537	9	16	2.89
·S	76	77	.497	14.5	534	543	170	60	12	.242	.306	185	231	119	.964	84	540	706	11	8	2.66
·I	36	117	.235	54.5	447	776	169	65	19	.242	.313	151	314	126	.951	94	715	575	11	3	3.84
AGUE TOTAL				4599	4599	1539	552	143	.248	.324	1425	1841	966	.965	629	4122	4698	104	101	2.81

INDIVIDUAL PITCHING

TCHER	T	W	L	PCT	ERA	SV	G	GS	CG	IP	H	BB	SO	R	ER	ShO	H/9	BB/9	SO/9
rry Coveleski	L	21	11	.656	1.97	2	44	39	22	324.1	278	63	108	105	71	3	7.71	1.75	3.00
oks Dauss	R	19	12	.613	3.21	4	39	29	18	238.2	220	90	95	102	85	1	8.30	3.39	3.58
an Dubuc	R	10	10	.500	2.96	1	36	16	8	170.1	134	84	40	66	56	1	7.08	4.44	2.11
. James	R	8	12	.400	3.68	1	30	20	8	151.2	141	79	61	76	62	0	8.37	4.69	3.62
orge Cunningham	R	7	10	.412	2.75	2	35	14	5	150.1	146	74	68	71	46	0	8.74	4.43	4.07
rnie Boland	R	10	3	.769	3.94	3	46	9	5	130.1	111	73	59	69	57	1	7.66	5.04	4.07
lie Mitchell	L	7	5	.583	3.31	0	23	17	7	127.2	119	48	60	53	47	2	8.39	3.38	4.23
ward Ehmke	R	3	1	.750	3.13	0	5	4	4	37.1	34	15	15	16	13	0	8.20	3.62	3.62
rl Hamilton	L	1	2	.333	2.65	0	5	5	3	37.1	34	22	7	14	11	0	8.20	5.30	1.69
c Erickson	R	0	0	–	2.81	0	8	0	0	16	13	8	7	6	5	0	7.31	4.50	3.94
orge Boehler	R	1	1	.500	4.73	0	5	2	1	13.1	12	9	8	10	7	0	8.10	6.08	5.40
acon Jones	R	0	0	–	2.57	0	1	0	0	7	7	5	2	3	2	0	9.00	6.43	2.57
McTigue	L	0	0	–	5.06	0	3	0	0	5.1	5	5	1	6	3	0	8.44	8.44	1.69
over Lowdermilk	R	0	0	–	0.00	0	1	0	0	.1	0	3	0	3	0	0	0.00	81.00	0.00
AM TOTAL		87	67	.565	2.97	13	281	155	81	1410	1254	578	531	597	465	8	8.00	3.69	3.39

MANAGER	W	L	PCT
Hughie Jennings	78	75	.510

POS	Player	B	G	AB	H	2B	3B	HR	HR %	R	RBI	BB	SO	SB	Pinch Hit AB	Pinch Hit H	BA	SA
REGULARS																		
1B	George Burns	R	119	407	92	14	10	1	0.2	42	40	15	33	3	15	2	.226	.317
2B	Ralph Young	B	141	503	116	18	2	1	0.2	64	35	61	35	8	0	0	.231	.280
SS	Donie Bush	B	147	581	163	18	3	0	0.0	112	24	80	40	34	0	0	.281	.322
3B	Ossie Vitt	R	140	512	130	13	6	0	0.0	65	47	56	15	18	0	0	.254	.303
RF	Harry Heilmann	R	150	556	156	22	11	5	0.9	57	86	41	54	11	0	0	.281	.387
CF	Ty Cobb	L	152	588	225	44	23	7	1.2	107	102	61	34	55	0	0	.383	.571
LF	Bobby Veach	L	154	571	182	31	12	8	1.4	79	103	61	44	21	0	0	.319	.457
C	Oscar Stanage	R	99	297	61	14	1	0	0.0	19	30	20	35	3	4	1	.205	.259
SUBSTITUTES																		
1B	Sam Crawford	L	61	104	18	4	0	2	1.9	6	12	4	6	0	38	7	.173	.269
23	Bob Jones	L	46	77	12	1	2	0	0.0	16	2	4	8	3	10	2	.156	.221
S3	Ben Dyer	R	30	67	14	5	0	0	0.0	6	0	2	17	3	8	0	.209	.284
1B	Babe Ellison	R	9	29	5	1	2	1	3.4	2	4	6	3	0	0	0	.172	.448
2B	Tony DeFate	R	3	2	0	0	0	0	0.0	1	0	0	1	0	0	0	.000	.000
OF	George Harper	L	47	117	24	3	0	0	0.0	6	12	11	15	2	16	4	.205	.231
OF	Fred Nicholson	R	13	14	4	1	0	0	0.0	4	1	1	2	0	4	1	.286	.357
OF	Ira Flagstead	R	4	4	0	0	0	0	0.0	0	0	0	1	0	2	0	.000	.000
C	Tubby Spencer	R	70	192	46	8	3	0	0.0	13	22	15	15	0	8	0	.240	.313
C	Archie Yelle	R	25	51	7	1	0	0	0.0	4	0	5	4	2	1	0	.137	.157
PH	Frank Walker	R	2	2	0	0	0	0	0.0	0	0	0	1	0	0	0	.000	.000
PITCHERS																		
P	Hooks Dauss	R	38	87	11	3	0	0	0.0	7	2	13	24	0	0	0	.126	.161
P	Bernie Boland	R	45	72	4	1	1	0	0.0	8	2	4	19	0	0	0	.056	.097
P	Howard Ehmke	R	35	69	17	2	0	0	0.0	3	2	4	13	0	0	0	.246	.275
P	Willie Mitchell	R	31	59	7	0	0	0	0.0	3	4	1	11	0	0	0	.119	.119
P	Bill James	B	34	57	12	0	0	0	0.0	7	2	10	20	0	0	0	.211	.211
P	George Cunningham	R	44	34	6	0	1	1	2.9	5	3	3	13	0	0	0	.176	.265
P	Harry Coveleski	B	16	22	5	0	0	0	0.0	2	0	0	5	0	0	0	.227	.227
P	Deacon Jones	R	24	15	0	0	0	0	0.0	1	0	4	8	0	0	0	.000	.000
P	Johnny Couch	L	3	4	0	0	0	0	0.0	0	0	1	0	0	0	0	.000	.000
TEAM TOTAL				5093	1317	204	76	26	0.5	639	535	483	476	163	106	17	.259	.344

INDIVIDUAL FIELDING

POS	Player	T	G	PO	A	E	DP	TC/G	FA	POS	Player	T	G	PO	A	E	DP	TC/G	FA
1B	G. Burns	R	104	1127	57	12	44	11.5	.990	OF	T. Cobb	R	152	373	27	11	9	2.7	.973
	H. Heilmann	R	27	266	23	4	9	10.9	.986		B. Veach	R	154	356	17	17	5	2.5	.956
	S. Crawford	L	15	158	2	2	5	10.8	.988		H. Heilmann	R	123	200	17	9	4	1.8	.960
	B. Ellison	R	9	98	1	2	5	11.2	.980		G. Harper	R	31	48	2	1	0	1.6	.980
2B	R. Young	R	141	300	449	33	46	5.5	.958		B. Boland	R	1	0	0	0	0	0.0	.000
	B. Jones	R	18	19	41	4	1	3.6	.938		H. Dauss	R	1	0	0	0	0	0.0	.000
	T. DeFate	R	1	0	1	0	0	1.0	1.000		W. Mitchell	L	1	0	0	0	0	0.0	.000
SS	D. Bush	R	147	281	423	51	41	5.1	.932		I. Flagstead	R	2	0	0	0	0	0.0	.000
	B. Dyer	R	14	19	25	8	4	3.7	.846		S. Crawford	L	3	7	0	0	0	2.3	1.000
3B	O. Vitt	R	140	164	260	27	18	3.2	.940		F. Nicholson	R	3	3	0	0	0	1.0	1.000
	B. Dyer	R	8	6	21	2	0	3.6	.931	C	O. Stanage	R	95	385	88	11	13	5.1	.977
	B. Jones	R	8	7	16	2	1	3.1	.920		T. Spencer	R	62	250	57	7	10	5.1	.978
											A. Yelle	R	24	62	16	2	1	3.3	.975

America joined the European war during spring training, but baseball did not immediately suffer: Crowds stayed large and few players enlisted. So the Tigers had no excuse. Detroit languished in the second division through the first half of the season. The Tigers managed to finish fourth—just three games over .500, 22 games out—only when New York suffered a late-season collapse.

Ty Cobb hit in 35 straight games (still second-high in team history to his 40 in 1911) en route to recapturing the batting title. Cobb also led the league in total bases, slugging, and stolen bases (55). And he was second to teammate Donie Bush in runs.

Bobby Veach permanently replaced Sam Crawford as second half of the one-two punch, hitting .319 with a league-leading 103 RBIs, one ahead of Cobb. Crawford, meanwhile, rather ignominiously finished his Hall of Fame career, batting .173 in 61 games, mostly as a pinch hitter. On the mound Hooks Dauss led the Tigers at 17–14 with a 2.43 ERA, while Harry Coveleski, his arm withering, dropped to 4–6.

The season's most memorable encounter occurred in spring training, as the Tigers and John McGraw's Giants barnstormed north from Waxahachie, Texas. In Dallas, Cobb spiked New York second baseman Buck Herzog. Cobb and McGraw exchanged unpleasantries, and the benches emptied. That night Cobb spotted Herzog in the dining room of the Oriental Hotel. "If you didn't get enough this afternoon," Cobb said, "see me in my room. It's 404. I'll be there all evening." Herzog, joined by Giants third baseman Heinie Zimmerman, accepted the invitation. Cobb's door was open: Herzog charged in swinging, Cobb retaliated, and Herzog retreated with a torn shirt and a limp. "If anyone else wants anything," Cobb called after him, "tell him to come right up."

TEAM STATISTICS

	W	L	PCT	GB	R	OR	2B	3B	Batting HR	BA	SA	SB	E	Fielding DP	FA	CG	BB	Pitching SO	ShO	SV	ERA
I	100	54	.649		657	464	152	80	19	.253	.326	219	204	117	.967	78	413	517	22	21	2.16
S	90	62	.592	9	556	453	198	64	14	.246	.319	105	183	116	.972	115	413	509	15	7	2.20
E	88	66	.571	12	584	543	218	63	14	.245	.322	210	242	136	.964	73	438	451	20	22	2.52
T	78	75	.510	21.5	639	577	204	76	26	.259	.344	163	234	95	.964	78	504	516	20	15	2.56
S	74	79	.484	25.5	543	566	173	70	4	.241	.304	166	251	127	.961	84	536	637	21	10	2.77
	71	82	.464	28.5	524	560	172	52	27	.239	.308	136	225	129	.965	87	427	571	10	6	2.66
L	57	97	.370	43	511	687	183	63	15	.245	.315	157	281	139	.957	65	537	429	12	12	3.20
I	55	98	.359	44.5	527	691	177	62	17	.254	.322	112	251	106	.961	80	562	516	8	8	3.27
GUE TOTAL					4541	4541	1477	530	136	.248	.320	1268	1871	965	.964	660	3830	4146	128	101	2.66

INDIVIDUAL PITCHING

CHER	T	W	L	PCT	ERA	SV	G	GS	CG	IP	H	BB	SO	R	ER	ShO	H/9	BB/9	SO/9
oks Dauss	R	17	14	.548	2.43	2	37	31	22	270.2	243	87	102	105	73	6	8.08	2.89	3.39
rnie Boland	R	16	11	.593	2.68	6	43	28	13	238	192	95	89	89	71	3	7.26	3.59	3.37
ward Ehmke	R	10	15	.400	2.97	2	35	25	13	206	174	88	90	84	68	4	7.60	3.84	3.93
James	R	13	10	.565	2.09	1	34	23	10	198	163	96	62	71	46	2	7.41	4.36	2.82
lie Mitchell	L	12	8	.600	2.19	0	30	22	12	185.1	172	46	80	66	45	5	8.35	2.23	3.17
orge Cunningham	R	2	7	.222	2.91	4	44	8	4	139	113	51	49	73	45	0	7.32	3.30	3.17
acon Jones	R	4	4	.500	2.92	0	24	6	2	77	69	26	28	34	25	0	8.06	3.04	3.27
rry Coveleski	L	4	6	.400	2.61	0	16	11	2	69	70	14	15	39	20	0	9.13	1.83	1.96
nny Couch	R	0	0	–	2.70	0	3	0	0	13.1	13	1	1	16	4	0	8.78	0.68	0.68
AM TOTAL		78	75	.510	2.56	15	266	154	78	1396.1	1209	504	516	577	397	20	7.79	3.25	3.33

MANAGER	W	L	PCT
Hughie Jennings	55	71	.437

POS	Player	B	G	AB	H	2B	3B	HR	HR %	R	RBI	BB	SO	SB	Pinch Hit AB	Pinch Hit H	BA	SA
REGULARS																		
1B	Harry Heilmann	R	79	286	79	10	6	5	1.7	34	44	35	10	13	1	1	.276	.406
2B	Ralph Young	B	91	298	56	7	1	0	0.0	31	21	54	17	15	0	0	.188	.218
SS	Donie Bush	B	128	500	117	10	3	0	0.0	74	22	79	31	9	0	0	.234	.266
3B	Ossie Vitt	R	81	267	64	5	2	0	0.0	29	17	32	6	5	3	0	.240	.273
RF	George Harper	L	69	227	55	5	2	0	0.0	19	16	18	14	3	3	0	.242	.282
CF	Ty Cobb	L	111	421	161	19	14	3	0.7	83	64	41	21	34	3	1	.382	.515
LF	Bobby Veach	L	127	499	139	21	13	3	0.6	59	78	35	23	21	0	0	.279	.391
C	Archie Yelle	R	56	144	25	3	0	0	0.0	7	7	9	15	0	4	1	.174	.194
SUBSTITUTES																		
3B	Bob Jones	L	74	287	79	14	4	0	0.0	43	21	17	16	7	3	1	.275	.352
1B	Lee Dressen	L	31	107	19	1	2	0	0.0	10	3	21	10	2	1	0	.178	.224
1B	Art Griggs	R	28	99	36	8	0	0	0.0	11	16	10	5	2	2	2	.364	.444
2B	Jack Coffey	R	22	67	14	0	2	0	0.0	7	4	8	6	2	0	0	.209	.269
1B	Marty Kavanagh	R	13	44	12	3	0	0	0.0	2	9	11	6	0	1	0	.273	.341
2B	Jim Curry	R	5	20	5	1	0	0	0.0	1	0	0	0	0	0	0	.250	.300
1B	Hughie Jennings	R	1	0	0	0	0	0	–	0	0	0	0	0	0	0	–	–
OF	Frank Walker	R	55	167	33	10	3	1	0.6	10	20	7	29	3	7	1	.198	.311
PO	George Cunningham	R	56	112	25	4	1	0	0.0	11	2	16	34	2	8	3	.223	.277
O2	Babe Ellison	R	7	23	6	1	0	0	0.0	1	2	3	1	1	0	0	.261	.304
UT	Ben Dyer	R	13	18	5	0	0	0	0.0	1	2	0	6	0	6	2	.278	.278
C	Oscar Stanage	R	54	186	47	4	0	1	0.5	9	14	11	18	2	2	0	.253	.290
C	Tubby Spencer	R	66	155	34	8	1	0	0.0	11	8	19	18	1	17	3	.219	.284
PH	Joe Cobb	R	1	0	0	0	0	0	–	0	0	1	0	0	1	0	–	–
PITCHERS																		
P	Hooks Dauss	R	33	77	14	2	2	0	0.0	3	11	11	13	0	0	0	.182	.260
P	Bernie Boland	R	29	69	12	3	0	0	0.0	9	2	6	17	0	0	0	.174	.217
P	Rudy Kallio	R	31	56	9	0	0	0	0.0	5	3	6	23	0	0	0	.161	.161
P	Bill James	B	19	46	5	1	0	0	0.0	0	0	1	12	0	0	0	.109	.130
P	Eric Erickson	R	12	33	4	0	0	0	0.0	1	0	0	9	0	0	0	.121	.121
P	Deacon Jones	R	23	27	5	0	0	0	0.0	1	3	1	12	1	0	0	.185	.185
P	Bill Bailey	L	8	13	1	1	0	0	0.0	0	0	0	4	0	0	0	.077	.154
P	Harry Coveleski	B	3	4	1	0	0	0	0.0	0	2	0	2	0	0	0	.250	.250
P	Happy Finneran	B	6	3	0	0	0	0	0.0	0	2	0	0	1	0	0	.000	.000
P	Wild Bill Donovan	R	2	2	1	0	0	0	0.0	1	1	0	0	0	0	0	.500	.500
P	Charley Hall	L	6	2	0	0	0	0	0.0	0	0	0	0	0	0	0	.000	.000
P	Willie Mitchell	R	1	2	0	0	0	0	0.0	0	0	0	1	0	0	0	.000	.000
P	Herb Hall	B	3	1	0	0	0	0	0.0	0	1	0	1	0	0	0	.000	.000
	TEAM TOTAL			4262	1063	141	56	13	0.3	473	395	452	380	123	63	15	.249	.318

INDIVIDUAL FIELDING

POS	Player	T	G	PO	A	E	DP	TC/G	FA
1B	H. Heilmann	R	37	367	18	5	11	10.5	.987
	L. Dressen	L	30	322	11	4	12	11.2	.988
	A. Griggs	R	25	263	9	4	10	11.0	.986
	T. Spencer	R	1	0	0	0	0	0.0	.000
	T. Cobb	R	13	133	12	3	6	11.4	.980
	M. Kavanagh	R	12	129	6	5	6	11.7	.964
	B. Jones	R	6	62	0	0	2	10.3	1.000
	O. Stanage	R	5	46	2	3	1	10.2	.941
	B. Dyer	R	2	14	2	0	1	8.0	1.000
	H. Jennings	R	1	2	0	0	0	2.0	1.000
2B	R. Young	R	91	190	271	30	28	5.4	.939
	J. Coffey	R	22	62	69	6	6	6.2	.956
	J. Curry	R	5	0	0	0	0	0.0	.000
	O. Vitt	R	9	20	22	2	2	4.9	.955
	B. Ellison	R	3	2	14	0	1	5.3	1.000
	T. Cobb	R	1	1	3	1	0	5.0	.800
	H. Heilmann	R	2	0	4	0	1	2.0	1.000
	B. Dyer	R	1	0	1	0	0	1.0	1.000
SS	D. Bush	R	128	280	364	48	29	5.4	.931
3B	O. Vitt	R	66	106	137	12	15	3.9	.953
	B. Jones	R	63	81	83	11	6	2.8	.937
	T. Cobb	R	1	1	1	0	0	2.0	1.000

POS	Player	T	G	PO	A	E	DP	TC/G	FA
OF	B. Veach	R	127	277	14	7	3	2.3	.977
	T. Cobb	R	95	225	12	6	1	2.6	.975
	G. Harper	R	64	125	5	6	2	2.1	.956
	F. Walker	R	45	102	5	9	1	2.6	.922
	H. Heilmann	R	40	60	6	3	1	1.7	.957
	G. Cunningham	R	20	18	0	1	0	1.0	.947
	R. Kallio	R	1	0	0	0	0	0.0	.000
	B. Ellison	R	4	6	0	0	0	1.5	1.000
	D. Jones	R	2	2	0	0	0	1.0	1.000
	O. Vitt	R	3	2	0	0	0	0.7	1.000
	B. Dyer	R	2	0	1	0	0	0.5	1.000
C	A. Yelle	R	52	172	81	14	5	5.1	.948
	O. Stanage	R	47	188	54	5	9	5.3	.980
	T. Spencer	R	48	153	46	7	3	4.3	.966

The second season of wartime baseball proved bad for the game and worse for the Tigers. German springtime victories chilled the nation's enthusiasm for its pastime. Detroit plunged into the second division for the first time in five years, 16 games below .500, 20 behind eventual World Champion Boston. When the secretary of war issued his work-or-fight edict cutting the season short at Labor Day, Detroit baseball fans barely cared. Tiger home attendance was less than half of 1917, little more than 200,000.

Before the season, Frank Navin had peddled first baseman George Burns to Philadelphia (where he hit .352), which added to Detroit's infield confusion. Five players (including Cobb) pulled duty at first, two shared third, and two shared second. Only Donie Bush injected stability, playing the whole season at shortstop. As the Tigers dropped to sixth in team batting, only Cobb hit above .279, winning his 11th batting title in 12 years at .382. (He was second in slugging to Red Sox outfielder-pitcher Babe Ruth, the start of a magnificent rivalry that stokes arguments to this day.) Bobby Veach dropped 40 points to .279, but still won his second straight RBI crown with 78.

No Tiger pitcher exceeded 13 victories; Bernie Boland was tops at 14–10, 2.65, Hooks Dauss next at 12–16, 2.99. Fading Harry Coveleski, in his final major-league season, finished 0–1 in three appearances. That rendered manager Hughie Jennings desperate enough to employ a pair of improbable hurlers. Cobb pitched in two games: four innings, six hits, two walks, 4.50 ERA. And Wild Bill Donovan (1–0, 1.50 ERA in just six innings) returned to Detroit after being fired as the Yankees manager for one last hurrah as he approached his forty-second birthday.

As the Tigers swept the season-ending Labor Day doubleheader from Chciago, even 48-year-old Jennings donned a mitt to play first base. When it was mercifully over, some half-dozen Tigers went off war, including Cobb and Harry Heilmann. Capt. T. R. Cobb dabbled in the military equivalent of sharpened spikes: chemical warfare.

TEAM STATISTICS

W	L	PCT	GB	R	OR	Batting						Fielding			Pitching					
						2B	3B	HR	BA	SA	SB	E	DP	FA	CG	BB	SO	ShO	SV	ERA
75	51	.595	_	473	381	159	54	15	.249	.327	110	149	89	.971	105	380	392	26	2	2.31
73	54	.575	2.5	510	447	176	67	9	.260	.341	165	207	82	.962	78	343	364	5	13	2.63
72	56	.563	4	461	392	156	48	5	.256	.316	137	226	95	.960	75	395	505	19	8	2.14
60	63	.488	13.5	491	474	160	45	20	.257	.330	88	161	137	.970	59	463	369	8	13	3.03
58	64	.475	15	426	448	152	40	5	.259	.320	138	190	86	.963	67	402	346	8	8	2.75
57	67	.460	17	457	443	136	54	9	.256	.321	116	169	98	.967	76	300	349	9	8	2.69
55	71	.437	20	473	555	141	56	13	.249	.318	123	211	77	.960	74	437	374	8	5	3.40
52	76	.406	24	412	563	124	44	22	.243	.308	83	228	136	.959	80	479	279	13	8	3.22
GUE TOTAL				3703	3703	1204	408	98	.254	.323	960	1541	800	.964	614	3199	2978	96	65	2.77

INDIVIDUAL PITCHING

CHER	T	W	L	PCT	ERA	SV	G	GS	CG	IP	H	BB	SO	R	ER	ShO	H/9	BB/9	SO/9
ks Dauss	R	12	16	.429	2.99	3	33	26	21	249.2	243	58	73	105	83	1	8.76	2.09	2.63
nie Boland	R	14	10	.583	2.65	0	29	25	14	204	176	67	63	69	60	4	7.76	2.96	2.78
ly Kallio	R	8	14	.364	3.62	0	30	22	10	181.1	178	76	70	91	73	2	8.83	3.77	3.47
rge Cunningham	R	6	7	.462	3.15	1	27	14	10	140	131	38	39	68	49	0	8.42	2.44	2.51
James	R	6	11	.353	3.76	0	19	18	8	122	127	68	42	68	51	1	9.37	5.02	3.10
Erickson	R	4	5	.444	2.48	1	12	9	8	94.1	81	29	48	32	26	0	7.73	2.77	4.58
con Jones	R	3	1	.750	3.09	0	21	4	1	67	60	38	15	36	23	0	8.06	5.10	2.01
Bailey	L	1	2	.333	5.97	0	8	4	1	37.2	53	26	13	34	25	0	12.66	6.21	3.11
ry Coveleski	L	0	1	.000	3.86	0	3	1	1	14	17	6	3	9	6	0	10.93	3.86	1.93
py Finneran	R	0	2	.000	9.88	1	5	2	0	13.2	22	8	2	17	15	0	14.49	5.27	1.32
rley Hall	R	0	1	.000	6.75	0	6	1	0	13.1	14	6	2	10	10	0	9.45	4.05	1.35
Bill Donovan	R	1	0	1.000	1.50	0	2	1	0	6	5	1	1	1	1	0	7.50	1.50	1.50
Hall	R	0	0	–	15.00	0	3	0	0	6	12	7	1	11	10	0	18.00	10.50	1.50
Cobb	R	0	0	–	4.50	0	2	0	0	4	6	2	0	2	2	0	13.50	4.50	0.00
e Mitchell	L	0	1	.000	9.00	0	1	1	0	4	3	5	2	4	4	0	6.75	11.25	4.50
by Veach	R	0	0	–	4.50	1	1	0	0	2	2	2	0	1	1	0	9.00	9.00	0.00
Dyer	R	0	0	–	0.00	0	2	0	0	1.2	0	0	0	0	0	0	0.00	0.00	0.00
M TOTAL		55	71	.437	3.40	7	204	128	74	1160.2	1130	437	374	558	439	8	8.76	3.39	2.90

MANAGER	W	L	PCT
Hughie Jennings	80	60	.571

POS	Player	B	G	AB	H	2B	3B	HR	HR %	R	RBI	BB	SO	SB	Pinch Hit AB	Pinch Hit H	BA	SA
REGULARS																		
1B	Harry Heilmann	R	140	537	172	30	15	8	1.5	74	95	37	41	7	0	0	.320	.477
2B	Ralph Young	B	125	456	96	13	5	1	0.2	63	25	53	32	8	0	0	.211	.268
SS	Donie Bush	B	129	509	124	11	6	0	0.0	82	26	75	36	22	0	0	.244	.289
3B	Bob Jones	L	127	439	114	18	6	1	0.2	37	57	34	39	11	0	0	.260	.335
RF	Ira Flagstead	R	97	287	95	22	3	5	1.7	43	41	35	39	6	11	3	.331	.481
CF	Ty Cobb	L	124	497	191	36	13	1	0.2	92	70	38	22	28	0	0	.384	.515
LF	Bobby Veach	L	139	538	191	45	17	3	0.6	87	101	33	33	19	1	1	.355	.519
C	Eddie Ainsmith	R	114	364	99	17	12	3	0.8	42	32	45	30	9	8	1	.272	.409
SUBSTITUTES																		
2O	Babe Ellison	R	56	134	29	4	0	0	0.0	18	11	13	24	4	15	3	.216	.246
3S	Ben Dyer	R	44	85	21	4	0	0	0.0	11	15	8	19	0	8	3	.247	.294
OF	Chick Shorten	L	95	270	85	9	3	0	0.0	37	22	22	13	5	19	5	.315	.370
C	Oscar Stanage	R	38	120	29	4	1	1	0.8	9	15	7	12	1	1	0	.242	.317
C	Archie Yelle	R	5	4	0	0	0	0	0.0	1	0	1	0	0	0	0	.000	.000
PH	Snooks Dowd	R	1	0	0	0	0	0	–	0	0	0	0	0	0	0	–	–
PITCHERS																		
P	Hooks Dauss	R	34	97	14	2	1	0	0.0	7	14	5	24	1	0	0	.144	.186
P	Howard Ehmke	R	33	91	23	3	1	0	0.0	6	5	3	12	0	0	0	.253	.308
P	Bernie Boland	R	35	74	8	1	1	0	0.0	2	4	8	18	0	0	0	.108	.149
P	Dutch Leonard	L	29	71	11	0	0	0	0.0	2	4	2	8	0	0	0	.155	.155
P	Slim Love	L	22	27	6	2	0	0	0.0	1	0	0	10	0	0	0	.222	.296
P	Doc Ayers	R	24	24	3	1	0	0	0.0	1	1	0	2	0	0	0	.125	.167
P	George Cunningham	R	26	23	5	0	0	0	0.0	4	5	9	8	0	6	1	.217	.217
P	Eric Erickson	R	3	5	1	0	0	0	0.0	0	1	0	2	0	0	0	.200	.200
P	Willie Mitchell	R	3	5	1	0	0	0	0.0	0	1	1	1	0	0	0	.200	.200
P	Bill James	B	2	4	1	0	0	0	0.0	1	1	0	2	0	0	0	.250	.250
P	Rudy Kallio	R	12	4	0	0	0	0	0.0	0	0	0	0	0	0	0	.000	.000
	TEAM TOTAL			4665	1319	222	84	23	0.5	620	546	429	427	121	69	17	.283	.381

INDIVIDUAL FIELDING

POS	Player	T	G	PO	A	E	DP	TC/G	FA
1B	H. Heilmann	R	140	1402	78	31	61	10.8	.979
	O. Stanage	R	1	1	0	0	0	1.0	1.000
2B	R. Young	R	121	300	389	22	38	5.9	.969
	B. Ellison	R	25	48	64	4	7	4.6	.966
SS	D. Bush	R	129	290	376	40	38	5.5	.943
	B. Ellison	R	1	0	0	0	0	0.0	.000
	B. Dyer	R	11	16	20	3	3	3.5	.923
	R. Young	R	4	12	16	1	1	7.3	.966
3B	B. Jones	R	127	134	219	21	14	2.9	.944
	B. Dyer	R	23	19	42	3	0	2.8	.953

POS	Player	T	G	PO	A	E	DP	TC/G	FA
OF	B. Veach	R	138	338	14	12	3	2.6	.967
	T. Cobb	R	123	272	19	8	3	2.4	.973
	I. Flagstead	R	83	140	15	8	4	2.0	.951
	C. Shorten	L	75	143	2	4	2	2.0	.973
	B. Ellison	R	10	11	1	0	0	1.2	1.000
	B. Dyer	R	1	1	0	0	0	1.0	1.000
C	E. Ainsmith	R	106	456	107	22	7	5.5	.962
	O. Stanage	R	36	149	39	5	8	5.4	.974
	A. Yelle	R	5	3	1	1	0	1.0	.800

The Tigers didn't grant their legions a pennant race. But they did give them a bizarre and chaotic third-place battle that would last until the following February.

It started when Red Sox owner Harry Frazee, who would unload Babe Ruth to the Yankees, sold submarine-ball pitcher Carl Mays to New York. American League president Ban Johnson nixed the deal, but the Yankees obtained an injunction and pitched Mays anyway. Amid the confusion, newspapers printed two sets of league statistics and standings, one with Mays, one without. Not till the league finally okayed Mays's games at the winter meetings did Detroit know it had finished fourth (out of the World Series money), five percentage points behind New York.

Overall, baseball flourished in the first postwar season. To a modest degree, so did the Tigers. After an unremarkable start, Detroit closed within four games of first with an August rally, then faded during a miserable final eastern trip. Still, fourth place marked the Tigers' return to the first division, 20 games over .500, eight behind the first-place White Sox. Frank Navin had improved matters when he traded Ossie Vitt to the Red Sox for catcher Eddie Ainsmith, outfielder Chick Shorten, and pitcher Slim Love; and purchased pitcher Dutch Leonard (who couldn't come to terms with the Yankees) for $7500. Overflow crowds flocked to Navin Field.

They saw an outfield that hit a cumulative .361. Centerfielder Ty Cobb won his 12th (and last) batting title in 13 years at .384. Leftfielder Bobby Veach was second in the league at .355. And rookie rightfielder Ira Flagstead hit .331, when he wasn't spelled by Shorten (.315). First baseman Harry Heilmann gave Detroit a fourth .300-hitting regular at .320, as the Tigers finished second in the league in team batting. Hooks Dauss, at 21–9, became Detroit's first 20-game winner in five years. And Howard Ehmke won 17, lost 10.

Baseball, however, would soon shake at its foundations. Despite the postwar prosperity, team owners had cut the schedule back to 140 games and trimmed player salaries. That October eight White Sox players opted for some extra money by throwing the World Series, to be forever branded Black Sox.

TEAM STATISTICS

	W	L	PCT	GB	R	OR	2B	3B	Batting HR	BA	SA	SB	E	Fielding DP	FA	CG	BB	Pitching SO	ShO	SV	ERA
:HI	88	52	.629		668	534	218	70	25	.287	.380	150	176	116	.969	88	342	468	14	3	3.04
:LE	84	55	.604	3.5	634	535	254	71	25	.278	.381	113	201	102	.965	80	362	432	10	10	2.92
:Y	80	59	.576	7.5	582	514	193	49	45	.267	.356	101	192	108	.968	85	433	500	14	6	2.78
•ET	80	60	.571	8	620	582	222	84	23	.283	.381	121	205	81	.964	85	431	428	10	4	3.30
:TL	67	72	.482	20.5	535	567	187	73	31	.264	.355	74	216	98	.963	77	421	415	14	5	3.13
.OS	66	71	.482	20.5	565	552	181	49	33	.261	.344	108	141	118	.975	89	420	380	15	8	3.30
✓AS	56	84	.400	32	533	570	177	63	24	.260	.339	142	227	86	.960	69	451	536	12	8	3.01
:HI	36	104	.257	52	459	742	175	71	35	.244	.334	103	259	96	.956	72	503	417	1	3	4.26
:EAGUE TOTAL					4596	4596	1607	530	241	.268	.359	912	1617	805	.965	645	3363	3576	90	47	3.21

INDIVIDUAL PITCHING

·ITCHER	T	W	L	PCT	ERA	SV	G	GS	CG	IP	H	BB	SO	R	ER	ShO	H/9	BB/9	SO/9
﹐ooks Dauss	R	21	9	.700	3.55	0	34	32	22	256.1	262	63	73	125	101	2	9.20	2.21	2.56
﹐oward Ehmke	R	17	10	.630	3.18	0	33	31	20	248.2	255	107	79	114	88	2	9.23	3.87	2.86
﹒ernie Boland	R	14	16	.467	3.04	1	35	30	18	242.2	222	80	71	93	82	1	8.23	2.97	2.63
·utch Leonard	L	14	13	.519	2.77	0	29	28	18	217.1	212	65	102	89	67	4	8.78	2.69	4.22
·oc Ayers	R	5	3	.625	2.69	0	24	5	3	93.2	88	28	32	34	28	1	8.46	2.69	3.07
﹐im Love	L	6	4	.600	3.01	1	22	8	4	89.2	92	40	46	40	30	0	9.23	4.01	4.62
﹐eorge Cunningham	R	1	1	.500	4.91	1	17	0	0	47.2	54	15	11	36	26	0	10.20	2.83	2.08
·udy Kallio	R	0	0	–	5.64	1	12	1	0	22.1	28	8	3	15	14	0	11.28	3.22	1.21
﹒ric Erickson	R	0	2	.000	6.75	0	3	2	0	14.2	17	10	4	17	11	0	10.43	6.14	2.45
﹒illie Mitchell	L	1	2	.333	5.27	0	3	2	0	13.2	12	10	4	8	8	0	7.90	6.59	2.63
﹒ill James	R	1	0	1.000	5.79	0	2	1	0	9.1	12	5	3	6	6	0	11.57	4.82	2.89
﹒EAM TOTAL		80	60	.571	3.30	4	214	140	85	1256	1254	431	428	577	461	10	8.99	3.09	3.07

MANAGER	W	L	PCT
Hughie Jennings	61	93	.396

POS	Player	B	G	AB	H	2B	3B	HR	HR %	R	RBI	BB	SO	SB	Pinch Hit AB	Pinch Hit H	BA	SA
REGULARS																		
1B	Harry Heilmann	R	145	543	168	28	5	9	1.7	66	89	39	32	3	1	0	.309	.429
2B	Ralph Young	B	150	594	173	21	6	0	0.0	84	33	85	30	8	0	0	.291	.347
SS	Donie Bush	B	141	506	133	18	5	1	0.2	85	33	73	32	15	1	1	.263	.324
3B	Babe Pinelli	R	102	284	65	9	3	0	0.0	33	21	25	16	6	4	0	.229	.282
RF	Chick Shorten	L	116	364	105	9	6	1	0.3	35	40	28	14	2	15	5	.288	.354
CF	Ty Cobb	L	112	428	143	28	8	2	0.5	86	63	58	28	14	0	0	.334	.451
LF	Bobby Veach	L	154	612	188	39	15	11	1.8	92	113	36	22	11	0	0	.307	.474
C	Oscar Stanage	R	78	238	55	17	0	0	0.0	12	17	14	21	0	1	0	.231	.303
SUBSTITUTES																		
3B	Bob Jones	L	81	265	66	6	3	1	0.4	35	18	22	13	3	5	0	.249	.306
1B	Babe Ellison	R	61	155	34	7	2	0	0.0	11	21	8	26	4	17	3	.219	.290
3O	Sammy Hale	R	76	116	34	3	3	1	0.9	13	14	5	15	2	52	17	.293	.397
3B	Clarence Huber	R	11	42	9	2	1	0	0.0	4	5	0	5	0	0	0	.214	.310
SS	Danny Claire	R	3	7	1	0	0	0	0.0	1	0	0	0	0	0	0	.143	.143
OF	Ira Flagstead	R	110	311	73	13	5	3	1.0	40	35	37	27	3	26	6	.235	.338
C	Eddie Ainsmith	R	69	186	43	5	3	1	0.5	19	19	14	19	4	7	2	.231	.306
C	Clyde Manion	R	32	80	22	4	1	0	0.0	4	8	4	7	0	2	1	.275	.350
C	Larry Woodall	R	18	49	12	1	0	0	0.0	4	5	2	6	0	2	0	.245	.265
PITCHERS																		
P	Howard Ehmke	R	38	105	25	7	2	0	0.0	4	5	0	10	0	0	0	.238	.343
P	Hooks Dauss	R	38	83	14	2	2	0	0.0	7	5	14	27	0	0	0	.169	.241
P	Red Oldham	L	39	69	12	0	1	0	0.0	7	7	6	13	0	0	0	.174	.203
P	Doc Ayers	R	46	59	9	4	0	0	0.0	2	3	2	6	0	0	0	.153	.220
P	Dutch Leonard	L	28	57	12	3	0	0	0.0	2	5	8	8	0	0	0	.211	.263
P	Roy Crumpler	L	4	9	3	1	1	0	0.0	1	0	0	0	0	1	1	.333	.667
P	John Bogart	R	4	8	2	0	0	0	0.0	1	0	0	1	0	0	0	.250	.250
P	Bill Morrisette	R	8	8	0	0	0	0	0.0	2	0	0	3	0	0	0	.000	.000
P	Bernie Boland	R	4	7	1	1	0	0	0.0	0	0	0	1	0	0	0	.143	.286
P	Frank Okrie	L	21	5	1	0	0	0	0.0	1	0	0	3	0	0	0	.200	.200
P	Harry Baumgartner	R	9	4	1	0	0	0	0.0	0	1	1	1	0	0	0	.250	.250
P	Red Conkwright	R	5	4	1	0	0	0	0.0	1	0	3	1	0	0	0	.250	.250
P	Mutt Wilson	R	3	4	1	0	0	0	0.0	0	1	0	1	0	0	0	.250	.250
P	Ernie Alten	R	14	3	0	0	0	0	0.0	0	0	0	0	0	0	0	.000	.000
P	John Glaiser	R	9	3	0	0	0	0	0.0	1	0	1	0	0	0	0	.000	.000
P	Jack Coombs	B	2	2	0	0	0	0	0.0	0	0	0	0	0	0	0	.000	.000
P	Red Cox	L	3	1	0	0	0	0	0.0	0	0	0	1	0	0	0	.000	.000
P	Cy Fried	L	2	0	0	0	0	0	–	0	0	0	0	0	0	0	–	–
P	Slim Love	L	1	0	0	0	0	0	–	0	0	0	0	0	0	0	–	–
P	Lou Vedder	R	1	0	0	0	0	0	–	0	0	0	0	0	0	0	–	–
TEAM TOTAL				5211	1406	228	72	30	0.6	653	561	485	389	75	134	36	.270	.358

INDIVIDUAL FIELDING

POS	Player	T	G	PO	A	E	DP	TC/G	FA
1B	H. Heilmann	R	122	1207	80	19	52	10.7	.985
	B. Ellison	R	38	363	26	1	13	10.3	.997
2B	R. Young	R	150	405	436	27	46	5.8	.969
	S. Hale	R	1	0	0	0	0	0.0	.000
	B. Jones	R	5	10	10	1	2	4.2	.952
	B. Pinelli	R	1	2	3	1	0	6.0	.833
SS	D. Bush	R	140	258	421	45	39	5.2	.938
	B. Pinelli	R	18	32	40	8	0	4.4	.900
	D. Claire	R	3	2	6	2	0	3.3	.800
	B. Jones	R	1	0	2	0	0	2.0	1.000
3B	B. Pinelli	R	74	110	183	14	20	4.1	.954
	B. Jones	R	67	80	146	14	7	3.6	.942
	S. Hale	R	16	8	31	5	2	2.8	.886
	C. Huber	R	11	21	28	5	0	4.9	.907
	B. Ellison	R	1	1	1	1	0	3.0	.667
OF	B. Veach	R	154	357	26	13	4	2.6	.967
	T. Cobb	R	112	246	8	9	2	2.3	.966
	C. Shorten	L	99	168	14	2	3	1.9	.989
	I. Flagstead	R	82	164	13	6	4	2.2	.967
	H. Heilmann	R	21	27	6	0	0	1.6	1.000
	S. Hale	R	4	6	1	0	0	1.8	1.000
	B. Ellison	R	4	1	2	0	1	0.8	1.000
C	O. Stanage	R	78	248	75	14	4	4.3	.958
	E. Ainsmith	R	61	219	55	13	4	4.7	.955
	C. Manion	R	30	83	27	7	3	3.9	.940
	L. Woodall	R	15	59	20	1	0	5.3	.988

The Tigers started the Roaring Twenties with a roaring collapse. Hughie Jennings's inability to develop young pitchers finally proved fatal. No Tiger won more than he lost; Hooks Dauss lost 21, Howard Ehmke lost 18, and Dutch Leonard, who didn't win his first game until May, lost 17. As Babe Ruth ushered in the live-ball era with 54 home runs, Detroit pitchers did their part by surrendering 10 of them, Dauss giving up four and Ehmke three to the Yankee slugger. The Tigers finished seventh, 37 games out, 32 games below .500.

From the start, the season was a disaster. After a long southern barnstorming trip with the Braves through wretched weather and worse playing fields, the Tigers lost their first 13, smothering Detroit's baseball enthusiasm at the onset.

Ty Cobb suffered his worst season yet. While St. Louis first baseman George Sisler won the batting title at .407, Cobb finished 10th at .334. And on June 7, he collided with Ira Flagstead in the Tiger outfield, tearing knee ligaments that slowed him for the duration. Two other Tigers exceeded .300, but not by much: Harry Heilmann at .309 and Bobby Veach at .307. Beyond that, the year that saw Detroit finish second-to-last in batting brought only two notable offensive accomplishments. On July 25 the Tigers scored 21 runs against the Browns to equal the still-standing club record. And in a 12-inning game against the Red Sox in Detroit, Veach became the first Tiger to hit for the cycle.

Frank Navin, in vain attempts to salvage the season, imported a litany of ineffective pitchers. At third base he tried Sammy Hale (who led the league in pinch hits) and Ralph "Babe" Pinelli, later a National League umpire. None helped significantly.

The winter brought two incidents. One was trivial: for three days in November— during the dispute over naming an all-powerful baseball commissioner—the Tigers and three other AL teams defied Ban Johnson by joining the National League. The other was major: Jennings, Tiger manager for 14 seasons, was fired. He was replaced by Tyrus Raymond Cobb.

TEAM STATISTICS

	W	L	PCT	GB	R	OR	Batting 2B	3B	HR	BA	SA	SB	Fielding E	DP	FA	CG	BB	Pitching SO	ShO	SV	ERA
E	98	56	.636		857	642	301	95	35	.303	.417	73	185	124	.971	93	401	466	10	7	3.41
l	96	58	.623	2	794	666	263	97	37	.295	.402	108	198	142	.968	112	405	440	9	10	3.59
	95	59	.617	3	839	629	268	71	115	.280	.426	64	193	129	.970	88	420	480	16	11	3.31
	76	77	.497	21.5	797	766	278	84	50	.308	.419	121	232	119	.963	84	578	444	9	14	4.03
S	72	81	.471	25.5	651	699	216	71	22	.269	.351	98	183	131	.972	91	461	481	11	6	3.82
S	68	84	.447	29	723	802	232	81	36	.290	.386	161	232	95	.963	80	520	418	10	10	4.17
T	61	93	.396	37	651	832	228	72	30	.270	.358	75	229	95	.965	76	561	483	9	7	4.04
I	48	106	.312	50	555	831	218	49	44	.252	.337	51	267	126	.959	81	461	423	5	2	3.93
GUE TOTAL					5867	5867	2004	620	369	.283	.387	751	1719	961	.966	705	3807	3635	79	67	3.79

INDIVIDUAL   PITCHING

CHER	T	W	L	PCT	ERA	SV	G	GS	CG	IP	H	BB	SO	R	ER	ShO	H/9	BB/9	SO/9
oks Dauss	R	13	21	.382	3.56	0	38	32	18	270.1	308	84	82	158	107	0	10.25	2.80	2.73
ward Ehmke	R	15	18	.455	3.29	3	38	33	23	268.1	250	124	98	133	98	2	8.39	4.16	3.29
d Oldham	L	8	13	.381	3.85	1	39	23	11	215.1	248	91	62	132	92	1	10.37	3.80	2.59
c Ayers	R	7	14	.333	3.88	0	46	22	9	208.2	217	62	103	115	90	3	9.36	2.67	4.44
tch Leonard	L	10	17	.370	4.33	0	28	27	10	191.1	192	63	76	107	92	3	9.03	2.96	3.57
nk Okrie	L	1	2	.333	5.27	0	21	1	1	41	44	18	9	29	24	0	9.66	3.95	1.98
Morrisette	R	1	1	.500	4.33	0	8	3	1	27	25	19	15	21	13	0	8.33	6.33	5.00
n Bogart	R	2	1	.667	3.04	0	4	3	0	23.2	16	18	5	12	8	0	6.08	6.85	1.90
ie Alten	L	0	1	.000	9.00	0	14	1	0	23	40	9	4	27	23	0	15.65	3.52	1.57
Conkwright	R	2	1	.667	6.98	1	5	2	0	19.1	29	16	4	16	15	0	13.50	7.45	1.86
rry Baumgartner	R	0	1	.000	4.00	0	9	0	0	18	18	6	7	10	8	0	9.00	3.00	3.50
nie Boland	R	0	2	.000	7.79	0	4	3	1	17.1	23	14	4	18	15	0	11.94	7.27	2.08
n Glaiser	R	0	0	—	6.35	1	9	1	0	17	23	8	3	15	12	0	12.18	4.24	1.59
y Crumpler	L	1	0	1.000	5.54	0	3	2	1	13	17	11	2	13	8	0	11.77	7.62	1.38
tt Wilson	R	1	1	.500	3.46	0	3	2	1	13	12	5	4	10	5	0	8.31	3.46	2.77
k Coombs	R	0	0	—	3.18	0	2	0	0	5.2	7	2	1	5	2	0	11.12	3.18	1.59
d Cox	R	0	0	—	5.40	0	3	0	0	5	9	3	1	4	3	0	16.20	5.40	1.80
n Love	L	0	0	—	8.31	0	1	0	0	4.1	6	4	2	4	4	0	12.46	8.31	4.15
Vedder	R	0	0	—	0.00	0	1	0	0	2	0	0	1	0	0	0	0.00	0.00	4.50
Fried	L	0	0	—	16.20	0	2	0	0	1.2	3	4	0	4	3	0	16.20	21.60	0.00
AM TOTAL		61	93	.396	4.04	7	278	155	76	1385	1487	561	483	833	622	9	9.66	3.65	3.14

MANAGER	W	L	PCT
Ty Cobb	71	82	.464

POS	Player	B	G	AB	H	2B	3B	HR	HR %	R	RBI	BB	SO	SB	Pinch Hit AB	Pinch Hit H	BA	SA
REGULARS																		
1B	Lu Blue	B	153	585	180	33	11	5	0.9	103	75	103	47	13	1	0	.308	.427
2B	Ralph Young	B	107	401	120	8	3	0	0.0	70	29	69	23	11	1	0	.299	.334
SS	Donie Bush	B	104	402	113	6	5	0	0.0	72	27	45	23	8	0	0	.281	.321
3B	Bob Jones	L	141	554	168	23	9	1	0.2	82	72	37	24	8	0	0	.303	.383
RF	Harry Heilmann	R	149	602	**237**	43	14	19	3.2	114	139	53	37	2	1	1	**.394**	.606
CF	Ty Cobb	L	128	507	197	37	16	12	2.4	124	101	56	19	22	7	1	.389	.596
LF	Bobby Veach	L	150	612	207	43	13	16	2.6	110	128	48	31	14	1	0	.338	.529
C	Johnny Bassler	L	119	388	119	18	5	0	0.0	37	56	58	16	2	3	1	.307	.379
SUBSTITUTES																		
UT	Ira Flagstead	R	85	259	79	15	1	0	0.0	40	31	21	21	7	7	2	.305	.371
UT	Joe Sargent	R	66	178	45	8	5	2	1.1	21	22	24	26	2	1	0	.253	.388
SS	Herm Merritt	R	20	46	17	1	2	0	0.0	3	6	1	5	1	1	0	.370	.478
2B	Sam Barnes	L	7	11	2	1	0	0	0.0	2	0	2	1	0	2	0	.182	.273
SS	Jackie Tavener	L	2	4	0	0	0	0	0.0	0	0	0	1	0	0	0	.000	.000
3B	Clarence Huber	R	1	0	0	0	0	0	–	0	0	0	0	0	0	0	–	–
OF	Chick Shorten	L	92	217	59	11	3	0	0.0	33	23	20	11	2	**37**	**9**	.272	.350
OF	George Cunningham	R	1	0	0	0	0	0	–	0	0	0	0	0	0	0	–	–
C	Eddie Ainsmith	R	35	98	27	5	2	0	0.0	6	12	13	7	1	1	0	.276	.367
C	Larry Woodall	R	46	80	29	4	1	0	0.0	10	14	6	7	1	18	5	.363	.438
C	Clyde Manion	R	12	18	2	0	0	0	0.0	0	2	2	2	0	6	1	.111	.111
PH	Sammy Hale	R	9	2	0	0	0	0	0.0	2	0	0	1	0	2	0	.000	.000
PITCHERS																		
P	Hooks Dauss	R	32	88	23	2	1	1	1.1	8	11	4	15	0	0	0	.261	.341
P	Red Oldham	L	42	85	19	1	3	2	2.4	12	7	5	23	0	0	0	.224	.376
P	Dutch Leonard	L	36	82	14	1	0	0	0.0	6	5	5	13	0	0	0	.171	.183
P	Howard Ehmke	R	30	74	21	3	1	0	0.0	9	9	1	7	0	0	0	.284	.351
P	Carl Holling	R	35	48	13	2	0	0	0.0	4	5	3	4	0	0	0	.271	.313
P	Bert Cole	L	30	46	13	2	3	0	0.0	12	8	1	4	0	2	1	.283	.457
P	Jim Middleton	R	38	34	5	1	0	0	0.0	2	4	2	0	0	0	0	.147	.176
P	Suds Sutherland	R	17	27	11	1	0	0	0.0	4	7	1	4	0	2	1	.407	.444
P	Slicker Parks	R	10	9	1	0	0	0	0.0	1	0	1	1	0	0	0	.111	.111
P	Pol Perritt	R	4	5	2	0	0	0	0.0	0	0	0	0	0	0	0	.400	.400
P	Danny Boone	R	1	1	0	0	0	0	0.0	0	0	0	0	0	0	0	.000	.000
P	Lefty Stewart	R	5	1	0	0	0	0	0.0	0	0	0	0	0	0	0	.000	.000
P	Doc Ayers	R	2	0	0	0	0	0	–	0	0	0	0	0	0	0	–	–
P	Jim Walsh	L	3	0	0	0	0	0	–	0	0	0	0	0	0	0	–	–
	TEAM TOTAL			5464	1723	269	98	58	1.1	887	793	581	373	94	93	22	.315	.432

INDIVIDUAL FIELDING

POS	Player	T	G	PO	A	E	DP	TC/G	FA		POS	Player	T	G	PO	A	E	DP	TC/G	FA
1B	L. Blue	L	152	1478	85	16	75	10.4	.990		OF	B. Veach	R	149	**384**	21	11	4	2.8	.974
	H. Heilmann	R	4	24	3	1	1	7.0	.964			T. Cobb	R	121	301	27	10	2	2.8	.970
2B	R. Young	R	106	285	270	31	44	5.5	.947			H. Heilmann	R	143	233	10	10	1	1.8	.960
	D. Bush	R	23	45	69	7	0	5.3	.942			C. Shorten	L	52	101	3	2	2	2.0	.981
	J. Sargent	R	24	51	51	8	10	4.6	.927			I. Flagstead	R	12	22	4	0	1	2.2	1.000
	I. Flagstead	R	8	17	18	1	13	4.5	.972			G. Cunningham	R	1	1	0	0	0	1.0	1.000
	S. Barnes	R	2	6	11	1	0	9.0	.944		C	J. Bassler	R	115	433	113	14	7	4.9	.975
SS	D. Bush	R	81	172	260	23	35	5.6	.949			E. Ainsmith	R	34	99	25	7	0	3.9	.947
	I. Flagstead	R	55	111	139	27	8	5.0	.903			L. Woodall	R	24	48	8	2	1	2.4	.966
	J. Sargent	R	19	34	41	8	9	4.4	.904			C. Shorten	L	1	0	0	0	0	0.0	.000
	H. Merritt	R	17	25	20	6	0	3.0	.882			C. Manion	R	4	5	3	0	0	2.0	1.000
	J. Tavener	R	2	3	4	0	0	3.5	1.000											
3B	B. Jones	R	141	194	324	**27**	12	**3.9**	.950											
	J. Sargent	R	23	27	42	5	2	3.2	.932											
	I. Flagstead	R	1	0	4	0	0	4.0	1.000											
	C. Huber	R	1	1	0	0	0	1.0	1.000											

During their first year under player-manager Ty Cobb, the Tigers greatly improved their stature as hitters, if not their stature in the standings. Seventh in team batting during Hughie Jennings's final season, the Tigers vaulted to first at a still-standing team-record .316, with a still-standing league-record 1,724 hits. Six Detroit regulars topped .300. Much-improved right-hander Harry Heilmann won the batting title at .394 (and would continue to win it every odd year through 1927). And for the first time, three Tigers—Heilmann, Bobby Veach, and Cobb—drove in 100-plus runs.

Cobb motivated as he sometimes played: dirty. In an attempt to incite the easygoing Veach, Cobb enlisted Heilmann to goad the leftfielder with nasty insults from on deck. Heilmann didn't want to lose Veach's friendship, but Cobb assured him he'd explain the plan to Veach after the season. So Heilmann abused Veach, who in turn developed a hefty batting average and a frenzied hate for Heilmann. The season over, Cobb took off with his hunting dogs without a word. When Heilmann tried to explain on his own, Veach told him to "not come sucking around me with that phony line." And the two were forever enemies.

But the new Tigers finished sixth, 27 games out, because of old problems: pitching and defense. Second baseman Pep Young (.299) and shortstop Donie Bush (.281) hit, but didn't field. Bush's unreliable glove earned him a late-season exile to the Senators. And no pitcher finished above .500, Hooks Dauss leading the staff at 13–14. Significantly, Detroit pitching managed to lead the league only in saves with 17; Jim Middleton had seven, Carl Holling four.

TEAM STATISTICS

	W	L	PCT	GB	R	OR	2B	Batting 3B	HR	BA	SA	SB	E	Fielding DP	FA	CG	Pitching BB	SO	ShO	SV	ERA
Y	98	55	.641		948	708	285	87	134	.300	.464	89	222	138	.965	92	470	481	7	15	3.79
LE	94	60	.610	4.5	925	712	355	90	42	.308	.430	58	204	124	.967	81	430	475	11	14	3.90
TL	81	73	.526	17.5	835	845	246	106	66	.304	.425	92	224	127	.964	79	557	478	9	9	4.62
AS	80	73	.523	18	704	738	240	96	42	.277	.383	111	235	153	.963	80	442	452	8	10	3.97
OS	75	79	.487	23.5	668	696	248	69	17	.277	.361	83	157	151	.975	88	452	446	9	5	3.98
ET	71	82	.464	27	883	852	268	100	58	.316	.433	95	232	107	.963	73	495	452	4	17	4.40
HI	62	92	.403	36.5	683	858	242	82	35	.283	.379	97	200	155	.969	86	549	392	7	9	4.94
HI	53	100	.346	45	657	894	256	64	83	.274	.390	68	274	144	.958	75	548	431	1	7	4.60
AGUE TOTAL					6303	6303	2140	694	477	.292	.408	693	1748	1099	.965	654	3943	3607	56	86	4.28

INDIVIDUAL PITCHING

TCHER	T	W	L	PCT	ERA	SV	G	GS	CG	IP	H	BB	SO	R	ER	ShO	H/9	BB/9	SO/9
utch Leonard	L	11	13	.458	3.75	1	36	32	16	245	273	63	120	125	102	1	10.03	2.31	4.41
ooks Dauss	R	10	15	.400	4.33	1	32	28	16	233	275	81	68	141	112	0	10.62	3.13	2.63
ed Oldham	L	11	14	.440	4.24	1	40	28	12	229.1	258	81	67	129	108	1	10.13	3.18	2.63
oward Ehmke	R	13	14	.481	4.54	0	30	22	13	196.1	220	81	68	123	99	1	10.08	3.71	3.12
arl Holling	R	3	7	.300	4.30	4	35	11	4	136	162	58	38	95	65	0	10.72	3.84	2.51
m Middleton	R	6	11	.353	5.03	7	38	10	2	121.2	149	44	31	83	68	0	11.02	3.25	2.29
ert Cole	L	7	4	.636	4.27	1	20	11	7	109.2	134	36	22	66	52	1	11.00	2.95	1.81
ds Sutherland	R	6	2	.750	4.97	0	13	8	3	58	80	18	18	43	32	0	12.41	2.79	2.79
icker Parks	R	3	2	.600	5.68	0	10	1	0	25.1	33	16	10	17	16	0	11.72	5.68	3.55
ol Perritt	R	1	0	1.000	4.85	0	4	2	0	13	18	7	3	9	7	0	12.46	4.85	2.08
fty Stewart	L	0	0	–	12.00	1	5	0	0	9	20	5	4	12	12	0	20.00	5.00	4.00
oc Ayers	R	0	0	–	9.00	0	2	1	0	4	9	2	0	6	4	0	20.25	4.50	0.00
m Walsh	L	0	0	–	2.25	0	3	0	0	4	2	1	3	2	1	0	4.50	2.25	6.75
anny Boone	R	0	0	–	0.00	1	1	0	0	2	1	2	0	1	0	0	4.50	9.00	0.00
AM TOTAL		71	82	.464	4.40	17	269	154	73	1386.1	1634	495	452	852	678	4	10.61	3.21	2.93

MANAGER	W	L	PCT
Ty Cobb	79	75	.513

POS	Player	B	G	AB	H	2B	3B	HR	HR %	R	RBI	BB	SO	SB	Pinch Hit AB	Pinch Hit H	BA	SA
REGULARS																		
1B	Lu Blue	B	145	584	175	31	9	6	1.0	131	45	82	48	8	1	1	.300	.414
2B	George Cutshaw	R	132	499	133	14	8	2	0.4	57	61	20	13	11	0	0	.267	.339
SS	Topper Rigney	R	155	536	161	17	7	2	0.4	68	63	68	44	17	0	0	.300	.369
3B	Bob Jones	L	124	455	117	10	6	3	0.7	65	44	36	18	8	3	0	.257	.325
RF	Harry Heilmann	R	118	455	162	27	10	21	4.6	92	92	58	28	8	0	0	.356	.598
CF	Ty Cobb	L	137	526	211	42	16	4	0.8	99	99	55	24	9	3	0	.401	.565
LF	Bobby Veach	L	155	618	202	34	13	9	1.5	96	126	42	27	9	0	0	.327	.468
C	Johnny Bassler	L	121	372	120	14	0	0	0.0	41	41	62	12	2	2	0	.323	.360
SUBSTITUTES																		
31	Fred Haney	R	81	213	75	7	4	0	0.0	41	25	32	14	3	9	3	.352	.423
2B	Danny Clark	L	83	185	54	11	3	3	1.6	31	26	15	11	1	36	8	.292	.432
S3	Chick Gagnon	R	10	4	1	0	0	0	0.0	2	0	0	2	0	2	1	.250	.250
OF	Bob Fothergill	R	42	152	49	12	4	0	0.0	20	29	8	9	1	3	1	.322	.454
OF	Ira Flagstead	R	44	91	28	5	3	3	3.3	21	8	14	16	0	8	2	.308	.527
OF	John Mohardt	R	5	1	1	0	0	0	0.0	0	0	1	0	0	0	0	1.000	1.000
C	Larry Woodall	R	50	125	43	2	2	0	0.0	19	18	8	11	0	11	4	.344	.392
C	Clyde Manion	R	42	69	19	4	1	0	0.0	9	12	4	6	0	13	4	.275	.362
PITCHERS																		
P	Howard Ehmke	R	45	102	16	4	1	0	0.0	6	8	2	10	0	0	0	.157	.216
P	Herman Pillette	R	40	99	17	3	0	0	0.0	5	11	4	28	0	0	0	.172	.202
P	Red Oldham	L	43	73	19	4	1	0	0.0	11	13	6	10	1	0	0	.260	.342
P	Hooks Dauss	R	39	72	15	3	0	1	1.4	4	7	8	20	0	0	0	.208	.292
P	Ole Olsen	R	39	39	7	2	0	0	0.0	1	2	1	6	0	0	0	.179	.231
P	Syl Johnson	R	29	36	8	0	1	0	0.0	5	1	0	10	0	0	0	.222	.278
P	Bert Cole	L	27	25	4	0	0	0	0.0	2	1	2	9	0	1	0	.160	.160
P	Lil Stoner	R	17	20	2	1	0	0	0.0	0	3	2	4	0	0	0	.100	.150
P	Roy Moore	B	9	7	3	0	0	0	0.0	0	0	0	1	0	0	0	.429	.429
P	Carl Holling	R	7	2	0	0	0	0	0.0	0	0	0	1	0	0	0	.000	.000
P	Ken Holloway	R	1	0	0	0	0	0	–	0	0	0	0	0	0	0	–	–
	TEAM TOTAL			5360	1642	247	89	54	1.0	828	735	530	382	78	92	24	.306	.416

INDIVIDUAL FIELDING

POS	Player	T	G	PO	A	E	DP	TC/G	FA
1B	L. Blue	L	144	1506	75	15	107	11.1	.991
	F. Haney	R	11	115	7	2	6	11.3	.984
	H. Heilmann	R	5	25	5	0	1	6.0	1.000
	C. Manion	R	1	0	1	0	0	1.0	1.000
2B	G. Cutshaw	R	132	334	390	21	69	5.6	.972
	D. Clark	R	38	72	99	10	16	4.8	.945
SS	T. Rigney	R	155	262	493	50	74	5.2	.938
	C. Gagnon	R	1	0	0	0	0	0.0	.000
	F. Haney	R	2	0	0	0	0	0.0	.000
3B	B. Jones	R	119	161	267	17	22	3.7	.962
	F. Haney	R	42	43	105	10	11	3.8	.937
	D. Clark	R	1	0	1	0	0	1.0	1.000
	C. Gagnon	R	1	0	0	1	0	1.0	.000

POS	Player	T	G	PO	A	E	DP	TC/G	FA
OF	B. Veach	R	154	375	16	7	3	2.6	.982
	T. Cobb	R	134	330	14	7	3	2.6	.980
	H. Heilmann	R	115	175	6	10	2	1.7	.948
	I. Flagstead	R	31	54	4	2	1	1.9	.967
	B. Fothergill	R	39	50	2	3	1	1.4	.945
	D. Clark	R	5	6	0	0	0	1.2	1.000
	B. Cole	L	1	3	0	0	0	3.0	1.000
	J. Mohardt	R	3	1	0	0	0	0.3	1.000
C	J. Bassler	R	118	421	113	11	12	4.6	.980
	L. Woodall	R	39	117	11	3	1	3.4	.977
	C. Manion	R	21	61	7	5	0	3.5	.932

As usual, Ty Cobb found himself embroiled in controversy. For a change, it wasn't his fault. The case of the two-percentage-point base hit started innocently during a drizzly midsummer game against the Yankees at the Polo Grounds. Cobb hit a grounder that was muffed by New York shortstop Everett Scott. The official scorer ruled it an error. The Associated Press scorer called it a hit. After the season, the league chose the AP version, which pushed Cobb's average to .401, his third .400-plus season, instead of the official scorer's, which would have left Cobb at .399. The incident elicited the predictable furor, particularly in New York. League president Ban Johnson eventually ruled to accept hit over error. But Cobb's average stayed second-best to George Sisler's .420 anyway.

The Tigers, meanwhile, compiled their first winning season in three years. After another slow start, Detroit edged ahead of Chicago and Cleveland into third place, four games over .500, 15 games behind Miller Huggins's Yankees. Newcomers fueled the improvement. Pitcher Herman "Old Folks" Pillette led the staff at 19–12 with a 2.85 ERA. Topper Rigney joined the team from Fort Worth, became the regular shortstop, and hit .300. George Cutshaw was purchased from the Pirates to man second base. During the season, outfielder Robert "Fat" Fothergill jumped from the minors to hit a part-time .322.

Among the veterans, Tiger outfielders kept slugging, batting an aggregate .372. In all, six Tiger regulars hit .300 for the second straight year. On the mound, Howard Ehmke kept opposing hitters preoccupied with ducking: Ehmke plunked 23 batters, still a Detroit record.

TEAM STATISTICS

W	L	PCT	GB	R	OR	2B	3B	HR	BA	SA	SB	E	DP	FA	CG	BB	SO	ShO	SV	ERA
94	60	.610		758	618	220	75	95	.287	.412	62	157	122	.975	98	423	458	7	14	3.39
93	61	.604	1	867	643	291	94	98	.313	.455	132	201	158	.968	79	421	534	8	22	3.38
79	75	.513	15	828	791	250	87	54	.305	.414	78	191	135	.970	67	473	461	7	15	4.27
78	76	.506	16	768	817	320	73	32	.292	.398	89	202	140	.968	76	464	489	14	7	4.60
77	77	.500	17	691	691	243	62	45	.278	.373	106	155	132	.975	86	529	484	13	8	3.93
69	85	.448	25	650	706	229	76	45	.268	.367	94	196	161	.969	84	500	422	11	10	3.81
65	89	.422	29	705	830	229	63	111	.269	.400	60	215	119	.966	73	469	373	4	6	4.59
61	93	.396	33	598	769	250	55	45	.263	.357	60	224	139	.965	71	503	359	10	6	4.30
GUE TOTAL				5865	5865	2032	585	525	.284	.397	681	1541	1106	.969	634	3782	3580	74	88	4.03

INDIVIDUAL PITCHING

CHER	T	W	L	PCT	ERA	SV	G	GS	CG	IP	H	BB	SO	R	ER	ShO	H/9	BB/9	SO/9
ward Ehmke	R	17	17	.500	4.22	1	45	30	16	279.2	299	101	108	146	131	1	9.62	3.25	3.48
rman Pillette	R	19	12	.613	2.85	1	40	37	18	274.2	270	95	71	112	87	4	8.85	3.11	2.33
oks Dauss	R	13	13	.500	4.20	4	39	25	12	218.2	251	59	78	123	102	1	10.33	2.43	3.21
Oldham	L	10	13	.435	4.67	3	43	27	9	212	256	59	72	130	110	0	10.87	2.50	3.06
Olsen	R	7	6	.538	4.53	3	37	15	5	137	147	40	52	84	69	0	9.66	2.63	3.42
Johnson	R	7	3	.700	3.71	1	29	8	3	97	99	30	29	52	40	0	9.19	2.78	2.69
t Cole	L	1	6	.143	4.88	0	23	5	2	79.1	105	39	21	60	43	0	11.91	4.42	2.38
Stoner	R	4	4	.500	7.04	0	17	7	2	62.2	76	35	18	53	49	0	10.91	5.03	2.59
Moore	L	0	0	–	5.95	2	9	0	0	19.2	29	10	9	14	13	0	13.27	4.58	4.12
l Holling	R	1	1	.500	15.43	0	5	1	0	9.1	21	5	2	16	16	0	20.25	4.82	1.93
n Holloway	R	0	0	–	0.00	0	1	0	0	1	1	0	1	1	0	0	9.00	0.00	9.00
AM TOTAL		79	75	.513	4.27	15	288	155	67	1391	1554	473	461	791	660	7	10.05	3.06	2.98

MANAGER	W	L	PCT
Ty Cobb	83	71	.539

POS	Player	B	G	AB	H	2B	3B	HR	HR %	R	RBI	BB	SO	SB	Pinch Hit AB	Pinch Hit H	BA	SA
REGULARS																		
1B	Lu Blue	B	129	504	143	27	7	1	0.2	100	46	96	40	9	0	0	.284	.371
2B	Fred Haney	R	142	503	142	13	4	4	0.8	85	67	45	23	12	0	0	.282	.348
SS	Topper Rigney	R	129	470	148	24	11	1	0.2	63	74	55	35	7	0	0	.315	.419
3B	Bob Jones	L	100	372	93	15	4	1	0.3	51	40	29	13	7	0	0	.250	.320
RF	Harry Heilmann	R	144	524	211	44	11	18	3.4	121	115	74	40	8	1	1	**.403**	.632
CF	Ty Cobb	L	145	556	189	40	7	6	1.1	103	88	66	14	9	2	1	.340	.469
LF	Heinie Manush	L	109	308	103	20	5	4	1.3	59	54	20	21	3	27	6	.334	.471
C	Johnny Bassler	L	135	383	114	12	3	0	0.0	45	49	76	13	2	5	2	.298	.345
SUBSTITUTES																		
UT	Del Pratt	R	101	297	92	18	3	0	0.0	43	40	25	9	5	8	4	.310	.391
2B	George Cutshaw	R	45	143	32	1	2	0	0.0	15	13	9	5	2	0	0	.224	.259
SS	John Kerr	B	19	42	9	1	0	0	0.0	4	1	4	5	0	1	0	.214	.238
UT	Les Burke	L	7	10	1	0	0	0	0.0	2	2	0	1	0	1	0	.100	.100
OF	Bobby Veach	L	114	293	94	13	3	2	0.7	45	39	29	21	10	22	8	.321	.406
OF	Bob Fothergill	R	101	241	76	18	2	1	0.4	34	49	12	19	4	30	9	.315	.419
PO	Roy Moore	L	4	5	0	0	0	0	0.0	1	0	1	3	0	0	0	.000	.000
C	Larry Woodall	R	71	148	41	12	2	1	0.7	20	19	22	9	2	9	4	.277	.405
C1	Clyde Manion	R	23	22	3	0	0	0	0.0	0	2	2	2	0	17	2	.136	.136
C	Fred Carisch	R	2	0	0	0	0	0	–	0	0	0	0	0	0	0	–	–
PH	Ira Flagstead	R	1	1	0	0	0	0	0.0	0	0	0	0	0	1	0	.000	.000
PITCHERS																		
P	Hooks Dauss	R	50	104	24	5	0	0	0.0	10	13	17	27	0	0	0	.231	.279
P	Herman Pillette	R	47	85	21	2	2	0	0.0	7	10	5	21	0	0	0	.247	.318
P	Ken Holloway	R	42	65	8	1	0	0	0.0	4	3	1	11	0	0	0	.123	.138
P	Syl Johnson	R	37	62	10	1	2	1	1.6	6	5	1	19	0	0	0	.161	.290
P	Bert Cole	L	58	55	14	1	1	1	1.8	7	6	0	12	1	0	0	.255	.364
P	Rip Collins	B	17	27	3	1	0	0	0.0	1	2	2	9	0	0	0	.111	.148
P	Ray Francis	L	37	21	3	0	0	0	0.0	5	1	0	6	0	0	0	.143	.143
P	Earl Whitehill	L	8	11	4	0	0	0	0.0	2	0	1	3	1	0	0	.364	.364
P	Ole Olsen	R	17	8	1	0	0	0	0.0	0	1	0	2	0	0	0	.125	.125
P	Ed Wells	L	7	1	0	0	0	0	0.0	0	0	0	1	0	0	0	.000	.000
P	Rufe Clarke	R	5	0	0	0	0	0	–	0	0	0	0	0	0	0	–	–
TEAM TOTAL				5261	1579	269	69	41	0.8	833	739	592	384	82	124	37	.300	.401

INDIVIDUAL FIELDING

POS	Player	T	G	PO	A	E	DP	TC/G	FA
1B	L. Blue	L	129	1347	93	12	74	11.3	.992
	D. Pratt	R	17	169	10	0	10	10.5	1.000
	C. Manion	R	1	0	0	0	0	0.0	.000
	H. Heilmann	R	12	101	8	1	5	9.2	.991
2B	F. Haney	R	69	162	178	16	29	5.2	.955
	D. Pratt	R	60	108	140	14	21	4.4	.947
	G. Cutshaw	R	43	103	150	3	2	6.0	.988
	L. Burke	R	1	0	2	0	0	2.0	1.000
SS	T. Rigney	R	129	209	383	35	46	4.9	.944
	F. Haney	R	16	29	54	3	6	5.4	.965
	J. Kerr	R	15	19	45	9	5	4.9	.877
3B	B. Jones	R	97	109	224	16	17	3.6	.954
	F. Haney	R	55	70	119	9	12	3.6	.955
	D. Pratt	R	12	4	29	4	1	3.1	.892
	L. Burke	R	2	1	1	2	0	2.0	.500
	G. Cutshaw	R	2	1	1	0	0	1.0	1.000

POS	Player	T	G	PO	A	E	DP	TC/G	FA
OF	T. Cobb	R	141	362	14	12	2	2.8	.969
	H. Heilmann	R	130	272	13	12	2	2.3	.960
	H. Manush	L	79	158	6	8	0	2.2	.953
	B. Veach	R	85	127	6	8	0	1.7	.943
	B. Fothergill	R	68	121	4	3	0	1.9	.977
	R. Moore	L	1	0	0	0	0	0.0	.000
C	J. Bassler	R	128	447	133	7	8	4.6	.988
	L. Woodall	R	60	140	32	3	2	2.9	.983
	L. Burke	R	1	0	0	0	0	0.0	.000
	B. Veach	R	1	0	0	0	0	0.0	.000
	C. Manion	R	3	5	1	1	0	2.3	.857
	F. Carisch	R	2	1	0	0	0	0.5	1.000

Ty Cobb forged his highest finish as manager: the Tigers edged the Indians for second place, 16 games behind the soon-to-be World Champion Yankees. The summer might have proved even more pleasant if not for a damaging preseason trade. Detroit dispatched pitchers Howard Ehmke and Carl Holling, rookie first baseman Babe Herman, and cash to the Red Sox for second baseman Del Pratt and pitcher Tip "Two-Gun" Collins. The 35-year-old Pratt could hit, but by July his ever-decreasing range had cost him the starting job. Collins squabbled with Cobb, frequently sat with injuries, and finished 3–7. Meanwhile, Ehmke went 20–7, including a no-hitter and a one-hitter back-to-back, for last-place Boston.

Detroit finished 12 games above .500 with help from Harry Heilmann, who won his second batting title with a career-high .403, 10 points ahead of second-place Babe Ruth. Cobb dropped 61 points to .340. The Tigers also came up with yet another slugging outfielder in Heinie Manush, who hit .334—good enough to take the left-field job from the 35-year-old Veach, who hit .321 as a pinch-hitter in his final Detroit season.

Early in the year, in a tryout arranged by Veach, 20-year-old Charlie Gehringer nervously took batting practice while the entire Tigers team watched and complained about lost time in the cage. "Cobb wouldn't take his eyes off me," Gehringer remembered. "I could feel him staring at me. They were all watching me—Heilmann, Manush, Veach. They liked what they saw, because they stopped grumbling about me being in there. It was eerie. The only sound in that big, empty ballpark was me standing there hitting line drives, with the whole Tiger club watching me." Still in uniform, Cobb clomped straight from the field to the offices to fetch owner Frank Navin. Gehringer would be back.

TEAM STATISTICS

W	L	PCT	GB	R	OR	Batting						Fielding			Pitching				
						2B	3B	HR	BA	SA	SB	E	DP	FA	CG	BB	SO	ShO	SV	ERA
98	54	.645		823	622	231	79	105	.291	.422	69	144	131	.977	102	491	506	9	10	3.66
83	71	.539	16	831	741	270	69	41	.300	.401	87	200	103	.968	61	459	447	9	12	4.09
82	71	.536	16.5	888	746	301	75	59	.301	.420	79	226	143	.964	76	466	407	10	11	3.91
75	78	.490	23.5	720	747	224	93	26	.274	.367	102	216	182	.966	70	559	474	8	16	3.99
74	78	.487	24	688	720	248	62	82	.281	.398	64	177	145	.971	83	528	488	10	10	3.93
69	83	.454	29	661	761	229	65	52	.271	.370	72	221	127	.965	65	550	400	6	12	4.08
69	85	.448	30	692	741	254	57	42	.279	.373	191	184	138	.971	74	534	467	5	11	4.03
61	91	.401	37	584	809	253	54	34	.261	.351	77	232	126	.963	78	520	412	3	11	4.20
GUE TOTAL				5887	5887	2010	554	441	.282	.388	741	1600	1095	.968	609	4107	3601	60	93	3.99

INDIVIDUAL PITCHING

CHER	T	W	L	PCT	ERA	SV	G	GS	CG	IP	H	BB	SO	R	ER	ShO	H/9	BB/9	SO/9
oks Dauss	R	21	13	.618	3.62	3	50	39	22	316	331	78	105	140	127	4	9.43	2.22	2.99
rman Pillette	R	14	19	.424	3.85	1	47	37	14	250.1	280	83	64	138	107	0	10.07	2.98	2.30
n Holloway	R	11	10	.524	4.45	1	42	24	7	194	232	75	55	117	96	1	10.76	3.48	2.55
Johnson	R	12	7	.632	3.98	0	37	18	7	176.1	181	47	93	82	78	1	9.24	2.40	4.75
t Cole	L	13	5	.722	4.14	5	52	13	5	163	183	61	32	95	75	1	10.10	3.37	1.77
Collins	R	3	7	.300	4.87	0	17	13	3	92.1	104	32	25	61	50	1	10.14	3.12	2.44
y Francis	L	5	8	.385	4.42	1	33	6	0	79.1	95	28	27	51	39	0	10.78	3.18	3.06
Olsen	R	1	1	.500	6.31	0	17	2	1	41.1	42	17	12	30	29	0	9.15	3.70	2.61
l Whitehill	L	2	0	1.000	2.73	0	8	3	2	33	22	15	19	14	10	1	6.00	4.09	5.18
y Moore	L	0	0	–	3.00	1	3	0	0	12	15	11	7	4	4	0	11.25	8.25	5.25
Wells	L	0	0	–	5.40	0	7	0	0	10	11	6	6	6	6	0	9.90	5.40	5.40
e Clarke	R	1	1	.500	4.50	0	5	0	0	6	6	6	2	3	3	0	9.00	9.00	3.00
AM TOTAL		83	71	.539	4.09	12	318	155	61	1373.2	1502	459	447	741	624	9	9.84	3.01	2.93

MANAGER	W	L	PCT
Ty Cobb	86	68	.558

POS	Player	B	G	AB	H	2B	3B	HR	HR %	R	RBI	BB	SO	SB	Pinch Hit AB	Pinch Hit H	BA	SA
REGULARS																		
1B	Lu Blue	B	108	395	123	26	7	2	0.5	81	50	64	26	9	0	0	.311	.428
2B	Del Pratt	R	121	429	130	32	3	1	0.2	56	77	31	10	6	1	0	.303	.399
SS	Topper Rigney	R	147	499	144	29	9	4	0.8	81	93	102	39	11	1	0	.289	.407
3B	Bob Jones	L	110	393	107	27	4	0	0.0	52	47	20	20	1	3	1	.272	.361
RF	Harry Heilmann	R	153	570	197	45	16	10	1.8	107	113	78	41	13	2	0	.346	.533
CF	Ty Cobb	L	155	625	211	38	10	4	0.6	115	74	85	18	23	0	0	.338	.450
LF	Heinie Manush	L	120	422	122	24	8	9	2.1	83	68	27	30	14	11	1	.289	.448
C	Johnny Bassler	L	124	379	131	20	3	1	0.3	43	68	62	11	2	3	1	.346	.422
SUBSTITUTES																		
3B	Fred Haney	R	86	256	79	11	1	1	0.4	54	30	39	13	7	13	4	.309	.371
2B	Les Burke	L	72	241	61	10	4	0	0.0	30	17	22	20	2	7	4	.253	.328
2B	Frank O'Rourke	R	47	181	50	11	2	0	0.0	28	19	12	19	7	0	0	.276	.359
2B	Charlie Gehringer	L	5	13	6	0	0	0	0.0	2	1	0	2	1	0	0	.462	.462
3O	John Kerr	B	17	11	3	0	0	0	0.0	3	1	0	0	0	7	2	.273	.273
OF	Bob Fothergill	R	54	166	50	8	3	0	0.0	28	15	5	13	2	9	3	.301	.386
OF	Al Wingo	L	78	150	43	12	2	1	0.7	21	26	21	13	2	29	10	.287	.413
C	Larry Woodall	R	67	165	51	9	2	0	0.0	23	24	21	5	0	4	0	.309	.388
C1	Clyde Manion	R	14	13	3	0	0	0	0.0	1	2	1	1	0	9	3	.231	.231
PITCHERS																		
P	Earl Whitehill	L	37	89	19	1	1	0	0.0	11	7	9	18	0	1	1	.213	.247
P	Lil Stoner	R	37	77	15	5	0	2	2.6	3	7	4	15	0	0	0	.195	.338
P	Rip Collins	R	37	76	11	1	0	0	0.0	5	2	1	23	0	0	0	.145	.158
P	Ken Holloway	R	49	58	11	1	1	0	0.0	2	5	2	10	0	0	0	.190	.241
P	Hooks Dauss	R	40	38	5	1	0	0	0.0	5	2	4	15	0	0	0	.132	.158
P	Bert Cole	L	33	37	10	0	0	0	0.0	4	2	4	6	0	1	0	.270	.270
P	Syl Johnson	R	29	34	7	2	0	0	0.0	1	3	2	6	0	0	0	.206	.265
P	Ed Wells	L	29	33	7	2	0	0	0.0	2	3	0	11	0	0	0	.212	.273
P	Dutch Leonard	L	9	19	4	0	0	0	0.0	2	2	1	4	0	0	0	.211	.211
P	Herman Pillette	R	19	11	4	0	0	0	0.0	4	0	0	4	0	0	0	.364	.364
P	Rufe Clarke	R	2	1	0	0	0	0	0.0	0	0	0	1	0	0	0	.000	.000
P	Willie Ludolph	R	3	1	0	0	0	0	0.0	0	0	0	1	0	0	0	.000	.000
P	Ken Jones	R	1	0	0	0	0	0	–	0	0	0	0	0	0	0	–	–
TEAM TOTAL				5382	1604	315	76	35	0.7	847	758	617	395	100	101	30	.298	.404

INDIVIDUAL FIELDING

POS	Player	T	G	PO	A	E	DP	TC/G	FA
1B	L. Blue	L	108	1099	85	17	72	11.1	.986
	D. Pratt	R	51	486	25	5	35	10.1	.990
	H. Heilmann	R	4	54	4	1	4	14.8	.983
	C. Manion	R	1	1	0	0	0	1.0	1.000
	H. Manush	L	1	1	0	0	0	1.0	1.000
2B	D. Pratt	R	63	133	192	18	38	5.4	.948
	L. Burke	R	58	125	167	13	30	5.3	.957
	F. O'Rourke	R	40	115	140	8	27	6.6	.970
	L. Stoner	R	1	0	0	0	0	0.0	.000
	R. Collins	R	2	0	0	0	0	0.0	.000
	C. Gehringer	R	5	12	17	1	2	6.0	.967
	F. Haney	R	3	4	7	0	0	3.7	1.000
SS	T. Rigney	R	146	273	463	25	72	5.2	**.967**
	F. O'Rourke	R	7	12	25	3	1	5.7	.925
	L. Burke	R	6	8	17	2	2	4.5	.926
	F. Haney	R	4	5	10	4	1	4.8	.789
3B	B. Jones	R	106	108	196	14	12	3.0	.956
	F. Haney	R	59	48	146	14	9	3.5	.933
	J. Kerr	R	3	0	0	0	0	0.0	.000
	D. Pratt	R	4	2	8	0	0	2.5	1.000

POS	Player	T	G	PO	A	E	DP	TC/G	FA
OF	T. Cobb	R	155	417	12	6	8	2.8	**.986**
	H. Heilmann	R	147	263	31	9	6	2.1	.970
	H. Manush	L	106	224	4	5	1	2.2	.970
	B. Fothergill	R	45	89	2	3	1	2.1	.968
	A. Wingo	R	43	59	3	5	2	1.6	.925
	B. Cole	L	2	2	0	0	0	1.0	1.000
	J. Kerr	R	2	1	0	0	0	0.5	1.000
C	J. Bassler	R	122	402	103	11	11	4.2	.979
	L. Woodall	R	62	174	41	3	5	3.5	.986
	C. Manion	R	3	3	0	1	0	1.3	.750

Before the season Navin Field acquired a grandstand upper deck to push capacity past 40,000, and just in time. Detroit boomed with the automobile industry and buzzed about the Tigers, who fought their fiercest pennant race in nine years, drawing 1 million–plus at home for the first time in team history.

The Tigers compiled their best record and most exciting season of Ty Cobb's management. Through July they dipped in and out of first place, holding it for three days as late as mid-August. Cobb got his preseason wish, beating the hated Yankees in the season series, 13–9. Still, the Tigers finished third, four games behind second-place New York, six behind the hitherto perennial last-place Washington Senators. Detroit again led the league in hitting, but Harry Heilmann suffered sinus trouble and dropped 57 points to .346, and 37-year-old Cobb—after hitting .450 in the first month of the season—finished at .338.

Silent, smooth-fielding, sweet-hitting Charlie Gehringer visited the club for five games. The Mechanical Man would return for eight more in 1925, then stick in 1926, staying for 19 summers and 2,323 games on his way to the Hall of Fame. Another valuable acquisition produced more immediate results. Left-hander Earl Whitehill joined the Tigers from Birmingham to lead Cobb's staff at 17–9, 3.86.

In June the simmering rivalry with Babe Ruth's Yankees exploded at Navin Field. Cobb habitually taunted Ruth on his way to right field. "Something around here really stinks. Like a polecat." So when King Cole drilled Bob Meusel and the benches emptied, the twentieth century's two greatest players took the opportunity to tackle each other at home plate. About 1000 spectators—some uprooting seats from their concrete moorings and tossing them onto the field—joined the fray, which lasted 30 minutes before the game was forfeited to New York.

TEAM STATISTICS

	W	L	PCT	GB	R	OR	Batting 2B	3B	HR	BA	SA	SB	Fielding E	DP	FA	Pitching CG	BB	SO	ShO	SV	ERA
AS	92	62	.597		755	613	255	88	22	.294	.387	115	171	149	.972	74	505	469	12	**25**	**3.35**
Y	89	63	.586	2	798	667	248	86	**98**	.289	**.426**	69	**156**	131	**.974**	76	522	**487**	**13**	13	3.86
:T	86	68	.558	6	849	796	315	76	35	**.298**	.404	100	187	142	.971	60	**466**	441	5	20	4.19
'L	74	78	.487	17	764	797	265	62	67	.294	.408	85	183	141	.969	66	512	382	11	7	4.55
HI	71	81	.467	20	685	778	251	59	63	.281	.389	79	180	**157**	.971	68	597	371	7	10	4.39
E	67	86	.438	24.5	755	814	306	59	41	.296	.399	84	205	130	.967	**87**	503	315	7	7	4.40
)S	67	87	.435	25	725	801	300	61	30	.277	.374	79	210	124	.967	73	519	414	8	16	4.36
HI	66	87	.431	25.5	793	858	254	58	41	.288	.382	**138**	229	136	.963	76	512	360	1	11	4.75
AGUE TOTAL					6124	6124	2194	549	397	.290	.396	749	1521	1110	.969	580	4136	3239	64	109	4.23

INDIVIDUAL PITCHING

TCHER	T	W	L	PCT	ERA	SV	G	GS	CG	IP	H	BB	SO	R	ER	ShO	H/9	BB/9	SO/9
rl Whitehill	L	17	9	.654	3.86	0	35	32	16	233	260	79	65	125	100	2	10.04	3.05	2.51
o Collins	R	14	7	.667	3.21	0	34	30	11	216	199	63	75	99	77	1	8.29	2.63	3.13
Stoner	R	11	11	.500	4.72	0	36	25	10	215.2	271	65	66	130	113	1	11.31	2.71	2.75
n Holloway	R	14	6	.700	4.07	3	49	14	5	181.1	209	61	46	105	82	0	10.37	3.03	2.28
oks Dauss	R	12	11	.522	4.59	6	40	10	5	131.1	155	40	44	78	67	0	10.62	2.74	3.02
rt Cole	L	3	9	.250	4.69	2	28	11	2	109.1	135	35	16	69	57	1	11.11	2.88	1.32
I Johnson	R	5	4	.556	4.93	3	29	9	2	104	117	42	55	63	57	0	10.13	3.63	4.76
Wells	L	6	8	.429	4.06	4	29	15	5	102	117	42	33	58	46	0	10.32	3.71	2.91
tch Leonard	L	3	2	.600	4.56	1	9	7	3	51.1	69	17	26	32	26	0	12.10	2.98	4.56
rman Pillette	R	1	1	.500	4.78	1	19	3	1	37.2	46	14	13	30	20	0	10.99	3.35	3.11
lie Ludolph	R	0	0	–	4.76	0	3	0	0	5.2	5	2	1	3	3	0	7.94	3.18	1.59
fe Clarke	R	0	0	–	3.38	0	2	0	0	5.1	3	5	1	2	2	0	5.06	8.44	1.69
n Jones	R	0	0	–	0.00	0	1	0	0	2	1	1	0	0	0	0	4.50	4.50	0.00
AM TOTAL		86	68	.558	4.19	20	314	156	60	1394.2	1587	466	441	794	650	5	10.24	3.01	2.85

MANAGER	W	L	PCT
Ty Cobb	81	73	.526

POS	Player	B	G	AB	H	2B	3B	HR	HR %	R	RBI	BB	SO	SB	Pinch Hit AB	Pinch Hit H	BA	SA
REGULARS																		
1B	Lu Blue	B	150	532	163	18	9	3	0.6	91	94	83	29	19	2	0	.306	.391
2B	Frank O'Rourke	R	124	482	141	40	7	5	1.0	88	57	32	37	5	0	0	.293	.436
SS	Jackie Tavener	L	134	453	111	11	11	0	0.0	45	47	39	60	5	0	0	.245	.318
3B	Fred Haney	R	114	398	111	15	3	0	0.0	84	40	66	29	11	5	1	.279	.332
RF	Harry Heilmann	R	150	573	225	40	11	13	2.3	97	133	67	27	6	2	1	**.393**	.569
CF	Ty Cobb	L	121	415	157	31	12	12	2.9	97	102	65	12	13	12	2	.378	.598
LF	Al Wingo	L	130	440	163	34	10	5	1.1	104	68	69	31	14	7	1	.370	.527
C	Johnny Bassler	L	121	344	96	19	3	0	0.0	40	52	74	6	1	3	0	.279	.352
SUBSTITUTES																		
2B	Les Burke	L	77	180	52	6	3	0	0.0	32	24	17	8	4	22	4	.289	.356
3B	Bob Jones	L	50	148	35	6	0	0	0.0	18	15	9	5	1	3	1	.236	.277
SS	Topper Rigney	R	62	146	36	5	2	2	1.4	21	18	21	15	2	6	0	.247	.349
1B	Johnny Neun	B	60	75	20	3	3	0	0.0	15	4	9	12	2	33	8	.267	.387
3B	Jack Warner	R	10	39	13	0	0	0	0.0	7	2	3	6	0	0	0	.333	.333
2B	Charlie Gehringer	L	8	18	3	0	0	0	0.0	3	0	2	0	0	2	0	.167	.167
OF	Heinie Manush	L	99	277	84	14	3	5	1.8	46	47	24	21	8	22	6	.303	.430
OF	Bob Fothergill	R	71	204	72	14	4	2	1.0	38	28	6	3	2	11	5	.353	.451
C	Larry Woodall	R	75	171	35	4	1	0	0.0	20	13	24	8	1	0	0	.205	.240
C	Oscar Stanage	R	3	5	1	0	0	0	0.0	0	0	0	0	0	0	0	.200	.200
PH	Andy Harrington	R	1	1	0	0	0	0	0.0	0	0	0	0	0	1	0	.000	.000
PITCHERS																		
P	Earl Whitehill	L	36	87	19	1	0	0	0.0	7	7	8	11	1	0	0	.218	.230
P	Hooks Dauss	R	35	81	15	3	1	1	1.2	10	12	10	18	0	0	0	.185	.284
P	Lil Stoner	R	34	55	16	6	1	0	0.0	10	8	3	5	1	0	0	.291	.436
P	Dutch Leonard	L	18	50	10	3	0	0	0.0	6	6	2	7	0	0	0	.200	.260
P	Ken Holloway	R	38	48	11	0	1	0	0.0	3	2	1	3	0	0	0	.229	.271
P	Ed Wells	L	35	43	12	1	2	0	0.0	8	6	2	9	0	0	0	.279	.395
P	Rip Collins	R	26	42	5	0	0	0	0.0	0	3	1	15	0	0	0	.119	.119
P	Jess Doyle	R	45	33	8	2	1	2	6.1	6	4	1	3	0	0	0	.242	.545
P	Ownie Carroll	R	11	16	6	1	0	0	0.0	4	4	0	1	0	0	0	.375	.438
P	Bert Cole	L	14	11	3	0	0	0	0.0	1	1	1	2	0	0	0	.273	.273
P	Syl Johnson	R	6	3	0	0	0	0	0.0	0	0	0	1	0	0	0	.000	.000
P	Bill Moore	R	1	0	0	0	0	0	–	0	0	0	0	0	0	0	–	–
	TEAM TOTAL			5370	1623	277	84	50	0.9	901	797	639	384	96	131	29	.302	.413

INDIVIDUAL FIELDING

POS	Player	T	G	PO	A	E	DP	TC/G	FA	POS	Player	T	G	PO	A	E	DP	TC/G	FA
1B	L. Blue	L	148	1480	101	19	115	10.8	.988	OF	A. Wingo	R	122	282	16	9	6	2.5	.971
	J. Neun	L	13	99	4	1	5	8.0	.990		H. Heilmann	R	148	278	9	9	1	2.0	.970
2B	F. O'Rourke	R	118	309	382	21	67	6.0	.971		T. Cobb	R	105	267	9	15	1	2.8	.948
	L. Burke	R	52	100	130	9	27	4.6	.962		H. Manush	L	73	153	7	3	0	2.2	.982
	C. Gehringer	R	6	8	20	0	5	4.7	1.000		B. Fothergill	R	59	120	6	3	2	2.2	.977
SS	J. Tavener	R	134	229	398	24	73	4.9	.963		O. Carroll	R	1	0	1	0	0	1.0	1.000
	T. Rigney	R	51	51	91	10	7	3.0	.934	C	J. Bassler	R	118	375	87	8	14	4.0	.983
3B	F. Haney	R	107	115	207	16	22	3.2	.953		L. Woodall	R	75	165	38	7	4	2.8	.967
	B. Jones	R	46	43	91	2	5	3.0	.985		O. Stanage	R	3	2	0	0	0	0.7	1.000
	J. Warner	R	10	3	15	0	3	1.8	1.000										
	F. O'Rourke	R	6	7	9	1	0	2.8	.941										
	T. Rigney	R	4	5	4	0	1	2.3	1.000										

Tiger fans were thrilled by a magnificent batting-title stretch-run battle between Harry Heilmann and Cleveland's Tris Speaker. The Indians centerfielder held a 50-point lead at Labor Day, but the 37-year-old player-manager's ailing legs forced him to sit or pinch-hit through the rest of September. Heilmann, meanwhile, steadily whittled the formidable lead. On the last day of the season, Speaker still led by a point. The Tigers finished with a doubleheader at St. Louis. In the first game, Heilmann went three-for-six, good enough to cinch the crown by a fraction of a percentage point. Teammates urged him to sit out the second game. But Heilmann insisted, "I'll win it fairly or not at all." In game two he went three-for-three, winning his third batting title in five years (the 15th by a Tiger in 19 years), .393 to .389.

It contributed to the most overpowering Detroit outfield yet: with Ty Cobb at .378 and newcomer Red Wingo at .370, they combined with Heilmann for a .382 total. The firepower erupted on June 17 to give Detroit its biggest inning in team history: 13 runs against the Yankees.

Thanks to the usual problems, the Tigers slipped to fourth, 16 1/2 games behind first-place Washington. Except for Lu Blue (.306) at first, the rest of the infield stayed unstable. Only Hooks Dauss (16–11, 3.16) finished with more than 13 victories and less than a 4.00 ERA. At one point the 38-year-old Cobb resorted to pitching himself and hurled one perfect inning to pick up a save.

TEAM STATISTICS

	W	L	PCT	GB	R	OR	2B	3B	HR	BA	SA	SB	E	DP	FA	CG	BB	SO	ShO	SV	ERA
AS	96	55	.636		829	669	251	71	56	.303	.411	134	170	166	.972	69	543	464	9	21	3.67
II	88	64	.579	8.5	830	714	298	79	76	.307	.434	67	211	148	.966	61	544	495	8	18	3.89
L	82	71	.536	15	897	909	304	68	110	.298	.439	85	226	164	.964	67	675	419	7	10	4.85
T	81	73	.526	16.5	903	829	277	84	50	.302	.413	97	173	143	.972	66	556	419	2	18	4.61
II	79	75	.513	18.5	811	771	299	59	38	.284	.385	129	200	162	.968	71	489	374	12	13	4.34
E	70	84	.455	27.5	782	810	285	58	52	.297	.399	90	210	146	.967	93	493	345	6	9	4.49
'	69	85	.448	28.5	706	774	247	74	110	.275	.410	67	160	150	.974	80	505	492	8	13	4.33
IS	47	105	.309	49.5	639	921	257	64	41	.266	.364	42	271	150	.957	68	510	310	6	6	4.97
AGUE TOTAL					6397	6397	2218	557	533	.292	.407	711	1621	1229	.968	575	4315	3318	58	108	4.39

INDIVIDUAL PITCHING

TCHER	T	W	L	PCT	ERA	SV	G	GS	CG	IP	H	BB	SO	R	ER	ShO	H/9	BB/9	SO/9
rl Whitehill	L	11	11	.500	4.66	2	35	33	15	239.1	267	88	83	135	124	1	10.04	3.31	3.12
oks Dauss	R	16	11	.593	3.16	1	35	30	16	228	238	85	58	110	80	1	9.39	3.36	2.29
n Holloway	R	13	4	.765	4.62	2	38	14	6	157.2	170	67	29	90	81	0	9.70	3.82	1.66
Stoner	R	10	9	.526	4.26	1	34	18	8	152	166	53	51	79	72	0	9.83	3.14	3.02
Collins	R	6	11	.353	4.56	0	26	20	5	140	149	52	33	86	71	0	9.58	3.34	2.12
Wells	L	6	9	.400	6.23	2	35	14	5	134.1	190	62	45	106	93	0	12.73	4.15	3.01
tch Leonard	L	11	4	.733	4.51	0	18	18	9	125.2	143	43	65	73	63	0	10.24	3.08	4.66
ss Doyle	R	4	7	.364	5.93	8	45	3	0	118.1	158	50	31	83	78	0	12.02	3.80	2.36
rnie Carroll	R	2	2	.500	3.76	0	10	4	1	40.2	46	28	12	30	17	0	10.18	3.80	2.66
rt Cole	L	2	3	.400	5.88	1	14	2	1	33.2	44	15	7	27	22	0	11.76	4.01	1.87
Johnson	R	0	2	.000	3.46	0	6	0	0	13	11	10	5	7	5	0	7.62	6.92	3.46
Cobb	R	0	0	—	0.00	1	1	0	0	1	0	0	0	0	0	0	0.00	0.00	0.00
Moore	R	0	0	—	0.00	0	1	0	0	0	0	3	0	2	2	0	—	∞	
AM TOTAL		81	73	.526	4.61	18	298	156	66	1383.2	1582	556	419	828	708	2	10.29	3.62	2.73

MANAGER	W	L	PCT
Ty Cobb	79	75	.513

POS	Player	B	G	AB	H	2B	3B	HR	HR %	R	RBI	BB	SO	SB	Pinch Hit AB	Pinch Hit H	BA	SA
REGULARS																		
1B	Lu Blue	B	128	429	123	24	14	1	0.2	92	52	90	18	13	12	5	.287	.415
2B	Charlie Gehringer	L	123	459	127	19	17	1	0.2	62	48	30	42	9	6	0	.277	.399
SS	Jackie Tavener	L	156	532	141	22	14	1	0.2	65	58	52	53	8	0	0	.265	.365
3B	Jack Warner	R	100	311	78	8	6	0	0.0	41	34	38	24	8	2	0	.251	.315
RF	Harry Heilmann	R	141	502	184	41	8	9	1.8	90	103	67	19	6	6	1	.367	.534
CF	Heinie Manush	L	136	498	188	35	8	14	2.8	95	86	31	28	11	14	5	**.378**	.564
LF	Bob Fothergill	R	110	387	142	31	7	3	0.8	63	73	33	23	4	6	4	.367	.506
C	Clyde Manion	R	75	176	35	4	0	0	0.0	15	14	24	16	1	1	0	.199	.222
SUBSTITUTES																		
32	Frank O'Rourke	R	111	363	88	16	1	1	0.3	43	41	35	33	8	3	0	.242	.300
1B	Johnny Neun	B	97	242	72	14	0	0	0.0	47	15	27	26	4	42	12	.298	.388
23	Les Burke	L	38	75	17	1	0	0	0.0	9	4	7	3	1	13	1	.227	.240
3B	Billy Mullen	R	11	13	1	0	0	0	0.0	2	0	5	1	1	2	0	.077	.077
OF	Al Wingo	L	108	298	84	19	0	1	0.3	45	45	52	32	4	24	6	.282	.356
OF	Ty Cobb	L	79	233	79	18	5	4	1.7	48	62	26	2	9	18	6	.339	.511
C	Johnny Bassler	L	66	174	53	8	1	0	0.0	20	22	45	6	0	2	0	.305	.362
C	Larry Woodall	R	67	146	34	5	0	0	0.0	18	15	15	2	0	5	1	.233	.267
C	Ray Hayworth	R	12	11	3	0	0	0	0.0	1	5	1	1	0	3	0	.273	.273
PITCHERS																		
P	Earl Whitehill	L	36	91	23	1	3	0	0.0	6	10	6	24	0	0	0	.253	.330
P	Ed Wells	L	36	73	15	3	1	0	0.0	6	7	1	12	1	0	0	.205	.274
P	Sam Gibson	L	36	72	18	4	0	0	0.0	6	2	1	4	0	1	0	.250	.306
P	Lil Stoner	R	32	53	9	1	0	0	0.0	5	5	2	13	0	0	0	.170	.189
P	Ken Holloway	R	36	46	11	1	0	0	0.0	1	1	1	8	0	0	0	.239	.261
P	Hooks Dauss	R	35	42	10	5	1	1	2.4	6	5	3	11	0	0	0	.238	.476
P	Rip Collins	R	31	39	6	1	0	0	0.0	2	5	2	16	0	0	0	.154	.179
P	Augie Johns	L	35	28	4	0	0	0	0.0	3	3	2	3	0	0	0	.143	.143
P	Clyde Barfoot	R	11	5	1	0	0	0	0.0	1	0	1	0	0	0	0	.200	.200
P	Rudy Kneisch	R	2	5	0	0	0	0	0.0	0	0	0	2	0	0	0	.000	.000
P	George Smith	R	23	5	0	0	0	0	0.0	1	1	1	1	0	0	0	.000	.000
P	Wilbur Cooper	R	8	4	0	0	0	0	0.0	0	1	0	0	0	0	0	.000	.000
P	Jess Doyle	R	2	1	1	0	0	0	0.0	0	0	0	0	0	0	0	1.000	1.000
	TEAM TOTAL			5313	1547	281	90	36	0.7	793	717	598	423	88	160	41	.291	.398

INDIVIDUAL FIELDING

POS	Player	T	G	PO	A	E	DP	TC/G	FA	POS	Player	T	G	PO	A	E	DP	TC/G	FA
1B	L. Blue	L	109	1153	56	17	95	11.2	.986	OF	H. Manush	L	120	283	7	10	3	2.5	.967
	J. Neun	L	49	433	22	3	34	9.3	.993		B. Fothergill	R	103	245	3	10	0	2.5	.961
2B	C. Gehringer	R	112	255	323	16	56	5.3	.973		H. Heilmann	R	134	228	18	7	4	1.9	.972
	F. O'Rourke	R	41	101	139	9	29	6.1	.964		A. Wingo	R	74	155	13	14	2	2.5	.923
	L. Burke	R	15	27	38	4	8	4.6	.942		T. Cobb	R	55	109	4	6	2	2.2	.950
SS	J. Tavener	R	156	300	470	39	92	5.2	.952		L. Blue	L	1	3	1	2	0	6.0	.667
	F. O'Rourke	R	10	10	8	1	1	1.9	.947										
	J. Warner	R	3	3	2	0	1	1.7	1.000	C	J. Bassler	R	63	223	61	0	6	4.5	1.000
	L. Burke	R	1	1	0	0	0	1.0	1.000		C. Manion	R	74	227	48	8	2	3.8	.972
3B	J. Warner	R	95	105	175	13	9	3.1	.956		L. Woodall	R	59	149	37	4	3	3.2	.979
	F. O'Rourke	R	58	80	117	14	13	3.6	.934		R. Hayworth	R	8	9	0	0	0	1.1	1.000
	A. Wingo	R	2	0	0	0	0	0.0	.000										
	C. Gehringer	R	6	9	17	0	0	4.3	1.000										
	L. Burke	R	7	7	16	2	0	3.6	.920										
	B. Mullen	R	9	6	8	2	0	1.8	.875										

Despite boasting three of the league's top four hitters, the Tigers tumbled into the second division to sixth place, 12 games behind the first-place Yankees.

In his last Detroit season, Ty Cobb, nagged by eye ailments, demoted himself to fourth outfielder and hit .339. Not bad, but Heinie Manush replaced Cobb in center, hit .378, and won the batting crown. Also noteworthy: in his first season as regular second baseman, Charlie Gehringer batted .277.

The Tigers failed to muster a bona fide pennant run because of mediocre pitching. Earl Whitehill led the staff at 16–13. In June, Babe Ruth blasted a home run off Hooks Dauss over Navin Field's right-field wall, the ball coming to rest two blocks away on Plum Street. Meanwhile, down on the Tigers' Toronto farm, but destined for greatness elsewhere, was southpaw Carl Hubbell. "I belonged to the Detroit club three years," the Giants ace later said, "and never once saw Navin Field."

In October, Navin announced Cobb's retirement as player and manager. "Maybe I was not a managerial success, but just as surely I was not a managerial failure," Cobb said. "What we could have done with a couple of pitchers! If I'd had them, the Yankees would have had to wait a few years to become the terrors of baseball. In every other way but pitching, we spit in their eye." In November, the baseball world shook when Tris Speaker was similarly let go in Cleveland. In December it was revealed that both stars were eased out because of alleged participation in a fixed game in 1919. Early in 1927, both were cleared. But neither returned to his former team. Detroit's 22-year Cobb era was over.

TEAM STATISTICS

	W	L	PCT	GB	R	OR	2B	3B	HR	BA	SA	SB	E	DP	FA	CG	BB	SO	ShO	SV	ERA
								Batting						Fielding				Pitching			
Y	91	63	.591		847	713	262	75	121	.289	.437	79	210	117	.966	64	478	486	4	20	3.86
LE	88	66	.571	3	738	612	333	49	27	.289	.386	88	173	153	.972	96	450	381	11	4	3.40
HI	83	67	.553	6	677	570	259	65	61	.269	.383	56	171	131	.972	62	451	571	10	16	**3.00**
AS	81	69	.540	8	802	761	244	97	43	.292	.401	122	184	129	.969	65	566	418	5	26	4.34
HI	81	72	.529	9.5	730	665	314	60	32	.289	.390	121	165	122	.973	85	506	458	11	12	3.74
ET	79	75	.513	12	793	830	281	90	36	.291	.398	88	193	151	.969	57	555	469	10	18	4.41
TL	62	92	.403	29	682	845	253	78	72	.276	.394	62	235	167	.963	64	654	337	5	9	4.66
OS	46	107	.301	44.5	562	835	249	54	32	.256	.343	48	193	143	.970	53	546	336	6	5	4.72
AGUE TOTAL					5831	5831	2195	568	424	.281	.392	664	1524	1113	.969	546	4206	3456	62	110	4.02

INDIVIDUAL PITCHING

TCHER	T	W	L	PCT	ERA	SV	G	GS	CG	IP	H	BB	SO	R	ER	ShO	H/9	BB/9	SO/9
arl Whitehill	L	16	13	.552	3.99	0	36	34	13	252.1	271	79	109	**136**	112	0	9.67	2.82	3.89
am Gibson	R	12	9	.571	3.48	2	35	24	16	196.1	199	75	61	94	76	2	9.12	3.44	2.80
d Wells	L	12	10	.545	4.15	0	36	26	9	178	201	76	58	101	82	4	10.16	3.84	2.93
l Stoner	R	7	10	.412	5.47	0	32	22	7	159.2	179	63	57	115	97	0	10.09	3.55	3.21
en Holloway	R	4	6	.400	5.12	2	36	12	3	139	192	42	43	94	79	0	12.43	2.72	2.78
ooks Dauss	R	12	6	**.667**	4.20	9	35	5	0	124.1	135	49	27	63	58	0	9.77	3.55	1.95
p Collins	R	8	8	.500	2.73	1	30	13	5	122	128	44	44	57	37	3	9.44	3.25	3.25
ugie Johns	L	6	4	.600	5.35	1	35	14	3	112.2	117	69	40	77	67	1	9.35	5.51	3.20
eorge Smith	R	1	2	.333	6.95	0	23	1	0	44	55	33	15	37	34	0	11.25	6.75	3.07
yde Barfoot	R	1	2	.333	4.88	2	11	1	0	31.1	42	9	7	27	17	0	12.06	2.59	2.01
udy Kneisch	L	0	1	.000	2.65	0	2	2	1	17	18	6	4	7	5	0	9.53	3.18	2.12
ilbur Cooper	L	0	4	.000	11.20	0	8	3	0	13.2	27	9	2	18	17	0	17.78	5.93	1.32
ss Doyle	R	0	0	–	4.15	1	2	0	0	4.1	6	1	2	3	2	0	12.46	2.08	4.15
AM TOTAL		79	75	.513	4.41	18	321	157	57	1394.2	1570	555	469	829	683	10	10.13	3.58	3.03

MANAGER	W	L	PCT
George Moriarty	82	71	.536

POS	Player	B	G	AB	H	2B	3B	HR	HR %	R	RBI	BB	SO	SB	Pinch Hit AB	Pinch Hit H	BA	SA
REGULARS																		
1B	Lu Blue	B	112	365	95	17	9	1	0.3	71	42	71	28	13	5	2	.260	.364
2B	Charlie Gehringer	L	133	508	161	29	11	4	0.8	110	61	52	31	17	9	3	.317	.441
SS	Jackie Tavener	L	116	419	115	22	9	5	1.2	60	59	36	38	20	1	0	.274	.406
3B	Jack Warner	R	139	559	149	22	9	1	0.2	78	45	47	45	15	1	0	.267	.343
RF	Harry Heilmann	R	141	505	201	50	9	14	2.8	106	120	72	16	11	5	1	.398	.616
CF	Heinie Manush	L	152	593	177	31	18	6	1.0	102	80	47	29	12	1	1	.298	.442
LF	Bob Fothergill	R	143	527	189	38	9	9	1.7	93	114	47	31	9	5	2	.359	.516
C	Larry Woodall	R	88	246	69	8	6	0	0.0	28	39	37	9	9	2	0	.280	.362
SUBSTITUTES																		
UT	Marty McManus	R	108	369	99	19	7	9	2.4	60	69	34	38	8	9	4	.268	.431
1B	Johnny Neun	B	79	204	66	9	4	0	0.0	38	27	35	13	22	17	6	.324	.407
SS	Bernie DeViveiros	R	24	22	5	1	0	0	0.0	4	2	2	8	1	2	0	.227	.273
OF	Al Wingo	L	75	137	32	8	2	0	0.0	15	20	25	14	1	33	6	.234	.321
OF	Art Ruble	L	56	91	15	4	2	0	0.0	16	11	14	15	2	3	0	.165	.253
C	Johnny Bassler	L	81	200	57	7	0	0	0.0	19	24	45	9	1	12	2	.285	.320
C	Merv Shea	R	34	85	15	6	3	0	0.0	5	9	7	15	0	3	0	.176	.318
PH	Clyde Manion	R	1	0	0	0	0	0	–	0	0	1	0	0	1	0	–	–
PITCHERS																		
P	Earl Whitehill	L	41	78	16	2	1	0	0.0	4	3	5	9	0	0	0	.205	.256
P	Lil Stoner	R	38	74	8	0	0	0	0.0	2	5	3	16	0	0	0	.108	.108
P	Ownie Carroll	R	37	69	12	2	1	0	0.0	11	5	2	5	0	2	0	.174	.232
P	Sam Gibson	L	33	66	14	4	0	0	0.0	6	4	0	8	0	0	0	.212	.273
P	Ken Holloway	R	36	62	8	0	0	0	0.0	2	2	1	13	0	0	0	.129	.129
P	Rip Collins	R	30	54	11	1	1	0	0.0	5	6	6	12	0	0	0	.204	.259
P	Haskell Billings	R	10	27	7	1	0	0	0.0	4	1	1	8	0	0	0	.259	.296
P	George Smith	R	29	19	7	0	0	2	10.5	5	6	0	4	0	0	0	.368	.684
P	Don Hankins	R	20	7	1	0	0	0	0.0	0	0	0	2	0	0	0	.143	.143
P	Ed Wells	L	8	7	2	0	0	0	0.0	1	0	0	1	0	0	0	.286	.286
P	Jess Doyle	R	7	3	1	0	0	0	0.0	0	1	0	1	0	0	0	.333	.333
P	Rufus Smith	R	1	3	0	0	0	0	0.0	0	0	0	2	0	0	0	.000	.000
P	Jim Walkup	R	2	1	0	0	0	0	0.0	0	0	0	0	0	0	0	.000	.000
P	Augie Johns	L	1	0	0	0	0	0	–	0	0	0	0	0	0	0	–	–
TEAM TOTAL				5300	1532	281	101	51	1.0	845	755	590	420	141	111	27	.289	.409

INDIVIDUAL FIELDING

POS	Player	T	G	PO	A	E	DP	TC/G	FA	POS	Player	T	G	PO	A	E	DP	TC/G	FA
1B	L. Blue	L	104	1019	68	18	99	10.6	.984	OF	H. Manush	L	150	361	9	11	3	2.5	.971
	J. Neun	L	53	548	30	12	45	11.1	.980		B. Fothergill	R	137	315	3	13	1	2.4	.961
	M. McManus	R	6	40	5	0	2	7.5	1.000		H. Heilmann	R	135	218	11	8	5	1.8	.966
2B	C. Gehringer	R	121	304	438	27	84	6.4	.965		A. Ruble	R	43	62	3	2	2	1.6	.970
	M. McManus	R	35	102	106	6	29	6.1	.972		A. Wingo	R	34	43	6	6	2	1.6	.891
SS	J. Tavener	R	114	246	356	33	79	5.6	.948	C	L. Woodall	R	86	265	72	1	6	3.9	.997
	M. McManus	R	39	82	112	8	21	5.2	.960		J. Bassler	R	67	206	56	7	8	4.0	.974
	DeViveiros	R	14	7	14	2	4	1.6	.913		M. Shea	R	31	94	17	6	1	3.8	.949
3B	J. Warner	R	138	156	277	24	34	3.3	.947										
	M. McManus	R	22	21	40	3	2	2.9	.953										
	DeViveiros	R	1	0	0	0	0	0.0	.000										

May brought to Navin Field the eerie sight of an old favorite in a new uniform: Ty Cobb, the Tigers' all-time leader in hits, RBIs, average, and stolen bases, the man who would own baseball's best lifetime average at .367, came to town wearing the elephant insignia of Connie Mack's Athletics.

Cobb nearly missed his celebrated Detroit homecoming. Five days before, he and Al Simmons had roughed up an umpire for the heinous act of ruling a Cobb home run foul. League president Ban Johnson suspended the pair, but reinstated them under fan pressure. As 35,000 cheered thanks for his remarkable 22 Detroit years, Cobb helped his new team to a 6–3 victory with a double and two RBIs.

Former Detroit third baseman George Moriarty gave up his job as an American League umpire to manage the Tigers, who jumped back into the first division in fourth place, 27 1/2 games behind the Murderer's Row Yankees. The new manager inherited Cobb's heavy hitters. Although Heinie Manush failed to defend his batting title, falling 80 points to .298, teammate Harry Heilmann snatched the crown, his fourth batting title in seven years. In another dramatic last day performance, he edged Simmons, securing the crown with seven hits, two of them homers, in a doubleheader against Cleveland.

Despite the usual infield woes, the Tigers notched one of eight unassisted triple plays in major-league history during a May 20 home game against Cleveland. With runners on first and second, Tigers' backup first baseman Johnny Neun caught Homer Summa's liner, scrambled to tag Charlie Jamieson between first and second, then stepped on second base before Glenn Myatt could return.

TEAM STATISTICS

W	L	PCT	GB	R	OR	2B	3B	Batting HR	BA	SA	SB	E	Fielding DP	FA	CG	BB	Pitching SO	ShO	SV	ERA
.	110	44	.714		975	599	291	103	158	.307	.489	90	195	123	.969	82	**409**	431	11	20	**3.20**
·I	91	63	.591	19	841	726	281	70	56	.303	.414	98	190	124	.970	66	442	**553**	8	**24**	3.95
AS	85	69	.552	25	782	730	268	87	29	.287	.386	133	195	125	.969	62	491	497	10	23	3.95
T	82	71	.536	27.5	845	805	282	100	51	.289	.409	141	206	**173**	.968	75	577	421	5	17	4.12
·I	70	83	.458	39.5	662	708	285	61	36	.278	.378	90	178	131	**.971**	85	440	365	10	8	3.91
E	66	87	.431	43.5	668	766	**321**	52	26	.283	.379	63	201	146	.968	72	508	366	5	8	4.27
·L	59	94	.386	50.5	724	904	262	59	55	.276	.380	91	248	166	.960	80	604	385	4	8	4.95
)S	51	103	.331	59	597	856	271	78	28	.259	.357	82	228	162	.964	63	558	381	6	7	4.68
AGUE TOTAL				6094	6094	2261	610	439	.285	.399	788	1641	1150	.967	585	4029	3399	59	115	4.12

INDIVIDUAL PITCHING

TCHER	T	W	L	PCT	ERA	SV	G	GS	CG	IP	H	BB	SO	R	ER	ShO	H/9	BB/9	SO/9
·rl Whitehill	L	16	14	.533	3.36	3	41	31	17	236	238	**105**	95	110	88	3	9.08	4.00	3.62
· Stoner	R	10	13	.435	3.98	5	38	24	13	215	251	77	63	118	95	0	10.51	3.22	2.64
m Gibson	R	11	12	.478	3.69	0	33	26	11	190.1	201	86	76	113	78	0	9.50	4.07	3.59
·n Holloway	R	11	12	.478	4.07	6	36	23	11	183.1	210	61	36	103	83	1	10.31	2.99	1.77
·p Collins	R	13	7	.650	4.69	0	30	25	10	172.2	207	59	37	116	90	1	10.79	3.08	1.93
·nie Carroll	R	10	6	.625	3.98	0	31	15	8	172	186	73	41	99	76	0	9.73	3.82	2.15
·orge Smith	R	4	1	.800	3.91	0	29	0	0	71.1	62	50	32	38	31	0	7.82	6.31	4.04
·skell Billings	R	5	4	.556	4.84	0	10	9	5	67	64	39	18	36	36	0	8.60	5.24	2.42
·n Hankins	R	2	1	.667	6.48	2	20	1	0	41.2	67	13	10	39	30	0	14.47	2.81	2.16
· Wells	L	0	1	.000	6.75	1	8	1	0	20	28	5	5	16	15	0	12.60	2.25	2.25
·ss Doyle	R	0	0	–	8.03	0	7	0	0	12.1	16	5	5	11	11	0	11.68	3.65	3.65
·fus Smith	L	0	0	–	3.38	0	1	1	0	8	8	3	2	4	3	0	9.00	3.38	2.25
·n Walkup	L	0	0	–	5.40	0	2	0	0	1.2	3	0	0	1	1	0	16.20	0.00	0.00
·gie Johns	L	0	0	–	9.00	0	1	0	0	1	1	1	1	1	1	0	9.00	9.00	9.00
·AM TOTAL		82	71	.536	4.12	17	287	156	75	1392.1	1542	577	421	805	638	5	9.97	3.73	2.72

MANAGER	W	L	PCT
George Moriarty	68	86	.442

POS	Player	B	G	AB	H	2B	3B	HR	HR %	R	RBI	BB	SO	SB	Pinch Hit AB	Pinch Hit H	BA	SA
REGULARS																		
1B	Bill Sweeney	R	89	309	78	15	5	0	0.0	47	19	15	28	12	8	1	.252	.333
2B	Charlie Gehringer	L	154	603	193	29	16	6	1.0	108	74	69	22	15	0	0	.320	.451
SS	Jackie Tavener	L	132	473	123	24	15	5	1.1	59	52	33	51	13	0	0	.260	.406
3B	Marty McManus	R	139	500	144	37	5	8	1.6	78	73	51	32	11	4	1	.288	.430
RF	Harry Heilmann	R	151	558	183	38	10	14	2.5	83	107	57	45	7	1	0	.328	.507
CF	Harry Rice	L	131	510	154	21	12	6	1.2	87	81	44	27	20	2	0	.302	.425
LF	Bob Fothergill	R	111	347	110	28	10	3	0.9	49	63	24	19	8	19	4	.317	.481
C	Pinky Hargrave	B	121	321	88	13	5	10	3.1	38	63	32	28	4	25	9	.274	.439
SUBSTITUTES																		
3B	Jack Warner	R	75	206	44	4	4	0	0.0	33	13	16	15	4	1	0	.214	.272
S3	Chick Galloway	R	53	148	39	5	2	1	0.7	17	17	15	3	7	4	2	.264	.345
1B	Johnny Neun	R	36	108	23	3	1	0	0.0	15	5	7	10	2	11	3	.213	.259
OF	Al Wingo	L	87	242	69	13	2	2	0.8	30	30	40	17	2	12	0	.285	.380
OF	Paul Easterling	R	43	114	37	7	1	3	2.6	17	12	8	24	2	8	3	.325	.482
OF	John Stone	L	26	113	40	10	3	2	1.8	20	21	5	8	1	0	0	.354	.549
C	Larry Woodall	R	65	186	39	5	1	0	0.0	19	13	24	10	3	3	0	.210	.247
C	Merv Shea	R	39	85	20	2	3	0	0.0	8	9	9	11	2	7	0	.235	.329
PITCHERS																		
P	Ownie Carroll	R	43	98	19	3	1	0	0.0	7	9	7	14	0	1	0	.194	.245
P	Earl Whitehill	L	31	67	13	0	0	0	0.0	4	3	5	11	0	0	0	.194	.194
P	Elam Vangilder	R	38	58	15	0	0	2	3.4	4	6	0	11	0	0	0	.259	.362
P	Vic Sorrell	R	29	55	6	2	0	0	0.0	2	1	0	14	0	0	0	.109	.145
P	Sam Gibson	L	20	42	12	1	0	0	0.0	4	6	2	2	0	0	0	.286	.310
P	Lil Stoner	R	36	39	7	2	0	0	0.0	4	3	1	6	0	0	0	.179	.231
P	Haskell Billings	R	21	35	10	2	1	0	0.0	7	5	3	6	0	0	0	.286	.400
P	Ken Holloway	R	30	33	4	2	0	0	0.0	2	1	0	7	0	0	0	.121	.182
P	George Smith	R	39	27	3	0	0	0	0.0	2	0	1	8	0	0	0	.111	.111
P	Phil Page	R	3	9	2	0	0	0	0.0	0	0	0	4	0	0	0	.222	.222
P	Charlie Sullivan	L	3	4	0	0	0	0	0.0	0	0	0	0	0	0	0	.000	.000
TEAM TOTAL				5290	1475	266	97	62	1.2	744	686	468	433	113	106	23	.279	.401

INDIVIDUAL FIELDING

POS	Player	T	G	PO	A	E	DP	TC/G	FA
1B	B. Sweeney	R	75	675	55	5	51	9.8	.993
	M. McManus	R	45	376	28	5	33	9.1	.988
	H. Heilmann	R	25	234	17	2	20	10.1	.992
	J. Neun	L	25	180	16	5	16	8.0	.975
	C. Galloway	R	1	1	0	0	0	1.0	1.000
2B	C. Gehringer	R	154	377	507	35	101	6.0	.962
SS	J. Tavener	R	131	302	405	42	81	5.7	.944
	C. Galloway	R	22	49	51	9	11	5.0	.917
	J. Warner	R	7	9	13	2	4	3.4	.917
	M. McManus	R	1	0	2	0	0	2.0	1.000
3B	M. McManus	R	92	114	183	14	12	3.4	.955
	J. Warner	R	52	62	107	10	6	3.4	.944
	C. Galloway	R	21	26	41	2	3	3.3	.971
	H. Rice	R	2	1	1	0	0	1.0	1.000

POS	Player	T	G	PO	A	E	DP	TC/G	FA
OF	H. Rice	R	129	346	9	14	0	2.9	.962
	H. Heilmann	R	126	215	17	7	2	1.9	.971
	B. Fothergill	R	90	179	6	8	0	2.1	.959
	A. Wingo	R	71	144	5	5	1	2.2	.968
	P. Easterling	R	34	68	2	6	0	2.2	.921
	J. Stone	R	26	49	2	2	0	2.0	.962
	C. Galloway	R	1	0	0	0	0	0.0	.000
	O. Carroll	R	5	10	1	0	0	2.2	1.000
	B. Sweeney	R	3	2	0	0	0	0.7	1.000
C	P. Hargrave	R	88	301	35	8	5	3.9	.977
	L. Woodall	R	62	218	44	2	3	4.3	.992
	M. Shea	R	30	93	24	6	2	4.1	.951

Frank Navin ushered in another forgettable season with a regrettable trade. During the winter, Detroit sent outfielder Heinie Manush and first baseman Lu Blue to the Browns for pitcher Elam Vangilder, outfielder Harry Rice, and shortstop Chick Galloway. The hope: to bolster the struggling pitching staff. The result: for Detroit, Vangilder won 11 and lost 10, Galloway hit .264 in 53 games, and Rice hit .302. For St. Louis, Blue hit .281 and Manush .378, second to league-leader Goose Goslin. Detroit in turn tumbled out of the first division, 33 games out. Home attendance declined proportionately, dropping nearly 300,000 to 475,000.

Even the heavy hitting was gone. Harry Heilmann slid 70 points to .328 and Fat Fothergill 40 points to .317 as the Tigers plunged to fifth in team batting. Modest good news came from second baseman Charlie Gehringer, who improved to .320. Among pitchers, once-heralded Owen Carroll compiled his only good season in Detroit to lead the staff at 16–12, 3.27. But no other pitcher won more than he lost or dipped below 4.00 in ERA. Farm-team pitcher and future Hall of Famer Carl Hubbell, in the meantime, was sold to the Giants for $40,000.

Securely out of the race entering the final month, the Tigers nevertheless experienced two memorable events in September. On the 29th against the Yankees, the Tigers totaled a still-standing team-record 28 hits. On the negative side, four days earlier against the Red Sox, they played before only 404 at Navin Field, the smallest home gathering in club history. When it was over, Moriarty was fired, free to resume umpiring in 1929.

TEAM STATISTICS

	W	L	PCT	GB	R	OR	2B	3B	HR	BA	SA	SB	E	DP	FA	CG	BB	SO	ShO	SV	ERA
Y	101	53	.656		**894**	685	269	79	**133**	**.296**	.450	51	194	136	.968	83	452	487	13	**21**	3.74
HI	98	55	.641	2.5	829	**615**	**323**	75	89	.295	.436	59	181	124	.970	81	**424**	**607**	15	16	**3.36**
TL	82	72	.532	19	772	742	276	76	63	.274	.393	76	189	146	.969	80	454	456	6	15	4.17
WAS	75	79	.487	26	718	705	277	93	40	.284	.393	110	**178**	146	**.972**	77	466	462	**15**	10	3.88
HI	72	82	.468	29	656	725	231	77	24	.270	.358	**139**	186	149	.970	**88**	501	418	6	11	3.98
ET	68	86	.442	33	744	804	265	**97**	62	.279	.401	113	218	140	.965	65	567	451	5	16	4.32
LE	62	92	.403	39	674	830	299	61	34	.285	.382	50	221	**187**	.965	71	511	416	4	15	4.47
OS	57	96	.373	43.5	589	770	260	62	38	.264	.361	99	**178**	139	.971	70	452	407	5	9	4.39
LEAGUE TOTAL					5876	5876	2200	620	483	.281	.397	697	1545	1167	.969	615	3827	3704	69	113	4.04

INDIVIDUAL PITCHING

PITCHER	T	W	L	PCT	ERA	SV	G	GS	CG	IP	H	BB	SO	R	ER	ShO	H/9	BB/9	SO/9
wnie Carroll	R	16	12	.571	3.27	2	34	28	19	231	219	87	51	100	84	2	8.53	3.39	1.99
arl Whitehill	L	11	16	.407	4.31	0	31	30	12	196.1	214	78	93	131	94	1	9.81	3.58	4.26
ic Sorrell	R	8	11	.421	4.79	0	29	23	8	171	182	83	67	106	91	0	9.58	4.37	3.53
am Vangilder	R	11	10	.524	3.91	5	38	11	7	156.1	163	68	43	82	68	0	9.38	3.91	2.48
l Stoner	R	5	8	.385	4.35	4	36	11	4	126.1	151	42	29	75	61	0	10.76	2.99	2.07
en Holloway	R	4	8	.333	4.34	2	30	11	5	120.1	137	32	32	67	58	0	10.25	2.39	2.39
am Gibson	R	5	8	.385	5.42	0	20	18	5	119.2	155	52	29	83	72	1	11.66	3.91	2.18
askell Billings	R	5	10	.333	5.12	0	21	16	3	110.2	118	59	48	83	63	1	9.60	4.80	3.90
eorge Smith	R	1	1	.500	4.42	3	39	2	0	106	103	50	54	55	52	0	8.75	4.25	4.58
il Page	L	2	0	1.000	2.45	0	3	2	2	22	21	10	3	9	6	0	8.59	4.09	1.23
harlie Sullivan	R	0	2	.000	6.57	0	3	2	0	12.1	18	6	2	12	9	0	13.14	4.38	1.46
EAM TOTAL		68	86	.442	4.32	16	284	154	65	1372	1481	567	451	803	658	5	9.72	3.72	2.96

MANAGER	W	L	PCT
Bucky Harris	70	84	.455

POS	Player	B	G	AB	H	2B	3B	HR	HR %	R	RBI	BB	SO	SB	Pinch Hit AB	Pinch Hit H	BA	SA
REGULARS																		
1B	Dale Alexander	R	155	626	**215**	43	15	25	4.0	110	137	56	63	5	0	0	.343	.580
2B	Charlie Gehringer	L	155	634	**215**	45	19	13	2.1	131	106	64	19	28	1	0	.339	.532
SS	Heinie Schuble	R	92	258	60	11	7	2	0.8	35	28	19	23	3	1	0	.233	.353
3B	Marty McManus	R	154	599	168	32	8	18	3.0	99	90	60	52	17	0	0	.280	.451
RF	Harry Heilmann	R	125	453	156	41	7	15	3.3	86	120	50	39	5	7	1	.344	.565
CF	Harry Rice	L	130	536	163	33	7	6	1.1	97	69	61	23	6	1	0	.304	.425
LF	Roy Johnson	L	146	**640**	201	45	14	10	1.6	128	69	67	60	20	2	0	.314	.475
C	Eddie Phillips	R	68	221	52	13	1	2	0.9	24	21	20	16	0	4	1	.235	.330
SUBSTITUTES																		
SS	Yats Wuestling	R	54	150	30	4	1	0	0.0	13	16	9	24	0	0	0	.200	.240
SS	Bill Akers	R	24	83	22	4	1	1	1.2	15	9	10	9	2	0	0	.265	.373
3S	Frank Sigafoos	R	14	23	4	1	0	0	0.0	3	2	5	4	0	1	0	.174	.217
SS	Nolen Richardsen	R	13	21	4	0	0	0	0.0	2	2	2	1	1	0	0	.190	.190
2B	Bucky Harris	R	7	11	1	0	0	0	0.0	3	0	2	2	1	0	0	.091	.091
OF	Bob Fothergill	R	115	277	98	24	9	6	2.2	42	62	11	11	3	53	19	.354	.570
OF	John Stone	L	51	150	39	11	2	2	1.3	23	15	11	13	1	15	4	.260	.400
C	Pinky Hargrave	B	76	185	61	12	0	3	1.6	26	26	20	24	2	26	5	.330	.443
C	Merv Shea	R	50	162	47	6	0	3	1.9	23	24	19	18	2	3	0	.290	.383
C	Ray Hayworth	R	14	43	11	0	0	0	0.0	5	4	3	8	0	0	0	.256	.256
PH	Larry Woodall	R	1	1	0	0	0	0	0.0	0	0	0	0	0	1	0	.000	.000
PITCHERS																		
P	George Uhle	R	40	108	37	1	1	0	0.0	18	13	6	6	0	7	1	.343	.370
P	Earl Whitehill	L	38	90	23	2	0	3	3.3	8	11	6	17	0	0	0	.256	.378
P	Vic Sorrell	R	36	83	12	1	0	0	0.0	9	6	1	28	0	0	0	.145	.157
P	Ownie Carroll	R	37	74	17	2	2	0	0.0	9	11	4	4	0	0	0	.230	.311
P	Emil Yde	B	46	48	16	1	1	0	0.0	8	3	3	6	0	13	5	.333	.396
P	Augie Prudhomme	R	34	21	5	2	0	0	0.0	2	0	3	8	0	0	0	.238	.333
P	Kyle Graham	R	13	19	2	0	0	1	5.3	1	1	0	6	0	0	0	.105	.263
P	Lil Stoner	R	24	15	1	0	0	0	0.0	0	0	0	3	0	0	0	.067	.067
P	Art Herring	R	4	14	3	2	1	0	0.0	2	3	0	1	0	0	0	.214	.500
P	George Smith	R	14	12	5	1	0	0	0.0	3	2	2	1	0	0	0	.417	.500
P	Chief Hogsett	L	4	10	2	0	0	0	0.0	0	1	0	2	0	0	0	.200	.200
P	Whit Wyatt	R	4	10	1	0	0	0	0.0	0	0	0	1	0	0	0	.100	.100
P	Phil Page	R	10	8	1	0	0	0	0.0	0	1	0	0	0	0	0	.125	.125
P	Haskell Billings	R	8	6	0	0	0	0	0.0	0	0	1	1	0	0	0	.000	.000
P	Frank Barnes	L	4	1	0	0	0	0	0.0	0	0	0	0	0	0	0	.000	.000
P	Elam Vangilder	R	6	1	0	0	0	0	0.0	0	0	0	0	0	0	0	.000	.000
TEAM TOTAL				5593	1672	337	96	110	2.0	925	851	515	493	96	135	36	.299	.453

INDIVIDUAL FIELDING

POS	Player	T	G	PO	A	E	DP	TC/G	FA
1B	D. Alexander	R	155	1443	90	**18**	129	10.0	.988
	H. Heilmann	R	1	0	0	0	0	0.0	.000
2B	C. Gehringer	R	154	**404**	501	23	93	6.0	**.975**
	B. Harris	R	4	5	13	2	0	5.0	.900
	Y. Wuestling	R	1	1	0	0	0	1.0	1.000
SS	H. Schuble	R	86	141	216	46	43	4.7	.886
	Y. Wuestling	R	52	76	139	13	19	4.4	.943
	B. Akers	R	24	43	57	7	13	4.5	.935
	B. Harris	R	1	0	0	0	0	0.0	.000
	M. McManus	R	9	13	19	1	2	3.7	.970
	N. Richardsen	R	13	15	11	5	2	2.4	.839
	F. Sigafoos	R	5	10	6	2	2	3.6	.889
3B	M. McManus	R	150	206	289	14	29	3.4	.972
	F. Sigafoos	R	6	6	4	1	0	1.8	.909
	H. Rice	R	3	2	4	0	0	2.0	1.000
	H. Schuble	R	2	1	1	1	0	1.5	.667
	Y. Wuestling	R	1	1	1	0	0	2.0	1.000

POS	Player	T	G	PO	A	E	DP	TC/G	FA
OF	R. Johnson	R	146	377	**25**	**31**	5	3.0	.928
	H. Rice	R	127	345	16	15	6	3.0	.960
	H. Heilmann	R	113	193	8	7	3	1.8	.966
	B. Fothergill	R	59	116	2	4	1	2.1	.967
	J. Stone	R	36	68	4	1	0	2.0	.986
C	E. Phillips	R	63	255	34	10	4	4.7	.967
	P. Hargrave	R	48	175	38	6	7	4.6	.973
	M. Shea	R	50	157	32	7	4	3.9	.964
	R. Hayworth	R	14	46	12	3	1	4.4	.951

As the young manager of the Senators, Bucky Harris had been called Boy Wonder. For his unremarkable reign in Detroit, he resembled Boy Slumber. In his first of five straight soporific second-division finishes, Harris (who would manage Detroit again for two more forgettable seasons in the '50s) trudged the Tigers into sixth place, 14 games under .500, 36 games behind first-place Philadelphia. "What do we do wrong here?" sighed an exasperated Frank Navin on the 20th anniversary of Detroit's previous pennant. "Don't we live right?"

The Tigers at least resumed hitting right, again leading the league. Harry Heilmann led the team at .344. Close behind was rookie Dale Alexander, a good-hitting, hatchet-fielding rookie first baseman purchased from Toronto, who batted .343 with a then-team record 25 home runs. Roy Johnson, a free-spirited outfielder purchased from San Francisco, hit .314. Charlie Gehringer kept improving to .339, and Harry Rice hit .304. And for only the second time in team history, three Tigers collected more than 100 RBIs: Alexander (137), Heilmann (120), and Gehringer (106).

Again Detroit hitters scored runs, but again Detroit pitching and defense quickly gave them back. Veteran right-hander George Uhle, acquired from Cleveland, led the staff at 15–11, followed by Earl Whitehill and Vic Sorrell, each at 14–15.

Shortly after the season in October, already restless Detroit disciples were further incited when Heilmann, bothered both by arthritis and Harris, was sold to Cincinnati. Later that month Navin was struck by an appropriate epilogue to the miserable season: he lost a sizable portion of his personal fortune in the stock market crash.

TEAM STATISTICS

W	L	PCT	GB	R	OR	2B	3B	HR	BA	SA	SB	E	DP	FA	CG	BB	SO	ShO	SV	ERA
104	46	.693		901	615	288	76	122	.296	.451	61	146	117	.975	72	487	573	8	24	3.44
88	66	.571	18	899	775	262	74	142	.295	.450	51	178	152	.971	64	485	484	12	18	4.17
81	71	.533	24	717	736	294	79	62	.294	.417	75	198	162	.968	80	488	389	8	10	4.05
79	73	.520	26	733	713	276	63	46	.276	.380	72	156	148	.975	83	462	415	15	10	4.08
71	81	.467	34	730	776	244	66	48	.276	.375	86	195	156	.968	61	496	494	3	17	4.34
70	84	.455	36	926	928	339	97	110	.299	.453	95	242	149	.961	82	646	467	5	9	4.96
59	93	.388	46	627	792	240	74	37	.268	.363	106	188	153	.970	78	505	328	5	7	4.41
58	96	.377	48	605	803	285	69	28	.267	.365	85	218	159	.965	84	496	416	9	5	4.43
LEAGUE TOTAL				6138	6138	2228	598	595	.284	.407	631	1521	1196	.969	604	4065	3566	65	100	4.24

INDIVIDUAL PITCHING

TCHER	T	W	L	PCT	ERA	SV	G	GS	CG	IP	H	BB	SO	R	ER	ShO	H/9	BB/9	SO/9
George Uhle	R	15	11	.577	4.08	0	32	30	23	249	283	58	100	141	113	1	10.23	2.10	3.61
Earl Whitehill	L	14	15	.483	4.62	1	38	28	18	245.1	267	96	103	147	126	1	9.79	3.52	3.78
Vic Sorrell	R	14	15	.483	5.18	1	36	31	13	226	270	106	81	152	130	1	10.75	4.22	3.23
Ownie Carroll	R	9	17	.346	4.63	1	34	26	12	202	249	86	54	133	104	0	11.09	3.83	2.41
Augie Prudhomme	R	1	6	.143	6.22	1	34	6	2	94	119	53	26	78	65	0	11.39	5.07	2.49
Phil Yde	L	7	3	.700	5.30	0	29	6	4	86.2	100	63	23	60	51	1	10.38	6.54	2.39
Stoner	R	3	3	.500	5.26	4	24	3	1	53	57	31	12	37	31	0	9.68	5.26	2.04
le Graham	R	1	3	.250	5.57	1	13	6	2	51.2	70	33	7	41	32	0	12.19	5.75	1.22
George Smith	R	3	2	.600	5.80	0	14	2	1	35.2	42	36	13	33	23	0	10.60	9.08	3.28
Herring	R	2	1	.667	4.78	0	4	4	2	32	38	19	15	17	17	0	10.69	5.34	4.22
ief Hogsett	L	1	2	.333	2.83	0	4	4	2	28.2	34	9	9	10	9	1	10.67	2.83	2.83
il Page	L	0	2	.000	8.17	0	10	4	1	25.1	29	19	6	24	23	0	10.30	6.75	2.13
hit Wyatt	R	0	1	.000	6.75	0	4	4	1	25.1	30	18	14	22	19	0	10.66	6.39	4.97
skell Billings	R	0	1	.000	5.12	0	8	0	0	19.1	27	9	1	14	11	0	12.57	4.19	0.47
m Vangilder	R	0	1	.000	6.35	0	6	0	0	11.1	16	7	3	11	8	0	12.71	5.56	2.38
nk Barnes	L	0	1	.000	7.20	0	4	1	0	5	10	3	0	8	4	0	18.00	5.40	0.00
AM TOTAL		70	84	.455	4.96	9	294	155	82	1390.1	1641	646	467	928	766	5	10.62	4.18	3.02

MANAGER	W	L	PCT
Bucky Harris	75	79	.487

POS	Player	B	G	AB	H	2B	3B	HR	HR %	R	RBI	BB	SO	SB	Pinch Hit AB	Pinch Hit H	BA	SA
REGULARS																		
1B	Dale Alexander	R	154	602	196	33	8	20	3.3	86	135	42	56	6	0	0	.326	.507
2B	Charlie Gehringer	L	154	610	201	47	15	16	2.6	144	98	69	17	19	0	0	.330	.534
SS	Mark Koenig	B	76	267	64	9	2	1	0.4	37	16	20	15	2	2	0	.240	.300
3B	Marty McManus	R	132	484	155	40	4	9	1.9	74	89	59	28	23	0	0	.320	.475
RF	Roy Johnson	L	125	462	127	30	13	2	0.4	84	35	40	46	17	6	2	.275	.409
CF	Liz Funk	L	140	527	145	26	11	4	0.8	74	65	29	39	12	10	0	.275	.389
LF	John Stone	L	126	422	132	29	11	3	0.7	60	56	32	49	6	18	4	.313	.455
C	Ray Hayworth	R	77	227	63	15	4	0	0.0	24	22	20	19	0	0	0	.278	.379
SUBSTITUTES																		
S3	Bill Akers	R	85	233	65	8	5	9	3.9	36	40	36	34	5	5	2	.279	.472
S3	Billy Rogell	B	54	144	24	4	2	0	0.0	20	9	15	23	1	2	0	.167	.222
1B	Jimmy Shevlin	L	28	14	2	0	0	0	0.0	4	2	2	3	0	2	0	.143	.143
SS	Johnny Watson	L	4	12	3	2	0	0	0.0	1	3	1	2	0	0	0	.250	.417
SS	Yats Wuestling	R	4	9	0	0	0	0	0.0	0	0	2	3	0	0	0	.000	.000
OF	Bob Fothergill	R	55	143	37	9	3	2	1.4	14	14	6	10	1	15*	4	.259	.406
OF	Harry Rice	L	37	128	39	6	0	2	1.6	16	24	19	8	0	1	1	.305	.398
OF	Paul Easterling	R	29	79	16	6	0	1	1.3	7	14	6	18	0	2	0	.203	.316
OF	Frank Doljack	R	20	74	19	5	1	3	4.1	10	17	2	11	0	0	0	.257	.473
OF	Tom Hughes	L	17	59	22	2	3	0	0.0	8	5	4	8	0	0	0	.373	.508
C	Pinky Hargrave	B	55	137	39	8	0	5	3.6	18	18	20	12	2	14	2	.285	.453
C	Gene Desautels	R	42	126	24	4	2	0	0.0	13	9	7	9	2	0	0	.190	.254
C	Tony Rensa	R	20	37	10	2	1	1	2.7	6	3	6	7	1	1	0	.270	.459
C	Hughie Wise	B	2	6	2	0	0	0	0.0	0	0	0	0	0	0	0	.333	.333
PH	Hank Greenberg	R	1	1	0	0	0	0	0.0	0	0	0	0	0	1	0	.000	.000
PITCHERS																		
P	George Uhle	R	59	117	36	4	2	2	1.7	15	21	8	13	0	21	5	.308	.427
P	Earl Whitehill	L	34	83	16	1	0	0	0.0	3	7	3	14	0	0	0	.193	.205
P	Vic Sorrell	R	35	80	15	3	0	0	0.0	9	5	5	25	0	0	0	.188	.225
P	Chief Hogsett	L	33	58	17	2	1	1	1.7	6	5	1	12	0	0	0	.293	.414
P	Waite Hoyt	R	26	46	9	0	0	0	0.0	2	3	1	6	0	0	0	.196	.196
P	Whit Wyatt	R	22	34	12	1	1	1	2.9	3	9	0	7	0	1	0	.353	.529
P	Charlie Sullivan	L	40	24	7	1	1	0	0.0	5	3	2	1	0	0	0	.292	.417
P	Art Herring	R	23	23	3	0	0	0	0.0	2	0	1	4	0	0	0	.130	.130
P	Tommy Bridges	R	8	10	3	1	0	0	0.0	1	0	1	3	0	0	0	.300	.400
P	Guy Cantrell	R	16	9	0	0	0	0	0.0	0	0	0	3	0	0	0	.000	.000
P	Ownie Carroll	R	6	7	1	0	0	0	0.0	1	1	0	2	0	0	0	.143	.143
P	Joe Samuels	R	2	1	0	0	0	0	0.0	0	0	0	0	0	0	0	.000	.000
P	Phil Page	R	12	0	0	0	0	0	–	0	0	0	0	0	0	0	–	–
TEAM TOTAL				5295	1504	298	90	82	1.5	783	728	459	507	97	101	16	.284	.421

INDIVIDUAL FIELDING

POS	Player	T	G	PO	A	E	DP	TC/G	FA	POS	Player	T	G	PO	A	E	DP	TC/G	FA
1B	D. Alexander	R	154	1338	71	22	132	9.3	.985	OF	L. Funk	L	129	354	8	13	4	2.9	.965
	J. Shevlin	L	25	55	3	0	0	2.3	1.000		R. Johnson	R	118	218	15	16	4	2.1	.936
	M. McManus	R	1	1	0	0	1	1.0	1.000		J. Stone	R	108	222	5	8	1	2.2	.966
											H. Rice	R	35	66	2	4	0	2.1	.944
2B	C. Gehringer	R	154	399	501	19	97	6.0	.979		B. Fothergill	R	38	53	1	3	0	1.5	.947
SS	M. Koenig	R	70	115	181	25	40	4.6	.922		F. Doljack	R	20	38	2	3	1	2.2	.930
	B. Akers	R	49	97	155	15	38	5.4	.944		P. Easterling	R	25	29	3	0	2	1.3	1.000
	B. Rogell	R	33	55	95	10	16	4.8	.938		T. Hughes	R	16	26	0	3	0	1.8	.897
	J. Watson	R	4	6	10	3	2	4.8	.842		M. Koenig	R	1	0	0	0	0	0.0	.000
	Y. Wuestling	R	4	7	7	1	3	3.8	.933		B. Rogell	R	1	0	0	0	0	0.0	.000
	M. McManus	R	3	3	8	0	2	3.7	1.000	C	R. Hayworth	R	76	277	27	7	4	4.1	.977
3B	M. McManus	R	130	152	241	14	23	3.1	.966		G. Desautels	R	42	209	23	1	3	5.5	.996
	B. Akers	R	26	22	29	5	5	2.2	.911		P. Hargrave	R	40	175	14	3	3	4.8	.984
	B. Rogell	R	13	7	19	0	4	2.0	1.000		T. Rensa	R	18	46	7	2	1	3.1	.964
	M. Koenig	R	2	2	3	0	0	2.5	1.000		H. Wise	R	2	9	2	0	0	5.5	1.000

The thought can still chill Tiger lovers: Hank Greenberg was nearly a Yankee. And New York might have landed the slugging first baseman if Yankee scout Paul Krichell hadn't squired Greenberg to Yankee Stadium a year before. From a box seat by the dugout, Greenberg watched in awe as Lou Gehrig emerged to kneel in the on-deck circle. "No way I'm going to sign with this team," he thought to himself, watching the Yankees' formidable Iron Man. "Not with *him* playing first base."

In his first pro season, the new Tiger didn't get a chance to hint at his future greatness: Greenburg came up to the big club to go 0-for-1 as a pinch hitter. But he'd be back in 1933.

Another future star—curveballing right-hander Tommy Bridges—debuted in relief at Yankee Stadium after the New Yorkers had battered two Tiger pitchers for 10 runs in less than five innings. Ready to greet the youngster: Babe Ruth, Tony Lazzeri, and Lou Gehrig. No wonder Bridges threw his warmup pitches outlandishly wild, one sailing over catcher Ray Hayworth's head. But he soon calmed down and gained his form. Ruth popped out, Lazzeri got a cheap hit, Gehrig struck out and Harry Rice grounded out.

Detroit could hardly wait for the talented youngsters. The Tigers in their second year under Bucky Harris barely improved, moving up one notch in the standings to fifth, 27 games behind first-place Philadelphia. Four Tigers batted above .300, but none edged near the league leaders. Charlie Gehringer led the team at .330. Fat Fothergill, more than ever living up to his nickname, was waived to the White Sox. Earl Whitehill led the pitching staff at 17–13, followed by Vic Sorrell at 16–11 and George Uhle at 12–12.

TEAM STATISTICS

	W	L	PCT	GB	R	OR	2B	3B	HR	BA	SA	SB	E	DP	FA	CG	BB	SO	ShO	SV	ERA
								Batting						Fielding				Pitching			
HI	102	52	.662		951	751	319	74	125	.294	.452	48	**145**	121	**.975**	72	488	672	**8**	**21**	4.28
AS	94	60	.610	8	892	**689**	300	98	57	.302	.426	**101**	159	150	.974	**78**	504	524	4	14	**3.96**
Y	86	68	.558	16	**1062**	898	298	110	**152**	**.309**	**.488**	91	207	132	.965	65	524	572	6	15	4.88
LE	81	73	.526	21	890	915	**358**	59	72	.304	.431	51	237	156	.962	69	528	441	4	14	4.88
ET	75	79	.487	27	783	833	298	90	82	.284	.421	98	192	156	.967	68	570	574	3	17	4.70
TL	64	90	.416	38	751	886	289	67	75	.268	.391	93	188	152	.970	68	449	470	5	10	5.07
HI	62	92	.403	40	729	884	255	90	63	.276	.391	74	235	136	.962	67	**407**	471	2	10	4.71
OS	52	102	.338	50	612	814	257	68	47	.264	.365	42	196	**161**	.968	**78**	488	356	4	5	4.70
EAGUE TOTAL					6670	6670	2374	656	673	.288	.421	598	1559	1164	.968	565	3958	4080	36	106	4.65

INDIVIDUAL PITCHING

ITCHER	T	W	L	PCT	ERA	SV	G	GS	CG	IP	H	BB	SO	R	ER	ShO	H/9	BB/9	SO/9
eorge Uhle	R	12	12	.500	3.65	3	33	29	18	239	239	75	117	110	97	1	9.00	2.82	4.41
c Sorrell	R	16	11	.593	3.86	1	35	30	14	233.1	245	106	97	116	100	2	9.45	4.09	3.74
arl Whitehill	L	17	13	.567	4.24	1	34	31	16	220.2	248	80	109	139	104	0	10.11	3.26	4.45
hief Hogsett	L	9	8	.529	5.42	1	33	17	4	146	174	63	54	102	88	0	10.73	3.88	3.33
aite Hoyt	R	9	8	.529	4.78	4	26	20	8	135.2	176	47	25	89	72	1	11.68	3.12	1.66
harlie Sullivan	R	1	5	.167	6.53	5	40	3	2	93.2	112	53	38	73	68	0	10.76	5.09	3.65
hit Wyatt	R	4	5	.444	3.57	2	21	7	2	85.2	76	35	68	41	34	0	7.98	3.68	7.14
rt Herring	R	3	3	.500	5.33	0	23	6	1	77.2	97	36	16	54	46	0	11.24	4.17	1.85
ommy Bridges	R	3	2	.600	4.06	0	8	5	2	37.2	28	23	17	18	17	0	6.69	5.50	4.06
uy Cantrell	R	1	5	.167	5.66	0	16	2	1	35	38	20	20	30	22	0	9.77	5.14	5.14
wnie Carroll	R	0	5	.000	10.62	0	6	3	0	20.1	30	9	4	24	24	0	13.28	3.98	1.77
nil Page	L	0	1	.000	9.75	0	12	0	0	12	23	9	2	16	13	0	17.25	6.75	1.50
ark Koenig	R	0	1	.000	10.00	0	2	1	0	9	11	8	6	10	10	0	11.00	8.00	6.00
e Samuels	R	0	0	–	16.50	0	2	0	0	6	10	6	1	11	11	0	15.00	9.00	1.50
EAM TOTAL		75	79	.487	4.70	17	291	154	68	1351.2	1507	570	574	833	706	4	10.03	3.80	3.82

MANAGER	W	L	PCT
Bucky Harris	61	93	.396

POS	Player	B	G	AB	H	2B	3B	HR	HR %	R	RBI	BB	SO	SB	Pinch Hit AB	Pinch Hit H	BA	SA
REGULARS																		
1B	Dale Alexander	R	135	517	168	47	3	3	0.6	75	87	64	35	5	6	0	.325	.445
2B	Charlie Gehringer	L	101	383	119	24	5	4	1.0	67	53	29	15	13	12	1	.311	.431
SS	Billy Rogell	B	48	185	56	12	3	2	1.1	21	24	24	17	8	0	0	.303	.432
3B	Marty McManus	R	107	362	98	17	3	3	0.8	39	53	49	22	7	4	0	.271	.359
RF	Roy Johnson	L	151	621	173	37	19	8	1.3	107	55	72	51	33	1	1	.279	.438
CF	Hub Walker	L	90	252	72	13	1	0	0.0	27	16	23	25	10	12	2	.286	.345
LF	John Stone	L	147	584	191	28	11	10	1.7	86	76	56	48	13	0	0	.327	.464
C	Ray Hayworth	R	88	273	70	10	3	0	0.0	28	25	19	27	0	0	0	.256	.315
SUBSTITUTES																		
UT	Marv Owen	R	105	377	84	11	6	3	0.8	35	39	29	38	2	3	1	.223	.308
2S	Mark Koenig	B	106	364	92	24	4	1	0.3	33	39	14	12	8	15	4	.253	.349
3B	Nolen Richardsen	R	38	148	40	9	2	0	0.0	13	16	6	3	2	0	0	.270	.358
SS	Bill Akers	R	29	66	13	2	2	0	0.0	5	3	7	6	0	5	2	.197	.288
SS	Lou Brower	R	21	62	10	1	0	0	0.0	3	6	8	5	1	0	0	.161	.177
3B	Joe Dugan	R	8	17	4	0	0	0	0.0	1	0	0	3	0	3	1	.235	.235
2B	Bucky Harris	R	4	8	1	1	0	0	0.0	1	0	1	1	0	0	0	.125	.250
OF	Gee Walker	R	59	189	56	17	2	1	0.5	20	28	14	21	10	9	4	.296	.423
OF	Frank Doljack	R	63	187	52	13	3	4	2.1	20	20	15	17	3	7	0	.278	.444
OF	George Quellich	R	13	54	12	5	0	1	1.9	6	11	3	4	1	0	0	.222	.370
OF	Ivey Shiver	R	2	9	1	0	0	0	0.0	2	0	0	3	0	0	0	.111	.111
C	Johnny Grabowski	R	40	136	32	7	1	1	0.7	9	14	6	19	0	1	1	.235	.324
C	Wally Schang	B	30	76	14	2	0	0	0.0	9	2	14	11	1	0	0	.184	.211
C	Muddy Ruel	R	14	50	6	1	0	0	0.0	1	3	5	1	0	0	0	.120	.140
C	Gene Desautels	R	3	11	1	0	0	0	0.0	1	0	1	1	0	0	0	.091	.091
PITCHERS																		
P	Earl Whitehill	L	34	97	15	0	1	0	0.0	7	5	3	10	0	0	0	.155	.175
P	George Uhle	R	53	90	22	6	0	2	2.2	8	7	8	8	0	21	3	.244	.378
P	Vic Sorrell	R	35	88	14	1	0	0	0.0	4	4	4	12	0	0	0	.159	.170
P	Art Herring	R	55	55	11	2	0	0	0.0	10	3	3	6	0	0	0	.200	.236
P	Tommy Bridges	R	35	54	8	0	0	0	0.0	4	1	5	23	0	0	0	.148	.148
P	Chief Hogsett	L	22	47	11	1	0	0	0.0	7	1	1	10	0	0	0	.234	.255
P	Waite Hoyt	R	16	30	4	0	0	0	0.0	1	5	0	4	0	0	0	.133	.133
P	Charlie Sullivan	L	31	24	4	0	0	0	0.0	1	3	1	6	0	0	0	.167	.167
P	Whit Wyatt	R	4	7	2	1	0	0	0.0	0	0	0	1	0	0	0	.286	.429
P	Orlin Collier	R	2	3	0	0	0	0	0.0	0	0	0	1	0	0	0	.000	.000
TEAM TOTAL				5426	1456	292	69	43	0.8	651	599	484	466	117	99	20	.268	.371

INDIVIDUAL FIELDING

POS	Player	T	G	PO	A	E	DP	TC/G	FA	POS	Player	T	G	PO	A	E	DP	TC/G	FA
1B	D. Alexander	R	126	1197	53	16	91	10.0	.987	OF	R. Johnson	R	150	332	25	15	8	2.5	.960
	M. Owen	R	27	185	12	2	14	7.4	.990		J. Stone	R	147	319	11	14	6	2.3	.959
	M. McManus	R	1	0	0	0	0	0.0	.000		H. Walker	R	66	170	4	7	1	2.7	.961
	C. Gehringer	R	9	68	6	1	3	8.3	.987		F. Doljack	R	54	140	8	12	1	3.0	.925
											G. Walker	R	44	99	2	5	1	2.4	.953
2B	C. Gehringer	R	78	224	236	10	54	6.0	.979		G. Quellich	R	13	27	2	0	0	2.2	1.000
	M. Koenig	R	55	132	146	13	28	5.3	.955		D. Alexander	R	4	8	0	0	0	2.0	1.000
	M. McManus	R	21	47	66	3	11	5.5	.974		I. Shiver	R	2	3	0	0	0	1.5	1.000
	M. Owen	R	4	9	14	0	1	5.8	1.000										
	B. Harris	R	3	5	6	0	1	3.7	1.000	C	R. Hayworth	R	88	334	61	11	5	4.6	.973
	B. Akers	R	2	2	0	1	0	1.5	.667		J. Grabowski	R	39	160	28	3	5	4.9	.984
	L. Brower	R	2	1	2	0	1	1.5	1.000		W. Schang	R	30	91	20	4	6	3.8	.965
											M. Ruel	R	14	60	17	2	2	5.6	.975
SS	B. Rogell	R	48	91	182	12	26	5.9	.958		G. Desautels	R	3	7	3	0	0	3.3	1.000
	M. Owen	R	37	81	113	13	22	5.6	.937										
	M. Koenig	R	35	59	90	15	13	4.7	.909										
	B. Akers	R	21	44	42	6	8	4.4	.935										
	L. Brower	R	20	39	38	10	10	4.4	.885										
3B	M. McManus	R	79	92	172	14	18	3.5	.950										
	M. Owen	R	37	33	81	9	9	3.3	.927										
	N. Richardsen	R	38	31	75	6	2	2.9	.946										
	J. Dugan	R	5	4	5	1	0	2.0	.900										

During his third season as Tigers manager, Bucky Harris achieved a dubious distinction: Detroit recorded its farthest finish from first place in team history at 47 games out, in seventh place. It was a balanced nosedive. The pitching sagged deeper into mediocrity, and the hitting—diluted by the departure of Harry Heilmann and Fat Fothergill—lost its once-vaunted punch.

No Tiger won more than 13 games, but two lost 16: Tommy Bridges and Earl Whitehall. Bridges, in his first full season, won only eight as he used his nasty curve to strike out 105, but also to walk 108. Beyond Roy Johnson's 33 stolen bases (second in the league), no Detroit player finished near the top of any significant offensive category, although four Tigers batted .300. Outfielder Rocky Stone led the team at .327; first baseman Dale Alexander, whose hitting was again nearly outweighed by his butchery afield, batted .325; shortstop Billy Rogell hit .303 in 48 games; Charlie Gehringer, who sat out 50 games with injuries, managed .311. The first of Gehringer's numerous ailments forced him to the bench on May 7—the only game he'd missed since September 3, 1927, a franchise-record 511 consecutive games.

Detroit spent 36 games in last place, ultimately avoiding the bottom spot by just four-and-a-half games. Good news was hard to find: at 32 games under .500, Detroit lost every season series but one. Most damaging was their record against the first-place Athletics: the Tigers won four, lost 18.

TEAM STATISTICS

	W	L	PCT	GB	R	OR	2B	3B	Batting HR	BA	SA	SB	Fielding E	DP	FA	CG	BB	Pitching SO	ShO	SV	ERA
HI	107	45	.704		858	626	311	64	118	.287	.435	27	141	151	.976	97	457	574	12	16	3.47
Y	94	59	.614	13.5	1067	760	277	78	155	.297	.457	138	169	131	.972	78	543	686	4	17	4.20
AS	92	62	.597	16	843	691	308	93	49	.285	.400	72	142	148	.976	60	498	582	6	24	3.76
LE	78	76	.506	30	885	833	321	69	71	.296	.419	63	232	143	.963	76	561	470	6	9	4.63
TL	63	91	.409	45	722	870	287	62	76	.271	.390	73	232	160	.963	65	448	436	4	10	4.76
OS	62	90	.408	45	625	800	289	34	37	.262	.349	43	188	127	.970	61	473	365	5	10	4.60
ET	61	93	.396	47	651	836	292	69	43	.268	.371	117	220	139	.964	93	597	511	5	6	4.56
HI	56	97	.366	51.5	704	939	238	69	27	.260	.343	94	245	131	.961	54	588	420	6	10	5.05
EAGUE TOTAL					6355	6355	2323	538	576	.278	.396	627	1569	1130	.968	584	4165	4044	48	102	4.38

INDIVIDUAL PITCHING

ITCHER	T	W	L	PCT	ERA	SV	G	GS	CG	IP	H	BB	SO	R	ER	ShO	H/9	BB/9	SO/9
arl Whitehill	L	13	16	.448	4.06	0	34	34	22	272.1	287	118	81	152	123	0	9.48	3.90	2.68
ic Sorrell	R	13	14	.481	4.12	1	35	32	19	247	267	114	99	131	113	1	9.73	4.15	3.61
eorge Uhle	R	11	12	.478	3.50	2	29	18	15	193	190	49	63	88	75	2	8.86	2.28	2.94
ommy Bridges	R	8	16	.333	4.99	0	35	23	15	173	182	108	105	120	96	1	9.47	5.62	5.46
rt Herring	R	7	13	.350	4.31	1	35	16	9	165	186	67	64	95	79	0	10.15	3.65	3.49
hief Hogsett	L	3	9	.250	5.93	2	22	12	5	112.1	150	33	47	80	74	0	12.02	2.64	3.77
harlie Sullivan	R	3	2	.600	4.73	0	31	4	2	99	109	46	28	60	52	0	9.91	4.18	2.55
aite Hoyt	R	3	8	.273	5.87	0	16	12	5	92	124	32	10	70	60	0	12.13	3.13	0.98
hit Wyatt	R	0	2	.000	8.44	0	4	1	1	21.1	30	12	8	23	20	0	12.66	5.06	3.38
rlin Collier	R	0	1	.000	7.84	0	2	2	0	10.1	17	7	3	12	9	0	14.81	6.10	2.61
ark Koenig	R	0	0	–	6.43	0	3	0	0	7	7	11	5	5	5	0	9.00	14.14	3.86
EAM TOTAL		61	93	.396	4.56	6	246	154	93	1392.1	1549	597	511	836	706	5	10.01	3.86	3.30

MANAGER	W	L	PCT
Bucky Harris	76	75	.503

POS	Player	B	G	AB	H	2B	3B	HR	HR %	R	RBI	BB	SO	SB	Pinch Hit AB	Pinch Hit H	BA	SA
REGULARS																		
1B	Harry Davis	L	140	590	159	32	13	4	0.7	92	74	60	53	12	0	0	.269	.388
2B	Charlie Gehringer	L	152	618	184	44	11	19	3.1	112	107	68	34	9	0	0	.298	.497
SS	Billy Rogell	B	143	554	150	29	6	9	1.6	88	61	50	38	14	0	0	.271	.394
3B	Heinie Schuble	R	101	340	92	20	6	5	1.5	57	52	24	37	14	2	0	.271	.409
RF	Earl Webb	L	87	338	97	19	8	3	0.9	49	51	39	18	1	1	0	.287	.417
CF	Gee Walker	R	126	480	155	32	6	8	1.7	71	78	13	38	30	8	1	.323	.465
LF	John Stone	L	144	582	173	35	12	17	2.9	106	108	58	64	2	3	0	.297	.486
C	Ray Hayworth	R	108	338	99	20	2	2	0.6	41	44	31	22	1	3	1	.293	.382
SUBSTITUTES																		
UT	Billy Rhiel	R	84	250	70	13	3	3	1.2	30	38	17	23	2	27	13	.280	.392
3B	Nolen Richardsen	R	69	155	34	5	2	0	0.0	13	12	9	13	5	0	0	.219	.277
1B	Dale Alexander	R	23	16	4	0	0	0	0.0	0	4	6	2	0	15	4	.250*	.250
OF	Jo-Jo White	L	79	208	54	6	3	2	1.0	25	21	22	19	6	25	9	.260	.346
OF	Roy Johnson	L	49	195	49	14	2	3	1.5	33	22	20	26	7	0	0	.251	.390
OF	Bill Lawrence	R	25	46	10	1	0	0	0.0	10	3	5	5	0	2	0	.217	.239
OF	Frank Doljack	R	8	26	10	1	0	1	3.8	5	7	2	2	1	1	0	.385	.538
C	Muddy Ruel	R	50	136	32	4	2	0	0.0	10	18	17	6	1	3	1	.235	.294
C	Gene Desautels	R	28	72	17	2	0	0	0.0	8	2	13	11	0	3	0	.236	.264
C	George Susce	R	2	0	0	0	0	0	—	0	0	0	0	0	0	0	—	—
PITCHERS																		
P	Earl Whitehill	L	33	90	22	4	0	0	0.0	9	7	4	19	0	0	0	.244	.289
P	Whit Wyatt	R	43	78	15	2	0	2	2.6	7	9	2	16	0	1	0	.192	.295
P	Vic Sorrell	R	33	76	9	0	1	0	0.0	7	8	8	18	0	0	0	.118	.145
P	Tommy Bridges	R	34	67	11	1	1	0	0.0	5	4	7	24	0	0	0	.164	.209
P	Chief Hogsett	L	48	57	14	2	0	2	3.5	11	5	4	18	0	0	0	.246	.386
P	George Uhle	R	38	55	10	3	1	0	0.0	2	4	6	5	0	5	1	.182	.273
P	Buck Marrow	R	18	19	3	1	1	0	0.0	2	0	0	6	0	0	0	.158	.316
P	Izzy Goldstein	B	16	17	5	1	0	0	0.0	3	3	0	1	0	0	0	.294	.353
P	Art Herring	R	12	4	0	0	0	0	0.0	1	0	1	2	0	0	0	.000	.000
P	Rip Sewell	R	5	2	1	0	0	0	0.0	0	0	0	1	0	0	0	.500	.500
TEAM TOTAL				5409	1479	291	80	80	1.5	797	742	486	521	105	99	30	.273	.401

INDIVIDUAL FIELDING

POS	Player	T	G	PO	A	E	DP	TC/G	FA
1B	H. Davis	L	140	1327	75	16	123	10.1	.989
	B. Rhiel	R	12	96	10	1	13	8.9	.991
	D. Alexander	R	2	4	0	0	0	2.0*	1.000
2B	C. Gehringer	R	152	396	495	30	110	6.1	.967
	B. Rhiel	R	1	2	1	0	0	3.0	1.000
SS	B. Rogell	R	139	275	433	42	88	5.4	.944
	H. Schuble	R	15	42	52	5	14	6.6	.949
	N. Richardsen	R	4	5	10	1	1	4.0	.938
3B	H. Schuble	R	76	70	152	14	10	3.1	.941
	N. Richardsen	R	65	51	92	2	8	2.2	.986
	B. Rhiel	R	36	33	53	4	8	2.5	.956
	B. Rogell	R	4	1	4	0	0	1.3	1.000

POS	Player	T	G	PO	A	E	DP	TC/G	FA
OF	J. Stone	R	141	334	11	14	2	2.5	.961
	G. Walker	R	116	309	9	17	1	2.9	.949
	E. Webb	R	84	163	8	8	0	2.1	.955
	R. Johnson	R	48	102	3	8	0	2.4	.929
	J. White	R	47	96	6	4	2	2.3	.962
	B. Lawrence	R	15	39	2	0	1	2.7	1.000
	B. Rhiel	R	8	19	1	0	0	2.5	1.000
	F. Doljack	R	6	6	0	0	0	1.0	1.000
C	R. Hayworth	R	105	399	59	4	8	4.4	.991
	M. Ruel	R	49	150	25	2	3	3.6	.989
	G. Desautels	R	24	109	13	2	0	5.2	.984
	G. Susce	R	2	1	0	0	0	0.5	1.000

Good news: Detroit for the first time in five years finished above .500. Bad news: the Tigers sold the batting title to the Red Sox. At the time, it seemed a good idea. First baseman Dale Alexander, never a nifty fielder, was hitting just .250 over the season's first 34 games. So Frank Navin peddled him to the Red Sox. And as Alexander's replacement, Harry "Stinky" Davis, finished with 16 errors and batted .269, Alexander finished with seven fewer errors and won the batting title at .372. It was the first time in the majors, and still the only time in the American League, that a batting champion split his season between teams.

Earl Whitehill was 16–12 in his last season in Detroit. Reliever Elon "Chief" Hogsett, a left-handed Indian (American, not Cleveland), totaled 11–9. But the best news came from Tommy Bridges, the slight right-hander with the big curve, who finished 14–12 with a 3.36 earned run average and four shutouts (tied for league-high with Lefty Grove).

One of those shutouts particularly frustrated Bridges. On August 5 in Washington, with two outs in the ninth, he owned a 13–0 lead and a perfect game. Washington manager Walter Johnson pinch hit Dave Harris for pitcher Bob Burke. Curveball-lover Harris got one on the first pitch and lined it cleanly to left for a single. End of perfect game, end of no-hitter. After the 28th batter grounded out, Bridges waxed philosophical. "I didn't want the perfect game to be given to me on a platter," he said. "I wanted it with the opposition doing its best. And that's all there is to it." Bridges would have to get used to such near-misses; within two years, he would pitch two more one-hitters.

TEAM STATISTICS

W	L	PCT	GB	R	OR	2B	3B	Batting HR	BA	SA	SB	E	Fielding DP	FA	CG	BB	Pitching SO	ShO	SV	ERA
107	47	.695		1002	724	279	82	160	.286	.454	77	188	124	.969	95	561	770	11	15	3.98
94	60	.610	13	981	752	303	51	173	.290	.457	38	124	142	.979	95	511	595	10	10	4.45
93	61	.604	14	840	716	303	100	61	.284	.408	70	125	157	.979	66	526	437	10	22	4.16
87	65	.572	19	845	747	310	74	78	.285	.413	52	191	129	.969	94	446	439	6	8	4.12
76	75	.503	29.5	799	787	291	80	80	.273	.401	103	187	154	.969	67	592	521	9	17	4.30
63	91	.409	44	736	898	274	69	67	.276	.388	69	188	156	.969	63	574	496	8	11	5.01
49	102	.325	56.5	667	897	274	56	36	.267	.360	89	264	170	.958	50	580	379	2	12	4.82
43	111	.279	64	566	915	253	57	53	.251	.351	46	233	165	.963	42	612	365	2	7	5.02
GUE TOTAL				6436	6436	2287	569	708	.277	.404	544	1500	1197	.969	572	4402	4002	58	102	4.48

INDIVIDUAL PITCHING

CHER	T	W	L	PCT	ERA	SV	G	GS	CG	IP	H	BB	SO	R	ER	ShO	H/9	BB/9	SO/9
Whitehill	L	16	12	.571	4.54	0	33	31	17	244	255	93	81	136	123	3	9.41	3.43	2.99
Sorrell	R	14	14	.500	4.03	0	32	31	13	234.1	234	77	84	136	105	1	8.99	2.96	3.23
t Wyatt	R	9	13	.409	5.03	1	43	22	10	205.2	228	102	82	136	115	0	9.98	4.46	3.59
nmy Bridges	R	14	12	.538	3.36	1	34	26	10	201	174	119	108	95	75	4	7.79	5.33	4.84
ef Hogsett	L	11	9	.550	3.54	7	47	15	7	178	201	66	56	97	70	0	10.16	3.34	2.83
rge Uhle	R	6	6	.500	4.48	0	33	15	6	146.2	152	42	51	84	73	1	9.33	2.58	3.13
k Marrow	R	2	5	.286	4.81	1	18	7	2	63.2	70	29	31	40	34	0	9.90	4.10	4.38
Goldstein	R	3	2	.600	4.47	0	16	6	2	56.1	63	41	14	42	28	0	10.07	6.55	2.24
Herring	R	1	2	.333	5.24	2	12	0	0	22.1	25	15	12	18	13	0	10.07	6.04	4.84
Sewell	R	0	0	–	12.66	0	5	0	0	10.2	19	8	2	15	15	0	16.03	6.75	1.69
M TOTAL		76	75	.503	4.30	17	273	153	67	1362.2	1421	592	521	787	651	9	9.39	3.91	3.44

MANAGER	W	L	PCT
Bucky Harris	73	79	.480
Del Baker	2	0	1.000

POS	Player	B	G	AB	H	2B	3B	HR	HR %	R	RBI	BB	SO	SB	Pinch Hit AB	Pinch Hit H	BA	SA
REGULARS																		
1B	Hank Greenberg	R	117	449	135	33	3	12	2.7	59	87	46	78	6	1	0	.301	.468
2B	Charlie Gehringer	L	155	628	204	42	6	12	1.9	103	105	68	27	5	0	0	.325	.468
SS	Billy Rogell	B	155	587	173	42	11	0	0.0	67	57	79	33	6	0	0	.295	.404
3B	Marv Owen	R	138	550	144	24	9	2	0.4	77	65	44	56	2	1	0	.262	.349
RF	John Stone	L	148	574	161	33	11	11	1.9	86	80	54	37	1	5	3	.280	.434
CF	Pete Fox	R	128	535	154	26	13	7	1.3	82	57	23	38	9	3	0	.288	.424
LF	Gee Walker	R	127	483	135	29	7	9	1.9	68	64	15	49	26	12	2	.280	.424
C	Ray Hayworth	R	134	425	104	14	3	1	0.2	37	45	35	28	0	1	0	.245	.299
SUBSTITUTES																		
1B	Harry Davis	L	66	173	37	8	2	0	0.0	24	14	22	8	2	19	3	.214	.283
3B	Heinie Schuble	R	49	96	21	4	1	0	0.0	12	6	5	17	2	9	4	.219	.281
OF	Jo-Jo White	L	91	234	59	9	5	2	0.9	43	34	27	26	5	26	10	.252	.359
OF	Frank Doljack	R	42	147	42	5	2	0	0.0	18	22	14	13	2	5	1	.286	.347
OF	Billy Rhiel	R	19	17	3	0	1	0	0.0	1	1	5	4	0	13	3	.176	.294
OF	Earl Webb	L	6	11	3	0	0	0	0.0	1	3	3	0	0	2*	0	.273	.273
C	Johnny Pasek	R	28	61	15	4	0	0	0.0	6	4	7	7	2	0	0	.246	.311
C	Gene Desautels	R	30	42	6	1	0	0	0.0	5	4	4	6	0	0	0	.143	.167
C	Frank Reiber	R	13	18	5	0	1	1	5.6	3	3	2	3	0	6	1	.278	.556
PITCHERS																		
P	Firpo Marberry	R	37	90	11	4	0	0	0.0	6	3	1	20	0	0	0	.122	.167
P	Tommy Bridges	R	33	78	16	2	2	0	0.0	5	5	7	17	0	0	0	.205	.282
P	Vic Sorrell	R	36	74	11	1	0	0	0.0	2	3	5	16	0	0	0	.149	.162
P	Carl Fischer	R	35	62	9	0	0	0	0.0	1	0	2	12	0	0	0	.145	.145
P	Schoolboy Rowe	R	21	50	11	1	0	0	0.0	6	6	1	4	0	1	0	.220	.240
P	Chief Hogsett	L	45	38	8	0	0	0	0.0	2	2	1	12	0	0	0	.211	.211
P	Vic Frazier	R	20	37	7	0	0	0	0.0	3	5	3	8	0	0	0	.189	.189
P	Eldon Auker	R	15	17	2	0	0	0	0.0	1	1	0	5	0	0	0	.118	.118
P	Art Herring	R	24	13	1	0	0	0	0.0	2	0	2	1	0	0	0	.077	.077
P	Luke Hamlin	L	3	5	2	1	1	0	0.0	1	0	0	1	0	0	0	.400	1.000
P	Roxie Lawson	R	4	5	0	0	0	0	0.0	1	0	0	1	0	0	0	.000	.000
P	Whit Wyatt	R	10	2	0	0	0	0	0.0	0	0	0	0	0	0	0	.000	.000
P	Bots Nekola	L	2	0	0	0	0	0	–	0	0	0	0	0	0	0	–	–
P	George Uhle	R	1	0	0	0	0	0	–	0	0	0	0	0	0	0	–	–
TEAM TOTAL				5501	1479	283	78	57	1.0	722	676	475	527	68	104	27	.269	.380

INDIVIDUAL FIELDING

POS	Player	T	G	PO	A	E	DP	TC/G	FA
1B	H. Greenberg	R	117	1133	63	14	111	10.3	.988
	H. Davis	L	44	433	13	10	33	10.4	.978
2B	C. Gehringer	R	155	358	542	17	111	5.9	.981
	H. Schuble	R	1	0	0	0	0	0.0	.000
SS	B. Rogell	R	155	326	526	51	116	5.8	.944
	H. Schuble	R	2	3	4	1	0	4.0	.875
3B	M. Owen	R	136	143	226	22	19	2.9	.944
	H. Schuble	R	23	16	42	3	1	2.7	.951

POS	Player	T	G	PO	A	E	DP	TC/G	FA
OF	P. Fox	R	124	313	5	7	0	2.6	.978
	J. Stone	R	141	280	11	9	1	2.1	.970
	G. Walker	R	113	234	10	15	3	2.3	.942
	J. White	R	54	122	4	3	1	2.4	.977
	F. Doljack	R	37	74	6	5	3	2.3	.941
	B. Rhiel	R	1	4	0	0	0	4.0	1.000
	E. Webb	R	2	1	0	0	0	0.5	1.000
C	R. Hayworth	R	133	546	79	4	14	4.7	.994
	J. Pasek	R	28	75	13	1	3	3.2	.989
	G. Desautels	R	30	75	5	2	0	2.7	.976
	F. Reiber	R	6	13	0	1	0	2.3	.929

If baseball was supposed to provide a bit of depression escapism, Detroit fans likely longed for a new deal. For the sixth straight season, the standings proved as discouraging as the stock tables: second division again, 25 games out, in fifth place. Detroit was sixth in the league in batting. And only two Tigers hit .300. But one of them was Hank Greenberg, who at .301 with 12 home runs claimed the first base job for the first of 11 Hall of Fame seasons in Detroit. To bolster the pitching, Harris traded Earl Whitehill to the Senators for Fred "Firpo" Marberry, and he led Detroit in wins at 16–11, tied for fourth in the league. (The bad news was that Whitehill finished third in the league in wins at 22–8.)

But after the season, in December, the course of Tiger history was most severely changed. With two weeks to go in his fifth season of lifeless management, Harris had resigned. At season's end team president Frank Navin telephoned Babe Ruth and asked him to come to Detroit immediately to confer about the job. In what Ruth would later term "one of the great boners in my career," the Babe chose a trip to Hawaii instead and fell out of contention for the job.

Navin then directed his attention to Philadelphia, where Connie Mack was hocking players to pay overdue bills. Needing an inspirational catcher as well as a manager, Navin inquired about Mickey Cochrane, the former Boston University football star who had backboned Mack's three straight championship teams. Mack wanted $100,-000. Navin, himself hurt by the economic collapse, went to half-owner Walter Briggs. "If Cochrane's a success here, he may be a bargain at that price," Briggs said, and agreed to furnish the money. Thus Black Mike became a Tiger, the best thing to happen to Detroit since the assembly line.

TEAM STATISTICS

W	L	PCT	GB	R	OR	2B	Batting 3B	HR	BA	SA	SB	E	Fielding DP	FA	CG	BB	Pitching SO	ShO	SV	ERA
99	53	.651		850	665	281	86	60	.287	.402	65	131	149	.979	68	452	447	5	26	3.82
91	59	.607	7	927	768	241	75	144	.283	.440	74	165	122	.972	70	612	711	8	22	4.36
79	72	.523	19.5	875	853	297	56	140	.285	.441	33	203	121	.966	69	644	423	6	14	4.81
75	76	.497	23.5	654	669	218	77	50	.261	.360	36	156	127	.974	74	465	437	12	5	3.71
75	79	.487	25	722	733	283	78	57	.269	.380	68	178	167	.971	69	561	575	6	17	3.96
67	83	.447	31	683	814	231	53	43	.272	.360	43	186	143	.970	53	519	423	8	13	4.45
63	86	.423	34.5	700	758	294	56	50	.271	.377	62	204	133	.966	60	591	473	4	14	4.35
55	96	.364	43.5	669	820	244	64	64	.253	.360	70	149	162	.976	55	531	426	7	10	4.82
LGUE TOTAL				6080	6080	2089	545	608	.273	.390	451	1372	1124	.972	518	4375	3915	56	123	4.28

INDIVIDUAL PITCHING

CHER	T	W	L	PCT	ERA	SV	G	GS	CG	IP	H	BB	SO	R	ER	ShO	H/9	BB/9	SO/9
o Marberry	R	16	11	.593	3.29	2	37	32	15	238.1	232	61	84	98	87	1	8.76	2.30	3.17
nmy Bridges	R	14	12	.538	3.09	2	33	28	17	233	192	110	120	102	80	2	7.42	4.25	4.64
Sorrell	R	11	15	.423	3.79	1	36	28	13	232.2	233	78	75	112	98	2	9.01	3.02	2.90
l Fischer	L	11	15	.423	3.55	3	35	22	9	182.2	176	84	93	88	72	0	8.67	4.14	4.58
oolboy Rowe	R	7	4	.636	3.58	0	19	15	8	123.1	129	31	75	60	49	1	9.41	2.26	5.47
ef Hogsett	L	6	10	.375	4.50	9	45	2	0	116	137	56	39	78	58	0	10.63	4.34	3.03
Frazier	R	5	5	.500	6.64	0	20	14	4	104.1	129	59	26	85	77	0	11.13	5.09	2.24
Herring	R	1	2	.333	3.84	0	24	3	1	61	61	20	20	34	26	0	9.00	2.95	2.95
n Auker	R	3	3	.500	5.24	0	15	6	2	55	63	25	17	34	32	1	10.31	4.09	2.78
t Wyatt	R	0	1	.000	4.24	0	10	0	0	17	20	9	9	9	8	0	10.59	4.76	4.76
e Hamlin	R	1	0	1.000	4.86	0	3	3	0	16.2	20	10	10	11	9	0	10.80	5.40	5.40
ie Lawson	R	0	1	.000	7.31	0	4	2	0	16	17	17	6	16	13	0	9.56	9.56	3.38
s Nekola	L	0	0	–	27.00	0	2	0	0	1.1	4	1	0	4	4	0	27.00	6.75	0.00
rge Uhle	R	0	0	–	27.00	0	1	0	0	.2	2	0	1	2	2	0	27.00	0.00	13.50
M TOTAL		75	79	.487	3.96	17	284	155	69	1398	1415	561	575	733	615	7	9.11	3.61	3.70

MANAGER	W	L	PCT
Mickey Cochrane	101	53	.656

POS	Player	B	G	AB	H	2B	3B	HR	HR %	R	RBI	BB	SO	SB	Pinch Hit AB	Pinch Hit H	BA	SA
REGULARS																		
1B	Hank Greenberg	R	153	593	201	**63**	7	26	4.4	118	139	63	93	9	0	0	.339	.600
2B	Charlie Gehringer	L	154	601	**214**	50	7	11	1.8	**134**	127	99	25	11	0	0	.356	.517
SS	Billy Rogell	B	154	592	175	32	8	3	0.5	114	100	74	36	13	0	0	.296	.392
3B	Marv Owen	R	154	565	179	34	9	8	1.4	79	96	59	37	3	0	0	.317	.451
RF	Pete Fox	R	128	516	147	31	2	2	0.4	101	45	49	53	25	6	1	.285	.364
CF	Jo-Jo White	L	115	384	120	18	5	0	0.0	97	44	69	39	28	12	2	.313	.385
LF	Goose Goslin	L	151	614	187	38	7	13	2.1	106	100	65	38	5	2	0	.305	.453
C	Mickey Cochrane	L	129	437	140	32	1	2	0.5	74	76	78	26	8	8	1	.320	.412
SUBSTITUTES																		
3B	Flea Clifton	R	16	16	1	0	0	0	0.0	3	1	1	2	0	8	1	.063	.063
UT	Heinie Schuble	R	11	15	4	2	0	0	0.0	2	2	1	4	0	4	0	.267	.400
OF	Gee Walker	R	98	347	104	19	2	6	1.7	54	39	19	20	20	17	5	.300	.418
OF	Frank Doljack	R	56	120	28	7	1	1	0.8	15	19	13	15	2	22	4	.233	.333
C	Ray Hayworth	R	54	167	49	5	2	0	0.0	20	27	16	22	0	1	0	.293	.347
C	Rudy York	R	3	6	1	0	0	0	0.0	0	0	1	3	0	2	1	.167	.167
PH	Cy Perkins	R	1	1	0	0	0	0	0.0	0	0	0	0	0	1	0	.000	.000
PH	Frank Reiber	R	3	1	0	0	0	0	0.0	0	0	2	0	0	1	0	.000	.000
PH	Icehouse Wilson	R	1	1	0	0	0	0	0.0	0	0	0	0	0	1	0	.000	.000
PITCHERS																		
P	Schoolboy Rowe	R	51	109	33	8	1	2	1.8	15	22	6	20	0	6	1	.303	.450
P	Tommy Bridges	R	36	98	12	2	0	0	0.0	7	10	7	25	0	0	0	.122	.143
P	Eldon Auker	R	43	74	11	2	0	0	0.0	3	8	4	28	0	0	0	.149	.176
P	Firpo Marberry	R	38	55	12	4	0	0	0.0	7	9	4	4	0	0	0	.218	.291
P	Vic Sorrell	R	28	37	4	0	0	0	0.0	1	0	5	9	0	0	0	.108	.108
P	Carl Fischer	R	20	31	2	0	0	0	0.0	1	3	1	6	0	0	0	.065	.065
P	General Crowder	L	9	30	4	0	0	0	0.0	1	0	0	4	0	0	0	.133	.133
P	Luke Hamlin	L	20	26	6	0	0	0	0.0	1	2	0	8	0	0	0	.231	.231
P	Chief Hogsett	L	26	13	3	0	0	0	0.0	0	1	0	5	0	0	0	.231	.231
P	Red Phillips	R	7	12	3	1	1	0	0.0	2	1	0	0	0	0	0	.250	.500
P	Vic Frazier	R	8	7	2	0	0	0	0.0	2	1	0	2	0	0	0	.286	.286
P	Steve Larkin	R	2	3	1	1	0	0	0.0	0	0	0	2	1	0	0	.333	.667
TEAM TOTAL				5471	1643	349	53	74	1.4	957	872	636	526	125	91	16	.300	.424

INDIVIDUAL FIELDING

POS	Player	T	G	PO	A	E	DP	TC/G	FA
1B	H. Greenberg	R	153	1454	84	16	124	10.2	.990
	F. Doljack	R	3	20	1	1	0	7.3	.955
2B	C. Gehringer	R	154	355	**516**	17	100	5.8	.981
	F. Clifton	R	1	1	2	1	0	4.0	.750
	H. Schuble	R	1	1	2	0	1	3.0	1.000
SS	B. Rogell	R	154	259	**518**	31	99	5.2	.962
	H. Schuble	R	3	3	5	0	0	2.7	1.000
3B	M. Owen	R	154	**202**	253	21	33	3.1	.956
	F. Clifton	R	4	2	5	0	0	1.8	1.000
	H. Schuble	R	2	0	2	0	0	1.0	1.000

POS	Player	T	G	PO	A	E	DP	TC/G	FA
OF	G. Goslin	R	149	290	15	15	2	2.1	.953
	P. Fox	R	121	245	13	7	4	2.2	.974
	J. White	R	100	225	9	10	2	2.4	.959
	G. Walker	R	80	191	5	11	2	2.6	.947
	F. Doljack	R	30	47	3	3	0	1.8	.943
C	M. Cochrane	R	124	517	69	7	7	4.8	.988
	R. Hayworth	R	54	226	23	4	3	4.7	.984
	R. York	R	2	4	2	0	0	3.0	1.000

After a 25-year wait, the pennant came to Detroit with unusual ease. Two days after acquiring Mickey Cochrane as catcher-manager, Frank Navin traded outfielder Rocky Stone to the the Senators for Goose Goslin to complete the Tigers' lethal G-man trio: Goslin, Hank Greenberg and Charlie Gehringer. With Cochrane (the league's Most Valuable Player over Triple Crown winner Lou Gehrig), shortstop Billy Rogell, third baseman Marv Owen, and centerfielder Jo-Jo White, Detroit's old slugging reputation was revived. The pitching was better than ever. Schoolboy Rowe used his fastball to finish 24–8, winning 16 straight to tie the league record shared by Walter Johnson, Smoky Joe Wood, and Lefty Grove. Tommy Bridges totaled 22–11, Firpo Marberry 15–5, and young submariner Eldon Auker 15–7.

The Tigers electrified their long-dormant disciples with a 101-victory season. They took first place for keeps on August 1 and finished seven games ahead of the second-place Yankees. October nearly brought the ultimate award. In the World Series against Frank Frisch's Cardinals, Detroit split the first two games at home, then took two of three in St. Louis. That sent the Tigers back to Navin Field a victory away from their first World Championship. But Paul Dean pitched the distance to keep the Cardinals alive in Game 6.

The 40,902 attending Game 7 were disappointed early. By the third inning, when the Cardinals hammered four Tiger pitchers for seven runs, the Tigers were dead and their legions were simmering. They exploded in the sixth after Cardinal outfielder Ducky Medwick spiked Owen at third, sparking a melee. When Medwick went out to take his position in left, the partisan fans greeted him with a barrage of apples, oranges, paper, scorecards, pop bottles, and even shoes. Commissioner Kenesaw Mountain Landis had to direct Frisch to remove Medwick. The Cardinals won, 11–0, and Navin spent the winter brokenhearted. "Are we never destined," he lamented, "to win one of these things?"

TEAM STATISTICS

W	L	PCT	GB	R	OR	2B	3B	Batting HR	BA	SA	SB	E	Fielding DP	FA	CG	BB	Pitching SO	ShO	SV	ERA
101	53	.656		958	708	349	53	74	.300	.424	124	159	150	.974	74	488	640	10	14	4.06
94	60	.610	7	842	669	226	60	135	.278	.419	71	157	151	.973	83	542	656	13	10	3.76
85	69	.552	16	814	763	340	46	100	.287	.423	52	172	164	.972	72	582	554	8	19	4.28
76	76	.500	24	820	775	287	70	51	.274	.383	116	188	141	.969	68	543	538	8	9	4.32
68	82	.453	31	764	838	236	50	144	.280	.425	57	196	166	.967	68	693	480	8	8	5.01
67	85	.441	33	674	800	252	59	62	.268	.373	42	187	160	.969	50	632	499	6	20	4.49
66	86	.434	34	729	806	278	70	51	.278	.382	49	162	167	.974	61	503	412	3	12	4.68
53	99	.349	47	704	946	237	40	71	.263	.363	36	207	126	.966	72	628	506	4	8	5.41
GUE TOTAL				6305	6305	2205	449	688	.279	.399	547	1428	1225	.970	548	4611	4285	60	100	4.50

INDIVIDUAL PITCHING

CHER	T	W	L	PCT	ERA	SV	G	GS	CG	IP	H	BB	SO	R	ER	ShO	H/9	BB/9	SO/9
my Bridges	R	22	11	.667	3.67	1	36	35	23	275	249	104	151	117	112	3	8.15	3.40	4.94
olboy Rowe	R	24	8	.750	3.45	1	45	30	20	266	259	81	149	110	102	4	8.76	2.74	5.04
n Auker	R	15	7	.682	3.42	1	43	18	10	205	234	56	86	103	78	2	10.27	2.46	3.78
o Marberry	R	15	5	.750	4.57	3	38	19	6	155.2	174	48	64	92	79	1	10.06	2.78	3.70
Sorrell	R	6	9	.400	4.79	2	28	19	6	129.2	146	45	46	76	69	0	10.13	3.12	3.19
Fischer	L	6	4	.600	4.37	1	20	15	4	94.2	107	38	39	50	46	1	10.17	3.61	3.71
Hamlin	R	2	3	.400	5.38	1	20	5	1	75.1	87	44	30	48	45	0	10.39	5.26	3.58
eral Crowder	R	5	1	.833	4.19	0	9	9	3	66.2	81	20	30	35	31	0	10.94	2.70	4.05
f Hogsett	L	3	2	.600	4.29	3	26	0	0	50.1	61	19	23	34	24	0	10.91	3.40	4.11
Phillips	R	2	0	1.000	6.17	1	7	1	1	23.1	31	16	3	17	16	0	11.96	6.17	1.16
razier	R	1	3	.250	5.96	0	8	2	0	22.2	30	12	11	19	15	0	11.91	4.76	4.37
e Larkin	R	0	0	–	1.50	0	2	1	0	6	8	5	8	7	1	0	12.00	7.50	12.00
M TOTAL		101	53	.656	4.06	14	282	154	74	1370.1	1467	488	640	708	618	11	9.63	3.21	4.20

MANAGER	W	L	PCT
Mickey Cochrane	93	58	.616

POS	Player	B	G	AB	H	2B	3B	HR	HR %	R	RBI	BB	SO	SB	Pinch Hit AB	Pinch Hit H	BA	SA
REGULARS																		
1B	Hank Greenberg	R	152	619	203	46	16	**36**	5.8	121	170	87	91	4	0	0	.328	.628
2B	Charlie Gehringer	L	150	610	201	32	8	19	3.1	123	108	79	16	11	2	1	.330	.502
SS	Billy Rogell	B	150	560	154	23	11	6	1.1	88	71	80	29	3	0	0	.275	.388
3B	Marv Owen	R	134	483	127	24	5	2	0.4	52	71	43	37	1	2	1	.263	.346
RF	Pete Fox	R	131	517	166	38	8	15	2.9	116	73	45	52	14	6	3	.321	.513
CF	Jo-Jo White	L	114	412	99	13	12	2	0.5	82	32	68	42	19	13	4	.240	.345
LF	Goose Goslin	L	147	590	172	34	6	9	1.5	88	109	56	31	5	3	1	.292	.415
C	Mickey Cochrane	L	115	411	131	33	3	5	1.2	93	47	96	15	5	3	1	.319	.450
SUBSTITUTES																		
UT	Flea Clifton	R	43	110	28	5	0	0	0.0	15	9	5	13	2	7	1	.255	.300
32	Heinie Schuble	R	11	8	2	0	0	0	0.0	3	0	1	0	0	2	1	.250	.250
OF	Gee Walker	R	98	362	109	22	6	7	1.9	52	53	15	21	6	14	7	.301	.453
OF	Hub Walker	L	9	25	4	3	0	0	0.0	4	1	3	4	0	2	1	.160	.280
OF	Chet Morgan	L	14	23	4	1	0	0	0.0	2	1	5	0	0	9	1	.174	.217
OF	Hugh Shelley	R	7	8	2	0	0	0	0.0	1	1	2	1	0	2	1	.250	.250
C	Ray Hayworth	R	51	175	54	14	2	0	0.0	22	22	9	14	0	3	1	.309	.411
C	Frank Reiber	R	8	11	3	0	0	0	0.0	3	1	3	3	0	2	0	.273	.273
PITCHERS																		
P	Tommy Bridges	R	36	109	26	5	1	0	0.0	9	10	6	24	0	0	0	.239	.303
P	Schoolboy Rowe	R	45	109	34	3	2	3	2.8	19	28	12	12	0	3	1	.312	.459
P	General Crowder	L	33	93	17	0	1	0	0.0	6	8	5	3	0	0	0	.183	.204
P	Eldon Auker	R	36	74	16	3	2	0	0.0	8	8	2	17	0	0	0	.216	.311
P	Joe Sullivan	R	25	43	7	1	0	0	0.0	6	5	4	9	0	0	0	.163	.186
P	Chief Hogsett	L	40	23	6	0	0	2	8.7	4	4	0	5	0	0	0	.261	.522
P	Vic Sorrell	R	12	18	0	0	0	0	0.0	0	0	0	7	0	0	0	.000	.000
P	Roxie Lawson	R	7	13	4	1	0	0	0.0	1	3	1	2	0	0	0	.308	.385
P	Clyde Hatter	R	8	10	3	0	0	0	0.0	1	1	0	4	0	0	0	.300	.300
P	Firpo Marberry	R	5	5	1	0	0	0	0.0	0	0	1	0	0	0	0	.200	.200
P	Carl Fischer	R	3	2	0	0	0	0	0.0	0	0	0	1	0	0	0	.000	.000
TEAM TOTAL				5423	1573	301	83	106	2.0	919	836	628	453	70	73	25	.290	.435

INDIVIDUAL FIELDING

POS	Player	T	G	PO	A	E	DP	TC/G	FA	POS	Player	T	G	PO	A	E	DP	TC/G	FA
1B	H. Greenberg	R	152	1437	99	13	142	10.2	.992	OF	G. Goslin	R	144	326	6	12	2	2.4	.965
2B	C. Gehringer	R	149	349	489	13	99	5.7	.985		J. White	R	98	247	7	10	1	2.7	.962
	H. Schuble	R	1	0	0	0	0	0.0	.000		P. Fox	R	125	244	9	3	1	2.0	.988
	F. Clifton	R	5	12	19	0	6	6.2	1.000		G. Walker	R	85	204	2	10	1	2.5	.954
SS	B. Rogell	R	150	280	512	24	104	5.4	.971		H. Walker	R	7	19	0	0	0	2.7	1.000
	F. Clifton	R	4	0	5	0	1	1.3	1.000		C. Morgan	R	4	10	0	1	0	2.8	.909
3B	M. Owen	R	131	148	215	16	19	2.9	.958		H. Shelley	R	5	5	0	0	0	1.0	1.000
	F. Clifton	R	21	22	35	4	2	2.9	.934	C	M. Cochrane	R	110	504	50	6	6	5.1	.989
	H. Schuble	R	2	1	4	2	2	3.5	.714		R. Hayworth	R	48	211	35	1	4	5.1	.996
											F. Reiber	R	5	10	0	0	1	2.0	1.000

On the morning of October 8, Detroit awoke with a mighty hangover. The Tigers the day before had given the city its first modern-day baseball World Championship, and the celebration began immediately after the final out. Delirious fans at Navin Field yelled themselves hoarse for 45 minutes after the game, then noisily paraded through town. Detroit bars accommodated the revelers till dawn.

The Tigers, who drew a million fans for the second time in team history, had started their pennant defense sluggishly, languishing in sixth place as late as May 28 before mounting a steady midsummer run at the Yankees, whom they caught, then passed for good in late July. They won their second straight pennant as they did the first: with fearsome hitting. Hank Greenberg tied Jimmie Foxx for the league lead in home runs with 36, won his first of four RBI crowns at 170, and batted .328 during his first of two MVP seasons. Charlie Gehringer, who in August ended a 504-consecutive-game streak (second in team history to his own 511), hit .330. Tommy Bridges won 21-plus for the second straight year, and topped the league in strikeouts with 163.

October brought a World Series foe of a past generation: the Cubs, who had dispatched Detroit in 1907 and '08. The Tigers split the first two games at Navin Field. Bridges won the second on a 12th-inning RBI single by Goslin. Detroit took the next two at Wrigley Field: Game 3 on Jo-Jo White's RBI single in the 11th, Game 4 on 36-year-old General Crowder's five-hitter. Chicago postponed the celebration, 3–1, in Game 5 to send the Series back to Detroit. But the following afternoon, 48,420 watched Bridges win his second game, 4–3, in the bottom of the ninth when Cochrane singled, went to second on Gehringer's groundout, then scored on Goslin's hit. Black Mike sprinted home and jumped up and down on the plate to make sure the run registered. "This is the happiest day of my life," said Cochrane. "My greatest thrill in baseball was scoring that run." Even Frank Navin cracked his poker face, exclaiming again and again, "I have waited 30 years for this day."

TEAM STATISTICS

W	L	PCT	GB	R	OR	2B	3B	HR	BA	SA	SB	E	DP	FA	CG	BB	SO	ShO	SV	ERA
						Batting						Fielding					Pitching			
:T	93	58	.616		919	665	301	83	106	.290	.435	70	128	154	.978	87	522	584	**16**	11	3.82
Y	89	60	.597	3	818	632	255	70	104	.280	.416	68	151	114	.974	76	516	**594**	12	13	**3.60**
:E	82	71	.536	12	776	739	**324**	77	93	.284	.421	63	177	147	.972	67	**457**	498	11	**21**	4.15
)S	78	75	.510	16	718	732	281	63	69	.276	.392	**89**	194	136	.969	82	520	470	6	11	4.05
-I	74	78	.487	19.5	738	750	262	42	74	.275	.382	46	146	133	.976	80	574	436	8	8	4.38
AS	67	86	.438	27	823	903	255	**95**	32	.285	.381	54	171	**186**	.972	67	613	456	5	12	5.25
L	65	87	.428	28.5	718	930	291	51	73	.270	.384	45	187	138	.970	42	640	435	4	15	5.26
-II	58	91	.389	34	710	869	243	44	**112**	.279	.406	42	190	150	.968	58	704	469	7	10	5.12
AGUE TOTAL				6220	6220	2212	525	663	.280	.402	477	1344	1158	.972	559	4546	3942	69	101	4.45

INDIVIDUAL PITCHING

TCHER	T	W	L	PCT	ERA	SV	G	GS	CG	IP	H	BB	SO	R	ER	ShO	H/9	BB/9	SO/9
hoolboy Rowe	R	19	13	.594	3.69	3	42	34	21	275.2	272	68	140	121	113	**6**	8.88	2.22	4.57
mmy Bridges	R	21	10	.677	3.51	1	36	34	23	274.1	277	113	**163**	129	107	4	9.09	3.71	5.35
eneral Crowder	R	16	10	.615	4.26	0	33	32	16	241	269	67	59	127	114	2	10.05	2.50	2.20
don Auker	R	18	7	**.720**	3.83	0	36	25	13	195	213	61	63	86	83	2	9.83	2.82	2.91
e Sullivan	L	6	6	.500	3.51	0	25	12	5	125.2	119	71	53	66	49	0	8.52	5.08	3.80
ief Hogsett	L	6	6	.500	3.54	5	40	0	0	96.2	109	49	39	45	38	0	10.15	4.56	3.63
: Sorrell	R	4	3	.571	4.03	0	12	6	4	51.1	65	25	22	28	23	0	11.40	4.38	3.86
xie Lawson	R	3	1	.750	1.58	2	7	4	4	40	34	24	16	11	7	2	7.65	5.40	3.60
yde Hatter	L	0	0	–	7.56	0	8	2	0	33.1	44	30	15	33	28	0	11.88	8.10	4.05
po Marberry	R	0	1	.000	4.26	0	5	2	1	19	22	9	7	11	9	0	10.42	4.26	3.32
rl Fischer	L	0	1	.000	6.00	0	3	1	0	12	16	5	7	8	8	0	12.00	3.75	5.25
AM TOTAL		93	58	.616	3.82	11	247	152	87	1364	1440	522	584	665	579	16	9.50	3.44	3.85

MANAGER	W	L	PCT
Mickey Cochrane	83	71	.539

POS	Player	B	G	AB	H	2B	3B	HR	HR %	R	RBI	BB	SO	SB	Pinch Hit AB	Pinch Hit H	BA	SA
REGULARS																		
1B	Jack Burns	R	138	558	158	36	3	4	0.7	96	63	79	45	4	0	0	.283	.380
2B	Charlie Gehringer	L	154	641	227	60	12	15	2.3	144	116	83	13	4	0	0	.354	.555
SS	Billy Rogell	B	146	585	160	27	5	6	1.0	85	68	73	41	14	1	0	.274	.368
3B	Marv Owen	R	154	583	172	20	4	9	1.5	72	105	53	41	9	0	0	.295	.389
RF	Gee Walker	R	134	550	194	55	5	12	2.2	105	93	23	30	17	9	1	.353	.536
CF	Al Simmons	R	143	568	186	38	6	13	2.3	96	112	49	35	6	4	1	.327	.484
LF	Goose Goslin	L	147	572	180	33	8	24	4.2	122	125	85	50	14	3	0	.315	.526
C	Ray Hayworth	R	81	250	60	10	0	1	0.4	31	30	39	18	0	1	0	.240	.292
SUBSTITUTES																		
1B	Hank Greenberg	R	12	46	16	6	2	1	2.2	10	16	9	6	1	0	0	.348	.630
UT	Flea Clifton	R	13	26	5	1	0	0	0.0	5	1	4	3	0	1	1	.192	.231
S1	Salty Parker	R	11	25	7	2	0	0	0.0	6	4	2	3	0	0	0	.280	.360
3B	Gil English	R	1	1	0	0	0	0	0.0	0	0	0	1	0	0	0	.000	.000
OF	Pete Fox	R	73	220	67	12	1	4	1.8	46	26	34	23	1	15	2	.305	.423
OF	Jo-Jo White	L	58	51	14	3	0	0	0.0	11	6	9	10	2	30	10	.275	.333
C	Mickey Cochrane	L	44	126	34	8	0	2	1.6	24	17	46	15	1	1	0	.270	.381
C	Glenn Myatt	L	27	78	17	1	0	0	0.0	5	5	9	4	0	1	1	.218	.231
C	Frank Reiber	R	20	55	15	2	0	1	1.8	7	5	5	7	0	2	0	.273	.364
C	Birdie Tebbetts	R	10	33	10	1	2	1	3.0	7	4	5	3	0	0	0	.303	.545
PITCHERS																		
P	Tommy Bridges	R	39	118	25	4	1	0	0.0	10	15	3	26	0	0	0	.212	.263
P	Schoolboy Rowe	R	45	90	23	2	1	1	1.1	16	12	13	15	0	4	2	.256	.333
P	Eldon Auker	R	35	78	24	1	2	0	0.0	7	15	7	24	0	0	0	.308	.372
P	Roxie Lawson	R	41	45	10	0	1	0	0.0	2	5	2	6	0	0	0	.222	.267
P	Vic Sorrell	R	30	39	6	2	0	0	0.0	1	1	7	13	0	0	0	.154	.205
P	Red Phillips	R	22	33	10	1	0	0	0.0	3	1	1	4	0	0	0	.303	.333
P	Jake Wade	L	13	29	5	0	0	0	0.0	3	1	3	11	0	0	0	.172	.172
P	Joe Sullivan	L	26	28	5	0	0	0	0.0	3	1	1	9	0	0	0	.179	.179
P	General Crowder	L	9	20	3	0	1	0	0.0	1	0	0	1	0	0	0	.150	.250
P	Chad Kimsey	L	22	16	5	1	1	0	0.0	3	1	1	5	0	0	0	.313	.500
P	Chief Hogsett	L	3	0	0	0	0	0	–	0	0	1	0	0	0	0	–	–
	TEAM TOTAL			5464	1638	326	55	94	1.7	921	848	646	462	73	72	18	.300	.431

INDIVIDUAL FIELDING

POS	Player	T	G	PO	A	E	DP	TC/G	FA
1B	J. Burns	R	138	1280	73	8	126	9.9	.994
	H. Greenberg	R	12	119	9	1	14	10.8	.992
	S. Parker	R	2	19	3	0	1	11.0	1.000
	A. Simmons	R	1	12	0	0	1	12.0	1.000
	M. Owen	R	2	12	0	0	1	6.0	1.000
2B	C. Gehringer	R	154	397	524	25	116	6.1	.974
	F. Clifton	R	1	0	1	0	0	1.0	1.000
SS	B. Rogell	R	146	286	462	27	98	5.3	.965
	S. Parker	R	7	11	18	3	5	4.6	.906
	F. Clifton	R	6	12	13	2	3	4.5	.926
3B	M. Owen	R	153	190	281	24	28	3.2	.952
	B. Rogell	R	1	1	2	0	1	3.0	1.000
	F. Clifton	R	2	0	2	1	1	1.5	.667
	G. English	R	1	1	1	0	0	2.0	1.000

POS	Player	T	G	PO	A	E	DP	TC/G	FA
OF	A. Simmons	R	138	352	8	5	1	2.6	.986
	G. Walker	R	125	280	14	16	5	2.5	.948
	G. Goslin	R	144	266	11	13	1	2.0	.955
	P. Fox	R	55	118	3	4	0	2.3	.968
	J. White	R	18	14	1	1	0	0.9	.938
	F. Reiber	R	1	0	0	0	0	0.0	.000
C	R. Hayworth	R	81	305	28	4	5	4.2	.988
	M. Cochrane	R	42	159	13	3	1	4.2	.983
	G. Myatt	R	27	79	12	0	1	3.4	1.000
	F. Reiber	R	17	47	7	1	0	3.2	.982
	B. Tebbetts	R	10	51	5	1	0	5.7	.982

The best news would come from the past—Ty Cobb led all vote-getters as one of the five original inductees into the Hall of Fame. Otherwise the Tigers saw their World Series champagne quickly lose its bubble. A month after his team's first World Championship, Frank Navin suffered a fatal heart attack. Partner Walter O. Briggs, Sr., who became full owner, watched 1935 MVP Hank Greenberg sit out the summer with his wrist in a cast, Mickey Cochrane suffer a nervous breakdown, and the Tigers weakly defend their title with a distant second-place finish, 19 1/2 games out.

First came a mistake. Briggs purchased Al Simmons from the White Sox. Simmons hit .327, but proved too disruptive. Then came the injuries. Besides Greenberg, Schoolboy Rowe had a season's worth of arm trouble and General Crowder retired with stomach problems. Cochrane's breakdown, exacerbated by injuries of his own, forced him to leave the team for hospitalization, then an extended rest on a Wyoming ranch. Del Baker, former Tiger catcher and a coach since 1933, took over as interim manager. By early August Cochrane returned, but curtailed his catching.

Complete collapse was avoided as four Tigers—Charlie Gehringer, Gee Walker, Simmons, and Goose Goslin—hit .300. On July 1 the Tigers exploded for 21 runs against the White Sox, equaling a team record not duplicated since. Among pitchers, Tommy Bridges compensated for his ailing colleagues with his third straight 20-win season at 23–11, leading the league in wins and strikeouts. The Tigers finished percentage points away from fourth. On the last day of the season, Detroit nosed out Chicago by .003, Washington by .004. There was no celebration in the Motor City streets.

TEAM STATISTICS

	W	L	PCT	GB	R	OR	2B	Batting 3B	HR	BA	SA	SB	E	Fielding DP	FA	CG	BB	Pitching SO	ShO	SV	ERA
	102	51	.667		1065	731	315	83	182	.300	.483	76	163	148	.973	77	663	624	6	21	4.17
T	83	71	.539	19.5	921	871	326	55	94	.300	.431	72	153	159	.975	76	562	526	13	13	5.00
I	81	70	.536	20	920	873	282	56	60	.292	.397	66	168	174	.973	80	578	414	5	8	5.06
S	82	71	.536	20	889	799	293	84	62	.295	.414	103	182	163	.970	78	588	462	8	14	4.58
E	80	74	.519	22.5	921	862	357	82	123	.304	.461	66	178	154	.971	80	607	619	6	12	4.83
S	74	80	.481	28.5	775	764	288	62	86	.276	.400	54	165	139	.972	78	552	584	11	9	4.39
	57	95	.375	44.5	804	1064	299	66	79	.279	.403	62	188	143	.969	54	609	399	3	13	6.24
I	53	100	.346	49	714	1045	240	60	72	.269	.376	59	209	152	.965	68	696	405	3	12	6.08
GUE TOTAL					7009	7009	2400	548	758	.289	.421	558	1406	1232	.971	591	4855	4033	55	102	5.04

INDIVIDUAL PITCHING

CHER	T	W	L	PCT	ERA	SV	G	GS	CG	IP	H	BB	SO	R	ER	ShO	H/9	BB/9	SO/9
mmy Bridges	R	23	11	.676	3.60	0	39	38	26	294.2	289	115	175	141	118	5	8.83	3.51	5.35
hoolboy Rowe	R	19	10	.655	4.51	3	41	35	19	245.1	266	64	115	134	123	4	9.76	2.35	4.22
on Auker	R	13	16	.448	4.89	0	35	31	14	215.1	263	83	66	140	117	2	10.99	3.47	2.76
Sorrell	R	6	7	.462	5.28	3	30	14	5	131.1	153	64	37	86	77	1	10.48	4.39	2.54
kie Lawson	R	8	6	.571	5.48	3	41	8	3	128	139	71	34	87	78	0	9.77	4.99	2.39
d Phillips	R	2	4	.333	6.49	0	22	6	3	87.1	124	22	15	67	63	0	12.78	2.27	1.55
Sullivan	L	2	5	.286	6.78	1	26	4	1	79.2	111	40	32	70	60	0	12.54	4.52	3.62
e Wade	L	4	5	.444	5.29	0	13	11	4	78.1	93	52	30	60	46	1	10.69	5.97	3.45
ad Kimsey	R	2	3	.400	4.85	3	22	0	0	52	58	29	11	36	28	0	10.04	5.02	1.90
neral Crowder	R	4	3	.571	8.39	0	9	7	1	44	64	21	10	42	41	0	13.09	4.30	2.05
ef Hogsett	L	0	1	.000	9.00	0	3	0	0	4	8	1	1	7	4	0	18.00	2.25	2.25
AM TOTAL		83	71	.539	5.00	13	281	154	76	1360	1568	562	526	870	755	13	10.38	3.72	3.48

MANAGER	W	L	PCT
Mickey Cochrane	89	65	.578

POS	Player	B	G	AB	H	2B	3B	HR	HR %	R	RBI	BB	SO	SB	Pinch Hit AB	Pinch Hit H	BA	SA
REGULARS
1B	Hank Greenberg	R	154	594	200	49	14	40	6.7	137	183	102	101	8	0	0	.337	.668
2B	Charlie Gehringer	L	144	564	209	40	1	14	2.5	133	96	90	25	11	1	0	.371	.520
SS	Billy Rogell	B	146	536	148	30	7	8	1.5	85	64	83	48	5	0	0	.276	.403
3B	Marv Owen	R	107	396	114	22	5	1	0.3	48	45	41	24	3	1	0	.288	.376
RF	Pete Fox	R	148	628	208	39	8	12	1.9	116	82	41	43	12	3	2	.331	.476
CF	Jo-Jo White	L	94	305	75	5	7	0	0.0	50	21	50	40	12	5	2	.246	.305
LF	Gee Walker	R	151	635	213	42	4	18	2.8	105	113	41	74	23	0	0	.335	.499
C	Rudy York	R	104	375	115	18	3	35	9.3	72	103	41	52	3	7	1	.307	.651
SUBSTITUTES
23	Gil English	R	18	65	17	1	0	1	1.5	6	6	6	4	1	1	1	.262	.323
SS	Charley Gelbert	R	20	47	4	2	0	0	0.0	4	1	4	11	0	5	0	.085	.128
UT	Flea Clifton	R	15	43	5	1	0	0	0.0	4	2	7	10	3	0	0	.116	.140
OF	Chet Laabs	R	72	242	58	13	5	8	3.3	31	37	24	66	6	9	2	.240	.434
OF	Goose Goslin	L	79	181	43	11	1	4	2.2	30	35	35	18	0	29	9	.238	.376
OF	Babe Herman	L	17	20	6	3	0	0	0.0	2	3	1	6	2	14	3	.300	.450
C	Birdie Tebbetts	R	50	162	31	4	3	2	1.2	15	16	10	13	0	2	0	.191	.290
C	Mickey Cochrane	L	27	98	30	10	1	2	2.0	27	12	25	4	0	0	0	.306	.490
C	Ray Hayworth	R	30	78	21	2	0	1	1.3	9	8	14	15	0	1	0	.269	.333
C	Cliff Bolton	L	27	57	15	2	0	1	1.8	6	7	8	6	0	13	3	.263	.351
PITCHERS
P	Tommy Bridges	R	34	96	23	2	1	0	0.0	9	8	5	26	0	0	0	.240	.281
P	Eldon Auker	R	43	91	18	4	2	3	3.3	14	16	8	36	0	0	0	.198	.385
P	Roxie Lawson	R	37	81	21	3	0	0	0.0	11	6	6	14	0	0	0	.259	.296
P	Jake Wade	L	33	59	11	1	0	0	0.0	4	1	3	31	0	0	0	.186	.203
P	Boots Poffenberger	R	29	51	11	3	0	0	0.0	5	3	0	8	0	0	0	.216	.275
P	George Gill	R	31	50	7	1	0	0	0.0	6	2	1	12	0	0	0	.140	.160
P	Slick Coffman	R	28	29	5	1	0	0	0.0	3	2	5	13	0	0	0	.172	.207
P	Pat McLaughlin	R	11	10	1	0	0	0	0.0	0	0	1	2	0	0	0	.100	.100
P	Schoolboy Rowe	R	10	10	2	0	0	0	0.0	2	1	1	4	0	0	0	.200	.200
P	Jack Russell	R	25	7	0	0	0	0	0.0	0	0	2	2	0	0	0	.000	.000
P	Clyde Hatter	R	3	3	0	0	0	0	0.0	1	0	1	2	0	0	0	.000	.000
P	Vic Sorrell	R	7	3	0	0	0	0	0.0	0	0	0	2	0	0	0	.000	.000
P	Bob Logan	R	1	0	0	0	0	0	–	0	0	0	0	0	0	0	–	–
	TEAM TOTAL			5516	1611	309	62	150	2.7	935	873	656	712	89	91	23	.292	.452

INDIVIDUAL FIELDING

POS	Player	T	G	PO	A	E	DP	TC/G	FA		POS	Player	T	G	PO	A	E	DP	TC/G	FA
1B	H. Greenberg	R	154	**1477**	102	13	133	10.3	.992		OF	G. Walker	R	151	316	9	15	2	2.3	.956
	G. Goslin	R	1	12	1	1	0	14.0	.929			P. Fox	R	143	321	6	8	0	2.3	.976
2B	C. Gehringer	R	142	331	485	12	102	5.8	**.986**			J. White	R	82	216	4	6	0	2.8	.973
	G. English	R	12	23	28	2	5	4.4	.962			C. Laabs	R	62	133	2	4	0	2.2	.971
	F. Clifton	R	3	6	6	3	2	5.0	.800			G. Goslin	R	40	81	2	4	1	2.2	.954
SS	B. Rogell	R	146	323	451	26	103	5.5	**.968**			B. Herman	L	2	3	0	0	0	1.5	1.000
	C. Gelbert	R	16	22	35	4	7	3.8	.934		C	R. York	R	54	190	27	9	6	4.2	.960
	F. Clifton	R	4	6	9	0	1	3.8	1.000			B. Tebbetts	R	48	155	25	7	1	3.9	.963
3B	M. Owen	R	106	108	219	10	17	3.2	**.970**			R. Hayworth	R	28	118	14	1	2	4.8	.992
	R. York	R	41	45	66	9	5	2.9	.925			M. Cochrane	R	27	103	13	0	1	4.3	1.000
	F. Clifton	R	7	9	14	1	1	3.4	.958			C. Bolton	R	13	47	9	1	2	4.4	.982
	G. English	R	6	3	6	0	0	1.5	1.000											

Ghastly luck continued to stalk Mickey Cochrane. This season it caught him on May 25 at Yankee Stadium, and nearly killed him. The Tigers had come to the Bronx battling New York for first place. Cochrane was batting in the fifth when Bump Hadley's pitch sailed high and tight. Cochrane frantically ducked away and threw his hands up to protect his head, but the ball struck him above the left temple with a sickening thud. The unconscious Cochrane was rushed to a hospital, where he was pronounced in critical condition with a triple skull fracture. Not until four days later were doctors certain he'd live. But his playing career was finished at 34. Del Baker again took over as interim manager, and by the time Cochrane returned on July 25 the team was in second place. But again there would be no serious run at the Yankees.

Charlie Gehringer captured the third MVP Award by a Tiger in four years, winning the batting title at .371 while again leading the league's second basemen in fielding average. After recovering from his broken wrist, Hank Greenberg authored what he would later call his best year, hitting .337, becoming the first Tiger to slam 40 homers, and driving home 183 runs, one short of Lou Gehrig's AL record. Rudy York joined the team from the minors to hit .307 with a career-high 35 home runs, 18 in August— still a major-league record for homers in one month. During an August 14 doubleheader against the Browns, Detroit scored a still-standing league record 36 runs. But Schoolboy Rowe led the pitching staff's decline, reporting out of shape and finishing 1–4. Late-blooming Roxie Lawson, in his second full season in Detroit at age 31, led the staff at 18–7, no doubt boosted by timely slugging—his ERA was 5.26.

TEAM STATISTICS

	W	L	PCT	GB	R	OR	Batting 2B	3B	HR	BA	SA	SB	Fielding E	DP	FA	Pitching CG	BB	SO	ShO	SV	ERA
Y	102	52	.662		979	671	282	73	174	.283	.456	60	170	134	.972	82	506	652	15	21	3.65
ET	89	65	.578	13	935	841	309	62	150	.292	.452	89	147	149	.976	70	635	485	6	11	4.87
HI	86	68	.558	16	780	730	280	76	67	.280	.400	70	174	173	.971	70	532	533	15	21	4.17
LE	83	71	.539	19	817	768	304	76	103	.280	.423	76	159	153	.974	64	563	630	4	15	4.39
OS	80	72	.526	21	821	775	269	64	100	.281	.411	79	177	139	.970	74	597	682	6	14	4.48
AS	73	80	.477	28.5	757	841	245	84	47	.279	.379	61	170	181	.972	75	676	535	5	14	4.58
HI	54	97	.358	46.5	699	854	278	60	94	.267	.397	95	198	150	.967	65	613	469	6	9	4.85
L	46	108	.299	56	715	1023	327	44	71	.285	.399	30	173	166	.972	55	653	468	2	8	6.00
AGUE TOTAL					6503	6503	2294	539	806	.281	.415	560	1368	1245	.972	555	4775	4454	59	113	4.62

INDIVIDUAL PITCHING

TCHER	T	W	L	PCT	ERA	SV	G	GS	CG	IP	H	BB	SO	R	ER	ShO	H/9	BB/9	SO/9
don Auker	R	17	9	.654	3.88	1	39	32	19	252.2	250	97	73	127	109	1	8.91	3.46	2.60
mmy Bridges	R	15	12	.556	4.07	0	34	31	18	245.1	267	91	138	129	111	3	9.79	3.34	5.06
xie Lawson	R	18	7	.720	5.26	1	37	29	15	217.1	236	115	68	141	127	0	9.77	4.76	2.82
ke Wade	L	7	10	.412	5.39	0	33	25	7	165.1	160	107	69	106	99	1	8.71	5.82	3.76
ots Poffenberger	R	10	5	.667	4.65	3	29	16	5	137.1	147	79	35	83	71	0	9.63	5.18	2.29
orge Gill	R	11	4	.733	4.51	1	31	10	4	127.2	146	42	40	74	64	1	10.29	2.96	2.82
ck Coffman	R	7	5	.583	4.37	0	28	5	1	101	121	39	22	61	49	0	10.78	3.48	1.96
ck Russell	R	2	5	.286	7.59	4	25	0	0	40.1	63	20	10	35	34	0	14.06	4.46	2.23
t McLaughlin	R	0	2	.000	6.34	0	10	3	0	32.2	39	16	8	23	23	0	10.74	4.41	2.20
hoolboy Rowe	R	1	4	.200	8.62	0	10	2	1	31.1	49	9	6	32	30	0	14.07	2.59	1.72
: Sorrell	R	0	2	.000	9.00	1	7	2	0	17	25	8	11	18	17	0	13.24	4.24	5.82
yde Hatter	L	1	0	1.000	11.57	0	3	0	0	9.1	17	11	4	12	12	0	16.39	10.61	3.86
b Logan	L	0	0	–	0.00	0	1	0	0	.2	1	1	1	0	0	0	13.50	13.50	13.50
AM TOTAL		89	65	.578	4.87	11	287	155	70	1378	1521	635	485	841	746	6	9.93	4.15	3.17

MANAGER	W	L	PCT
Mickey Cochrane	47	50	.485
Del Baker	37	20	.649

POS	Player	B	G	AB	H	2B	3B	HR	HR %	R	RBI	BB	SO	SB	Pinch Hit AB	Pinch Hit H	BA	SA
REGULARS																		
1B	Hank Greenberg	R	155	556	175	23	4	58	10.4	144	146	119	92	7	0	0	.315	.683
2B	Charlie Gehringer	L	152	568	174	32	5	20	3.5	133	107.	112	21	14	0	0	.306	.486
SS	Billy Rogell	B	136	501	130	22	8	3	0.6	76	55	86	37	9	2	0	.259	.353
3B	Don Ross	R	77	265	69	7	1	1	0.4	22	30	28	11	1	2	0	.260	.306
RF	Pete Fox	R	155	634	186	35	10	7	1.1	91	96	31	39	16	0	0	.293	.413
CF	Chet Morgan	L	74	306	87	6	1	0	0.0	50	27	20	12	5	0	0	.284	.310
LF	Dixie Walker	L	127	454	140	27	6	6	1.3	84	43	65	32	5	10	3	.308	.434
C	Rudy York	R	135	463	138	27	2	33	7.1	85	127	92	74	1	3	0	.298	.579
SUBSTITUTES																		
3S	Mark Christman	R	95	318	79	6	4	1	0.3	35	44	27	21	5	0	0	.248	.302
3B	Tony Piet	R	41	80	17	6	0	0	0.0	9	14	15	11	2	17	3	.213	.288
2B	Benny McCoy	L	7	15	3	1	0	0	0.0	2	0	1	2	0	0	0	.200	.267
OF	Chet Laabs	R	64	211	50	7	3	7	3.3	26	37	15	52	3	11	3	.237	.398
OF	Jo-Jo White	L	78	206	54	6	1	0	0.0	40	15	28	15	3	18	3	.262	.301
OF	Roy Cullenbine	L	25	67	19	1	3	0	0.0	12	9	12	9	2	7	2	.284	.388
C	Birdie Tebbetts	R	53	143	42	6	2	1	0.7	16	25	12	13	1	9	3	.294	.385
C	Ray Hayworth	R	8	19	4	0	0	0	0.0	1	5	3	4	1	1	1	.211	.211
PH	George Archie	R	3	2	0	0	0	0	0.0	0	0	0	1	0	2	0	.000	.000
PITCHERS																		
P	Vern Kennedy	L	37	79	23	3	0	0	0.0	10	8	1	11	0	4	1	.291	.329
P	Eldon Auker	R	27	57	5	0	0	0	0.0	6	2	4	24	1	0	0	.088	.088
P	George Gill	R	24	57	6	1	1	0	0.0	4	1	0	15	0	0	0	.105	.158
P	Tommy Bridges	R	25	54	7	1	1	0	0.0	5	3	6	17	0	0	0	.130	.185
P	Roxie Lawson	R	27	45	2	0	0	0	0.0	1	1	1	9	0	0	0	.044	.044
P	Boots Poffenberger	R	25	44	8	0	0	0	0.0	0	2	2	9	0	0	0	.182	.182
P	Harry Eisenstat	L	32	36	5	0	0	0	0.0	4	1	4	16	0	0	0	.139	.139
P	Al Benton	R	19	33	4	0	0	0	0.0	1	1	0	13	0	0	0	.121	.121
P	Slick Coffman	R	39	24	4	1	0	0	0.0	2	5	3	7	0	0	0	.167	.208
P	Jake Wade	L	27	21	1	0	0	0	0.0	0	0	1	8	0	0	0	.048	.048
P	Schoolboy Rowe	R	4	6	1	1	0	0	0.0	1	0	0	1	0	0	0	.167	.333
P	Bob Harris	R	3	3	1	0	0	0	0.0	1	0	0	2	0	0	0	.333	.333
P	Joe Rogalski	R	2	2	0	0	0	0	0.0	0	0	0	0	0	0	0	.000	.000
P	Woody Davis	L	2	1	0	0	0	0	0.0	0	0	0	1	0	0	0	.000	.000
TEAM TOTAL				5270	1434	219	52	137	2.6	861	804	688	579	76	86	21	.272	.411

INDIVIDUAL FIELDING

POS	Player	T	G	PO	A	E	DP	TC/G	FA
1B	H. Greenberg	R	155	1484	120	14	146	10.4	.991
	R. York	R	1	4	0	0	1	4.0	1.000
2B	C. Gehringer	R	152	393	455	21	115	5.7	.976
	T. Piet	R	1	0	0	0	0	0.0	.000
	B. McCoy	R	6	10	16	1	4	4.5	.963
SS	B. Rogell	R	134	291	431	31	101	5.6	.959
	M. Christman	R	21	46	66	6	17	5.6	.949
3B	D. Ross	R	75	90	157	14	15	3.5	.946
	M. Christman	R	69	86	146	4	14	3.4	.983
	T. Piet	R	18	12	45	5	3	3.4	.919
	B. McCoy	R	1	0	0	2	0	2.0	.000

POS	Player	T	G	PO	A	E	DP	TC/G	FA
OF	P. Fox	R	154	301	13	2	2	2.1	**.994**
	D. Walker	R	114	224	8	5	1	2.1	.979
	C. Morgan	R	74	192	6	4	2	2.7	.980
	J. White	R	55	141	4	5	0	2.7	.967
	C. Laabs	R	53	128	4	4	1	2.6	.971
	R. Cullenbine	R	17	34	1	0	0	2.1	1.000
	R. York	R	14	21	1	5	0	1.9	.815
C	R. York	R	116	406	70	5	10	4.1	.990
	B. Tebbetts	R	53	108	20	2	4	2.5	.985
	R. Hayworth	R	7	32	1	1	0	4.9	.971

Their home park added outfield upper decks to completely enclose the playing field, and got a new name: Briggs Stadium (new capacity, 56,000). But the Tigers' post-1935 malaise dragged on. Mickey Cochrane tried to improve the pitching by dealing popular outfielder Gee Walker, third baseman Marv Owen, and catcher Mike Tresh to the White Sox for 21-game winner Vern Kennedy, outfielder Dixie Walker, and infielder Tony Piet. The trade infuriated Detroit; the fans roundly denounced the deal and circulated petitions signed by thousands threatening to boycott the club unless the deal was rescinded. The fans were right: Kennedy won his first nine starts, but from June 9 on won three while losing 12. Walker was not the People's Cherce in the Motor City as he would be in Brooklyn, and Piet's final major-league season was dismal.

Thus relations between Cochrane and Walter O. Briggs, Sr. and Jr. deteriorated, then completely unraveled in August, with the club in fifth place. After two tough home losses to the Red Sox, Briggs the elder summoned the manager to his office. Little more than a year after he was nearly killed by a pitch, and just three years after leading the Tigers to their first world championship, Cochrane was fired.

Del Baker again took field leadership of the team, which eventually trudged home fourth, 16 games out. Tiger fans could only get excited about Rudy York's collection of four grand slams and Hank Greenberg's assault on Babe Ruth's home-run record. Greenberg, who became the first and only Tiger to top 50 homers, slammed his 58th with five games left in the season, but couldn't manage another. Still, Greenberg's total remains a major-league record for first basemen, and is tied for most ever by a right-handed batter (with Jimmie Foxx's 58 in 1932).

TEAM STATISTICS

W	L	PCT	GB	R	OR	2B	3B	HR	BA	SA	SB	E	DP	FA	CG	BB	SO	ShO	SV	ERA
99	53	.651		966	710	283	63	174	.274	.446	91	169	169	.973	91	566	567	10	13	3.91
88	61	.591	9.5	902	751	298	56	98	.299	.434	55	190	172	.968	67	528	484	10	15	4.46
86	66	.566	13	847	782	300	89	113	.281	.434	83	151	145	.974	68	681	717	5	17	4.60
84	70	.545	16	862	795	219	52	137	.272	.411	76	147	172	.976	75	608	435	2	11	4.79
75	76	.497	23.5	814	873	278	72	85	.293	.416	65	180	179	.970	59	655	515	6	11	4.94
65	83	.439	32	709	752	239	55	67	.277	.383	56	196	155	.967	83	550	432	5	9	4.36
55	97	.362	44	755	962	273	36	92	.281	.397	51	145	163	.975	71	737	632	3	7	5.80
53	99	.349	46	726	956	243	62	98	.270	.396	65	206	119	.965	56	599	473	4	12	5.48
GUE TOTAL				6581	6581	2133	485	864	.281	.415	542	1384	1274	.971	570	4924	4255	45	95	4.79

INDIVIDUAL PITCHING

CHER	T	W	L	PCT	ERA	SV	G	GS	CG	IP	H	BB	SO	R	ER	ShO	H/9	BB/9	SO/9
n Kennedy	R	12	9	.571	5.06	2	33	26	11	190.1	215	113	53	123	107	0	10.17	5.34	2.51
orge Gill	R	12	9	.571	4.12	0	24	23	13	164	195	50	30	82	75	1	10.70	2.74	1.65
on Auker	R	11	10	.524	5.27	0	27	24	12	160.2	184	56	46	97	94	1	10.31	3.14	2.58
nmy Bridges	R	13	9	.591	4.59	1	25	20	13	151	171	58	101	83	77	0	10.19	3.46	6.02
ie Lawson	R	8	9	.471	5.46	1	27	16	5	127	154	82	39	85	77	0	10.91	5.81	2.76
ry Eisenstat	L	9	6	.600	3.73	4	32	9	5	125.1	131	29	37	60	52	0	9.41	2.08	2.66
ts Poffenberger	R	6	7	.462	4.82	1	25	15	8	125	147	66	28	74	67	0	10.58	4.75	2.02
k Coffman	R	4	4	.500	6.02	2	39	6	1	95.2	120	48	31	70	64	0	11.29	4.52	2.92
Benton	R	5	3	.625	3.30	0	19	10	6	95.1	93	39	33	40	35	0	8.78	3.68	3.12
e Wade	L	3	2	.600	6.56	0	27	2	0	70	73	48	23	56	51	0	9.39	6.17	2.96
oolboy Rowe	R	0	2	.000	3.00	0	4	3	0	21	20	11	4	11	7	0	8.57	4.71	1.71
Harris	R	1	0	1.000	7.20	0	3	1	1	10	14	4	7	9	8	0	12.60	3.60	6.30
Rogalski	R	0	0	–	2.57	0	2	0	0	7	12	0	2	4	2	0	15.43	0.00	2.57
dy Davis	R	0	0	–	1.50	0	2	0	0	6	3	4	1	1	1	0	4.50	6.00	1.50
M TOTAL		84	70	.545	4.79	11	289	155	75	1348.1	1532	608	435	795	717	2	10.23	4.06	2.90

MANAGER	W	L	PCT
Del Baker	81	73	.526

POS	Player	B	G	AB	H	2B	3B	HR	HR %	R	RBI	BB	SO	SB	Pinch Hit AB	Pinch Hit H	BA	SA
REGULARS																		
1B	Hank Greenberg	R	138	500	156	42	7	33	6.6	112	112	91	95	8	1	0	.312	.622
2B	Charlie Gehringer	L	118	406	132	29	6	16	3.9	86	86	68	16	4	9	4	.325	.544
SS	Frank Croucher	R	97	324	87	15	0	5	1.5	38	40	16	42	2	2	2	.269	.361
3B	Pinky Higgins	R	132	489	135	23	2	8	1.6	57	76	56	41	7	2	1	.276	.380
RF	Pete Fox	R	141	519	153	24	6	7	1.3	69	66	35	41	23	14	2	.295	.405
CF	Barney McCosky	L	147	611	190	33	14	4	0.7	120	58	70	45	20	2	1	.311	.430
LF	Earl Averill	L	87	309	81	20	6	10	3.2	58	58	43	30	4	7	0	.262	.463
C	Birdie Tebbetts	R	106	341	89	22	2	4	1.2	37	53	25	20	2	6	1	.261	.372
SUBSTITUTES																		
2S	Benny McCoy	L	55	192	58	13	6	1	0.5	38	33	29	26	3	5	0	.302	.448
S3	Billy Rogell	B	74	174	40	6	3	2	1.1	24	23	26	14	3	3	0	.230	.333
S2	Red Kress	R	51	157	38	7	0	1	0.6	19	22	17	16	2	6	4	.242	.306
3B	Mark Christman	R	6	16	4	2	0	0	0.0	0	0	0	2	0	0	0	.250	.375
OF	Roy Cullenbine	B	75	179	43	9	2	6	3.4	31	23	34	29	0	25	7	.240	.413
OF	Dixie Walker	L	43	154	47	4	5	4	2.6	30	19	15	8	4	4	1	.305	.494
OF	Beau Bell	R	54	134	32	4	2	0	0.0	14	24	24	16	0	15	3	.239	.299
OF	Les Fleming	L	8	16	0	0	0	0	0.0	0	1	0	4	0	5	0	.000	.000
OF	Chet Laabs	R	5	16	5	1	1	0	0.0	1	2	2	0	0	0	0	.313	.500
C1	Rudy York	R	102	329	101	16	1	20	6.1	66	68	41	50	5	16	2	.307	.544
C	Merv Shea	R	4	2	0	0	0	0	0.0	0	0	0	1	0	0	0	.000	.000
C	Dixie Parsons	R	5	1	0	0	0	0	0.0	0	0	1	1	0	1	0	.000	.000
PITCHERS																		
P	Bobo Newsom	R	35	97	18	0	1	0	0.0	6	7	1	16	0	0	0	.186	.206
P	Tommy Bridges	R	29	71	14	2	0	0	0.0	11	6	8	24	0	0	0	.197	.225
P	Schoolboy Rowe	R	31	61	15	0	1	1	1.6	7	12	5	7	1	3	1	.246	.328
P	Dizzy Trout	R	35	57	12	2	1	0	0.0	7	1	2	9	0	0	0	.211	.281
P	Al Benton	R	37	44	4	0	0	0	0.0	5	1	0	15	0	0	0	.091	.091
P	Archie McKain	B	32	41	9	2	1	2	4.9	7	5	8	12	0	0	0	.220	.463
P	Fred Hutchinson	L	13	34	13	1	0	0	0.0	5	6	2	0	0	0	0	.382	.412
P	Bud Thomas	R	27	9	1	0	0	0	0.0	0	0	0	6	0	0	0	.111	.111
P	Harry Eisenstat	L	10	8	3	0	0	0	0.0	0	0	0	2	0	0	0	.375	.375
P	Vern Kennedy	L	4	7	2	0	0	0	0.0	0	0	0	1	0	0	0	.286	.286
P	Bob Harris	R	5	5	2	0	0	0	0.0	1	0	0	0	0	0	0	.400	.400
P	Cotton Pippen	R	3	5	2	0	0	0	0.0	0	0	0	0	0	0	0	.400	.400
P	Slick Coffman	R	23	5	0	0	0	0	0.0	0	0	1	1	0	0	0	.000	.000
P	Roxie Lawson	R	2	4	0	0	0	0	0.0	0	0	0	0	0	0	0	.000	.000
P	Floyd Giebell	L	9	2	0	0	0	0	0.0	0	0	0	0	0	0	0	.000	.000
P	George Gill	R	3	2	0	0	0	0	0.0	0	0	0	2	0	0	0	.000	.000
P	Red Lynn	R	4	2	0	0	0	0	0.0	0	0	0	0	0	0	0	.000	.000
P	Jim Walkup	R	7	2	1	0	0	0	0.0	0	0	0	1	0	0	0	.500	.500
P	Hal Newhouser	L	1	1	0	0	0	0	0.0	0	0	0	0	0	0	0	.000	.000
TEAM TOTAL				5326	1487	277	67	124	2.3	849	802	620	593	88	126	29	.279	.426

INDIVIDUAL FIELDING

POS	Player	T	G	PO	A	E	DP	TC/G	FA
1B	H. Greenberg	R	136	1205	75	9	108	9.5	.993
	R. York	R	19	151	1	0	17	8.0	1.000
	R. Cullenbine	R	2	23	2	0	4	12.5	1.000
2B	C. Gehringer	R	107	245	312	13	67	5.3	.977
	B. McCoy	R	34	79	104	8	19	5.6	.958
	R. Kress	R	16	29	47	6	13	5.1	.927
	B. Rogell	R	2	8	5	1	2	7.0	.929
	F. Croucher	R	3	5	8	1	3	4.7	.929
SS	F. Croucher	R	93	139	256	28	47	4.5	.934
	B. Rogell	R	43	59	90	11	21	3.7	.931
	R. Kress	R	25	48	69	5	15	4.9	.959
	B. McCoy	R	16	29	46	3	6	4.9	.962
3B	P. Higgins	R	130	140	241	36	22	3.2	.914
	B. Rogell	R	21	17	40	4	3	2.9	.934
	R. Kress	R	4	7	7	1	1	3.8	.933
	M. Christman	R	6	4	5	1	1	1.7	.900

POS	Player	T	G	PO	A	E	DP	TC/G	FA
OF	B. McCosky	R	145	428	7	6	2	3.0	.986
	P. Fox	R	126	275	12	9	3	2.3	.970
	E. Averill	R	80	157	3	4	0	2.1	.976
	D. Walker	R	37	93	4	3	1	2.7	.970
	R. Cullenbine	R	46	81	2	9	1	2.0	.902
	B. Bell	R	37	73	4	0	1	2.1	1.000
	C. Laabs	R	5	13	1	1	0	3.0	.933
	L. Fleming	L	3	6	0	0	0	2.0	1.000
C	B. Tebbetts	R	100	449	64	16	10	5.3	.970
	R. York	R	67	283	38	5	5	4.9	.985
	D. Parsons	R	4	2	0	0	0	0.5	1.000
	M. Shea	R	4	1	0	1	0	0.5	.500

The regression was complete. In his first full season as manager, Del Baker took the Tigers back to the Bucky Harris years: Detroit sank into the second division for the first time in six seasons. Hank Greenberg missed 17 games with an injury and his home run production slipped from 58 to 33 (still second in the league). Charlie Gehringer sat out 36 games, but hit .325 and became the fourth Tiger to hit for the cycle on May 27 versus the Browns, this one in perfect single-double-triple-homer succession. Tommy Bridges finished 17–7 and became the first Tiger pitcher to win the All-Star Game. Also of note: Detroit played under the lights for the first time, winning 5–0, at Philadelphia on June 20.

Some of the best news came from newcomers. Mike "Pinky" Higgins filled the third-base void. Hometown rookie Barney McCosky stepped into center field for his first of three .300 seasons. Two pitchers with exceptional futures also made their major-league debuts: right-hander Dizzy Trout and 18-year-old Detroit-born left-hander Hal Newhouser, after working his way up in one season from Class D.

The strangest trade came in May, appropriately involving colorful, well-traveled pitcher Bobo Newsom. On a Saturday morning, Zeller and Browns general manager Bill Dewitt held a meeting at St. Louis's Sportman's Park that lasted into the night. The next morning Newsom was a Tiger and Vern Kennedy a Brown as part of a 10-player swap. For the Tigers, it was a fruitful marathon: Newsom, already 3–1 with St. Louis, finished at 20–11, tied for the league lead in complete games, and was second in strikeouts. Kennedy finished 9–20.

TEAM STATISTICS

	W	L	PCT	GB	R	OR	Batting						Fielding			CG	BB	Pitching			
							2B	3B	HR	BA	SA	SB	E	DP	FA			SO	ShO	SV	ERA
	106	45	.702		967	556	259	55	166	.287	.451	72	126	159	.978	87	567	565	12	26	3.31
S	89	62	.589	17	890	795	287	57	124	.291	.436	42	180	147	.970	52	543	539	4	20	4.56
E	87	67	.565	20.5	797	700	291	79	85	.280	.413	72	180	148	.970	69	602	614	9	13	4.08
l	85	69	.552	22.5	755	737	220	56	64	.275	.374	113	167	140	.972	62	454	535	5	21	4.31
T	81	73	.526	26.5	849	762	277	67	124	.279	.426	88	198	147	.967	64	574	633	6	16	4.29
S	65	87	.428	41.5	702	797	249	79	44	.278	.379	94	205	167	.966	72	602	521	4	10	4.60
l	55	97	.362	51.5	711	1022	282	55	98	.271	.400	60	210	131	.964	50	579	397	5	12	5.79
_	43	111	.279	64.5	733	1035	242	50	91	.268	.381	48	199	144	.968	56	739	516	3	3	6.01
GUE TOTAL					6404	6404	2107	498	796	.279	.407	589	1465	1183	.969	512	4660	4320	48	121	4.62

INDIVIDUAL PITCHING

CHER	T	W	L	PCT	ERA	SV	G	GS	CG	IP	H	BB	SO	R	ER	ShO	H/9	BB/9	SO/9
Bo Newsom	R	17	10	.630	3.37	2	35	31*	21*	246	222	104	164	100	92	3	8.12	3.80	6.00
mmy Bridges	R	17	7	.708	3.50	2	29	26	16	198	186	61	129	87	77	2	8.45	2.77	5.86
hoolboy Rowe	R	10	12	.455	4.99	0	28	24	8	164	192	61	51	113	91	1	10.54	3.35	2.80
zy Trout	R	9	10	.474	3.61	2	33	22	6	162	168	74	72	82	65	0	9.33	4.11	4.00
Benton	R	6	8	.429	4.56	5	37	16	3	150	182	58	67	94	76	0	10.92	3.48	4.02
hie McKain	L	5	6	.455	3.68	4	32	11	4	129.2	120	54	49	66	53	1	8.33	3.75	3.40
d Hutchinson	R	3	6	.333	5.21	0	13	12	3	84.2	95	51	22	56	49	0	10.10	5.42	2.34
d Thomas	R	7	0	1.000	4.18	1	27	0	0	47.1	45	20	14	25	22	0	8.56	3.80	2.66
k Coffman	R	2	1	.667	6.38	0	23	1	0	42.1	51	22	10	36	30	0	10.84	4.68	2.13
ry Eisenstat	L	2	2	.500	6.98	0	10	2	1	29.2	39	9	6	24	23	0	11.83	2.73	1.82
n Kennedy	R	0	3*	.000	6.43	0	4	4	1	21	25	9	9	15	15	0	10.71	3.86	3.86
Harris	R	1	1	.500	4.00	0	5	1	0	18	18	8	9	8	8	0	9.00	4.00	4.50
yd Giebell	R	1	1	.500	2.93	0	9	0	0	15.1	19	12	9	7	5	0	11.15	7.04	5.28
ton Pippen	R	0	1	.000	7.07	0	3	2	0	14	18	6	5	13	11	0	11.57	3.86	3.21
Walkup	R	0	1	.000	7.50	0	7	0	0	12	15	8	5	10	10	0	11.25	6.00	3.75
ie Lawson	R	1	1	.500	4.76	0	2	1	0	11.1	7	7	4	7	6	0	5.56	5.56	3.18
rge Gill	R	0	1	.000	8.31	0	3	1	0	8.2	14	3	1	8	8	0	14.54	3.12	1.04
Lynn	R	0	1	.000	8.64	0	4	0	0	8.1	11	3	3	8	8	0	11.88	3.24	3.24
Newhouser	L	0	1	.000	5.40	0	1	1	1	5	3	4	4	3	3	0	5.40	7.20	7.20
AM TOTAL		81	73	.526	4.29	16	305	155	64	1367.1	1430	574	633	762	652	7	9.41	3.78	4.17

MANAGER	W	L	PCT
Del Baker	90	64	.584

POS	Player	B	G	AB	H	2B	3B	HR	HR %	R	RBI	BB	SO	SB	Pinch Hit AB	Pinch Hit H	BA	SA
REGULARS																		
1B	Rudy York	R	155	588	186	46	6	33	5.6	105	134	89	88	3	0	0	.316	.583
2B	Charlie Gehringer	L	139	515	161	33	3	10	1.9	108	81	101	17	10	1	0	.313	.447
SS	Dick Bartell	R	139	528	123	24	3	7	1.3	76	53	76	53	12	0	0	.233	.330
3B	Pinky Higgins	R	131	480	130	24	3	13	2.7	70	76	61	31	4	1	0	.271	.415
RF	Pete Fox	R	93	350	101	17	4	5	1.4	49	48	21	30	7	9	1	.289	.403
CF	Barney McCosky	L	143	589	200	39	19	4	0.7	123	57	67	41	13	2	1	.340	.491
LF	Hank Greenberg	R	148	573	195	50	8	41	7.2	129	150	93	75	6	0	0	.340	.670
C	Birdie Tebbetts	R	111	379	112	24	4	4	1.1	46	46	35	14	4	2	0	.296	.412
SUBSTITUTES																		
3S	Red Kress	R	33	99	22	3	1	1	1.0	13	11	10	12	0	5	3	.222	.303
2B	Dutch Meyer	R	23	58	15	3	0	0	0.0	12	6	4	10	2	3	0	.259	.310
S2	Frank Croucher	R	37	57	6	0	0	0	0.0	3	2	4	5	0	5	0	.105	.105
23	Scat Metha	R	26	37	9	0	1	0	0.0	6	3	2	8	0	2	0	.243	.297
OF	Bruce Campbell	L	103	297	84	15	5	8	2.7	56	44	45	28	2	23	9	.283	.448
OF	Earl Averill	L	64	118	33	4	1	2	1.7	10	20	5	14	0	38	12	.280	.381
OF	Tuck Stainback	R	15	40	9	2	0	0	0.0	4	1	1	9	0	5	1	.225	.275
OF	Pat Mullin	L	4	4	0	0	0	0	0.0	0	0	0	0	0	3	0	.000	.000
C	Billy Sullivan	L	78	220	68	14	4	3	1.4	36	41	31	11	2	15	5	.309	.450
PH	Frank Secory	R	1	1	0	0	0	0	0.0	0	0	0	1	0	1	0	.000	.000
PITCHERS																		
P	Bobo Newsom	R	36	107	23	5	0	0	0.0	9	16	1	17	0	0	0	.215	.262
P	Tommy Bridges	R	29	68	12	2	0	0	0.0	5	4	3	23	0	0	0	.176	.206
P	Schoolboy Rowe	R	27	67	18	6	1	1	1.5	7	18	5	13	1	0	0	.269	.433
P	Johnny Gorsica	R	29	62	12	0	2	1	1.6	6	7	3	15	0	0	0	.194	.306
P	Hal Newhouser	L	28	40	8	0	0	0	0.0	3	2	3	4	0	0	0	.200	.200
P	Dizzy Trout	R	33	31	4	0	0	0	0.0	4	4	2	9	0	0	0	.129	.129
P	Fred Hutchinson	L	17	30	8	1	0	0	0.0	1	2	0	0	0	0	0	.267	.300
P	Lynn Nelson	L	19	23	8	0	0	1	4.3	4	3	0	6	0	14	5	.348	.478
P	Al Benton	R	42	17	0	0	0	0	0.0	0	0	0	8	0	0	0	.000	.000
P	Tom Seats	B	26	12	1	0	0	0	0.0	0	0	0	2	0	0	0	.083	.083
P	Cotton Pippen	R	4	8	0	0	0	0	0.0	0	0	0	2	0	0	0	.000	.000
P	Archie McKain	B	27	7	1	0	0	0	0.0	3	0	2	4	0	0	0	.143	.143
P	Clay Smith	R	14	7	0	0	0	0	0.0	0	0	0	4	0	0	0	.000	.000
P	Floyd Giebell	L	2	6	0	0	0	0	0.0	0	0	0	0	0	0	0	.000	.000
P	Dick Conger	R	2	0	0	0	0	0	–	0	0	0	0	0	0	0	–	–
P	Bud Thomas	R	3	0	0	0	0	0	–	0	0	0	0	0	0	0	–	–
P	Bob Uhle	B	1	0	0	0	0	0	–	0	0	0	0	0	0	0	–	–
	TEAM TOTAL			5418	1549	312	65	134	2.5	888	829	664	554	66	129	37	.286	.442

INDIVIDUAL FIELDING

POS	Player	T	G	PO	A	E	DP	TC/G	FA
1B	R. York	R	155	1390	107	15	101	9.8	.990
2B	C. Gehringer	R	138	276	374	19	72	4.8	.972
	D. Meyer	R	21	28	44	3	6	3.6	.960
	S. Metha	R	10	9	15	1	3	2.5	.960
	F. Croucher	R	7	4	2	0	1	0.9	1.000
SS	D. Bartell	R	139	295	394	34	74	5.2	.953
	F. Croucher	R	26	17	27	3	2	1.8	.936
	R. Kress	R	12	25	33	3	5	5.1	.951
3B	P. Higgins	R	129	133	239	29	16	3.1	.928
	R. Kress	R	17	20	41	5	1	3.9	.924
	B. Sullivan	R	6	4	14	2	1	3.3	.900
	S. Metha	R	6	1	12	1	0	2.3	.929
	F. Croucher	R	1	2	1	2	0	5.0	.600

POS	Player	T	G	PO	A	E	DP	TC/G	FA
OF	B. McCosky	R	141	349	7	6	2	2.6	.983
	H. Greenberg	R	148	298	14	15	1	2.2	.954
	P. Fox	R	85	169	6	6	0	2.1	.967
	B. Campbell	R	74	133	6	6	0	2.0	.959
	E. Averill	R	22	23	2	1	0	1.2	.962
	P. Mullin	R	1	0	0	0	0	0.0	.000
	T. Stainback	R	9	26	4	1	0	3.4	.968
C	B. Tebbetts	R	107	572	89	17	10	6.3	.975
	B. Sullivan	R	57	292	29	8	4	5.8	.976

During the winter general manager Jack Zeller gave a dubious Hank Greenberg an extra $10,000 to play left field. The experiment, designed to find a home for Rudy York at first base, proved a magnificent success. Greenberg-York became a mighty one-two punch. Greenberg won his second MVP Award (the only American Leaguer ever to win it at different positions), batting .340 with a league-leading 41 home runs and 150 RBI. York batted .316 with 33 home runs and a league second-best 134 RBI. Leading the league in batting average and runs, the Tigers, 26 1/2 games out the previous season, won the pennant.

Detroit also was helped by the Indians, who were fighting the Tigers for the pennant. On June 13, a number of players had petitioned the Cleveland owner to fire manager (and former Tiger) Ossie Vitt. The turmoil hampered the Indians' pennant run, and branded them the Cry Babies for the rest of the summer. During one late-season trip to Briggs Stadium, baby bottles—complete with nipples—were attached to strings, lowered from the upper deck, and dangled before the Cleveland dugout.

Still, the pennant hinged on a final three-game series in Cleveland. With a two-game lead, Detroit needed to win just one. With deadly fireballer Bob Feller pitching the opener, Del Baker surprisingly countered with little-known rookie Floyd Giebell. The result: the crowd repeatedly showered the field with garbage—in the bullpen, Birdie Tebbetts was knocked out when a fan dropped a basket of bottles and fruit on him—but Giebell outdueled Feller, 2–0, to clinch the flag. Against the Reds in the World Series, Newsom won two games, Tommy Bridges one to set up a Game 7 showdown in Cincinnati. But pitching on one day's rest, Newsom lost the World Championship to Paul Derringer, 2–1, on seventh-inning doubles by Frank McCormick and Jim Ripple and a sacrifice fly by Billy Myers.

TEAM STATISTICS

	W	L	PCT	GB	R	OR	Batting 2B	3B	HR	BA	SA	SB	Fielding E	DP	FA	Pitching CG	BB	SO	ShO	SV	ERA
T	90	64	.584		888	717	312	65	134	.286	.442	66	194	116	.968	59	570	752	10	23	4.01
E	89	65	.578	1	710	637	287	61	101	.265	.398	53	149	164	.975	72	512	686	13	22	3.63
	88	66	.571	2	817	671	243	66	155	.259	.418	59	152	158	.975	76	511	559	10	14	3.89
S	82	72	.532	8	872	825	301	80	145	.286	.449	55	173	158	.972	51	625	613	4	16	4.89
I	82	72	.532	8	735	672	238	63	73	.278	.387	52	185	125	.969	83	480	574	10	18	3.74
	67	87	.435	23	757	882	278	58	118	.263	.401	51	158	179	.974	64	646	439	4	9	5.12
S	64	90	.416	26	665	811	266	67	52	.271	.374	94	194	166	.968	74	618	618	6	7	4.59
	54	100	.351	36	703	932	242	53	105	.262	.387	48	238	131	.960	72	534	488	4	12	5.22
GUE TOTAL					6147	6147	2167	513	883	.271	.407	478	1443	1195	.970	551	4496	4729	61	121	4.38

INDIVIDUAL PITCHING

CHER	T	W	L	PCT	ERA	SV	G	GS	CG	IP	H	BB	SO	R	ER	ShO	H/9	BB/9	SO/9
o Newsom	R	21	5	.808	2.83	0	36	34	20	264	235	100	164	110	83	3	8.01	3.41	5.59
nmy Bridges	R	12	9	.571	3.37	0	29	28	12	197.2	171	88	133	89	74	2	7.79	4.01	6.06
oolboy Rowe	R	16	3	.842	3.46	0	27	23	11	169	170	43	61	68	65	1	9.05	2.29	3.25
nny Gorsica	R	7	7	.500	4.33	0	29	20	5	160	170	57	68	85	77	2	9.56	3.21	3.83
Newhouser	L	9	9	.500	4.86	0	28	20	7	133.1	149	76	89	81	72	0	10.06	5.13	6.01
zy Trout	R	3	7	.300	4.47	2	33	10	1	100.2	125	54	64	60	50	0	11.18	4.83	5.72
3enton	R	6	10	.375	4.42	17	42	0	0	79.1	93	36	50	44	39	0	10.55	4.08	5.67
d Hutchinson	R	3	7	.300	5.68	0	17	10	1	76	85	26	32	52	48	0	10.07	3.08	3.79
n Seats	L	2	2	.500	4.69	1	26	2	0	55.2	67	21	25	43	29	0	10.83	3.40	4.04
hie McKain	L	5	0	1.000	2.82	3	27	0	0	51	48	25	24	18	16	0	8.47	4.41	4.24
y Smith	R	1	1	.500	5.08	0	14	1	0	28.1	32	13	14	18	16	0	10.16	4.13	4.45
ton Pippen	R	1	2	.333	6.75	0	4	3	0	21.1	29	10	9	16	16	0	12.23	4.22	3.80
vd Giebell	R	2	0	1.000	1.00	0	2	2	2	18	14	4	11	2	2	1	7.00	2.00	5.50
n Nelson	R	1	1	.500	10.93	0	6	2	0	14	23	9	7	19	17	0	14.79	5.79	4.50
Thomas	R	0	1	.000	9.00	0	3	0	0	4	8	3	0	5	4	0	18.00	6.75	0.00
x Conger	R	1	0	1.000	3.00	0	2	0	0	3	2	3	1	1	1	0	6.00	9.00	3.00
Uhle	L	0	0	–	0.00	0	1	0	0	4	2	0	0	5	4	0	∞	∞	–
M TOTAL		90	64	.584	4.01	23	326	155	59	1375.1	1425	570	752	716	613	9	9.33	3.73	4.92

MANAGER	W	L	PCT
Del Baker	75	79	.487

POS	Player	B	G	AB	H	2B	3B	HR	HR %	R	RBI	BB	SO	SB	Pinch Hit AB	Pinch Hit H	BA	SA
REGULARS																		
1B	Rudy York	R	155	590	153	29	3	27	4.6	91	111	92	88	3	0	0	.259	.456
2B	Charlie Gehringer	L	127	436	96	19	4	3	0.7	65	46	95	26	1	10	3	.220	.303
SS	Frank Croucher	R	136	489	124	21	4	2	0.4	51	39	33	72	2	0	0	.254	.325
3B	Pinky Higgins	R	147	540	161	28	3	11	2.0	79	73	67	45	5	2	0	.298	.422
RF	Bruce Campbell	L	141	512	141	28	10	15	2.9	72	93	68	67	3	5	2	.275	.457
CF	Barney McCosky	L	127	494	160	25	8	3	0.6	80	55	61	33	8	4	4	.324	.425
LF	Rip Radcliff	L	96	379	120	14	5	3	0.8	47	39	19	13	4	8	0	.317	.404
C	Birdie Tebbetts	R	110	359	102	19	4	2	0.6	28	47	38	29	1	12	3	.284	.376
SUBSTITUTES																		
2B	Dutch Meyer	R	46	153	29	9	1	1	0.7	12	14	8	13	1	6	2	.190	.281
S2	Boyd Perry	R	36	83	15	5	0	0	0.0	9	11	10	9	1	0	0	.181	.241
3S	Eric McNair	R	23	59	11	1	0	0	0.0	5	3	4	4	0	9	3	.186	.203
SS	Dick Bartell	R	5	12	2	1	0	0	0.0	0	1	2	2	0	0	0	.167	.250
SS	Murray Franklin	R	13	10	3	1	0	0	0.0	1	0	2	2	0	7	2	.300	.400
OF	Pat Mullin	L	54	220	76	11	5	5	2.3	42	23	18	18	5	2	0	.345	.509
OF	Tuck Stainback	R	94	200	49	8	1	2	1.0	19	10	3	21	6	8	1	.245	.325
OF	Hank Greenberg	R	19	67	18	5	1	2	3.0	12	12	16	12	1	0	0	.269	.463
OF	Bob Harris	L	26	61	13	3	1	1	1.6	11	4	6	13	1	11	1	.213	.344
OF	Bob Patrick	R	5	7	2	0	0	0	0.0	2	0	0	1	0	2	1	.286	.286
OF	Dick Wakefield	L	7	7	1	0	0	0	0.0	0	0	0	1	0	6	1	.143	.143
OF	Hoot Evers	R	1	4	0	0	0	0	0.0	0	0	0	2	0	0	0	.000	.000
C	Billy Sullivan	L	85	234	66	15	1	3	1.3	29	29	35	11	0	21	6	.282	.393
PH	Fred Hutchinson	L	2	2	0	0	0	0	0.0	0	0	0	2	0	2	0	.000	.000
PITCHERS																		
P	Bobo Newsom	R	43	88	9	0	0	0	0.0	3	3	2	20	0	0	0	.102	.102
P	Hal Newhouser	L	33	60	9	0	0	0	0.0	3	2	3	8	1	0	0	.150	.150
P	Johnny Gorsica	R	33	57	17	1	0	0	0.0	5	3	6	7	0	0	0	.298	.316
P	Schoolboy Rowe	R	32	55	15	0	3	1	1.8	10	12	5	8	0	5	3	.273	.436
P	Al Benton	R	38	50	3	1	0	0	0.0	0	2	0	20	0	0	0	.060	.080
P	Dizzy Trout	R	40	50	9	1	1	0	0.0	5	5	4	10	0	0	0	.180	.240
P	Tommy Bridges	R	25	47	4	1	0	0	0.0	2	1	4	11	0	0	0	.085	.106
P	Bud Thomas	R	26	19	2	1	0	0	0.0	0	0	0	4	0	0	0	.105	.158
P	Archie McKain	L	15	11	0	0	0	0	0.0	1	0	1	5	0	0	0	.000	.000
P	Floyd Giebell	L	17	6	2	0	0	0	0.0	0	0	0	1	0	0	0	.333	.333
P	Hal Manders	R	8	4	0	0	0	0	0.0	0	0	0	1	0	0	0	.000	.000
P	Les Mueller	R	4	3	0	0	0	0	0.0	0	0	0	3	0	0	0	.000	.000
P	Hal White	L	4	2	0	0	0	0	0.0	0	0	0	1	0	0	0	.000	.000
P	Earl Cook	R	1	0	0	0	0	0	–	0	0	0	0	0	0	0	–	–
P	Virgil Trucks	R	1	0	0	0	0	0	–	0	0	0	0	0	0	0	–	–
	TEAM TOTAL			5370	1412	247	55	81	1.5	686	636	602	583	43	120	32	.263	.375

INDIVIDUAL FIELDING

POS	Player	T	G	PO	A	E	DP	TC/G	FA
1B	R. York	R	155	1393	110	**21**	111	9.8	.986
2B	C. Gehringer	R	116	279	324	11	59	5.3	**.982**
	D. Meyer	R	40	107	101	6	19	5.4	.972
	B. Perry	R	11	18	15	2	2	3.2	.943
SS	F. Croucher	R	136	270	361	44	85	5.0	.935
	B. Perry	R	25	28	47	2	10	3.1	.974
	D. Bartell	R	5	12	11	2	2	5.0	.920
	E. McNair	R	3	2	4	1	1	2.3	.857
	M. Franklin	R	4	1	2	1	1	1.0	.750
3B	P. Higgins	R	145	153	304	26	14	3.3	.946
	M. Franklin	R	1	0	0	0	0	0.0	.000
	E. McNair	R	11	12	20	1	0	3.0	.970

POS	Player	T	G	PO	A	E	DP	TC/G	FA
OF	B. McCosky	R	122	328	6	5	2	2.8	.985
	B. Campbell	R	133	241	5	6	1	1.9	.976
	R. Radcliff	L	87	155	6	5	1	1.9	.970
	P. Mullin	R	51	117	2	7	0	2.5	.944
	T. Stainback	R	80	107	3	6	0	1.5	.948
	H. Greenberg	R	19	32	0	3	0	1.8	.914
	H. Evers	R	1	0	0	0	0	0.0	.000
	B. Harris	L	12	16	0	0	0	1.3	1.000
	B. Patrick	R	3	3	0	1	0	1.3	.750
	D. Wakefield	R	1	1	0	0	0	1.0	1.000
C	B. Tebbetts	R	98	461	**83**	13	11	**5.7**	.977
	B. Sullivan	R	63	339	33	9	7	6.0	.976

On May 7, 19 games into the season, Hank Greenberg answered greetings from Uncle Sam; he was the first American Leaguer drafted. As U.S. involvement in the war loomed closer, Detroit fans were livid, but Greenberg served. Meanwhile, his Tiger mates forged a forgettable postpennant season, tying for fourth, 26 games out. Detroit fans in turn stayed away from the ballpark, attendance plunging nearly a half-million.

The biggest disappointment was Bobo Newsom, who had secured a substantial raise. He responded by leading the league in losses at 12–20 with a 4.60 ERA. With their best hitter away in khaki, the Tigers lost much of their punch. Only two hit .300: centerfielder Barney McCosky (.324) and leftfielder Rip Radcliff (.311), obtained early in the season from the Browns. The summer's finest moment at Briggs Stadium came during the All-Star Game. The 54,674 attending erupted in celebration when the Americans won on a two-out, three-run, bottom-of-the-ninth home run by Boston's Ted Williams.

Detroit also made history in late June when the Tigers outbid at least 10 other teams to sign baseball's first bonus baby. Michigan State star Dick Wakefield was offered $52,000 and a car to become a Tiger. So Wakefield, who beforehand didn't know how to drive, signed, and then unwisely selected a Ford Lincoln, apparently not knowing that team owner Briggs made Chryslers and Packards.

TEAM STATISTICS

W	L	PCT	GB	R	OR	2B	Batting 3B	HR	BA	SA	SB	E	Fielding DP	FA	CG	BB	Pitching SO	ShO	SV	ERA
101	53	.656		830	631	243	60	151	.269	.419	51	165	196	.973	75	598	589	13	26	3.53
S 84	70	.545	17	865	750	304	55	124	.283	.430	67	172	139	.972	70	611	574	8	11	4.19
77	77	.500	24	638	649	245	47	47	.255	.343	91	180	145	.971	106	521	564	14	4	3.52
75	79	.487	26	677	668	249	84	103	.256	.393	63	142	158	.976	68	660	617	10	19	3.90
T 75	79	.487	26	686	743	247	55	81	.263	.375	43	186	129	.969	52	645	697	8	16	4.18
70	84	.455	31	765	823	281	58	91	.266	.390	50	151	156	.975	65	549	454	7	10	4.72
S 70	84	.455	31	728	798	257	80	52	.272	.376	79	187	169	.969	69	603	544	8	7	4.35
64	90	.416	37	713	840	240	69	85	.268	.387	27	200	150	.967	64	557	386	3	18	4.83
GUE TOTAL				5902	5902	2066	508	734	.266	.389	471	1383	1242	.972	569	4744	4425	71	111	4.15

INDIVIDUAL PITCHING

CHER	T	W	L	PCT	ERA	SV	G	GS	CG	IP	H	BB	SO	R	ER	ShO	H/9	BB/9	SO/9
o Newsom	R	12	20	.375	4.60	2	43	36	12	250.1	265	118	175	140	128	2	9.53	4.24	6.29
Newhouser	L	9	11	.450	4.79	0	33	27	5	173	166	137	106	109	92	1	8.64	7.13	5.51
nny Gorsica	R	9	11	.450	4.47	2	33	21	8	171	193	55	59	98	85	1	10.16	2.89	3.11
Benton	R	15	6	.714	2.97	7	38	14	7	157.2	130	65	63	63	52	1	7.42	3.71	3.60
zy Trout	R	9	9	.500	3.74	2	37	18	6	151.2	144	84	88	76	63	1	8.55	4.98	5.22
nmy Bridges	R	9	12	.429	3.41	0	25	22	10	147.2	128	70	90	66	56	1	7.80	4.27	5.49
oolboy Rowe	R	8	6	.571	4.14	1	27	14	4	139	155	33	54	70	64	0	10.04	2.14	3.50
Thomas	R	1	3	.250	4.21	2	26	1	0	72.2	74	22	17	45	34	0	9.17	2.72	2.11
hie McKain	L	2	1	.667	5.02	0	15	0	0	43	58	11	14	24	24	0	12.14	2.30	2.93
d Giebell	R	0	0	–	6.03	0	17	2	0	34.1	45	26	10	29	23	0	11.80	6.82	2.62
Manders	R	1	0	1.000	2.35	0	8	0	0	15.1	13	8	7	5	4	0	7.63	4.70	4.11
Mueller	R	0	0	–	4.85	0	4	0	0	13	9	10	8	9	7	0	6.23	6.92	5.54
White	R	0	0	–	6.00	0	4	0	0	9	11	6	2	6	6	0	11.00	6.00	2.00
Cook	R	0	0	–	4.50	0	1	0	0	2	4	0	1	1	1	0	18.00	0.00	4.50
il Trucks	R	0	0	–	9.00	0	1	0	0	2	4	0	3	2	2	0	18.00	0.00	13.50
M TOTAL		75	79	.487	4.18	16	312	155	52	1381.2	1399	645	697	743	641	7	9.11	4.20	4.54

MANAGER	W	L	PCT
Del Baker	73	81	.474

POS	Player	B	G	AB	H	2B	3B	HR	HR %	R	RBI	BB	SO	SB	Pinch Hit AB	Pinch Hit H	BA	SA
REGULARS																		
1B	Rudy York	R	153	577	150	26	4	21	3.6	81	90	73	71	3	1	1	.260	.428
2B	Jimmy Bloodworth	R	137	533	129	23	1	13	2.4	62	57	35	63	2	1	0	.242	.362
SS	Billy Hitchcock	R	85	280	59	8	1	0	0.0	27	29	26	21	2	0	0	.211	.246
3B	Pinky Higgins	R	143	499	133	34	2	11	2.2	65	79	72	21	3	5	0	.267	.409
RF	Bob Harris	L	121	398	108	16	10	9	2.3	53	45	49	35	5	15	6	.271	.430
CF	Doc' Cramer	L	151	630	166	26	4	0	0.0	71	43	43	18	4	1	1	.263	.317
LF	Barney McCosky	L	154	600	176	28	11	7	1.2	75	50	68	37	11	0	0	.293	.412
C	Birdie Tebbetts	R	99	308	76	11	0	1	0.3	24	27	39	17	4	2	2	.247	.292
SUBSTITUTES																		
SS	Murray Franklin	R	48	154	40	7	0	2	1.3	24	16	7	5	0	5	0	.260	.344
SS	Johnny Lipon	R	34	131	25	2	0	0	0.0	5	9	7	7	1	0	0	.191	.206
SS	Eric McNair	R	26	68	11	2	0	1	1.5	5	4	3	5	0	5	1	.162	.235
2B	Dutch Meyer	R	14	52	17	3	0	2	3.8	5	9	4	4	0	0	0	.327	.423
2B	Charlie Gehringer	L	45	45	12	0	0	1	2.2	6	7	7	4	0	38	11	.267	.333
O3	Don Ross	R	87	226	62	10	2	3	1.3	29	30	36	16	2	22	8	.274	.376
OF	Rip Radcliff	L	62	144	36	5	0	1	0.7	13	20	9	6	0	29	3	.250	.306
OF	Bob Patrick	R	4	8	2	1	0	1	12.5	1	3	1	0	0	1	0	.250	.750
C	Dixie Parsons	R	63	188	37	4	0	2	1.1	8	11	13	22	1	1	0	.197	.250
C	Hank Riebe	R	11	35	11	2	0	0	0.0	1	2	0	6	0	0	0	.314	.371
C	Al Unser	R	4	8	3	0	0	0	0.0	2	0	0	2	0	0	0	.375	.375
PITCHERS																		
P	Hal White	L	34	77	13	1	0	0	0.0	7	2	3	25	0	0	0	.169	.182
P	Dizzy Trout	R	36	75	16	3	0	1	1.3	9	7	4	16	1	0	0	.213	.293
P	Al Benton	R	35	67	5	1	0	0	0.0	3	0	0	32	0	0	0	.075	.090
P	Virgil Trucks	R	28	65	8	1	0	0	0.0	4	3	0	12	0	0	0	.123	.138
P	Tommy Bridges	R	23	63	6	1	1	0	0.0	5	2	5	12	0	0	0	.095	.143
P	Hal Newhouser	L	39	52	8	2	0	0	0.0	3	1	3	8	0	0	0	.154	.192
P	Charlie Fuchs	B	9	13	1	0	0	0	0.0	0	1	0	3	0	0	0	.077	.077
P	Roy Henshaw	R	23	12	1	0	0	0	0.0	0	0	1	2	0	0	0	.083	.083
P	Johnny Gorsica	R	31	10	1	0	1	0	0.0	2	0	0	1	0	0	0	.100	.300
P	Hal Manders	R	18	4	1	0	0	0	0.0	1	0	0	0	0	0	0	.250	.250
P	Schoolboy Rowe	R	2	4	0	0	0	0	0.0	0	0	0	0	0	0	0	.000	.000
P	Jack Wilson	R	9	1	0	0	0	0	0.0	0	0	0	1	0	0	0	.000	.000
TEAM TOTAL				5327	1313	217	37	76	1.4	589	547	508	472	39	126	33	.246	.344

INDIVIDUAL FIELDING

POS	Player	T	G	PO	A	E	DP	TC/G	FA		POS	Player	T	G	PO	A	E	DP	TC/G	FA
1B	R. York	R	152	1413	146	19	117	10.4	.988		OF	D. Cramer	R	150	352	15	7	6	2.5	.981
	R. Radcliff	L	4	40	5	0	0	11.3	1.000			B. McCosky	R	154	351	7	7	2	2.4	.981
2B	J. Bloodworth	R	134	334	431	22	66	5.9	.972			B. Harris	L	104	164	5	10	2	1.7	.944
	D. Meyer	R	14	31	56	1	14	6.3	.989			D. Ross	R	38	77	4	3	2	2.2	.964
	M. Franklin	R	7	15	13	1	3	4.1	.966			R. Radcliff	L	24	43	1	1	1	1.9	.978
	C. Gehringer	R	3	7	9	0	1	5.3	1.000			B. Patrick	R	3	5	0	0	0	1.7	1.000
SS	B. Hitchcock	R	80	157	199	21	39	4.7	.944		C	B. Tebbetts	R	97	446	69	12	10	5.4	.977
	J. Lipon	R	34	85	103	11	24	5.9	.945			D. Parsons	R	62	274	44	6	6	5.2	.981
	M. Franklin	R	32	67	79	5	14	4.7	.967			H. Riebe	R	11	42	5	0	1	4.3	1.000
	E. McNair	R	21	27	32	8	6	3.2	.881			A. Unser	R	4	11	3	0	0	3.5	1.000
	J. Bloodworth	R	2	2	0	0	0	1.0	1.000											
3B	P. Higgins	R	137	134	243	30	24	3.0	.926											
	D. Ross	R	20	17	26	4	2	2.4	.915											
	B. Hitchcock	R	1	0	0	0	0	0.0	.000											

World War II started taking its toll. Owner Walter O. Briggs, Sr., his automobile factories turning out tanks, concentrated on war business, leaving general manager Jack Zeller to run the team. Attendance dropped another 100,000 to 580,000, lowest in ten years. Hank Greenberg was already in the military; Charlie Gehringer followed in the fall, playing his 2,323rd and final game and finishing with a .320 lifetime average. The Tigers fell out of the first division to fifth place, 30 games out. For the first time since 1906, no Tiger hit .300. Barney McCosky led at .293. The Tigers as a team hit .246, tied for worst in the league. Zeller tried to help. Before the season, the Tigers had forged a helpful trade: outfielder Bruce Campbell and shortstop Frank Crowder to Washington for centerfielder Doc Cramer and second baseman Jimmy Bloodworth.

Bobo Newsom's salary was cut $20,000 in the spring, prompting a holdout. Zeller responded by selling the 35-year-old right-hander to the Senators. In the spring, 32-year-old Schoolboy Rowe had proved ineffective again and was sold to Brooklyn. Thus the pitching fell to Virgil Trucks, Hal White, and Hal Newhouser, all hurt by their mates' weak hitting; each owned ERAs under three, but Trucks finished 14–8, White 12–12, and Newhouser 8–14. Reliever Al Benton started almost exclusively and pitched five brilliant innings in the All-Star Game, but wasn't nearly as effective against the American League (7–13). And to punctuate the season, manager Del Baker was fired.

TEAM STATISTICS

	W	L	PCT	GB	R	OR	2B	3B	HR	BA	SA	SB	E	DP	FA	CG	BB	SO	ShO	SV	ERA
	103	51	.669		801	507	223	57	108	.269	.394	69	142	190	.976	88	431	558	18	17	2.91
S	93	59	.612	9	761	594	244	55	103	.276	.403	68	157	156	.974	84	553	500	11	17	3.44
L	82	69	.543	19.5	730	637	239	62	98	.259	.385	37	167	143	.972	68	505	488	12	13	3.59
E	75	79	.487	28	590	659	223	58	50	.253	.345	69	163	175	.974	61	560	448	12	11	3.59
T	73	81	.474	30	589	587	217	37	76	.246	.344	39	194	142	.969	65	598	671	12	14	3.13
ll	66	82	.446	34	538	609	214	36	25	.246	.318	114	173	144	.970	86	473	432	8	8	3.58
S	62	89	.411	39.5	653	817	224	49	40	.258	.341	98	222	133	.962	68	558	496	12	11	4.58
l	55	99	.357	48	549	801	213	46	33	.249	.325	44	188	124	.969	67	639	546	5	9	4.48
GUE TOTAL					5211	5211	1797	400	533	.257	.357	538	1406	1207	.971	587	4317	4139	90	100	3.66

INDIVIDUAL PITCHING

CHER	T	W	L	PCT	ERA	SV	G	GS	CG	IP	H	BB	SO	R	ER	ShO	H/9	BB/9	SO/9
Benton	R	7	13	.350	2.90	2	35	30	9	226.2	210	84	110	87	73	1	8.34	3.34	4.37
zy Trout	R	12	18	.400	3.43	0	35	29	13	223	214	89	91	98	85	1	8.64	3.59	3.67
White	R	12	12	.500	2.91	1	34	25	12	216.2	212	82	93	80	70	4	8.81	3.41	3.86
Newhouser	L	8	14	.364	2.45	5	38	23	11	183.2	137	114	103	73	50	1	6.71	5.59	5.05
mmy Bridges	R	9	7	.563	2.74	1	23	22	11	174	164	61	97	66	53	2	8.48	3.16	5.02
gil Trucks	R	14	8	.636	2.74	0	28	20	8	167.2	147	74	91	64	51	2	7.89	3.97	4.88
Henshaw	L	2	4	.333	4.09	1	23	2	0	61.2	63	27	24	32	28	0	9.19	3.94	3.50
nny Gorsica	R	3	2	.600	4.75	4	28	0	0	53	63	26	19	31	28	0	10.70	4.42	3.23
arlie Fuchs	R	3	3	.500	6.63	0	9	4	1	36.2	43	19	15	27	27	1	10.55	4.66	3.68
Manders	R	2	0	1.000	4.09	0	18	0	0	33	39	15	14	19	15	0	10.64	4.09	3.82
k Wilson	R	0	0	–	4.85	0	9	0	0	13	20	5	7	8	7	0	13.85	3.46	4.85
oolboy Rowe	R	1	0	1.000	0.00	0	2	1	0	10.1	9	2	7	2	0	0	7.84	1.74	6.10
AM TOTAL		73	81	.474	3.13	14	282	156	65	1399.1	1321	598	671	587	487	12	8.50	3.85	4.32

MANAGER	W	L	PCT
Steve O'Neill	78	76	.506

POS	Player	B	G	AB	H	2B	3B	HR	HR%	R	RBI	BB	SO	SB	Pinch Hit AB	Pinch Hit H	BA	SA
REGULARS																		
1B	Rudy York	R	155	571	155	22	11	34	6.0	90	118	84	88	5	0	0	.271	**.527**
2B	Jimmy Bloodworth	R	129	474	114	23	4	6	1.3	41	52	29	59	4	0	0	.241	.344
SS	Joe Hoover	R	144	575	140	15	8	4	0.7	78	38	36	101	6	0	0	.243	.318
3B	Pinky Higgins	R	138	523	145	20	1	10	1.9	62	84	57	31	2	0	0	.277	.377
RF	Bob Harris	L	114	354	90	14	3	6	1.7	43	32	47	29	6	18	5	.254	.362
CF	Doc Cramer	L	140	606	182	18	4	1	0.2	79	43	31	13	4	2	1	.300	.348
LF	Dick Wakefield	L	155	**633**	**200**	38	8	7	1.1	91	79	62	60	4	0	0	.316	.434
C	Paul Richards	R	100	313	69	7	1	5	1.6	32	33	38	35	1	0	0	.220	.297
SUBSTITUTES																		
23	Joe Wood	R	60	164	53	4	4	1	0.6	22	17	6	13	2	10	3	.323	.415
UT	Don Ross	R	89	247	66	13	0	0	0.0	19	18	20	3	2	24	5	.267	.320
OF	Rip Radcliff	L	70	115	30	4	0	0	0.0	3	10	13	3	1	44	11	.261	.296
OF	Jimmy Outlaw	R	20	67	18	1	0	1	1.5	8	6	8	4	0	4	1	.269	.328
OF	Charlie Metro	R	44	40	8	0	0	0	0.0	12	2	3	6	1	2	0	.200	.200
C	Dixie Parsons	R	40	106	15	3	0	0	0.0	2	4	6	16	0	0	0	.142	.170
C	Al Unser	R	38	101	25	5	0	0	0.0	14	4	15	15	0	0	0	.248	.297
PH	John McHale	L	4	3	0	0	0	0	0.0	0	0	1	1	0	3	0	.000	.000
PITCHERS																		
P	Dizzy Trout	R	45	91	20	5	0	1	1.1	9	6	2	8	2	0	0	.220	.308
P	Virgil Trucks	R	33	72	13	1	0	0	0.0	7	7	2	4	0	0	0	.181	.194
P	Hal Newhouser	L	37	65	12	2	0	0	0.0	4	5	3	8	0	0	0	.185	.215
P	Tommy Bridges	R	25	64	14	3	0	0	0.0	4	3	5	14	0	0	0	.219	.266
P	Hal White	L	32	57	8	0	0	0	0.0	4	2	7	18	0	0	0	.140	.140
P	Stubby Overmire	R	29	42	7	0	1	0	0.0	1	2	5	7	0	0	0	.167	.214
P	Prince Oana	R	20	26	10	2	1	1	3.8	5	7	1	2	0	9	3	.385	.654
P	Johnny Gorsica	R	36	23	4	0	1	0	0.0	2	0	1	6	0	0	0	.174	.261
P	Roy Henshaw	R	26	18	2	0	0	0	0.0	0	0	0	2	0	0	0	.111	.111
P	Rufe Gentry	R	4	10	0	0	0	0	0.0	0	0	1	5	0	0	0	.000	.000
P	Joe Orrell	R	10	4	1	0	0	0	0.0	0	0	0	1	0	0	0	.250	.250
TEAM TOTAL				5364	1401	200	47	77	1.4	632	572	483	552	40	116	29	.261	.359

INDIVIDUAL FIELDING

POS	Player	T	G	PO	A	E	DP	TC/G	FA	POS	Player	T	G	PO	A	E	DP	TC/G	FA
1B	R. York	R	155	1349	**149**	15	105	9.8	.990	OF	D. Cramer	R	138	346	9	4	3	2.6	.989
	R. Radcliff	L	1	2	2	0	0	4.0	1.000		D. Wakefield	R	155	314	11	14	1	2.2	.959
2B	J. Bloodworth	R	129	349	393	21	74	5.9	.972		B. Harris	L	96	192	6	8	2	2.1	.961
	J. Wood	R	22	54	41	11	6	4.8	.896		D. Ross	R	38	62	3	1	0	1.7	.985
	D. Ross	R	7	14	19	4	3	5.3	.892		R. Radcliff	L	19	37	1	0	1	2.0	1.000
SS	J. Hoover	R	144	301	393	**41**	84	5.1	.944		J. Outlaw	R	16	32	2	0	0	2.1	1.000
	D. Ross	R	18	29	41	4	7	4.1	.946		C. Metro	R	14	28	0	1	0	2.1	.966
3B	P. Higgins	R	138	156	253	**26**	22	3.2	.940	C	P. Richards	R	100	**537**	86	9	**12**	**6.3**	**.986**
	J. Wood	R	18	16	23	1	0	2.2	.975		D. Parsons	R	40	167	31	5	2	5.1	.975
	D. Ross	R	1	1	2	0	0	3.0	1.000		A. Unser	R	37	143	20	3	4	4.5	.982

The call to arms continued. Besides Charlie Gehringer and Hank Greenberg, Tigers in the military included Barney McCosky, Pat Mullin, Birdie Tebbetts, Al Benton, Freddie Hutchinson, and Johnny Lipon. Former Cleveland skipper Steve O'Neill became manager of Detroit's watered-down collection and nudged the Tigers two games over .500 into fifth place, 20 games out.

The synthetic wartime baseball deflated averages throughout the majors. Of only four American Leaguers who hit .300, two were Tigers: 38-year-old centerfielder Doc Cramer (.300), and bonus baby Dick Wakefield, who distracted Detroit fans with a run at the batting crown before losing to Chicago shortstop Luke Appling in the final week, .328 to .316. Wakefield was nevertheless the only American Leaguer to notch 200 hits. Rudy York, meanwhile, won his sole home-run title with 34 and his only RBI crown with 118, also leading the league in slugging and total bases. Dizzy Trout became Detroit's first 20-game winner in three years at 20–12 with a 2.48 ERA, and tied for first in victories and shutouts (five).

Like everyone on the home front, major leaguers were expected to bear a few burdens. Required to train near home at Evansville, Indiana, the Tigers saw their exhibition schedule wiped out by strict nonessential travel cutbacks. Unable to get to any games without violating edicts of the Office of Defense Transportation, Jack Zeller came up with an idea: the Tigers could play by walking to the White Sox camp in Terre Haute—112 miles away. "Have them carry their uniforms and bats on their backs," Zeller told O'Neill. "There are a few million boys who aren't athletes and are walking 10 to 20 miles a day and they're carrying something heavier than uniforms and bats. You could take five or six days to get there, stopping along the way."

"If they walk," responded O'Neill, "they'll have to go without the manager."

TEAM STATISTICS

	W	L	PCT	GB	R	OR	2B	Batting 3B	HR	BA	SA	SB	Fielding E	DP	FA	CG	BB	Pitching SO	ShO	SV	ERA
Y	98	56	.636		669	542	218	59	100	.256	.376	46	160	166	.974	83	489	653	14	13	**2.93**
AS	84	69	.549	13.5	666	595	245	50	47	.254	.347	142	179	145	.971	61	540	495	16	**21**	3.18
LE	82	71	.536	15.5	600	577	**246**	45	55	.255	.350	47	157	**183**	.975	64	606	585	14	20	3.15
HI	82	72	.532	16	573	594	193	46	33	.247	.320	**173**	166	167	.973	70	501	476	12	19	3.20
ET	78	76	.506	20	632	604	200	47	77	**.261**	.359	40	177	130	.971	67	549	**706**	18	20	3.00
TL	72	80	.474	25	596	604	229	36	78	.245	.349	37	**152**	127	.975	64	**488**	572	10	14	3.41
OS	68	84	.447	29	563	607	223	42	57	.244	.332	86	153	179	**.976**	62	615	513	13	16	3.45
HI	49	105	.318	49	497	717	174	44	26	.232	.297	55	162	148	.973	73	536	503	5	13	4.05
EAGUE TOTAL					4796	4796	1728	369	473	.249	.341	626	1306	1245	.973	544	4324	4503	102	136	3.30

INDIVIDUAL PITCHING

ITCHER	T	W	L	PCT	ERA	SV	G	GS	CG	IP	H	BB	SO	R	ER	ShO	H/9	BB/9	SO/9
izzy Trout	R	**20**	12	.625	2.48	6	44	30	18	246.2	204	101	111	83	68	5	7.44	3.69	4.05
rgil Trucks	R	16	10	.615	2.84	2	33	25	10	202.2	170	52	118	72	64	3	7.55	2.31	5.24
al Newhouser	L	8	17	.320	3.04	1	37	25	10	195.2	163	**111**	144	88	66	1	7.50	5.11	6.62
ommy Bridges	R	12	7	.632	2.39	0	25	22	11	191.2	159	61	124	57	51	3	7.47	2.86	5.82
al White	R	7	12	.368	3.39	2	32	24	7	177.2	150	71	58	84	67	2	7.60	3.60	2.94
ubby Overmire	L	7	6	.538	3.18	1	29	18	8	147	135	38	48	56	52	3	8.27	2.33	2.94
ohnny Gorsica	R	4	5	.444	3.36	5	35	4	1	96.1	88	40	45	43	36	0	8.22	3.74	4.20
oy Henshaw	L	0	2	.000	3.79	2	26	3	0	71.1	75	33	33	35	30	0	9.46	4.16	4.16
rince Oana	R	3	2	.600	4.50	0	10	0	0	34	34	19	15	21	17	0	9.00	5.03	3.97
ufe Gentry	R	1	3	.250	3.68	0	4	4	2	29.1	30	12	8	12	12	0	9.20	3.68	2.45
e Orrell	R	0	0	–	3.72	1	10	0	0	19.1	18	11	2	9	8	0	8.38	5.12	0.93
EAM TOTAL		78	76	.506	3.00	20	285	155	67	1411.2	1226	549	706	560	471	17	7.82	3.50	4.50

MANAGER	W	L	PCT
Steve O'Neill	88	66	.571

POS	Player	B	G	AB	H	2B	3B	HR	HR %	R	RBI	BB	SO	SB	Pinch Hit AB	Pinch Hit H	BA	SA
REGULARS																		
1B	Rudy York	R	151	583	161	27	7	18	3.1	77	98	68	73	5	0	0	.276	.439
2B	Eddie Mayo	L	154	607	151	18	3	5	0.8	76	63	57	23	9	0	0	.249	.313
SS	Joe Hoover	R	120	441	104	20	2	0	0.0	67	29	35	66	7	0	0	.236	.290
3B	Pinky Higgins	R	148	543	161	32	4	7	1.3	79	76	81	34	4	2	1	.297	.409
RF	Jimmy Outlaw	R	139	535	146	20	6	3	0.6	69	57	41	40	7	3	0	.273	.350
CF	Doc Cramer	L	143	578	169	20	9	2	0.3	69	42	37	21	6	2	0	.292	.369
LF	Dick Wakefield	L	78	276	98	15	5	12	4.3	53	53	55	29	2	0	0	.355	.576
C	Paul Richards	R	95	300	71	13	0	3	1.0	24	37	35	30	8	3	0	.237	.310
SUBSTITUTES																		
UT	Joe Orengo	R	46	154	31	10	0	0	0.0	14	10	20	29	1	1	0	.201	.266
2B	Al Unser	R	11	25	3	0	1	1	4.0	2	5	3	2	0	5	2	.120	.320
2B	Don Heffner	R	6	19	4	1	0	0	0.0	0	1	5	1	0	1	0	.211	.263
2B	Red Borom	L	7	14	1	0	0	0	0.0	1	1	2	2	0	2	0	.071	.071
SS	Bubba Floyd	R	3	9	4	1	0	0	0.0	1	0	1	0	0	0	0	.444	.556
2B	Jack Sullivan	R	1	1	0	0	0	0	0.0	0	0	0	0	0	0	0	.000	.000
OF	Chuck Hostetler	L	90	265	79	9	2	0	0.0	42	20	21	31	4	19	4	.298	.347
OF	Don Ross	R	66	167	35	5	0	2	1.2	14	15	14	9	2	24	8	.210	.275
OF	Charlie Metro	R	38	78	15	0	1	0	0.0	8	5	3	10	1	5	2	.192	.218
C	Bob Swift	R	80	247	63	11	4	1	0.4	15	19	27	27	2	4	1	.255	.320
C	Hack Miller	R	5	5	1	0	0	1	20.0	1	3	1	1	0	0	0	.200	.800
PH	John McHale	L	1	1	0	0	0	0	0.0	0	0	0	0	0	1	1	.000	.000
PITCHERS																		
P	Dizzy Trout	R	51	133	36	4	1	5	3.8	18	24	9	28	2	1	0	.271	.429
P	Hal Newhouser	L	47	120	29	4	0	0	0.0	10	5	6	12	1	0	0	.242	.275
P	Rufe Gentry	R	37	76	15	2	0	0	0.0	1	10	1	11	0	0	0	.197	.224
P	Stubby Overmire	R	32	63	11	3	1	0	0.0	4	8	6	8	0	0	0	.175	.254
P	Johnny Gorsica	R	40	52	7	2	1	0	0.0	7	4	2	6	0	0	0	.135	.212
P	Boom-Boom Beck	R	28	22	7	3	0	0	0.0	3	3	0	2	0	0	0	.318	.455
P	Zeb Eaton	R	9	10	1	0	0	0	0.0	1	2	1	1	0	4	0	.100	.100
P	Jake Mooty	R	15	7	1	0	0	0	0.0	0	0	0	0	0	0	0	.143	.143
P	Roy Henshaw	R	7	5	0	0	0	0	0.0	1	0	0	1	0	0	0	.000	.000
P	Joe Orrell	R	10	4	1	0	0	0	0.0	1	0	1	1	0	0	0	.250	.250
P	Bob Gillespie	R	7	2	0	0	0	0	0.0	0	0	0	2	0	0	0	.000	.000
P	Chief Hogsett	L	3	2	0	0	0	0	0.0	0	1	0	0	0	0	0	.000	.000
TEAM TOTAL				5344	1405	220	44	60	1.1	658	591	532	500	61	77	19	.263	.354

INDIVIDUAL FIELDING

POS	Player	T	G	PO	A	E	DP	TC/G	FA	POS	Player	T	G	PO	A	E	DP	TC/G	FA
1B	R. York	R	151	1453	107	17	163	10.4	.989	OF	D. Cramer	R	141	337	13	7	2	2.5	.980
	J. Orengo	R	5	55	3	1	2	11.8	.983		J. Outlaw	R	137	254	14	10	2	2.0	.964
	D. Ross	R	1	17	1	0	0	18.0	1.000		D. Wakefield	R	78	155	3	6	1	2.1	.963
											C. Hostetler	R	65	129	5	2	1	2.1	.985
2B	E. Mayo	R	143	384	458	19	120	6.0	.978		D. Ross	R	37	67	2	3	1	1.9	.958
	D. Heffner	R	5	12	13	1	4	5.2	.962		C. Metro	R	20	44	1	0	0	2.3	1.000
	A. Unser	R	5	12	7	3	2	4.4	.864										
	R. Borom	R	4	5	14	1	1	5.0	.950	C	P. Richards	R	90	413	60	10	13	5.4	.979
	J. Orengo	R	2	4	5	0	1	4.5	1.000		B. Swift	R	76	288	48	6	4	4.5	.982
	J. Hoover	R	1	2	1	0	1	3.0	1.000		A. Unser	R	1	0	0	0	0	0.0	.000
	J. Sullivan	R	1	1	0	0	0	1.0	1.000		H. Miller	R	5	7	1	0	0	1.6	1.000
SS	J. Hoover	R	119	256	405	48	102	6.0	.932										
	J. Orengo	R	29	54	86	15	20	5.3	.903										
	E. Mayo	R	11	17	40	2	5	5.4	.966										
	B. Floyd	R	3	1	8	0	1	3.0	1.000										
	D. Ross	R	2	1	4	0	0	2.5	1.000										
	R. Borom	R	1	1	0	1	0	2.0	.500										
3B	P. Higgins	R	146	146	311	22	21	3.3	.954										
	J. Orengo	R	11	11	30	4	1	4.1	.911										

Hal Newhouser had a reputation as a good pitcher with a bad temper. Manager Steve O'Neill soothed his irascible left-hander with patient encouragement. At the end of 1943, Newhouser promised him, "I won't let you down. I'm going to win for you next year." Indeed. Hometown-bred Prince Hal won the Most Valuable Player Award, led the majors in victories at 29–9 (still the most ever by a Detroit left-hander) and in strikeouts, and notched the second-best ERA (2.22). Close behind was Dizzy Trout at 27–14 with a league-best 2.12 ERA. The slugging Tigers uncharacteristically owned the best one-two pitching punch since Christy Mathewson and Joe McGinnity of the 1904 Giants.

Still, the pennant race proved a tough fight. Largely because of conscription, no full-timer hit .300. The Tigers stumbled to a woeful start, losing 12 of their first 13 at home, sagging similarly on the road. By the All-Star break, they sat in seventh place—one-half game from last, but crazily, only eight and a half from first.

Then Detroit got lucky. The Navy granted Dick Wakefield a 90-day leave prior to reassignment. Wakefield—though he didn't collect enough plate appearances to qualify for the batting title—returned to lead the league at .355. And the Tigers climbed into the pennant race. They captured first place on September 17, then entered a season-ending four-game set against the last-place Senators, owning a one-game lead. It seemed safe enough: the second-place Browns were finishing against the still-tough Yankees. But Detroit split with Washington while St. Louis swept New York, and the Browns—in the ultimate statement on wartime baseball—won their only pennant by a game.

TEAM STATISTICS

W	L	PCT	GB	R	OR	2B	3B	HR	BA	SA	SB	E	DP	FA	CG	BB	SO	ShO	SV	ERA
L	89	65	.578		684	587	223	45	72	.252	.352	44	171	142	.972	71	469	581	16	17	3.17
T	88	66	.571	1	658	581	220	44	60	.263	.354	61	190	184	.970	87	452	568	20	8	3.09
	83	71	.539	6	674	617	216	74	96	.264	.387	91	156	170	.974	78	532	529	9	13	3.39
S	77	77	.500	12	739	676	277	56	69	.270	.380	60	171	154	.972	58	592	524	5	17	3.82
E	72	82	.468	17	643	677	270	50	70	.266	.372	48	165	192	.974	48	621	524	7	18	3.65
I	72	82	.468	17	525	594	169	47	36	.257	.327	42	176	127	.971	72	390	534	9	14	3.26
I	71	83	.461	18	543	662	210	55	23	.247	.320	66	183	154	.970	64	420	481	5	17	3.58
S	64	90	.416	25	592	664	186	42	33	.261	.330	127	218	156	.964	83	475	503	12	11	3.49
AGUE TOTAL				5058	5058	1771	413	459	.260	.353	539	1430	1279	.971	561	3951	4244	83	115	3.43

INDIVIDUAL PITCHING

TCHER	T	W	L	PCT	ERA	SV	G	GS	CG	IP	H	BB	SO	R	ER	ShO	H/9	BB/9	SO/9
zy Trout	R	27	14	.659	2.12	0	49	40	33	352.1	314	83	144	104	83	7	8.02	2.12	3.68
l Newhouser	L	29	9	.763	2.22	2	47	34	25	312.1	264	102	187	94	77	6	7.61	2.94	5.39
fe Gentry	R	12	14	.462	4.24	0	37	30	10	203.2	211	108	68	104	96	4	9.32	4.77	3.00
ubby Overmire	L	11	11	.500	3.07	1	32	28	11	199.2	214	41	57	84	68	3	9.65	1.85	2.57
nny Gorsica	R	6	14	.300	4.11	4	34	19	8	162	192	32	47	88	74	1	10.67	1.78	2.61
om-Boom Beck	R	1	2	.333	3.89	1	28	2	0	74	67	27	25	36	32	0	8.15	3.28	3.04
ke Mooty	R	0	0	—	4.45	0	15	0	0	28.1	35	18	7	20	14	0	11.12	5.72	2.22
e Orrell	R	2	1	.667	2.42	0	10	2	0	22.1	26	11	10	13	6	0	10.48	4.43	4.03
b Eaton	R	0	0	—	5.74	0	6	0	0	15.2	19	8	4	12	10	0	10.91	4.60	2.30
y Henshaw	L	0	0	—	8.76	0	7	1	0	12.1	17	6	10	12	12	0	12.41	4.38	7.30
b Gillespie	R	0	1	.000	6.55	0	7	0	0	11	7	12	4	8	8	0	5.73	9.82	3.27
ief Hogsett	L	0	0	—	0.00	0	3	0	0	6.1	7	4	5	6	0	0	9.95	5.68	7.11
AM TOTAL		88	66	.571	3.09	8	275	156	87	1400	1373	452	568	581	480	21	8.83	2.91	3.65

MANAGER	W	L	PCT
Steve O'Neill	88	65	.575

POS	Player	B	G	AB	H	2B	3B	HR	HR %	R	RBI	BB	SO	SB	Pinch Hit AB	Pinch Hit H	BA	SA
REGULARS																		
1B	Rudy York	R	155	595	157	25	5	18	3.0	71	87	59	85	6	0	0	.264	.413
2B	Eddie Mayo	L	134	501	143	24	3	10	2.0	71	54	48	29	7	9	4	.285	.405
SS	Skeeter Webb	R	118	407	81	12	2	0	0.0	43	21	30	35	8	0	0	.199	.238
3B	Bob Maier	R	132	486	128	25	7	1	0.2	58	34	37	32	7	2	1	.263	.350
RF	Roy Cullenbine	B	146	523	145	27	5	18	3.4	80	93	101*	36	2	0	0	.277	.451
CF	Doc Cramer	L	141	541	149	22	8	6	1.1	62	58	35	21	2	1	0	.275	.379
LF	Jimmy Outlaw	R	132	446	121	16	5	0	0.0	56	34	45	33	6	7	0	.271	.330
C	Bob Swift	R	95	279	65	5	0	0	0.0	19	24	25	22	1	1	0	.233	.251
SUBSTITUTES																		
SS	Joe Hoover	R	74	222	57	10	5	1	0.5	33	17	21	35	6	0	0	.257	.360
2B	Red Borom	L	55	130	35	4	0	0	0.0	19	9	7	8	4	12	2	.269	.300
3B	Don Ross	R	8	29	11	4	0	0	0.0	3	4	5	1	2	0	0	.379	.517
1B	John McHale	L	19	14	2	0	0	0	0.0	0	1	1	4	0	14	2	.143	.143
OF	Hank Greenberg	R	78	270	84	20	2	13	4.8	47	60	42	40	3	5	2	.311	.544
OF	Chuck Hostetler	L	42	44	7	3	0	0	0.0	3	2	7	8	0	30	6	.159	.227
OF	Hub Walker	L	28	23	3	0	0	0	0.0	4	1	9	4	1	15	1	.130	.130
OF	Ed Mierkowicz	R	10	15	2	2	0	0	0.0	0	2	1	3	0	3	1	.133	.267
C	Paul Richards	R	83	234	60	12	1	3	1.3	26	32	19	31	4	0	0	.256	.355
C	Hack Miller	R	2	4	3	0	0	0	0.0	0	1	0	0	0	0	0	.750	.750
C	Milt Welch	R	1	2	0	0	0	0	0.0	0	0	0	1	0	0	0	.000	.000
PH	Russ Kerns	L	1	1	0	0	0	0	0.0	0	0	0	0	0	1	0	.000	.000
PH	Carl McNabb	R	1	1	0	0	0	0	0.0	0	0	0	1	0	1	0	.000	.000
PITCHERS																		
P	Hal Newhouser	L	40	109	28	5	1	0	0.0	9	17	7	10	0	0	0	.257	.321
P	Dizzy Trout	R	42	102	25	3	2	2	2.0	11	11	2	23	1	1	0	.245	.373
P	Al Benton	R	31	63	4	2	0	0	0.0	2	3	2	21	0	0	0	.063	.095
P	Stubby Overmire	R	31	53	10	2	1	0	0.0	5	3	4	6	0	0	0	.189	.264
P	Les Mueller	R	26	44	8	3	0	1	2.3	5	4	2	10	0	0	0	.182	.318
P	Zeb Eaton	R	26	32	8	1	0	2	6.3	2	10	0	7	0	9	3	.250	.469
P	Jim Tobin	R	17	25	3	0	0	2	8.0	2	5	5	5	0	3	0	.120	.360
P	Walter Wilson	L	25	19	1	0	0	0	0.0	1	0	0	9	0	0	0	.053	.053
P	Joe Orrell	R	12	15	2	0	0	0	0.0	0	0	0	6	0	0	0	.133	.133
P	George Caster	R	22	11	2	0	0	0	0.0	0	1	2	3	0	0	0	.182	.182
P	Art Houtteman	R	13	5	0	0	0	0	0.0	0	0	0	2	0	0	0	.000	.000
P	Prince Oana	R	4	5	1	0	0	0	0.0	0	0	0	0	0	1	0	.200	.200
P	Tommy Bridges	R	4	3	0	0	0	0	0.0	0	0	0	0	0	0	0	.000	.000
P	Billy Pierce	L	5	2	0	0	0	0	0.0	0	0	0	0	0	0	0	.000	.000
P	Virgil Trucks	R	1	2	0	0	0	0	0.0	1	0	1	1	0	0	0	.000	.000
P	Pat McLaughlin	R	1	0	0	0	0	0	—	0	0	0	0	0	0	0	—	—
TEAM TOTAL				5257	1345	227	47	77	1.5	633	588	517	533	60	115	22	.256	.361

INDIVIDUAL FIELDING

POS	Player	T	G	PO	A	E	DP	TC/G	FA	POS	Player	T	G	PO	A	E	DP	TC/G	FA
1B	R. York	R	155	**1464**	113	**19**	142	10.3	.988	OF	R. Cullenbine	R	146	321	23*	7	3	2.4	.980
	J. McHale	R	3	5	1	0	0	2.0	1.000		D. Cramer	R	140	314	7	3	4	2.3	**.991**
2B	E. Mayo	R	124	326	393	15	91	5.9	**.980**		J. Outlaw	R	105	192	13	7	6	2.0	.967
	R. Borom	R	28	62	82	5	15	5.3	.966		H. Greenberg	R	72	129	3	0	0	1.8	1.000
	S. Webb	R	11	30	25	0	8	5.0	1.000		C. Hostetler	R	8	8	0	1	0	1.1	.889
SS	S. Webb	R	104	215	343	25	71	5.6	.957		E. Mierkowicz	R	6	8	0	0	0	1.3	1.000
	J. Hoover	R	68	126	163	17	35	4.5	.944		H. Walker	R	7	5	0	0	0	0.7	1.000
	R. Borom	R	2	3	4	0	1	3.5	1.000		B. Maier	R	5	2	0	0	0	0.4	1.000
3B	B. Maier	R	124	142	226	25	19	3.2	.936	C	B. Swift	R	94	358	60	5	12	4.5	.988
	J. Outlaw	R	21	18	42	4	5	3.0	.938		P. Richards	R	83	361	44	2	7	4.9	.995
	D. Ross	R	8	6	18	1	0	3.1	.960		H. Miller	R	2	4	1	0	0	2.5	1.000
	R. Borom	R	4	1	7	1	0	2.3	.889		M. Welch	R	1	3	1	0	1	4.0	1.000

The Scene: a season-ending doubleheader at St. Louis, Detroit needing one victory to win the pennant. The Senators finished their schedule early, a game-and-a-half behind the Tigers, who in turn had one week to play. Detroit needed three victories in its final eight games. Entering the final doubleheader, the Tigers had won two. Trailing, 2–1, in the ninth inning of the doubleheader's first game, Detroit loaded the bases for Hank Greenberg, who had returned from four-and-a-half years in the service on July 1. With one out, Greenberg lined Nelson Potter's second pitch deep into the left-field bleachers for the Tigers' seventh pennant. "That was my biggest thrill of all," said Greenberg. "What was going through my mind is that only a few months before I was in India, wondering if the war would ever end. Now I had just hit a pennant-winning grand-slam home run. I wasn't sure whether I was awake or dreaming."

Hal Newhouser led the majors in wins at 25–9 and ERA at 1.81 (still the lowest ever by a Tiger), and won his second-straight MVP Award—the sixth by a Tiger in 12 years, the last until 1968. National League castoff Eddie Mayo led league second basemen in fielding, and was named *The Sporting News'* AL Most Valuable Player.

In a World Series that one cynic predicted neither team could win, the Tigers beat the Cubs in seven games. Newhouser struck out 22 while winning two, losing one. Greenberg collected two homers and three doubles while hitting .304. And Detroit won its first seven-game Series in four tries. Unlike 1935, Detroit fans didn't celebrate this World Championship through the night. Perhaps they should have: they'd have to wait 23 years for another.

TEAM STATISTICS

W	L	PCT	GB	R	OR	2B	3B	HR	BA	SA	SB	E	DP	FA	CG	BB	SO	ShO	SV	ERA
T	88	65	.575		633	565	227	47	77	.256	.361	60	158	173	.975	78	538	588	19	16	2.99
S	87	67	.565	1.5	622	562	197	63	27	.258	.334	110	183	124	.970	82	440	550	19	11	2.92
L	81	70	.536	6	597	548	215	37	63	.249	.341	25	143	123	.976	91	506	570	10	8	3.14
	81	71	.533	6.5	676	606	189	61	93	.259	.373	64	175	170	.971	78	485	474	9	14	3.45
E	73	72	.503	11	557	548	216	48	65	.255	.359	19	126	149	.977	76	501	497	14	12	3.31
I	71	78	.477	15	596	633	204	55	22	.262	.337	78	180	139	.970	84	448	486	13	13	3.69
S	71	83	.461	17.5	599	674	225	44	50	.260	.346	72	169	198	.973	71	656	490	15	13	3.80
I	52	98	.347	34.5	494	638	201	37	33	.245	.316	25	168	160	.973	65	571	531	11	8	3.62
GUE TOTAL				4774	4774	1674	392	430	.255	.346	453	1302	1236	.973	625	4145	4186	110	95	3.36

INDIVIDUAL PITCHING

CHER	T	W	L	PCT	ERA	SV	G	GS	CG	IP	H	BB	SO	R	ER	ShO	H/9	BB/9	SO/9
Newhouser	L	25	9	.735	1.81	2	40	36	29	313.1	239	110	212	73	63	8	6.86	3.16	6.09
zy Trout	R	18	15	.545	3.14	2	41	31	18	246.1	252	79	97	108	86	4	9.21	2.89	3.54
Benton	R	13	8	.619	2.02	3	31	27	12	191.2	175	63	76	68	43	5	8.22	2.96	3.57
bby Overmire	L	9	9	.500	3.88	4	31	22	9	162.1	189	42	36	81	70	0	10.48	2.33	2.00
s Mueller	R	6	8	.429	3.68	1	26	18	6	134.2	117	58	42	63	55	2	7.82	3.88	2.81
lter Wilson	R	1	3	.250	4.61	0	25	4	1	70.1	76	35	28	40	36	0	9.73	4.48	3.58
n Tobin	R	4	5	.444	3.55	1	14	6	2	58.1	61	28	14	31	23	0	9.41	4.32	2.16
Eaton	R	4	2	.667	4.05	0	17	3	0	53.1	48	40	15	28	24	0	8.10	6.75	2.53
orge Caster	R	5	1	.833	3.86	2	22	0	0	51.1	47	27	23	25	22	0	8.24	4.73	4.03
e Orrell	R	2	3	.400	3.00	0	12	5	1	48	46	24	14	18	16	0	8.63	4.50	2.63
Houtteman	R	0	2	.000	5.33	0	13	0	0	25.1	27	11	9	17	15	0	9.59	3.91	3.20
nce Oana	R	0	0	–	1.59	1	3	1	0	11.1	3	7	3	2	2	0	2.38	5.56	2.38
mmy Bridges	R	1	0	1.000	3.27	0	4	1	0	11	14	2	6	6	4	0	11.45	1.64	4.91
y Pierce	L	0	0	–	1.80	0	5	0	0	10	6	10	10	2	2	0	5.40	9.00	9.00
gil Trucks	R	0	0	–	1.69	0	1	1	0	5.1	3	2	3	1	1	0	5.06	3.38	5.06
McLaughlin	R	0	0	–	9.00	0	1	0	0	1	2	0	0	2	1	0	18.00	0.00	0.00
AM TOTAL		88	65	.575	2.99	16	286	155	78	1393.2	1305	538	588	565	463	19	8.43	3.47	3.80

MANAGER	W	L	PCT
Steve O'Neill	92	62	.597

POS	Player	B	G	AB	H	2B	3B	HR	HR %	R	RBI	BB	SO	SB	Pinch Hit AB	Pinch Hit H	BA	SA
REGULARS																		
1B	Hank Greenberg	R	142	523	145	29	5	44	8.4	91	127	80	88	5	2	0	.277	.604
2B	Jimmy Bloodworth	R	76	249	61	8	1	5	2.0	25	36	12	26	3	4	0	.245	.345
SS	Eddie Lake	R	155	587	149	24	1	8	1.4	105	31	103	69	15	0	0	.254	.339
3B	George Kell	R	105	434	142	19	9	4	0.9	67	41	30	14	3	0	0	.327	.440
RF	Roy Cullenbine	B	113	328	110	21	0	15	4.6	63	56	88	39	3	9	2	.335	.537
CF	Hoot Evers	R	81	304	81	8	4	4	1.3	42	33	34	43	7	2	0	.266	.359
LF	Dick Wakefield	L	111	396	106	11	5	12	3.0	64	59	59	55	3	4	0	.268	.412
C	Birdie Tebbetts	R	87	280	68	11	2	1	0.4	20	34	28	23	1	0	0	.243	.307
SUBSTITUTES																		
2B	Eddie Mayo	L	51	202	51	9	2	0	0.0	21	22	14	12	6	2	0	.252	.317
2B	Skeeter Webb	R	64	169	37	1	1	0	0.0	12	17	9	18	3	1	0	.219	.237
3B	Pinky Higgins	R	18	60	13	3	1	0	0.0	2	8	5	6	0	0	0	.217	.300
SS	Johnny Lipon	R	14	20	6	0	0	0	0.0	4	1	5	3	0	1	0	.300	.300
2B	Billy Hitchcock	R	3	3	0	0	0	0	0.0	0	0	1	0	0	1	0	.000	.000
O3	Jimmy Outlaw	R	92	299	78	14	2	2	0.7	36	31	29	24	5	5	1	.261	.341
OF	Pat Mullin	L	93	276	68	13	4	3	1.1	34	35	25	36	3	14	1	.246	.355
OF	Doc Cramer	L	68	204	60	8	2	1	0.5	26	26	15	8	3	16	4	.294	.368
OF	Anse Moore	L	51	134	28	4	0	1	0.7	16	8	12	9	1	16	4	.209	.261
OF	Barney McCosky	L	25	91	18	5	0	1	1.1	11	11	17	9	0	0	0	.198	.286
OF	Johnny Groth	R	4	9	0	0	0	0	0.0	1	0	0	3	0	0	0	.000	.000
C	Paul Richards	R	57	139	28	5	2	0	0.0	13	11	23	18	2	3	2	.201	.266
C	Bob Swift	R	42	107	25	2	0	2	1.9	13	10	14	7	0	0	0	.234	.308
PH	Bob Harris	L	1	1	0	0	0	0	0.0	0	0	0	0	0	1	0	.000	.000
PITCHERS																		
P	Hal Newhouser	L	37	103	13	3	0	2	1.9	6	11	6	27	1	0	0	.126	.214
P	Dizzy Trout	R	40	103	20	3	0	3	2.9	7	10	4	34	1	1	0	.194	.311
P	Virgil Trucks	R	32	95	17	4	0	0	0.0	4	5	0	13	0	0	0	.179	.221
P	Fred Hutchinson	L	40	89	28	4	0	0	0.0	11	13	6	1	0	9	2	.315	.360
P	Al Benton	R	28	49	9	1	0	0	0.0	3	3	0	17	0	0	0	.184	.204
P	Stubby Overmire	R	24	33	5	0	0	0	0.0	4	3	2	2	0	0	0	.152	.152
P	George Caster	R	26	7	1	0	0	0	0.0	0	0	0	0	0	0	0	.143	.143
P	Hal White	L	11	7	0	0	0	0	0.0	0	0	0	5	0	0	0	.000	.000
P	Lou Kretlow	R	1	4	2	1	0	0	0.0	1	1	0	1	0	0	0	.500	.750
P	Tommy Bridges	R	9	3	0	0	0	0	0.0	1	0	2	2	0	0	0	.000	.000
P	Johnny Gorsica	R	14	3	2	1	0	0	0.0	1	0	0	0	0	0	0	.667	1.000
P	Ted Gray	B	3	3	0	0	0	0	0.0	0	0	1	2	0	0	0	.000	.000
P	Art Houtteman	R	1	2	1	0	0	0	0.0	0	1	0	0	0	0	0	.500	.500
P	Hal Manders	R	2	2	1	0	0	0	0.0	0	0	0	0	0	0	0	.500	.500
P	Rufe Gentry	R	2	0	0	0	0	0	0.0	0	0	0	0	0	0	0	—	—
	TEAM TOTAL			5318	1373	212	41	108	2.0	704	644	624	616	65	91	16	.258	.374

INDIVIDUAL FIELDING

POS	Player	T	G	PO	A	E	DP	TC/G	FA		POS	Player	T	G	PO	A	E	DP	TC/G	FA
1B	H. Greenberg	R	140	1272	93	15	110	9.9	.989		OF	D. Wakefield	R	104	210	6	8	1	2.2	.964
	R. Cullenbine	R	21	168	18	3	14	9.0	.984			H. Evers	R	76	196	2	5	0	2.7	.975
	G. Kell	R	1	2	0	0	0	2.0	1.000			R. Cullenbine	R	81	125	12	5	1	1.8	.965
2B	J. Bloodworth	R	71	157	184	9	46	4.9	.974			P. Mullin	R	75	121	8	7	1	1.8	.949
	S. Webb	R	50	97	143	7	28	4.9	.972			D. Cramer	L	50	89	2	0	0	1.8	1.000
	E. Mayo	R	49	96	125	8	28	4.7	.965			J. Outlaw	R	43	71	5	0	0	1.8	1.000
	B. Hitchcock	R	1	1	2	0	0	3.0	1.000			A. Moore	R	32	65	2	2	1	2.2	.971
SS	E. Lake	R	155	232	391	35	85	4.2	.947			B. McCosky	R	24	56	1	2	0	2.5	.966
	J. Lipon	R	8	14	14	2	5	3.8	.933			J. Groth	R	4	6	0	0	0	1.5	1.000
	S. Webb	R	8	8	12	0	2	2.5	1.000		C	B. Tebbetts	R	87	486	53	10	4	6.3	.982
3B	G. Kell	R	105	105*	210*	5	22*	3.0*	.984*			P. Richards	R	54	311	35	1	6	6.4	.997
	J. Outlaw	R	38	30	59	7	4	2.5	.927			B. Swift	R	42	187	14	4	2	4.9	.980
	P. Higgins	R	17	12	25	2	2	2.3	.949											
	J. Lipon	R	1	0	1	0	0	1.0	1.000											

In one of many postwar alterations, new Tiger general manager George Trautman had engineered the deal that sent home-grown favorite Barney McCosky to the Athletics in return for the smooth-fielding third baseman George Kell, who would average well over .300 and win a batting title during his seven seasons in Detroit. In all, only 13 Tigers from the previous season's World Championship team would remain, as prewar regulars returned from the service. But Detroit didn't resume its prewar sluging. Only Kell (.327) and rightfielder Roy Cullenbine (.335) hit .300, although 35-year-old Hank Greenberg's .277 was accompanied by his fourth home-run (44) and RBI (127) titles. Greenberg was nevertheless left off the All-Star squad, and rumors flew that Greenberg, so miffed by the snub, would retire and join with his in-laws (the department store Gimbels) to buy their own ballclub.

The biggest disappointment was Dick Wakefield. During the spring, the Tiger leftfielder had wagered Ted Williams $1000 on who would finish with a higher average. Commissioner Happy Chandler later canceled the bet, saving Wakefield (.268) from sending a chunk of his bonus money to Williams (.342). For the most part, the Tigers stayed close because of pitching. Hal Newhouser notched 25-plus victories for the third straight year at 26–9 (80–27 over those three seasons) to lead the majors in wins and ERA (1.94).

Detroit lingered in third before finishing second, 12 games behind the fast-starting Red Sox. The hottest team in the majors over the final six weeks at 28–10, the Tigers garnered mild satisfaction from back-to-back victories over the Red Sox on September 10 and 11, postponing Boston's pennant victory. Detroit also finished second in the league in attendance behind New York. Cashing in on baseball's postwar prosperity, the Tigers drew a then–team record 1,722,590.

TEAM STATISTICS

	W	L	PCT	GB	R	OR	Batting 2B	3B	HR	BA	SA	SB	Fielding E	DP	FA	Pitching CG	BB	SO	ShO	SV	ERA
)S	104	50	.675		792	594	268	50	109	.271	.402	45	139	165	.977	79	501	667	16	20	3.38
T	92	62	.597	12	704	567	212	41	108	.258	.374	65	155	138	.974	94	497	896	18	15	3.22
	87	67	.565	17	684	547	208	50	136	.248	.387	48	150	174	.975	68	552	653	17	17	3.13
AS	76	78	.494	28	608	706	260	63	60	.260	.366	51	211	162	.966	71	547	537	8	10	3.74
Hl	74	80	.481	30	562	595	206	44	37	.257	.333	78	175	170	.972	62	508	550	9	16	3.10
E	68	86	.442	36	537	637	233	56	79	.245	.356	57	147	147	.975	63	649	789	16	13	3.62
L	66	88	.429	38	621	711	220	46	84	.251	.356	23	159	157	.974	63	573	574	13	12	3.95
Il	49	105	.318	55	529	680	220	51	40	.253	.338	39	167	141	.971	61	577	562	10	5	3.90
AGUE TOTAL					5037	5037	1827	401	653	.256	.364	406	1303	1254	.973	561	4404	5228	106	108	3.50

INDIVIDUAL PITCHING

TCHER	T	W	L	PCT	ERA	SV	G	GS	CG	IP	H	BB	SO	R	ER	ShO	H/9	BB/9	SO/9
l Newhouser	L	26	9	.743	1.94	1	37	34	29	292.1	215	98	275	77	63	6	6.62	3.02	8.47
zzy Trout	R	17	13	.567	2.34	3	38	32	23	276.1	244	97	151	85	72	5	7.95	3.16	4.92
gil Trucks	R	14	9	.609	3.23	0	32	29	15	236.2	217	75	161	94	85	3	8.25	2.85	6.12
ed Hutchinson	R	14	11	.560	3.09	2	28	26	16	207	184	66	138	78	71	3	8.00	2.87	6.00
Benton	R	11	7	.611	3.65	1	28	15	6	140.2	132	58	60	69	57	1	8.45	3.71	3.84
ubby Overmire	L	5	7	.417	4.62	1	24	13	3	97.1	106	29	34	54	50	0	9.80	2.68	3.14
orge Caster	R	2	1	.667	5.66	4	26	0	0	41.1	42	24	19	26	26	0	9.15	5.23	4.14
l White	R	1	1	.500	5.60	0	11	1	1	27.1	34	15	12	20	17	0	11.20	4.94	3.95
nny Gorsica	R	0	0	–	4.56	1	14	0	0	23.2	28	11	14	13	12	0	10.65	4.18	5.32
mmy Bridges	R	1	1	.500	5.91	1	9	1	0	21.1	24	8	17	16	14	0	10.13	3.38	7.17
d Gray	L	0	2	.000	8.49	1	3	2	0	11.2	17	5	5	12	11	0	13.11	3.86	3.86
u Kretlow	R	1	0	1.000	3.00	0	1	1	1	9	7	2	4	3	3	0	7.00	2.00	4.00
Houtteman	R	0	1	.000	9.00	0	1	1	0	8	15	0	2	8	8	0	16.88	0.00	2.25
l Manders	R	0	0	–	10.50	0	2	0	0	6	8	2	3	7	7	0	12.00	3.00	4.50
e Gentry	R	0	0	–	15.00	0	2	0	0	3	4	7	1	5	5	0	12.00	21.00	3.00
AM TOTAL		92	62	.597	3.22	15	256	155	94	1401.2	1277	497	896	567	501	18	8.20	3.19	5.75

MANAGER	W	L	PCT
Steve O'Neill	85	69	.552

POS	Player	B	G	AB	H	2B	3B	HR	HR %	R	RBI	BB	SO	SB	Pinch Hit AB	H	BA	SA
REGULARS																		
1B	Roy Cullenbine	B	142	464	104	18	1	24	5.2	82	78	137	51	3	4	0	.224	.422
2B	Eddie Mayo	L	142	535	149	28	4	6	1.1	66	48	48	28	3	1	1	.279	.379
SS	Eddie Lake	R	158	602	127	19	6	12	2.0	96	46	120	54	11	0	0	.211	.322
3B	George Kell	R	152	588	188	29	5	5	0.9	75	93	61	16	9	0	0	.320	.412
RF	Pat Mullin	L	116	398	102	28	6	15	3.8	62	62	63	66	3	9	3	.256	.470
CF	Hoot Evers	R	126	460	136	24	5	10	2.2	67	67	45	49	8	2	1	.296	.435
LF	Dick Wakefield	L	112	368	104	15	5	8	2.2	59	51	80	44	1	10	4	.283	.416
C	Bob Swift	R	97	279	70	11	0	1	0.4	23	21	33	16	2	1	0	.251	.301
SUBSTITUTES																		
1B	John McHale	L	39	95	20	1	0	3	3.2	10	11	7	24	1	15	4	.211	.316
2B	Skeeter Webb	R	50	79	16	3	0	0	0.0	13	6	7	9	3	2	0	.203	.241
OF	Vic Wertz	L	102	333	96	22	4	6	1.8	60	44	47	66	2	18	5	.288	.432
OF	Doc Cramer	L	73	157	42	2	2	2	1.3	21	30	20	5	0	33	9	.268	.344
OF	Jimmy Outlaw	R	70	127	29	7	1	0	0.0	20	15	21	14	3	3	0	.228	.299
OF	Ed Mierkowicz	R	21	42	8	1	0	1	2.4	6	1	1	12	1	9	1	.190	.286
OF	Johnny Groth	R	2	4	1	0	0	0	0.0	1	0	2	1	0	1	0	.250	.250
C	Hal Wagner	L	71	191	55	10	0	5	2.6	19	33	28	16	0	1	1	.288	.419
C	Birdie Tebbetts	R	20	53	5	1	0	0	0.0	0	1	3	3	0	0	0	.094	.113
C	Hank Riebe	R	8	7	0	0	0	0	0.0	0	2	0	2	0	5	0	.000	.000
PH	Ben Steiner	L	1	0	0	0	0	0	–	1	0	0	0	0	0	0	–	–
PITCHERS																		
P	Fred Hutchinson	L	56	106	32	5	2	2	1.9	8	15	6	6	2	22	6	.302	.443
P	Hal Newhouser	L	40	96	19	0	0	0	0.0	5	9	15	20	0	0	0	.198	.198
P	Virgil Trucks	R	36	70	19	2	0	0	0.0	7	5	1	7	0	0	0	.271	.300
P	Dizzy Trout	R	34	68	11	2	1	3	4.4	5	15	8	19	0	2	0	.162	.353
P	Stubby Overmire	R	28	47	7	0	0	0	0.0	2	2	5	8	0	0	0	.149	.149
P	Art Houtteman	R	23	40	12	2	0	0	0.0	2	3	0	3	0	0	0	.300	.350
P	Al Benton	R	36	39	6	1	0	0	0.0	1	2	0	10	0	0	0	.154	.179
P	Hal White	L	35	18	3	2	0	0	0.0	2	1	2	7	0	0	0	.167	.278
P	Johnny Gorsica	R	31	10	2	1	0	0	0.0	0	0	1	7	0	0	0	.200	.300
P	Rufe Gentry	R	1	0	0	0	0	0	–	0	0	0	0	0	0	0	–	–
TEAM TOTAL				5276	1363	234	42	103	2.0	714	662	761	563	52	138	35	.258	.377

INDIVIDUAL FIELDING

POS	Player	T	G	PO	A	E	DP	TC/G	FA	POS	Player	T	G	PO	A	E	DP	TC/G	FA
1B	R. Cullenbine	R	138	1184	139	15	111	9.7	.989	OF	H. Evers	R	123	354	10	8	2	3.0	.978
	J. McHale	R	25	195	12	1	12	8.3	.995		P. Mullin	R	106	229	10	3	2	2.3	.988
2B	E. Mayo	R	142	326	365	12	80	5.0	.983		D. Wakefield	R	101	197	10	11	2	2.2	.950
	S. Webb	R	30	52	74	1	9	4.2	.992		V. Wertz	R	82	160	6	6	0	2.1	.965
SS	E. Lake	R	158	268	441	43	94	4.8	.943		D. Cramer	R	35	79	3	3	0	2.4	.965
	S. Webb	R	6	0	4	1	1	0.8	.800		J. Outlaw	R	37	58	0	1	0	1.6	.983
3B	G. Kell	R	152	167	333	20	25	3.4	.962		E. Mierkowicz	R	10	18	0	1	0	1.9	.947
	J. Outlaw	R	9	11	7	1	0	2.1	.947		J. Groth	R	1	5	0	0	0	5.0	1.000
										C	B. Swift	R	97	401	45	5	6	4.6	.989
											H. Wagner	R	71	275	25	3	4	4.3	.990
											B. Tebbetts	R	20	95	15	0*	4	5.5	1.000
											H. Riebe	R	3	2	0	0	0	0.7	1.000

Hank Greenberg was bitter. Little more than a year after slamming a pennant-winning home run on the last day of the season, and mere months after winning the home-run and RBI crowns, the 12-year Tiger switched on his radio one cold January morning and heard he'd been sold to Pittsburgh. "It was one of the biggest shocks of my whole life," said Greenberg, who'd batted .319 and hit 306 home runs despite missing more than five prime seasons to injury and the war. "I was dumped without even the courtesy of a phone call."

At first the Tigers didn't miss him. While the Yankees and Red Sox stalled, Detroit raced to a fast start, took first place, and built a four-game lead by early July. Then came a 10-game losing streak. New York, meanwhile, embarked on a 19-game winning streak to bury Boston and Detroit. The Tigers finished the same as in 1946, in second place, 12 games behind the Yankees.

Roy Cullenbine replaced Greenberg at first base and hit 24 home runs and drew a still-standing team-record 137 walks in his final major league season. George Kell (.320) was the only Tiger to hit .300. On September 14 at Washington's Griffith Stadium, rookie Vic Wertz became the fifth Tiger—the first on the road—to hit for the cycle. Hal Newhouser showed signs of his old temperament—once refusing to leave the mound when O'Neill called for a relief pitcher—and fell short of the 20-win plateau for the first time in four years at 17–17 (leading the league in losses), but with a 2.87 ERA. Fred Hutchinson led the staff at 18–10, 3.03.

Partially because of dismal early-season weather, home attendance dropped more than 300,000. Still, on July 20, Detroit drew its biggest home crowd ever, 58,369, for a doubleheader against the Yankees.

TEAM STATISTICS

W	L	PCT	GB	R	OR	Batting 2B	3B	HR	BA	SA	SB	Fielding E	DP	FA	CG	Pitching BB	SO	ShO	SV	ERA
97	57	.630		794	568	230	72	115	.271	.407	27	109	151	.981	73	628	691	14	21	3.39
85	69	.552	12	714	642	234	42	103	.258	.377	52	155	142	.975	77	531	648	15	18	3.57
83	71	.539	14	720	669	206	54	103	.265	.382	41	137	172	.977	64	575	586	13	19	3.81
80	74	.519	17	687	588	234	51	112	.259	.385	29	104	178	.983	55	628	590	13	29	3.44
78	76	.506	19	633	614	218	52	61	.252	.349	37	143	161	.976	70	597	493	12	15	3.51
70	84	.455	27	553	661	211	41	53	.256	.342	91	155	180	.975	47	603	522	11	27	3.64
64	90	.416	33	496	675	186	48	42	.241	.321	53	143	151	.977	67	579	551	15	12	3.97
59	95	.383	38	564	744	189	52	90	.241	.350	69	134	169	.977	50	604	552	7	13	4.33
LEAGUE TOTAL				5161	5161	1708	412	679	.256	.364	399	1080	1304	.977	503	4745	4633	100	154	3.71

INDIVIDUAL PITCHING

PITCHER	T	W	L	PCT	ERA	SV	G	GS	CG	IP	H	BB	SO	R	ER	ShO	H/9	BB/9	SO/9
Hal Newhouser	L	17	17	.500	2.87	2	40	36	24	285	268	110	176	105	91	3	8.46	3.47	5.56
Fred Hutchinson	R	18	10	.643	3.03	2	33	25	18	219.2	211	61	113	84	74	3	8.64	2.50	4.63
Dizzy Trout	R	10	11	.476	3.48	2	32	26	9	186.1	186	65	74	85	72	2	8.98	3.14	3.57
Virgil Trucks	R	10	12	.455	4.53	2	36	26	8	180.2	186	79	108	105	91	2	9.27	3.94	5.38
Stubby Overmire	L	11	5	.688	3.77	0	28	17	7	140.2	142	44	33	62	59	3	9.09	2.82	2.11
Al Benton	R	6	7	.462	4.40	7	31	14	4	133	147	61	33	77	65	0	9.95	4.13	2.23
Art Houtteman	R	7	2	.778	3.42	0	23	9	7	110.2	106	36	58	51	42	2	8.62	2.93	4.72
Hal White	R	4	5	.444	3.61	2	35	5	0	84.2	91	47	33	43	34	0	9.67	5.00	3.51
Johnny Gorsica	R	2	0	1.000	3.75	1	31	0	0	57.2	44	26	20	27	24	0	6.87	4.06	3.12
Rube Gentry	R	0	0	–	81.00	0	1	0	0	.1	2	2	0	3	3	0	27.00	54.00	0.00
TEAM TOTAL		85	69	.552	3.57	18	290	158	77	1398.2	1382	531	648	642	555	15	8.89	3.42	4.17

MANAGER	W	L	PCT
Steve O'Neill	78	76	.506

POS	Player	B	G	AB	H	2B	3B	HR	HR %	R	RBI	BB	SO	SB	Pinch Hit AB	Pinch Hit H	BA	SA
REGULARS																		
1B	George Vico	L	144	521	139	23	9	8	1.5	50	58	39	39	2	2	0	.267	.392
2B	Eddie Mayo	L	106	370	92	20	1	2	0.5	35	42	30	19	1	10	2	.249	.324
SS	Johnny Lipon	R	121	458	133	18	8	5	1.1	65	52	68	22	4	1	0	.290	.397
3B	George Kell	R	92	368	112	24	3	2	0.5	47	44	33	15	2	0	0	.304	.402
RF	Pat Mullin	L	138	496	143	16	11	23	4.6	91	80	77	57	1	4	0	.288	.504
CF	Hoot Evers	R	139	538	169	33	6	10	1.9	81	103	51	31	3	1	0	.314	.454
LF	Vic Wertz	L	119	391	97	19	9	7	1.8	49	67	48	70	0	19	4	.248	.396
C	Bob Swift	R	113	292	65	6	0	4	1.4	23	33	51	29	1	1	0	.223	.284
SUBSTITUTES																		
S2	Neil Berry	R	87	256	68	8	1	0	0.0	46	16	37	23	1	5	1	.266	.305
23	Eddie Lake	R	64	198	52	6	0	2	1.0	51	18	57	20	3	0	0	.263	.323
3O	Jimmy Outlaw	R	74	198	56	12	0	0	0.0	33	25	31	15	0	11	4	.283	.343
1B	Paul Campbell	L	59	83	22	1	1	1	1.2	15	11	1	10	0	13	1	.265	.337
2B	Johnny Bero	L	4	9	0	0	0	0	0.0	2	0	1	1	0	1	0	.000	.000
OF	Dick Wakefield	L	110	322	89	20	5	11	3.4	50	53	70	55	0	22	7	.276	.472
OF	Johnny Groth	R	6	17	8	3	0	1	5.9	3	5	1	1	0	1	0	.471	.824
OF	Ed Mierkowicz	R	3	5	1	0	0	0	0.0	0	1	2	2	0	2	0	.200	.200
OF	Doc Cramer	L	4	4	0	0	0	0	0.0	1	1	3	0	0	2	0	.000	.000
C	Hal Wagner	L	54	109	22	3	0	0	0.0	10	10	20	11	1	1	0	.202	.229
C	Hank Riebe	R	25	62	12	0	0	0	0.0	0	5	3	5	0	1	0	.194	.194
C	Joe Ginsberg	L	11	36	13	0	0	0	0.0	7	1	3	1	0	0	0	.361	.361
PH	John McHale	L	1	1	0	0	0	0	0.0	0	0	0	0	0	1	0	.000	.000
PITCHERS																		
P	Fred Hutchinson	L	76	112	23	1	0	1	0.9	11	12	23	9	3	32	7	.205	.241
P	Hal Newhouser	L	39	92	19	0	1	0	0.0	6	6	10	14	0	0	0	.207	.228
P	Virgil Trucks	R	43	79	13	0	1	0	0.0	6	2	2	14	0	0	0	.165	.190
P	Dizzy Trout	R	32	69	15	3	0	1	1.4	6	2	5	14	0	0	0	.217	.304
P	Art Houtteman	R	43	56	11	0	0	0	0.0	2	7	0	2	0	0	0	.196	.196
P	Ted Gray	B	26	29	7	1	0	0	0.0	2	1	2	7	0	0	0	.241	.276
P	Billy Pierce	L	22	17	5	0	2	0	0.0	5	2	0	4	0	0	0	.294	.529
P	Stubby Overmire	R	37	14	1	0	0	0	0.0	0	1	2	1	0	0	0	.071	.071
P	Hal White	L	27	13	2	1	0	0	0.0	1	1	2	6	0	0	0	.154	.231
P	Al Benton	R	30	11	2	1	0	0	0.0	1	1	0	6	0	0	0	.182	.273
P	Lou Kretlow	R	5	8	4	0	0	0	0.0	0	1	0	1	0	0	0	.500	.500
P	Rufe Gentry	R	4	1	1	0	0	0	0.0	1	0	0	0	0	0	0	1.000	1.000
TEAM TOTAL				5235	1396	219	58	78	1.5	700	661	672	504	22	130	26	.267	.375

INDIVIDUAL FIELDING

POS	Player	T	G	PO	A	E	DP	TC/G	FA		POS	Player	T	G	PO	A	E	DP	TC/G	FA
1B	G. Vico	R	142	1169	85	15	112	8.9	.988		OF	H. Evers	R	138	392	8	11	0	3.0	.973
	P. Campbell	L	27	172	18	6	11	7.3	.969			P. Mullin	R	131	274	7	8	0	2.2	.972
2B	E. Mayo	R	86	202	223	11	48	5.1	.975			V. Wertz	R	98	196	11	10	3	2.2	.954
	E. Lake	R	45	110	132	7	31	5.5	.972			D. Wakefield	R	86	198	3	11	1	2.5	.948
	N. Berry	R	26	71	79	3	15	5.9	.980			J. Outlaw	R	13	19	1	0	0	1.5	1.000
	J. Lipon	R	1	0	0	0	0	0.0	.000			J. Groth	R	4	8	1	1	1	2.5	.900
	J. Bero	R	2	5	3	0	0	4.0	1.000			E. Mierkowicz	R	1	4	0	0	0	4.0	1.000
SS	J. Lipon	R	117	211	346	17	63	4.9	.970			D. Cramer	R	1	2	0	0	0	2.0	1.000
	N. Berry	R	41	67	120	14	31	4.9	.930		C	B. Swift	R	112	476	55	5	13	4.8	.991
3B	G. Kell	R	92	108	146	8	15	2.8	.969			H. Wagner	R	52	162	12	2	4	3.4	.989
	J. Outlaw	R	47	39	87	11	8	2.9	.920			H. Riebe	R	24	90	6	0	1	4.0	1.000
	E. Lake	R	17	12	15	1	0	1.6	.964			J. Ginsberg	R	11	46	4	3	3	4.8	.943
	E. Mayo	R	10	9	19	0	1	2.8	1.000											
	J. Lipon	R	1	1	1	0	0	2.0	1.000											

For the most part, it was a season for Briggs Stadium trivia. The Tigers finally installed lights to become the last American League team to recognize night baseball. But they did so reluctantly, scheduling only seven evening performances, the first a 4–1 victory over the Athletics on June 15. On September 26, with nothing at stake, the Tigers drew 57,888 to a day game against the pennant-contending Indians—still a franchise record for a single home game. And the Tigers drew 56,586 against Cleveland on August 9 —still team-high for a night home game.

Trivial pursuits aside, the Tigers did not significantly inject themselves into the pennant race. Steve O'Neill marked the end of his six-year managerial reign with a slide back to the second division into fifth, two games under .500 and 18 1/2 games out of first place. Hal Newhouser edged back into the 20-victory circle to lead the league at 21–12 with a 3.01 ERA; he would be the last Tiger pitcher to win 20 games for eight seasons. Only two Tigers hit .300: centerfielder Hoot Evers (.314) and oft-injured third baseman George Kell (.304). Outfielder Pat Mullin led the team in home runs with 23.

Detroit appropriately punctuated the season with a significantly bad trade. Considered expendable, homegrown southpaw Billy Pierce was sent to the White Sox for lefty-hitting catcher Aaron Robinson. Pierce proceeded to win more than 200 games in 18 seasons with Chicago and San Francisco. Robinson would remain best known as one-third of the answer to a popular trivia question: Name the Yankee catchers between Bill Dickey and Yogi Berra.

TEAM STATISTICS

W	L	PCT	GB	R	OR	2B	Batting 3B	HR	BA	SA	SB	Fielding E	DP	FA	CG	BB	Pitching SO	ShO	SV	ERA
E	97	58	.626		840	568	242	54	155	.282	.431	54	114	183	.982	66	628	595	26	30	3.22
S	96	59	.619	1	907	720	277	40	121	.274	.409	38	116	174	.981	70	592	513	11	13	4.20
	94	60	.610	2.5	857	633	251	75	139	.278	.432	24	120	161	.979	62	641	654	16	24	3.75
I	84	70	.545	12.5	729	735	231	47	68	.260	.362	39	113	180	.981	74	638	486	7	18	4.43
T	78	76	.506	18.5	700	726	219	58	78	.267	.375	22	155	143	.974	60	589	678	5	22	4.15
	59	94	.386	37	671	849	251	62	63	.271	.378	42	168	190	.972	35	737	531	4	20	5.01
S	56	97	.366	40	578	796	203	75	31	.244	.331	76	154	144	.974	42	734	446	4	22	4.65
I	51	101	.336	44.5	559	814	172	39	55	.251	.331	46	160	176	.974	35	673	403	2	23	4.89
GUE TOTAL				5841	5841	1846	450	710	.266	.382	362	1100	1351	.977	444	5232	4306	75	172	4.28

INDIVIDUAL   PITCHING

CHER	T	W	L	PCT	ERA	SV	G	GS	CG	IP	H	BB	SO	R	ER	ShO	H/9	BB/9	SO/9
Newhouser	L	21	12	.636	3.01	1	39	35	19	272.1	249	99	143	109	91	2	8.23	3.27	4.73
d Hutchinson	R	13	11	.542	4.32	0	33	28	15	221	223	48	92	119	106	0	9.08	1.95	3.75
gil Trucks	R	14	13	.519	3.78	2	43	26	7	211.2	190	85	123	97	89	0	8.08	3.61	5.23
zy Trout	R	10	14	.417	3.43	2	32	23	11	183.2	193	73	91	87	70	2	9.46	3.58	4.46
Houtteman	R	2	16	.111	4.66	10	43	20	4	164.1	186	52	74	101	85	0	10.19	2.85	4.05
Gray	L	6	2	.750	4.22	0	26	11	3	85.1	73	72	60	43	40	1	7.70	7.59	6.33
bby Overmire	L	3	4	.429	5.97	3	37	4	0	66.1	89	31	14	48	44	0	12.08	4.21	1.90
Pierce	L	3	0	1.000	6.34	0	22	5	0	55.1	47	51	36	40	39	0	7.64	8.30	5.86
Benton	R	2	2	.500	5.68	3	30	0	0	44.1	45	36	18	34	28	0	9.14	7.31	3.65
White	R	2	1	.667	6.12	1	27	0	0	42.2	46	26	17	31	29	0	9.70	5.48	3.59
Kretlow	R	2	1	.667	4.63	0	5	2	1	23.1	21	11	9	14	12	0	8.10	4.24	3.47
e Gentry	R	0	0	–	2.70	0	4	0	0	6.2	5	5	1	2	2	0	6.75	6.75	1.35
M TOTAL		78	76	.506	4.15	22	341	154	60	1377	1367	589	678	725	635	5	8.93	3.85	4.43

MANAGER	W	L	PCT
Red Rolfe	87	67	.565

POS	Player	B	G	AB	H	2B	3B	HR	HR %	R	RBI	BB	SO	SB	Pinch Hit AB	Pinch Hit H	BA	SA
REGULARS																		
1B	Paul Campbell	L	87	255	71	15	4	3	1.2	38	30	24	32	3	9	5	.278	.404
2B	Neil Berry	R	109	329	78	9	1	0	0.0	38	18	27	24	4	4	0	.237	.271
SS	Johnny Lipon	R	127	439	110	14	6	3	0.7	57	59	75	24	2	5	0	.251	.330
3B	George Kell	R	134	522	179	38	9	3	0.6	97	59	71	13	7	0	0	**.343**	.467
RF	Vic Wertz	L	155	608	185	26	6	20	3.3	96	133	80	61	2	0	0	.304	.465
CF	Johnny Groth	R	103	348	102	19	5	11	3.2	60	73	65	27	3	3	0	.293	.471
LF	Hoot Evers	R	132	432	131	21	6	7	1.6	68	72	70	38	6	10	2	.303	.428
C	Aaron Robinson	L	110	331	89	12	0	13	3.9	38	56	73	21	0	2	0	.269	.423
SUBSTITUTES																		
21	Don Kolloway	R	126	483	142	19	3	2	0.4	71	47	49	25	7	9	2	.294	.358
UT	Eddie Lake	R	94	240	47	9	1	1	0.4	38	15	61	33	2	12	2	.196	.254
1B	George Vico	L	67	142	27	5	2	4	2.8	15	18	21	17	0	13	2	.190	.338
OF	Pat Mullin	L	104	310	83	8	6	12	3.9	55	59	42	29	1	26	6	.268	.448
OF	Dick Wakefield	L	59	126	26	3	1	6	4.8	17	19	32	24	0	18	3	.206	.389
C	Bob Swift	R	74	189	45	6	0	2	1.1	16	18	26	20	0	6	1	.238	.302
C	Hank Riebe	R	17	33	6	2	0	0	0.0	1	2	0	5	1	6	1	.182	.242
PH	Jimmy Outlaw	R	5	4	1	0	0	0	0.0	1	0	0	1	0	4	1	.250	.250
PH	Don Lund	R	2	2	0	0	0	0	0.0	0	0	0	1	0	2	0	.000	.000
PH	Bob Mavis	L	1	0	0	0	0	0	–	0	0	0	0	0	0	0	–	–
PH	Earl Rapp	L	1	0	0	0	0	0	–	0	0	1	0	0	0	0	–	–
PITCHERS																		
P	Virgil Trucks	R	41	100	12	2	0	0	0.0	6	3	1	15	0	0	0	.120	.140
P	Hal Newhouser	L	38	91	18	3	0	0	0.0	8	6	12	19	0	0	0	.198	.231
P	Art Houtteman	R	36	78	19	2	0	0	0.0	8	7	1	14	0	0	0	.244	.269
P	Fred Hutchinson	L	38	73	18	2	1	0	0.0	12	7	8	5	1	4	1	.247	.301
P	Ted Gray	B	36	63	8	0	0	0	0.0	5	0	6	27	0	0	0	.127	.127
P	Lou Kretlow	R	25	26	0	0	0	0	0.0	0	1	1	16	0	0	0	.000	.000
P	Dizzy Trout	R	33	14	2	0	0	1	7.1	2	4	0	2	0	0	0	.143	.357
P	Marv Grissom	R	27	9	2	0	0	0	0.0	2	0	1	3	0	0	0	.222	.222
P	Marlin Stuart	L	15	6	2	0	0	0	0.0	2	1	1	1	0	0	0	.333	.333
P	Stubby Overmire	R	14	3	1	0	0	0	0.0	0	0	0	2	0	0	0	.333	.333
P	Hal White	L	10	3	1	0	0	0	0.0	0	0	0	2	0	0	0	.333	.333
P	Saul Rogovin	R	5	0	0	0	0	0	–	0	0	0	0	0	0	0	–	–
	TEAM TOTAL			5259	1405	215	51	88	1.7	751	707	748	501	39	133	26	.267	.378

INDIVIDUAL FIELDING

POS	Player	T	G	PO	A	E	DP	TC/G	FA
1B	D. Kolloway	R	57	472	35	5	49	9.0	.990
	P. Campbell	L	74	461	38	7	67	6.8	.986
	G. Vico	R	53	372	32	6	36	7.7	.985
2B	N. Berry	R	95	225	234	14	56	5.0	.970
	D. Kolloway	R	62	135	149	13	44	4.8	.956
	E. Lake	R	19	25	31	2	6	3.1	.966
SS	J. Lipon	R	120	240	364	22	92	5.2	.965
	E. Lake	R	38	71	114	8	28	5.1	.959
	N. Berry	R	4	2	3	0	0	1.3	1.000
3B	G. Kell	R	134	154	271	11	23	3.3	.975
	E. Lake	R	18	17	22	0	3	2.2	1.000
	D. Kolloway	R	7	6	12	0	1	2.6	1.000

POS	Player	T	G	PO	A	E	DP	TC/G	FA
OF	H. Evers	R	123	319	12	2	2	2.7	.994
	V. Wertz	R	155	302	14	6	4	2.1	.981
	J. Groth	R	99	247	8	9	3	2.7	.966
	P. Mullin	R	79	169	4	2	0	2.2	.989
	D. Wakefield	R	32	71	3	0	1	2.3	1.000
C	A. Robinson	R	108	458	44	7	9	4.7	.986
	B. Swift	R	69	232	26	3	6	3.8	.989
	H. Riebe	R	11	21	3	1	1	2.3	.960

After showing a marked propensity for breaking bones for the better part of two seasons, George Kell decided it was time to break records. The 27-year-old Tiger—who had broken his lower jaw and a wrist the previous season—broke a bone in his right foot and fractured his left thumb en route to becoming the first third baseman to win the American League batting title, shading Boston's Ted Williams on the last day of the season, .3429 to .3428. By that thinnest of margins, Kell kept Williams from winning his third Triple Crown. On the final day of the season, Williams went 0-for-2 with two walks at Yankee Stadium as the Red Sox lost the pennant to New York. Meanwhile, at Briggs Stadium, Kell went 2-for-3 against 22-game winner Bob Lemon.

Under new manager and former Yankees third baseman Red Rolfe, Detroit won nine more than the previous season, improved a notch in the standings, and climbed out of the second division into fourth place, 10 games behind the first-place Yankees.

Beyond Kell, only two others hit .300: rightfielder Vic Wertz (.304, also third in RBIs and total bases) and left fielder Hoot Evers (.303). Reserve outfielder Pat Mullin, who smacked 12 home runs for the season, hit three in one game.

Solid pitching aided the club's improvement. Virgil Trucks led Detroit pitchers at 19–11 with a league second-best 2.81 ERA. First in the league in strikeouts, tied for first in shutouts, Trucks was the All-Star Game's winning pitcher in Brooklyn—the first Tiger to win it since Tommy Bridges in 1939. Hal Newhouser finished the year with an 18–11 record, finished second in the league in strikeouts, and tied for second in complete games.

TEAM STATISTICS

	W	L	PCT	GB	R	OR	2B	3B	HR	BA	SA	SB	E	DP	FA	CG	BB	SO	ShO	SV	ERA
	97	57	.630		829	637	215	60	115	.269	.400	58	138	195	.977	59	812	671	12	36	3.69
S	96	58	.623	1	896	667	272	36	131	.282	.420	43	120	207	.980	84	661	598	16	16	3.97
E	89	65	.578	8	675	574	194	58	112	.260	.384	44	103	192	.983	65	611	594	10	19	3.36
T	87	67	.565	10	751	655	215	51	88	.267	.378	39	131	174	.978	70	628	631	19	12	3.77
I	81	73	.526	16	726	725	214	49	82	.260	.369	36	140	217	.976	85	758	490	9	11	4.23
I	63	91	.409	34	648	737	207	66	43	.257	.347	62	141	180	.977	57	693	502	10	17	4.30
L	53	101	.344	44	667	913	213	30	117	.254	.377	38	166	154	.971	43	685	432	3	16	5.21
S	50	104	.325	47	584	868	207	41	81	.254	.356	46	161	168	.973	44	779	451	9	9	5.10
GUE TOTAL					5776	5776	1737	391	769	.263	.379	366	1100	1487	.977	507	5627	4369	88	136	4.20

INDIVIDUAL PITCHING

CHER	T	W	L	PCT	ERA	SV	G	GS	CG	IP	H	BB	SO	R	ER	ShO	H/9	BB/9	SO/9
Newhouser	L	18	11	.621	3.36	1	38	35	22	292	277	111	144	118	109	3	8.54	3.42	4.44
gil Trucks	R	19	11	.633	2.81	4	41	32	17	275	209	124	153	95	86	6	6.84	4.06	5.01
Houtteman	R	15	10	.600	3.71	0	34	25	13	203.2	227	59	85	101	84	2	10.03	2.61	3.76
Gray	L	10	10	.500	3.51	1	34	27	8	195	163	103	96	83	76	3	7.52	4.75	4.43
d Hutchinson	R	15	7	.682	2.96	1	33	21	9	188.2	167	52	54	70	62	4	7.97	2.48	2.58
Kretlow	R	3	2	.600	6.16	0	25	10	1	76	85	69	40	58	52	0	10.07	8.17	4.74
zy Trout	R	3	6	.333	4.40	3	33	0	0	59.1	68	21	19	35	29	0	10.31	3.19	2.88
rv Grissom	R	2	4	.333	6.41	0	27	2	0	39.1	56	34	17	32	28	0	12.81	7.78	3.89
rlin Stuart	R	0	2	.000	9.10	0	14	2	0	29.2	39	35	14	33	30	0	11.83	10.62	4.25
bby Overmire	L	1	3	.250	9.87	0	14	1	0	17.1	29	9	3	21	19	0	15.06	4.67	1.56
White	R	1	0	1.000	0.00	2	9	0	0	12	5	4	4	0	0	0	3.75	3.00	3.00
l Rogovin	R	0	1	.000	14.29	0	5	0	0	5.2	13	7	2	9	9	0	20.65	11.12	3.18
AM TOTAL		87	67	.565	3.77	12	307	155	70	1393.2	1338	628	631	655	584	18	8.64	4.06	4.07

MANAGER	W	L	PCT
Red Rolfe	95	59	.617

POS	Player	B	G	AB	H	2B	3B	HR	HR %	R	RBI	BB	SO	SB	Pinch Hit AB	Pinch Hit H	BA	SA
REGULARS																		
1B	Don Kolloway	R	125	467	135	20	4	6	1.3	55	62	29	28	1	5	1	.289	.388
2B	Gerry Priddy	R	157	618	171	26	6	13	2.1	104	75	95	95	2	0	0	.277	.401
SS	Johnny Lipon	R	147	601	176	27	6	2	0.3	104	63	81	26	9	0	0	.293	.368
3B	George Kell	R	157	**641**	**218**	**56**	6	8	1.2	114	101	66	18	3	0	0	.340	.484
RF	Vic Wertz	L	149	559	172	37	4	27	4.8	99	123	91	55	0	4	2	.308	.533
CF	Johnny Groth	R	157	566	173	30	8	12	2.1	95	85	95	27	1	0	0	.306	.451
LF	Hoot Evers	R	143	526	170	35	11	21	4.0	100	103	71	40	5	1	0	.323	.551
C	Aaron Robinson	L	107	283	64	7	0	9	3.2	37	37	75	35	0	3	3	.226	.346
SUBSTITUTES																		
1B	Dick Kryhoski	L	53	169	37	10	0	4	2.4	20	19	8	11	0	5	2	.219	.349
S2	Neil Berry	R	38	39	10	1	0	0	0.0	9	7	6	11	0	4	0	.256	.282
S3	Eddie Lake	R	20	7	0	0	0	0	0.0	3	1	1	3	0	7	0	.000	.000
OF	Pat Mullin	L	69	142	31	5	0	6	4.2	16	23	20	23	1	33	6	.218	.380
OF	Charlie Keller	L	50	51	16	1	3	2	3.9	7	16	13	6	0	32	9	.314	.569
C	Bob Swift	R	67	132	30	4	0	2	1.5	14	9	25	6	0	1	0	.227	.303
C	Joe Ginsberg	L	36	95	22	6	0	0	0.0	12	12	11	6	1	4	1	.232	.295
C	Frank House	L	5	5	2	1	0	0	0.0	1	0	0	1	0	1	0	.400	.600
PH	Paul Campbell	L	3	1	0	0	0	0	0.0	1	0	0	0	0	1	0	.000	.000
PITCHERS																		
P	Fred Hutchinson	L	44	95	31	7	0	0	0.0	15	20	12	3	0	4	1	.326	.400
P	Art Houtteman	R	41	93	14	4	1	0	0.0	5	3	5	20	0	0	0	.151	.215
P	Hal Newhouser	L	35	74	13	2	0	0	0.0	6	8	5	8	0	0	0	.176	.203
P	Dizzy Trout	R	34	63	12	1	1	1	1.6	6	10	6	20	0	0	0	.190	.286
P	Ted Gray	B	27	50	7	2	0	0	0.0	4	3	4	22	0	0	0	.140	.180
P	Hal White	L	42	33	4	2	0	0	0.0	1	1	0	10	0	0	0	.121	.182
P	Virgil Trucks	R	7	20	3	1	0	0	0.0	2	0	0	2	0	0	0	.150	.200
P	Saul Rogovin	R	11	16	3	0	0	1	6.3	2	5	0	3	0	0	0	.188	.375
P	Marlin Stuart	L	19	12	1	0	0	0	0.0	2	0	1	1	0	0	0	.083	.083
P	Hank Borowy	R	13	7	1	0	0	0	0.0	1	1	0	1	0	0	0	.143	.143
P	Paul Calvert	R	32	7	0	0	0	0	0.0	2	1	1	0	0	0	0	.000	.000
P	Ray Herbert	R	8	7	2	0	0	0	0.0	0	0	0	0	0	0	0	.286	.286
P	Bill Connelly	L	2	1	0	0	0	0	0.0	0	0	0	0	0	0	0	.000	.000
	TEAM TOTAL			5380	1518	285	50	114	2.1	837	788	722	481	23	105	25	.282	.417

INDIVIDUAL FIELDING

POS	Player	T	G	PO	A	E	DP	TC/G	FA		POS	Player	T	G	PO	A	E	DP	TC/G	FA
1B	D. Kolloway	R	118	1087	85	13	133	10.0	.989		OF	J. Groth	R	157	374	9	6	0	2.5	.985
	D. Kryhoski	L	47	409	27	4	44	9.4	.991			H. Evers	R	139	325	15	1	3	2.5	**.997**
2B	G. Priddy	R	157	440	**542**	19	**150**	6.4	.981			V. Wertz	R	145	286	5	10	3	2.1	.967
	N. Berry	R	2	2	4	1	1	3.0	1.000			P. Mullin	R	32	62	4	0	1	2.1	1.000
	D. Kolloway	R	1	1	3	0	0	4.0	1.000			C. Keller	R	6	10	0	0	0	1.7	1.000
SS	J. Lipon	R	147	273	**483**	33	126	5.4	.958		C	A. Robinson	R	103	355	42	3	4	3.9	.993
	E. Lake	R	1	0	0	0	0	0.0	.000			B. Swift	R	66	201	20	1	3	3.4	.995
	N. Berry	R	11	19	30	3	13	4.7	.942			J. Ginsberg	R	31	97	8	2	3	3.5	.981
3B	G. Kell	R	157	186	315	9	30	3.2	**.982**			F. House	R	5	4	1	0	0	1.0	1.000
	E. Lake	R	1	0	0	0	0	0.0	.000											
	N. Berry	R	1	0	1	0	0	1.0	1.000											

The Tigers were sluggers again. Four hit over .300: third baseman George Kell (.340) and the entire outfield—Hoot Evers in left (.323), Vic Wertz in right (.308), and Johnny Groth in center (.306). For the first time in 12 seasons, three notched 100 RBIs: Wertz, Evers, and Kell. Two hit for the cycle: Kell and Evers. Four authored hitting streaks: Kell (20 games), Evers (19), shortstop Johnny Lipon (19), and Groth (18). And against the Yankees on June 23, four slammed home runs in one inning: pitcher Dizzy Trout, second baseman Jerry Priddy, Wertz, and Evers.

Among pitchers, Art Houtteman had his best major league season, the 23-year-old right-hander finishing 19–12 with a 3.54 ERA and a league-high four shutouts.

En route to 95 victories—their most in 16 years—the Tigers climbed into first place on June 10 and stayed there tenuously but continuously entering September. And on August 30 still only two games separated the top four clubs: Detroit, New York, Boston, and Cleveland. Then the Yankees surged into first. No one would depose them, although for a time it stayed close—on September 19, the Tigers and Red Sox were a half game behind, and two days later Detroit and New York were tied. But the Indians became spoilers, beating the Tigers three straight in Cleveland.

During the final, fatal loss of that pennant-losing sweep, the Tigers beat themselves with a bit of botchery. In the bottom of the 10th, with the bases loaded and one out, Luke Easter grounded to first baseman Don Kolloway, who stepped on the bag and threw home to Aaron Robinson. But the Detroit catcher hadn't seen the play at first base, and instead of making an easy tag on Lemon chugging home from third, Robinson simply stepped on the plate for what he thought was a force out. It wasn't, and Lemon scored the winning run. Thus the Tigers, who had spent 119 days in first place, finished second, three games behind the pennant-winning Yankees.

TEAM STATISTICS

W	L	PCT	GB	R	OR	2B	3B	HR	BA	SA	SB	E	DP	FA	CG	BB	SO	ShO	SV	ERA
98	56	.636		914	691	234	70	159	.282	.441	41	119	188	.980	66	708	712	12	31	4.15
95	59	.617	3	837	713	285	50	114	.282	.417	23	120	194	.981	72	553	576	9	20	4.12
94	60	.610	4	1027	804	287	61	161	.302	.464	32	111	181	.981	66	748	630	6	28	4.88
92	62	.597	6	806	654	222	46	164	.269	.422	40	129	160	.978	69	647	674	11	16	3.74
67	87	.435	31	690	813	190	53	76	.260	.360	42	167	181	.972	59	648	486	7	18	4.66
60	94	.390	38	625	749	172	47	93	.260	.364	19	140	181	.977	62	734	566	7	9	4.41
58	96	.377	40	684	916	235	43	106	.246	.370	39	196	155	.967	56	651	448	7	14	5.20
52	102	.338	46	670	913	204	53	100	.261	.378	42	155	208	.974	50	729	466	3	18	5.49
GUE TOTAL				6253	6253	1829	423	973	.271	.402	278	1137	1448	.976	500	5418	4558	62	154	4.58

INDIVIDUAL PITCHING

CHER	T	W	L	PCT	ERA	SV	G	GS	CG	IP	H	BB	SO	R	ER	ShO	H/9	BB/9	SO/9
Houtteman	R	19	12	.613	3.54	4	41	34	21	274.2	257	99	88	112	108	4	8.42	3.24	2.88
d Hutchinson	R	17	8	.680	3.96	0	39	26	10	231.2	269	48	71	119	102	1	10.45	1.86	2.76
Newhouser	L	15	13	.536	4.34	3	35	30	15	213.2	232	81	87	110	103	1	9.77	3.41	3.66
ty Trout	R	13	5	.722	3.75	4	34	20	11	184.2	190	64	88	84	77	1	9.26	3.12	4.29
Gray	L	10	7	.588	4.40	1	27	21	7	149.1	139	72	102	85	73	0	8.38	4.34	6.15
White	R	9	6	.600	4.54	1	42	8	3	111	96	65	53	59	56	1	7.78	5.27	4.30
l Calvert	R	2	2	.500	6.31	4	32	0	0	51.1	71	25	14	42	36	0	12.45	4.38	2.45
il Trucks	R	3	1	.750	3.54	0	7	7	2	48.1	45	21	25	20	19	1	8.38	3.91	4.66
in Stuart	R	3	1	.750	5.56	2	19	1	0	43.2	59	22	19	32	27	0	12.16	4.53	3.92
Rogovin	R	2	1	.667	4.50	0	11	5	1	40	39	26	11	21	20	0	8.78	5.85	2.48
k Borowy	R	1	1	.500	3.31	0	13	2	1	32.2	23	16	12	15	12	0	6.34	4.41	3.31
Herbert	R	1	2	.333	3.63	1	8	3	1	22.1	20	12	5	11	9	0	8.06	4.84	2.01
Connelly	R	0	0	–	6.75	0	2	0	0	4	4	2	1	3	3	0	9.00	4.50	2.25
M TOTAL		95	59	.617	4.12	20	310	157	72	1407.1	1444	553	576	713	645	9	9.23	3.54	3.68

MANAGER	W	L	PCT
Red Rolfe	73	81	.474

POS	Player	B	G	AB	H	2B	3B	HR	HR %	R	RBI	BB	SO	SB	Pinch Hit AB	Pinch Hit H	BA	SA
REGULARS																		
1B	Dick Kryhoski	L	119	421	121	19	4	12	2.9	58	57	28	29	1	10	4	.287	.437
2B	Gerry Priddy	R	154	584	152	22	6	8	1.4	73	57	69	73	4	0	0	.260	.360
SS	Johnny Lipon	R	129	487	129	15	1	0	0.0	56	38	49	27	7	2	0	.265	.300
3B	George Kell	R	147	598	191	36	3	2	0.3	92	59	61	18	10	0	0	.319	.400
RF	Vic Wertz	L	138	501	143	24	4	27	5.4	86	94	78	61	0	6	0	.285	.511
CF	Johnny Groth	R	118	428	128	29	1	3	0.7	41	49	31	32	1	6	2	.299	.393
LF	Hoot Evers	R	116	393	88	15	2	11	2.8	47	46	40	47	5	8	2	.224	.356
C	Joe Ginsberg	L	102	304	79	10	2	8	2.6	44	37	43	21	0	8	2	.260	.385
SUBSTITUTES																		
1B	Don Kolloway	R	78	212	54	7	0	1	0.5	28	17	15	12	2	17	4	.255	.302
UT	Neil Berry	R	67	157	36	5	2	0	0.0	17	9	10	15	4	4	0	.229	.287
2B	Al Federoff	R	2	4	0	0	0	0	0.0	0	0	0	0	0	0	0	.000	.000
OF	Pat Mullin	L	110	295	83	11	6	12	4.1	41	51	40	38	2	30	5	.281	.481
OF	Steve Souchock	R	91	188	46	10	3	11	5.9	33	28	18	27	0	34	7	.245	.505
OF	Charlie Keller	L	54	62	16	2	0	3	4.8	6	21	11	12	0	38	9	.258	.435
OF	Russ Sullivan	L	7	26	5	1	0	1	3.8	2	1	2	1	0	0	0	.192	.346
C	Bob Swift	R	44	104	20	0	0	0	0.0	8	5	12	10	0	1	0	.192	.192
C	Aaron Robinson	L	36	82	17	6	0	0	0.0	3	9	17	9	0	1	1	.207	.293
C	Frank House	L	18	41	9	2	0	1	2.4	3	4	6	2	1	0	0	.220	.341
PH	Doc Daugherty	R	1	1	0	0	0	0	0.0	0	0	0	1	0	1	0	.000	.000
PITCHERS																		
P	Fred Hutchinson	L	47	85	16	2	0	0	0.0	7	7	7	4	0	13	2	.188	.212
P	Ted Gray	B	35	63	9	1	0	0	0.0	3	3	6	27	0	0	0	.143	.159
P	Virgil Trucks	R	37	55	13	3	0	0	0.0	5	14	0	12	0	0	0	.236	.291
P	Bob Cain	L	35	53	13	3	0	0	0.0	9	9	6	9	0	0	0	.245	.302
P	Dizzy Trout	R	42	52	14	1	0	1	1.9	6	7	11	13	0	0	0	.269	.346
P	Marlin Stuart	L	29	43	10	2	1	1	2.3	4	3	0	8	0	0	0	.233	.395
P	Gene Bearden	L	37	32	6	2	0	2	6.3	7	6	0	4	0	0	0	.188	.438
P	Hal Newhouser	L	17	29	9	0	0	0	0.0	4	3	5	3	0	0	0	.310	.310
P	Hal White	L	38	16	4	1	0	0	0.0	0	0	0	3	0	0	0	.250	.313
P	Hank Borowy	R	26	8	0	0	0	0	0.0	0	0	0	3	0	0	0	.000	.000
P	Saul Rogovin	R	5	7	2	2	0	0	0.0	2	2	1	1	0	0	0	.286	.571
P	Ray Herbert	R	5	4	0	0	0	0	0.0	0	0	1	1	0	0	0	.000	.000
P	Wayne McLeland	R	6	1	0	0	0	0	0.0	0	0	0	0	0	0	0	.000	.000
P	Paul Calvert	R	1	0	0	0	0	0	–	0	0	0	0	0	0	0	–	–
P	Earl Johnson	L	6	0	0	0	0	0	0.0	0	0	0	0	0	0	0	–	–
P	Dick Marlowe	R	2	0	0	0	0	0	–	0	0	0	0	0	0	0	–	–
	TEAM TOTAL			5336	1413	231	35	104	1.9	685	636	567	523	37	179	38	.265	.380

INDIVIDUAL FIELDING

POS	Player	T	G	PO	A	E	DP	TC/G	FA	POS	Player	T	G	PO	A	E	DP	TC/G	FA
1B	D. Kryhoski	L	112	964	81	9	95	9.4	.991	OF	J. Groth	R	112	266	12	2	3	2.5	.993
	D. Kolloway	R	59	452	49	4	53	8.6	.992		V. Wertz	R	131	254	7	3	1	2.0	.989
	S. Souchock	R	1	1	0	0	0	1.0	1.000		H. Evers	R	108	234	9	6	1	2.3	.976
2B	G. Priddy	R	154	437	463	18	118	6.0	.980		P. Mullin	R	83	151	4	10	1	2.0	.939
	N. Berry	R	10	9	9	0	2	1.8	1.000		S. Souchock	R	59	92	3	6	1	1.7	.941
	A. Federoff	R	1	3	5	1	0	9.0	.889		C. Keller	R	8	22	0	0	0	2.8	1.000
	S. Souchock	R	1	1	1	0	0	2.0	1.000		R. Sullivan	R	7	14	1	1	0	2.3	.938
SS	J. Lipon	R	125	244	364	33	80	5.1	.949	C	J. Ginsberg	R	95	388	56	10	7	4.8	.978
	N. Berry	R	38	63	106	10	19	4.7	.944		B. Swift	R	43	146	17	3	3	3.9	.982
	G. Priddy	R	1	1	1	0	0	2.0	1.000		A. Robinson	R	35	100	17	0	0	3.3	1.000
3B	G. Kell	R	147	175	310	20	34	3.4	.960		F. House	R	18	56	11	3	1	3.9	.957
	N. Berry	R	7	6	12	2	1	2.9	.900										

The first inning of the second game of a mid-August doubleheader at St. Louis brought out of the Browns dugout three-foot-seven, 67-pound pinch hitter Eddie Gaedel. Tigers catcher Bob Swift called time, walked to the mound bewildered and conferred with pitcher Bob Cain on how to pitch to a batter with a one-and-a-half-inch strike zone. Swift returned, dropped to his knees behind Gaedel and a still-astonished Cain pitched. The first two easily sailed over Gaedel's head. By the third pitch, Cain was laughing too hard even to come close, walking the midget on four pitches. Gaedel was taken out for a pinch runner and trotted out of baseball, but forever into baseball lore.

The Tigers found little else to laugh about. Never rising above third place, Detroit dropped below .500 and out of the first division into fifth place—25 games behind the first-place Yankees. Pitching and hitting were equally devastated by a series of slumps, injuries, and inductions as selective service geared up for the Korean War. Third baseman George Kell led the league in hits, was tied for second in doubles, and finished third in hitting at .319. But he was the only Tiger above .300, as Detroit's team batting average dropped 37 points from a major league-leading .302 the previous season to .265. During the winter, 19-game winner Art Houtteman had been drafted. Ray Herbert looked as if he'd fill the void by winning his first four games, but the army snatched him, too, on May 16. One other staff member was lost in an early-season trade. Saul Rogovin left the Tigers at 1–1 and finished with the White Sox at 12–8 with a league-leading 2.78 ERA.

Even the arrival of the All-Star Game barely cheered the Motor City. Briggs Stadium hosted its second midsummer classic, but this time there were no Ted Williams heroics to save the Americans, who lost, 8–3. Tiger fans were consoled by a home run each from hometown starters Kell and Vic Wertz. And less than a month later, an all-star from the past returned to Detroit: Charlie Gehringer took over as vice-president and general manager.

TEAM STATISTICS

W	L	PCT	GB	R	OR	2B	3B	Batting HR	BA	SA	SB	E	Fielding DP	FA	CG	BB	Pitching SO	ShO	SV	ERA
98	56	.636		798	621	208	48	140	.269	.408	78	144	190	.975	66	562	664	24	22	3.56
93	61	.604	5	696	594	208	35	140	.256	.389	52	134	151	.978	76	577	642	10	19	3.38
87	67	.565	11	804	725	233	32	127	.266	.392	20	141	184	.977	46	599	658	7	24	4.14
81	73	.526	17	714	644	229	64	86	.270	.385	99	151	176	.975	74	549	572	11	14	3.50
73	81	.474	25	685	741	231	35	104	.265	.380	37	163	166	.973	51	602	597	8	17	4.29
70	84	.455	28	736	745	262	43	102	.262	.386	48	136	204	.978	52	569	437	7	22	4.47
62	92	.403	36	672	764	242	45	54	.263	.355	45	160	148	.973	58	630	475	6	13	4.49
52	102	.338	46	611	882	223	47	86	.247	.357	35	172	179	.971	56	801	550	5	9	5.17
AGUE TOTAL				5716	5716	1836	349	839	.262	.381	414	1201	1398	.975	479	4889	4595	78	140	4.12

INDIVIDUAL PITCHING

TCHER	T	W	L	PCT	ERA	SV	G	GS	CG	IP	H	BB	SO	R	ER	ShO	H/9	BB/9	SO/9
d Gray	L	7	14	.333	4.06	1	34	28	9	197.1	194	95	131	103	89	1	8.85	4.33	5.97
zzy Trout	R	9	14	.391	4.04	5	42	22	7	191.2	172	75	89	98	86	0	8.08	3.52	4.18
ed Hutchinson	R	10	10	.500	3.68	2	31	20	9	188.1	204	27	53	84	77	2	9.75	1.29	2.53
gil Trucks	R	13	8	.619	4.33	1	37	18	6	153.2	153	75	89	81	74	1	8.96	4.39	5.21
b Cain	L	11	10	.524	4.70	2	35	22	6	149.1	135	82	58	88	78	1	8.14	4.94	3.50
arlin Stuart	R	4	6	.400	3.77	1	29	15	5	124	119	71	46	60	52	0	8.64	5.15	3.34
ne Bearden	L	3	4	.429	4.33	0	37	4	2	106	112	58	38	58	51	1	9.51	4.92	3.23
l Newhouser	L	6	6	.500	3.92	0	15	14	7	96.1	98	19	37	47	42	1	9.16	1.78	3.46
l White	R	3	4	.429	4.74	4	38	4	0	76	74	49	23	45	40	0	8.76	5.80	2.72
nk Borowy	R	2	2	.500	6.95	0	26	1	0	45.1	58	27	16	39	35	0	11.51	5.36	3.18
ul Rogovin	R	1	1	.500	5.25*	0	5	4	0	24	23	7	5	15	14	0	8.63	2.63	1.88
Herbert	R	4	0	1.000	1.42	0	5	0	0	12.2	8	9	9	2	2	0	5.68	6.39	6.39
ayne McLeland	R	0	0	.000	8.18	0	6	1	0	11	20	4	0	10	10	0	16.36	3.27	0.00
rl Johnson	L	0	0	–	6.35	1	6	0	0	5.2	9	2	2	5	4	0	14.29	3.18	3.18
ck Marlowe	R	0	1	.000	32.40	0	2	1	0	1.2	5	2	1	6	6	0	27.00	10.80	5.40
ul Calvert	R	0	0	–	0.00	0	1	0	0	1	1	0	0	0	0	0	9.00	0.00	0.00
AM TOTAL		73	81	.474	4.29	17	349	154	51	1384	1385	602	597	741	660	7	9.01	3.91	3.88

MANAGER	W	L	PCT
Red Rolfe	23	49	.319
Fred Hutchinson	27	55	.329

POS	Player	B	G	AB	H	2B	3B	HR	HR %	R	RBI	BB	SO	SB	Pinch Hit AB	Pinch Hit H	BA	SA
REGULARS																		
1B	Walt Dropo	R	115	459	128	17	3	23	5.0	56	70	26	63	2	0	0	.279	.479
2B	Gerry Priddy	R	75	279	79	23	3	4	1.4	37	20	42	29	1	0	0	.283	.430
SS	Neil Berry	R	73	189	43	4	3	0	0.0	22	13	22	19	1	1	1	.228	.280
3B	Fred Hatfield	L	112	441	104	12	2	2	0.5	42	25	35	52	2	0	0	.236	.286
RF	Vic Wertz	L	85	285	70	15	3	17	6.0	46	51	46	44	1	7	2	.246	.498
CF	Johnny Groth	R	141	524	149	22	2	4	0.8	56	51	51	39	2	3	0	.284	.357
LF	Pat Mullin	L	97	255	64	13	5	7	2.7	29	35	31	30	4	30	6	.251	.424
C	Joe Ginsberg	L	113	307	68	13	2	6	2.0	29	36	51	21	1	16	2	.221	.336
SUBSTITUTES																		
2B	Al Federoff	R	74	231	56	4	2	0	0.0	14	14	16	13	1	0	0	.242	.277
S2	Johnny Pesky	L	69	177	45	4	0	1	0.6	26	9	42	11	1	10	1	.254	.294
1B	Don Kolloway	R	65	173	42	9	0	2	1.2	19	21	7	19	0	25	5	.243	.329
3B	George Kell	R	39	152	45	8	0	1	0.7	11	17	14	13	0	0	0	.296	.368
SS	Johnny Lipon	R	39	136	30	4	2	0	0.0	17	12	16	6	3	0	0	.221	.279
SS	Harvey Kuenn	R	19	80	26	2	2	0	0.0	2	8	2	1	2	0	0	.325	.400
1B	Bennie Taylor	L	7	18	3	0	0	0	0.0	0	0	0	5	0	3	0	.167	.167
UT	Steve Souchock	R	92	265	66	16	4	13	4.9	40	45	21	28	1	17	4	.249	.487
OF	Cliff Mapes	L	86	193	38	7	0	9	4.7	26	23	27	42	0	23	6	.197	.373
OF	Don Lenhardt	R	45	144	27	2	1	3	2.1	18	13	28	18	0	2	0	.188	.278
OF	Jim Delsing	L	33	113	31	2	1	3	2.7	14	15	11	8	1	1	1	.274	.389
OF	Russ Sullivan	L	15	52	17	2	1	3	5.8	7	5	3	5	1	1	1	.327	.577
OF	Johnny Hopp	L	42	46	10	1	0	0	0.0	5	3	6	7	0	31	8	.217	.239
OF	George Lerchen	B	14	32	5	1	0	1	3.1	1	3	7	10	1	7	2	.156	.281
OF	Bill Tuttle	R	7	25	6	0	0	0	0.0	2	2	0	1	0	1	0	.240	.240
OF	Don Lund	R	8	23	7	0	0	0	0.0	1	1	3	3	0	1	0	.304	.304
C	Matt Batts	R	56	173	41	4	1	3	1.7	11	13	14	22	1	2	0	.237	.324
C	Bob Swift	R	28	58	8	1	0	0	0.0	3	4	7	7	0	0	0	.138	.155
PH	Carl Linhart	L	3	2	0	0	0	0	0.0	0	0	0	0	0	2	0	.000	.000
PH	Hoot Evers	R	1	1	1	0	0	0	0.0	0	0	0	0	0	1	1	1.000	1.000
PH	Alex Garbowski	R	2	0	0	0	0	0	–	0	0	0	0	0	0	0	–	–
PITCHERS																		
P	Ted Gray	B	36	76	13	0	0	0	0.0	3	2	1	19	0	0	0	.171	.171
P	Art Houtteman	R	36	69	7	0	0	0	0.0	2	2	2	10	0	0	0	.101	.101
P	Virgil Trucks	R	35	64	12	0	0	1	1.6	3	3	1	11	1	0	0	.188	.234
P	Bill Wight	L	23	50	11	2	0	0	0.0	2	4	1	7	0	0	0	.220	.260
P	Hal Newhouser	L	26	46	10	1	0	0	0.0	5	4	10	9	0	0	0	.217	.239
P	Billy Hoeft	L	34	40	6	1	0	0	0.0	3	1	2	15	0	0	0	.150	.175
P	Marlin Stuart	L	30	23	2	0	0	0	0.0	3	2	3	6	0	0	0	.087	.087
P	Fred Hutchinson	L	17	18	1	0	0	0	0.0	0	0	3	0	0	5	1	.056	.056
P	Hal White	L	41	11	2	0	0	0	0.0	0	0	0	5	0	0	0	.182	.182
P	Dizzy Trout	R	10	9	3	0	0	0	0.0	1	0	0	3	0	0	0	.333	.333
P	Dick Littlefield	L	28	7	1	0	0	0	0.0	1	0	0	2	0	0	0	.143	.143
P	Bill Black	R	2	3	0	0	0	0	0.0	0	0	0	0	0	0	0	.000	.000
P	Ken Johnson	L	9	3	1	0	0	0	0.0	0	2	0	0	0	0	0	.333	.333
P	Ned Garver	R	1	2	0	0	0	0	0.0	0	0	1	0	0	0	0	.000	.000
P	Dave Madison	R	10	2	0	0	0	0	0.0	0	0	0	1	0	0	0	.000	.000
P	Dick Marlowe	R	4	2	0	0	0	0	0.0	0	0	0	0	0	0	0	.000	.000
P	Wayne McLeland	R	4	0	0	0	0	0	–	0	0	0	0	0	0	0	–	–
	TEAM TOTAL			5258	1278	190	37	103	2.0	557	529	553	603	27	189	41	.243	.352

INDIVIDUAL FIELDING

POS	Player	T	G	PO	A	E	DP	TC/G	FA	POS	Player	T	G	PO	A	E	DP	TC/G	FA
1B	W. Dropo	R	115	1005	78	12	104	9.5	.989	OF	J. Groth	R	139	329	14	5	3	2.5	.986
	D. Kolloway	R	32	252	28	6	15	8.9	.979		V. Wertz	R	79	134	8	2	3	1.8	.986
	S. Souchock	R	9	81	6	1	4	9.8	.989		P. Mullin	R	65	131	6	3	2	2.2	.979
	B. Taylor	L	4	36	2	0	4	9.5	1.000		S. Souchock	R	56	103	4	4	2	2.0	.964
	B. Hoeft	L	1	1	0	0	0	1.0	1.000		D. Lenhardt	R	43	89	5	1	1	2.2	.989
	J. Hopp	L	1	1	0	0	0	1.0	1.000		C. Mapes	R	62	86	3	3	1	1.5	.967
											J. Delsing	R	32	67	1	3	0	2.2	.958
2B	G. Priddy	R	75	211	209	14	48	5.8	.968		R. Sullivan	R	14	17	2	4	0	1.6	.826
	A. Federoff	R	70	136	184	8	42	4.7	.976		B. Tuttle	R	6	19	0	0	0	3.2	1.000
	J. Pesky	R	22	27	36	2	12	3.0	.969		G. Lerchen	R	7	15	0	0	0	2.1	1.000
	D. Kolloway	R	8	14	16	1	4	3.9	.968		D. Lund	R	7	10	1	0	0	1.6	1.000
											J. Hopp	L	4	6	0	0	0	1.5	1.000
SS	N. Berry	R	66	90	158	9	26	3.9	.965										
	J. Pesky	R	41	78	101	9	25	4.6	.952	C	J. Ginsberg	R	101	442	41	8	7	4.9	.984
	J. Lipon	R	39	80	101	4	12	4.7	.978*		M. Batts	R	55	262	36	5	4	5.5	.983
	H. Kuenn	R	19	44	57	4	12	5.5	.962		B. Swift	R	28	118	12	3	1	4.8	.977
	A. Federoff	R	7	12	19	1	3	4.6	.969										
	F. Hatfield	R	9	11	13	2	3	2.9	.923										
3B	F. Hatfield	R	107	114	253*	12	32	3.5	.968*										
	G. Kell	R	39	38	78	5	7	3.1	.959										
	S. Souchock	R	13	11	21	3	1	2.7	.914										
	J. Pesky	R	3	2	5	0	0	2.3	1.000										
	N. Berry	R	2	1	2	0	0	1.5	1.000										

For Detroit fans, it was a year that will live in infamy. The Tigers—who had been the only American League team never to finish last—crashed to their first eighth-place finish in team history. Their 50 victories are still a franchise low, their 104 losses still a franchise high. They were bad from the start, losing their first eight, 10 of their first 13, and dropping into the cellar for keeps on May 2. Nothing helped. Manager Red Rolfe engineered a poor nine-player deal with the Red Sox—George Kell, Dizzy Trout, Hoot Evers, and Johnny Lipon to Boston for Johnny Pesky, Walt Dropo, Fred Hatfield, Bill Wight, and Don Lenhardt. A month later on July 5, Rolfe was fired by Spike Briggs—who had taken over as team president after the off-season death of his father, Walter O., Sr.—as Detroit foundered at 23–49. He was replaced by pitcher Fred Hutchinson, who shortly removed himself from the active list to end a 10-year Tiger career.

With no Tiger hitter exceeding .284—centerfielder Johnny Groth led at that mark—team batting plummeted to .243, second-worst in the league. Meanwhile, in Boston, Kell finished third-best in the league at .311. For the Tigers, Dropo—who strung together 12 straight hits, still tied for the major-league record—finished fourth in the league with 29 home runs. At one point Detroit resorted to trading with the Browns, including an eight-player waiver deal that dispatched Vic Wertz.

The pitching was worse. Detroit's 4.25 team ERA was highest in the league; Art Houttman lost nine straight en route to leading the league in losses at 8–20; and Virgil Trucks lost 19, won five—but two of his victories were the second and third no-hitters in team history. The right-hander notched No. 1 on May 15 against Washington at Briggs Stadium—the first no-hitter by a Tiger in 40 years—and No. 2 on August 25 against New York at Yankee Stadium. There was nearly a third. Trucks hurled a one-hitter on July 22 against the Senators; Eddie Yost singled on the first pitch of the game, and Trucks proceeded to retire the next 27 batters.

TEAM STATISTICS

W	L	PCT	GB	R	OR	2B	3B	HR	BA	SA	SB	E	DP	FA	CG	BB	SO	ShO	SV	ERA
95	59	.617		727	557	221	56	129	.267	.403	52	127	199	.979	72	581	666	17	27	3.14
93	61	.604	2	763	606	211	49	148	.262	.404	46	155	141	.975	80	556	671	16	18	3.32
81	73	.526	14	610	568	199	38	80	.252	.348	61	123	158	.980	53	578	774	13	28	3.25
79	75	.513	16	664	723	212	35	89	.253	.359	52	140	148	.977	73	526	562	11	16	4.15
78	76	.506	17	598	608	225	44	50	.239	.326	48	132	152	.978	75	577	574	10	15	3.37
76	78	.494	19	668	658	233	34	113	.255	.377	59	145	181	.976	53	623	624	7	24	3.80
64	90	.416	31	604	733	225	46	82	.250	.356	30	155	176	.974	48	598	581	6	18	4.12
50	104	.325	45	557	738	190	37	103	.243	.352	27	152	145	.975	51	591	702	10	14	4.25
LGUE TOTAL				5191	5191	1716	339	794	.253	.365	375	1129	1300	.977	505	4630	5154	90	160	3.67

INDIVIDUAL PITCHING

CHER	T	W	L	PCT	ERA	SV	G	GS	CG	IP	H	BB	SO	R	ER	ShO	H/9	BB/9	SO/9
Gray	L	12	17	.414	4.14	0	35	32	13	224	212	101	138	118	103	2	8.52	4.06	5.54
Houtteman	R	8	20	.286	4.36	1	35	28	10	221	218	65	109	116	107	2	8.88	2.65	4.44
gil Trucks	R	5	19	.208	3.97	1	35	29	8	197	190	82	129	99	87	3	8.68	3.75	5.89
Newhouser	L	9	9	.500	3.74	0	25	19	8	154	148	47	57	72	64	0	8.65	2.75	3.33
Wight	L	5	9	.357	3.88	0	23	19	8	143.2	167	55	65	71	62	3	10.46	3.45	4.07
Hoeft	L	2	7	.222	4.32	4	34	10	1	125	123	63	67	66	60	0	8.86	4.54	4.82
rlin Stuart	R	3	2	.600	4.93	1	30	9	2	91.1	91	48	32	60	50	0	8.97	4.73	3.15
White	R	1	8	.111	3.69	0	41	0	0	63.1	53	39	18	29	26	0	7.53	5.54	2.56
k Littlefield	L	0	3	.000	4.34	1	28	1	0	47.2	46	25	32	24	23	0	8.69	4.72	6.04
d Hutchinson	R	2	1	.667	3.38	0	12	1	0	37.1	40	9	12	16	14	0	9.64	2.17	2.89
zy Trout	R	1	5	.167	5.33	1	10	2	0	27	30	19	20	16	16	0	10.00	6.33	6.67
e Madison	R	1	1	.500	7.80	0	10	1	0	15	16	10	7	14	13	0	9.60	6.00	4.20
Johnson	L	0	0	–	6.35	0	9	1	0	11.1	12	11	10	11	8	0	9.53	8.74	7.94
Marlowe	R	0	2	.000	7.36	0	4	1	0	11	21	3	3	10	9	0	17.18	2.45	2.45
Garver	R	1	0	1.000	2.00	0	1	1	1	9	9	3	3	2	2	0	9.00	3.00	3.00
Black	R	0	1	.000	10.57	0	2	2	0	7.2	14	5	0	11	9	0	16.43	5.87	0.00
yne McLeland	R	0	0	–	10.13	0	4	0	0	2.2	4	6	0	3	3	0	13.50	20.25	0.00
M TOTAL		50	104	.325	4.25	14	338	156	51	1388	1394	591	702	738	656	10	9.04	3.83	4.55

MANAGER	W	L	PCT
Fred Hutchinson	60	94	.390

POS	Player	B	G	AB	H	2B	3B	HR	HR %	R	RBI	BB	SO	SB	Pinch Hit AB	Pinch Hit H	BA	SA
REGULARS																		
1B	Walt Dropo	R	152	606	150	30	3	13	2.1	61	96	29	69	2	2	1	.248	.371
2B	Johnny Pesky	L	103	308	90	22	1	2	0.6	43	24	27	10	3	30	12	.292	.390
SS	Harvey Kuenn	R	155	679	209	33	7	2	0.3	94	48	50	31	6	0	0	.308	.386
3B	Ray Boone	R	101	385	120	16	6	22	5.7	73	93	48	47	2	1	1	.312	.556
RF	Don Lund	R	131	421	108	21	4	9	2.1	51	47	39	65	3	8	2	.257	.390
CF	Jim Delsing	L	138	479	138	26	6	11	2.3	77	62	66	39	1	6	1	.288	.453
LF	Bob Nieman	R	142	508	143	32	5	15	3.0	72	69	57	57	0	7	1	.281	.453
C	Matt Batts	R	116	374	104	24	3	6	1.6	38	42	24	36	2	12	4	.278	.406
SUBSTITUTES																		
32	Fred Hatfield	L	109	311	79	11	1	3	1.0	41	19	40	34	3	19	7	.254	.325
21	Gerry Priddy	R	65	196	46	6	2	1	0.5	14	24	17	19	1	9	2	.235	.301
2B	Owen Friend	R	31	96	17	4	0	3	3.1	10	10	6	9	0	2	1	.177	.313
3B	Billy Hitchcock	R	22	38	8	0	0	0	0.0	8	0	3	3	0	6	1	.211	.211
3B	John Baumgartner	R	7	27	5	0	0	0	0.0	3	2	0	5	0	0	0	.185	.185
P1	Fred Hutchinson	L	4	6	1	0	0	1	16.7	1	1	0	0	0	0	0	.167	.667
2B	Reno Bertoia	R	1	1	0	0	0	0	0.0	0	0	0	1	0	0	0	.000	.000
OF	Steve Souchock	R	89	278	84	13	3	11	4.0	29	46	8	35	5	10	3	.302	.489
OF	Pat Mullin	L	79	97	26	1	0	4	4.1	11	17	14	15	0	57	13	.268	.402
OF	Russ Sullivan	L	23	72	18	5	1	1	1.4	7	6	13	5	0	3	0	.250	.389
OF	Al Kaline	R	30	28	7	0	0	1	3.6	9	2	1	5	1	1	0	.250	.357
OF	Frank Carswell	R	16	15	4	0	0	0	0.0	2	2	3	1	0	12	4	.267	.267
C	Johnny Bucha	R	60	158	35	9	0	1	0.6	17	14	20	14	1	2	0	.222	.297
C	Joe Ginsberg	L	18	53	16	2	0	0	0.0	6	3	10	1	0	3	0	.302	.340
C	Bob Swift	R	2	3	1	1	0	0	0.0	0	1	2	1	0	0	0	.333	.667
PH	George Freese	R	1	1	0	0	0	0	0.0	0	0	0	0	0	1	0	.000	.000
PITCHERS																		
P	Ned Garver	R	30	72	11	0	0	1	1.4	3	6	6	12	0	0	0	.153	.194
P	Billy Hoeft	L	30	64	11	1	0	0	0.0	8	4	9	17	0	0	0	.172	.188
P	Ted Gray	B	32	61	14	0	1	0	0.0	5	7	6	14	0	0	0	.230	.262
P	Steve Gromek	B	19	41	3	0	0	0	0.0	0	2	0	10	0	0	0	.073	.073
P	Ralph Branca	R	17	34	4	0	1	0	0.0	3	4	2	14	0	0	0	.118	.176
P	Dick Marlowe	R	42	32	7	0	0	0	0.0	0	2	0	13	0	0	0	.219	.219
P	Al Aber	L	17	23	3	0	0	0	0.0	2	2	1	6	0	0	0	.130	.130
P	Ray Herbert	R	43	19	3	0	0	0	0.0	0	0	2	7	0	0	0	.158	.158
P	Art Houtteman	R	16	19	3	1	0	1	5.3	4	2	0	2	0	0	0	.158	.368
P	Dave Madison	R	32	11	1	0	0	0	0.0	1	0	0	2	0	0	0	.091	.091
P	Bob Miller	R	13	8	1	0	0	0	0.0	0	0	0	0	0	0	0	.125	.125
P	Hal Newhouser	L	7	8	4	0	0	0	0.0	1	1	1	0	0	0	0	.500	.500
P	Bill Wight	L	13	7	3	0	0	0	0.0	0	1	0	1	0	0	0	.429	.429
P	Hal Erickson	R	18	4	0	0	0	0	0.0	0	0	0	0	0	0	0	.000	.000
P	Earl Harrist	R	8	3	0	0	0	0	0.0	0	0	1	0	0	0	0	.000	.000
P	Milt Jordan	R	8	2	1	0	0	0	0.0	0	0	0	0	0	0	0	.500	.500
P	Ray Scarborough	R	13	2	0	0	0	0	0.0	0	0	0	0	0	0	0	.000	.000
P	Dick Weik	R	12	2	1	1	0	0	0.0	1	1	0	1	0	0	0	.500	1.000
P	Paul Foytack	R	6	1	0	0	0	0	0.0	0	0	0	1	0	0	0	.000	.000
TEAM TOTAL				5553	1479	259	44	108	1.9	695	660	505	602	30	191	53	.266	.387

INDIVIDUAL FIELDING

POS	Player	T	G	PO	A	E	DP	TC/G	FA	POS	Player	T	G	PO	A	E	DP	TC/G	FA
1B	W. Dropo	R	150	1260	127	14	121	9.3	.990	OF	J. Delsing	R	133	354	7	3	2	2.7	.992
	G. Priddy	R	11	92	9	0	7	9.2	1.000		D. Lund	R	123	275	12	6	0	2.4	.980
	F. Hutchinson	R	1	4	0	0	0	4.0	1.000		B. Nieman	R	135	271	10	6	1	2.1	.979
	S. Souchock	R	1	3	0	0	0	3.0	1.000		S. Souchock	R	80	144	7	6	3	2.0	.962
											R. Sullivan	R	20	42	4	2	1	2.4	.958
2B	J. Pesky	R	73	166	183	3	49	4.8	.991		A. Kaline	R	20	11	1	0	0	0.6	1.000
	G. Priddy	R	45	111	106	5	28	4.9	.977		P. Mullin	R	14	16	1	1	0	1.3	.944
	F. Hatfield	R	28	64	87	5	21	5.6	.968		F. Carswell	R	3	1	0	0	0	0.3	1.000
	O. Friend	R	26	74	69	8	22	5.8	.947										
	B. Hitchcock	R	1	0	0	0	0	0.0	.000	C	M. Batts	R	103	463	44	7	7	5.0	.986
	R. Bertoia	R	1	1	0	1	0	2.0	.500		J. Bucha	R	56	218	22	4	4	4.4	.984
											J. Ginsberg	R	15	71	12	1	2	5.6	.988
SS	H. Kuenn	R	155	308	441	21	78	5.0	.973		B. Swift	R	2	13	0	0	0	6.5	1.000
	F. Hatfield	R	1	0	0	0	0	0.0	.000										
	R. Boone	R	3	4	8	1	2	4.3	.923										
	B. Hitchcock	R	1	1	1	0	1	2.0	1.000										
3B	R. Boone	R	97	111	211	14	32	3.5	.958										
	F. Hatfield	R	54	56	121	4	13	3.4	.978										
	B. Hitchcock	R	12	9	17	2	1	2.3	.929										
	Baumgartner	R	7	10	11	2	2	3.3	.913										
	G. Priddy	R	2	0	3	0	0	1.5	1.000										

As general manager Charlie Gehringer continued to shuffle personnel as mechanically as he had fielded ground balls, only five Tigers who went to spring training the year before returned to Lakeland, Florida: Pat Mullin, Hal Newhouser, Ted Gray, Gerry Priddy, and Steve Souchock. Six deals, four with the Browns, had moved 40 players: 20 coming, 20 going. And those who survived didn't stay long. The 32-year-old Newhouser would be released during the season; Mullin and Priddy would retire after the season.

Not surprisingly, an influx of St. Louis Browns didn't save the Tigers from another embarrassing summer as Fred Hutchinson's charges moved out of the basement into sixth and 40 1/2 behind first-place New York. Poor performances were plentiful. In his Tiger debut on June 18 at Fenway Park, pitcher Steve Gromek was shelled as the Red Sox collected a major league-record 17 runs and 14 hits—all in one inning.

But a few of the newcomers sparkled. Signed out of the University of Wisconsin the year before for $55,000, shortstop Harvey Kuenn led the majors in hits at 209 (most ever by a right-hand–hitting Tiger, two short of Ty Cobb's team mark), batted .308, and became the first Tiger to win the Rookie of the Year Award. Acquired early in the season from Cleveland, third baseman Ray Boone hit .312 in 101 games for Detroit—.296 overall, finishing third in the league in RBI (114), and cracking 26 home runs (including four grand slams to equal Rudy York's 15-year-old team record). And an 18-year-old rookie outfielder without an inning of minor-league experience joined the team to hit just .250 with one home run in 28 at bats in 30 games. But it was still a historic arrival. The games were the first of a team-record 2,834 and the home run the first of a team-record 399 for the Baltimore schoolboy, eventual 22-year Tiger, and Hall of Famer Albert Kaline.

TEAM STATISTICS

W	L	PCT	GB	R	OR	2B	Batting 3B	HR	BA	SA	SB	Fielding E	DP	FA	CG	BB	Pitching SO	ShO	SV	ERA
99	52	.656		801	547	226	52	139	.273	.417	34	126	182	.979	50	500	604	16	39	3.20
92	62	.597	8.5	770	627	201	29	160	.270	.410	33	127	197	.979	81	519	586	11	15	3.64
89	65	.578	11.5	716	592	226	53	74	.258	.364	73	125	144	.980	57	583	714	16	33	3.41
84	69	.549	16	656	632	255	37	101	.264	.384	33	148	173	.975	41	584	642	14	37	3.59
76	76	.500	23.5	687	614	230	53	69	.263	.368	65	120	173	.979	76	478	515	16	10	3.66
60	94	.390	40.5	695	923	259	44	108	.266	.387	30	135	149	.978	50	585	645	2	16	5.25
59	95	.383	41.5	632	799	205	38	116	.256	.372	41	137	161	.977	51	594	566	6	11	4.67
54	100	.351	46.5	555	778	214	25	112	.249	.363	17	152	165	.974	28	626	639	7	24	4.48
GUE TOTAL				5512	5512	1816	331	879	.262	.383	326	1070	1344	.978	434	4469	4911	88	185	4.00

INDIVIDUAL PITCHING

CHER	T	W	L	PCT	ERA	SV	G	GS	CG	IP	H	BB	SO	R	ER	ShO	H/9	BB/9	SO/9
Garver	R	11	11	.500	4.45	1	30	26	13	198.1	228	66	69	107	98	0	10.35	2.99	3.13
Hoeft	L	9	14	.391	4.83	2	29	27	9	197.2	223	58	90	113	106	0	10.15	2.64	4.10
Gray	L	10	15	.400	4.60	0	30	28	8	176	166	76	115	102	90	0	8.49	3.89	5.88
ve Gromek	R	6	8	.429	4.51	1	19	17	6	125.2	138	36	59	70	63	1	9.88	2.58	4.23
Marlowe	R	6	7	.462	5.26	0	42	11	2	119.2	152	42	52	74	70	0	11.43	3.16	3.91
oh Branca	R	4	7	.364	4.15	1	17	14	7	102	98	31	50	55	47	0	8.65	2.74	4.41
Herbert	R	4	6	.400	5.24	6	43	3	0	87.2	109	46	37	58	51	0	11.19	4.72	3.80
Houtteman	R	2	6	.250	5.90	1	16	9	3	68.2	87	29	28	50	45	1	11.40	3.80	3.67
ber	L	4	3	.571	4.46	0	17	10	2	66.2	63	41	34	35	33	0	8.51	5.54	4.59
e Madison	R	3	4	.429	6.82	0	32	1	0	62	76	44	27	55	47	0	11.03	6.39	3.92
Miller	L	1	2	.333	5.94	0	13	1	0	36.1	43	21	9	25	24	0	10.65	5.20	2.23
Erickson	R	0	1	.000	4.73	1	18	0	0	32.1	43	10	19	23	17	0	11.97	2.78	5.29
Wight	L	0	3	.000	8.88	0	13	4	0	25.1	35	14	10	33	25	0	12.43	4.97	3.55
Newhouser	L	0	1	.000	7.06	1	7	4	0	21.2	31	8	6	22	17	0	12.88	3.32	2.49
Scarborough	R	0	2	.000	8.27	2	13	0	0	20.2	34	11	12	24	19	0	14.81	4.79	5.23
Weik	R	0	1	.000	13.97	0	12	1	0	19.1	32	23	6	30	30	0	14.90	10.71	2.79
Harrist	R	0	2	.000	8.68	0	8	1	0	18.2	25	15	7	19	18	0	12.05	7.23	3.38
Jordan	R	0	1	.000	5.82	0	8	1	0	17	26	5	4	13	11	0	13.76	2.65	2.12
Foytack	R	0	0	–	11.17	0	6	0	0	9.2	15	9	7	12	12	0	13.97	6.39	6.52
Hutchinson	R	0	0	–	2.79	0	3	0	0	9.2	9	0	4	3	3	0	8.38	0.00	3.72
M TOTAL		60	94	.390	5.25	16	376	158	50	1415	1633	585	645	923	826	2	10.39	3.72	4.10

MANAGER	W	L	PCT
Fred Hutchinson	68	86	.442

POS	Player	B	G	AB	H	2B	3B	HR	HR %	R	RBI	BB	SO	SB	Pinch Hit AB	H	BA	SA
REGULARS																		
1B	Walt Dropo	R	107	320	90	14	2	4	1.3	27	44	24	41	0	18	5	.281	.375
2B	Frank Bolling	R	117	368	87	15	2	6	1.6	46	38	36	51	3	3	0	.236	.337
SS	Harvey Kuenn	R	155	656	201	28	6	5	0.8	81	48	29	13	9	0	0	.306	.390
3B	Ray Boone	R	148	543	160	19	7	20	3.7	76	85	71	53	4	0	0	.295	.466
RF	Al Kaline	R	138	504	139	18	3	4	0.8	42	43	22	45	9	3	1	.276	.347
CF	Bill Tuttle	R	147	530	141	20	11	7	1.3	64	58	62	60	5	3	1	.266	.385
LF	Jim Delsing	L	122	371	92	24	2	6	1.6	39	38	49	38	4	13	5	.248	.372
C	Frank House	L	114	352	88	12	1	9	2.6	35	38	31	34	2	9	1	.250	.366
SUBSTITUTES																		
1B	Wayne Belardi	L	88	250	58	7	1	11	4.4	27	24	33	34	1	12	2	.232	.400
23	Fred Hatfield	L	81	218	64	12	0	2	0.9	31	25	28	24	4	17	5	.294	.376
UT	Reno Bertoia	R	54	37	6	2	0	1	2.7	13	2	5	9	1	2	0	.162	.297
1B	Charlie Kress	L	24	37	7	0	1	0	0.0	4	3	1	4	0	15	2	.189	.243
SS	George Bullard	R	4	1	0	0	0	0	0.0	0	0	0	0	0	0	0	.000	.000
OF	Bob Nieman	R	91	251	66	14	1	8	3.2	24	35	22	32	0	26	8	.263	.422
OF	Hoot Evers	R	30	60	11	4	0	0	0.0	5	5	5	8	1	5	0	.183	.250
OF	Don Lund	R	35	54	7	2	0	0	0.0	4	3	4	3	1	9	1	.130	.167
OF	Steve Souchock	R	25	39	7	0	1	3	7.7	6	8	2	10	1	14	2	.179	.462
OF	Charlie King	R	11	28	6	0	1	0	0.0	4	3	3	8	0	4	0	.214	.286
C	Red Wilson	R	54	170	48	11	1	2	1.2	22	22	27	12	3	1	0	.282	.394
C	Matt Batts	R	12	21	6	1	0	0	0.0	1	5	2	4	0	5	2	.286	.333
C	Al Lakeman	R	5	6	0	0	0	0	0.0	0	0	0	1	0	1	0	.000	.000
C	Walt Streuli	R	1	0.	0	0	0	0	–	0	0	1	0	0	0	0	–	–
PH	Johnny Pesky	L	20	17	3	0	0	1	5.9	5	1	3	1	0	17	3	.176	.353
PITCHERS																		
P	Ned Garver	R	36	79	13	2	0	0	0.0	3	4	6	15	0	0	0	.165	.190
P	Steve Gromek	B	36	79	15	0	0	0	0.0	6	3	8	21	0	0	0	.190	.190
P	George Zuverink	R	35	64	8	1	0	0	0.0	1	3	1	14	0	0	0	.125	.141
P	Billy Hoeft	L	35	52	10	6	0	0	0.0	5	6	10	24	0	0	0	.192	.308
P	Al Aber	L	32	39	5	0	0	0	0.0	3	3	2	17	0	0	0	.128	.128
P	Ted Gray	B	19	22	1	0	0	0	0.0	0	0	0	4	0	0	0	.045	.045
P	Dick Marlowe	R	38	18	3	1	0	0	0.0	1	1	1	11	0	0	0	.167	.222
P	Ray Herbert	R	42	17	3	0	1	1	5.9	5	3	2	4	0	0	0	.176	.471
P	Bob Miller	R	34	15	2	1	0	0	0.0	2	0	0	4	0	0	0	.133	.200
P	Ralph Branca	R	17	13	4	1	0	0	0.0	2	1	2	3	0	0	0	.308	.385
P	Dick Donovan	L	2	1	0	0	0	0	0.0	0	0	0	1	0	0	0	.000	.000
P	Dick Weik	R	9	1	0	0	0	0	0.0	0	0	0	0	0	0	0	.000	.000
P	Frank Lary	R	3	0	0	0	0	0	–	0	0	0	0	0	0	0	–	–
	TEAM TOTAL			5233	1351	215	41	90	1.7	584	552	492	603	48	177	38	.258	.367

INDIVIDUAL FIELDING

POS	Player	T	G	PO	A	E	DP	TC/G	FA	POS	Player	T	G	PO	A	E	DP	TC/G	FA
1B	W. Dropo	R	95	681	54	3	60	7.8	.996	OF	B. Tuttle	R	145	364	18	6	3	2.7	.985
	W. Belardi	L	79	636	51	8	54	8.8	.988		A. Kaline	R	135	283	16	9	0	2.3	.971
	C. Kress	L	7	63	5	2	4	10.0	.971		J. Delsing	R	108	221	5	1	0	2.1	.996
2B	F. Bolling	R	113	248	232	13	54	4.4	.974		B. Nieman	R	62	119	2	2	0	2.0	.984
	F. Hatfield	R	54	114	126	7	29	4.6	.972		H. Evers	R	24	33	1	0	0	1.4	1.000
	R. Bertoia	R	15	26	36	2	6	4.3	.969		D. Lund	R	31	32	1	1	0	1.1	.971
SS	H. Kuenn	R	155	294	496	28	85	5.3	.966		C. Kress	L	1	0	0	0	0	0.0	.000
	R. Boone	R	1	0	0	0	0	0.0	.000		C. King	R	7	22	1	1	1	3.4	.958
	G. Bullard	R	1	2	2	1	0	5.0	.800		S. Souchock	R	9	13	0	0	1	1.4	1.000
	R. Bertoia	R	3	0	3	1	1	1.3	.750	C	F. House	R	107	434	56	4	7	4.6	.992
3B	R. Boone	R	148	170	332	19	22	3.5	.964		R. Wilson	R	53	245	25	1	7	5.1	.996
	F. Hatfield	R	15	15	26	4	4	3.0	.911		M. Batts	R	8	24	5	1	1	3.8	.967
	S. Souchock	R	2	2	4	0	0	3.0	1.000		A. Lakeman	R	4	10	0	0	0	2.5	1.000
	R. Bertoia	R	8	1	2	0	0	0.4	1.000		W. Streuli	R	1	1	0	0	0	1.0	1.000

Tiger fans likely wondered what was so fabulous about the fifties. Detroit improved a notch to fifth place—just a game behind fourth-place Boston—but hardly tantalized its legions with another sub-.500 summer, 43 games away from the pennant. The Tigers and the White Sox both had raced to fast starts, each winning 11 of their first 16. Detroit veteran Steve Gromek won seven of his first eight decisions, while several of his fresh, young teammates sparkled in the spring. But by mid-May the Indians streaked past en route to their league-record 111 victories. After his exceptional start, Gromek went 11–15, and by the All-Star break the fourth-place Detroits were 19 games out and fading.

Not long after the team dropped out of the pennant race, Harvey Kuenn broke out of his slump. Having fallen to .252 on July 19, he erupted to hit .375 the rest of the season to finish at .306 with 201 hits—tied with Chicago's Nellie Fox for league-most. Kuenn also struck out just 13 times in 656 at bats to tie Charlie Gehringer (1936) for fewest in a season by a Tiger. No other Tiger edged into the .300 circle: third baseman Ray Boone finished closest at .295, though a flurry of power came on June 11, when the Tigers equaled a team record with six home runs in a game versus the Athletics.

After the season, Spike Briggs rejected Fred Hutchinson's demand for a two-year contract and offered a one-year renewal. Hutchinson in turn resigned on September 30. The Tigers, apparently feeling nostalgic, immediately reached back into time to hire Bucky Harris, the man who had piloted Detroit to five straight second-division finishes in the '30s.

TEAM STATISTICS

W	L	PCT	GB	R	OR	2B	3B	HR	BA	SA	SB	E	DP	FA	CG	BB	SO	ShO	SV	ERA
111	43	.721		746	504	188	39	156	.262	.403	30	128	148	.979	77	486	678	12	36	2.78
103	51	.669	8	805	563	215	59	133	.268	.408	34	126	198	.979	51	655	655	15	37	3.26
94	60	.610	17	711	521	203	47	94	.267	.379	98	108	149	.982	60	517	701	21	33	3.05
69	85	.448	42	700	728	244	41	123	.266	.395	51	176	163	.972	41	612	707	9	22	4.01
68	86	.442	43	584	664	215	41	90	.258	.367	48	129	131	.978	58	506	603	13	13	3.81
66	88	.429	45	632	680	188	41	81	.246	.355	37	137	172	.977	69	573	562	10	7	3.84
54	100	.351	57	483	668	195	49	52	.251	.338	30	147	152	.975	58	688	668	6	8	3.88
51	103	.331	60	542	875	191	41	94	.236	.342	30	169	163	.972	49	685	555	3	13	5.18
GUE TOTAL				5203	5203	1639	386	823	.257	.373	358	1120	1276	.977	463	4619	5129	89	169	3.72

INDIVIDUAL PITCHING

CHER	T	W	L	PCT	ERA	SV	G	GS	CG	IP	H	BB	SO	R	ER	ShO	H/9	BB/9	SO/9
ve Gromek	R	18	16	.529	2.74	1	36	32	17	252.2	236	57	102	85	77	4	8.41	2.03	3.63
Garver	R	14	11	.560	2.81	1	35	32	16	246.1	216	62	93	93	77	3	7.89	2.27	3.40
rge Zuverink	R	9	13	.409	3.59	4	35	25	9	203	201	62	70	93	81	2	8.91	2.75	3.10
Hoeft	L	7	15	.318	4.58	1	34	25	10	175	180	59	114	93	89	4	9.26	3.03	5.86
,ber	L	5	11	.313	3.97	3	32	18	4	124.2	121	40	54	63	55	0	8.74	2.89	3.90
Herbert	R	3	6	.333	5.87	0	42	4	0	84.1	114	50	44	64	55	0	12.17	5.34	4.70
Marlowe	R	5	4	.556	4.18	2	38	2	0	84	76	40	39	45	39	0	8.14	4.29	4.18
Gray	L	3	5	.375	5.38	0	19	10	2	72	70	56	29	48	43	0	8.75	7.00	3.63
Miller	L	1	1	.500	2.45	1	32	1	0	69.2	62	26	27	25	19	0	8.01	3.36	3.49
h Branca	R	3	3	.500	5.76	0	17	5	0	45.1	63	30	15	33	29	0	12.51	5.96	2.98
Weik	R	0	1	.000	7.16	0	9	1	0	16.1	23	16	9	14	13	0	12.67	8.82	4.96
Donovan	R	0	0	–	10.50	0	2	0	0	6	9	5	2	7	7	0	13.50	7.50	2.45
k Lary	R	0	0	–	2.45	0	3	0	0	3.2	4	3	5	1	1	0	9.82	7.36	12.27
M TOTAL		68	86	.442	3.81	13	334	155	58	1383	1375	506	603	664	585	13	8.95	3.29	3.92

MANAGER	W	L	PCT
Bucky Harris	79	75	.513

POS	Player	B	G	AB	H	2B	3B	HR	HR %	R	RBI	BB	SO	SB	Pinch Hit AB	H	BA	SA
REGULARS																		
1B	Earl Torgeson	L	89	300	85	10	1	9	3.0	58	50	61	29	9	6	2	.283	.413
2B	Fred Hatfield	L	122	413	96	15	3	8	1.9	51	33	61	49	3	3	0	.232	.341
SS	Harvey Kuenn	R	145	620	190	38	5	8	1.3	101	62	40	27	8	4	1	.306	.423
3B	Ray Boone	R	135	500	142	22	7	20	4.0	61	116	50	49	1	8	2	.284	.476
RF	Al Kaline	R	152	588	**200**	24	8	27	4.6	121	102	82	57	6	0	0	**.340**	.546
CF	Bill Tuttle	R	154	603	168	23	4	14	2.3	102	78	76	54	6	1	0	.279	.400
LF	Jim Delsing	L	114	356	85	14	2	10	2.8	49	60	48	40	2	14	3	.239	.374
C	Frank House	L	102	328	85	11	1	15	4.6	37	53	22	25	0	12	3	.259	.436
SUBSTITUTES																		
2B	Harry Malmberg	R	67	208	45	5	2	0	0.0	25	19	29	19	0	0	0	.216	.260
1B	Ferris Fain	L	58	140	37	8	0	2	1.4	23	23	52	12	2	9	3	.264	.364
1B	Jack Phillips	R	55	117	37	8	2	1	0.9	15	20	10	12	0	17	8	.316	.444
UT	Reno Bertoia	R	38	68	14	2	1	1	1.5	13	10	5	11	0	6	0	.206	.309
UT	J. W. Porter	R	24	55	13	2	0	0	0.0	6	3	8	15	0	8	2	.236	.273
SS	Ron Samford	R	1	1	0	0	0	0	0.0	0	0	0	1	0	0	0	.000	.000
OF	Bubba Phillips	R	95	184	43	4	0	3	1.6	18	23	14	20	2	17	1	.234	.304
OF	Charlie Maxwell	L	55	109	29	7	1	7	6.4	19	18	8	20	0	26	7	.266	.541
OF	Charlie King	R	7	21	5	0	0	0	0.0	3	0	1	2	0	0	0	.238	.238
OF	Jim Small	L	12	4	0	0	0	0	0.0	2	0	1	1	0	2	0	.000	.000
C	Red Wilson	R	78	241	53	9	0	2	0.8	26	17	26	23	1	8	1	.220	.282
C	Walt Streuli	R	2	4	1	1	0	0	0.0	1	1	0	0	0	0	0	.250	.500
PH	Wayne Belardi	L	3	3	0	0	0	0	0.0	0	0	0	1	0	3	0	.000	.000
PH	Steve Souchock	R	1	1	1	0	0	0	0.0	0	1	0	0	0	1	1	1.000	1.000
PITCHERS																		
P	Billy Hoeft	L	36	82	17	2	0	0	0.0	9	4	10	25	0	0	0	.207	.232
P	Frank Lary	R	36	82	16	2	0	0	0.0	4	2	4	29	0	0	0	.195	.220
P	Ned Garver	R	33	76	17	1	0	1	1.3	11	13	9	5	1	0	0	.224	.276
P	Steve Gromek	B	28	54	9	1	0	0	0.0	10	5	16	12	0	0	0	.167	.185
P	Duke Maas	R	18	30	5	0	1	0	0.0	2	2	1	12	0	0	0	.167	.233
P	Babe Birrer	R	36	19	3	1	0	2	10.5	3	6	2	4	0	0	0	.158	.526
P	Al Aber	L	39	17	1	0	0	0	0.0	0	0	0	9	0	0	0	.059	.059
P	Jim Bunning	R	15	15	3	0	0	0	0.0	0	0	0	5	0	0	0	.200	.200
P	Paul Foytack	R	22	11	1	0	0	0	0.0	0	1	0	2	0	0	0	.091	.091
P	Bob Miller	R	9	9	2	0	0	0	0.0	1	2	0	1	0	0	0	.222	.222
P	Leo Cristante	R	20	7	0	0	0	0	0.0	0	0	0	5	0	0	0	.000	.000
P	Bill Black	R	3	4	1	0	0	0	0.0	1	0	0	1	0	0	0	.250	.250
P	Joe Coleman	R	17	4	3	0	0	0	0.0	2	0	0	0	0	0	0	.750	.750
P	Dick Marlowe	R	4	4	0	0	0	0	0.0	1	0	1	1	0	0	0	.000	.000
P	George Zuverink	R	14	4	0	0	0	0	0.0	0	0	0	2	0	0	0	.000	.000
P	Ben Flowers	R	4	1	0	0	0	0	0.0	0	0	0	1	0	0	0	.000	.000
P	Van Fletcher	R	9	0	0	0	0	0	–	0	0	1	0	0	0	0	–	–
P	Bill Froats	L	1	0	0	0	0	0	–	0	0	0	0	0	0	0	–	–
P	Bob Schultz	R	1	0	0	0	0	0	–	0	0	0	0	0	0	0	–	–
TEAM TOTAL				5283	1407	210	38	130	2.5	775	724	638	581	41	145	34	.266	.394

INDIVIDUAL FIELDING

POS	Player	T	G	PO	A	E	DP	TC/G	FA	POS	Player	T	G	PO	A	E	DP	TC/G	FA
1B	E. Torgeson	L	83	695	53	6	79	9.1	.992	OF	B. Tuttle	R	154	**442**	12	7	2	**3.0**	.985
	F. Fain	L	44	370	29	5	42	9.2	.988		A. Kaline	R	152	306	14	7	4	2.2	.979
	J. Phillips	R	35	236	13	2	16	7.2	.992		J. Delsing	R	101	178	3	1	1	1.8	.995
	J. Porter	R	6	52	1	0	5	8.8	1.000		B. Phillips	R	65	128	2	1	0	2.0	.992
	C. Maxwell	L	2	21	2	1	0	12.0	.958		C. Maxwell	L	26	55	3	2	0	2.3	.967
											C. King	R	6	12	0	1	0	2.2	.923
2B	F. Hatfield	R	92	216	251	12	74	5.2	.975		J. Porter	R	4	4	0	0	0	1.0	1.000
	H. Malmberg	R	65	155	181	5	42	5.2	.985		J. Small	L	4	2	1	0	0	0.8	1.000
	R. Bertoia	R	6	7	22	1	4	5.0	.967										
										C	F. House	R	93	423	35	6	5	5.0	.987
SS	H. Kuenn	R	141	253	378	29	83	4.7	.956		R. Wilson	R	72	292	25	5	5	4.5	.984
	F. Hatfield	R	14	19	43	4	4	4.7	.939		J. Porter	R	4	16	1	0	0	4.3	1.000
	R. Bertoia	R	5	4	6	0	0	2.0	1.000		W. Streuli	R	2	7	0	0	0	3.5	1.000
	R. Samford	R	1	0	2	0	0	2.0	1.000										
3B	R. Boone	R	126	135	252	19	33	3.2	.953										
	F. Hatfield	R	16	17	30	5	2	3.3	.904										
	R. Bertoia	R	14	12	24	3	4	2.8	.923										
	B. Phillips	R	4	3	9	2	1	3.5	.857										
	J. Phillips	R	3	3	2	0	0	1.7	1.000										

Bucky Harris returned after a 21-year absence to become the only manager in Tiger history to serve separate terms. He picked up where he had left off: Detroit finished in the second division, 17 games out, in fifth place. While the Tigers weren't great, they at least improved. For the first time since 1950, they finished above .500. At age 20, Al Kaline joined Ty Cobb as the youngest batting champions ever, with a major league-high .340, but lost the Most Valuable Player award to Yankees catcher Yogi Berra. Kaline, who would never be named MVP or win another batting title, also led the majors in hits with 200 and the league in total bases. He was second in slugging and in runs, tied for fourth in home runs (27), and was fifth in RBIs (102). Shortstop Harvey Kuenn hit .306 (fifth in the league), while third baseman Ray Boone tied Red Sox outfielder Jackie Jensen for the RBI crown with 116. And finally living up to expectations after three losing seasons, Billy Hoeft led Tiger pitchers at 16–7 with a 2.99 ERA, led the majors in shutouts, finished second in the league in complete games, and was third in winning percentage.

Detroit's front office came up with a big play on May 11. With general manager Muddy Ruel out of town, team president Spike Briggs checked the waiver wire and saw listed Charlie Maxwell, whom the Orioles were trying to slip through to the Braves to complete an earlier trade. Briggs ruined the gambit and snatched Maxwell, who embarked on a slugging spree late in the season: seven of his 29 hits were homers. And that was just the start of Maxwell's Tiger heroics.

TEAM STATISTICS

W	L	PCT	GB	R	OR	2B	Batting 3B	HR	BA	SA	SB	E	Fielding DP	FA	CG	BB	Pitching SO	ShO	SV	ERA
96	58	.623		762	569	179	55	175	.260	.418	55	128	180	.978	52	689	731	18	33	3.23
93	61	.604	3	698	601	195	31	148	.257	.394	28	108	152	.981	45	558	877	13	36	3.39
91	63	.591	5	725	557	204	36	116	.268	.388	69	111	147	.981	55	499	.720	17	23	3.37
84	70	.545	12	755	652	241	39	137	.264	.402	43	136	140	.977	44	582	674	9	34	3.72
79	75	.513	17	775	658	211	38	130	.266	.394	41	139	159	.976	66	517	629	15	12	3.79
63	91	.409	33	638	911	189	46	121	.261	.382	22	146	174	.976	29	707	572	7	23	5.35
57	97	.370	39	540	754	177	39	54	.240	.320	34	167	159	.972	35	625	595	9	22	4.21
53	101	.344	43	598	789	178	54	80	.248	.351	25	154	170	.974	37	637	607	9	16	4.62
GUE TOTAL				5491	5491	1574	338	961	.258	.381	317	1089	1281	.977	363	4814	5405	97	199	3.96

INDIVIDUAL PITCHING

CHER	T	W	L	PCT	ERA	SV	G	GS	CG	IP	H	BB	SO	R	ER	ShO	H/9	BB/9	SO/9
nk Lary	R	14	15	.483	3.10	1	36	31	16	235	232	89	98	100	81	2	8.89	3.41	3.75
Garver	R	12	16	.429	3.98	0	33	32	16	230.2	251	67	83	115	102	1	9.79	2.61	3.24
y Hoeft	L	16	7	.696	2.99	0	32	29	17	220	187	75	133	75	73	7	7.65	3.07	5.44
ve Gromek	R	13	10	.565	3.98	0	28	25	8	181	183	37	73	89	80	2	9.10	1.84	3.63
ke Maas	R	5	6	.455	4.88	0	18	16	5	86.2	91	50	42	52	47	2	9.45	5.19	4.36
e Birrer	R	4	3	.571	4.15	3	36	3	1	80.1	77	29	28	39	37	0	8.63	3.25	3.14
ber	L	6	3	.667	3.38	3	39	1	0	80	86	28	37	32	30	0	9.68	3.15	4.16
Bunning	R	3	5	.375	6.35	1	15	8	0	51	59	32	37	38	36	0	10.41	5.65	6.53
l Foytack	R	0	1	.000	5.26	0	22	1	0	49.2	48	36	38	29	29	0	8.70	6.52	6.89
Cristante	R	0	1	.000	3.19	0	20	1	0	36.2	37	14	9	15	13	0	9.08	3.44	2.21
rge Zuverink	R	0	5	.000	6.99	0	14	1	0	28.1	38	14	13	27	22	0	12.07	4.45	4.13
Coleman	R	2	1	.667	3.20	0	17	0	0	25.1	22	14	5	9	9	0	7.82	4.97	1.78
Miller	L	2	1	.667	2.49	0	7	3	1	25.1	26	12	11	12	7	0	9.24	4.26	3.91
k Marlowe	R	1	0	1.000	1.80	1	4	1	0	15	12	4	9	4	3	0	7.20	2.40	5.40
Black	R	1	1	.500	1.26	0	3	2	1	14.1	12	8	7	5	2	1	7.53	5.02	4.40
Fletcher	R	0	0	–	3.00	0	9	0	0	12	13	2	4	10	4	0	9.75	1.50	3.00
Flowers	R	0	0	–	6.00	0	4	0	0	6	5	2	2	4	4	0	7.50	3.00	3.00
Froats	L	0	0	–	0.00	0	1	0	0	2	0	2	0	0	0	0	0.00	9.00	0.00
Schultz	L	0	0	–	20.25	0	1	0	0	1.1	2	2	0	3	3	0	13.50	13.50	0.00
M TOTAL		79	75	.513	3.79	12	339	154	66	1380.2	1381	517	629	658	582	15	9.00	3.37	4.10

MANAGER	W	L	PCT
Bucky Harris	82	72	.532

POS	Player	B	G	AB	H	2B	3B	HR	HR %	R	RBI	BB	SO	SB	Pinch Hit AB	Pinch Hit H	BA	SA
REGULARS																		
1B	Earl Torgeson	L	117	318	84	9	3	12	3.8	61	42	78	47	6	27	10	.264	.425
2B	Frank Bolling	R	102	366	103	21	7	7	1.9	53	45	42	51	6	0	0	.281	.434
SS	Harvey Kuenn	R	146	591	**196**	32	7	12	2.0	96	88	55	34	9	6	1	.332	.470
3B	Ray Boone	R	131	481	148	14	6	25	5.2	77	81	77	46	0	0	0	.308	.518
RF	Al Kaline	R	153	617	194	32	10	27	4.4	96	128	70	55	7	0	0	.314	.530
CF	Bill Tuttle	R	140	546	138	22	4	9	1.6	61	65	38	48	5	4	2	.253	.357
LF	Charlie Maxwell	L	141	500	163	14	3	28	5.6	96	87	79	74	1	7	4	.326	.554
C	Frank House	L	94	321	77	6	2	10	3.1	44	44	21	19	1	9	3	.240	.364
SUBSTITUTES																		
1B	Jack Phillips	R	67	224	66	13	2	1	0.4	31	20	21	19	1	9	3	.295	.384
S2	Jim Brideweser	R	70	156	34	4	0	0	0.0	23	10	20	19	3	1	1	.218	.244
1B	Wayne Belardi	L	79	154	43	3	1	6	3.9	24	15	15	13	0	37	8	.279	.429
2B	Reno Bertoia	R	22	66	12	2	0	1	1.5	7	5	6	12	0	0	0	.182	.258
S2	Buddy Hicks	B	26	47	10	2	0	0	0.0	5	5	3	2	0	2	0	.213	.255
2B	Fred Hatfield	L	8	12	3	0	0	0	0.0	2	2	2	1	0	1	0	.250	.250
O3	Bob Kennedy	R	69	177	41	5	0	4	2.3	17	22	24	19	2	16	2	.232	.328
OF	Jim Small	L	58	91	29	4	2	0	0.0	13	10	6	10	0	15	7	.319	.407
OF	Jim Delsing	L	10	12	0	0	0	0	0.0	0	0	3	3	0	4	0	.000	.000
OF	Charlie King	R	7	9	2	0	0	0	0.0	0	0	1	4	0	2	0	.222	.222
C	Red Wilson	R	78	228	66	12	2	7	3.1	32	38	42	18	2	1	0	.289	.452
CO	J. W. Porter	R	14	21	2	0	0	0	0.0	0	3	0	8	0	10	0	.095	.095
C	Charlie Lau	L	3	9	2	0	0	0	0.0	1	0	1	0	0	0	0	.222	.222
C	Walt Streuli	R	3	8	2	1	0	0	0.0	0	1	1	2	0	0	0	.250	.375
PITCHERS																		
P	Frank Lary	R	41	103	19	2	0	1	1.0	14	12	8	25	0	0	0	.184	.233
P	Paul Foytack	R	43	90	11	2	0	0	0.0	7	7	2	30	0	0	0	.122	.144
P	Billy Hoeft	L	42	80	20	3	1	0	0.0	16	9	12	22	0	0	0	.250	.313
P	Virgil Trucks	R	22	45	11	2	0	0	0.0	4	2	0	4	0	0	0	.244	.289
P	Steve Gromek	B	40	27	4	0	0	0	0.0	3	1	11	10	0	0	0	.148	.148
P	Jim Bunning	R	15	18	6	2	0	0	0.0	4	1	0	5	0	0	0	.333	.444
P	Duke Maas	R	26	16	3	1	0	0	0.0	1	1	2	8	0	0	0	.188	.250
P	Al Aber	L	42	10	3	0	0	0	0.0	0	0	1	4	0	0	0	.300	.300
P	Bob Miller	R	11	7	1	1	0	0	0.0	0	0	1	2	0	0	0	.143	.286
P	Ned Garver	R	6	5	0	0	0	0	0.0	0	0	1	1	0	0	0	.000	.000
P	Walt Masterson	R	35	4	1	0	0	0	0.0	0	1	0	1	0	0	0	.250	.250
P	Bill Black	R	5	2	0	0	0	0	0.0	0	0	0	0	0	0	0	.000	.000
P	Gene Host	B	1	2	0	0	0	0	0.0	0	0	0	0	0	0	0	.000	.000
P	Dick Marlowe	R	7	1	0	0	0	0	0.0	0	0	0	1	0	0	0	.000	.000
P	Jim Brady	L	6	0	0	0	0	0	–	1	0	1	0	0	0	0	–	–
P	Pete Wojey	R	2	0	0	0	0	0	–	0	0	0	0	0	0	0	–	–
P	Hal Woodeshick	R	2	0	0	0	0	0	–	0	0	0	0	0	0	0	–	–
	TEAM TOTAL			5364	1494	209	50	150	2.8	789	745	643	618	43	151	41	.279	.420

INDIVIDUAL FIELDING

POS	Player	T	G	PO	A	E	DP	TC/G	FA	POS	Player	T	G	PO	A	E	DP	TC/G	FA
1B	E. Torgeson	L	83	623	32	5	62	8.0	.992	OF	B. Tuttle	R	137	348	13	9	2	2.7	.976
	J. Phillips	R	56	422	32	9	49	8.3	.981		A. Kaline	R	153	343	18	6	4	2.4	.984
	W. Belardi	L	31	240	17	3	21	8.4	.988		C. Maxwell	L	136	281	12	4	1	2.2	.987
2B	F. Bolling	R	102	223	260	11	72	4.8	.978		B. Kennedy	R	29	52	2	4	0	2.0	.931
	J. Brideweser	R	31	84	83	4	20	5.5	.977		J. Small	L	26	47	0	3	0	1.9	.940
	R. Bertoia	R	18	51	57	2	18	6.1	.982		H. Kuenn	R	1	0	0	0	0	0.0	.000
	B. Hicks	R	6	15	13	0	2	4.7	1.000		W. Belardi	L	2	3	0	2	0	2.5	.600
	F. Hatfield	R	4	7	6	0	1	3.3	1.000		C. King	R	4	4	0	1	0	1.3	.800
	J. Phillips	R	1	1	0	1	0	2.0	.500		J. Porter	R	2	2	0	1	0	1.5	.667
SS	H. Kuenn	R	141	219	388	20	86	4.4	**.968**		J. Delsing	R	3	3	0	0	0	1.0	1.000
	J. Brideweser	R	32	27	51	1	12	2.5	.987		J. Phillips	R	1	2	0	0	0	2.0	1.000
	B. Hicks	R	16	6	18	0	3	1.5	1.000	C	F. House	R	88	450	33	7	8	5.6	.986
3B	R. Boone	R	130	151	243	17	23	3.2	.959		R. Wilson	R	78	393	34	4	7	5.5	.991
	B. Kennedy	R	27	35	38	8	3	3.0	.901		C. Lau	R	3	17	0	0	0	5.7	1.000
	B. Hicks	R	1	0	0	0	0	0.0	.000		W. Streuli	R	3	13	1	1	1	5.0	.933
	R. Bertoia	R	2	3	4	0	1	3.5	1.000		J. Porter	R	2	7	0	0	1	3.5	1.000
	J. Brideweser	R	4	2	5	0	1	1.8	1.000										

Charlie Maxwell had never hit more than seven home runs in a season. "I knew it was now or never," the 29-year-old outfielder said of his first full Detroit season "The next stop figured to be the minors again." But for Maxwell there'd be no more rickety buses: he hit .326 with 28 home runs, then the most ever by a lefty batter in Tiger history.

There were other sluggers. As Detroit led the league in hitting, for the first time in team history three Tigers hit 25 home runs: Maxwell, Al Kaline (27), and third baseman Ray Boone (25). And three hit .300: shortstop Harvey Kuenn (.332), Kaline (.314), and Boone (.308). Third in the MVP balloting, Kuenn led the league in hits (196). Fourth on the MVP balloting, Kaline was second in hits (194) and RBI (128). The pitching also fell into line. The Tigers, who hadn't boasted a 20-game winner in eight years, had two for the first time in 12 years: Frank Lary (21–13) and Billy Hoeft (20–14).

Still, the Tigers finished fifth for the third straight season, 15 games behind the first-place Yankees. Detroit lay in the cellar as late as May 25, but edged toward the first division, winning 12 of 13 in the middle weeks of September—though still falling two games short of fourth-place Boston. As a consolation, The Tigers went 12–10 against New York, only the second time the Bombers had dropped a season series under Casey Stengel.

Meanwhile, a syndicate led by broadcast executive John Fetzer acquired the club for a reported $5.5 million. Spike Briggs was retained as general manager, but Bucky Harris was not kept on as manager. His 29-year, five-team managing career ended with a postseason resignation.

TEAM STATISTICS

W	L	PCT	GB	R	OR	2B	3B	Batting HR	BA	SA	SB	E	Fielding DP	FA	CG	BB	Pitching SO	ShO	SV	ERA
97	57	.630		857	631	193	55	190	.270	.434	51	136	214	.977	50	652	732	9	35	3.63
88	66	.571	9	712	581	199	23	153	.244	.381	40	129	130	.978	67	564	845	17	24	3.32
85	69	.552	12	776	634	218	43	128	.267	.397	70	122	160	.979	65	524	722	11	13	3.73
84	70	.545	13	780	751	261	45	139	.275	.419	28	169	168	.972	50	668	712	8	20	4.17
82	72	.532	15	789	699	209	50	150	.279	.420	43	140	151	.976	62	655	788	10	15	4.06
69	85	.448	28	571	705	198	34	91	.244	.350	39	137	142	.977	38	547	715	10	24	4.20
59	95	.383	38	652	924	198	62	112	.250	.377	37	171	173	.972	36	730	663	1	18	5.33
52	102	.338	45	619	831	204	41	112	.252	.370	40	166	187	.973	30	679	636	3	18	4.86
LEAGUE TOTAL						5756	5756	1680	353	1075	.260	.394	348	1170	1325	.975	398	5019	5813	69	167	4.16

INDIVIDUAL PITCHING

PITCHER	T	W	L	PCT	ERA	SV	G	GS	CG	IP	H	BB	SO	R	ER	ShO	H/9	BB/9	SO/9
Frank Lary	R	21	13	.618	3.15	1	41	38	20	294	289	116	165	116	103	3	8.85	3.55	5.05
Paul Foytack	R	15	13	.536	3.59	1	43	33	16	256	211	142	184	114	102	1	7.42	4.99	6.47
Billy Hoeft	L	20	14	.588	4.06	0	38	34	18	248	276	104	172	127	112	4	10.02	3.77	6.24
Steve Gromek	R	8	6	.571	4.28	4	40	13	4	141	142	47	64	74	67	0	9.06	3.00	4.09
Virgil Trucks	R	6	5	.545	3.83	1	22	16	3	120	104	63	43	56	51	1	7.80	4.73	3.23
Duke Maas	R	0	7	.000	6.54	0	26	7	0	63.1	81	32	34	51	46	0	11.51	4.55	4.83
Al Aber	L	4	4	.500	3.43	7	42	0	0	63	65	25	21	30	24	0	9.29	3.57	3.00
Jim Bunning	R	5	1	.833	3.71	1	15	3	0	53.1	55	28	34	24	22	0	9.28	4.73	5.74
Walt Masterson	R	1	1	.500	4.17	0	35	0	0	49.2	54	32	28	28	23	0	9.79	5.80	5.07
Bob Miller	L	0	2	.000	5.68	0	11	3	0	31.2	37	22	16	23	20	0	10.52	6.25	4.55
Ned Garver	R	0	2	.000	4.08	0	6	3	1	17.2	15	13	6	10	8	0	7.64	6.62	3.06
Dick Marlowe	R	1	1	.500	5.73	0	7	1	0	11	12	9	4	8	7	0	9.82	7.36	3.27
Black	R	1	1	.500	3.60	0	5	1	0	10	10	5	7	4	4	0	9.00	4.50	6.30
Brady	L	0	0	–	28.42	0	6	0	0	6.1	15	11	3	21	20	0	21.32	15.63	4.26
Woodeshick	L	0	2	.000	13.50	0	2	2	0	5.1	3	1	8	8	0	20.25	5.06	1.69
Gene Host	L	0	0	–	7.71	0	1	1	0	4.2	9	2	5	4	4	0	17.36	3.86	9.64
Joe Wojey	R	0	0	–	2.25	0	2	0	0	4	2	1	1	1	1	0	4.50	2.25	2.25
TEAM TOTAL		82	72	.532	4.06	15	342	155	62	1379	1389	655	788	699	622	9	9.07	4.27	5.14

MANAGER	W	L	PCT
Jack Tighe	78	76	.506

POS	Player	B	G	AB	H	2B	3B	HR	HR %	R	RBI	BB	SO	SB	Pinch Hit AB	Pinch Hit H	BA	SA
REGULARS																		
1B	Ray Boone	R	129	462	126	25	3	12	2.6	48	65	57	47	1	5	1	.273	.418
2B	Frank Bolling	R	146	576	149	27	6	15	2.6	72	40	57	64	4	0	0	.259	.405
SS	Harvey Kuenn	R	151	624	173	30	6	9	1.4	74	44	47	28	5	1	0	.277	.388
3B	Reno Bertoia	R	97	295	81	16	2	4	1.4	28	28	19	43	2	9	0	.275	.383
RF	Al Kaline	R	149	577	170	29	4	23	4.0	83	90	43	38	11	5	1	.295	.478
CF	Bill Tuttle	R	133	451	113	12	4	5	1.1	49	47	44	41	2	3	1	.251	.328
LF	Charlie Maxwell	L	138	492	136	23	3	24	4.9	75	82	76	84	3	3	3	.276	.482
C	Frank House	L	106	348	90	9	0	7	2.0	31	36	35	26	1	7	2	.259	.345
SUBSTITUTES																		
3B	Jim Finigan	R	64	174	47	4	2	0	0.0	20	17	23	18	1	3	0	.270	.316
1O	Dave Philley	B	65	173	49	8	1	2	1.2	15	16	7	16	3	25	10	.283	.376
S2	Ron Samford	R	54	91	20	1	2	0	0.0	6	5	6	15	1	0	0	.220	.275
1B	Earl Torgeson	L	30	50	12	2	1	1	2.0	5	5	12	10	0	12	3	.240	.380
3S	Steve Boros	R	24	41	6	1	0	0	0.0	4	2	1	8	0	4	0	.146	.171
32	Jack Dittmer	L	16	22	5	1	0	0	0.0	3	2	2	1	0	12	4	.227	.273
1B	Eddie Robinson	L	13	9	0	0	0	0	0.0	0	0	3	0	0	8	0	.000	.000
3B	George Thomas	R	1	1	0	0	0	0	0.0	0	0	0	1	0	1	0	.000	.000
OC	J. W. Porter	R	58	140	35	8	0	2	1.4	14	18	14	20	0	17	4	.250	.350
OF	Johnny Groth	R	38	103	30	10	0	0	0.0	11	16	6	7	0	1	0	.291	.388
OF	Jim Small	L	36	42	9	2	0	0	0.0	7	0	2	11	0	13	2	.214	.262
O1	Bobo Osborne	L	11	27	4	1	0	0	0.0	4	1	3	7	0	2	0	.148	.185
OF	Bill Taylor	L	9	23	8	2	0	1	4.3	4	3	0	3	0	4	2	.348	.565
OF	Karl Olson	R	8	14	2	0	0	0	0.0	1	1	0	6	0	3	0	.143	.143
OF	Mel Clark	R	5	7	0	0	0	0	0.0	0	1	0	3	0	3	0	.000	.000
C	Red Wilson	R	59	178	43	8	1	3	1.7	21	13	24	19	2	0	0	.242	.348
C	Tom Yewcic	R	1	1	0	0	0	0	0.0	0	0	0	0	0	0	0	.000	.000
PH	Jack Phillips	R	1	1	0	0	0	0	0.0	1	0	0	0	0	1	0	.000	.000
PITCHERS																		
P	Jim Bunning	R	45	94	20	2	1	1	1.1	10	4	5	29	0	0	0	.213	.287
P	Frank Lary	R	40	73	9	0	1	0	0.0	4	4	2	22	0	0	0	.123	.151
P	Duke Maas	R	45	71	6	1	0	1	1.4	2	8	3	27	0	0	0	.085	.141
P	Billy Hoeft	L	42	67	10	2	0	3	4.5	13	10	5	14	0	0	0	.149	.313
P	Paul Foytack	R	38	63	14	0	0	0	0.0	4	5	4	17	0	0	0	.222	.222
P	Lou Sleater	L	41	20	5	0	0	3	15.0	4	7	1	2	0	1	0	.250	.700
P	Don Lee	R	11	12	2	0	0	0	0.0	1	3	0	3	0	0	0	.167	.167
P	Al Aber	L	28	8	1	0	0	0	0.0	0	1	1	4	0	0	0	.125	.125
P	Harry Byrd	R	37	8	0	0	0	0	0.0	0	0	0	2	0	0	0	.000	.000
P	Steve Gromek	B	15	2	0	0	0	0	0.0	0	0	0	2	0	0	0	.000	.000
P	Bob Shaw	R	7	2	0	0	0	0	0.0	0	0	0	1	0	0	0	.000	.000
P	Jim Stump	R	6	2	1	0	0	0	0.0	0	0	0	1	0	0	0	.500	.500
P	Joe Presko	R	7	1	0	0	0	0	0.0	0	0	0	1	0	0	0	.000	.000
P	John Tsitouris	R	2	1	0	0	0	0	0.0	0	0	0	1	0	0	0	.000	.000
P	Jack Crimian	R	4	0	0	0	0	0	–	0	0	0	0	0	0	0	–	–
P	Chuck Daniel	R	1	0	0	0	0	0	–	0	0	0	0	0	0	0	–	–
P	Pete Wojey	R	2	0	0	0	0	0	–	0	0	0	0	0	0	0	–	–
TEAM TOTAL				5346	1376	224	37	116	2.2	614	574	502	641	36	143	33	.257	.378

INDIVIDUAL FIELDING

POS	Player	T	G	PO	A	E	DP	TC/G	FA
1B	R. Boone	R	117	972	45	10	103	8.8	.990
	D. Philley	R	27	203	25	1	19	8.5	.996
	E. Torgeson	L	17	98	7	0	11	6.2	1.000
	J. Porter	R	3	28	3	1	2	10.7	.969
	B. Osborne	R	4	20	1	0	1	5.3	1.000
	E. Robinson	R	1	4	1	0	0	5.0	1.000
	H. Kuenn	R	1	2	0	0	1	2.0	1.000
2B	F. Bolling	R	146	394	401	16	112	5.6	.980
	R. Samford	R	11	17	21	1	5	3.5	.974
	J. Finigan	R	3	8	4	1	2	4.3	.923
	R. Bertoia	R	2	2	1	0	0	1.5	1.000
	J. Dittmer	R	1	1	1	0	0	2.0	1.000
SS	H. Kuenn	R	136	225	354	27	86	4.5	.955
	R. Samford	R	35	34	72	4	18	3.1	.964
	S. Boros	R	5	1	5	0	0	1.2	1.000
	R. Bertoia	R	7	1	2	0	0	0.4	1.000
3B	R. Bertoia	R	83	76	125	10	8	2.5	.953
	J. Finigan	R	59	58	108	8	9	2.9	.954
	H. Kuenn	R	17	24	33	3	4	3.5	.950
	D. Philley	R	1	0	0	0	0	0.0	.000
	S. Boros	R	9	7	22	3	1	3.6	.906
	R. Boone	R	4	5	12	2	0	4.8	.895
	J. Dittmer	R	3	3	3	0	0	2.0	1.000
	R. Samford	R	4	2	2	1	0	1.3	.800
	G. Thomas	R	1	0	0	1	0	1.0	.000

POS	Player	T	G	PO	A	E	DP	TC/G	FA
OF	B. Tuttle	R	128	331	5	6	1	2.7	.982
	A. Kaline	R	145	319	13	5	2	2.3	.985
	C. Maxwell	L	137	317	6	1	1	2.4	.997
	J. Groth	R	36	73	0	0	0	2.0	1.000
	J. Porter	R	27	40	1	2	0	1.6	.953
	D. Philley	R	12	16	0	1	0	1.4	.941
	J. Small	L	14	15	0	0	0	1.1	1.000
	B. Osborne	R	5	8	0	0	0	1.6	1.000
	K. Olson	R	5	6	0	0	0	1.2	1.000
	B. Taylor	L	5	5	0	0	0	1.0	1.000
	M. Clark	R	2	4	0	0	0	2.0	1.000
C	F. House	R	97	535	54	2	5	6.1	.997
	R. Wilson	R	59	277	29	0	5	5.2	1.000
	J. Porter	R	12	50	7	3	5	5.0	.950
	T. Yewcic	R	1	4	1	1	0	6.0	.833

In a preseason national vote by baseball writers, the Tigers were picked as the Yankees' most serious challengers. But the scheduled pennant run was canceled by weak hitting. No Tiger topped .300, as the team average dropped from a league-leading .279 to .257. Al Kaline and Harvey Kuenn spearheaded the slump, particularly in the first half. Kuenn dropped 55 points to .277; Kaline managed to reach .295, but only with a second-half surge that included 17 of his 23 home runs in the final 54 games. Jim Bunning was promoted to the big club and finished 20–8, his only 20-victory season in Detroit, to tie former Tiger Billy Pierce of the White Sox for the league lead in victories. No other Detroit pitcher surpassed 14 wins; still, under rookie manager Jack Tighe, Detroit managed to move into fourth place, 20 games out to finish in the first division for the first time since 1950.

A pair of Detroit heroes impressed in the All-Star Game in St. Louis. Starter Bunning retired all nine batters he faced to become the third Tiger pitcher (Tommy Bridges, 1939; Virgil Trucks, 1949) to beat the Nationals. And Kaline contributed a spectacular catch and two singles to the 6–5 victory, driving in two runs and scoring another in the American League's three-run ninth.

Early in the season Spike Briggs, team president from his father's death in 1952 until 1956, resigned as general manager to end his family's four-decade association with the club. He was replaced by 35-year-old Detroit native and onetime Tiger substitute John McHale, who after the season engineered a 13-player swap with the Kansas City Athletics. None of the principals immediately helped either team. However, one would manage the Tigers to first place 16 years later: Billy Martin.

TEAM STATISTICS

W	L	PCT	GB	R	OR	2B	3B	HR	BA	SA	SB	E	DP	FA	CG	BB	SO	ShO	SV	ERA
										Batting			Fielding				Pitching			
98	56	.636		723	534	200	54	145	.268	.409	49	123	183	.980	41	580	810	13	42	3.00
90	64	.584	8	707	566	208	41	106	.260	.375	109	107	169	.982	59	470	665	16	27	3.35
82	72	.532	16	721	668	231	32	153	.262	.405	29	149	179	.976	55	498	692	9	23	3.88
78	76	.506	20	614	614	224	37	116	.257	.378	36	121	151	.980	52	505	756	9	21	3.56
76	76	.500	21	597	588	191	39	87	.252	.353	57	112	159	.981	44	493	767	13	25	3.46
76	77	.497	21.5	682	722	199	26	140	.252	.382	40	153	154	.974	46	618	807	7	23	4.05
59	94	.386	38.5	563	710	195	40	166	.244	.394	35	125	162	.979	26	565	626	6	19	4.19
55	99	.357	43	603	808	215	38	111	.244	.363	13	128	159	.979	31	580	691	5	16	4.85
AGUE TOTAL				5210	5210	1663	307	1024	.255	.382	368	1018	1316	.979	354	4309	5814	78	196	3.79

INDIVIDUAL PITCHING

TCHER	T	W	L	PCT	ERA	SV	G	GS	CG	IP	H	BB	SO	R	ER	ShO	H/9	BB/9	SO/9
n Bunning	R	20	8	.714	2.69	1	45	30	14	267.1	214	72	182	91	80	1	7.20	2.42	6.13
ank Lary	R	11	16	.407	3.98	3	40	35	12	237.2	250	72	107	111	105	2	9.47	2.73	4.05
ke Maas	R	10	14	.417	3.28	6	45	26	8	219.1	210	65	116	92	80	2	8.62	2.67	4.76
ul Foytack	R	14	11	.560	3.14	1	38	27	8	212	175	104	118	79	74	1	7.43	4.42	5.01
ly Hoeft	L	9	11	.450	3.48	1	34	28	10	207	188	69	111	85	80	1	8.17	3.00	4.83
u Sleater	L	3	3	.500	3.76	2	41	0	0	69.1	61	28	43	33	29	0	7.92	3.63	5.58
rry Byrd	R	4	3	.571	3.36	5	37	1	0	59	53	28	20	23	22	0	8.08	4.27	3.05
n Lee	R	1	3	.250	4.66	0	11	6	0	38.2	48	18	19	22	20	0	11.17	4.19	4.42
Aber	L	3	3	.500	6.81	1	28	0	0	37	46	11	15	33	28	0	11.19	2.68	3.65
eve Gromek	R	0	1	.000	6.08	1	15	1	0	23.2	32	13	11	16	16	0	12.17	4.94	4.18
n Stump	R	1	0	1.000	2.03	0	6	0	0	13.1	11	8	2	4	3	0	7.43	5.40	1.35
e Presko	R	1	1	.500	1.64	0	7	0	0	11	10	4	3	3	2	0	8.18	3.27	2.45
b Shaw	R	0	1	.000	7.45	0	7	0	0	9.2	11	7	4	9	8	0	10.24	6.52	3.72
ck Crimian	R	0	1	.000	12.71	0	4	0	0	5.2	9	4	1	8	8	0	14.29	6.35	1.59
n Tsitouris	R	1	0	1.000	8.10	0	2	0	0	3.1	8	2	2	3	3	0	21.60	5.40	5.40
uck Daniel	R	0	0	–	7.71	0	2	0	0	2.1	3	0	2	2	2	0	11.57	0.00	7.71
te Wojey	R	0	0	–	0.00	0	2	0	0	1.1	1	0	0	0	0	0	6.75	0.00	0.00
AM TOTAL		78	76	.506	3.56	21	363	154	52	1417.2	1330	505	756	614	560	7	8.44	3.21	4.80

MANAGER	W	L	PCT
Jack Tighe	21	28	.429
Bill Norman	56	49	.533

POS	Player	B	G	AB	H	2B	3B	HR	HR %	R	RBI	BB	SO	SB	Pinch Hit AB	Pinch Hit H	BA	SA
REGULARS																		
1B	Gail Harris	L	134	451	123	18	8	20	4.4	63	83	36	60	1	14	5	.273	.481
2B	Frank Bolling	R	154	610	164	25	4	14	2.3	91	75	54	54	6	0	0	.269	.392
SS	Billy Martin	R	131	498	127	19	1	7	1.4	56	42	16	62	5	2	0	.255	.339
3B	Reno Bertoia	R	86	240	56	6	0	6	2.5	28	27	20	35	5	5	0	.233	.333
RF	Al Kaline	R	146	543	170	34	7	16	2.9	84	85	54	47	7	2	0	.313	.490
CF	Harvey Kuenn	R	139	561	179	39	3	8	1.4	73	54	51	34	5	1	1	.319	.442
LF	Charlie Maxwell	L	131	397	108	14	4	13	3.3	56	65	64	54	6	8	1	.272	.426
C	Red Wilson	R	103	298	89	13	1	3	1.0	31	29	35	30	10	3	0	.299	.379
SUBSTITUTES																		
SS	Coot Veal	R	58	207	53	10	2	0	0.0	29	16	14	21	1	0	0	.256	.324
3B	Ozzie Virgil	R	49	193	47	10	2	3	1.6	19	19	8	20	1	1	0	.244	.363
1B	Ray Boone	R	39	114	27	4	1	6	5.3	16	20	14	13	0	7	1	.237	.447
SS	Milt Bolling	R	24	31	6	2	0	0	0.0	3	0	5	7	0	4	0	.194	.258
2B	Steve Boros	R	6	2	0	0	0	0	0.0	0	0	0	0	0	0	0	.000	.000
OF	Johnny Groth	R	88	146	41	5	2	2	1.4	24	11	13	19	0	16	6	.281	.384
OF	Gus Zernial	R	66	124	40	7	1	5	4.0	8	23	6	25	0	38	15	.323	.516
OF	Tito Francona	L	45	69	17	5	0	0	0.0	11	10	15	16	0	22	8	.246	.319
OF	Bob Hazle	L	43	58	14	2	0	2	3.4	5	5	5	13	0	28	5	.241	.379
O3	Lou Skizas	R	23	33	8	2	0	1	3.0	4	2	5	1	0	13	2	.242	.394
OF	Bill Taylor	L	8	8	3	0	0	0	0.0	0	1	0	2	0	6	3	.375	.375
OF	George Alusik	R	2	2	0	0	0	0	0.0	0	0	0	1	0	1	0	.000	.000
OF	George Thomas	R	1	0	0	0	0	0	–	0	0	0	0	0	0	0	–	–
C	Jim Hegan	R	45	130	25	6	0	1	0.8	14	7	10	32	0	0	0	.192	.262
C	Charlie Lau	L	30	68	10	1	2	0	0.0	8	6	12	15	0	4	1	.147	.221
C	Tim Thompson	L	4	6	1	0	0	0	0.0	1	0	3	2	0	1	0	.167	.167
C	Jack Feller	R	1	0	0	0	0	0	–	0	0	0	0	0	0	0	–	–
PH	Bobo Osborne	L	2	2	0	0	0	0	0.0	0	0	0	0	0	2	0	.000	.000
PITCHERS																		
P	Frank Lary	R	39	88	15	1	1	1	1.1	6	6	3	20	0	0	0	.170	.239
P	Jim Bunning	R	36	75	14	2	0	0	0.0	7	3	3	24	0	0	0	.187	.213
P	Paul Foytack	R	39	75	18	2	0	0	0.0	5	9	6	20	1	0	0	.240	.267
P	Billy Hoeft	L	43	44	12	0	2	0	0.0	10	5	4	11	0	0	0	.273	.364
P	Herb Moford	R	25	37	1	0	0	0	0.0	1	1	1	9	0	0	0	.027	.027
P	George Susce	R	27	24	3	1	0	0	0.0	0	3	1	11	0	0	0	.125	.167
P	Al Cicotte	R	15	17	3	0	0	0	0.0	1	0	0	5	0	0	0	.176	.176
P	Hank Aguirre	R	44	14	3	1	0	0	0.0	1	1	1	5	0	0	0	.214	.286
P	Tom Morgan	R	39	10	2	0	0	0	0.0	3	1	0	6	0	0	0	.200	.200
P	Bob Shaw	R	12	8	3	0	0	0	0.0	0	0	1	0	0	0	0	.375	.375
P	Herm Wehmeier	R	7	6	0	0	0	0	0.0	0	0	1	2	0	0	0	.000	.000
P	Mickey McDermott	L	4	3	1	0	0	0	0.0	0	1	0	2	0	2	1	.333	.333
P	Bill Fischer	R	22	1	0	0	0	0	0.0	0	0	1	0	0	0	0	.000	.000
P	Lou Sleater	L	4	1	1	0	0	1	0.0	1	1	0	0	0	0	0	1.000	4.000
P	Don Lee	R	1	0	0	0	0	0	–	0	0	0	0	0	0	0	–	–
P	Joe Presko	R	7	0	0	0	0	0	–	0	0	1	0	0	0	0	–	–
P	George Spencer	R	7	0	0	0	0	0	–	0	0	0	0	0	0	0	–	–
P	Vito Valentinetti	R	15	0	0	0	0	0	–	0	0	0	0	0	0	0	–	–
	TEAM TOTAL			5194	1384	229	41	109	2.1	659	612	463	678	48	180	49	.266	.389

INDIVIDUAL FIELDING

POS	Player	T	G	PO	A	E	DP	TC/G	FA	POS	Player	T	G	PO	A	E	DP	TC/G	FA
1B	G. Harris	L	122	942	79	15	90	8.5	.986	OF	H. Kuenn	R	138	**358**	9	6	1	**2.7**	.984
	R. Boone	R	32	236	15	3	26	7.9	.988		A. Kaline	R	145	316	**23**	2	4	2.4	.994
	C. Maxwell	L	14	89	4	1	9	6.7	.989		C. Maxwell	L	114	201	4	3	0	1.8	.986
	T. Francona	L	1	1	0	0	0	1.0	1.000		J. Groth	R	80	95	2	1	1	1.2	.990
2B	F. Bolling	R	154	342	**445**	12	109	5.2	**.985**		G. Zernial	R	24	30	1	2	0	1.4	.939
	M. Bolling	R	1	1	2	0	0	3.0	1.000		T. Francona	L	18	23	0	0	0	1.3	1.000
	S. Boros	R	1	2	0	0	0	2.0	1.000		R. Bertoia	R	1	0	0	0	0	0.0	.000
											G. Thomas	R	1	0	0	0	0	0.0	.000
SS	B. Martin	R	88	159	229	17	58	4.6	.958		B. Hazle	R	12	12	0	0	0	1.0	1.000
	C. Veal	R	58	95	160	5	30	4.5	.981		L. Skizas	R	5	3	0	1	0	0.8	.750
	M. Bolling	R	13	14	21	2	7	2.8	.946		G. Alusik	R	1	1	0	0	0	1.0	1.000
	R. Bertoia	R	5	2	3	1	0	1.2	.833		B. Taylor	L	1	1	0	0	0	1.0	1.000
3B	R. Bertoia	R	68	70	139	11	13	3.2	.950	C	R. Wilson	R	101	565	34	5	6	6.0	.992
	O. Virgil	R	49	55	101	3	7	3.2	.981		J. Hegan	R	45	211	19	1	4	5.1	.996
	B. Martin	R	41	47	59	3	5	2.7	.972		C. Lau	R	27	120	10	2	3	4.9	.985
	L. Skizas	R	4	1	7	2	0	2.5	.800		T. Thompson	R	4	8	1	0	0	2.3	1.000
	M. Bolling	R	1	0	1	0	0	1.0	1.000		J. Feller	R	1	0	0	0	0	1.0	1.000

"Don't unpack" rapidly became the best advice for Tiger managers. Jack Tighe was succeeded by minor-league manager Bill Norman—who within a year would be replaced by Jimmy Dykes—as the Tigers again settled where they'd spent most of the decade: in the second division. This time they finsished in fifth place at 77–77, 15 games behind the first-place Yankees. Shifting from infield to outfield, Kuenn led Tiger hitters and finished third in the league at .319. Al Kaline was fourth in the league at .313. But no other Tiger hit .300. The tempestuous Billy Martin played 88 games at shortstop and 41 at third base while batting .255 during his only playing season in Detroit.

The pitching staff mirrored the overall mediocrity. Frank Lary led at 16–15 (with a 2.90 ERA, tied for league best). But in the first game of a June 20 doubleheader against the Red Sox at Fenway Park, Jim Bunning notched the fourth of five no-hitters in Tiger history. It didn't come easy. Gene Stephens led off the first inning with a fly to Kaline at the warning track, and Pete Runnels followed with a sharp grounder behind third, Ozzie Virgil's throw barely beating him at first. From there, Bunning defied superstition with unabashed dugout discussion of his no-hitter in progress. "I was going for it from the sixth inning on," he said. "In fact, I told some of the fellows to keep digging those balls because I was going to make it."

Detroit general manager John McHale rallied in December to overtake Cleveland GM Frank Lane as most prolific trader of the year. In a six-player deal, the Tigers sent Reno Bertoia, Ron Samford, and Jim Delsing to the Senators for Eddie Yost, Rocky Bridges, and Neil Chrisley.

TEAM STATISTICS

W	L	PCT	GB	R	OR	Batting						Fielding					Pitching			
						2B	3B	HR	BA	SA	SB	E	DP	FA	CG	BB	SO	ShO	SV	ERA
92	62	.597		759	577	212	39	164	.268	.416	48	128	182	.978	53	557	796	21	33	3.22
82	72	.532	10	634	615	191	42	101	.257	.367	101	114	160	.981	55	515	751	15	25	3.61
79	75	.513	13	697	691	229	30	155	.256	.400	29	145	172	.976	44	521	695	5	28	3.92
77	76	.503	14.5	694	635	210	31	161	.258	.403	50	152	171	.974	51	604	766	2	20	3.73
77	77	.500	15	659	606	229	41	109	.266	.389	48	106	140	.982	59	437	797	8	19	3.59
74	79	.484	17.5	521	575	195	19	108	.241	.350	33	114	159	.980	55	403	749	15	28	3.40
73	81	.474	19	642	713	196	50	138	.247	.381	22	125	166	.979	42	467	720	9	25	4.15
61	93	.396	31	553	747	161	38	121	.240	.357	22	118	163	.980	28	558	762	6	28	4.53
AGUE TOTAL				5159	5159	1623	290	1057	.254	.383	353	1002	1313	.979	387	4062	6036	81	206	3.77

INDIVIDUAL PITCHING

TCHER	T	W	L	PCT	ERA	SV	G	GS	CG	IP	H	BB	SO	R	ER	ShO	H/9	BB/9	SO/9
ank Lary	R	16	15	.516	2.90	1	39	34	19	260.1	249	68	131	91	84	3	8.61	2.35	4.53
ul Foytack	R	15	13	.536	3.44	1	39	33	16	230	198	77	135	98	88	2	7.75	3.01	5.28
n Bunning	R	14	12	.538	3.52	0	35	34	10	219.2	188	79	177	96	86	3	7.70	3.24	7.25
ly Hoeft	L	10	9	.526	4.15	3	36	21	6	143	148	49	94	70	66	0	9.31	3.08	5.92
rb Moford	R	4	9	.308	3.61	1	25	11	6	109.2	83	42	58	45	44	0	6.81	3.45	4.76
orge Susce	R	4	3	.571	3.67	1	27	10	2	90.2	90	26	42	45	37	0	8.93	2.58	4.17
nk Aguirre	L	3	4	.429	3.75	5	44	3	0	69.2	67	27	38	31	29	0	8.66	3.49	4.91
m Morgan	R	2	5	.286	3.16	1	39	1	0	62.2	70	4	32	28	22	0	10.05	0.57	4.60
Cicotte	R	3	1	.750	3.56	0	14	2	0	43	50	15	21	19	17	0	10.47	3.14	4.40
l Fischer	R	2	4	.333	7.63	2	22	0	0	30.2	46	13	16	34	26	0	13.50	3.82	4.70
b Shaw	R	1	2	.333	5.06	0	11	2	0	26.2	32	13	17	16	15	0	10.80	4.39	5.74
rm Wehmeier	R	1	0	1.000	2.38	0	7	3	0	22.2	21	5	11	8	6	0	8.34	1.99	4.37
o Valentinetti	R	1	0	1.000	3.38	2	15	0	0	18.2	18	5	10	7	7	0	8.68	2.41	4.82
e Presko	R	0	0	–	3.38	2	7	0	0	10.2	13	1	6	4	4	0	10.97	0.84	5.06
orge Spencer	R	1	0	1.000	2.70	0	7	0	0	10	11	4	5	4	3	0	9.90	3.60	4.50
u Sleater	L	0	0	–	6.75	0	4	0	0	5.1	3	6	4	4	4	0	5.06	10.13	6.75
n Lee	R	0	0	–	9.00	0	1	0	0	2	1	1	0	2	2	0	4.50	4.50	0.00
ckey McDermott	L	0	0	–	9.00	0	2	0	0	2	6	2	0	4	2	0	27.00	9.00	0.00
AM TOTAL		77	77	.500	3.59	19	374	154	59	1357.1	1294	437	797	606	542	8	8.58	2.90	5.28

MANAGER	W	L	PCT
Bill Norman	2	15	.118
Jimmy Dykes	74	63	.540

POS	Player	B	G	AB	H	2B	3B	HR	HR %	R	RBI	BB	SO	SB	Pinch Hit AB	Pinch Hit H	BA	SA
REGULARS																		
1B	Gail Harris	L	114	349	77	4	3	9	2.6	39	39	29	49	0	22	4	.221	.327
2B	Frank Bolling	R	127	459	122	18	3	13	2.8	56	55	45	37	2	1	0	.266	.403
SS	Rocky Bridges	R	116	381	102	16	3	3	0.8	38	35	30	35	1	2	0	.268	.349
3B	Eddie Yost	R	148	521	145	19	0	21	4.0	115	61	135	77	9	3	0	.278	.436
RF	Harvey Kuenn	R	139	561	198	42	7	9	1.6	99	71	48	37	7	1	0	.353	.501
CF	Al Kaline	R	136	511	167	19	2	27	5.3	86	94	72	42	10	0	0	.327	.530
LF	Charlie Maxwell	L	145	518	130	12	2	31	6.0	81	95	81	91	0	8	3	.251	.461
C	Lou Berberet	L	100	338	73	8	2	13	3.8	38	44	35	59	0	3	0	.216	.367
SUBSTITUTES																		
UT	Ted Lepcio	R	76	215	60	8	0	7	3.3	25	24	17	49	2	14	4	.279	.414
1B	Bobo Osborne	L	86	209	40	7	1	3	1.4	27	21	16	41	1	23	0	.191	.278
1B	Gus Zernial	R	60	132	30	4	0	7	5.3	11	26	7	27	0	27	6	.227	.417
SS	Coot Veal	R	77	89	18	1	0	1	1.1	12	15	8	7	0	0	0	.202	.247
3B	Steve Demeter	R	11	18	2	1	0	0	0.0	1	1	0	1	0	9	1	.111	.167
OF	Neil Chrisley	L	65	106	14	3	0	6	5.7	7	11	12	10	0	43	5	.132	.330
OF	Johnny Groth	R	55	102	24	7	1	1	1.0	12	10	7	14	0	13	4	.235	.353
OF	Larry Doby	L	18	55	12	3	1	0	0.0	5	3	8	9	0	1	0	.218	.309
C	Red Wilson	R	67	228	60	17	2	4	1.8	28	35	10	23	2	3	0	.263	.408
C	Ron Shoop	R	3	7	1	0	0	0	0.0	1	1	0	1	0	0	0	.143	.143
C	Charlie Lau	L	2	6	1	0	0	0	0.0	0	0	0	2	0	1	0	.167	.167
PH	Ossie Alvarez	R	8	2	1	0	0	0	0.0	0	0	0	1	0	2	1	.500	.500
PITCHERS																		
P	Jim Bunning	R	40	89	17	0	1	1	1.1	7	7	5	25	0	0	0	.191	.247
P	Paul Foytack	R	39	81	9	1	0	0	0.0	6	2	5	20	0	0	0	.111	.123
P	Frank Lary	R	32	80	10	1	1	1	1.3	7	2	4	26	0	0	0	.125	.200
P	Don Mossi	L	36	77	13	4	0	1	1.3	6	8	3	28	0	0	0	.169	.260
P	Tom Morgan	R	46	23	9	0	0	2	8.7	3	4	0	6	0	0	0	.391	.652
P	Ray Narleski	R	42	21	2	0	1	0	0.0	0	0	0	4	0	0	0	.095	.190
P	Pete Burnside	R	30	10	0	0	0	0	0.0	0	0	1	5	0	0	0	.000	.000
P	Jerry Davie	R	11	10	4	0	0	0	0.0	1	2	2	3	0	0	0	.400	.400
P	Dave Sisler	R	32	5	1	0	0	0	0.0	1	0	0	0	0	0	0	.200	.200
P	Billy Hoeft	L	3	3	1	0	0	0	0.0	0	0	0	0	0	0	0	.333	.333
P	Barney Schultz	R	13	2	2	0	0	0	0.0	0	0	0	0	0	0	0	1.000	1.000
P	Bob Smith	R	9	1	0	0	0	0	0.0	0	0	0	1	0	0	0	.000	.000
P	Jim Stump	R	5	1	1	1	0	0	0.0	1	0	0	0	0	0	0	1.000	2.000
P	George Susce	R	9	1	0	0	0	0	0.0	0	0	0	1	0	0	0	.000	.000
P	Hank Aguirre	R	3	0	0	0	0	0	–	0	0	0	0	0	0	0	–	–
P	Bob Bruce	R	2	0	0	0	0	0	–	0	0	0	0	0	0	0	–	–
P	Jim Proctor	R	2	0	0	0	0	0	–	0	0	0	0	0	0	0	–	–
TEAM TOTAL				5211	1346	196	30	160	3.1	713	666	580	735	34	176	28	.258	.400

INDIVIDUAL FIELDING

POS	Player	T	G	PO	A	E	DP	TC/G	FA	POS	Player	T	G	PO	A	E	DP	TC/G	FA
1B	G. Harris	L	93	728	57	6	59	8.5	.992	OF	A. Kaline	R	136	364	4	4	0	2.7	.989
	B. Osborne	R	56	377	27	7	36	7.3	.983		C. Maxwell	L	136	285	6	4	1	2.2	.986
	G. Zernial	R	32	197	10	6	20	6.7	.972		H. Kuenn	R	137	247	6	3	0	1.9	.988
											J. Groth	R	41	58	0	1	0	1.4	.983
2B	F. Bolling	R	126	281	340	8	81	5.0	.987		N. Chrisley	R	21	28	0	0	0	1.3	1.000
	T. Lepcio	R	24	59	58	5	18	5.1	.959		L. Doby	R	16	23	1	1	1	1.6	.960
	R. Bridges	R	5	16	15	0	4	6.2	1.000		B. Osborne	R	1	1	0	1	0	2.0	.500
	E. Yost	R	1	0	1	0	0	1.0	1.000		G. Zernial	R	1	1	0	0	0	1.0	1.000
SS	R. Bridges	R	110	179	293	24	66	4.5	.952	C	L. Berberet	R	95	511	39	6	4	5.9	.989
	C. Veal	R	72	57	96	6	16	2.2	.962		R. Wilson	R	64	374	25	5	8	6.3	.988
	T. Lepcio	R	35	32	65	5	12	2.9	.951		C. Lau	R	2	11	1	0	1	6.0	1.000
3B	E. Yost	R	146	168	259	17	21	3.0	.962		R. Shoop	R	3	8	0	0	0	2.7	1.000
	T. Lepcio	R	11	5	20	1	0	2.4	.962										
	S. Demeter	R	4	4	6	1	1	2.8	.909										

Detroit began the final year of the frustrating fifties with a 2–15 start. With the Motor City waiting till next year just two weeks into the season, the Tigers fired manager Bill Norman on May 2 and the next day hired Pirates coach and 18-year major-league manager Jimmy Dykes. And within six weeks, the Tigers had won 32 of 46 to move a half game out of first on June 20. But then injuries hit and the Tigers steadily slipped away. By the All-Star break they were in fifth place at 40–40. Eventually the Tigers squeezed into fourth with their first losing season in five years, 18 games behind the first-place White Sox.

Like Tigers of a previous era, Harvey Kuenn, Al Kaline, and Charlie Maxwell teamed to give Detroit a slugging outfield. In his final season as a Tiger, Kuenn led the league in hits, authored hitting streaks of 22 and 18 straight games, and won his only batting crown at .353. Second in the league at .327, Kaline was the only other Tiger in the .300 club. Maxwell hit .251, but slammed 31 home runs—the first Tiger to reach 30 in 13 years. And three hit 20-plus: Maxwell, Kaline (27), and third baseman Eddie Yost (21).

Left-handed reliever Don Mossi was obtained from Cleveland, became a starter, and led the staff at 17–9, 3.36. Jim Bunning led the league in strikeouts and finished 17–13, 3.89. They were backed up by exceptional fielding. Yost led American League third baseman in putouts and fielding percentage. And second baseman Frank Bolling fell one short of tying the major-league record for second baseman with 72 straight games without an error, from May 18 until August 29. The front office, meanwhile, still featured revolving doors. General manager John McHale left to join the Milwaukee Braves and was replaced by Rick Ferrell; William O. DeWitt was elected team president.

TEAM STATISTICS

	W	L	PCT	GB	R	OR	Batting 2B	3B	HR	BA	SA	SB	Fielding E	DP	FA	Pitching CG	BB	SO	ShO	SV	ERA
HI	94	60	.610		669	588	220	46	97	.250	.364	113	130	141	.979	44	525	761	13	36	3.29
LE	89	65	.578	5	745	646	216	25	167	.263	.408	33	126	138	.978	58	635	799	7	23	3.75
Y	79	75	.513	15	687	647	224	40	153	.260	.402	45	131	160	.978	38	594	836	15	28	3.60
ET	76	78	.494	18	713	732	196	30	160	.258	.400	34	124	131	.978	53	432	829	9	24	4.20
OS	75	79	.487	19	726	696	248	28	125	.256	.385	68	131	167	.978	38	589	724	9	25	4.17
AL	74	80	.481	20	551	621	182	23	109	.238	.345	36	147	163	.976	45	476	735	15	30	3.56
C	66	88	.429	28	681	760	231	43	117	.263	.390	34	159	156	.973	44	492	703	8	21	4.35
AS	63	91	.409	31	619	701	173	32	163	.237	.379	51	162	140	.973	46	467	694	10	21	4.01
AGUE TOTAL					5391	5391	1690	267	1091	.253	.384	414	1110	1196	.977	366	4210	6081	86	208	3.86

INDIVIDUAL PITCHING

TCHER	T	W	L	PCT	ERA	SV	G	GS	CG	IP	H	BB	SO	R	ER	ShO	H/9	BB/9	SO/9
m Bunning	R	17	13	.567	3.89	1	40	35	14	249.2	220	75	201	111	108	1	7.93	2.70	7.25
aul Foytack	R	14	14	.500	4.64	1	39	37	11	240.1	239	64	110	137	124	2	8.95	2.40	4.12
on Mossi	L	17	9	.654	3.36	0	34	30	15	228	210	49	125	92	85	3	8.29	1.93	4.93
ank Lary	R	17	10	.630	3.55	0	32	32	11	223	225	46	137	109	88	3	9.08	1.86	5.53
ay Narleski	R	4	12	.250	5.78	5	42	10	1	104.1	105	59	71	83	67	0	9.06	5.09	6.12
m Morgan	R	1	4	.200	3.98	9	46	1	0	92.2	94	18	39	48	41	0	9.13	1.75	3.79
ete Burnside	L	1	3	.250	3.77	1	30	0	0	62	55	25	49	31	26	0	7.98	3.63	7.11
ave Sisler	R	1	3	.250	4.01	7	32	0	0	51.2	46	36	29	28	23	0	8.01	6.27	5.05
erry Davie	R	2	2	.500	4.17	0	11	5	1	36.2	40	17	20	25	17	0	9.82	4.17	4.91
arney Schultz	R	1	2	.333	4.42	0	13	0	0	18.1	17	14	17	12	9	0	8.35	6.87	8.35
eorge Susce	R	0	0	–	12.89	0	9	0	0	14.2	24	9	9	22	21	0	14.73	5.52	5.52
m Stump	R	0	0	–	2.38	0	5	0	0	11.1	12	4	6	3	3	0	9.53	3.18	4.76
ob Smith	L	0	3	.000	8.18	0	9	0	0	11	20	3	10	15	10	0	16.36	2.45	8.18
lly Hoeft	L	1	1	.500	5.00	0	2	2	0	9	6	4	2	5	5	0	6.00	4.00	2.00
ank Aguirre	L	0	0	–	3.38	0	2	0	0	2.2	4	3	3	1	1	0	13.50	10.13	10.13
m Proctor	R	0	1	.000	16.88	0	2	1	0	2.2	8	3	0	5	5	0	27.00	10.13	0.00
ob Bruce	R	0	1	.000	9.00	0	2	1	0	2	2	3	1	5	2	0	9.00	13.50	4.50
EAM TOTAL		76	78	.494	4.20	24	351	154	53	1360	1327	432	829	732	635	9	8.78	2.86	5.49

MANAGER	W	L	PCT
Jimmy Dykes	44	52	.458
Billy Hitchcock	1	0	1.000
Joe Gordon	26	31	.456

POS	Player	B	G	AB	H	2B	3B	HR	HR %	R	RBI	BB	SO	SB	Pinch Hit AB	Pinch Hit H	BA	SA
REGULARS																		
1B	Norm Cash	L	121	353	101	16	3	18	5.1	64	63	65	58	4	23	9	.286	.501
2B	Frank Bolling	R	139	536	136	20	4	9	1.7	64	59	40	48	7	1	0	.254	.356
SS	Chico Fernandez	R	133	435	105	13	3	4	0.9	44	35	39	50	13	2	0	.241	.313
3B	Eddie Yost	R	143	497	129	23	2	14	2.8	78	47	125	69	5	5	1	.260	.398
RF	Rocky Colavito	R	145	555	138	18	1	35	6.3	67	87	53	80	3	2	0	.249	.474
CF	Al Kaline	R	147	551	153	29	4	15	2.7	77	68	65	47	19	4	2	.278	.426
LF	Charlie Maxwell	L	134	482	114	16	5	24	5.0	70	81	58	75	5	14	1	.237	.440
C	Lou Berberet	L	85	232	45	4	0	5	2.2	18	23	41	31	2	4	1	.194	.276
SUBSTITUTES																		
1B	Steve Bilko	R	78	222	46	11	2	9	4.1	20	25	27	31	0	17	1	.207	.396
UT	Ozzie Virgil	R	62	132	30	4	2	3	2.3	16	13	4	14	1	8	2	.227	.356
2S	Casey Wise	B	30	68	10	0	2	2	2.9	6	5	4	9	1	3	0	.147	.294
SS	Coot Veal	R	27	64	19	5	1	0	0.0	8	8	11	7	0	2	1	.297	.406
1O	Dick Gernert	R	21	50	15	4	0	1	2.0	6	5	4	5	0	4	1	.300	.440
SS	Dick McAuliffe	L	8	27	7	0	1	0	0.0	2	1	2	6	0	0	0	.259	.333
3S	Rocky Bridges	R	10	5	1	0	0	0	0.0	0	0	0	0	0	0	0	.200	.200
1B	Gail Harris	L	8	5	0	0	0	0	0.0	0	0	2	1	0	3	0	.000	.000
OF	Neil Chrisley	L	96	220	56	10	3	5	2.3	27	24	19	26	2	44	10	.255	.395
OF	Sandy Amoros	L	65	67	10	0	0	1	1.5	7	7	12	10	0	44	8	.149	.194
OF	Johnny Groth	R	25	19	7	1	0	0	0.0	3	2	3	1	0	8	3	.368	.421
C	Red Wilson	R	45	134	29	4	0	1	0.7	17	14	16	14	3	0	0	.216	.269
C	Harry Chiti	R	37	104	17	0	0	2	1.9	9	5	10	12	0	1	0	.163	.221
C	Hank Foiles	R	26	56	14	3	0	0	0.0	5	3	1	8	1	2	0	.250	.304
PH	Em Lindbeck	L	2	1	0	0	0	0	0.0	0	0	1	0	0	1	0	.000	.000
PITCHERS																		
P	Frank Lary	R	39	93	17	4	1	2	2.2	11	13	7	32	0	0	0	.183	.312
P	Jim Bunning	R	38	81	13	1	0	0	0.0	2	4	3	22	0	0	0	.160	.173
P	Don Mossi	L	23	43	5	0	0	0	0.0	0	2	7	12	0	0	0	.116	.116
P	Bob Bruce	R	34	39	7	0	0	0	0.0	4	0	4	11	0	0	0	.179	.179
P	Hank Aguirre	R	37	28	1	0	0	0	0.0	0	0	0	19	0	0	0	.036	.036
P	Pete Burnside	R	31	27	4	0	0	0	0.0	2	1	2	6	0	0	0	.148	.148
P	Paul Foytack	R	29	25	7	1	0	0	0.0	4	4	3	9	0	0	0	.280	.320
P	Phil Regan	R	17	17	1	0	0	0	0.0	0	1	2	7	0	0	0	.059	.059
P	Dave Sisler	R	41	16	2	0	0	0	0.0	0	0	2	5	0	0	0	.125	.125
P	Bill Fischer	R	20	11	4	1	0	0	0.0	2	1	3	0	0	0	0	.364	.455
P	Ray Semproch	R	17	4	0	0	0	0	0.0	0	0	1	3	0	0	0	.000	.000
P	Clem Labine	R	14	2	0	0	0	0	0.0	0	0	0	0	0	0	0	.000	.000
P	George Spencer	R	5	1	0	0	0	0	0.0	0	0	0	0	0	0	0	.000	.000
P	Tom Morgan	R	22	0	0	0	0	0	—	0	0	0	0	0	0	0	—	—
TEAM TOTAL				5202	1243	188	34	150	2.9	633	601	636	728	66	192	40	.239	.375

INDIVIDUAL FIELDING

POS	Player	T	G	PO	A	E	DP	TC/G	FA
1B	N. Cash	L	99	739	59	7	68	8.1	.991
	S. Bilko	R	62	501	36	5	47	8.7	.991
	D. Gernert	R	13	93	4	0	13	7.5	1.000
	N. Chrisley	R	2	8	0	1	0	4.5	.889
	G. Harris	L	5	8	1	0	1	1.8	1.000
2B	F. Bolling	R	138	375	377	17	93	5.6	.978
	C. Wise	R	17	21	37	1	8	3.5	.983
	O. Virgil	R	8	11	24	0	2	4.4	1.000
	C. Veal	R	1	2	1	0	0	3.0	1.000
SS	C. Fernandez	R	130	226	381	34	67	4.9	.947
	C. Veal	R	22	26	53	1	10	3.6	.988
	D. McAuliffe	R	7	12	26	5	7	6.1	.884
	C. Wise	R	10	12	22	0	4	3.4	1.000
	O. Virgil	R	5	11	14	2	4	5.4	.926
	R. Bridges	R	3	2	3	0	1	1.7	1.000
3B	E. Yost	R	142	155	208	26	18	2.7	.933
	O. Virgil	R	42	28	46	2	7	1.8	.974
	C. Wise	R	1	0	0	0	0	0.0	.000
	R. Bridges	R	7	2	5	0	0	1.0	1.000
	C. Veal	R	3	2	1	0	0	1.0	1.000

POS	Player	T	G	PO	A	E	DP	TC/G	FA
OF	A. Kaline	R	142	367	5	5	1	2.7	.987
	R. Colavito	R	144	271	11	7	5	2.0	.976
	C. Maxwell	L	120	254	5	1	0	2.2	**.996**
	N. Chrisley	R	47	101	2	2	0	2.2	.981
	S. Amoros	L	10	17	0	0	0	1.7	1.000
	D. Gernert	R	6	7	0	1	0	1.3	.875
	J. Groth	R	8	6	0	0	0	0.8	1.000
	N. Cash	L	4	4	0	0	0	1.0	1.000
C	L. Berberet	R	81	396	36	3	4	5.4	.993
	R. Wilson	R	45	229	17	5	0	5.6	.980
	H. Chiti	R	36	173	17	3	0	5.4	.984
	H. Foiles	R	22	96	11	0	1	4.9	1.000
	O. Virgil	R	1	2	1	0	0	3.0	1.000

On August 2, Detroit and Cleveland created baseball history as the first and only major league teams to trade managers in midseason: the Tigers sent Jim Dykes to the Indians in return for Joe Gordon. It couldn't hurt. The sixth-place Tigers had lost 12 of their last 15, the fourth-place Indians 18 of their previous 25. But it didn't help either. Cleveland stayed fourth and the Tigers stayed sixth to finish 26 games behind the first-place Yankees.

A pair of trades concocted by Bill DeWitt and Cleveland general manager Frank "Trader"Lane proved less bizarre, but no less momentous. In one of the most fortuitous deals in Detroit history the Tigers sent third baseman Steve Demeter to the Indians for first baseman Norm Cash. Demeter wouldn't stick in the majors. Cash would win the batting title the following season and hit 373 home runs during a 2,018-game, 15-year career in Detroit. Five days later as spring training ended, the Tigers dispatched defending batting champion Harvey Kuenn for defending home run co-champ Rocky Colavito. When the stunning deal was announced, Cleveland fans were outraged while baseball fans across the nation debated trading 135 singles for 42 home runs. Kuenn hit .308 and was sent to San Francisco the following season. Colavito hit .249 with 35 home runs.

Starting the season 5–0 before losing 10 straight, the Tigers compiled their worst record since 1954, mostly via subpar hitting. Detroit was last in team batting at .239 and lost 31 games by one run. Al Kaline hit .278 with 15 home runs as no Tiger reached .300; Cash came closest at .286. Thus Jim Bunning's 2.79 ERA was good for only an 11–14 record. After the season Detroit lost seven players in the expansion draft, including third baseman Eddie Yost to the Los Angeles Angels. The unlucky draftees would soon miss Detroit's first bona fide pennant race in 11 years.

TEAM STATISTICS

W	L	PCT	GB	R	OR	Batting 2B	3B	HR	BA	SA	SB	Fielding E	DP	FA	CG	BB	Pitching SO	ShO	SV	ERA
97	57	.630		746	627	215	40	193	.260	.426	37	129	162	.979	38	609	712	16	42	3.52
89	65	.578	8	682	606	206	33	123	.253	.377	37	108	172	.982	48	552	785	11	22	3.52
87	67	.565	10	741	617	242	38	112	.270	.396	122	109	175	.982	42	533	695	11	26	3.60
76	78	.494	21	667	693	218	20	127	.267	.388	58	128	165	.978	32	636	771	10	30	3.95
73	81	.474	24	672	696	205	43	147	.244	.384	52	165	159	.973	34	538	775	10	35	3.77
71	83	.461	26	633	644	188	34	150	.239	.375	66	138	138	.977	40	474	824	7	25	3.64
65	89	.422	32	658	775	234	32	124	.261	.389	34	141	156	.976	34	580	767	6	23	4.62
58	96	.377	39	615	756	212	34	110	.249	.366	16	127	149	.979	44	525	664	4	14	4.38
GUE TOTAL				5414	5414	1720	274	1086	.255	.388	422	1045	1276	.978	312	4447	5993	75	217	3.87

INDIVIDUAL PITCHING

CHER	T	W	L	PCT	ERA	SV	G	GS	CG	IP	H	BB	SO	R	ER	ShO	H/9	BB/9	SO/9
nk Lary	R	15	15	.500	3.51	1	38	36	15	274.1	262	62	149	125	107	2	8.60	2.03	4.89
Bunning	R	11	14	.440	2.79	0	36	34	10	252	217	64	201	92	78	3	7.75	2.29	7.18
Mossi	L	9	8	.529	3.47	0	23	22	9	158.1	158	32	69	68	61	2	8.98	1.82	3.92
Bruce	R	4	7	.364	3.74	0	34	15	1	130	127	56	76	68	54	0	8.79	3.88	5.26
te Burnside	L	7	7	.500	4.28	2	31	15	2	113.2	122	50	71	56	54	0	9.66	3.96	5.62
Jl Foytack	R	2	11	.154	6.14	2	28	13	1	96.2	108	49	38	70	66	0	10.06	4.56	3.54
nk Aguirre	L	5	3	.625	2.85	10	37	6	1	94.2	75	30	80	31	30	0	7.13	2.85	7.61
ve Sisler	R	7	5	.583	2.48	6	41	0	0	80	56	45	47	23	22	0	6.30	5.06	5.29
l Regan	R	0	4	.000	4.50	1	17	7	0	68	70	25	38	39	34	0	9.26	3.31	5.03
Fischer	R	5	3	.625	3.44	0	20	6	1	55	50	18	24	23	21	0	8.18	2.95	3.93
m Morgan	R	3	2	.600	4.66	1	22	0	0	29	33	10	12	17	15	0	10.24	3.10	3.72
y Semproch	R	3	0	1.000	4.00	0	17	0	0	27	29	16	9	17	12	0	9.67	5.33	3.00
m Labine	R	0	3	.000	5.12	2	14	0	0	19.1	19	12	6	12	11	0	8.84	5.59	2.79
orge Spencer	R	0	1	.000	3.52	0	5	0	0	7.2	10	5	4	3	3	0	11.74	5.87	4.70
AM TOTAL		71	83	.461	3.64	25	363	154	40	1405.2	1336	474	824	644	568	7	8.55	3.03	5.28

MANAGER	W	L	PCT
Bob Scheffing	101	61	.623

POS	Player	B	G	AB	H	2B	3B	HR	HR %	R	RBI	BB	SO	SB	Pinch Hit AB	Pinch Hit H	BA	SA
REGULARS
1B	Norm Cash	L	159	535	**193**	22	8	41	7.7	119	132	124	85	11	1	0	**.361**	.662
2B	Jake Wood	R	162	663	171	17	**14**	11	1.7	96	69	58	141	30	1	0	.258	.376
SS	Chico Fernandez	R	133	435	108	15	4	3	0.7	41	40	36	45	8	4	2	.248	.322
3B	Steve Boros	R	116	396	107	18	2	5	1.3	51	62	68	42	4	0	0	.270	.364
RF	Al Kaline	R	153	586	190	41	7	19	3.2	116	82	66	42	14	5	3	.324	.515
CF	Bill Bruton	L	160	596	153	15	5	17	2.9	99	63	61	66	22	6	1	.257	.384
LF	Rocky Colavito	R	163	583	169	30	2	45	7.7	129	140	113	75	1	2	0	.290	.580
C	Dick Brown	R	98	308	82	12	2	16	5.2	32	45	22	57	0	3	2	.266	.474
SUBSTITUTES
S3	Dick McAuliffe	L	80	285	73	12	4	6	2.1	36	33	24	39	2	7	3	.256	.389
13	Bobo Osborne	L	71	93	20	7	0	2	2.2	8	13	20	15	1	41	10	.215	.355
32	Reno Bertoia	R	24	46	10	1	0	1	2.2	6	4	3	8	2	0	0	.217	.304
UT	Ozzie Virgil	R	20	30	4	0	0	1	3.3	1	1	1	5	0	7	2	.133	.233
SS	Chuck Cottier	R	10	7	2	0	0	0	0.0	2	1	1	1	0	0	0	.286	.286
OF	Charlie Maxwell	L	79	131	30	4	2	5	3.8	11	18	20	24	0	45	12	.229	.405
OF	Bubba Morton	R	77	108	31	5	1	2	1.9	26	19	9	25	3	37	11	.287	.407
OF	George Alusik	R	15	14	2	0	0	0	0.0	0	2	1	4	0	12	2	.143	.143
OS	George Thomas	R	17	6	0	0	0	0	0.0	2	0	0	4	0	4	0	.000	.000
C	Mike Roarke	R	86	229	51	6	1	2	0.9	21	22	20	31	0	1	0	.223	.284
C	Frank House	L	17	22	5	1	1	0	0.0	3	3	4	2	0	3	0	.227	.364
C	Harry Chiti	R	5	12	1	0	0	0	0.0	0	0	1	2	0	0	0	.083	.083
C	Bill Freehan	R	4	10	4	0	0	0	0.0	1	4	1	0	0	0	0	.400	.400
PH	Vic Wertz	L	8	6	1	0	0	0	0.0	0	1	0	1	0	6	1	.167	.167
PH	Dick Gernert	R	6	5	1	0	0	1	20.0	1	1	1	2	0	5	1	.200	.800
PITCHERS
P	Frank Lary	R	42	108	25	2	0	1	0.9	13	5	3	27	0	0	0	.231	.278
P	Jim Bunning	R	38	100	13	1	0	0	0.0	6	4	2	30	0	0	0	.130	.140
P	Don Mossi	L	35	79	13	2	0	1	1.3	8	8	6	28	0	0	0	.165	.228
P	Paul Foytack	R	32	54	12	1	0	1	1.9	4	2	1	11	0	0	0	.222	.296
P	Phil Regan	R	33	40	3	1	0	0	0.0	4	1	3	15	0	0	0	.075	.100
P	Ron Kline	R	10	18	3	1	0	0	0.0	2	2	0	8	0	0	0	.167	.222
P	Terry Fox	R	39	12	2	0	0	0	0.0	1	0	1	7	0	0	0	.167	.167
P	Bob Bruce	R	14	9	1	1	0	0	0.0	1	1	2	2	0	0	0	.111	.222
P	Bill Fischer	R	26	7	0	0	0	0	0.0	0	0	0	2	0	0	0	.000	.000
P	Howie Koplitz	R	4	4	0	0	0	0	0.0	0	0	0	1	0	0	0	.000	.000
P	Hal Woodeshick	R	12	4	0	0	0	0	0.0	1	0	1	1	0	0	0	.000	.000
P	Jerry Casale	R	3	3	0	0	0	0	0.0	0	0	0	3	0	0	0	.000	.000
P	Fred Gladding	L	8	3	0	0	0	0	0.0	0	0	0	3	0	0	0	.000	.000
P	Ron Nischwitz	B	6	2	0	0	0	0	0.0	0	0	0	2	0	0	0	.000	.000
P	Jim Donohue	R	14	1	0	0	0	0	0.0	0	0	0	0	0	0	0	.000	.000
P	Joe Grzenda	R	4	1	1	0	0	0	0.0	0	0	0	0	0	0	0	1.000	1.000
P	Gerry Staley	R	13	1	0	0	0	0	0.0	0	0	0	1	0	0	0	.000	.000
P	Manny Montejo	R	12	0	0	0	0	0	–	0	0	0	0	0	0	0	–	–
	TEAM TOTAL			5561	1481	215	53	180	3.2	841	779	673	865	98	190	50	.266	.421

INDIVIDUAL FIELDING

POS	Player	T	G	PO	A	E	DP	TC/G	FA
1B	N. Cash	L	157	**1231**	127	11	121	8.7	.992
	B. Osborne	R	11	50	3	0	4	4.8	1.000
2B	J. Wood	R	162	380	396	**25**	83	4.9	.969
	O. Virgil	R	1	0	0	0	0	0.0	.000
	R. Bertoia	R	7	7	7	0	3	2.0	1.000
	C. Cottier	R	2	2	6	0	2	4.0	1.000
SS	C. Fernandez	R	121	207	312	23	59	4.5	.958
	D. McAuliffe	R	55	79	115	14	29	3.8	.933
	R. Bertoia	R	1	0	0	0	0	0.0	.000
	C. Cottier	R	8	7	1	1	1	1.1	.889
	G. Thomas	R	1	3	1	0	1	4.0	1.000
	O. Virgil	R	1	2	2	0	0	4.0	1.000
3B	S. Boros	R	116	115	192	15	15	2.8	.953
	D. McAuliffe	R	22	13	39	5	3	2.6	.912
	R. Bertoia	R	13	8	16	2	1	2.0	.923
	B. Osborne	R	8	10	12	1	2	2.9	.957
	C. Fernandez	R	8	10	10	0	2	2.5	1.000
	O. Virgil	R	9	9	6	1	0	1.8	.938
	A. Kaline	R	1	1	1	0	0	2.0	1.000
OF	B. Bruton	R	155	**410**	4	5	2	2.7	.988
	A. Kaline	R	147	378	9	4	3	2.7	.990
	R. Colavito	R	161	329	**16**	9	4	2.2	.975
	C. Maxwell	L	25	53	2	2	0	2.3	.965
	B. Morton	R	30	39	1	2	1	1.4	.952
	G. Alusik	R	1	0	0	0	0	0.0	.000
	G. Thomas	R	2	0	0	0	0	0.0	.000
C	D. Brown	R	91	460	38	5	7	5.5	.990
	M. Roarke	R	85	383	22	5	5	4.8	.988
	F. House	R	14	36	1	1	0	2.7	.974
	H. Chiti	R	5	19	3	0	0	4.4	1.000
	B. Freehan	R	3	14	4	0	0	6.0	1.000
	O. Virgil	R	3	2	1	0	0	1.0	1.000

The Tigers fielded two sluggers with 40-plus home runs, won 101 games, and won back the hearts of their fans, who ballooned attendance at newly named Tiger Stadium by nearly half a million to 1,600,710. They did not, however, win the pennant: the Yankees fielded two sluggers with 50-plus home runs and won 109 games. In baseball's first 162-game season, the Tigers stayed in the pennant race into September. Under new manager Bob Scheffing, Detroit owned first place through much of the first half. Then New York—with Mickey Mantle (54) and Roger Maris (61) conducting a spectacular home run duel—won 16 of 20 to move into first.

But the Tigers kept up. Never trailing by more than four, they sat just one-and-a-half games out before losing three in a row in a September showdown at Yankee Stadium. New York proceeded to win 13 straight while the Tigers skidded to finish eight games out.

Norm Cash, Al Kaline, and Rocky Colavito blessed Detroit with its hardest-hitting trio since the G-men of the thirties. First baseman Cash won his only batting title at .361 (the highest by a Tiger since 1937) and pounded 41 home runs (most ever by a Tiger lefty) with 132 RBI. He also became the first Tiger to hit a home run completely out of Tiger Stadium since it was double-decked in 1938. Rightfielder Kaline followed at .324. And leftfielder Colavito chipped in .290 with 45 home runs and 140 RBI. Weakest in the league in hitting the previous year, Detroit led the AL in batting and the majors in runs. But the Tigers, despite strong starters Frank Lary (career-best 23–9), Jim Bunning (17–11), and Don Mossi (15–7), couldn't keep pace with the Yankees' pitching depth.

Amid the frenzied pennant race, Detroit disciples stopped to grieve on July 17 when 74-year-old Ty Cobb died of cancer in Atlanta.

TEAM STATISTICS

W	L	PCT	GB	R	OR	2B	3B	HR	BA	SA	SB	E	DP	FA	CG	BB	SO	ShO	SV	ERA
109	53	.673		827	612	194	40	240	.263	.442	28	124	180	.980	47	542	866	14	39	3.46
101	61	.623	8	841	671	215	53	180	.266	.421	98	146	147	.976	62	469	836	12	30	3.55
95	67	.586	14	691	588	227	36	149	.254	.390	39	128	173	.980	54	617	926	21	33	3.22
86	76	.531	23	765	726	216	46	138	.265	.395	100	128	138	.980	39	498	814	3	33	4.06
78	83	.484	30.5	737	752	257	39	150	.266	.406	34	139	142	.977	35	599	801	12	23	4.15
76	86	.469	33	729	792	251	37	112	.254	.374	56	144	170	.977	35	679	831	6	30	4.29
70	90	.438	38	707	778	215	40	167	.250	.397	47	174	150	.971	49	570	914	14	23	4.28
70	91	.435	38.5	744	784	218	22	189	.245	.398	37	192	154	.969	25	713	973	5	34	4.31
61	100	.379	47.5	683	863	216	47	90	.247	.354	58	175	160	.972	32	629	703	5	23	4.74
61	100	.379	47.5	618	776	217	44	119	.244	.367	81	156	171	.975	39	586	666	8	21	4.23
AGUE TOTAL				7342	7342	2226	404	1534	.256	.395	578	1506	1585	.976	417	5902	8330	100	289	4.02

INDIVIDUAL PITCHING

CHER	T	W	L	PCT	ERA	SV	G	GS	CG	IP	H	BB	SO	R	ER	ShO	H/9	BB/9	SO/9
ank Lary	R	23	9	.719	3.24	0	36	36	22	275.1	252	66	146	117	99	4	8.24	2.16	4.77
Bunning	R	17	11	.607	3.19	1	38	37	12	268	232	71	194	113	95	4	7.79	2.38	6.51
n Mossi	L	15	7	.682	2.96	1	35	34	12	240.1	237	47	137	97	79	1	8.88	1.76	5.13
ul Foytack	R	11	10	.524	3.93	0	32	20	6	169.2	152	56	89	81	74	0	8.06	2.97	4.72
l Regan	R	10	7	.588	5.25	2	32	16	6	120	134	41	46	70	70	0	10.05	3.08	3.45
ry Fox	R	5	2	.714	1.41	12	39	0	0	57.1	42	16	32	12	9	0	6.59	2.51	5.02
n Kline	R	5	3	.625	2.72	0	10	8	3	56.1	53	17	27	25	17	1	8.47	2.72	4.31
nk Aguirre	L	4	4	.500	3.25	8	45	0	0	55.1	44	38	32	22	20	0	7.16	6.18	5.20
Fischer	R	3	2	.600	5.01	3	26	1	0	46.2	54	17	18	28	26	0	10.41	3.28	3.47
b Bruce	R	1	2	.333	4.43	0	14	6	0	44.2	57	24	25	28	22	0	11.49	4.84	5.04
n Donohue	R	1	1	.500	3.54	1	14	0	0	20.1	23	15	20	10	8	0	10.18	6.64	8.85
l Woodeshick	L	1	1	.500	7.85	0	12	2	0	18.1	25	17	13	17	16	0	12.27	8.35	6.38
ed Gladding	R	1	0	1.000	3.31	0	8	0	0	16.1	18	11	11	7	6	0	9.92	6.06	6.06
nny Montejo	R	0	0	—	3.86	0	12	0	0	16.1	13	6	15	7	7	0	7.16	3.31	8.27
rry Staley	R	1	1	.500	3.38	2	13	0	0	13.1	15	6	8	6	5	0	10.13	4.05	5.40
ry Casale	R	0	0	—	5.25	0	3	1	0	12	15	3	6	8	7	0	11.25	2.25	4.50
wie Koplitz	R	2	0	1.000	2.25	0	4	1	1	12	16	8	9	6	3	0	12.00	6.00	6.75
l Nischwitz	L	0	1	.000	5.56	0	6	1	0	11.1	13	8	8	12	7	0	10.32	6.35	6.35
e Grzenda	L	1	0	1.000	7.94	0	4	0	0	5.2	9	2	0	5	5	0	14.29	3.18	0.00
AM TOTAL		101	61	.623	3.55	30	383	163	62	1459.1	1404	469	836	671	575	10	8.66	2.89	5.16

MANAGER

	W	L	PCT
Bob Scheffing	85	76	.528

POS	Player	B	G	AB	H	2B	3B	HR	HR %	R	RBI	BB	SO	SB	Pinch Hit AB	Pinch Hit H	BA	SA
REGULARS																		
1B	Norm Cash	L	148	507	123	16	2	39	7.7	94	89	104	82	6	2	1	.243	.513
2B	Jake Wood	R	111	367	83	10	5	8	2.2	68	30	33	59	24	11	2	.226	.346
SS	Chico Fernandez	R	141	503	125	17	2	20	4.0	64	59	42	69	10	1	0	.249	.410
3B	Steve Boros	R	116	356	81	14	1	16	4.5	46	47	53	62	3	8	0	.228	.407
RF	Al Kaline	R	100	398	121	16	6	29	7.3	78	94	47	39	4	0	0	.304	.593
CF	Bill Bruton	L	147	561	156	27	5	16	2.9	90	74	55	67	14	5	1	.278	.430
LF	Rocky Colavito	R	161	601	164	30	2	37	6.2	90	112	96	68	2	0	0	.273	.514
C	Dick Brown	R	134	431	104	12	0	12	2.8	40	40	21	66	0	3	1	.241	.353
SUBSTITUTES																		
UT	Dick McAuliffe	L	139	471	124	20	5	12	2.5	50	63	64	76	4	6	1	.263	.403
1B	Vic Wertz	L	74	105	34	2	0	5	4.8	7	18	5	13	0	53	17	.324	.486
S2	Don Buddin	R	31	83	19	3	0	0	0.0	14	4	20	16	1	4	1	.229	.265
31	Bobo Osborne	L	64	74	17	1	0	0	0.0	12	7	16	25	0	29	6	.230	.243
3B	Frank Kostro	R	16	41	11	3	0	0	0.0	5	3	1	6	0	4	1	.268	.341
UT	Reno Bertoia	R	5	0	0	0	0	0	–	3	0	0	0	0	0	0	–	–
OF	Bubba Morton	R	90	195	51	6	3	4	2.1	30	17	32	32	1	21	5	.262	.385
OF	Purnal Goldy	R	20	70	16	1	1	3	4.3	8	12	0	12	0	3	1	.229	.400
OF	Charlie Maxwell	L	30	67	13	2	0	1	1.5	5	9	8	10	0	11	2	.194	.269
O1	Bob Farley	L	36	50	8	2	0	1	2.0	9	4	14	10	0	13	3	.160	.260
C	Mike Roarke	R	56	136	29	4	1	4	2.9	11	14	13	17	0	3	1	.213	.346
PH	George Alusik	R	2	2	0	0	0	0	0.0	0	0	0	0	0	2	0	.000	.000
PITCHERS																		
P	Jim Bunning	R	43	95	23	2	1	1	1.1	9	5	1	19	0	0	0	.242	.316
P	Hank Aguirre	R	42	75	2	0	0	0	0.0	0	1	1	46	0	0	0	.027	.027
P	Phil Regan	R	35	63	13	2	0	0	0.0	4	6	2	22	0	0	0	.206	.238
P	Don Mossi	L	36	55	9	0	0	0	0.0	5	3	10	20	0	1	0	.164	.164
P	Paul Foytack	R	29	42	6	0	0	0	0.0	4	5	2	11	0	0	0	.143	.143
P	Frank Lary	R	22	24	4	0	1	0	0.0	3	1	2	9	0	0	0	.167	.250
P	Sam Jones	R	30	21	2	0	0	1	4.8	1	1	0	9	0	0	0	.095	.238
P	Ron Kline	R	36	16	2	0	0	0	0.0	1	0	0	5	0	0	0	.125	.125
P	Howie Koplitz	R	12	13	3	0	0	0	0.0	3	0	2	7	0	0	0	.231	.231
P	Ron Nischwitz	B	48	12	5	0	1	0	0.0	1	1	0	5	0	0	0	.417	.583
P	Jerry Casale	R	18	8	0	0	0	0	0.0	0	0	1	4	0	0	0	.000	.000
P	Terry Fox	R	47	8	2	1	0	0	0.0	3	0	4	4	0	0	0	.250	.375
P	Doug Gallagher	R	9	6	2	0	0	0	0.0	0	0	2	4	0	0	0	.333	.333
P	Bill Faul	R	1	0	0	0	0	0	–	0	0	0	0	0	0	0	–	–
P	Tom Fletcher	B	1	0	0	0	0	0	–	0	0	0	0	0	0	0	–	–
P	Fred Gladding	L	6	0	0	0	0	0	–	0	0	0	0	0	0	0	–	–
P	Bob Humphreys	R	4	0	0	0	0	0	–	0	0	0	0	0	0	0	–	–
TEAM TOTAL				5456	1352	191	36	209	3.8	758	719	651	894	69	180	43	.248	.411

INDIVIDUAL FIELDING

POS	Player	T	G	PO	A	E	DP	TC/G	FA
1B	N. Cash	L	146	1081	116	10	94	8.3	.992
	V. Wertz	R	16	75	9	1	5	5.3	.988
	B. Farley	L	6	21	2	2	3	4.2	.920
	B. Morton	R	3	14	0	0	0	4.7	1.000
	B. Osborne	R	7	11	2	0	1	1.9	1.000
	C. Maxwell	L	1	1	1	0	0	2.0	1.000
	C. Fernandez	R	1	1	0	0	0	1.0	1.000
2B	J. Wood	R	90	185	197	20	33	4.5	.950
	D. McAuliffe	R	70	186	146	12	32	4.9	.965
	S. Boros	R	6	13	12	2	4	4.5	.926
	D. Buddin	R	5	8	6	0	1	2.8	1.000
	R. Bertoia	R	1	0	1	0	0	1.0	1.000
SS	C. Fernandez	R	138	235	336	24	53	4.3	.960
	D. Buddin	R	19	40	49	2	13	4.8	.978
	D. McAuliffe	R	16	13	32	4	3	3.1	.918
	R. Bertoia	R	1	0	0	0	0	0.0	.000
3B	S. Boros	R	105	105	151	19	15	2.6	.931
	D. McAuliffe	R	49	61	79	14	10	3.1	.909
	D. Buddin	R	2	0	0	0	0	0.0	.000
	B. Osborne	R	13	11	19	5	0	2.7	.857
	F. Kostro	R	11	9	20	1	2	2.7	.967
	C. Fernandez	R	2	3	2	0	0	2.5	1.000
	R. Bertoia	R	1	0	1	0	0	1.0	1.000

POS	Player	T	G	PO	A	E	DP	TC/G	FA
OF	B. Bruton	R	145	394	5	7	2	2.8	.983
	R. Colavito	R	161	359	10	3	1	2.3	.992
	A. Kaline	R	100	225	8	4	1	2.4	.983
	B. Morton	R	62	110	4	1	1	1.9	.991
	C. Maxwell	L	15	28	0	1	0	1.9	.966
	P. Goldy	R	15	26	1	1	0	1.9	.964
	N. Cash	L	3	10	0	0	0	3.3	1.000
	B. Farley	L	6	6	0	1	0	1.2	.857
C	D. Brown	R	132	742	42	5	8	6.0	.994
	M. Roarke	R	53	247	24	5	1	5.2	.982
	B. Osborne	R	1	0	0	0	0	0.0	.000

During one 22-game stretch, Detroit won 16, lost four, and tied two. Unfortunately for Tiger fans, that was during a postseason tour through Hawaii and Japan. Their heroes had proved far less successful when it counted. Detroit barely finished fourth, 10 1/2 games behind the first-place Yankees, a half game behind the third-place expansion Angels, and a half game ahead of the White Sox. The Tigers hit them far, but not necessarily often. Detroit led the majors in home runs with 209 (their most in a season), but was also tied for league-worst in batting at .248. First baseman Norm Cash ripped 39 home runs, including three completely out of Tiger Stadium. For the first time, four Tigers hit 20-plus home runs: Cash, Rocky Colavito (37), Al Kaline (29), and shortstop Chico Fernandez (20). And there were other homeric feats: Detroit tied a team record with six home runs against Kansas City on July 20; Colavito homered three times in succession against the Indians on July 5; and third baseman Steve Boros homered three times in succession, also against Cleveland on August 6. But Cash feebly defended his batting title, his average diving 118 points to .243; only Kaline, who was hitting .361 on May 26 before sitting 61 games with a severely broken right collarbone, topped .300 at .304. Jim Bunning finished 19–10, and Hank Aguirre, 16–8, led the majors in ERA at 2.21 (best by a Tiger in 16 years).

Sometimes the Tigers had to go to great lengths even to lose. On June 24, Detroit helped set an American League record for the longest game (in time) with a seven-hour, 9–7 loss to the Yankees in 22 innings. Colavito earned his overtime with six singles in 10 at bats. But the game's biggest hit came in the 22nd inning, when New York reserve outfielder Jack Reed mercifully ended the Tiger Stadium marathon with his only major-league home run.

TEAM STATISTICS

W	L	PCT	GB	R	OR	2B	3B	HR	BA	SA	SB	E	DP	FA	CG	BB	SO	ShO	SV	ERA
96	66	.593		817	680	240	29	199	**.267**	**.426**	42	131	151	.979	33	499	838	10	42	3.70
91	71	.562	5	798	713	215	39	185	.260	.412	33	129	**173**	.979	**53**	**493**	**948**	11	27	3.89
86	76	.531	10	718	706	232	35	137	.250	.380	46	175	153	.972	23	616	858	**15**	**47**	3.70
85	76	.528	10.5	758	692	191	36	**209**	.248	.411	69	156	114	.974	46	503	873	8	35	3.81
85	77	.525	11	707	658	250	56	92	.257	.372	76	110	153	**.982**	50	537	821	13	28	3.73
80	82	.494	16	682	745	202	22	180	.245	.388	35	139	168	.977	45	594	780	12	31	4.14
77	85	.475	19	652	680	225	34	156	.248	.387	45	122	152	.980	32	549	898	8	33	**3.69**
76	84	.475	19	707	756	**257**	53	146	.258	.403	45	131	152	.979	34	632	923	10	40	4.22
72	90	.444	24	745	837	220	**58**	116	.263	.386	76	132	131	.979	32	655	825	4	33	4.79
60	101	.373	35.5	599	716	206	38	132	.250	.373	**99**	139	160	.978	38	593	771	11	13	4.04
AGUE TOTAL				7183	7183	2238	400	1552	.255	.394	560	1364	1507	.978	386	5671	8535	102	329	3.97

INDIVIDUAL PITCHING

TCHER	T	W	L	PCT	ERA	SV	G	GS	CG	IP	H	BB	SO	R	ER	ShO	H/9	BB/9	SO/9
h Bunning	R	19	10	.655	3.59	6	41	35	12	258	262	74	184	112	103	2	9.14	2.58	6.42
nk Aguirre	L	16	8	.667	**2.21**	3	42	22	11	216	162	65	156	67	53	2	**6.75**	2.71	6.50
n Mossi	L	11	13	.458	4.19	1	35	27	8	180.1	195	36	121	92	84	1	9.73	1.80	6.04
il Regan	R	11	9	.550	4.04	0	35	23	6	171.1	169	64	87	89	77	0	8.88	3.36	4.57
ul Foytack	R	10	7	.588	4.39	0	29	21	5	143.2	145	86	63	80	70	1	9.08	5.39	3.95
m Jones	R	2	4	.333	3.65	1	30	6	1	81.1	77	35	73	39	33	0	8.52	3.87	8.08
nk Lary	R	2	6	.250	5.74	0	17	14	2	80	98	21	41	59	51	1	11.03	2.36	4.61
n Kline	R	3	6	.333	4.31	2	36	4	0	77.1	88	28	47	40	37	0	10.24	3.26	5.47
n Nischwitz	L	4	5	.444	3.90	4	48	0	0	64.2	73	26	28	30	28	0	10.16	3.62	3.90
rry Fox	R	3	1	.750	1.71	16	44	0	0	58	48	16	23	13	11	0	7.45	2.48	3.57
wie Koplitz	R	3	0	1.000	5.26	0	10	6	1	37.2	54	10	10	24	22	0	12.90	2.39	2.39
ry Casale	R	1	2	.333	4.66	0	18	1	0	36.2	33	18	16	19	19	0	8.10	4.42	3.93
ug Gallagher	L	0	4	.000	4.68	1	9	2	0	25	31	15	14	18	13	0	11.16	5.40	5.04
d Gladding	R	0	0	–	0.00	0	6	0	0	5	3	2	4	0	0	0	5.40	3.60	7.20
o Humphreys	R	0	1	.000	7.20	1	4	0	0	5	8	2	3	4	4	0	14.40	3.60	5.40
m Fletcher	L	0	0	–	0.00	0	1	0	0	2	2	2	1	0	0	0	9.00	9.00	4.50
Faul	R	0	0	–	32.40	0	1	0	0	1.2	4	3	2	6	6	0	21.60	16.20	10.80
AM TOTAL		85	76	.528	3.81	35	406	161	46	1443.2	1452	503	873	692	611	7	9.05	3.14	5.44

MANAGER

	W	L	PCT
Bob Scheffing	24	36	.400
Chuck Dressen	55	47	.539

POS	Player	B	G	AB	H	2B	3B	HR	HR %	R	RBI	BB	SO	SB	Pinch Hit AB	Pinch Hit H	BA	SA
REGULARS																		
1B	Norm Cash	L	147	493	133	19	1	26	5.3	67	79	89	76	2	7	0	.270	.471
2B	Jake Wood	R	85	351	95	11	2	11	3.1	50	27	24	61	18	1	0	.271	.407
SS	Dick McAuliffe	L	150	568	149	18	6	13	2.3	77	61	64	75	11	2	1	.262	.384
3B	Bubba Phillips	R	128	464	114	11	2	5	1.1	42	45	19	42	6	6	2	.246	.310
RF	Al Kaline	R	145	551	172	24	3	27	4.9	89	101	54	48	6	5	3	.312	.514
CF	Bill Bruton	L	145	524	134	21	8	8	1.5	84	48	59	70	14	11	6	.256	.372
LF	Rocky Colavito	R	160	597	162	29	2	22	3.7	91	91	84	78	0	1	0	.271	.407
C	Gus Triandos	R	106	327	78	13	0	14	4.3	28	41	32	67	0	13	3	.239	.407
SUBSTITUTES																		
UT	Don Wert	R	78	251	65	6	2	7	2.8	31	25	24	51	3	4	0	.259	.382
2B	George Smith	R	52	171	37	8	2	0	0.0	16	17	18	34	4	0	0	.216	.287
1O	Whitey Herzog	L	52	53	8	2	1	0	0.0	5	7	11	17	0	35	4	.151	.226
UT	Frank Kostro	R	31	52	12	1	0	0	0.0	4	4	9	13	0	20	5	.231	.250
SS	Chico Fernandez	R	15	49	7	1	0	0	0.0	3	2	6	11	0	1	0	.143	.163
SS	Coot Veal	R	15	32	7	0	0	0	0.0	5	4	4	4	0	4	2	.219	.219
OF	George Thomas	R	44	109	26	4	1	1	0.9	13	11	11	22	2	8	0	.239	.321
OF	Gates Brown	L	55	82	22	3	1	2	2.4	16	14	8	13	2	30	6	.268	.402
OF	Willie Horton	R	15	43	14	2	1	1	2.3	6	4	0	8	2	5	3	.326	.488
OF	Bubba Morton	R	6	11	1	0	0	0	0.0	2	2	2	1	0	1	0	.091	.091
C1	Bill Freehan	R	100	300	73	12	2	9	3.0	37	36	39	56	2	9	3	.243	.387
C	Mike Roarke	R	23	44	14	0	0	0	0.0	5	1	2	3	0	7	1	.318	.318
C	John Sullivan	L	3	5	0	0	0	0	0.0	0	0	2	1	0	0	0	.000	.000
PH	Purnal Goldy	R	9	8	2	0	0	0	0.0	1	0	0	4	0	8	2	.250	.250
PH	Vic Wertz	L	6	5	0	0	0	0	0.0	0	0	0	1	0	5	0	.000	.000
PITCHERS																		
P	Jim Bunning	R	41	84	13	1	1	0	0.0	4	5	4	15	0	0	0	.155	.190
P	Hank Aguirre	R	38	76	10	3	0	0	0.0	5	6	3	48	1	0	0	.132	.171
P	Phil Regan	R	38	63	9	0	0	1	1.6	5	5	3	21	0	0	0	.143	.190
P	Don Mossi	L	24	39	8	2	0	0	0.0	2	4	6	12	0	0	0	.205	.256
P	Mickey Lolich	B	33	36	2	0	0	0	0.0	3	1	9	20	0	0	0	.056	.056
P	Frank Lary	R	16	35	8	0	1	0	0.0	2	6	1	10	0	0	0	.229	.286
P	Bill Faul	R	28	27	4	2	0	0	0.0	1	1	2	11	0	0	0	.148	.222
P	Terry Fox	R	46	11	1	0	0	0	0.0	1	0	2	7	0	0	0	.091	.091
P	Bob Anderson	R	32	9	4	1	0	0	0.0	1	2	0	3	0	0	0	.444	.556
P	Tom Sturdivant	L	28	9	0	0	0	0	0.0	0	0	0	2	0	0	0	.000	.000
P	Willie Smith	L	17	8	1	0	0	0	0.0	2	0	0	1	0	2	0	.125	.125
P	Denny McLain	R	3	5	1	0	0	1	20.0	1	2	0	1	0	0	0	.200	.800
P	Paul Foytack	R	9	4	0	0	0	0	0.0	0	0	1	1	0	0	0	.000	.000
P	Alan Koch	R	8	3	2	1	0	0	0.0	1	1	0	0	0	0	0	.667	1.000
P	Fred Gladding	L	22	1	0	0	0	0	0.0	0	0	0	0	0	0	0	.000	.000
P	Bob Dustal	R	7	0	0	0	0	0	–	0	0	0	0	0	0	0	–	–
P	Dick Egan	L	20	0	0	0	0	0	–	0	0	0	0	0	0	0	–	–
P	Larry Foster	L	1	0	0	0	0	0	–	0	0	0	0	0	0	0	–	–
	TEAM TOTAL			5500	1388	195	36	148	2.7	700	649	592	908	73	185	41	.252	.382

INDIVIDUAL FIELDING

POS	Player	T	G	PO	A	E	DP	TC/G	FA
1B	N. Cash	L	142	1161	99	7	93	8.9	.994
	B. Freehan	R	19	147	16	1	14	8.6	.994
	W. Herzog	L	7	40	1	1	2	6.0	.976
	F. Kostro	R	3	21	3	0	0	8.0	1.000
2B	J. Wood	R	81	188	202	17	47	5.0	.958
	G. Smith	R	52	120	157	5	28	5.4	.982
	D. Wert	R	21	36	54	3	10	4.4	.968
	D. McAuliffe	R	15	36	32	2	8	4.7	.971
	G. Thomas	R	1	0	0	0	0	0.0	.000
SS	D. McAuliffe	R	133	220	356	22	68	4.5	.963
	C. Fernandez	R	14	30	42	4	8	5.4	.947
	C. Veal	R	12	14	35	1	1	4.2	.980
	D. Wert	R	8	16	20	1	4	4.6	.973
3B	B. Phillips	R	117	116	226	14	26	3.0	.961
	D. Wert	R	47	33	99	6	6	2.9	.957
	F. Kostro	R	6	1	12	1	0	2.3	.929
	J. Wood	R	1	2	0	0	0	2.0	1.000

POS	Player	T	G	PO	A	E	DP	TC/G	FA
OF	B. Bruton	R	138	339	6	3	3	2.5	.991
	R. Colavito	R	159	319	10	4	0	2.1	.988
	A. Kaline	R	140	257	5	2	0	1.9	.992
	G. Thomas	R	40	83	0	0	0	2.1	1.000
	G. Brown	R	16	35	3	0	1	2.4	1.000
	W. Horton	R	9	13	0	0	0	1.4	1.000
	B. Phillips	R	5	9	0	1	0	2.0	.900
	B. Morton	R	3	7	0	1	0	2.7	.875
	W. Herzog	L	4	4	0	0	0	1.0	1.000
	F. Kostro	R	3	3	0	0	0	1.0	1.000
C	G. Triandos	R	90	535	29	1	4	6.3	.998
	B. Freehan	R	73	407	22	2	5	5.9	.995
	M. Roarke	R	16	67	5	1	1	4.6	.986
	J. Sullivan	R	2	9	1	0	0	5.0	1.000

Overall, it was a good year for losing. The Tigers lost four more than they won, manager Bob Scheffing lost his job, and the franchise lost $800,000 as Detroit fans lost interest: attendance dropped 400,000 to a 20-year low of 821,952. The Tigers slid gradually but surely. After a 5–2 start, they dropped 17 of their next 34. Then, with his charges settled into ninth place amid a 10-game losing streak, Scheffing was fired on June 17. He was replaced by Dodger scout and former Brooklyn manager Chuck Dressen. But Detroit improved little at first: under their new leader, the Tigers lost nine of their first 13. But soon they offered a glimmer of encouragement, albeit too late. From June 30 on, Detroit went 51–38 to squeeze into a fifth-place tie with the Indians, 25 1/2 games behind the champion Yankees.

Phil Regan prospered under Dressen, winning 13 of 16 decisions after the managerial switch, to lead the staff at 15–9. Still, no other Tiger pitcher topped .500.

Despite limping through the final two months on a bad knee, Al Kaline ranked second in the league in batting at .312, second in RBIs with 101, and second in the MVP balloting to New York's Elston Howard. Again, three Tigers hit 20-plus home runs— Kaline (27), Norm Cash (26) and Rocky Colavito (22).

Newcomers only hinted at future glory. Rookie left-hander Mickey Lolich finished 5–9 as a starter-reliever. Rookie catcher Bill Freehan hit .243 in 100 games. And in his first major-league at-bat, Gates Brown homered as a pinch hitter off Boston's Don Heffner at Fenway Park. Brown would hit 16 pinch homers among 107 pinch hits during a 13-year Tiger career, retiring in 1975 as the premier pinch hitter in American League history.

TEAM STATISTICS

	W	L	PCT	GB	R	OR	Batting 2B	3B	HR	BA	SA	SB	Fielding E	DP	FA	Pitching CG	BB	SO	ShO	SV	ERA
Y	104	57	.646		714	547	197	35	188	.252	.403	42	110	162	.982	59	476	965	17	31	3.07
HI	94	68	.580	10.5	683	544	208	40	114	.250	.365	64	131	163	.979	49	440	932	19	39	2.97
N	91	70	.565	13	767	602	223	35	225	.255	.430	32	144	140	.976	58	459	941	12	30	3.28
AL	86	76	.531	18.5	644	621	207	32	146	.249	.380	97	99	157	.984	35	507	913	8	43	3.45
E	79	83	.488	25.5	635	702	214	29	169	.239	.381	59	143	129	.977	40	478	1018	11	25	3.79
ET	79	83	.488	25.5	700	703	195	36	148	.252	.382	73	113	124	.981	42	477	930	6	28	3.90
OS	76	85	.472	28	666	704	247	34	171	.252	.400	27	135	119	.978	29	539	1009	6	32	3.97
C	73	89	.451	31.5	615	704	225	38	95	.247	.353	47	127	131	.980	35	540	887	9	29	3.92
A	70	91	.435	34	597	660	208	38	95	.250	.354	43	163	155	.974	30	578	889	9	31	3.52
AS	56	106	.346	48.5	578	812	190	35	138	.227	.351	68	182	165	.971	29	537	744	8	25	4.42
AGUE TOTAL					6599	6599	2114	352	1489	.247	.380	552	1347	1445	.978	406	5031	9228	105	313	3.63

INDIVIDUAL PITCHING

TCHER	T	W	L	PCT	ERA	SV	G	GS	CG	IP	H	BB	SO	R	ER	ShO	H/9	BB/9	SO/9
n Bunning	R	12	13	.480	3.88	1	39	35	6	248.1	245	69	196	119	107	2	8.88	2.50	7.10
nk Aguirre	L	14	15	.483	3.67	0	38	33	14	225.2	222	68	134	96	92	3	8.85	2.71	5.34
il Regan	R	15	9	.625	3.86	1	38	27	5	189	179	59	115	95	81	1	8.52	2.81	5.48
ckey Lolich	L	5	9	.357	3.55	0	33	18	4	144.1	145	56	103	64	57	0	9.04	3.49	6.42
n Mossi	L	7	7	.500	3.74	2	24	16	3	122.2	110	17	68	58	51	0	8.07	1.25	4.99
nk Lary	R	4	9	.308	3.27	0	16	14	6	107.1	90	26	46	40	39	0	7.55	2.18	3.86
l Faul	R	5	6	.455	4.64	1	28	10	2	97	93	48	64	55	50	0	8.63	4.45	5.94
rry Fox	R	8	6	.571	3.59	11	46	0	0	80.1	81	20	35	37	32	0	9.07	2.24	3.92
b Anderson	R	3	1	.750	3.30	0	32	3	0	60	58	21	38	28	22	0	8.70	3.15	5.70
m Sturdivant	R	1	2	.333	3.76	2	28	0	0	55	43	24	36	26	23	0	7.04	3.93	5.89
ed Gladding	R	1	1	.500	1.98	7	22	0	0	27.1	19	14	24	6	6	0	6.26	4.61	7.90
lie Smith	L	1	0	1.000	4.57	2	11	2	0	21.2	24	13	16	13	11	0	9.97	5.40	6.65
k Egan	L	0	1	.000	5.14	0	20	0	0	21	25	3	16	12	12	0	10.71	1.29	6.86
nny McLain	R	2	1	.667	4.29	0	3	3	2	21	20	16	22	12	10	0	8.57	6.86	9.43
ul Foytack	R	0	0	.000	8.66	1	9	0	0	17.2	18	8	7	18	17	0	9.17	4.08	3.57
n Koch	R	1	1	.500	10.80	0	7	1	0	10	21	9	5	12	12	0	18.90	8.10	4.50
o Dustal	R	0	0	.000	9.00	0	7	0	0	6	10	5	4	9	6	0	15.00	7.50	6.00
ry Foster	R	0	0	—	13.50	0	1	0	0	2	4	1	1	3	3	0	18.00	4.50	4.50
AM TOTAL		79	83	.488	3.90	28	402	162	42	1456.1	1407	477	930	703	631	6	8.70	2.95	5.75

MANAGER	W	L	PCT
Chuck Dressen	85	77	.525

POS	Player	B	G	AB	H	2B	3B	HR	HR %	R	RBI	BB	SO	SB	Pinch Hit AB	Pinch Hit H	BA	SA
REGULARS																		
1B	Norm Cash	L	144	479	123	15	5	23	4.8	63	83	70	66	2	10	1	.257	.453
2B	Jerry Lumpe	L	158	624	160	21	6	6	1.0	75	46	50	61	2	0	0	.256	.338
SS	Dick McAuliffe	L	162	557	134	18	7	24	4.3	85	66	77	96	8	2	1	.241	.427
3B	Don Wert	R	148	525	135	18	5	9	1.7	63	55	50	74	3	3	0	.257	.362
RF	Al Kaline	R	146	525	154	31	5	17	3.2	77	68	75	51	4	9	2	.293	.469
CF	George Thomas	R	105	308	88	15	2	12	3.9	39	44	18	53	4	18	6	.286	.464
LF	Gates Brown	L	123	426	116	22	6	15	3.5	65	54	31	53	11	19	4	.272	.458
C	Bill Freehan	R	144	520	156	14	8	18	3.5	69	80	36	68	5	6	1	.300	.462
SUBSTITUTES																		
UT	Jake Wood	R	64	125	29	2	2	1	0.8	11	7	4	24	0	29	7	.232	.304
3B	Bubba Phillips	R	46	87	22	1	0	3	3.4	14	6	10	13	1	17	4	.253	.368
1B	Bill Roman	L	3	8	3	0	0	1	12.5	2	1	0	2	0	2	1	.375	.750
2B	George Smith	R	5	7	2	0	0	0	0.0	1	2	1	4	1	1	1	.286	.286
O1	Don Demeter	R	134	441	113	22	1	22	5.0	57	80	17	85	4	27	5	.256	.460
OF	Bill Bruton	L	106	296	82	11	5	5	1.7	42	33	32	54	14	26	6	.277	.399
OF	Willie Horton	R	25	80	13	1	3	1	1.3	6	10	11	20	0	3	1	.163	.288
OF	Jim Northrup	L	5	12	1	1	0	0	0.0	0	0	0	3	1	3	0	.083	.167
OF	Mickey Stanley	R	4	11	3	0	0	0	0.0	3	1	0	1	0	0	0	.273	.273
C	Mike Roarke	R	29	82	19	1	0	0	0.0	4	7	10	10	0	2	1	.232	.244
C	John Sullivan	L	2	3	0	0	0	0	0.0	0	0	0	1	0	0	0	.000	.000
PITCHERS																		
P	Dave Wickersham	R	40	82	6	1	0	0	0.0	1	1	2	27	0	0	0	.073	.085
P	Mickey Lolich	B	44	64	7	0	0	0	0.0	9	4	11	32	0	0	0	.109	.109
P	Hank Aguirre	R	32	53	3	1	0	0	0.0	1	3	1	32	0	0	0	.057	.075
P	Phil Regan	R	33	41	13	2	0	0	0.0	3	1	5	13	0	0	0	.317	.366
P	Ed Rakow	B	42	39	0	0	0	0	0.0	3	0	3	16	0	0	0	.000	.000
P	Denny McLain	R	20	37	5	0	0	0	0.0	2	2	1	15	0	0	0	.135	.135
P	Joe Sparma	R	23	25	4	0	2	0	0.0	3	4	1	11	0	0	0	.160	.320
P	Larry Sherry	R	38	14	0	0	0	0	0.0	0	0	0	6	0	0	0	.000	.000
P	Terry Fox	R	32	12	3	2	0	0	0.0	0	0	0	7	0	0	0	.250	.417
P	Fred Gladding	L	42	9	0	0	0	0	0.0	0	0	0	6	0	0	0	.000	.000
P	Frank Lary	R	6	7	0	0	0	0	0.0	0	0	1	1	0	0	0	.000	.000
P	Julio Navarro	R	26	5	0	0	0	0	0.0	0	0	0	0	0	0	0	.000	.000
P	Dick Egan	L	23	3	0	0	0	0	0.0	0	0	0	3	0	0	0	.000	.000
P	Jack Hamilton	R	5	3	0	0	0	0	0.0	0	0	0	2	0	0	0	.000	.000
P	Bill Faul	R	1	2	0	0	0	0	0.0	0	0	0	1	0	0	0	.000	.000
P	Johnnie Seale	L	4	1	0	0	0	0	0.0	0	0	0	1	0	0	0	.000	.000
P	Fritz Fisher	L	1	0	0	0	0	0	–	0	0	0	0	0	0	0	–	–
P	Alan Koch	R	3	0	0	0	0	0	–	0	0	0	0	0	0	0	–	–
TEAM TOTAL				5513	1394	199	57	157	2.8	699	658	517	912	60	177	41	.253	.395

INDIVIDUAL FIELDING

POS	Player	T	G	PO	A	E	DP	TC/G	FA
1B	N. Cash	L	137	1105	92	4	97	8.8	**.997**
	D. Demeter	R	23	202	12	2	12	9.4	.991
	J. Wood	R	11	81	7	1	6	8.1	.989
	B. Roman	L	2	13	1	0	2	7.0	1.000
	B. Freehan	R	1	7	0	0	0	7.0	1.000
2B	J. Lumpe	R	158	339	394	13	95	4.7	.983
	J. Wood	R	10	17	13	0	4	3.0	1.000
	G. Smith	R	3	2	5	0	2	2.3	1.000
SS	D. McAuliffe	R	160	262	467	32	84	4.8	.958
	D. Wert	R	4	8	10	1	3	4.8	.947
3B	D. Wert	R	142	126	283	15	30	3.0	.965
	B. Phillips	R	22	18	40	1	5	2.7	.983
	J. Wood	R	6	5	10	3	3	3.0	.833
	G. Thomas	R	1	1	1	0	0	2.0	1.000

POS	Player	T	G	PO	A	E	DP	TC/G	FA
OF	A. Kaline	R	136	278	6	3	2	2.1	.990
	G. Brown	R	106	205	4	4	0	2.0	.981
	G. Thomas	R	90	164	4	2	1	1.9	.988
	D. Demeter	R	88	164	3	0	1	1.9	1.000
	B. Bruton	R	81	143	7	2	3	1.9	.987
	W. Horton	R	23	33	0	2	0	1.5	.943
	B. Phillips	R	1	0	0	0	0	0.0	.000
	M. Stanley	R	4	5	0	0	0	1.3	1.000
	J. Northrup	R	2	4	0	0	0	2.0	1.000
	J. Wood	R	1	2	0	1	0	3.0	.667
C	B. Freehan	R	141	923	61	7	7	7.0	.993
	M. Roarke	R	27	165	11	1	0	6.6	.994
	J. Sullivan	R	2	2	2	0	0	2.0	1.000

Obtained from the Kansas City Athletics in the off season, Tiger right-hander Dave Wickersham entered his last start of the season 19–12 at Yankee Stadium on October 1. With the game tied 1–1 in the seventh, Wickersham got into a dispute with the umpire over a close play at first base, and was sent to the showers. Detroit proceeded to prevail, 4–2, but the victory went to reliever Mickey Lolich, denying Wickersham 20 victories. For the rest of his career, Wickersham would never win more than nine in a season.

It was that kind of year in Detroit. Charlie Dressen's first full season as Tiger manager started poorly: by July, Detroit sat in eighth place. Summoning too little too late for the second straight season, the Tigers then went 20–10 in August to finish fourth, 14 games behind the first-place Yankees. Attendance dropped again, this time to 816,139—the lowest since 1943.

Beyond Wickersham, only Lolich (18–9) posted more than eight victories. But the April 9 purchase of Larry Sherry from the Dodgers helped. The veteran right-hander became Detroit's bullpen ace, winning seven, saving 11.

Sophomore catcher Bill Freehan led the team at .300—the only .300 season of his 14-year Tiger career. Al Kaline slipped to .293 with 17 home runs. And the Tigers again boasted a litany of players with above-average averages. Three hit 20 or more home runs: shortstop Dick McAuliffe (24), first baseman Norm Cash (23), and outfielder Don Demeter (22), but none among the three topped .257.

TEAM STATISTICS

W	L	PCT	GB	R	OR	2B	3B	HR	BA	SA	SB	E	DP	FA	CG	BB	SO	ShO	SV	ERA
99	63	.611		730	577	208	35	162	.253	.387	54	109	158	.983	46	504	989	18	45	3.15
98	64	.605	1	642	501	184	40	106	.247	.353	75	122	164	.981	44	401	955	20	45	2.72
97	65	.599	2	679	567	229	20	162	.248	.387	78	95	159	.985	44	456	939	17	41	3.16
85	77	.525	14	699	678	199	57	157	.253	.395	60	111	137	.982	35	536	993	11	35	3.84
82	80	.506	17	544	551	186	27	102	.242	.344	49	138	168	.978	30	530	965	28	41	2.91
79	83	.488	20	689	693	208	22	164	.247	.380	79	118	149	.981	37	565	1162	16	37	3.75
79	83	.488	20	737	678	227	46	221	.252	.427	46	145	131	.977	47	545	1099	4	29	3.57
72	90	.444	27	688	793	253	29	186	.258	.416	18	138	123	.977	21	571	1094	9	38	4.50
62	100	.383	37	578	733	199	28	125	.231	.348	47	127	145	.979	27	505	794	5	26	3.98
57	105	.352	42	621	836	216	29	166	.239	.379	34	158	152	.974	18	614	966	6	27	4.71
GUE TOTAL				6607	6607	2109	333	1551	.247	.382	540	1261	1486	.980	349	5227	9956	134	364	3.63

INDIVIDUAL PITCHING

CHER	T	W	L	PCT	ERA	SV	G	GS	CG	IP	H	BB	SO	R	ER	ShO	H/9	BB/9	SO/9
e Wickersham	R	19	12	.613	3.44	1	40	36	11	254	224	81	164	108	97	1	7.94	2.87	5.81
key Lolich	L	18	9	.667	3.26	2	44	33	12	232	196	64	192	88	84	6	7.60	2.48	7.45
nk Aguirre	L	5	10	.333	3.79	1	32	27	3	161.2	134	59	88	76	68	0	7.46	3.28	4.90
Rakow	R	8	9	.471	3.72	3	42	13	1	152.1	155	59	96	70	63	0	9.16	3.49	5.67
Regan	R	5	10	.333	5.03	1	32	21	2	146.2	162	49	91	87	82	0	9.94	3.01	5.58
ny McLain	R	4	5	.444	4.05	0	19	16	3	100	84	37	70	48	45	0	7.56	3.33	6.30
Sparma	R	5	6	.455	3.00	0	21	11	3	84	62	45	71	33	28	2	6.64	4.82	7.61
d Gladding	R	7	4	.636	3.07	7	42	0	0	67.1	57	27	59	23	23	0	7.62	3.61	7.89
ry Sherry	R	7	5	.583	3.66	11	38	0	0	66.1	52	37	58	29	27	0	7.06	5.02	7.87
ry Fox	R	4	3	.571	3.39	5	32	0	0	61	77	16	28	26	23	0	11.36	2.36	4.13
o Navarro	R	2	1	.667	3.95	2	26	0	0	41	40	16	36	19	18	0	8.78	3.51	7.90
k Egan	L	0	0	–	4.46	2	23	0	0	34.1	33	17	21	22	17	0	8.65	4.46	5.50
nk Lary	R	0	2	.000	7.00	0	6	4	0	18	24	10	6	15	14	0	12.00	5.00	3.00
k Hamilton	R	0	1	.000	8.40	0	5	1	0	15	24	8	5	17	14	0	14.40	4.80	3.00
nnie Seale	L	1	0	1.000	3.60	0	4	0	0	10	6	4	5	4	4	0	5.40	3.60	4.50
Faul	R	0	0	–	10.80	0	1	1	0	5	5	2	1	6	6	0	9.00	3.60	1.80
n Koch	R	0	0	–	6.75	0	3	0	0	4	6	3	1	3	3	0	13.50	6.75	2.25
z Fisher	L	0	0	–	0.00	0	1	0	0	.1	2	2	1	4	4	0	54.00	54.00	27.00
M TOTAL		85	77	.525	3.84	35	411	163	35	1453	1343	536	993	678	620	9	8.32	3.32	6.15

MANAGER	W	L	PCT
Chuck Dressen	89	73	.549

POS	Player	B	G	AB	H	2B	3B	HR	HR %	R	RBI	BB	SO	SB	Pinch Hit AB	Pinch Hit H	BA	SA
REGULARS																		
1B	Norm Cash	L	142	467	124	23	1	30	6.4	79	82	77	62	6	5	0	.266	.512
2B	Jerry Lumpe	L	145	502	129	15	3	4	0.8	72	39	56	34	7	10	1	.257	.323
SS	Dick McAuliffe	L	113	404	105	13	6	15	3.7	61	54	49	62	6	2	0	.260	.433
3B	Don Wert	R	162	609	159	22	2	12	2.0	81	54	73	71	5	0	0	.261	.363
RF	Al Kaline	R	125	399	112	18	2	18	4.5	72	72	72	49	6	11	4	.281	.471
CF	Don Demeter	R	122	389	108	16	4	16	4.1	50	58	23	65	4	15	6	.278	.463
LF	Willie Horton	R	143	512	140	20	2	29	5.7	69	104	48	101	5	3	0	.273	.490
C	Bill Freehan	R	130	431	101	15	0	10	2.3	45	43	39	63	4	3	1	.234	.399
SUBSTITUTES																		
SS	Ray Oyler	R	82	194	36	6	0	5	2.6	22	13	21	61	1	11	3	.186	.294
2B	Jake Wood	R	58	104	30	3	0	2	1.9	12	7	10	19	3	25	9	.288	.375
UT	George Smith	R	32	53	5	0	0	1	1.9	6	1	3	18	0	5	0	.094	.151
1B	Bill Roman	L	21	27	2	0	0	0	0.0	0	0	2	7	0	13	2	.074	.074
OF	Gates Brown	L	96	227	58	14	2	10	4.4	33	43	17	33	6	34	9	.256	.467
OF	Jim Northrup	L	80	219	45	12	3	2	0.9	20	16	12	50	1	24	3	.205	.315
OF	George Thomas	R	79	169	36	5	1	3	1.8	19	10	12	39	2	17	2	.213	.308
OF	Mickey Stanley	R	30	117	28	6	0	3	2.6	14	13	3	12	1	0	0	.239	.368
OF	Wayne Redmond	R	4	4	0	0	0	0	0.0	1	0	1	1	0	0	0	.000	.000
C	John Sullivan	L	34	86	23	0	0	2	2.3	5	11	9	13	0	4	1	.267	.337
C	Jackie Moore	R	21	53	5	0	0	0	0.0	2	2	6	12	0	1	0	.094	.094
PITCHERS																		
P	Mickey Lolich	B	43	86	5	0	0	0	0.0	3	0	2	37	0	0	0	.058	.058
P	Denny McLain	R	33	74	4	0	0	0	0.0	2	3	6	32	0	0	0	.054	.054
P	Hank Aguirre	B	32	70	6	1	0	0	0.0	4	4	4	43	0	0	0	.086	.100
P	Dave Wickersham	R	34	58	4	0	0	0	0.0	2	1	1	20	0	0	0	.069	.069
P	Joe Sparma	R	30	52	7	1	0	0	0.0	4	3	3	25	0	0	0	.135	.154
P	Terry Fox	R	42	15	0	0	0	0	0.0	1	2	1	9	0	0	0	.000	.000
P	Phil Regan	R	16	12	1	0	0	0	0.0	1	0	1	4	0	0	0	.083	.083
P	Larry Sherry	R	39	10	3	0	1	0	0.0	0	0	1	4	0	0	0	.300	.500
P	Orlando Pena	R	30	8	2	0	0	0	0.0	0	0	1	0	0	0	0	.250	.250
P	Fred Gladding	L	46	7	0	0	0	0	0.0	0	0	0	2	0	0	0	.000	.000
P	Julio Navarro	R	15	4	0	0	0	0	0.0	0	0	0	1	0	0	0	.000	.000
P	Ron Nischwitz	B	20	3	0	0	0	0	0.0	0	0	0	2	0	0	0	.000	.000
P	Ed Rakow	B	6	3	0	0	0	0	0.0	0	0	1	1	0	0	0	.000	.000
P	Jack Hamilton	R	4	0	0	0	0	0	–	0	0	0	0	0	0	0	–	–
P	John Hiller	R	5	0	0	0	0	0	–	0	0	0	0	0	0	0	–	–
P	Vern Holtgrave	R	1	0	0	0	0	0	–	0	0	0	0	0	0	0	–	–
P	Leo Marentette	R	2	0	0	0	0	0	–	0	0	0	0	0	0	0	–	–
P	Johnnie Seale	L	4	0	0	0	0	0	–	0	0	0	0	0	0	0	–	–
	TEAM TOTAL			5368	1278	190	27	162	3.0	680	635	554	952	57	183	41	.238	.374

INDIVIDUAL FIELDING

POS	Player	T	G	PO	A	E	DP	TC/G	FA
1B	N. Cash	L	139	1091	**97**	9	96	8.6	.992
	D. Demeter	R	34	219	10	2	19	6.8	.991
	B. Roman	L	6	38	1	0	2	6.5	1.000
	J. Wood	R	1	10	0	0	1	10.0	1.000
	R. Oyler	R	1	1	1	0	0	2.0	1.000
2B	J. Lumpe	R	139	281	308	9	69	4.3	.985
	J. Wood	R	20	47	38	2	11	4.4	.977
	G. Smith	R	22	30	31	1	10	2.8	.984
	R. Oyler	R	11	12	6	0	1	1.6	1.000
	G. Thomas	R	1	1	0	0	0	1.0	1.000
	D. Wert	R	1	1	0	0	0	1.0	1.000
SS	D. McAuliffe	R	112	190	286	22	58	4.4	.956
	R. Oyler	R	57	79	156	11	17	4.3	.955
	J. Wood	R	1	0	0	0	0	.000	.000
	D. Wert	R	3	0	6	0	1	2.0	1.000
	G. Smith	R	3	1	1	0	0	0.7	1.000
3B	D. Wert	R	161	163	331	12	33	3.1	**.976**
	J. Wood	R	1	0	0	0	0	0.0	.000
	A. Kaline	R	1	2	1	0	0	3.0	1.000
	R. Oyler	R	1	0	3	0	0	3.0	1.000
	G. Smith	R	3	2	1	0	0	1.0	1.000
	W. Horton	R	1	0	2	0	0	2.0	1.000

POS	Player	T	G	PO	A	E	DP	TC/G	FA
OF	W. Horton	R	141	249	7	3	1	1.8	.988
	A. Kaline	R	112	193	2	3	0	1.8	.985
	D. Demeter	R	81	158	1	2	1	2.0	.988
	G. Brown	R	56	108	1	3	0	2.0	.973
	G. Thomas	R	59	87	4	5	0	1.6	.948
	J. Northrup	R	54	82	0	2	0	1.6	.976
	M. Stanley	R	29	69	1	1	0	2.4	.986
	W. Redmond	R	2	3	0	0	0	1.5	1.000
C	B. Freehan	R	129	**865**	57	4	4	**7.2**	.996
	J. Sullivan	R	29	163	14	1	1	6.1	.994
	J. Moore	R	20	128	6	2	1	6.8	.985

"If I could point to the one game that turned my confidence around," said Denny McLain, "it would be the night I pitched in relief against the Red Sox." Two springs earlier, Detroit had acquired McLain on waivers from the White Sox. After two part-time seasons, McLain was largely unheralded prior to that June night at Fenway Park when he stepped to the mound to relieve Dave Wickersham in the first inning. He proceeded to strike out 14 (including the first seven straight, a major-league record for relief pitchers) in six-and-two-thirds innings. And the meteoric rise of Dennis Dale McLain had begun.

McLain at one juncture won eight straight en route to leading the staff at 16–6 with a 2.61 ERA. He was third in the league in strikeouts, fourth in complete games. Creditable pitching also came from Mickey Lolich, who finished second in the league in strikeouts with a 15–9 record, Hank Aguirre (14–10, two 1–0 losses), and Joe Sparma (13–8, 3.18).

But they weren't good enough to save Detroit—and Chuck Dressen, who suffered a heart attack during the season, replaced in the interim by coach Bob Swift—from its second straight fourth-place finish at 89–73, 13 games behind the division champ Twins. The lineup still lacked consistent punch. Norm Cash improved his batting average nine points to .266, his slugging average 59 points to .512, and his home-run total seven to 30 to win his first American League Comeback of the Year Award. Don Wert hit .261 and led AL third basemen with a .976 fielding average. And in his first full season in Detroit, Willie Horton finished third in the league in homers with 29 and drove in 104 runs (four behind league-leader Rocky Colavito). But no Tiger hit .300, Al Kaline leading the team at .281.

TEAM STATISTICS

W	L	PCT	GB	R	OR	2B	3B	HR	BA	SA	SB	E	DP	FA	CG	BB	SO	ShO	SV	ERA
102	60	.630		774	600	257	42	150	.254	.399	92	172	158	.973	32	503	934	12	45	3.14
95	67	.586	7	647	555	200	38	125	.246	.364	50	127	156	.980	21	460	946	14	53	2.99
94	68	.580	8	641	578	227	38	125	.238	.363	67	126	152	.980	32	510	939	15	41	2.98
89	73	.549	13	680	602	190	27	162	.238	.374	57	116	126	.981	45	509	1069	14	31	3.35
87	75	.537	15	663	613	198	21	156	.250	.379	109	114	127	.981	41	500	1156	13	41	3.30
77	85	.475	25	611	604	196	31	149	.235	.364	35	137	166	.978	41	511	1001	11	31	3.28
75	87	.463	27	527	569	200	36	92	.239	.341	107	123	149	.981	39	563	847	14	33	3.17
70	92	.432	32	591	721	179	33	136	.228	.350	30	143	148	.976	21	633	867	8	40	3.93
62	100	.383	40	669	791	244	40	165	.251	.400	47	162	129	.974	33	543	993	9	25	4.24
59	103	.364	43	585	755	186	59	110	.240	.358	110	139	142	.977	18	574	882	7	32	4.24
GUE TOTAL				6388	6388	2077	365	1370	.242	.369	704	1359	1453	.978	323	5306	9634	117	372	3.46

INDIVIDUAL PITCHING

CHER	T	W	L	PCT	ERA	SV	G	GS	CG	IP	H	BB	SO	R	ER	ShO	H/9	BB/9	SO/9
key Lolich	L	15	9	.625	3.44	3	43	37	7	243.2	216	72	226	103	93	3	7.98	2.66	8.35
ny McLain	R	16	6	.727	2.61	1	33	29	13	220.1	174	62	192	73	64	4	7.11	2.53	7.84
k Aguirre	L	14	10	.583	3.59	0	32	32	10	208.1	185	60	141	89	83	2	7.99	2.59	6.09
e Wickersham	R	9	14	.391	3.78	0	34	27	8	195.1	179	61	109	91	82	3	8.25	2.81	5.02
Sparma	R	13	8	.619	3.18	0	30	28	6	167	142	75	127	69	59	0	7.65	4.04	6.84
y Sherry	R	3	6	.333	3.10	5	39	0	0	78.1	71	40	46	30	27	0	8.16	4.60	5.29
y Fox	R	6	4	.600	2.78	10	42	0	0	77.2	59	31	34	26	24	0	6.84	3.59	3.94
Gladding	R	6	2	.750	2.83	5	46	0	0	70	63	29	43	22	22	0	8.10	3.73	5.53
ndo Pena	R	4	6	.400	2.51	4	30	0	0	57.1	54	20	55	18	16	0	8.48	3.14	8.63
Regan	R	1	5	.167	5.05	0	16	7	1	51.2	57	20	37	31	29	0	9.93	3.48	6.45
) Navarro	R	0	2	.000	4.20	1	15	1	0	30	25	12	22	16	14	0	7.50	3.60	6.60
Nischwitz	L	1	0	1.000	2.78	1	20	0	0	22.2	21	6	12	10	7	0	8.34	2.38	4.76
Rakow	R	0	0	—	6.08	0	6	0	0	13.1	14	11	10	11	9	0	9.45	7.43	6.75
Hiller	L	0	0	—	0.00	1	5	0	0	6	5	1	4	0	0	0	7.50	1.50	6.00
Hamilton	R	1	1	.500	14.54	0	4	1	0	4.1	6	4	3	7	7	0	12.46	8.31	6.23
Holtgrave	R	0	0	—	6.00	0	1	0	0	3	4	2	2	2	2	0	12.00	6.00	6.00
Marentette	R	0	0	—	0.00	0	2	0	0	3	1	1	3	0	0	0	3.00	3.00	9.00
nie Seale	L	0	0	—	12.00	0	4	0	0	3	7	2	3	4	4	0	21.00	6.00	9.00
M TOTAL		89	73	.549	3.35	31	402	162	45	1455	1283	509	1069	602	542	12	7.94	3.15	6.61

MANAGER	W	L	PCT
Chuck Dressen	16	10	.615
Bob Swift	32	25	.561
Frank Skaff	40	39	.506

POS	Player	B	G	AB	H	2B	3B	HR	HR %	R	RBI	BB	SO	SB	Pinch Hit AB	Pinch Hit H	BA	SA
REGULARS																		
1B	Norm Cash	L	160	603	168	18	3	32	5.3	98	93	66	91	2	3	1	.279	.478
2B	Jerry Lumpe	L	113	385	89	14	3	1	0.3	30	26	24	44	0	20	2	.231	.291
SS	Dick McAuliffe	L	124	430	118	16	8	23	5.3	83	56	66	80	5	8	2	.274	.509
3B	Don Wert	R	150	559	150	20	2	11	2.0	56	70	64	69	6	0	0	.268	.370
RF	Jim Northrup	L	123	419	111	24	6	16	3.8	53	58	33	52	4	10	4	.265	.465
CF	Al Kaline	R	142	479	138	29	1	29	6.1	85	88	81	66	5	3	1	.288	.534
LF	Willie Horton	R	146	526	138	22	6	27	5.1	72	100	44	103	1	9	2	.262	.481
C	Bill Freehan	R	136	492	115	22	0	12	2.4	47	46	40	72	5	1	1	.234	.352
SUBSTITUTES																		
2B	Jake Wood	R	98	230	58	9	3	2	0.9	39	27	28	48	4	40	6	.252	.343
SS	Ray Oyler	R	71	210	36	8	3	1	0.5	16	9	23	62	0	1	0	.171	.252
2B	Dick Tracewski	R	81	124	24	1	1	0	0.0	15	7	10	32	1	7	0	.194	.218
1B	Don Pepper	L	4	3	0	0	0	0	0.0	0	0	0	1	0	3	0	.000	.000
OF	Mickey Stanley	R	92	235	68	15	4	3	1.3	28	19	17	20	2	9	3	.289	.426
OF	Gates Brown	L	88	169	45	5	1	7	4.1	27	27	18	19	3	40	13	.266	.432
OF	Don Demeter	R	32	99	21	5	0	5	5.1	12	12	3	19	1	4	0	.212	.414
C	Orlando McFarlane	R	49	138	35	7	0	5	3.6	16	13	9	46	0	15	2	.254	.413
C	Arlo Brunsberg	L	2	3	1	1	0	0	0.0	1	0	0	0	0	0	0	.333	.667
PITCHERS																		
P	Denny McLain	R	38	93	17	2	0	0	0.0	10	5	5	39	1	0	0	.183	.204
P	Mickey Lolich	B	40	64	9	0	1	0	0.0	12	3	7	28	0	0	0	.141	.172
P	Earl Wilson	R	27	64	15	0	2	5	7.8	13	17	4	25	0	4	1	.234	.531
P	Dave Wickersham	R	38	45	2	1	0	0	0.0	1	1	2	17	0	0	0	.044	.067
P	Johnny Podres	L	36	30	7	3	0	0	0.0	5	2	2	5	0	0	0	.233	.333
P	Bill Monbouquette	R	30	26	4	0	0	0	0.0	0	1	1	14	1	0	0	.154	.154
P	Hank Aguirre	B	30	25	3	1	0	0	0.0	0	0	4	16	0	0	0	.120	.160
P	Joe Sparma	R	29	23	5	1	0	0	0.0	0	1	0	5	0	0	0	.217	.261
P	Orlando Pena	R	54	18	2	0	0	0	0.0	0	0	0	8	0	0	0	.111	.111
P	Larry Sherry	R	55	10	4	0	1	0	0.0	0	1	0	1	0	0	0	.400	.600
P	Terry Fox	R	4	3	0	0	0	0	0.0	0	0	0	3	0	0	0	.000	.000
P	Fred Gladding	L	51	2	0	0	0	0	0.0	0	0	0	1	0	0	0	.000	.000
P	Bill Graham	R	1	0	0	0	0	0	–	0	0	0	0	0	0	0	–	–
P	John Hiller	R	1	0	0	0	0	0	–	0	0	0	0	0	0	0	–	–
P	George Korince	R	2	0	0	0	0	0	–	0	0	0	0	0	0	0	–	–
P	Julio Navarro	R	1	0	0	0	0	0	–	0	0	0	0	0	0	0	–	–
TEAM TOTAL				5507	1383	224	45	179	3.3	719	682	551	986	41	177	38	.251	.406

INDIVIDUAL FIELDING

POS	Player	T	G	PO	A	E	DP	TC/G	FA
1B	N. Cash	L	158	1271	114	17	118	8.9	.988
	B. Freehan	R	5	44	4	0	3	9.6	1.000
	D. Demeter	R	4	15	4	0	1	4.8	1.000
	J. Wood	R	2	14	0	0	1	7.0	1.000
	D. Pepper	L	1	2	0	0	0	2.0	1.000
2B	J. Lumpe	R	95	202	223	4	51	4.5	.991
	J. Wood	R	52	109	100	7	25	4.2	.968
	D. Tracewski	R	70	69	91	9	25	2.4	.947
SS	D. McAuliffe	R	105	160	292	17	49	4.5	.964
	R. Oyler	R	69	107	194	11	42	4.5	.965
	D. Tracewski	R	3	2	9	1	2	4.0	.917
3B	D. Wert	R	150	128	253	11	20	2.6	.972
	D. McAuliffe	R	15	14	29	2	3	3.0	.956
	J. Wood	R	4	1	0	2	0	0.8	.333

POS	Player	T	G	PO	A	E	DP	TC/G	FA
OF	A. Kaline	R	136	279	7	2	1	2.1	.993
	J. Northrup	R	113	241	8	5	1	2.2	.980
	W. Horton	R	137	233	4	5	1	1.8	.979
	M. Stanley	R	82	163	6	0	1	2.1	1.000
	D. Demeter	R	27	65	2*	1	2	2.5	.985
	G. Brown	R	43	46	4	1	1	1.2	.980
C	B. Freehan	R	132	898	56	4	11	7.3	.996
	O. McFarlane	R	33	205	21	2	2	6.9	.991
	A. Brunsberg	R	2	4	0	0	0	2.0	1.000

For long, solemn stretches in Detroit, baseball seemed relatively unimportant to Detroit fans. The Tigers had played under three managers over the season; by year's end, two were dead. With the team in third place on May 16, Charlie Dressen suffered his second heart attack in two years. Coach and former Tiger catcher Bob Swift took over as interim manager and led a surge as Detroit won 19 of 24 in June to close within a game and a half of first-place Baltimore. But over the next nine days the Orioles won 10 of 11. And in early July the Tigers lost five straight to drop eight games out. By mid-July it didn't seem to matter: Swift was dying—hospitalized with lung cancer. He died on October 17. Under replacement Frank Skaff Detroit came home third, 10 games behind the first-place Orioles, just one game behind the second-place Twins.

Detroit led the league in home runs with 179, but for the second straight season no Tiger hit .300. Al Kaline again came closest at .288 (with 29 home runs). Posting his best average since winning the 1961 batting title, Norm Cash hit .279 with a team-high 32 home runs. Willie Horton slammed 27 homers, Dick McAuliffe 23.

Despite allowing a still-standing team-record 42 home runs, Denny McLain became Detroit's first 20-game winner in five years at 20–14 with a 3.92 ERA. In five of his victories, McLain allowed two hits or less: one-hitters against the White Sox and Athletics, two-hitters against the Yankees, Twins, and White Sox. McLain started for the American League in the All-Star Game, and in 109-degree weather in St. Louis retired the first nine batters in order. Obtained in a trade with Boston, veteran pitcher Earl Wilson racked up nine straight victories en route to an 18–11, 3.07 ERA season. Wilson won another game on July 15, but it didn't go on his record: he beat eventual World Champion Baltimore with a pinch-hit three-run homer.

TEAM STATISTICS

W	L	PCT	GB	R	OR	2B	3B	HR	BA	SA	SB	E	DP	FA	CG	BB	SO	ShO	SV	ERA
97	63	.606		755	601	243	35	175	.258	.409	55	115	142	.981	23	514	1070	13	51	3.32
89	73	.549	9	663	581	219	33	144	.249	.382	67	139	118	.977	52	392	1015	11	28	3.13
88	74	.543	10	719	698	224	45	179	.251	.406	41	120	142	.980	36	520	1026	11	38	3.85
83	79	.512	15	574	517	193	40	87	.231	.331	153	159	149	.976	38	403	896	22	34	2.68
81	81	.500	17	574	586	156	25	155	.237	.360	53	138	132	.977	49	489	1111	15	28	3.23
80	82	.494	18	604	643	179	54	122	.232	.354	80	136	186	.979	31	511	836	12	40	3.56
74	86	.463	23	564	648	212	56	70	.236	.337	132	138	154	.977	19	630	854	11	47	3.55
71	88	.447	25.5	557	659	185	40	126	.234	.355	53	142	139	.977	25	448	866	6	35	3.70
72	90	.444	26	655	731	228	44	145	.240	.376	35	155	153	.975	32	577	977	10	31	3.92
70	89	.440	26.5	611	612	182	36	162	.235	.374	49	142	142	.977	29	443	842	7	32	3.42
GUE TOTAL				6276	6276	2021	408	1365	.240	.369	718	1384	1457	.978	334	4927	9493	118	364	3.44

INDIVIDUAL PITCHING

CHER	T	W	L	PCT	ERA	SV	G	GS	CG	IP	H	BB	SO	R	ER	ShO	H/9	BB/9	SO/9
ny McLain	R	20	14	.588	3.92	0	38	38	14	264.1	205	104	192	120	115	4	6.98	3.54	6.54
ey Lolich	L	14	14	.500	4.77	3	40	33	5	203.2	204	83	173	119	108	1	9.01	3.67	7.64
Wilson	R	13	6	.684	2.59	0	23	23	8	163.1	126	38	133	49	47	2	6.94	2.09	7.33
Wickersham	R	8	3	.727	3.20	1	38	14	3	140.2	139	54	93	64	50	0	8.89	3.45	5.95
do Pena	R	4	2	.667	3.08	7	54	0	0	108	105	35	79	47	37	0	8.75	2.92	6.58
ny Podres	L	4	5	.444	3.43	4	36	13	2	107.2	106	34	53	48	41	1	8.86	2.84	4.43
Aguirre	L	3	9	.250	3.82	0	30	14	2	103.2	104	26	50	50	44	0	9.03	2.26	4.34
onbouquette	R	7	8	.467	4.73	0	30	14	2	102.2	120	22	61	60	54	1	10.52	1.93	5.35
Sparma	R	2	7	.222	5.30	0	29	13	0	91.2	103	52	61	57	54	0	10.11	5.11	5.99
Sherry	R	8	5	.615	3.82	20	55	0	0	77.2	66	36	63	38	33	0	7.65	4.17	7.30
Gladding	R	5	0	1.000	3.28	2	51	0	0	74	62	29	57	33	27	0	7.54	3.53	6.93
Fox	R	0	1	.000	6.30	1	4	0	0	10	9	2	6	8	7	0	8.10	1.80	5.40
ge Korince	R	0	0	—	0.00	0	2	0	0	3	1	3	2	0	0	0	3.00	9.00	6.00
raham	R	0	0	—	0.00	0	1	0	0	2	2	0	2	0	0	0	9.00	0.00	9.00
Hiller	L	0	0	—	9.00	0	1	0	0	2	2	2	1	2	2	0	9.00	9.00	4.50
Navarro	R	0	0	—	0.00	0	1	0	0		2	0	0	3	3	0	∞	—	—
M TOTAL		88	74	.543	3.85	38	433	162	36	1454.1	1356	520	1026	698	622	9	8.39	3.22	6.35

MANAGER	W	L	PCT
Mayo Smith	91	71	.562

POS	Player	B	G	AB	H	2B	3B	HR	HR %	R	RBI	BB	SO	SB	Pinch Hit AB	H	BA	SA
REGULARS																		
1B	Norm Cash	L	152	488	118	16	5	22	4.5	64	72	81	100	3	7	1	.242	.430
2B	Dick McAuliffe	L	153	557	133	16	7	22	3.9	92	65	105	118	6	0	0	.239	.411
SS	Ray Oyler	R	148	367	76	14	2	1	0.3	33	29	37	91	0	0	0	.207	.264
3B	Don Wert	R	142	534	137	23	2	6	1.1	60	40	44	59	1	2	0	.257	.341
RF	Al Kaline	R	131	458	141	28	2	25	5.5	94	78	83	47	8	1	0	.308	.541
CF	Jim Northrup	L	144	495	134	18	6	10	2.0	63	61	43	83	7	5	1	.271	.392
LF	Willie Horton	R	122	401	110	20	3	19	4.7	47	67	36	80	0	11	3	.274	.481
C	Bill Freehan	R	155	517	146	23	1	20	3.9	66	74	73	71	1	2	2	.282	.447
SUBSTITUTES																		
2B	Jerry Lumpe	L	81	177	41	4	0	4	2.3	19	17	16	18	0	29	3	.232	.322
31	Eddie Mathews	L	36	108	25	3	0	6	5.6	14	19	15	23	0	5	0	.231	.426
UT	Dick Tracewski	R	74	107	30	4	2	1	0.9	19	9	8	20	1	9	3	.280	.383
12	Jake Wood	R	14	20	1	1	0	0	0.0	2	0	1	7	0	9	0	.050	.100
SS	Tommy Matchick	L	8	6	1	0	0	0	0.0	1	0	0	2	0	5	0	.167	.167
1B	Dave Campbell	R	2	2	0	0	0	0	0.0	0	0	0	1	0	1	0	.000	.000
OF	Mickey Stanley	R	145	333	70	7	3	7	2.1	38	24	29	46	9	13	1	.210	.312
OF	Lenny Green	L	58	151	42	8	1	1	0.7	22	13	9	17	1	11	1	.278	.364
OF	Gates Brown	L	51	91	17	1	1	2	2.2	17	9	13	15	0	26	4	.187	.363
OF	Jim Landis	R	25	48	10	0	0	2	4.2	4	4	7	12	0	10	1	.208	.333
OF	Wayne Comer	R	4	3	1	0	0	0	0.0	0	0	0	0	0	1	1	.333	.333
C	Jim Price	R	44	92	24	4	0	0	0.0	9	8	4	10	0	20	5	.261	.304
C	Bill Heath	L	20	32	4	0	0	0	0.0	0	4	1	4	0	14	2	.125	.125
PITCHERS																		
P	Earl Wilson	R	52	108	20	2	0	4	3.7	8	15	8	39	0	12	2	.185	.315
P	Denny McLain	R	38	85	10	0	0	0	0.0	3	0	2	37	0	0	0	.118	.118
P	Joe Sparma	R	37	74	4	0	0	0	0.0	1	1	3	33	0	0	0	.054	.054
P	Mickey Lolich	B	32	61	12	0	0	0	0.0	4	4	7	25	0	0	0	.197	.197
P	Johnny Podres	L	21	20	2	0	0	0	0.0	1	0	0	4	0	0	0	.100	.100
P	Fred Gladding	L	42	18	0	0	0	0	0.0	0	0	0	9	0	0	0	.000	.000
P	John Hiller	R	23	15	2	0	0	0	0.0	0	2	1	5	0	0	0	.133	.133
P	Dave Wickersham	R	36	15	0	0	0	0	0.0	0	0	0	5	0	0	0	.000	.000
P	Fred Lasher	R	17	9	1	0	0	0	0.0	0	0	0	6	0	0	0	.111	.111
P	Mike Marshall	R	37	9	2	0	0	0	0.0	2	1	0	3	0	2	1	.222	.222
P	Pat Dobson	R	28	5	0	0	0	0	0.0	0	0	0	2	0	0	0	.000	.000
P	Hank Aguirre	B	31	2	1	0	1	0	0.0	0	3	0	1	0	0	0	.500	1.500
P	George Korince	R	9	1	0	0	0	0	0.0	0	0	0	1	0	0	0	.000	.000
P	Larry Sherry	R	20	1	0	0	0	0	0.0	0	0	0	0	0	0	0	.000	.000
P	Johnny Klippstein	R	5	0	0	0	0	0	–	0	0	0	0	0	0	0	–	–
P	Bill Monbouquette	R	2	0	0	0	0	0	–	0	0	0	0	0	0	0	–	–
P	Orlando Pena	R	2	0	0	0	0	0	0.0	0	0	0	0	0	0	0	–	–
	TEAM TOTAL			5410	1315	192	36	152	2.8	683	619	626	994	37	195	31	.243	.376

INDIVIDUAL FIELDING

POS	Player	T	G	PO	A	E	DP	TC/G	FA
1B	N. Cash	L	146	1135	112	6	89	8.6	.995
	E. Mathews	R	13	106	12	1	9	9.2	.992
	B. Freehan	R	11	77	5	0	6	7.5	1.000
	M. Stanley	R	8	48	4	0	3	6.5	1.000
	J. Wood	R	2	9	0	0	2	4.5	1.000
	D. Campbell	R	1	1	0	1	0	2.0	.500
2B	D. McAuliffe	R	145	270	307	21	74	4.1	.965
	J. Lumpe	R	54	70	85	6	12	3.0	.963
	D. Tracewski	R	12	14	25	0	5	3.3	1.000
	J. Wood	R	2	3	5	1	1	4.5	.889
SS	R. Oyler	R	146	185	374	21	61	4.0	.964
	D. McAuliffe	R	43	30	67	7	8	2.4	.933
	D. Tracewski	R	44	31	52	3	12	2.0	.965
	D. Wert	R	1	1	2	0	1	3.0	1.000
	T. Matchick	R	1	1	0	0	0	1.0	1.000
3B	D. Wert	R	140	112	280	9	21	2.9	.978
	E. Mathews	R	21	14	28	3	0	2.1	.933
	D. Tracewski	R	10	9	13	0	0	2.2	1.000
	J. Lumpe	R	6	3	8	1	0	2.0	.917

POS	Player	T	G	PO	A	E	DP	TC/G	FA
OF	J. Northrup	R	143	271	3	8	1	2.0	.972
	A. Kaline	R	130	217	14	4	2	1.8	.983
	M. Stanley	R	128	216	3	4	2	1.7	.982
	W. Horton	R	110	165	5	5	2	1.6	.971
	L. Green	L	44	57	0	1	0	1.3	.983
	G. Brown	R	20	22	1	0	0	1.2	1.000
	W. Comer	R	1	0	0	0	0	0.0	.000
	J. Landis	R	12	18	2	1	0	1.8	.952
C	B. Freehan	R	147	950	63	8	9	6.9	.992
	J. Price	R	24	139	8	4	1	6.3	.974
	B. Heath	R	7	38	3	0	1	5.9	1.000

On the night of October 1, Dick McAuliffe grounded into a double play to seal a Tiger off-season of nightmares. "Losing the pennant on the last day of the season," said first-year Detroit manager Mayo Smith, "made for an awfully long winter." Earlier that day Boston had culminated its participation in a furious four-team pennant race with a victory over Minnesota. Meanwhile, in Detroit, the Tigers had won the first game of doubleheader against the Angels; a nightcap victory would have forced a one-game pennant playoff against the Red Sox the following day at Tiger Stadium. But as the Red Sox listened gleefully to radios back in Boston, the Tigers lost, 8–5, to drop into a second-place tie with the Twins, one game behind.

Detroit's closest near-miss since its previous pennant 22 years earlier was forged by pitching, undoubtedly improved by the arrival of coach Johnny Sain. In his first full Tiger season, Earl Wilson became Detroit's top winner in six years at 22–11, 3.27, to tie for the major-league lead in wins. Bill Freehan became the league's dominant catcher with a .282 season, placing third in the Most Valuable Player voting. On August 17 slugging third baseman–first baseman Eddie Mathews was acquired from Houston for the pennant stretch; he hit just .231 but in crucial late games drove in six game-winning runs. Al Kaline led the team in average at .308 (Detroit's first .300 hitter in three years, its last till 1973), and won his 10th Gold Glove in 11 years. But after striking out against Cleveland's Sam McDowell in a June 27 game, Kaline angrily slammed his bat into a dugout rack and broke a bone in his hand, forcing him to sit out 26 games.

TEAM STATISTICS

W	L	PCT	GB	R	OR	Batting						Fielding			Pitching					
						2B	3B	HR	BA	SA	SB	E	DP	FA	CG	BB	SO	ShO	SV	ERA
S	92	70	.568		722	614	216	39	158	.255	.395	68	142	142	.977	41	477	1010	9	44	3.36
T	91	71	.562	1	683	587	192	36	152	.243	.376	37	131	126	.979	46	472	1038	17	40	3.32
N	91	71	.562	1	671	590	216	48	131	.240	.369	55	132	123	.978	58	396	1089	18	24	3.14
I	89	73	.549	3	531	491	181	34	89	.225	.320	124	138	149	.979	36	465	927	24	39	2.45
L	84	77	.522	7.5	567	587	170	37	114	.238	.349	40	111	135	.982	19	525	892	14	46	3.19
L	76	85	.472	15.5	654	592	215	44	138	.240	.372	54	124	144	.980	29	566	1034	17	36	3.32
S	76	85	.472	15.5	550	637	168	25	115	.223	.326	53	144	167	.978	24	495	878	14	39	3.38
E	75	87	.463	17	559	613	213	35	131	.235	.359	53	117	138	.981	49	559	1189	14	27	3.25
	72	90	.444	20	522	621	166	17	100	.225	.317	63	154	144	.976	37	480	898	16	27	3.24
	62	99	.385	29.5	533	660	212	50	69	.233	.330	132	132	120	.978	26	558	990	10	34	3.68
GUE TOTAL				5992	5992	1949	365	1197	.236	.351	679	1325	1388	.979	365	4993	9945	153	356	3.23

INDIVIDUAL PITCHING

CHER	T	W	L	PCT	ERA	SV	G	GS	CG	IP	H	BB	SO	R	ER	ShO	H/9	BB/9	SO/9
l Wilson	R	22	11	.667	3.27	0	39	38	12	264	216	92	184	103	96	0	7.36	3.14	6.27
nny McLain	R	17	16	.515	3.79	0	37	37	10	235	209	73	161	110	99	3	8.00	2.80	6.17
e Sparma	R	16	9	.640	3.76	0	37	37	11	217.2	186	85	153	103	91	5	7.69	3.51	6.33
ckey Lolich	L	14	13	.519	3.04	0	31	30	11	204	165	56	174	71	69	6	7.28	2.47	7.68
ve Wickersham	R	4	5	.444	2.74	4	36	4	0	85.1	72	33	44	30	26	0	7.59	3.48	4.64
d Gladding	R	6	4	.600	1.99	12	42	1	0	77	62	19	64	20	17	0	7.25	2.22	7.48
n Hiller	L	4	3	.571	2.63	3	23	6	2	65	57	9	49	20	19	2	7.89	1.25	6.78
nny Podres	L	3	1	.750	3.84	1	21	8	0	63.1	58	11	34	29	27	0	8.24	1.56	4.83
e Marshall	R	1	3	.250	1.98	10	37	0	0	59	51	20	41	15	13	0	7.78	3.05	6.25
Dobson	R	1	2	.333	2.92	0	28	1	0	49.1	38	27	34	20	16	0	6.93	4.93	6.20
nk Aguirre	L	0	1	.000	2.40	0	31	1	0	41.1	34	17	33	15	11	0	7.40	3.70	7.19
d Lasher	R	2	1	.667	3.90	9	17	0	0	30	25	11	28	14	13	0	7.50	3.30	8.40
ry Sherry	R	0	1	.000	6.43	1	20	0	0	28	35	7	20	22	20	0	11.25	2.25	6.43
orge Korince	R	1	0	1.000	5.14	0	9	0	0	14	10	11	11	8	8	0	6.43	7.07	7.07
nny Klippstein	R	0	0	–	5.40	0	5	0	0	6.2	6	1	4	4	4	0	8.10	1.35	5.40
Monbouquette	R	0	0	–	0.00	0	2	0	0	2	1	0	2	0	0	0	4.50	0.00	9.00
ando Pena	R	0	1	.000	13.50	0	2	0	0	2	5	0	2	3	3	0	22.50	0.00	9.00
M TOTAL		91	71	.562	3.32	40	417	163	46	1443.2	1230	472	1038	587	532	16	7.67	2.94	6.47

MANAGER	W	L	PCT
Mayo Smith	103	59	.636

POS	Player	B	G	AB	H	2B	3B	HR	HR %	R	RBI	BB	SO	SB	Pinch Hit AB	Pinch Hit H	BA	SA
REGULARS																		
1B	Norm Cash	L	127	411	108	15	1	25	6.1	50	63	39	70	1	15	2	.263	.487
2B	Dick McAuliffe	L	151	570	142	24	10	16	2.8	95	56	82	99	8	3	2	.249	.411
SS	Ray Oyler	R	111	215	29	6	1	1	0.5	13	12	20	59	0	0	0	.135	.186
3B	Don Wert	R	150	536	107	15	1	12	2.2	44	37	37	79	0	1	1	.200	.299
RF	Jim Northrup	L	154	580	153	29	7	21	3.6	76	90	50	87	4	4	0	.264	.447
CF	Mickey Stanley	R	153	583	151	16	6	11	1.9	88	60	42	57	4	6	0	.259	.364
LF	Willie Horton	R	143	512	146	20	2	36	7.0	68	85	49	110	0	5	1	.285	.543
C	Bill Freehan	R	155	540	142	24	2	25	4.6	73	84	65	64	0	3	1	.263	.454
SUBSTITUTES																		
S2	Tommy Matchick	L	80	227	46	6	2	3	1.3	18	14	10	46	0	13	5	.203	.286
UT	Dick Tracewski	R	90	212	33	3	1	4	1.9	30	15	24	51	3	9	1	.156	.236
13	Eddie Mathews	L	31	52	11	0	0	3	5.8	4	8	5	12	0	16	3	.212	.385
2B	Dave Campbell	R	9	8	1	0	0	1	12.5	1	2	1	3	0	3	0	.125	.500
O1	Al Kaline	R	102	327	94	14	1	10	3.1	49	53	55	39	6	10	5	.287	.428
OF	Gates Brown	L	67	92	34	7	2	6	6.5	15	15	12	4	0	39	18	.370	.685
OF	Wayne Comer	R	48	48	6	0	1	1	2.1	8	3	2	7	0	18	2	.125	.229
OF	Lenny Green	L	6	4	1	0	0	0	0.0	0	0	1	0	0	3	1	.250	.250
O1	Bob Christian	R	3	3	1	1	0	0	0.0	0	0	0	0	0	1	0	.333	.667
C	Jim Price	R	64	132	23	4	0	3	2.3	12	13	13	14	0	22	5	.174	.273
PITCHERS																		
P	Denny McLain	R	44	111	18	1	1	0	0.0	7	4	1	37	0	0	0	.162	.189
P	Earl Wilson	R	40	88	20	0	1	7	8.0	9	17	2	35	0	6	0	.227	.489
P	Mickey Lolich	B	41	70	8	3	0	0	0.0	5	3	6	25	0	1	0	.114	.157
P	Joe Sparma	R	34	60	8	1	0	0	0.0	2	2	1	24	0	0	0	.133	.150
P	John Hiller	R	39	37	3	0	0	0	0.0	1	2	0	14	0	0	0	.081	.081
P	Pat Dobson	R	47	28	4	0	0	0	0.0	2	1	2	7	0	0	0	.143	.143
P	Daryl Patterson	L	38	13	0	0	0	0	0.0	0	1	1	8	0	0	0	.000	.000
P	Fred Lasher	R	34	9	1	0	0	0	0.0	0	0	0	4	0	0	0	.111	.111
P	Les Cain	L	8	7	1	1	0	0	0.0	0	0	0	2	0	0	0	.143	.143
P	Dennis Ribant	R	16	5	1	0	0	0	0.0	1	0	1	1	0	0	0	.200	.200
P	Don McMahon	R	20	4	0	0	0	0	0.0	0	0	0	2	0	0	0	.000	.000
P	John Wyatt	R	22	2	0	0	0	0	0.0	0	0	0	2	0	0	0	.000	.000
P	Jon Warden	B	28	2	0	0	0	0	0.0	0	0	0	1	0	0	0	.000	.000
P	Jim Rooker	R	2	2	0	0	0	0	0.0	0	0	0	1	0	0	0	.000	.000
P	Roy Face	B	2	0	0	0	0	0	–	0	0	0	0	0	0	0		
	TEAM TOTAL			5490	1292	190	39	185	3.4	671	640	521	964	26	178	47	.235	.385

INDIVIDUAL FIELDING

POS	Player	T	G	PO	A	E	DP	TC/G	FA
1B	N. Cash	L	117	924	88	8	66	8.7	.992
	B. Freehan	R	21	162	10	1	11	8.2	.994
	A. Kaline	R	22	152	13	4	15	7.7	.976
	M. Stanley	R	15	99	8	2	9	7.3	.982
	E. Mathews	R	6	34	3	1	5	6.3	.974
	T. Matchick	R	6	28	2	0	4	5.0	1.000
	G. Brown	R	1	3	0	0	0	3.0	1.000
	B. Christian	R	1	3	0	0	0	3.0	1.000
2B	D. McAuliffe	R	148	288	348	9	79	4.4	.986
	M. Stanley	R	1	0	0	0	0	0.0	.000
	T. Matchick	R	13	25	34	1	7	4.6	.983
	D. Tracewski	R	14	15	30	0	5	3.2	1.000
	D. Campbell	R	5	4	3	0	1	1.4	1.000
SS	R. Oyler	R	111	139	207	8	31	3.2	.977
	T. Matchick	R	59	53	118	9	20	3.1	.950
	D. Tracewski	R	51	60	108	3	19	3.4	.982
	M. Stanley	R	9	9	25	2	2	4.0	.944
	D. McAuliffe	R	5	4	4	0	1	1.6	1.000
	D. Wert	R	2	2	0	0	0	1.0	1.000
3B	D. Wert	R	150	142	284	15	22	2.9	.966
	D. Tracewski	R	16	7	19	2	3	1.8	.929
	E. Mathews	R	6	3	11	0	0	2.3	1.000

POS	Player	T	G	PO	A	E	DP	TC/G	FA
OF	J. Northrup	R	151	321	7	7	1	2.2	.979
	M. Stanley	R	130	297	7	0	2	2.3	**1.000**
	W. Horton	R	139	212	6	6	2	1.6	.973
	A. Kaline	R	74	131	1	3	0	1.8	.978
	W. Comer	R	27	20	0	0	0	0.7	1.000
	G. Brown	R	17	18	1	0	0	1.1	1.000
	B. Freehan	R	1	0	0	0	0	0.0	.000
	B. Christian	R	1	0	0	0	0	0.0	.000
	L. Green	L	2	0	0	0	0	0.0	.000
C	B. Freehan	R	138	**971**	73	6	**15**	7.6	.994
	J. Price	R	42	223	14	1	1	5.7	.996
	W. Comer	R	1	2	0	0	0	2.0	1.000

It was clearly Denny McLain's year. The 24-year-old righthander won 31 of 37 decisions—Detroit's first and only 30-game winner, the major leagues' biggest winner in 37 years, and the majors' first 30-game winner since Dizzy Dean in 1934. The team's fourth starter entering spring training, McLain won the Cy Young Award (unanimously), the Most Valuable Player Award, and *The Sporting News'* Pitcher of the Year and Player of the Year Awards.

Detroit captured first place for keeps on May 10, won 103 games, and breezed to the pennant by 12 games. The Tigers led the majors in home runs with 185 (52 more than any other club), led the American League in scoring and fewest runs allowed, and led the majors in fielding. Attendance soared nearly 600,000 to over 2,000,000. In a season that saw only one American Leaguer hit .300, leftfielder Willie Horton led Tiger regulars at .285 with 36 home runs. Rightfielder Jim Northrup finished third in the league with 90 RBIs; four of his 21 home runs were grand slams, three in one week. Al Kaline (.287) started the season in right, was out five weeks after being hit on the hand by a pitch, then returned to alternate with Cash at first base.

For the World Series against the defending World Champion Cardinals, Smith gambled and moved centerfielder Mickey Stanley, errorless through the season, to shortstop to make outfield room for Kaline, who after a 16-season wait hit .379 in his only Fall Classic. Cardinal ace Bob Gibson struck out a Series-record 17 in Game 1, and St. Louis won three of the first four to back the Tigers to the brink of elimination. Then Mickey Lolich won Game 5, McLain won Game 6, and Lolich captured the Series MVP award with a 4–1 five-hitter in Game 7 at St. Louis. Motown exploded in celebration. "The entire downtown area was jammed," said McLain. "There were so many people waiting to meet our plane, they had to close the airport. At the time, the world seemed wonderfully warm."

TEAM STATISTICS

W	L	PCT	GB	R	OR	2B	3B	HR	BA	SA	SB	E	DP	FA	CG	BB	SO	ShO	SV	ERA
T 103	59	.636		671	492	190	39	185	.235	.385	26	105	133	.983	59	486	1115	19	29	2.71
91	71	.562	12	579	497	215	28	133	.225	.352	78	120	131	.981	53	502	1044	16	31	2.66
86	75	.534	16.5	516	504	210	36	75	.234	.327	115	127	130	.979	48	540	1157	23	32	2.66
S 86	76	.531	17	614	611	207	17	125	.236	.352	76	128	147	.979	55	523	972	17	31	3.33
83	79	.512	20	536	531	154	34	109	.214	.318	90	139	142	.979	45	424	831	14	27	2.79
K 82	80	.506	21	569	544	192	40	94	.240	.343	147	145	136	.976	45	505	997	18	29	2.94
N 79	83	.488	24	562	546	207	41	105	.237	.350	98	170	117	.973	46	414	996	14	29	2.89
L 67	95	.414	36	498	615	170	33	83	.227	.318	62	140	156	.977	29	519	869	11	31	3.43
67	95	.414	36	463	527	169	33	71	.228	.311	90	151	152	.977	20	451	834	11	40	2.75
S 65	96	.404	37.5	524	665	160	37	124	.224	.336	29	148	144	.976	26	517	826	11	28	3.64
GUE TOTAL				5532	5532	1874	338	1104	.230	.339	811	1373	1388	.978	426	4881	9641	154	307	2.98

INDIVIDUAL PITCHING

CHER	T	W	L	PCT	ERA	SV	G	GS	CG	IP	H	BB	SO	R	ER	ShO	H/9	BB/9	SO/9
nny McLain	R	31	6	.838	1.96	0	41	41	28	336	241	63	280	86	73	6	6.46	1.69	7.50
l Wilson	R	13	12	.520	2.85	0	34	33	10	224.1	192	65	168	77	71	3	7.70	2.61	6.74
key Lolich	L	17	9	.654	3.19	1	39	32	8	220	178	65	197	84	78	4	7.28	2.66	8.06
Sparma	R	10	10	.500	3.70	0	34	31	7	182.1	169	77	110	81	75	1	8.34	3.80	5.43
n Hiller	L	9	6	.600	2.39	2	39	12	4	128	92	51	78	37	34	1	6.47	3.59	5.48
Dobson	R	5	8	.385	2.66	7	47	10	2	125	89	48	93	39	37	1	6.41	3.46	6.70
yl Patterson	R	2	3	.400	2.12	7	38	1	0	68	53	27	49	19	16	0	7.01	3.57	6.49
d Lasher	R	5	1	.833	3.33	5	34	0	0	48.2	37	22	32	19	18	0	6.84	4.07	5.92
Warden	L	4	1	.800	3.62	3	28	0	0	37.1	30	15	25	15	15	0	7.23	3.62	6.03
McMahon	R	3	1	.750	2.02	1	20	0	0	35.2	22	10	33	8	8	0	5.55	2.52	8.33
n Wyatt	R	1	0	1.000	2.37	2	22	0	0	30.1	26	11	25	9	8	0	7.71	3.26	7.42
nis Ribant	R	2	2	.500	2.22	1	14	0	0	24.1	20	10	7	7	6	0	7.40	3.70	2.59
Cain	L	1	0	1.000	3.00	0	8	4	0	24	25	20	13	9	8	0	9.38	7.50	4.88
Rooker	L	0	0	–	3.86	0	2	0	0	4.2	4	1	4	2	2	0	7.71	1.93	7.71
Face	R	0	0	–	0.00	0	2	0	0	1	2	1	1	0	0	0	18.00	9.00	9.00
M TOTAL		103	59	.636	2.71	29	402	164	59	1489.2	1180	486	1115	492	449	16	7.13	2.94	6.74

MANAGER	W	L	PCT
Mayo Smith	90	72	.556

POS	Player	B	G	AB	H	2B	3B	HR	HR %	R	RBI	BB	SO	SB	Pinch Hit AB	Pinch Hit H	BA	SA
REGULARS																		
1B	Norm Cash	L	142	483	135	15	4	22	4.6	81	74	63	80	2	9	2	.280	.464
2B	Dick McAuliffe	L	74	271	71	10	5	11	4.1	49	33	47	41	2	2	1	.262	.458
SS	Tom Tresh	B	94	331	74	13	1	13	3.9	46	37	39	47	2	6	1	.224	.387
3B	Don Wert	R	132	423	95	11	1	14	3.3	46	50	49	60	3	2	0	.225	.355
RF	Al Kaline	R	131	456	124	17	0	21	4.6	74	69	54	61	1	7	2	.272	.447
CF	Jim Northrup	L	148	543	160	31	5	25	4.6	79	66	52	83	4	5	0	.295	.508
LF	Willie Horton	R	141	508	133	17	1	28	5.5	66	91	52	93	3	5	1	.262	.465
C	Bill Freehan	R	143	489	128	16	3	16	3.3	61	49	53	55	1	8	1	.262	.405
SUBSTITUTES																		
23	Tommy Matchick	L	94	298	72	11	2	0	0.0	25	32	15	51	3	16	8	.242	.292
23	Ike Brown	R	70	170	39	4	3	5	2.9	24	12	26	43	2	12	0	.229	.376
S2	Dick Tracewski	R	66	79	11	2	0	0	0.0	10	4	15	20	3	3	1	.139	.165
SS	Cesar Gutierrez	R	17	49	12	1	0	0	0.0	5	0	5	3	1	1	0	.245	.265
12	Dave Campbell	R	32	39	4	1	0	0	0.0	4	2	4	15	0	14	2	.103	.128
OS	Mickey Stanley	R	149	592	139	28	1	16	2.7	73	70	52	56	8	7	2	.235	.367
OF	Gates Brown	L	60	93	19	1	2	1	1.1	13	6	5	17	0	39	8	.204	.290
OF	Ron Woods	R	17	15	4	0	0	1	6.7	3	3	2	3	0	5	0	.267	.467
C	Jim Price	R	72	192	45	8	0	9	4.7	21	28	18	20	0	21	2	.234	.417
PH	Wayne Redmond	R	5	3	0	0	0	0	0.0	0	0	0	2	0	3	0	.000	.000
PITCHERS																		
P	Denny McLain	R	42	106	17	0	0	0	0.0	5	8	4	41	0	0	0	.160	.160
P	Mickey Lolich	B	38	91	8	0	1	0	0.0	6	5	9	41	0	0	0	.088	.110
P	Earl Wilson	R	37	76	10	0	0	0	0.0	6	6	10	37	0	2	0	.132	.132
P	Mike Kilkenny	R	39	37	2	0	0	0	0.0	1	4	2	21	0	0	0	.054	.054
P	Joe Sparma	R	23	29	4	0	0	0	0.0	1	0	1	8	0	0	0	.138	.138
P	Pat Dobson	R	49	22	2	1	0	0	0.0	0	0	0	6	0	0	0	.091	.136
P	John Hiller	R	41	21	6	1	0	0	0.0	1	0	1	3	0	0	0	.286	.333
P	Tom Timmerman	R	31	9	1	0	0	0	0.0	0	0	0	4	0	0	0	.111	.111
P	Don McMahon	R	34	6	0	0	0	0	0.0	0	0	0	5	0	0	0	.000	.000
P	Fred Lasher	R	32	4	0	0	0	0	0.0	1	0	0	1	0	0	0	.000	.000
P	Dick Radatz	R	11	2	0	0	0	0	0.0	0	0	0	2	0	0	0	.000	.000
P	Bob Reed	R	8	2	1	0	0	0	0.0	0	0	0	1	0	0	0	.500	.500
P	Daryl Patterson	L	18	1	0	0	0	0	0.0	0	0	0	1	0	0	0	.000	.000
P	Gary Taylor	R	7	1	0	0	0	0	0.0	0	0	0	1	0	0	0	.000	.000
P	Fred Scherman	L	4	0	0	0	0	0	–	0	0	0	0	0	0	0	–	–
P	Norm McRae	R	3	0	0	0	0	0	–	0	0	0	0	0	0	0	–	–
	TEAM TOTAL			5441	1316	188	29	182	3.3	701	649	578	922	35	167	31	.242	.387

INDIVIDUAL FIELDING

POS	Player	T	G	PO	A	E	DP	TC/G	FA	POS	Player	T	G	PO	A	E	DP	TC/G	FA
1B	N. Cash	L	134	1016	96	7	99	8.4	.994	OF	J. Northrup	R	143	323	8	5	2	2.3	.985
	B. Freehan	R	20	138	7	3	7	7.4	.980		W. Horton	R	136	272	8	8	0	2.1	.972
	A. Kaline	R	9	65	2	0	3	7.4	1.000		A. Kaline	R	118	192	9	7	4	1.8	.966
	M. Stanley	R	4	42	1	0	2	10.8	1.000		M. Stanley	R	101	190	2	3	0	1.9	.985
	D. Campbell	R	13	28	1	1	4	2.3	.967		G. Brown	R	14	28	1	3	0	2.3	.906
	T. Matchick	R	2	11	1	0	0	6.0	1.000		T. Tresh	R	11	20	1	1	0	2.0	.955
2B	D. McAuliffe	R	72	167	196	9	40	5.2	.976		R. Woods	R	7	6	0	0	0	0.9	1.000
	T. Matchick	R	47	89	122	6	32	4.6	.972		I. Brown	R	3	2	0	0	0	0.7	1.000
	I. Brown	R	45	75	100	7	18	4.0	.962	C	B. Freehan	R	120	821	49	7	7	7.3	.992
	D. Tracewski	R	13	19	24	1	4	3.4	.977		J. Price	R	51	337	18	4	4	7.0	.989
	D. Campbell	R	5	10	7	1	1	3.6	.944										
SS	T. Tresh	R	77	118	187	11	38	4.1	.965										
	M. Stanley	R	59	110	135	7	22	4.3	.972										
	D. Tracewski	R	41	37	53	4	15	2.3	.957										
	C. Gutierrez	R	16	25	45	4	6	4.6	.946										
	I. Brown	R	1	0	0	0	0	0.0	.000										
	T. Matchick	R	6	6	8	1	2	2.5	.933										
3B	D. Wert	R	129	114	259	13	20	3.0	.966										
	T. Matchick	R	27	15	45	1	2	2.3	.984										
	I. Brown	R	12	10	16	2	0	2.3	.929										
	D. Tracewski	R	6	3	10	0	1	2.2	1.000										
	T. Tresh	R	1	1	3	1	0	5.0	.800										
	D. Campbell	R	1	0	1	0	0	1.0	1.000										

In May, booing at Tiger Stadium drove Willie Horton to go AWOL. In June, the Orioles were running away with the American League East. In July, scheduled All-Star Game starter Denny McLain showed up in the second inning. In August, pitching coach Johnny Sain quit. And by October, attendance had dropped 400,000 as the Tigers finished a distant second, 19 games out. The post–World Championship malaise was back.

There was some good news, mostly from the pitching staff, which led the league in complete games and in strikeouts and tied for the league lead in shutouts. McLain shared with Baltimore's Mike Cuellar his second straight Cy Young Award at 24–9 with a 2.80 ERA; he led the league in victories and the majors in shutouts (nine). Mickey Lolich totaled 19–11 and finished second in the league in strikeouts—twice striking out a team-record 16 in a game.

Nine Tigers finished in double figures in home runs, but for the second straight year no Tiger hit .300. Jim Northrup led at .295. After Horton had angrily disappeared for four days (the team in turn docked him $1360 in pay) in mid-May, he returned calm enough to lead the team in RBIs with 91 and home runs with 28.

McLain embroiled himself in the first of a series of celebrated controversies with his late arrival at the All-Star Game in Washington. When the gala salute to baseball's centennial was delayed a day by torrential rains, McLain took the opportunity to fly back to Detroit for dental work. When his starter didn't return in time, American League manager Mayo Smith substituted Yankees right-hander Mel Stottlemyre. By the time McLain got to the mound in the fourth, the National League had rolled up eight runs. McLain would soon start rolling up trouble.

TEAM STATISTICS

	W	L	PCT	GB	R	OR	Batting 2B	3B	HR	BA	SA	SB	Fielding E	DP	FA	CG	BB	Pitching SO	ShO	SV	ERA
ST																					
L	109	53	.673		779	517	234	29	175	.265	.414	82	101	145	.984	50	498	897	20	36	2.83
T	90	72	.556	19	701	601	188	29	182	.242	.387	35	130	130	.979	55	586	1032	20	28	3.32
S	87	75	.537	22	743	736	234	37	197	.251	.415	41	157	178	.975	30	685	935	7	41	3.93
S	86	76	.531	23	694	644	171	40	148	.251	.378	52	140	159	.978	28	656	835	10	41	3.49
	80	81	.497	28.5	562	587	210	44	94	.235	.344	119	131	158	.979	53	522	801	13	20	3.23
E	62	99	.385	46.5	573	717	173	24	119	.237	.345	85	145	153	.976	35	681	1000	7	22	3.94
ST																					
N	97	65	.599		790	618	246	32	163	.268	.408	115	150	177	.977	41	524	906	8	43	3.25
K	88	74	.543	9	740	678	210	28	148	.249	.376	100	137	162	.978	42	586	887	14	36	3.71
L	71	91	.438	26	528	652	151	29	88	.230	.319	54	136	164	.978	25	517	885	9	39	3.55
	69	93	.426	28	586	688	179	32	98	.240	.338	129	157	114	.975	42	560	894	10	25	3.72
I	68	94	.420	29	625	723	210	27	112	.247	.357	54	122	163	.981	29	564	810	10	25	4.21
A	64	98	.395	33	639	799	179	27	125	.234	.346	167	167	149	.974	21	653	963	6	33	4.35
GUE TOTAL					7960	7960	2385	378	1649	.246	.369	1033	1673	1852	.978	451	7032	10845	134	389	3.63

INDIVIDUAL PITCHING

CHER	T	W	L	PCT	ERA	SV	G	GS	CG	IP	H	BB	SO	R	ER	ShO	H/9	BB/9	SO/9
nny McLain	R	24	9	.727	2.80	0	42	41	23	325	288	67	181	105	101	9	7.98	1.86	5.01
key Lolich	L	19	11	.633	3.14	1	37	36	15	280.2	214	122	271	111	98	1	6.86	3.91	8.69
l Wilson	R	12	10	.545	3.31	0	35	35	5	214.2	209	69	150	93	79	1	8.76	2.89	6.29
ke Kilkenny	L	8	6	.571	3.37	2	39	15	6	128.1	99	63	97	54	48	4	6.94	4.42	6.80
: Dobson	R	5	10	.333	3.60	9	49	9	1	105	100	39	64	48	42	0	8.57	3.34	5.49
n Hiller	L	4	4	.500	3.99	4	40	8	1	99.1	97	44	74	50	44	1	8.79	3.99	6.70
e Sparma	R	6	8	.429	4.76	0	23	16	3	92.2	78	77	41	55	49	2	7.58	7.48	3.98
n Timmerman	R	4	3	.571	2.75	1	31	1	1	55.2	50	26	42	22	17	0	8.08	4.20	6.79
d Lasher	R	2	1	.667	3.07	0	32	0	0	44	34	22	26	16	15	0	6.95	4.50	5.32
n McMahon	R	3	5	.375	3.89	11	34	0	0	37	25	18	38	17	16	0	6.08	4.38	9.24
yl Patterson	R	0	2	.000	2.82	0	18	0	0	22.1	15	19	12	8	7	0	6.04	7.66	4.84
k Radatz	R	2	2	.500	3.38	0	11	0	0	18.2	14	5	18	8	7	0	6.75	2.41	8.68
o Reed	R	0	0	–	1.84	0	8	1	0	14.2	9	8	9	3	3	0	5.52	4.91	5.52
y Taylor	R	0	1	.000	5.23	0	7	0	0	10.1	10	6	3	6	6	0	8.71	5.23	2.61
d Scherman	L	1	0	1.000	6.75	0	4	0	0	4	6	0	3	3	3	0	13.50	0.00	6.75
rm McRae	R	0	0	–	6.00	0	3	0	0	3	2	1	3	2	2	0	6.00	3.00	9.00
AM TOTAL		90	72	.556	3.32	28	413	162	55	1455.1	1250	586	1032	601	537	18	7.73	3.62	6.38

MANAGER	W	L	PCT
Mayo Smith	79	83	.488

POS	Player	B	G	AB	H	2B	3B	HR	HR %	R	RBI	BB	SO	SB	Pinch Hit AB	Pinch Hit H	BA	SA
REGULARS																		
1B	Norm Cash	L	130	370	96	18	2	15	4.1	58	53	72	58	0	17	6	.259	.441
2B	Dick McAuliffe	L	146	530	124	21	1	12	2.3	73	50	101	62	5	8	0	.234	.345
SS	Cesar Gutierrez	R	135	415	101	11	6	0	0.0	40	22	18	39	4	0	0	.243	.299
3B	Don Wert	R	128	363	79	13	0	6	1.7	34	33	44	56	1	15	2	.218	.303
RF	Al Kaline	R	131	467	130	24	4	16	3.4	64	71	77	49	2	3	0	.278	.450
CF	Mickey Stanley	R	142	568	143	21	11	13	2.3	83	47	45	56	10	5	2	.252	.396
LF	Jim Northrup	L	139	504	132	21	3	24	4.8	71	80	58	68	3	3	1	.262	.458
C	Bill Freehan	R	117	395	95	17	3	16	4.1	44	52	52	48	0	3	1	.241	.420
SUBSTITUTES																		
UT	Elliott Maddox	R	109	258	64	13	4	3	1.2	30	24	30	42	2	20	2	.248	.364
UT	Dalton Jones	L	89	191	42	7	0	6	3.1	29	21	33	33	1	29	11	.220	.351
2B	Ike Brown	R	56	94	27	5	0	4	4.3	17	15	13	26	0	21	7	.287	.468
SS	Ken Szotkiewicz	L	47	84	9	1	0	3	3.6	9	9	12	29	0	3	0	.107	.226
1B	Kevin Collins	L	25	24	5	1	0	1	4.2	2	3	1	10	0	21	4	.208	.375
OF	Willie Horton	R	96	371	113	18	2	17	4.6	53	69	28	43	0	0	0	.305	.501
OF	Gates Brown	L	81	124	28	3	0	3	2.4	18	24	20	14	0	41	10	.226	.323
OF	Rusty Nagelson	L	28	32	6	0	0	0	0.0	5	2	5	6	0	20	5	.188	.188
C	Jim Price	R	52	132	24	4	0	5	3.8	12	15	21	23	0	12	1	.182	.326
C	Gene Lamont	L	15	44	13	3	1	1	2.3	3	4	2	9	0	0	0	.295	.477
C	Tim Hosley	R	7	12	2	0	0	1	8.3	1	2	0	6	0	4	1	.167	.417
PITCHERS																		
P	Mickey Lolich	B	42	82	11	0	0	0	0.0	4	3	12	29	1	0	0	.134	.134
P	Les Cain	L	29	68	11	1	0	1	1.5	2	9	1	18	0	0	0	.162	.221
P	Joe Niekro	R	39	66	13	3	1	0	0.0	8	7	7	17	0	1	1	.197	.273
P	Mike Kilkenny	R	37	39	3	0	0	0	0.0	0	1	0	19	0	0	0	.077	.077
P	Denny McLain	R	14	31	2	1	0	0	0.0	2	0	0	13	0	0	0	.065	.097
P	Earl Wilson	R	18	31	6	1	0	1	3.2	2	3	2	16	0	0	0	.194	.323
P	John Hiller	R	47	23	0	0	0	0	0.0	0	0	1	9	0	0	0	.000	.000
P	Tom Timmerman	R	61	16	0	0	0	0	0.0	0	0	0	9	0	0	0	.000	.000
P	Fred Scherman	L	48	12	2	0	0	0	0.0	1	0	0	1	0	0	0	.167	.167
P	Bob Reed	R	17	12	1	0	0	0	0.0	1	0	1	4	0	0	0	.083	.083
P	Daryl Patterson	L	43	11	0	0	0	0	0.0	0	0	0	9	0	0	0	.000	.000
P	Dennis Saunders	B	8	5	0	0	0	0	0.0	0	0	0	3	0	0	0	.000	.000
P	Fred Lasher	R	12	1	0	0	0	0	0.0	0	0	0	1	0	0	0	.000	.000
P	Norm McRae	R	19	1	0	0	0	0	0.0	0	0	0	0	0	0	0	.000	.000
P	Lerrin LaGrow	R	10	1	0	0	0	0	0.0	0	0	0	0	0	0	0	.000	.000
P	Jerry Robertson	R	11	0	0	0	0	0	–	0	0	0	0	0	0	0	–	–
	TEAM TOTAL			5377	1282	207	38	148	2.8	666	619	656	825	29	226	54	.238	.374

INDIVIDUAL FIELDING

POS	Player	T	G	PO	A	E	DP	TC/G	FA
1B	N. Cash	L	114	868	70	10	76	8.3	.989
	A. Kaline	R	52	374	31	4	39	7.9	.990
	M. Stanley	R	9	67	6	1	10	8.2	.986
	D. Jones	R	10	43	4	0	4	4.7	1.000
	K. Collins	R	1	5	1	0	0	6.0	1.000
	R. Nagelson	R	1	4	0	0	0	4.0	1.000
2B	D. McAuliffe	R	127	280	333	16	75	5.0	.975
	D. Jones	R	35	59	70	2	18	3.7	.985
	I. Brown	R	23	41	31	5	8	3.3	.935
	E. Maddox	R	1	2	1	0	1	3.0	1.000
	D. Wert	R	2	1	2	0	0	1.5	1.000
SS	C. Gutierrez	R	135	183	326	23	60	3.9	.957
	Szotkiewicz	R	44	32	101	4	20	3.1	.971
	D. McAuliffe	R	15	16	34	3	3	3.5	.943
	E. Maddox	R	19	6	14	2	0	1.2	.909
3B	D. Wert	R	117	94	191	14	20	2.6	.953
	E. Maddox	R	40	41	83	11	8	3.4	.919
	D. Jones	R	18	9	25	2	4	2.0	.944
	D. McAuliffe	R	12	3	24	2	5	2.4	.931
	I. Brown	R	1	1	2	2	0	5.0	.600

POS	Player	T	G	PO	A	E	DP	TC/G	FA
OF	M. Stanley	R	132	317	3	0	0	2.4	**1.000**
	J. Northrup	R	136	284	4	2	1	2.1	.993
	W. Horton	R	96	154	10	3	1	1.7	.982
	A. Kaline	R	91	156	3	2	1	1.8	.988
	E. Maddox	R	37	55	2	1	1	1.6	.983
	G. Brown	R	26	37	1	2	0	1.5	.950
	I. Brown	R	4	7	0	1	0	2.0	.875
	R. Nagelson	R	4	5	0	0	0	1.3	1.000
C	B. Freehan	R	114	742	42	2	6	6.9	**.997**
	J. Price	R	38	266	8	6	2	7.4	.979
	G. Lamont	R	15	87	8	0	0	6.3	1.000
	T. Hosley	R	4	22	3	0	0	6.3	1.000

Denny McLain led the majors—in trouble. Having compiled a 55–15 mark over the previous two seasons, he embarked on his celebrated slide with fervor. First he was suspended by baseball Commissioner Bowie Kuhn in February for alleged participation in a Michigan bookmaking operation in 1967. Less than two months later, McLain was suspended a week by Tigers general manager Jim Campbell for dousing two sportswriters with a bucket of ice water. And when McLain was due to return the first week of September, Kuhn suspended him a third time for carrying a gun and allegedly brandishing it in a Chicago restaurant. Between suspensions, McLain—who had also suffered tendinitis in his pitching arm since 1968—went 3–5 with a 4.65 ERA. Then on the eve of the World Series, Detroit finally washed away its troubles, shipping McLain to the Senators.

Other Detroit pitchers, in effect, took much of the summer off, too. The staff's 4.09 ERA was the team's worst in 20 years. Glimmers of encouragement came from reliever Tom Timmerman, who won six and tied for third in the league in saves with 27; bullpen colleague Daryl Patterson, who won seven straight to finish 7–1; and John Hiller, who struck out seven straight to tie McLain's record (set in 1965). The hitting proved equally discouraging. Tied with Washington for league-worst batting average at .238, Detroit for the third straight year didn't have a .300-hitting regular. Al Kaline led regulars at .278; Willie Horton hit .305 before incurring an ankle injury in late July that sidelined him for the season; shortstop Cesar Gutierrez hit just .243, but did set a major-league record with a 7-for-7 performance on June 21 against Cleveland.

Thus the Tigers fell below .500 for the first time in seven years at 79–83, tumbling to fourth place, 29 games out. And after the season Mayo Smith was fired. He'd be replaced by former Tigers infielder and Twins manager Billy Martin. "I am the leader," Martin would tell his new team on opening day of the following spring training. "And I am a very, very bad loser."

TEAM STATISTICS

W	L	PCT	GB	R	OR	2B	3B	HR	BA	SA	SB	E	DP	FA	CG	BB	SO	ShO	SV	ERA
108	54	.667		792	574	213	25	179	.257	.401	84	117	148	.981	60	469	941	12	31	**3.15**
93	69	.574	15	680	612	208	41	111	.251	.365	105	130	146	.980	36	**451**	777	6	49	3.25
87	75	.537	21	786	722	**252**	28	**203**	.262	**.428**	50	156	131	.974	38	594	1003	8	44	3.90
79	83	.488	29	666	731	207	38	148	.238	.374	29	133	142	.978	33	623	1045	9	39	4.09
76	86	.469	32	649	675	197	23	183	.249	.394	25	133	168	.979	34	689	**1076**	8	35	3.91
70	92	.432	38	626	689	184	28	138	.238	.358	72	**116**	173	**.982**	20	611	823	11	40	3.80
98	64	.605		744	605	230	41	153	**.262**	.403	57	123	130	.980	26	486	940	12	**58**	3.23
89	73	.549	9	678	593	208	24	171	.249	.392	131	141	152	.977	33	542	858	15	40	3.30
86	76	.531	12	631	630	197	40	114	.251	.363	69	127	169	.980	21	559	922	10	49	3.48
65	97	.401	33	611	705	202	41	97	.244	.348	97	152	162	.976	30	641	915	11	25	3.78
65	97	.401	33	613	751	202	24	126	.242	.358	91	136	142	.978	31	587	895	2	27	4.20
56	106	.346	42	633	822	192	20	123	.253	.362	54	165	**187**	.975	20	556	762	6	30	4.54
GUE TOTAL				8109	8109	2492	373	1746	.250	.379	864	1629	1850	.978	382	6808	10957	110	467	3.72

INDIVIDUAL PITCHING

CHER	T	W	L	PCT	ERA	SV	G	GS	CG	IP	H	BB	SO	R	ER	ShO	H/9	BB/9	SO/9
key Lolich	L	14	19	.424	3.79	0	40	39	13	273	272	109	230	125	115	3	8.97	3.59	7.58
Niekro	R	12	13	.480	4.06	0	38	34	6	213	221	72	101	107	96	2	9.34	3.04	4.27
Cain	L	12	7	.632	3.83	0	29	29	5	181	167	98	156	92	77	0	8.30	4.87	7.76
e Kilkenny	L	7	6	.538	5.16	0	36	21	3	129	141	70	105	77	74	0	9.84	4.88	7.33
n Hiller	L	6	6	.500	3.03	3	47	5	1	104	82	46	89	39	35	1	7.10	3.98	7.70
Wilson	R	4	6	.400	4.41	0	18	16	4	96	87	32	74	53	47	1	8.16	3.00	6.94
ny McLain	R	3	5	.375	4.65	0	14	14	1	91	100	28	52	51	47	0	9.89	2.77	5.14
n Timmerman	R	6	7	.462	4.13	27	61	0	0	85	90	34	49	44	39	0	9.53	3.60	5.19
yl Patterson	R	7	1	.875	4.85	2	43	0	0	78	81	39	55	47	42	0	9.35	4.50	6.35
d Scherman	L	4	4	.500	3.21	1	48	0	0	70	61	28	58	28	25	0	7.84	3.60	7.46
Reed	R	2	4	.333	4.89	2	16	4	0	46	54	14	26	25	25	0	10.57	2.74	5.09
m McRae	R	0	0	—	2.90	0	19	0	0	31	26	25	16	13	10	0	7.55	7.26	4.65
y Robertson	R	0	0	—	3.60	0	11	0	0	15	19	5	11	8	6	0	11.40	3.00	6.60
nis Saunders	R	1	1	.500	3.21	1	8	0	0	14	16	5	8	5	5	0	10.29	3.21	5.14
in LaGrow	R	0	1	.000	7.50	0	10	0	0	12	16	6	7	11	10	0	12.00	4.50	5.25
d Lasher	R	1	3	.250	5.00	3	12	0	0	9	10	12	8	6	5	0	10.00	12.00	8.00
M TOTAL		79	83	.488	4.09	39	450	162	33	1447	1443	623	1045	731	658	7	8.98	3.87	6.50

MANAGER	W	L	PCT
Billy Martin	91	71	.562

POS	Player	B	G	AB	H	2B	3B	HR	HR %	R	RBI	BB	SO	SB	Pinch Hit AB	Pinch Hit H	BA	SA
REGULARS																		
1B	Norm Cash	L	135	452	128	10	3	32	7.1	72	91	59	86	1	7	1	.283	.531
2B	Dick McAuliffe	L	128	477	99	16	6	18	3.8	67	57	53	67	4	4	2	.208	.379
SS	Ed Brinkman	R	159	527	120	18	2	1	0.2	40	37	44	54	1	0	0	.228	.275
3B	Aurelio Rodriguez	R	154	604	153	30	7	15	2.5	68	39	27	93	4	3	1	.253	.401
RF	Al Kaline	R	133	405	119	19	2	15	3.7	69	54	82	57	4	12	3	.294	.462
CF	Mickey Stanley	R	139	401	117	14	5	7	1.7	43	41	24	44	1	6	3	.292	.404
LF	Willie Horton	R	119	450	130	25	1	22	4.9	64	72	37	75	1	2	0	.289	.496
C	Bill Freehan	R	148	516	143	26	4	21	4.1	57	71	54	48	2	4	1	.277	.465
SUBSTITUTES																		
2B	Tony Taylor	R	55	181	52	10	2	3	1.7	27	19	12	11	5	9	4	.287	.414
UT	Ike Brown	R	59	110	28	1	0	8	7.3	20	19	19	25	0	19	6	.255	.482
UT	Kevin Collins	L	35	41	11	2	1	1	2.4	6	4	0	12	0	31	9	.268	.439
S3	Cesar Gutierrez	R	38	37	7	0	0	0	0.0	8	4	0	3	0	9	3	.189	.189
1B	John Young	L	2	4	2	1	0	0	0.0	1	1	0	0	0	1	0	.500	.750
O1	Jim Northrup	L	136	459	124	27	2	16	3.5	72	71	60	43	7	14	5	.270	.442
OF	Gates Brown	L	82	195	66	2	3	11	5.6	37	29	21	17	4	26	9	.338	.549
UT	Dalton Jones	L	83	138	35	5	0	5	3.6	15	11	9	21	1	45	13	.254	.399
OF	Marv Lane	R	8	14	2	0	0	0	0.0	0	1	1	3	0	2	0	.143	.143
C	Jim Price	R	29	54	13	2	0	1	1.9	4	7	6	3	0	2	0	.241	.333
C	Tim Hosley	R	7	16	3	0	0	2	12.5	2	6	0	1	0	4	0	.188	.563
C	Gene Lamont	L	7	15	1	0	0	0	0.0	2	1	0	5	0	0	0	.067	.067
PITCHERS																		
P	Mickey Lolich	B	45	115	15	2	0	0	0.0	9	7	16	55	0	0	0	.130	.148
P	Joe Coleman	R	39	96	9	2	0	0	0.0	1	2	6	39	0	0	0	.094	.115
P	Les Cain	L	27	55	8	1	0	1	1.8	7	2	1	23	0	1	0	.145	.218
P	Joe Niekro	R	32	30	4	1	0	0	0.0	5	2	2	9	0	0	0	.133	.167
P	Mike Kilkenny	R	30	24	2	0	0	0	0.0	0	0	0	14	0	0	0	.083	.083
P	Fred Scherman	L	69	24	5	0	0	0	0.0	3	4	3	9	0	0	0	.208	.208
P	Dean Chance	R	31	21	0	0	0	0	0.0	0	0	0	16	0	0	0	.000	.000
P	Tom Timmerman	R	52	19	1	0	0	0	0.0	2	0	1	11	0	0	0	.053	.053
P	Bill Gilbreth	L	9	11	2	0	0	0	0.0	0	0	0	7	0	0	0	.182	.182
P	Bill Zepp	R	16	4	0	0	0	0	0.0	0	0	0	2	0	0	0	.000	.000
P	Jim Hannan	R	7	2	0	0	0	0	0.0	0	0	0	0	0	0	0	.000	.000
P	Ron Perranoski	L	11	2	0	0	0	0	0.0	0	0	0	1	0	0	0	.000	.000
P	Bill Denehy	R	31	2	0	0	0	0	0.0	0	0	3	0	0	0	0	.000	.000
P	Jack Whillock	R	7	1	0	0	0	0	0.0	0	0	0	0	0	0	0	.000	.000
P	Dave Boswell	R	3	0	0	0	0	0	–	0	0	0	0	0	0	0	–	–
P	Daryl Patterson	L	12	0	0	0	0	0	–	0	0	0	0	0	0	0	–	–
P	Jim Foor	L	3	0	0	0	0	0	–	0	0	0	0	0	0	0	–	–
P	Chuck Seelbach	R	5	0	0	0	0	0	0.0	0	0	0	0	0	0	0	–	–
TEAM TOTAL				5502	1399	214	38	179	3.3	701	652	540	854	35	201	60	.254	.405

INDIVIDUAL FIELDING

POS	Player	T	G	PO	A	E	DP	TC/G	FA
1B	N. Cash	L	131	1020	75	9	105	8.4	.992
	J. Northrup	R	32	236	16	5	23	8.0	.981
	I. Brown	R	17	104	7	0	5	6.5	1.000
	A. Kaline	R	5	27	1	0	3	5.6	1.000
	J. Young	L	1	7	0	0	0	7.0	1.000
	T. Hosley	R	1	5	0	0	0	5.0	1.000
	D. Jones	R	3	4	0	0	0	1.3	1.000
2B	D. McAuliffe	R	123	322	308	8	86	5.2	.987
	T. Taylor	R	51	114	107	1	29	4.4	.995
	I. Brown	R	8	12	13	1	3	3.3	.962
	C. Gutierrez	R	2	2	1	0	1	1.5	1.000
	K. Collins	R	1	1	1	0	0	2.0	1.000
	D. Jones	R	1	0	1	0	0	1.0	1.000
SS	E. Brinkman	R	159	235	513	15	91	4.8	.980
	C. Gutierrez	R	14	11	22	1	2	2.4	.971
	D. McAuliffe	R	7	4	2	0	1	0.9	1.000
	A. Rodriguez	R	1	1	3	0	2	4.0	1.000
	I. Brown	R	1	1	1	0	0	2.0	1.000
3B	A. Rodriguez	R	153	127	341	23	33	3.2	.953
	D. Jones	R	13	4	16	2	2	1.7	.909
	I. Brown	R	4	6	6	1	2	3.3	.923
	K. Collins	R	4	1	5	0	0	1.5	1.000
	C. Gutierrez	R	5	1	3	0	1	0.8	1.000
	T. Taylor	R	3	1	2	0	0	1.0	1.000

POS	Player	T	G	PO	A	E	DP	TC/G	FA
OF	M. Stanley	R	139	315	10	4	3	2.4	.988
	J. Northrup	R	108	205	4	4	0	2.0	.981
	A. Kaline	R	129	207	6	0	0	1.7	1.000
	W. Horton	R	118	176	8	7	1	1.6	.963
	G. Brown	R	56	68	2	1	0	1.3	.986
	D. Jones	R	16	17	0	0	0	1.1	1.000
	B. Freehan	R	1	0	0	0	0	0.0	.000
	I. Brown	R	9	10	0	1	0	1.2	.909
	M. Lane	R	6	6	0	0	0	1.0	1.000
	K. Collins	R	2	3	0	0	0	1.5	1.000
C	B. Freehan	R	144	912	50	4	6	6.7	.996
	J. Price	R	25	99	7	2	2	4.3	.952
	G. Lamont	R	7	38	2	2	0	6.0	.952
	T. Hosley	R	4	21	0	0	0	5.3	1.000

Billy Martin immediately established Detroit's first priority: catch the World Champion Orioles. "Get your hellos over with fast," Martin told his charges during the season's first trip to Baltimore. "Then don't say anything to them. We've got a job to do against this club." And when the Tigers trailed the Orioles by seven-and-a-half games at the All-Star break, Detroit's fiery new manager didn't let up. "The world is full of quitters—people looking for the easy way out," he said. "Let's play so we can be proud of the name Detroit across our chests." By September the Tigers charged the Orioles, beating them five straight before Baltimore regrouped to win 11 in a row and finish first. Detroit ended a dozen games back in second.

The Tigers' inspired pursuit was led by Mickey Lolich. Replacing departed Denny McLain as staff leader, Lolich went from the league's losingest pitcher the previous year to the winningest at 25–14 with a 2.92 ERA. The portly left-hander led the league in complete games with 29 (most in the AL since 1946), set a still-standing team record with 308 strikeouts, notched two 14-strikeout games, won six straight in midseason and finished second in the Cy Young balloting. Detroit led the league in home runs. But for the fourth straight year no Tiger hit .300. At age 36, first baseman Norm Cash won his second American League Comeback Player of Year Award with .283 (a 24-point improvement) and 32 home runs. Catcher Bill Freehan rebounded from spinal surgery and hit .277 with 21 home runs. Kaline fielded 1.000 in right field, and shortstop Ed Brinkman and third baseman Aurelio Rodriguez solidified the infield's left side as the Tigers led the league in fielding and the majors in fewest errors.

TEAM STATISTICS

	W	L	PCT	GB	R	OR	2B	3B	HR	BA	SA	SB	E	DP	FA	CG	BB	SO	ShO	SV	ERA
ST																					
L	101	57	.639		742	530	207	25	158	.261	.398	66	112	148	.981	71	416	793	15	22	3.00
T	91	71	.562	12	701	645	214	38	179	.254	.405	35	106	156	.983	53	609	1000	11	32	3.64
S	85	77	.525	18	691	667	246	28	161	.252	.397	51	116	149	.981	44	535	871	11	35	3.83
'	82	80	.506	21	648	641	195	43	97	.254	.360	75	125	159	.981	67	423	707	15	12	3.45
S	63	96	.396	38.5	537	660	189	30	86	.230	.326	68	141	170	.977	30	554	762	10	26	3.70
E	60	102	.370	43	543	747	200	20	109	.238	.342	57	116	159	.981	21	770	937	7	32	4.28
ST																					
K	101	60	.627		691	564	195	25	160	.252	.384	80	117	157	.981	57	501	999	18	36	3.06
	85	76	.528	16	603	566	225	40	80	.250	.353	130	134	178	.978	34	496	775	15	44	3.25
I	79	83	.488	22.5	617	597	185	30	138	.250	.373	83	160	128	.975	46	468	976	19	32	3.13
L	76	86	.469	25.5	511	576	213	18	96	.231	.329	72	131	159	.980	39	607	904	11	32	3.10
N	74	86	.463	26.5	654	670	197	31	116	.260	.372	66	118	134	.980	43	529	895	9	25	3.82
L	69	92	.429	32	534	609	160	23	104	.229	.329	82	138	152	.977	32	569	795	23	32	3.38
AGUE TOTAL					7472	7472	2426	351	1484	.247	.364	865	1514	1849	.980	537	6477	10414	164	360	3.47

INDIVIDUAL PITCHING

TCHER	T	W	L	PCT	ERA	SV	G	GS	CG	IP	H	BB	SO	R	ER	ShO	H/9	BB/9	SO/9
ckey Lolich	L	25	14	.641	2.92	0	45	45	29	376	336	92	308	133	122	4	8.04	2.20	7.37
e Coleman	R	20	9	.690	3.15	0	39	38	16	286	241	96	100	106	100	3	7.58	3.02	7.43
s Cain	L	10	9	.526	4.34	0	26	26	3	145	121	91	118	77	70	1	7.51	5.65	7.32
e Niekro	R	6	7	.462	4.50	1	31	15	0	122	136	49	43	62	61	0	10.03	3.61	3.17
ed Scherman	L	11	6	.647	2.71	20	69	1	1	113	91	49	46	38	34	0	7.25	3.90	3.66
an Chance	R	4	6	.400	3.50	0	31	14	0	90	91	50	64	43	35	0	9.10	5.00	6.40
ke Kilkenny	L	4	5	.444	5.02	1	30	11	2	86	83	44	47	52	48	0	8.69	4.60	4.92
m Timmerman	R	7	6	.538	3.86	4	52	2	0	84	82	37	51	36	36	0	8.79	3.96	5.46
Denehy	R	0	3	.000	4.22	1	31	1	0	49	47	28	27	25	23	0	8.63	5.14	4.96
Zepp	R	1	1	.500	5.06	2	16	4	0	32	41	17	15	20	18	0	11.53	4.78	4.22
Gilbreth	L	2	1	.667	4.80	0	9	5	2	30	28	21	14	17	16	0	8.40	6.30	4.20
n Perranoski	L	0	1	.000	2.50	2	11	0	0	18	16	3	8	9	5	0	8.00	1.50	4.00
n Hannan	R	1	0	1.000	3.27	0	7	0	0	11	7	7	6	4	4	0	5.73	5.73	4.91
ryl Patterson	R	0	1	.000	4.82	0	12	0	0	9.1	6	6	5	7	5	0	13.50	5.79	4.82
ck Whillock	R	0	2	.000	5.63	1	7	0	0	8	10	2	6	5	5	0	11.25	2.25	6.75
ve Boswell	R	0	0	–	6.23	0	3	0	0	4.1	3	6	3	3	3	0	6.23	12.46	6.23
uck Seelbach	R	0	0	–	13.50	0	5	0	0	4	6	7	1	6	6	0	13.50	15.75	2.25
n Foor	L	0	0	–	18.00	0	3	0	0	1	2	4	2	2	2	0	18.00	36.00	18.00
AM TOTAL		91	71	.562	3.63	32	427	162	53	1468.2	1355	609	1000	645	593	8	8.30	3.73	6.13

MANAGER	W	L	PCT
Billy Martin	86	70	.551

POS	Player	B	G	AB	H	2B	3B	HR	HR %	R	RBI	BB	SO	SB	Pinch Hit AB	Pinch Hit H	BA	SA
REGULARS																		
1B	Norm Cash	L	137	440	114	16	0	22	5.0	51	61	50	64	0	11	0	.259	.445
2B	Dick McAuliffe	L	122	408	98	16	3	8	2.0	47	30	59	59	0	8	0	.240	.353
SS	Ed Brinkman	R	156	516	105	19	1	6	1.2	42	49	38	51	0	0	0	.203	.279
3B	Aurelio Rodriguez	R	153	601	142	23	5	13	2.2	65	56	28	104	2	1	0	.236	.356
RF	Jim Northrup	L	134	426	111	15	2	8	1.9	40	42	38	47	4	14	2	.261	.362
CF	Mickey Stanley	R	142	435	102	16	6	14	3.2	45	55	29	49	1	5	3	.234	.395
LF	Willie Horton	R	108	333	77	9	5	11	3.3	44	36	27	47	0	12	1	.231	.387
C	Bill Freehan	R	111	374	98	18	2	10	2.7	51	56	48	51	0	8	3	.262	.401
SUBSTITUTES																		
2B	Tony Taylor	R	78	228	69	12	4	1	0.4	33	20	14	34	5	20	6	.303	.404
1O	Paul Jata	R	32	74	17	2	0	0	0.0	8	3	7	14	0	12	4	.230	.257
1B	Frank Howard	R	14	33	8	1	0	1	3.0	1	7	4	8	0	5	1	.242	.364
2B	John Knox	L	14	13	1	1	0	0	0.0	1	0	1	2	0	9	1	.077	.154
SS	John Gamble	R	6	3	0	0	0	0	0.0	0	0	0	0	0	1	0	.000	.000
1B	Joe Staton	L	6	2	0	0	0	0	0.0	1	0	0	1	0	0	0	.000	.000
OF	Al Kaline	R	106	278	87	11	2	10	3.6	46	32	28	33	1	24	10	.313	.475
OF	Gates Brown	L	103	252	58	5	0	10	4.0	33	31	26	28	3	28	4	.230	.369
UT	Ike Brown	R	51	84	21	3	0	2	2.4	12	10	17	23	1	12	1	.250	.357
OF	Wayne Comer	R	27	9	1	0	0	0	0.0	1	1	0	1	0	6	1	.111	.111
OF	Marv Lane	R	8	6	0	0	0	0	0.0	2	0	0	2	0	1	0	.000	.000
OF	Ike Blessitt	R	4	5	0	0	0	0	0.0	0	0	0	2	0	3	0	.000	.000
C	Tom Haller	L	59	121	25	5	2	2	1.7	7	13	15	14	0	20	2	.207	.331
C	Duke Sims	L	38	98	31	4	0	4	4.1	11	19	19	18	0	6	1	.316	.480
C	Gene Lamont	L	1	0	0	0	0	0	–	0	0	0	0	0	0	0	–	–
PH	Dalton Jones	L	7	7	0	0	0	0	0.0	0	0	0	2	0	7	0	.000	.000
PITCHERS																		
P	Mickey Lolich	B	41	89	6	0	0	0	0.0	3	0	20	39	0	0	0	.067	.067
P	Joe Coleman	R	40	82	9	0	0	0	0.0	5	5	5	30	0	0	0	.110	.110
P	Tom Timmerman	R	35	44	6	0	0	0	0.0	3	1	3	25	0	0	0	.136	.136
P	Woodie Fryman	R	16	40	5	0	0	0	0.0	0	3	0	7	0	0	0	.125	.125
P	Bill Slayback	R	23	23	4	0	0	0	0.0	1	0	0	6	0	0	0	.174	.174
P	Fred Scherman	L	57	22	2	0	0	0	0.0	1	0	1	8	0	0	0	.091	.091
P	Chuck Seelbach	R	61	21	3	2	0	0	0.0	1	0	4	11	0	0	0	.143	.238
P	Joe Niekro	R	18	12	3	1	0	0	0.0	2	1	1	4	0	0	0	.250	.333
P	Les Cain	L	5	7	1	0	0	0	0.0	0	0	2	0	0	0	0	.143	.143
P	John Hiller	R	24	4	0	0	0	0	0.0	0	0	0	3	0	0	0	.000	.000
P	Fred Holdsworth	R	2	3	1	0	0	0	0.0	1	0	0	1	0	0	0	.333	.333
P	Chris Zachary	L	25	2	1	0	0	0	0.0	0	0	1	1	0	0	0	.500	.500
P	Phil Meeler	R	7	2	0	0	0	0	0.0	0	0	0	2	0	0	0	.000	.000
P	Ron Perranoski	L	17	1	0	0	0	0	0.0	0	0	0	0	0	0	0	.000	.000
P	Bill Gilbreth	L	2	1	0	0	0	0	0.0	0	0	0	0	0	0	0	.000	.000
P	Mike Kilkenny	R	1	0	0	0	0	0	–	0	0	0	0	0	0	0	–	–
P	Jim Foor	L	7	0	0	0	0	0	–	0	0	0	0	0	0	0	–	–
P	Lerrin LaGrow	R	16	0	0	0	0	0	–	0	0	0	0	0	0	0	–	–
P	Don Leshnock	R	1	0	0	0	0	0	–	0	0	0	0	0	0	0	–	–
P	Bob Strampe	B	7	0	0	0	0	0	–	0	0	0	0	0	0	0	–	–
	TEAM TOTAL			5099	1206	179	32	122	2.4	558	531	483	793	17	213	40	.237	.356

INDIVIDUAL FIELDING

POS	Player	T	G	PO	A	E	DP	TC/G	FA	POS	Player	T	G	PO	A	E	DP	TC/G	FA
1B	N. Cash	L	134	1060	70	8	102	8.5	.993	OF	M. Stanley	R	139	309	9	2	1	2.3	.994
	P. Jata	R	12	100	6	1	6	8.9	.991		J. Northrup	R	127	215	8	5	2	1.8	.978
	I. Brown	R	13	70	2	0	5	5.5	1.000		W. Horton	R	98	131	6	0	0	1.4	1.000
	F. Howard	R	10	54	5	3	5	6.2	.952		G. Brown	R	72	122	5	3	1	1.8	.977
	A. Kaline	R	11	37	4	0	3	3.7	1.000		A. Kaline	R	84	111	5	1	0	1.4	.991
	J. Northrup	R	2	9	1	0	0	5.0	1.000		I. Brown	R	22	43	1	0	0	2.0	1.000
	B. Freehan	R	1	6	3	0	0	9.0	1.000		W. Comer	R	17	5	0	0	0	0.3	1.000
	J. Staton	L	2	5	0	0	0	2.5	1.000		P. Jata	R	10	16	0	0	0	1.6	1.000
	T. Taylor	R	1	4	0	0	0	4.0	1.000		D. Sims	R	4	6	0	2	0	2.0	.750
2B	D. McAuliffe	R	116	266	249	13	63	4.6	.975		M. Lane	R	3	3	0	0	0	1.0	1.000
	T. Taylor	R	67	121	108	8	25	3.5	.966		I. Blessitt	R	1	2	0	0	0	2.0	1.000
	I. Brown	R	3	7	6	0	1	4.3	1.000		F. Howard	R	1	1	0	0	0	1.0	1.000
	J. Knox	R	4	3	10	0	3	3.3	1.000										
SS	E. Brinkman	R	156	233	495	7	81	4.7	**.990**	C	B. Freehan	R	105	648	57	8	9	6.8	.989
	J. Gamble	R	1	3	2	0	0	5.0	1.000		T. Haller	R	36	220	15	0	1	6.5	1.000
	A. Rodriguez	R	2	0	2	1	1	1.5	.667		D. Sims	R	25	145	10	1	1	6.2	.994
	D. McAuliffe	R	3	1	2	0	0	1.0	1.000		P. Jata	R	1	0	0	0	0	0.0	.000
	I. Brown	R	1	1	1	0	1	2.0	1.000		G. Lamont	R	1	1	0	0	0	1.0	1.000
3B	A. Rodriguez	R	153	**150**	348	16	33	**3.4**	.969										
	D. McAuliffe	R	1	0	0	0	0	0.0	.000										
	T. Taylor	R	8	5	14	0	1	2.4	1.000										
	I. Brown	R	1	1	1	1	0	3.0	.667										

The Tigers and the Red Sox concluded baseball's first strike-shortened schedule with a pennant-deciding three-game series at Tiger Stadium. Boston came to Motown in first place by a half game, but left with a winter's worth of frustration: Detroit clinched the AL East title by winning the first two games; the Red Sox won the third to finish a half game behind (the strike had left the schedule uneven).

Detroit secured its first trip to an American League Championship Series via impressive pitching, crafty managing, and tight defense. The staff ERA was 2.96; Mickey Lolich recorded his second straight 20-victory season at 22–14. The Tigers again led the league in fielding and the majors in fewest errors as shortstop Ed Brinkman played 72 straight games without an error and committed just seven all season—both still major-league records—to win the Gold Glove. And 37-year-old Al Kaline extended his errorless string to 242 (spread over three seasons) before erring. Detroit clearly couldn't afford to give away runs; as a team, the Tigers hit .237. For the fifth straight year no Detroit regular hit .300, although part-timer Kaline, hobbled by a knee injury through most of the year, rallied in the September stretch to hit .313 (his best since 1961). During one offensive lull, manager Billy Martin resorted to picking his lineup out of a hat. And with .203-hitting Brinkman batting cleanup, the Tigers won.

In the ALCS, the A's captured the first two games from the Tigers in Oakland. In Game 2 when a pitch from Detroit reliever Lerrin LaGrow hit A's shortstop Bert Campaneris on the ankle, Campaneris responded by flinging his bat at LaGrow, and both benches cleared. Three umpires restrained Martin from getting at Campaneris, who was fined $500 and suspended for the rest of the playoffs. The Tigers proceeded to win the next two in Detroit, but lost decisive Game 5 at Tiger Stadium. "We got beat by an umpire's bad call in the final game," said Martin. "But it was a pretty damn good year."

TEAM STATISTICS

W	L	PCT	GB	R	OR	Batting						Fielding			Pitching					
						2B	3B	HR	BA	SA	SB	E	DP	FA	CG	BB	SO	ShO	SV	ERA
ST																				
86	70	.551		558	514	179	32	122	.237	.356	17	96	137	.984	46	465	952	11	33	2.96
85	70	.548	0.5	640	620	229	34	124	.248	.376	66	130	141	.978	48	512	918	20	25	3.47
80	74	.519	5	519	430	193	29	100	.229	.339	78	100	150	.983	62	395	788	20	21	2.54
79	76	.510	6.5	557	527	201	24	103	.249	.357	71	134	179	.978	35	419	625	19	39	3.05
72	84	.462	14	472	519	187	18	91	.234	.330	49	116	157	.981	47	534	846	13	25	2.97
65	91	.417	21	493	595	167	22	88	.235	.328	64	139	145	.977	37	486	740	14	32	3.45
ST																				
93	62	.600		604	457	195	29	134	.240	.366	87	130	146	.979	42	418	862	23	43	2.58
87	67	.565	5.5	566	538	170	28	108	.238	.346	100	135	136	.977	36	431	936	14	42	3.12
77	77	.500	15.5	537	535	182	31	93	.244	.344	53	159	133	.974	37	444	838	17	34	2.86
76	78	.494	16.5	580	545	220	26	78	.255	.353	85	120	164	.980	44	405	801	16	28	3.24
75	80	.484	18	454	533	171	26	78	.242	.330	57	114	135	.981	57	620	1000	18	16	3.06
54	100	.351	38.5	461	628	166	17	56	.217	.290	126	166	147	.972	11	613	868	8	34	3.53
AGUE TOTAL				6441	6441	2260	316	1175	.239	.343	853	1539	1770	.979	502	5742	10174	193	372	3.07

INDIVIDUAL PITCHING

TCHER	T	W	L	PCT	ERA	SV	G	GS	CG	IP	H	BB	SO	R	ER	ShO	H/9	BB/9	SO/9
ckey Lolich	L	22	14	.611	2.50	0	41	41	23	327	282	74	250	100	91	4	7.76	2.04	6.88
e Coleman	R	19	14	.576	2.80	0	40	39	9	279.2	216	110	222	99	87	3	6.95	3.54	7.14
m Timmerman	R	8	10	.444	2.89	0	34	25	3	149.2	121	41	88	57	48	2	7.28	2.47	5.29
odie Fryman	L	10	3	.769	2.05	0	16	14	6	114	93	31	72	31	26	1	7.34	2.45	5.68
uck Seelbach	R	9	8	.529	2.89	14	61	3	0	112	96	39	76	39	36	0	7.71	3.13	6.11
d Scherman	L	7	3	.700	3.64	12	57	3	0	94	91	53	53	43	38	0	8.71	5.07	5.07
Slayback	R	5	6	.455	3.18	0	23	13	3	82	74	25	65	36	29	1	8.12	2.74	7.13
e Niekro	R	3	2	.600	3.83	1	18	7	1	47	62	8	24	20	20	0	11.87	1.53	4.60
n Hiller	L	1	2	.333	2.05	3	24	3	1	44	39	13	26	13	10	0	7.98	2.66	5.32
ris Zachary	R	1	1	.500	1.42	1	25	1	0	38	27	15	21	6	6	0	6.39	3.55	4.97
rrin LaGrow	R	0	1	.000	1.33	2	16	0	0	27	22	6	9	4	4	0	7.33	2.00	3.00
s Cain	L	0	3	.000	3.75	0	5	5	0	24	18	16	16	12	10	0	6.75	6.00	6.00
n Perranoski	L	0	1	.000	7.58	0	17	0	0	19	23	8	10	16	16	0	10.89	3.79	4.74
il Meeler	R	0	1	.000	4.50	0	7	0	0	8	10	7	5	6	4	0	11.25	7.88	5.63
d Holdsworth	R	0	1	.000	12.86	0	2	2	0	7	13	2	5	10	10	0	16.71	2.57	6.43
Gilbreth		0	0	—	16.20	0	2	0	0	5	10	4	2	9	9	0	18.00	7.20	3.60
b Strampe	R	0	0	—	10.80	0	7	0	0	5	6	7	4	6	6	0	10.80	12.60	7.20
n Foor	L	1	0	1.000	13.50	0	7	0	0	4	6	6	2	6	6	0	13.50	13.50	4.50
ke Kilkenny	L	0	0	—	9.00	0	1	0	0	1	1	0	0	1	1	0	9.00	0.00	0.00
n Leshnock	L	0	0	—	0.00	0	1	0	0	1	2	0	2	0	0	0	18.00	0.00	18.00
AM TOTAL		86	70	.551	2.96	33	404	156	46	1388.1	1212	465	952	514	457	11	7.86	3.01	6.17

MANAGER	W	L	PCT
Billy Martin	76	67	.531
Joe Schultz	9	10	.474

POS	Player	B	G	AB	H	2B	3B	HR	HR %	R	RBI	BB	SO	SB	Pinch Hit AB	Pinch Hit H	BA	SA
REGULARS																		
1B	Norm Cash	L	121	363	95	19	0	19	5.2	51	40	47	73	1	8	2	.262	.471
2B	Dick McAuliffe	L	106	343	94	18	1	12	3.5	39	47	49	52	0	6	2	.274	.437
SS	Ed Brinkman	R	162	515	122	16	4	7	1.4	55	40	34	79	0	0	0	.237	.324
3B	Aurelio Rodriguez	R	160	555	123	27	3	9	1.6	46	58	31	85	3	0	0	.222	.330
RF	Jim Northrup	L	119	404	124	14	7	12	3.0	55	44	38	41	4	8	2	.307	.465
CF	Mickey Stanley	R	157	602	147	23	5	17	2.8	81	57	48	65	0	0	0	.244	.384
LF	Willie Horton	R	111	411	130	19	3	17	4.1	42	53	23	57	1	3	1	.316	.501
C	Bill Freehan	R	110	380	89	10	1	6	1.6	33	29	40	30	0	3	0	.234	.313
DH	Gates Brown	L	125	377	89	11	1	12	3.2	48	50	52	41	1	4	0	.236	.366
SUBSTITUTES																		
2B	Tony Taylor	R	84	275	63	9	3	5	1.8	35	24	17	29	9	9	0	.229	.338
DH	Frank Howard	R	85	227	58	9	1	12	5.3	26	29	24	28	0	7	1	.256	.463
1O	Rich Reese	L	59	102	14	1	0	2	2.0	10	4	7	17	0	8	0	.137	.206
UT	Ike Brown	R	42	76	22	2	1	1	1.3	12	9	15	13	0	7	1	.289	.382
2B	John Knox	L	12	32	9	1	0	0	0.0	1	3	3	3	1	0	0	.281	.313
SS	Tom Veryzer	R	18	20	6	0	1	0	0.0	1	2	2	4	0	0	0	.300	.400
1B	Joe Staton	L	9	17	4	0	0	0	0.0	2	3	0	3	1	2	0	.235	.235
O1	Al Kaline	R	91	310	79	13	0	10	3.2	40	45	29	28	4	9	0	.255	.394
OF	Dick Sharon	R	91	178	43	9	0	7	3.9	20	16	10	31	2	3	1	.242	.410
O3	Ron Cash	R	14	39	16	1	1	0	0.0	8	6	5	5	0	0	0	.410	.487
OF	Marv Lane	R	6	8	2	0	0	1	12.5	2	2	2	2	0	0	0	.250	.625
C	Duke Sims	L	80	252	61	10	0	8	3.2	31	30	30	36	1	9	1	.242	.377
C	Bob Didier	B	7	22	10	1	0	0	0.0	3	1	3	0	0	0	0	.455	.500
PH	John Gamble	R	7	0	0	0	0	0	—	1	0	0	0	0	0	0	—	—
PITCHERS																		
P	Joe Coleman	R	40	0	0	0	0	0	—	0	0	0	0	0	0	0	—	—
P	Woodie Fryman	R	34	0	0	0	0	0	—	0	0	0	0	0	0	0	—	—
P	John Hiller	R	65	0	0	0	0	0	—	0	0	0	0	0	0	0	—	—
P	Mickey Lolich	B	42	0	0	0	0	0	—	0	0	0	0	0	0	0	—	—
P	Bob Miller	R	22	0	0	0	0	0	—	0	0	0	0	0	0	0	—	—
P	Jim Perry	B	35	0	0	0	0	0	—	0	0	0	0	0	0	0	—	—
P	Fred Scherman	L	34	0	0	0	0	0	—	0	0	0	0	0	0	0	—	—
P	Tom Timmerman	R	17	0	0	0	0	0	—	0	0	0	0	0	0	0	—	—
P	Ed Farmer	R	24	0	0	0	0	0	—	0	0	0	0	0	0	0	—	—
P	Lerrin LaGrow	R	21	0	0	0	0	0	—	0	0	0	0	0	0	0	—	—
P	Chuck Seelbach	R	5	0	0	0	0	0	—	0	0	0	0	0	0	0	—	—
P	Mike Strahler	R	22	0	0	0	0	0	—	0	0	0	0	0	0	0	—	—
P	Fred Holdsworth	R	5	0	0	0	0	0	—	0	0	0	0	0	0	0	—	—
P	Bill Slayback	R	3	0	0	0	0	0	—	0	0	0	0	0	0	0	—	—
P	Gary Ignasiak	R	3	0	0	0	0	0	—	0	0	0	0	0	0	0	—	—
P	Dave Lemanczyk	R	1	0	0	0	0	0	—	0	0	0	0	0	0	0	—	—
	TEAM TOTAL			5508	1400	213	32	157	2.9	642	592	509	722	28	86	11	.254	.390

INDIVIDUAL FIELDING

POS	Player	T	G	PO	A	E	DP	TC/G	FA	POS	Player	T	G	PO	A	E	DP	TC/G	FA
1B	N. Cash	L	114	856	64	8	72	8.1	.991	OF	M. Stanley	R	157	420	10	3	3	2.8	.993
	A. Kaline	R	36	245	12	1	32	7.2	.996		J. Northrup	R	116	207	6	4	2	1.9	.982
	I. Brown	R	21	105	9	2	9	5.5	.983		W. Horton	R	107	160	2	10	0	1.6	.942
	R. Reese	L	37	106	7	0	7	3.1	1.000		D. Sharon	R	91	124	5	4	1	1.5	.970
	B. Freehan	R	7	54	3	0	2	8.1	1.000		A. Kaline	R	63	102	1	0	0	1.6	1.000
	J. Staton	L	5	25	6	1	1	6.4	.969		R. Reese	L	21	28	0	1	0	1.4	.966
	T. Taylor	R	6	17	2	0	0	3.2	1.000		I. Brown	R	12	10	1	0	0	0.9	1.000
	F. Howard	R	2	12	0	1	0	6.5	.923		R. Cash	R	7	8	1	1	0	1.4	.900
2B	D. McAuliffe	R	102	217	265	7	62	4.8	.986		M. Lane	R	4	7	0	0	0	1.8	1.000
	T. Taylor	R	72	134	165	4	37	4.2	.987		D. Sims	R	6	6	0	0	0	1.0	1.000
	J. Knox	R	9	17	17	0	3	3.8	1.000		G. Brown	R	2	1	0	0	0	0.5	1.000
SS	E. Brinkman	R	162	249	480	24	89	4.6	.968	C	B. Freehan	R	98	584	50	3	3	6.5	**.995**
	T. Veryzer	R	18	6	12	3	1	1.2	.857		D. Sims	R	68	375	39	9	7	6.2	.979
	A. Rodriguez	R	1	2	3	0	1	5.0	1.000		B. Didier	R	7	38	5	0	2	6.1	1.000
	D. McAuliffe	R	2	0	1	0	0	0.5	1.000										
3B	A. Rodriguez	R	160	135	335	14	30	3.0	.971										
	R. Cash	R	6	5	9	0	0	2.3	1.000										
	I. Brown	R	2	2	2	0	0	2.0	1.000										
	T. Taylor	R	4	0	1	0	0	0.3	1.000										

During the first two-thirds of the season, the Tigers bobbed in and out of contention. Detroit lost eight straight in June to slide into fifth, rallied to take first, faded before the All-Star break, then surged again. Embarking on a West Coast swing in late August, the Tigers sat one-and-a-half games ahead of the pack. But they would return two weeks later hopelessly settled in third place, six games out.

Detroit was introduced to the dark side of Billy Martin, who during a spring training tantrum quit for a day. Later in the season, Martin did not arrive at the park for a series opener against Chicago until 35 minutes before the game, leaving everyone to guess at the evening's starting lineup. After the Tigers dropped a Sunday doubleheader to the White Sox, effectively to fall out of the race, Martin blasted Detroit's farm system. Campbell reprimanded his manager, but didn't fire him—yet. When Cleveland's reputed spitballer Gaylord Perry beat the Tigers three days later, Martin claimed he had ordered Tiger pitchers to throw spitters in retaliation. American League president Joe Cronin suspended him for three days. But before Martin could return, Campbell fired him and promoted third base coach Joe Schultz to take over for the final 19 games.

The Tigers hastened Martin's departure. Leftfielder Willie Horton led the hitters at .316, as Detroit finally cracked the .300 circle for the first time since 1967, but managed just 53 RBI. Mickey Lolich became the first $100,000 pitcher in team history and responded with a 16–15, 3.82 season. Joe Coleman authored his best season at 23–15, but lost seven straight in the stretch. The best news came from relief pitcher John Hiller. Returning from a January 1971 heart attack, the 30-year-old left-hander notched a 10–5 record, a 1.44 ERA, and a still-standing team-record 38 saves. That earned him Comeback Player of the Year, Fireman of the Year, the Hutch Award, and fourth-place finishes in the Cy Young and MVP balloting.

TEAM STATISTICS

W	L	PCT	GB	R	OR	2B	3B	HR	BA	SA	SB	E	DP	FA	CG	BB	SO	ShO	SV	ERA
								Batting					Fielding				Pitching			
EAST																				
97	65	.599		754	561	229	48	119	.266	.389	**146**	119	184	.981	67	475	715	14	26	**3.07**
89	73	.549	8	738	647	235	30	147	.267	**.401**	114	127	162	.979	67	499	808	10	33	3.65
85	77	.525	12	642	674	213	32	157	.254	.390	28	**112**	144	**.982**	39	493	911	11	**46**	3.90
80	82	.494	17	641	610	212	17	131	.261	.378	47	156	172	.976	47	**457**	708	16	39	3.34
74	88	.457	23	708	731	229	40	145	.253	.388	110	145	167	.977	50	623	671	11	28	3.98
71	91	.438	26	679	826	205	29	**158**	.256	.387	60	139	174	.978	55	602	883	9	21	4.58
WEST																				
94	68	.580		**758**	615	216	28	147	.260	.389	4	137	170	.978	46	494	797	16	41	3.29
88	74	.543	6	754	752	239	40	114	.261	.381	105	167	**192**	.974	40	617	790	7	41	4.21
81	81	.500	13	738	692	**240**	44	120	**.270**	.393	87	139	147	.978	48	519	880	**18**	34	3.77
79	83	.488	15	629	657	183	29	93	.253	.348	59	156	153	.975	**72**	614	**1010**	13	19	3.57
77	85	.475	17	652	705	228	38	111	.256	.372	83	144	165	.977	48	574	848	15	35	3.86
57	105	.352	37	619	844	195	29	110	.255	.361	91	161	164	.974	35	680	831	10	27	4.64
LEAGUE TOTAL				8312	8314	2624	404	1552	.259	.381	934	1702	1994	.977	614	6647	9852	150	390	3.82

INDIVIDUAL PITCHING

PITCHER	T	W	L	PCT	ERA	SV	G	GS	CG	IP	H	BB	SO	R	ER	ShO	H/9	BB/9	SO/9
Mickey Lolich	L	16	15	.516	3.82	0	42	42	17	309	315	79	214	143	131	3	9.17	2.30	6.23
Joe Coleman	R	23	15	.605	3.53	0	40	40	13	288	283	93	202	125	113	2	8.84	2.91	6.31
Jim Perry	R	14	13	.519	4.03	0	35	34	7	203	225	55	66	96	91	1	9.98	2.44	2.93
Woodie Fryman	L	6	13	.316	5.35	0	34	29	1	170	200	64	119	106	101	0	10.59	3.39	6.30
John Hiller	L	10	5	.667	1.44	38	65	0	0	125	89	39	124	21	20	0	6.41	2.81	8.93
Mike Strahler	R	4	5	.444	4.39	0	22	11	1	80	84	39	37	45	39	0	9.45	4.39	4.16
Fred Scherman	L	2	2	.500	4.21	1	34	0	0	62	59	30	28	30	29	0	8.56	4.35	4.06
Lerrin LaGrow	R	1	5	.167	4.33	3	21	3	0	54	54	23	33	26	26	0	9.00	3.83	5.50
Ed Farmer	R	3	0	1.000	5.00	2	24	0	0	45	52	27	28	26	25	0	10.40	5.40	5.60
Bob Miller	R	4	2	.667	3.43	1	22	0	0	42	34	22	23	16	16	0	7.29	4.71	4.93
Tom Timmerman	R	1	1	.500	3.69	1	17	1	0	39	39	11	21	17	16	0	9.00	2.54	4.85
Fred Holdsworth	R	0	1	.000	6.60	0	5	2	0	15	13	6	9	11	11	0	7.80	3.60	5.40
Chuck Seelbach	R	1	0	1.000	3.86	0	5	0	0	7	7	2	2	3	3	0	9.00	2.57	2.57
Gary Ignasiak	L	0	0	–	3.60	0	3	0	0	5	5	3	4	2	2	0	9.00	5.40	7.20
Bill Slayback	R	0	0	–	4.50	0	3	0	0	2	5	0	1	4	1	0	22.50	0.00	4.50
Dave Lemanczyk	R	0	0	–	13.50	0	1	0	0	2	4	0	0	3	3	0	18.00	0.00	0.00
TEAM TOTAL		85	77	.525	3.90	46	373	162	39	1448	1468	493	911	674	627	6	9.12	3.06	5.66

MANAGER	W	L	PCT
Ralph Houk	72	90	.444

POS	Player	B	G	AB	H	2B	3B	HR	HR %	R	RBI	BB	SO	SB	Pinch Hit AB	Pinch Hit H	BA	SA
REGULARS																		
1B	Bill Freehan	R	130	445	132	17	5	18	4.0	58	60	42	44	2	1	0	.297	.479
2B	Gary Sutherland	R	149	619	157	20	1	5	0.8	60	49	26	37	1	2	1	.254	.313
SS	Ed Brinkman	R	153	502	111	15	3	14	2.8	55	54	29	71	2	0	0	.221	.347
3B	Aurelio Rodriguez	R	159	571	127	23	5	5	0.9	54	49	26	70	2	0	0	.222	.306
RF	Jim Northrup	L	97	376	89	12	1	11	2.9	41	42	36	46	0	0	0	.237	.362
CF	Mickey Stanley	R	99	394	87	13	2	8	2.0	40	34	26	63	5	1	0	.221	.325
LF	Willie Horton	R	72	238	71	8	1	15	6.3	32	47	21	36	0	6	3	.298	.529
C	Gerry Moses	R	74	198	47	6	3	4	2.0	19	19	11	38	0	1	0	.237	.359
DH	Al Kaline	R	147	558	146	28	2	13	2.3	71	64	65	75	2	1	0	.262	.389
SUBSTITUTES																		
1B	Norm Cash	L	53	149	34	3	2	7	4.7	17	12	19	30	1	9	3	.228	.416
DH	Gates Brown	L	73	99	24	2	0	4	4.0	7	17	10	15	0	53	16	.242	.384
1B	Reggie Sanders	R	26	99	27	7	0	3	3.0	12	10	5	20	1	0	0	.273	.434
2B	John Knox	L	55	88	27	1	1	0	0.0	11	6	6	13	5	4	1	.307	.341
13	Ron Cash	R	20	62	14	2	0	0	0.0	6	5	0	11	0	1	0	.226	.258
SS	Tom Veryzer	R	22	55	13	2	0	2	3.6	4	9	5	8	1	1	0	.236	.382
3B	Ike Brown	R	2	2	0	0	0	0	0.0	0	0	0	0	0	0	0	.000	.000
OF	Ron LeFlore	R	59	254	66	8	1	2	0.8	37	13	13	58	23	0	0	.260	.323
OF	Ben Oglivie	L	92	252	68	11	3	4	1.6	28	29	34	38	12	19	5	.270	.385
OF	Jim Nettles	L	43	141	32	5	1	6	4.3	20	17	15	26	3	1	1	.227	.404
OF	Dick Sharon	R	60	129	28	4	0	2	1.6	12	10	14	29	4	5	0	.217	.295
OF	Marv Lane	R	50	103	24	4	1	2	1.9	16	9	19	24	2	5	3	.233	.350
OF	Leon Roberts	R	17	63	17	3	2	0	0.0	5	7	3	10	0	1	0	.270	.381
OF	Dan Meyer	L	13	50	10	1	1	3	6.0	5	7	1	1	1	1	0	.200	.440
C	Gene Lamont	L	60	92	20	4	0	3	3.3	9	8	7	19	0	0	0	.217	.359
C	John Wockenfuss	R	13	29	4	1	0	0	0.0	1	2	3	2	0	0	0	.138	.172
PITCHERS																		
P	Joe Coleman	R	41	0	0	0	0	0	–	0	0	0	0	0	0	0	–	–
P	Woodie Fryman	R	27	0	0	0	0	0	–	0	0	0	0	0	0	0	–	–
P	John Hiller	R	59	0	0	0	0	0	–	0	0	0	0	0	0	0	–	–
P	Mickey Lolich	B	41	0	0	0	0	0	–	0	0	0	0	0	0	0	–	–
P	Jim Ray	R	28	0	0	0	0	0	–	0	0	0	0	0	0	0	–	–
P	Luke Walker	L	28	0	0	0	0	0	–	0	0	0	0	0	0	0	–	–
P	Vern Ruhle	R	5	0	0	0	0	0	–	0	0	0	0	0	0	0	–	–
P	Lerrin LaGrow	R	37	0	0	0	0	0	–	0	0	0	0	0	0	0	–	–
P	Chuck Seelbach	R	4	0	0	0	0	0	–	0	0	0	0	0	0	0	–	–
P	Fred Holdsworth	R	8	0	0	0	0	0	–	0	0	0	0	0	0	0	–	–
P	Bill Slayback	R	16	0	0	0	0	0	–	0	0	0	0	0	0	0	–	–
P	Dave Lemanczyk	R	22	0	0	0	0	0	–	0	0	0	0	0	0	0	–	–
TEAM TOTAL				5568	1375	200	35	131	2.4	620	579	436	784	67	112	33	.247	.366

INDIVIDUAL FIELDING

POS	Player	T	G	PO	A	E	DP	TC/G	FA
1B	B. Freehan	R	65	590	36	4	49	9.7	.994
	N. Cash	L	44	368	24	6	32	9.0	.985
	R. Sanders	R	25	218	17	3	19	9.5	.987
	R. Cash	R	15	136	7	3	12	9.7	.979
	M. Stanley	R	12	89	10	2	9	8.4	.980
	B. Oglivie	L	10	75	8	0	13	8.3	1.000
2B	G. Sutherland	R	147	337	360	17	101	4.9	.976
	J. Knox	R	33	54	54	5	20	3.4	.956
	M. Stanley	R	1	0	0	0	0	0.0	.000
SS	E. Brinkman	R	151	237	493	21	88	5.0	.972
	T. Veryzer	R	20	18	33	4	4	2.8	.927
	G. Sutherland	R	10	2	7	1	1	1.0	.900
3B	A. Rodriguez	R	159	132	389	21	40	3.4	.961
	G. Sutherland	R	4	1	13	0	1	3.5	1.000
	E. Brinkman	R	2	2	5	0	1	3.5	1.000
	R. Cash	R	4	3	2	1	0	1.5	.833
	I. Brown	R	2	2	1	0	0	1.5	1.000
	J. Knox	R	1	1	0	0	0	1.0	1.000

POS	Player	T	G	PO	A	E	DP	TC/G	FA
OF	M. Stanley	R	91	252	4	2	2	2.8	.992
	J. Northrup	R	97	209	5	6	0	2.3	.973
	R. LeFlore	R	59	151	8	11	3	2.9	.935
	W. Horton	R	64	106	2	6	0	1.8	.947
	B. Oglivie	L	63	87	3	5	0	1.5	.947
	D. Sharon	R	56	84	3	1	1	1.6	.989
	J. Nettles	L	41	80	1	0	0	2.0	1.000
	M. Lane	R	46	70	3	1	0	1.6	.986
	L. Roberts	R	17	25	0	2	0	1.6	.926
	D. Meyer	R	12	29	0	1	0	2.5	.967
C	G. Moses	R	74	377	26	6	6	5.5	.985
	B. Freehan	R	63	312	45	5	6	5.7	.986
	G. Lamont	R	60	204	21	6	0	3.9	.974
	J. Wockenfuss	R	13	45	10	4	2	4.5	.932

After 22 Hall of Fame summers as a Tiger, 39-year-old Al Kaline was moved to designated hitter, exceeded 3000 career hits, and retired after the season. Norm Cash, a Detroit fixture at first base for 15 years and the second all-time homer-hitting Tiger, was released outright in August. Outfielder Jim Northrup was sold to Montreal. And Ralph Houk, who had resigned as Yankees manager the previous autumn, marked his first season in Detroit with a last-place finish—the Tigers' second cellar season ever, their first in 22 years.

The old corps Tigers obviously could no longer contend. Mickey Lolich at 16–21 became the losingest Detroit pitcher in 54 years. Only John Hiller lived up to expectations, setting an American League record for victories (17) and losses (14) in relief with 13 saves. Detroit pitchers often found themselves fighting uphill—the Tigers were outscored in the first inning, 136 to 66. No Tiger regular hit .300, though Willie Horton, who injured his knee in May and missed half the season, managed to finish at .298.

In August, centerfielder Mickey Stanley broke his hand, the Tigers looked to the minors for help, and on August 1 brought up a Detroit-born 22-year-old outfielder. Discovered in prison, where he had been serving a term for armed robbery and where he had played his first organized baseball game, Ron LeFlore joined the Tigers in Milwaukee after a meteoric rise through the minors. In his debut, LeFlore went 0-for-4 with three strikeouts. But he would hit .260 in 59 games with 23 stolen bases—the first Tiger to steal 20 or more since 1962.

TEAM STATISTICS

	W	L	PCT	GB	R	OR	2B	3B	Batting HR	BA	SA	SB	E	Fielding DP	FA	CG	BB	Pitching SO	ShO	SV	ERA
ST																					
L	91	71	.562		659	612	226	27	116	.256	.370	145	128	174	**.980**	57	480	701	16	25	3.27
	89	73	.549	2	671	623	220	30	101	.263	.368	53	142	158	.977	53	528	829	13	24	3.31
S	84	78	.519	7	**696**	661	**236**	31	109	.264	.377	104	145	156	.977	71	463	751	12	18	3.72
E	77	85	.475	14	662	694	201	19	131	.255	.370	79	146	157	.977	45	479	650	8	27	3.80
L	76	86	.469	15	647	660	228	**49**	120	.244	.369	106	**127**	168	.980	43	493	621	11	24	3.77
T	72	90	.444	19	620	768	200	35	131	.247	.366	67	158	155	.975	54	621	869	7	15	4.17
EST																					
K	90	72	.556		689	**551**	205	37	132	.247	.373	**164**	141	154	.977	49	**430**	755	12	28	**2.95**
X	84	76	.525	5	690	698	198	39	99	**.272**	.377	113	163	164	.974	62	449	871	16	12	3.82
N	82	80	.506	8	673	669	190	37	111	.272	.378	74	151	164	.976	43	513	934	11	**29**	3.64
I	80	80	.500	9	684	721	225	23	**135**	.268	**.389**	64	147	**188**	.977	55	548	826	11	**29**	3.94
	77	85	.475	13	667	662	232	42	89	.259	.364	146	152	166	.976	54	482	731	14	17	3.51
L	68	94	.420	22	618	657	203	31	95	.254	.356	119	147	150	.977	64	649	**986**	13	12	3.52
AGUE TOTAL					7976	7976	2564	400	1369	.258	.371	1234	1747	1954	.977	650	6135	9524	144	260	3.62

INDIVIDUAL PITCHING

TCHER	T	W	L	PCT	ERA	SV	G	GS	CG	IP	H	BB	SO	R	ER	ShO	H/9	BB/9	SO/9
ckey Lolich	L	16	**21**	.432	4.15	0	41	41	27	308	310	78	202	155	**142**	3	9.06	2.28	5.90
e Coleman	R	14	12	.538	4.31	0	41	41	11	286	272	158	177	**160**	137	2	8.56	4.97	5.57
rrin LaGrow	R	8	19	.296	4.67	0	37	34	11	216	245	80	85	132	112	0	10.21	3.33	3.54
hn Hiller	L	17	14	.548	2.64	13	59	0	0	150	127	62	134	51	44	0	7.62	3.72	8.04
oodie Fryman	L	6	9	.400	4.31	0	27	22	4	142	120	67	92	73	68	1	7.61	4.25	5.83
ke Walker	L	5	5	.500	4.99	0	28	9	0	92	100	54	52	56	51	0	9.78	5.28	5.09
ve Lemanczyk	R	2	1	.667	3.99	0	22	3	0	79	79	44	52	43	35	0	9.00	5.01	5.92
Slayback	R	1	3	.250	4.75	0	16	4	0	55	57	26	23	34	29	0	9.33	4.25	3.76
n Ray	R	1	3	.250	4.50	2	28	0	0	52	49	29	26	27	26	0	8.48	5.02	4.50
ed Holdsworth	R	0	3	.000	4.25	0	8	5	0	36	40	14	16	20	17	0	10.00	3.50	4.00
rn Ruhle	R	2	0	1.000	2.73	0	5	3	1	33	35	6	10	13	10	0	9.55	1.64	2.73
uck Seelbach	R	0	0	–	4.50	0	4	0	0	8	9	3	0	4	4	0	10.13	3.38	0.00
AM TOTAL		72	90	.444	4.17	15	316	162	54	1457	1443	621	869	768	675	6	8.91	3.84	5.37

MANAGER	W	L	PCT
Ralph Houk	57	102	.358

POS	Player	B	G	AB	H	2B	3B	HR	HR %	R	RBI	BB	SO	SB	Pinch Hit AB	Pinch Hit H	BA	SA
REGULARS																		
1B	Dan Meyer	L	122	470	111	17	3	8	1.7	56	47	26	25	8	2	1	.236	.336
2B	Gary Sutherland	R	129	503	130	12	3	6	1.2	51	39	45	41	0	1	0	.258	.330
SS	Tom Veryzer	R	128	404	102	13	1	5	1.2	37	48	23	76	2	0	0	.252	.327
3B	Aurelio Rodriguez	R	151	507	124	20	6	13	2.6	47	60	30	63	1	0	0	.245	.385
RF	Leon Roberts	R	129	447	115	17	5	10	2.2	51	38	36	94	3	3	1	.257	.385
CF	Ron LeFlore	R	136	550	142	13	6	8	1.5	66	37	33	139	28	0	0	.258	.347
LF	Ben Oglivie	L	100	332	95	14	1	9	2.7	45	36	16	62	11	3	0	.286	.416
C	Bill Freehan	R	120	427	105	17	3	14	3.3	42	47	32	56	2	2	1	.246	.398
DH	Willie Horton	R	159	615	169	13	1	25	4.1	62	92	44	109	1	0	0	.275	.421
SUBSTITUTES																		
1B	Jack Pierce	B	53	170	40	6	1	8	4.7	19	22	20	40	0	4	0	.235	.424
1B	Nate Colbert	R	45	156	23	4	2	4	2.6	16	18	17	52	0	0	0	.147	.276
SS	Gene Michael	B	56	145	31	2	0	3	2.1	15	13	8	28	0	1	1	.214	.290
UT	John Knox	L	43	86	23	1	0	0	0.0	8	2	10	9	1	5	2	.267	.279
2B	Jerry Manuel	B	6	18	1	0	0	0	0.0	0	0	0	4	0	0	0	.056	.056
3S	Chuck Scrivener	R	4	16	4	1	0	0	0.0	0	0	0	1	1	0	0	.250	.313
UT	Mickey Stanley	R	52	164	42	7	3	3	1.8	26	19	15	27	1	3	2	.256	.390
OF	Bobby Baldwin	L	30	95	21	3	0	4	4.2	8	8	5	14	2	0	0	.221	.379
OF	Art James	L	11	40	9	2	0	0	0.0	2	1	1	3	1	0	0	.225	.275
OF	Bob Molinaro	L	6	19	5	0	1	0	0.0	2	1	1	0	0	0	0	.263	.368
C	John Wockenfuss	R	35	118	27	6	3	4	3.4	15	13	10	15	0	1	0	.229	.432
C	Terry Humphrey	R	18	41	10	0	0	0	0.0	0	1	2	6	0	0	0	.244	.244
C	Gene Lamont	L	4	8	3	1	0	0	0.0	1	1	0	2	1	0	0	.375	.500
PITCHERS																		
P	Joe Coleman	R	31	0	0	0	0	0	–	0	0	0	0	0	0	0	–	–
P	John Hiller	R	36	0	0	0	0	0	–	0	0	0	0	0	0	0	–	–
P	Mickey Lolich	B	32	0	0	0	0	0	–	0	0	0	0	0	0	0	–	–
P	Bob Reynolds	R	21	0	0	0	0	0	–	0	0	0	0	0	0	0	–	–
P	Vern Ruhle	R	32	0	0	0	0	0	–	0	0	0	0	0	0	0	–	–
P	Fernando Arroyo	R	14	0	0	0	0	0	–	0	0	0	0	0	0	0	–	–
P	Ed Brookens	R	3	0	0	0	0	0	–	0	0	0	0	0	0	0	–	–
P	Ed Glynn	R	3	0	0	0	0	0	–	0	0	0	0	0	0	0	–	–
P	Steve Grilli	R	3	0	0	0	0	0	–	0	0	0	0	0	0	0	–	–
P	Tom Makowski	R	3	0	0	0	0	0	–	0	0	0	0	0	0	0	–	–
P	Gene Pentz	R	13	0	0	0	0	0	–	0	0	0	0	0	0	0	–	–
P	Lerrin LaGrow	R	32	0	0	0	0	0	–	0	0	0	0	0	0	0	–	–
P	Ray Bare	R	29	0	0	0	0	0	–	0	0	0	0	0	0	0	–	–
P	Tom Walker	R	36	0	0	0	0	0	–	0	0	0	0	0	0	0	–	–
P	Dave Lemanczyk	R	26	0	0	0	0	0	–	0	0	0	0	0	0	0	–	–
TEAM TOTAL				5331	1332	169	39	124	2.3	569	543	374	866	63	25	8	.250	.366

INDIVIDUAL FIELDING

POS	Player	T	G	PO	A	E	DP	TC/G	FA
1B	D. Meyer	R	46	441	37	5	39	10.5	.990
	J. Pierce	R	49	407	26	13	38	9.1	.971
	N. Colbert	R	44	407	22	8	31	9.9	.982
	M. Stanley	R	14	119	7	0	8	9.0	1.000
	B. Freehan	R	5	53	4	0	4	11.0	1.000
	B. Oglivie	L	5	40	4	0	4	8.8	1.000
2B	G. Sutherland	R	128	278	365	21	83	5.2	.968
	J. Knox	R	23	38	61	2	10	4.4	.980
	J. Manuel	R	6	11	23	2	4	6.0	.944
	G. Michael	R	7	9	23	0	5	4.6	1.000
SS	T. Veryzer	R	128	215	358	24	62	4.7	.960
	G. Michael	R	44	52	99	10	23	3.7	.938
	C. Scrivener	R	2	2	4	0	0	3.0	1.000
3B	A. Rodriguez	R	151	136	375	25	33	3.5	.953
	M. Stanley	R	7	6	14	1	1	3.0	.952
	G. Michael	R	4	2	3	0	0	1.3	1.000
	C. Scrivener	R	3	0	4	0	0	1.3	1.000
	J. Knox	R	3	0	1	3	0	1.3	.250

POS	Player	T	G	PO	A	E	DP	TC/G	FA
OF	R. LeFlore	R	134	317	13	9	3	2.5	.973
	L. Roberts	R	127	268	10	5	2	2.2	.982
	B. Oglivie	L	86	192	4	5	1	2.3	.975
	D. Meyer	R	74	130	4	7	0	1.9	.950
	M. Stanley	R	28	58	1	1	0	2.1	.983
	B. Baldwin	L	25	53	4	1	1	2.3	.983
	A. James	L	11	33	0	0	0	3.0	1.000
	B. Molinaro	R	6	8	1	0	0	1.5	1.000
C	B. Freehan	R	113	582	64	6	8	5.8	.991
	J. Wockenfuss	R	34	195	23	4	4	6.5	.982
	T. Humphrey	R	18	61	9	0	1	3.9	1.000
	G. Lamont	R	4	14	3	1	0	4.5	.944

Finishing last for the second straight season—and for just the third time in team history—the Tigers stumbled through a summer that featured several notable low achievements. They lost 102, second most in club history, the most by a Tiger team in 23 years; they finished 37 1/2 games behind eventual pennant-winner Boston, their furthest finish from first place in 21 years; they committed more errors than any Tiger team in 31 years; their pitchers allowed more earned runs than any Detroit staff in 22 years; they scored the fewest runs and stole the fewest bases in the league; they set an all-time Tiger record for consecutive losses with 19; and they managed to get worse as the season progressed, winning just six of 26 in August and five of 26 in September while losing 47 of their last 58 games.

All of this was a team effort. No Tiger hit .300. First baseman Nate Colbert was acquired in the off-season from San Diego to add right-handed power, but hit .147 with four home runs and eventually lost his job to rookie Danny Meyer. And in his first full major-league season, Ron LeFlore stole 28 bases and batted .258. "The Tigers were the laughingstock of baseball," said LeFlore, "and I was the number one clown." Meanwhile, only three Tiger pitchers won more than eight—Mickey Lolich at 12–18 with a 3.78 ERA, rookie Vern Ruhle at 11–12, 4.03, and Joe Coleman at 10–18, 5.55.

The Tigers needed a savior.

TEAM STATISTICS

	W	L	PCT	GB	R	OR	Batting 2B	3B	HR	BA	SA	SB	Fielding E	DP	FA	Pitching CG	BB	SO	ShO	SV	ERA
AST																					
OS	95	65	.594		796	709	284	44	134	.275	.417	66	139	142	.977	62	490	720	11	31	3.99
AL	90	69	.566	4.5	682	553	224	33	124	.252	.373	104	107	175	.983	70	500	717	19	21	3.17
Y	83	77	.519	12	681	588	230	39	110	.264	.382	102	135	148	.978	70	502	809	11	20	3.29
LE	79	80	.497	15.5	688	703	201	25	153	.261	.392	106	134	156	.978	37	599	800	6	32	3.84
IL	68	94	.420	28	675	792	242	34	146	.250	.389	65	180	162	.971	36	624	643	10	34	4.34
ET	57	102	.358	37.5	570	786	171	39	125	.249	.366	63	173	141	.972	52	533	787	10	17	4.29
EST																					
AK	98	64	.605		758	606	220	33	151	.254	.391	183	143	140	.977	36	523	784	10	44	3.29
C	91	71	.562	7	710	649	263	58	118	.261	.394	155	154	151	.976	52	498	815	11	25	3.49
EX	79	83	.488	19	714	733	208	17	134	.256	.371	102	191	173	.971	60	518	792	16	17	3.90
IN	76	83	.478	20.5	724	736	215	28	121	.271	.386	81	170	147	.973	57	617	846	7	22	4.05
HI	75	86	.466	22.5	655	703	209	38	94	.255	.358	101	140	155	.978	34	657	802	7	39	3.94
AL	72	89	.447	25.5	628	723	195	41	55	.246	.328	220	184	164	.971	59	613	975	19	16	3.89
EAGUE TOTAL					8281	8281	2662	429	1465	.258	.379	1348	1850	1854	.975	625	6674	9490	137	318	3.79

INDIVIDUAL PITCHING

ITCHER	T	W	L	PCT	ERA	SV	G	GS	CG	IP	H	BB	SO	R	ER	ShO	H/9	BB/9	SO/9
Mickey Lolich	L	12	18	.400	3.78	0	32	32	19	240.2	260	64	139	119	101	1	9.72	2.39	5.20
oe Coleman	R	10	18	.357	5.55	0	31	31	6	201	234	85	125	137	124	1	10.48	3.81	5.60
ern Ruhle	R	11	12	.478	4.03	0	32	31	8	190	199	65	67	104	85	3	9.43	3.08	3.17
errin LaGrow	R	7	14	.333	4.38	0	32	26	7	164.1	183	66	75	105	80	2	10.02	3.61	4.11
ay Bare	R	8	13	.381	4.48	0	29	21	6	150.2	174	47	71	81	75	1	10.39	2.81	4.24
om Walker	R	3	8	.273	4.45	0	36	9	1	115.1	116	40	60	69	57	0	9.05	3.12	4.68
ave Lemanczyk	R	2	7	.222	4.46	0	26	6	4	109	120	46	67	62	54	0	9.91	3.80	5.53
ohn Hiller	L	2	3	.400	2.17	14	36	0	0	70.2	52	36	87	20	17	0	6.62	4.58	11.08
ernando Arroyo	R	2	1	.667	4.56	0	14	2	1	53.1	56	22	25	28	27	0	9.45	3.71	4.22
ob Reynolds	R	0	2	.000	4.67	3	21	0	0	34.2	40	14	26	20	18	0	10.38	3.63	6.75
ene Pentz	R	0	4	.000	3.20	0	13	0	0	25.1	27	20	21	14	9	0	9.59	7.11	7.46
d Glynn	L	0	2	.000	4.30	0	3	1	0	14.2	11	8	8	8	7	0	6.75	4.91	4.91
d Brookens	R	0	0	–	5.40	0	3	0	0	10	11	5	8	6	6	0	9.90	4.50	7.20
om Makowski	L	0	0	–	4.82	0	3	0	0	9.1	10	9	3	11	5	0	9.64	8.68	2.89
teve Grilli	R	0	0	–	1.35	0	3	0	0	6.2	3	6	5	2	1	0	4.05	8.10	6.75
EAM TOTAL		57	102	.358	4.29	17	314	159	52	1395.2	1496	533	787	786	666	8	9.65	3.44	5.07

MANAGER	W	L	PCT
Ralph Houk	74	87	.460

POS	Player	B	G	AB	H	2B	3B	HR	HR %	R	RBI	BB	SO	SB	Pinch Hit AB	Pinch Hit H	BA	SA
REGULARS																		
1B	Jason Thompson	L	123	412	90	12	1	17	4.1	45	54	68	72	2	3	0	.218	.376
2B	Pedro Garcia	R	77	227	45	10	2	3	1.3	21	20	9	40	2	0	0	.198	.300
SS	Tom Veryzer	R	97	354	83	8	2	1	0.3	31	25	21	44	1	0	0	.234	.277
3B	Aurelio Rodriguez	R	128	480	115	13	2	8	1.7	40	50	19	61	0	0	0	.240	.325
CF	Ron LeFlore	R	135	544	172	23	8	4	0.7	93	39	51	111	58	1	0	.316	.410
LF	Alex Johnson	R	125	429	115	15	2	6	1.4	41	45	19	49	14	16	5	.268	.354
C	Bill Freehan	R	71	237	64	10	1	5	2.1	22	27	12	27	0	6	0	.270	.384
DH	Willie Horton	R	114	401	105	17	0	14	3.5	40	56	49	63	0	6	1	.262	.409
SUBSTITUTES																		
2S	Chuck Scrivener	R	80	222	49	7	1	2	0.9	28	16	19	34	1	2	0	.221	.288
2B	Gary Sutherland	R	42	117	24	5	2	0	0.0	10	6	7	12	0	2	1	.205	.282
SS	Mark Wagner	R	39	115	30	2	3	0	0.0	9	12	6	18	0	0	0	.261	.330
3B	Phil Mankowski	L	24	85	23	2	1	1	1.2	9	4	4	8	0	1	0	.271	.353
2B	Jerry Manuel	B	54	43	6	1	0	0	0.0	4	2	3	9	1	0	0	.140	.163
OD	Rusty Staub	L	161	589	176	28	3	15	2.5	73	96	83	49	3	0	0	.299	.433
OF	Ben Oglivie	L	115	305	87	12	3	15	4.9	36	47	11	44	9	38	9	.285	.492
O1	Dan Meyer	L	105	294	74	8	4	2	0.7	37	16	17	22	10	36	8	.252	.327
UT	Mickey Stanley	R	84	214	55	17	1	4	1.9	34	29	14	19	2	19	6	.257	.402
OF	Marv Lane	R	18	48	9	1	0	0	0.0	3	5	6	11	0	3	0	.188	.208
C	Bruce Kimm	R	63	152	40	8	0	1	0.7	13	6	15	20	4	0	0	.263	.336
C	John Wockenfuss	R	60	144	32	7	2	3	2.1	18	10	17	14	0	1	0	.222	.361
C	Milt May	L	6	25	7	1	0	0	0.0	2	1	0	1	0	0	0	.280	.320
PITCHERS																		
P	Frank MacCormick	R	9	3	0	0	0	0	0.0	0	0	0	2	0	0	0	.000	.000
P	John Hiller	R	56	1	0	0	0	0	0.0	0	0	0	0	0	0	0	.000	.000
P	Joe Coleman	R	12	0	0	0	0	0	—	0	0	0	0	0	0	0	—	—
P	Dave Roberts	L	36	0	0	0	0	0	—	0	0	0	0	0	0	0	—	—
P	Vern Ruhle	R	32	0	0	0	0	0	—	0	0	0	0	0	0	0	—	—
P	Ed Glynn	R	5	0	0	0	0	0	—	0	0	0	0	0	0	0	—	—
P	Steve Grilli	R	36	0	0	0	0	0	—	0	0	0	0	0	0	0	—	—
P	Mark Fidrych	R	31	0	0	0	0	0	—	0	0	0	0	0	0	0	—	—
P	Bill Laxton	L	26	0	0	0	0	0	—	0	0	0	0	0	0	0	—	—
P	Ray Bare	R	30	0	0	0	0	0	—	0	0	0	0	0	0	0	—	—
P	Jim Crawford	L	32	0	0	0	0	0	—	0	0	0	0	0	0	0	—	—
P	Dave Lemanczyk	R	20	0	0	0	0	0	—	0	0	0	0	0	0	0	—	—
TEAM TOTAL				5441	1401	207	38	101	1.9	609	566	450	730	107	134	30	.257	.365

INDIVIDUAL   FIELDING

POS	Player	T	G	PO	A	E	DP	TC/G	FA
1B	J. Thompson	L	117	1157	88	8	104	10.7	.994
	D. Meyer	R	19	168	10	1	15	9.4	.994
	M. Stanley	R	17	117	9	1	10	7.5	.992
	B. Oglivie	L	9	98	1	1	13	11.1	.990
	B. Freehan	R	2	16	6	0	2	11.0	1.000
2B	P. Garcia	R	77	168	219	17	53	5.2	.958
	C. Scrivener	R	43	86	120	5	22	4.9	.976
	G. Sutherland	R	42	73	117	3	31	4.6	.984
	J. Manuel	R	47	36	57	8	8	2.1	.921
	M. Stanley	R	2	3	2	1	1	3.0	.833
SS	T. Veryzer	R	97	164	313	17	53	5.1	.966
	M. Wagner	R	39	60	135	11	25	5.3	.947
	C. Scrivener	R	37	48	101	6	24	4.2	.961
	J. Manuel	R	4	4	7	0	0	2.8	1.000
	M. Stanley	R	3	0	2	0	0	0.7	1.000
3B	A. Rodriguez	R	128	120	280	9	21	3.2	.978
	P. Mankowski	R	23	20	47	2	8	3.0	.971
	M. Stanley	R	11	7	32	1	3	3.6	.975
	C. Scrivener	R	5	3	9	1	1	2.6	.923

POS	Player	T	G	PO	A	E	DP	TC/G	FA
OF	R. LeFlore	R	132	381	14	11	1	3.1	.973
	R. Staub	R	126	218	8	7	3	1.8	.970
	A. Johnson	R	90	159	7	8	1	1.9	.954
	B. Oglivie	L	64	136	7	2	0	2.3	.986
	D. Meyer	R	47	76	4	1	1	1.7	.970
	M. Stanley	R	38	60	2	2	0	1.7	.969
	M. Lane	R	15	23	1	1	0	1.7	.960
C	B. Freehan	R	61	312	28	6	2	5.7	.973
	B. Kimm	R	61	256	33	9	5	4.9	.970
	J. Wockenfuss	R	59	221	19	15	5	4.3	.941
	M. May	R	6	33	5	0	0	6.3	1.000

There had never been a rookie quite like him—this skinny, frizzy-haired phenom of a pitcher who talked to the baseball. At age 21, he captivated not only Tiger fans, but all of America. He dropped to his hands and knees to landscape the mound. He applauded teammates after each putout, and after every victory he danced off the field. His enthusiasm was contagious—not only among his fellow Tigers, but among frenzied fans. Mark Steven Fidrych, nicknamed for his resemblance to *Sesame Street*'s Big Bird, had it all: color, charisma, magic. And best of all, he could pitch.

It was pure storybook stuff. Less than two years out of high school, Fidrych wasn't even on the major-league roster during spring training. After two brief relief appearances, he got his first start in mid-May, a 2–1 two-hitter over the Indians in Detroit. Then there was no stopping him. Compiling one complete-game win atop another (including eight straight victories), by early August Fidrych was 11–3 and had been only the second rookie pitcher to start the All-Star Game. He was the Tigers' hottest drawing card ever. *The Wall Street Journal* estimated Fidrych brought the Tigers $1 million, about 60 times his salary. And turnstile figures didn't include the vast television audiences he attracted as the networks planned their schedules around the Tigers, a team struggling to avoid a third straight last-place finish.

Detroit did climb out of the cellar, although just one notch to fifth place, 24 games behind the pennant-winning Yankees. Catcher Bill Freehan had retired; Mickey Lolich was also gone, dealt to the Mets in the off-season after leaving an imprint on Detroit pitching records (including most starts, shutouts, and strikeouts, and near the top in victories, games, and innings).

Centerfielder Ron LeFlore was Detroit's only .300 hitter (.316). LeFlore opened the season with a 30-game hitting streak (the Tigers' longest in 42 years) and stole 58 bases, Detroit's most since Ty Cobb's 68 in 1916.

Still, the spotlight belonged to The Bird. Fidrych was AL Rookie of the Year and runner-up for the Cy Young Award as he led the majors in ERA (2.34) and tied for fourth in league victories at 19–9 (most wins by a Tiger rookie in 68 years) while completing an AL high 24 of 29 starts. Almost as though it couldn't last, it didn't.

TEAM STATISTICS

	W	L	PCT	GB	R	OR	Batting 2B	3B	HR	BA	SA	SB	Fielding E	DP	FA	Pitching CG	BB	SO	ShO	SV	ERA
AST																					
Y	97	62	.610		730	575	231	36	120	.269	.389	163	126	141	.980	62	448	674	15	37	3.19
AL	88	74	.543	10.5	619	598	213	28	119	.243	.358	150	118	157	.982	59	489	678	16	23	3.31
OS	83	79	.512	15.5	716	660	257	53	134	.263	.402	95	141	148	.978	49	409	673	13	27	3.52
LE	81	78	.509	16	615	615	189	38	85	.263	.359	75	121	159	.980	30	533	928	17	46	3.48
ET	74	87	.460	24	609	709	207	38	101	.257	.365	107	168	161	.974	55	550	738	12	20	3.87
IL	66	95	.410	32	570	655	170	38	88	.246	.340	62	152	160	.975	45	567	677	10	27	3.64
EST																					
C	90	72	.556		713	611	259	57	65	.269	.371	218	139	147	.978	41	493	735	12	35	3.21
AK	87	74	.540	2.5	686	598	208	33	113	.246	.361	341	144	130	.977	39	415	711	15	29	3.26
IN	85	77	.525	5	743	704	222	51	81	.274	.375	146	172	182	.973	29	610	762	11	23	3.72
AL	76	86	.469	14	550	631	210	23	63	.235	.318	126	150	139	.977	64	553	992	15	17	3.36
EX	76	86	.469	14	616	652	213	26	80	.250	.341	87	156	142	.976	63	461	773	15	15	3.47
HI	64	97	.398	25.5	586	745	209	46	73	.255	.349	120	130	155	.979	54	600	802	10	22	4.25
LEAGUE TOTAL					7753	7753	2588	467	1122	.256	.361	1690	1717	1821	.977	590	6128	9143	161	321	3.52

INDIVIDUAL PITCHING

PITCHER	T	W	L	PCT	ERA	SV	G	GS	CG	IP	H	BB	SO	R	ER	ShO	H/9	BB/9	SO/9
Dave Roberts	L	16	17	.485	4.00	0	36	36	18	252	254	63	79	122	112	4	9.07	2.25	2.82
Mark Fidrych	R	19	9	.679	2.34	0	31	29	24	250	217	53	97	76	65	4	7.81	1.91	3.49
Vern Ruhle	R	9	12	.429	3.92	0	32	32	5	200	227	59	88	99	87	1	10.22	2.66	3.96
Ray Bare	R	7	8	.467	4.63	0	30	21	3	134	157	51	59	85	69	2	10.54	3.43	3.96
John Hiller	L	12	8	.600	2.38	13	56	1	1	121	93	67	117	37	32	1	6.92	4.98	8.70
Jim Crawford	L	1	8	.111	4.53	2	32	5	1	109.1	115	43	68	65	55	0	9.47	3.54	5.60
Bill Laxton	L	0	5	.000	4.09	2	26	3	0	94.2	77	51	74	49	43	0	7.32	4.85	7.04
Dave Lemanczyk	R	4	6	.400	5.11	0	20	10	1	81	86	34	51	47	46	0	9.56	3.78	5.67
Joe Coleman	R	2	5	.286	4.84	0	12	10	1	67	80	34	38	44	36	0	10.75	4.57	5.10
Steve Grilli	R	3	1	.750	4.64	3	36	0	0	66	63	41	36	43	34	0	8.59	5.59	4.91
Frank MacCormick	R	0	5	.000	5.73	0	9	8	0	33	35	34	14	24	21	0	9.55	9.27	3.82
Ed Glynn	L	1	3	.250	6.00	0	5	4	1	24	22	20	17	18	16	0	8.25	7.50	6.38
TEAM TOTAL		74	87	.460	3.87	20	325	161	55	1432	1426	550	738	709	616	12	8.96	3.46	4.64

MANAGER	W	L	PCT
Ralph Houk	74	88	.457

POS	Player	B	G	AB	H	2B	3B	HR	HR %	R	RBI	BB	SO	SB	Pinch Hit AB	Pinch Hit H	BA	SA
REGULARS																		
1B	Jason Thompson	L	158	585	158	24	5	31	5.3	87	105	73	91	0	0	0	.270	.487
2B	Tito Fuentes	R	151	615	190	19	10	5	0.8	83	51	38	61	4	1	0	.309	.397
SS	Tom Veryzer	R	125	350	69	12	1	2	0.6	31	28	16	44	0	0	0	.197	.254
3B	Aurelio Rodriguez	R	96	306	67	14	1	10	3.3	30	32	16	36	1	10	1	.219	.369
RF	Ben Oglivie	L	132	450	118	24	2	21	4.7	63	61	40	80	9	12	4	.262	.464
CF	Ron LeFlore	R	154	652	212	30	10	16	2.5	100	57	37	121	39	3	2	.325	.475
LF	Steve Kemp	L	151	552	142	29	4	18	3.3	75	88	71	93	3	3	0	.257	.422
C	Milt May	L	115	397	99	9	3	12	3.0	32	46	26	31	0	5	2	.249	.378
DH	Rusty Staub	L	158	623	173	34	3	22	3.5	84	101	59	47	1	2	0	.278	.448
SUBSTITUTES																		
3B	Phil Mankowski	L	94	286	79	7	3	3	1.0	21	27	16	41	1	10	3	.276	.353
SS	Chuck Scrivener	R	61	72	6	0	0	0	0.0	10	2	5	9	0	0	0	.083	.083
SS	Mark Wagner	R	22	48	7	0	1	1	2.1	4	3	4	12	0	0	0	.146	.250
SS	Alan Trammell	R	19	43	8	0	0	0	0.0	6	0	4	12	0	0	0	.186	.186
2B	Lou Whitaker	L	11	32	8	1	0	0	0.0	5	2	4	6	2	0	0	.250	.281
1C	Bob Adams	R	15	24	6	1	0	2	8.3	2	2	0	5	0	12	4	.250	.542
3B	Luis Alvarado	R	2	1	0	0	0	0	0.0	0	0	0	0	0	0	0	.000	.000
OF	Mickey Stanley	R	75	222	51	9	1	8	3.6	30	23	18	30	0	13	3	.230	.387
OF	Tim Corcoran	L	55	103	29	3	0	3	2.9	13	15	6	9	0	32	10	.282	.398
OF	Willie Horton	R	1	4	1	0	0	0	0.0	0	0	0	0	0	0	0	.250	.250
CO	John Wockenfuss	R	53	164	45	8	1	9	5.5	26	25	14	18	0	9	2	.274	.500
C	Lance Parrish	R	12	46	9	2	0	3	6.5	10	7	5	12	0	0	0	.196	.435
C	Bruce Kimm	R	14	25	2	1	0	0	0.0	2	1	0	4	0	0	0	.080	.120
PITCHERS																		
P	John Hiller	R	45	0	0	0	0	0	—	0	0	0	0	0	0	0	—	—
P	Dave Roberts	L	22	0	0	0	0	0	—	0	0	0	0	0	0	0	—	—
P	Vern Ruhle	R	14	0	0	0	0	0	—	0	0	0	0	0	0	0	—	—
P	Fernando Arroyo	R	38	0	0	0	0	0	—	0	0	0	0	0	0	0	—	—
P	Ed Glynn	R	8	0	0	0	0	0	—	0	0	0	0	0	0	0	—	—
P	Steve Grilli	R	30	0	0	0	0	0	—	0	0	0	0	0	0	0	—	—
P	Mark Fidrych	R	11	0	0	0	0	0	—	0	0	0	0	0	0	0	—	—
P	Jack Morris	R	7	0	0	0	0	0	—	0	0	0	0	0	0	0	—	—
P	Dave Rozema	R	28	0	0	0	0	0	—	0	0	0	0	0	0	0	—	—
P	Bob Sykes	B	32	0	0	0	0	0	—	0	0	0	0	0	0	0	—	—
P	Bruce Taylor	R	19	0	0	0	0	0	—	0	0	0	0	0	0	0	—	—
P	Milt Wilcox	R	20	0	0	0	0	0	—	0	0	0	0	0	0	0	—	—
P	Ray Bare	R	5	0	0	0	0	0	—	0	0	0	0	0	0	0	—	—
P	Jim Crawford	L	37	0	0	0	0	0	—	0	0	0	0	0	0	0	—	—
P	Steve Foucault	L	44	0	0	0	0	0	—	0	0	0	0	0	0	0	—	—
TEAM TOTAL				5600	1479	227	45	166	3.0	714	676	452	762	60	112	31	.264	.410

INDIVIDUAL   FIELDING

POS	Player	T	G	PO	A	E	DP	TC/G	FA
1B	J. Thompson	L	158	**1599**	97	16	135	10.8	.991
	M. Stanley	R	3	26	0	0	3	8.7	1.000
	B. Adams	R	2	20	1	0	1	10.5	1.000
2B	T. Fuentes	R	151	**379**	459	26	115	5.7	.970
	P. Mankowski	R	1	0	0	0	0	0.0	.000
	L. Whitaker	R	9	17	18	0	2	3.9	1.000
	C. Scrivener	R	8	9	22	0	2	3.9	1.000
	M. Wagner	R	1	0	1	0	0	1.0	1.000
SS	T. Veryzer	R	124	185	377	18	62	4.7	.969
	C. Scrivener	R	50	41	65	2	13	2.2	.981
	M. Wagner	R	21	15	57	6	10	3.7	.923
	A. Trammell	R	19	15	34	2	5	2.7	.961
	A. Rodriguez	R	1	0	0	0	0	0.0	.000
	M. Stanley	R	3	1	3	1	0	1.7	.800
3B	A. Rodriguez	R	95	60	222	8	19	3.1	.972
	P. Mankowski	R	85	73	196	10	15	3.3	.964
	L. Alvarado	R	2	0	0	0	0	0.0	.000
	C. Scrivener	R	3	0	2	1	1	1.0	.667

POS	Player	T	G	PO	A	E	DP	TC/G	FA
OF	R. LeFlore	R	154	365	12	11	0	2.5	.972
	S. Kemp	L	148	252	10	5	1	1.8	.981
	B. Oglivie	L	118	236	10	6	3	2.1	.976
	M. Stanley	R	57	101	2	3	0	1.9	.972
	T. Corcoran	L	18	38	0	0	0	2.1	1.000
	J. Wockenfuss	R	9	6	0	0	0	0.7	1.000
	W. Horton	R	1	1	0	0	0	1.0	1.000
C	M. May	R	111	551	78	9	12	5.7	.986
	J. Wockenfuss	R	37	175	20	3	2	5.4	.985
	L. Parrish	R	12	76	6	0	0	6.8	1.000
	B. Kimm	R	12	43	3	2	0	4.0	.958
	B. Adams	R	1	6	0	0	0	6.0	1.000

Mark Fidrych's meteor crashed as suddenly as it had risen—the ultimate sophomore jinx. During spring training at Lakeland, he vaulted a fence to take a shortcut to the Tiger clubhouse. The pitching prodigy felt "something funny" happen in his left knee. The next day The Bird leaped for a ball in the outfield and felt it again. Ten days later he underwent surgery to repair torn cartilage. It was the beginning of the end—at age 22.

Rushing back in May, Fidrych lost his first two decisions, then won six in a row. He was 6–4 with a 2.89 ERA on July 12, when during a game against Toronto at Tiger Stadium, intense pain in his right shoulder forced him to the sidelines after throwing just 15 pitches. The diagnosis: tendinitis.

Fidrych was through for the season— and in effect, for his career. He would pitch in only 16 more big-league games as he bounced between the majors and the minors the next four years trying to recapture the magic. On October 5, 1981, general manager Jim Campbell would telephone Northboro, Massachusetts, to tell Mark Fidrych the Tigers were releasing him.

Without Fidrych, the Tigers were essentially forgettable. Detroit finished below .500 for the fourth straight year, occupying fourth place, 26 games behind eventual World Champion New York. Two Tigers hit .300: centerfielder Ron LeFlore (.325) and second baseman Tito Fuentes (.309). First baseman Jason Thompson became only the third Tiger to hit a home run completely out of Tiger Stadium since it was double-decked in 1938, and did it twice against the Yankees within a month. Dave Rozema was the Tigers' second straight American League Rookie Pitcher of the Year. The only Tiger to exceed eight victories at 15–7 with a 3.10 ERA, the right-hander issued the fewest walks per nine innings in the majors and was third in AL winning percentage.

TEAM STATISTICS

	W	L	PCT	GB	R	OR	Batting 2B	3B	HR	BA	SA	SB	Fielding E	DP	FA	Pitching CG	BB	SO	ShO	SV	ERA
ST																					
'	100	62	.617		831	651	267	47	184	.281	.444	93	132	151	.979	52	486	758	16	34	3.61
L	97	64	.602	2.5	719	653	231	25	148	.261	.393	90	106	189	.983	65	494	737	11	23	3.74
S	97	64	.602	2.5	859	712	258	56	213	.281	.465	66	133	162	.978	40	378	758	13	40	4.16
T	74	88	.457	26	714	751	228	45	166	.264	.410	60	142	153	.978	44	470	784	3	23	4.13
E	71	90	.441	28.5	676	739	221	46	100	.269	.380	87	130	145	.979	45	550	876	8	30	4.10
_	67	95	.414	33	639	765	255	46	125	.258	.389	85	139	165	.978	38	566	719	6	25	4.32
R	54	107	.335	45.5	605	822	230	41	100	.252	.365	65	164	133	.974	40	623	771	3	20	4.57
ST																					
	102	60	.630		822	651	299	77	146	.277	.436	170	137	145	.978	41	499	850	15	42	3.52
X	94	68	.580	8	767	657	265	39	135	.270	.405	154	117	156	.982	49	471	864	17	31	3.56
II	90	72	.556	12	844	771	254	52	192	.278	.444	42	159	125	.974	34	516	842	3	40	4.25
N	84	77	.522	17.5	867	776	273	60	123	.282	.417	105	143	184	.978	35	507	737	4	25	4.38
L	74	88	.457	28	675	695	233	40	131	.255	.386	159	147	137	.976	53	572	965	13	26	3.76
A	64	98	.395	38	624	855	218	33	133	.256	.381	110	147	162	.976	18	578	785	1	34	4.83
K	63	98	.391	38.5	605	749	176	37	117	.240	.352	176	190	136	.970	32	560	788	4	26	4.05
GUE TOTAL					10247	10247	3408	644	2013	.266	.405	1462	1986	2143	.977	586	7270	11234	117	416	4.07

INDIVIDUAL PITCHING

CHER	T	W	L	PCT	ERA	SV	G	GS	CG	IP	H	BB	SO	R	ER	ShO	H/9	BB/9	SO/9
ve Rozema	R	15	7	.682	3.10	0	28	28	16	218	222	34	92	87	75	1	9.17	1.40	3.80
nando Arroyo	R	8	18	.308	4.18	0	38	28	8	209	227	52	60	102	97	1	9.78	2.24	2.58
b Sykes	L	5	7	.417	4.40	0	32	20	3	133	141	50	58	74	65	0	9.54	3.38	3.92
ve Roberts	L	4	10	.286	5.16	0	22	22	5	129	143	41	46	88	74	0	9.98	2.86	3.21
1 Crawford	L	7	8	.467	4.79	1	37	7	0	126	156	50	91	82	67	0	11.14	3.57	6.50
n Hiller	L	8	14	.364	3.56	7	45	8	3	124	120	61	115	59	49	0	8.71	4.43	8.35
t Wilcox	R	6	2	.750	3.65	0	20	13	1	106	96	37	82	46	43	0	8.15	3.14	6.96
rk Fidrych	R	6	4	.600	2.89	0	11	11	7	81	82	12	42	29	26	1	9.11	1.33	4.67
ve Foucault	R	7	7	.500	3.16	13	44	0	0	74	64	17	58	29	26	0	7.78	2.07	7.05
ve Grilli	R	1	2	.333	4.81	0	30	2	0	73	71	49	49	42	39	0	8.75	6.04	6.04
rn Ruhle	R	3	5	.375	5.73	0	14	10	0	66	83	15	27	44	42	0	11.32	2.05	3.68
k Morris	R	1	1	.500	3.72	0	7	6	1	46	38	23	28	20	19	0	7.43	4.50	5.48
ice Taylor	R	1	0	1.000	3.41	2	19	0	0	29	23	10	19	11	11	0	7.14	3.10	5.90
Glynn	L	2	1	.667	5.33	0	8	3	0	27	36	12	13	17	16	0	12.00	4.00	4.33
y Bare	R	0	2	.000	12.86	0	5	4	0	14	24	7	4	21	20	0	15.43	4.50	2.57
AM TOTAL		74	88	.457	4.14	23	360	162	44	1455	1526	470	784	751	669	3	9.44	2.91	4.85

MANAGER	W	L	PCT
Ralph Houk	86	76	.531

POS	Player	B	G	AB	H	2B	3B	HR	HR %	R	RBI	BB	SO	SB	Pinch Hit AB	Pinch Hit H	BA	SA
REGULARS																		
1B	Jason Thompson	L	153	589	169	25	3	26	4.4	79	96	74	96	0	1	0	.287	.472
2B	Lou Whitaker	L	139	484	138	12	7	3	0.6	71	58	61	65	7	6	3	.285	.357
SS	Alan Trammell	R	139	448	120	14	6	2	0.4	49	34	45	56	3	0	0	.268	.339
3B	Aurelio Rodriguez	R	134	385	102	25	2	7	1.8	40	43	19	37	0	20	7	.265	.395
RF	Tim Corcoran	L	116	324	86	13	1	1	0.3	37	27	24	27	3	12	2	.265	.321
CF	Ron LeFlore	R	155	666	198	30	3	12	1.8	126	62	65	104	68	0	0	.297	.405
LF	Steve Kemp	L	159	582	161	18	4	15	2.6	75	79	97	87	2	2	1	.277	.399
C	Milt May	L	105	352	88	9	0	10	2.8	24	37	27	26	0	12	1	.250	.361
DH	Rusty Staub	L	162	642	175	30	1	24	3.7	75	121	76	35	3	0	0	.273	.435
SUBSTITUTES																		
3B	Phil Mankowski	L	88	222	61	8	0	4	1.8	28	20	22	28	2	9	2	.275	.365
2B	Steve Dillard	R	56	130	29	5	2	0	0.0	21	7	6	11	1	1	0	.223	.292
SS	Mark Wagner	R	39	109	26	1	2	0	0.0	10	6	3	11	1	1	1	.239	.284
OF	John Wockenfuss	R	71	187	53	5	0	7	3.7	23	22	21	14	0	17	6	.283	.422
O1	Mickey Stanley	R	53	151	40	9	0	3	2.0	15	8	9	19	0	12	2	.265	.384
OF	Charlie Spikes	R	10	28	7	1	0	0	0.0	1	2	2	6	0	0	0	.250	.286
OF	Dave Stegman	R	8	14	4	2	0	1	7.1	3	3	1	2	0	0	0	.286	.643
C	Lance Parrish	R	85	288	63	11	3	14	4.9	37	41	11	71	0	6	1	.219	.424
PITCHERS																		
P	John Hiller	R	51	0	0	0	0	0	–	0	0	0	0	0	0	0	–	–
P	Jack Billingham	R	30	0	0	0	0	0	–	0	0	0	0	0	0	0	–	–
P	Fernando Arroyo	R	2	0	0	0	0	0	–	0	0	0	0	0	0	0	–	–
P	Ed Glynn	R	10	0	0	0	0	0	–	0	0	0	0	0	0	0	–	–
P	Mark Fidrych	R	3	0	0	0	0	0	–	0	0	0	0	0	0	0	–	–
P	Jack Morris	R	28	0	0	0	0	0	–	0	0	0	0	0	0	0	–	–
P	Dave Rozema	R	28	0	0	0	0	0	–	0	0	0	0	0	0	0	–	–
P	Bob Sykes	B	22	0	0	0	0	0	–	0	0	0	0	0	0	0	–	–
P	Bruce Taylor	R	1	0	0	0	0	0	–	0	0	0	0	0	0	0	–	–
P	Steve Baker	R	15	0	0	0	0	0	–	0	0	0	0	0	0	0	–	–
P	Sheldon Burnside	R	2	0	0	0	0	0	–	0	0	0	0	0	0	0	–	–
P	Dave Tobik	R	5	0	0	0	0	0	–	0	0	0	0	0	0	0	–	–
P	Kip Young	R	14	0	0	0	0	0	–	0	0	0	0	0	0	0	–	–
P	Jim Slaton	R	35	0	0	0	0	0	–	0	0	0	0	0	0	0	–	–
P	Milt Wilcox	R	29	0	0	0	0	0	–	0	0	0	0	0	0	0	–	–
P	Jim Crawford	L	20	0	0	0	0	0	–	0	0	0	0	0	0	0	–	–
P	Steve Foucault	L	24	0	0	0	0	0	–	0	0	0	0	0	0	0	–	–
TEAM TOTAL				5601	1520	218	34	129	2.3	714	666	563	695	90	99	26	.271	.392

INDIVIDUAL FIELDING

POS	Player	T	G	PO	A	E	DP	TC/G	FA		POS	Player	T	G	PO	A	E	DP	TC/G	FA
1B	J. Thompson	L	151	1503	92	11	153	10.6	.993		OF	R. LeFlore	R	155	440	9	11	4	3.0	.976
	M. Stanley	R	12	126	8	0	8	11.2	1.000			S. Kemp	L	157	325	11	8	2	2.2	.977
												T. Corcoran	L	109	186	6	3	4	1.8	.985
2B	L. Whitaker	R	136	301	458	17	95	5.7	.978			J. Wockenfuss	R	60	89	2	2	0	1.6	.978
	S. Dillard	R	41	88	118	9	31	5.2	.958			M. Stanley	R	34	47	1	2	8	1.5	.960
	M. Wagner	R	4	2	2	0	0	1.0	1.000			D. Stegman	R	7	11	0	0	0	1.6	1.000
SS	A. Trammell	R	139	239	421	14	95	4.8	.979			C. Spikes	R	9	9	1	1	1	1.2	.909
	M. Wagner	R	35	55	79	5	18	4.0	.964		C	M. May	R	94	406	58	10	5	5.0	.979
3B	A. Rodriguez	R	131	79	228	4	20	2.4	.987			L. Parrish	R	79	353	39	5	5	5.0	.987
	P. Mankowski	R	80	42	129	5	17	2.2	.972											

Detroit won 12 more games than the previous year, vaulted over .500 for the first time in the Houk Era, and compiled its best record in six seasons, but dropped a notch in the standings into fifth place, 13 1/2 games behind the Yankees.

Many contributed to the improvement. Ron LeFlore started slowly, but led the team in hitting at .297, led the majors in runs with 126, led the league with in stolen bases with 68 (the most by a Tiger since Ty Cobb in 1916), and was second in the league in hits with 198. Designated hitter Rusty Staub finished second in the league in RBI with 121. First baseman Jason Thompson was hampered by injuries through the second half of the season, but still managed to reach .287 with 26 home runs. And most importantly, the Tigers acquired an enviable double-play combination in rookies Lou Whitaker at second base and Alan Trammell at shortstop. Whitaker hit .285 and won Detroit's second AL Rookie of the Year Award in three years; Trammell hit .268; and Detroit led the majors in executing double plays with 177. In his only Detroit season, once and future Brewer Jim Slaton led the pitching staff at 17–11 with a 4.12 ERA. John Hiller was the most reliable reliever at 9–4 with 15 saves and a 2.34 ERA.

The improvement would have proved more dramatic if not for a mid-May collapse (Detroit lost seven straight and 11 of 14 to plummet from first place into third, seven games back), and if not for pitcher Mark Fidyrch's continuing ailment (he made just three starts, winning two). After the season, Ralph Houk said, "It's time for me to go fishing," then retired. And the Tigers spent the winter calling themselves the "best fifth-place team in baseball."

TEAM STATISTICS

	W	L	PCT	GB	R	OR	2B	3B	HR	BA	SA	SB	E	DP	FA	CG	BB	SO	ShO	SV	ERA
							Batting						Fielding			Pitching					
EAST																					
Y	100	63	.613		735	582	228	38	125	.267	.388	98	113	136	.982	39	478	817	16	**36**	3.18
OS	99	64	.607	1	796	657	270	46	172	.267	.424	74	146	172	.977	57	464	706	15	26	3.54
IL	93	69	.574	6.5	**804**	650	265	38	**173**	**.276**	**.432**	95	150	144	.977	62	**398**	577	**19**	24	3.65
AL	90	71	.559	9	659	633	248	19	154	.258	.396	75	**110**	166	**.982**	65	509	754	16	33	3.56
ET	86	76	.531	13.5	714	653	218	34	129	.271	.392	90	118	**177**	.981	60	503	684	12	21	3.64
E	69	90	.434	29	639	694	223	45	106	.261	.379	64	123	142	.980	36	568	739	6	28	3.97
OR	59	102	.366	40	590	775	217	39	98	.250	.359	28	131	163	.979	35	614	758	5	23	4.55
WEST																					
C	92	70	.568		743	634	**305**	**59**	98	.268	.399	**216**	150	152	.976	53	478	657	14	33	3.44
AL	87	75	.537	5	691	666	226	28	108	.259	.370	86	136	136	.978	44	599	**892**	13	33	3.65
X	87	75	.537	5	692	632	216	36	132	.253	.381	196	153	140	.976	54	421	776	12	25	3.42
N	73	89	.451	19	666	678	259	47	82	.267	.375	99	146	171	.977	48	520	703	9	26	3.69
HI	71	90	.441	20.5	634	731	221	41	106	.264	.379	83	139	130	.977	38	586	710	9	33	4.22
AK	69	93	.426	23	532	690	200	31	100	.245	.351	144	179	142	.971	26	582	750	11	29	3.62
A	56	104	.350	35	614	834	229	37	97	.248	.359	123	141	172	.978	28	567	630	4	20	4.72
AGUE TOTAL					9509	9509	3325	538	1680	.261	.385	1471	1935	2143	.978	645	7287	10153	161	390	3.77

INDIVIDUAL PITCHING

TCHER	T	W	L	PCT	ERA	SV	G	GS	CG	IP	H	BB	SO	R	ER	ShO	H/9	BB/9	SO/9
n Slaton	R	17	11	.607	4.12	0	35	34	11	233.2	235	85	92	117	107	2	9.05	3.27	3.54
lt Wilcox	R	13	12	.520	3.76	0	29	27	16	215.1	208	68	132	94	90	2	8.69	2.84	5.52
ve Rozema	R	9	12	.429	3.14	0	28	28	11	209.1	205	41	57	83	73	2	8.81	1.76	2.45
ck Billingham	R	15	8	.652	3.88	0	30	30	10	201.2	218	65	59	95	87	4	9.73	2.90	2.63
ck Morris	R	3	5	.375	4.33	0	28	7	0	106	107	49	48	57	51	0	9.08	4.16	4.08
o Young	R	6	7	.462	2.81	0	14	13	7	105.2	94	30	49	34	33	0	8.01	2.56	4.17
b Sykes	L	6	6	.500	3.94	2	22	10	3	93.2	99	34	58	43	41	2	9.51	3.27	5.57
hn Hiller	L	9	4	.692	2.34	15	51	0	0	92.1	64	35	74	27	24	0	6.24	3.41	7.21
ve Baker	R	2	4	.333	4.55	0	15	10	0	63.1	66	42	39	37	32	0	9.38	5.97	5.54
n Crawford	L	2	3	.400	4.35	0	20	0	0	39.1	45	19	24	24	19	0	10.30	4.35	5.49
ve Foucault	R	2	4	.333	3.16	4	24	0	0	37	48	21	18	18	13	0	11.68	5.11	4.38
ark Fidrych	R	2	0	1.000	2.45	0	3	3	2	22	17	5	10	6	6	0	6.95	2.05	4.09
Glynn	L	0	0	—	3.07	0	10	0	0	14.2	11	4	9	5	5	0	6.75	2.45	5.52
ve Tobik	R	0	0	—	3.75	0	10	0	0	12	12	3	11	5	5	0	9.00	2.25	8.25
rnando Arroyo	R	0	0	—	8.31	0	2	0	0	4.1	8	0	1	4	4	0	16.62	0.00	2.08
eldon Burnside	L	0	0	—	9.00	0	2	0	0	4	4	2	3	4	4	0	9.00	4.50	6.75
uce Taylor	R	0	0	—	0.00	0	1	0	0	0	1	0	0	0	0	0	0.00	0.00	0.00
AM TOTAL		86	76	.531	3.67	21	319	162	60	1455.1	1441	503	684	653	594	12	8.91	3.11	4.23

MANAGER

	W	L	PCT
Les Moss	27	26	.509
Dick Tracewski	2	1	.667
Sparky Anderson	56	49	.533

POS	Player	B	G	AB	H	2B	3B	HR	HR %	R	RBI	BB	SO	SB	Pinch Hit AB	Pinch Hit H	BA	SA
REGULARS																		
1B	Jason Thompson	L	145	492	121	16	1	20	4.1	58	79	70	90	2	8	2	.246	.404
2B	Lou Whitaker	L	127	423	121	14	8	3	0.7	75	42	78	66	20	5	0	.286	.378
SS	Alan Trammell	R	142	460	127	11	4	6	1.3	68	50	43	55	17	0	0	.276	.357
3B	Aurelio Rodriguez	R	106	343	87	18	0	5	1.5	27	36	11	40	0	3	0	.254	.350
RF	Jerry Morales	R	129	440	93	23	1	14	3.2	50	56	30	56	10	7	0	.211	.364
CF	Ron LeFlore	R	148	600	180	22	10	9	1.5	110	57	52	95	78	1	1	.300	.415
LF	Steve Kemp	L	134	490	156	26	3	26	5.3	88	105	68	70	5	4	1	.318	.543
C	Lance Parrish	R	143	493	136	26	3	19	3.9	65	65	49	105	6	3	1	.276	.456
DH	Rusty Staub	L	68	246	58	12	1	9	3.7	32	40	32	18	1	2	0	.236	.402
SUBSTITUTES																		
UT	John Wockenfuss	R	87	231	61	9	1	15	6.5	27	46	18	40	2	20	5	.264	.506
32	Tom Brookens	R	60	190	50	5	2	4	2.1	23	21	11	40	10	0	0	.263	.374
S2	Mark Wagner	R	75	146	40	3	0	1	0.7	16	13	16	25	3	1	1	.274	.315
3B	Phil Mankowski	L	42	99	22	4	0	0	0.0	11	8	10	16	0	9	1	.222	.263
DO	Al Greene	L	29	59	8	1	0	3	5.1	9	6	10	15	0	6	2	.136	.305
2B	Dave Machemer	R	19	26	5	1	0	0	0.0	8	2	3	2	0	0	0	.192	.231
UT	Ricky Peters	B	12	19	5	0	0	0	0.0	3	2	5	3	0	1	0	.263	.263
OF	Champ Summers	L	90	246	77	12	1	20	8.1	47	51	40	33	7	13	4	.313	.614
OF	Lynn Jones	R	95	213	63	8	0	4	1.9	33	26	17	22	9	11	2	.296	.390
OF	Kirk Gibson	L	12	38	9	3	0	1	2.6	3	4	1	3	3	2	0	.237	.395
OF	Dave Stegman	R	12	31	6	0	0	3	9.7	6	5	2	3	1	1	0	.194	.484
UT	Tim Corcoran	L	18	22	5	1	0	0	0.0	4	6	4	2	1	2	1	.227	.273
OD	Dan Gonzalez	L	7	18	4	1	0	0	0.0	1	2	0	2	1	3	0	.222	.278
C1	Ed Putman	R	21	39	9	3	0	2	5.1	4	4	4	12	0	3	0	.231	.462
C	Milt May	L	6	11	3	2	0	0	0.0	1	3	1	1	0	1	0	.273	.455
PITCHERS																		
P	John Hiller	R	43	0	0	0	0	0	–	0	0	0	0	0	0	0	–	–
P	Jack Billingham	R	35	0	0	0	0	0	–	0	0	0	0	0	0	0	–	–
P	Aurelio Lopez	R	61	0	0	0	0	0	–	0	0	0	0	0	0	0	–	–
P	Fernando Arroyo	R	6	0	0	0	0	0	–	0	0	0	0	0	0	0	–	–
P	Mark Fidrych	R	4	0	0	0	0	0	–	0	0	0	0	0	0	0	–	–
P	Jack Morris	R	28	0	0	0	0	0	–	1	0	0	0	0	0	0	–	–
P	Dave Rozema	R	16	0	0	0	0	0	–	0	0	0	0	0	0	0	–	–
P	Bruce Taylor	R	10	0	0	0	0	0	–	0	0	0	0	0	0	0	–	–
P	Steve Baker	R	21	0	0	0	0	0	–	0	0	0	0	0	0	0	–	–
P	Sheldon Burnside	R	10	0	0	0	0	0	–	0	0	0	0	0	0	0	–	–
P	Dave Tobik	R	37	0	0	0	0	0	–	0	0	0	0	0	0	0	–	–
P	Kip Young	R	13	0	0	0	0	0	–	0	0	0	0	0	0	0	–	–
P	Mike Chris	L	13	0	0	0	0	0	–	0	0	0	0	0	0	0	–	–
P	Dan Petry	R	15	0	0	0	0	0	–	0	0	0	0	0	0	0	–	–
P	Bruce Robbins	L	10	0	0	0	0	0	–	0	0	0	0	0	0	0	–	–
P	Pat Underwood	L	27	0	0	0	0	0	–	0	0	0	0	0	0	0	–	–
P	Milt Wilcox	R	33	0	0	0	0	0	–	0	0	0	0	0	0	0	–	–
TEAM TOTAL				5375	1446	221	35	164	3.1	770	729	575	814	176	106	21	.269	.415

INDIVIDUAL FIELDING

POS	Player	T	G	PO	A	E	DP	TC/G	FA
1B	J. Thompson	L	140	1176	91	8	135	9.1	.994
	J. Wockenfuss	R	31	205	18	1	22	7.2	.996
	A. Rodriguez	R	1	0	0	0	0	0.0	.000
	E. Putman	R	5	35	3	1	5	7.8	.974
	T. Corcoran	L	5	35	1	0	2	7.2	1.000
	C. Summers	R	4	23	1	0	1	6.0	1.000
2B	L. Whitaker	R	126	280	369	9	103	5.2	.986
	M. Wagner	R	29	57	63	5	10	4.3	.960
	T. Brookens	R	19	37	42	3	10	4.3	.963
	D. Machemer	R	11	15	20	1	6	3.3	.972
	R. Peters	R	2	1	0	0	0	0.5	1.000
SS	A. Trammell	R	142	245	388	26	99	4.6	.961
	M. Wagner	R	41	31	83	3	18	2.9	.974
3B	A. Rodriguez	R	106	72	211	13	23	2.8	.956
	T. Brookens	R	42	39	99	8	11	3.5	.945
	P. Mankowski	R	36	22	56	3	6	2.3	.963
	M. Wagner	R	2	0	0	0	0	0.0	.000
	R. Peters	R	3	0	0	2	0	0.7	.000
OF	R. LeFlore	R	113	293	6	3	3	2.7	.990
	S. Kemp	L	120	229	12	6	2	2.1	.976
	J. Morales	R	119	206	6	3	2	1.8	.986
	L. Jones	R	84	142	3	3	1	1.8	.980
	C. Summers	R	69	87	3	1	0	1.3	.989
	D. Stegman	R	12	35	0	0	0	2.9	1.000
	K. Gibson	L	10	15	0	0	0	1.5	1.000
	A. Greene	R	6	14	0	0	0	2.3	1.000
	T. Corcoran	L	9	10	1	0	0	1.2	1.000
	J. Wockenfuss	R	6	4	0	0	0	0.7	1.000
	D. Machemer	R	1	3	0	0	0	3.0	1.000
	R. Peters	R	1	3	0	0	0	3.0	1.000
	D. Gonzalez	R	3	3	0	0	0	1.0	1.000
C	L. Parrish	R	142	707	79	9	10	5.6	.989
	J. Wockenfuss	R	20	109	8	2	0	6.0	.983
	E. Putman	R	16	40	4	0	0	2.8	1.000
	M. May	R	5	19	1	0	0	4.0	1.000

The Tigers switched managers in midseason and traded their highest-paid player. But the bottom line stayed the same: the Tigers finished fifth for the third time in four years, 18 games behind the first-place Orioles.

Rusty Staub sat out spring training hoping to extend his already team-high contract, finally settled on May 1, but was traded to Montreal after 68 games. And following a successful two-week road trip in June, Les Moss, who had taken over after Ralph Houk's retirement, was dumped in favor of Sparky Anderson, fired by the Reds the previous winter.

Anderson spoke of catching "lightning in a bottle" with his new club, but instead the Tigers flickered: Detroit lost nine of its first 11 under the new manager to take fifth place for keeps by the end of June.

Mark Fidrych failed in another comeback attempt (0–3, 10.20 ERA), Dave Rozema suffered arm problems for the second straight year, and first baseman Jason Thompson slumped 24 points to .246. Still, Anderson's enthusiasm wasn't completely unfounded. The Tigers assumed a style unseen in Detroit since World War I, stealing 176 bases, second in the league and team-high since the Ty Cobb era. Ron LeFlore led Detroit base stealers with 78. Leftfielder Steve Kemp's average jumped 41 points to .318 with 26 home runs and 105 RBI. Outfielder–first baseman Champ Summers was acquired in May and became a fan favorite, using Tiger Stadium's short right field to hit 20 home runs and hit .313 in 90 games. The pitching staff enjoyed excellent defensive support as Detroit led the league in fewest errors. Jack Morris spent the season's first month in the minors, but would lead the staff at 17–7 with a 3.27 ERA. And portly reliever Aurelio Lopez, acquired from St. Louis in the off-season, flourished under Anderson, finishing 10–5 with 21 saves.

TEAM STATISTICS

	W	L	PCT	GB	R	OR	2B	3B	HR	BA	SA	SB	E	DP	FA	CG	BB	SO	ShO	SV	ERA
ST									Batting					Fielding				Pitching			
L	102	57	.642		757	**582**	258	24	181	.261	.419	99	125	161	.980	52	467	786	**12**	30	**3.26**
L	95	66	.590	8	807	722	291	41	185	.280	.448	100	127	153	.980	**61**	381	580	**12**	23	4.03
S	91	69	.569	11.5	841	711	**310**	34	**194**	**.283**	**.456**	60	142	166	.977	47	463	731	11	29	4.03
	89	71	.556	13.5	734	672	226	40	150	.266	.406	65	122	183	**.981**	43	455	731	10	37	3.83
T	85	76	.528	18	770	738	221	35	164	.269	.415	176	**120**	184	**.981**	25	547	802	5	37	4.28
E	81	80	.503	22	760	805	206	29	138	.258	.384	143	134	149	.978	28	570	781	7	32	4.57
R	53	109	.327	50.5	613	862	253	34	95	.251	.363	75	159	187	.975	44	594	613	7	11	4.82
EST																					
L	88	74	.543		866	768	242	43	164	.282	.429	100	135	172	.978	46	573	**820**	9	33	4.34
	85	77	.525	3	851	816	286	**79**	116	.282	.422	**207**	146	160	.977	42	536	640	7	27	4.45
X	83	79	.512	5	750	698	252	26	140	.278	.409	79	130	151	.979	26	532	773	10	**42**	3.86
l	82	80	.506	6	764	725	256	46	112	.278	.402	66	134	**203**	.979	31	452	721	6	33	4.13
l	73	87	.456	14	730	748	290	33	127	.275	.410	97	173	142	.972	28	618	675	9	37	4.10
A	67	95	.414	21	711	820	250	52	132	.269	.404	126	141	170	.978	37	571	736	7	26	4.58
K	54	108	.333	34	573	860	188	32	108	.239	.346	104	174	137	.972	41	654	726	4	20	4.75
AGUE TOTAL					10527	10527	3529	548	2006	.270	.408	1497	1962	2318	.978	551	7413	10115	116	417	4.22

INDIVIDUAL PITCHING

TCHER	T	W	L	PCT	ERA	SV	G	GS	CG	IP	H	BB	SO	R	ER	ShO	H/9	BB/9	SO/9
ck Morris	R	17	7	.708	3.27	0	27	27	9	198	179	59	113	76	72	1	8.14	2.68	5.14
t Wilcox	R	12	10	.545	4.36	0	33	29	7	196	201	73	109	105	95	0	9.23	3.35	5.01
ck Billingham	R	10	7	.588	3.30	3	35	19	2	158	163	60	59	74	58	0	9.28	3.42	3.36
relio Lopez	R	10	5	.667	2.41	21	61	0	0	127	95	51	106	37	34	0	6.73	3.61	7.51
t Underwood	L	6	4	.600	4.57	0	27	15	1	122	126	29	83	64	62	0	9.30	2.14	6.12
n Petry	R	6	5	.545	3.95	0	15	15	2	98	90	33	43	46	43	0	8.27	3.03	3.95
ve Rozema	R	4	4	.500	3.53	0	16	16	4	97	101	30	33	52	38	1	9.37	2.78	3.06
ve Baker	R	1	7	.125	6.64	1	21	12	0	84	97	51	54	63	62	0	10.39	5.46	5.79
n Hiller	L	4	7	.364	5.24	9	43	0	0	79	83	55	46	47	46	0	9.46	6.27	5.24
ve Tobik	R	3	5	.375	4.30	3	37	0	0	69	59	25	48	34	33	0	7.70	3.26	6.26
ice Robbins	L	3	3	.500	3.91	0	10	8	0	46	45	21	22	21	20	0	8.80	4.11	4.30
Young	R	2	2	.500	6.34	0	13	7	0	44	60	11	22	32	31	0	12.27	2.25	4.50
ke Chris	L	3	3	.500	6.92	0	13	8	0	39	46	21	31	30	30	0	10.62	4.85	7.15
eldon Burnside	L	1	1	.500	6.43	0	10	0	0	21	28	8	13	16	15	0	12.00	3.43	5.57
ice Taylor	R	1	2	.333	4.74	0	10	0	0	19	16	7	8	13	10	0	7.58	3.32	3.79
rk Fidrych	R	0	3	.000	10.20	0	4	4	0	15	23	9	5	17	17	0	13.80	5.40	3.00
nando Arroyo	R	1	1	.500	8.25	0	6	0	0	12	17	4	7	11	11	0	12.75	3.00	5.25
AM TOTAL		84	76	.525	4.28	37	381	160	25	1424	1429	547	802	738	677	2	9.03	3.46	5.07

MANAGER	W	L	PCT
Sparky Anderson	84	78	.519

POS	Player	B	G	AB	H	2B	3B	HR	HR %	R	RBI	BB	SO	SB	Pinch Hit AB	Pinch Hit H	BA	SA
REGULARS																		
1B	Richie Hebner	L	104	341	99	10	7	12	3.5	48	82	38	45	0	11	6	.290	.466
2B	Lou Whitaker	L	145	477	111	19	1	1	0.2	68	45	73	79	8	8	2	.233	.283
SS	Alan Trammell	R	146	560	168	21	5	9	1.6	107	65	69	63	12	2	0	.300	.404
3B	Tom Brookens	R	151	509	140	25	9	10	2.0	64	66	32	71	13	4	1	.275	.418
RF	Al Cowens	R	108	403	113	15	3	5	1.2	58	42	37	40	5	2	0	.280	.370
CF	Ricky Peters	B	133	477	139	19	7	2	0.4	79	42	54	48	13	13	3	.291	.373
LF	Steve Kemp	L	135	508	149	23	3	21	4.1	88	101	69	64	5	6	2	.293	.474
C	Lance Parrish	R	144	553	158	34	6	24	4.3	79	82	31	109	6	4	1	.286	.499
DH	Champ Summers	L	120	347	103	19	1	17	4.9	61	60	52	52	4	26	7	.297	.504
SUBSTITUTES																		
UT	John Wockenfuss	R	126	372	102	13	2	16	4.3	56	65	68	64	1	17	4	.274	.449
1O	Tim Corcoran	L	84	153	44	7	1	3	2.0	20	18	22	10	0	16	3	.288	.405
1B	Jason Thompson	L	36	126	27	5	0	4	3.2	10	20	13	26	0	0	0	.214	.349
UT	Stan Papi	R	46	114	27	3	4	3	2.6	12	17	5	24	0	4	1	.237	.412
UT	Mark Wagner	R	45	72	17	1	0	0	0.0	5	3	7	11	0	2	0	.236	.250
DO	Dan Gonzalez	L	2	7	1	0	0	0	0.0	1	0	0	1	0	1	0	.143	.143
OF	Kirk Gibson	L	51	175	46	2	1	9	5.1	23	16	10	45	4	5	1	.263	.440
OF	Jim Lentine	R	67	161	42	8	1	1	0.6	19	17	28	30	2	7	2	.261	.342
OF	Dave Stegman	R	65	130	23	5	0	2	1.5	12	9	14	23	1	6	1	.177	.262
OD	Lynn Jones	R	30	55	14	2	2	0	0.0	9	6	10	5	1	4	1	.255	.364
CD	Duffy Dyer	R	48	108	20	1	0	4	3.7	11	11	13	34	0	3	0	.185	.306
PITCHERS																		
P	John Hiller	R	11	0	0	0	0	0	–	0	0	0	0	0	0	0	–	–
P	Jack Billingham	R	8	0	0	0	0	0	–	0	0	0	0	0	0	0	–	–
P	Aurelio Lopez	R	67	0	0	0	0	0	–	0	0	0	0	0	0	0	–	–
P	Mark Fidrych	R	10	0	0	0	0	0	–	0	0	0	0	0	0	0	–	–
P	Jack Morris	R	44	0	0	0	0	0	–	0	0	0	0	0	0	0	–	–
P	Dave Rozema	R	42	0	0	0	0	0	–	0	0	0	0	0	0	0	–	–
P	Dan Schatzeder	L	32	0	0	0	0	0	–	0	0	0	0	0	0	0	–	–
P	Dave Tobik	R	17	0	0	0	0	0	–	0	0	0	0	0	0	0	–	–
P	Dan Petry	R	27	0	0	0	0	0	–	0	0	0	0	0	0	0	–	–
P	Bruce Robbins	L	15	0	0	0	0	0	–	0	0	0	0	0	0	0	–	–
P	Pat Underwood	L	49	0	0	0	0	0	–	0	0	0	0	0	0	0	–	–
P	Roger Weaver	R	19	0	0	0	0	0	–	0	0	0	0	0	0	0	–	–
P	Jerry Ujdur	R	9	0	0	0	0	0	–	0	0	0	0	0	0	0	–	–
P	Milt Wilcox	R	33	0	0	0	0	0	0	0	0	0	0	0	0	0	–	–
TEAM TOTAL				5648	1543	232	53	143	2.5	830	767	645	844	75	141	35	.273	.409

INDIVIDUAL FIELDING

POS	Player	T	G	PO	A	E	DP	TC/G	FA	POS	Player	T	G	PO	A	E	DP	TC/G	FA
1B	R. Hebner	R	61	466	35	1	35	8.2	.998	OF	R. Peters	R	109	296	1	7	1	2.8	.977
	J. Wockenfuss	R	52	415	35	8	41	8.8	.983		A. Cowens	R	107	199	8	3	2	2.0	.986
	J. Thompson	L	36	328	30	0	33	9.9	1.000		S. Kemp	L	85	197	4	1	3	2.4	.995
	T. Corcoran	R	48	249	18	4	32	5.6	.985		K. Gibson	L	49	122	1	1	0	2.5	.992
	C. Summers	R	1	0	0	0	0	0.0	.000		J. Lentine	R	55	98	5	4	0	1.9	.963
	L. Parrish	R	5	42	1	1	7	8.8	.977		D. Stegman	R	57	82	1	1	0	1.5	.988
	S. Papi	R	1	5	0	0	1	5.0	1.000		C. Summers	R	47	60	1	3	0	1.4	.953
2B	L. Whitaker	R	143	340	428	12	93	5.5	.985		J. Wockenfuss	R	23	37	2	0	1	1.7	1.000
	S. Papi	R	31	53	55	3	14	3.6	.973		L. Jones	R	17	31	0	0	0	1.8	1.000
	T. Brookens	R	9	13	26	0	10	4.3	1.000		T. Corcoran	L	18	25	1	1	0	1.5	.963
	M. Wagner	R	6	4	5	0	1	1.5	1.000		L. Parrish	R	5	8	0	0	0	1.6	1.000
SS	A. Trammell	R	144	225	412	13	89	4.5	.980		D. Gonzalez	R	1	3	0	1	0	4.0	.750
	M. Wagner	R	28	39	47	6	7	3.3	.935	C	L. Parrish	R	121	557	66	6	8	5.2	.990
	S. Papi	R	5	4	12	0	3	3.2	1.000		D. Dyer	R	37	129	10	2	0	3.8	.986
	T. Brookens	R	1	2	2	0	1	4.0	1.000		J. Wockenfuss	R	25	123	10	3	2	5.4	.978
3B	T. Brookens	R	138	112	279	29	27	3.0	.931										
	R. Hebner	R	32	19	49	3	10	2.2	.958										
	S. Papi	R	11	6	13	2	1	1.9	.905										
	M. Wagner	R	9	0	9	1	0	1.1	.900										

On the threshold of his first full Detroit season, manager George Lee Anderson issued a prediction. "If our pitching comes through we'll contend," declared Sparky. "If not, then we'll disappear." The Tigers lost seven of their first eight, and were soon invisible.

Ron LeFlore was traded to Montreal in the off-season, and heralded Michigan State rookie Kirk Gibson was sidelined by a wrist injury, but the Tigers didn't worry about scoring runs—they led the majors with 830, although shortstop Alan Trammell was the only Tiger to hit .300. The Tigers hit pitchers in more ways than one: Al Cowens was suspended for seven games when he charged Ed Farmer, who had broken his jaw with a pitch the previous season, on the mound on June 20 in Chicago. Farmer filed criminal charges, preventing Cowens from making an August return trip to Chicago lest he be picked up by the authorities. But the pair shook hands at home plate when the White Sox visited Detroit in September, and the complaint was dropped.

The Tigers did worry about opponents scoring runs; the team ERA was 4.25, as Detroit finished fifth for the third straight year, 19 games behind the first-place Yankees. Jack Morris led the staff at 16–15 with a 4.18 ERA. Sophomore Dan Petry (10–9) was the only Tiger starter to crack the 4.00 ERA barrier—but just barely at 3.93. John Hiller retired in midseason at age 37, concluding his career as the top reliever in Tiger history, with 125 saves. Aurelio Lopez picked up some of the bullpen slack but proved inconsistent. "We scored more than five runs a game on the average," said Anderson. "We just have to find a way to keep the other team from scoring six."

TEAM STATISTICS

	W	L	PCT	GB	R	OR	2B	3B	HR	BA	SA	SB	E	DP	FA	CG	BB	SO	ShO	SV	ERA
AST																					
Y	103	59	.636		820	662	239	34	189	.267	.425	86	138	160	.978	29	463	845	15	50	3.58
AL	100	62	.617	3	805	640	258	29	156	.273	.413	111	95	178	.985	42	507	789	10	41	3.64
IL	86	76	.531	17	811	682	298	36	203	.275	.448	131	147	189	.977	48	420	575	14	30	3.71
OS	83	77	.519	19	757	767	297	36	162	.283	.436	79	149	206	.977	30	481	696	8	43	4.38
ET	84	78	.519	19	830	757	232	53	143	.273	.409	75	133	165	.979	40	558	741	9	30	4.25
LE	79	81	.494	23	738	807	221	40	89	.277	.381	118	105	143	.983	35	552	842	8	32	4.68
OR	67	95	.414	36	624	762	249	53	126	.251	.383	67	133	206	.979	39	635	705	9	23	4.19
EST																					
	97	65	.599		809	694	266	59	115	.286	.413	185	141	150	.978	37	465	614	10	42	3.83
AK	83	79	.512	14	686	642	212	35	137	.259	.385	175	130	115	.979	94	521	769	9	13	3.46
IN	77	84	.478	19.5	670	724	252	46	99	.265	.381	62	148	192	.977	35	468	744	9	30	3.93
EX	76	85	.472	20.5	756	752	263	27	124	.284	.405	91	147	169	.977	35	519	890	6	25	4.02
HI	70	90	.438	26	587	722	255	38	91	.259	.370	68	171	162	.973	32	563	724	12	42	3.92
AL	65	95	.406	31	698	797	236	32	106	.265	.378	91	134	144	.978	22	529	725	6	30	4.52
EA	59	103	.364	38	610	793	211	35	104	.248	.356	116	149	189	.977	31	540	703	7	26	4.38
AGUE TOTAL					10201	10201	3489	553	1844	.269	.399	1455	1920	2368	.978	549	7221	10362	132	457	4.03

INDIVIDUAL PITCHING

TCHER	T	W	L	PCT	ERA	SV	G	GS	CG	IP	H	BB	SO	R	ER	ShO	H/9	BB/9	SO/9
ck Morris	R	16	15	.516	4.18	0	36	36	11	250	252	87	112	125	116	2	9.07	3.13	4.03
lt Wilcox	R	13	11	.542	4.48	0	32	31	13	199	201	68	97	112	99	1	9.09	3.08	4.39
an Schatzeder	L	11	13	.458	4.01	0	32	26	9	193	178	58	94	88	86	2	8.30	2.70	4.38
an Petry	R	10	9	.526	3.93	0	27	25	4	165	156	83	88	82	72	3	8.51	4.53	4.80
ave Rozema	R	6	9	.400	3.91	4	42	13	2	145	152	49	49	68	63	1	9.43	3.04	3.04
relio Lopez	R	13	6	.684	3.77	21	67	1	0	124	125	45	97	56	52	0	9.07	3.27	7.04
t Underwood	L	3	6	.333	3.58	5	49	7	0	113	121	35	60	51	45	0	9.64	2.79	4.78
ger Weaver	R	3	4	.429	4.08	0	19	6	0	64	56	34	42	32	29	0	7.88	4.78	5.91
ave Tobik	R	1	0	1.000	3.98	0	17	1	0	61	61	21	34	27	27	0	9.00	3.10	5.02
uce Robbins	L	4	2	.667	6.58	0	15	6	0	52	60	28	23	40	38	0	10.38	4.85	3.98
ark Fidrych	R	2	3	.400	5.73	0	9	9	1	44	58	20	16	35	28	0	11.86	4.09	3.27
hn Hiller	L	1	0	1.000	4.35	0	11	0	0	31	38	14	18	15	15	0	11.03	4.06	5.23
rry Ujdur	R	1	0	1.000	7.71	0	9	2	0	21	36	10	8	20	18	0	15.43	4.29	3.43
ck Billingham	R	0	0	–	7.71	0	8	0	0	7	11	6	3	6	6	0	14.14	7.71	3.86
AM TOTAL		84	78	.519	4.25	30	373	163	40	1469	1505	558	741	757	694	9	9.22	3.42	4.54

MANAGER	W	L	PCT
Sparky Anderson	31	26	.544
Sparky Anderson	29	23	.558

POS	Player	B	G	AB	H	2B	3B	HR	HR %	R	RBI	BB	SO	SB	Pinch Hit AB	H	BA	SA
REGULARS																		
1B	Richie Hebner	L	78	226	51	8	2	5	2.2	19	28	27	28	1	11	1	.226	.345
2B	Lou Whitaker	L	109	335	88	14	4	5	1.5	48	36	40	42	5	2	1	.263	.373
SS	Alan Trammell	R	105	392	101	15	3	2	0.5	52	31	49	31	10	1	1	.258	.327
3B	Tom Brookens	R	71	239	58	10	1	4	1.7	19	25	14	43	5	1	0	.243	.343
RF	Kirk Gibson	L	83	290	95	11	3	9	3.1	41	40	18	64	17	8	1	.328	.479
CF	Al Cowens	R	85	253	66	11	4	1	0.4	27	18	22	36	3	12	3	.261	.348
LF	Steve Kemp	L	105	372	103	18	4	9	2.4	52	49	70	48	9	3	1	.277	.419
C	Lance Parrish	R	96	348	85	18	2	10	2.9	39	46	34	52	2	0	0	.244	.394
DH	Champ Summers	L	64	165	42	8	0	3	1.8	16	21	19	35	1	14	3	.255	.358
SUBSTITUTES																		
D1	John Wockenfuss	R	70	172	37	4	0	9	5.2	20	25	28	22	0	13	1	.215	.395
1B	Ron Jackson	R	31	95	27	8	1	1	1.1	12	12	8	11	4	7	1	.284	.421
3B	Stan Papi	R	40	93	19	2	1	3	3.2	8	12	3	18	1	4	1	.204	.344
1O	Rick Leach	L	54	83	16	3	1	1	1.2	9	11	16	15	0	10	2	.193	.289
UT	Mick Kelleher	R	61	77	17	4	0	0	0.0	10	6	7	10	0	3	1	.221	.273
UT	Marty Castillo	R	6	8	1	0	0	0	0.0	1	0	0	2	0	0	0	.125	.125
OD	Ricky Peters	B	63	207	53	7	3	0	0.0	26	15	29	28	1	5	1	.256	.319
OF	Lynn Jones	R	71	174	45	5	0	2	1.1	19	19	18	10	1	13	4	.259	.322
OD	Darrell Brown	B	16	4	1	0	0	0	0.0	4	0	0	1	1	2	1	.250	.250
C	Bill Fahey	L	27	67	17	2	0	1	1.5	5	9	2	4	0	0	0	.254	.328
C	Duffy Dyer	R	2	0	0	0	0	0	—	0	0	0	0	0	0	0	—	—
PITCHERS																		
P	Aurelio Lopez	R	29	0	0	0	0	0	—	0	0	0	0	0	0	0	—	—
P	Jack Morris	R	25	0	0	0	0	0	—	0	0	0	0	0	0	0	—	—
P	Dave Rozema	R	28	0	0	0	0	0	—	0	0	0	0	0	0	0	—	—
P	Dan Schatzeder	L	17	0	0	0	0	0	—	0	0	0	0	0	0	0	—	—
P	Dennis Kinney	L	6	0	0	0	0	0	—	0	0	0	0	0	0	0	—	—
P	Dave Tobik	R	27	0	0	0	0	0	—	0	0	0	0	0	0	0	—	—
P	Kevin Saucier	R	38	0	0	0	0	0	—	0	0	0	0	0	0	0	—	—
P	Dan Petry	R	23	0	0	0	0	0	—	0	0	0	0	0	0	0	—	—
P	Jerry Ujdur	R	4	0	0	0	0	0	—	0	0	0	0	0	0	0	—	—
P	Milt Wilcox	R	24	0	0	0	0	0	—	0	0	0	0	0	0	0	—	—
P	Howard Bailey	R	9	0	0	0	0	0	—	0	0	0	0	0	0	0	—	—
P	George Cappuzzello	R	18	0	0	0	0	0	—	0	0	0	0	0	0	0	—	—
P	Larry Rothschild	R	5	0	0	0	0	0	—	0	0	0	0	0	0	0	—	—
P	Dave Rucker	L	2	0	0	0	0	0	—	0	0	0	0	0	0	0	—	—
TEAM TOTAL				3600	922	148	29	65	1.8	427	403	404	500	61	109	23	.256	.368

INDIVIDUAL FIELDING

POS	Player	T	G	PO	A	E	DP	TC/G	FA
1B	R. Hebner	R	61	531	29	3	36	9.2	.995
	R. Jackson	R	29	218	15	0	20	8.0	1.000
	J. Wockenfuss	R	25	179	5	3	27	7.5	.984
	R. Leach	L	32	133	14	0	15	4.6	1.000
	S. Papi	R	1	1	0	0	0	1.0	1.000
2B	L. Whitaker	R	108	227	354	9	77	5.5	.985
	M. Kelleher	R	11	9	16	1	5	2.4	.962
	S. Papi	R	1	1	1	0	0	2.0	1.000
SS	A. Trammell	R	105	181	347	9	65	5.1	.983
	M. Kelleher	R	9	9	31	0	5	4.4	1.000
3B	T. Brookens	R	71	58	139	10	13	2.9	.952
	S. Papi	R	32	14	50	4	3	2.1	.941
	M. Kelleher	R	39	12	28	3	2	1.1	.930
	M. Castillo	R	4	3	8	0	3	2.8	1.000

POS	Player	T	G	PO	A	E	DP	TC/G	FA
OF	S. Kemp	L	92	207	4	3	0	2.3	.986
	A. Cowens	R	83	166	3	1	0	2.0	.994
	K. Gibson	L	67	142	1	4	0	2.2	.973
	R. Peters	R	38	103	3	1	1	2.8	.991
	L. Jones	R	60	85	5	1	2	1.5	.989
	C. Summers	R	18	26	1	1	0	1.6	.964
	R. Leach	L	15	16	0	0	0	1.1	1.000
	S. Papi	R	1	0	0	0	0	0.0	.000
	J. Wockenfuss	R	1	3	0	0	0	3.0	1.000
	D. Brown	R	6	2	0	0	0	0.3	1.000
	M. Castillo	R	1	1	0	0	0	1.0	1.000
C	L. Parrish	R	90	407	40	3	6	5.0	.993
	B. Fahey	R	27	96	9	2	3	4.0	.981
	D. Dyer	R	2	0	0	0	0	0.0	.000
	J. Wockenfuss	R	5	15	1	0	0	3.2	1.000
	M. Castillo	R	1	1	0	0	0	1.0	1.000

A June 12 baseball strike that lasted 50 days forced players to find other work (Tiger Richie Hebner dug graves), forced fans to get their baseball fixes elsewhere (Japanese games were televised), and forced the Lords of Baseball to split the season (more playoffs were a quick way to recoup lost TV money). After finishing fourth in the first half, the poststrike Tigers trailed the first-place Brewers by a game when they visited Milwaukee for a schedule-ending three-game series. For the first time in nine years, Detroit was embroiled in a pennant race. But Dan Petry lost the opener, 8–2, to Moose Haas, and Rollie Fingers came on in relief to shut down and eliminate the Tigers in the second game, 2–1. Detroit won the meaningless third game to finish one game out in a second-half second-place tie with the Red Sox; overall the Tigers finished 60–49 in fourth place, two wins fewer then the league's best.

Leading Detroit's second-half success was outfielder Kirk Gibson, who hit .234 before the strike, but led poststrike major-leaguers at .375 to finish at .328 overall. Pitching was not the problem it was the year before. Jack Morris (14–7, 3.05), Milt Wilcox (12–9, 3.04), and Dan Petry (10–9, 3.00) proved three reliable starters; newly obtained reliever Kevin Saucier finished 4–2 with a 1.65 ERA and 13 saves. Saucier's wild dances off the mound following final outs became a new attraction at Tiger Stadium and earned him the nickname "Hot Sauce."

The Tigers knew they needed more runs, preferably produced by right-handed batters. By Christmas the team would have them: Chet Lemon and Larry Herndon, obtained in trades with the White Sox and the Giants respectively.

TEAM STATISTICS

	W	L	PCT	GB	R	OR	2B	3B	HR	BA	SA	SB	E	DP	FA	CG	BB	SO	ShO	SV	ERA
ST																					
	62	47	.569		493	459	173	20	96	.257	.391	39	79	135	.982	11	352	448	4	35	3.91
	59	46	.562	1	429	437	165	11	88	.251	.379	41	68	114	.983	25	347	489	10	23	3.70
	59	48	.551	2	421	343	148	22	100	.252	.391	46	72	100	.982	16	287	606	13	30	2.90
T	60	49	.550	2	427	404	148	29	65	.256	.368	61	67	109	.984	33	373	476	13	22	3.53
S	59	49	.546	2.5	519	481	168	17	90	.275	.399	32	91	108	.979	19	354	536	4	24	3.81
E	52	51	.505	7	431	442	150	21	39	.263	.351	119	87	91	.978	33	311	569	10	13	3.88
R	37	69	.349	23.5	329	466	137	23	61	.226	.330	66	105	102	.975	20	377	451	4	18	3.82
ST																					
K	64	45	.587	.	458	403	119	26	104	.247	.379	98	81	74	.980	60	370	505	11	10	3.30
K	57	48	.543	5	452	389	178	15	49	.270	.369	46	69	102	.984	23	322	488	13	18	3.40
I	54	52	.509	8.5	476	423	135	27	76	.272	.387	86	87	113	.979	20	336	529	8	23	3.47
	50	53	.485	11	397	405	169	29	61	.267	.383	100	72	94	.982	24	273	404	8	24	3.56
	51	59	.464	13.5	426	453	134	16	97	.256	.380	44	101	120	.977	27	323	426	8	19	3.70
A	44	65	.404	20	426	521	148	13	89	.251	.368	100	91	122	.979	10	360	478	5	23	4.23
N	41	68	.376	23	378	486	147	36	47	.240	.338	34	96	103	.978	13	376	500	6	22	3.98
GUE TOTAL					6112	6112	2119	305	1062	.256	.373	912	1166	1487	.980	334	4761	6905	117	304	3.66

INDIVIDUAL PITCHING

CHER	T	W	L	PCT	ERA	SV	G	GS	CG	IP	H	BB	SO	R	ER	ShO	H/9	BB/9	SO/9
k Morris	R	14	7	.667	3.05	0	25	25	15	198	153	78	97	69	67	1	6.95	3.55	4.41
t Wilcox	R	12	9	.571	3.04	0	24	24	8	166	152	52	79	61	56	1	8.24	2.82	4.28
n Petry	R	10	9	.526	3.00	0	23	22	7	141	115	57	79	53	47	2	7.34	3.64	5.04
ve Rozema	R	5	5	.500	3.63	3	28	9	2	104	99	25	46	42	42	2	8.57	2.16	3.98
elio Lopez	R	5	2	.714	3.62	3	29	3	0	82	70	31	53	34	33	0	7.68	3.40	5.82
n Schatzeder	L	6	8	.429	6.08	0	17	14	1	71	74	29	20	49	48	0	9.38	3.68	2.54
e Tobik	R	2	2	.500	2.70	1	27	0	0	60	47	33	32	19	18	0	7.05	4.95	4.80
in Saucier	L	4	2	.667	1.65	13	38	0	0	49	26	21	23	11	9	0	4.78	3.86	4.22
vard Bailey	L	1	4	.200	7.30	0	9	5	0	37	45	13	17	31	30	0	10.95	3.16	4.14
rge Cappuzzello	L	1	1	.500	3.44	1	18	3	0	34	28	18	19	14	13	0	7.41	4.76	5.03
ry Ujdur	R	0	0	–	6.43	0	4	4	0	14	19	5	5	12	10	0	12.21	3.21	3.21
ry Rothschild	R	0	0	–	1.50	1	5	0	0	6	4	6	1	1	1	0	6.00	9.00	1.50
nis Kinney	L	0	0	–	9.00	0	6	0	0	4	5	4	3	4	4	0	11.25	9.00	6.75
e Rucker	L	0	0	–	6.75	0	2	0	0	4	3	1	2	4	3	0	6.75	2.25	4.50
M TOTAL		60	49	.550	3.54	22	255	109	33	970	840	373	476	404	381	6	7.79	3.46	4.42

MANAGER	W	L	PCT
Sparky Anderson	83	79	.512

POS	Player	B	G	AB	H	2B	3B	HR	HR %	R	RBI	BB	SO	SB	Pinch Hit AB	Pinch Hit H	BA	SA
REGULARS																		
1B	Enos Cabell	R	125	464	121	17	3	2	0.4	45	37	15	48	15	10	2	.261	.323
2B	Lou Whitaker	L	152	560	160	22	8	15	2.7	76	65	48	58	11	4	1	.286	.434
SS	Alan Trammell	R	157	489	126	34	3	9	1.8	66	57	52	47	19	0	0	.258	.395
3B	Tom Brookens	R	140	398	92	15	3	9	2.3	40	58	27	63	5	6	2	.231	.352
RF	Chet Lemon	R	125	436	116	20	1	19	4.4	75	52	56	69	1	2	1	.266	.447
CF	Glenn Wilson	R	84	322	94	15	1	12	3.7	39	34	15	51	2	2	0	.292	.457
LF	Larry Herndon	R	157	614	179	21	13	23	3.7	92	88	38	92	12	3	0	.292	.480
C	Lance Parrish	R	133	486	138	19	2	32	6.6	75	87	40	99	3	2	1	.284	.529
DH	Mike Ivie	R	80	259	60	12	1	14	5.4	35	38	24	51	0	11	2	.232	.448
SUBSTITUTES																		
1O	Rick Leach	L	82	218	52	7	2	3	1.4	23	12	21	29	4	14	2	.239	.330
DO	Jerry Turner	L	85	210	52	3	0	8	3.8	21	27	20	37	1	24	4	.248	.376
1D	Richie Hebner	L	68	179	49	6	0	8	4.5	25	18	25	21	1	14	3	.274	.441
UT	Howard Johnson	B	54	155	49	5	0	4	2.6	23	14	16	30	7	7	1	.316	.426
1D	Mike Laga	L	27	88	23	9	0	3	3.4	6	11	4	23	1	4	1	.261	.466
SS	Mark DeJohn	B	24	21	4	2	0	0	0.0	1	1	4	4	1	0	0	.190	.286
23	Mick Kelleher	R	2	1	0	0	0	0	0.0	0	0	0	0	0	1	0	.000	.000
OF	Kirk Gibson	L	69	266	74	16	2	8	3.0	34	35	25	41	9	1	0	.278	.444
OF	Lynn Jones	R	58	139	31	3	1	0	0.0	15	14	7	14	0	7	2	.223	.259
OF	Eddie Miller	B	14	25	1	0	0	0	0.0	3	0	4	4	1	1	0	.040	.040
UT	John Wockenfuss	R	70	193	58	9	0	8	4.1	28	32	29	21	0	11	4	.301	.472
C	Bill Fahey	L	28	67	10	2	0	0	0.0	7	4	0	5	1	2	0	.149	.179
C	Marty Castillo	R	1	0	0	0	0	0	–	0	0	0	0	0	0	0	–	–
PITCHERS																		
P	Aurelio Lopez	R	19	0	0	0	0	0	–	0	0	0	0	0	0	0	–	–
P	Jack Morris	R	37	0	0	0	0	0	–	0	0	0	0	0	0	0	–	–
P	Dave Rozema	R	8	0	0	0	0	0	–	0	0	0	0	0	0	0	–	–
P	Dave Tobik	R	51	0	0	0	0	0	–	0	0	0	0	0	0	0	–	–
P	Juan Berenguer	R	2	0	0	0	0	0	–	0	0	0	0	0	0	0	–	–
P	Bob James	R	12	0	0	0	0	0	–	0	0	0	0	0	0	0	–	–
P	Kevin Saucier	R	31	0	0	0	0	0	–	0	0	0	0	0	0	0	–	–
P	Dan Petry	R	35	0	0	0	0	0	–	0	0	0	0	0	0	0	–	–
P	Jerry Ujdur	R	25	0	0	0	0	0	–	0	0	0	0	0	0	0	–	–
P	Pat Underwood	L	33	0	0	0	0	0	–	0	0	0	0	0	0	0	–	–
P	Milt Wilcox	R	29	0	0	0	0	0	–	0	0	0	0	0	0	0	–	–
P	Howard Bailey	R	8	0	0	0	0	0	–	0	0	0	0	0	0	0	–	–
P	Larry Rothschild	R	2	0	0	0	0	0	–	0	0	0	0	0	0	0	–	–
P	Dave Rucker	L	27	0	0	0	0	0	–	0	0	0	0	0	0	0	–	–
P	Dave Gumpert	R	5	0	0	0	0	0	–	0	0	0	0	0	0	0	–	–
P	Larry Pashnick	R	28	0	0	0	0	0	–	0	0	0	0	0	0	0	–	–
P	Elias Sosa	R	38	0	0	0	0	0	–	0	0	0	0	0	0	0	–	–
	TEAM TOTAL			5590	1489	237	40	177	3.2	729	684	470	807	93	126	26	.266	.418

INDIVIDUAL FIELDING

POS	Player	T	G	PO	A	E	DP	TC/G	FA
1B	E. Cabell	R	83	548	52	5	62	7.3	.992
	R. Leach	L	56	410	28	2	36	7.9	.995
	R. Hebner	R	40	286	25	3	15	7.9	.990
	M. Laga	L	19	163	4	1	18	8.8	.994
	J. Wockenfuss	R	17	122	3	0	9	7.4	1.000
2B	L. Whitaker	R	149	331	470	10	120	5.4	.988
	T. Brookens	R	26	37	57	2	7	3.7	.979
	M. DeJohn	R	1	1	1	0	1	2.0	1.000
	M. Kelleher	R	1	0	1	0	0	1.0	1.000
SS	A. Trammell	R	157	259	459	16	97	4.7	.978
	M. DeJohn	R	20	19	26	1	7	2.3	.978
	T. Brookens	R	9	7	13	0	0	2.2	1.000
3B	T. Brookens	R	113	72	206	18	20	2.6	.939
	E. Cabell	R	59	44	91	11	7	2.5	.925
	H. Johnson	R	33	25	39	7	6	2.2	.901
	J. Wockenfuss	R	1	0	0	0	0	0.0	.000
	M. Kelleher	R	1	0	0	0	0	0.0	.000
	M. DeJohn	R	4	0	4	1	2	1.3	.800

POS	Player	T	G	PO	A	E	DP	TC/G	FA
OF	L. Herndon	R	155	328	11	6	3	2.2	.983
	C. Lemon	R	121	242	11	4	2	2.1	.984
	G. Wilson	R	80	215	8	3	1	2.8	.987
	K. Gibson	L	64	167	4	1	3	2.7	.994
	L. Jones	R	56	86	3	0	2	1.6	1.000
	L. Parrish	R	1	0	0	0	0	0.0	.000
	E. Cabell	R	3	0	0	0	0	0.0	.000
	R. Leach	L	14	20	1	0	0	1.5	1.000
	J. Wockenfuss	R	10	15	1	0	0	1.6	1.000
	E. Miller	R	8	13	1	0	0	1.8	1.000
	H. Johnson	R	9	11	1	0	0	1.3	1.000
	J. Turner	L	13	10	0	1	0	0.8	.909
	T. Brookens	R	1	3	0	0	0	3.0	1.000
C	L. Parrish	R	132	627	76	8	8	5.4	.989
	J. Wockenfuss	R	24	91	10	2	0	4.3	.981
	B. Fahey	R	28	85	16	0	2	3.6	1.000
	M. Castillo	R	1	1	0	0	0	1.0	1.000

The Tigers longed for relief—all season. "We lost 28 games from the seventh inning on," said manager Sparky Anderson. "One relief pitcher would have made the difference." It was not to be. Kevin Saucier slumped his way back to the Florida Instructional League, Dave Rozema tore knee ligaments during a May 14 brawl with the Twins, and Aurelio Lopez suffered an early-season sore shoulder. Dave Tobik provided the most reliable relief at 4–9 with nine saves. And Detroit lost 15 of 17 during a June swoon en route to locking up another fourth-place season, 12 games behind the pennant-winning Brewers.

The starting rotation combined for 54 victories. Jack Morris, for the fourth straight year, led the team in wins at 17–16, and Dan Petry had the club's lowest ERA for the third straight year at 3.22. Leftfielder Larry Herndon batted a team high .292 with 23 home runs and 88 RBIs, and tied the major-league mark of four home runs in consecutive plate appearances on May 16 and 18, including three home runs with seven RBIs on May 18 versus the A's. Second baseman Lou Whitaker hit .286 providing Detroit with its first creditable leadoff man since the departure of LeFlore. Lance Parrish hit .284 and set the American League record for home runs by a catcher with 32. Howard Johnson, a rookie sent back to the minors for three months, returned and batted .347, winning the starting third-base job. And rookie outfielder Glenn Wilson hit .292 in 84 games (including a 19-game hitting streak) with 12 home runs.

TEAM STATISTICS

	W	L	PCT	GB	R	OR	Batting 2B	3B	HR	BA	SA	SB	Fielding E	DP	FA	Pitching CG	BB	SO	ShO	SV	ERA
ST																					
L	95	67	.586		891	717	277	41	216	.279	.455	84	125	184	.980	34	511	717	6	47	3.98
L	94	68	.580	1	774	687	259	27	179	.266	.419	49	101	140	.984	38	488	719	8	34	3.99
S	89	73	.549	6	753	713	271	31	136	.274	.407	42	121	172	.981	23	478	816	11	33	4.03
T	83	79	.512	12	729	685	237	40	177	.266	.418	93	117	164	.981	45	554	740	5	27	3.80
	79	83	.488	16	709	716	225	37	161	.256	.398	69	128	157	.979	24	589	882	9	30	3.99
E	78	84	.481	17	683	748	225	32	109	.262	.373	151	123	127	.980	31	589	882	9	30	4.11
R	78	84	.481	17	651	701	262	45	106	.262	.383	118	136	146	.978	41	493	776	13	25	3.95
ST																					
L	93	69	.574		814	670	268	26	186	.274	.433	55	108	171	.983	40	482	728	10	27	3.82
	90	72	.556	3	784	717	295	58	132	.285	.428	133	127	140	.979	16	471	650	12	45	4.08
l	87	75	.537	6	786	710	266	52	136	.273	.413	136	154	173	.976	30	460	753	10	41	3.87
A	76	86	.469	17	651	712	259	33	130	.254	.381	131	139	157	.978	23	547	1002	11	39	3.88
K	68	94	.420	25	691	819	211	27	149	.236	.367	232	160	135	.974	42	648	697	6	22	4.54
X	64	98	.395	29	590	749	204	26	115	.249	.359	63	121	168	.981	32	483	690	5	24	4.28
N	60	102	.370	33	657	819	234	44	148	.257	.396	38	108	162	.982	26	643	812	7	30	4.72
AGUE TOTAL					10163	10163	3493	519	2080	.264	.402	1394	1768	2196	.980	445	7338	10921	121	463	4.07

INDIVIDUAL PITCHING

TCHER	T	W	L	PCT	ERA	SV	G	GS	CG	IP	H	BB	SO	R	ER	ShO	H/9	BB/9	SO/9
ck Morris	R	17	16	.515	4.06	0	37	37	17	266.1	247	96	135	131	120	3	8.35	3.24	4.56
n Petry	R	15	9	.625	3.22	0	35	35	8	246	220	100	132	98	88	1	8.05	3.66	4.83
t Wilcox	R	12	10	.545	3.62	0	29	29	9	193.2	187	85	112	91	78	1	8.69	3.95	5.20
ry Ujdur	R	10	10	.500	3.69	0	25	25	7	178	150	69	86	76	73	0	7.58	3.49	4.35
Underwood	L	4	8	.333	4.73	3	33	12	2	99	108	22	43	66	52	0	9.82	2.00	3.91
ve Tobik	R	4	9	.308	3.56	9	51	1	0	98.2	86	38	63	45	39	0	7.84	3.47	5.75
rry Pashnick	R	4	4	.500	4.01	0	28	13	1	94.1	110	25	19	46	42	0	10.49	2.39	1.81
ve Rucker	L	5	6	.455	3.38	0	27	4	1	64	62	23	31	26	24	0	8.72	3.23	4.36
as Sosa	R	3	3	.500	4.43	4	38	0	0	61	64	18	24	31	30	0	9.44	2.66	3.54
relio Lopez	R	3	1	.750	5.27	3	19	0	0	41	41	19	26	27	24	0	9.00	4.17	5.71
vin Saucier	L	3	1	.750	3.12	5	31	1	0	40.1	35	29	23	15	14	0	7.81	6.47	5.13
ve Rozema	R	3	0	1.000	1.63	1	8	2	0	27.2	17	7	15	5	5	0	5.53	2.28	4.88
b James	R	0	2	.000	5.03	0	12	1	0	19.2	22	8	20	13	11	0	10.07	3.66	9.15
ward Bailey	L	0	0	—	0.00	1	8	0	0	10	6	2	3	0	0	0	5.40	1.80	2.70
an Berenguer	R	0	0	—	6.75	0	2	1	0	6.2	5	9	8	5	5	0	6.75	12.15	10.80
rry Rothschild	R	0	0	—	13.50	0	2	0	0	2.2	4	2	0	4	4	0	13.50	6.75	0.00
ve Gumpert	R	0	0	—	27.00	1	5	1	0	2	7	2	0	6	6	0	31.50	9.00	0.00
AM TOTAL		83	79	.512	3.81	27	390	162	45	1451	1371	554	740	685	615	5	8.50	3.44	4.59

MANAGER	W	L	PCT
Sparky Anderson	92	70	.568

POS	Player	B	G	AB	H	2B	3B	HR	HR %	R	RBI	BB	SO	SB	Pinch Hit AB	Pinch Hit H	BA	SA
REGULARS																		
1B	Enos Cabell	R	121	392	122	23	5	5	1.3	62	46	16	41	4	11	4	.311	.434
2B	Lou Whitaker	L	161	643	206	40	6	12	1.9	94	72	67	70	17	7	3	.320	.457
SS	Alan Trammell	R	142	505	161	31	2	14	2.8	83	66	57	64	30	0	0	.319	.471
3B	Tom Brookens	R	138	332	71	13	3	6	1.8	50	32	29	46	10	10	1	.214	.325
RF	Glenn Wilson	R	144	503	135	25	6	11	2.2	55	65	25	79	1	7	3	.268	.408
CF	Chet Lemon	R	145	491	125	21	5	24	4.9	78	69	54	70	0	2	1	.255	.464
LF	Larry Herndon	R	153	603	182	28	9	20	3.3	88	92	46	95	9	5	1	.302	.478
C	Lance Parrish	R	155	605	163	42	3	27	4.5	80	114	44	106	1	2	0	.269	.483
DH	Kirk Gibson	L	128	401	91	12	9	15	3.7	60	51	53	96	14	20	5	.227	.414
SUBSTITUTES																		
UT	John Wockenfuss	R	92	245	66	8	1	9	3.7	32	44	31	37	1	24	7	.269	.420
1B	Rick Leach	L	99	242	60	17	0	3	1.2	22	26	19	21	2	18	4	.248	.355
UT	Wayne Krenchicki	L	59	133	37	7	0	1	0.8	18	16	11	27	0	7	1	.278	.353
3B	Marty Castillo	R	67	119	23	4	0	2	1.7	10	10	7	22	2	2	0	.193	.277
3B	Howard Johnson	B	27	66	14	0	0	3	4.5	11	5	7	10	0	6	.2	.212	.348
1B	Mike Ivie	R	12	42	9	4	0	0	0.0	4	7	2	4	0	0	0	.214	.310
S2	Julio Gonzalez	R	12	21	3	1	0	0	0.0	0	2	1	7	0	0	0	.143	.190
D1	Mike Laga	L	12	21	4	0	0	0	0.0	2	2	1	9	0	3	1	.190	.190
DH	Bob Molinaro	L	8	2	0	0	0	0	0.0	3	0	1	1	1	2	0	.000	.000
OD	Johnny Grubb	L	57	134	34	5	2	4	3.0	20	22	28	17	0	10	4	.254	.410
OF	Lynn Jones	R	49	64	17	1	2	0	0.0	9	6	3	6	1	15	3	.266	.344
C	Bill Fahey	L	19	22	6	1	0	0	0.0	4	2	5	3	0	1	0	.273	.318
C	Sal Butera	R	4	5	1	0	0	0	0.0	1	0	0	0	0	0	0	.200	.200
PITCHERS																		
P	Aurelio Lopez	R	57	0	0	0	0	0	–	0	0	0	0	0	0	0	–	–
P	Doug Bair	R	27	0	0	0	0	0	–	0	0	0	0	0	0	0	–	–
P	Jack Morris	R	44	0	0	0	0	0	–	3	0	0	0	0	0	0	–	–
P	Dave Rozema	R	29	0	0	0	0	0	–	0	0	0	0	0	0	0	–	–
P	Juan Berenguer	R	37	0	0	0	0	0	–	0	0	0	0	0	0	0	–	–
P	Bob James	R	4	0	0	0	0	0	–	0	0	0	0	0	0	0	–	–
P	Dan Petry	R	38	0	0	0	0	0	–	0	0	0	0	0	0	0	–	–
P	Pat Underwood	L	4	0	0	0	0	0	–	0	0	0	0	0	0	0	–	–
P	John Martin	B	15	0	0	0	0	0	–	0	0	0	0	0	0	0	–	–
P	Jerry Ujdur	R	11	0	0	0	0	0	–	0	0	0	0	0	0	0	–	–
P	Milt Wilcox	R	26	0	0	0	0	0	–	0	0	0	0	0	0	0	–	–
P	Howard Bailey	L	33	0	0	0	0	0	–	0	0	0	0	0	0	0	–	–
P	Dave Rucker	L	4	0	0	0	0	0	–	0	0	0	0	0	0	0	–	–
P	Dave Gumpert	R	26	0	0	0	0	0	–	0	0	0	0	0	0	0	–	–
P	Larry Pashnick	R	12	0	0	0	0	0	–	0	0	0	0	0	0	0	–	–
P	Glenn Abbott	R	7	0	0	0	0	0	–	0	0	0	0	0	0	0	–	–
TEAM TOTAL				5591	1530	283	53	156	2.8	789	749	507	831	93	152	40	.274	.427

INDIVIDUAL FIELDING

POS	Player	T	G	PO	A	E	DP	TC/G	FA
1B	E. Cabell	R	106	830	79	3	76	8.6	.997
	R. Leach	L	73	447	45	3	37	6.8	.994
	J. Wockenfuss	R	13	84	10	2	8	7.7	.979
	M. Ivie	R	12	86	6	0	6	7.7	1.000
	M. Laga	L	5	9	1	0	2	2.0	1.000
	W. Krenchicki	R	3	7	1	0	0	2.7	1.000
2B	L. Whitaker	R	160	299	447	13	92	4.7	.983
	T. Brookens	R	10	8	28	1	4	3.7	.973
	W. Krenchicki	R	6	5	10	1	2	2.7	.938
	J. Gonzalez	R	5	5	7	1	2	2.6	.923
SS	A. Trammell	R	140	236	367	13	71	4.4	.979
	T. Brookens	R	30	35	62	4	9	3.4	.960
	E. Cabell	R	1	0	0	0	0	0.0	.000
	J. Gonzalez	R	6	5	19	3	1	4.5	.889
	W. Krenchicki	R	6	2	8	1	1	1.8	.909
3B	T. Brookens	R	103	54	164	17	21	2.3	.928
	M. Castillo	R	58	35	68	1	6	1.8	.990
	W. Krenchicki	R	48	29	56	6	8	1.9	.934
	H. Johnson	R	21	10	30	7	2	2.2	.851
	J. Wockenfuss	R	1	0	0	0	0	0.0	.000
	J. Gonzalez	R	1	0	0	0	0	0.0	.000
	E. Cabell	R	4	0	0	0	0	0.0	.000

POS	Player	T	G	PO	A	E	DP	TC/G	FA
OF	C. Lemon	R	145	406	6	5	3	2.9	.988
	L. Herndon	R	133	283	6	15	1	2.3	.951
	G. Wilson	R	143	225	12	3	2	1.7	.988
	K. Gibson	L	54	116	2	3	0	2.2	.975
	J. Grubb	R	26	34	1	0	0	1.3	1.000
	L. Jones	R	31	28	2	1	0	1.0	.968
	J. Wockenfuss	R	1	0	0	0	0	0.0	.000
	R. Leach	L	13	18	0	1	0	1.5	.947
C	L. Parrish	R	131	695	73	4	8	5.9	.995
	J. Wockenfuss	R	29	141	11	0	2	5.2	1.000
	B. Fahey	R	18	39	2	0	0	2.3	1.000
	M. Castillo	R	10	38	1	0	0	3.9	1.000
	S. Butera	R	4	12	1	1	0	3.5	.929

Good times returned to Detroit; the auto industry finally broke out of the red, and the Tigers finally broke out of mediocrity. Detroit enjoyed its most successful season since winning the American League East flag in 1972, notching its first finish above fourth place in 10 years and its most victories in 15 years. But despite 92 wins, the Tigers still finished second, six games behind the Orioles, who proceeded to win their first World Championship in 13 years.

Motown baseball fans believed something special was impending. As Detroit finished third in the league in batting, four Tigers hit .300: second baseman Lou Whitaker (third in the league at .320), shortstop Alan Trammell (fourth at .319), first baseman Enos Cabell (.311), and leftfielder Larry Herndon (.302). The first lefty-hitting Tiger to notch 200 hits since Dick Wakefield in 1943, Whitaker joined Trammell to form the AL's first second base-shortstop combination to hit .300 in 24 years.

Leading the league in strikeouts with 232, Jack Morris won 10 straight from July 14 to September 1, but lost five of his final seven starts to finish at 20–13 with a 3.34 ERA. Milt Wilcox was an out away from a perfect game on April 15 in Chicago when White Sox pinch hitter Jerry Hairston singled to center field. Supporting all of them was reliever Aurelio Lopez; despite being sidelined two weeks in August with a hand injury, he finished 9–8 with 18 saves and a 2.81 ERA as opposing batters hit a league-low .210 against him.

After sitting in last place on May 25 with a 17–22 start, the Tigers roared at 75–48 for the remainder of the season. And they had a chance in September: seven of their final 13 games were against the Orioles. But Detroit went 2–5 against Baltimore and lost four of six against other teams in the final two weeks.

"Overall, I was very pleased," said Sparky Anderson, "But we have to pick up six games somewhere." Within a year, they'd pick up their six games—and much, much more.

TEAM STATISTICS

	W	L	PCT	GB	R	OR	2B	3B	HR	BA	SA	SB	E	DP	FA	CG	BB	SO	ShO	SV	ERA
								Batting						Fielding				Pitching			
ST																					
L	98	64	.605		799	652	283	27	**168**	.269	.421	61	121	159	.981	36	452	774	**15**	38	3.63
T	92	70	.568	6	789	679	283	53	156	.274	.427	93	125	142	.980	42	522	875	9	28	3.80
Y	91	71	.562	7	770	703	269	40	153	.273	.416	84	139	157	.978	**47**	455	892	12	32	3.85
R	89	73	.549	9	795	726	268	**58**	167	**.277**	**.436**	131	115	148	.981	43	517	835	8	32	4.12
L	87	75	.537	11	764	708	281	57	132	.277	.418	101	**113**	162	.982	35	491	689	10	43	4.02
S	78	84	.481	20	724	775	**287**	32	142	.270	.409	30	130	168	.979	29	493	767	7	42	4.34
E	70	92	.432	28	704	785	249	31	86	.265	.369	109	122	174	.980	34	529	794	8	25	4.43
ST																					
HI	99	63	.611		**800**	650	270	42	157	.262	.413	165	120	158	.981	35	**447**	877	12	48	3.67
C	79	83	.488	20	696	767	273	54	109	.271	.397	182	165	178	.974	19	471	593	8	**49**	4.25
X	77	85	.475	22	639	**609**	242	33	106	.255	.366	119	**113**	150	**.982**	43	471	826	11	32	**3.31**
K	74	88	.457	25	708	782	237	28	121	.262	.381	**235**	157	157	.974	22	626	719	12	33	4.35
L	70	92	.432	29	722	779	241	22	154	.260	.393	41	154	**190**	.977	39	496	668	7	23	4.31
N	70	92	.432	29	709	822	280	41	141	.261	.401	44	121	170	.980	20	580	748	5	39	4.67
A	60	102	.370	39	558	740	247	31	111	.240	.360	144	136	159	.978	25	544	**910**	9	39	4.12
AGUE TOTAL					10177	10177	3710	549	1903	.266	.401	1539	1831	2272	.979	469	7094	10967	133	503	4.06

INDIVIDUAL PITCHING

TCHER	T	W	L	PCT	ERA	SV	G	GS	CG	IP	H	BB	SO	R	ER	ShO	H/9	BB/9	SO/9
ck Morris	R	20	13	.606	3.34	0	37	37	20	293.2	257	83	**232**	117	109	1	7.88	2.54	7.11
n Petry	R	19	11	.633	3.92	0	38	**38**	9	266.1	256	99	122	126	116	2	8.65	3.35	4.12
lt Wilcox	R	11	10	.524	3.97	0	26	26	9	186	164	74	101	89	82	2	7.94	3.58	4.89
an Berenguer	R	9	5	.643	3.14	1	37	19	2	157.2	110	71	129	58	55	1	6.28	4.05	7.36
relio Lopez	R	9	8	.529	2.81	18	57	0	0	115.1	87	49	90	36	36	0	6.79	3.82	7.02
ve Rozema	R	8	3	.727	3.43	2	29	16	1	105	100	29	63	50	40	0	8.57	2.49	5.40
ward Bailey	L	5	5	.500	4.88	0	33	3	0	72	69	25	21	45	39	0	8.63	3.13	2.63
ug Bair	R	7	3	.700	3.88	4	27	1	0	55.2	51	19	39	27	24	0	8.25	3.07	6.31
enn Abbott	R	2	1	.667	1.93	0	7	7	1	46.2	43	7	11	12	10	1	8.29	1.35	2.12
ve Gumpert	R	0	2	.000	2.64	2	26	0	0	44.1	43	7	14	16	13	0	8.73	1.42	2.84
rry Pashnick	R	1	3	.250	5.26	0	12	6	0	37.2	48	18	17	27	22	0	11.47	4.30	4.06
rry Ujdur	R	0	4	.000	7.15	0	11	6	0	34	41	20	13	33	27	0	10.85	5.29	3.44
hn Martin	L	0	0	–	7.43	1	15	0	0	13.1	15	4	11	11	11	0	10.13	2.70	7.43
t Underwood	L	0	0	–	8.71	0	4	0	0	10.1	11	6	2	10	10	0	9.58	5.23	1.74
ve Rucker	L	1	2	.333	17.00	0	4	3	0	9	18	8	6	17	17	0	18.00	8.00	6.00
b James	R	0	0	–	11.25	0	4	0	0	4	5	3	4	5	5	0	11.25	6.75	9.00
AM TOTAL		92	70	.568	3.82	28	367	162	42	1451	1318	522	875	679	616	7	8.18	3.24	5.43

MANAGER	W	L	PCT
Sparky Anderson	104	58	.642

POS	Player	B	G	AB	H	2B	3B	HR	HR %	R	RBI	BB	SO	SB	Pinch Hit AB	Pinch Hit H	BA	SA
REGULARS																		
1B	Dave Bergman	L	120	271	74	8	5	7	2.6	42	44	33	40	3	21	6	.273	.417
2B	Lou Whitaker	L	143	558	161	25	1	13	2.3	90	56	62	63	6	6	1	.289	.407
SS	Alan Trammell	R	139	555	174	34	5	14	2.5	85	69	60	63	19	3	1	.314	.468
3B	Howard Johnson	B	116	355	88	14	1	12	3.4	43	50	40	67	10	7	2	.248	.394
RF	Kirk Gibson	L	149	531	150	23	10	27	5.1	92	91	63	103	29	11	1	.282	.516
CF	Chet Lemon	R	141	509	146	34	6	20	3.9	77	76	51	83	5	3	1	.287	.495
LF	Larry Herndon	R	125	407	114	18	5	7	1.7	52	43	32	63	6	24	7	.280	.400
C	Lance Parrish	R	147	578	137	16	2	33	5.7	75	98	41	120	2	3	1	.237	.443
DH	Darrell Evans	L	131	401	93	11	1	16	4.0	60	63	77	70	2	18	3	.232	.384
SUBSTITUTES																		
UT	Barbaro Garbey	R	110	327	94	17	1	5	1.5	45	52	17	35	6	25	8	.287	.391
UT	Tom Brookens	R	113	224	55	11	4	5	2.2	32	26	19	33	6	3	2	.246	.397
SS	Doug Baker	B	43	108	20	4	1	0	0.0	15	11	7	22	3	1	1	.185	.241
2B	Scottie Earl	R	14	35	4	0	1	0	0.0	3	1	0	9	1	0	0	.114	.171
DH	Rod Allen	R	15	27	8	1	0	0	0.0	6	3	2	8	1	3	1	.296	.333
D1	Mike Laga	L	9	11	6	0	0	0	0.0	1	1	1	2	0	3	3	.545	.545
OF	Ruppert Jones	L	79	215	61	12	1	12	5.6	26	37	21	47	2	15	6	.284	.516
OD	Johnny Grubb	L	86	176	47	5	0	8	4.5	25	17	36	36	1	22	8	.267	.432
OF	Rusty Kuntz	R	84	140	40	12	0	2	1.4	32	22	25	28	2	12	5	.286	.414
OD	Nelson Simmons	B	9	30	13	2	0	0	0.0	4	3	2	5	1	1	0	.433	.500
C3	Marty Castillo	R	70	141	33	5	2	4	2.8	16	17	10	33	1	1	0	.234	.383
C	Dwight Lowry	L	32	45	11	2	0	2	4.4	8	7	3	11	0	4	1	.244	.422
PITCHERS																		
P	Aurelio Lopez	R	71	0	0	0	0	0	–	0	0	0	0	0	0	0	–	–
P	Sid Monge	B	19	0	0	0	0	0	–	0	0	0	0	0	0	0	–	–
P	Doug Bair	R	47	0	0	0	0	0	–	0	0	0	0	0	0	0	–	–
P	Jack Morris	R	35	0	0	0	0	0	–	0	0	0	0	0	0	0	–	–
P	Dave Rozema	R	29	0	0	0	0	0	–	0	0	0	0	0	0	0	–	–
P	Willie Hernandez	L	80	0	0	0	0	0	–	0	0	0	0	0	0	0	–	–
P	Juan Berenguer	R	31	0	0	0	0	0	–	0	0	0	0	0	0	0	–	–
P	Dan Petry	R	35	0	0	0	0	0	–	0	0	0	0	0	0	0	–	–
P	Milt Wilcox	R	33	0	0	0	0	0	–	0	0	0	0	0	0	0	–	–
P	Bill Scherrer	L	18	0	0	0	0	0	–	0	0	0	0	0	0	0	–	–
P	Glenn Abbott	R	13	0	0	0	0	0	–	0	0	0	0	0	0	0	–	–
P	Roger Mason	R	4	0	0	0	0	0	–	0	0	0	0	0	0	0	–	–
P	Randy O'Neal	R	4	0	0	0	0	0	–	0	0	0	0	0	0	0	–	–
P	Carl Willis	L	10	0	0	0	0	0	–	0	0	0	0	0	0	0	–	–
TEAM TOTAL				5644	1529	254	46	187	3.3	829	787	602	941	106	186	58	.271	.432

INDIVIDUAL FIELDING

POS	Player	T	G	PO	A	E	DP	TC/G	FA
1B	D. Bergman	L	114	657	75	8	63	6.5	.989
	B. Garbey	R	65	391	42	5	50	6.7	.989
	D. Evans	R	47	324	44	1	33	7.9	.997
	M. Laga	L	4	12	1	0	1	3.3	1.000
	H. Johnson	R	1	1	0	0	1	1.0	1.000
2B	L. Whitaker	R	142	290	405	15	83	5.0	.979
	T. Brookens	R	26	28	48	4	14	3.1	.950
	S. Earl	R	14	23	24	2	9	3.5	.959
	D. Baker	R	5	10	7	1	2	3.6	.944
	B. Garbey	R	3	2	2	0	2	1.3	1.000
SS	A. Trammell	R	114	180	314	10	71	4.4	.980
	D. Baker	R	39	46	79	4	18	3.3	.969
	T. Brookens	R	28	38	76	5	11	4.3	.958
	H. Johnson	R	9	3	7	2	4	1.3	.833
3B	H. Johnson	R	108	58	143	12	16	2.0	.944
	T. Brookens	R	68	32	63	3	10	1.4	.969
	M. Castillo	R	33	12	26	2	1	1.2	.950
	B. Garbey	R	20	7	14	7	1	1.4	.750
	D. Evans	R	19	7	18	1	1	1.4	.962

POS	Player	T	G	PO	A	E	DP	TC/G	FA
OF	C. Lemon	R	140	427	6	2	1	3.1	.995
	K. Gibson	L	139	245	4	12	2	1.9	.954
	L. Herndon	R	117	199	7	3	0	1.8	.986
	R. Jones	L	73	150	4	0	1	2.1	1.000
	R. Kuntz	R	67	74	2	1	1	1.1	.987
	J. Grubb	R	36	47	0	0	0	1.3	1.000
	B. Garbey	R	10	11	0	0	0	1.1	1.000
	N. Simmons	R	5	8	0	0	0	1.6	1.000
	R. Allen	R	2	2	0	0	0	1.0	1.000
	H. Johnson	R	1	1	0	0	0	1.0	1.000
	D. Bergman	L	2	1	0	0	0	0.5	1.000
C	L. Parrish	R	127	720	67	7	11	6.3	.991
	M. Castillo	R	36	149	11	5	2	4.6	.970
	D. Lowry	R	31	87	8	0	2	3.1	1.000

By mid-October, baseball fans and headline writers nationwide agreed: the Tigers were *grrrrrreat*. Detroit jumped into first place on opening day and never left—they won their first nine, 18 of their first 20, 26 of 30, and 35 of 40 en route to a franchise-record 104 victories, finishing 16 games ahead of the second-place Blue Jays. "I knew in my heart," said Sparky Anderson, "that the 1984 Tigers would be the best baseball team Detroit has ever seen."

The most important step to the pennant came on March 24, when Detroit traded handyman John Wockenfuss and outfielder Glenn Wilson to the Phillies for first baseman Dave Bergman and eventual Most Valuable Player and Cy Young award winner Willie Hernandez. The left-handed reliever was just what the Tigers needed. He led the league in appearances with 80, saved 32 in 33 save opportunities, won nine, lost three, and notched a 1.92 ERA.

Others joined Hernandez in helping to give new owner–pizza baron Tom Monaghan a season with everything on it. Jack Morris led Detroit starters at 19–11 with a 3.65 ERA, including a 4–0 no-hitter over the White Sox at Comiskey Park on April 7, the first by a Tiger in 26 years. Providing a right-handed alternative to Hernandez in the bullpen, Aurelio Lopez won 10, lost one, and saved 14 with a 2.94 ERA. Only shortstop Alan Trammell hit .300 (.314 with 14 home runs despite shoulder and knee ailments), but seven other Tigers—Lance Parrish, Kirk Gibson, Chet Lemon, Darrell Evans, Lou Whitaker, Howard Johnson, and Ruppert Jones—reached double digits in home runs.

The Tigers, who drew 2,704,794 at home and 4,864,943 overall—both club records—swept the Royals 3–0 for the pennant, and then pounced upon the Padres in the World Series, splitting the first two games in San Diego before sweeping the next three at Tiger Stadium for Detroit's first World Championship in 16 years. The celebration had barely subsided when Anderson looked ahead. "We must win in '85," he insisted. "As Vince Lombardi once said, 'Any squirrel can find an acorn once. . . .'"

TEAM STATISTICS

	W	L	PCT	GB	R	OR	Batting 2B	3B	HR	BA	SA	SB	Fielding E	DP	FA	CG	BB	Pitching SO	ShO	SV	ERA
ST																					
T	104	58	.642		829	643	254	46	187	.271	.432	106	127	162	.979	19	489	914	8	51	3.49
R	89	73	.549	15	750	696	275	68	143	.273	.421	193	123	166	.980	34	528	875	10	33	3.86
	87	75	.537	17	758	679	276	32	130	.276	.405	62	142	177	.977	15	518	992	12	43	3.78
S	86	76	.531	18	810	764	259	45	181	.283	.441	37	143	127	.977	40	517	927	12	32	4.18
E	85	77	.525	19	681	667	234	23	160	.252	.391	51	123	166	.981	48	512	713	13	32	3.72
	75	87	.463	29	761	766	222	39	123	.265	.384	126	146	163	.977	21	545	803	7	35	4.25
	67	94	.416	36.5	641	734	232	36	96	.262	.370	52	136	156	.978	13	480	785	7	41	4.06
ST																					
	84	78	.519		673	686	268	52	117	.268	.399	106	131	157	.979	18	433	724	9	50	3.91
L	81	81	.500	3	696	697	211	30	150	.249	.381	79	128	170	.980	36	474	754	12	26	3.96
N	81	81	.500	3	673	675	259	33	114	.265	.385	39	120	133	.980	32	463	713	9	38	3.86
K	77	85	.475	7	738	796	257	29	158	.259	.404	145	146	159	.975	15	592	695	6	44	4.49
	74	88	.457	10	679	736	225	38	172	.247	.395	109	122	160	.981	43	483	840	9	32	4.13
A	74	88	.457	10	682	774	244	34	129	.258	.384	116	128	141	.979	26	619	972	4	35	4.31
K	69	92	.429	14.5	656	714	227	29	120	.261	.377	80	138	137	.977	38	518	864	6	21	3.91
GUE TOTAL					10027	10027	3443	534	1980	.264	.398	1301	1853	2174	.979	398	7171	11571	124	513	3.99

INDIVIDUAL PITCHING

CHER	T	W	L	PCT	ERA	SV	G	GS	CG	IP	H	BB	SO	R	ER	ShO	H/9	BB/9	SO/9
k Morris	R	19	11	.633	3.65	0	35	35	9	241.1	224	87	149	110	98	1	8.35	14	5.56
n Petry	R	18	8	.692	3.24	0	35	35	7	233.1	231	66	144	94	84	2	8.91	2.55	5.55
t Wilcox	R	17	8	.680	4.00	0	33	33	0	193.2	183	66	119	99	86	0	8.50	3.07	5.53
in Berenguer	R	11	10	.524	3.48	0	31	27	2	168.1	146	79	118	75	65	1	7.81	4.22	6.31
lie Hernandez	L	9	3	.750	1.92	32	80	0	0	140.1	96	36	112	30	30	0	6.16	2.31	7.18
relio Lopez	R	10	1	.909	2.94	14	71	0	0	137.2	109	52	94	51	45	0	7.13	3.40	6.15
ve Rozema	R	7	6	.538	3.74	0	29	16	0	101	110	18	48	49	42	0	9.80	1.60	4.28
ug Bair	R	5	3	.625	3.75	4	47	1	0	93.2	82	36	57	42	39	0	7.88	3.46	5.48
nn Abbott	R	3	4	.429	5.93	0	13	8	0	44	62	8	8	39	29	0	12.68	1.64	1.64
Monge	L	1	0	1.000	4.25	0	19	0	0	36	40	12	19	21	17	0	10.00	3.00	4.75
ger Mason	R	1	1	.500	3.86	1	4	2	0	21	20	10	14	9	9	0	8.57	4.29	6.00
Scherrer	L	1	0	1.000	1.89	0	18	0	0	19	14	8	16	4	4	0	6.63	3.79	7.58
ndy O'Neal	R	2	1	.667	3.38	0	4	3	0	18.2	16	6	12	7	7	0	7.71	2.89	5.79
1 Willis	R	0	2	.000	7.31	0	10	2	0	16	25	5	4	13	13	0	14.06	2.81	2.25
AM TOTAL		104	58	.642	3.49	51	429	162	19	1464	1358	489	914	643	568	4	8.35	3.01	5.62

Tigers Graphics

Graphs are not everyone's cup of tea. That's a shame, because a clear, well-drawn graph can present an enormous amount of information faster than any other method. And baseball is the perfect subject for a graphic treatment that can make quick sense of the wealth of statistics and measures generated by that most measured of all sports.

The graphs that follow paint a clear picture of more than eighty years of accumulated results and communicate them at a glance. The graph below charts the Tigers' season finishes and won-lost percentage for every season from 1901 through 1984. Notice that the Tigers have had sustained periods at or near the top of the standings (the 1930s and '40s, and the '60s), and many stretches in the middle of the pack, but very few at the bottom. The Tigers have finished first ten times and second fourteen times in eighty-four seasons; in the same period, they have finished last just three times, and next-to-last six times.

Graphic History of the Detroit Tigers

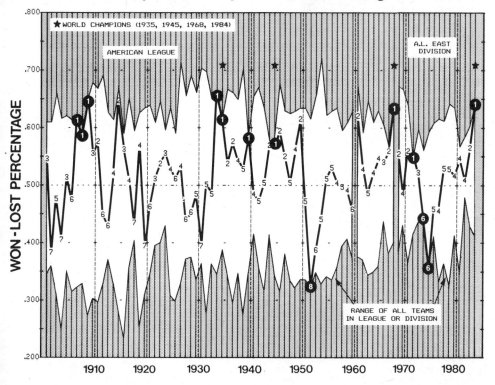

The white space indicates the range of won-lost percentages for all the teams in the league or division for a given season; the numbers represent the Tigers' final placement in each season.

Home Games

Defense

Offense

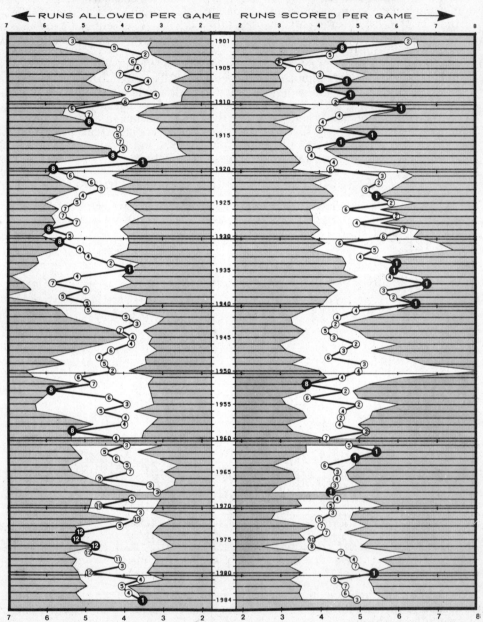

The graphs on these two pages show were Detroit has ranked, year by year, in runs scored and allowed at home and on the road. It is clear from a comparison of the two that Tiger Stadium does have a tendency to favor the hitters; in the past thirty years, the Tigers have ranked in the bottom half of the league in runs scored on the road fifteen times, but just six times in runs scored at home.

Road Games

Defense   ## Offense

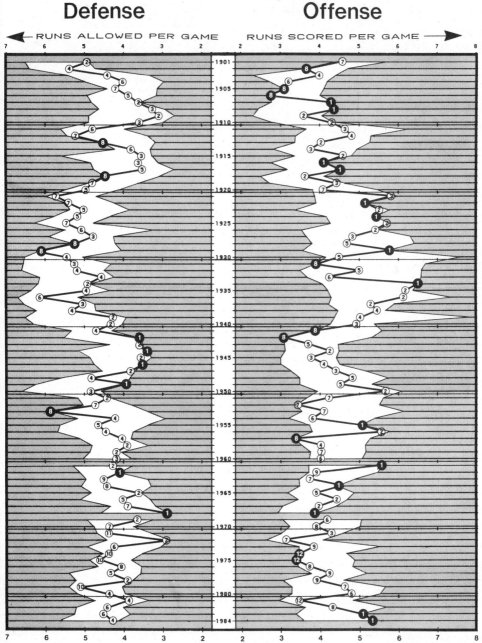

Similarly, the pitchers have been better than they looked to the home fans; while they ranked in the bottom three in runs allowed at home eight times since 1967, including three straight last-place finishes in the mid-'70s (despite Mark Fidrych), they were in the bottom three on the road just three times. But this shouldn't mislead anyone about the strength of the present team's hitters: they've led the league in road runs scored each of the past two seasons.

THE PENNANT RACES

Graphs prove an excellent way of showing the patterns and results of a pennant race. John Davenport's method is to chart each team's progress above or below the .500 mark. That way each win is a move up one step, and each loss a step down. It takes a two-game difference in record over or under .500 to make a one-game difference in the standing: a team with a 10-1 mark, nine games over .500, is one game ahead of one with a 9-2 mark, seven games over.

The graph below shows, as an example, the stretch drive of the 1972 pennant race, in which the Tigers edge out Boston for the Eastern Division crown under Billy Martin. Entering September, the Tigers, Red Sox, Yankees, and Orioles were all within a game of first. By the middle of the month, the Yankees had fallen off, and the Orioles soon followed (although, as we can tell from the absence of any steep rise, because the leaders were setting any blistering pace). Brief winning streaks by both the Tigers and Red Sox brought them to the final series with Boston a half game ahead. The Tigers took the first two games to clinch the pennant, which they won by a slender half-game margin.

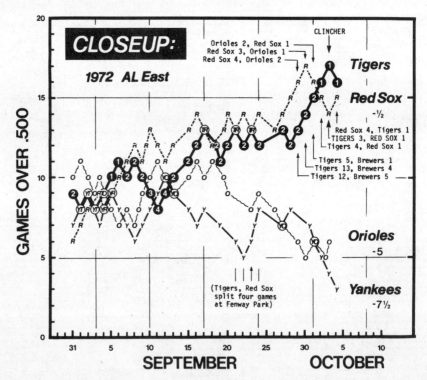

The graphs on the following pages track the Tigers' standing from start to finish for every season since 1901. The black space shows the range of all the clubs in the league (or division, since 1969).

197

Games over or under .500

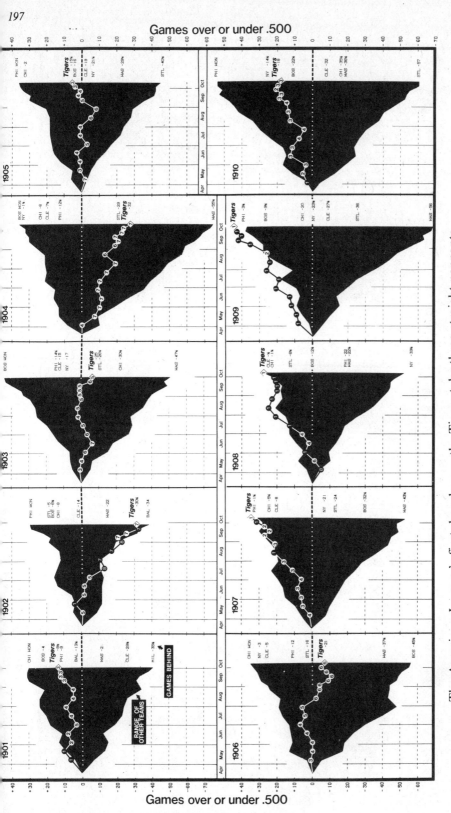

The American League's first decade saw the Tigers take three straight pennants, none of them by comfortable margins (though they did lead virtually wire to wire in 1909).

Games over or under .500

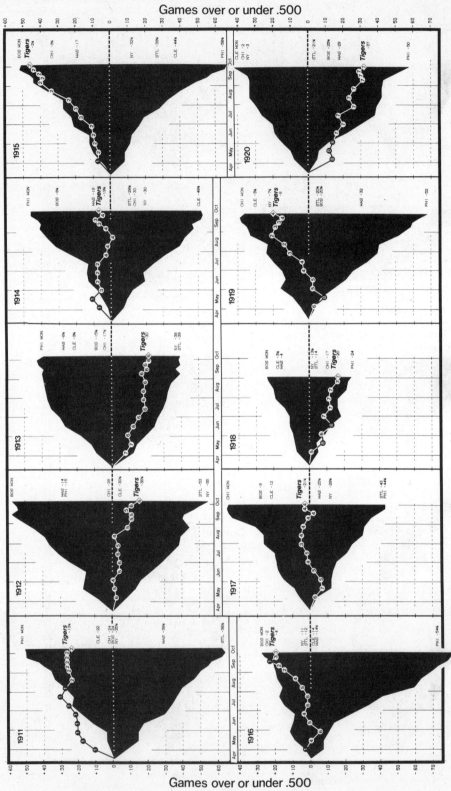

Games over or under .500

Games over or under .500

A fast start doesn't always mean a pennant; the Tigers were 21 games over .500 on Memorial Day in 1911, and ten games ahead of Philadelphia, but failed to hold the

Games over or under .500

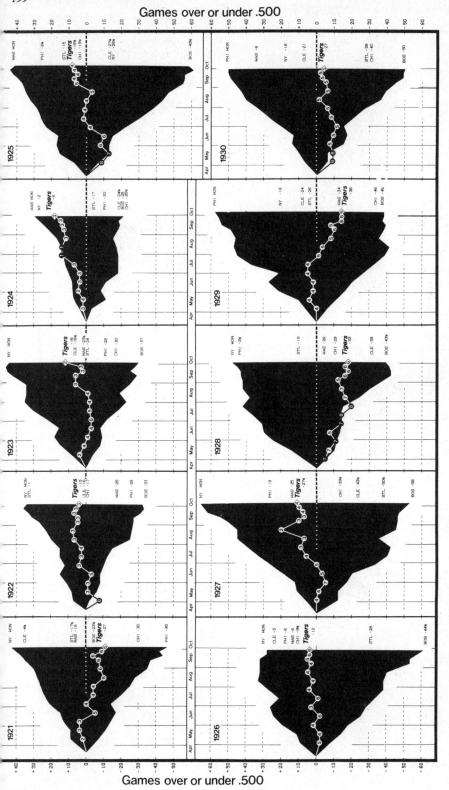

No cigar, and not close: over the ten-year period, the Tigers never finished more than twenty games above .500, and never further than twenty below.

Games over or under .500

Games over or under .500

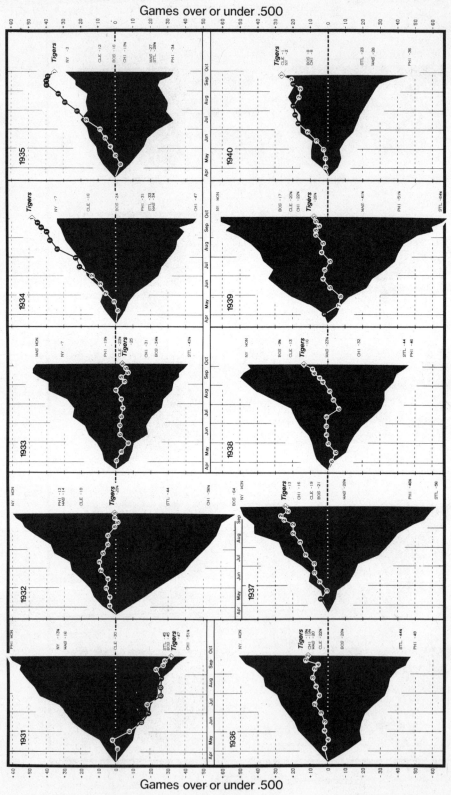

A feast-or-famine decade: Detroit won three pennants, and failed to finish within ten games of first in any of the other seven years.

Games over or under .500

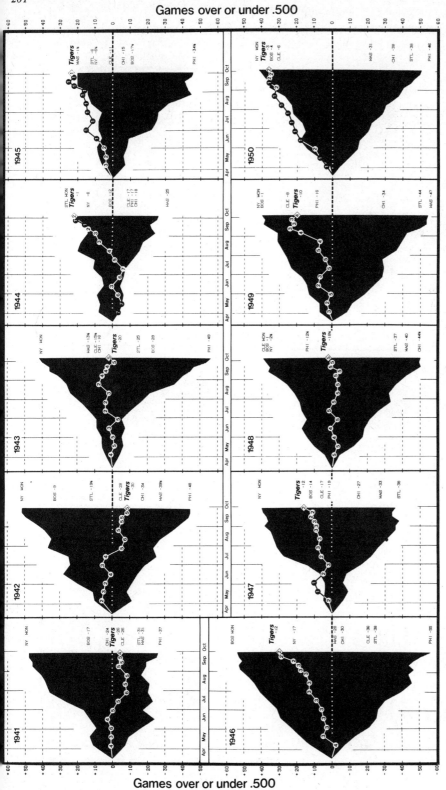

A split of back-to-back nail-biters in 1944 and '45 gave Detroit its last reason to celebrate until the 1968 World Champions.

Games over or under .500

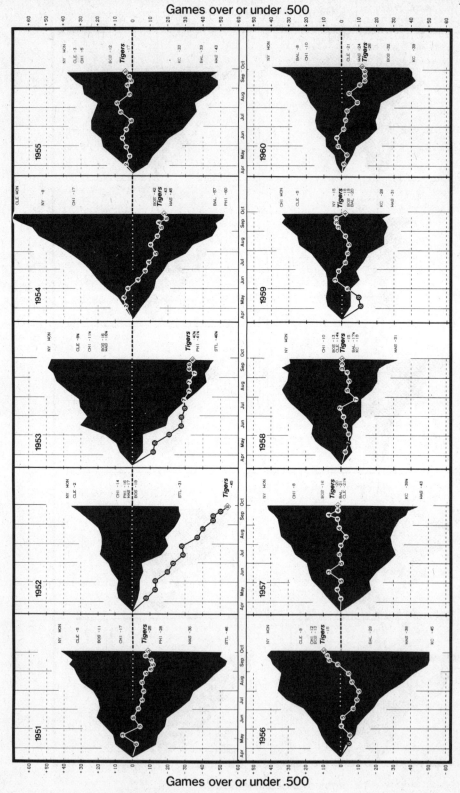

The Tigers hit low ebb with three straight years of finishing more than forty games out of first (1952-54). The rest of the '50s was spent fighting their way back to

Games over or under .500

Games over or under .500

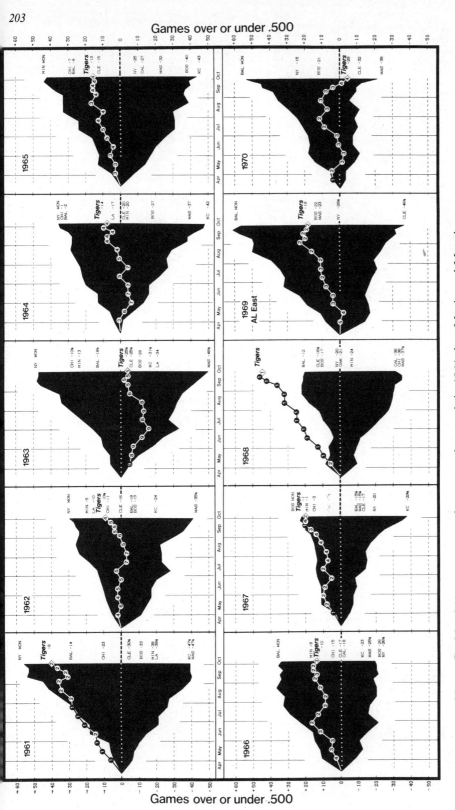

Norm Cash's .361 season was almost good enough in 1961, but Maris and Mantle proved too much; after another heartbreaking loss in '67, the Tigers took their first pennant in twenty-three years.

Games over or under .500

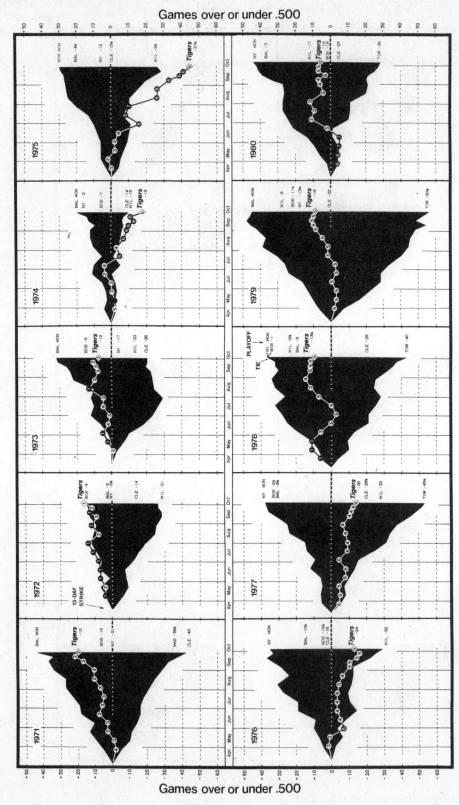

Games over or under .500

A rookie called The Bird brought Detroit out of the cellar in 1976, but the decade was one of the most dismal in Tigers history, brightened only the divisional title in

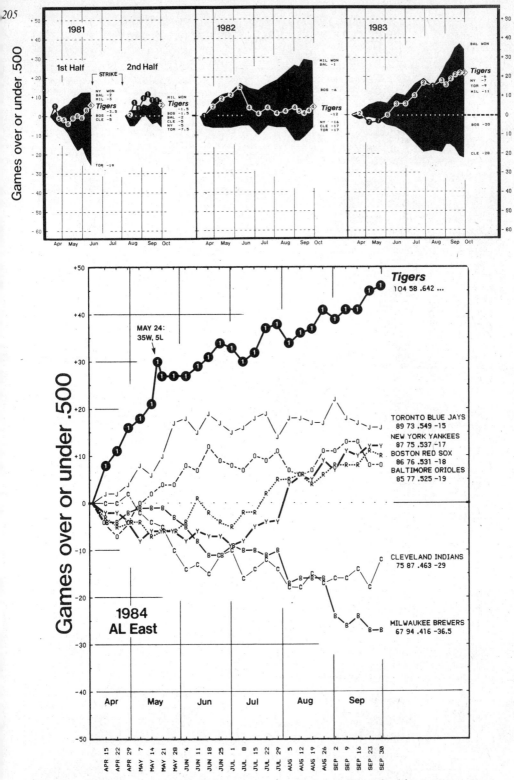

The Fantastic Forty start in 1984 (see next page) put Detroit thirty games over .500 on May 24. They blew as big a lead seventy-two years earlier, but '84 was truly the Year of the Tiger.

1984 DETROIT TIGERS -- FIRST FORTY GAMES

G# / DATE / W-L	POS. LEAD	LINE SCORE	HITTING LEADERS	PITCHERS
1 / 4/3 / 1-0	1st / ---	TIGERS 002 003 300 -- 8 10 0 *Minnesota 001 000 000 -- 1 5 0	Evans Parrish Johnson HR,3BI 2BI 2H	Morris 7 (W,1-0) Lopez, Hernandez
2 / 4/5 / 2-0	1st / ---	TIGERS 001 301 200 -- 7 9 1 *Minnesota 020 001 000 -- 3 5 0	Gibson Trammell Lemon HR,3BI 4H,HR 2H	Petry 7 (W,1-0) Hernandez 2
3 / 4/5 / 3-0	1st / ---	TIGERS 300 000 000 -- 3 5 0 *Chicago 000 100 010 -- 2 6 0	Bergman Evans 2BI GWBI	Wilcox 7 (W,1-0) Hernandez 2 (SV1)
4 / 4/7 / 4-0	1st / +.5	TIGERS 020 020 000 -- 4 5 0 *Chicago 000 000 000 -- 0 0 0	Lemon HR,2BI	MORRIS CG (W,2-0) NO-HITTER!
5 / 4/8 / 5-0	1st / +1.5	TIGERS 020 120 200 -- 7 11 0 *Chicago 011 000 010 -- 3 7 0	Garbey Gibson Whitaker 2H,3BI HR(2),2H 2H	Rozema 4; Hern'dez 1 Lopez 4 (W,1-0)
6 / 4/10 / 6-0	1st / +2.5	TIGERS 401 000 00x -- 5 5 0 Rangers 100 000 000 -- 1 4 0	Evans 3BI,HR(2)	Petry CG (W,2-0) (4-hitter)
7 / 4/12 / 7-0	1st / +3	TIGERS 200 104 11x -- 9 12 1 Rangers 001 000 120 -- 4 10 1	Lemon Trammell Whitaker HR(2),3BI HR(2),2H HR(1)	Morris 7 (W,3-0) Lopez, Hernandez
8 / 4/13 / 8-0	1st / +3	TIGERS 800 100 040 -- 13 16 0 *Boston 510 000 030 -- 9 14 3	Parrish Herndon Lemon HR(1),2BI 2H,2BI 2H,2BI	Bair (W,1-0); Wilcox Abbott, Hernandez
9 / 4/18 / 9-0	1st / +3	TIGERS 010 100 100 1 -- 3 12 0 Royals 000 000 030 0 -- 3 9 1	Parrish Brookens Lemon HR(2),2BI 2H 2H	Morris 9 Hernandez 1 (W,1-0)
10 / 4/19 / 9-1	1st / +1.5	Royals 002 001 020 -- 5 8 0 Tigers 100 000 001 -- 2 7 2	Gibson Evans HR(3),2H 2H	Petry 8 (L,2-1) Lopez 1
11 / 4/20 / 10-1	1st / +2.5	TIGERS 010 000 101 -- 3 11 0 White Sox 020 000 000 -- 2 8 1	Parrish Garbey Gibson 3H 2H 2H	Wilcox, 8 Lopez 1 (W,2-0)
12 / 4/21 / 11-1	1st / +3.5	TIGERS 101 000 20x -- 4 10 1 White Sox 000 000 001 -- 1 5 0	Whitaker Evans Trammell HR(2),2H 2H 3H	Rozema 6 (W,1-0) Bair 3 (SV1)
13 / 4/22 / 12-1	1st / +4.5	TIGERS 200 020 05x -- 9 18 0 White Sox 000 000 001 -- 1 5 0	Evans Garbey Lemon Gibson 3H,2BI 2H,3BI 4H HR(4)	Berenguer 7 (W,1-0) Lopez, 1; Hern'dez 1
14 / 4/24 / 13-1	1st / +5	TIGERS 001 020 003 -- 6 9 1 Twins 000 410 000 -- 5 7 0	Whitaker Trammell Lemon 2H,GWBI 2H,2BI HR(3)	Morris CG (W,4-0) (7-hitter)
15 / 4/24 / 14-1	1st / +5.5	TIGERS 001 030 000 -- 4 9 2 Twins 100 020 000 -- 3 6 1	Parrish Garbey HR(3),3BI 2H	Petry 3; Abbott 3 (W,1-0); Lopez (SV1)
16 / 4/25 / 15-1	1st / +6	TIGERS 010 200 501 -- 9 13 2 *Texas 000 020 020 -- 4 11 0	Parrish Whitaker Grubb John'n HR(4),3BI 3H HR HR(2)	Wilcox 6 (W,2-0) Hernandez 3 (SV2)
17 / 4/26 / 16-1	1st / +6	TIGERS 401 100 100 -- 7 13 1 *Texas 110 030 000 -- 5 11 0	Trammell Lemon Parrish Garbey 3H 2H,2BI HR(5) 2BI	Rozema 4.3; Bair 2 (W,2-0); Lopez (SV2)
18 / 4/27 / 16-2	1st / +5	Indians 120 000 100 000 000 4 -- 8 11 1 Tigers 300 000 000 100 000 000 0 -- 4 10 4	(won by Hargrove's GSHR in 19th)	Berenguer, Hernandez Lopez, Abbott (L,1-1)
19 / 4/28 / 17-2	1st / +5.5	TIGERS 120 300 00x -- 6 10 0 Indians 000 200 000 -- 2 3 0	Whitaker Lemon Trammell HR(3),2BI HR(4),2H 2BI	Morris CG (W,5-0) (3-hitter)
20 / 4/29 / 18-2	1st / +6	TIGERS 003 010 02x -- 6 11 0 Indians 000 000 100 -- 1 2 2	Gibson Whitaker 3H,3BI 2H	Petry (W,3-1, no-hit for 7.7); Hernandez
21 / 4/30 / 19-2	1st / +6.5	TIGERS 040 200 14x -- 11 16 0 Red Sox 100 100 000 -- 2 8 2	Lemon Garbey Kuntz HR(6),3H,4BI 3H,4BI 3H,3BI	Wilcox 8 (W,3-0) Lopez, 1
22 / 5/2 / 19-3	1st / +6.5	Red Sox 202 001 000 -- 5 8 0 Tigers 000 001 012 -- 4 13 0	Gibson Bergman 4H 3H	Berenguer 6 (L,1-1) Bair, Hernandez
23 / 5/3 / 19-4	1st / +5	Red Sox 000 000 010 -- 1 5 1 Tigers 000 000 000 -- 0 6 0	Parrish 2H	Morris CG, (L,5-1 (shutout by Ojeda)
24 / 5/4 / 20-4	1st / +5	*Cleveland 200 120 130 -- 9 13 2 TIGERS 200 000 00-- 2 8 4	Whitaker Herndon Johnson 4H 3H,2BI HR(2)	Petry 5 (W,4-1) Hernandez 4 (SV3)
25 / 5/5 / 21-4	1st / +5	TIGERS 200 102 010 -- 6 10 1 *Cleveland 220 000 001 -- 5 9 1	Lemon 4H,3BI,HR(7)	Abbott 5.3 (W,2-0) Bair, Lopez (SV3)
26 / 5/6 / 22-4	1st / +5	TIGERS 000 001 040 001 - 6 12 0 *Cleveland 010 220 000 -- 5 12 0	Grubb Bergman Trammell Whit'r HR,2BI 3H 3H 2BI	Wilcox 8, Rozema H'dez, Lopez (W,3-0)
27 / 5/7 / 23-4	1st / +5.5	*Kansas City 000 203 230 -- 10 12 0 Tigers 000 020 100 -- 3 7 1	Trammell Lemon Grubb 3H 2H,3BI HR(3),2BI	Berenguer 6.7 (W,2-1) Bair 2.3 (SV2)
28 / 5/8 / 24-4	1st / +6	TIGERS 000 000 500 -- 5 9 0 *Kansas City 000 011 000 -- 2 7 0	Trammell Lemon GSHR(3) 2H	Morris CG (W,6-1) (7-hitter)
29 / 5/9 / 25-4	1st / +7	TIGERS 020 000 000 -- 3 12 2 *Kansas City 000 001 000 -- 1 7 2	Trammell Evans Kuntz 3H 3H 2H	Petry 6.7 (W,5-1) Lopez 2.3 (SV4)
30 / 5/11 / 26-4	1st / +7.5	TIGERS 020 302 10x -- 8 14 1 Angels 000 000 011 -- 2 11 1	Bergman Evans Gibson 2H,3BI 2H,2BI HR(5),2H	Wilcox 6 (W,4-0) Hernandez 3 (SV4)
31 / 5/12 / 26-5	1st / +7.5	Angels 000 020 110 -- 4 11 1 Tigers 010 100 000 -- 2 8 2	Lemon Whitaker 2H 2H	Berenguer 6.7 (L,2-2) Lopez 2.3
32 / 5/14 / 27-5	1st / +8	TIGERS 120 110 02x -- 7 15 2 Mariners 000 201 020 -- 5 9 1	Trammell Kuntz Parrish HR(4),3H HR(2),3H 2H	Petry 5; Bair 2; Lopez 2 (W,4-0)
33 / 5/15 / 28-5	1st / +8	TIGERS 103 002 00x -- 6 5 0* Mariners 100 000 300 -- 4 5 2	Whitaker Gibson Johnson 2H 2BI 2BI	Morris 7 (W,7-1) Hernandez 2 (SV5)
34 / 5/16 / 29-5	1st / +8	TIGERS 501 010 03x -- 10 14 0 Mariners 001 000 100 -- 1 6 0	Kuntz Parrish Whit'r Grubb 2BI 2BI 2H HR(3)	Wilcox 6 (W,5-0) Bair, Hern'z, Lopez
35 / 5/18 / 30-5	1st / +7.5	TIGERS 511 10 -- 8 9 0 (rain) A's 001 300 -- 4 7 0	Parrish Gibson Garbey Evans 2H,2BI HR,2H HR(4)	Petry 5.3 (W,6-1) (one out at end)
36 / 5/19 / 31-5	1st / +8	TIGERS 101 011 10x -- 5 11 0 A's 100 000 021 -- 4 9 1	Evans Whitaker 3H,2BI HR(4),2BI	Morris 7.3 (W,8-1) Lopez 1.7 (SV5)
37 / 5/20 / 32-5	1st / +8	TIGERS 210 100 00x -- 4 10 1 A's 011 000 010 -- 3 4 1	Herndon Lowry 2H HR(1)	Wilcox 6 (W,6-0) Hernandez 3 (SV6)
38 / 5/22 / 33-5	1st / +8	TIGERS 110 000 010 -- 3 7 0 *California 100 000 000 -- 1 5 1	Whitaker 2H	Berenguer 6 (W,3-2) Lopez 3 (SV6)
39 / 5/23 / 34-5	1st / +8	TIGERS 020 000 200 -- 4 12 0 *California 000 200 000 -- 2 5 0	Parrish Lemon Castillo HR(6),2BI 2H 2H	Petry 7 (W,7-1) Hernandez 2 (SV7)
40 / 5/24 / 35-5	1st / +8.5	TIGERS 000 401 000 -- 5 7 1 *California 100 000 000 -- 1 4 2	Trammell Parrish HR(5),2BI HR(7),2H	Morris CG (W,9-1) (4-hitter)

* = ROAD GAMES

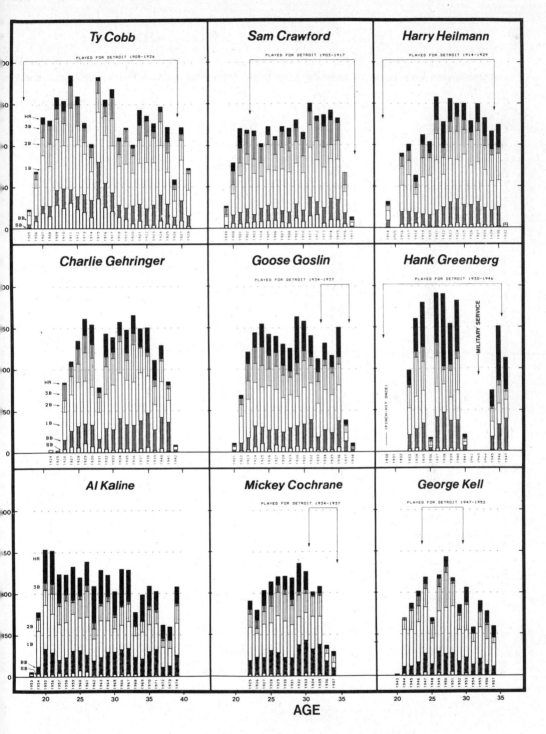

Tigers' all-time offensive stars: just as you'd expect, Hank Greenberg and Ty
Cobb tower above the rest, though by very different routes. Cobb got his bases
largely one at a time; Greenberg took his in fours.

CLIMBING THE ALL-TIME LADDERS—

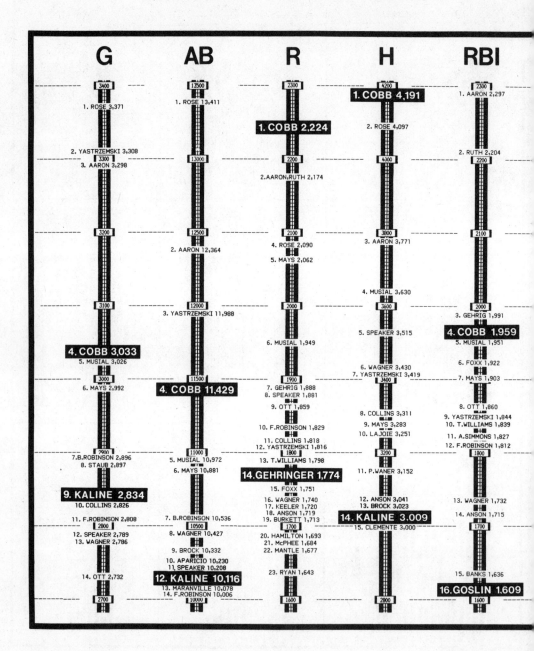

G	AB	R	H	RBI

G
- 3400
- 1. ROSE 3,371
- 3300
- 2. YASTRZEMSKI 3,308
- 3. AARON 3,298
- 3200
- 3100
- **4. COBB 3,033**
- 5. MUSIAL 3,026
- 3000
- 6. MAYS 2,992
- 2900
- 7. B.ROBINSON 2,896
- 8. STAUB 2,897
- **9. KALINE 2,834**
- 10. COLLINS 2,826
- 2800
- 11. F.ROBINSON 2,808
- 12. SPEAKER 2,789
- 13. WAGNER 2,786
- 14. OTT 2,732
- 2700

AB
- 13500
- 1. ROSE 13,411
- 13000
- 12500
- 2. AARON 12,364
- 12000
- 3. YASTRZEMSKI 11,988
- 11500
- **4. COBB 11,429**
- 11000
- 5. MUSIAL 10,972
- 6. MAYS 10,881
- 10500
- 7. B.ROBINSON 10,536
- 8. WAGNER 10,427
- 9. BROCK 10,332
- 10. APARICIO 10,230
- 11. SPEAKER 10,208
- **12. KALINE 10,116**
- 13. MARANVILLE 10,078
- 14. F.ROBINSON 10,006
- 10000

R
- 2300
- **1. COBB 2,224**
- 2200
- 2.AARON,RUTH 2,174
- 2100
- 4. ROSE 2,090
- 5. MAYS 2,062
- 2000
- 6. MUSIAL 1,949
- 1900
- 7. GEHRIG 1,888
- 8. SPEAKER 1,881
- 9. OTT 1,859
- 10. F.ROBINSON 1,829
- 11. COLLINS 1,818
- 12. YASTRZEMSKI 1,816
- 13. T.WILLIAMS 1,798
- 1800
- **14.GEHRINGER 1,774**
- 15. FOXX 1,751
- 16. WAGNER 1,740
- 17. KEELER 1,720
- 18. ANSON 1,719
- 19. BURKETT 1,713
- 1700
- 20. HAMILTON 1,693
- 21. McPHEE 1,684
- 22. MANTLE 1,677
- 23. RYAN 1,643
- 1600

H
- 4200
- **1. COBB 4,191**
- 2. ROSE 4,097
- 4000
- 3800
- 3. AARON 3,771
- 4. MUSIAL 3,630
- 3600
- 5. SPEAKER 3,515
- 6. WAGNER 3,430
- 7. YASTRZEMSKI 3,419
- 3400
- 8. COLLINS 3,311
- 9. MAYS 3,283
- 10. LAJOIE 3,251
- 3200
- 11. P.WANER 3,152
- 12. ANSON 3,041
- 13. BROCK 3,023
- **14. KALINE 3,009**
- 15. CLEMENTE 3,000
- 2800

RBI
- 2300
- 1. AARON 2,297
- 2200
- 2. RUTH 2,204
- 2100
- 3. GEHRIG 1,991
- 2000
- **4. COBB 1,959**
- 5. MUSIAL 1,951
- 6. FOXX 1,922
- 7. MAYS 1,903
- 1900
- 8. OTT 1,860
- 9. YASTRZEMSKI 1,844
- 10. T.WILLIAMS 1,839
- 11. A.SIMMONS 1,827
- 12. F.ROBINSON 1,812
- 1800
- 13. WAGNER 1,732
- 14. ANSON 1,715
- 1700
- 15. BANKS 1,636
- **16.GOSLIN 1,609**
- 1600

WHERE THE TIGERS ALL-STARS STAND

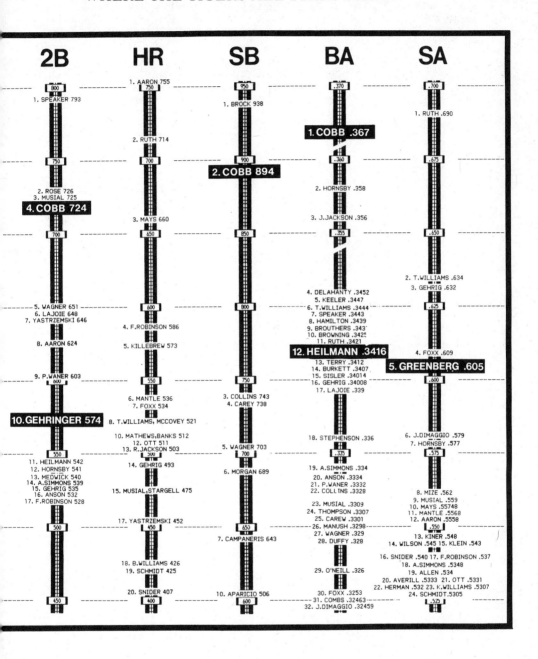

Here—for the last time?—a side-by-side look at all-time hits leader Ty Cobb and his pursuer, Pete Rose. Rose may have started at a later age, but his career has paralleled Cobb's at every step of the way. If we exclude Cobb's first year, when he had just 150 at bats, we can see how close they've been: after ten years, Rose was 15 hits behind; after 15 years, he was actually 108 hits ahead; at the twenty-year mark, he remained 46 hits up. At the start of the 1985 season, Rose stood twenty hits ahead of where Cobb stood at the end of his twenty-second full season. A thought: what would the Georgia Peach have to say about Rose's efforts? Something sharper than, "Records are made to be broken," perhaps?

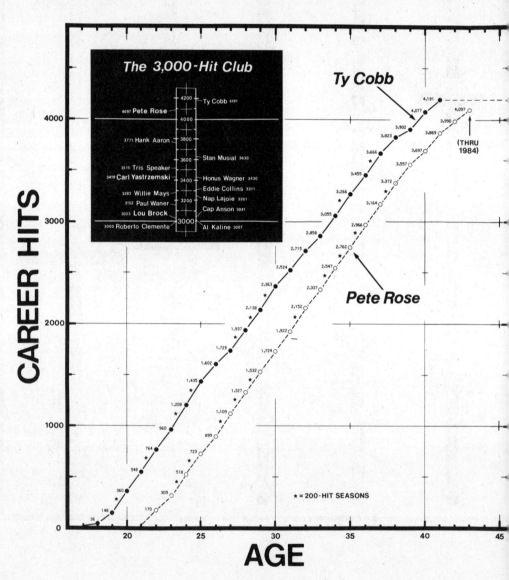

Player Register

The Player Register is an alphabetical listing of every man who has played in the major leagues and played or managed for the Detroit Tigers from 1901 through today, except those players who were primarily pitchers. However, pitchers who pinch-hit and played in other positions for a total of 25 games or more are listed in this Player Register. Included are facts about the players and their year-by-year batting records and their lifetime totals of League Championship Series and World Series.

Much of this information has never been compiled, especially for the period 1876 through 1919. For certain other years some statistics are still missing or incomplete. Research in this area is still in progress, and the years that lack complete information are indicated. In fact, all information and abbreviations that may appear unfamiliar are explained in the sample format presented below. John Doe, the player used in the sample, is fictitious and serves only to illustrate the information.

	G	AB	H	2B	3B	HR	HR %	R	RBI	BB	SO	SB	BA	SA	Pinch Hit AB	Pinch Hit H	G by POS

John Doe

DOE, JOHN LEE (Slim)   BR TR 6'2" 165 lbs.
Played as John Cherry part of 1900.   BB 1884 BL 1906
Born John Lee Doughnut.   Brother of Bill Doe.
B. Jan. 1,1850, New York, N. Y.   D. July 1, 1955, New York, N.Y.
Manager 1908-15.
Hall of Fame 1946.

Year/Team	G	AB	H	2B	3B	HR	HR %	R	RBI	BB	SO	SB	BA	SA	PH AB	PH H	G by POS
1884 STL U	125	435	121	18	1	3	0.7	44		37	42	7	.278	.345	9	2	SS-99, P-26
1885 LOU AA	155	547	138	22	3	3	0.6	50	58	42	48	8	.252	.320	8	4	SS-115, P-40
1886 CLE N	147	485	134	38	5	0	0.0	66	54	48	50	8	.276	.375	7	1	SS-107, P-40
1887 BOS N	129	418	117	15	3	1	0.2	38	52	32	37	1	.280	.337	1	0	SS-102, P-27
1888 NY N	144	506	135	26	2	6	1.2	50	63	43	50	1	.267	.362	10	8	SS-105, P-39
1889 3 teams	DET	N (10G – .300)		PIT	N (32G – .241)			PHI	N (41G – .364)								
" total	83	237	75	31	16	7	3.0	90	42	25	35	3	.316	.671	6	3	SS-61, P-22
1890 NY P	123	430	119	27	5	1	0.2	63	59	39	39	2	.277	.370	12	10	SS-85, P-38
1900 CHI N	146	498	116	29	4	3	0.6	51	46	59	53	1	.233	.325	13	8	SS-111, P-35
1901 NY N	149	540	147	19	6	4	0.7	57	74	49	58	3	.272	.352	23	15	SS-114, P-35
1906 DET A	144	567	143	26	4	4	0.7	70	43	37	54	1	.252	.333	7	1	SS-113, P-31
1907	134	515	140	31	2	5	1.0	61	70	37	42	0	.272	.369	13	8	SS-97, P-37
1908	106	372	92	10	2	4	1.1	36	40	4	55	1	.247	.317	1	0	SS-105, P-1
1914 CHI F	6	6	0	0	0	0	0.0	0	0	0	1	0	.000	.000	0	0	P-6
1915 NY A	1	0	0	0	0	0	–	0	0	0	0	0	–	–	0	0	SS-1
14 yrs.	1592	5556	1927	292	53 4th	41	0.7	676	601	452	564	36	.266	.360	110	60	SS-1215, P-377
3 yrs.	384	1454	375	67	8	13	0.9	167	153	78	151	2	.258	.342 6th	21	9	SS-315, P-96

LEAGUE CHAMPIONSHIP SERIES

Year/Team	G	AB	H	2B	3B	HR	HR %	R	RBI	BB	SO	SB	BA	SA	PH AB	PH H	G by POS
1901 NY N	3	14	5	2	0	3	21.4	3	7	0	1	0	.357	1.143	0	0	OF-3

WORLD SERIES

Year/Team	G	AB	H	2B	3B	HR	HR %	R	RBI	BB	SO	SB	BA	SA	PH AB	PH H	G by POS
1901 NY N	7	28	9	1	0	6	21.4	12	14	3	4	0	.321	1.000	0	0	SS-5, P-2
1906 DET A	5	10	5	1	0	1	10.0	3	2	0	2	0	.500	.900	2	0	P-4, SS-1
2 yrs.	12	38	14	2	0	7 5th	18.4	15	16 9th	3	6	0	.368	.974	2	0	SS-6, P-6

PLAYER INFORMATION

John Doe	This shortened version of the player's full name is the name most familiar to the fans. All players in this section are alphabetically arranged by the last name part of this name.
DOE, JOHN LEE	Player's full name. The arrangement is last name first, then first and middle name(s).
(Slim)	Player's nickname. Any name or names appearing in parentheses indicates a nickname.

The player's main batting and throwing style. Doe, for instance, batted and threw righthanded. The information listed directly below the main batting information indicates that at various times in a player's career he changed his batting style. The "BB" for Doe in 1884 means he was a switch hitter that year, and the "BL" means he batted lefthanded in 1906. For the years that are not shown it can be assumed that Doe batted right, as his main batting information indicates.

BR TR
BB 1884
BL 1906

Player's height. 6'2"

Player's average playing weight. 165 lbs

The player at one time in his major league career played under another name and can be found only in box scores or newspaper stories under that name.

Played as John Cherry part of 1900

The name the player was given at birth. (For the most part, the player never used this name while playing in the major leagues, but, if he did, it would be listed as "played as," which is explained above under the heading "Played as John Cherry part of 1900.")

Born John Lee Doughnut

The player's brother. (Relatives indicated here are fathers, sons, brothers, grandfathers, and grandsons who played or managed in the major leagues and the National Association.)

Brother of Bill Doe

Date and place of birth.

B. Jan. 1, 1850, New York, N.Y.

Date and place of death. (For those players who are listed simply as "deceased," it means that, although no certification of death or other information is presently available, it is reasonably certain they are dead.)

D. July 1, 1955, New York, N.Y.

Doe also served as a major league manager. All men who were managers for the Tigers can be found in the Manager Register, where their complete managerial record is shown.

Manager 1908–15

Doe was elected to the Baseball Hall of Fame in 1946.

Hall of Fame 1946

COLUMN HEADINGS INFORMATION

G	AB	H	2B	3B	HR	HR %	R	RBI	BB	SO	SB	BA	SA	Pinch Hit AB H	G by POS

G	Games
AB	At Bats
H	Hits
2B	Doubles
3B	Triples
HR	Home Runs
HR %	Home Run Percentage (the number of home runs per 100 times at bat)
R	Runs Scored
RBI	Runs Batted In
BB	Bases on Balls
SO	Strikeouts
SB	Stolen Bases
BA	Batting Average
SA	Slugging Average

Pinch Hit

AB	Pinch Hit At Bats
H	Pinch Hits
G by POS	Games by Position. (All fielding positions a man played within the given year are shown. The position where the most games were played is listed first. Any man who pitched, as Doe did, is listed also in the alphabetically arranged Pitcher Register, where his complete pitching record can be found.) If no fielding positions are shown in a particular year, it means the player only pinch-hit, pinch-ran, or was a "designated hitter."

TEAM AND LEAGUE INFORMATION

Doe's record has been exaggerated so that his playing career spans all the years of the six different major leagues. Directly alongside the year and team information is the symbol for the league:

N   National League (1876 to date)
A   American League (1901 to date)
F   Federal League (1914–15)
AA   American Association (1882–91)
P   Players' League (1890)
U   Union Association (1884)

STL—The abbreviation of the city in which the team played. Doe, for example, played for St. Louis in 1884. All teams in this section are listed by an abbreviation of the city in which the team played. The abbreviations follow:

ALT	Altoona		NWK	Newark
ATL	Atlanta		NY	New York
BAL	Baltimore		OAK	Oakland
BOS	Boston		PHI	Philadelphia
BKN	Brooklyn		PIT	Pittsburgh
BUF	Buffalo		PRO	Providence
CAL	California		RIC	Richmond
CHI	Chicago		ROC	Rochester
CIN	Cincinnati		SD	San Diego
CLE	Cleveland		SEA	Seattle
COL	Columbus		SF	San Francisco
DET	Detroit		STL	St. Louis
HAR	Hartford		STP	St. Paul
HOU	Houston		SYR	Syracuse
IND	Indianapolis		TEX	Texas
KC	Kansas City		TOL	Toledo
LA	Los Angeles		TOR	Toronto
LOU	Louisville		TRO	Troy
MIL	Milwaukee		WAS	Washington
MIN	Minnesota		WIL	Wilmington
MON	Montreal		WOR	Worcester

Three franchises in the history of major league baseball changed their location during the season. These teams are designated by the first letter of the two cities they represented. They are:

B-B   Brooklyn-Baltimore (American Association, 1890)
C-M   Cincinnati-Milwaukee (American Association, 1891)
C-P   Chicago-Pittsburgh (Union Association, 1884)

Blank space appearing beneath a team and league indicates that the team and league are the same. Doe, for example, played for Detroit in the American League from 1906 through 1908.

3 Teams Total. Indicates a player played for more than one team in the same year. Doe played for three teams in 1889. The number of games he played and his batting average for each team are also shown. Directly beneath this line, following the word "total," is Doe's combined record for all three teams for 1889.

Total Playing Years. This information, which appears as the first item on the player's lifetime total line, indicates the total number of years in which he played at least one game. Doe, for example, played in at least one game for fourteen years.

Tigers Playing Years. This information, which appears as the first item on the player's Tigers career total line, indicates the total number of years in which he played at least one game for the Tigers.

STATISTICAL INFORMATION

League Leaders. Statistics that appear in bold-faced print indicate the player led his league that year in a particular statistical category. Doe, for example, led the National League in doubles in 1889. When there is a tie for league lead, the figures for all the men who tied are shown in boldface.

All-Time Single Season Leaders. Indicated by the small number that appears next to the statistic. Doe, for example, is shown with a small number "1" next to his doubles total in 1889. This means he is first on the all-time major league list for hitting the most doubles in a single season. All players who tied for first are also shown by the same number.

Lifetime Leaders. Indicated by the figure that appears beneath the line showing the player's lifetime totals. Doe has a "4th" shown below his lifetime triples total. This means that, lifetime, Doe ranks fourth among major league players for hitting the most triples. Once again, only the top ten are indicated, and players who are tied receive the same number.

Unavailable Information. Any time a blank space is shown in a particular statistical column, such as in Doe's 1884 RBI total, it indicates the information was unavailable or incomplete.

Meaningless Averages. Indicated by use of a dash (—). In the case of Doe, a dash is shown for his 1915 batting average. This means that, although he played one game, he had no official at bats. A batting average of .000 would mean he had at least one at bat with no hits.

Tigers Career Totals. The statistical line appearing below Doe's major league career totals indicates his totals for his career with the Detroit Tigers. In Doe's case, the totals are for the years 1906–1908.

Tigers Lifetime Leaders. Indicated by the figure that appears beneath his Tigers career total. Doe has a "6th" shown below his Tigers career pinch hit as bats total. This means that he ranks sixth among Tigers in that category, counting only his years with the club.

World Series Lifetime Leaders. Indicated by the figure that appears beneath the player's lifetime World Series totals. Doe has a "5th" shown below his lifetime home run total. This means that, lifetime, Doe ranks fifth among major league players for hitting the most home runs in total World Series play. Players who tied for a position in the top ten are shown by the same number, so that, if two men tried for fourth and fifth place, the appropriate information for both men would be followed by the small number "4," and the next man would be considered sixth in the ranking. Tigers career totals are not provided for post-season play; the indicated totals are for Doe's entire career.

	G	AB	H	2B	3B	HR	HR %	R	RBI	BB	SO	SB	BA	SA	Pinch Hit AB	H	G by POS

Bob Adams

ADAMS, ROBERT MELVIN   BR TR 6'2"   200 lbs.
B. Jan. 6, 1952, Pittsburgh, Pa.

	G	AB	H	2B	3B	HR	HR %	R	RBI	BB	SO	SB	BA	SA	PH AB	PH H	G by POS
77 DET A	15	24	6	1	0	2	8.3	2	2	0	5	0	.250	.542	12	4	1B-2, C-1

Eddie Ainsmith

AINSMITH, EDWARD WILBUR   BR TR 5'11"   180 lbs.
B. Feb. 4, 1890, Cambridge, Mass.   D. Sept. 6, 1981, Fort Lauderdale, Fla.

	G	AB	H	2B	3B	HR	HR %	R	RBI	BB	SO	SB	BA	SA	PH AB	PH H	G by POS
10 WAS A	33	104	20	1	2	0	0.0	4	9	6		0	.192	.240	0	0	C-30
11	61	149	33	2	3	0	0.0	12	14	10		5	.221	.275	7	1	C-49
12	60	186	42	7	2	0	0.0	22	22	14		4	.226	.285	2	0	C-58
13	79	229	49	4	4	2	0.9	26	20	12	41	17	.214	.293	0	0	C-79, P-1
14	58	151	34	7	0	0	0.0	11	13	9	28	8	.225	.272	3	2	C-51
15	47	120	24	4	2	0	0.0	13	6	10	18	7	.200	.267	3	0	C-42
16	51	100	17	4	0	0	0.0	11	8	8	14	3	.170	.210	1	0	C-46
17	125	350	67	17	4	0	0.0	38	42	40	48	16	.191	.263	5	0	C-119
18	96	292	62	10	9	0	0.0	22	20	29	44	6	.212	.308	4	1	C-89
19 DET A	114	364	99	17	12	3	0.8	42	32	45	30	9	.272	.409	8	1	C-106
20	69	186	43	5	3	1	0.5	19	19	14	19	4	.231	.306	7	2	C-61
21 2 teams		DET A (35G – .276)				STL N (27G – .290)											
total	62	160	45	5	3	0	0.0	11	17	16	11	1	.281	.350	4	0	C-57, 1B-1
22 STL N	119	379	111	14	4	13	3.4	46	59	28	43	2	.293	.454	2	1	C-116
23 2 teams		STL N (82G – .213)				BKN N (2G – .200)											
total	84	273	58	11	6	3	1.1	22	36	22	19	4	.212	.330	2	1	C-82
24 NY N	10	5	3	0	0	0	0.0	0	0	0	0	0	.600	.600	1	1	C-9
15 yrs.	1068	3048	707	108	54	22	0.7	299	317	263	315	86	.232	.324	49	10	C-994, 1B-1, P-1
3 yrs.	218	648	169	27	17	4	0.6	67	63	72	56	14	.261	.373	16	3	C-201

Bill Akers

AKERS, THOMAS ERNEST   BR TR 5'11"   178 lbs.
B. Dec. 25, 1904, Chattanooga, Tenn.   D. Apr. 13, 1962, Chattanooga, Tenn.

	G	AB	H	2B	3B	HR	HR %	R	RBI	BB	SO	SB	BA	SA	PH AB	PH H	G by POS
29 DET A	24	83	22	4	1	1	1.2	15	9	10	9	2	.265	.373	0	0	SS-24
30	85	233	65	8	5	9	3.9	36	40	36	34	5	.279	.472	5	2	SS-49, 3B-26
31	29	66	13	2	2	0	0.0	5	3	7	6	0	.197	.288	5	2	SS-24
32 BOS N	36	93	24	3	1	1	1.1	8	17	10	15	0	.258	.344	6	1	3B-20, SS-5, 2B-5
4 yrs.	174	475	124	17	9	11	2.3	64	69	63	64	7	.261	.404	16	5	SS-99, 3B-46, 2B-7
3 yrs.	138	382	100	14	8	10	2.6	56	52	53	49	7	.262	.419	10	4	SS-94, 3B-26, 2B-2

Dale Alexander

ALEXANDER, DAVID DALE (Moose)   BR TR 6'3"   210 lbs.
B. Apr. 26, 1903, Greenville, Tenn.   D. Mar. 2, 1979, Greenville, Tenn.

	G	AB	H	2B	3B	HR	HR %	R	RBI	BB	SO	SB	BA	SA	PH AB	PH H	G by POS
29 DET A	155	626	215	43	15	25	4.0	110	137	56	63	5	.343	.580	0	0	1B-155
30	154	602	196	33	8	20	3.3	86	135	42	56	6	.326	.507	0	0	1B-154
31	135	517	168	47	3	3	0.6	75	87	64	35	5	.325	.445	6	0	1B-126, OF-4
32 2 teams		DET A (23G – .250)				BOS A (101G – .372)											
total	124	392	144	27	3	8	2.0	58	60	61	21	4	.367	.513	15	4	1B-103
33 BOS A	94	313	88	14	1	5	1.6	40	40	25	22	0	.281	.380	15	4	1B-79
5 yrs.	662	2450	811	164	30	61	2.5	369	459	248	197	20	.331	.497	36	8	1B-617, OF-4
4 yrs.	467	1761	583	123	26	48	2.7	271	363	168	156	16	.331	.512	21	4	1B-437, OF-4
								4th	**4th**								

Rod Allen

ALLEN, RODERICK BERNET   BR TR 6'1"   185 lbs.
B. Oct. 5, 1959, Los Angeles, Calif.

	G	AB	H	2B	3B	HR	HR %	R	RBI	BB	SO	SB	BA	SA	PH AB	PH H	G by POS
83 SEA A	11	12	2	0	0	0	0.0	1	0	0	1	0	.167	.167	4	1	DH-3, OF-2
84 DET A	15	27	8	1	0	0	0.0	6	3	2	8	1	.296	.333	3	1	DH-11, OF-2
2 yrs.	26	39	10	1	0	0	0.0	7	3	2	9	1	.256	.282	7	2	DH-14, OF-4
1 yr.	15	27	8	1	0	0	0.0	6	3	2	8	1	.296	.333	3	1	DH-11, OF-2

George Alusik

ALUSIK, GEORGE JOSEPH (Turk, Glider)   BR TR 6'3½"   175 lbs.
B. Feb. 11, 1935, Ashley, Pa.

	G	AB	H	2B	3B	HR	HR %	R	RBI	BB	SO	SB	BA	SA	PH AB	PH H	G by POS
58 DET A	2	2	0	0	0	0	0.0	0	0	0	1	0	.000	.000	1	0	OF-1
61	15	14	2	0	0	0	0.0	0	2	1	4	0	.143	.143	12	2	OF-1
62 2 teams		DET A (2G – .000)				KC A (90G – .273)											
total	92	211	57	10	1	11	5.2	29	35	16	29	1	.270	.483	38	11	OF-50, 1B-1
63 KC A	87	221	59	11	0	9	4.1	28	37	26	33	0	.267	.439	19	9	OF-63
64	102	204	49	10	1	3	1.5	18	19	30	36	0	.240	.343	40	6	OF-44, 1B-12
5 yrs.	298	652	167	31	2	23	3.5	75	93	73	103	1	.256	.416	110	28	OF-159, 1B-13
3 yrs.	19	18	2	0	0	0	0.0	0	2	1	5	0	.111	.111	15	2	OF-2

Luis Alvarado

ALVARADO, LUIS CESAR (Pimba)   BR TR 5'9"   162 lbs.
B. Jan. 15, 1949, La Jas, Puerto Rico

	G	AB	H	2B	3B	HR	HR %	R	RBI	BB	SO	SB	BA	SA	PH AB	PH H	G by POS
68 BOS A	11	46	6	2	0	0	0.0	3	1	1	11	0	.130	.174	0	0	SS-11
69	6	5	0	0	0	0	0.0	0	0	0	2	0	.000	.000	1	0	SS-5
70	59	183	41	11	0	1	0.5	19	10	9	30	1	.224	.301	0	0	3B-29, SS-27
71 CHI A	99	264	57	14	1	0	0.0	22	8	11	34	1	.216	.277	9	0	SS-71, 3B-20
72	103	254	54	4	1	4	1.6	30	29	13	36	2	.213	.283	7	2	SS-81, 2B-16, 3B-2
73	80	203	47	7	2	0	0.0	21	20	4	20	6	.232	.286	7	4	2B-45, SS-18, 3B-10
74 3 teams		CHI A (8G – .100)				CLE A (61G – .219)					STL N (17G – .139)						
total	86	160	31	4	0	0	0.0	16	13	8	21	5	.194	.219	5	1	2B-47, SS-28, DH-3, 3B-1
75 STL N	16	42	12	1	0	0	0.0	5	3	3	6	0	.286	.310	0	0	2B-16
77 2 teams		DET A (2G – .000)				NY N (1G – .000)											
total	3	3	0	0	0	0	0.0	0	0	0	0	0	.000	.000	0	0	3B-2, 2B-1
9 yrs.	463	1160	248	43	4	5	0.4	116	84	49	160	11	.214	.271	30	7	SS-241, 2B-141, 3B-44, DH-3
1 yr.	2	1	0	0	0	0	0.0	0	0	0	0	0	.000	.000	0	0	3B-2

Ossie Alvarez

ALVAREZ, OSWALDO GONZALEZ   BR TR 5'10"   165 lbs.
B. Oct. 19, 1933, Matanzas, Cuba

	G	AB	H	2B	3B	HR	HR %	R	RBI	BB	SO	SB	BA	SA	PH AB	PH H	G by POS
58 WAS A	87	196	41	3	0	0	0.0	20	5	16	26	1	.209	.224	3	0	SS-64, 2B-14, 3B-3

	G	AB	H	2B	3B	HR	HR %	R	RBI	BB	SO	SB	BA	SA	Pinch Hit AB	Pinch Hit H	G by POS

Ossie Alvarez continued

	G	AB	H	2B	3B	HR	HR%	R	RBI	BB	SO	SB	BA	SA	AB	H	G by POS
1959 DET A	8	2	1	0	0	0	0.0	0	0	0	1	0	.500	.500	2	1	
2 yrs.	95	198	42	3	0	0	0.0	20	5	16	27	1	.212	.227	5	1	SS-64, 2B-14, 3B-3
1 yr.	8	2	1	0	0	0	0.0	0	0	0	1	0	.500	.500	2	1	

Sandy Amoros

AMOROS, EDMUNDO ISASI
B. Jan. 30, 1930, Havana, Cuba
BL TL 5'7½" 170 lb

	G	AB	H	2B	3B	HR	HR%	R	RBI	BB	SO	SB	BA	SA	AB	H	G by POS
1952 BKN N	20	44	11	3	1	0	0.0	10	3	5	14	1	.250	.364	11	0	OF-10
1954	79	263	72	18	6	9	3.4	44	34	31	24	1	.274	.490	8	2	OF-70
1955	119	388	96	16	7	10	2.6	59	51	55	45	10	.247	.402	9	3	OF-109
1956	114	292	76	11	8	16	5.5	53	58	59	51	3	.260	.517	22	3	OF-86
1957	106	238	66	7	1	7	2.9	40	26	46	42	3	.277	.403	28	4	OF-66
1959 LA N	5	5	1	0	0	0	0.0	1	1	0	1	0	.200	.200	5	1	
1960 2 teams	LA	N	(9G –	.143)		DET	A	(65G –	.149)								
" total	74	81	12	0	0	1	1.2	8	7	15	12	0	.148	.185	48	8	OF-13
7 yrs.	517	1311	334	55	23	43	3.3	215.	180	211	189	18	.255	.430	131	21	OF-354
1 yr.	65	67	10	0	0	1	1.5	7	7	12	10	0	.149	.194	44	8	OF-10

WORLD SERIES

	G	AB	H	2B	3B	HR	HR%	R	RBI	BB	SO	SB	BA	SA	AB	H	G by POS
1952 BKN N	1	0	0	0	0	0	–	0	0	0	0	0	–	–	0	0	
1955	5	12	4	0	0	1	8.3	3	3	4	4	0	.333	.583	0	0	OF-5
1956	6	19	1	0	0	0	0.0	1	1	2	4	0	.053	.053	0	0	OF-6
3 yrs.	12	31	5	0	0	1	3.2	4	4	6	8	0	.161	.258	0	0	OF-11

Sparky Anderson

ANDERSON, GEORGE LEE
B. Feb. 22, 1934, Bridgewater, S. D.
Manager 1970-84.
BR TR 5'9" 170 lb

	G	AB	H	2B	3B	HR	HR%	R	RBI	BB	SO	SB	BA	SA	AB	H	G by POS
1959 PHI N	152	477	104	9	3	0	0.0	42	34	42	53	6	.218	.249	0	0	2B-152

Jimmy Archer

ARCHER, JAMES PETER
B. May 13, 1883, Dublin, Ireland   D. Mar. 29, 1958, Milwaukee, Wis.
BR TR 5'10" 168 lb

	G	AB	H	2B	3B	HR	HR%	R	RBI	BB	SO	SB	BA	SA	AB	H	G by POS
1904 PIT N	7	20	3	0	0	0	0.0	1	1	0		0	.150	.150	0	0	C-7, OF-1
1907 DET A	18	42	5	0	0	0	0.0	6	0	4		0	.119	.119	0	0	C-17, 2B-1
1909 CHI N	80	261	60	9	2	1	0.4	31	30	12		5	.230	.291	0	0	C-80
1910	98	313	81	17	6	2	0.6	36	41	14	49	6	.259	.371	8	3	C-49, 1B-40
1911	116	387	98	18	5	4	1.0	41	41	18	43	5	.253	.357	3	0	C-102, 1B-10, 2B-1
1912	120	385	109	20	2	5	1.3	35	58	22	36	7	.283	.384	1	0	C-118
1913	110	367	98	14	7	2	0.5	38	44	19	27	4	.267	.360	3	1	C-103, 1B-8
1914	79	248	64	9	2	0	0.0	17	19	9	9	1	.258	.310	3	1	C-76
1915	97	309	75	11	5	1	0.3	21	27	11	38	5	.243	.320	5	2	C-88
1916	77	205	45	6	2	1	0.5	11	30	12	24	3	.220	.283	16	2	C-65, 3B-1
1917	2	2	0	0	0	0	0.0	0	0	0	1	0	.000	.000	2	0	
1918 3 teams	PIT	N	(24G –	.155)		BKN	N	(9G –	.273)		CIN	N	(9G –	.269)			
" total	42	106	22	3	0	0	0.0	10	5	3	14	0	.208	.283	1	1	C-35, 1B-2
12 yrs.	846	2645	660	106	34	16	0.6	247	296	124	241	36	.250	.333	46	10	C-740, 1B-60, 2B-2, OF, 3B-1
1 yr.	18	42	5	0	0	0	0.0	6	0	4		0	.119	.119	0	0	C-17, 2B-1

WORLD SERIES

	G	AB	H	2B	3B	HR	HR%	R	RBI	BB	SO	SB	BA	SA	AB	H	G by POS
1907 DET A	1	3	0	0	0	0	0.0	0	0	0	0	0	.000	.000	0	0	C-1
1910 CHI N	3	11	2	1	0	0	0.0	1	0	0	4	0	.182	.273	0	0	1B-1
2 yrs.	4	14	2	1	0	0	0.0	1	0	0	5	0	.143	.214	0	0	1B-1, C-1

George Archie

ARCHIE, GEORGE ALBERT
B. Apr. 27, 1914, Nashville, Tenn.
BR TR 6' 170 lb

	G	AB	H	2B	3B	HR	HR%	R	RBI	BB	SO	SB	BA	SA	AB	H	G by POS
1938 DET A	3	2	0	0	0	0	0.0	0	0	0	1	0	.000	.000	2	0	
1941 2 teams	WAS	A	(105G –	.269)		STL	A	(9G –	.379)								
" total	114	408	113	23	4	3	0.7	48	53	37	45	10	.277	.375	9	1	3B-73, 1B-31
1946 STL A	4	11	2	1	0	0	0.0	1	0	0	1	0	.182	.273	0	0	1B-3
3 yrs.	121	421	115	24	4	3	0.7	49	53	37	47	10	.273	.371	11	1	3B-73, 1B-34
1 yr.	3	2	0	0	0	0	0.0	0	0	0	1	0	.000	.000	2	0	

Harry Arndt

ARNDT, HARRY J.
B. Feb. 12, 1879, South Bend, Ind.   D. Mar. 24, 1921, South Bend, Ind.
TR

	G	AB	H	2B	3B	HR	HR%	R	RBI	BB	SO	SB	BA	SA	AB	H	G by POS
1902 2 teams	DET	A	(10G –	.147)		BAL	A	(68G –	.254)								
" total	78	282	68	7	5	2	0.7	45	35	41		9	.241	.323	0	0	OF-72, 2B-4, 3B-2, SS-1, 1B-1
1905 STL N	113	415	101	11	6	2	0.5	40	36	24		13	.243	.313	2	1	2B-90, OF-9, 3B-7, SS-3
1906	69	256	69	7	9	2	0.8	30	26	19		5	.270	.391	1	0	3B-65, OF-1, 1B-1
1907	11	32	6	1	0	0	0.0	3	2	1		0	.188	.219	4	1	1B-4, 3B-3
4 yrs.	271	985	244	26	20	6	0.6	118	99	85		27	.248	.333	7	2	2B-94, OF-82, 3B-77, SS-6, 1B-6
1 yr.	10	34	5	0	1	0	0.0	4	7	6		0	.147	.206	0	0	OF-10, 1B-1

Earl Averill

AVERILL, HOWARD EARL
Father of Earl Averill.
B. May 21, 1902, Snohomish, Wash.   D. Aug. 16, 1983, Everett, Wash.
Hall of Fame 1975.
BL TR 5'9½" 172 lb

	G	AB	H	2B	3B	HR	HR%	R	RBI	BB	SO	SB	BA	SA	AB	H	G by POS
1929 CLE A	152	602	199	43	13	18	3.0	110	97	64	53	13	.331	.535	0	0	OF-152
1930	139	534	181	33	8	19	3.6	102	119	56	48	10	.339	.537	5	2	OF-134
1931	155	627	209	36	10	32	5.1	140	143	68	38	9	.333	.576	0	0	OF-155
1932	153	631	198	37	14	32	5.1	116	124	75	40	5	.314	.569	0	0	OF-153
1933	151	599	180	39	16	11	1.8	83	92	54	29	3	.301	.474	2	1	OF-149
1934	154	598	187	48	6	31	5.2	128	113	99	44	4	.313	.569	0	0	OF-154
1935	140	563	162	34	13	19	3.4	109	79	70	58	8	.288	.496	1	0	OF-139
1936	152	614	232	39	15	28	4.6	136	126	65	35	3	.378	.627	2	1	OF-150
1937	156	609	182	33	11	21	3.4	121	92	88	65	5	.299	.493	0	0	OF-156
1938	134	482	159	27	15	14	2.9	101	93	81	48	5	.330	.535	3	0	OF-131

	G	AB	H	2B	3B	HR	HR %	R	RBI	BB	SO	SB	BA	SA	Pinch Hit AB	Pinch Hit H	G by POS

Earl Averill continued

	G	AB	H	2B	3B	HR	HR %	R	RBI	BB	SO	SB	BA	SA	AB	H	G by POS
'39 2 teams	CLE A (24G – .273)			DET A (87G – .262)													
total	111	364	96	28	6	11	3.0	66	65	49	42	4	.264	.464	19	6	OF-91
'40 DET A	64	118	33	4	1	2	1.7	10	20	5	14	0	.280	.381	38	12	OF-22
'41 BOS N	8	17	2	0	0	0	0.0	2	2	1	4	0	.118	.118	3	0	OF-4
13 yrs.	1669	6358	2020	401	128	238	3.7	1224	1165	775	518	69	.318	.533	73	22	OF-1590
2 yrs.	151	427	114	24	7	12	2.8	68	78	48	44	4	.267	.440	45	12	OF-102
WORLD SERIES																	
'40 DET A	3	3	0	0	0	0	0.0	0	0	0	0	0	.000	.000	3	0	

Del Baker

BAKER, DELMAR DAVID
B. May 3, 1892, Sherwood, Ore.   D. Sept. 11, 1973, San Antonio, Tex.
Manager 1933, 1938-42.   BR TR 5'11½" 176 lbs.

	G	AB	H	2B	3B	HR	HR %	R	RBI	BB	SO	SB	BA	SA	AB	H	G by POS
'14 DET A	43	70	15	2	1	0	0.0	4	1	6	9	0	.214	.271	3	0	C-38
'15	68	134	33	3	3	0	0.0	16	15	15	15	3	.246	.313	3	0	C-61
'16	61	98	15	4	0	0	0.0	7	6	11	8	2	.153	.194	1	0	C-59
3 yrs.	172	302	63	9	4	0	0.0	27	22	32	32	5	.209	.265	7	0	C-158
3 yrs.	172	302	63	9	4	0	0.0	27	22	32	32	5	.209	.265	7	0	C-158

Doug Baker

BAKER, DOUGLAS
B. Apr. 13, 1961, Fullerton, Calif.   BB TR 5'9"   160 lbs.

	G	AB	H	2B	3B	HR	HR %	R	RBI	BB	SO	SB	BA	SA	AB	H	G by POS
'84 DET A	43	108	20	4	1	0	0.0	15	11	7	22	3	.185	.241	1	1	SS-39, 2B-5
LEAGUE CHAMPIONSHIP SERIES																	
'84 DET A	1	0	0	0	0	0	–	0	0	0	0	0	–	–	0	0	SS-1

Bobby Baldwin

BALDWIN, ROBERT HARVEY
B. June 9, 1951, Tazewell, Va.   BL TL 6'   175 lbs.

	G	AB	H	2B	3B	HR	HR %	R	RBI	BB	SO	SB	BA	SA	AB	H	G by POS
'75 DET A	30	95	21	3	0	4	4.2	8	8	5	14	2	.221	.379	0	0	OF-25, DH-1
'76 NY N	9	22	6	1	1	1	4.5	4	5	1	2	0	.273	.545	3	1	OF-5
2 yrs.	39	117	27	4	1	5	4.3	12	13	6	16	2	.231	.410	3	1	OF-30, DH-1
1 yr.	30	95	21	3	0	4	4.2	8	8	5	14	2	.221	.379	0	0	OF-25, DH-1

Sam Barnes

BARNES, SAMUEL THOMAS
B. Dec. 18, 1899, Suggsville, Ala.   D. Feb. 19, 1981, Montgomery, Ala.   BL TR 5'8"   150 lbs.

	G	AB	H	2B	3B	HR	HR %	R	RBI	BB	SO	SB	BA	SA	AB	H	G by POS
'21 DET A	7	11	2	1	0	0	0.0	2		2	1	0	.182	.273	2	0	2B-2

Jimmy Barrett

BARRETT, JAMES ERIGENA
B. Mar. 28, 1875, Athol, Mass.   D. Oct. 24, 1921, Detroit, Mich.   BL TL 5'9"   170 lbs.

	G	AB	H	2B	3B	HR	HR %	R	RBI	BB	SO	SB	BA	SA	AB	H	G by POS
'99 CIN N	26	92	34	2	4	0	0.0	30	10	18		4	.370	.478	0	0	OF-26
'00	137	545	172	11	7	5	0.9	114	42	72		44	.316	.389	0	0	OF-137
'01 DET A	135	542	159	16	9	4	0.7	110	65	76		26	.293	.378	0	0	OF-135
'02	136	509	154	19	6	4	0.8	93	44	74		24	.303	.387	0	0	OF-136
'03	136	517	163	13	10	2	0.4	95	31	74		27	.315	.391	0	0	OF-136
'04	162	624	167	10	5	0	0.0	83	31	79		15	.268	.300	0	0	OF-162
'05	20	67	17	1	0	0	0.0	2	3	6		0	.254	.269	2	0	OF-18
'06 CIN N	5	12	0	0	0	0	0.0	1	0	2		0	.000	.000	1	0	OF-4
'07 BOS N	106	390	95	11	6	1	0.3	52	28	38		3	.244	.310	7	3	OF-99
'08	2	8	1	0	0	0	0.0	0	1	1			.125	.125	0	0	OF-2
10 yrs.	865	3306	962	83	47	16	0.5	580	255	440		143	.291	.359	10	3	OF-855
5 yrs.	589	2259	660	59	30	10	0.4	383	174	309		92	.292	.358	2	0	OF-587

Dick Bartell

BARTELL, RICHARD WILLIAM (Rowdy Richard)
B. Nov. 22, 1907, Chicago, Ill.   BR TR 5'9"   160 lbs.

	G	AB	H	2B	3B	HR	HR %	R	RBI	BB	SO	SB	BA	SA	AB	H	G by POS
'27 PIT N	1	2	0	0	0	0	0.0	0	0	2	0	0	.000	.000	0	0	SS-1
'28	72	233	71	8	4	1	0.4	27	36	21	18	4	.305	.386	2	0	2B-39, SS-27, 3B-1
'29	143	610	184	40	13	2	0.3	101	57	40	29	11	.302	.420	0	0	SS-97, 2B-70
'30	129	475	152	32	13	4	0.8	69	75	39	34	8	.320	.467	3	0	SS-126
'31 PHI N	135	554	160	43	7	0	0.0	88	34	27	38	6	.289	.392	0	0	SS-133, 2B-3
'32	154	614	189	48	7	1	0.2	118	53	64	47	8	.308	.414	0	0	SS-154
'33	152	587	159	25	5	1	0.2	78	37	56	46	6	.271	.336	0	0	SS-152
'34	146	604	187	30	4	0	0.0	102	37	64	59	13	.310	.373	0	0	SS-146
'35 NY N	137	539	141	28	4	14	2.6	60	53	37	52	5	.262	.406	0	0	SS-137
'36	145	510	152	31	3	8	1.6	71	42	40	36	6	.298	.418	0	0	SS-144
'37	128	516	158	38	2	14	2.7	91	62	40	38	5	.306	.469	0	0	SS-128
'38	127	481	126	26	1	9	1.9	67	49	55	60	4	.262	.376	0	0	SS-127
'39 CHI N	105	336	80	24	2	3	0.9	37	34	42	25	6	.238	.348	3	1	SS-101, 3B-1
'40 DET A	139	528	123	24	3	7	1.3	76	53	76	53	12	.233	.330	0	0	SS-139
'41 2 teams	DET A (5G – .167)			NY N (104G – .303)													
total	109	385	115	21	0	5	1.3	44	36	54	31	6	.299	.392	3	0	3B-84, SS-26
'42 NY N	90	316	77	10	3	5	1.6	53	24	44	34	4	.244	.342	8	1	3B-52, SS-31
'43	99	337	91	14	0	5	1.5	48	28	47	27	5	.270	.356	10	1	3B-54, SS-33
'46	5	2	0	0	0	0	0.0	0	0	0	0	0	.000	.000	0	0	3B-4, 2B-2
18 yrs.	2016	7629	2165	442	71	79	1.0	1130	710	748	627	109	.284	.391	29	3	SS-1702, 3B-196, 2B-114
2 yrs.	144	540	125	25	3	7	1.3	76	54	78	55	12	.231	.328	0	0	SS-144
WORLD SERIES																	
'36 NY N	6	21	8	3	0	1	4.8	5	3	4	4	0	.381	.667	0	0	SS-6
'37	5	21	5	1	0	0	0.0	3	1	0	3	0	.238	.286	0	0	SS-5
'40 DET A	7	26	7	2	0	0	0.0	2	3	3	3	0	.269	.346	0	0	SS-7
3 yrs.	18	68	20	6	0	1	1.5	10	7	7	10	0	.294	.426	0	0	SS-18

Al Bashang

BASHANG, ALBERT C.
B. Aug. 22, 1888, Cincinnati, Ohio   D. June 23, 1967, Cincinnati, Ohio   BB TR 5'8"   150 lbs.

	G	AB	H	2B	3B	HR	HR %	R	RBI	BB	SO	SB	BA	SA	AB	H	G by POS
'12 DET A	5	12	1	0	0	0	0.0	3	0	3		0	.083	.083	0	0	OF-5

	G	AB	H	2B	3B	HR	HR %	R	RBI	BB	SO	SB	BA	SA	Pinch Hit AB	Pinch Hit H	G by POS

Al Bashang continued

	G	AB	H	2B	3B	HR	HR%	R	RBI	BB	SO	SB	BA	SA	PH AB	PH H	G by POS
1918 BKN N	2	5	1	0	0	0	0.0	0	0	0	0	0	.200	.200	1	0	OF-1
2 yrs.	7	17	2	0	0	0	0.0	3	0	3	0	0	.118	.118	1	0	OF-6
1 yr.	5	12	1	0	0	0	0.0	3	0	3		0	.083	.083	0	0	OF-5

Johnny Bassler

BASSLER, JOHN LANDIS   BL TR 5'9"   170 lb
B. June 3, 1895, Mechanics Grove, Pa.   D. June 29, 1979, Santa Monica, Calif.

	G	AB	H	2B	3B	HR	HR%	R	RBI	BB	SO	SB	BA	SA	PH AB	PH H	G by POS
1913 CLE A	1	2	0	0	0	0	0.0	0	0	0	0	0	.000	.000	0	0	C-1
1914	43	77	14	1	1	0	0.0	5	6	15	8	3	.182	.221	10	1	C-25, OF-1, 3B-1
1921 DET A	119	388	119	18	5	0	0.0	37	56	58	16	2	.307	.379	3	1	C-115
1922	121	372	120	14	0	0	0.0	41	41	62	12	2	.323	.360	2	0	C-118
1923	135	383	114	12	3	0	0.0	45	49	76	13	2	.298	.345	5	2	C-128
1924	124	379	131	20	3	1	0.3	43	68	62	11	2	.346	.422	3	1	C-122
1925	121	344	96	19	3	0	0.0	40	52	74	6	1	.279	.352	3	0	C-118
1926	66	174	53	8	1	0	0.0	20	22	45	6	0	.305	.362	2	0	C-63
1927	81	200	57	7	0	0	0.0	19	24	45	9	1	.285	.320	12	2	C-67
9 yrs.	811	2319	704	99	16	1	0.0	250	318	437	81	13	.304	.361	40	7	C-757, OF-1, 3B-1
7 yrs.	767	2240	690	98	15	1	0.0	245	312	422	73	10	.308	.367	30	6	C-731

Matt Batts

BATTS, MATTHEW DANIEL   BR TR 5'11"   200 lb
B. Oct. 16, 1921, San Antonio, Tex.

	G	AB	H	2B	3B	HR	HR%	R	RBI	BB	SO	SB	BA	SA	PH AB	PH H	G by POS
1947 BOS A	7	16	8	1	0	1	6.3	3	5	1	1	0	.500	.750	1	0	C-6
1948	46	118	37	12	0	1	0.8	13	24	15	9	0	.314	.441	6	1	C-41
1949	60	157	38	9	1	3	1.9	23	31	25	22	1	.242	.369	11	1	C-50
1950	75	238	65	15	3	4	1.7	27	34	18	19	0	.273	.412	2	1	C-73
1951 2 teams			BOS	A	(11G –	.138)		STL	A	(79G –	.302)						
" total	90	277	79	18	1	5	1.8	27	33	22	23	2	.285	.412	11	1	C-75
1952 DET A	56	173	41	4	1	3	1.7	11	13	14	22	1	.237	.324	2	0	C-55
1953	116	374	104	24	3	6	1.6	38	42	24	36	2	.278	.406	12	4	C-103
1954 2 teams			DET	A	(12G –	.286)		CHI	A	(55G –	.228)						
" total	67	179	42	8	1	3	1.7	17	24	19	19	0	.235	.341	17	4	C-50
1955 CIN N	26	71	18	4	1	0	0.0	4	13	4	11	0	.254	.338	5	1	C-21
1956	3	2	0	0	0	0	0.0	0	0	1	1	0	.000	.000	2	0	
10 yrs.	546	1605	432	95	11	26	1.6	163	219	143	163	6	.269	.391	69	13	C-474
3 yrs.	184	568	151	29	4	9	1.6	50	60	42	62	3	.266	.379	19	6	C-166

Paddy Baumann

BAUMANN, CHARLES JOHN   BR TR 5'9"   160 lb
B. Dec. 20, 1885, Indianapolis, Ind.   D. Nov. 20, 1969, Indianapolis, Ind.

	G	AB	H	2B	3B	HR	HR%	R	RBI	BB	SO	SB	BA	SA	PH AB	PH H	G by POS
1911 DET A	26	94	24	2	4	0	0.0	8	11	6		1	.255	.362	0	0	2B-23, OF-3
1912	13	42	11	1	0	0	0.0	3	7	6		4	.262	.286	1	0	3B-6, 2B-5, OF-1
1913	49	191	57	7	4	1	0.5	31	22	16	18	4	.298	.393	0	0	2B-49
1914	3	11	0	0	0	0	0.0	1	0	2	1	0	.000	.000	0	0	2B-3
1915 NY A	76	219	64	13	1	2	0.9	30	28	28	32	9	.292	.388	10	2	2B-43, 3B-19
1916	79	237	68	5	3	1	0.4	35	25	19	16	10	.287	.346	14	5	OF-28, 3B-26, 2B-9
1917	49	110	24	2	1	0	0.0	10	8	4	9	2	.218	.255	21	6	2B-18, OF-7, 3B-1
7 yrs.	295	904	248	30	13	4	0.4	118	101	81	76	30	.274	.350	46	13	2B-150, 3B-52, OF-39
4 yrs.	91	338	92	10	8	1	0.3	43	40	30	19	9	.272	.358	1	0	2B-80, 3B-6, OF-4

John Baumgartner

BAUMGARTNER, JOHN EDWARD   BR TR 6'1"   190 lb
B. May 29, 1931, Birmingham, Ala.

	G	AB	H	2B	3B	HR	HR%	R	RBI	BB	SO	SB	BA	SA	PH AB	PH H	G by POS
1953 DET A	7	27	5	0	0	0	0.0	3	2	0	5	0	.185	.185	0	0	3B-7

Erve Beck

BECK, ERVIN THOMAS (Dutch)   BR TR 5'10"   168 lb
B. July 19, 1878, Toledo, Ohio   D. Dec. 23, 1916, Toledo, Ohio

	G	AB	H	2B	3B	HR	HR%	R	RBI	BB	SO	SB	BA	SA	PH AB	PH H	G by POS
1899 BKN N	8	24	4	2	0	0	0.0	2	2	0		0	.167	.250	0	0	2B-6, SS-2
1901 CLE A	135	539	156	26	8	6	1.1	78	79	23		7	.289	.401	3	1	2B-132
1902 2 teams			CIN	N	(48G –	.305)		DET	A	(41G –	.296)						
" total	89	349	105	14	3	3	0.9	42	42	7		5	.301	.384	4	1	1B-42, 2B-32, OF-11
3 yrs.	232	912	265	42	11	9	1.0	122	123	30		12	.291	.390	7	2	2B-170, 1B-42, OF-11, SS-2
1 yr.	41	162	48	4	0	2	1.2	23	22	4		3	.296	.358	0	0	1B-36, OF-5

Heinie Beckendorf

BECKENDORF, HENRY WARD   BR TR 5'9"   174 lb
B. June 15, 1884, New York, N.Y.   D. Sept. 15, 1949, Jackson Heights, N.Y.

	G	AB	H	2B	3B	HR	HR%	R	RBI	BB	SO	SB	BA	SA	PH AB	PH H	G by POS
1909 DET A	15	27	7	1	0	0	0.0	1	1	2		0	.259	.296	0	0	C-15
1910 2 teams			DET	A	(3G –	.231)		WAS	A	(37G –	.155)						
" total	40	110	18	1	0	0	0.0	8	12	6		0	.164	.173	2	1	C-38
2 yrs.	55	137	25	2	0	0	0.0	9	13	8		0	.182	.197	2	1	C-53
2 yrs.	18	40	10	1	0	0	0.0	1	3	3		0	.250	.275	1	1	C-17

Wayne Belardi

BELARDI, CARROLL WAYNE (Footsie)   BL TL 6'1"   185 lb
B. Sept. 5, 1930, Calistoga, Calif.

	G	AB	H	2B	3B	HR	HR%	R	RBI	BB	SO	SB	BA	SA	PH AB	PH H	G by POS
1950 BKN N	10	10	0	0	0	0	0.0	0	0	0	4	0	.000	.000	9	0	1B-1
1951	3	3	1	0	1	0	0.0	1	0	0	2	0	.333	1.000	3	1	
1953	69	163	39	3	2	11	6.7	19	34	16	40	0	.239	.485	28	9	1B-38
1954 2 teams			BKN	N	(11G –	.222)		DET	A	(88G –	.232)						
" total	99	259	60	7	1	11	4.2	27	25	35	37	1	.232	.394	21	4	1B-79
1955 DET A	3	3	0	0	0	0	0.0	0	0	0	1	0	.000	.000	3	0	
1956	79	154	43	3	1	6	3.9	24	15	15	13	0	.279	.429	37	8	1B-31, OF-2
6 yrs.	263	592	143	13	5	28	4.7	71	74	66	97	1	.242	.422	101	22	1B-149, OF-2
3 yrs.	170	407	101	10	2	17	4.2	51	39	48	48	1	.248	.408	52	10	1B-110, OF-2

WORLD SERIES

	G	AB	H	2B	3B	HR	HR%	R	RBI	BB	SO	SB	BA	SA	PH AB	PH H	G by POS
1953 BKN N	2	2	0	0	0	0	0.0	0	0	0	1	0	.000	.000	2	0	

	G	AB	H	2B	3B	HR	HR %	R	RBI	BB	SO	SB	BA	SA	Pinch Hit AB	Pinch Hit H	G by POS

eau Bell

BELL, ROY CHESTER   BR TR 6'2" 185 lbs.
B. Aug. 20, 1907, Bellville, Tex. D. Sept. 14, 1977, College Station, Tex.

	G	AB	H	2B	3B	HR	HR %	R	RBI	BB	SO	SB	BA	SA	PH AB	PH H	G by POS
35 STL A	76	220	55	8	2	3	1.4	20	17	16	16	1	.250	.345	24	4	OF-37, 1B-15, 3B-3
36	155	616	212	40	12	11	1.8	100	123	60	55	4	.344	.502	0	0	OF-142, 1B-17
37	156	642	218	51	8	14	2.2	82	117	53	54	2	.340	.509	0	0	OF-131, 1B-26, 3B-2
38	147	526	138	35	3	13	2.5	91	84	71	46	1	.262	.414	8	3	OF-132, 1B-4
39 2 teams	STL	A (11G – .219)		DET	A (54G – .239)												
total	65	166	39	5	2	1	0.6	18	29	28	19	0	.235	.307	17	3	OF-46
40 CLE A	120	444	124	22	2	4	0.9	55	58	34	41	2	.279	.365	9	0	OF-97, 1B-14
41	48	104	20	4	3	0	0.0	12	9	10	8	1	.192	.288	23	3	OF-14, 1B-10
7 yrs.	767	2718	806	165	32	46	1.7	378	437	272	239	11	.297	.432	81	13	OF-599, 1B-86, 3B-5
1 yr.	54	134	32	4	2	0	0.0	14	24	24	16	0	.239	.299	15	3	OF-37

ou Berberet

BERBERET, LOUIS JOSEPH   BL TR 5'11" 200 lbs.
B. Nov. 20, 1929, Long Beach, Calif.

	G	AB	H	2B	3B	HR	HR %	R	RBI	BB	SO	SB	BA	SA	PH AB	PH H	G by POS
54 NY A	5	5	2	0	0	0	0.0	1	3	1	1	0	.400	.400	2	1	C-3
55	2	5	2	0	0	0	0.0	1	2	1	0	0	.400	.400	1	1	C-1
56 WAS A	95	207	54	6	3	4	1.9	25	27	46	33	0	.261	.377	33	6	C-59
57	99	264	69	11	2	7	2.7	24	36	41	38	0	.261	.398	16	3	C-77
58 2 teams	WAS	A (5G – .167)		BOS	A (57G – .210)												
total	62	173	36	5	3	2	1.2	11	18	35	33	0	.208	.306	8	0	C-51
59 DET A	100	338	73	8	2	13	3.8	38	44	35	59	0	.216	.367	3	0	C-95
60	85	232	45	4	0	5	2.2	18	23	41	31	2	.194	.276	4	1	C-81
7 yrs.	448	1224	281	34	10	31	2.5	118	153	200	195	2	.230	.350	67	12	C-367
2 yrs.	185	570	118	12	2	18	3.2	56	67	76	90	2	.207	.330	7	1	C-176

Dave Bergman

BERGMAN, DAVID BRUCE   BL TL 6'1½" 185 lbs.
B. June 6, 1953, Park Ridge, Ill.

	G	AB	H	2B	3B	HR	HR %	R	RBI	BB	SO	SB	BA	SA	PH AB	PH H	G by POS
75 NY A	7	17	0	0	0	0	0.0	0	0	2	4	0	.000	.000	0	0	OF-6
77	5	4	1	0	0	0	0.0	1	1	0	0	0	.250	.250	0	0	OF-3, 1B-2
78 HOU N	104	186	43	5	1	0	0.0	15	12	39	32	2	.231	.269	16	2	1B-66, OF-29
79	13	15	6	0	0	1	6.7	4	2	0	3	0	.400	.600	10	5	1B-4
80	90	78	20	6	1	0	0.0	12	3	10	10	1	.256	.359	24	4	1B-59, OF-5
81 2 teams	HOU	N (6G – .167)		SF	N (63G – .255)												
total	69	151	38	9	4	4	2.6	17	14	19	18	2	.252	.391	23	4	1B-34, OF-15
82 SF N	100	121	33	3	1	4	3.3	22	14	18	11	3	.273	.413	21	5	1B-69, OF-6
83	90	140	40	4	1	6	4.3	16	24	24	21	2	.286	.457	31	11	1B-50, OF-6
84 DET A	120	271	74	8	5	7	2.6	42	44	33	40	3	.273	.417	21	6	1B-114, OF-2
9 yrs.	598	983	255	35	9	22	2.2	129	114	145	139	13	.259	.380	146	37	1B-398, OF-72
1 yr.	120	271	74	8	5	7	2.6	42	44	33	40	3	.273	.417	21	6	1B-114, OF-2
LEAGUE CHAMPIONSHIP SERIES																	
80 HOU N	4	3	1	0	1	0	0.0	0	2	0	1	0	.333	1.000	0	0	1B-4
84 DET A	2	1	1	0	0	0	0.0	1	0	0	0	1	1.000	1.000	0	0	1B-1
2 yrs.	6	4	2	0	1	0	0.0	1	2	0	1	1	.500	1.000	0	0	1B-5
WORLD SERIES																	
84 DET A	5	5	0	0	0	0	0.0	0	0	0	1	0	.000	.000	0	0	1B-5

ohnny Bero

BERO, JOHN GEORGE   BL TR 6' 170 lbs.
B. Dec. 22, 1922, Gary, W. Va.

	G	AB	H	2B	3B	HR	HR %	R	RBI	BB	SO	SB	BA	SA	PH AB	PH H	G by POS
48 DET A	4	9	0	0	0	0	0.0	2	0	1	1	0	.000	.000	1	0	2B-2
51 STL A	61	160	34	5	0	5	3.1	24	17	26	30	1	.213	.338	7	2	SS-55, 2B-1
2 yrs.	65	169	34	5	0	5	3.0	26	17	27	31	1	.201	.320	8	2	SS-55, 2B-3
1 yr.	4	9	0	0	0	0	0.0	2	0	1	1	0	.000	.000	1	0	2B-2

eil Berry

BERRY, CORNELIUS JOHN   BR TR 5'10" 168 lbs.
B. Jan. 11, 1922, Kalamazoo, Mich.

	G	AB	H	2B	3B	HR	HR %	R	RBI	BB	SO	SB	BA	SA	PH AB	PH H	G by POS
48 DET A	87	256	68	8	1	0	0.0	46	16	37	23	1	.266	.305	5	1	SS-41, 2B-26
49	109	329	78	9	1	0	0.0	38	18	27	24	4	.237	.271	4	0	2B-95, SS-4
50	38	39	10	1	0	0	0.0	9	7	6	11	0	.256	.282	4	0	SS-11, 2B-2, 3B-1
51	67	157	36	5	2	0	0.0	17	9	10	15	4	.229	.287	4	0	SS-38, 2B-10, 3B-7
52	73	189	43	4	3	0	0.0	22	13	22	19	1	.228	.280	1	1	SS-66, 3B-2
53 2 teams	STL	A (57G – .283)		CHI	A (5G – .125)												
total	62	107	29	1	2	0	0.0	15	11	10	11	1	.271	.318	6	1	3B-18, 2B-18, SS-6
54 BAL A	9	9	1	0	0	0	0.0	1	0	1	2	0	.111	.111	0	0	SS-5
7 yrs.	441	1086	265	28	9	0	0.0	148	74	113	105	11	.244	.286	24	3	SS-171, 2B-151, 3B-28
5 yrs.	374	970	235	27	7	0	0.0	132	63	102	92	10	.242	.285	18	2	SS-160, 2B-133, 3B-10

eno Bertoia

BERTOIA, RENO PETER   BR TR 5'11½" 185 lbs.
B. Jan. 8, 1935, St. Vito Udine, Italy

	G	AB	H	2B	3B	HR	HR %	R	RBI	BB	SO	SB	BA	SA	PH AB	PH H	G by POS
53 DET A	1	1	0	0	0	0	0.0	0	0	0	1	0	.000	.000	0	0	2B-1
54	54	37	6	2	0	1	2.7	13	2	5	9	1	.162	.297	2	0	2B-15, 3B-8, SS-3
55	38	68	14	2	1	1	1.5	13	10	5	11	0	.206	.309	6	1	3B-14, 2B-6, SS-5
56	22	66	12	0	1	1	1.5	7	5	6	12	0	.182	.258	0	0	2B-18, 3B-2
57	97	295	81	16	2	4	1.4	28	28	19	43	2	.275	.383	9	0	3B-83, SS-7, 2B-2
58	86	240	56	6	0	6	2.5	28	27	20	35	5	.233	.333	5	0	3B-68, SS-5, OF-1
59 WAS A	90	308	73	10	0	8	2.6	33	29	29	48	2	.237	.347	14	3	2B-71, 3B-5, SS-1
60	121	460	122	17	7	4	0.9	44	45	26	58	3	.265	.359	5	1	3B-112, 2B-21
61 3 teams	MIN	A (35G – .212)		KC	A (39G – .242)		DET	A (24G – .217)									
total	98	270	61	5	0	2	0.7	35	25	32	35	3	.226	.267	6	2	3B-74, 2B-13, SS-1
62 DET A	5	0	0	0	0	0	–	0	3	0	0	0	–	–	0	0	SS-1, 3B-1, 2B-1
10 yrs.	612	1745	425	60	10	27	1.5	204	171	142	252	16	.244	.336	47	8	3B-367, 2B-148, SS-23, OF-1
8 yrs.	327	753	179	29	3	14	1.9	98	76	58	119	10	.238	.340	22	0	3B-189, 2B-50, SS-22, OF-1

	G	AB	H	2B	3B	HR	HR%	R	RBI	BB	SO	SB	BA	SA	Pinch Hit AB	Pinch Hit H	G by POS

Monte Beville

BEVILLE, HENRY MONTE
B. Feb. 24, 1875, Dublin, Ind. D. Jan. 24, 1955, Grand Rapids, Mich.
BL TR 5'11" 180 lb

	G	AB	H	2B	3B	HR	HR%	R	RBI	BB	SO	SB	BA	SA	PH AB	PH H	G by POS
1903 NY A	82	258	50	14	1	0	0.0	23	29	16		4	.194	.256	4	1	C-75, 1B-3
1904 2 teams	NY A (9G – .273)				DET A (54G – .207)												
" total	63	196	42	7	1	0	0.0	16	15	10		2	.214	.260	4	0	C-33, 1B-28
2 yrs.	145	454	92	21	2	0	0.0	39	44	26		6	.203	.258	8	1	C-108, 1B-31
1 yr.	54	174	36	5	1	0	0.0	14	13	8		2	.207	.247	2	0	C-30, 1B-24

Steve Bilko

BILKO, STEVEN THOMAS
B. Nov. 13, 1928, Nanticoke, Pa. D. Mar. 7, 1978, Wilkes Barre, Pa.
BR TR 6'1" 230 lb

	G	AB	H	2B	3B	HR	HR%	R	RBI	BB	SO	SB	BA	SA	PH AB	PH H	G by POS
1949 STL N	6	17	5	2	0	0	0.0	3	2	5	6	0	.294	.412	1	0	1B-5
1950	10	33	6	1	0	0	0.0	1	2	4	10	0	.182	.212	1	1	1B-9
1951	21	72	16	4	0	2	2.8	5	12	9	10	0	.222	.361	2	1	1B-19
1952	20	72	19	6	1	1	1.4	7	6	4	15	0	.264	.417	0	0	1B-20
1953	154	570	143	23	3	21	3.7	72	84	70	125	0	.251	.412	0	0	1B-154
1954 2 teams	STL N (8G – .143)				CHI N (47G – .239)												
" total	55	106	24	8	1	4	3.8	12	13	14	25	0	.226	.434	24	6	1B-28
1958 2 teams	CIN N (31G – .264)				LA N (47G – .208)												
" total	78	188	44	5	4	11	5.9	25	35	18	57	0	.234	.479	27	5	1B-46
1960 DET A	78	222	46	11	2	9	4.1	20	25	27	31	0	.207	.396	17	1	1B-62
1961 LA A	114	294	82	16	1	20	6.8	49	59	58	81	1	.279	.544	24	8	1B-86, OF-3
1962	64	164	47	9	1	8	4.9	26	38	25	35	1	.287	.500	14	3	1B-50
10 yrs.	600	1738	432	85	13	76	4.4	220	276	234	395	2	.249	.444	110	25	1B-479, OF-3
1 yr.	78	222	46	11	2	9	4.1	20	25	27	31	0	.207	.396	17	1	1B-62

Ike Blessitt

BLESSITT, ISIAH
B. Sept. 30, 1949, Detroit, Mich.
BR TR 5'11" 185 lb

	G	AB	H	2B	3B	HR	HR%	R	RBI	BB	SO	SB	BA	SA	PH AB	PH H	G by POS
1972 DET A	4	5	0	0	0	0	0.0	0	0	0	2	0	.000	.000	3	0	OF-1

Jimmy Bloodworth

BLOODWORTH, JAMES HENRY
B. July 26, 1917, Tallahassee, Fla.
BR TR 5'11" 180 lb

	G	AB	H	2B	3B	HR	HR%	R	RBI	BB	SO	SB	BA	SA	PH AB	PH H	G by POS
1937 WAS A	15	50	11	2	1	0	0.0	3	8	5	8	0	.220	.300	1	0	2B-14
1939	83	318	92	24	1	4	1.3	34	40	10	26	3	.289	.409	5	2	2B-73, OF-5
1940	119	469	115	17	8	11	2.3	47	70	16	71	3	.245	.386	0	0	2B-96, 1B-17, 3B-6
1941	142	506	124	24	4	7	1.4	59	66	41	58	1	.245	.346	4	0	2B-132, 3B-6, SS-1
1942 DET A	137	533	129	23	1	13	2.4	62	57	35	63	2	.242	.362	1	0	2B-134, SS-2
1943	129	474	114	23	4	6	1.3	41	52	29	59	4	.241	.344	0	0	2B-129
1946	76	249	61	8	1	5	2.0	25	36	12	26	3	.245	.345	4	0	2B-71
1947 PIT N	88	316	79	9	0	7	2.2	27	48	16	39	1	.250	.345	1	0	2B-87
1949 CIN N	134	452	118	27	4	9	2.0	40	59	27	36	1	.261	.385	14	8	2B-92, 1B-23, 3B-8
1950 2 teams	CIN N (4G – .214)				PHI N (54G – .229)												
" total	58	110	25	3	0	0	0.0	7	14	8	12	0	.227	.255	16	4	2B-31, 1B-7, 3B-2
1951 PHI N	21	42	6	0	0	0	0.0	2	3	1	9	1	.143	.143	7	3	2B-8, 1B-6
11 yrs.	1002	3519	874	160	20	62	1.8	347	453	200	407	19	.248	.358	53	17	2B-867, 1B-53, 3B-22, OF-5, SS-3
3 yrs.	342	1256	304	54	6	24	1.9	128	145	76	148	9	.242	.352	5	0	2B-334, SS-2

WORLD SERIES

	G	AB	H	2B	3B	HR	HR%	R	RBI	BB	SO	SB	BA	SA	PH AB	PH H	G by POS
1950 PHI N	1	0	0	0	0	0	–	0	0	0	0	0	–	–	0	0	2B-1

Lu Blue

BLUE, LUZERNE ATWELL
B. Mar. 5, 1897, Washington, D. C. D. July 28, 1958, Alexandria, Va.
BB TL 5'10" 165 lb

	G	AB	H	2B	3B	HR	HR%	R	RBI	BB	SO	SB	BA	SA	PH AB	PH H	G by POS
1921 DET A	153	585	180	33	11	5	0.9	103	75	103	47	13	.308	.427	1	0	1B-152
1922	145	584	175	31	9	6	1.0	131	45	82	48	8	.300	.414	1	1	1B-144
1923	129	504	143	27	7	1	0.2	100	46	96	40	9	.284	.371	0	0	1B-129
1924	108	395	123	26	7	2	0.5	81	50	64	26	9	.311	.428	0	0	1B-108
1925	150	532	163	18	9	3	0.6	91	94	83	29	19	.306	.391	2	0	1B-148
1926	128	429	123	24	14	1	0.2	92	52	90	18	13	.287	.415	12	5	1B-109, OF-1
1927	112	365	95	17	9	1	0.3	71	42	71	28	13	.260	.364	5	2	1B-104
1928 STL A	154	549	154	32	11	14	2.6	116	80	105	43	12	.281	.455	0	0	1B-154
1929	151	573	168	40	10	6	1.0	111	61	126	32	12	.293	.429	0	0	1B-151
1930	117	425	100	27	5	4	0.9	85	42	81	44	12	.235	.351	4	1	1B-111
1931 CHI A	155	589	179	23	15	1	0.2	119	62	127	60	13	.304	.399	0	0	1B-155
1932	112	373	93	21	2	0	0.0	51	43	64	21	17	.249	.316	6	1	1B-105
1933 BKN N	1	1	0	0	0	0	0.0	0	0	0	0	0	.000	.000	0	0	1B-1
13 yrs.	1615	5904	1696	319	109	44	0.7	1151	692	1092	436	150	.287	.401	31	10	1B-1571, OF-1
				10th													
7 yrs.	925	3394	1002	176	66	19	0.6	669	404	589	236	84	.295	.403	21	8	1B-894, OF-1

Frank Bolling

BOLLING, FRANK ELMORE
Brother of Milt Bolling.
B. Nov. 16, 1931, Mobile, Ala.
BR TR 6'1" 175 lb

	G	AB	H	2B	3B	HR	HR%	R	RBI	BB	SO	SB	BA	SA	PH AB	PH H	G by POS
1954 DET A	117	368	87	15	2	6	1.6	46	38	36	51	3	.236	.337	3	0	2B-113
1956	102	366	103	21	7	7	1.9	53	45	42	51	6	.281	.434	0	0	2B-102
1957	146	576	149	27	6	15	2.6	72	40	57	64	4	.259	.405	0	0	2B-146
1958	154	610	164	25	4	14	2.3	91	75	54	54	6	.269	.392	0	0	2B-154
1959	127	459	122	18	3	13	2.8	56	55	45	37	2	.266	.403	1	0	2B-126
1960	139	536	136	20	4	9	1.7	64	59	40	48	7	.254	.356	1	0	2B-138
1961 MIL N	148	585	153	16	4	15	2.6	86	56	57	62	7	.262	.379	0	0	2B-148
1962	122	406	110	17	4	9	2.2	45	43	35	45	2	.271	.399	5	1	2B-119
1963	142	542	132	18	2	5	0.9	73	43	41	47	2	.244	.312	0	0	2B-141
1964	120	352	70	11	1	5	1.4	35	34	21	44	0	.199	.278	7	0	2B-117
1965	148	535	141	26	3	7	1.3	55	50	24	41	0	.264	.363	1	0	2B-147
1966 ATL N	75	227	48	7	0	1	0.4	16	18	10	14	1	.211	.256	11	1	2B-67
12 yrs.	1540	5562	1415	221	40	106	1.9	692	556	462	558	40	.254	.366	29	2	2B-1518
6 yrs.	785	2915	761	126	26	64	2.2	382	312	274	305	28	.261	.388	5	0	2B-779

	G	AB	H	2B	3B	HR	HR%	R	RBI	BB	SO	SB	BA	SA	Pinch Hit AB	Pinch Hit H	G by POS

Milt Bolling

BOLLING, MILTON JOSEPH
Brother of Frank Bolling.
B. Aug. 9, 1930, Mississippi City, Miss.   BR TR 6'1"   177 lbs.

	G	AB	H	2B	3B	HR	HR%	R	RBI	BB	SO	SB	BA	SA	PH AB	PH H	G by POS
'52 BOS A	11	36	8	1	0	1	2.8	4	3	3	5	0	.222	.333	0	0	SS-11
'53	109	323	85	12	1	5	1.5	30	28	24	41	1	.263	.353	1	0	SS-109
'54	113	370	92	20	3	6	1.6	42	36	47	55	2	.249	.368	1	0	SS-107, 3B-5
'55	6	5	1	0	0	0	0.0	0	0	0	1	0	.200	.200	2	0	SS-2
'56	45	118	25	3	2	3	2.5	19	8	18	20	1	.212	.347	5	2	SS-26, 3B-11, 2B-1
'57 2 teams	BOS A (1G – .000)					WAS A (91G – .227)											
total	92	278	63	12	1	4	1.4	29	19	18	59	2	.227	.320	4	0	2B-53, SS-37, 3B-1
'58 DET A	24	31	6	2	0	0	0.0	3	0	5	7	0	.194	.258	4	0	SS-13, 3B-1, 2B-1
7 yrs.	400	1161	280	50	7	19	1.6	127	94	115	188	5	.241	.345	17	2	SS-305, 2B-55, 3B-18
1 yr.	24	31	6	2	0	0	0.0	3	0	5	7	0	.194	.258	4	0	SS-13, 3B-1, 2B-1

Cliff Bolton

BOLTON, WILLIAM CLIFTON
B. Apr. 10, 1907, High Point, N.C.   D. Apr. 21, 1979, Lexington, Ky.   BL TR 5'9"   160 lbs.

	G	AB	H	2B	3B	HR	HR%	R	RBI	BB	SO	SB	BA	SA	PH AB	PH H	G by POS
'31 WAS A	23	43	11	1	1	0	0.0	3	6	1	5	0	.256	.326	10	6	C-13
'33	33	39	16	1	1	0	0.0	4	6	6	3	0	.410	.487	22	9	C-9, OF-1
'34	42	148	40	9	1	1	0.7	12	17	11	9	2	.270	.365	3	2	C-39
'35	110	375	114	18	11	2	0.5	47	55	56	13	0	.304	.427	3	0	C-106
'36	86	289	84	18	4	2	0.7	41	51	25	12	1	.291	.401	5	1	C-83
'37 DET A	27	57	15	2	0	1	1.8	6	7	8	6	0	.263	.351	13	3	C-13
'41 WAS A	14	11	0	0	0	0	0.0	0	1	1	2	0	.000	.000	10	0	C-3
7 yrs.	335	962	280	49	18	6	0.6	113	143	108	50	3	.291	.398	66	21	C-266, OF-1
1 yr.	27	57	15	2	0	1	1.8	6	7	8	6	0	.263	.351	13	3	C-13

WORLD SERIES

	G	AB	H	2B	3B	HR	HR%	R	RBI	BB	SO	SB	BA	SA	PH AB	PH H	G by POS
'33 WAS A	2	2	0	0	0	0	0.0	0	0	0	0	0	.000	.000	2	0	

Ray Boone

BOONE, RAYMOND OTIS (Ike)
Father of Bob Boone.
B. July 27, 1923, San Diego, Calif.   BR TR 6'   172 lbs.

	G	AB	H	2B	3B	HR	HR%	R	RBI	BB	SO	SB	BA	SA	PH AB	PH H	G by POS
'48 CLE A	6	5	2	1	0	0	0.0	0	1	0	1	0	.400	.600	1	0	SS-4
'49	86	258	65	4	4	4	1.6	39	26	38	17	0	.252	.345	7	1	SS-76
'50	109	365	110	14	6	7	1.9	53	58	56	27	4	.301	.430	6	0	SS-102
'51	151	544	127	14	1	12	2.2	65	51	48	36	5	.233	.329	0	0	SS-151
'52	103	316	83	8	2	7	2.2	57	45	53	33	0	.263	.367	4	0	SS-96, 3B-2, 2B-1
'53 2 teams	CLE A (34G – .241)					DET A (101G – .312)											
total	135	497	147	17	8	26	5.2	94	114	72	68	3	.296	.519	4	1	3B-97, SS-34
'54 DET A	148	543	160	19	7	20	3.7	76	85	71	53	4	.295	.466	0	0	3B-148, SS-1
'55	135	500	142	22	7	20	4.0	61	116	50	49	1	.284	.476	8	2	3B-126
'56	131	481	148	14	6	25	5.2	77	81	77	46	0	.308	.518	0	0	3B-130
'57	129	462	126	25	3	12	2.6	48	65	57	47	1	.273	.418	5	1	1B-117, 3B-4
'58 2 teams	DET A (39G – .237)					CHI A (77G – .244)											
total	116	360	87	16	2	13	3.6	41	61	32	46	1	.242	.406	21	2	1B-95
'59 3 teams	CHI A (9G – .238)			KC A (61G – .273)			MIL N (13G – .200)										
total	83	168	44	6	0	4	2.4	25	19	38	24	2	.262	.369	37	11	1B-47, 3B-3
'60 2 teams	MIL N (7G – .250)					BOS A (34G – .205)											
total	41	90	19	2	0	1	1.1	9	15	16	16	0	.211	.267	15	3	1B-26
13 yrs.	1373	4589	1260	162	46	151	3.3	645	737	608	463	21	.275	.429	108	21	3B-510, SS-464, 1B-285, 2B-1
								10th						8th			
6 yrs.	683	2485	723	100	30	105	4.2	351	460	317	255	8	.291	.482	21	5	3B-505, 1B-149, SS-4

WORLD SERIES

	G	AB	H	2B	3B	HR	HR%	R	RBI	BB	SO	SB	BA	SA	PH AB	PH H	G by POS
'48 CLE A	1	1	0	0	0	0	0.0	0	0	0	1	0	.000	.000	1	0	

Ed Borom

BOROM, EDWARD JONES
B. Oct. 30, 1915, Spartanburg, S.C.   BL TR 5'11"   180 lbs.

	G	AB	H	2B	3B	HR	HR%	R	RBI	BB	SO	SB	BA	SA	PH AB	PH H	G by POS
'44 DET A	7	14	1	0	0	0	0.0	1	1	2	2	0	.071	.071	2	0	2B-4, SS-1
'45	55	130	35	4	0	0	0.0	19	9	7	8	4	.269	.300	12	2	2B-28, 3B-4, SS-2
2 yrs.	62	144	36	4	0	0	0.0	20	10	9	10	4	.250	.278	14	2	2B-32, 3B-4, SS-3
2 yrs.	62	144	36	4	0	0	0.0	20	10	9	10	4	.250	.278	14	2	2B-32, 3B-4, SS-3

WORLD SERIES

	G	AB	H	2B	3B	HR	HR%	R	RBI	BB	SO	SB	BA	SA	PH AB	PH H	G by POS
'45 DET A	2	1	0	0	0	0	0.0	0	0	0	0	0	.000	.000	1	0	

Steve Boros

BOROS, STEPHEN
B. Sept. 3, 1936, Flint, Mich.
Manager 1983-84.   BR TR 6'   185 lbs.

	G	AB	H	2B	3B	HR	HR%	R	RBI	BB	SO	SB	BA	SA	PH AB	PH H	G by POS
'57 DET A	24	41	6	1	0	0	0.0	4	2	1	8	0	.146	.171	4	0	3B-9, SS-5
'58	6	2	0	0	0	0	0.0	0	0	0	0	0	.000	.000	0	0	2B-1
'61	116	396	107	18	2	5	1.3	51	62	68	42	4	.270	.364	0	0	3B-116
'62	116	356	81	14	1	16	4.5	46	47	53	62	3	.228	.407	8	0	3B-105, 2B-6
'63 CHI N	41	90	19	5	1	3	3.3	9	7	12	19	0	.211	.389	17	2	1B-14, OF-11
'64 CIN N	117	370	95	12	3	2	0.5	31	31	47	43	4	.257	.322	1	0	3B-114
'65	0	0	0	0	0	0	0.0	–	0	0	0	0	–	–	0	0	3B-2
7 yrs.	422	1255	308	50	7	26	2.1	141	149	181	174	11	.245	.359	30	4	3B-346, 1B-14, OF-11, 2B-7, SS-5
4 yrs.	262	795	194	33	3	21	2.6	101	111	122	112	7	.244	.372	12	0	3B-230, 2B-7, SS-5

Jim Brideweser

BRIDEWESER, JAMES EHRENFELD
B. Feb. 13, 1927, Lancaster, Ohio   BR TR 6'   165 lbs.

	G	AB	H	2B	3B	HR	HR%	R	RBI	BB	SO	SB	BA	SA	PH AB	PH H	G by POS
'51 NY A	2	8	3	0	0	0	0.0	1	0	0	1	0	.375	.375	0	0	SS-2
'52	42	38	10	0	0	0	0.0	12	2	3	5	0	.263	.263	9	1	SS-22, 2B-4, 3B-1
'53	7	3	3	0	1	0	0.0	3	3	1	0	0	1.000	1.667	2	2	SS-3
'54 BAL A	73	204	54	7	2	0	0.0	18	12	15	27	1	.265	.319	11	2	SS-48, 2B-19
'55 CHI A	34	58	12	3	0	0	0.0	6	4	3	7	0	.207	.328	1	0	SS-26, 3B-3, 2B-2
'56 2 teams	CHI A (10G – .182)					DET A (70G – .218)											
total	80	167	36	5	0	0	0.0	23	11	20	22	3	.216	.246	1	1	SS-42, 2B-31, 3B-4

	G	AB	H	2B	3B	HR	HR %	R	RBI	BB	SO	SB	BA	SA	Pinch Hit AB	Pinch Hit H	G by POS

Jim Brideweser continued

	G	AB	H	2B	3B	HR	HR%	R	RBI	BB	SO	SB	BA	SA	AB	H	G by POS
1957 BAL A	91	142	38	6	1	1	0.7	16	18	21	16	2	.268	.345	5	1	SS-74, 3B-3, 2B-1
7 yrs.	329	620	156	21	6	1	0.2	79	50	63	78	6	.252	.310	29	7	SS-217, 2B-57, 3B-11
1 yr.	70	156	34	4	0	0	0.0	23	10	20	19	3	.218	.244	1	1	SS-32, 2B-31, 3B-4

Rocky Bridges

BRIDGES, EVERETT LAMAR
B. Aug. 7, 1927, Refugio, Tex.

BR TR 5'8" 170 lb

	G	AB	H	2B	3B	HR	HR%	R	RBI	BB	SO	SB	BA	SA	AB	H	G by POS
1951 BKN N	63	134	34	7	0	1	0.7	13	15	10	10	0	.254	.328	2	0	3B-40, 2B-10, SS-9
1952	51	56	11	3	0	0	0.0	9	2	7	9	0	.196	.250	3	1	2B-24, SS-13, 3B-6
1953 CIN N	122	432	98	13	2	1	0.2	52	21	37	42	6	.227	.273	4	0	2B-115, SS-6, 3B-3
1954	53	52	12	1	0	0	0.0	4	2	7	7	0	.231	.250	1	0	SS-20, 2B-19, 3B-13
1955	95	168	48	4	0	1	0.6	20	18	15	19	1	.286	.327	0	0	3B-59, SS-26, 2B-9
1956	71	19	4	0	0	0	0.0	9	1	4	3	1	.211	.211	2	0	3B-51, 2B-8, SS-7, OF
1957 2 teams	CIN	N (5G –	.000)		WAS	A	(120G –	.228)									
" total	125	392	89	17	2	3	0.8	41	47	41	33	0	.227	.304	0	0	SS-109, 2B-16, 3B-2
1958 WAS A	116	377	99	14	3	5	1.3	38	28	27	32	0	.263	.355	4	0	SS-112, 3B-3, 2B-3
1959 DET A	116	381	102	16	3	3	0.8	38	35	30	35	1	.268	.349	2	0	SS-110, 2B-5
1960 3 teams	DET	A (10G –	.200)		CLE	A	(10G –	.333)		STL	N	(3G –	.000)				
" total	23	32	10	0	0	0	0.0	1	3	1	2	0	.313	.313	0	0	SS-10, 3B-10, 2B-3
1961 LA A	84	229	55	5	1	2	0.9	20	15	26	37	1	.240	.297	1	0	2B-58, SS-25, 3B-4
11 yrs.	919	2272	562	80	11	16	0.7	245	187	205	229	10	.247	.313	19	1	SS-447, 2B-270, 3B-191, OF-1
2 yrs.	126	386	103	16	3	3	0.8	38	35	30	35	1	.267	.347	2	0	SS-113, 3B-7, 2B-5

Ed Brinkman

BRINKMAN, EDWIN ALBERT
Brother of Chuck Brinkman.
B. Dec. 8, 1941, Cincinnati, Ohio

BR TR 6' 170 lb

	G	AB	H	2B	3B	HR	HR%	R	RBI	BB	SO	SB	BA	SA	AB	H	G by POS
1961 WAS A	4	11	1	0	0	0	0.0	0	0	1	1	0	.091	.091	1	0	3B-3
1962	54	133	22	7	1	0	0.0	8	4	11	28	1	.165	.233	0	0	SS-38, 3B-10
1963	145	514	117	20	3	7	1.4	44	45	31	86	5	.228	.319	2	1	SS-143
1964	132	447	100	20	3	8	1.8	54	34	26	99	2	.224	.336	7	1	SS-125
1965	154	444	82	13	2	5	1.1	35	35	38	82	1	.185	.257	3	0	SS-150
1966	158	582	133	18	9	7	1.2	42	48	29	105	7	.229	.326	0	0	SS-158
1967	109	320	60	9	2	1	0.3	21	18	24	58	1	.188	.238	0	0	SS-109
1968	77	193	36	3	0	0	0.0	12	6	19	31	0	.187	.202	2	0	SS-74, 2B-2, OF-1
1969	151	576	153	18	5	2	0.3	71	43	50	42	2	.266	.325	1	1	SS-150
1970	158	625	164	17	2	1	0.2	63	40	60	41	8	.262	.301	2	1	SS-157
1971 DET A	159	527	120	18	2	1	0.2	40	37	44	54	1	.228	.275	0	0	SS-159
1972	156	516	105	19	1	6	1.2	42	49	38	51	0	.203	.279	0	0	SS-156
1973	162	515	122	16	4	7	1.4	55	40	34	79	0	.237	.324	0	0	SS-162
1974	153	502	111	15	3	14	2.8	55	54	29	71	2	.221	.347	0	0	SS-151, 3B-2
1975 3 teams	STL	N (28G –	.240)		TEX	A	(1G –	.000)		NY	A	(44G –	.175)				
" total	73	140	29	8	1	1	0.7	8	8	10	17	0	.207	.300	4	1	SS-63, 3B-4, 2B-3
15 yrs.	1845	6045	1355	201	38	60	1.0	550	461	444	845	30	.224	.300	22	5	SS-1795, 3B-19, 2B-5, OF-1
4 yrs.	630	2060	458	68	10	28	1.4	192	180	145	255	3	.222	.306	0	0	SS-628, 3B-2

LEAGUE CHAMPIONSHIP SERIES

	G	AB	H	2B	3B	HR	HR%	R	RBI	BB	SO	SB	BA	SA	AB	H	G by POS
1972 DET A	1	4	1	1	0	0	0.0	0	0	0	0	0	.250	.500	0	0	SS-1

Tom Brookens

BROOKENS, THOMAS DALE
B. Aug. 10, 1953, Chambersburg, Pa.

BR TR 5'10" 165 lb

	G	AB	H	2B	3B	HR	HR%	R	RBI	BB	SO	SB	BA	SA	AB	H	G by POS
1979 DET A	60	190	50	5	2	4	2.1	23	21	11	40	10	.263	.374	0	0	3B-42, 2B-19, DH-1
1980	151	509	140	25	9	10	2.0	64	66	32	71	13	.275	.418	4	1	3B-138, 2B-9, DH-1, S
1981	71	239	58	10	1	4	1.7	19	25	14	43	5	.243	.343	1	0	3B-71
1982	140	398	92	15	3	9	2.3	40	58	27	63	5	.231	.352	6	2	3B-113, 2B-26, SS-9, OF-1
1983	138	332	71	13	3	6	1.8	50	32	29	46	10	.214	.325	10	1	3B-103, SS-30, 2B-10, DH-1
1984	113	224	55	11	4	5	2.2	32	26	19	33	6	.246	.397	3	2	3B-68, SS-28, 2B-26, DH-1
6 yrs.	673	1892	466	79	22	38	2.0	228	228	132	296	49	.246	.372	24	6	3B-535, 2B-90, SS-68, DH-4, OF-1
6 yrs.	673	1892	466	79	22	38	2.0	228	228	132	296	49	.246	.372	24	6	3B-535, 2B-90, SS-68, DH-4, OF-1

LEAGUE CHAMPIONSHIP SERIES

	G	AB	H	2B	3B	HR	HR%	R	RBI	BB	SO	SB	BA	SA	AB	H	G by POS
1984 DET A	2	2	0	0	0	0	0.0	0	0	0	1	0	.000	.000	0	0	3B-2

WORLD SERIES

	G	AB	H	2B	3B	HR	HR%	R	RBI	BB	SO	SB	BA	SA	AB	H	G by POS
1984 DET A	3	3	0	0	0	0	0.0	0	0	0	1	0	.000	.000	2	0	3B-3

Lou Brower

BROWER, LOUIS LESTER
B. July 1, 1900, Cleveland, Ohio

BR TR 5'10" 155 lb

	G	AB	H	2B	3B	HR	HR%	R	RBI	BB	SO	SB	BA	SA	AB	H	G by POS
1931 DET A	21	62	10	1	0	0	0.0	3	6	8	5	1	.161	.177	0	0	SS-20, 2B-2

Darrell Brown

BROWN, DARRELL WAYNE
B. Oct. 29, 1955, Oklahoma City, Okla.

BB TR 6' 180 lb

	G	AB	H	2B	3B	HR	HR%	R	RBI	BB	SO	SB	BA	SA	AB	H	G by POS
1981 DET A	16	4	1	0	0	0	0.0	4	0	0	1	1	.250	.250	2	1	OF-6, DH-4
1982 OAK A	8	18	6	0	1	0	0.0	2	3	1	2	1	.333	.444	0	0	OF-7, DH-1
1983 MIN A	91	309	84	6	2	0	0.0	40	22	10	28	3	.272	.304	6	0	OF-81, DH-3
1984	95	260	71	9	3	1	0.4	36	19	14	16	4	.273	.342	35	10	OF-55, DH-13
4 yrs.	210	591	162	15	6	1	0.2	82	44	25	47	9	.274	.325	43	11	OF-149, DH-21
1 yr.	16	4	1	0	0	0	0.0	4	0	0	1	1	.250	.250	2	1	OF-6, DH-4

Dick Brown

BROWN, RICHARD ERNEST
Brother of Larry Brown.
B. Jan. 17, 1935, Shinnston, W. Va.   D. Apr. 12, 1970, Baltimore, Md.

BR TR 6'2" 176 lb

	G	AB	H	2B	3B	HR	HR%	R	RBI	BB	SO	SB	BA	SA	AB	H	G by POS
1957 CLE A	34	114	30	4	0	4	3.5	10	22	4	23	1	.263	.404	1	0	C-33

	G	AB	H	2B	3B	HR	HR %	R	RBI	BB	SO	SB	BA	SA	Pinch Hit AB	Pinch Hit H	G by POS

Dick Brown continued

	G	AB	H	2B	3B	HR	HR %	R	RBI	BB	SO	SB	BA	SA	AB	H	G by POS
'58	68	173	41	5	0	7	4.0	20	20	12	27	1	.237	.387	6	0	C-62
'59	48	141	31	7	0	5	3.5	15	16	11	39	0	.220	.376	2	0	C-48
'60 CHI A	16	43	7	0	0	3	7.0	4	5	3	11	0	.163	.372	2	1	C-14
'61 DET A	98	308	82	12	2	16	5.2	32	45	22	57	0	.266	.474	3	2	C-91
'62	134	431	104	12	0	12	2.8	40	40	21	66	0	.241	.353	3	1	C-132
'63 BAL A	59	171	42	7	0	2	1.2	13	13	15	35	1	.246	.322	1	1	C-58
'64	88	230	59	6	0	8	3.5	24	32	12	45	2	.257	.387	7	0	C-84
'65	96	255	59	9	1	5	2.0	17	30	17	53	2	.231	.333	7	1	C-92
9 yrs.	641	1866	455	62	3	62	3.3	175	223	117	356	7	.244	.380	32	6	C-614
2 yrs.	232	739	186	24	2	28	3.8	72	85	43	123	0	.252	.403	6	3	C-223

Gates Brown

BROWN, WILLIAM JAMES
B. May 2, 1939, Crestline, Ohio

BL TR 5'11" 220 lbs.

	G	AB	H	2B	3B	HR	HR %	R	RBI	BB	SO	SB	BA	SA	AB	H	G by POS
'63 DET A	55	82	22	3	1	2	2.4	16	14	8	13	2	.268	.402	30	6	OF-16
'64	123	426	116	22	6	15	3.5	65	54	31	53	11	.272	.458	19	4	OF-106
'65	96	227	58	14	2	10	4.4	33	43	17	33	6	.256	.467	34	9	OF-56
'66	88	169	45	5	1	7	4.1	27	27	18	19	3	.266	.432	40	13	OF-43
'67	51	91	17	1	1	2	2.2	17	9	13	15	0	.187	.286	26	4	OF-20
'68	67	92	34	7	2	6	6.5	15	15	12	4	0	.370	.685	39	18	OF-17, 1B-1
'69	60	93	19	1	2	1	1.1	13	6	5	17	0	.204	.290	39	8	OF-14
'70	81	124	28	3	0	3	2.4	18	24	20	14	0	.226	.323	41	10	OF-26
'71	82	195	66	2	3	11	5.6	37	29	21	17	4	.338	.549	26	9	OF-56
'72	103	252	58	5	0	10	4.0	33	31	26	28	3	.230	.369	28	4	OF-72
'73	125	377	89	11	1	12	3.2	48	50	52	41	1	.236	.366	4	1	DH-119, OF-2
'74	73	99	24	2	0	4	4.0	7	17	10	15	0	.242	.384	53	16	DH-13
'75	47	35	6	2	0	1	2.9	1	3	9	6	0	.171	.314	35	6	
13 yrs.	1051	2262	582	78	19	84	3.7	330	322	242	275	30	.257	.420	414	107	OF-428, DH-132, 1B-1
															8th	7th	
13 yrs.	1051	2262	582	78	19	84	3.7	330	322	242	275	30	.257	.420	414	107	OF-428, DH-132, 1B-1
															1st	1st	

LEAGUE CHAMPIONSHIP SERIES

	G	AB	H	2B	3B	HR	HR %	R	RBI	BB	SO	SB	BA	SA	AB	H	G by POS
'72 DET A	3	2	0	0	0	0	0.0	1	0	1	0	0	.000	.000	2	0	

WORLD SERIES

	G	AB	H	2B	3B	HR	HR %	R	RBI	BB	SO	SB	BA	SA	AB	H	G by POS
'68 DET A	1	1	0	0	0	0	0.0	0	0	0	0	0	.000	.000	1	0	

Ike Brown

BROWN, ISAAC
B. Apr. 13, 1942, Memphis, Tenn.

BR TR 6' 190 lbs.

	G	AB	H	2B	3B	HR	HR %	R	RBI	BB	SO	SB	BA	SA	AB	H	G by POS
'69 DET A	70	170	39	4	3	5	2.9	24	12	26	43	2	.229	.376	12	0	2B-45, 3B-12, OF-3, SS-1
'70	56	94	27	5	0	4	4.3	17	15	13	26	0	.287	.468	21	7	2B-23, OF-4, 3B-1
'71	59	110	28	1	0	8	7.3	20	19	19	25	0	.255	.482	19	6	1B-17, OF-9, 2B-8, 3B-4, SS-1
'72	51	84	21	3	0	2	2.4	12	10	17	23	1	.250	.357	12	1	OF-22, 1B-13, 2B-3, SS-1, 3B-1
'73	42	76	22	2	1	1	1.3	12	9	15	13	0	.289	.382	7	1	1B-21, OF-12, DH-2, 3B-2
'74	2	2	0	0	0	0	0.0	0	0	0	0	0	.000	.000	0	0	3B-2
6 yrs.	280	536	137	15	4	20	3.7	85	65	90	130	3	.256	.410	71	15	2B-79, 1B-51, OF-50, 3B-22, SS-3, DH-2
6 yrs.	280	536	137	15	4	20	3.7	85	65	90	130	3	.256	.410	71	15	2B-79, 1B-51, OF-50, 3B-22, SS-3, DH-2

LEAGUE CHAMPIONSHIP SERIES

	G	AB	H	2B	3B	HR	HR %	R	RBI	BB	SO	SB	BA	SA	AB	H	G by POS
'72 DET A	1	2	1	0	0	0	0.0	0	2	0	1	0	.500	.500	0	0	1B-1

Arlo Brunsberg

BRUNSBERG, ARLO ADOLPH
B. Aug. 15, 1940, Fertile, Minn.

BL TR 6' 195 lbs.

	G	AB	H	2B	3B	HR	HR %	R	RBI	BB	SO	SB	BA	SA	AB	H	G by POS
'66 DET A	2	3	1	1	0	0	0.0	1	0	0	0	0	.333	.667	0	0	C-2

Bill Bruton

BRUTON, WILLIAM HARON
B. Dec. 22, 1929, Panola, Ala.

BL TR 6'½" 169 lbs.

	G	AB	H	2B	3B	HR	HR %	R	RBI	BB	SO	SB	BA	SA	AB	H	G by POS
'53 MIL N	151	613	153	18	14	1	0.2	82	41	44	100	26	.250	.330	1	0	OF-150
'54	142	567	161	20	7	4	0.7	89	30	40	78	34	.284	.365	3	2	OF-141
'55	149	636	175	30	12	9	1.4	106	47	43	72	25	.275	.403	2	0	OF-149
'56	147	525	143	23	15	8	1.5	73	56	26	63	8	.272	.419	4	0	OF-145
'57	79	306	85	16	9	5	1.6	41	30	19	35	11	.278	.438	1	0	OF-79
'58	100	325	91	11	3	3	0.9	47	28	27	37	4	.280	.360	5	0	OF-96
'59	133	478	138	22	6	6	1.3	72	41	35	54	13	.289	.397	6	2	OF-133
'60	151	629	180	27	13	12	1.9	112	54	41	97	22	.286	.428	3	0	OF-149
'61 DET A	160	596	153	15	5	17	2.9	99	63	61	66	22	.257	.384	6	1	OF-155
'62	147	561	156	27	5	16	2.9	90	74	55	67	14	.278	.430	5	1	OF-145
'63	145	524	134	21	8	8	1.5	84	48	59	70	14	.256	.372	11	6	OF-138
'64	106	296	82	11	5	5	1.7	42	33	32	54	14	.277	.399	26	6	OF-81
12 yrs.	1610	6056	1651	241	102	94	1.6	937	545	482	793	207	.273	.393	73	18	OF-1561
4 yrs.	558	1977	525	74	23	46	2.3	315	218	207	257	64	.266	.396	48	14	OF-519

WORLD SERIES

	G	AB	H	2B	3B	HR	HR %	R	RBI	BB	SO	SB	BA	SA	AB	H	G by POS
'58 MIL N	7	17	7	0	0	1	5.9	2	2	5	5	0	.412	.588	1	0	OF-7

Johnny Bucha

BUCHA, JOHN GEORGE
B. Jan. 22, 1925, Allentown, Pa.

BR TR 5'11" 190 lbs.

	G	AB	H	2B	3B	HR	HR %	R	RBI	BB	SO	SB	BA	SA	AB	H	G by POS
'48 STL N	2	1	0	0	0	0	0.0	0	0	1	0	0	.000	.000	1	0	C-1
'50	22	36	5	1	0	0	0.0	1	1	4	7	0	.139	.167	5	2	C-17
'53 DET A	60	158	35	9	0	1	0.6	17	14	20	14	1	.222	.297	2	0	C-56
3 yrs.	84	195	40	10	0	1	0.5	18	15	25	21	1	.205	.272	8	2	C-74
1 yr.	60	158	35	9	0	1	0.6	17	14	20	14	1	.222	.297	2	0	C-56

	G	AB	H	2B	3B	HR	HR %	R	RBI	BB	SO	SB	BA	SA	Pinch Hit AB	Pinch Hit H	G by POS

Don Buddin

BUDDIN, DONALD THOMAS   BR TR 5'11"   178 lb
B. May 5, 1934, Turbeville, S. C.

	G	AB	H	2B	3B	HR	HR %	R	RBI	BB	SO	SB	BA	SA	AB	H	G by POS
1956 BOS A	114	377	90	24	0	5	1.3	49	37	65	62	2	.239	.342	1	0	SS-113
1958	136	497	118	25	2	12	2.4	74	43	82	106	0	.237	.368	0	0	SS-136
1959	151	485	117	24	1	10	2.1	75	53	92	99	6	.241	.357	0	0	SS-150
1960	124	428	105	21	5	6	1.4	62	36	62	59	4	.245	.360	0	0	SS-124
1961	115	339	89	22	3	6	1.8	58	42	72	45	2	.263	.398	4	1	SS-109
1962 2 teams		HOU N	(40G –	.163)		DET A	(31G –	.229)									
" total	71	163	32	7	1	2	1.2	24	14	37	33	1	.196	.288	12	3	SS-46, 3B-11, 2B-5
6 yrs.	711	2289	551	123	12	41	1.8	342	225	410	404	15	.241	.359	17	4	SS-678, 3B-11, 2B-5
1 yr.	31	83	19	3	0	0	0.0	14	4	20	16	1	.229	.265	4	1	SS-19, 2B-5, 3B-2

Fritz Buelow

BUELOW, FREDERICK WILLIAM   BR TR 5'9½"
B. Feb. 13, 1876, Berlin, Germany   D. Dec. 27, 1933, Detroit, Mich.

	G	AB	H	2B	3B	HR	HR %	R	RBI	BB	SO	SB	BA	SA	AB	H	G by POS
1899 STL N	7	15	7	0	2	0	0.0	4	2	2		0	.467	.733	1	0	C-4, OF-2
1900	6	17	4	0	0	0	0.0	2	3	0		0	.235	.235	1	1	C-4, OF-1
1901 DET A	70	231	52	5	5	2	0.9	28	29	11		2	.225	.316	1	0	C-69
1902	66	224	50	5	2	2	0.9	23	29	9		3	.223	.290	0	0	C-63, 1B-2
1903	63	192	41	3	6	1	0.5	24	13	6		4	.214	.307	0	0	C-60, 1B-2
1904 2 teams		DET A	(42G –	.110)		CLE A	(42G –	.176)									
" total	84	255	36	5	2	0	0.0	17	10	19		4	.141	.176	0	0	C-84
1905 CLE A	74	236	41	4	1	1	0.4	11	18	6		7	.174	.212	2	1	C-59, OF-8, 1B-3, 3B-2
1906	34	86	14	2	0	0	0.0	7	7	9		0	.163	.186	0	0	C-33, 1B-1
1907 STL A	26	75	11	1	0	0	0.0	9	1	7		0	.147	.160	1	0	C-25
9 yrs.	430	1331	256	25	18	6	0.5	125	112	69		20	.192	.252	6	2	C-401, OF-11, 1B-8, 3B
4 yrs.	241	783	158	14	14	5	0.6	81	76	34		11	.202	.275	1	0	C-234, 1B-4

George Bullard

BULLARD, GEORGE DONALD (Curly)   BR TR 5'9"   155 lb
B. Oct. 24, 1928, Lynn, Mass.

	G	AB	H	2B	3B	HR	HR %	R	RBI	BB	SO	SB	BA	SA	AB	H	G by POS
1954 DET A	4	1	0	0	0	0	0.0	0	0	0	0	0	.000	.000	0	0	SS-1

Les Burke

BURKE, LESLIE KINGSTON (Buck)   BL TR 5'9"   168 lb
B. Dec. 18, 1902, Lynn, Mass.   D. May 6, 1975, Danvers, Mass.

	G	AB	H	2B	3B	HR	HR %	R	RBI	BB	SO	SB	BA	SA	AB	H	G by POS
1923 DET A	7	10	1	0	0	0	0.0	2	2	0	1	0	.100	.100	1	0	3B-2, 2B-1, C-1
1924	72	241	61	10	4	0	0.0	30	17	22	20	2	.253	.328	7	4	2B-58, SS-6
1925	77	180	52	6	3	0	0.0	32	24	17	8	4	.289	.356	22	4	2B-52
1926	38	75	17	1	0	0	0.0	9	4	7	3	1	.227	.240	13	1	2B-15, 3B-7, SS-1
4 yrs.	194	506	131	17	7	0	0.0	73	47	46	32	7	.259	.320	43	9	2B-126, 3B-9, SS-7, C-
4 yrs.	194	506	131	17	7	0	0.0	73	47	46	32	7	.259	.320	43	9	2B-126, 3B-9, SS-7, C-

George Burns

BURNS, GEORGE HENRY (Tioga George)   BR TR 6'1½"   180 lb
B. Jan. 31, 1893, Niles, Ohio   D. Jan. 7, 1978, Kirkland, Wash.

	G	AB	H	2B	3B	HR	HR %	R	RBI	BB	SO	SB	BA	SA	AB	H	G by POS
1914 DET A	137	478	139	22	5	5	1.0	55	57	32	56	23	.291	.389	0	0	1B-137
1915	105	392	99	18	3	5	1.3	49	50	22	51	9	.253	.352	1	0	1B-104
1916	135	479	137	22	6	4	0.8	60	73	22	30	12	.286	.382	11	3	1B-124
1917	119	407	92	14	10	1	0.2	42	40	15	33	3	.226	.317	15	2	1B-104
1918 PHI A	130	505	178	22	9	6	1.2	61	70	23	25	8	.352	.467	0	0	1B-128, OF-2
1919	126	470	139	29	9	8	1.7	63	57	19	18	15	.296	.447	5	0	1B-86, OF-34
1920 2 teams		PHI A	(22G –	.233)		CLE A	(44G –	.268)									
" total	66	116	29	7	1	1	0.9	8	20	10	10	5	.250	.353	39	11	OF-13, 1B-12
1921 CLE A	84	244	88	21	4	0	0.0	52	48	13	19	2	.361	.480	10	2	1B-73
1922 BOS A	147	558	171	32	5	12	2.2	71	73	20	28	8	.306	.446	6	2	1B-140
1923	146	551	181	47	5	7	1.3	91	82	45	33	9	.328	.470	0	0	1B-146
1924 CLE A	129	462	143	37	5	4	0.9	64	66	29	27	14	.310	.437	2	0	1B-127
1925	127	488	164	41	4	6	1.2	69	79	24	24	16	.336	.473	1	1	1B-126
1926	151	603	216	64	3	4	0.7	97	114	28	33	13	.358	.494	0	0	1B-151
1927	140	549	175	51	2	3	0.5	84	78	42	27	13	.319	.435	1	0	1B-139
1928 2 teams		CLE A	(82G –	.249)		NY A	(4G –	.500)									
" total	86	213	54	12	1	5	2.3	30	30	17	12	2	.254	.390	30	6	1B-55
1929 2 teams		NY A	(9G –	.000)		PHI A	(29G –	.265)									
" total	38	58	13	5	0	1	1.7	5	11	2	7	1	.224	.362	17	0	1B-19
16 yrs.	1866	6573	2018	444	72	72	1.1	901	948	363	433	153	.307	.429	138	27	1B-1671, OF-49
4 yrs.	496	1756	467	76	24	15	0.9	206	220	91	170	47	.266	.362	27	5	1B-469

WORLD SERIES

	G	AB	H	2B	3B	HR	HR %	R	RBI	BB	SO	SB	BA	SA	AB	H	G by POS
1920 CLE A	5	10	3	1	0	0	0.0	1	3	3	3	0	.300	.400	1	1	1B-4
1929 PHI A	1	2	0	0	0	0	0.0	0	0	1	1	0	.000	.000	2	0	
2 yrs.	6	12	3	1	0	0	0.0	1	3	4	4	0	.250	.333	3	1	1B-4

Jack Burns

BURNS, JOHN IRVING (Slug)   BR TR 5'10½"   175 lb
B. Aug. 31, 1907, Cambridge, Mass.   D. Apr. 18, 1975, Boston, Mass.

	G	AB	H	2B	3B	HR	HR %	R	RBI	BB	SO	SB	BA	SA	AB	H	G by POS
1930 STL A	8	30	9	3	0	0	0.0	5	2	5	5	0	.300	.400	0	0	1B-8
1931	144	570	148	27	7	4	0.7	75	70	42	58	19	.260	.353	1	0	1B-143
1932	150	617	188	33	8	11	1.8	111	70	61	43	17	.305	.438	0	0	1B-150
1933	144	556	160	43	4	7	1.3	89	71	56	51	11	.288	.417	1	0	1B-143
1934	154	612	157	28	8	13	2.1	86	73	62	47	9	.257	.392	0	0	1B-154
1935	143	549	157	28	1	5	0.9	77	67	68	49	3	.286	.368	0	0	1B-141
1936 2 teams		STL A	(9G –	.214)		DET A	(138G –	.283)									
" total	147	572	161	37	3	4	0.7	98	64	82	46	4	.281	.378	6	3	1B-140
7 yrs.	890	3506	980	199	31	44	1.3	541	417	376	299	63	.280	.392	8	3	1B-879
1 yr.	138	558	158	36	3	4	0.7	96	63	79	45	4	.283	.380	0	0	1B-138

Joe Burns

BURNS, JOSEPH FRANCIS   BL TL 5'11"   170 lb
B. Mar. 26, 1889, Ipswich, Mass.

	G	AB	H	2B	3B	HR	HR %	R	RBI	BB	SO	SB	BA	SA	AB	H	G by POS
1910 CIN N	1	1	1	0	0	0	0.0	0	0	0	1	1.000	1.000	1	1		
1913 DET A	4	13	5	0	0	0	0.0	0	1	2	4	0	.385	.385	0	0	OF-4
2 yrs.	5	14	6	0	0	0	0.0	0	1	2	4	1	.429	.429	1	1	OF-4
1 yr.	4	13	5	0	0	0	0.0	0	1	2	4	0	.385	.385	0	0	OF-4

	G	AB	H	2B	3B	HR	HR %	R	RBI	BB	SO	SB	BA	SA	Pinch Hit AB	Pinch Hit H	G by POS

ohn Burns

BURNS, JOHN JOSEPH
B. May 13, 1877, Moosic, Pa.   D. June 24, 1957, Pleasure Beach, Conn.
BR TR 5'10" 160 lbs.

	G	AB	H	2B	3B	HR	HR %	R	RBI	BB	SO	SB	BA	SA	AB	H	G by POS
903 DET A	11	37	10	0	0	0	0.0	2	3	1		0	.270	.270	0	0	2B-11
904	4	16	2	0	0	0	0.0	3	1	1		1	.125	.125	0	0	2B-4
2 yrs.	15	53	12	0	0	0	0.0	5	4	2		1	.226	.226	0	0	2B-15
2 yrs.	15	53	12	0	0	0	0.0	5	4	2		1	.226	.226	0	0	2B-15

Donie Bush

BUSH, OWEN JOSEPH
B. Oct. 8, 1887, Indianapolis, Ind.   D. Mar. 28, 1972, Indianapolis, Ind.
Manager 1923, 1927-31, 1933.
BB TR 5'6" 140 lbs.

	G	AB	H	2B	3B	HR	HR %	R	RBI	BB	SO	SB	BA	SA	AB	H	G by POS
908 DET A	20	68	20	1	1	0	0.0	13	4	7		2	.294	.338	0	0	SS-20
909	157	532	145	18	2	0	0.0	114	33	88		53	.273	.314	0	0	SS-157
910	142	496	130	13	4	3	0.6	90	34	78		49	.262	.323	0	0	SS-141, 3B-1
911	150	561	130	18	5	1	0.2	126	36	98		40	.232	.287	0	0	SS-150
912	144	511	118	14	8	2	0.4	107	38	117		35	.231	.301	0	0	SS-144
913	153	593	149	19	10	1	0.2	98	40	80	32	44	.251	.322	0	0	SS-153
914	157	596	150	18	4	0	0.0	97	32	112	54	35	.252	.295	0	0	SS-157
915	155	561	128	12	8	1	0.2	99	44	118	44	35	.228	.283	0	0	SS-155
916	145	550	124	5	9	0	0.0	73	34	75	42	19	.225	.267	0	0	SS-144
917	147	581	163	18	3	0	0.0	112	24	80	40	34	.281	.322	0	0	SS-147
918	128	500	117	10	3	0	0.0	74	22	79	31	9	.234	.266	0	0	SS-128
919	129	509	124	11	6	0	0.0	82	26	75	36	22	.244	.289	0	0	SS-129
920	141	506	133	18	5	1	0.2	85	33	73	32	15	.263	.324	1	1	SS-140
921 2 teams		DET	A (104G –		.281)		WAS	A (23G –	.214)								
total	127	486	131	7	5	0	0.0	87	29	57	27	10	.270	.305	2	1	SS-102, 2B-23
922 WAS A	41	134	32	4	1	0	0.0	17	7	21	7	1	.239	.284	3	0	3B-37, 2B-1
923	10	22	9	0	0	0	0.0	6	0	1		0	.409	.409	1	0	3B-6, 2B-1
16 yrs.	1946	7206	1803	186	74	9	0.1	1280	436	1158	346	403	.250	.300	7	2	SS-1867, 3B-44, 2B-25
14 yrs.	1872	6966	1744	181	73	9	0.1	1242	427	1125	334	400	.250	.301	1	1	SS-1846, 2B-23, 3B-1
	7th	6th	8th		7th				4th			4th			2nd		

WORLD SERIES

	G	AB	H	2B	3B	HR	HR %	R	RBI	BB	SO	SB	BA	SA	AB	H	G by POS
909 DET A	7	23	6	1	0	0	0.0	5	2	5	3	1	.261	.304	0	0	SS-7

al Butera

BUTERA, SALVATORE PHILIP
B. Sept. 25, 1952, Richmond Hill, N. Y.
BR TR 6' 190 lbs.

	G	AB	H	2B	3B	HR	HR %	R	RBI	BB	SO	SB	BA	SA	AB	H	G by POS
980 MIN A	34	85	23	1	0	0	0.0	4	2	3	6	0	.271	.282	2	0	C-32, DH-2
981	62	167	40	7	1	0	0.0	13	18	22	14	0	.240	.293	1	0	C-59, DH-1, 1B-1
982	54	126	32	2	0	0	0.0	9	8	17	12	0	.254	.270	1	0	C-53
983 DET A	4	5	1	0	0	0	0.0	1	0	0	0	0	.200	.200	0	0	C-4
984 MON N	3	3	0	0	0	0	0.0	0	0	1	0	0	.000	.000	0	0	C-2
5 yrs.	157	386	96	10	1	0	0.0	27	28	43	32	0	.249	.280	4	0	C-150, DH-3, 1B-1
1 yr.	4	5	1	0	0	0	0.0	1	0	0	0	0	.200	.200	0	0	C-4

Enos Cabell

CABELL, ENOS MILTON
B. Oct. 8, 1949, Fort Riley, Kans.
BR TR 6'4" 170 lbs.

	G	AB	H	2B	3B	HR	HR %	R	RBI	BB	SO	SB	BA	SA	AB	H	G by POS
972 BAL A	3	5	0	0	0	0	0.0	0	1	0	0	0	.000	.000	1	0	1B-1
73	32	47	10	2	0	1	2.1	12	3	3	7	1	.213	.319	4	1	1B-23, 3B-1
74	80	174	42	4	2	3	1.7	24	17	7	20	5	.241	.339	4	0	1B-28, OF-22, 3B-19, 2B-1
75 HOU N	117	348	92	17	6	2	0.6	43	43	18	53	12	.264	.365	17	7	OF-67, 1B-25, 3B-22
76	144	586	160	13	7	2	0.3	85	43	29	79	35	.273	.329	1	0	3B-143, 1B-3
77	150	625	176	36	7	16	2.6	101	68	27	55	42	.282	.438	3	0	3B-144, 1B-8, SS-1
78	162	660	195	31	8	7	1.1	92	71	22	80	33	.295	.398	0	0	3B-153, 1B-14, SS-1
79	155	603	164	30	5	6	1.0	60	67	21	68	37	.272	.368	0	0	3B-132, 1B-51
80	152	604	167	23	8	2	0.3	69	55	26	84	21	.276	.351	1	1	3B-150, 1B-6
981 SF N	96	396	101	20	1	2	0.5	41	36	10	47	6	.255	.326	6	1	1B-69, 3B-22
982 DET A	125	464	121	17	3	2	0.4	45	37	15	48	15	.261	.323	10	2	1B-83, 3B-59, OF-3
983	121	392	122	23	5	5	1.3	62	46	16	41	4	.311	.434	11	4	1B-106, DH-8, 3B-4, SS-1
984 HOU N	127	436	135	17	3	8	1.8	52	44	21	47	8	.310	.417	17	5	1B-112
13 yrs.	1464	5340	1485	233	55	56	1.0	686	531	215	629	219	.278	.374	75	21	1B-849, 1B-524, OF-92, DH-8, SS-3, 2B-1
2 yrs.	246	856	243	40	8	7	0.8	107	83	31	89	19	.284	.374	21	6	1B-189, 3B-63, DH-8, OF-3, SS-1

LEAGUE CHAMPIONSHIP SERIES

	G	AB	H	2B	3B	HR	HR %	R	RBI	BB	SO	SB	BA	SA	AB	H	G by POS
974 BAL A	3	4	1	0	0	0	0.0	0	0	0	2	0	.250	.250	1	0	OF-1
980 HOU N	5	21	5	1	0	0	0.0	1	0	1	3	0	.238	.286	0	0	3B-5
2 yrs.	8	25	6	1	0	0	0.0	1	0	1	5	0	.240	.280	1	0	3B-5, OF-1

Bruce Campbell

CAMPBELL, BRUCE DOUGLAS
B. Oct. 20, 1909, Chicago, Ill.
BL TR 6'1" 185 lbs.

	G	AB	H	2B	3B	HR	HR %	R	RBI	BB	SO	SB	BA	SA	AB	H	G by POS
930 CHI A	5	10	5	1	1	0	0.0	4	5	1	2	0	.500	.800	1	1	OF-4
931	4	17	7	2	0	2	11.8	4	5	0	4	0	.412	.882	0	0	OF-4
932 2 teams		CHI	A (9G –		.154)		STL	A (137G –	.289)								
total	146	611	173	36	11	14	2.3	86	87	40	104	7	.283	.447	3	0	OF-143
933 STL A	148	567	157	38	8	16	2.8	87	106	69	77	10	.277	.457	4	1	OF-144
934	138	481	134	25	6	9	1.9	62	74	51	64	5	.279	.412	14	4	OF-123
935 CLE A	80	308	100	26	3	7	2.3	56	54	31	33	2	.325	.497	4	1	OF-75
936	76	172	64	15	2	6	3.5	35	30	19	17	2	.372	.587	25	9	OF-47
937	134	448	135	42	11	4	0.9	82	61	67	49	4	.301	.471	11	5	OF-123
938	133	511	148	27	12	12	2.3	90	72	53	57	11	.290	.460	11	2	OF-122
939	130	450	129	23	13	8	1.8	84	72	67	48	7	.287	.449	14	2	OF-115
940 DET A	103	297	84	15	5	8	2.7	56	44	45	28	2	.283	.448	23	9	OF-74
941	141	512	141	28	10	15	2.9	72	93	68	67	3	.275	.457	5	2	OF-133
942 WAS A	122	378	105	17	5	5	1.3	41	63	37	34	0	.278	.389	29	5	OF-87
13 yrs.	1360	4762	1382	295	87	106	2.2	759	766	548	584	53	.290	.455	144	41	OF-1194
2 yrs.	244	809	225	43	15	23	2.8	128	137	113	95	5	.278	.454	28	11	OF-207

WORLD SERIES

	G	AB	H	2B	3B	HR	HR %	R	RBI	BB	SO	SB	BA	SA	AB	H	G by POS
940 DET A	7	25	9	1	0	1	4.0	4	5	4	4	0	.360	.520	0	0	OF-7

	G	AB	H	2B	3B	HR	HR %	R	RBI	BB	SO	SB	BA	SA	Pinch Hit AB	Pinch Hit H	G by POS

Dave Campbell

CAMPBELL, DAVID WILSON
B. Jan. 14, 1942, Manistee, Mich.　　　　　BR TR 6'1" 180 lb

	G	AB	H	2B	3B	HR	HR %	R	RBI	BB	SO	SB	BA	SA	PH AB	PH H	G by POS
1967 DET A	2	2	0	0	0	0	0.0	0	0	0	1	0	.000	.000	1	0	1B-1
1968	9	8	1	0	0	1	12.5	1	2	1	3	0	.125	.500	3	0	2B-5
1969	32	39	4	1	0	0	0.0	4	2	4	15	0	.103	.128	14	2	1B-13, 2B-5, 3B-1
1970 SD N	154	581	127	28	2	12	2.1	71	40	40	115	18	.219	.336	1	0	2B-153
1971	108	365	83	14	2	7	1.9	38	29	37	75	9	.227	.334	1	0	2B-69, 3B-40, SS-4, OF-1B-2
1972	33	100	24	5	0	0	0.0	6	3	11	12	0	.240	.290	0	0	3B-31, 2B-1
1973 3 teams	SD	N (33G –	.224)		STL	N (13G –	.000)		HOU	N (9G –	.267)						
" total	55	134	26	5	0	0	0.0	4	11	8	25	1	.194	.231	10	0	2B-33, 3B-7, 1B-5, OF-
1974 HOU N	35	23	2	1	0	0	0.0	4	2	1	8	1	.087	.130	13	0	2B-9, 1B-6, 3B-2, OF-1
8 yrs.	428	1252	267	54	4	20	1.6	128	89	102	254	29	.213	.311	43	2	2B-275, 3B-81, 1B-27, OF-4, SS-4
3 yrs.	43	49	5	1	0	1	2.0	5	4	5	19	0	.102	.184	18	2	1B-14, 2B-10, 3B-1

Paul Campbell

CAMPBELL, PAUL McLAUGHLIN
B. Sept. 1, 1917, Paw Creek, N. C.　　　　　BL TL 5'10" 185 lb

	G	AB	H	2B	3B	HR	HR %	R	RBI	BB	SO	SB	BA	SA	PH AB	PH H	G by POS
1941 BOS A	1	0	0	0	0	0	–	0	0	0	0	0	–	–	0	0	
1942	26	15	1	0	0	0	0.0	4	0	1	5	1	.067	.067	13	1	OF-4
1946	28	26	3	1	0	0	0.0	3	0	2	7	0	.115	.154	14	2	1B-5
1948 DET A	59	83	22	1	1	1	1.2	15	11	1	10	0	.265	.337	13	1	1B-27
1949	87	255	71	15	4	3	1.2	38	30	24	32	3	.278	.404	9	5	1B-74
1950	3	1	0	0	0	0	0.0	1	0	0	0	0	.000	.000	1	0	
6 yrs.	204	380	97	17	5	4	1.1	61	41	28	54	4	.255	.358	50	9	1B-106, OF-4
3 yrs.	149	339	93	16	5	4	1.2	54	41	25	42	3	.274	.386	23	6	1B-101

WORLD SERIES

	G	AB	H	2B	3B	HR	HR %	R	RBI	BB	SO	SB	BA	SA	PH AB	PH H	G by POS
1946 BOS A	1	0	0	0	0	0	–	0	0	0	0	0	–	–	0	0	

Fred Carisch

CARISCH, FREDERICK BEHLMER
B. Nov. 14, 1881, Fountain City, Wis.　D. Apr. 19, 1977, San Gabriel, Calif.　　BR TR 5'10½" 174 lb

	G	AB	H	2B	3B	HR	HR %	R	RBI	BB	SO	SB	BA	SA	PH AB	PH H	G by POS
1903 PIT N	5	18	6	4	0	1	5.6	4	5	0		0	.333	.722	1	0	C-4
1904	37	125	31	3	1	0	0.0	9	8	9		3	.248	.288	1	0	C-22, 1B-14
1905	32	107	22	0	3	0	0.0	7	8	2		1	.206	.262	2	0	C-30
1906	4	12	1	0	0	0	0.0	0	0	1		1	.083	.083	0	0	C-4
1912 CLE A	25	69	19	3	1	0	0.0	4	5	1		3	.275	.348	2	0	C-23
1913	81	222	48	4	2	0	0.0	11	26	21	19	6	.216	.252	2	0	C-79
1914	40	102	22	3	2	0	0.0	8	5	12	18	2	.216	.284	2	0	C-38
1923 DET A	2	0	0	0	0	0	–	0	0	0	0	0	–	–	0	0	C-2
8 yrs.	226	655	149	17	9	1	0.2	43	57	46	37	16	.227	.285	10	0	C-202, 1B-14
1 yr.	2	0	0	0	0	0	–	0	0	0	0	0	–	–	0	0	C-2

Charlie Carr

CARR, CHARLES CARBITT
B. Dec. 27, 1876, Coatesville, Pa.　D. Nov. 26, 1932, Memphis, Tenn.　　BR TR 6'2" 195 lb

	G	AB	H	2B	3B	HR	HR %	R	RBI	BB	SO	SB	BA	SA	PH AB	PH H	G by POS
1898 WAS N	20	73	14	2	0	0	0.0	6	4	2		2	.192	.219	0	0	1B-20
1901 PHI A	2	8	1	0	0	0	0.0	0	0	0		0	.125	.125	0	0	1B-2
1903 DET A	135	548	154	23	11	2	0.4	59	79	10		10	.281	.374	0	0	1B-135
1904 2 teams	DET	A (92G –	.214)		CLE	A (32G –	.225)										
" total	124	480	104	18	4	0	0.0	38	47	18		6	.217	.271	0	0	1B-124
1905 CLE A	89	306	72	12	4	1	0.3	29	31	13		12	.235	.310	2	1	1B-87
1906 CIN N	22	94	18	2	3	0	0.0	9	10	2		0	.191	.277	0	0	1B-22
1914 IND F	115	441	129	11	10	3	0.7	44	69	26		19	.293	.383	0	0	1B-115
7 yrs.	507	1950	492	68	32	6	0.3	185	240	71		49	.252	.329	2	1	1B-505
2 yrs.	227	908	231	36	14	2	0.2	88	119	24		16	.254	.331	0	0	1B-227

Frank Carswell

CARSWELL, FRANK WILLIS (Tex, Wheels)
B. Nov. 6, 1919, Palestine, Tex.　　　　　BR TR 6' 195 lb

	G	AB	H	2B	3B	HR	HR %	R	RBI	BB	SO	SB	BA	SA	PH AB	PH H	G by POS
1953 DET A	16	15	4	0	0	0	0.0	2	3	1		0	.267	.267	12	4	OF-3

Doc Casey

CASEY, JAMES PETER
B. Mar. 15, 1871, Lawrence, Mass.　D. Dec. 30, 1936, Detroit, Mich.　　BL TR

	G	AB	H	2B	3B	HR	HR %	R	RBI	BB	SO	SB	BA	SA	PH AB	PH H	G by POS
1898 WAS N	28	112	31	2	0	0	0.0	13	15	3		15	.277	.295	0	0	3B-22, SS-4, C-3
1899 2 teams	WAS	N (9G –	.118)		BKN	N (134G –	.269)										
" total	143	559	145	16	8	0	0.0	78	45	27		28	.259	.322	0	0	3B-143
1900 BKN N	1	3	1	0	0	0	0.0	0	1	0		0	.333	.333	0	0	3B-1
1901 DET A	128	540	153	16	9	2	0.4	105	46	32		34	.283	.357	1	0	3B-127
1902	132	520	142	18	7	3	0.6	69	55	44		22	.273	.352	0	0	3B-132
1903 CHI N	112	435	126	8	3	1	0.2	56	40	19		11	.290	.329	0	0	3B-112
1904	136	548	147	20	4	1	0.2	71	43	18		21	.268	.325	0	0	3B-134, C-2
1905	144	526	122	21	10	1	0.2	66	56	41		22	.232	.316	2	0	3B-142, SS-1
1906 BKN N	149	571	133	17	8	0	0.0	71	34	52		22	.233	.291	0	0	3B-149
1907	141	527	122	19	3	0	0.0	55	19	34		16	.231	.279	3	0	3B-138
10 yrs.	1114	4341	1122	137	52	9	0.2	584	354	270		191	.258	.320	6	0	3B-1100, SS-5, C-5
2 yrs.	260	1060	295	34	16	5	0.5	174	101	76		56	.278	.355	1	0	3B-259

Joe Casey

CASEY, JOSEPH FELIX
B. Aug. 15, 1887, Boston, Mass.　D. June 2, 1966, Melrose, Mass.　　BR TR

	G	AB	H	2B	3B	HR	HR %	R	RBI	BB	SO	SB	BA	SA	PH AB	PH H	G by POS
1909 DET A	3	5	0	0	0	0	0.0	1	0	1		0	.000	.000	0	0	C-3
1910	23	62	12	3	0	0	0.0	3	2	2		1	.194	.242	0	0	C-22
1911	15	33	5	0	0	0	0.0	2	3	3		0	.152	.152	0	0	C-12, OF-3
1918 WAS A	9	17	4	0	0	0	0.0	3	2	2	2	0	.235	.235	0	0	C-8
4 yrs.	50	117	21	3	0	0	0.0	9	7	8	2	1	.179	.205	0	0	C-45, OF-3
3 yrs.	41	100	17	3	0	0	0.0	6	5	6		1	.170	.200	0	0	C-37, OF-3

Norm Cash

CASH, NORMAN DALTON
B. Nov. 10, 1934, Justiceburg, Tex.　　　　　BL TL 6' 185 lb

	G	AB	H	2B	3B	HR	HR %	R	RBI	BB	SO	SB	BA	SA	PH AB	PH H	G by POS
1958 CHI A	13	8	2	0	0	0	0.0	2	0	0	1	0	.250	.250	5	1	OF-4
1959	58	104	25	0	1	4	3.8	16	16	18	9	1	.240	.375	19	5	1B-31

	G	AB	H	2B	3B	HR	HR %	R	RBI	BB	SO	SB	BA	SA	Pinch Hit AB	Pinch Hit H	G by POS

Norm Cash continued

	G	AB	H	2B	3B	HR	HR %	R	RBI	BB	SO	SB	BA	SA	PH AB	PH H	G by POS
1960 DET A	121	353	101	16	3	18	5.1	64	63	65	58	4	.286	.501	23	9	1B-99, OF-4
1961	159	535	193	22	8	41	7.7	119	132	124	85	11	.361	.662	1	0	1B-157
1962	148	507	123	16	2	39	7.7	94	89	104	82	6	.243	.513	2	1	1B-146, OF-3
1963	147	493	133	19	1	26	5.3	67	79	89	76	2	.270	.471	7	0	1B-142
1964	144	479	123	15	5	23	4.8	63	83	70	66	2	.257	.453	10	1	1B-137
1965	142	467	124	23	1	30	6.4	79	82	77	62	6	.266	.512	5	0	1B-139
1966	160	603	168	18	3	32	5.3	98	93	66	91	2	.279	.478	3	1	1B-158
1967	152	488	118	16	5	22	4.5	64	72	81	100	3	.242	.430	7	1	1B-146
1968	127	411	108	15	1	25	6.1	50	63	39	70	1	.263	.487	15	2	1B-117
1969	142	483	135	15	4	22	4.6	81	74	63	80	2	.280	.464	9	2	1B-134
1970	130	370	96	18	2	15	4.1	58	53	72	58	0	.259	.441	17	6	1B-114
1971	135	452	128	10	3	32	7.1	72	91	59	86	1	.283	.531	7	1	1B-131
1972	137	440	114	16	0	22	5.0	51	61	50	64	0	.259	.445	11	0	1B-134
1973	121	363	95	19	0	19	5.2	51	40	47	73	1	.262	.471	8	2	1B-114, DH-3
1974	53	149	34	3	2	7	4.7	17	12	19	30	1	.228	.416	9	3	1B-44
17 yrs.	2089	6705	1820	241	41	377	5.6	1046	1103	1043	1091	43	.271	.488	158	35	1B-1943, OF-11, DH-3
15 yrs.	2018	6593	1793	241	40	373	5.7	1028	1087	1025	1081	42	.272	.490	134	29	1B-1912, OF-7, DH-3
	5th	7th	7th	9th		2nd	3rd	7th	7th	5th	1st		7th	4th	8th		

LEAGUE CHAMPIONSHIP SERIES

	G	AB	H	2B	3B	HR	HR %	R	RBI	BB	SO	SB	BA	SA	PH AB	PH H	G by POS
1972 DET A	5	15	4	0	0	1	6.7	1	2	2	3	0	.267	.467	1	0	1B-5

WORLD SERIES

	G	AB	H	2B	3B	HR	HR %	R	RBI	BB	SO	SB	BA	SA	PH AB	PH H	G by POS
1959 CHI A	4	4	0	0	0	0	0.0	0	0	0	2	0	.000	.000	4	0	
1968 DET A	7	26	10	0	0	1	3.8	5	5	3	5	0	.385	.500	0	0	1B-7
2 yrs.	11	30	10	0	0	1	3.3	5	5	3	7	0	.333	.433	4	0	1B-7

Ron Cash

CASH, RONALD FORREST   BR TR 6'   180 lbs.
B. Nov. 20, 1949, Decatur, Ga.

	G	AB	H	2B	3B	HR	HR %	R	RBI	BB	SO	SB	BA	SA	PH AB	PH H	G by POS
1973 DET A	14	39	16	1	1	0	0.0	8	6	5	5	0	.410	.487	0	0	OF-7, 3B-6
1974	20	62	14	2	0	0	0.0	6	5	0	11	0	.226	.258	1	0	1B-15, 3B-4
2 yrs.	34	101	30	3	1	0	0.0	14	11	5	16	0	.297	.347	1	0	1B-15, 3B-10, OF-7
2 yrs.	34	101	30	3	1	0	0.0	14	11	5	16	0	.297	.347	1	0	1B-15, 3B-10, OF-7

Marty Castillo

CASTILLO, MARTIN HORACE   BR TR 6'1"   190 lbs.
B. Jan. 16, 1957, Long Beach, Calif.

	G	AB	H	2B	3B	HR	HR %	R	RBI	BB	SO	SB	BA	SA	PH AB	PH H	G by POS
1981 DET A	6	8	1	0	0	0	0.0	1	0	0	2	0	.125	.125	0	0	3B-4, OF-1, C-1
1982	1	0	0	0	0	0	–	0	0	0	0	0	–	–	0	0	C-1
1983	67	119	23	4	0	2	1.7	10	10	7	22	2	.193	.277	2	0	3B-58, C-10
1984	70	141	33	5	2	4	2.8	16	17	10	33	1	.234	.383	1	0	C-36, 3B-33, DH-1
4 yrs.	144	268	57	9	2	6	2.2	27	27	17	57	3	.213	.328	3	0	3B-95, C-48, DH-1, OF-1
4 yrs.	144	268	57	9	2	6	2.2	27	27	17	57	3	.213	.328	3	0	3B-95, C-48, DH-1, OF-1

LEAGUE CHAMPIONSHIP SERIES

	G	AB	H	2B	3B	HR	HR %	R	RBI	BB	SO	SB	BA	SA	PH AB	PH H	G by POS
1984 DET A	3	8	2	0	0	0	0.0	0	2	0	3	1	.250	.250	0	0	3B-3

WORLD SERIES

	G	AB	H	2B	3B	HR	HR %	R	RBI	BB	SO	SB	BA	SA	PH AB	PH H	G by POS
1984 DET A	3	9	3	0	0	1	11.1	2	2	2	1	0	.333	.667	0	0	3B-3

Harry Chiti

CHITI, HARRY DOMINICK   BR TR 6'2½"   221 lbs.
B. Nov. 16, 1932, Kincaid, Ill.

	G	AB	H	2B	3B	HR	HR %	R	RBI	BB	SO	SB	BA	SA	PH AB	PH H	G by POS
1950 CHI N	3	6	2	0	0	0	0.0	0	0	0	0	0	.333	.333	2	0	C-1
1951	9	31	11	2	0	0	0.0	1	5	2	2	0	.355	.419	1	0	C-8
1952	32	113	31	5	0	5	4.4	14	13	5	8	0	.274	.451	0	0	C-32
1955	113	338	78	6	1	11	3.3	24	41	25	68	0	.231	.352	1	0	C-113
1956	72	203	43	6	4	4	2.0	17	18	19	35	0	.212	.340	5	2	C-67
1958 KC A	103	295	79	11	3	9	3.1	32	44	18	48	3	.268	.417	19	3	C-83
1959	55	162	44	11	1	5	3.1	20	25	17	26	0	.272	.444	8	4	C-47
1960 2 teams	KC	A (58G – .221)				DET	A (37G – .163)										
" total	95	294	59	7	0	7	2.4	25	33	27	45	1	.201	.296	8	2	C-88
1961 DET A	5	12	1	0	0	0	0.0	0	1	0	2	0	.083	.083	0	0	C-5
1962 NY N	15	41	8	1	0	0	0.0	2	0	1	8	0	.195	.220	2	0	C-14
10 yrs.	502	1495	356	49	9	41	2.7	135	179	115	242	4	.238	.365	46	11	C-458
2 yrs.	42	116	18	0	0	2	1.7	9	5	11	14	0	.155	.207	1	0	C-41

Neil Chrisley

CHRISLEY, BARBRA O'NEIL   BL TR 6'3"   187 lbs.
B. Dec. 16, 1931, Calhoun Falls, S. C.

	G	AB	H	2B	3B	HR	HR %	R	RBI	BB	SO	SB	BA	SA	PH AB	PH H	G by POS
1957 WAS A	26	51	8	2	1	0	0.0	6	3	7	7	0	.157	.235	13	2	OF-11
1958	105	233	50	7	4	5	2.1	19	26	16	18	1	.215	.343	38	10	OF-69, 3B-1
1959 DET A	65	106	14	3	0	6	5.7	7	11	12	10	0	.132	.330	43	5	OF-21
1960	96	220	56	10	3	5	2.3	27	24	19	26	2	.255	.395	44	10	OF-47, 1B-2
1961 MIL N	10	9	2	0	0	0	0.0	1	0	1	1	0	.222	.222	9	2	
5 yrs.	302	619	130	22	8	16	2.6	60	64	55	62	3	.210	.349	147	29	OF-148, 1B-2, 3B-1
2 yrs.	161	326	70	13	3	11	3.4	34	35	31	36	2	.215	.374	87	15	OF-68, 1B-2

Bob Christian

CHRISTIAN, ROBERT CHARLES   BR TR 5'10"   180 lbs.
B. Oct. 17, 1945, Chicago, Ill.   D. Feb. 20, 1974, San Diego, Calif.

	G	AB	H	2B	3B	HR	HR %	R	RBI	BB	SO	SB	BA	SA	PH AB	PH H	G by POS
1968 DET A	3	3	1	1	0	0	0.0	0	0	0	0	0	.333	.667	1	0	OF-1, 1B-1
1969 CHI A	39	129	28	4	0	3	2.3	11	16	10	19	3	.217	.318	1	1	OF-38
1970	12	15	4	0	0	1	6.7	3	3	1	4	0	.267	.467	9	3	OF-4
3 yrs.	54	147	33	5	0	4	2.7	14	19	11	23	3	.224	.340	11	4	OF-43, 1B-1
1 yr.	3	3	1	1	0	0	0.0	0	0	0	0	0	.333	.667	1	0	OF-1, 1B-1

Mark Christman

CHRISTMAN, MARK JOSEPH   BR TR 5'11"   175 lbs.
B. Oct. 21, 1913, Maplewood, Mo.   D. Oct. 9, 1976, St. Louis, Mo.

	G	AB	H	2B	3B	HR	HR %	R	RBI	BB	SO	SB	BA	SA	PH AB	PH H	G by POS
1938 DET A	95	318	79	6	4	1	0.3	35	44	27	21	5	.248	.302	0	0	3B-69, SS-21

	G	AB	H	2B	3B	HR	HR%	R	RBI	BB	SO	SB	BA	SA	Pinch Hit AB	Pinch Hit H	G by POS

Mark Christman continued

	G	AB	H	2B	3B	HR	HR%	R	RBI	BB	SO	SB	BA	SA	PH AB	PH H	G by POS
1939 2 teams	DET A (6G – .250)					STL A (79G – .216)											
" total	85	238	52	8	3	0	0.0	27	20	20	12	2	.218	.277	11	0	SS-64, 3B-6, 2B-1
1943 STL A	98	336	91	11	5	2	0.6	31	35	19	19	0	.271	.351	3	0	3B-37, SS-24, 1B-20, 2B-14
1944	148	547	148	25	1	6	1.1	56	83	47	37	5	.271	.353	0	0	3B-145, 1B-3
1945	78	289	80	7	4	4	1.4	32	34	19	19	1	.277	.370	1	0	3B-77
1946	128	458	118	22	2	1	0.2	40	41	22	29	0	.258	.321	6	1	3B-77, SS-47
1947 WAS A	110	374	83	15	2	1	0.3	27	33	33	16	4	.222	.281	3	1	SS-106, 2B-1
1948	120	409	106	17	2	1	0.2	38	40	25	19	0	.259	.318	8	2	SS-102, 3B-9, 2B-3
1949	49	112	24	2	0	3	2.7	8	18	8	7	0	.214	.313	16	2	3B-23, 1B-6, SS-4, 2B-1
9 yrs.	911	3081	781	113	23	19	0.6	294	348	220	179	17	.253	.324	48	6	3B-443, SS-368, 1B-29, 2B-20
2 yrs.	101	334	83	8	4	1	0.3	35	44	27	23	5	.249	.305	0	0	3B-75, SS-21

WORLD SERIES

	G	AB	H	2B	3B	HR	HR%	R	RBI	BB	SO	SB	BA	SA	PH AB	PH H	G by POS
1944 STL A	6	22	2	0	0	0	0.0	0	1	0	6	0	.091	.091	0	0	3B-6

Danny Claire

CLAIRE, DAVID MATTHEW   BR TR 5'8" 164 lbs
B. Nov. 18, 1897, Ludington, Mich.   D. Mar. 24, 1929, Battle Creek, Mich.

	G	AB	H	2B	3B	HR	HR%	R	RBI	BB	SO	SB	BA	SA	PH AB	PH H	G by POS
1920 DET A	3	7	1	0	0	0	0.0	1	0	0	0	0	.143	.143	0	0	SS-3

Danny Clark

CLARK, DANIEL CURRAN   BL TR 5'9" 167 lbs
B. Jan. 18, 1895, Meridian, Miss.   D. May 23, 1937, Meridian, Miss.

	G	AB	H	2B	3B	HR	HR%	R	RBI	BB	SO	SB	BA	SA	PH AB	PH H	G by POS
1922 DET A	83	185	54	11	3	3	1.6	31	26	15	11	1	.292	.432	36	8	2B-38, OF-5, 3B-1
1924 BOS A	104	325	90	23	3	2	0.6	36	54	50	18	4	.277	.385	10	1	3B-93
1927 STL N	58	72	17	2	2	0	0.0	8	13	8	7	0	.236	.319	40	12	OF-9
3 yrs.	245	582	161	36	8	5	0.9	75	93	73	36	5	.277	.392	86	21	3B-94, 2B-38, OF-14
1 yr.	83	185	54	11	3	3	1.6	31	26	15	11	1	.292	.432	36	8	2B-38, OF-5, 3B-1

Mel Clark

CLARK, MELVIN EARL   BR TR 6' 180 lbs
B. July 7, 1926, Letart, W. Va.

	G	AB	H	2B	3B	HR	HR%	R	RBI	BB	SO	SB	BA	SA	PH AB	PH H	G by POS
1951 PHI N	10	31	10	1	0	1	3.2	2	3	0	3	0	.323	.452	3	0	OF-7
1952	47	155	52	6	4	1	0.6	20	15	6	13	2	.335	.445	7	1	OF-38, 3B-1
1953	60	198	59	10	4	0	0.0	31	19	11	17	1	.298	.389	8	3	OF-51
1954	83	233	56	9	7	1	0.4	26	24	17	21	0	.240	.352	21	2	OF-63
1955	10	32	5	3	0	0	0.0	3	1	3	4	0	.156	.250	2	0	OF-8
1957 DET A	5	7	0	0	0	0	0.0	0	1	0	3	0	.000	.000	3	0	OF-2
6 yrs.	215	656	182	29	15	3	0.5	82	63	37	61	3	.277	.381	44	6	OF-169, 3B-1
1 yr.	5	7	0	0	0	0	0.0	0	1	0	3	0	.000	.000	3	0	OF-2

Nig Clarke

CLARKE, JAY JUSTIN   BB TR
B. Dec. 15, 1882, Amherstburg, Ont., Canada   D. June 15, 1949, Detroit, Mich.

	G	AB	H	2B	3B	HR	HR%	R	RBI	BB	SO	SB	BA	SA	PH AB	PH H	G by POS
1905 3 teams	CLE A (5G – .111)					DET A (3G – .429)			CLE A (37G – .202)								
" total	45	130	27	6	1	1	0.8	12	10	11			.208	.292	2	0	C-43
1906 CLE A	57	179	64	12	4	1	0.6	22	21	13		3	.358	.486	0	0	C-54
1907	120	390	105	19	6	3	0.8	44	33	35		3	.269	.372	5	0	C-115
1908	97	290	70	8	6	1	0.3	34	27	30		6	.241	.321	6	0	C-90
1909	55	164	45	4	2	0	0.0	15	14	9		1	.274	.323	10	0	C-44
1910	21	58	9	2	0	0	0.0	4	2	8		0	.155	.190	3	1	C-17
1911 STL A	82	256	55	10	1	0	0.0	22	18	26		2	.215	.262	4	0	C-73, 1B-4
1919 PHI N	26	62	15	3	0	0	0.0	4	2	4	5	1	.242	.290	4	0	C-22
1920 PIT N	3	7	0	0	0	0	0.0	0	0	2	4	0	.000	.000	1	0	C-3
9 yrs.	506	1536	390	64	20	6	0.4	157	127	138	9	16	.254	.333	35	1	C-461, 1B-4
1 yr.	3	7	3	0	0	1	14.3	1	1	0		0	.429	.857	1	0	C-2

Flea Clifton

CLIFTON, HERMAN EARL   BR TR 5'10" 160 lbs
B. Dec. 12, 1909, Cincinnati, Ohio

	G	AB	H	2B	3B	HR	HR%	R	RBI	BB	SO	SB	BA	SA	PH AB	PH H	G by POS
1934 DET A	16	16	1	0	0	0	0.0	3	1	1	2	0	.063	.063	8	1	3B-4, 2B-1
1935	43	110	28	5	0	0	0.0	15	9	5	13	2	.255	.300	7	1	3B-21, 2B-5, SS-4
1936	13	26	5	1	0	0	0.0	5	1	4	3	0	.192	.231	1	1	SS-6, 3B-2, 2B-1
1937	15	43	5	1	0	0	0.0	4	2	7	10	3	.116	.140	0	0	3B-7, SS-4, 2B-3
4 yrs.	87	195	39	7	0	0	0.0	27	13	17	28	5	.200	.236	16	3	3B-34, SS-14, 2B-10
4 yrs.	87	195	39	7	0	0	0.0	27	13	17	28	5	.200	.236	16	3	3B-34, SS-14, 2B-10

WORLD SERIES

	G	AB	H	2B	3B	HR	HR%	R	RBI	BB	SO	SB	BA	SA	PH AB	PH H	G by POS
1935 DET A	4	16	0	0	0	0	0.0	1	0	2	4	0	.000	.000	0	0	3B-4

Joe Cobb

COBB, JOSEPH STANLEY   BR TR 5'9" 170 lbs
Born Joseph Stanley Serafin.
B. Jan. 24, 1895, Hudson, Pa.   D. Dec. 24, 1947, Allentown, Pa.

	G	AB	H	2B	3B	HR	HR%	R	RBI	BB	SO	SB	BA	SA	PH AB	PH H	G by POS
1918 DET A	1	0	0	0	0	0	–	0	0	1	0	0	–	–	0	0	

Ty Cobb

COBB, TYRUS RAYMOND (The Georgia Peach)   BL TR 6'1" 175 lbs
B. Dec. 18, 1886, Narrows, Ga.   D. July 17, 1961, Atlanta, Ga.
Manager 1921-26.
Hall of Fame 1936.

	G	AB	H	2B	3B	HR	HR%	R	RBI	BB	SO	SB	BA	SA	PH AB	PH H	G by POS
1905 DET A	41	150	36	6	0	1	0.7	19	15	10		2	.240	.300	0	0	OF-41
1906	98	350	112	13	7	1	0.3	45	41	19		23	.320	.406	1	0	OF-96
1907	150	605	212	29	15	5	0.8	97	116	24		49	.350	.473	0	0	OF-150
1908	150	581	188	36	20	4	0.7	88	108	34		39	.324	.475	0	0	OF-150
1909	156	573	216	33	10	9	1.6	116	107	48		76	.377	.517	0	0	OF-156
1910	140	509	196	36	13	8	1.6	106	91	64		65	.385	.554	3	1	OF-137
1911	146	591	248	24	8	8	1.4	147	144	44		83	.420	.621	0	0	OF-146
1912	140	553	227	30	23	7	1.3	119	90	43		61	.410	.586	0	0	OF-140
1913	122	428	167	18	16	4	0.9	70	67	58	31	52	.390	.535	2	0	OF-118
1914	97	345	127	22	11	2	0.6	69	57	57	22	35	.368	.513	0	0	OF-96
1915	156	563	208	31	13	3	0.5	144	99	118	43	96	.369	.487	0	0	OF-156

	G	AB	H	2B	3B	HR	HR %	R	RBI	BB	SO	SB	BA	SA	Pinch Hit AB	Pinch Hit H	G by POS

y Cobb continued

	G	AB	H	2B	3B	HR	HR %	R	RBI	BB	SO	SB	BA	SA	AB	H	G by POS
'16	145	542	201	31	10	5	0.9	**113**	68	78	39	**68**	.371	.493	0	0	OF-143, 1B-1
'17	152	**588**	**225**	**44**	**23**	7	1.2	107	102	61	34	**55**	**.383**	**.571**	0	0	OF-152
'18	111	421	161	19	**14**	3	0.7	83	64	41	21	34	**.382**	.515	3	1	OF-95, 1B-13, P-2, 3B-1, 2B-1
'19	124	497	**191**	36	13	1	0.2	92	70	38	22	28	**.384**	.515	0	0	OF-112
'20	112	428	143	28	8	2	0.5	86	63	58	28	14	.334	.451	0	0	OF-112
'21	128	507	197	37	16	12	2.4	124	101	56	19	22	.389	.596	7	1	OF-121
'22	137	526	211	42	16	4	0.8	99	99	55	24	9	.401	.565	3	0	OF-134
'23	145	556	189	40	7	6	1.1	103	88	66	14	9	.340	.469	2	1	OF-141
'24	155	625	211	38	10	4	0.6	115	74	85	18	23	.338	.450	0	0	OF-155
'25	121	415	157	31	12	12	2.9	97	102	65	12	13	.378	.598	12	2	OF-105, P-1
'26	79	233	79	18	5	4	1.7	48	62	26	2	9	.339	.511	18	6	OF-55
'27 PHI A	134	490	175	32	7	5	1.0	104	93	67	12	22	.357	.482	8	2	OF-126
'28	95	353	114	27	4	1	0.3	54	40	34	16	5	.323	.431	10	1	OF-95
24 yrs.	3034	11429	4191	724	297	118	1.0	2245	1961	1249	357	892	.367	.513	69	15	OF-2943, 1B-14, P-3, 3B-1, 2B-1
	4th	**4th**	**1st**	**4th**	**2nd**			**1st**	**4th**			**2nd**	**1st**				
22 yrs.	2805	10586	3902	665	286	112	1.1	2087	1828	1148	329	865	.369	.517	51	12	OF-2722, 1B-14, P-3, 3B-1, 2B-1
	2nd	**1st**	**1st**	**1st**	**1st**			**1st**	**1st**	**3rd**		**1st**	**1st**	**3rd**			

ORLD SERIES

	G	AB	H	2B	3B	HR	HR %	R	RBI	BB	SO	SB	BA	SA	AB	H	G by POS
'07 DET A	5	20	4	0	1	0	0.0	1	1	0	3	0	.200	.300	0	0	OF-5
'08	5	19	7	1	0	0	0.0	3	4	1	2	2	.368	.421	0	0	OF-5
'09	7	26	6	3	0	0	0.0	3	6	2	2	2	.231	.346	0	0	OF-7
3 yrs.	17	65	17	4	1	0	0.0	7	11	3	7	4	.262	.354	0	0	OF-17

Mickey Cochrane

COCHRANE, GORDON STANLEY (Black Mike)   BL TR 5'10½" 180 lbs.
B. Apr. 6, 1903, Bridgewater, Mass.   D. June 28, 1962, Lake Forest, Ill.
Manager 1934-38.
Hall of Fame 1947.

	G	AB	H	2B	3B	HR	HR %	R	RBI	BB	SO	SB	BA	SA	AB	H	G by POS
'25 PHI A	134	420	139	21	5	6	1.4	69	55	44	19	7	.331	.448	1	1	C-133
'26	120	370	101	8	9	8	2.2	50	47	56	15	5	.273	.408	1	0	C-115
'27	126	432	146	20	6	12	2.8	80	80	50	7	9	.338	.495	3	1	C-123
'28	131	468	137	26	12	10	2.1	92	57	76	25	7	.293	.464	1	0	C-130
'29	135	514	170	37	8	7	1.4	113	95	69	8	7	.331	.475	0	0	C-135
'30	130	487	174	42	5	10	2.1	110	85	55	18	5	.357	.526	0	0	C-130
'31	122	459	160	31	6	17	3.7	87	89	56	21	2	.349	.553	5	0	C-117
'32	139	518	152	35	4	23	4.4	118	112	100	22	0	.293	.510	2	0	C-137, OF-1
'33	130	429	138	30	4	15	3.5	104	60	106	22	8	.322	.515	2	0	C-128
'34 DET A	129	437	140	32	1	2	0.5	74	76	78	26	8	.320	.412	8	1	C-124
'35	115	411	131	33	3	5	1.2	93	47	96	15	5	.319	.450	3	1	C-110
'36	44	126	34	8	0	2	1.6	24	17	46	15	1	.270	.381	1	0	C-42
'37	27	98	30	10	1	2	2.0	27	12	25	4	0	.306	.490	0	0	C-27
13 yrs.	1482	5169	1652	333	64	119	2.3	1041	832	857	217	64	.320	.478	27	4	C-1451, OF-1
4 yrs.	315	1072	335	83	5	11	1.0	218	152	245	60	14	.313	.430	12	2	C-303

ORLD SERIES

	G	AB	H	2B	3B	HR	HR %	R	RBI	BB	SO	SB	BA	SA	AB	H	G by POS
'29 PHI A	5	15	6	1	0	0	0.0	5	0	7	0	0	.400	.467	0	0	C-5
'30	6	18	4	1	0	2	11.1	5	3	5	2	0	.222	.611	0	0	C-6
'31	7	25	4	0	0	0	0.0	2	1	5	2	0	.160	.160	0	0	C-7
'34 DET A	7	28	6	1	0	0	0.0	2	1	4	3	0	.214	.250	0	0	C-7
'35	6	24	7	1	0	0	0.0	3	1	4	1	0	.292	.333	0	0	C-6
5 yrs.	31	110	27	4	0	2	1.8	17	6	25	8	0	.245	.336	0	0	C-31
										6th							

ack Coffey

COFFEY, JOHN FRANCIS   BR TR 5'11" 178 lbs.
B. Jan. 28, 1887, New York, N. Y.   D. Feb. 14, 1966, Bronx, N. Y.

	G	AB	H	2B	3B	HR	HR %	R	RBI	BB	SO	SB	BA	SA	AB	H	G by POS
'09 BOS N	73	257	48	4	4	0	0.0	21	20	11		2	.187	.233	0	0	SS-73
'18 2 teams		DET	A	(22G –	.209)		BOS	A	(15G –	.159)							
total	37	111	21	1	2	1	0.9	12	6	11	8	4	.189	.261	0	0	SS-23, 2B-23, 3B-14
2 yrs.	110	368	69	5	6	1	0.3	33	26	22	8	6	.188	.242	0	0	SS-73, 2B-23, 3B-14
1 yr.	22	67	14	0	2	0	0.0	7	4	8	6	2	.209	.269	0	0	2B-22

Rocky Colavito

COLAVITO, ROCCO DOMENICO   BR TR 6'3" 190 lbs.
B. Aug. 10, 1933, New York, N. Y.

	G	AB	H	2B	3B	HR	HR %	R	RBI	BB	SO	SB	BA	SA	AB	H	G by POS
'55 CLE A	5	9	4	2	0	0	0.0	3	0	0	2	0	.444	.667	2	0	OF-2
'56	101	322	89	11	4	21	6.5	55	65	49	46	0	.276	.531	5	0	OF-98
'57	134	461	116	26	0	25	5.4	66	84	71	80	1	.252	.471	3	1	OF-130
'58	143	489	148	26	3	41	**8.4**	80	113	84	89	0	.303	**.620**	5	1	OF-129, 1B-11, P-1
'59	154	588	151	24	0	**42**	7.1	90	111	71	86	3	.257	.512	0	0	OF-154
'60 DET A	145	555	138	18	1	35	6.3	67	87	53	80	3	.249	.474	2	0	OF-144
'61	163	583	169	30	2	45	7.7	129	140	113	75	1	.290	.580	2	0	OF-161
'62	161	601	164	30	2	37	6.2	90	112	96	68	2	.273	.514	0	0	OF-161
'63	160	597	162	29	2	22	3.7	91	91	84	78	0	.271	.437	1	0	OF-159
'64 KC A	160	588	161	31	2	34	5.8	89	102	83	56	3	.274	.507	1	1	OF-159
'65 CLE A	162	592	170	25	2	26	4.4	92	**108**	**93**	63	1	.287	.468	0	0	OF-162
'66	151	533	127	13	0	30	5.6	68	72	76	81	2	.238	.432	5	3	OF-146
'67 2 teams		CLE	A	(63G –	.241)		CHI	A	(60G –	.221)							
total	123	381	88	13	1	8	2.1	30	50	49	41	3	.231	.333	12	3	OF-108
'68 2 teams		LA	N	(40G –	.204)		NY	A	(39G –	.220)							
total	79	204	43	5	2	8	3.9	21	24	29	35	0	.211	.373	17	2	OF-61, P-1
14 yrs.	1841	6503	1730	283	21	374	5.8	971	1159	951	880	19	.266	.489	55	11	OF-1774, 1B-11, P-2
4 yrs.	629	2336	633	107	7	139	6.0	377	430	346	301	6	.271	.501	5	0	OF-625
							2nd							**6th**			

	G	AB	H	2B	3B	HR	HR %	R	RBI	BB	SO	SB	BA	SA	Pinch Hit AB	Pinch Hit H	G by POS

Nate Colbert

COLBERT, NATHAN
B. Apr. 9, 1946, St. Louis, Mo.   BR TR 6'2"   190 lbs

	G	AB	H	2B	3B	HR	HR %	R	RBI	BB	SO	SB	BA	SA	PH AB	PH H	G by POS
1966 HOU N	19	7	0	0	0	0	0.0	3	0	0	4	0	.000	.000	7	0	
1968	20	53	8	1	0	0	0.0	5	4	1	23	1	.151	.170	2	0	OF-11, 1B-5
1969 SD N	139	483	123	20	9	24	5.0	64	66	45	123	6	.255	.482	4	0	1B-134
1970	156	572	148	17	6	38	6.6	84	86	56	150	3	.259	.509	4	0	1B-153, 3B-1
1971	156	565	149	25	3	27	4.8	81	84	63	119	5	.264	.462	3	1	1B-153
1972	151	563	141	27	2	38	6.7	87	111	70	127	15	.250	.508	2	1	1B-150
1973	145	529	143	25	2	22	4.2	73	80	54	146	9	.270	.450	1	0	1B-144
1974	119	368	76	16	0	14	3.8	53	54	62	108	10	.207	.364	12	4	1B-79, OF-48
1975 2 teams	DET	A	(45G –	.147)		MON	N	(38G –	.173)								
" total	83	237	37	8	3	8	3.4	26	29	22	83	0	.156	.316	19	3	1B-66, DH-1
1976 2 teams	MON	N	(14G –	.200)		OAK	A	(2G –	.000)								
" total	16	45	8	2	0	2	4.4	5	6	10	19	3	.178	.356	3	1	OF-7, 1B-6, DH-2
10 yrs.	1004	3422	833	141	25	173	5.1	481	520	383	902	52	.243	.451	57	9	1B-890, OF-66, DH-3, 3B-1
1 yr.	45	156	23	4	2	4	2.6	16	18	17	52	0	.147	.276	0	0	1B-44, DH-1

Kevin Collins

COLLINS, KEVIN MICHAEL (Casey)
B. Aug. 4, 1946, Springfield, Mass.   BL TR 6'1"   180 lbs

	G	AB	H	2B	3B	HR	HR %	R	RBI	BB	SO	SB	BA	SA	PH AB	PH H	G by POS
1965 NY N	11	23	4	1	0	0	0.0	3	0	1	9	0	.174	.217	3	1	3B-7, SS-3
1967	4	10	1	0	0	0	0.0	1	0	0	3	1	.100	.100	2	0	2B-2
1968	58	154	31	5	2	1	0.6	12	13	7	37	0	.201	.279	14	0	3B-40, 2B-6, SS-1
1969 2 teams	NY	N	(16G –	.150)		MON	N	(52G –	.240)								
" total	68	136	29	8	1	3	2.2	6	14	11	26	0	.213	.353	30	9	3B-30, 2B-20
1970 DET A	25	24	5	1	0	1	4.2	2	3	1	10	0	.208	.375	21	4	1B-1
1971	35	41	11	2	1	1	2.4	6	4	0	12	0	.268	.439	31	9	3B-4, OF-2, 2B-1
6 yrs.	201	388	81	17	4	6	1.5	30	34	20	97	1	.209	.320	101	23	3B-81, 2B-29, SS-4, OF-1B-1
2 yrs.	60	65	16	3	1	2	3.1	8	7	1	22	0	.246	.415	52	13	3B-4, OF-2, 2B-1, 1B-1

Wayne Comer

COMER, HARRY WAYNE
B. Feb. 3, 1944, Shenandoah, Va.   BR TR 5'10"   175 lbs

	G	AB	H	2B	3B	HR	HR %	R	RBI	BB	SO	SB	BA	SA	PH AB	PH H	G by POS
1967 DET A	4	3	1	0	0	0	0.0	0	0	0	0	0	.333	.333	1	1	OF-1
1968	48	48	6	0	1	1	2.1	8	3	2	7	0	.125	.229	18	2	OF-27, C-1
1969 SEA A	147	481	118	18	2	15	3.1	88	54	82	79	18	.245	.380	12	1	OF-139, 3B-1, C-1
1970 2 teams	MIL	A	(13G –	.059)		WAS	A	(77G –	.233)								
" total	90	146	31	4	0	0	0.0	22	9	22	19	4	.212	.240	26	3	OF-63, 3B-1
1972 DET A	27	9	1	0	0	0	0.0	1	1	0	1	0	.111	.111	6	1	OF-17
5 yrs.	316	687	157	22	2	16	2.3	119	67	106	106	22	.229	.336	63	8	OF-247, 3B-2, C-2
3 yrs.	79	60	8	0	1	1	1.7	9	4	2	8	0	.133	.217	25	4	OF-45, C-1

WORLD SERIES

	G	AB	H	2B	3B	HR	HR %	R	RBI	BB	SO	SB	BA	SA	PH AB	PH H	G by POS
1968 DET A	1	1	1	0	0	0	0.0	0	0	0	0	0	1.000	1.000	1	1	

Duff Cooley

COOLEY, DICK GORDON (Sir Richard)
B. Mar. 14, 1873, Dallas, Tex.   D. Aug. 9, 1937, Dallas, Tex.   BL TR

	G	AB	H	2B	3B	HR	HR %	R	RBI	BB	SO	SB	BA	SA	PH AB	PH H	G by POS
1893 STL N	29	107	37	2	3	0	0.0	20	21	8	9	8	.346	.421	1	0	OF-15, C-10, SS-5
1894	54	206	61	3	1	1	0.5	35	21	12	16	7	.296	.335	0	0	OF-39, 3B-13, SS-1, 1B-
1895	132	563	191	9	21	6	1.1	106	75	36	29	27	.339	.462	1	0	OF-124, 3B-5, SS-3, C-1
1896 2 teams	STL	N	(40G –	.307)		PHI	N	(64G –	.307)								
" total	104	453	139	11	7	2	0.4	92	35	25	19	30	.307	.375	0	0	OF-104
1897 PHI N	133	566	186	14	13	4	0.7	124	40	51		31	.329	.420	0	0	OF-131, 1B-2
1898	149	629	196	24	12	4	0.6	123	55	48		17	.312	.407	0	0	OF-149
1899	94	406	112	15	8	1	0.2	75	31	29		15	.276	.360	1	0	1B-79, OF-14, 2B-1
1900 PIT N	66	249	50	8	1	0	0.0	30	22	14		9	.201	.241	0	0	1B-66
1901 BOS N	63	240	62	13	3	0	0.0	27	27	14		5	.258	.338	0	0	OF-53, 1B-10
1902	135	548	162	26	8	0	0.0	73	58	34		27	.296	.372	1	0	OF-127, 1B-7
1903	138	553	160	26	10	0	0.2	76	70	44		27	.289	.378	0	0	OF-126, 1B-13
1904	122	467	127	18	7	5	1.1	41	70	24		14	.272	.373	0	0	OF-116, 1B-6
1905 DET A	99	377	93	11	9	1	0.3	25	32	26		7	.247	.332	1	0	OF-97
13 yrs.	1318	5364	1576	180	103	25	0.5	847	557	365	73	224	.294	.380	5	1	OF-1095, 1B-184, 3B-18, C-11, SS-9, 2B-1
1 yr.	99	377	93	11	9	1	0.3	25	32	26		7	.247	.332	1	1	OF-97

Jack Coombs

COOMBS, JOHN WESLEY (Colby Jack)
B. Nov. 18, 1882, LeGrand, Iowa   D. Apr. 15, 1957, LeGrand, Iowa
Manager 1919.   BB TR 6'   185 lbs

	G	AB	H	2B	3B	HR	HR %	R	RBI	BB	SO	SB	BA	SA	PH AB	PH H	G by POS
1906 PHI A	24	67	16	2	0	0	0.0	9	3	1		2	.239	.269	1	0	P-23
1907	24	48	8	0	0	1	2.1	4	4	0		1	.167	.229	1	0	P-23
1908	78	220	56	9	5	1	0.5	24	23	9		5	.255	.355	5	4	OF-47, P-26
1909	37	83	14	4	0	0	0.0	4	10	4		6	.169	.217	6	1	P-31
1910	46	132	29	3	0	0	0.0	20	9	7		3	.220	.242	1	0	P-45
1911	52	141	45	6	1	2	1.4	31	23	8		1	.319	.418	4	1	P-47
1912	55	110	28	2	0	0	0.0	10	13	14		1	.255	.273	14	4	P-40
1913	2	3	1	1	0	0	0.0	1	0	0		0	.333	.667	0	0	P-2
1914	5	11	3	1	0	0	0.0	0	2	1		0	.273	.364	1	0	OF-2, P-2
1915 BKN N	29	75	21	1	1	0	0.0	8	5	2	17	0	.280	.320	0	0	P-29
1916	27	61	11	2	0	0	0.0	2	3	2	10	0	.180	.213	0	0	P-27
1917	32	44	10	0	1	0	0.0	4	2	4	9	1	.227	.273	0	0	P-31
1918	46	113	19	3	2	0	0.0	6	3	7	5	1	.168	.230	3	1	P-27, OF-13
1920 DET A	2	2	0	0	0	0	0.0	0	0	0	0	0	.000	.000	0	0	P-2
14 yrs.	459	1110	261	34	10	4	0.4	123	100	59	44	21	.235	.295	36	11	P-355, OF-62
1 yr.	2	2	0	0	0	0	0.0	0	0	0	0	0	.000	.000	0	0	P-2

WORLD SERIES

	G	AB	H	2B	3B	HR	HR %	R	RBI	BB	SO	SB	BA	SA	PH AB	PH H	G by POS
1910 PHI A	3	13	5	1	0	0	0.0	3	3	0	3	0	.385	.462	0	0	P-3
1911	2	8	2	1	0	0	0.0	1	0	0	0	0	.250	.250	0	0	P-2

	G	AB	H	2B	3B	HR	HR %	R	RBI	BB	SO	SB	BA	SA	Pinch Hit AB	Pinch Hit H	G by POS

Jack Coombs continued

	G	AB	H	2B	3B	HR	HR %	R	RBI	BB	SO	SB	BA	SA	AB	H	G by POS
1916 BKN N	1	3	1	0	0	0	0.0	0	1	0	0	0	.333	.333	0	0	P-1
3 yrs.	6	24	8	1	0	0	0.0	1	4	0	3	0	.333	.375	0	0	P-6

Tim Corcoran

CORCORAN, TIMOTHY MICHAEL
B. Mar. 19, 1953, Glendale, Calif.   BL TL 5'11" 175 lbs.

	G	AB	H	2B	3B	HR	HR %	R	RBI	BB	SO	SB	BA	SA	AB	H	G by POS
1977 DET A	55	103	29	3	0	3	2.9	13	15	6	9	0	.282	.398	32	10	OF-18, DH-3
1978	116	324	86	13	1	1	0.3	37	27	24	27	3	.265	.321	12	2	OF-109, DH-1
1979	18	22	5	1	0	0	0.0	4	6	4	2	1	.227	.273	2	1	OF-9, 1B-5, DH-2
1980	84	153	44	7	1	3	2.0	20	18	22	10	0	.288	.405	16	3	1B-48, OF-18, DH-5
1981 MIN A	22	51	9	3	0	0	0.0	4	4	6	7	0	.176	.235	4	0	1B-16, DH-3
1983 PHI N	3	0	0	0	0	0	–	0	0	0	0	0	–	–	0	0	1B-3
1984	102	208	71	13	1	5	2.4	30	36	37	27	0	.341	.486	37	10	1B-51, OF-17
7 yrs.	400	861	244	40	3	12	1.4	108	106	99	82	4	.283	.379	103	26	OF-171, 1B-123, DH-14
4 yrs.	273	602	164	24	2	7	1.2	74	66	56	48	4	.272	.354	62	16	OF-154, 1B-53, DH-11

Red Corriden

CORRIDEN, JOHN MICHAEL, SR.
Father of John Corriden.   BR TR 5'9" 165 lbs.
B. Sept. 4, 1887, Logansport, Ind.   D. Sept. 28, 1959, Indianapolis, Ind.
Manager 1950.

	G	AB	H	2B	3B	HR	HR %	R	RBI	BB	SO	SB	BA	SA	AB	H	G by POS
1910 STL A	26	84	13	3	0	1	1.2	19	4	13		5	.155	.226	0	0	SS-14, 3B-12
1912 DET A	38	138	28	6	0	0	0.0	22	5	15		4	.203	.246	3	0	3B-25, 2B-7, SS-3
1913 CHI N	45	97	17	3	0	2	2.1	13	9	9	14	4	.175	.268	4	1	SS-36, 2B-2, 3B-1
1914	107	318	73	9	5	3	0.9	42	29	35	33	13	.230	.318	6	2	SS-96, 3B-8, 2B-3
1915	6	3	0	0	0	0	0.0	1	0	2	1	0	.000	.000	2	0	OF-1, 3B-1
5 yrs.	222	640	131	21	5	6	0.9	97	47	74	48	26	.205	.281	15	3	SS-149, 3B-47, 2B-12, OF-1
1 yr.	38	138	28	6	0	0	0.0	22	5	15		4	.203	.246	3	0	3B-25, 2B-7, SS-3

Chuck Cottier

COTTIER, CHARLES KEITH
B. Jan. 8, 1936, Delta, Colo.   BR TR 5'10½" 175 lbs.
Manager 1984.

	G	AB	H	2B	3B	HR	HR %	R	RBI	BB	SO	SB	BA	SA	AB	H	G by POS
1959 MIL N	10	24	3	1	0	0	0.0	1	1	3	7	0	.125	.167	0	0	2B-10
1960	95	229	52	8	0	3	1.3	29	19	14	21	1	.227	.301	1	1	2B-92
1961 2 teams		DET	A	(10G –	.286)			WAS	A	(101G –	.234)						
" total	111	344	81	14	4	2	0.6	39	35	31	52	9	.235	.317	1	0	2B-102, SS-8
1962 WAS A	136	443	107	14	6	6	1.4	50	40	44	57	14	.242	.341	0	0	2B-134
1963	113	337	69	16	4	5	1.5	30	21	24	63	2	.205	.320	2	0	2B-85, SS-24, 3B-1
1964	73	137	23	6	2	3	2.2	16	10	19	33	2	.168	.307	5	1	2B-53, 3B-3, SS-2
1965	7	1	0	0	0	0	0.0	1	0	0	0	0	.000	.000	1	0	
1968 CAL A	33	67	13	4	1	0	0.0	2	1	2	15	0	.194	.284	2	0	3B-27, 2B-4
1969	2	0	0	0	0	0	–	0	0	0	0	0	.000	.000	0	0	2B-2
9 yrs.	580	1584	348	63	17	19	1.2	168	127	137	248	28	.220	.317	12	2	2B-482, SS-34, 3B-31
1 yr.	10	7	2	0	0	0	0.0	2	1	1	1	0	.286	.286	0	0	SS-8, 2B-2

Bill Coughlin

COUGHLIN, WILLIAM PAUL
B. Aug. 12, 1877, Scranton, Pa.   D. May 7, 1943, Scranton, Pa.   BR TR 5'9" 140 lbs.

	G	AB	H	2B	3B	HR	HR %	R	RBI	BB	SO	SB	BA	SA	AB	H	G by POS
1899 WAS N	6	24	3	0	1	0	0.0	2	3	1		1	.125	.208	0	0	3B-6
1901 WAS A	137	506	139	17	13	6	1.2	75	68	25		16	.275	.395	0	0	3B-137
1902	123	469	141	27	4	6	1.3	84	71	26		29	.301	.414	0	0	3B-66, SS-31, 2B-26
1903	125	470	118	18	3	1	0.2	56	31	9		30	.251	.309	0	0	3B-119, SS-4, 2B-2
1904 2 teams		WAS	A	(65G –	.275)			DET	A	(56G –	.228)						
" total	121	471	120	21	4	0	0.0	50	34	14		11	.255	.316	1	1	3B-120
1905 DET A	138	489	123	20	6	0	0.0	48	44	34		16	.252	.317	1	0	3B-137
1906	147	498	117	15	5	2	0.4	54	60	36		31	.235	.297	0	0	3B-147
1907	134	519	126	10	2	0	0.0	80	46	35		15	.243	.270	0	0	3B-133
1908	119	405	87	5	1	0	0.0	32	23	23		10	.215	.232	0	0	3B-119
9 yrs.	1050	3851	974	133	39	15	0.4	481	380	203		159	.253	.319	2	1	3B-984, SS-35, 2B-28
5 yrs.	594	2117	500	56	14	2	0.1	236	190	133		73	.236	.279	1	0	3B-592

WORLD SERIES

	G	AB	H	2B	3B	HR	HR %	R	RBI	BB	SO	SB	BA	SA	AB	H	G by POS
1907 DET A	5	20	5	0	0	0	0.0	0	0	1	4	1	.250	.250	0	0	3B-5
1908	3	8	1	0	0	0	0.0	0	1	0	1	0	.125	.125	0	0	3B-3
2 yrs.	8	28	6	0	0	0	0.0	0	1	1	5	1	.214	.214	0	0	3B-8

Ernie Courtney

COURTNEY, ERNEST E.
B. Jan. 20, 1875, Los Angeles, Calif.   D. Feb. 29, 1920, Buffalo, N. Y.   BL TR 5'10"

	G	AB	H	2B	3B	HR	HR %	R	RBI	BB	SO	SB	BA	SA	AB	H	G by POS
1902 2 teams		BOS	N	(48G –	.218)			BAL	A	(1G –	.500)						
" total	49	169	38	3	1	0	0.0	26	18	14		3	.225	.254	6	2	OF-39, SS-3, 3B-1
1903 2 teams		NY	A	(25G –	.266)			DET	A	(23G –	.230)						
" total	48	153	38	3	3	1	0.7	14	14	12		2	.248	.327	2	0	SS-28, 3B-13, 2B-4, 1B-1
1905 PHI N	155	601	165	14	7	2	0.3	77	77	47		17	.275	.331	0	0	3B-155
1906	116	398	94	12	2	0	0.0	53	42	45		6	.236	.276	4	0	3B-96, 1B-13, OF-3, SS-1
1907	130	440	107	17	4	2	0.5	42	43	55		6	.243	.314	0	0	3B-75, 1B-48, OF-4, SS-2, 2B-2
1908	60	160	29	3	0	0	0.0	14	6	15		1	.181	.200	17	3	3B-22, 1B-13, 2B-5, SS-2
6 yrs.	558	1921	471	52	17	5	0.3	226	200	188		35	.245	.298	29	5	3B-362, 1B-75, OF-46, SS-36, 2B-11
1 yr.	23	74	17	0	0	0	0.0	7	6	5		1	.230	.230	1	0	3B-13, SS-9

Al Cowens

COWENS, ALFRED EDWARD
B. Oct. 25, 1951, Los Angeles, Calif.   BR TR 6'1" 197 lbs.

	G	AB	H	2B	3B	HR	HR %	R	RBI	BB	SO	SB	BA	SA	AB	H	G by POS
1974 KC A	110	269	65	7	1	1	0.4	28	25	23	38	5	.242	.286	8	4	OF-102, DH-4, 3B-2
1975	120	328	91	13	8	4	1.2	44	42	28	36	12	.277	.402	7	2	OF-113, DH-2
1976	152	581	154	23	6	3	0.5	71	59	26	50	23	.265	.341	5	2	OF-148, DH-1
1977	162	606	189	32	14	23	3.8	98	112	41	64	16	.312	.525	6	2	OF-159, DH-1
1978	132	485	133	24	8	5	1.0	63	63	31	54	14	.274	.388	2	0	OF-127, 3B-5, DH-2
1979	136	516	152	18	7	9	1.7	69	73	40	44	10	.295	.409	3	2	OF-134, DH-1

	G	AB	H	2B	3B	HR	HR %	R	RBI	BB	SO	SB	BA	SA	Pinch Hit AB	Pinch Hit H	G by POS

Al Cowens continued

	G	AB	H	2B	3B	HR	HR%	R	RBI	BB	SO	SB	BA	SA	AB	H	G by POS
1980 2 teams	CAL A (34G – .227)				DET A (108G – .280)												
" total	142	522	140	20	3	6	1.1	69	59	49	61	6	.268	.352	5	1	OF-137, DH-2
1981 DET A	85	253	66	11	4	1	0.4	27	18	22	36	3	.261	.348	12	3	OF-83
1982 SEA A	146	560	151	39	8	20	3.6	72	78	46	81	11	.270	.475	0	0	OF-145, DH-1
1983	110	356	73	19	2	7	2.0	39	35	23	38	10	.205	.329	6	1	OF-70, DH-34
1984	139	524	145	34	2	15	2.9	60	78	27	83	9	.277	.435	8	1	OF-130, DH-7
11 yrs.	1434	5000	1359	240	63	94	1.9	640	642	356	585	119	.272	.401	62	18	OF-1348, DH-55, 3B-7
2 yrs.	193	656	179	26	7	6	0.9	85	60	59	76	8	.273	.361	14	3	OF-190, DH-1
LEAGUE CHAMPIONSHIP SERIES																	
1976 KC A	5	21	4	0	1	0	0.0	3	0	1	1	2	.190	.286	0	0	OF-5
1977	5	19	5	0	0	1	5.3	2	5	1	3	0	.263	.421	0	0	OF-5
1978	4	15	2	0	0	0	0.0	2	1	0	2	0	.133	.133	0	0	OF-4
3 yrs.	14	55	11	0	1	1	1.8	7	6	2	6	2	.200	.291	0	0	OF-14

Doc Cramer

CRAMER, ROGER MAXWELL (Flit)
B. July 22, 1905, Beach Haven, N. J.   BL TR 6'2" 185 lbs.

	G	AB	H	2B	3B	HR	HR%	R	RBI	BB	SO	SB	BA	SA	AB	H	G by POS
1929 PHI A	2	6	0	0	0	0	0.0	0	0	0	2	0	.000	.000	1	0	OF-1
1930	30	82	19	1	1	0	0.0	12	6	2	8	0	.232	.268	8	0	OF-21, SS-1
1931	65	223	58	8	2	2	0.9	37	20	11	15	2	.260	.341	10	3	OF-55
1932	92	384	129	27	6	3	0.8	73	46	17	27	3	.336	.461	4	2	OF-86
1933	152	661	195	27	8	8	1.2	109	75	36	24	5	.295	.396	0	0	OF-152
1934	153	649	202	29	9	6	0.9	99	46	40	35	1	.311	.411	0	0	OF-152
1935	149	644	214	37	4	3	0.5	96	70	37	34	6	.332	.416	0	0	OF-149
1936 BOS A	154	643	188	31	7	0	0.0	99	41	49	20	4	.292	.362	0	0	OF-154
1937	133	560	171	22	11	0	0.0	90	51	35	14	8	.305	.384	0	0	OF-133
1938	148	658	198	36	8	0	0.0	116	71	51	19	4	.301	.380	0	0	OF-148, P-1
1939	137	589	183	30	6	0	0.0	110	56	36	17	3	.311	.382	2	1	OF-135
1940	150	661	200	27	12	1	0.2	94	51	36	29	3	.303	.384	0	0	OF-149
1941 WAS A	154	660	180	25	6	2	0.3	93	66	37	15	4	.273	.338	2	0	OF-152
1942 DET A	151	630	166	26	4	0	0.0	71	43	43	18	4	.263	.317	1	1	OF-150
1943	140	606	182	18	4	1	0.2	79	43	31	13	4	.300	.348	2	1	OF-138
1944	143	578	169	20	9	2	0.3	69	42	37	21	6	.292	.369	2	0	OF-141
1945	141	541	149	22	8	6	1.1	62	58	35	21	2	.275	.379	1	0	OF-140
1946	68	204	60	8	2	1	0.5	26	26	15	8	3	.294	.368	16	4	OF-50
1947	73	157	42	2	2	2	1.3	21	30	20	5	0	.268	.344	33	9	OF-35
1948	4	4	0	0	0	0	0.0	1	1	3	0	0	.000	.000	2	0	OF-1
20 yrs.	2239	9140	2705	396	109	37	0.4	1357	842	571	345	62	.296	.375	84	21	OF-2142, SS-1, P-1
7 yrs.	720	2720	768	96	29	12	0.4	329	243	184	86	19	.282	.352	57	15	OF-655
WORLD SERIES																	
1931 PHI A	2	2	1	0	0	0	0.0	0	0	0	0	0	.500	.500	2	1	
1945 DET A	7	29	11	0	0	0	0.0	7	4	1	0	1	.379	.379	0	0	OF-7
2 yrs.	9	31	12	0	0	0	0.0	7	6	1	0	1	.387	.387	2	1	OF-7

Sam Crawford

CRAWFORD, SAMUEL EARL (Wahoo Sam)
B. Apr. 18, 1880, Wahoo, Neb.   D. June 15, 1968, Hollywood, Calif.
Hall of Fame 1957.   BL TL 6' 190 lbs.

	G	AB	H	2B	3B	HR	HR%	R	RBI	BB	SO	SB	BA	SA	AB	H	G by POS
1899 CIN N	31	127	39	2	8	1	0.8	25	20	2		6	.307	.472	0	0	OF-31
1900	101	389	104	14	15	7	1.8	68	59	28		14	.267	.434	6	1	OF-94
1901	131	515	170	22	16	16	3.1	91	104	37		13	.330	.528	4	2	OF-126
1902	140	555	185	16	23	3	0.5	94	78	47		16	.333	.461	0	0	OF-140
1903 DET A	137	550	184	23	25	4	0.7	88	89	25		18	.335	.489	0	0	OF-137
1904	150	571	143	21	17	2	0.4	49	73	44		20	.250	.357	0	0	OF-150
1905	154	575	171	40	10	6	1.0	73	75	50		22	.297	.433	0	0	OF-103, 1B-51
1906	145	563	166	25	16	2	0.4	65	72	38		24	.295	.407	0	0	OF-116, 1B-32
1907	144	582	188	34	17	4	0.7	102	81	37		18	.323	.460	0	0	OF-144, 1B-2
1908	152	591	184	33	16	7	1.2	102	80	37		15	.311	.457	1	0	OF-134, 1B-17
1909	156	589	185	35	14	6	1.0	83	97	47		30	.314	.452	0	0	OF-139, 1B-17
1910	154	588	170	26	19	5	0.9	83	120	37		20	.289	.423	0	0	OF-153, 1B-1
1911	146	574	217	36	14	7	1.2	109	115	61		37	.378	.526	0	0	OF-146
1912	149	581	189	30	21	4	0.7	81	109	42		41	.325	.470	0	0	OF-149
1913	153	610	193	32	23	9	1.5	78	83	52	28	13	.316	.489	0	0	OF-140, 1B-13
1914	157	582	183	22	26	8	1.4	74	104	69	31	25	.314	.483	0	0	OF-157
1915	156	612	183	31	19	4	0.7	81	112	66	29	24	.299	.431	0	0	OF-156
1916	100	322	92	11	13	0	0.0	41	42	37	10	10	.286	.401	15	8	OF-79, 1B-2
1917	61	104	18	4	0	2	1.9	6	12	4	6	0	.173	.269	38	7	1B-15, OF-3
19 yrs.	2517	9580	2964	457 1st	312	97	1.0	1393	1525	760	104	366	.309	.453	64	18	OF-2297, 1B-150
15 yrs.	2114 4th	7994 4th	2466 5th	403 5th	312 2nd	70	0.9	1115 6th	1264 5th	646 9th	104	317 3rd	.308	.448	54	15	OF-1906, 1B-150
WORLD SERIES																	
1907 DET A	5	21	5	1	0	0	0.0	1	2	0	3	0	.238	.286	0	0	OF-5
1908	5	21	5	1	0	0	0.0	2	1	1	2	0	.238	.286	0	0	OF-5
1909	7	28	7	3	0	1	3.6	4	3	1	1	1	.250	.464	0	0	OF-7
3 yrs.	17	70	17	5	0	1	1.4	7	6	2	6	1	.243	.357	0	0	OF-17

Davey Crockett

CROCKETT, DAVID SOLOMON
B. Oct. 5, 1875, Roanoke, Va.   D. Feb. 23, 1961, Charlottesville, Va.   6'1" 175 lbs.

	G	AB	H	2B	3B	HR	HR%	R	RBI	BB	SO	SB	BA	SA	AB	H	G by POS
1901 DET A	28	102	29	2	2	0	0.0	10	14	6		1	.284	.343	1	0	1B-27

Frank Croucher

CROUCHER, FRANK DONALD (Dingle)
B. July 23, 1914, San Antonio, Tex.   D. May 21, 1980, Houston, Tex.   BR TR 5'11" 165 lbs.

	G	AB	H	2B	3B	HR	HR%	R	RBI	BB	SO	SB	BA	SA	AB	H	G by POS
1939 DET A	97	324	87	15	6	5	1.5	38	40	16	42	2	.269	.361	2	2	SS-93, 2B-3
1940	37	57	6	0	0	0	0.0	3	2	4	5	0	.105	.105	5	0	SS-26, 2B-7, 3B-1
1941	136	489	124	21	4	2	0.4	51	39	33	72	2	.254	.325	0	0	SS-136

	G	AB	H	2B	3B	HR	HR %	R	RBI	BB	SO	SB	BA	SA	Pinch Hit AB	Pinch Hit H	G by POS

Frank Croucher continued

	G	AB	H	2B	3B	HR	HR %	R	RBI	BB	SO	SB	BA	SA	PH AB	PH H	G by POS
'42 WAS A	26	65	18	1	1	0	0.0	2	5	3	9	0	.277	.323	7	2	2B-18
4 yrs.	296	935	235	37	5	7	0.7	94	86	56	128	4	.251	.324	14	4	SS-255, 2B-28, 3B-1
3 yrs.	270	870	217	36	4	7	0.8	92	81	53	119	4	.249	.324	7	2	SS-255, 2B-10, 3B-1
WORLD SERIES																	
'40 DET A	1	0	0	0	0	0	–	0	0	0	0	0	–	–	0	0	SS-1

Roy Cullenbine

CULLENBINE, ROY JOSEPH
B. Oct. 18, 1915, Nashville, Tenn.
BB TR 6'1" 195 lbs.
BL 1938,1941

	G	AB	H	2B	3B	HR	HR %	R	RBI	BB	SO	SB	BA	SA	PH AB	PH H	G by POS
'38 DET A	25	67	19	1	3	0	0.0	12	9	12	9	2	.284	.388	7	2	OF-17
'39	75	179	43	9	2	6	3.4	31	23	34	29	0	.240	.413	25	7	OF-46, 1B-2
'40 2 teams		BKN N (22G – .180)			STL A (86G – .230)												
total	108	318	70	12	2	8	2.5	49	40	73	45	2	.220	.346	21	3	OF-76, 1B-6
'41 STL A	149	501	159	29	9	9	1.8	82	98	121	43	6	.317	.465	9	3	OF-120, 1B-22
'42 3 teams		STL A (38G – .193)		WAS A (64G – .286)			NY A (21G – .364)										
total	123	427	118	33	1	6	1.4	61	66	92	40	1	.276	.400	6	1	OF-77, 3B-28, 1B-6
'43 CLE A	138	488	141	24	4	8	1.6	66	56	96	58	3	.289	.404	5	0	OF-121, 1B-13
'44	154	571	162	34	5	16	2.8	98	80	87	49	4	.284	.445	2	0	OF-151
'45 2 teams		CLE A (8G – .077)		DET A (146G – .277)													
total	154	536	146	28	5	18	3.4	83	93	112	36	2	.272	.444	1	0	OF-150, 3B-3
'46 DET A	113	328	110	21	0	15	4.6	63	56	88	39	3	.335	.537	9	2	OF-81, 1B-21
'47	142	464	104	18	1	24	5.2	82	78	137	51	3	.224	.422	4	0	1B-138
10 yrs.	1181	3879	1072	209	32	110	2.8	627	599	852	399	26	.276	.432	89	18	OF-839, 1B-208, 3B-31
5 yrs.	501	1561	421	76	11	63	4.0	268	259	372	164	10	.270	.454	45	11	OF-290, 1B-161
WORLD SERIES																	
'42 NY A	5	19	5	1	0	0	0.0	3	2	1	2	1	.263	.316	0	0	OF-5
'45 DET A	7	22	5	2	0	0	0.0	5	4	8	2	1	.227	.318	0	0	OF-7
2 yrs.	12	41	10	3	0	0	0.0	8	6	9	4	2	.244	.317	0	0	OF-12

George Cunningham

CUNNINGHAM, GEORGE HAROLD
B. July 13, 1894, Sturgeon Lake, Minn.   D. Mar. 10, 1972, Chattanooga, Tenn.
BR TR 5'11" 185 lbs.

	G	AB	H	2B	3B	HR	HR %	R	RBI	BB	SO	SB	BA	SA	PH AB	PH H	G by POS
'16 DET A	35	41	11	2	2	0	0.0	7	3	8	12	0	.268	.415	0	0	P-35
'17	44	34	6	0	0	1	2.9	5	3	3	13	0	.176	.265	0	0	P-44
'18	56	112	25	4	1	0	0.0	11	2	16	34	2	.223	.277	8	3	P-27, OF-20
'19	26	23	5	0	0	0	0.0	4	5	9	8	0	.217	.217	6	1	P-17
'21	1	0	0	0	0	0	–	0	0	0	0	0	–	–	0	0	OF-1
5 yrs.	162	210	47	6	3	1	0.5	27	13	36	67	2	.224	.295	14	4	P-123, OF-21
5 yrs.	162	210	47	6	3	1	0.5	27	13	36	67	2	.224	.295	14	4	P-123, OF-21

Jim Curry

CURRY, JAMES L.
B. Mar. 10, 1893, Camden, N. J.   D. Aug. 1, 1938, Lakefield, N. J.
BR TR 5'11" 160 lbs.

	G	AB	H	2B	3B	HR	HR %	R	RBI	BB	SO	SB	BA	SA	PH AB	PH H	G by POS
'09 PHI A	1	4	1	0	0	0	0.0	1	0	0		0	.250	.250	0	0	2B-1
'11 NY A	4	11	2	0	0	0	0.0	3	0	1		0	.182	.182	0	0	2B-4
'18 DET A	5	20	5	1	0	0	0.0	1	0	0		0	.250	.300	0	0	2B-5
3 yrs.	10	35	8	1	0	0	0.0	5	0	1	0	0	.229	.257	0	0	2B-10
1 yr.	5	20	5	1	0	0	0.0	1	0	0	0	0	.250	.300	0	0	2B-5

George Cutshaw

CUTSHAW, GEORGE WILLIAM (Clancy)
B. July 29, 1887, Wilmington, Ill.   D. Aug. 22, 1973, San Diego, Calif.
BR TR 5'9" 160 lbs.

	G	AB	H	2B	3B	HR	HR %	R	RBI	BB	SO	SB	BA	SA	PH AB	PH H	G by POS
'12 BKN N	102	357	100	14	4	0	0.0	41	28	31	16	16	.280	.342	5	1	2B-91, 3B-5, SS-1
'13	147	592	158	23	13	7	1.2	72	80	39	22	39	.267	.385	0	0	2B-147
'14	153	583	150	22	12	2	0.3	69	78	30	32	34	.257	.346	0	0	2B-153
'15	154	566	139	18	9	0	0.0	68	62	34	35	28	.246	.309	0	0	2B-154
'16	154	581	151	21	4	2	0.3	58	63	25	32	27	.260	.320	0	0	2B-154
'17	135	487	126	17	7	4	0.8	42	49	21	26	22	.259	.347	1	0	2B-134
'18 PIT N	126	463	132	16	10	5	1.1	56	68	27	18	25	.285	.395	0	0	2B-126
'19	139	512	124	15	8	3	0.6	49	51	30	22	36	.242	.320	0	0	2B-139
'20	131	488	123	16	8	0	0.0	56	47	23	10	17	.252	.318	2	0	2B-129
'21	98	350	119	18	4	0	0.0	46	53	11	11	14	.340	.414	14	2	2B-84
'22 DET A	132	499	133	14	8	2	0.4	57	61	20	13	11	.267	.339	0	0	2B-132
'23	45	143	32	1	2	0	0.0	15	13	9	5	2	.224	.259	0	0	2B-43, 3B-2
12 yrs.	1516	5621	1487	195	89	25	0.4	629	653	300	242	271	.265	.344	22	3	2B-1486, 3B-7, SS-1
2 yrs.	177	642	165	15	10	2	0.3	72	74	29	18	13	.257	.321	0	0	2B-175, 3B-2
WORLD SERIES																	
'16 BKN N	5	19	2	1	0	0	0.0	2	2	1	1	0	.105	.158	0	0	2B-5

Jack Dalton

DALTON, TALBOT PERCY
B. July 3, 1885, Henderson, Tenn.
BR TR 5'10½" 187 lbs.

	G	AB	H	2B	3B	HR	HR %	R	RBI	BB	SO	SB	BA	SA	PH AB	PH H	G by POS
'10 BKN N	77	273	62	9	4	1	0.4	33	21	26	30	5	.227	.300	4	1	OF-72
'14	128	442	141	13	8	1	0.2	65	45	53	39	19	.319	.391	10	4	OF-116
'15 BUF F	132	437	128	17	3	2	0.5	68	46	50		28	.293	.359	12	4	OF-119
'16 DET A	8	11	2	0	0	0	0.0	1	0	0	5	0	.182	.182	2	1	OF-4
4 yrs.	345	1163	333	39	15	4	0.3	167	112	129	74	52	.286	.356	28	10	OF-311
1 yr.	8	11	2	0	0	0	0.0	1	0	0	5	0	.182	.182	2	1	OF-4

Doc Daugherty

DAUGHERTY, HAROLD RAY
B. Oct. 12, 1927, Paris, Pa.
BR TR 6' 180 lbs.

	G	AB	H	2B	3B	HR	HR %	R	RBI	BB	SO	SB	BA	SA	PH AB	PH H	G by POS
'51 DET A	1	1	0	0	0	0	0	0	0	1	0	.000	.000	1	0		

Harry Davis

DAVIS, HARRY ALBERT (Stinky)
B. May 7, 1908, Shreveport, La.
BL TL 5'10½" 175 lbs.

	G	AB	H	2B	3B	HR	HR %	R	RBI	BB	SO	SB	BA	SA	PH AB	PH H	G by POS
'32 DET A	140	590	159	32	13	4	0.7	92	74	60	53	12	.269	.388	0	0	1B-140
'33	66	173	37	8	2	0	0.0	24	14	22	8	2	.214	.283	19	3	1B-44

	G	AB	H	2B	3B	HR	HR %	R	RBI	BB	SO	SB	BA	SA	Pinch Hit AB	Pinch Hit H	G by POS

Harry Davis continued

	G	AB	H	2B	3B	HR	HR%	R	RBI	BB	SO	SB	BA	SA	PH AB	PH H	G by POS
1937 STL A	120	450	124	25	3	3	0.7	89	35	71	26	7	.276	.364	7	2	1B-112, OF-1
3 yrs.	326	1213	320	65	18	7	0.6	205	123	153	87	21	.264	.364	26	5	1B-296, OF-1
2 yrs.	206	763	196	40	15	4	0.5	116	88	82	61	14	.257	.364	19	3	1B-184

Charlie Deal

DEAL, CHARLES ALBERT   BR TR 5'11"   160 lbs.
B. Oct. 30, 1891, Wilkinsburg, Pa.   D. Sept. 16, 1979, Covina, Calif.

	G	AB	H	2B	3B	HR	HR%	R	RBI	BB	SO	SB	BA	SA	PH AB	PH H	G by POS
1912 DET A	41	142	32	4	2	0	0.0	13	11	9		4	.225	.282	0	0	3B-41
1913 2 teams		DET	A (16G – .220)			BOS	N (10G – .306)										
" total	26	86	22	1	2	0	0.0	9	6	3	8	3	.256	.314	1	0	3B-15, 2B-10
1914 BOS N	79	257	54	13	2	0	0.0	17	23	20	23	4	.210	.276	4	0	3B-74, SS-1
1915 STL F	65	223	72	12	4	1	0.4	21	27	12		10	.323	.426	0	0	3B-65
1916 2 teams		STL	A (23G – .135)			CHI	N (2G – .250)										
" total	25	82	12	2	0	0	0.0	9	13	6	8	4	.146	.171	0	0	3B-24, 2B-1
1917 CHI N	135	449	114	11	3	0	0.0	46	47	19	18	10	.254	.292	5	1	3B-130
1918	119	414	99	9	3	2	0.5	43	34	21	13	11	.239	.290	1	0	3B-118
1919	116	405	117	23	5	2	0.5	57	52	12	12	11	.289	.385	0	0	3B-116
1920	129	450	108	10	5	3	0.7	48	39	20	14	5	.240	.304	1	1	3B-128
1921	115	422	122	19	8	3	0.7	52	66	13	9	3	.289	.393	2	0	3B-113
10 yrs.	850	2930	752	104	34	11	0.4	295	318	135	105	65	.257	.327	14	2	3B-824, 2B-11, SS-1
2 yrs.	57	192	43	4	4	0	0.0	16	14	10	7	6	.224	.286	1	0	3B-56

WORLD SERIES

	G	AB	H	2B	3B	HR	HR%	R	RBI	BB	SO	SB	BA	SA	PH AB	PH H	G by POS
1914 BOS N	4	16	2	2	0	0	0.0	1	0	0	0	2	.125	.250	0	0	3B-4
1918 CHI N	6	17	3	0	0	0	0.0	0	0	0	1	0	.176	.176	0	0	3B-6
2 yrs.	10	33	5	2	0	0	0.0	1	0	0	1	2	.152	.212	0	0	3B-10

Tony DeFate

DeFATE, CLYDE HERBERT   BR TR 5'8½"   158 lbs.
B. Feb. 22, 1898, Kansas City, Mo.   D. Sept. 3, 1963, New Orleans, La.

	G	AB	H	2B	3B	HR	HR%	R	RBI	BB	SO	SB	BA	SA	PH AB	PH H	G by POS
1917 2 teams		STL	N (14G – .143)			DET	A (3G – .000)										
" total	17	16	2	0	0	0	0.0	1	1	4	6	1	.125	.125	6	1	3B-5, 2B-2

Mark DeJohn

DeJOHN, MARK STEPHEN   BB TR 5'11"   170 lbs.
B. Sept. 18, 1953, Middletown, Conn.

	G	AB	H	2B	3B	HR	HR%	R	RBI	BB	SO	SB	BA	SA	PH AB	PH H	G by POS
1982 DET A	24	21	4	2	0	0	0.0	1	1	4	4	1	.190	.286	0	0	SS-20, 3B-4, 2B-1

Jim Delahanty

DELAHANTY, JAMES CHRISTOPHER   BR TR 5'10½" 170 lbs.
Brother of Ed Delahanty.   Brother of Frank Delahanty.
Brother of Tom Delahanty.   Brother of Joe Delahanty.
B. June 20, 1879, Cleveland, Ohio   D. Oct. 17, 1953, Cleveland, Ohio

	G	AB	H	2B	3B	HR	HR%	R	RBI	BB	SO	SB	BA	SA	PH AB	PH H	G by POS
1901 CHI N	17	63	12	2	0	0	0.0	4	4	3		5	.190	.222	0	0	3B-17, 2B-1
1902 NY N	7	26	6	1	0	0	0.0	3	3	1		0	.231	.269	0	0	OF-7
1904 BOS N	142	499	142	27	8	3	0.6	56	60	27		16	.285	.389	0	0	3B-113, 2B-18, OF-9, P-
1905	125	461	119	11	8	5	1.1	50	55	28		12	.258	.349	1	0	OF-124, P-1
1906 CIN N	115	379	106	21	4	1	0.3	63	39	45		21	.280	.364	3	1	3B-105, SS-5, OF-2
1907 2 teams		STL	A (33G – .221)			WAS	A (109G – .292)										
" total	142	499	139	21	7	2	0.4	52	60	41		24	.279	.361	8	0	2B-70, 3B-48, OF-13, 1
1908 WAS A	83	287	91	11	4	1	0.3	33	30	24		16	.317	.394	2	0	2B-79
1909 2 teams		WAS	A (90G – .222)			DET	A (46G – .253)										
" total	136	452	105	23	6	1	0.2	47	41	40		13	.232	.316	5	0	2B-131
1910 DET A	106	378	111	16	3	2	0.5	67	45	43		15	.294	.368	0	0	2B-106
1911	144	542	184	30	14	3	0.6	83	94	56		15	.339	.463	1	0	1B-72, 2B-59, 3B-12
1912	78	266	76	14	1	0	0.0	34	41	42		9	.286	.346	1	0	2B-44, OF-33
1914 BKN F	74	214	62	13	5	0	0.0	28	15	25		4	.290	.397	13	2	2B-55, 1B-5
1915	17	25	6	1	0	0	0.0	0	2	3		1	.240	.280	11	1	2B-4
13 yrs.	1186	4091	1159	191	60	18	0.4	520	489	378		151	.283	.373	45	4	2B-567, 3B-295, OF-188, 1B-81, SS-5, P-2
4 yrs.	374	1336	409	70	19	5	0.4	213	200	158		48	.306	.398	2	0	2B-255, 1B-72, OF-33, 3B-12

WORLD SERIES

	G	AB	H	2B	3B	HR	HR%	R	RBI	BB	SO	SB	BA	SA	PH AB	PH H	G by POS
1909 DET A	7	26	9	4	0	0	0.0	2	4	2	5	0	.346	.500	0	0	2B-7

Jim Delsing

DELSING, JAMES HENRY   BL TR 5'10"   175 lbs.
B. Nov. 13, 1925, Rudolph, Wis.

	G	AB	H	2B	3B	HR	HR%	R	RBI	BB	SO	SB	BA	SA	PH AB	PH H	G by POS
1948 CHI A	20	63	12	0	0	0	0.0	5	5	5	12	0	.190	.190	4	0	OF-15
1949 NY A	9	20	7	1	0	1	5.0	5	3	1	2	0	.350	.550	4	2	OF-5
1950 2 teams		NY	A (12G – .400)			STL	A (69G – .263)										
" total	81	219	59	5	2	0	0.0	27	17	22	23	1	.269	.311	24	8	OF-53
1951 STL A	131	449	112	20	2	8	1.8	59	45	56	39	2	.249	.356	4	1	OF-124
1952 2 teams		STL	A (93G – .255)			DET	A (33G – .274)										
" total	126	411	107	15	7	4	1.0	48	49	36	37	4	.260	.360	11	4	OF-117
1953 DET A	138	479	138	26	6	11	2.3	77	62	66	39	1	.288	.436	6	1	OF-133
1954	122	371	92	24	2	6	1.6	39	38	49	38	4	.248	.372	13	5	OF-108
1955	114	356	85	14	2	10	2.8	49	60	48	40	2	.239	.374	14	3	OF-101
1956 2 teams		DET	A (10G – .000)			CHI	A (55G – .122)										
" total	65	53	5	3	0	0	0.0	11	2	13	16	1	.094	.151	21	3	OF-32
1960 KC A	16	40	10	3	0	0	0.0	2	2	5	3	0	.250	.325	6	1	OF-10
10 yrs.	822	2461	627	111	21	40	1.6	322	286	299	251	15	.255	.366	107	28	OF-698
5 yrs.	417	1331	346	66	11	30	2.3	179	175	177	128	8	.260	.394	38	10	OF-377

Don Demeter

DEMETER, DONALD LEE   BR TR 6'4"   190 lbs.
B. June 25, 1935, Oklahoma City, Okla.

	G	AB	H	2B	3B	HR	HR%	R	RBI	BB	SO	SB	BA	SA	PH AB	PH H	G by POS
1956 BKN N	3	3	1	0	0	1	33.3	1	1	0	1	0	.333	1.333	2	0	OF-1
1958 LA N	43	106	20	2	0	5	4.7	11	8	5	32	2	.189	.349	4	0	OF-39
1959	139	371	95	11	1	18	4.9	55	70	16	87	5	.256	.437	22	3	OF-124
1960	64	168	46	7	1	9	5.4	23	29	8	34	0	.274	.488	8	2	OF-62
1961 2 teams		LA	N (15G – .172)			PHI	N (106G – .257)										
" total	121	411	103	18	4	21	5.1	57	70	22	80	2	.251	.467	13	2	OF-93, 1B-22
1962 PHI N	153	550	169	24	3	29	5.3	85	107	41	93	2	.307	.520	6	2	3B-105, OF-63, 1B-1

	G	AB	H	2B	3B	HR	HR %	R	RBI	BB	SO	SB	BA	SA	Pinch Hit AB	Pinch Hit H	G by POS

Don Demeter continued

	G	AB	H	2B	3B	HR	HR %	R	RBI	BB	SO	SB	BA	SA	AB	H	G by POS
963	154	515	133	20	2	22	4.3	63	83	31	93	1	.258	.433	11	2	OF-119, 3B-43, 1B-26
964 DET A	134	441	113	22	1	22	5.0	57	80	17	85	4	.256	.460	27	5	OF-88, 1B-23
965	122	389	108	16	4	16	4.1	50	58	23	65	4	.278	.463	15	6	OF-81, 1B-34
966 2 teams		DET	A (32G –	.212)		BOS	A (73G –	.292)									
" total	105	325	87	18	1	14	4.3	43	41	8	61	2	.268	.458	21	2	OF-84, 1B-6
967 2 teams		BOS	A (20G –	.279)		CLE	A (51G –	.207)									
" total	71	164	37	9	0	6	3.7	22	16	9	27	0	.226	.390	26	7	OF-47, 3B-2
11 yrs.	1109	3443	912	147	17	163	4.7	467	563	180	658	22	.265	.459	155	31	OF-801, 3B-150, 1B-112
3 yrs.	288	929	242	43	5	43	4.6	119	150	43	169	9	.260	.456	46	11	OF-196, 1B-61
WORLD SERIES																	
959 LA N	6	12	3	0	0	0	0.0	2	0	1	3	0	.250	.250	0	0	OF-6

Steve Demeter

DEMETER, STEPHEN
B. Jan. 27, 1935, Homer City, Pa.
BR TR 5'9½" 185 lbs.

	G	AB	H	2B	3B	HR	HR %	R	RBI	BB	SO	SB	BA	SA	AB	H	G by POS
959 DET A	11	18	2	1	0	0	0.0	1	1	0	1	0	.111	.167	9	1	3B-4
960 CLE A	4	5	0	0	0	0	0.0	0	0	0	1	0	.000	.000	2	0	3B-3
2 yrs.	15	23	2	1	0	0	0.0	1	1	0	2	0	.087	.130	11	1	3B-7
1 yr.	11	18	2	1	0	0	0.0	1	1	0	1	0	.111	.167	9	1	3B-4

Ray Demmitt

DEMMITT, CHARLES RAYMOND
B. Feb. 2, 1884, Illiopolis, Ill.   D. Feb. 19, 1956, Glen Ellyn, Ill.
BL TR 5'8½" 170 lbs.

	G	AB	H	2B	3B	HR	HR %	R	RBI	BB	SO	SB	BA	SA	AB	H	G by POS
909 NY A	123	427	105	12	12	4	0.9	68	30	55		16	.246	.358	0	0	OF-109
910 STL A	10	23	4	1	0	0	0.0	4	2	3		0	.174	.217	2	0	OF-8
914 2 teams		DET	A (1G –	.000)		CHI	A (146G –	.258)									
" total	147	515	133	13	12	2	0.4	63	46	61	48	12	.258	.342	3	1	OF-142
915 CHI A	9	6	0	0	0	0	0.0	0	0	1	2	0	.000	.000	6	0	OF-3
917 STL A	14	53	15	1	2	0	0.0	6	7	0	8	1	.283	.377	0	0	OF-14
918	116	405	114	23	5	1	0.2	45	61	38	35	10	.281	.370	1	0	OF-114
919	79	202	48	11	2	1	0.5	19	19	14	27	3	.238	.327	27	6	OF-49
7 yrs.	498	1631	419	61	33	8	0.5	205	165	172	120	42	.257	.349	39	7	OF-439
1 yr.	1	0	0	0	0	0	–	0	0	0	0	0	–	–	0	0	

Gene Desautels

DESAUTELS, EUGENE ABRAHAM (Red)
B. June 13, 1907, Worcester, Mass.
BR TR 5'11" 170 lbs.

	G	AB	H	2B	3B	HR	HR %	R	RBI	BB	SO	SB	BA	SA	AB	H	G by POS
930 DET A	42	126	24	4	2	0	0.0	13	9	7	9	2	.190	.254	0	0	C-42
931	3	11	1	0	0	0	0.0	1	0	1	1	0	.091	.091	0	0	C-3
932	28	72	17	2	0	0	0.0	8	2	13	11	0	.236	.264	3	0	C-24
933	30	42	6	1	0	0	0.0	5	4	4	6	0	.143	.167	0	0	C-30
937 BOS A	96	305	74	10	3	0	0.0	33	27	36	26	1	.243	.295	1	1	C-94
938	108	333	97	16	2	2	0.6	47	48	57	31	1	.291	.369	0	0	C-108
939	76	226	55	14	0	0	0.0	26	21	33	13	3	.243	.305	2	1	C-73
940	71	222	50	7	1	0	0.0	19	17	32	13	0	.225	.266	0	0	C-70
941 CLE A	66	189	38	5	1	1	0.5	20	17	14	12	1	.201	.254	0	0	C-66
942	62	162	40	5	0	0	0.0	14	9	12	13	1	.247	.278	1	0	C-61
943	68	185	38	6	1	0	0.0	14	19	11	16	2	.205	.249	2	0	C-66
945	10	9	1	0	0	0	0.0	1	0	1	1	0	.111	.111	0	0	C-10
946 PHI A	52	130	28	3	1	0	0.0	10	13	12	16	1	.215	.254	0	0	C-52
13 yrs.	712	2012	469	73	11	3	0.1	211	186	233	168	12	.233	.285	9	2	C-699
4 yrs.	103	251	48	7	2	0	0.0	27	15	25	27	2	.191	.235	3	0	C-99

Bernie DeViveiros

DeVIVEIROS, BERNARD JOHN
B. Apr. 19, 1901, Oakland, Calif.
BR TR 5'7" 160 lbs.

	G	AB	H	2B	3B	HR	HR %	R	RBI	BB	SO	SB	BA	SA	AB	H	G by POS
924 CHI A	1	1	0	0	0	0	0.0	0	0	0	0	0	.000	.000	0	0	SS-1
927 DET A	24	22	5	1	0	0	0.0	4	2	2	8	1	.227	.273	2	0	SS-14, 3B-1
2 yrs.	25	23	5	1	0	0	0.0	4	2	2	8	1	.217	.261	2	0	SS-15, 3B-1
1 yr.	24	22	5	1	0	0	0.0	4	2	2	8	1	.227	.273	2	0	SS-14, 3B-1

Bob Didier

DIDIER, ROBERT DANIEL
B. Feb. 16, 1949, Hattiesburg, Miss.
BB TR 6' 190 lbs.

	G	AB	H	2B	3B	HR	HR %	R	RBI	BB	SO	SB	BA	SA	AB	H	G by POS
969 ATL N	114	352	90	16	1	0	0.0	30	32	34	39	1	.256	.307	0	0	C-114
970	57	168	25	2	1	0	0.0	9	7	12	11	1	.149	.173	0	0	C-57
971	51	155	34	4	1	0	0.0	9	5	6	17	0	.219	.258	2	1	C-50
972	13	40	12	2	1	0	0.0	5	5	2	4	0	.300	.400	2	0	C-11
973 DET A	7	22	10	1	0	0	0.0	3	1	3	0	0	.455	.500	0	0	C-7
974 BOS A	5	14	1	0	0	0	0.0	0	1	2	1	0	.071	.071	0	0	C-5
6 yrs.	247	751	172	25	4	0	0.0	56	51	59	72	2	.229	.273	4	1	C-244
1 yr.	7	22	10	1	0	0	0.0	3	1	3	0	0	.455	.500	0	0	C-7

| LEAGUE CHAMPIONSHIP SERIES | | | | | | | | | | | | | | | | | |
| 969 ATL N | 3 | 11 | 0 | 0 | 0 | 0 | 0.0 | 0 | 0 | 0 | 2 | 0 | .000 | .000 | 0 | 0 | C-3 |

Steve Dillard

DILLARD, STEPHEN BRADLEY
B. Dec. 8, 1951, Memphis, Tenn.
BR TR 6'1" 171 lbs.

	G	AB	H	2B	3B	HR	HR %	R	RBI	BB	SO	SB	BA	SA	AB	H	G by POS
975 BOS A	1	5	2	0	0	0	0.0	2	0	0	0	1	.400	.400	0	0	2B-1
976	57	167	46	14	0	1	0.6	22	15	17	20	6	.275	.377	3	1	3B-18, 2B-17, SS-12, DH-7
977	66	141	34	7	0	1	0.7	22	13	7	13	4	.241	.312	7	1	2B-45, SS-9, DH-6
978 DET A	56	130	29	5	2	0	0.0	21	7	6	11	1	.223	.292	1	0	2B-41, DH-4
979 CHI N	89	166	47	6	1	5	3.0	31	24	17	24	1	.283	.422	17	6	2B-60, 3B-9
980	100	244	55	8	1	4	1.6	31	27	20	54	2	.225	.316	13	3	3B-51, 2B-38, SS-2
981	53	119	26	7	1	2	1.7	18	11	8	20	0	.218	.345	11	3	2B-32, 3B-7, SS-2
982 CHI A	16	41	7	3	1	0	0.0	1	5	1	5	0	.171	.293	0	0	2B-16
8 yrs.	438	1013	246	50	6	13	1.3	148	102	76	147	15	.243	.343	52	14	2B-250, 3B-85, SS-25, DH-17
1 yr.	56	130	29	5	2	0	0.0	21	7	6	11	1	.223	.292	1	0	2B-41, DH-4

	G	AB	H	2B	3B	HR	HR %	R	RBI	BB	SO	SB	BA	SA	Pinch Hit AB	H	G by POS

Pop Dillon

DILLON, FRANK EDWARD
B. Oct. 17, 1873, Normal, Ill.   D. Sept. 12, 1931, Pasadena, Calif.   BL TR

	G	AB	H	2B	3B	HR	HR%	R	RBI	BB	SO	SB	BA	SA	AB	H	G by POS
1899 PIT N	30	121	31	5	0	0	0.0	21	20	5		5	.256	.298	0	0	1B-30
1900	5	18	2	1	0	0	0.0	3	1	0		0	.111	.167	0	0	1B-5
1901 DET A	74	281	81	14	6	1	0.4	40	42	15		14	.288	.391	0	0	1B-74
1902 2 teams					DET	A	(66G –	.206)		BAL	A	(2G –	.286)				
" total	68	250	52	6	4	0	0.0	22	22	18		2	.208	.264	0	0	1B-68
1904 BKN N	135	511	132	18	6	0	0.0	60	31	40		13	.258	.317	0	0	1B-134
5 yrs.	312	1181	298	44	16	1	0.1	146	116	78		34	.252	.319	0	0	1B-311
2 yrs.	140	524	131	20	9	1	0.2	61	64	31		16	.250	.328	0	0	1B-140

Jack Dittmer

DITTMER, JOHN DOUGLAS
B. Jan. 10, 1928, Elkader, Iowa   BL TR 6'1"   175 lbs.

	G	AB	H	2B	3B	HR	HR%	R	RBI	BB	SO	SB	BA	SA	AB	H	G by POS
1952 BOS N	93	326	63	7	2	7	2.1	26	41	26	26	1	.193	.291	3	0	2B-90
1953 MIL N	138	504	134	22	1	9	1.8	54	63	18	35	1	.266	.367	0	0	2B-138
1954	66	192	47	8	0	6	3.1	22	20	19	17	0	.245	.380	11	2	2B-55
1955	38	72	9	1	1	1	1.4	4	4	4	15	0	.125	.208	11	1	2B-28
1956	44	102	25	4	0	1	1.0	8	6	8	8	0	.245	.314	4	2	2B-42
1957 DET A	16	22	5	1	0	0	0.0	3	2	2	1	0	.227	.273	12	4	3B-3, 2B-1
6 yrs.	395	1218	283	43	4	24	2.0	117	136	77	102	2	.232	.333	41	9	2B-354, 3B-3
1 yr.	16	22	5	1	0	0	0.0	3	2	2	1	0	.227	.273	12	4	3B-3, 2B-1

Larry Doby

DOBY, LAWRENCE EUGENE
B. Dec. 13, 1923, Camden, S. C.   BL TR 6'1"   180 lbs.
Manager 1978.

	G	AB	H	2B	3B	HR	HR%	R	RBI	BB	SO	SB	BA	SA	AB	H	G by POS
1947 CLE A	29	32	5	1	0	0	0.0	3	2	1	11	0	.156	.188	21	4	2B-4, SS-1, 1B-1
1948	121	439	132	23	9	14	3.2	83	66	54	77	9	.301	.490	6	2	OF-114
1949	147	547	153	25	3	24	4.4	106	85	91	90	10	.280	.468	0	0	OF-147
1950	142	503	164	25	5	25	5.0	110	102	98	71	8	.326	.545	2	1	OF-140
1951	134	447	132	27	5	20	4.5	84	69	101	81	4	.295	.512	2	0	OF-132
1952	140	519	143	26	8	**32**	6.2	**104**	104	90	**111**	5	.276	**.541**	3	1	OF-136
1953	149	513	135	18	5	29	5.7	92	102	96	**121**	3	.263	.487	3	1	OF-146
1954	153	577	157	18	4	**32**	5.5	94	**126**	85	94	3	.272	.484	0	0	OF-153
1955	131	491	143	17	5	26	5.3	91	75	61	100	2	.291	.505	2	0	OF-129
1956 CHI A	140	504	135	22	3	24	4.8	89	102	102	105	0	.268	.466	3	1	OF-137
1957	119	416	120	27	2	14	3.4	57	79	56	79	2	.288	.464	9	1	OF-110
1958 CLE A	89	247	70	10	1	13	5.3	41	45	26	49	0	.283	.490	18	5	OF-68
1959 2 teams	39	DET	A	(18G –	.218)			CHI	A	(21G –	.241)						
" total	39	113	26	4	2	0	0.0	6	12	10	22	1	.230	.301	9	2	OF-28, 1B-2
13 yrs.	1533	5348	1515	243	52	253	4.7	960	969	871	1011	47	.283	.490	78	18	OF-1440, 2B-4, 3B-3, SS-1
1 yr.	18	55	12	3	1	0	0.0	5	3	8	9	0	.218	.309	1	0	OF-16
WORLD SERIES
1948 CLE A	6	22	7	1	0	1	4.5	1	2	2	4	0	.318	.500	0	0	OF-6
1954	4	16	2	0	0	0	0.0	0	0	2	4	0	.125	.125	0	0	OF-4
2 yrs.	10	38	9	1	0	1	2.6	1	2	4	8	0	.237	.342	0	0	OF-10

Frank Doljack

DOLJACK, FRANK JOSEPH
B. Oct. 5, 1907, Cleveland, Ohio   D. Jan. 23, 1948, Cleveland, Ohio   BR TR 5'11"   175 lbs.

	G	AB	H	2B	3B	HR	HR%	R	RBI	BB	SO	SB	BA	SA	AB	H	G by POS
1930 DET A	20	74	19	5	1	3	4.1	10	17	2	11	0	.257	.473	0	0	OF-20
1931	63	187	52	13	3	4	2.1	20	20	15	17	3	.278	.444	7	0	OF-54
1932	8	26	10	1	0	1	3.8	5	7	2	2	1	.385	.538	1	0	OF-6
1933	42	147	42	5	2	0	0.0	18	22	14	13	2	.286	.347	5	1	OF-37
1934	56	120	28	7	1	1	0.8	15	19	13	15	2	.233	.333	22	4	OF-30, 1B-3
1943 CLE A	3	7	0	0	0	0	0.0	0	0	1	2	0	.000	.000	1	0	OF-3
6 yrs.	192	561	151	31	7	9	1.6	68	85	47	60	8	.269	.398	36	5	OF-150, 1B-3
5 yrs.	189	554	151	31	7	9	1.6	68	85	46	58	8	.273	.403	35	5	OF-147, 1B-3
WORLD SERIES
1934 DET A	2	2	0	0	0	0	0.0	0	0	0	0	0	.000	.000	1	0	OF-1

Wild Bill Donovan

DONOVAN, WILLIAM EDWARD
B. Oct. 13, 1876, Lawrence, Mass.   D. Dec. 9, 1923, Forsyth, N. Y.   BR TR 5'11"   190 lbs.
Manager 1915-17, 1921.

	G	AB	H	2B	3B	HR	HR%	R	RBI	BB	SO	SB	BA	SA	AB	H	G by POS
1898 WAS N	39	103	17	2	3	1	1.0	11	8	4		2	.165	.272	2	1	OF-20, P-17, SS-1, 2B-1
1899 BKN N	5	13	3	1	0	0	0.0	2	0	0		0	.231	.308	0	0	P-5
1900	5	13	0	0	0	0	0.0	0	2	0		0	.000	.000	0	0	P-5
1901	46	135	23	3	0	2	1.5	16	13	8		1	.170	.237	0	0	P-45
1902	48	161	27	3	2	1	0.6	16	16	9		7	.168	.230	0	0	P-35, 1B-8, OF-4, 2B-1
1903 DET A	40	124	30	3	2	0	0.0	11	12	4		3	.242	.298	2	0	P-35, SS-2, OF-1, 2B-1
1904	46	140	38	2	1	0	0.7	12	6	3		2	.271	.321	2	1	P-34, 1B-8, OF-1
1905	46	130	25	4	0	0	0.0	16	5	12		8	.192	.223	0	0	P-34, OF-8, 2B-2
1906	28	91	11	0	1	0	0.0	5	0	1		6	.121	.143	0	0	P-25, 2B-3, OF-1
1907	37	109	29	7	2	0	0.0	20	19	6		4	.266	.367	4	0	P-32
1908	30	82	13	1	0	0	0.0	5	2	10		2	.159	.171	0	0	P-29
1909	22	45	9	0	0	0	0.0	6	1	2		0	.200	.200	0	0	P-21
1910	26	69	10	1	0	0	0.0	6	2	5		0	.145	.159	0	0	P-26
1911	24	60	12	3	1	1	1.7	11	6	11		0	.200	.333	1	1	P-20
1912	6	13	1	0	0	0	0.0	3	0	1		0	.077	.077	0	0	P-3, OF-2, 1B-2
1915 NY A	10	12	1	0	0	0	0.0	1	0	1	6	0	.083	.083	0	0	P-9
1916	1	0	0	0	0	0	–	0	0	0	0	0	–	–	0	0	P-1
1918 DET A	2	2	1	0	0	0	0.0	1	1	0	0	0	.500	.500	0	0	P-2
18 yrs.	461	1302	250	30	12	6	0.5	142	93	77	6	36	.192	.247	11	3	P-378, OF-37, 1B-18, 2B-8, SS-3
11 yrs.	307	865	179	21	7	2	0.2	96	54	55		26	.207	.254	9	2	P-261, OF-13, 1B-10, 2B-6, SS-2
WORLD SERIES
1907 DET A	2	8	0	0	0	0	0.0	0	0	0	3	0	.000	.000	0	0	P-2

	G	AB	H	2B	3B	HR	HR %	R	RBI	BB	SO	SB	BA	SA	Pinch Hit AB	Pinch Hit H	G by POS

Wild Bill Donovan continued

'08	2	4	0	0	0	0	0.0	0	0	1	1	1	.000	.000	0	0	P-2
'09	2	4	0	0	0	0	0.0	0	0	0	1	0	.000	.000	0	0	P-2
3 yrs.	6	16	0	0	0	0	0.0	0	0	1	5	1	.000	.000	0	0	P-6

Tom Doran

DORAN, THOMAS J.
B. Feb. 2, 1880, Westchester County, N. Y.   D. June 22, 1910, New York, N. Y.   TL

	G	AB	H	2B	3B	HR	HR %	R	RBI	BB	SO	SB	BA	SA	AB	H	G by POS
'04 BOS A	12	32	4	0	1	0	0.0	1	0	4		1	.125	.188	1	0	C-11
'05 2 teams		BOS A (2G – .000)				DET A (34G – .160)											
'' total	36	96	15	3	0	0	0.0	8	4	8		2	.156	.188	3	1	C-33
'06 BOS A	2	3	0	0	0	0	0.0	1	0	0		0	.000	.000	0	0	C-2
3 yrs.	50	131	19	3	1	0	0.0	10	4	12		3	.145	.183	4	1	C-46
1 yr.	34	94	15	3	0	0	0.0	8	4	8		2	.160	.191	2	1	C-32

Snooks Dowd

DOWD, RAYMOND BERNARD
B. Dec. 20, 1897, Springfield, Mass.   D. Apr. 4, 1962, Springfield, Mass.   BR TR 5'8" 163 lbs.

	G	AB	H	2B	3B	HR	HR %	R	RBI	BB	SO	SB	BA	SA	AB	H	G by POS
'19 2 teams		DET A (1G – .000)				PHI A (13G – .167)											
'' total	14	18	3	0	0	0	0.0	4	6	0	5	2	.167	.167	1	0	2B-3, SS-2, OF-1, 3B-1
'26 BKN N	2	8	0	0	0	0	0.0	0	0	0	0	0	.000	.000	0	0	2B-2
2 yrs.	16	26	3	0	0	0	0.0	4	6	0	5	2	.115	.115	1	0	2B-5, SS-2, OF-1, 3B-1
1 yr.	1	0	0	0	0	0	–	0	0	0	0	0	–	–	0	0	

Red Downs

DOWNS, JEROME WILLIS
B. Aug. 23, 1883, Neola, Iowa   D. Oct. 19, 1939, Council Bluffs, Iowa   BR TR

	G	AB	H	2B	3B	HR	HR %	R	RBI	BB	SO	SB	BA	SA	AB	H	G by POS
'07 DET A	105	374	82	13	5	1	0.3	28	42	13		3	.219	.289	4	1	2B-80, OF-20, SS-1, 3B-1
'08	84	289	64	10	3	1	0.3	29	35	5		2	.221	.287	1	0	2B-82, 3B-1
'12 2 teams		BKN N (9G – .250)				CHI N (43G – .263)											
'' total	52	127	33	7	3	1	0.8	11	17	10	22	8	.260	.386	11	2	2B-25, SS-9, 3B-5
3 yrs.	241	790	179	30	11	3	0.4	68	94	28	22	13	.227	.304	16	3	2B-187, OF-20, SS-10, 3B-7
2 yrs.	189	663	146	23	8	2	0.3	57	77	18		5	.220	.288	5	1	2B-162, OF-20, 3B-2, SS-1
WORLD SERIES																	
'08 DET A	2	6	1	1	0	0	0.0	1	1	1	2	0	.167	.333	0	0	2B-2

Delos Drake

DRAKE, DELOS DANIEL
B. Dec. 3, 1886, Girard, Ohio   D. Oct. 3, 1965, Findlay, Ohio   BR TL 5'11½" 170 lbs.

	G	AB	H	2B	3B	HR	HR %	R	RBI	BB	SO	SB	BA	SA	AB	H	G by POS
'11 DET A	91	315	88	9	9	1	0.3	37	36	17		20	.279	.375	9	3	OF-83, 1B-2
'14 STL F	138	514	129	18	8	3	0.6	51	42	31		17	.251	.335	4	0	OF-116, 1B-18
'15	102	343	91	23	4	1	0.3	32	41	23		6	.265	.364	4	0	OF-99, 1B-1
3 yrs.	331	1172	308	50	21	5	0.4	120	119	71		43	.263	.354	17	3	OF-298, 1B-21
1 yr.	91	315	88	9	9	1	0.3	37	36	17		20	.279	.375	9	3	OF-83, 1B-2

Lee Dressen

DRESSEN, LEE AUGUST
B. July 23, 1889, Ellinwood, Kans.   D. June 30, 1931, Diller, Neb.   BL TL 6' 165 lbs.

	G	AB	H	2B	3B	HR	HR %	R	RBI	BB	SO	SB	BA	SA	AB	H	G by POS
'14 STL N	46	103	24	2	1	0	0.0	16	7	11	20	2	.233	.272	7	1	1B-38
'18 DET A	31	107	19	1	2	0	0.0	10	3	21	10	2	.178	.224	1	0	1B-30
2 yrs.	77	210	43	3	3	0	0.0	26	10	32	30	4	.205	.248	8	1	1B-68
1 yr.	31	107	19	1	2	0	0.0	10	3	21	10	2	.178	.224	1	0	1B-30

Lew Drill

DRILL, LEWIS L
B. May 9, 1877, Browerville, Minn.   D. July 4, 1969, St. Paul, Minn.   BR TR 5'6" 186 lbs.

	G	AB	H	2B	3B	HR	HR %	R	RBI	BB	SO	SB	BA	SA	AB	H	G by POS
'02 2 teams		BAL A (2G – .250)				WAS A (71G – .262)											
'' total	73	229	60	10	4	1	0.4	35	29	26		5	.262	.354	4	0	C-54, OF-8, 2B-5, 3B-1, 1B-1
'03 WAS A	51	154	39	9	3	0	0.0	11	23	15		4	.253	.351	1	0	C-47, 1B-3
'04 2 teams		WAS A (46G – .268)				DET A (51G – .244)											
'' total	97	302	77	13	3	1	0.3	24	24	41		5	.255	.328	2	1	C-78, OF-14, 1B-2
'05 DET A	71	211	55	9	0	0	0.0	17	24	32		7	.261	.303	1	0	C-70
4 yrs.	292	896	231	41	10	2	0.2	87	100	114		21	.258	.333	8	1	C-249, OF-22, 1B-6, 2B-5, 3B-1
2 yrs.	122	371	94	15	1	0	0.0	24	37	52		9	.253	.299	1	0	C-119, 1B-2

Walt Dropo

DROPO, WALTER (Moose)
B. Jan. 30, 1923, Moosup, Conn.   BR TR 6'5" 220 lbs.

	G	AB	H	2B	3B	HR	HR %	R	RBI	BB	SO	SB	BA	SA	AB	H	G by POS
'49 BOS A	11	41	6	2	0	0	0.0	3	1	3	7	0	.146	.195	0	0	1B-11
'50	136	559	180	28	8	34	6.1	101	144	45	75	0	.322	.583	2	0	1B-134
'51	99	360	86	14	0	11	3.1	37	57	38	52	0	.239	.369	7	2	1B-93
'52 2 teams		BOS A (37G – .265)				DET A (115G – .279)											
'' total	152	591	163	24	4	29	4.9	69	97	37	85	2	.276	.477	2	0	1B-150
'53 DET A	152	606	150	30	3	13	2.1	61	96	29	69	2	.248	.371	2	1	1B-150
'54	107	320	90	14	2	4	1.3	27	44	24	41	0	.281	.375	18	5	1B-95
'55 CHI A	141	453	127	15	2	19	4.2	55	79	42	71	0	.280	.448	2	1	1B-140
'56	125	361	96	13	1	8	2.2	42	52	37	51	1	.266	.374	10	2	1B-117
'57	93	223	57	2	0	13	5.8	24	49	16	40	0	.256	.439	31	11	1B-69
'58 2 teams		CHI A (28G – .192)				CIN N (63G – .290)											
'' total	91	214	57	8	2	9	4.2	21	39	17	42	0	.266	.449	31	7	1B-59
'59 2 teams		CIN N (26G – .103)				BAL A (62G – .278)											
'' total	88	190	46	10	0	7	3.7	21	23	16	27	0	.242	.405	11	1	1B-77, 3B-2
'60 BAL A	79	179	48	8	0	4	2.2	16	21	20	19	0	.268	.380	14	2	1B-67, 3B-1
'61	14	27	7	0	0	1	3.7	1	2	4	3	0	.259	.370	2	1	1B-12
13 yrs.	1288	4124	1113	168	22	152	3.7	478	704	328	582	5	.270	.432	132	33	1B-1174, 3B-3
3 yrs.	374	1385	368	61	8	40	2.9	144	210	79	173	4	.266	.408	20	6	1B-360

	G	AB	H	2B	3B	HR	HR %	R	RBI	BB	SO	SB	BA	SA	Pinch Hit AB	H	G by POS

Jean Dubuc

DUBUC, JEAN JOSEPH OCTAVE (Chauncey)
Born Jean Baptiste Arthur Dubuc.
B. Sept. 15, 1888, St. Johnsbury, Vt.   D. Aug. 29, 1958, Ft. Myers, Fla.   BR TR 5'10½" 185 lbs.

	G	AB	H	2B	3B	HR	HR %	R	RBI	BB	SO	SB	BA	SA	AB	H	G by POS
1908 CIN N	15	29	4	1	0	0	0.0	2	2	0		0	.138	.172	0	0	P-15
1909	19	18	3	0	0	0	0.0	1	0	2		0	.167	.167	0	0	P-19
1912 DET A	40	108	29	6	2	1	0.9	16	9	3		0	.269	.389	1	0	P-37, OF-2
1913	68	135	36	5	3	2	1.5	17	11	2	17	1	.267	.393	28	3	P-36, OF-3
1914	70	124	28	8	1	1	0.8	9	11	7	11	1	.226	.331	32	6	P-36
1915	60	112	23	2	1	0	0.0	7	14	8	15	0	.205	.241	17	5	P-39
1916	52	78	20	0	2	0	0.0	3	7	7	12	0	.256	.308	12	2	P-36
1918 BOS A	5	6	1	0	0	0	0.0	0	0	1	2	0	.167	.167	2	0	P-2
1919 NY N	36	42	6	1	1	0	0.0	2	2	0	6	0	.143	.214	1	0	P-36
9 yrs.	365	652	150	23	10	4	0.6	57	56	30	63	2	.230	.314	93	16	P-256, OF-5
5 yrs.	290	557	136	21	9	4	0.7	52	52	27	55	2	.244	.336	90	16	P-184, OF-5

WORLD SERIES

	G	AB	H	2B	3B	HR	HR %	R	RBI	BB	SO	SB	BA	SA	AB	H	G by POS
1918 BOS A	1	1	0	0	0	0	0.0	0	0	0	1	0	.000	.000	1	0	

Joe Dugan

DUGAN, JOSEPH ANTHONY (Jumping Joe)
B. May 12, 1897, Mahanoy City, Pa.   D. July 7, 1982, Norwood, Mass.   BR TR 5'11" 160 lbs.

	G	AB	H	2B	3B	HR	HR %	R	RBI	BB	SO	SB	BA	SA	AB	H	G by POS
1917 PHI A	43	134	26	8	0	0	0.0	9	16	3	16	0	.194	.254	0	0	SS-39, 2B-2
1918	120	406	79	11	3	3	0.7	25	34	16	55	4	.195	.259	0	0	SS-85, 2B-35
1919	104	387	105	17	2	1	0.3	25	30	11	30	9	.271	.333	0	0	SS-98, 2B-4, 3B-2
1920	123	491	158	40	5	3	0.6	65	60	19	51	5	.322	.442	0	0	3B-59, SS-32, 2B-32
1921	119	461	136	22	6	10	2.2	54	58	28	45	5	.295	.434	0	0	3B-119
1922 2 teams		BOS	A (84G –	.287)		NY	A	(60G –	.286)								
" total	144	593	170	31	4	6	1.0	89	63	22	49	3	.287	.383	1	0	3B-123, SS-20
1923 NY A	146	644	182	30	7	7	1.1	111	67	25	41	4	.283	.384	0	0	3B-146
1924	148	610	184	31	7	3	0.5	105	56	31	32	1	.302	.390	0	0	3B-148, 2B-2
1925	102	404	118	19	4	0	0.0	50	31	19	20	2	.292	.359	5	1	3B-96
1926	123	434	125	19	5	1	0.2	39	64	25	16	2	.288	.362	1	0	3B-122
1927	112	387	104	24	3	2	0.5	44	43	27	37	1	.269	.362	1	1	3B-111
1928	94	312	86	15	0	6	1.9	33	34	16	15	1	.276	.381	2	0	3B-91
1929 BOS N	60	125	38	10	0	0	0.0	14	15	8	8	0	.304	.384	26	9	3B-24, SS-5, OF-2, 2B-2
1931 DET A	8	17	4	0	0	0	0.0	1	0	0	3	0	.235	.235	3	1	3B-5
14 yrs.	1446	5405	1515	277	46	42	0.8	664	571	250	418	37	.280	.372	39	12	3B-1046, SS-279, 2B-77, OF-2
1 yr.	8	17	4	0	0	0	0.0	1	0	0	3	0	.235	.235	3	1	3B-5

WORLD SERIES

	G	AB	H	2B	3B	HR	HR %	R	RBI	BB	SO	SB	BA	SA	AB	H	G by POS
1922 NY A	5	20	5	1	0	0	0.0	4	0	0	1	0	.250	.300	0	0	3B-5
1923	6	25	7	2	1	1	4.0	5	5	3	0	0	.280	.560	0	0	3B-6
1926	7	24	8	1	0	0	0.0	2	2	1	1	0	.333	.375	0	0	3B-7
1927	4	15	3	0	0	0	0.0	2	0	0	0	0	.200	.200	0	0	3B-4
1928	3	6	1	0	0	0	0.0	0	1	0	0	0	.167	.167	0	0	3B-3
5 yrs.	25	90	24	4	1	1	1.1	13	8	4	2	0	.267	.367	0	0	3B-25

Ben Dyer

DYER, BENJAMIN FRANKLIN
B. Feb. 13, 1893, Chicago, Ill.   D. Aug. 7, 1959, Kenosha, Wis.   BR TR 5'10" 170 lbs.

	G	AB	H	2B	3B	HR	HR %	R	RBI	BB	SO	SB	BA	SA	AB	H	G by POS
1914 NY N	7	4	1	0	0	0	0.0	1	0	0	1	1	.250	.250	0	0	SS-6, 2B-1
1915	7	19	4	0	1	0	0.0	4	0	4	3	0	.211	.316	0	0	3B-6, SS-1
1916 DET A	4	14	4	1	0	0	0.0	4	1	1	1	0	.286	.357	0	0	SS-4
1917	30	67	14	5	0	0	0.0	6	0	2	17	3	.209	.284	8	0	SS-14, 3B-8
1918	13	18	5	0	0	0	0.0	1	2	0	6	0	.278	.278	6	2	OF-2, 1B-2, P-2, 2B-1
1919	44	85	21	4	0	0	0.0	11	15	8	19	0	.247	.294	8	3	3B-23, SS-11, OF-1
6 yrs.	105	207	49	10	1	0	0.0	27	18	15	47	4	.237	.295	22	5	3B-37, SS-36, OF-3, 2B-2, 1B-2, P-2
4 yrs.	91	184	44	10	0	0	0.0	22	18	11	43	3	.239	.293	22	5	3B-31, SS-29, OF-3, 1B-2, P-2, 2B-1

Duffy Dyer

DYER, DON ROBERT
B. Aug. 15, 1945, Dayton, Ohio   BR TR 6' 187 lbs.

	G	AB	H	2B	3B	HR	HR %	R	RBI	BB	SO	SB	BA	SA	AB	H	G by POS
1968 NY N	1	3	1	0	0	0	0.0	0	0	1	1	0	.333	.333	0	0	C-1
1969	29	74	19	3	1	3	4.1	5	12	4	22	0	.257	.446	8	3	C-19
1970	59	148	31	6	0	2	1.4	8	12	21	32	1	.209	.257	1	1	C-57
1971	59	169	39	7	1	2	1.2	13	18	14	45	1	.231	.320	9	4	C-53
1972	94	325	75	17	3	8	2.5	33	36	28	71	0	.231	.375	3	2	C-91, OF-1
1973	70	189	35	6	1	1	0.5	9	9	13	40	0	.185	.243	10	2	C-60
1974	63	142	30	1	1	0	0.0	14	10	18	15	0	.211	.232	17	8	C-45
1975 PIT N	48	132	30	5	2	3	2.3	8	16	6	22	0	.227	.364	11	3	C-36
1976	69	184	41	8	0	3	1.6	12	9	29	35	0	.223	.315	12	5	C-58
1977	94	270	65	11	1	3	1.1	27	19	54	49	6	.241	.322	3	0	C-93
1978	58	175	37	8	1	0	0.0	7	13	18	32	2	.211	.269	3	2	C-55
1979 MON N	28	74	18	6	0	1	1.4	4	8	9	17	0	.243	.365	1	0	C-27
1980 DET A	48	108	20	1	0	4	3.7	11	11	13	34	0	.185	.306	3	0	C-37, DH-10
1981	2	0	0	0	0	0	0	0	0	0	0	0	–	–	0	0	C-2
14 yrs.	722	1993	441	74	11	30	1.5	151	173	228	415	10	.221	.315	81	30	C-634, DH-10, OF-1
2 yrs.	50	108	20	1	0	4	3.7	11	11	13	34	0	.185	.306	3	0	C-39, DH-10

LEAGUE CHAMPIONSHIP SERIES

	G	AB	H	2B	3B	HR	HR %	R	RBI	BB	SO	SB	BA	SA	AB	H	G by POS
1975 PIT N	1	0	0	0	0	0	–	0	1	1	0	0	–	–	0	0	

WORLD SERIES

	G	AB	H	2B	3B	HR	HR %	R	RBI	BB	SO	SB	BA	SA	AB	H	G by POS
1969 NY N	1	1	0	0	0	0	0.0	0	0	0	0	0	.000	.000	1	0	

Scottie Earl

EARL, WILLIAM SCOTT
B. Sept. 18, 1960, Seymour, Ind.   BR TR 5'11" 165 lbs.

	G	AB	H	2B	3B	HR	HR %	R	RBI	BB	SO	SB	BA	SA	AB	H	G by POS
1984 DET A	14	35	4	0	1	0	0.0	3	1	0	9	1	.114	.171	0	0	2B-14

	G	AB	H	2B	3B	HR	HR %	R	RBI	BB	SO	SB	BA	SA	Pinch Hit AB	Pinch Hit H	G by POS

Paul Easterling

EASTERLING, PAUL BR TR 5'11" 180 lbs.
B. Sept. 28, 1905, Reidsville, Ga.

	G	AB	H	2B	3B	HR	HR %	R	RBI	BB	SO	SB	BA	SA	AB	H	G by POS
'28 DET A	43	114	37	7	1	3	2.6	17	12	8	24	2	.325	.482	8	3	OF-34
'30	29	79	16	6	0	1	1.3	7	14	6	18	0	.203	.316	2	0	OF-25
'38 PHI A	4	7	2	0	0	0	0.0	1	0	1	2	0	.286	.286	3	0	OF-1
3 yrs.	76	200	55	13	1	4	2.0	25	26	15	44	2	.275	.410	13	3	OF-60
2 yrs.	72	193	53	13	1	4	2.1	24	26	14	42	2	.275	.415	10	3	OF-59

Kid Elberfeld

ELBERFELD, NORMAN ARTHUR (The Tabasco Kid) BR TR 5'5½" 134 lbs.
B. Apr. 13, 1875, Pomeroy, Ohio   D. Jan. 13, 1944, Chattanooga, Tenn.
Manager 1908.

	G	AB	H	2B	3B	HR	HR %	R	RBI	BB	SO	SB	BA	SA	AB	H	G by POS
'98 PHI N	14	38	9	4	0	0	0.0	1	7	5		0	.237	.342	0	0	3B-14
'99 CIN N	41	138	36	4	2	0	0.0	23	22	15		5	.261	.319	0	0	SS-24, 3B-18
'01 DET A	122	436	135	21	11	3	0.7	76	76	57		24	.310	.429	0	0	SS-121
'02	130	488	127	17	6	1	0.2	70	64	55		19	.260	.326	0	0	SS-130
'03 2 teams		DET	A	(35G –	.341)		NY	A	(90G –	.287)							
" total	125	481	145	23	8	0	0.0	78	64	33		22	.301	.383	0	0	SS-124, 3B-1
'04 NY A	122	445	117	13	5	2	0.4	55	46	37		18	.263	.328	0	0	SS-122
'05	111	390	102	18	2	0	0.0	48	53	23		18	.262	.318	2	0	SS-108
'06	99	346	106	11	5	2	0.6	59	31	30		19	.306	.384	0	0	SS-98
'07	120	447	121	17	6	0	0.0	61	51	36		22	.271	.336	2	2	SS-118
'08	19	56	11	3	0	0	0.0	11	5	6		1	.196	.250	2	0	SS-17
'09	106	379	90	9	5	0	0.0	47	26	28		23	.237	.288	2	0	SS-61, 3B-43
'10 WAS A	127	455	114	9	2	2	0.4	53	42	35		19	.251	.292	3	0	3B-113, 2B-10, SS-3
'11	127	404	110	19	4	0	0.0	58	47	65		24	.272	.339	7	1	2B-66, 3B-54
'14 BKN N	30	62	14	1	0	0	0.0	7	1	2		4	0	.226	.242	6	1	SS-18, 2B-1
14 yrs.	1293	4565	1237	169	56	10	0.2	647	535	427	4	214	.271	.339	24	4	SS-944, 3B-243, 2B-77
3 yrs.	287	1056	307	43	20	4	0.4	175	159	123		49	.291	.381	0	0	SS-285, 3B-1

Babe Ellison

ELLISON, HERBERT SPENCER BR TR 5'11" 170 lbs.
B. Nov. 15, 1896, Ola, Ark.   D. Aug. 11, 1955, San Francisco, Calif.

	G	AB	H	2B	3B	HR	HR %	R	RBI	BB	SO	SB	BA	SA	AB	H	G by POS
'16 DET A	2	7	1	0	0	0	0.0	0	1	0	1	0	.143	.143	0	0	3B-2
'17	9	29	5	1	2	1	3.4	2	4	6	3	0	.172	.448	0	0	1B-9
'18	7	23	6	1	0	0	0.0	1	2	3	1	0	.261	.304	0	0	OF-4, 2B-3
'19	56	134	29	4	0	0	0.0	18	11	13	24	4	.216	.246	15	3	2B-25, OF-10, SS-1
'20	61	155	34	7	2	0	0.0	11	21	8	26	4	.219	.290	17	3	1B-38, OF-4, 3B-1
5 yrs.	135	348	75	13	4	1	0.3	32	39	30	55	9	.216	.284	32	6	1B-47, 2B-28, OF-18, 3B-3, SS-1
5 yrs.	135	348	75	13	4	1	0.3	32	39	30	55	9	.216	.284	32	6	1B-47, 2B-28, OF-18, 3B-3, SS-1

Gil English

ENGLISH, GILBERT RAYMOND BR TR 5'11" 180 lbs.
B. July 2, 1909, Glenola, N. C.

	G	AB	H	2B	3B	HR	HR %	R	RBI	BB	SO	SB	BA	SA	AB	H	G by POS
'31 NY N	3	8	0	0	0	0	0.0	0	0	1	3	0	.000	.000	0	0	3B-3
'32	59	204	46	7	5	2	1.0	22	19	5	20	0	.225	.338	1	0	3B-39, SS-23
'36 DET A	1	1	0	0	0	0	0.0	0	0	1	0	0	.000	.000	0	0	3B-1
'37 2 teams		DET	A	(18G –	.262)		BOS	N	(79G –	.290)							
' total	97	334	95	6	2	3	0.9	31	43	29	31	4	.284	.341	6	4	3B-77, 2B-12
'38 BOS N	53	165	41	6	0	2	1.2	17	21	15	16	1	.248	.321	4	2	3B-43, OF-3, SS-2, 2B-2
'44 BKN N	27	79	12	3	0	1	1.3	4	7	6	7	0	.152	.228	1	0	SS-13, 3B-11, 2B-2
6 yrs.	240	791	194	22	7	8	1.0	74	90	56	78	5	.245	.321	12	6	3B-174, SS-38, 2B-16, OF-3
2 yrs.	19	66	17	1	0	1	1.5	6	6	6	5	1	.258	.318	1	1	2B-12, 3B-7

Tex Erwin

ERWIN, ROSS EMIL BL TR 6' 185 lbs.
B. Dec. 22, 1885, Forney, Tex.   D. Apr. 5, 1953, Rochester, N. Y.

	G	AB	H	2B	3B	HR	HR %	R	RBI	BB	SO	SB	BA	SA	AB	H	G by POS
'07 DET A	4	5	1	0	0	0	0.0	0	1	1		0	.200	.200	0	0	C-4
'10 BKN N	81	202	38	3	1	1	0.5	15	10	24	12	3	.188	.228	12	1	C-68
'11	91	218	59	13	2	7	3.2	30	34	31	23	5	.271	.445	15	4	C-74
'12	59	133	28	3	0	2	1.5	14	14	18	16	1	.211	.278	12	2	C-41
'13	20	31	8	1	0	0	0.0	6	3	4	5	0	.258	.290	7	1	C-13
'14 2 teams		BKN	N	(9G –	.455)		CIN	N	(12G –	.314)							
' total	21	46	16	3	0	1	2.2	5	8	4	4	1	.348	.478	6	3	C-16
6 yrs.	276	635	150	23	3	11	1.7	70	70	82	60	10	.236	.334	52	11	C-216
1 yr.	4	5	1	0	0	0	0.0	0	1	1		0	.200	.200	0	0	C-4

Darrell Evans

EVANS, DARRELL WAYNE BL TR 6'2" 200 lbs.
B. May 26, 1947, Pasadena, Calif.

	G	AB	H	2B	3B	HR	HR %	R	RBI	BB	SO	SB	BA	SA	AB	H	G by POS
'69 ATL N	12	26	6	0	0	0	0.0	3	1	1	8	0	.231	.231	4	0	3B-6
'70	12	44	14	1	0	0	0.0	4	9	7	5	0	.318	.386	0	0	3B-12
'71	89	260	63	11	1	12	4.6	42	38	39	54	2	.242	.431	10	1	3B-72, OF-3
'72	125	418	106	12	0	19	4.5	67	71	90	58	4	.254	.419	1	0	3B-123
'73	161	595	167	25	8	41	6.9	114	104	124	104	6	.281	.556	2	0	3B-146, 1B-20
'74	160	571	137	21	3	25	4.4	99	79	126	88	4	.240	.419	0	0	3B-160
'75	156	567	138	22	2	22	3.9	82	73	105	106	12	.243	.406	3	1	3B-156, 1B-3
'76 2 teams		ATL	N	(44G –	.173)		SF	N	(92G –	.222)							
' total	136	396	81	9	1	11	2.8	53	46	72	71	9	.205	.356	7	0	1B-119, 3B-12
'77 SF N	144	461	117	18	3	17	3.7	64	72	69	50	9	.254	.416	16	4	OF-81, 1B-41, 3B-35
'78	159	547	133	24	2	20	3.7	82	78	105	64	4	.243	.404	5	1	3B-155
'79	160	562	142	23	2	17	3.0	68	70	91	80	6	.253	.391	2	1	3B-159
'80	154	556	147	23	4	20	3.6	69	78	83	65	17	.264	.414	4	1	3B-140, 1B-14
'81	102	357	92	13	4	12	3.4	51	48	54	33	2	.258	.417	2	0	3B-87, 1B-12
'82	141	465	119	20	4	16	3.4	64	61	77	64	5	.256	.419	12	2	3B-84, 1B-49, SS-13
'83	142	523	145	29	3	30	5.7	94	82	84	81	6	.277	.516	2	1	1B-113, 3B-32, SS-9
'84 DET A	131	401	93	11	1	16	4.0	60	63	77	70	2	.232	.384	18	3	DH-62, 1B-47, 3B-19
16 yrs.	1984	6749	1700	262	35	278	4.1	1016	973	1204	1001	88	.252	.425	88	15	3B-1398, 1B-418, OF-84, DH-62, SS-22
1 yr.	131	401	93	11	1	16	4.0	60	63	77	70	2	.232	.384	18	3	DH-62, 1B-47, 3B-19

LEAGUE CHAMPIONSHIP SERIES

	G	AB	H	2B	3B	HR	HR %	R	RBI	BB	SO	SB	BA	SA	AB	H	G by POS
'84 DET A	3	10	3	1	0	0	0.0	1	1	1	0	1	.300	.400	0	0	1B-3

	G	AB	H	2B	3B	HR	HR %	R	RBI	BB	SO	SB	BA	SA	Pinch Hit AB	Pinch Hit H	G by POS

Darrell Evans continued

WORLD SERIES

		G	AB	H	2B	3B	HR	HR %	R	RBI	BB	SO	SB	BA	SA	PH AB	PH H	G by POS
1984 DET A		5	15	1	0	0	0	0.0	1	1	4	4	0	.067	.067	0	0	1B-4

Hoot Evers

EVERS, WALTER ARTHUR
B. Feb. 8, 1921, St. Louis, Mo.　　　　　　　BR TR 6'2"　180 lbs.

	G	AB	H	2B	3B	HR	HR %	R	RBI	BB	SO	SB	BA	SA	PH AB	PH H	G by POS
1941 DET A	1	4	0	0	0	0	0.0	0	0	0	2	0	.000	.000	0	0	OF-1
1946	81	304	81	8	4	4	1.3	42	33	34	43	7	.266	.359	2	0	OF-76
1947	126	460	136	24	5	10	2.2	67	67	45	49	8	.296	.435	2	1	OF-123
1948	139	538	169	33	6	10	1.9	81	103	51	31	3	.314	.454	1	0	OF-138
1949	132	432	131	21	6	7	1.6	68	72	70	38	6	.303	.428	10	2	OF-123
1950	143	526	170	35	11	21	4.0	100	103	71	40	5	.323	.551	1	0	OF-139
1951	116	393	88	15	2	11	2.8	47	46	40	47	5	.224	.356	8	2	OF-108
1952 2 teams		DET	A	(1G – 1.000)		BOS	A	(106G – .262)									
" total	107	402	106	17	4	14	3.5	53	59	29	55	5	.264	.430	2	1	OF-105
1953 BOS A	99	300	72	10	1	11	3.7	39	31	23	41	2	.240	.390	7	1	OF-93
1954 3 teams		BOS	A	(6G – .000)	NY	N	(12G – .091)		DET	A	(30G – .183)					
" total	48	79	12	4	0	1	1.3	7	8	5	16	1	.152	.241	17	1	OF-29
1955 2 teams		BAL	A	(60G – .238)		CLE	A	(39G – .288)									
" total	99	251	63	17	2	8	3.2	31	39	22	40	2	.251	.430	16	6	OF-80
1956 2 teams		CLE	A	(3G – .000)		BAL	A	(48G – .241)									
" total	51	112	27	3	0	1	0.9	21	4	25	18	1	.241	.295	10	2	OF-36
12 yrs.	1142	3801	1055	187	41	98	2.6	556	565	415	420	45	.278	.426	76	16	OF-1051
9 yrs.	769	2718	787	140	34	63	2.3	410	429	316	258	35	.290	.436	30	6	OF-732

Bill Fahey

FAHEY, WILLIAM ROGER
B. June 14, 1950, Detroit, Mich.　　　　　　　BL TR 6'　200 lbs.

	G	AB	H	2B	3B	HR	HR %	R	RBI	BB	SO	SB	BA	SA	PH AB	PH H	G by POS
1971 WAS A	2	8	0	0	0	0	0.0	0	0	0	0	0	.000	.000	0	0	C-2
1972 TEX A	39	119	20	2	0	1	0.8	8	10	12	23	4	.168	.210	1	1	C-39
1974	6	16	4	0	0	0	0.0	1	0	0	1	0	.250	.250	0	0	C-6
1975	21	37	11	1	1	0	0.0	3	3	1	10	0	.297	.378	2	0	C-21
1976	38	80	20	2	0	1	1.3	12	9	11	6	1	.250	.313	1	0	C-38
1977	37	68	15	4	0	0	0.0	3	5	1	8	0	.221	.279	1	0	C-34
1979 SD N	73	209	60	8	1	3	1.4	14	19	21	17	1	.287	.378	6	1	C-68
1980	93	241	62	4	0	1	0.4	18	22	21	16	2	.257	.286	11	2	C-85
1981 DET A	27	67	17	2	0	1	1.5	5	9	2	4	0	.254	.328	0	0	C-27
1982	28	67	10	2	0	0	0.0	7	4	0	5	1	.149	.179	2	0	C-28
1983	19	22	6	1	0	0	0.0	4	2	5	3	0	.273	.318	1	0	C-18
11 yrs.	383	934	225	26	2	7	0.7	75	83	74	93	9	.241	.296	25	4	C-366
3 yrs.	74	156	33	5	0	1	0.6	16	15	7	12	1	.212	.263	3	0	C-73

Ferris Fain

FAIN, FERRIS ROY (Burrhead)
B. Mar. 29, 1921, San Antonio, Tex.　　　　　　　BL TL 5'11"　180 lbs.

	G	AB	H	2B	3B	HR	HR %	R	RBI	BB	SO	SB	BA	SA	PH AB	PH H	G by POS
1947 PHI A	136	461	134	28	6	7	1.5	70	71	95	34	4	.291	.423	4	0	1B-132
1948	145	520	146	27	6	7	1.3	81	88	113	37	10	.281	.396	0	0	1B-145
1949	150	525	138	21	5	3	0.6	81	78	136	51	8	.263	.339	0	0	1B-150
1950	151	522	147	25	4	10	1.9	83	83	132	26	8	.282	.402	0	0	1B-151
1951	117	425	146	30	3	6	1.4	63	57	80	20	0	.344	.471	0	0	1B-108, OF-11
1952	145	538	176	43	3	2	0.4	82	59	105	26	3	.327	.429	1	0	1B-144
1953 CHI A	128	446	114	18	2	6	1.3	73	52	108	28	3	.256	.345	1	1	1B-127
1954	65	235	71	10	1	5	2.1	30	51	40	14	5	.302	.417	0	0	1B-64
1955 2 teams		DET	A	(58G – .264)		CLE	A	(56G – .254)									
" total	114	258	67	11	2	0	0.8	32	31	94	25	5	.260	.326	13	4	1B-95
9 yrs.	1151	3930	1139	213	30	48	1.2	595	570	903	261	46	.290	.396	19	5	1B-1116, OF-11
1 yr.	58	140	37	8	0	2	1.4	23	22	52	12	2	.264	.364	9	3	1B-44

Bob Farley

FARLEY, ROBERT JACOB
B. Nov. 15, 1937, Watsontown, Pa.　　　　　　　BL TL 6'2"　200 lbs.

	G	AB	H	2B	3B	HR	HR %	R	RBI	BB	SO	SB	BA	SA	PH AB	PH H	G by POS
1961 SF N	13	20	2	0	0	0	0.0	3	1	3	5	0	.100	.100	8	1	OF-3, 1B-1
1962 2 teams		CHI	A	(35G – .189)		DET	A	(36G – .160)									
" total	71	103	18	3	1	2	1.9	16	8	27	23	0	.175	.282	33	4	1B-20, OF-6
2 yrs.	84	123	20	3	1	2	1.6	19	9	30	28	0	.163	.252	41	5	1B-21, OF-9
1 yr.	36	50	8	2	0	1	2.0	9	4	14	10	0	.160	.260	13	3	OF-6, 1B-6

Al Federoff

FEDEROFF, ALFRED (Whitey)
B. July 11, 1924, Bairford, Pa.　　　　　　　BR TR 5'10½" 165 lbs.

	G	AB	H	2B	3B	HR	HR %	R	RBI	BB	SO	SB	BA	SA	PH AB	PH H	G by POS
1951 DET A	2	4	0	0	0	0	0.0	0	0	0	0	0	.000	.000	0	0	2B-1
1952	74	231	56	4	2	0	0.0	14	14	16	13	1	.242	.277	0	0	2B-70, SS-7
2 yrs.	76	235	56	4	2	0	0.0	14	14	16	13	1	.238	.272	0	0	2B-71, SS-7
2 yrs.	76	235	56	4	2	0	0.0	14	14	16	13	1	.238	.272	0	0	2B-71, SS-7

Jack Feller

FELLER, JACK LELAND
B. Dec. 10, 1936, Adrian, Mich.　　　　　　　BR TR 5'10½" 185 lbs.

	G	AB	H	2B	3B	HR	HR %	R	RBI	BB	SO	SB	BA	SA	PH AB	PH H	G by POS
1958 DET A	1	0	0	0	0	0	–	0	0	0	0	0	–	–	0	0	C-1

Chico Fernandez

FERNANDEZ, HUMBERTO PEREZ
B. Mar. 2, 1932, Havana, Cuba　　　　　　　BR TR 6'　165 lbs.

	G	AB	H	2B	3B	HR	HR %	R	RBI	BB	SO	SB	BA	SA	PH AB	PH H	G by POS
1956 BKN N	34	66	15	2	0	1	1.5	11	9	3	10	2	.227	.303	1	0	SS-25
1957 PHI N	149	500	131	14	4	5	1.0	42	51	31	64	18	.262	.336	0	0	SS-149
1958	148	522	120	18	5	6	1.1	38	51	37	48	12	.230	.318	0	0	SS-148
1959	45	123	26	5	1	0	0.0	15	3	10	11	2	.211	.268	0	0	SS-40, 2B-2
1960 DET A	133	435	105	13	3	4	0.9	44	35	39	50	13	.241	.313	2	0	SS-130
1961	133	435	108	15	4	3	0.7	41	40	36	45	8	.248	.322	4	2	SS-121, 3B-8
1962	141	503	125	17	2	20	4.0	64	59	42	69	10	.249	.410	1	0	SS-138, 3B-2, 1B-1

	G	AB	H	2B	3B	HR	HR %	R	RBI	BB	SO	SB	BA	SA	Pinch Hit AB	Pinch Hit H	G by POS

Chico Fernandez continued

	G	AB	H	2B	3B	HR	HR %	R	RBI	BB	SO	SB	BA	SA	AB	H	G by POS
63 2 teams	DET A (15G – .143)					NY	N	(58G – .200)									
total	73	194	36	7	0	1	0.5	15	11	15	41	3	.186	.237	15	1	SS-59, 3B-5, 2B-3
8 yrs.	856	2778	666	91	19	40	1.4	270	259	213	338	68	.240	.329	23	3	SS-810, 3B-15, 2B-5, 1B-1
4 yrs.	422	1422	345	46	9	27	1.9	152	136	123	175	31	.243	.345	8	2	SS-403, 3B-10, 1B-1

Jim Finigan

FINIGAN, JAMES LEROY   BR TR 5'11" 175 lbs.
B. Aug. 19, 1928, Quincy, Ill.   D. May 16, 1981, Quincy, Ill.

	G	AB	H	2B	3B	HR	HR %	R	RBI	BB	SO	SB	BA	SA	AB	H	G by POS
54 PHI A	136	487	147	25	6	7	1.4	57	51	64	66	2	.302	.421	1	0	3B-136
55 KC A	150	545	139	30	7	9	1.7	72	68	61	49	1	.255	.385	2	1	2B-90, 3B-59
56	91	250	54	7	2	2	0.8	29	21	30	28	3	.216	.284	9	0	2B-52, 3B-32
57 DET A	64	174	47	4	2	0	0.0	20	17	23	18	1	.270	.316	3	0	3B-59, 2B-3
58 SF N	23	25	5	2	0	0	0.0	3	1	3	5	0	.200	.280	12	2	2B-8, 3B-4
59 BAL A	48	119	30	6	0	1	0.8	14	10	9	10	1	.252	.328	5	2	3B-42, 2B-6, SS-2
6 yrs.	512	1600	422	74	17	19	1.2	195	168	190	176	8	.264	.367	32	5	3B-332, 2B-159, SS-2
1 yr.	64	174	47	4	2	0	0.0	20	17	23	18	1	.270	.316	3	0	3B-59, 2B-3

Ira Flagstead

FLAGSTEAD, IRA JAMES (Pete)   BR TR 5'9" 165 lbs.
B. Sept. 22, 1893, Montague, Mich.   D. Mar. 13, 1940, Olympia, Wash.

	G	AB	H	2B	3B	HR	HR %	R	RBI	BB	SO	SB	BA	SA	AB	H	G by POS
17 DET A	4	4	0	0	0	0	0.0	0	0	1	0	0	.000	.000	2	0	OF-2
19	97	287	95	22	3	5	1.7	43	41	35	39	6	.331	.481	11	3	OF-83
20	110	311	73	13	5	3	1.0	40	35	37	27	3	.235	.338	26	6	OF-82
21	85	259	79	15	1	0	0.0	40	31	21	21	7	.305	.371	7	2	SS-55, OF-12, 2B-8, 3B-1
22	44	91	28	5	3	3	3.3	21	8	14	16	0	.308	.527	8	2	OF-31
23 2 teams	DET A (1G – .000)					BOS	A	(109G – .312)									
total	110	383	119	23	4	8	2.1	55	53	37	26	8	.311	.454	6	0	OF-102
24 BOS A	149	560	171	35	7	5	0.9	106	43	75	41	10	.305	.420	5	2	OF-143
25	148	572	160	38	2	6	1.0	84	61	63	30	5	.280	.385	3	1	OF-144
26	98	415	124	31	7	3	0.7	65	31	36	22	4	.299	.429	0	0	OF-98
27	131	466	133	26	8	4	0.9	63	69	57	25	12	.285	.401	2	0	OF-129
28	140	510	148	41	4	1	0.2	84	39	60	23	12	.290	.392	4	0	OF-135
29 3 teams	BOS A (14G – .306)					WAS	A	(18G – .179)			PIT	N	(26G – .280)				
total	58	125	32	5	1	0	0.0	22	18	13	8	3	.256	.312	23	9	OF-33
30 PIT N	44	156	39	7	4	2	1.3	21	21	17	9	1	.250	.385	3	0	OF-40
13 yrs.	1218	4139	1201	261	49	40	1.0	644	450	465	288	71	.290	.406	100	25	OF-1034, SS-55, 2B-8, 3B-1
6 yrs.	341	953	275	55	12	11	1.2	144	115	107	104	16	.289	.406	55	13	OF-210, SS-55, 2B-8, 3B-1

Les Fleming

FLEMING, LESLIE HARVEY (Moe)   BL TL 5'10" 185 lbs.
B. Aug. 7, 1915, Singleton, Tex.   D. Mar. 5, 1980, Cleveland, Tex.

	G	AB	H	2B	3B	HR	HR %	R	RBI	BB	SO	SB	BA	SA	AB	H	G by POS
39 DET A	8	16	0	0	0	0	0.0	0	1	0	4	0	.000	.000	5	0	OF-3
41 CLE A	2	8	2	1	0	0	0.0	0	2	0	0	0	.250	.375	0	0	1B-2
42	156	548	160	27	4	14	2.6	71	82	106	57	6	.292	.432	0	0	1B-156
45	42	140	46	10	2	3	2.1	18	22	11	5	0	.329	.493	3	1	OF-33, 1B-5
46	99	306	85	17	5	8	2.6	40	42	50	42	1	.278	.444	17	5	1B-80, OF-1
47	103	281	68	14	2	4	1.4	39	43	53	42	0	.242	.349	20	6	1B-77
49 PIT N	24	31	8	0	2	0	0.0	0	7	6	2	0	.258	.387	16	4	1B-5
7 yrs.	434	1330	369	69	15	29	2.2	168	199	226	152	7	.277	.417	61	16	1B-325, OF-37
1 yr.	8	16	0	0	0	0	0.0	0	1	0	4	0	.000	.000	5	0	OF-3

Bubba Floyd

FLOYD, LESLIE ROE   BR TR 5'11" 160 lbs.
B. June 23, 1917, Dallas, Tex.

	G	AB	H	2B	3B	HR	HR %	R	RBI	BB	SO	SB	BA	SA	AB	H	G by POS
44 DET A	3	9	4	1	0	0	0.0	1	0	1	0	0	.444	.556	0	0	SS-3

Hank Foiles

FOILES, HENRY LEE   BR TR 6' 195 lbs.
B. June 10, 1929, Richmond, Va.

	G	AB	H	2B	3B	HR	HR %	R	RBI	BB	SO	SB	BA	SA	AB	H	G by POS
53 2 teams	CIN N (5G – .154)					CLE	A	(7G – .143)									
total	12	20	3	0	0	0	0.0	3	0	2	3	0	.150	.150	2	0	C-10
55 CLE A	62	111	29	9	0	1	0.9	13	7	17	18	0	.261	.369	20	6	C-41
56 2 teams	CLE A (1G – .000)					PIT	N	(79G – .212)									
total	80	222	47	10	2	7	3.2	24	25	17	56	0	.212	.369	5	1	C-74
57 PIT N	109	281	76	10	4	9	3.2	32	36	37	53	1	.270	.431	4	0	C-109
58	104	264	54	10	2	8	3.0	31	30	45	53	0	.205	.348	0	0	C-103
59	53	80	18	3	0	3	3.8	10	4	7	16	0	.225	.375	1	0	C-51
60 3 teams	KC A (6G – .571)					CLE	A	(24G – .279)			DET	A	(26G – .250)				
total	56	131	37	4	0	1	0.8	15	10	11	15	1	.282	.336	6	1	C-46
61 BAL A	43	124	34	6	0	6	4.8	18	19	12	27	0	.274	.468	4	0	C-38
62 CIN N	43	131	36	6	1	7	5.3	17	25	13	39	0	.275	.496	5	2	C-41
63 2 teams	CIN N (1G – .000)					LA	A	(41G – .214)									
total	42	87	18	1	1	4	4.6	8	10	9	13	1	.207	.379	11	2	C-31
64 LA A	4	4	1	0	0	0	0.0	0	0	0	2	0	.250	.250	4	1	
11 yrs.	608	1455	353	59	10	46	3.2	171	166	170	295	3	.243	.392	62	13	C-544
1 yr.	26	56	14	3	0	0	0.0	5	3	1	8	1	.250	.304	2	0	C-22

Pat Foley

Playing record listed under Willie Greene

Bob Fothergill

FOTHERGILL, ROBERT ROY (Fat)   BR TR 5'10½" 230 lbs.
B. Aug. 16, 1897, Massillon, Ohio   D. Mar. 20, 1938, Detroit, Mich.

	G	AB	H	2B	3B	HR	HR %	R	RBI	BB	SO	SB	BA	SA	AB	H	G by POS
22 DET A	42	152	49	12	4	0	0.0	20	29	8	9	1	.322	.454	3	1	OF-39
23	101	241	76	18	2	1	0.4	34	49	12	19	4	.315	.419	30	9	OF-68
24	54	166	50	8	3	0	0.0	28	15	5	13	2	.301	.386	9	3	OF-45
25	71	204	72	14	0	2	1.0	38	28	6	3	2	.353	.451	11	5	OF-59
26	110	387	142	31	7	3	0.8	63	73	33	23	4	.367	.506	6	4	OF-103
27	143	527	189	38	9	9	1.7	93	114	47	31	9	.359	.516	5	2	OF-137
28	111	347	110	28	10	3	0.9	49	63	24	19	8	.317	.481	19	4	OF-90

Bob Fothergill continued

	G	AB	H	2B	3B	HR	HR%	R	RBI	BB	SO	SB	BA	SA	Pinch Hit AB	Pinch Hit H	G by POS
1929	115	277	98	24	9	6	2.2	42	62	11	11	3	.354	.570	53	19	OF-59
1930 2 teams	DET A (55G – .259)		CHI A (51G – .305)														
" total	106	274	77	18	3	2	0.7	24	38	10	18	1	.281	.391	34	6	OF-68
1931 CHI A	108	312	88	9	4	3	1.0	25	56	17	17	2	.282	.365	31	8	OF-74
1932	116	346	102	24	1	7	2.0	36	50	27	10	4	.295	.431	29	8	OF-86
1933 BOS A	28	32	11	1	0	0	0.0	1	5	2	4	0	.344	.375	23	7	OF-4
12 yrs.	1105	3265	1064	225	52	36	1.1	453	582	202	177	40	.326	.460	253	76	OF-832
9 yrs.	802	2444	823	182	47	26	1.1	381	447	152	138	34	.337	.482	151	47	OF-638
													3rd	9th	3rd	2nd	

Pete Fox

FOX, ERVIN. B. Mar. 8, 1909, Evansville, Ind. D. July 5, 1966, Detroit, Mich. BR TR 5'11" 165 lb

	G	AB	H	2B	3B	HR	HR%	R	RBI	BB	SO	SB	BA	SA	Pinch Hit AB	Pinch Hit H	G by POS
1933 DET A	128	535	154	26	13	7	1.3	82	57	23	38	9	.288	.424	3	0	OF-124
1934	128	516	147	31	2	2	0.4	101	45	49	53	25	.285	.364	6	1	OF-121
1935	131	517	166	38	8	15	2.9	116	73	45	52	14	.321	.513	6	3	OF-125
1936	73	220	67	12	1	4	1.8	46	26	34	23	1	.305	.423	15	2	OF-55
1937	148	628	208	39	8	12	1.9	116	82	41	43	12	.331	.476	3	2	OF-143
1938	155	634	186	35	10	7	1.1	91	96	31	39	16	.293	.413	0	0	OF-154
1939	141	519	153	24	6	7	1.3	69	66	35	41	23	.295	.405	14	2	OF-126
1940	93	350	101	17	4	5	1.4	49	48	21	30	7	.289	.403	9	1	OF-85
1941 BOS A	73	268	81	12	7	0	0.0	38	31	21	32	9	.302	.399	7	0	OF-62
1942	77	256	67	15	5	3	1.2	42	42	20	28	8	.262	.395	3	1	OF-71
1943	127	489	141	24	4	2	0.4	54	44	34	40	22	.288	.366	1	0	OF-125
1944	121	496	156	38	6	1	0.2	70	64	27	34	10	.315	.421	2	0	OF-119
1945	66	208	51	4	1	0	0.0	21	20	11	18	2	.245	.274	5	0	OF-57
13 yrs.	1461	5636	1678	315	75	65	1.2	895	694	392	471	158	.298	.415	74	12	OF-1367
8 yrs.	997	3919	1182	222	52	59	1.5	670	493	279	319	107	.302	.430	56	11	OF-933

WORLD SERIES

	G	AB	H	2B	3B	HR	HR%	R	RBI	BB	SO	SB	BA	SA	Pinch Hit AB	Pinch Hit H	G by POS
1934 DET A	7	28	8	6	0	0	0.0	1	2	1	4	0	.286	.500	0	0	OF-7
1935	6	26	10	3	1	0	0.0	1	4	0	1	0	.385	.577	0	0	OF-6
1940	1	1	0	0	0	0	0.0	0	0	0	0	0	.000	.000	1	0	
3 yrs.	14	55	18	9	1	0	0.0	2	6	1	5	0	.327	.527	1	0	OF-13
				3rd													

Tito Francona

FRANCONA, JOHN PATSY. Father of Terry Francona. B. Nov. 4, 1933, Aliquippa, Pa. BL TL 5'11" 190 lbs

	G	AB	H	2B	3B	HR	HR%	R	RBI	BB	SO	SB	BA	SA	Pinch Hit AB	Pinch Hit H	G by POS
1956 BAL A	139	445	115	16	4	9	2.0	62	57	51	60	11	.258	.373	18	4	OF-122, 1B-21
1957	97	279	65	8	3	7	2.5	35	38	29	48	7	.233	.358	23	3	OF-73, 1B-4
1958 2 teams	CHI A (41G – .258)		DET A (45G – .246)														
" total	86	197	50	8	2	1	0.5	21	20	29	40	2	.254	.330	29	11	OF-53, 1B-1
1959 CLE A	122	399	145	17	2	20	5.0	68	79	35	42	2	.363	.566	20	5	OF-64, 1B-35
1960	147	544	159	36	2	17	3.1	84	79	67	67	4	.292	.460	3	0	OF-138, 1B-13
1961	155	592	178	30	8	16	2.7	87	85	56	52	2	.301	.459	7	1	OF-138, 1B-14
1962	158	621	169	28	5	14	2.3	82	70	47	74	3	.272	.401	0	0	1B-158
1963	142	500	114	29	0	10	2.0	57	41	47	77	9	.228	.346	13	4	OF-122, 1B-11
1964	111	270	67	13	2	8	3.0	35	24	44	46	1	.248	.400	29	6	OF-69, 1B-7
1965 STL N	81	174	45	6	2	5	2.9	15	19	17	30	0	.259	.402	35	9	OF-34, 1B-13
1966	83	156	33	4	1	4	2.6	14	17	7	27	0	.212	.327	41	7	1B-30, OF-9
1967 2 teams	PHI N (27G – .205)		ATL N (82G – .248)														
" total	109	327	78	6	1	6	1.8	35	28	27	44	1	.239	.318	27	3	1B-80, OF-7
1968 ATL N	122	346	99	13	1	2	0.6	32	47	51	45	3	.286	.347	24	5	OF-65, 1B-33
1969 2 teams	ATL N (51G – .295)		OAK A (32G – .341)														
" total	83	173	55	7	1	5	2.9	17	42	25	21	0	.318	.457	32	8	1B-26, OF-16
1970 2 teams	OAK A (32G – .242)		MIL A (52G – .231)														
" total	84	98	23	3	0	1	1.0	6	10	12	21	1	.235	.296	64	15	1B-19, OF-1
15 yrs.	1719	5121	1395	224	34	125	2.4	650	656	544	694	46	.272	.403	365	81	OF-911, 1B-475
1 yr.	45	69	17	5	0	0	0.0	11	10	15	16	0	.246	.319	22	8	OF-18, 1B-1

Murray Franklin

FRANKLIN, MURRAY ASHER (Moe). B. Apr. 1, 1914, Chicago, Ill. D. Mar. 16, 1978, Harbor City, Calif. BR TR 6' 175 lbs

	G	AB	H	2B	3B	HR	HR%	R	RBI	BB	SO	SB	BA	SA	Pinch Hit AB	Pinch Hit H	G by POS
1941 DET A	13	10	3	1	0	0	0.0	1	0	2	2	0	.300	.400	7	2	SS-4, 3B-1
1942	48	154	40	7	0	2	1.3	24	16	7	5	0	.260	.344	5	0	SS-32, 2B-7
2 yrs.	61	164	43	8	0	2	1.2	25	16	9	7	0	.262	.348	12	2	SS-36, 2B-7, 3B-1
2 yrs.	61	164	43	8	0	2	1.2	25	16	9	7	0	.262	.348	12	2	SS-36, 2B-7, 3B-1

Bill Freehan

FREEHAN, WILLIAM ASHLEY. B. Nov. 29, 1941, Detroit, Mich. BR TR 6'3" 203 lbs

	G	AB	H	2B	3B	HR	HR%	R	RBI	BB	SO	SB	BA	SA	Pinch Hit AB	Pinch Hit H	G by POS
1961 DET A	4	10	4	0	0	0	0.0	0	4	1	0	0	.400	.400	0	0	C-3
1963	100	300	73	12	2	9	3.0	37	36	39	56	2	.243	.387	9	3	C-73, 1B-19
1964	144	520	156	14	8	18	3.5	69	80	36	68	5	.300	.462	6	1	C-141, 1B-1
1965	130	431	101	15	0	10	2.3	45	43	39	63	4	.234	.339	3	1	C-129
1966	136	492	115	22	0	12	2.4	47	46	40	72	5	.234	.352	1	1	C-132, 1B-5
1967	155	517	146	23	1	20	3.9	66	74	73	71	1	.282	.447	2	2	C-147, 1B-11
1968	155	540	142	24	2	25	4.6	73	84	65	64	0	.263	.454	3	1	C-138, 1B-21, OF-1
1969	143	489	128	16	3	16	3.3	61	49	53	55	1	.262	.405	8	1	C-120, 1B-20
1970	117	395	95	17	3	16	4.1	44	52	52	48	0	.241	.420	3	1	C-114
1971	148	516	143	26	4	21	4.1	57	71	54	48	2	.277	.465	4	1	C-144, OF-1
1972	111	374	98	18	2	10	2.7	51	56	48	51	0	.262	.401	8	3	C-105, 1B-1
1973	110	380	89	10	1	6	1.6	33	29	40	30	0	.234	.313	3	0	C-98, 1B-7
1974	130	445	132	17	5	18	4.0	58	60	42	44	2	.297	.479	1	0	1B-65, C-63, DH-1
1975	120	427	105	17	3	14	3.3	42	47	32	56	2	.246	.398	2	1	C-113, 1B-5
1976	71	237	64	10	1	5	2.1	22	27	12	27	0	.270	.384	6	0	C-61, DH-3, 1B-2
15 yrs.	1774	6073	1591	241	35	200	3.3	706	758	626	753	24	.262	.412	59	16	C-1581, 1B-157, DH-4, OF-2
15 yrs.	1774	6073	1591	241	35	200	3.3	706	758	626	753	24	.262	.412	59	16	C-1581, 1B-157, DH-4, OF-2
	8th	8th	9th	9th		6th					6th						

	G	AB	H	2B	3B	HR	HR %	R	RBI	BB	SO	SB	BA	SA	Pinch Hit AB	H	G by POS

Bill Freehan continued

LEAGUE CHAMPIONSHIP SERIES

| '72 DET A | 3 | 12 | 3 | 1 | 0 | 1 | 8.3 | 2 | 3 | 0 | 1 | 0 | .250 | .583 | 0 | 0 | C-3 |

WORLD SERIES

| '68 DET A | 7 | 24 | 2 | 1 | 0 | 0 | 0.0 | 0 | 2 | 4 | 8 | 0 | .083 | .125 | 0 | 0 | C-7 |

George Freese

FREESE, GEORGE WALTER (Bud)
Brother of Gene Freese.
B. Sept. 12, 1926, Wheeling, W. Va.   BR TR 6' 190 lbs.

'53 DET A	1	1	0	0	0	0	0.0	0	0	0	0	0	.000	.000	1	0	
'55 PIT N	51	179	46	8	2	3	1.7	17	22	17	18	1	.257	.374	1	0	3B-50
'61 CHI N	9	7	2	0	0	0	0.0	0	1	1	4	0	.286	.286	7	2	
3 yrs.	61	187	48	8	2	3	1.6	17	23	18	22	1	.257	.369	9	2	3B-50
1 yr.	1	1	0	0	0	0	0.0	0	0	0	0	0	.000	.000	1	0	

Owen Friend

FRIEND, OWEN LACEY (Red)
B. Mar. 21, 1927, Granite City, Ill.   BR TR 6'1" 180 lbs.

'49 STL A	2	8	3	0	0	0	0.0	1	1	0	0	0	.375	.375	0	0	2B-2
'50	119	372	88	15	2	8	2.2	48	50	40	68	2	.237	.352	1	1	2B-93, 3B-24, SS-3
'53 2 teams	DET A (31G – .177)							CLE A (34G – .235)									
total	65	164	33	6	0	5	3.0	17	23	11	25	0	.201	.329	2	1	2B-45, SS-8, 3B-1
'55 2 teams	BOS A (14G – .262)							CHI N (6G – .100)									
total	20	52	12	3	0	0	0.0	3	2	4	14	0	.231	.288	3	0	SS-15, 3B-2, 2B-1
'56 CHI N	2	2	0	0	0	0	0.0	0	0	0	2	0	.000	.000	2	0	
5 yrs.	208	598	136	24	2	13	2.2	69	76	55	109	2	.227	.339	8	2	2B-141, 3B-27, SS-26
1 yr.	31	96	17	4	0	3	3.1	10	10	6	9	0	.177	.313	2	1	2B-26

Emil Frisk

FRISK, JOHN EMIL
B. Oct. 15, 1874, Kalkaska, Mich.   D. Jan. 27, 1922, Seattle, Wash.   BL TR 6'1" 190 lbs.

'99 CIN N	9	25	7	1	0	0	0.0	5	2	2		0	.280	.320	0	0	P-9
'01 DET A	20	48	15	3	0	1	2.1	10	7	3		0	.313	.438	6	2	P-11, OF-2
'05 STL A	127	429	112	11	6	3	0.7	58	36	42		7	.261	.336	7	1	OF-116
'07	4	4	1	0	0	0	0.0	0	0	1		0	.250	.250	4	1	
4 yrs.	160	506	135	15	6	4	0.8	73	45	48		7	.267	.344	17	4	OF-118, P-20
1 yr.	20	48	15	3	0	1	2.1	10	7	3		0	.313	.438	6	2	P-11, OF-2

Tito Fuentes

FUENTES, RIGOBERTO PEAT
B. Jan. 4, 1944, Havana, Cuba   BR TR 5'11" 175 lbs.
BB 1969

'65 SF N	26	72	15	1	0	0	0.0	12	1	5	14	0	.208	.222	0	0	SS-18, 2B-7, 3B-1
'66	133	541	141	21	3	9	1.7	63	40	9	57	6	.261	.360	1	0	SS-76, 2B-60
'67	133	344	72	12	1	5	1.5	27	29	27	61	4	.209	.294	0	0	2B-130, SS-5
'69	67	183	54	4	3	1	0.5	28	14	15	25	2	.295	.366	1	0	3B-36, SS-30
'70	123	435	116	13	7	2	0.5	49	32	36	52	4	.267	.343	7	0	2B-78, SS-36, 3B-24
'71	152	630	172	28	6	4	0.6	63	52	18	46	12	.273	.356	1	0	2B-152
'72	152	572	151	33	6	7	1.2	64	53	39	56	16	.264	.379	1	0	2B-152
'73	160	656	182	25	5	6	0.9	78	63	45	62	12	.277	.358	0	0	2B-160, 3B-1
'74	108	390	97	15	2	0	0.0	33	22	22	32	7	.249	.297	7	2	2B-103
'75 SD N	146	565	158	21	3	4	0.7	57	43	25	51	8	.280	.349	2	0	2B-142
'76	135	520	137	18	0	2	0.4	48	36	18	38	5	.263	.310	8	2	2B-127
'77 DET A	151	615	190	19	10	5	0.8	83	51	38	61	4	.309	.397	1	0	2B-151
'78 OAK A	13	43	6	1	0	0	0.0	5	2	1	6	0	.140	.163	0	0	2B-13
13 yrs.	1499	5566	1491	211	46	45	0.8	610	438	298	561	80	.268	.347	31	4	2B-1275, SS-165, 3B-62
1 yr.	151	615	190	19	10	5	0.8	83	51	38	61	4	.309	.397	1	0	2B-151

LEAGUE CHAMPIONSHIP SERIES

| '71 SF N | 4 | 16 | 5 | 1 | 0 | 1 | 6.3 | 4 | 2 | 1 | 3 | 0 | .313 | .563 | 0 | 0 | 2B-4 |

Frank Fuller

FULLER, FRANK EDWARD (Rabbit)
B. Jan. 1, 1893, Detroit, Mich.   D. Oct. 29, 1965, Warren, Mich.   BB TR 5'7" 150 lbs.

'15 DET A	14	32	5	0	0	0	0.0	6	2	9	7	2	.156	.156	2	1	2B-9, SS-1
'16	20	10	1	0	0	0	0.0	2	1	1	4	3	.100	.100	1	0	2B-8, SS-1
'23 BOS A	6	21	5	0	0	0	0.0	3	0	1	1	1	.238	.238	0	0	2B-6
3 yrs.	40	63	11	0	0	0	0.0	11	3	11	12	6	.175	.175	3	1	2B-23, SS-2
2 yrs.	34	42	6	0	0	0	0.0	8	3	10	11	5	.143	.143	3	1	2B-17, SS-2

Liz Funk

FUNK, ELIAS CALVIN
B. Oct. 28, 1904, La Cygne, Kans.   D. Jan. 16, 1968, Norman, Okla.   BL TL 5'8½" 160 lbs.

'29 NY A	1	0	0	0	0	0	–	0	0	0	0	0	–	–	0	0	
'30 DET A	140	527	145	26	11	4	0.8	74	65	29	39	12	.275	.389	10	0	OF-129
'32 CHI A	122	440	114	21	5	2	0.5	59	40	43	19	17	.259	.343	1	0	OF-120
'33	10	9	2	0	0	0	0.0	1	0	1	0	0	.222	.222	8	2	OF-2
4 yrs.	273	976	261	47	16	6	0.6	134	105	73	58	29	.267	.367	19	2	OF-251
1 yr.	140	527	145	26	11	4	0.8	74	65	29	39	12	.275	.389	10	0	OF-129

Chick Gagnon

GAGNON, HAROLD DENNIS
B. Sept. 27, 1897, Millbury, Mass.   D. Apr. 30, 1970, Wilmington, Del.   BR TR 5'7½" 158 lbs.

'22 DET A	10	4	1	0	0	0	0.0	2	0	0	2	0	.250	.250	2	1	SS-1, 3B-1
'24 WAS A	4	5	1	0	0	0	0.0	1	1	0	0	0	.200	.200	2	1	SS-2
2 yrs.	14	9	2	0	0	0	0.0	3	1	0	2	0	.222	.222	4	2	SS-3, 3B-1
1 yr.	10	4	1	0	0	0	0.0	2	0	0	2	0	.250	.250	2	1	SS-1, 3B-1

Del Gainor

GAINOR, DELOS CLINTON (Sheriff)
B. Nov. 10, 1886, Montrose, W. Va.   D. Jan. 29, 1947, Elkins, W. Va.   BR TR 6' 180 lbs.

'09 DET A	2	5	1	0	0	0	0.0	0	0	0		0	.200	.200	0	0	1B-2
'11	70	248	75	11	4	2	0.8	32	25	20		10	.302	.403	0	0	1B-69
'12	51	179	43	5	6	0	0.0	28	20	18		14	.240	.335	0	0	1B-50
'13	104	363	97	16	8	2	0.6	47	25	30	45	10	.267	.372	2	1	1B-102

	G	AB	H	2B	3B	HR	HR %	R	RBI	BB	SO	SB	BA	SA	Pinch Hit AB	Pinch Hit H	G by POS

Del Gainor continued

	G	AB	H	2B	3B	HR	HR %	R	RBI	BB	SO	SB	BA	SA	AB	H	G by POS
1914 **2 teams**	**DET** A (1G – .000)					**BOS** A (38G – .238)											
" total	39	84	20	9	2	2	2.4	11	13	8	14	2	.238	.464	8	1	1B-19, 2B-11
1915 **BOS** A	82	200	59	5	8	1	0.5	30	29	21	31	7	.295	.415	14	4	1B-56, OF-6
1916	56	142	36	6	0	3	2.1	14	18	10	24	5	.254	.359	4	0	1B-48, 2B-2
1917	52	172	53	10	2	2	1.2	28	19	15	21	1	.308	.424	1	0	1B-50
1919	47	118	28	6	2	0	0.0	9	13	13	15	5	.237	.322	6	1	1B-21, OF-18
1922 **STL** N	43	97	26	7	4	2	2.1	19	23	14	6	0	.268	.485	9	1	1B-26, OF-10
10 yrs.	546	1608	438	75	36	14	0.9	218	185	149	156	54	.272	.390	44	8	1B-443, OF-34, 2B-13
5 yrs.	228	795	216	32	18	4	0.5	107	70	68	45	34	.272	.372	2	1	1B-224

WORLD SERIES

	G	AB	H	2B	3B	HR	HR %	R	RBI	BB	SO	SB	BA	SA	AB	H	G by POS
1915 **BOS** A	1	3	1	0	0	0	0.0	1	0	0	0	0	.333	.333	1	0	1B-1
1916	1	1	1	0	0	0	0.0	0	1	0	0	0	1.000	1.000	1	1	
2 yrs.	2	4	2	0	0	0	0.0	1	1	0	0	0	.500	.500	2	1	1B-1

Chick Galloway

GALLOWAY, CLARENCE EDWARD
B. Aug. 4, 1896, Manning, S. C.   D. Nov. 7, 1969, Clinton, S. C.
BR TR 5'8"   160 lb

	G	AB	H	2B	3B	HR	HR %	R	RBI	BB	SO	SB	BA	SA	AB	H	G by POS
1919 **PHI** A	17	63	9	0	0	0	0.0	2	4	1	8	0	.143	.143	0	0	SS-17
1920	98	298	60	9	3	0	0.0	28	18	22	22	2	.201	.252	6	0	SS-84, 2B-4, 3B-3
1921	131	465	123	28	5	3	0.6	42	47	29	43	12	.265	.366	0	0	SS-110, 3B-20, 2B-1
1922	155	571	185	26	9	6	1.1	83	69	39	38	10	.324	.433	0	0	SS-155
1923	134	504	140	18	9	2	0.4	64	62	37	30	12	.278	.361	0	0	SS-134
1924	129	464	128	16	4	2	0.4	41	48	23	23	11	.276	.341	0	0	SS-129
1925	149	481	116	11	4	3	0.6	52	71	59	28	16	.241	.299	1	0	SS-148
1926	133	408	98	13	6	0	0.0	37	49	31	20	8	.240	.301	0	0	SS-133
1927	77	181	48	10	4	0	0.0	15	22	18	9	1	.265	.365	9	6	SS-61, 3B-7
1928 **DET** A	53	148	39	5	2	1	0.7	17	17	15	3	7	.264	.345	4	2	SS-22, 3B-21, OF-1, 1B
10 yrs.	1076	3583	946	136	46	17	0.5	381	407	274	224	79	.264	.342	20	8	SS-993, 3B-51, 2B-5, OF-1, 1B-1
1 yr.	53	148	39	5	2	1	0.7	17	17	15	3	7	.264	.345	4	2	SS-22, 3B-21, OF-1, 1B

John Gamble

GAMBLE, JOHN ROBERT JR.
B. Feb. 10, 1948, Reno, Nev.
BR TR 5'10"   165 lb

	G	AB	H	2B	3B	HR	HR %	R	RBI	BB	SO	SB	BA	SA	AB	H	G by POS
1972 **DET** A	6	3	0	0	0	0	0.0	0	0	0	0	0	.000	.000	1	0	SS-1
1973	7	0	0	0	0	0	–	1	0	0	0	0	–	–	0	0	
2 yrs.	13	3	0	0	0	0	0.0	1	0	0	0	0	.000	.000	1	0	SS-1
2 yrs.	13	3	0	0	0	0	0.0	1	0	0	0	0	.000	.000	1	0	SS-1

Barbaro Garbey

GARBEY, BARBARO GARBEY
B. Dec. 4, 1956, Santiagoà Cuba
BR TR 5'9"   165 lb

	G	AB	H	2B	3B	HR	HR %	R	RBI	BB	SO	SB	BA	SA	AB	H	G by POS
1984 **DET** A	110	327	94	17	1	5	1.5	45	52	17	35	6	.287	.391	25	8	1B-65, 3B-20, DH-18, OF-10, 2B-3

LEAGUE CHAMPIONSHIP SERIES

	G	AB	H	2B	3B	HR	HR %	R	RBI	BB	SO	SB	BA	SA	AB	H	G by POS
1984 **DET** A	3	9	3	0	0	0	0.0	1	0	0	1	0	.333	.333	1	0	DH-2

WORLD SERIES

	G	AB	H	2B	3B	HR	HR %	R	RBI	BB	SO	SB	BA	SA	AB	H	G by POS
1984 **DET** A	4	12	0	0	0	0	0.0	0	0	0	2	0	.000	.000	1	0	DH-3

Alex Garbowski

GARBOWSKI, ALEXANDER
B. June 25, 1925, Yonkers, N. Y.
BR TR 6'1"   185 lb

	G	AB	H	2B	3B	HR	HR %	R	RBI	BB	SO	SB	BA	SA	AB	H	G by POS
1952 **DET** A	2	0	0	0	0	0	–	0	0	0	0	0	–	–	0	0	

Pedro Garcia

GARCIA, PEDRO DELFI
B. Apr. 17, 1950, Guayama, Puerto Rico
BR TR 5'10"   175 lb

	G	AB	H	2B	3B	HR	HR %	R	RBI	BB	SO	SB	BA	SA	AB	H	G by POS
1973 **MIL** A	160	580	142	32	5	15	2.6	67	54	40	119	11	.245	.395	0	0	2B-160
1974	141	452	90	15	4	12	2.7	46	54	26	67	8	.199	.330	0	0	2B-140
1975	98	302	68	15	2	6	2.0	40	38	18	59	12	.225	.348	1	0	2B-94, DH-1
1976 **2 teams**	**MIL** A (41G – .217)					**DET** A (77G – .198)											
" total	118	333	68	17	3	4	1.2	33	29	13	63	4	.204	.309	3	0	2B-116
1977 **TOR** A	41	130	27	10	1	0	0.0	10	9	5	21	0	.208	.300	2	0	2B-34, DH-4
5 yrs.	558	1797	395	89	15	37	2.1	196	184	102	329	35	.220	.348	6	0	2B-544, DH-5
1 yr.	77	227	45	10	2	3	1.3	21	20	9	40	2	.198	.300	0	0	2B-77

Charlie Gehringer

GEHRINGER, CHARLES LEONARD
B. May 11, 1903, Fowlerville, Mich.
Hall of Fame 1949.
BL TR 5'11"   180 lb

	G	AB	H	2B	3B	HR	HR %	R	RBI	BB	SO	SB	BA	SA	AB	H	G by POS
1924 **DET** A	5	13	6	0	0	0	0.0	2	1	0	2	1	.462	.462	0	0	2B-5
1925	8	18	3	0	0	0	0.0	3	0	2	0	0	.167	.167	2	0	2B-6
1926	123	459	127	19	17	1	0.2	62	48	30	42	9	.277	.399	6	0	2B-112, 3B-6
1927	133	508	161	29	11	4	0.8	110	61	52	31	17	.317	.441	9	3	2B-121
1928	154	603	193	29	16	6	1.0	108	74	69	22	15	.320	.451	0	0	2B-154
1929	155	634	215	45	19	13	2.1	131	106	64	19	28	.339	.532	1	0	2B-154
1930	154	610	201	47	15	16	2.6	144	98	69	17	19	.330	.534	0	0	2B-154
1931	101	383	119	24	5	4	1.0	67	53	29	15	13	.311	.431	12	1	2B-78, 1B-9
1932	152	618	184	44	11	19	3.1	112	107	68	34	9	.298	.497	0	0	2B-152
1933	155	628	204	42	6	12	1.9	103	105	68	27	5	.325	.468	0	0	2B-155
1934	154	601	214	50	7	11	1.8	134	127	99	25	11	.356	.517	0	0	2B-154
1935	150	610	201	32	8	19	3.1	123	108	79	16	11	.330	.502	2	1	2B-149
1936	154	641	227	60	12	15	2.3	144	116	83	13	4	.354	.555	0	0	2B-154
1937	144	564	209	40	1	14	2.5	133	96	90	25	11	.371	.520	1	0	2B-142
1938	152	568	174	32	5	20	3.5	133	107	112	21	14	.306	.486	0	0	2B-154
1939	118	406	132	29	6	16	3.9	86	86	68	16	4	.325	.544	9	4	2B-107
1940	139	515	161	33	3	10	1.9	108	81	101	17	10	.313	.447	1	0	2B-138
1941	127	436	96	19	4	3	0.7	65	46	95	26	1	.220	.303	10	3	2B-116

	G	AB	H	2B	3B	HR	HR %	R	RBI	BB	SO	SB	BA	SA	Pinch Hit AB	Pinch Hit H	G by POS

Charlie Gehringer continued

	G	AB	H	2B	3B	HR	HR %	R	RBI	BB	SO	SB	BA	SA	PH AB	PH H	G by POS
'42	45	45	12	0	0	1	2.2	6	7	7	4	0	.267	.333	38	11	2B-3
19 yrs.	2323	8860	2839	574	146	184	2.1	1774	1427	1185	372	182	.320	.480	91	23	2B-2206, 1B-9, 3B-6
			10th														
19 yrs.	2323	8860	2839	574	146	184	2.1	1774	1427	1185	372	182	.320	.480	91	23	2B-2206, 1B-9, 3B-6
	3rd	3rd	3rd	2nd	3rd	8th		2nd	4th	2nd		7th	7th	10th			

WORLD SERIES

	G	AB	H	2B	3B	HR	HR %	R	RBI	BB	SO	SB	BA	SA	PH AB	PH H	G by POS
'34 DET A	7	29	11	1	0	1	3.4	5	2	3	0	1	.379	.517	0	0	2B-7
'35	6	24	9	3	0	0	0.0	4	4	2	1	1	.375	.500	0	0	2B-6
'40	7	28	6	0	0	0	0.0	3	1	2	0	0	.214	.214	0	0	2B-7
3 yrs.	20	81	26	4	0	1	1.2	12	7	7	1	2	.321	.407	0	0	2B-20

Charley Gelbert

GELBERT, CHARLES MAGNUS   BR TR 5'11" 170 lbs.
B. Jan. 26, 1906, Scranton, Pa.   D. Jan. 13, 1967, Easton, Pa.

	G	AB	H	2B	3B	HR	HR %	R	RBI	BB	SO	SB	BA	SA	PH AB	PH H	G by POS
'29 STL N	146	512	134	29	8	3	0.6	60	65	51	46	8	.262	.367	0	0	SS-146
'30	139	513	156	39	11	3	0.6	92	72	43	41	6	.304	.441	0	0	SS-139
'31	131	447	129	29	5	1	0.2	61	62	54	31	7	.289	.383	0	0	SS-131
'32	122	455	122	28	9	1	0.2	60	45	39	30	8	.268	.376	0	0	SS-122
'35	62	168	49	7	2	2	1.2	24	21	17	18	0	.292	.393	5	1	3B-37, SS-21, 2B-3
'36	93	280	64	15	2	3	1.1	33	27	25	26	2	.229	.329	2	0	3B-60, SS-28, 2B-8
'37 2 teams	CIN N (43G – .193)			DET A (20G – .085)													
total	63	161	26	6	0	1	0.6	16	14	19	23	1	.161	.217	6	0	SS-53, 2B-9, 3B-1
'39 WAS A	68	188	48	7	5	3	1.6	36	29	30	11	2	.255	.394	16	2	SS-28, 3B-20, 2B-1
'40 2 teams	WAS A (22G – .370)			BOS A (30G – .198)													
total	52	145	38	9	1	0	0.0	16	15	12	19	0	.262	.338	4	0	3B-29, SS-13, P-2, 2B-1
9 yrs.	876	2869	766	169	43	17	0.6	398	350	290	245	34	.267	.374	33	3	SS-681, 3B-147, 2B-22, P-2
1 yr.	20	47	4	2	0	0	0.0	4	1	4	11	0	.085	.128	5	0	SS-16

WORLD SERIES

	G	AB	H	2B	3B	HR	HR %	R	RBI	BB	SO	SB	BA	SA	PH AB	PH H	G by POS
'30 STL N	6	17	6	0	1	0	0.0	2	2	3	3	0	.353	.471	0	0	SS-6
'31	7	23	6	1	0	0	0.0	0	3	0	4	0	.261	.304	0	0	SS-7
2 yrs.	13	40	12	1	1	0	0.0	2	5	3	7	0	.300	.375	0	0	SS-13

Dick Gernert

GERNERT, RICHARD EDWARD   BR TR 6'3" 209 lbs.
B. Sept. 28, 1928, Reading, Pa.

	G	AB	H	2B	3B	HR	HR %	R	RBI	BB	SO	SB	BA	SA	PH AB	PH H	G by POS
'52 BOS A	102	367	89	20	2	19	5.2	58	67	35	83	4	.243	.463	4	1	1B-99
'53	139	494	125	15	1	21	4.3	73	71	88	82	0	.253	.415	3	0	1B-136
'54	14	23	6	2	0	0	0.0	2	1	6	4	0	.261	.348	7	1	1B-6
'55	7	20	4	2	0	0	0.0	6	1	1	5	0	.200	.300	1	0	1B-5
'56	106	306	89	11	0	16	5.2	53	68	56	57	1	.291	.484	22	4	OF-50, 1B-37
'57	99	316	75	13	3	14	4.4	45	58	39	62	1	.237	.430	18	6	1B-71, OF-16
'58	122	431	102	19	1	20	4.6	59	69	59	78	2	.237	.425	7	3	1B-114
'59	117	298	78	14	1	11	3.7	41	42	52	49	1	.262	.426	21	4	1B-75, OF-25
'60 2 teams	CHI N (52G – .250)			DET A (21G – .300)													
total	73	146	39	7	0	1	0.7	14	16	14	24	1	.267	.336	31	8	1B-31, OF-11
'61 2 teams	DET A (6G – .200)			CIN N (40G – .302)													
total	46	68	20	1	0	1	1.5	8	8	8	11	0	.294	.353	25	6	1B-21
'62 HOU N	10	24	5	0	0	0	0.0	1	1	5	7	0	.208	.208	1	0	1B-9
11 yrs.	835	2493	632	104	8	103	4.1	357	402	363	462	10	.254	.426	140	33	1B-604, OF-102
2 yrs.	27	55	16	4	0	2	3.6	7	6	5	7	0	.291	.473	9	2	1B-13, OF-6

WORLD SERIES

	G	AB	H	2B	3B	HR	HR %	R	RBI	BB	SO	SB	BA	SA	PH AB	PH H	G by POS
'61 CIN N	4	4	0	0	0	0	0.0	0	0	0	1	0	.000	.000	4	0	

Doc Gessler

GESSLER, HARRY HOMER   BL TR
B. Dec. 23, 1880, Indiana, Pa.   D. Dec. 26, 1924, Indiana, Pa.
Manager 1914.

	G	AB	H	2B	3B	HR	HR %	R	RBI	BB	SO	SB	BA	SA	PH AB	PH H	G by POS
'03 2 teams	DET A (29G – .238)			BKN N (49G – .247)													
total	78	259	63	13	7	0	0.0	29	30	20		10	.243	.347	4	1	OF-71
'04 BKN N	104	341	99	18	4	2	0.6	41	28	30		13	.290	.384	12	2	OF-88, 2B-1, 1B-1
'05	126	431	125	17	4	3	0.7	44	46	38		26	.290	.369	7	2	1B-107, OF-12
'06 2 teams	BKN N (9G – .242)			CHI N (34G – .253)													
total	43	116	29	4	2	0	0.0	11	14	15		7	.250	.319	11	2	OF-21, 1B-10
'08 BOS A	128	435	134	13	14	3	0.7	55	63	51		19	.308	.423	2	2	OF-126
'09 2 teams	BOS A (111G – .298)			WAS A (17G – .241)													
total	128	440	128	26	2	0	0.0	66	54	43		20	.291	.359	1	0	OF-127, 1B-2
'10 WAS A	145	487	126	17	11	2	0.4	58	50	62		18	.259	.351	1	0	OF-144
'11	128	450	127	19	5	4	0.9	65	78	74		29	.282	.373	1	0	OF-126, 1B-1
8 yrs.	880	2959	831	127	49	14	0.5	369	363	333		142	.281	.371	39	9	OF-715, 1B-121, 2B-1
1 yr.	29	105	25	5	4	0	0.0	9	12	3		1	.238	.362	1	0	OF-28

WORLD SERIES

	G	AB	H	2B	3B	HR	HR %	R	RBI	BB	SO	SB	BA	SA	PH AB	PH H	G by POS
'06 CHI N	2	1	0	0	0	0	0.0	0	0	1		0	.000	.000	1	0	

Frank Gibson

GIBSON, FRANK GILBERT   BB TR 6'½" 172 lbs.
B. Sept. 27, 1890, Omaha, Neb.   BL 1921-22,1924
D. Apr. 27, 1961, Austin, Tex.

	G	AB	H	2B	3B	HR	HR %	R	RBI	BB	SO	SB	BA	SA	PH AB	PH H	G by POS
'13 DET A	20	57	8	1	0	0	0.0	8	2	3	9	2	.140	.158	0	0	C-19, OF-1
'21 BOS N	63	125	33	5	4	2	1.6	14	13	3	17	0	.264	.416	17	4	C-41
'22	66	164	49	7	2	3	1.8	15	20	10	27	4	.299	.421	15	2	C-29, 1B-20
'23	41	50	15	1	0	0	0.0	13	5	7	7	0	.300	.320	15	6	C-20
'24	90	229	71	15	6	1	0.4	25	30	10	23	1	.310	.441	31	6	C-46, 1B-10, 3B-2
'25	104	316	88	23	5	2	0.6	36	50	15	28	3	.278	.402	15	7	C-88, 1B-2
'26	24	47	16	4	0	0	0.0	3	7	4	6	0	.340	.426	12	6	C-12
'27	60	167	37	1	2	0	0.0	7	19	3	10	2	.222	.251	12	4	C-47
8 yrs.	468	1155	317	57	19	8	0.7	121	146	55	127	12	.274	.377	117	29	C-302, 1B-32, 3B-2, OF-1
1 yr.	20	57	8	1	0	0	0.0	8	2	3	9	2	.140	.158	0	0	C-19, OF-1

	G	AB	H	2B	3B	HR	HR%	R	RBI	BB	SO	SB	BA	SA	Pinch Hit AB	Pinch Hit H	G by POS

Kirk Gibson

GIBSON, KIRK HAROLD
B. May 28, 1957, Pontiac, Mich.
BL TL 6'3" 215 lb

	G	AB	H	2B	3B	HR	HR%	R	RBI	BB	SO	SB	BA	SA	AB	H	G by POS
1979 DET A	12	38	9	3	0	1	2.6	3	4	1	3	3	.237	.395	2	0	OF-10
1980	51	175	46	2	1	9	5.1	23	16	10	45	4	.263	.440	5	1	OF-49, DH-1
1981	83	290	95	11	3	9	3.1	41	40	18	64	17	.328	.479	8	1	OF-67, DH-9
1982	69	266	74	16	2	8	3.0	34	35	25	41	9	.278	.444	1	0	OF-64, DH-4
1983	128	401	91	12	9	15	3.7	60	51	53	96	14	.227	.414	20	5	DH-66, OF-54
1984	149	531	150	23	10	27	5.1	92	91	63	103	29	.282	.516	11	1	OF-139, DH-6
6 yrs.	492	1701	465	67	25	69	4.1	253	237	170	352	76	.273	.464	47	8	OF-383, DH-86
6 yrs.	492	1701	465	67	25	69	4.1	253	237	170	352	76	.273	.464	47	8	OF-383, DH-86

LEAGUE CHAMPIONSHIP SERIES

	G	AB	H	2B	3B	HR	HR%	R	RBI	BB	SO	SB	BA	SA	AB	H	G by POS
1984 DET A	3	12	5	1	0	1	8.3	2	2	2	1	1	.417	.750	0	0	OF-3

WORLD SERIES

	G	AB	H	2B	3B	HR	HR%	R	RBI	BB	SO	SB	BA	SA	AB	H	G by POS
1984 DET A	5	18	6	0	0	2	11.1	4	7	4	4	3	.333	.667	0	0	OF-5

Joe Ginsberg

GINSBERG, MYRON NATHAN
B. Oct. 11, 1926, New York, N. Y.
BL TR 5'11" 180 lb

	G	AB	H	2B	3B	HR	HR%	R	RBI	BB	SO	SB	BA	SA	AB	H	G by POS
1948 DET A	11	36	13	0	0	0	0.0	7	1	3	1	0	.361	.361	0	0	C-11
1950	36	95	22	6	0	0	0.0	12	12	11	6	1	.232	.295	4	1	C-31
1951	102	304	79	10	2	8	2.6	44	37	43	21	0	.260	.385	8	2	C-95
1952	113	307	68	13	2	6	2.0	29	36	51	21	1	.221	.336	16	2	C-101
1953 2 teams				DET A (18G – .302)				CLE A (46G – .284)									
" total	64	162	47	6	0	0	0.0	16	13	24	5	0	.290	.327	12	2	C-54
1954 CLE A	3	2	1	0	1	0	0.0	0	1	0	0	0	.500	1.500	2	1	C-1
1956 2 teams				KC A (71G – .246)				BAL A (15G – .071)									
" total	86	223	50	8	1	1	0.4	15	14	25	21	1	.224	.283	18	3	C-65
1957 BAL A	85	175	48	8	2	1	0.6	15	18	18	19	2	.274	.360	18	3	C-66
1958	61	109	23	1	0	3	2.8	4	16	13	14	0	.211	.303	20	4	C-39
1959	65	166	30	2	0	1	0.6	14	14	21	3	1	.181	.211	5	1	C-62
1960 2 teams				BAL A (14G – .267)				CHI A (28G – .253)									
" total	42	105	27	5	0	0	0.0	11	15	16	9	1	.257	.305	2	0	C-39
1961 2 teams				CHI A (6G – .000)				BOS A (19G – .250)									
" total	25	27	6	0	0	0	0.0	1	5	1	4	0	.222	.222	16	3	C-8
1962 NY N	2	5	0	0	0	0	0.0	0	0	0	2	0	.000	.000	0	0	C-2
13 yrs.	695	1716	414	59	8	20	1.2	168	182	226	125	7	.241	.320	121	22	C-574
5 yrs.	280	795	198	31	4	14	1.8	98	89	118	50	2	.249	.351	31	5	C-253

Kid Gleason

GLEASON, WILLIAM J.
Brother of Harry Gleason.
B. Oct. 26, 1866, Camden, N. J.   D. Jan. 2, 1933, Philadelphia, Pa.
Manager 1919-23.
BL TR 5'7" 158 lb

	G	AB	H	2B	3B	HR	HR%	R	RBI	BB	SO	SB	BA	SA	AB	H	G by POS
1888 PHI N	24	83	17	2	0	0	0.0	4	5	3	16	3	.205	.229	0	0	P-24, OF-1
1889	30	99	25	5	0	0	0.0	11	8	8	12	4	.253	.303	0	0	P-28, OF-3, 2B-2
1890	63	224	47	3	0	0	0.0	22	17	12	21	10	.210	.223	0	0	P-60, 2B-2
1891	65	214	53	5	2	0	0.0	31	17	20	17	6	.248	.290	0	0	P-53, OF-9, SS-4
1892 STL N	66	233	50	4	2	3	1.3	35	25	34	23	7	.215	.288	0	0	P-47, OF-11, 2B-10, 1B-1, C-1
1893	59	199	51	6	4	0	0.0	25	20	19	8	2	.256	.327	2	1	P-48, OF-11, SS-1
1894 2 teams				STL N (9G – .250)				BAL N (26G – .349)									
" total	35	114	37	5	2	0	0.0	25	18	9	3	1	.325	.404	4	2	P-29, 1B-2
1895 BAL N	112	421	130	14	12	0	0.0	90	74	33	18	19	.309	.399	3	0	2B-85, 3B-12, P-9, OF-
1896 NY N	133	541	162	17	5	4	0.7	79	89	42	13	46	.299	.372	0	0	2B-130, 3B-3, OF-1
1897	131	540	172	16	4	1	0.2	85	106	26		43	.319	.369	0	0	2B-129, SS-3
1898	150	570	126	8	5	0	0.0	78	62	39		21	.221	.253	0	0	2B-144, SS-6
1899	146	576	152	14	4	0	0.0	72	59	24		29	.264	.302	0	0	2B-146
1900	111	420	104	11	3	1	0.2	60	29	17		23	.248	.295	0	0	2B-111, SS-1
1901 DET A	135	547	150	16	12	3	0.5	82	75	41		32	.274	.364	0	0	2B-135
1902	118	441	109	11	4	1	0.2	42	38	25		17	.247	.297	0	0	2B-118
1903 PHI N	106	412	117	19	6	1	0.2	65	49	23		12	.284	.367	0	0	2B-102, OF-4
1904	153	587	161	23	6	0	0.0	61	42	37		17	.274	.334	0	0	2B-152, 3B-1
1905	155	608	150	17	7	1	0.2	95	50	45		16	.247	.303	0	0	2B-155
1906	135	494	112	17	2	0	0.0	47	34	36		17	.227	.269	0	0	2B-135
1907	36	126	18	3	0	0	0.0	11	6	7		3	.143	.167	1	0	2B-26, SS-4, 1B-4, OF-
1908	2	1	0	0	0	0	0.0	0	0	0		0	.000	.000	0	0	OF-1, 2B-1
1912 CHI A	1	2	1	0	0	0	0.0	0	0	0		0	.500	.500	0	0	2B-1
22 yrs.	1966	7452	1944	216	80	15	0.2	1020	823	500	131	328	.261	.317	10	3	2B-1584, P-298, OF-46, SS-19, 3B-16, 1B-7, C-2
2 yrs.	253	988	259	27	16	4	0.4	124	113	66		49	.262	.334	0	0	2B-253

Purnal Goldy

GOLDY, PURNAL WILLIAM
B. Nov. 28, 1937, Camden, N. J.
BR TR 6'5" 200 lb

	G	AB	H	2B	3B	HR	HR%	R	RBI	BB	SO	SB	BA	SA	AB	H	G by POS
1962 DET A	20	70	16	1	1	3	4.3	8	12	0	12	0	.229	.400	3	1	OF-15
1963	9	8	2	0	0	0	0.0	1	0	0	4	0	.250	.250	8	2	
2 yrs.	29	78	18	1	1	3	3.8	9	12	0	16	0	.231	.385	11	3	OF-15
2 yrs.	29	78	18	1	1	3	3.8	9	12	0	16	0	.231	.385	11	3	OF-15

Dan Gonzalez

GONZALEZ, DANIEL DAVID
B. Sept. 30, 1953, Whittier, Calif.
BL TR 6'1" 195 lb

	G	AB	H	2B	3B	HR	HR%	R	RBI	BB	SO	SB	BA	SA	AB	H	G by POS
1979 DET A	7	18	4	1	0	0	0.0	1	2	0	2	1	.222	.278	3	0	OF-3, DH-1
1980	2	7	1	0	0	0	0.0	1	0	0	1	0	.143	.143	1	0	DH-1, OF-1
2 yrs.	9	25	5	1	0	0	0.0	2	2	0	3	1	.200	.240	4	0	OF-4, DH-2
2 yrs.	9	25	5	1	0	0	0.0	2	2	0	3	1	.200	.240	4	0	OF-4, DH-2

Julio Gonzalez

GONZALEZ, JULIO CESAR
Also known as Julio Cesar Hernandez.
B. Dec. 25, 1953, Caguas, Puerto Rico
BR TR 5'11" 162 lb

	G	AB	H	2B	3B	HR	HR%	R	RBI	BB	SO	SB	BA	SA	AB	H	G by POS
1977 HOU N	110	383	94	18	3	1	0.3	34	27	19	45	3	.245	.316	7	1	SS-63, 2B-45
1978	78	223	52	3	1	1	0.4	24	16	8	31	6	.233	.269	12	1	2B-54, SS-17, 3B-4

	G	AB	H	2B	3B	HR	HR %	R	RBI	BB	SO	SB	BA	SA	Pinch Hit AB	H	G by POS

ulio Gonzalez continued

	G	AB	H	2B	3B	HR	HR%	R	RBI	BB	SO	SB	BA	SA	PH AB	PH H	G by POS
79	68	181	45	5	2	0	0.0	16	10	5	14	2	.249	.298	7	3	2B-32, SS-21, 3B-9
80	40	52	6	1	0	0	0.0	5	1	1	8	1	.115	.135	10	0	SS-16, 3B-11, 2B-2
81 STL N	20	22	7	1	0	1	4.5	2	3	1	3	0	.318	.500	10	2	SS-5, 2B-4, 3B-2
82	42	87	21	3	2	1	1.1	9	7	1	24	1	.241	.356	12	1	3B-21, 2B-9, SS-1
83 DET A	12	21	3	1	0	0	0.0	0	2	1	7	0	.143	.190	0	0	SS-6, 2B-5, 3B-1
7 yrs.	370	969	228	32	8	4	0.4	90	66	36	132	13	.235	.297	58	8	2B-151, SS-129, 3B-48
1 yr.	12	21	3	1	0	0	0.0	2	1	7	0	.143	.190	0	0	SS-6, 2B-5, 3B-1

oose Goslin

GOSLIN, LEON ALLEN BL TR 5'11½" 185 lbs.
B. Oct. 16, 1900, Salem, N. J.   D. May 15, 1971, Bridgeton, N. J.
Hall of Fame 1968.

	G	AB	H	2B	3B	HR	HR%	R	RBI	BB	SO	SB	BA	SA	PH AB	PH H	G by POS
21 WAS A	14	50	13	1	1	1	2.0	8	6	6	5	0	.260	.380	0	0	OF-14
22	101	358	116	19	7	3	0.8	44	53	25	26	4	.324	.441	5	0	OF-93
23	150	600	180	29	18	9	1.5	86	99	40	53	7	.300	.453	1	1	OF-149
24	154	579	199	30	17	12	2.1	100	129	68	29	16	.344	.516	0	0	OF-154
25	150	601	201	34	20	18	3.0	116	113	53	50	26	.334	.547	0	0	OF-150
26	147	567	201	26	15	17	3.0	105	108	63	38	8	.354	.543	0	0	OF-147
27	148	581	194	37	15	13	2.2	96	120	50	28	21	.334	.516	0	0	OF-148
28	135	456	173	36	10	17	3.7	80	102	48	19	16	.379	.614	7	2	OF-125
29	145	553	159	28	7	18	3.3	82	91	66	33	10	.288	.461	3	3	OF-142
30 2 teams total	WAS A (47G – .271)	STL A (101G – .326)														
	148	584	180	36	12	37	6.3	115	138	67	54	17	.308	.601	0	0	OF-148
31 STL A	151	591	194	42	10	24	4.1	114	105	80	41	9	.328	.555	0	0	OF-151
32	150	572	171	28	9	17	3.0	88	104	92	35	12	.299	.469	0	0	OF-149, 3B-1
33 WAS A	132	549	163	35	10	10	1.8	97	64	42	32	5	.297	.452	4	2	OF-128
34 DET A	151	614	187	38	7	13	2.1	106	100	65	38	5	.305	.453	2	0	OF-149
35	147	590	172	34	6	9	1.5	88	109	56	31	5	.292	.415	3	1	OF-144
36	147	572	180	33	8	24	4.2	122	125	85	50	14	.315	.526	3	0	OF-144
37	79	181	43	11	1	4	2.2	30	35	35	18	0	.238	.376	29	9	OF-40, 1B-1
38 WAS A	38	57	9	3	0	2	3.5	6	8	8	5	0	.158	.316	18	4	OF-13
18 yrs.	2287	8655	2735	500	173	248	2.9	1483	1609	949	585	175	.316	.500	75	22	OF-2188, 3B-1, 1B-1
4 yrs.	524	1957	582	116	22	50	2.6	346	369	241	137	24	.297	.456	37	10	OF-477, 1B-1
ORLD SERIES																	
24 WAS A	7	32	11	1	0	3	9.4	4	7	0	7	0	.344	.656	0	0	OF-7
25	7	26	8	1	0	3	11.5	6	5	3	3	1	.308	.692	0	0	OF-7
33	5	20	5	1	0	1	5.0	2	1	1	3	0	.250	.450	0	0	OF-5
34 DET A	7	29	7	1	0	0	0.0	2	2	3	1	0	.241	.276	0	0	OF-7
35	6	22	6	1	0	0	0.0	2	3	5	0	0	.273	.318	0	0	OF-6
5 yrs.	32	129	37	5	0	7	5.4	16	18	12	14	1	.287	.488	0	0	OF-32
							10th										

ohnny Grabowski

GRABOWSKI, JOHN PATRICK (Nig) BR TR 5'10" 185 lbs.
B. Jan. 7, 1900, Ware, Mass.   D. May 23, 1946, Albany, N. Y.

	G	AB	H	2B	3B	HR	HR%	R	RBI	BB	SO	SB	BA	SA	PH AB	PH H	G by POS
24 CHI A	20	56	14	3	0	0	0.0	10	3	2	4	0	.250	.304	0	0	C-19
25	21	46	14	4	1	0	0.0	5	10	2	4	0	.304	.435	0	0	C-21
26	48	122	32	1	1	1	0.8	6	11	4	15	0	.262	.311	8	4	C-38, 1B-1
27 NY A	70	195	54	2	4	0	0.0	29	25	20	15	0	.277	.328	2	0	C-68
28	75	202	48	7	1	1	0.5	21	21	10	21	0	.238	.297	0	0	C-75
29	22	59	12	1	0	0	0.0	4	2	3	6	1	.203	.220	0	0	C-22
31 DET A	40	136	32	7	1	1	0.7	9	14	6	19	0	.235	.324	1	1	C-39
7 yrs.	296	816	206	25	8	3	0.4	84	86	47	84	1	.252	.314	11	5	C-282, 1B-1
1 yr.	40	136	32	7	1	1	0.7	9	14	6	19	0	.235	.324	1	1	C-39
ORLD SERIES																	
27 NY A	1	2	0	0	0	0	0.0	0	0	0	0	0	.000	.000	0	0	C-1

enny Green

GREEN, LEONARD CHARLES BL TL 5'11" 170 lbs.
B. Jan. 6, 1934, Detroit, Mich.

	G	AB	H	2B	3B	HR	HR%	R	RBI	BB	SO	SB	BA	SA	PH AB	PH H	G by POS
57 BAL A	19	33	6	1	1	1	3.0	2	5	1	4	0	.182	.364	2	0	OF-15
58	69	91	21	4	0	0	0.0	10	4	9	10	0	.231	.275	9	1	OF-53
59 2 teams total	BAL A (27G – .292)	WAS A (88G – .242)														
	115	214	53	6	1	3	1.4	32	17	21	18	9	.248	.327	35	11	OF-81
60 WAS A	127	330	97	16	7	5	1.5	62	33	43	25	21	.294	.430	29	8	OF-100
61 MIN A	156	600	171	28	7	9	1.5	92	50	81	50	17	.285	.400	2	1	OF-153
62	158	619	168	33	3	14	2.3	97	63	88	36	8	.271	.402	3	1	OF-156
63	145	280	67	10	1	4	1.4	41	27	31	21	11	.239	.325	23	4	OF-119
64 3 teams total	MIN A (26G – .000)	LA A (39G – .250)	BAL A (14G – .190)													
	79	128	27	2	0	2	1.6	16	5	21	17	3	.211	.273	33	4	OF-38
65 BOS A	119	373	103	24	6	7	1.9	69	24	48	43	8	.276	.429	24	7	OF-95
66	85	133	32	6	0	1	0.8	18	12	15	19	0	.241	.308	52	14	OF-27
67 DET A	58	151	42	8	1	1	0.7	22	13	9	17	1	.278	.364	11	1	OF-47
68	6	4	1	0	0	0	0.0	0	0	1	1	0	.250	.250	3	1	OF-2
12 yrs.	1136	2956	788	138	27	47	1.6	461	253	368	260	78	.267	.379	226	53	OF-883
2 yrs.	64	155	43	8	1	1	0.6	22	13	10	17	1	.277	.361	14	2	OF-46

ank Greenberg

GREENBERG, HENRY BENJAMIN (Hammerin' Hank) BR TR 6'3½" 210 lbs.
B. Jan. 1, 1911, New York, N. Y.
Hall of Fame 1956.

	G	AB	H	2B	3B	HR	HR%	R	RBI	BB	SO	SB	BA	SA	PH AB	PH H	G by POS
30 DET A	1	1	0	0	0	0	0.0	0	0	0	0	0	.000	.000	1	0	
33	117	449	135	33	3	12	2.7	59	87	46	78	6	.301	.468	1	0	1B-117
34	153	593	201	63	7	26	4.4	118	139	63	93	9	.339	.600	0	0	1B-153
35	152	619	203	46	16	36	5.8	121	170	87	91	4	.328	.628	0	0	1B-152
36	12	46	16	6	2	1	2.2	10	16	9	6	1	.348	.630	0	0	1B-12
37	154	594	200	49	14	40	6.7	137	183	102	101	8	.337	.668	0	0	1B-154
38	155	556	175	23	4	58	10.4	144	146	119	92	7	.315	.683	0	0	1B-155
39	138	500	156	42	7	33	6.6	112	112	91	95	8	.312	.622	1	0	1B-136
40	148	573	195	50	8	41	7.2	129	150	93	75	6	.340	.670	0	0	OF-148

	G	AB	H	2B	3B	HR	HR %	R	RBI	BB	SO	SB	BA	SA	Pinch Hit AB	Pinch Hit H	G by POS

Hank Greenberg continued

	G	AB	H	2B	3B	HR	HR %	R	RBI	BB	SO	SB	BA	SA	Pinch Hit AB	Pinch Hit H	G by POS
1941	19	67	18	5	1	2	3.0	12	12	16	12	1	.269	.463	0	0	OF-19
1945	78	270	84	20	2	13	4.8	47	60	42	40	3	.311	.544	5	2	OF-72
1946	142	523	145	29	5	**44**	8.4	91	**127**	80	88	5	.277	.604	2	0	1B-140
1947 PIT N	125	402	100	13	2	25	6.2	71	74	**104**	73	0	.249	.478	6	1	1B-119
13 yrs.	1394	5193	1628	379	71	331	6.4 **9th**	1051	1276	852	844	58	.313	.605 **5th**	16	3	1B-1138, OF-239
12 yrs.	1269	4791	1528	366 **6th**	69 **9th**	306 **3rd**	6.4 **1st**	980 **8th**	1202 **6th**	748 **8th**	771 **5th**	58	.319 **8th**	.616 **1st**	10	2	1B-1019, OF-239
				10th													

WORLD SERIES

	G	AB	H	2B	3B	HR	HR %	R	RBI	BB	SO	SB	BA	SA	Pinch Hit AB	Pinch Hit H	G by POS
1934 DET A	7	28	9	2	1	1	3.6	4	7	4	9	1	.321	.571	0	0	1B-7
1935	2	6	1	0	0	1	16.7	1	2	1	0	0	.167	.667	0	0	1B-2
1940	7	28	10	2	1	1	3.6	5	6	2	5	0	.357	.607	0	0	OF-7
1945	7	23	7	3	0	2	8.7	7	7	6	5	0	.304	.696	0	0	OF-7
4 yrs.	23	85	27	7 **8th**	2	5	5.9	17	22	13	19	1	.318	.624 **7th**	0	0	OF-14, 1B-9

Al Greene

GREENE, ALTAR ALPHONSE
B. Nov. 9, 1954, Detroit, Mich.
BL TR 5'11" 190 lb

	G	AB	H	2B	3B	HR	HR %	R	RBI	BB	SO	SB	BA	SA	Pinch Hit AB	Pinch Hit H	G by POS
1979 DET A	29	59	8	1	0	3	5.1	9	6	10	15	0	.136	.305	6	2	DH-15, OF-6

Willie Greene

GREENE, PATRICK JOSEPH
Played as Pat Foley 1902.
B. Mar. 20, 1875, Providence, R. I.   D. Oct. 20, 1934, Providence, R. I.

	G	AB	H	2B	3B	HR	HR %	R	RBI	BB	SO	SB	BA	SA	Pinch Hit AB	Pinch Hit H	G by POS
1902 PHI N	19	65	11	1	0	0	0.0	6	1	2		2	.169	.185	0	0	3B-19
1903 2 teams	NY	A (4G –	.308)			DET	A (1G –	.000)									
" total	5	16	4	1	0	0	0.0	1	0	0		0	.250	.313	1	0	3B-3, SS-1
2 yrs.	24	81	15	2	0	0	0.0	7	1	2		2	.185	.210	1	0	3B-22, SS-1
1 yr.	1	3	0	0	0	0	0.0	0	0	0		0	.000	.000	0	0	3B-1

Ed Gremminger

GREMMINGER, LORENZO EDWARD (Battleship)
B. Mar. 30, 1874, Canton, Ohio   D. May 26, 1942, Canton, Ohio
BR TR 6'1" 200 lb

	G	AB	H	2B	3B	HR	HR %	R	RBI	BB	SO	SB	BA	SA	Pinch Hit AB	Pinch Hit H	G by POS
1895 CLE N	20	78	21	1	0	0	0.0	10	15	5	13	0	.269	.282	0	0	3B-20
1902 BOS N	140	522	134	20	12	1	0.2	55	66	39		7	.257	.347	0	0	3B-140
1903	140	511	135	24	9	5	1.0	57	56	31		12	.264	.376	0	0	3B-140
1904 DET A	83	309	66	13	3	1	0.3	18	28	14		3	.214	.285	0	0	3B-83
4 yrs.	383	1420	356	58	24	7	0.5	140	165	89	13	22	.251	.340	0	0	3B-383
1 yr.	83	309	66	13	3	1	0.3	18	28	14		3	.214	.285	0	0	3B-83

Art Griggs

GRIGGS, ART CARLE
B. Dec. 10, 1883, Topeka, Kans.   D. Dec. 19, 1938, Los Angeles, Calif.
BR TR 5'11" 185 lb

	G	AB	H	2B	3B	HR	HR %	R	RBI	BB	SO	SB	BA	SA	Pinch Hit AB	Pinch Hit H	G by POS
1909 STL A	108	364	102	17	5	0	0.0	38	43	24		11	.280	.354	9	1	1B-49, OF-40, 2B-8, S
1910	123	416	98	22	5	2	0.5	28	30	25		11	.236	.327	10	1	OF-49, 2B-41, 1B-17, SS-3, 3B-3
1911 CLE A	27	68	17	3	2	1	1.5	7	7	5		1	.250	.397	5	1	2B-11, OF-4, 3B-3, 1B-
1912	89	273	83	16	7	0	0.0	29	39	33		10	.304	.414	18	3	1B-71
1914 BKN F	40	112	32	6	1	1	0.9	10	15	5		1	.286	.384	12	2	1B-27, OF-1
1915	27	38	11	1	0	1	2.6	4	2	3		0	.289	.395	16	5	1B-5, OF-1
1918 DET A	28	99	36	8	0	0	0.0	11	16	10	5	2	.364	.444	2	2	1B-25
7 yrs.	442	1370	379	73	20	5	0.4	127	152	105	5	36	.277	.370	72	15	1B-195, OF-95, 2B-60, 3B-6, SS-4
1 yr.	28	99	36	8	0	0	0.0	11	16	10	5	2	.364	.444	2	2	1B-25

Johnny Groth

GROTH, JOHN THOMAS
B. July 23, 1926, Chicago, Ill.
BR TR 6' 182 lb

	G	AB	H	2B	3B	HR	HR %	R	RBI	BB	SO	SB	BA	SA	Pinch Hit AB	Pinch Hit H	G by POS
1946 DET A	4	9	0	0	0	0	0.0	1	0	1	0	0	.000	.000	0	0	OF-4
1947	2	4	1	0	0	0	0.0	1	0	2	1	0	.250	.250	1	0	OF-1
1948	6	17	8	3	0	1	5.9	3	5	1	1	0	.471	.824	1	0	OF-4
1949	103	348	102	19	5	11	3.2	60	73	65	27	3	.293	.471	3	0	OF-99
1950	157	566	173	30	8	12	2.1	95	85	95	27	1	.306	.451	0	0	OF-157
1951	118	428	128	29	1	3	0.7	41	49	31	32	1	.299	.393	6	2	OF-112
1952	141	524	149	22	2	4	0.8	56	51	51	39	2	.284	.357	3	0	OF-139
1953 STL A	141	557	141	27	4	10	1.8	65	57	42	53	5	.253	.370	0	0	OF-141
1954 CHI A	125	422	116	20	0	7	1.7	41	60	42	37	3	.275	.372	1	0	OF-125
1955 2 teams	CHI	A (32G –	.338)			WAS	A (63G –	.219)									
" total	95	260	66	11	5	4	1.5	35	28	24	31	3	.254	.381	14	5	OF-74
1956 KC A	95	244	63	13	3	5	2.0	22	37	30	31	1	.258	.398	13	4	OF-84
1957 2 teams	KC	A (55G –	.254)			DET	A (38G –	.291)									
" total	93	162	45	10	0	0	0.0	21	18	13	13	0	.278	.340	4	0	OF-86
1958 DET A	88	146	41	5	2	2	1.4	24	11	13	19	0	.281	.384	16	6	OF-80
1959	55	102	24	7	1	1	1.0	12	10	7	14	0	.235	.353	13	4	OF-41
1960	25	19	7	1	0	0	0.0	3	2	3	1	0	.368	.421	8	3	OF-8
15 yrs.	1248	3808	1064	197	31	60	1.6	480	486	419	329	19	.279	.395	83	24	OF-1155
11 yrs.	737	2266	663	126	19	34	1.5	307	302	274	171	7	.293	.410	52	15	OF-681

Johnny Grubb

GRUBB, JOHN MAYWOOD JR.
B. Aug. 4, 1948, Richmond, Va.
BL TR 6'3" 175 lb

	G	AB	H	2B	3B	HR	HR %	R	RBI	BB	SO	SB	BA	SA	Pinch Hit AB	Pinch Hit H	G by POS
1972 SD N	7	21	7	1	1	0	0.0	4	1	1	3	0	.333	.476	1	0	OF-6
1973	113	389	121	22	3	8	2.1	52	37	37	50	9	.311	.445	12	7	OF-102, 3B-2
1974	140	444	127	20	4	8	1.8	53	42	46	47	4	.286	.403	17	3	OF-122, 3B-2
1975	144	553	149	36	2	4	0.7	72	38	59	59	2	.269	.363	6	0	OF-139
1976	109	384	109	22	1	5	1.3	54	27	65	53	1	.284	.385	5	0	OF-98, 1B-9, 3B-3
1977 CLE A	34	93	28	3	2	2	2.2	8	14	19	18	0	.301	.462	1	0	OF-28, DH-4
1978 2 teams	CLE	A (113G –	.265)			TEX	A (21G –	.394)									
" total	134	411	113	19	6	15	3.6	62	67	70	65	6	.275	.460	11	5	OF-123, DH-11
1979 TEX A	102	289	79	14	0	10	3.5	42	37	34	44	2	.273	.426	24	6	OF-82, DH-6
1980	110	274	76	12	1	9	3.3	40	32	42	35	2	.277	.427	28	7	OF-77, DH-8

Johnny Grubb continued

	G	AB	H	2B	3B	HR	HR%	R	RBI	BB	SO	SB	BA	SA	Pinch Hit AB	Pinch Hit H	G by POS
1981	67	199	46	9	1	3	1.5	26	26	23	25	0	.231	.332	9	2	OF-58
1982	103	308	86	13	3	3	1.0	35	26	39	37	0	.279	.370	14	4	OF-77, DH-18
1983 DET A	57	134	34	5	2	4	3.0	20	22	28	17	0	.254	.410	10	4	OF-26, DH-18
1984	86	176	47	5	0	8	4.5	25	17	36	36	1	.267	.432	22	8	OF-36, DH-33
13 yrs	1206	3675	1022	181	27	79	2.1	493	386	499	489	27	.278	.407	160	46	OF-974, DH-90, 1B-9, 3B-7
2 yrs	143	310	81	10	2	12	3.9	45	39	64	53	1	.261	.423	32	12	OF-62, DH-51

LEAGUE CHAMPIONSHIP SERIES

	G	AB	H	2B	3B	HR	HR%	R	RBI	BB	SO	SB	BA	SA	Pinch Hit AB	Pinch Hit H	G by POS
1984 DET A	1	4	1	1	0	0	0.0	0	2	0	0	0	.250	.500	0	0	

WORLD SERIES

	G	AB	H	2B	3B	HR	HR%	R	RBI	BB	SO	SB	BA	SA	Pinch Hit AB	Pinch Hit H	G by POS
1984 DET A	4	3	1	0	0	0	0.0	0	0	0	0	0	.333	.333	0	0	DH-2

Cesar Gutierrez

GUTIERREZ, CESAR DARIO (Coca) B. Jan. 26, 1943, Coro, Venezuela   BR TR 5'9" 155 lbs.

	G	AB	H	2B	3B	HR	HR%	R	RBI	BB	SO	SB	BA	SA	Pinch Hit AB	Pinch Hit H	G by POS
1967 SF N	18	21	3	0	0	0	0.0	4	0	1	4	1	.143	.143	1	1	SS-15, 2B-1
1969 2 teams	SF N (15G – .217)					DET A (17G – .245)											
" total	32	72	17	2	0	0	0.0	9	0	11	5	2	.236	.264	2	1	SS-20, 3B-7
1970 DET A	135	415	101	11	6	0	0.0	40	22	18	39	4	.243	.299	0	0	SS-135
1971	38	37	7	0	0	0	0.0	8	4	0	3	0	.189	.189	9	3	SS-14, 3B-5, 2B-2
4 yrs	223	545	128	13	6	0	0.0	61	26	30	51	7	.235	.281	12	5	SS-184, 3B-12, 2B-3
3 yrs	190	501	120	12	6	0	0.0	53	26	23	45	5	.240	.287	10	3	SS-165, 3B-5, 2B-2

Sammy Hale

HALE, SAMUEL DOUGLAS B. Sept. 10, 1896, Glen Rose, Tex. D. Sept. 6, 1974, Wheeler, Tex.   BR TR 5'8½" 160 lbs.

	G	AB	H	2B	3B	HR	HR%	R	RBI	BB	SO	SB	BA	SA	Pinch Hit AB	Pinch Hit H	G by POS
1920 DET A	76	116	34	3	3	1	0.9	13	14	5	15	2	.293	.397	52	17	3B-16, OF-4, 2B-1
1921	9	2	0	0	0	0	0.0	2	0	0	1	0	.000	.000	2	0	
1923 PHI A	115	434	125	22	8	3	0.7	68	51	17	31	8	.288	.396	5	2	3B-107
1924	80	261	83	14	2	2	0.8	41	17	17	19	3	.318	.410	14	2	3B-55, OF-5, SS-1, C-1
1925	110	391	135	30	11	8	2.0	62	63	17	27	7	.345	.540	12	4	3B-96, 2B-1
1926	111	327	92	22	9	4	1.2	49	43	13	36	1	.281	.440	28	6	3B-77, OF-1
1927	131	501	157	24	8	5	1.0	77	81	32	32	11	.313	.423	1	0	3B-128
1928	88	314	97	20	9	4	1.3	38	58	9	21	2	.309	.468	8	3	3B-79
1929	101	379	105	14	3	1	0.3	51	40	12	18	6	.277	.338	0	0	3B-99, 2B-1
1930 STL A	62	190	52	8	1	2	1.1	21	25	8	18	1	.274	.358	12	2	3B-47
10 yrs	883	2915	880	157	54	30	1.0	422	392	130	218	41	.302	.424	134	36	3B-704, OF-10, 2B-3, SS-1, C-1
2 yrs	85	118	34	3	3	1	0.8	15	14	5	16	2	.288	.390	54	17	3B-16, OF-4, 2B-1

Charley Hall

HALL, CHARLES LOUIS (Sea Lion) Born Carlos Clolo. B. July 27, 1885, Ventura, Calif. D. Dec. 6, 1943, Ventura, Calif.   BL TR 6'2" 185 lbs.

	G	AB	H	2B	3B	HR	HR%	R	RBI	BB	SO	SB	BA	SA	Pinch Hit AB	Pinch Hit H	G by POS
1906 CIN N	17	47	6	2	0	0	0.0	7	2	2		0	.128	.170	1	0	P-14, 1B-2
1907	12	26	7	0	1	0	0.0	1	1	0		0	.269	.346	1	0	P-11
1909 BOS A	11	19	3	0	0	0	0.0	0	4	0		0	.158	.158	0	0	P-11
1910	47	82	17	2	4	0	0.0	6	8	6		1	.207	.329	8	1	P-35, OF-3
1911	39	64	9	1	1	1	1.6	6	8	4		0	.141	.234	7	1	P-32
1912	34	75	20	4	2	1	1.3	10	14	4		0	.267	.413	0	0	P-34
1913	43	42	9	1	1	0	0.0	2	2	1	10	0	.214	.286	7	0	P-35, 3B-1
1916 STL A	10	14	2	0	0	0	0.0	0	1	0	6	0	.143	.143	0	0	P-10
1918 DET A	6	2	0	0	0	0	0.0	0	0	0	0	0	.000	.000	0	0	P-6
9 yrs	219	371	73	10	9	2	0.5	32	40	17	16	1	.197	.288	24	2	P-188, OF-3, 1B-2, 3B-1
1 yr	6	2	0	0	0	0	0.0	0	0	0	0	0	.000	.000	0	0	P-6

WORLD SERIES

	G	AB	H	2B	3B	HR	HR%	R	RBI	BB	SO	SB	BA	SA	Pinch Hit AB	Pinch Hit H	G by POS
1912 BOS A	2	4	3	1	0	0	0.0	0	0	1	0	0	.750	1.000	0	0	P-2

Tom Haller

HALLER, THOMAS FRANK B. June 23, 1937, Lockport, Ill.   BL TR 6'4" 195 lbs.

	G	AB	H	2B	3B	HR	HR%	R	RBI	BB	SO	SB	BA	SA	Pinch Hit AB	Pinch Hit H	G by POS
1961 SF N	30	62	9	1	0	2	3.2	5	8	9	23	0	.145	.258	4	0	C-25
1962	99	272	71	13	1	18	6.6	53	55	51	59	1	.261	.515	9	0	C-91
1963	98	298	76	8	1	14	4.7	32	44	34	45	4	.255	.430	8	2	C-85, OF-7
1964	117	388	98	14	3	16	4.1	43	48	55	51	4	.253	.428	7	1	C-113, OF-3
1965	134	422	106	4	3	16	3.8	40	49	47	67	0	.251	.389	3	1	C-133
1966	142	471	113	19	2	27	5.7	74	67	53	74	1	.240	.461	10	1	C-136, 1B-8
1967	141	455	114	23	5	14	3.1	54	49	62	61	0	.251	.415	12	5	C-136, OF-1
1968 LA N	144	474	135	27	5	4	0.8	37	53	46	76	1	.285	.388	12	1	C-139
1969	134	445	117	18	3	6	1.3	46	39	48	58	0	.263	.357	7	3	C-132
1970	112	325	93	16	6	10	3.1	47	47	32	35	3	.286	.465	12	5	C-106
1971	84	202	54	5	0	5	2.5	23	32	25	30	0	.267	.366	17	6	C-67
1972 DET A	59	121	25	5	2	2	1.7	7	13	15	14	0	.207	.331	20	2	C-36
12 yrs	1294	3935	1011	153	31	134	3.4	461	504	477	593	14	.257	.414	121	27	C-1199, OF-11, 1B-4
1 yr	59	121	25	5	2	2	1.7	7	13	15	14	0	.207	.331	20	2	C-36

LEAGUE CHAMPIONSHIP SERIES

	G	AB	H	2B	3B	HR	HR%	R	RBI	BB	SO	SB	BA	SA	Pinch Hit AB	Pinch Hit H	G by POS
1972 DET A	1	1	0	0	0	0	0.0	0	0	0	0	0	.000	.000	1	0	

WORLD SERIES

	G	AB	H	2B	3B	HR	HR%	R	RBI	BB	SO	SB	BA	SA	Pinch Hit AB	Pinch Hit H	G by POS
1962 SF N	4	14	4	1	0	1	7.1	1	3	2	0	0	.286	.571	0	0	C-4

Fred Haney

HANEY, FRED GIRARD (Pudge) B. Apr. 25, 1898, Albuquerque, N. M. D. Nov. 9, 1977, Beverly Hills, Calif. Manager 1939-41, 1953-59.   BR TR 5'6" 170 lbs.

	G	AB	H	2B	3B	HR	HR%	R	RBI	BB	SO	SB	BA	SA	Pinch Hit AB	Pinch Hit H	G by POS
1922 DET A	81	213	75	7	4	0	0.0	41	25	32	14	3	.352	.423	9	3	3B-42, 1B-11, SS-2
1923	142	503	142	13	4	4	0.8	85	67	45	23	12	.282	.348	0	0	2B-69, 3B-55, SS-16
1924	86	256	79	11	1	1	0.4	54	30	39	13	7	.309	.371	13	4	3B-59, SS-4, 2B-3
1925	114	398	111	15	3	0	0.0	84	40	66	29	11	.279	.332	5	1	3B-107
1926 BOS A	138	462	102	15	7	0	0.0	47	52	74	28	13	.221	.284	1	0	3B-137

	G	AB	H	2B	3B	HR	HR%	R	RBI	BB	SO	SB	BA	SA	Pinch Hit AB	Pinch Hit H	G by POS

Fred Haney continued

	G	AB	H	2B	3B	HR	HR%	R	RBI	BB	SO	SB	BA	SA	PH AB	PH H	G by POS
1927 2 teams	BOS A (47G – .276)					CHI N (4G – .000)											
" total	51	119	32	4	1	3	2.5	23	12	25	14	4	.269	.395	14	4	3B-34, OF-1
1929 STL N	10	26	3	1	1	0	0.0	4	2	1	2	0	.115	.231	2	1	3B-6
7 yrs.	622	1977	544	66	21	8	0.4	338	228	282	123	50	.275	.342	44	13	3B-440, 2B-72, SS-22, 1B-11, OF-1
4 yrs.	423	1370	407	46	12	5	0.4	264	162	182	79	33	.297	.359	27	8	3B-263, 2B-72, SS-22, 1B-11

Pinky Hargrave

HARGRAVE, WILLIAM McKINLEY
Brother of Bubbles Hargrave.
B. Jan. 31, 1896, New Haven, Ind.   D. Oct. 3, 1942, Fort Wayne, Ind.
BB TR 5'8½" 180 lb
BR 1923-26, BL 1933

	G	AB	H	2B	3B	HR	HR%	R	RBI	BB	SO	SB	BA	SA	PH AB	PH H	G by POS
1923 WAS A	33	59	17	2	0	0	0.0	4	8	2	6	0	.288	.322	18	7	3B-8, C-5, OF-1
1924	24	33	5	1	1	0	0.0	3	5	1	4	0	.152	.242	14	1	C-8
1925 2 teams	WAS A (5G – .500)					STL A (67G – .284)											
" total	72	231	67	15	2	8	3.5	34	43	14	15	2	.290	.476	9	5	C-63
1926 STL A	92	235	66	16	3	7	3.0	20	37	10	38	3	.281	.464	33	9	C-59
1928 DET A	121	321	88	13	5	10	3.1	38	63	32	28	4	.274	.439	25	9	C-88
1929	76	185	61	12	0	3	1.6	26	26	20	24	2	.330	.443	26	5	C-48
1930 2 teams	DET A (55G – .285)					WAS A (10G – .194)											
" total	65	168	45	10	2	6	3.6	21	25	23	13	3	.268	.458	15	2	C-49
1931 WAS A	40	80	26	8	0	1	1.3	6	19	9	12	1	.325	.463	15	4	C-25
1932 BOS N	82	217	57	14	3	4	1.8	20	33	24	18	1	.263	.410	7	2	C-73
1933	45	73	13	0	0	0	0.0	5	6	5	7	1	.178	.178	18	1	C-25
10 yrs.	650	1602	445	91	16	39	2.4	177	265	140	165	17	.278	.428	180	45	C-443, 3B-8, OF-1
3 yrs.	252	643	188	33	5	18	2.8	82	107	72	64	8	.292	.443	65	16	C-176

Dick Harley

HARLEY, RICHARD JOSEPH
B. Sept. 25, 1872, Blue Bell, Pa.   D. Apr. 3, 1952, Philadelphia, Pa.
BL TR 5'10½" 150 lb

	G	AB	H	2B	3B	HR	HR%	R	RBI	BB	SO	SB	BA	SA	PH AB	PH H	G by POS
1897 STL N	89	330	96	6	4	3	0.9	43	35	36		23	.291	.361	0	0	OF-89
1898	142	549	135	6	5	0	0.0	74	42	34		13	.246	.275	1	1	OF-141
1899 CLE N	142	567	142	15	7	1	0.2	70	50	40		15	.250	.307	0	0	OF-143
1900 CIN N	5	21	9	1	0	0	0.0	2	5	1		4	.429	.476	0	0	OF-5
1901	133	535	146	13	2	4	0.7	69	27	31		37	.273	.327	0	0	OF-133
1902 DET A	125	491	138	9	8	2	0.4	59	44	36		20	.281	.344	0	0	OF-125
1903 CHI N	104	386	89	9	1	0	0.0	72	33	45		27	.231	.259	2	2	OF-103
7 yrs.	740	2879	755	59	27	10	0.3	389	236	223		139	.262	.312	3	3	OF-739
1 yr.	125	491	138	9	8	2	0.4	59	44	36		20	.281	.344	0	0	OF-125

George Harper

HARPER, GEORGE WASHINGTON
B. June 24, 1892, Arlington, Ky.   D. Aug. 18, 1978, Magnolia, Ark.
BL TR 5'8" 167 lb

	G	AB	H	2B	3B	HR	HR%	R	RBI	BB	SO	SB	BA	SA	PH AB	PH H	G by POS
1916 DET A	44	56	9	1	0	0	0.0	4	3	5	8	0	.161	.179	24	4	OF-14
1917	47	117	24	3	0	0	0.0	6	12	11	15	2	.205	.231	16	4	OF-31
1918	69	227	55	5	2	0	0.0	19	16	18	14	3	.242	.282	3	0	OF-64
1922 CIN N	128	430	146	22	8	2	0.5	67	68	35	22	11	.340	.442	14	3	OF-109
1923	61	125	32	4	2	3	2.4	14	16	11	9	0	.256	.392	28	7	OF-29
1924 2 teams	CIN N (28G – .270)					PHI N (109G – .294)											
" total	137	485	141	29	6	16	3.3	75	58	51	28	11	.291	.474	2	0	OF-131
1925 PHI N	132	495	173	35	7	18	3.6	86	97	28	32	10	.349	.558	6	3	OF-126
1926	56	194	61	6	5	7	3.6	32	38	16	7	6	.314	.505	1	1	OF-55
1927 NY N	145	483	160	19	6	16	3.3	85	87	84	27	7	.331	.495	3	1	OF-142
1928 2 teams	NY N (19G – .228)					STL N (99G – .305)											
" total	118	329	96	9	2	19	5.8	52	65	61	19	3	.292	.505	13	4	OF-103
1929 BOS N	136	457	133	25	5	10	2.2	65	68	69	27	5	.291	.433	5	0	OF-130
11 yrs.	1073	3398	1030	158	43	91	2.7	505	528	389	208	58	.303	.455	115	27	OF-934
3 yrs.	160	400	88	9	2	0	0.0	29	31	34	37	5	.220	.253	43	8	OF-109

WORLD SERIES

	G	AB	H	2B	3B	HR	HR%	R	RBI	BB	SO	SB	BA	SA	PH AB	PH H	G by POS
1928 STL N	3	9	1	0	0	0	0.0	1	0	2	2	0	.111	.111	0	0	OF-3

Andy Harrington

HARRINGTON, ANDREW MATTHEW
B. Feb. 12, 1903, Mountain View, Calif.   D. Jan. 29, 1979, Boise, Ida.
BR TR 5'11" 170 lb

	G	AB	H	2B	3B	HR	HR%	R	RBI	BB	SO	SB	BA	SA	PH AB	PH H	G by POS
1925 DET A	1	1	0	0	0	0	0.0	0	0	0	0	0	.000	.000	1	0	

Bob Harris

HARRIS, ROBERT NED
B. July 9, 1916, Ames, Iowa   D. Dec. 18, 1976, West Palm Beach, Fla.
BL TL 5'11" 175 lb

	G	AB	H	2B	3B	HR	HR%	R	RBI	BB	SO	SB	BA	SA	PH AB	PH H	G by POS
1941 DET A	26	61	13	3	1	1	1.6	11	4	6	13	1	.213	.344	11	1	OF-12
1942	121	398	108	16	10	9	2.3	53	45	49	35	5	.271	.430	15	6	OF-104
1943	114	354	90	14	3	6	1.7	43	32	47	29	6	.254	.362	18	5	OF-96
1946	1	1	0	0	0	0	0.0	0	0	0	0	0	.000	.000	1	0	
4 yrs.	262	814	211	33	14	16	2.0	107	81	102	77	12	.259	.393	45	12	OF-212
4 yrs.	262	814	211	33	14	16	2.0	107	81	102	77	12	.259	.393	45	12	OF-212

Bucky Harris

HARRIS, STANLEY RAYMOND
B. Nov. 8, 1896, Port Jervis, N. Y.   D. Nov. 8, 1977, Bethesda, Md.
Manager 1924-43, 1947-48, 1950-56.
Hall of Fame 1975.
BR TR 5'9½" 156 lb

	G	AB	H	2B	3B	HR	HR%	R	RBI	BB	SO	SB	BA	SA	PH AB	PH H	G by POS
1919 WAS A	8	28	6	2	0	0	0.0	0	4	1	3	0	.214	.286	0	0	2B-8
1920	137	506	152	26	6	1	0.2	76	68	41	36	16	.300	.381	1	1	2B-135
1921	154	584	169	22	8	0	0.0	82	54	54	39	29	.289	.354	0	0	2B-154
1922	154	602	162	24	8	2	0.3	95	40	52	38	25	.269	.346	0	0	2B-154
1923	145	532	150	21	13	2	0.4	60	70	50	29	23	.282	.382	0	0	2B-144, SS-1
1924	143	544	146	28	9	1	0.2	88	58	56	41	19	.268	.358	0	0	2B-143
1925	144	551	158	30	3	1	0.2	91	66	64	21	14	.287	.358	0	0	2B-144
1926	141	537	152	39	9	1	0.2	94	63	58	41	16	.283	.395	0	0	2B-141
1927	128	475	127	20	3	1	0.2	98	55	66	33	18	.267	.328	0	0	2B-128
1928	99	358	73	11	5	0	0.0	34	28	27	26	5	.204	.263	0	0	2B-96, OF-1, 3B-1
1929 DET A	7	11	1	0	0	0	0.0	3	0	2	2	1	.091	.091	0	0	2B-4, SS-1

Cobb.

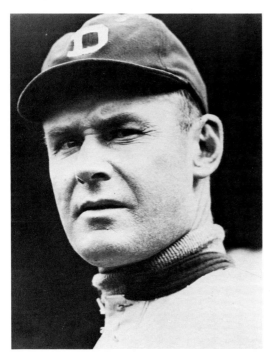

Sam Crawford.

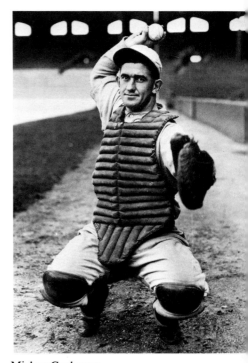

Mickey Cochrane.

Hughie Jennings.

Hank Greenberg.

Charlie Gehringer.

Hal Newhouser.

George Kell.

Al Kaline.

Harvey Kuenn.

Rocky Colavito.

Denny McLain.

Mickey Lolich.

Mark Fidrych.

Alan Trammell.

Lou Whitaker.

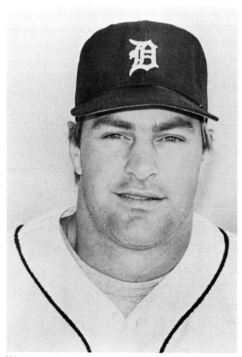

Kirk Gibson.

	G	AB	H	2B	3B	HR	HR %	R	RBI	BB	SO	SB	BA	SA	Pinch Hit AB	Pinch Hit H	G by POS

~~B~~ucky Harris continued

	G	AB	H	2B	3B	HR	HR %	R	RBI	BB	SO	SB	BA	SA	AB	H	G by POS
~~31~~	4	8	1	1	0	0	0.0	1	0	1	1	0	.125	.250	0	0	2B-3
12 yrs.	1264	4736	1297	224	64	9	0.2	722	506	472	310	166	.274	.354	1	1	2B-1254, SS-2, OF-1, 3B-1
2 yrs.	11	19	2	1	0	0	0.0	4	0	3	3	1	.105	.158	0	0	2B-7, SS-1
~~W~~ORLD SERIES																	
~~19~~24 WAS A	7	33	11	0	0	2	6.1	5	7	1	4	0	.333	.515	0	0	2B-7
~~19~~25	7	23	2	0	0	0	0.0	2	0	1	3	0	.087	.087	0	0	2B-7
2 yrs.	14	56	13	0	0	2	3.6	7	7	2	7	0	.232	.339	0	0	2B-14

~~G~~ail Harris

HARRIS, BOYD GAIL
B. Oct. 15, 1931, Abingdon, Va.   BL TL 6'   195 lbs.

	G	AB	H	2B	3B	HR	HR %	R	RBI	BB	SO	SB	BA	SA	AB	H	G by POS
~~19~~55 NY N	79	263	61	9	0	12	4.6	27	36	20	46	0	.232	.403	4	2	1B-75
~~19~~56	12	38	5	0	1	1	2.6	2	1	3	10	0	.132	.263	1	0	1B-11
~~19~~57	90	225	54	7	3	9	4.0	28	31	16	28	1	.240	.418	25	2	1B-61
~~19~~58 DET A	134	451	123	18	8	20	4.4	63	83	36	60	1	.273	.481	14	5	1B-122
~~19~~59	114	349	77	4	3	9	2.6	39	39	29	49	0	.221	.327	22	4	1B-93
~~19~~60	8	5	0	0	0	0	0.0	0	0	2	1	0	.000	.000	3	0	1B-5
6 yrs.	437	1331	320	38	15	51	3.8	159	190	106	194	2	.240	.406	69	13	1B-367
3 yrs.	256	805	200	22	11	29	3.6	102	122	67	110	1	.248	.411	39	9	1B-220

~~F~~red Hatfield

HATFIELD, FRED JAMES
B. Mar. 18, 1925, Lanett, Ala.   BL TR 6'1"   171 lbs.

	G	AB	H	2B	3B	HR	HR %	R	RBI	BB	SO	SB	BA	SA	AB	H	G by POS
~~19~~50 BOS A	10	12	3	0	0	0	0.0	3	2	3	1	0	.250	.250	1	0	3B-3
~~19~~51	80	163	28	4	2	2	1.2	23	14	22	27	1	.172	.258	14	2	3B-49
~~19~~52 2 teams		BOS A (19G – .320)				DET A (112G – .236)											
total	131	466	112	13	3	3	0.6	48	28	39	54	2	.240	.300	0	0	3B-124, SS-9
~~19~~53 DET A	109	311	79	11	1	3	1.0	41	19	40	34	3	.254	.325	19	7	3B-54, 2B-28, SS-1
~~19~~54	81	218	64	12	0	2	0.9	31	25	28	24	4	.294	.376	17	5	2B-54, 3B-15
~~19~~55	122	413	96	15	3	8	1.9	51	33	61	49	3	.232	.341	3	0	2B-92, 3B-16, SS-14
~~19~~56 2 teams		DET A (8G – .250)				CHI A (106G – .262)											
total	114	333	87	9	1	7	2.1	48	35	39	37	1	.261	.357	12	2	3B-100, 2B-4, SS-3
~~19~~57 CHI A	69	114	23	3	0	0	0.0	14	8	15	20	1	.202	.228	23	4	3B-44
~~19~~58 2 teams		CLE A (3G – .125)				CIN N (3G – .000)											
total	6	9	1	0	0	0	0.0	0	1	1	1	0	.111	.111	2	0	3B-2
9 yrs.	722	2039	493	67	10	25	1.2	259	165	248	247	15	.242	.321	91	20	3B-407, 2B-178, SS-27
5 yrs.	432	1395	346	50	6	15	1.1	167	104	166	160	12	.248	.325	40	12	3B-192, 2B-178, SS-24

~~R~~ay Hayworth

HAYWORTH, RAYMOND HALL
Brother of Red Hayworth.
B. Jan. 29, 1904, High Point, N. C.   BR TR 6'   180 lbs.

	G	AB	H	2B	3B	HR	HR %	R	RBI	BB	SO	SB	BA	SA	AB	H	G by POS
~~19~~26 DET A	12	11	3	0	0	0	0.0	1	5	1	1	0	.273	.273	3	0	C-8
~~19~~29	14	43	11	0	0	0	0.0	5	4	3	8	0	.256	.256	0	0	C-14
~~19~~30	77	227	63	15	4	0	0.0	24	22	20	19	0	.278	.379	0	0	C-76
~~19~~31	88	273	70	10	3	0	0.0	28	25	19	27	0	.256	.315	0	0	C-88
~~19~~32	108	338	99	20	2	2	0.6	41	44	31	22	1	.293	.382	3	1	C-105
~~19~~33	134	425	104	14	3	1	0.2	37	45	35	28	0	.245	.299	1	0	C-133
~~19~~34	54	167	49	5	2	0	0.0	20	27	16	22	0	.293	.347	1	0	C-54
~~19~~35	51	175	54	14	2	0	0.0	22	22	9	14	0	.309	.411	3	1	C-48
~~19~~36	81	250	60	10	0	1	0.4	31	30	39	18	0	.240	.292	1	0	C-81
~~19~~37	30	78	21	0	1	1	1.3	9	8	14	15	0	.269	.333	1	0	C-28
~~19~~38 2 teams		DET A (8G – .211)				BKN N (5G – .000)											
total	13	23	4	0	0	0	0.0	1	5	4	5	1	.174	.174	2	1	C-10
~~19~~39 2 teams		BKN N (21G – .154)				NY N (5G – .231)											
total	26	39	7	2	0	0	0.0	1	1	4	8	0	.179	.231	2	0	C-23
~~19~~42 STL A	1	1	1	0	0	0	0.0	0	0	0	0	0	1.000	1.000	1	1	
~~19~~44 BKN N	7	10	0	0	0	0	0.0	1	0	2	1	0	.000	.000	1	0	C-6
~~19~~45	2	2	0	0	0	0	0.0	0	0	1	0	0	.000	.000	2	0	C-2
15 yrs.	698	2062	546	92	16	5	0.2	221	238	198	188	2	.265	.332	19	4	C-676
11 yrs.	657	2006	538	90	16	5	0.2	219	237	190	178	2	.268	.336	14	3	C-642
~~W~~ORLD SERIES																	
~~19~~34 DET A	1	0	0	0	0	0	–	0	0	0	0	0	–	–	0	0	C-1

~~B~~ob Hazle

HAZLE, ROBERT SIDNEY (Hurricane)
B. Dec. 9, 1930, Laurens, S. C.   BL TR 6'   190 lbs.

	G	AB	H	2B	3B	HR	HR %	R	RBI	BB	SO	SB	BA	SA	AB	H	G by POS
~~19~~55 CIN N	6	13	3	0	0	0	0.0	0	0	0	3	0	.231	.231	3	1	OF-4
~~19~~57 MIL N	41	134	54	12	0	7	5.2	26	27	18	15	1	.403	.649	1	1	OF-40
~~19~~58 2 teams		MIL N (20G – .179)				DET A (43G – .241)											
total	63	114	24	2	0	2	1.8	11	10	14	17	0	.211	.281	29	6	OF-32
3 yrs.	110	261	81	14	0	9	3.4	37	37	32	35	1	.310	.467	33	8	OF-76
1 yr.	43	58	14	2	0	2	3.4	5	5	5	13	0	.241	.379	28	5	OF-12
~~W~~ORLD SERIES																	
~~19~~57 MIL N	4	13	2	0	0	0	0.0	2	0	1	2	0	.154	.154	0	0	OF-4

~~Bi~~ll Heath

HEATH, WILLIAM CHRIS
B. Mar. 10, 1939, Yuba City, Calif.   BL TR 5'8"   175 lbs.

	G	AB	H	2B	3B	HR	HR %	R	RBI	BB	SO	SB	BA	SA	AB	H	G by POS
~~196~~5 CHI A	1	1	0	0	0	0	0.0	0	0	0	0	0	.000	.000	1	0	
~~196~~6 HOU N	55	123	37	6	0	0	0.0	12	8	9	11	1	.301	.350	16	4	C-37
~~196~~7 2 teams		HOU N (9G – .091)				DET A (20G – .125)											
total	29	43	5	0	0	0	0.0	4	4	5	7	0	.116	.116	19	2	C-12
~~196~~9 CHI N	27	32	5	0	1	0	0.0	1	1	12	4	0	.156	.219	12	2	C-9
4 yrs.	112	199	47	6	1	0	0.0	13	13	26	22	1	.236	.276	48	8	C-58
1 yr.	20	32	4	0	0	0	0.0	0	4	1	4	0	.125	.125	14	2	C-7

	G	AB	H	2B	3B	HR	HR %	R	RBI	BB	SO	SB	BA	SA	Pinch Hit AB	H	G by POS

Richie Hebner

HEBNER, RICHARD JOSEPH
B. Nov. 26, 1947, Brighton, Mass.
BL TR 6'1" 195 lb

	G	AB	H	2B	3B	HR	HR %	R	RBI	BB	SO	SB	BA	SA	Pinch Hit AB	H	G by POS
1968 PIT N	2	1	0	0	0	0	0.0	0	0	0	0	0	.000	.000	1	0	
1969	129	459	138	23	4	8	1.7	72	47	53	53	4	.301	.420	4	1	3B-124, 1B-1
1970	120	420	122	24	8	11	2.6	60	46	42	48	2	.290	.464	6	2	3B-117
1971	112	388	105	17	8	17	4.4	50	67	32	68	2	.271	.487	7	5	3B-108
1972	124	427	128	24	4	19	4.4	63	72	52	54	0	.300	.508	5	1	3B-121
1973	144	509	138	28	1	25	4.9	73	74	56	60	0	.271	.477	7	1	3B-139
1974	146	550	160	21	6	18	3.3	97	68	60	53	0	.291	.449	7	1	3B-141
1975	128	472	116	16	4	15	3.2	65	57	43	48	0	.246	.392	3	1	3B-126
1976	132	434	108	21	3	8	1.8	60	51	47	39	1	.249	.366	7	0	3B-126
1977 PHI N	118	397	113	17	4	18	4.5	67	62	61	46	7	.285	.484	10	3	1B-103, 3B-13, 2B-1
1978	137	435	123	22	3	17	3.9	61	71	53	58	4	.283	.464	9	5	1B-117, 3B-19, 2B-1
1979 NY N	136	473	127	25	2	10	2.1	54	79	59	59	3	.268	.393	4	1	3B-134, 1B-6
1980 DET A	104	341	99	10	7	12	3.5	48	82	38	45	0	.290	.466	11	6	1B-61, 3B-32, DH-5
1981	78	226	51	8	2	5	2.2	19	28	27	28	1	.226	.345	11	1	1B-61, DH-11
1982 2 teams	DET A (68G – .274)					PIT N (25G – .300)											
" total	93	249	70	8	0	10	4.0	31	30	30	24	5	.281	.434	17	3	1B-44, OF-21, DH-20, 3B-1
1983 PIT N	78	162	43	4	1	5	3.1	23	26	17	28	8	.265	.395	27	7	3B-40, OF-7, 1B-7
1984 CHI N	44	81	27	3	0	2	2.5	12	8	10	15	1	.333	.444	26	8	3B-14, OF-3, 1B-3
17 yrs.	1825	6024	1668	271	57	200	3.3	855	868	680	726	38	.277	.440	162	43	3B-1255, 1B-403, DH-OF-31, 2B-2
3 yrs.	250	746	199	24	9	25	3.4	92	128	90	94	2	.267	.424	36	10	1B-162, DH-36, 3B-32

LEAGUE CHAMPIONSHIP SERIES

	G	AB	H	2B	3B	HR	HR %	R	RBI	BB	SO	SB	BA	SA	Pinch Hit AB	H	G by POS
1970 PIT N	2	6	4	2	0	0	0.0	0	0	2	1	0	.667	1.000	0	0	3B-2
1971	4	17	5	1	0	2	11.8	3	4	0	4	0	.294	.706	1	0	3B-4
1972	5	16	3	1	0	0	0.0	2	1	1	3	0	.188	.250	0	0	3B-5
1974	4	13	3	0	0	1	7.7	1	4	1	4	0	.231	.462	0	0	3B-4
1975	3	12	4	1	0	0	0.0	2	2	1	1	0	.333	.417	0	0	3B-3
1977 PHI N	4	14	5	2	0	0	0.0	2	0	0	1	0	.357	.500	1	0	1B-3
1978	3	9	1	0	0	0	0.0	0	1	0	0	0	.111	.111	1	0	1B-2
1984 CHI N	1	1	0	0	0	0	0.0	0	0	0	0	0	.000	.000	1	0	
8 yrs.	26	88	25	7	0	3	3.4	10	12	5	14	0	.284	.466	4	0	3B-18, 1B-5

WORLD SERIES

	G	AB	H	2B	3B	HR	HR %	R	RBI	BB	SO	SB	BA	SA	Pinch Hit AB	H	G by POS
1971 PIT N	3	12	2	0	0	1	8.3	2	3	3	3	0	.167	.417	0	0	3B-3

Don Heffner

HEFFNER, DONALD HENRY (Jeep)
B. Feb. 8, 1911, Rouzerville, Pa.
Manager 1966.
BR TR 5'10" 155 lb

	G	AB	H	2B	3B	HR	HR %	R	RBI	BB	SO	SB	BA	SA	Pinch Hit AB	H	G by POS
1934 NY A	72	241	63	8	3	0	0.0	29	25	25	18	1	.261	.320	2	2	2B-68
1935	10	36	11	3	1	0	0.0	3	8	4	1	0	.306	.444	0	0	2B-10
1936	19	48	11	2	1	0	0.0	7	6	6	5	0	.229	.313	2	1	3B-8, 2B-5, SS-3
1937	60	201	50	6	5	0	0.0	23	21	19	19	1	.249	.328	4	1	2B-38, SS-13, 3B-3, C, 1B-1
1938 STL A	141	473	116	23	3	2	0.4	47	69	65	53	1	.245	.319	0	0	2B-141
1939	110	375	100	10	2	1	0.3	45	35	48	39	1	.267	.312	4	2	SS-73, 2B-32
1940	126	487	115	23	2	3	0.6	52	53	39	37	5	.236	.310	1	0	2B-125
1941	110	399	93	14	2	0	0.0	48	17	38	27	5	.233	.278	6	1	2B-105
1942	19	36	6	2	0	0	0.0	2	3	1	4	1	.167	.222	7	2	2B-6, 1B-4
1943 2 teams	STL A (18G – .121)					PHI A (52G – .208)											
" total	70	211	41	7	0	0	0.0	19	10	20	14	3	.194	.227	6	0	2B-60, 1B-2
1944 DET A	6	19	4	1	0	0	0.0	0	1	5	1	0	.211	.263	1	0	2B-5
11 yrs.	743	2526	610	99	19	6	0.2	275	248	270	218	18	.241	.303	33	10	2B-595, SS-89, 3B-11, 1B-7, OF-1
1 yr.	6	19	4	1	0	0	0.0	0	1	5	1	0	.211	.263	1	0	2B-5

Jim Hegan

HEGAN, JAMES EDWARD
Father of Mike Hegan.
B. Aug. 3, 1920, Lynn, Mass.   D. June 17, 1984, Swampscott, Mass.
BR TR 6'2" 195 lb

	G	AB	H	2B	3B	HR	HR %	R	RBI	BB	SO	SB	BA	SA	Pinch Hit AB	H	G by POS
1941 CLE A	16	47	15	2	0	1	2.1	4	5	4	7	0	.319	.426	0	0	C-16
1942	68	170	33	5	0	0	0.0	10	11	11	31	1	.194	.224	2	1	C-66
1946	88	271	64	11	5	0	0.0	29	17	17	44	1	.236	.314	0	0	C-87
1947	135	378	94	14	5	4	1.1	38	42	41	49	3	.249	.344	1	0	C-133
1948	144	472	117	21	6	14	3.0	60	61	48	74	6	.248	.407	3	0	C-142
1949	152	468	105	19	5	8	1.7	54	55	49	89	1	.224	.338	0	0	C-152
1950	131	415	91	16	5	14	3.4	53	58	42	52	1	.219	.383	0	0	C-129
1951	133	416	99	17	5	6	1.4	60	43	38	72	0	.238	.346	2	0	C-129
1952	112	333	75	17	2	4	1.2	39	41	29	47	0	.225	.324	3	0	C-107
1953	112	299	65	10	1	9	3.0	37	37	25	41	1	.217	.348	0	0	C-106
1954	139	423	99	12	7	11	2.6	56	40	34	48	0	.234	.374	2	0	C-137
1955	116	304	67	5	2	9	3.0	30	40	34	33	0	.220	.339	2	0	C-111
1956	122	315	70	15	2	6	1.9	42	34	49	54	1	.222	.340	3	1	C-118
1957	58	148	32	7	0	4	2.7	14	15	16	23	0	.216	.345	0	0	C-58
1958 2 teams	DET A (45G – .192)					PHI N (25G – .220)											
" total	70	189	38	12	0	1	0.5	19	13	14	48	0	.201	.280	0	0	C-70
1959 2 teams	PHI N (25G – .196)					SF N (21G – .133)											
" total	46	81	14	2	0	0	0.0	1	8	4	20	0	.173	.198	0	0	C-46
1960 CHI N	24	43	9	2	1	1	2.3	4	5	7	10	0	.209	.372	2	0	C-22
17 yrs.	1666	4772	1087	187	46	92	1.9	550	525	456	742	15	.228	.344	20	2	C-1629
1 yr.	45	130	25	6	0	1	0.8	14	7	10	32	0	.192	.262	0	0	C-45

WORLD SERIES

	G	AB	H	2B	3B	HR	HR %	R	RBI	BB	SO	SB	BA	SA	Pinch Hit AB	H	G by POS
1948 CLE A	6	19	4	0	0	1	5.3	2	5	1	4	1	.211	.368	0	0	C-6
1954	4	13	2	1	0	0	0.0	1	0	1	1	0	.154	.231	0	0	C-4
2 yrs.	10	32	6	1	0	1	3.1	3	5	2	5	1	.188	.313	0	0	C-10

Harry Heilmann

HEILMANN, HARRY EDWIN (Slug)   BR TR 6'1"   195 lbs.
B. Aug. 3, 1894, San Francisco, Calif.   D. July 9, 1951, Southfield, Mich.
Hall of Fame 1952.

	G	AB	H	2B	3B	HR	HR%	R	RBI	BB	SO	SB	BA	SA	Pinch Hit AB	Pinch Hit H	G by POS
1914 DET A	67	182	41	8	1	2	1.1	25	22	22	29	1	.225	.313	11	3	OF-29, 1B-16, 2B-6
1916	136	451	127	30	11	2	0.4	57	76	42	40	9	.282	.410	16	5	OF-77, 1B-30, 2B-9
1917	150	556	156	22	11	5	0.9	57	86	41	54	11	.281	.387	0	0	OF-123, 1B-27
1918	79	286	79	10	6	5	1.7	34	44	35	10	13	.276	.406	1	1	OF-40, 1B-37, 2B-2
1919	140	537	172	30	15	8	1.5	74	95	37	41	7	.320	.477	0	0	1B-140
1920	145	543	168	28	5	9	1.7	66	89	39	32	3	.309	.429	1	0	1B-122, OF-21
1921	149	602	**237**	43	14	19	3.2	114	139	53	37	2	**.394**	.606	1	1	OF-143, 1B-4
1922	118	455	162	27	10	21	4.6	92	92	58	28	8	.356	.598	0	0	OF-115, 1B-5
1923	144	524	211	44	11	18	3.4	121	115	74	40	8	**.403**	.632	1	1	OF-130, 1B-12
1924	153	570	197	**45**	16	10	1.8	107	113	78	41	13	.346	.533	2	0	OF-147, 1B-4
1925	150	573	225	40	11	13	2.3	97	133	67	27	6	**.393**	.569	2	1	OF-148
1926	141	502	184	41	8	9	1.8	90	103	67	19	6	.367	.534	6	1	OF-134
1927	141	505	201	50	9	14	2.8	106	120	72	16	11	**.398**	.616	5	1	OF-135
1928	151	558	183	38	10	14	2.5	83	107	57	45	7	.328	.507	1	0	OF-126, 1B-25
1929	125	453	156	41	7	15	3.3	86	120	50	39	5	.344	.565	7	1	OF-113, 1B-1
1930 CIN N	142	459	153	43	6	19	4.1	79	91	64	50	2	.333	.577	12	5	OF-106, 1B-19
1932	15	31	8	2	0	0	0.0	3	6	0	2	0	.258	.323	9	3	1B-6
17 yrs.	2146	7787	2660	542	151	183	2.4	1291	1551	856	550	112	.342	.520	75	23	OF-1587, 1B-448, 2B-17
15 yrs.	1989	7297	2499	497	145	164	2.2	1209	1454	792	498	110	.342	.518	54	15	OF-1481, 1B-423, 2B-17
	6th	5th	4th	4th	4th	9th		5th	3rd	7th			2nd	2nd			

Les Hennessy

HENNESSY, LESTER BAKER   BR TR 6'   190 lbs.
B. Dec. 12, 1893, Lynn, Mass.   D. Nov. 20, 1976, New York, N. Y.

	G	AB	H	2B	3B	HR	HR%	R	RBI	BB	SO	SB	BA	SA	Pinch Hit AB	Pinch Hit H	G by POS
1913 DET A	12	22	3	0	0	0	0.0	2	0	3	6	2	.136	.136	2	0	2B-9

Babe Herman

HERMAN, FLOYD CAVES   BL TL 6'4"   190 lbs.
B. June 26, 1903, Buffalo, N. Y.

	G	AB	H	2B	3B	HR	HR%	R	RBI	BB	SO	SB	BA	SA	Pinch Hit AB	Pinch Hit H	G by POS
1926 BKN N	137	496	158	35	11	11	2.2	64	81	44	53	8	.319	.500	6	2	1B-101, OF-35
1927	130	412	112	26	9	14	3.4	65	73	39	41	4	.272	.481	20	7	1B-105, OF-1
1928	134	486	165	37	6	12	2.5	64	91	38	36	1	.340	.514	6	1	OF-127
1929	146	569	217	42	13	21	3.7	105	113	55	45	21	.381	.612	3	2	OF-141, 1B-2
1930	153	614	241	48	11	35	5.7	143	130	66	56	18	.393	.678	0	0	OF-153
1931	151	610	191	43	16	18	3.0	93	97	50	65	17	.313	.525	0	0	OF-150
1932 CIN N	148	577	188	38	19	16	2.8	87	87	60	45	7	.326	.541	2	1	OF-146
1933 CHI N	137	508	147	36	12	16	3.1	77	93	50	57	6	.289	.502	5	4	OF-131
1934	125	467	142	34	5	14	3.0	65	84	35	71	1	.304	.488	6	2	OF-113, 1B-7
1935 2 teams		PIT N (26G – .235)				CIN N (92G – .335)											
" total	118	430	136	31	6	10	2.3	52	65	38	35	5	.316	.484	10	0	OF-91, 1B-17
1936 CIN N	119	380	106	25	2	13	3.4	59	71	39	36	4	.279	.458	19	4	OF-92, 1B-4
1937 DET A	17	20	6	3	0	0	0.0	2	3	1	6	2	.300	.450	14	3	OF-2
1945 BKN N	37	34	9	1	0	1	2.9	6	9	5	7	0	.265	.382	29	6	OF-3
13 yrs.	1552	5603	1818	399	110	181	3.2	882	997	520	553	94	.324	.532	120	32	OF-1185, 1B-236
1 yr.	17	20	6	3	0	0	0.0	2	3	1	6	2	.300	.450	14	3	OF-2

Larry Herndon

HERNDON, LARRY DARNELL   BR TR 6'3"   190 lbs.
B. Nov. 3, 1953, Sunflower, Miss.

	G	AB	H	2B	3B	HR	HR%	R	RBI	BB	SO	SB	BA	SA	Pinch Hit AB	Pinch Hit H	G by POS
1974 STL N	12	1	1	0	0	0	0.0	3	0	0	0	0	1.000	1.000	0	0	OF-1
1976 SF N	115	337	97	11	3	2	0.6	42	23	23	45	12	.288	.356	6	2	OF-110
1977	49	109	26	4	3	1	0.9	13	5	5	20	4	.239	.358	5	1	OF-44
1978	151	471	122	15	9	1	0.2	52	32	35	71	13	.259	.335	4	2	OF-149
1979	132	354	91	14	5	7	2.0	35	36	29	70	8	.257	.384	19	7	OF-122
1980	139	493	127	17	11	8	1.6	54	49	19	91	8	.258	.385	21	6	OF-122
1981	96	364	105	15	8	5	1.4	48	41	20	55	15	.288	.415	4	0	OF-93
1982 DET A	157	614	179	21	13	23	3.7	92	88	38	92	12	.292	.480	3	0	OF-155, DH-2
1983	153	603	182	28	9	20	3.3	88	92	46	95	9	.302	.478	5	1	OF-133, DH-19
1984	125	407	114	18	5	7	1.7	52	43	32	63	6	.280	.400	24	7	OF-117, DH-4
10 yrs.	1129	3753	1044	143	66	74	2.0	479	409	247	602	87	.278	.411	91	26	OF-1046, DH-26
3 yrs.	435	1624	475	67	27	50	3.1	232	223	116	250	27	.292	.459	32	8	OF-405, DH-26

LEAGUE CHAMPIONSHIP SERIES

	G	AB	H	2B	3B	HR	HR%	R	RBI	BB	SO	SB	BA	SA	Pinch Hit AB	Pinch Hit H	G by POS
1984 DET A	2	5	1	0	0	1	20.0	1	1	1	2	0	.200	.800	0	0	OF-2

WORLD SERIES

	G	AB	H	2B	3B	HR	HR%	R	RBI	BB	SO	SB	BA	SA	Pinch Hit AB	Pinch Hit H	G by POS
1984 DET A	5	15	5	0	0	1	6.7	1	3	3	2	0	.333	.533	2	0	OF-5

Whitey Herzog

HERZOG, DORREL NORMAN ELVERT   BL TL 5'11"   182 lbs.
B. Nov. 9, 1931, New Athens, Ill.
Manager 1973, 1975-84.

	G	AB	H	2B	3B	HR	HR%	R	RBI	BB	SO	SB	BA	SA	Pinch Hit AB	Pinch Hit H	G by POS
1956 WAS A	117	421	103	13	7	4	1.0	49	35	35	74	8	.245	.337	11	5	OF-103, 1B-5
1957	36	78	13	3	0	0	0.0	7	4	13	12	1	.167	.205	10	0	OF-28
1958 2 teams		WAS A (8G – .000)				KC A (88G – .240)											
" total	96	101	23	1	2	0	0.0	11	9	17	26	0	.228	.277	32	7	OF-44, 1B-22
1959 KC A	38	123	36	7	1	1	0.8	25	9	34	23	1	.293	.390	2	1	OF-34, 1B-5
1960	83	252	67	10	2	8	3.2	43	38	40	32	0	.266	.417	12	5	OF-69, 1B-2
1961 BAL A	113	323	94	11	6	5	1.5	39	35	50	41	1	.291	.409	18	6	OF-98
1962	99	263	70	13	1	7	2.7	34	35	41	36	2	.266	.403	26	5	OF-70
1963 DET A	52	53	8	2	1	0	0.0	5	7	11	17	0	.151	.226	35	4	1B-7, OF-4
8 yrs.	634	1614	414	60	20	25	1.5	213	172	241	261	13	.257	.365	146	33	OF-450, 1B-37
1 yr.	52	53	8	2	1	0	0.0	5	7	11	17	0	.151	.226	35	4	1B-7, OF-4

Gus Hetling

HETLING, AUGUST JULIUS   BR TR 5'10"   165 lbs.
B. Nov. 21, 1885, St. Louis, Mo.   D. Oct. 13, 1962, Wichita, Kans.

	G	AB	H	2B	3B	HR	HR%	R	RBI	BB	SO	SB	BA	SA	Pinch Hit AB	Pinch Hit H	G by POS
1906 DET A	2	7	1	0	0	0	0.0	0	0			0	.143	.143	0	0	3B-2

	G	AB	H	2B	3B	HR	HR %	R	RBI	BB	SO	SB	BA	SA	Pinch Hit AB	Pinch Hit H	G by POS

Piano Legs Hickman

HICKMAN, CHARLES TAYLOR   BR TR 5'9" 185 lbs
B. Mar. 4, 1876, Taylortown, Pa.   D. Apr. 19, 1934, Morgantown, W. Va.

	G	AB	H	2B	3B	HR	HR%	R	RBI	BB	SO	SB	BA	SA	PH AB	PH H	G by POS
1897 BOS N	2	3	2	0	0	1	33.3	1	2	0		0	.667	1.667	0	0	P-2
1898	19	58	15	2	0	0	0.0	4	7	1		0	.259	.293	0	0	OF-7, 1B-6, P-6
1899	19	63	25	2	7	0	0.0	15	15	2		1	.397	.651	0	0	P-11, OF-7, 1B-1
1900 NY N	127	473	148	19	17	9	1.9	65	91	17		10	.313	.482	0	0	3B-120, OF-7
1901	112	401	113	20	6	4	1.0	44	62	15		5	.282	.392	8	1	OF-50, SS-23, 3B-15, P 2B-7, 1B-2
1902 2 teams							BOS A (28G – .296)			CLE A (102G – .380)							
" total	130	534	194	36	13	11	2.1	74	110	15		9	.363	.541	1	0	1B-98, OF-27, 2B-3, P-1
1903 CLE A	130	518	171	31	11	12	2.3	67	97	17		14	.330	.502	0	0	1B-125, 2B-7
1904 2 teams							CLE A (86G – .288)			DET A (42G – .243)							
" total	128	481	132	28	16	6	1.2	52	67	24		12	.274	.437	1	1	1B-79, 2B-45, OF-1
1905 2 teams							DET A (59G – .221)			WAS A (88G – .311)							
" total	147	573	159	37	12	4	0.7	69	66	21		6	.277	.405	0	0	2B-85, OF-47, 1B-15
1906 WAS A	120	451	128	25	5	9	2.0	53	57	14		9	.284	.421	1	0	OF-95, 1B-18, 3B-5, 2B-
1907 2 teams							WAS A (60G – .285)			CHI A (21G – .261)							
" total	81	216	61	12	4	1	0.5	23	24	18		4	.282	.389	22	4	1B-30, OF-21, 2B-3, P-1
1908 CLE A	65	197	46	6	1	2	1.0	16	16	9		2	.234	.305	16	4	OF-28, 1B-20, 2B-1
12 yrs.	1080	3968	1194	218	92	59	1.5	483	614	153		72	.301	.447	49	10	1B-394, OF-290, 2B-152 3B-140, P-30, SS-23
2 yrs.	101	357	82	18	9	4	1.1	39	42	23		6	.230	.364	1	1	1B-51, OF-47

Buddy Hicks

HICKS, CLARENCE WALTER   BB TR 5'10" 170 lbs
B. Feb. 15, 1927, Belvedere, Calif.

	G	AB	H	2B	3B	HR	HR%	R	RBI	BB	SO	SB	BA	SA	PH AB	PH H	G by POS
1956 DET A	26	47	10	2	0	0	0.0	5	5	3	2	0	.213	.255	2	0	SS-16, 2B-6, 3B-1

Pinky Higgins

HIGGINS, MICHAEL FRANKLIN   BR TR 6'1" 185 lbs
B. May 27, 1909, Red Oak, Tex.   D. Mar. 21, 1969, Dallas, Tex.
Manager 1955-62.

	G	AB	H	2B	3B	HR	HR%	R	RBI	BB	SO	SB	BA	SA	PH AB	PH H	G by POS
1930 PHI A	14	24	6	2	0	0	0.0	1	0	4	5	0	.250	.333	4	0	3B-5, 2B-2, SS-1
1933	152	567	178	34	11	14	2.5	85	99	61	53	2	.314	.487	0	0	3B-152
1934	144	543	179	37	6	16	2.9	89	90	56	70	9	.330	.508	0	0	3B-144
1935	133	524	155	32	4	23	4.4	69	94	42	62	6	.296	.504	1	1	3B-131
1936	146	550	159	32	2	12	2.2	89	80	67	61	7	.289	.420	1	1	3B-145
1937 BOS A	153	570	172	33	5	9	1.6	88	106	76	51	2	.302	.425	1	1	3B-152
1938	139	524	159	29	5	5	1.0	77	106	71	55	10	.303	.406	1	0	3B-138
1939 DET A	132	489	135	23	2	8	1.6	57	76	56	41	7	.276	.380	2	1	3B-130
1940	131	480	130	24	3	13	2.7	70	76	61	31	4	.271	.415	1	0	3B-129
1941	147	540	161	28	3	11	2.0	79	73	67	45	5	.298	.422	2	0	3B-145
1942	143	499	133	34	2	11	2.2	65	79	72	21	3	.267	.409	5	0	3B-137
1943	138	523	145	20	1	10	1.9	62	84	57	31	2	.277	.337	0	0	3B-138
1944	148	543	161	32	4	7	1.3	79	76	81	34	4	.297	.409	2	1	3B-146
1946 2 teams							DET A (18G – .217)			BOS A (64G – .275)							
" total	82	260	68	14	2	2	0.8	20	36	29	30	0	.262	.354	5	1	3B-76
14 yrs.	1802	6636	1941	374	50	141	2.1	930	1075	800	590	61	.292	.428	25	5	3B-1768, 2B-2, SS-1
7 yrs.	857	3134	878	164	16	60	1.9	414	472	399	209	25	.280	.400	12	2	3B-842

WORLD SERIES

	G	AB	H	2B	3B	HR	HR%	R	RBI	BB	SO	SB	BA	SA	PH AB	PH H	G by POS
1940 DET A	7	24	8	3	1	1	4.2	2	6	3	3	0	.333	.667	0	0	3B-7
1946 BOS A	7	24	5	1	0	0	0.0	1	2	2	0	0	.208	.250	0	0	3B-7
2 yrs.	14	48	13	4	1	1	2.1	3	8	5	3	0	.271	.458	0	0	3B-14

Hugh High

HIGH, HUGH JENKEN (Bunny, Lefty)   BL TL 5'7½" 155 lbs
Brother of Andy High.   Brother of Charlie High.
B. Oct. 24, 1887, Pottstown, Pa.   D. Nov. 16, 1962, St. Louis, Mo.

	G	AB	H	2B	3B	HR	HR%	R	RBI	BB	SO	SB	BA	SA	PH AB	PH H	G by POS
1913 DET A	80	183	42	6	1	0	0.0	18	16	28	24	6	.230	.273	19	5	OF-50
1914	80	184	49	5	3	0	0.0	25	17	26	21	7	.266	.326	19	3	OF-53
1915 NY A	119	427	110	19	7	1	0.2	51	43	62	47	22	.258	.342	1	1	OF-117
1916	115	377	99	13	4	1	0.3	44	28	47	44	13	.263	.326	5	1	OF-109
1917	103	365	86	11	6	1	0.3	37	19	48	31	8	.236	.307	2	0	OF-100
1918	7	10	0	0	0	0	0.0	1	0	1	1	0	.000	.000	3	0	OF-4
6 yrs.	504	1546	386	54	21	3	0.2	176	123	212	168	56	.250	.318	49	10	OF-433
2 yrs.	160	367	91	11	4	0	0.0	43	33	54	45	13	.248	.300	38	8	OF-103

Billy Hitchcock

HITCHCOCK, WILLIAM CLYDE   BR TR 6'1½" 185 lbs
Brother of Jim Hitchcock.
B. July 31, 1916, Inverness, Ala.
Manager 1960, 1962-63, 1966-67.

	G	AB	H	2B	3B	HR	HR%	R	RBI	BB	SO	SB	BA	SA	PH AB	PH H	G by POS
1942 DET A	85	280	59	8	1	0	0.0	27	29	26	21	2	.211	.246	0	0	SS-80, 3B-1
1946 2 teams							DET A (3G – .000)			WAS A (98G – .212)							
" total	101	357	75	8	3	0	0.0	27	25	27	52	2	.210	.249	1	0	SS-53, 3B-46, 2B-1
1947 STL A	80	275	61	2	2	1	0.4	25	28	21	34	3	.222	.255	5	0	2B-46, 3B-17, SS-7, 1B-
1948 BOS A	49	124	37	3	2	1	0.8	15	20	7	9	0	.298	.379	12	3	3B-15, 2B-15
1949	55	147	30	6	1	0	0.0	22	9	17	11	2	.204	.259	16	0	1B-29, 2B-8
1950 PHI A	115	399	109	22	5	1	0.3	35	54	44	32	3	.273	.361	8	3	2B-107, SS-1
1951	77	222	68	10	4	1	0.5	27	36	21	23	2	.306	.401	11	3	3B-45, 2B-23, 1B-1
1952	119	407	100	8	4	1	0.2	45	56	39	45	1	.246	.292	4	0	3B-104, 1B-13
1953 DET A	22	38	8	0	0	0	0.0	8	0	3	3	0	.211	.211	6	1	3B-12, SS-1, 2B-1
9 yrs.	703	2249	547	67	22	5	0.2	231	257	205	230	15	.243	.299	63	10	3B-240, 2B-201, SS-142, 1B-48
3 yrs.	110	321	67	8	1	0	0.0	35	29	30	24	2	.209	.240	7	1	SS-81, 3B-13, 2B-2

Ducky Holmes

HOLMES, JAMES WILLIAM   BL TR 5'6" 170 lbs
B. Jan. 28, 1869, Des Moines, Iowa   D. Aug. 6, 1932, Truro, Iowa

	G	AB	H	2B	3B	HR	HR%	R	RBI	BB	SO	SB	BA	SA	PH AB	PH H	G by POS
1895 LOU N	40	161	60	10	2	3	1.9	33	20	12	9	9	.373	.516	0	0	OF-29, SS-8, 3B-4, 1B-1
1896	47	141	38	3	2	0	0.0	22	18	13	5	8	.270	.319	10	3	OF-33, P-2, SS-1, 2B-1

	G	AB	H	2B	3B	HR	HR %	R	RBI	BB	SO	SB	BA	SA	Pinch Hit AB	Pinch Hit H	G by POS

Ducky Holmes continued

	G	AB	H	2B	3B	HR	HR %	R	RBI	BB	SO	SB	BA	SA	AB	H	G by POS
'97 2 teams	LOU N (2G – .000)			NY N (79G – .268)													
total	81	310	82	8	6	1	0.3	51	44	19		30	.265	.339	2	0	OF-77, SS-2
'98 2 teams	STL N (23G – .238)			BAL N (113G – .285)													
total	136	543	150	11	10	1	0.2	63	64	25		29	.276	.339	1	1	OF-135
'99 BAL N	138	553	177	31	7	4	0.7	80	66	39		50	.320	.423	0	0	OF-138
'01 DET A	131	537	158	28	10	4	0.7	90	62	37		35	.294	.406	0	0	OF-131
'02	92	362	93	15	4	2	0.6	50	33	28		16	.257	.337	0	0	OF-92
'03 2 teams	WAS A (21G – .225)			CHI A (86G – .279)													
total	107	415	112	10	6	1	0.2	66	26	30		35	.270	.330	3	0	OF-96, 3B-7, 2B-2
'04 CHI A	68	251	78	11	9	1	0.4	42	19	14		13	.311	.438	5	2	OF-63
'05	92	328	66	15	2	0	0.0	42	22	19		11	.201	.259	3	2	OF-89
10 yrs.	932	3601	1014	142	58	17	0.5	539	374	236	14	236	.282	.367	24	8	OF-883, SS-11, 3B-11, P-4, 2B-3
2 yrs.	223	899	251	43	14	6	0.7	140	95	65		51	.279	.378	0	0	OF-223

Joe Hoover

HOOVER, ROBERT JOE   BR TR 5'11"   175 lbs.
B. Apr. 15, 1915, Brawley, Calif.   D. Sept. 2, 1965, Los Angeles, Calif.

	G	AB	H	2B	3B	HR	HR %	R	RBI	BB	SO	SB	BA	SA	AB	H	G by POS
'43 DET A	144	575	140	15	8	4	0.7	78	38	36	101	6	.243	.318	0	0	SS-144
'44	120	441	104	20	2	0	0.0	67	29	35	66	7	.236	.290	0	0	SS-119, 2B-1
'45	74	222	57	10	5	1	0.5	33	17	21	35	6	.257	.360	0	0	SS-68
3 yrs.	338	1238	301	45	15	5	0.4	178	84	92	202	19	.243	.316	0	0	SS-331, 2B-1
3 yrs.	338	1238	301	45	15	5	0.4	178	84	92	202	19	.243	.316	0	0	SS-331, 2B-1
WORLD SERIES																	
'45 DET A	1	3	1	0	0	0	0.0	1	1	0	0	0	.333	.333	0	0	SS-1

Johnny Hopp

HOPP, JOHN LEONARD (Hippity)   BL TL 5'10"   170 lbs.
B. July 18, 1916, Hastings, Neb.

	G	AB	H	2B	3B	HR	HR %	R	RBI	BB	SO	SB	BA	SA	AB	H	G by POS
'39 STL N	6	4	2	1	0	0	0.0	1	1	2	1	0	.500	.750	3	2	1B-1
'40	80	152	41	7	4	1	0.7	24	14	9	21	3	.270	.388	23	4	OF-39, 1B-10
'41	134	445	135	25	11	4	0.9	83	50	50	63	15	.303	.436	6	1	OF-91, 1B-39
'42	95	314	81	16	7	3	1.0	41	37	36	40	14	.258	.382	3	1	1B-88
'43	91	241	54	10	2	2	0.8	33	25	24	22	8	.224	.307	4	0	OF-52, 1B-27
'44	139	527	177	35	9	11	2.1	106	72	58	47	15	.336	.499	2	0	OF-131, 1B-6
'45	124	446	129	22	8	3	0.7	67	44	49	24	14	.289	.395	6	1	OF-104, 1B-15
'46 BOS N	129	445	148	23	8	3	0.7	71	48	34	34	21	.333	.440	8	3	1B-68, OF-58
'47	134	430	124	20	2	2	0.5	74	32	58	30	13	.288	.358	7	0	OF-125
'48 PIT N	120	392	109	15	12	1	0.3	64	31	40	25	5	.278	.385	14	7	OF-80, 1B-25
'49 2 teams	PIT N (105G – .318)			BKN N (8G – .000)													
total	113	385	118	14	5	5	1.3	55	39	37	32	9	.306	.408	13	5	1B-79, OF-20
'50 2 teams	PIT N (106G – .340)			NY A (19G – .333)													
total	125	345	117	26	6	9	2.6	60	55	52	18	7	.339	.528	28	8	1B-82, OF-13
'51 NY A	46	63	13	1	0	2	3.2	10	4	9	11	2	.206	.317	19	4	1B-25
'52 2 teams	NY A (15G – .160)			DET A (42G – .217)													
total	57	71	14	1	0	0	0.0	9	5	8	10	2	.197	.211	33	8	1B-13, OF-4
14 yrs.	1393	4260	1262	216	74	46	1.1	698	458	465	378	128	.296	.414	169	44	OF-717, 1B-478
1 yr.	42	46	10	1	0	0	0.0	5	3	6	7	0	.217	.239	31	8	OF-4, 1B-1
WORLD SERIES																	
'42 STL N	5	17	3	0	0	0	0.0	3	0	1	1	0	.176	.176	0	0	1B-5
'43	1	4	0	0	0	0	0.0	0	0	0	1	0	.000	.000	0	0	OF-1
'44	6	27	5	0	0	0	0.0	2	0	0	8	0	.185	.185	0	0	OF-6
'50 NY A	3	2	0	0	0	0	0.0	0	0	0	0	0	.000	.000	0	0	1B-3
'51	1	0	0	0	0	0	–	0	0	1	0	0	–	–	0	0	
5 yrs.	16	50	8	0	0	0	0.0	5	0	2	10	0	.160	.160	0	0	1B-8, OF-7

Willie Horton

HORTON, WILLIE WATTERSON   BR TR 5'11"   209 lbs.
B. Oct. 18, 1942, Arno, Va.

	G	AB	H	2B	3B	HR	HR %	R	RBI	BB	SO	SB	BA	SA	AB	H	G by POS
'63 DET A	15	43	14	2	1	1	2.3	6	4	0	8	2	.326	.488	5	3	OF-9
'64	25	80	13	1	3	1	1.3	6	10	11	20	0	.163	.288	3	1	OF-23
'65	143	512	140	20	2	29	5.7	69	104	48	101	5	.273	.490	3	0	OF-141, 3B-1
'66	146	526	138	22	6	27	5.1	72	100	44	103	1	.262	.481	9	2	OF-137
'67	122	401	110	20	3	19	4.7	47	67	36	80	0	.274	.481	11	3	OF-110
'68	143	512	146	20	2	36	7.0	68	85	49	110	0	.285	.543	5	1	OF-139
'69	141	508	133	17	1	28	5.5	66	91	52	93	3	.262	.465	5	1	OF-136
'70	96	371	113	18	2	17	4.6	53	69	28	43	0	.305	.501	0	0	OF-96
'71	119	450	130	25	1	22	4.9	64	72	37	75	1	.289	.496	2	0	OF-118
'72	108	333	77	9	5	11	3.3	44	36	27	47	0	.231	.387	12	1	OF-98
'73	111	411	130	19	3	17	4.1	42	53	23	57	1	.316	.501	3	1	OF-107, DH-1
'74	72	238	71	8	1	15	6.3	32	47	21	36	0	.298	.529	6	3	OF-64, DH-1
'75	159	615	169	13	1	25	4.1	62	92	44	109	1	.275	.421	0	0	DH-159
'76	114	401	105	17	0	14	3.5	40	56	49	63	0	.262	.409	6	1	DH-105
'77 2 teams	DET A (1G – .250)			TEX A (139G – .289)													
total	140	523	151	23	3	15	2.9	55	75	42	117	2	.289	.430	6	2	DH-128, OF-11
'78 3 teams	CLE A (50G – .249)			OAK A (32G – .314)				TOR A (33G – .205)									
total	119	393	99	21	0	11	2.8	38	60	28	69	3	.252	.389	9	3	DH-105, OF-1
'79 SEA A	162	646	180	19	5	29	4.5	77	106	42	112	1	.279	.458	0	0	DH-162
'80	97	335	74	10	1	8	2.4	32	36	39	70	0	.221	.328	5	2	DH-92
18 yrs.	2028	7298	1993	284	40	325	4.5	873	1163	620	1313	20	.273	.457	90	24	OF-1190, DH-753, 3B-1
15 yrs.	1515	5405	1490	211	31	262	4.8	671	886	469	945	14	.276	.472	70	17	OF-1179, DH-266, 3B-1
							4th	6th			10th			3rd			
LEAGUE CHAMPIONSHIP SERIES																	
'72 DET A	5	10	1	0	0	0	0.0	0	0	1	3	0	.100	.100	2	1	OF-3
WORLD SERIES																	
'68 DET A	7	23	7	1	1	1	4.3	6	3	5	6	0	.304	.565	0	0	OF-7

	G	AB	H	2B	3B	HR	HR %	R	RBI	BB	SO	SB	BA	SA	Pinch Hit AB	Pinch Hit H	G by POS

Tim Hosley

HOSLEY, TIMOTHY KENNETH BR TR 5'11" 185 lb
B. May 10, 1947, Spartanburg, S. C.

	G	AB	H	2B	3B	HR	HR %	R	RBI	BB	SO	SB	BA	SA	AB	H	G by POS
1970 DET A	7	12	2	0	0	1	8.3	1	2	0	6	0	.167	.417	4	1	C-4
1971	7	16	3	0	0	2	12.5	2	6	0	1	0	.188	.563	4	0	C-4, 1B-1
1973 OAK A	13	14	3	0	0	0	0.0	3	2	2	3	0	.214	.214	4	1	C-12
1974	11	7	2	0	0	0	0.0	3	1	1	2	0	.286	.286	4	1	C-8, 1B-1
1975 CHI N	62	141	36	7	0	6	4.3	22	20	27	25	1	.255	.433	10	2	C-53
1976 2 teams	CHI	N (1G –	.000)			OAK	A (37G –	.164)									
" total	38	56	9	2	0	1	1.8	4	4	8	12	0	.161	.250	12	2	C-37
1977 OAK A	39	78	15	0	0	1	1.3	5	10	16	13	0	.192	.231	5	1	C-19, DH-12, 1B-3
1978	13	23	7	2	0	0	0.0	1	3	1	6	0	.304	.391	7	2	C-2, DH-1
1981	18	21	2	0	0	1	4.8	2	5	2	5	0	.095	.238	14	1	DH-4, 1B-1
9 yrs.	208	368	79	11	0	12	3.3	43	53	57	73	1	.215	.342	64	11	C-139, DH-17, 1B-6
2 yrs.	14	28	5	0	0	3	10.7	3	8	0	7	0	.179	.500	8	1	C-8, 1B-1

Chuck Hostetler

HOSTETLER, CHARLES CLOYD BL TR 6' 175 lb
B. Sept. 22, 1903, McClellandtown, Pa.   D. Feb. 18, 1971, Fort Collins, Colo.

	G	AB	H	2B	3B	HR	HR %	R	RBI	BB	SO	SB	BA	SA	AB	H	G by POS
1944 DET A	90	265	79	9	2	0	0.0	42	20	21	31	4	.298	.347	19	4	OF-65
1945	42	44	7	3	0	0	0.0	3	2	7	8	0	.159	.227	30	6	OF-8
2 yrs.	132	309	86	12	2	0	0.0	45	22	28	39	4	.278	.330	49	10	OF-73
2 yrs.	132	309	86	12	2	0	0.0	45	22	28	39	4	.278	.330	49	10	OF-73

WORLD SERIES

	G	AB	H	2B	3B	HR	HR %	R	RBI	BB	SO	SB	BA	SA	AB	H	G by POS
1945 DET A	3	3	0	0	0	0	0.0	0	0	0	0	0	.000	.000	3	0	

Frank House

HOUSE, HENRY FRANKLIN (Pig) BL TR 6'1½" 190 lb
B. Feb. 18, 1930, Bessemer, Ala.

	G	AB	H	2B	3B	HR	HR %	R	RBI	BB	SO	SB	BA	SA	AB	H	G by POS
1950 DET A	5	5	2	1	0	0	0.0	1	0	0	1	0	.400	.600	1	0	C-5
1951	18	41	9	2	0	1	2.4	3	4	6	2	1	.220	.341	0	0	C-18
1954	114	352	88	12	1	9	2.6	35	38	31	34	2	.250	.366	9	1	C-107
1955	102	328	85	11	1	15	4.6	37	53	22	25	0	.259	.436	12	3	C-93
1956	94	321	77	6	2	10	3.1	44	44	21	19	1	.240	.364	9	3	C-88
1957	106	348	90	9	0	7	2.0	31	36	35	26	1	.259	.345	7	2	C-97
1958 KC A	76	202	51	6	3	4	2.0	16	24	12	13	1	.252	.371	19	7	C-55
1959	98	347	82	14	3	1	0.3	32	30	20	23	0	.236	.303	4	1	C-95
1960 CIN N	23	28	5	2	0	0	0.0	0	3	0	2	0	.179	.250	17	3	C-8
1961 DET A	17	22	5	1	1	0	0.0	3	3	4	2	0	.227	.364	3	0	C-14
10 yrs.	653	1994	494	64	11	47	2.4	202	235	151	147	6	.248	.362	81	20	C-580
7 yrs.	456	1417	356	42	5	42	3.0	154	178	119	109	5	.251	.377	41	9	C-422

Frank Howard

HOWARD, FRANK OLIVER (The Capital Punisher, Hondo) BR TR 6'7" 255 lb
B. Aug. 8, 1936, Columbus, Ohio
Manager 1981, 1983.

	G	AB	H	2B	3B	HR	HR %	R	RBI	BB	SO	SB	BA	SA	AB	H	G by POS
1958 LA N	8	29	7	1	0	1	3.4	3	2	1	11	0	.241	.379	0	0	OF-8
1959	9	21	3	0	1	1	4.8	2	6	2	9	0	.143	.381	4	1	OF-6
1960	117	448	120	15	2	23	5.1	54	77	32	108	0	.268	.464	2	0	OF-115, 1B-4
1961	99	267	79	10	2	15	5.6	36	45	21	50	0	.296	.517	19	7	OF-65, 1B-7
1962	141	493	146	25	6	31	6.3	80	119	39	108	1	.296	.560	11	2	OF-131
1963	123	417	114	16	1	28	6.7	58	64	33	116	1	.273	.518	15	3	OF-111
1964	134	433	98	13	2	24	5.5	60	69	51	113	1	.226	.432	10	0	OF-122
1965 WAS A	149	516	149	22	6	21	4.1	53	84	55	112	0	.289	.477	10	1	OF-138
1966	146	493	137	19	4	18	3.7	52	71	53	104	1	.278	.442	9	1	OF-135
1967	149	519	133	20	2	36	6.9	71	89	60	155	0	.256	.511	5	0	OF-141, 1B-4
1968	158	598	164	28	3	44	7.4	79	106	54	141	0	.274	.552	1	1	OF-107, 1B-55
1969	161	592	175	17	2	48	8.1	111	111	102	96	1	.296	.574	0	0	OF-114, 1B-70
1970	161	566	160	15	1	44	7.8	90	126	132	125	1	.283	.546	0	0	OF-120, 1B-48
1971	153	549	153	25	2	26	4.7	60	83	77	121	0	.279	.474	5	0	OF-100, 1B-68
1972 2 teams	TEX	A (95G –	.244)			DET	A (14G –	.242)									
" total	109	320	78	10	0	10	3.1	29	38	46	63	1	.244	.369	17	3	1B-76, OF-22
1973 DET A	85	227	58	9	1	12	5.3	26	29	24	28	0	.256	.463	7	1	DH-76, 1B-2
16 yrs.	1902	6488	1774	245	35	382	5.9	864	1119	782	1460	8	.273	.499	116	20	OF-1435, 1B-334, DH-?
2 yrs.	99	260	66	10	1	13	5.0	27	36	28	36	0	.254	.450	12	2	DH-76, 1B-12, OF-1

WORLD SERIES

	G	AB	H	2B	3B	HR	HR %	R	RBI	BB	SO	SB	BA	SA	AB	H	G by POS
1963 LA N	3	10	3	1	0	1	10.0	2	1	0	2	0	.300	.700	0	0	OF-3

Clarence Huber

HUBER, CLARENCE BILL (Gilly) BR TR 5'10" 165 lb
B. Oct. 28, 1897, Tyler, Tex.   D. Feb. 22, 1965, Laredo, Tex.

	G	AB	H	2B	3B	HR	HR %	R	RBI	BB	SO	SB	BA	SA	AB	H	G by POS
1920 DET A	11	42	9	2	1	0	0.0	4	5	0	5	0	.214	.310	0	0	3B-11
1921	1	0	0	0	0	0	–	0	0	0	0	0	–	–	0	0	3B-1
1925 PHI N	124	436	124	28	5	5	1.1	46	54	17	33	3	.284	.406	4	2	3B-120
1926	118	376	92	17	7	1	0.3	45	34	42	29	9	.245	.335	2	2	3B-115
4 yrs.	254	854	225	47	13	6	0.7	95	93	59	67	12	.263	.370	6	4	3B-247
2 yrs.	12	42	9	2	1	0	0.0	4	5	0	5	0	.214	.310	0	0	3B-12

Frank Huelsman

HUELSMAN, FRANK ELMER BR TR 6'2" 210 lb
B. June 5, 1874, St. Louis, Mo.   D. June 9, 1959, Affton, Mo.

	G	AB	H	2B	3B	HR	HR %	R	RBI	BB	SO	SB	BA	SA	AB	H	G by POS
1897 STL N	2	7	2	1	0	0	0.0	0	0	0		0	.286	.429	0	0	OF-2
1904 4 teams	CHI	A (4G –	.143)			DET	A (4G –	.333)		STL	A (20G –	.221)		WAS	A (84G –	.248)	
" total	112	396	97	23	5	2	0.5	28	35	31		7	.245	.343	4	0	OF-107
1905 WAS A	126	421	114	28	8	3	0.7	48	62	31		11	.271	.397	4	1	OF-123
3 yrs.	240	824	213	52	13	5	0.6	76	97	62		18	.258	.371	8	1	OF-232
1 yr.	4	18	6	1	0	0	0.0	4	5	1		1	.333	.389	0	0	OF-4

Tom Hughes

HUGHES, THOMAS FRANKLIN BL TR 6'1" 190 lb
B. Aug. 6, 1907, Emmet, Ark.

	G	AB	H	2B	3B	HR	HR %	R	RBI	BB	SO	SB	BA	SA	AB	H	G by POS
1930 DET A	17	59	22	2	3	0	0.0	8	5	4	8	0	.373	.508	0	0	OF-16

	G	AB	H	2B	3B	HR	HR %	R	RBI	BB	SO	SB	BA	SA	Pinch Hit AB	Pinch Hit H	G by POS

erry Humphrey

HUMPHREY, TERRYAL GENE   BR TR 6'3" 185 lbs.
B. Aug. 4, 1949, Chickasha, Okla.

	G	AB	H	2B	3B	HR	HR %	R	RBI	BB	SO	SB	BA	SA	PH AB	PH H	G by POS
'71 MON N	9	26	5	1	0	0	0.0	1	1	0	4	0	.192	.231	1	0	C-9
'72	69	215	40	8	0	1	0.5	13	9	16	38	4	.186	.237	4	1	C-65
'73	43	90	15	2	0	1	1.1	5	9	5	16	0	.167	.222	5	0	C-35
'74	20	52	10	3	0	0	0.0	3	3	4	9	0	.192	.250	2	2	C-17
'75 DET A	18	41	10	0	0	0	0.0	0	1	2	6	0	.244	.244	0	0	C-18
'76 CAL A	71	196	48	10	0	1	0.5	17	19	13	30	0	.245	.311	1	0	C-71
'77	123	304	69	11	0	2	0.7	17	34	21	58	1	.227	.283	0	0	C-123
'78	53	114	25	4	1	1	0.9	11	9	6	12	0	.219	.298	0	0	C-52, 3B-1, 2B-1
'79	9	17	1	0	0	0	0.0	2	0	1	2	0	.059	.059	0	0	C-9
9 yrs.	415	1055	223	39	1	6	0.6	69	85	68	175	5	.211	.267	13	3	C-399, 3B-1, 2B-1
1 yr.	18	41	10	0	0	0	0.0	0	1	2	6	0	.244	.244	0	0	C-18

red Hutchinson

HUTCHINSON, FREDERICK CHARLES   BL TR 6'2" 190 lbs.
B. Aug. 12, 1919, Seattle, Wash.   D. Nov. 12, 1964, Bradenton, Fla.
Manager 1952-54, 1956-64.

	G	AB	H	2B	3B	HR	HR %	R	RBI	BB	SO	SB	BA	SA	PH AB	PH H	G by POS
'39 DET A	13	34	13	1	0	0	0.0	5	6	2	0	0	.382	.412	0	0	P-13
'40	17	30	8	1	0	0	0.0	1	2	0	0	0	.267	.300	0	0	P-17
'41	2	2	0	0	0	0	0.0	0	0	0	2	0	.000	.000	2	0	
'46	40	89	28	4	0	0	0.0	11	13	6	1	0	.315	.360	9	2	P-28
'47	56	106	32	5	2	2	1.9	8	15	6	6	2	.302	.443	22	6	P-33
'48	76	112	23	1	0	1	0.9	11	12	23	9	3	.205	.241	32	7	P-33
'49	38	73	18	2	1	0	0.0	12	7	8	5	1	.247	.301	4	1	P-33
'50	44	95	31	7	0	0	0.0	15	20	12	3	0	.326	.400	4	1	P-39
'51	47	85	16	2	0	0	0.0	7	7	7	4	0	.188	.212	13	2	P-31
'52	17	18	1	0	0	0	0.0	4	0	3	0	0	.056	.056	5	1	P-12
'53	4	6	1	0	0	1	16.7	1	1	0	0	0	.167	.667	0	0	P-3, 1B-1
11 yrs.	354	650	171	23	3	4	0.6	71	83	67	30	6	.263	.326	91	20	P-242, 1B-1
11 yrs.	354	650	171	23	3	4	0.6	71	83	67	30	6	.263	.326	91	20	P-242, 1B-1

WORLD SERIES

	G	AB	H	2B	3B	HR	HR %	R	RBI	BB	SO	SB	BA	SA	PH AB	PH H	G by POS
'40 DET A	1	0	0	0	0	0	–	0	0	0	0	0	–	–	0	0	P-1

d Irvin

IRVIN, WILLIAM EDWARD   TR
B. 1882, Philadelphia, Pa.   D. Feb. 18, 1916, Philadelphia, Pa.

	G	AB	H	2B	3B	HR	HR %	R	RBI	BB	SO	SB	BA	SA	PH AB	PH H	G by POS
'12 DET A	1	3	2	0	2	0	0.0	0		0		0	.667	2.000	0	0	3B-1

Mike Ivie

IVIE, MICHAEL WILSON   BR TR 6'3" 205 lbs.
B. Aug. 8, 1952, Atlanta, Ga.

	G	AB	H	2B	3B	HR	HR %	R	RBI	BB	SO	SB	BA	SA	PH AB	PH H	G by POS
'71 SD N	6	17	8	0	0	0	0.0	0	3	1	1	0	.471	.471	1	0	C-6
'74	12	34	3	0	0	1	2.9	1	3	2	8	0	.088	.176	1	0	1B-11
'75	111	377	94	16	2	8	2.1	36	46	20	63	4	.249	.366	9	3	1B-78, 3B-61, C-1
'76	140	405	118	19	5	7	1.7	51	70	30	41	6	.291	.415	4	0	1B-135, 3B-2, C-2
'77	134	489	133	29	2	9	1.8	66	66	39	57	3	.272	.395	15	2	1B-105, 3B-25
'78 SF N	117	318	98	14	3	11	3.5	34	55	27	45	3	.308	.475	31	12	1B-76, OF-22
'79	133	402	115	18	3	27	6.7	58	89	47	80	5	.286	.547	23	9	1B-98, OF-24, 3B-4, 2B-1
'80	79	286	69	16	1	4	1.4	21	25	19	40	1	.241	.346	6	1	1B-72
'81 2 teams	SF N (7G – .294)				HOU N (19G – .238)												
total	26	59	15	5	0	0	0.0	3	9	2	12	0	.254	.339	13	4	1B-15
'82 2 teams	HOU N (7G – .333)				DET A (80G – .232)												
total	87	265	62	12	1	14	5.3	35	38	25	51	0	.234	.445	17	4	DH-79
'83 DET A	12	42	9	4	0	0	0.0	4	7	2	4	0	.214	.310	0	0	1B-12
1 yrs.	857	2694	724	133	17	81	3.0	309	411	214	402	22	.269	.421	120	35	1B-602, 3B-92, DH-79, OF-46, C-9, 2B-1
2 yrs.	92	301	69	16	1	14	4.7	39	45	26	55	0	.229	.429	11	2	DH-79, 1B-12

on Jackson

JACKSON, RONNIE DAMIEN   BR TR 6' 200 lbs.
B. May 9, 1953, Birmingham, Ala.

	G	AB	H	2B	3B	HR	HR %	R	RBI	BB	SO	SB	BA	SA	PH AB	PH H	G by POS
'75 CAL A	13	39	9	2	0	0	0.0	2	2	1	10	1	.231	.282	1	0	OF-9, 3B-3, DH-1
'76	127	410	93	18	3	8	2.0	44	40	30	58	5	.227	.344	5	1	3B-114, 2B-7, DH-6, OF-4
'77	106	292	71	15	2	8	2.7	38	28	24	42	3	.243	.390	20	8	1B-43, 3B-30, DH-20, OF-3, SS-1
'78	105	387	115	18	6	6	1.6	49	57	16	31	2	.297	.421	5	1	1B-75, 3B-31, DH-1, OF-1
'79 MIN A	159	583	158	40	5	14	2.4	85	68	51	59	3	.271	.429	4	0	1B-157, OF-1, SS-1, 3B-1
'80	131	396	105	29	3	5	1.3	48	42	28	41	1	.265	.391	21	4	1B-119, OF-15, 3B-2, DH-1
'81 2 teams	MIN A (54G – .263)				DET A (31G – .284)												
total	85	270	73	17	1	5	1.9	29	40	18	26	6	.270	.396	10	1	1B-65, OF-7, DH-6, 3B-3
'82 CAL A	53	142	47	6	0	2	1.4	15	19	10	12	0	.331	.415	8	4	1B-37, 3B-9
'83	102	348	80	16	1	8	2.3	41	39	27	33	2	.230	.351	12	2	3B-38, 1B-35, DH-16, OF-15
'84 2 teams	CAL A (33G – .165)				BAL A (12G – .286)												
total	45	119	23	4	1	0	0.0	5	7	7	17	0	.193	.244	8	1	1B-21, 3B-19, OF-1
10 yrs.	926	2986	774	165	22	56	1.9	356	342	213	329	23	.259	.385	94	22	1B-552, 3B-250, OF-56, DH-51, 2B-7, SS-2
1 yr.	31	95	27	8	1	1	1.1	12	12	8	11	4	.284	.421	7	1	1B-29

LEAGUE CHAMPIONSHIP SERIES

	G	AB	H	2B	3B	HR	HR %	R	RBI	BB	SO	SB	BA	SA	PH AB	PH H	G by POS
'82 CAL A	1	1	1	0	0	0	0.0	0	0	0	0	0	1.000	1.000	1	1	

aby Doll Jacobson

JACOBSON, WILLIAM CHESTER   BR TR 6'3" 215 lbs.
B. Aug. 16, 1890, Cable, Ill.   D. Jan. 16, 1977, Orion, Ill.

	G	AB	H	2B	3B	HR	HR %	R	RBI	BB	SO	SB	BA	SA	PH AB	PH H	G by POS
'15 2 teams	DET A (37G – .215)				STL A (34G – .209)												
total	71	180	38	12	3	2	1.1	18	13	15	40	3	.211	.344	22	5	OF-39, 1B-10
'17 STL A	148	529	131	23	7	4	0.8	53	55	31	67	10	.248	.340	6	1	OF-131, 1B-11
'19	120	455	147	31	8	4	0.9	70	51	24	47	9	.323	.453	5	2	OF-105, 1B-8
'20	154	609	216	34	14	9	1.5	97	122	46	37	11	.355	.501	0	0	OF-154, 1B-1
'21	151	599	211	38	14	5	0.8	90	90	42	30	8	.352	.487	0	0	OF-141, 1B-11
'22	145	555	176	22	16	9	1.6	88	102	46	36	19	.317	.463	1	0	OF-137, 1B-7

	G	AB	H	2B	3B	HR	HR %	R	RBI	BB	SO	SB	BA	SA	Pinch Hit AB	H	G by POS

Baby Doll Jacobson continued

	G	AB	H	2B	3B	HR	HR %	R	RBI	BB	SO	SB	BA	SA	PH AB	PH H	G by POS
1923	147	592	183	29	6	8	1.4	76	81	29	27	6	.309	.419	1	0	OF-146
1924	152	579	184	41	12	19	3.3	103	97	35	45	6	.318	.528	0	0	OF-151
1925	142	540	184	30	9	15	2.8	103	76	45	26	8	.341	.513	2	1	OF-139
1926 2 teams		STL	A	(50G –	.286)			BOS	A	(98G –	.305)						
" total	148	576	172	51	2	8	1.4	62	90	31	36	5	.299	.436	0	0	OF-148
1927 3 teams		BOS	A	(45G –	.245)			CLE	A	(32G –	.252)		PHI	A	(17G –	.229)	
" total	94	293	72	17	3	1	0.3	27	42	11	19	1	.246	.334	9	0	OF-84
11 yrs.	1472	5507	1714	328	94	84	1.5	787	819	355	410	86	.311	.451	46	9	OF-1375, 1B-48
1 yr.	37	65	14	6	2	0	0.0	5	4	5	14	0	.215	.369	20	5	1B-10, OF-7

Art James

JAMES, ARTHUR, JR.
B. Aug. 2, 1952, Detroit, Mich.
BL TL 6' 170 lb

	G	AB	H	2B	3B	HR	HR %	R	RBI	BB	SO	SB	BA	SA	PH AB	PH H	G by POS
1975 DET A	11	40	9	2	0	0	0.0	2	1	1	3	1	.225	.275	0	0	OF-11

Paul Jata

JATA, PAUL
B. Sept. 4, 1949, Astoria, N. Y.
BR TR 6'1" 190 lb

	G	AB	H	2B	3B	HR	HR %	R	RBI	BB	SO	SB	BA	SA	PH AB	PH H	G by POS
1972 DET A	32	74	17	2	0	0	0.0	8	3	7	14	0	.230	.257	12	4	1B-12, OF-10, C-1

Hughie Jennings

JENNINGS, HUGH AMBROSE (Ee-Yah)
B. Apr. 2, 1869, Pittston, Pa.   D. Feb. 1, 1928, Scranton, Pa.
Manager 1907-20.
Hall of Fame 1945.
BR TR 5'8½" 165 lb

	G	AB	H	2B	3B	HR	HR %	R	RBI	BB	SO	SB	BA	SA	PH AB	PH H	G by POS
1891 LOU AA	90	360	105	10	8	1	0.3	53	58	17	36	12	.292	.372	0	0	SS-70, 1B-17, 3B-3
1892 LOU N	152	594	132	16	4	2	0.3	65	61	30	30	28	.222	.273	0	0	SS-152
1893 2 teams		LOU	N	(23G –	.136)			BAL	N	(16G –	.255)						
" total	39	143	26	3	0	1	0.7	12	15	7	6	0	.182	.224	0	0	SS-38, OF-1
1894 BAL N	128	501	168	28	16	4	0.8	134	109	37	17	37	.335	.479	0	0	SS-128
1895	131	529	204	41	7	4	0.8	159	125	24	17	53	.386	.512	0	0	SS-131
1896	130	523	208	27	9	0	0.0	125	121	19	11	70	.398	.484	0	0	SS-130
1897	117	439	156	26	9	2	0.5	133	79	42		60	.355	.469	1	0	SS-116
1898	143	534	175	25	11	1	0.2	135	87	78		28	.328	.421	0	0	SS-115, 2B-27, OF-1
1899 2 teams		BAL	N	(2G –	.375)			BKN	N	(67G –	.296)						
" total	69	224	67	3	12	0	0.0	44	42	22		18	.299	.420	1	1	1B-50, SS-12, 2B-3
1900 BKN N	115	441	120	18	6	1	0.2	61	69	31		31	.272	.347	1	1	1B-112, 2B-2
1901 PHI N	82	302	83	21	2	1	0.3	38	39	25		13	.275	.368	0	0	1B-80, SS-1, 2B-1
1902	78	289	80	16	3	1	0.3	31	32	14		8	.277	.363	0	0	1B-69, SS-5, 2B-4
1903 BKN N	6	17	4	0	0	0	0.0	2	1	1		1	.235	.235	2	0	OF-4
1907 DET A	1	4	1	1	0	0	0.0	0	0	0		0	.250	.500	0	0	SS-1, 2B-1
1909	2	4	2	0	0	0	0.0	1	2	0		0	.500	.500	0	0	1B-2
1912	1	1	0	0	0	0	0.0	0	0	0		0	.000	.000	1	0	
1918	1	0	0	0	0	0	–	0	0	0		0	–	–	0	0	1B-1
17 yrs.	1285	4905	1531	235	87	18	0.4	993	840	347	117	359	.312	.407	6	2	SS-899, 1B-331, 2B-38, OF-6, 3B-3
4 yrs.	5	9	3	1	0	0	0.0	1	2	0	0	0	.333	.444	1	0	1B-3, SS-1, 2B-1

Alex Johnson

JOHNSON, ALEXANDER
B. Dec. 7, 1942, Helena, Ark.
BR TR 6' 205 lb

	G	AB	H	2B	3B	HR	HR %	R	RBI	BB	SO	SB	BA	SA	PH AB	PH H	G by POS
1964 PHI N	43	109	33	7	4	3.7		18	18	6	26	1	.303	.495	7	2	OF-35
1965	97	262	77	9	3	8	3.1	27	28	15	60	4	.294	.443	27	8	OF-82
1966 STL N	25	86	16	0	1	2	2.3	7	6	5	18	1	.186	.279	2	0	OF-22
1967	81	175	39	9	2	1	0.6	20	12	9	26	6	.223	.314	20	5	OF-57
1968 CIN N	149	603	188	32	6	2	0.3	79	58	26	71	16	.312	.395	9	1	OF-140
1969	139	523	165	18	4	17	3.3	86	88	25	69	11	.315	.463	9	3	OF-132
1970 CAL A	156	614	202	26	6	14	2.3	85	86	35	68	17	**.329**	.459	0	0	OF-156
1971	65	242	63	8	0	2	0.8	19	21	15	34	5	.260	.318	5	0	OF-61
1972 CLE A	108	356	85	10	1	8	2.2	31	37	22	40	6	.239	.340	10	0	OF-95
1973 TEX A	158	624	179	26	3	8	1.3	62	68	32	82	10	.287	.377	1	1	DH-116, OF-47
1974 2 teams		TEX	A	(114G –	.291)			NY	A	(10G –	.214)						
" total	124	481	138	15	3	5	1.0	60	43	28	62	20	.287	.362	6	0	OF-82, DH-36
1975 NY A	52	119	31	5	1	1	0.8	15	15	7	21	2	.261	.345	14	5	DH-28, OF-7
1976 DET A	125	429	115	15	2	6	1.4	41	45	19	49	14	.268	.354	16	5	OF-90, DH-19
13 yrs.	1322	4623	1331	180	33	78	1.7	550	525	244	626	113	.288	.392	126	30	OF-1006, DH-199
1 yr.	125	429	115	15	2	6	1.4	41	45	19	49	14	.268	.354	16	5	OF-90, DH-19

Howard Johnson

JOHNSON, HOWARD MICHAEL
B. Nov. 29, 1960, Clearwater, Fla.
BB TR 5'11" 175 lb

	G	AB	H	2B	3B	HR	HR %	R	RBI	BB	SO	SB	BA	SA	PH AB	PH H	G by POS
1982 DET A	54	155	49	5	0	4	2.6	23	14	16	30	7	.316	.426	7	1	3B-33, DH-10, OF-9
1983	27	66	14	0	0	3	4.5	11	5	7	10	0	.212	.348	6	2	3B-21, DH-2
1984	116	355	88	14	1	12	3.4	43	50	40	67	10	.248	.394	7	2	3B-108, SS-9, DH-4, OF-1, 1B-1
3 yrs.	197	576	151	19	1	19	3.3	77	69	63	107	17	.262	.398	20	5	3B-162, DH-16, OF-10, SS-9, 1B-1
3 yrs.	197	576	151	19	1	19	3.3	77	69	63	107	17	.262	.398	20	5	3B-162, DH-16, OF-10, SS-9, 1B-1

WORLD SERIES
| 1984 DET A | 1 | 1 | 0 | 0 | 0 | 0 | 0.0 | 0 | 0 | 0 | 0 | 0 | .000 | .000 | 1 | 0 | |

Roy Johnson

JOHNSON, ROY CLEVELAND
Brother of Bob Johnson.
B. Feb. 23, 1903, Pryor, Okla.   D. Sept. 11, 1973, Tacoma, Wash.
Manager 1944.
BL TR 5'9" 175 lb

	G	AB	H	2B	3B	HR	HR %	R	RBI	BB	SO	SB	BA	SA	PH AB	PH H	G by POS
1929 DET A	146	640	201	**45**	14	10	1.6	128	69	67	60	20	.314	.475	2	0	OF-146
1930	125	462	127	30	13	2	0.4	84	35	40	46	17	.275	.409	6	2	OF-118
1931	151	621	173	37	**19**	8	1.3	107	55	72	51	33	.279	.438	1	1	OF-150

	G	AB	H	2B	3B	HR	HR %	R	RBI	BB	SO	SB	BA	SA	Pinch Hit AB	H	G by POS

Roy Johnson continued

	G	AB	H	2B	3B	HR	HR %	R	RBI	BB	SO	SB	BA	SA	AB	H	G by POS
32 2 teams	DET A (49G – .251)			BOS A (94G – .299)													
total	143	543	153	38	6	14	2.6	103	69	64	67	20	.282	.451	9	4	OF-133
33 BOS A	133	483	151	30	7	10	2.1	88	95	55	36	13	.313	.466	7	1	OF-125
34	143	569	182	43	10	7	1.2	85	119	54	36	11	.320	.467	5	1	OF-137
35	145	553	174	33	9	3	0.5	70	66	74	34	11	.315	.423	3	2	OF-142
36 NY A	63	147	39	8	2	1	0.7	21	19	21	14	3	.265	.367	20	3	OF-33
37 2 teams	NY A (12G – .294)			BOS N (85G – .277)													
total	97	311	87	11	3	3	1.0	29	28	41	31	6	.280	.363	20	4	OF-75, 3B-1
38 BOS N	7	29	5	0	0	0	0.0	2	1	1	5	1	.172	.172	0	0	OF-7
10 yrs.	1153	4358	1292	275	83	58	1.3	717	556	489	380	135	.296	.438	73	18	OF-1066, 3B-1
4 yrs.	471	1918	550	126	48	23	1.2	352	181	199	183	77	.287	.438	9	3	OF-462

WORLD SERIES

	G	AB	H	2B	3B	HR	HR %	R	RBI	BB	SO	SB	BA	SA	AB	H	G by POS
36 NY A	2	1	0	0	0	0	0.0	0	0	0	1	0	.000	.000	1	0	

Bob Jones

JONES, ROBERT WALTER (Ducky)   BL TR 6'   170 lbs.
B. Dec. 2, 1889, Clayton, Calif.   D. Aug. 30, 1964, San Diego, Calif.

	G	AB	H	2B	3B	HR	HR %	R	RBI	BB	SO	SB	BA	SA	AB	H	G by POS
17 DET A	46	77	12	1	2	0	0.0	16	2	4	8	3	.156	.221	10	2	2B-18, 3B-8
18	74	287	79	14	4	0	0.0	43	21	17	16	7	.275	.352	3	1	3B-63, 1B-6
19	127	439	114	18	6	1	0.2	37	57	34	39	11	.260	.335	0	0	3B-127
20	81	265	66	6	3	1	0.4	35	18	22	13	3	.249	.306	5	0	3B-67, 2B-5, SS-1
21	141	554	168	23	9	1	0.2	82	72	37	24	8	.303	.383	0	0	3B-141
22	124	455	117	10	6	3	0.7	65	44	36	18	8	.257	.325	3	0	3B-119
23	100	372	93	15	4	1	0.3	51	40	29	13	7	.250	.320	0	0	3B-97
24	110	393	107	27	4	0	0.0	52	47	20	20	1	.272	.361	3	1	3B-106
25	50	148	35	6	0	0	0.0	18	15	9	5	1	.236	.277	3	1	3B-46
9 yrs.	853	2990	791	120	38	7	0.2	399	316	208	156	49	.265	.337	27	5	3B-774, 2B-23, 1B-6, SS-1
9 yrs.	853	2990	791	120	38	7	0.2	399	316	208	156	49	.265	.337	27	5	3B-774, 2B-23, 1B-6, SS-1

Dalton Jones

JONES, JAMES DALTON   BL TR 6'1"   180 lbs.
B. Dec. 10, 1943, McComb, Miss.

	G	AB	H	2B	3B	HR	HR %	R	RBI	BB	SO	SB	BA	SA	AB	H	G by POS
64 BOS A	118	374	86	16	4	6	1.6	37	39	22	38	6	.230	.342	35	11	2B-85, SS-1, 3B-1
65	112	367	99	13	5	5	1.4	41	37	28	45	8	.270	.373	28	4	3B-81, 2B-8
66	115	252	59	11	5	4	1.6	26	23	25	27	1	.234	.365	48	13	2B-70, 3B-3
67	89	159	46	6	2	3	1.9	18	25	11	23	0	.289	.409	47	13	3B-30, 2B-19, 1B-1
68	111	354	83	13	0	5	1.4	38	29	17	53	1	.234	.314	28	11	1B-56, 2B-26, 3B-8
69	111	336	74	18	3	3	0.9	50	33	39	36	1	.220	.318	18	3	1B-81, 3B-9, 2B-1
70 DET A	89	191	42	7	0	6	3.1	29	21	33	33	1	.220	.351	29	11	2B-35, 3B-18, 1B-10
71	83	138	35	5	0	5	3.6	15	11	9	21	1	.254	.399	45	13	OF-16, 3B-13, 1B-3, 2B-1
72 2 teams	DET A (7G – .000)			TEX A (72G – .159)													
total	79	158	24	2	0	4	2.5	14	19	10	33	1	.152	.241	32	2	3B-23, 2B-17, 1B-7, OF-2
9 yrs.	907	2329	548	91	19	41	1.8	268	237	191	309	20	.235	.343	310	81	2B-262, 3B-186, 1B-158, OF-18, SS-1
3 yrs.	179	336	77	12	0	11	3.3	44	32	42	56	2	.229	.363	81	24	2B-36, 3B-31, OF-16, 1B-13

WORLD SERIES

	G	AB	H	2B	3B	HR	HR %	R	RBI	BB	SO	SB	BA	SA	AB	H	G by POS
67 BOS A	6	18	7	0	0	0	0.0	2	1	1	3	0	.389	.389	1	1	3B-4

Davy Jones

JONES, DAVID JEFFERSON (Kangaroo)   BL TR 5'10"   165 lbs.
B. June 30, 1880, Cambria, Wis.   D. Mar. 30, 1972, Mankato, Minn.

	G	AB	H	2B	3B	HR	HR %	R	RBI	BB	SO	SB	BA	SA	AB	H	G by POS
01 MIL A	14	52	9	0	3	3	5.8	12	5	11		4	.173	.346	0	0	OF-14
02 2 teams	STL A (15G – .224)			CHI N (64G – .305)													
total	79	292	85	13	4	0	0.0	45	17	44		17	.291	.363	0	0	OF-79
03 CHI N	130	497	140	18	3	1	0.2	64	62	53		15	.282	.336	0	0	OF-130
04	98	336	82	11	5	3	0.9	44	39	41		14	.244	.333	0	0	OF-97
06 DET A	84	323	84	12	2	0	0.0	41	24	41		21	.260	.310	0	0	OF-84
07	126	491	134	10	6	0	0.0	101	27	60		30	.273	.318	0	0	OF-126
08	56	121	25	2	1	0	0.0	17	10	13		11	.207	.240	21	3	OF-32
09	69	204	57	2	2	0	0.0	44	10	28		12	.279	.309	10	1	OF-57
10	113	377	100	6	6	0	0.0	77	24	51		25	.265	.313	9	0	OF-101
11	98	341	93	10	0	0	0.0	78	19	41		25	.273	.302	4	1	OF-92
12	97	316	93	5	2	0	0.0	54	24	38		16	.294	.323	15	4	OF-81
13 CHI A	10	21	6	0	0	0	0.0	2	0	9	0	1	.286	.286	1	0	OF-8
14 PIT F	97	352	96	9	8	2	0.6	58	24	42		15	.273	.361	4	2	OF-93
15	14	49	16	0	1	0	0.0	6	4	6		1	.327	.367	0	0	OF-13
14 yrs.	1085	3772	1020	98	40	9	0.2	643	289	478		207	.270	.325	64	11	OF-1007
7 yrs.	643	2173	586	47	19	0	0.0	412	138	272		140 8th	.270	.309	59	6	OF-573

WORLD SERIES

	G	AB	H	2B	3B	HR	HR %	R	RBI	BB	SO	SB	BA	SA	AB	H	G by POS
07 DET A	5	17	6	0	0	0	0.0	1	0	4	0	3	.353	.353	0	0	OF-5
08	3	2	0	0	0	0	0.0	1	0	1	1	0	.000	.000	2	0	
09	7	30	7	0	0	1	3.3	6	2	2	1	1	.233	.333	0	0	OF-7
3 yrs.	15	49	13	0	0	1	2.0	8	2	7	2	4	.265	.327	2	0	OF-12

Lynn Jones

JONES, LYNN MORRIS   BR TR 5'9"   175 lbs.
Brother of Darryl Jones.
B. Jan. 1, 1953, Meadville, Pa.

	G	AB	H	2B	3B	HR	HR %	R	RBI	BB	SO	SB	BA	SA	AB	H	G by POS
79 DET A	95	213	63	8	0	4	1.9	33	26	17	22	9	.296	.390	11	2	OF-84, DH-6
80	30	55	14	2	2	0	0.0	9	6	10	5	1	.255	.364	4	1	OF-17, DH-6
81	71	174	45	5	0	2	1.1	19	19	18	10	1	.259	.322	13	4	OF-60, DH-4
82	58	139	31	3	1	0	0.0	15	14	7	14	0	.223	.259	7	2	OF-56, DH-1
83	49	64	17	1	2	0	0.0	9	6	3	6	1	.266	.344	15	3	OF-31, DH-6
84 KC A	47	103	31	6	0	1	1.0	11	10	4	9	1	.301	.388	7	2	OF-45
6 yrs.	350	748	201	25	5	7	0.9	96	81	59	66	13	.269	.344	57	14	OF-293, DH-23
5 yrs.	303	645	170	19	5	6	0.9	85	71	55	57	12	.264	.336	50	12	OF-248, DH-23

LEAGUE CHAMPIONSHIP SERIES

	G	AB	H	2B	3B	HR	HR %	R	RBI	BB	SO	SB	BA	SA	AB	H	G by POS
84 KC A	3	5	1	0	0	0	0.0	1	0	0	0	0	.200	.200	3	1	OF-2

	G	AB	H	2B	3B	HR	HR %	R	RBI	BB	SO	SB	BA	SA	Pinch Hit AB	H	G by POS

Ruppert Jones

JONES, RUPPERT SANDERSON
B. Mar. 12, 1955, Dallas, Tex.   BL TL 5'10"   170 lb

	G	AB	H	2B	3B	HR	HR %	R	RBI	BB	SO	SB	BA	SA	Pinch Hit AB	H	G by POS
1976 KC A	28	51	11	1	1	1	2.0	9	7	3	16	0	.216	.333	9	1	OF-17, DH-3
1977 SEA A	160	597	157	26	8	24	4.0	85	76	55	120	13	.263	.454	1	0	OF-155, DH-4
1978	129	472	111	24	3	6	1.3	48	46	55	85	22	.235	.337	1	0	OF-128
1979	162	622	166	29	9	21	3.4	109	78	85	78	33	.267	.444	1	0	OF-161
1980 NY A	83	328	73	11	3	9	2.7	38	42	34	50	18	.223	.357	0	0	OF-82
1981 SD N	105	397	99	34	1	4	1.0	53	39	43	66	7	.249	.370	0	0	OF-104
1982	116	424	120	20	2	12	2.8	69	61	62	90	18	.283	.425	2	0	OF-114
1983	133	335	78	12	3	12	3.6	42	49	35	58	11	.233	.394	18	3	OF-111, 1B-5
1984 DET A	79	215	61	12	1	12	5.6	26	37	21	47	2	.284	.516	15	6	OF-73, DH-2
9 yrs.	995	3441	876	169	31	101	2.9	479	435	393	610	124	.255	.410	47	10	OF-945, DH-9, 1B-5
1 yr.	79	215	61	12	1	12	5.6	26	37	21	47	2	.284	.516	15	6	OF-73, DH-2

LEAGUE CHAMPIONSHIP SERIES

1984 DET A	2	5	0	0	0	0	0.0	1	0	1	1	0	.000	.000	1	0	OF-2

WORLD SERIES

1984 DET A	2	3	0	0	0	0	0.0	0	0	0	1	0	.000	.000	0	0	OF-2

Tom Jones

JONES, THOMAS
B. Jan. 22, 1877, Honesdale, Pa.   D. June 21, 1923, Danville, Pa.   BR TR 6'1"   195 lb

	G	AB	H	2B	3B	HR	HR %	R	RBI	BB	SO	SB	BA	SA	Pinch Hit AB	H	G by POS
1902 BAL A	37	159	45	8	4	0	0.0	22	14	2		1	.283	.384	0	0	1B-37, 2B-1
1904 STL A	156	625	152	15	10	2	0.3	53	68	15		16	.243	.309	0	0	1B-134, 2B-23, OF-4
1905	135	504	122	16	2	0	0.0	44	48	30		5	.242	.282	0	0	1B-135
1906	144	539	136	22	6	0	0.0	51	30	24		27	.252	.315	1	0	1B-143
1907	155	549	137	17	3	0	0.0	53	34	34		24	.250	.291	0	0	1B-155
1908	155	549	135	14	2	1	0.2	43	50	30		18	.246	.284	0	0	1B-155
1909 2 teams		STL A	(97G – .249)			DET A	(44G – .281)										
" total	141	490	127	18	3	0	0.0	43	47	23		22	.259	.308	0	0	1B-139, 3B-2
1910 DET A	135	432	110	13	4	0	0.0	32	45	35		22	.255	.303	0	0	1B-135
8 yrs.	1058	3847	964	123	34	3	0.1	341	336	193		135	.251	.303	1	0	1B-1033, 2B-24, OF-4, 3B-2
2 yrs.	179	585	153	22	4	0	0.0	45	63	40		31	.262	.313	0	0	1B-179

WORLD SERIES

1909 DET A	7	24	6	1	0	0	0.0	3	2	2		1	.250	.292	0	0	1B-7

Al Kaline

KALINE, ALBERT WILLIAM
B. Dec. 19, 1934, Baltimore, Md.
Hall of Fame 1980.   BR TR 6'1½"   175 lb

	G	AB	H	2B	3B	HR	HR %	R	RBI	BB	SO	SB	BA	SA	Pinch Hit AB	H	G by POS
1953 DET A	30	28	7	0	0	1	3.6	9	2	1	5	1	.250	.357	1	0	OF-20
1954	138	504	139	18	3	4	0.8	42	43	22	45	9	.276	.347	3	1	OF-135
1955	152	588	**200**	24	8	27	4.6	121	102	82	57	6	**.340**	.546	0	0	OF-152
1956	153	617	194	32	10	27	4.4	96	128	70	55	7	.314	.530	0	0	OF-153
1957	149	577	170	29	4	23	4.0	83	90	43	38	11	.295	.478	5	1	OF-145
1958	146	543	170	34	7	16	2.9	84	85	54	47	7	.313	.490	2	0	OF-145
1959	136	511	167	19	2	27	5.3	86	94	72	42	10	.327	**.530**	0	0	OF-136
1960	147	551	153	29	4	15	2.7	77	68	65	47	19	.278	.426	4	2	OF-142
1961	153	586	190	41	7	19	3.2	116	82	66	42	14	.324	.515	5	3	OF-147, 3B-1
1962	100	398	121	16	6	29	7.3	78	94	47	39	4	.304	.593	0	0	OF-100
1963	145	551	172	24	3	27	4.9	89	101	54	48	6	.312	.514	5	3	OF-140
1964	146	525	154	31	5	17	3.2	77	68	75	51	4	.293	.469	9	2	OF-136
1965	125	399	112	18	2	18	4.5	72	72	72	49	6	.281	.471	11	4	OF-112, 3B-1
1966	142	479	138	29	1	29	6.1	85	88	81	66	5	.288	.534	3	1	OF-136
1967	131	458	141	28	2	25	5.5	94	78	83	47	8	.308	.541	1	0	OF-130
1968	102	327	94	14	1	10	3.1	49	53	55	39	6	.287	.428	10	5	OF-74, 1B-22
1969	131	456	124	17	0	21	4.6	74	69	54	61	1	.272	.447	7	2	OF-118, 1B-9
1970	131	467	130	24	4	16	3.4	64	71	77	49	2	.278	.450	3	0	OF-91, 1B-52
1971	133	405	119	19	2	15	3.7	69	54	82	57	4	.294	.462	12	3	OF-129, 1B-5
1972	106	278	87	11	2	10	3.6	46	32	28	33	1	.313	.475	24	10	OF-84, 1B-11
1973	91	310	79	13	0	10	3.2	40	45	29	28	4	.255	.394	9	0	OF-63, 1B-36
1974	147	558	146	28	2	13	2.3	71	64	65	75	2	.262	.389	1	0	DH-146
22 yrs.	2834 9th	10116	3007	498	75	399	3.9	1622	1583	1277	1020	137	.297	.480	115	37	OF-2488, DH-146, 1B-135, 3B-2
22 yrs.	2834 1st	10116 2nd	3007 2nd	498 3rd	75 6th	399 1st	3.9	1622 3rd	1583 2nd	1277 1st	1020 2nd	137 9th	.297	.480	115 9th	37 5th	OF-2488, DH-146, 1B-135, 3B-2

LEAGUE CHAMPIONSHIP SERIES

1972 DET A	5	19	5	0	0	1	5.3	3	1	2	2	0	.263	.421	0	0	OF-5

WORLD SERIES

1968 DET A	7	29	11	2	0	2	6.9	6	8	0	7	0	.379	.655	0	0	OF-7

Marty Kavanagh

KAVANAGH, MARTIN JOSEPH
B. June 13, 1891, Harrison, N. J.   D. July 28, 1960, Taylor, Mich.   BR TR 6'   187 lbs

	G	AB	H	2B	3B	HR	HR %	R	RBI	BB	SO	SB	BA	SA	Pinch Hit AB	H	G by POS
1914 DET A	127	439	109	21	6	4	0.9	60	35	41	42	16	.248	.351	8	1	2B-115, 1B-4
1915	113	332	98	14	13	4	1.2	55	49	42	44	8	.295	.452	20	10	1B-44, 2B-42, OF-2, SS-1
1916 2 teams		DET A	(58G – .141)			CLE A	(19G – .250)										
" total	77	122	22	6	1	0	0.8	10	15	11	20	0	.180	.270	46	7	OF-11, 2B-11, 3B-3, 1B-3
1917 CLE A	14	14	0	0	0	0	0.0	3	2	0		0	.000	.000	4	0	OF-2
1918 3 teams		CLE A	(13G – .211)			STL N	(12G – .182)			DET A	(13G – .273)						
" total	38	126	28	6	0	1	0.8	12	23	21	14	2	.222	.294	2	0	1B-24, OF-8, 2B-4
5 yrs.	369	1033	257	47	20	10	1.0	138	122	118	122	26	.249	.362	85	18	2B-172, 1B-73, OF-23, 3B-3, SS-2
4 yrs.	311	893	230	42	19	8	0.9	123	98	103	107	24	.258	.374	68	17	2B-159, 1B-60, OF-13, SS-2, 3B-2

	G	AB	H	2B	3B	HR	HR%	R	RBI	BB	SO	SB	BA	SA	Pinch Hit AB	Pinch Hit H	G by POS

George Kell

KELL, GEORGE CLYDE
Brother of Skeeter Kell.
B. Aug. 23, 1922, Swifton, Ark.
Hall of Fame 1983.
BR TR 5'9" 175 lbs.

	G	AB	H	2B	3B	HR	HR%	R	RBI	BB	SO	SB	BA	SA	PH AB	PH H	G by POS
'43 PHI A	1	5	1	0	1	0	0.0	1	1	0	0	0	.200	.600	0	0	3B-1
'44	139	514	138	15	3	0	0.0	51	44	22	23	5	.268	.309	0	0	3B-139
'45	147	567	154	30	3	4	0.7	50	56	27	15	2	.272	.356	0	0	3B-147
'46 2 teams	PHI A (26G – .299)			DET A (105G – .327)													
total	131	521	168	25	10	4	0.8	70	52	40	20	3	.322	.432	0	0	3B-131, 1B-1
'47 DET A	152	588	188	29	5	5	0.9	75	93	61	16	9	.320	.412	0	0	3B-152
'48	92	368	112	24	3	2	0.5	47	44	33	15	2	.304	.402	0	0	3B-92
'49	134	522	179	38	9	3	0.6	97	59	71	13	7	.343	.467	0	0	3B-134
'50	157	641	218	56	6	8	1.2	114	101	66	18	3	.340	.484	0	0	3B-157
'51	147	598	191	36	3	2	0.3	92	59	61	18	10	.319	.400	0	0	3B-147
'52 2 teams	DET A (39G – .296)			BOS A (75G – .319)													
total	114	428	133	23	2	7	1.6	52	57	45	23	0	.311	.423	1	0	3B-112
'53 BOS A	134	460	141	41	2	12	2.6	68	73	52	22	5	.307	.483	8	4	3B-124, OF-7
'54 2 teams	BOS A (26G – .258)			CHI A (71G – .283)													
total	97	326	90	13	0	5	1.5	40	58	33	15	1	.276	.362	9	1	3B-56, 1B-32, OF-2
'55 CHI A	128	429	134	24	1	8	1.9	44	81	51	36	2	.312	.429	8	2	3B-105, 1B-24, OF-1
'56 2 teams	CHI A (21G – .313)			BAL A (102G – .261)													
total	123	425	115	22	2	9	2.1	52	48	33	37	0	.271	.395	6	0	3B-115, 1B-6, 2B-1
'57 BAL A	99	310	92	9	0	9	2.9	28	44	25	16	2	.297	.413	11	4	3B-80, 1B-22
15 yrs.	1795	6702	2054	385	50	78	1.2	881	870	620	287	51	.306	.414	43	11	3B-1692, 1B-85, OF-10, 2B-1
7 yrs.	826	3303	1075	210	35	25	0.8	503	414	336	107	34	.325 5th	.433	0	0	3B-826, 1B-1

Mick Kelleher

KELLEHER, MICHAEL DENNIS
B. July 25, 1947, Seattle, Wash.
BR TR 5'9" 176 lbs.

	G	AB	H	2B	3B	HR	HR%	R	RBI	BB	SO	SB	BA	SA	PH AB	PH H	G by POS
'72 STL N	23	63	10	2	1	0	0.0	5	1	6	15	0	.159	.222	0	0	SS-23
'73	43	38	7	2	0	0	0.0	4	2	4	11	0	.184	.237	0	0	SS-42
'74 HOU N	19	57	9	0	0	0	0.0	4	2	5	10	1	.158	.158	0	0	SS-18
'75 STL N	7	4	0	0	0	0	0.0	0	0	0	1	0	.000	.000	0	0	SS-7
'76 CHI N	124	337	77	12	1	0	0.0	28	22	15	32	0	.228	.270	3	1	SS-101, 3B-22, 2B-5
'77	63	122	28	5	2	0	0.0	14	11	9	12	0	.230	.303	0	0	2B-40, SS-14, 3B-1
'78	68	95	24	1	0	0	0.0	8	6	7	11	4	.253	.263	3	1	3B-37, 2B-17, SS-10
'79	73	142	36	4	1	0	0.0	14	10	7	9	2	.254	.296	0	0	3B-32, 2B-29, SS-14
'80	105	96	14	1	1	0	0.0	12	4	9	17	1	.146	.177	3	1	2B-57, 3B-31, SS-17
'81 DET A	61	77	17	4	0	0	0.0	10	6	7	10	0	.221	.273	3	1	3B-39, 2B-11, SS-9
'82 2 teams	DET A (2G – .000)			CAL A (34G – .163)													
total	36	50	8	1	0	0	0.0	9	1	5	5	1	.160	.180	1	0	SS-28, 3B-7, 2B-1
11 yrs.	622	1081	230	32	6	0	0.0	108	65	74	133	9	.213	.253	13	4	SS-283, 3B-169, 2B-160
2 yrs.	63	78	17	4	0	0	0.0	10	6	7	10	0	.218	.269	4	1	3B-40, 2B-12, SS-9

Charlie Keller

KELLER, CHARLES ERNEST (King Kong)
Brother of Hal Keller.
B. Sept. 12, 1916, Middletown, Md.
BL TR 5'10" 185 lbs.

	G	AB	H	2B	3B	HR	HR%	R	RBI	BB	SO	SB	BA	SA	PH AB	PH H	G by POS
'39 NY A	111	398	133	21	6	11	2.8	87	83	81	49	6	.334	.500	4	2	OF-105
'40	138	500	143	18	15	21	4.2	102	93	106	65	8	.286	.508	0	0	OF-136
'41	140	507	151	24	10	33	6.5	102	122	102	65	6	.298	.580	0	0	OF-137
'42	152	544	159	24	9	26	4.8	106	108	114	61	14	.292	.513	0	0	OF-141
'43	141	512	139	15	11	31	6.1	97	86	106	60	7	.271	.525	0	0	OF-141
'45	44	163	49	7	4	10	6.1	26	34	31	21	0	.301	.577	4	0	OF-44
'46	150	538	148	29	10	30	5.6	98	101	113	101	1	.275	.533	1	0	OF-149
'47	45	151	36	6	1	13	8.6	36	36	41	18	0	.238	.550	2	0	OF-43
'48	83	247	66	15	2	6	2.4	41	44	41	25	1	.267	.417	15	2	OF-66
'49	60	116	29	4	1	3	2.6	17	16	25	15	2	.250	.379	27	3	OF-31
'50 DET A	50	51	16	1	3	2	3.9	7	16	13	6	0	.314	.569	32	9	OF-6
'51	54	62	16	2	0	3	4.8	6	21	11	12	0	.258	.435	38	9	OF-8
'52 NY A	2	1	0	0	0	0	0.0	0	0	0	1	0	.000	.000	1	0	OF-1
13 yrs.	1170	3790	1085	166	72	189	5.0	725	760	784	499	45	.286	.518	123	25	OF-1019
2 yrs.	104	113	32	3	3	5	4.4	13	37	24	18	0	.283	.496	70	18	OF-14

WORLD SERIES

	G	AB	H	2B	3B	HR	HR%	R	RBI	BB	SO	SB	BA	SA	PH AB	PH H	G by POS
'39 NY A	4	16	7	1	1	3	18.8	8	6	1	2	0	.438	1.188	0	0	OF-4
'41	5	18	7	2	0	0	0.0	5	5	3	1	0	.389	.500	0	0	OF-5
'42	5	20	4	0	0	2	10.0	2	5	1	3	0	.200	.500	0	0	OF-5
'43	5	18	4	0	1	0	0.0	3	2	2	5	1	.222	.333	0	0	OF-5
4 yrs.	19	72	22	3	2	5	6.9	18	18	7	11	1	.306	.611 8th	0	0	OF-19

Steve Kemp

KEMP, STEVEN F.
B. Aug. 7, 1954, San Angelo, Tex.
BL TL 6' 195 lbs.

	G	AB	H	2B	3B	HR	HR%	R	RBI	BB	SO	SB	BA	SA	PH AB	PH H	G by POS
'77 DET A	151	552	142	29	4	18	3.3	75	88	71	93	3	.257	.422	3	0	OF-148
'78	159	582	161	18	4	15	2.6	75	79	97	87	2	.277	.399	2	1	OF-157
'79	134	490	156	26	3	26	5.3	88	105	68	70	5	.318	.543	4	1	OF-120, DH-11
'80	135	508	149	23	3	21	4.1	88	101	69	64	5	.293	.474	6	2	OF-85, DH-46
'81	105	372	103	18	4	9	2.4	52	49	70	48	9	.277	.419	3	1	OF-92, DH-12
'82 CHI A	160	580	166	23	1	19	3.3	91	98	89	83	7	.286	.428	3	1	OF-154, DH-2
'83 NY A	109	373	90	17	3	12	3.2	53	49	41	37	1	.241	.399	9	2	OF-101, DH-2
'84	94	313	91	12	1	7	2.2	37	41	40	54	4	.291	.403	9	2	OF-75, DH-12
8 yrs.	1047	3770	1058	166	23	127	3.4	559	610	545	536	36	.281	.438	39	10	OF-932, DH-85
5 yrs.	684	2504	711	114	18	89	3.6	378	422	375	362	24	.284	.450	18	5	OF-602, DH-69

	G	AB	H	2B	3B	HR	HR %	R	RBI	BB	SO	SB	BA	SA	Pinch Hit AB	H	G by POS

Bob Kennedy

KENNEDY, ROBERT DANIEL
Father of Terry Kennedy.
B. Aug. 18, 1920, Chicago, Ill.
Manager 1963-65, 1968.

BR TR 6'2" 193 lbs

	G	AB	H	2B	3B	HR	HR %	R	RBI	BB	SO	SB	BA	SA	AB	H	G by POS
1939 CHI A	3	8	2	0	0	0	0.0	0	1	0	0	0	.250	.250	1	0	3B-2
1940	154	606	153	23	3	3	0.5	74	52	42	58	3	.252	.315	0	0	3B-154
1941	76	257	53	9	3	1	0.4	16	29	17	23	5	.206	.276	0	0	3B-71
1942	113	412	95	18	5	0	0.0	37	38	22	41	11	.231	.299	1	0	3B-96, OF-16
1946	113	411	106	13	5	5	1.2	43	34	24	42	6	.258	.350	5	2	OF-75, 3B-29
1947	115	428	112	19	3	6	1.4	47	48	18	38	3	.262	.362	4	0	OF-106, 3B-1
1948 2 teams	CHI	A	(30G –	.248)		CLE	A	(66G –	.301)								
" total	96	186	50	11	3	0	0.0	14	19	8	23	0	.269	.360	12	6	OF-80, 2B-2, 3B-1
1949 CLE A	121	424	117	23	5	9	2.1	49	57	37	40	5	.276	.417	2	0	OF-98, 3B-21
1950	146	540	157	27	5	9	1.7	79	54	53	31	3	.291	.409	2	0	OF-144
1951	108	321	79	15	4	7	2.2	30	29	34	33	4	.246	.383	4	0	OF-106
1952	22	40	12	3	1	0	0.0	6	12	9	5	1	.300	.425	5	0	OF-13, 3B-3
1953	100	161	38	5	0	3	1.9	22	22	19	11	0	.236	.323	6	2	OF-89
1954 2 teams	CLE	A	(1G –	.000)		BAL	A	(106G –	.251)								
" total	107	323	81	13	2	6	1.9	37	45	28	43	2	.251	.359	17	4	3B-71, OF-22
1955 2 teams	BAL	A	(26G –	.143)		CHI	A	(83G –	.304)								
" total	109	284	75	11	2	9	3.2	38	48	26	26	0	.264	.412	23	4	3B-56, OF-34, 1B-9
1956 2 teams	CHI	A	(8G –	.077)		DET	A	(69G –	.232)								
" total	77	190	42	5	0	4	2.1	17	22	26	23	2	.221	.311	19	2	3B-33, OF-29
1957 2 teams	CHI	A	(4G –	.000)		BKN	N	(19G –	.129)								
" total	23	33	4	1	0	1	3.0	5	4	1	6	0	.121	.242	7	1	OF-9, 3B-3
16 yrs.	1483	4624	1176	196	41	63	1.4	514	514	364	443	45	.254	.355	108	21	OF-821, 3B-540, 1B-10, 2B-2
1 yr.	69	177	41	5	0	4	2.3	17	22	24	19	2	.232	.328	16	2	OF-29, 3B-27
WORLD SERIES																	
1948 CLE A	3	2	1	0	0	0	0.0	0	1	0	1	0	.500	.500	0	0	OF-3

Russ Kerns

KERNS, RUSSELL ELDON
B. Nov. 10, 1920, Fremont, Ohio

BL TR 6' 188 lbs

	G	AB	H	2B	3B	HR	HR %	R	RBI	BB	SO	SB	BA	SA	AB	H	G by POS
1945 DET A	1	1	0	0	0	0	0.0	0	0	0	0	0	.000	.000	1	0	

John Kerr

KERR, JOHN FRANCIS
B. Nov. 26, 1898, San Francisco, Calif.

BR TR 5'8" 158 lbs
BB 1923-24

	G	AB	H	2B	3B	HR	HR %	R	RBI	BB	SO	SB	BA	SA	AB	H	G by POS
1923 DET A	19	42	9	1	0	0	0.0	4	1	4	5	0	.214	.238	1	0	SS-15
1924	17	11	3	0	0	0	0.0	3	1	0	0	0	.273	.273	7	2	3B-3, OF-2
1929 CHI A	127	419	108	20	4	1	0.2	50	39	31	24	9	.258	.332	1	1	2B-122
1930	70	266	77	11	6	3	1.1	37	27	21	23	4	.289	.410	0	0	2B-51, SS-19
1931	128	444	119	17	2	2	0.5	51	50	35	22	9	.268	.329	4	1	2B-117, 3B-7, SS-1
1932 WAS A	51	132	36	6	1	0	0.0	14	15	13	3	3	.273	.333	10	1	2B-17, SS-14, 3B-8
1933	28	40	8	0	0	0	0.0	5	0	3	2	0	.200	.200	5	1	2B-16, 3B-1
1934	31	103	28	4	0	0	0.0	8	12	8	13	1	.272	.311	1	1	3B-17, 2B-13
8 yrs.	471	1457	388	59	13	6	0.4	172	145	115	92	26	.266	.337	29	7	2B-336, SS-49, 3B-36, OF-2
2 yrs.	36	53	12	1	0	0	0.0	7	2	4	5	0	.226	.245	8	2	SS-15, 3B-3, OF-2
WORLD SERIES																	
1933 WAS A	1	0	0	0	0	0	–	0	0	0	0	0	–	–	0	0	

Red Killefer

KILLEFER, WADE (Lollypop)
Brother of Bill Killefer.
B. Apr. 13, 1884, Bloomingdale, Mich. D. Sept. 4, 1958, Los Angeles, Calif.

BR TR 5'9½" 175 lbs

	G	AB	H	2B	3B	HR	HR %	R	RBI	BB	SO	SB	BA	SA	AB	H	G by POS
1907 DET A	1	4	0	0	0	0	0.0	0	0	0		0	.000	.000	0	0	OF-1
1908	28	75	16	1	0	0	0.0	9	11	3		4	.213	.227	0	0	2B-16, SS-7, 3B-4
1909 2 teams	DET	A	(23G –	.279)		WAS	A	(40G –	.174)								
" total	63	182	38	3	2	1	0.5	17	9	16		6	.209	.264	7	3	OF-25, 2B-20, 3B-6, C-3, SS-1
1910 WAS A	106	345	79	17	1	0	0.0	35	24	29		17	.229	.284	4	1	OF-88, OF-12
1914 CIN N	42	141	39	6	1	0	0.0	16	12	20	18	11	.277	.333	1	0	OF-37, 2B-5, 3B-1
1915	155	555	151	21	11	1	0.2	75	41	38	33	12	.272	.362	2	0	OF-153, 1B-2
1916 2 teams	CIN	N	(70G –	.244)		NY	N	(2G –	1.000)								
" total	72	235	58	9	1	1	0.4	29	19	22	8	7	.247	.306	3	2	OF-68
7 yrs.	467	1537	381	61	16	3	0.2	181	116	128	59	57	.248	.314	17	6	OF-296, 2B-129, 3B-11, SS-8, C-3, 1B-2
3 yrs.	52	140	33	3	2	1	0.7	15	15	15		6	.236	.307	4	1	2B-33, SS-7, 3B-4, OF-2

Bruce Kimm

KIMM, BRUCE EDWARD
B. June 29, 1951, Norway, Iowa

BR TR 5'11" 175 lbs

	G	AB	H	2B	3B	HR	HR %	R	RBI	BB	SO	SB	BA	SA	AB	H	G by POS
1976 DET A	63	152	40	8	0	1	0.7	13	6	15	20	4	.263	.336	0	0	C-61, DH-2
1977	14	25	2	1	0	0	0.0	2	1	0	4	0	.080	.120	0	0	C-12, DH-2
1979 CHI N	9	11	1	0	0	0	0.0	0	0	0	0	0	.091	.091	0	0	C-9
1980 CHI A	100	251	61	10	1	0	0.0	20	19	17	26	1	.243	.291	3	0	C-98
4 yrs.	186	439	104	19	1	1	0.2	35	26	32	50	5	.237	.292	3	0	C-180, DH-4
2 yrs.	77	177	42	9	0	1	0.6	15	7	15	24	4	.237	.305	0	0	C-73, DH-4

Chad Kimsey

KIMSEY, CLYDE ELIAS
B. Aug. 6, 1905, Copperhill, Tenn. D. Dec. 3, 1942, Pryor, Okla.

BL TR 6'3½" 200 lbs

	G	AB	H	2B	3B	HR	HR %	R	RBI	BB	SO	SB	BA	SA	AB	H	G by POS
1929 STL A	29	30	8	2	0	2	6.7	6	4	1	8	0	.267	.533	5	1	P-24
1930	60	70	24	4	1	2	2.9	14	14	5	16	1	.343	.514	16	2	P-42
1931	47	37	10	1	0	2	5.4	5	5	8	11	1	.270	.459	4	0	P-42
1932 2 teams	STL	A	(34G –	.333)		CHI	A	(7G –	.000)								
" total	41	20	6	1	0	0	0.0	1	1	1	4	0	.300	.350	1	0	P-40
1933 CHI A	28	33	5	0	0	0	0.0	1	1	0	9	0	.152	.152	1	0	P-28
1936 DET A	22	16	5	1	1	0	0.0	3	1	1	5	0	.313	.500	0	0	P-22
6 yrs.	227	206	58	9	2	6	2.9	30	26	16	53	2	.282	.432	27	3	P-198
1 yr.	22	16	5	1	1	0	0.0	3	1	1	5	0	.313	.500	0	0	P-22

	G	AB	H	2B	3B	HR	HR %	R	RBI	BB	SO	SB	BA	SA	Pinch Hit AB	H	G by POS

Charlie King

KING, CHARLES GILBERT (Chick)   BR TR 6'2"   190 lbs.
B. Nov. 10, 1930, Paris, Tenn.

	G	AB	H	2B	3B	HR	HR %	R	RBI	BB	SO	SB	BA	SA	PH AB	PH H	G by POS
1954 DET A	11	28	6	0	1	0	0.0	4	3	3	8	0	.214	.286	4	0	OF-7
1955	7	21	5	0	0	0	0.0	3	0	1	2	0	.238	.238	0	0	OF-6
1956	7	9	2	0	0	0	0.0	0	0	1	4	0	.222	.222	2	0	OF-4
1958 CHI N	8	8	2	0	0	0	0.0	1	1	3	1	0	.250	.250	1	0	OF-7
1959 2 teams	CHI N (7G – .000)		STL N (5G – .429)														
" total	12	10	3	0	0	0	0.0	3	1	0	3	0	.300	.300	0	0	OF-5
5 yrs.	45	76	18	0	1	0	0.0	11	5	8	18	0	.237	.263	7	0	OF-29
3 yrs.	25	58	13	0	1	0	0.0	7	3	5	14	0	.224	.259	6	0	OF-17

Jay Kirke

KIRKE, JUDSON FABIAN   BL TR 6'   195 lbs.
B. June 16, 1888, Fleichmans, N. Y.   D. Aug. 31, 1968, New Orleans, La.

	G	AB	H	2B	3B	HR	HR %	R	RBI	BB	SO	SB	BA	SA	PH AB	PH H	G by POS
1910 DET A	8	25	5	1	0	0	0.0	3	3	1		1	.200	.240	0	0	2B-7, OF-1
1911 BOS N	20	89	32	5	5	0	0.0	9	12	2	6	3	.360	.528	0	0	OF-14, 1B-3, SS-1, 3B-1, 2B-1
1912	103	359	115	11	4	4	1.1	53	62	9	46	7	.320	.407	17	4	OF-71, 3B-32, 1B-1
1913	18	38	9	2	0	0	0.0	3	3	1	6	0	.237	.289	5	1	OF-13
1914 CLE A	67	242	66	10	2	1	0.4	18	25	7	30	5	.273	.343	7	3	OF-42, 1B-18
1915	87	339	105	19	2	2	0.6	35	40	14	21	5	.310	.395	0	0	1B-87
1918 NY N	17	56	14	1	0	0	0.0	1	3	1	3	0	.250	.268	1	0	1B-16
7 yrs.	320	1148	346	49	13	7	0.6	122	148	35	112	21	.301	.385	30	8	OF-141, 1B-125, 3B-33, 2B-8, SS-1
1 yr.	8	25	5	1	0	0	0.0	3	3	1		1	.200	.240	0	0	2B-7, OF-1

Frank Kitson

KITSON, FRANK L   BL TR 5'11"   165 lbs.
B. Apr. 11, 1872, Hopkins, Mich.   D. Apr. 14, 1930, Allegan, Mich.

	G	AB	H	2B	3B	HR	HR %	R	RBI	BB	SO	SB	BA	SA	PH AB	PH H	G by POS
1898 BAL N	31	86	27	1	3	0	0.0	13	16	5		2	.314	.395	3	2	P-17, OF-11
1899	45	134	27	7	1	0	0.0	13	8	6		7	.201	.269	4	0	P-40
1900 BKN N	43	109	32	5	1	0	0.0	20	16	6		2	.294	.358	2	0	P-40, OF-1
1901	47	133	35	5	2	1	0.8	22	16	4		0	.263	.353	6	2	P-38, OF-2, 1B-1
1902	39	113	30	3	4	1	0.9	9	11	3		0	.265	.389	7	3	P-31
1903 DET A	36	116	21	0	2	0	0.0	12	4	2		2	.181	.216	0	0	P-31, OF-5
1904	27	72	15	0	0	1	1.4	9	4	1		0	.208	.250	1	0	P-26
1905	33	87	16	2	0	0	0.0	8	4	3		0	.184	.207	0	0	P-33
1906 WAS A	31	90	22	4	4	1	1.1	9	12	8		1	.244	.411	1	0	P-30
1907 2 teams	WAS A (5G – .125)		NY A (12G – .261)														
" total	17	31	7	0	0	0	0.0	4	4	1		0	.226	.226	0	0	P-17
10 yrs.	349	971	232	27	17	4	0.4	119	95	39		14	.239	.314	24	7	P-303, OF-19, 1B-1
3 yrs.	96	275	52	2	2	1	0.4	29	12	6		2	.189	.222	1	0	P-90, OF-5

John Knox

KNOX, JOHN CLINTON   BL TR 6'   170 lbs.
B. July 26, 1948, Newark, N. J.

	G	AB	H	2B	3B	HR	HR %	R	RBI	BB	SO	SB	BA	SA	PH AB	PH H	G by POS
1972 DET A	14	13	1	1	0	0	0.0	1	0	1	2	0	.077	.154	9	1	2B-4
1973	12	32	9	1	0	0	0.0	1	3	3	3	1	.281	.313	0	0	2B-9
1974	55	88	27	1	1	0	0.0	11	6	6	13	5	.307	.341	4	1	2B-33, DH-1, 3B-1
1975	43	86	23	1	0	0	0.0	8	2	10	9	1	.267	.279	5	2	2B-23, DH-3, 3B-3
4 yrs.	124	219	60	4	1	0	0.0	21	11	20	27	7	.274	.301	18	4	2B-69, DH-4, 3B-4
4 yrs.	124	219	60	4	1	0	0.0	21	11	20	27	7	.274	.301	18	4	2B-69, DH-4, 3B-4

LEAGUE CHAMPIONSHIP SERIES

	G	AB	H	2B	3B	HR	HR %	R	RBI	BB	SO	SB	BA	SA	PH AB	PH H	G by POS
1972 DET A	1	0	0	0	0	0	–	0	0	0	0	0	–	–	0	0	

Brad Kocher

KOCHER, BRADLEY WILSON   BR TR 5'11"   188 lbs.
B. Jan. 16, 1888, White Haven, Pa.   D. Feb. 13, 1965, White Haven, Pa.

	G	AB	H	2B	3B	HR	HR %	R	RBI	BB	SO	SB	BA	SA	PH AB	PH H	G by POS
1912 DET A	24	63	13	3	1	0	0.0	5	9	2		0	.206	.286	1	0	C-23
1915 NY N	4	11	5	0	1	0	0.0	3	2	0	1	0	.455	.636	1	0	C-3
1916	34	65	7	2	0	0	0.0	1	1	2	10	0	.108	.138	4	1	C-30
3 yrs.	62	139	25	5	2	0	0.0	9	12	4	11	0	.180	.245	6	1	C-56
1 yr.	24	63	13	3	1	0	0.0	5	9	2		0	.206	.286	1	0	C-23

Mark Koenig

KOENIG, MARK ANTHONY   BB TR 6'   180 lbs.
B. July 19, 1902, San Francisco, Calif.   BL 1928

	G	AB	H	2B	3B	HR	HR %	R	RBI	BB	SO	SB	BA	SA	PH AB	PH H	G by POS
1925 NY A	28	110	23	6	1	0	0.0	14	4	5	4	0	.209	.282	0	0	SS-28
1926	147	617	167	26	8	5	0.8	93	62	43	37	4	.271	.363	6	1	SS-141
1927	123	526	150	20	11	3	0.6	99	62	25	21	3	.285	.382	1	0	SS-122
1928	132	533	170	19	10	4	0.8	89	63	32	19	3	.319	.415	7	3	SS-125
1929	116	373	109	27	5	3	0.8	44	41	23	17	1	.292	.416	16	1	SS-61, 3B-37, 2B-1
1930 2 teams	NY A (21G – .230)		DET A (76G – .240)														
" total	97	341	81	14	2	1	0.3	46	25	26	20	2	.238	.299	4	0	SS-89, 3B-2, P-2, OF-1
1931 DET A	106	364	92	24	4	1	0.3	46	39	14	12	8	.253	.349	15	4	2B-55, SS-35, P-3
1932 CHI N	33	102	36	5	1	3	2.9	15	11	3	5	0	.353	.510	2	0	SS-33
1933	80	218	62	12	1	3	1.4	32	25	15	9	5	.284	.390	15	4	3B-37, SS-26, 2B-2
1934 CIN N	151	633	172	26	6	1	0.2	60	67	15	24	5	.272	.336	2	0	3B-64, SS-58, 2B-26, 1B-4
1935 NY N	107	396	112	12	0	3	0.8	40	37	13	18	0	.283	.336	9	1	2B-64, SS-21, 3B-15
1936	42	58	16	4	0	1	1.7	7	7	8	4	0	.276	.397	17	4	SS-10, 2B-8, 3B-3
12 yrs.	1162	4271	1190	195	49	28	0.7	572	443	222	190	31	.279	.367	94	18	SS-749, 3B-158, 2B-156, P-5, 1B-4, OF-1
2 yrs.	182	631	156	33	6	2	0.3	70	55	34	27	10	.247	.328	17	4	SS-105, 2B-55, P-5, 3B-2, OF-1

WORLD SERIES

	G	AB	H	2B	3B	HR	HR %	R	RBI	BB	SO	SB	BA	SA	PH AB	PH H	G by POS
1926 NY A	7	32	4	1	0	0	0.0	2	2	0	6	0	.125	.156	0	0	SS-7
1927	4	18	9	2	0	0	0.0	5	2	0	0	0	.500	.611	0	0	SS-4
1928	4	19	3	0	0	0	0.0	1	0	0	1	0	.158	.158	0	0	SS-4
1932 CHI N	2	4	1	0	1	0	0.0	1	1	1	0	0	.250	.750	0	0	SS-1
1936 NY N	3	3	1	0	0	0	0.0	0	0	1	0	0	.333	.333	3	1	2B-1
5 yrs.	20	76	18	3	1	0	0.0	9	5	1	10	0	.237	.303	3	1	SS-16, 2B-1

	G	AB	H	2B	3B	HR	HR%	R	RBI	BB	SO	SB	BA	SA	Pinch Hit AB	Pinch Hit H	G by POS

Don Kolloway

KOLLOWAY, DONALD MARTIN (Butch, Cab)
B. Aug. 4, 1918, Posen, Ill.
BR TR 6'3" 200 lbs.

	G	AB	H	2B	3B	HR	HR%	R	RBI	BB	SO	SB	BA	SA	AB	H	G by POS
1940 CHI A	10	40	9	1	0	0	0.0	5	3	0	3	1	.225	.250	0	0	2B-10
1941	71	280	76	8	3	3	1.1	33	24	6	12	11	.271	.354	3	1	2B-62, 1B-4
1942	147	601	164	40	4	3	0.5	72	60	30	39	16	.273	.368	0	0	2B-116, 1B-33
1943	85	348	75	14	4	1	0.3	29	33	9	30	11	.216	.287	0	0	2B-85
1946	123	482	135	23	4	3	0.6	45	53	9	29	14	.280	.363	1	0	2B-90, 3B-31
1947	124	485	135	25	4	2	0.4	49	35	17	34	11	.278	.359	7	2	2B-99, 1B-11, 3B-8
1948	119	417	114	14	4	6	1.4	60	38	18	18	2	.273	.369	12	3	2B-83, 3B-18
1949 2 teams	130																CHI A (4G – .000) DET A (126G – .294)
" total	130	487	142	19	3	2	0.4	71	47	49	26	7	.292	.353	12	5	2B-62, 1B-57, 3B-9
1950 DET A	125	467	135	20	4	6	1.3	55	62	29	28	1	.289	.388	5	1	1B-118, 2B-1
1951	78	212	54	7	0	1	0.5	28	17	15	12	2	.255	.302	17	4	1B-59
1952	65	173	42	9	0	2	1.2	19	21	7	19	0	.243	.329	25	5	1B-32, 2B-8
1953 PHI A	2	1	0	0	0	0	0.0	0	0	0	1	0	.000	.000	1	0	3B-1
12 yrs.	1079	3993	1081	180	30	29	0.7	466	393	189	251	76	.271	.353	83	18	2B-616, 1B-314, 3B-67
4 yrs.	394	1335	373	55	7	11	0.8	173	147	100	84	10	.279	.356	56	12	1B-266, 2B-71, 3B-7

Frank Kostro

KOSTRO, FRANK JERRY
B. Aug. 4, 1937, Windber, Pa.
BR TR 6'2" 190 lbs.

	G	AB	H	2B	3B	HR	HR%	R	RBI	BB	SO	SB	BA	SA	AB	H	G by POS
1962 DET A	16	41	11	3	0	0	0.0	5	3	1	6	0	.268	.341	4	1	3B-11
1963 2 teams	74																DET A (31G – .231) LA A (43G – .222)
" total	74	151	34	3	1	2	1.3	10	10	15	30	0	.225	.298	36	7	3B-25, 1B-8, OF-6
1964 MIN A	59	103	28	5	0	3	2.9	10	12	4	21	0	.272	.408	35	10	3B-12, 2B-7, OF-2, 1B-1
1965	20	31	5	2	0	0	0.0	2	1	4	5	0	.161	.226	4	1	2B-7, 3B-6, OF-2
1967	32	31	10	0	0	0	0.0	4	2	3	2	0	.323	.323	23	9	OF-3, 3B-1
1968	63	108	26	4	1	0	0.0	9	9	6	20	0	.241	.296	36	7	OF-24, 1B-5
1969	2	2	0	0	0	0	0.0	0	0	0	1	0	.000	.000	2	0	
7 yrs.	266	467	114	17	2	5	1.1	40	37	33	85	0	.244	.321	142	34	3B-55, OF-37, 2B-14, 1B-14
2 yrs.	47	93	23	4	0	0	0.0	9	3	10	19	0	.247	.290	24	6	3B-17, OF-3, 1B-3

Wayne Krenchicki

KRENCHICKI, WAYNE RICHARD
B. Sept. 17, 1954, Trenton, N. J.
BL TR 6'1" 180 lbs.

	G	AB	H	2B	3B	HR	HR%	R	RBI	BB	SO	SB	BA	SA	AB	H	G by POS
1979 BAL A	16	21	4	1	0	0	0.0	1	0	0	0	0	.190	.238	0	0	SS-7, 2B-6
1980	9	14	2	0	0	0	0.0	1	0	1	3	0	.143	.143	1	0	SS-6, DH-1, 2B-1
1981	33	56	12	4	0	0	0.0	7	6	4	9	0	.214	.286	1	0	SS-16, 2B-7, 3B-6, DH-1
1982 CIN N	94	187	53	6	1	2	1.1	19	21	13	23	5	.283	.358	28	7	3B-70, 2B-9
1983 2 teams	110																CIN N (51G – .273) DET A (59G – .278)
" total	110	210	58	9	0	1	0.5	24	27	19	31	0	.276	.333	18	2	3B-87, 2B-7, SS-6, 1B-3
1984 CIN N	97	181	54	9	2	6	3.3	18	22	19	23	0	.298	.470	36	7	3B-62, 2B-3, 1B-3
6 yrs.	359	669	183	29	3	9	1.3	70	76	56	89	5	.274	.366	84	16	3B-225, SS-35, 2B-33, 1B-6, DH-2
1 yr.	59	133	37	7	0	1	0.8	18	16	11	27	0	.278	.353	7	1	3B-48, SS-6, 2B-6, 1B-3

Charlie Kress

KRESS, CHARLES STEVEN (Chuck)
B. Dec. 9, 1921, Philadelphia, Pa.
BL TL 6' 190 lbs.

	G	AB	H	2B	3B	HR	HR%	R	RBI	BB	SO	SB	BA	SA	AB	H	G by POS
1947 CIN N	11	27	4	0	0	0	0.0	4	0	6	4	0	.148	.148	2	1	1B-8
1949 2 teams	124																CIN N (27G – .207) CHI A (97G – .278)
" total	124	382	104	20	6	1	0.3	48	47	42	49	6	.272	.364	11	3	1B-111
1950 CHI A	3	8	0	0	0	0	0.0	0	0	0	2	0	.000	.000	1	0	1B-2
1954 2 teams	37																DET A (24G – .189) BKN N (13G – .083)
" total	37	49	8	0	1	0	0.0	5	5	1	4	0	.163	.204	27	3	1B-8, OF-1
4 yrs.	175	466	116	20	7	1	0.2	57	52	49	59	6	.249	.328	41	7	1B-129, OF-1
1 yr.	24	37	7	0	1	0	0.0	4	3	1	4	0	.189	.243	15	2	1B-7, OF-1

Red Kress

KRESS, RALPH
B. Jan. 2, 1907, Columbia, Calif. D. Nov. 29, 1962, Los Angeles, Calif.
BR TR 5'11½" 165 lbs.

	G	AB	H	2B	3B	HR	HR%	R	RBI	BB	SO	SB	BA	SA	AB	H	G by POS
1927 STL A	7	23	7	2	1	1	4.3	3	3	3	3	0	.304	.609	0	0	SS-7
1928	150	560	153	26	10	3	0.5	78	81	48	70	5	.273	.371	0	0	SS-150
1929	147	557	170	38	4	9	1.6	82	107	52	54	5	.305	.436	1	0	SS-146
1930	154	614	192	43	8	16	2.6	94	112	50	56	3	.313	.487	0	0	SS-123, 3B-31
1931	150	605	188	46	8	16	2.6	87	114	46	48	3	.311	.493	1	0	3B-84, OF-40, SS-38, 1B-10
1932 2 teams	149																STL A (14G – .173) CHI A (135G – .285)
" total	149	567	156	42	5	11	1.9	85	66	51	42	7	.275	.425	0	0	OF-64, SS-53, 3B-33
1933 CHI A	129	467	116	20	5	10	2.1	47	78	37	40	4	.248	.377	12	6	1B-111, OF-8
1934 2 teams	64																CHI A (8G – .286) WAS A (56G – .228)
" total	64	185	43	4	3	4	2.2	21	25	20	22	3	.232	.351	9	2	1B-30, OF-10, 2B-9, SS-1, 3B-1
1935 WAS A	84	252	75	13	4	2	0.8	32	42	25	16	3	.298	.405	18	4	SS-53, 1B-5, P-3, OF-2, 2B-1
1936	109	391	111	20	6	8	2.0	51	51	39	25	6	.284	.427	5	0	SS-64, 2B-33, 1B-5
1938 STL A	150	566	171	33	7	7	1.2	74	79	69	47	5	.302	.408	1	0	SS-150
1939 2 teams	64																STL A (13G – .279) DET A (51G – .242)
" total	64	200	50	8	0	1	0.5	24	30	23	18	3	.250	.305	6	4	SS-38, 2B-16, 3B-4
1940 DET A	33	99	22	3	1	1	1.0	13	11	10	12	0	.222	.303	5	3	3B-17, SS-12
1946 NY N	1	1	0	0	0	0	0.0	0	0	0	1	0	.000	.000	0	0	P-1
14 yrs.	1391	5087	1454	298	58	89	1.7	691	799	474	453	47	.286	.420	58	20	SS-835, 3B-170, 1B-161, OF-124, 2B-59, P-4
2 yrs.	84	256	60	10	1	2	0.8	32	33	27	28	2	.234	.305	11	7	SS-37, 3B-21, 2B-16

Dick Kryhoski

KRYHOSKI, RICHARD DAVID
B. Mar. 24, 1925, Leonia, N. J.
BL TL 6'2" 182 lbs.

	G	AB	H	2B	3B	HR	HR%	R	RBI	BB	SO	SB	BA	SA	AB	H	G by POS
1949 NY A	54	177	52	10	3	1	0.6	18	27	9	17	2	.294	.401	2	0	1B-51
1950 DET A	53	169	37	10	0	4	2.4	20	19	8	11	0	.219	.349	5	2	1B-47
1951	119	421	121	19	4	12	2.9	58	57	28	29	1	.287	.437	10	4	1B-112
1952 STL A	111	342	83	13	1	11	3.2	38	42	23	42	2	.243	.383	25	8	1B-86
1953	104	338	94	18	4	16	4.7	35	50	26	33	0	.278	.497	19	4	1B-88
1954 BAL A	100	300	78	13	2	1	0.3	32	34	19	24	0	.260	.327	23	3	1B-69

	G	AB	H	2B	3B	HR	HR%	R	RBI	BB	SO	SB	BA	SA	Pinch Hit AB	Pinch Hit H	G by POS

Dick Kryhoski continued

	G	AB	H	2B	3B	HR	HR%	R	RBI	BB	SO	SB	BA	SA	AB	H	G by POS
55 KC A	28	47	10	2	0	0	0.0	2	2	6	7	0	.213	.255	13	3	1B-14
7 yrs.	569	1794	475	85	14	45	2.5	203	231	119	163	5	.265	.403	97	24	1B-467
2 yrs.	172	590	158	29	4	16	2.7	78	76	36	40	1	.268	.412	15	6	1B-159

Harvey Kuenn

KUENN, HARVEY EDWARD
B. Dec. 4, 1930, Milwaukee, Wis.
Manager 1975, 1982-83.

BR TR 6'2" 187 lbs.

	G	AB	H	2B	3B	HR	HR%	R	RBI	BB	SO	SB	BA	SA	AB	H	G by POS
52 DET A	19	80	26	2	2	0	0.0	2	8	2	1	2	.325	.400	0	0	SS-19
53	155	679	209	33	7	2	0.3	94	48	50	31	6	.308	.386	0	0	SS-155
54	155	656	201	28	6	5	0.8	81	48	29	13	9	.306	.390	0	0	SS-155
55	145	620	190	38	5	8	1.3	101	62	40	27	8	.306	.423	4	1	SS-141
56	146	591	196	32	7	12	2.0	96	88	55	34	9	.332	.470	6	1	SS-141, OF-1
57	151	624	173	30	6	9	1.4	74	44	47	28	5	.277	.388	1	0	SS-136, 3B-17, 1B-1
58	139	561	179	39	3	8	1.4	73	54	51	34	5	.319	.442	1	1	OF-138
59	139	561	198	42	7	9	1.6	99	71	48	37	7	.353	.501	1	0	OF-137
60 CLE A	126	474	146	24	0	9	1.9	65	54	55	25	3	.308	.416	4	1	OF-119, 3B-5
61 SF N	131	471	125	22	4	5	1.1	60	46	47	34	5	.265	.361	10	4	OF-93, 3B-32, SS-1
62	130	487	148	23	5	10	2.1	73	68	49	37	3	.304	.433	9	2	OF-105, 3B-30
63	120	417	121	13	2	6	1.4	61	31	44	38	2	.290	.374	15	2	OF-64, 3B-53
64	111	351	92	16	2	4	1.1	42	22	35	32	0	.262	.353	17	5	OF-88, 1B-11, 3B-2
65 2 teams	SF	N	(23G –	.237)		CHI	N	(54G –	.217)								
" total	77	179	40	5	0	0	0.0	15	12	32	16	4	.223	.251	25	7	OF-49, 1B-8
66 2 teams	CHI	N	(3G –	.333)		PHI	N	(86G –	.296)								
" total	89	162	48	9	0	0	0.0	15	15	10	17	0	.296	.352	48	11	OF-32, 1B-13, 3B-1
15 yrs.	1833	6913	2092	356	56	87	1.3	951	671	594	404	68	.303	.408	141	35	OF-826, SS-748, 3B-140, 1B-33
8 yrs.	1049	4372	1372	244 8th	43	53	1.2	620	423	322	205	51	.314	.426 10th	13	3	SS-747, OF-276, 3B-17, 1B-1

WORLD SERIES

	G	AB	H	2B	3B	HR	HR%	R	RBI	BB	SO	SB	BA	SA	AB	H	G by POS
62 SF N	4	12	1	0	0	0	0.0	1	0	1	1	0	.083	.083	0	0	OF-4

Rusty Kuntz

KUNTZ, RUSSELL JAY
B. Feb. 4, 1955, Orange, Calif.

BR TR 6'3" 190 lbs.

	G	AB	H	2B	3B	HR	HR%	R	RBI	BB	SO	SB	BA	SA	AB	H	G by POS
79 CHI A	5	11	1	0	0	0	0.0	0	0	2	6	0	.091	.091	0	0	OF-5
80	36	62	14	4	0	0	0.0	5	3	5	13	1	.226	.290	3	2	OF-34
81	67	55	14	2	0	0	0.0	15	4	6	8	1	.255	.291	3	0	OF-51, DH-5
82	21	26	5	1	0	0	0.0	4	3	2	8	0	.192	.231	0	0	OF-21, P-1
83 2 teams	CHI	A	(28G –	.262)		MIN	A	(31G –	.190)								
" total	59	142	30	4	0	3	2.1	19	6	18	41	1	.211	.303	4	1	OF-57, DH-1
84 DET A	84	140	40	12	0	2	1.4	32	22	25	28	2	.286	.414	12	5	OF-67, DH-10
6 yrs.	272	436	104	23	0	5	1.1	75	38	58	104	5	.239	.326	22	8	OF-235, DH-16, P-1
1 yr.	84	140	40	12	0	2	1.4	32	22	25	28	2	.286	.414	12	5	OF-67, DH-10

LEAGUE CHAMPIONSHIP SERIES

	G	AB	H	2B	3B	HR	HR%	R	RBI	BB	SO	SB	BA	SA	AB	H	G by POS
84 DET A	1	1	0	0	0	0	0.0	0	0	0	0	0	.000	.000	1	0	OF-1

WORLD SERIES

	G	AB	H	2B	3B	HR	HR%	R	RBI	BB	SO	SB	BA	SA	AB	H	G by POS
84 DET A	2	1	0	0	0	0	0.0	0	1	0	1	0	.000	.000	1	0	

Chet Laabs

LAABS, CHESTER PETER
B. Apr. 30, 1912, Milwaukee, Wis.   D. Jan. 26, 1983, Warren, Mich.

BR TR 5'8" 175 lbs.

	G	AB	H	2B	3B	HR	HR%	R	RBI	BB	SO	SB	BA	SA	AB	H	G by POS
37 DET A	72	242	58	13	5	8	3.3	31	37	24	66	6	.240	.434	9	2	OF-62
38	64	211	50	7	3	7	3.3	26	37	15	52	3	.237	.398	11	3	OF-53
39 2 teams	DET	A	(5G –	.313)		STL	A	(95G –	.300)								
" total	100	333	100	21	6	10	3.0	53	64	35	62	4	.300	.489	16	4	OF-84
40 STL A	105	218	59	11	5	10	4.6	32	40	34	59	3	.271	.505	35	14	OF-63
41	118	392	109	23	6	15	3.8	64	59	51	59	5	.278	.482	16	5	OF-100
42	144	520	143	21	7	27	5.2	90	99	88	88	0	.275	.498	3	1	OF-144
43	151	580	145	27	7	17	2.9	83	85	73	105	5	.250	.409	1	0	OF-150
44	66	201	47	10	2	5	2.5	28	23	29	33	3	.234	.378	11	0	OF-55
45	35	109	26	4	3	1	0.9	15	8	16	17	0	.239	.358	0	0	OF-35
46	80	264	69	13	0	16	6.1	40	52	20	50	3	.261	.492	6	0	OF-72
47 PHI A	15	32	7	1	0	1	3.1	5	5	4	4	0	.219	.344	7	1	OF-7
11 yrs.	950	3102	813	151	44	117	3.8	467	509	389	595	32	.262	.452	115	30	OF-820
3 yrs.	141	469	113	21	9	15	3.2	58	76	41	118	9	.241	.420	20	5	OF-120

WORLD SERIES

	G	AB	H	2B	3B	HR	HR%	R	RBI	BB	SO	SB	BA	SA	AB	H	G by POS
44 STL A	5	15	3	1	1	0	0.0	1	0	2	6	0	.200	.400	1	0	OF-4

Mike Laga

LAGA, MICHAEL RUSSELL
B. June 4, 1960, Ridgewood, N. J.

BL TL 6'3" 198 lbs.

	G	AB	H	2B	3B	HR	HR%	R	RBI	BB	SO	SB	BA	SA	AB	H	G by POS
82 DET A	27	88	23	9	0	3	3.4	6	11	4	23	1	.261	.466	4	1	1B-19, DH-8
83	12	21	4	0	0	0	0.0	2	2	1	9	0	.190	.190	3	1	DH-6, 1B-5
84	9	11	6	0	0	0	0.0	1	1	1	2	0	.545	.545	3	3	DH-4, 1B-4
3 yrs.	48	120	33	9	0	3	2.5	9	14	6	34	1	.275	.425	10	5	1B-28, DH-18
3 yrs.	48	120	33	9	0	3	2.5	9	14	6	34	1	.275	.425	10	5	1B-28, DH-18

Eddie Lake

LAKE, EDWARD ERVING
B. Mar. 18, 1916, Antioch, Calif.

BR TR 5'7" 159 lbs.

	G	AB	H	2B	3B	HR	HR%	R	RBI	BB	SO	SB	BA	SA	AB	H	G by POS
39 STL N	2	4	1	0	0	0	0.0	0	0	1	0	0	.250	.250	0	0	SS-2
40	32	66	14	3	0	2	3.0	12	7	12	17	1	.212	.348	5	0	2B-17, SS-6
41	45	76	8	2	0	0	0.0	9	0	15	22	3	.105	.132	6	1	SS-15, 3B-15, 2B-5
43 BOS A	75	216	43	10	0	3	1.4	26	16	47	35	3	.199	.287	2	0	SS-63
44	57	126	26	5	0	0	0.0	21	8	23	22	5	.206	.246	1	0	SS-41, P-6, 2B-3, 3B-1
45	133	473	132	27	1	11	2.3	81	51	106	37	9	.279	.410	1	0	SS-130, 2B-1
46 DET A	155	587	149	24	1	8	1.4	105	31	103	69	15	.254	.339	0	0	SS-155
47	158	602	127	19	6	12	2.0	96	46	120	54	11	.211	.322	0	0	SS-158

	G	AB	H	2B	3B	HR	HR %	R	RBI	BB	SO	SB	BA	SA	Pinch Hit AB	Pinch Hit H	G by POS

Eddie Lake continued

	G	AB	H	2B	3B	HR	HR %	R	RBI	BB	SO	SB	BA	SA	PH AB	PH H	G by POS
1948	64	198	52	6	0	2	1.0	51	18	57	20	3	.263	.323	0	0	2B-45, 3B-17
1949	94	240	47	9	1	1	0.4	38	15	61	33	2	.196	.254	12	2	SS-38, 2B-19, 3B-18
1950	20	7	0	0	0	0	0.0	3	1	1	3	0	.000	.000	7	0	SS-1, 3B-1
11 yrs.	835	2595	599	105	9	39	1.5	442	193	546	312	52	.231	.323	34	3	SS-609, 2B-90, 3B-52, P
5 yrs.	491	1634	375	58	8	23	1.4	293	111	342	179	31	.229	.317	19	2	SS-352, 2B-64, 3B-36

Al Lakeman

LAKEMAN, ALBERT WESLEY (Moose) BR TR 6'2" 195 lbs
B. Dec. 31, 1918, Cincinnati, Ohio   D. May 25, 1976, Spartanburg, S. C.

	G	AB	H	2B	3B	HR	HR %	R	RBI	BB	SO	SB	BA	SA	PH AB	PH H	G by POS
1942 CIN N	20	38	6	1	0	0	0.0	0	2	3	10	0	.158	.184	2	0	C-17
1943	22	55	14	2	0	0	0.0	5	6	3	11	0	.255	.327	1	0	C-21
1944	1	1	0	0	0	0	0.0	0	0	0	1	0	.000	.000	1	0	
1945	76	258	66	9	4	8	3.1	22	31	17	45	0	.256	.415	2	1	C-74
1946	23	30	4	0	0	0	0.0	0	4	2	7	0	.133	.133	16	1	C-6
1947 2 teams	CIN N (2G – .000)				PHI N (55G – .159)												
" total	57	184	29	3	0	6	3.3	11	19	5	40	0	.158	.272	5	0	1B-29, C-23
1948 PHI N	32	68	11	2	0	1	1.5	2	4	5	22	0	.162	.235	9	1	C-22, P-1
1949 BOS N	3	6	1	0	0	0	0.0	0	0	1	0	0	.167	.167	1	0	1B-2
1954 DET A	5	6	0	0	0	0	0.0	0	0	0	1	0	.000	.000	1	0	C-4
9 yrs.	239	646	131	17	5	15	2.3	40	66	36	137	0	.203	.314	38	3	C-167, 1B-31, P-1
1 yr.	5	6	0	0	0	0	0.0	0	0	0	1	0	.000	.000	1	0	C-4

Gene Lamont

LAMONT, GENE WILLIAM BL TR 6'1" 195 lbs
B. Dec. 25, 1946, Rockford, Ill.

	G	AB	H	2B	3B	HR	HR %	R	RBI	BB	SO	SB	BA	SA	PH AB	PH H	G by POS
1970 DET A	15	44	13	3	1	1	2.3	3	4	2	9	0	.295	.477	0	0	C-15
1971	7	15	1	0	0	0	0.0	2	1	0	5	0	.067	.067	0	0	C-7
1972	1	0	0	0	0	0	–	0	0	0	0	0	–	–	0	0	C-1
1974	60	92	20	4	0	3	3.3	9	8	7	19	0	.217	.359	0	0	C-60
1975	4	8	3	1	0	0	0.0	1	1	0	2	1	.375	.500	0	0	C-4
5 yrs.	87	159	37	8	1	4	2.5	15	14	9	35	1	.233	.371	0	0	C-87
5 yrs.	87	159	37	8	1	4	2.5	15	14	9	35	1	.233	.371	0	0	C-87

Jim Landis

LANDIS, JAMES HENRY BR TR 6'1" 180 lbs
B. Mar. 9, 1934, Fresno, Calif.

	G	AB	H	2B	3B	HR	HR %	R	RBI	BB	SO	SB	BA	SA	PH AB	PH H	G by POS
1957 CHI A	96	274	58	11	3	2	0.7	38	16	45	61	14	.212	.296	4	1	OF-90
1958	142	523	145	23	7	15	2.9	72	64	52	80	19	.277	.434	1	0	OF-142
1959	149	515	140	26	7	5	1.0	78	60	78	68	20	.272	.379	0	0	OF-148
1960	148	494	125	25	6	10	2.0	89	49	80	84	23	.253	.389	0	0	OF-147
1961	140	534	151	18	8	22	4.1	87	85	65	71	19	.283	.470	2	0	OF-139
1962	149	534	122	21	6	15	2.8	82	61	80	105	19	.228	.375	4	1	OF-144
1963	133	396	89	6	6	13	3.3	56	45	47	75	8	.225	.369	11	3	OF-124
1964	106	298	62	8	4	1	0.3	30	18	36	64	5	.208	.272	7	1	OF-101
1965 KC A	118	364	87	15	1	3	0.8	46	36	57	84	8	.239	.310	13	3	OF-108
1966 CLE A	85	158	35	5	1	3	1.9	23	14	20	25	2	.222	.323	22	4	OF-61
1967 3 teams	HOU N (50G – .252)				DET A (25G – .208)				BOS A (5G – .143)								
" total	80	198	47	11	4	4	2.0	24	19	28	50	2	.237	.364	16	1	OF-61
11 yrs.	1346	4288	1061	169	50	93	2.2	625	467	588	767	139	.247	.375	80	14	OF-1265
1 yr.	25	48	10	0	0	2	4.2	4	4	7	12	0	.208	.333	10	1	OF-12

WORLD SERIES

	G	AB	H	2B	3B	HR	HR %	R	RBI	BB	SO	SB	BA	SA	PH AB	PH H	G by POS
1959 CHI A	6	24	7	0	0	0	0.0	6	1	1	7	1	.292	.292	0	0	OF-6

Marv Lane

LANE, MARVIN BR TR 5'11" 180 lbs
B. Jan. 18, 1950, Sandersville, Ga.

	G	AB	H	2B	3B	HR	HR %	R	RBI	BB	SO	SB	BA	SA	PH AB	PH H	G by POS
1971 DET A	8	14	2	0	0	0	0.0	0	1	1	3	0	.143	.143	2	0	OF-6
1972	8	6	0	0	0	0	0.0	2	0	1	2	0	.000	.000	1	0	OF-3
1973	6	8	2	0	0	1	12.5	2	2	2	2	0	.250	.625	0	0	OF-4
1974	50	103	24	4	1	2	1.9	16	9	19	24	2	.233	.350	5	3	OF-46, DH-1
1976	18	48	9	1	0	0	0.0	3	5	6	11	0	.188	.208	3	0	OF-15
5 yrs.	90	179	37	5	1	3	1.7	23	17	28	42	2	.207	.296	11	3	OF-74, DH-1
5 yrs.	90	179	37	5	1	3	1.7	23	17	28	42	2	.207	.296	11	3	OF-74, DH-1

Chick Lathers

LATHERS, CHARLES TEN EYCK BL TR 6' 180 lbs
B. Oct. 22, 1888, Detroit, Mich.   D. July 26, 1971, Petoskey, Mich.

	G	AB	H	2B	3B	HR	HR %	R	RBI	BB	SO	SB	BA	SA	PH AB	PH H	G by POS
1910 DET A	41	82	19	2	0	0	0.0	4	3	8		0	.232	.256	14	3	3B-13, 2B-7, SS-4
1911	29	45	10	1	0	0	0.0	5	4	5		0	.222	.244	4	2	2B-9, 3B-8, SS-4, 1B-3
2 yrs.	70	127	29	3	0	0	0.0	9	7	13		0	.228	.252	18	5	3B-21, 2B-16, SS-8, 1B-3
2 yrs.	70	127	29	3	0	0	0.0	9	7	13		0	.228	.252	18	5	3B-21, 2B-16, SS-8, 1B-3

Charlie Lau

LAU, CHARLES RICHARD BL TR 6' 190 lbs
B. Apr. 12, 1933, Romulus, Mich.   D. Mar. 18, 1984, Key Colony Beach, Fla.

	G	AB	H	2B	3B	HR	HR %	R	RBI	BB	SO	SB	BA	SA	PH AB	PH H	G by POS
1956 DET A	3	9	2	0	0	0	0.0	1	0	0	1	0	.222	.222	0	0	C-3
1958	30	68	10	1	2	0	0.0	8	6	12	15	0	.147	.221	4	1	C-27
1959	2	6	1	0	0	0	0.0	0	0	0	2	0	.167	.167	1	0	C-2
1960 MIL N	21	53	10	2	0	0	0.0	4	2	6	10	0	.189	.226	7	0	C-16
1961 2 teams	MIL N (28G – .207)				BAL A (17G – .170)												
" total	45	129	25	5	0	1	0.8	6	9	15	14	1	.194	.256	2	0	C-42
1962 BAL A	81	197	58	11	2	6	3.0	21	37	7	11	1	.294	.462	30	11	C-56
1963 2 teams	BAL A (29G – .188)				KC A (62G – .294)												
" total	91	235	64	13	0	3	1.3	19	32	15	22	1	.272	.366	29	4	C-58
1964 2 teams	KC A (43G – .271)				BAL A (62G – .259)												
" total	105	276	73	22	2	3	1.1	27	23	27	45	0	.264	.391	28	7	C-82
1965 BAL A	68	132	39	5	2	2	1.5	15	18	17	18	0	.295	.409	29	8	C-35
1966	18	12	6	2	1	0	0.0	1	5	4	1	0	.500	.833	12	6	
1967 2 teams	BAL A (11G – .125)				ATL N (52G – .200)												
" total	63	53	10	2	0	1	1.9	3	8	6	11	0	.189	.283	53	10	
11 yrs.	527	1170	298	63	9	16	1.4	105	140	109	150	3	.255	.365	195	47	C-321
3 yrs.	35	83	13	1	2	0	0.0	9	6	12	18	0	.157	.217	5	1	C-32

	G	AB	H	2B	3B	HR	HR %	R	RBI	BB	SO	SB	BA	SA	Pinch Hit AB	Pinch Hit H	G by POS

Bill Lawrence

LAWRENCE, WILLIAM HENRY   BR TR 6'4" 194 lbs.
B. Mar. 11, 1906, San Mateo, Calif.

	G	AB	H	2B	3B	HR	HR%	R	RBI	BB	SO	SB	BA	SA	PH AB	PH H	G by POS
1932 DET A	25	46	10	1	0	0	0.0	10	3	5	5	0	.217	.239	2	0	OF-15

Rick Leach

LEACH, RICHARD MAX   BL TL 6'1" 180 lbs.
B. May 4, 1957, Ann Arbor, Mich.

	G	AB	H	2B	3B	HR	HR%	R	RBI	BB	SO	SB	BA	SA	PH AB	PH H	G by POS
1981 DET A	54	83	16	3	1	1	1.2	9	11	16	15	0	.193	.289	10	2	1B-32, OF-15, DH-2
1982	82	218	52	7	2	3	1.4	23	12	21	29	4	.239	.330	14	2	1B-56, OF-14, DH-4
1983	99	242	60	17	0	3	1.2	22	26	19	21	2	.248	.355	18	4	1B-73, OF-13, DH-3
1984 TOR A	65	88	23	6	2	0	0.0	11	7	8	14	0	.261	.375	22	8	OF-23, 1B-15, DH-6, P-1
4 yrs.	300	631	151	33	5	7	1.1	65	56	64	79	6	.239	.341	64	16	1B-176, OF-65, DH-15, P-1
3 yrs.	235	543	128	27	3	7	1.3	54	49	56	65	6	.236	.335	42	8	1B-161, OF-42, DH-9

Ron LeFlore

LeFLORE, RONALD   BR TR 6' 200 lbs.
B. June 16, 1948, Detroit, Mich.

	G	AB	H	2B	3B	HR	HR%	R	RBI	BB	SO	SB	BA	SA	PH AB	PH H	G by POS
1974 DET A	59	254	66	8	1	2	0.8	37	13	13	58	23	.260	.323	0	0	OF-59
1975	136	550	142	13	6	8	1.5	66	37	33	139	28	.258	.347	0	0	OF-134
1976	135	544	172	23	8	4	0.7	93	39	51	111	58	.316	.410	1	0	OF-132, DH-1
1977	154	652	212	30	10	16	2.5	100	57	57	121	39	.325	.475	3	2	OF-154
1978	155	666	198	30	3	12	1.8	126	62	65	104	68	.297	.405	0	0	OF-155
1979	148	600	180	22	10	9	1.5	110	57	52	95	78	.300	.415	1	1	OF-113, DH-34
1980 MON N	139	521	134	21	11	4	0.8	95	39	62	99	97	.257	.363	1	1	OF-130
1981 CHI A	82	337	83	10	4	0	0.0	46	24	28	70	36	.246	.300	0	0	OF-82
1982	91	334	96	15	4	4	1.2	58	25	22	91	28	.287	.392	5	1	OF-83, DH-2
9 yrs.	1099	4458	1283	172	57	59	1.3	731	353	363	888	455	.288	.392	11	5	OF-1042, DH-37
6 yrs.	787	3266	970	126	38	51	1.6	532	265	251	628	294	.297	.406	5	3	OF-747, DH-35
								9th			4th						

Bill Leinhauser

LEINHAUSER, WILLIAM CHARLES   BR TR 5'10" 150 lbs.
B. Nov. 4, 1893, Philadelphia, Pa.   D. Apr. 14, 1978, Elkins Park, Pa.

	G	AB	H	2B	3B	HR	HR%	R	RBI	BB	SO	SB	BA	SA	PH AB	PH H	G by POS
1912 DET A	1	4	0	0	0	0	0.0	0	0	0	0	0	.000	.000	0	0	OF-1

Chet Lemon

LEMON, CHESTER EARL   BR TR 6' 190 lbs.
B. Feb. 12, 1955, Jackson, Miss.

	G	AB	H	2B	3B	HR	HR%	R	RBI	BB	SO	SB	BA	SA	PH AB	PH H	G by POS
1975 CHI A	9	35	9	2	0	0	0.0	2	1	2	6	1	.257	.314	1	0	3B-6, DH-2, OF-1
1976	132	451	111	15	5	4	0.9	46	38	28	65	13	.246	.328	1	0	OF-131
1977	150	553	151	38	4	19	3.4	99	67	52	88	8	.273	.459	0	0	OF-149
1978	105	357	107	24	6	13	3.6	51	55	39	46	5	.300	.510	1	0	OF-95, DH-10
1979	148	556	177	44	2	17	3.1	79	86	56	68	7	.318	.496	0	0	OF-147, DH-1
1980	147	514	150	32	6	11	2.1	76	51	71	56	6	.292	.442	1	0	OF-139, DH-6, 2B-1
1981	94	328	99	23	6	9	2.7	50	50	33	48	5	.302	.491	0	0	OF-93
1982 DET A	125	436	116	20	1	19	4.4	75	52	56	69	1	.266	.447	2	1	OF-121, DH-1
1983	145	491	125	21	5	24	4.9	78	69	54	70	0	.255	.464	2	1	OF-145
1984	141	509	146	34	6	20	3.9	77	76	51	83	5	.287	.495	3	1	OF-140, DH-1
10 yrs.	1196	4230	1191	253	41	136	3.2	633	545	442	599	51	.282	.457	11	3	OF-1161, DH-21, 3B-6, 2B-1
3 yrs.	411	1436	387	75	12	63	4.4	230	197	161	222	6	.269	.470	7	3	OF-406, DH-2

LEAGUE CHAMPIONSHIP SERIES

	G	AB	H	2B	3B	HR	HR%	R	RBI	BB	SO	SB	BA	SA	PH AB	PH H	G by POS
1984 DET A	3	13	0	0	0	0	0.0	1	0	0	1	0	.000	.000	0	0	OF-3

WORLD SERIES

	G	AB	H	2B	3B	HR	HR%	R	RBI	BB	SO	SB	BA	SA	PH AB	PH H	G by POS
1984 DET A	5	17	5	0	0	0	0.0	1	1	2	2	2	.294	.294	0	0	OF-5

Don Lenhardt

LENHARDT, DONALD EUGENE (Footsie)   BR TR 6'3" 190 lbs.
B. Oct. 4, 1922, Alton, Ill.

	G	AB	H	2B	3B	HR	HR%	R	RBI	BB	SO	SB	BA	SA	PH AB	PH H	G by POS
1950 STL A	139	480	131	22	6	22	4.6	75	81	90	94	3	.273	.481	10	3	1B-86, OF-39, 3B-10
1951 2 teams	STL A (31G – .262)				CHI A (64G – .266)												
" total	95	302	80	12	1	15	5.0	32	63	30	38	2	.265	.460	13	3	OF-80, 1B-3
1952 3 teams	BOS A (30G – .295)				DET A (45G – .188)			STL A (18G – .271)									
" total	93	297	71	10	2	11	3.7	41	42	47	44	0	.239	.397	10	2	OF-81, 1B-2
1953 STL A	97	303	96	15	0	10	3.3	37	35	41	41	1	.317	.465	17	4	OF-77, 3B-6
1954 2 teams	BAL A (13G – .152)				BOS A (44G – .273)												
" total	57	99	23	5	0	3	3.0	7	18	6	18	0	.232	.374	35	6	OF-20, 1B-2, 3B-1
5 yrs.	481	1481	401	64	9	61	4.1	192	239	214	235	6	.271	.450	85	18	OF-297, 1B-93, 3B-17
1 yr.	45	144	27	2	1	3	2.1	18	13	28	18	0	.188	.278	2	0	OF-43

Jim Lentine

LENTINE, JAMES MATTHEW   BR TR 6' 175 lbs.
B. July 16, 1954, Los Angeles, Calif.

	G	AB	H	2B	3B	HR	HR%	R	RBI	BB	SO	SB	BA	SA	PH AB	PH H	G by POS
1978 STL N	8	11	2	0	0	0	0.0	1	1	0	0	1	.182	.182	1	0	OF-3
1979	11	23	9	1	0	0	0.0	2	1	3	6	0	.391	.435	3	2	OF-8
1980 2 teams	STL N (9G – .100)				DET A (67G – .261)												
" total	76	171	43	8	1	1	0.6	20	18	28	32	2	.251	.327	10	2	OF-61, DH-9
3 yrs.	95	205	54	9	1	1	0.5	23	20	31	38	3	.263	.332	14	4	OF-72, DH-9
1 yr.	67	161	42	8	1	1	0.6	19	17	28	30	2	.261	.342	7	2	OF-55, DH-9

Ted Lepcio

LEPCIO, THADDEUS STANLEY   BR TR 5'10" 177 lbs.
B. July 28, 1930, Utica, N. Y.

	G	AB	H	2B	3B	HR	HR%	R	RBI	BB	SO	SB	BA	SA	PH AB	PH H	G by POS
1952 BOS A	84	274	72	17	2	5	1.8	34	26	24	41	3	.263	.394	0	0	2B-57, 3B-25, SS-1
1953	66	161	38	4	2	4	2.5	17	11	17	24	0	.236	.360	4	1	2B-34, SS-20, 3B-11
1954	116	398	102	19	4	8	2.0	42	45	42	62	3	.256	.384	2	0	2B-80, 3B-24, SS-14
1955	51	134	31	9	0	6	4.5	19	15	13	36	1	.231	.433	4	0	3B-45
1956	83	284	74	10	0	15	5.3	34	51	30	77	1	.261	.454	9	3	2B-57, 3B-22
1957	79	232	56	10	2	9	3.9	24	37	29	61	0	.241	.418	10	2	2B-68
1958	50	136	27	3	0	6	4.4	10	14	12	47	0	.199	.353	10	3	2B-40
1959 2 teams	BOS A (3G – .333)				DET A (76G – .279)												
" total	79	218	61	9	0	7	3.2	26	25	17	51	2	.280	.417	16	5	SS-35, 2B-25, 3B-11
1960 PHI N	69	141	32	7	0	2	1.4	16	8	17	41	0	.227	.319	9	1	3B-50, SS-14, 2B-5

	G	AB	H	2B	3B	HR	HR %	R	RBI	BB	SO	SB	BA	SA	Pinch Hit AB	Pinch Hit H	G by POS

Ted Lepcio continued

	G	AB	H	2B	3B	HR	HR %	R	RBI	BB	SO	SB	BA	SA	PH AB	PH H	G by POS
1961 2 teams		CHI A (5G – .000)				MIN A (47G – .170)											
" total	52	114	19	3	1	7	6.1	11	19	9	31	1	.167	.395	5	0	3B-36, 2B-22, SS-6
10 yrs.	729	2092	512	91	11	69	3.3	233	251	210	471	11	.245	.398	69	15	2B-388, 3B-224, SS-90
1 yr.	76	215	60	8	0	7	3.3	25	24	17	49	2	.279	.414	14	4	SS-35, 2B-24, 3B-11

Pete LePine

LePINE, LOUIS JOSEPH
B. Sept. 5, 1876, Montreal, Que., Canada   D. Dec. 4, 1949, Woonsocket, R. I.   BL TL

	G	AB	H	2B	3B	HR	HR %	R	RBI	BB	SO	SB	BA	SA	PH AB	PH H	G by POS
1902 DET A	30	96	20	3	2	1	1.0	8	19	8		1	.208	.313	2	0	OF-19, 1B-8

George Lerchen

LERCHEN, GEORGE EDWARD
Son of Dutch Lerchen.
B. Dec. 1, 1922, Detroit, Mich.   BB TR 5'11" 175 lbs.
BL 1953

	G	AB	H	2B	3B	HR	HR %	R	RBI	BB	SO	SB	BA	SA	PH AB	PH H	G by POS
1952 DET A	14	32	5	1	0	1	3.1	1	3	7	10	1	.156	.281	7	2	OF-7
1953 CIN N	22	17	5	1	0	0	0.0	2	2	5	6	0	.294	.353	17	6	OF-1
2 yrs.	36	49	10	2	0	1	2.0	3	5	12	16	1	.204	.306	24	8	OF-8
1 yr.	14	32	5	1	0	1	3.1	1	3	7	10	1	.156	.281	7	2	OF-7

Em Lindbeck

LINDBECK, EMERIT DESMOND
B. Aug. 27, 1935, Kewanee, Ill.   BL TR 6' 185 lbs.

	G	AB	H	2B	3B	HR	HR %	R	RBI	BB	SO	SB	BA	SA	PH AB	PH H	G by POS
1960 DET A	2	1	0	0	0	0	0.0	0	0	0		0	.000	.000	1	0	

Pinky Lindsay

LINDSAY, CHRISTIAN HALLER
B. July 24, 1878, Moon Township, Pa.   D. Jan. 25, 1941, Cleveland, Ohio

	G	AB	H	2B	3B	HR	HR %	R	RBI	BB	SO	SB	BA	SA	PH AB	PH H	G by POS
1905 DET A	88	329	88	14	1	0	0.0	38	31	18		10	.267	.316	0	0	1B-88
1906	141	499	112	16	2	0	0.0	59	33	45		18	.224	.265	2	0	1B-122, 2B-17, 3B-1
2 yrs.	229	828	200	30	3	0	0.0	97	64	63		28	.242	.285	2	0	1B-210, 2B-17, 3B-1
2 yrs.	229	828	200	30	3	0	0.0	97	64	63		28	.242	.285	2	0	1B-210, 2B-17, 3B-1

Carl Linhart

LINHART, CARL JAMES
B. Dec. 14, 1929, Zborov, Czechoslovakia   BL TR 5'11" 184 lbs.

	G	AB	H	2B	3B	HR	HR %	R	RBI	BB	SO	SB	BA	SA	PH AB	PH H	G by POS
1952 DET A	3	2	0	0	0	0	0.0	0	0	0	0	0	.000	.000	2	0	

Johnny Lipon

LIPON, JOHN JOSEPH (Skids)
B. Nov. 10, 1922, Martin's Ferry, Ohio   BR TR 6' 175 lbs.
Manager 1971.

	G	AB	H	2B	3B	HR	HR %	R	RBI	BB	SO	SB	BA	SA	PH AB	PH H	G by POS
1942 DET A	34	131	25	2	0	0	0.0	9	5	9	7	1	.191	.206	0	0	SS-34
1946	14	20	6	0	0	0	0.0	4	1	5	3	0	.300	.300	1	0	SS-8, 3B-1
1948	121	458	133	18	8	5	1.1	65	52	68	22	4	.290	.397	1	0	SS-117, 3B-1, 2B-1
1949	127	439	110	14	6	3	0.7	57	59	75	24	2	.251	.330	5	0	SS-120
1950	147	601	176	27	6	2	0.3	104	63	81	26	9	.293	.368	0	0	SS-147
1951	129	487	129	15	1	0	0.0	56	38	49	27	7	.265	.300	2	0	SS-125
1952 2 teams		DET A (39G – .221)				BOS A (79G – .205)											
" total	118	370	78	12	3	0	0.0	42	30	48	26	4	.211	.259	1	0	SS-108, 3B-7
1953 2 teams		BOS A (60G – .214)				STL A (7G – .222)											
" total	67	154	33	7	0	0	0.0	18	14	14	17	1	.214	.260	2	0	SS-58, 3B-6, 2B-1
1954 CIN N	1	1	0	0	0	0	0.0	0	0	0	0		.000	.000	1	0	
9 yrs.	758	2661	690	95	24	10	0.4	351	266	347	152	28	.259	.324	13	0	SS-717, 3B-15, 2B-2
7 yrs.	611	2272	609	80	23	10	0.4	308	234	301	115	26	.268	.337	9	0	SS-590, 3B-2, 2B-1

Harry Lochhead

LOCHHEAD, HARRY ROBERT
B. Mar. 29, 1876, Stockton, Calif.   D. Aug. 22, 1909, Stockton, Calif.   TR

	G	AB	H	2B	3B	HR	HR %	R	RBI	BB	SO	SB	BA	SA	PH AB	PH H	G by POS
1899 CLE N	148	541	129	7	1	1	0.2	52	43	21		23	.238	.261	0	0	SS-146, 2B-1, P-1
1901 2 teams		DET A (1G – .500)				PHI A (9G – .088)											
" total	10	38	5	0	0	0	0.0	5	2	3		0	.132	.132	0	0	SS-10
2 yrs.	158	579	134	7	1	1	0.2	57	45	24		23	.231	.252	0	0	SS-156, 2B-1, P-1
1 yr.	1	4	2	0	0	0	0.0	2	0	0		0	.500	.500	0	0	SS-1

Herman Long

LONG, HERMAN C. (Germany)
B. Apr. 13, 1866, Chicago, Ill.   D. Sept. 17, 1909, Denver, Colo.   BL TR 5'8½" 160 lbs.

	G	AB	H	2B	3B	HR	HR %	R	RBI	BB	SO	SB	BA	SA	PH AB	PH H	G by POS
1889 KC AA	136	574	160	32	6	3	0.5	137	60	64	63	89	.279	.371	0	0	SS-128, 2B-8, OF-1
1890 BOS N	101	431	108	15	3	8	1.9	95	52	40	34	49	.251	.355	0	0	SS-101
1891	139	577	166	21	12	10	1.7	129	74	80	51	60	.288	.418	0	0	SS-139
1892	151	647	185	33	6	6	0.9	115	77	44	36	57	.286	.383	0	0	SS-141, OF-12, 3B-1
1893	128	552	159	22	6	6	1.1	149	58	73	32	38	.288	.382	0	0	SS-123, 2B-5
1894	104	475	154	28	11	12	2.5	137	79	35	17	24	.324	.505	0	0	SS-98, OF-5, 2B-3
1895	124	540	172	23	10	9	1.7	110	75	31	12	35	.319	.448	0	0	SS-122, 2B-2
1896	120	508	172	26	8	6	1.2	108	100	26	16	36	.339	.457	0	0	SS-120
1897	107	452	148	32	7	3	0.7	89	69	23		22	.327	.449	0	0	SS-107, OF-1
1898	144	589	156	21	10	6	1.0	99	99	39		20	.265	.365	0	0	SS-142, 2B-2
1899	145	578	153	30	8	6	1.0	91	100	45		20	.265	.375	0	0	SS-143, 1B-2
1900	125	486	127	19	4	12	2.5	80	66	44		26	.261	.391	0	0	SS-125
1901	138	518	118	14	6	3	0.6	55	68	25		20	.228	.295	0	0	SS-138
1902	118	429	98	11	0	2	0.5	39	44	31		24	.228	.268	0	0	SS-105, 2B-13
1903 2 teams		NY A (22G – .188)				DET A (69G – .222)											
" total	91	319	68	15	0	0	0.0	27	31	12		14	.213	.260	1	1	SS-60, 2B-31
1904 PHI N	1	4	1	0	0	0	0.0	0		0			.250	.250	0	0	2B-1
16 yrs.	1872	7679	2145	342	97	92	1.2	1460	1052	612	261	534	.279	.385	1	1	SS-1792, 2B-65, OF-19, 1B-2, 3B-1
1 yr.	69	239	53	12	0	0	0.0	21	23	10		11	.222	.272	1	1	SS-38, 2B-31

Baldy Louden

LOUDEN, WILLIAM
B. Aug. 27, 1885, Piedmont, W. Va.   D. Dec. 8, 1935, Piedmont, W. Va.   BR TR 5'11" 175 lbs.

	G	AB	H	2B	3B	HR	HR %	R	RBI	BB	SO	SB	BA	SA	PH AB	PH H	G by POS
1907 NY A	5	9	1	0	0	0	0.0	4	0	2		1	.111	.111	0	0	3B-3
1912 DET A	121	403	97	12	4	1	0.2	57	36	58		28	.241	.298	2	1	2B-86, 3B-26, SS-5
1913	72	191	46	4	5	0	0.0	28	23	24	22	6	.241	.314	2	0	2B-32, 3B-26, SS-6, OF-5

	G	AB	H	2B	3B	HR	HR %	R	RBI	BB	SO	SB	BA	SA	Pinch Hit AB	Pinch Hit H	G by POS

Baldy Louden continued

	G	AB	H	2B	3B	HR	HR%	R	RBI	BB	SO	SB	BA	SA	PH AB	PH H	G by POS
'14 BUF F	126	431	135	11	4	6	1.4	73	63	52		35	.313	.399	10	4	SS-115
'15	141	469	132	18	5	4	0.9	67	48	64		30	.281	.367	2	0	2B-88, SS-27, 3B-19
'16 CIN N	134	439	96	16	4	1	0.2	38	32	54	54	12	.219	.280	5	0	2B-108, SS-23
6 yrs.	599	1942	507	61	22	12	0.6	267	202	254	76	112	.261	.334	21	5	2B-314, SS-176, 3B-74, OF-5
2 yrs.	193	594	143	16	9	1	0.2	85	59	82	22	34	.241	.303	4	1	2B-118, 3B-52, SS-11, OF-5

Bobby Lowe

LOWE, ROBERT LINCOLN (Link)
B. July 10, 1868, Pittsburgh, Pa.   D. Dec. 8, 1951, Detroit, Mich.
Manager 1904.
BR TR 5'10" 150 lbs.

	G	AB	H	2B	3B	HR	HR%	R	RBI	BB	SO	SB	BA	SA	PH AB	PH H	G by POS
'90 BOS N	52	207	58	13	2	2	1.0	35	21	26	32	15	.280	.391	0	0	SS-24, OF-15, 3B-12
'91	125	497	129	19	5	6	1.2	92	74	53	54	43	.260	.354	1	0	OF-107, 2B-17, SS-2, 3B-1, P-1
'92	124	475	115	16	7	3	0.6	79	57	37	46	36	.242	.324	0	0	OF-90, 3B-14, SS-13, 2B-10
'93	126	526	157	19	5	13	2.5	130	89	55	29	22	.298	.428	0	0	2B-121, SS-5
'94	133	613	212	34	11	17	2.8	158	115	50	25	23	.346	.520	0	0	2B-130, SS-2, 3B-1
'95	99	412	122	12	7	7	1.7	101	62	40	16	24	.296	.410	0	0	2B-99
'96	73	305	98	11	4	2	0.7	59	48	20	11	15	.321	.403	0	0	2B-73
'97	123	499	154	24	8	5	1.0	87	106	32		16	.309	.419	0	0	2B-123
'98	149	566	154	13	7	4	0.7	69	94	29		12	.272	.341	0	0	2B-145, SS-2
'99	152	559	152	5	9	4	0.7	81	88	35		17	.272	.335	0	0	2B-148, SS-4
'00	127	474	132	11	5	3	0.6	65	71	26		15	.278	.342	0	0	2B-127
'01	129	491	125	11	1	3	0.6	47	47	17		22	.255	.299	0	0	3B-111, 2B-18
'02 CHI N	121	472	116	13	3	0	0.0	41	31	11		16	.246	.286	0	0	2B-117, 3B-2
'03	32	105	28	5	3	0	0.0	14	15	4		5	.267	.371	1	1	2B-22, 1B-6, 3B-1
'04 2 teams		PIT N (1G – .000)			DET A (140G – .208)												
'' total	141	507	105	14	6	0	0.0	47	40	17		15	.207	.258	1	0	2B-140
'05 DET A	60	181	35	7	2	0	0.0	17	9	13		3	.193	.254	2	0	OF-25, 3B-22, 2B-6, SS-4, 1B-1
'06	41	145	30	3	0	1	0.7	11	12	4		3	.207	.248	2	0	SS-19, 2B-17, 3B-5
'07	17	37	9	2	0	0	0.0	2	5	4		0	.243	.297	2	0	3B-10, OF-4, SS-2
18 yrs.	1824	7071	1931	232	85	70	1.0	1135	984	473	213	302	.273	.360	9	1	2B-1313, OF-241, 3B-179, SS-77, 1B-7, P-1
4 yrs.	258	869	179	26	8	3	0.1	77	66	38		21	.206	.258	6	0	2B-163, 3B-37, OF-29, SS-25, 1B-1

Dwight Lowry

LOWRY, DWIGHT
B. Oct. 23, 1957, Robeson County, N. C.
BL TR 6'3" 210 lbs.

	G	AB	H	2B	3B	HR	HR%	R	RBI	BB	SO	SB	BA	SA	PH AB	PH H	G by POS
'84 DET A	32	45	11	2	0	2	4.4	8	7	3	11	0	.244	.422	4	1	C-31

Jerry Lumpe

LUMPE, JERRY DEAN
B. June 2, 1933, Lincoln, Mo.
BL TR 6'2" 185 lbs.

	G	AB	H	2B	3B	HR	HR%	R	RBI	BB	SO	SB	BA	SA	PH AB	PH H	G by POS
'56 NY A	20	62	16	3	0	0	0.0	12	4	5	11	1	.258	.306	4	0	SS-17, 3B-1
'57	40	103	35	6	2	0	0.0	15	11	9	13	2	.340	.437	7	2	3B-30, SS-6
'58	81	232	59	8	4	3	1.3	34	32	23	21	1	.254	.362	16	4	3B-65, SS-5
'59 2 teams		NY A (18G – .222)			KC A (108G – .243)												
'' total	126	448	108	11	5	3	0.7	49	30	47	39	2	.241	.308	4	1	2B-62, SS-60, 3B-16
'60 KC A	146	574	156	19	3	8	1.4	69	53	48	49	1	.272	.357	5	0	2B-134, SS-15
'61	148	569	167	29	9	3	0.5	81	54	48	39	1	.293	.392	1	0	2B-147
'62	156	641	193	34	10	10	1.6	89	83	44	38	0	.301	.432	1	1	2B-156, SS-2
'63	157	595	161	26	7	5	0.8	75	59	58	44	3	.271	.363	2	0	2B-155
'64 DET A	158	624	160	21	6	6	1.0	75	46	50	61	2	.256	.338	0	0	2B-158
'65	145	502	129	15	3	4	0.8	72	39	56	34	7	.257	.323	10	1	2B-139
'66	113	385	89	14	3	1	0.3	30	26	24	44	0	.231	.291	20	2	2B-95
'67	81	177	41	4	0	4	2.3	19	17	16	18	0	.232	.322	29	3	2B-54, 3B-6
12 yrs.	1371	4912	1314	190	52	47	1.0	620	454	428	411	20	.268	.356	99	14	2B-1100, 3B-118, SS-105
4 yrs.	497	1688	419	54	12	15	0.9	196	128	146	157	9	.248	.321	59	6	2B-446, 3B-6
WORLD SERIES																	
'57 NY A	6	14	4	0	0	0	0.0	0	2	1	1	0	.286	.286	3	2	3B-3
'58	6	12	2	0	0	0	0.0	0	0	1	2	0	.167	.167	3	0	3B-3
2 yrs.	12	26	6	0	0	0	0.0	0	2	2	3	0	.231	.231	6	2	3B-6

Don Lund

LUND, DONALD ANDREW
B. May 18, 1923, Detroit, Mich.
BR TR 6' 200 lbs.

	G	AB	H	2B	3B	HR	HR%	R	RBI	BB	SO	SB	BA	SA	PH AB	PH H	G by POS
'45 BKN N	4	3	0	0	0	0	0.0	0	0	1	1	0	.000	.000	3	0	
'47	11	20	6	2	0	2	10.0	5	5	3	7	0	.300	.700	5	2	OF-5
'48 2 teams		BKN N (27G – .188)			STL A (63G – .248)												
'' total	90	230	53	11	4	4	1.7	30	30	15	33	1	.230	.365	16	0	OF-70
'49 DET A	2	2	0	0	0	0	0.0	0	0	0	1	0	.000	.000	2	0	
'52	8	23	7	0	0	0	0.0	1	1	3	3	0	.304	.304	1	0	OF-7
'53	131	421	108	21	4	9	2.1	51	47	39	65	3	.257	.390	8	2	OF-123
'54	35	54	7	2	0	0	0.0	4	3	4	3	1	.130	.167	9	1	OF-31
7 yrs.	281	753	181	36	8	15	2.0	91	86	65	113	5	.240	.369	44	5	OF-236
4 yrs.	176	500	122	23	4	9	1.8	56	51	46	72	4	.244	.360	20	3	OF-161

Billy Lush

LUSH, WILLIAM LUCAS
Brother of Ernie Lush.
B. Nov. 10, 1873, Bridgeport, Conn.   D. Aug. 28, 1951, Hawthorne, N. Y.
BB TR 5'8" 165 lbs.

	G	AB	H	2B	3B	HR	HR%	R	RBI	BB	SO	SB	BA	SA	PH AB	PH H	G by POS
'95 WAS N	5	18	6	0	0	0	0.0	2	2	2	1	0	.333	.333	0	0	OF-5
'96	97	352	87	9	11	4	1.1	74	45	66	49	28	.247	.369	3	1	OF-91, 2B-3
'97	3	12	0	0	0	0	0.0	1	0	2		0	.000	.000	0	0	OF-3
'01 BOS N	7	27	5	1	1	0	0.0	2	3	3		0	.185	.296	0	0	OF-7
'02	120	413	92	8	1	2	0.5	68	19	76		30	.223	.262	3	1	OF-116, 3B-1
'03 DET A	119	423	116	18	14	1	0.2	71	33	70		14	.274	.390	1	0	OF-101, 3B-12, SS-3, 2B-3

	G	AB	H	2B	3B	HR	HR %	R	RBI	BB	SO	SB	BA	SA	Pinch Hit AB	Pinch Hit H	G by POS

Billy Lush continued

	G	AB	H	2B	3B	HR	HR%	R	RBI	BB	SO	SB	BA	SA	PH AB	PH H	G by POS
1904 CLE A	138	477	123	13	8	1	0.2	76	50	72		12	.258	.325	0	0	OF-138
7 yrs.	489	1722	429	49	35	8	0.5	294	152	291	50	84	.249	.332	7	2	OF-461, 3B-13, 2B-6, SS-3
1 yr.	119	423	116	18	14	1	0.2	71	33	70		14	.274	.390	1	0	OF-101, 3B-12, SS-3, 2B-3

Dave Machemer

MACHEMER, DAVID RITCHIE
B. May 24, 1951, St. Joseph, Mich.

BR TR 5'11½" 180 lbs.

	G	AB	H	2B	3B	HR	HR%	R	RBI	BB	SO	SB	BA	SA	PH AB	PH H	G by POS
1978 CAL A	10	22	6	1	0	1	4.5	6	2	2	1	0	.273	.455	0	0	2B-5, 3B-3, SS-1
1979 DET A	19	26	5	1	0	0	0.0	8	2	3	2	0	.192	.231	0	0	2B-11, DH-1, OF-1
2 yrs.	29	48	11	2	0	1	2.1	14	4	5	3	0	.229	.333	0	0	2B-16, 3B-3, DH-1, OF-SS-1
1 yr.	19	26	5	1	0	0	0.0	8	2	3	2	0	.192	.231	0	0	2B-11, DH-1, OF-1

Elliott Maddox

MADDOX, ELLIOTT
B. Dec. 21, 1947, Orange, N. J.

BR TR 5'11" 180 lbs.

	G	AB	H	2B	3B	HR	HR%	R	RBI	BB	SO	SB	BA	SA	PH AB	PH H	G by POS
1970 DET A	109	258	64	13	4	3	1.2	30	24	30	42	2	.248	.364	20	2	3B-40, OF-37, SS-19, 2B-1
1971 WAS A	128	258	56	8	2	1	0.4	38	18	51	42	10	.217	.275	19	7	OF-103, 3B-12
1972 TEX A	98	294	74	7	2	0	0.0	40	10	49	53	20	.252	.289	1	0	OF-94
1973	100	172	41	1	0	1	0.6	24	17	29	28	5	.238	.262	3	0	OF-89, 3B-7, DH-1
1974 NY A	137	466	141	26	2	3	0.6	75	45	69	48	6	.303	.386	3	2	OF-135, 2B-2, 3B-1
1975	55	218	67	10	3	1	0.5	36	23	21	24	9	.307	.394	0	0	OF-55, 2B-1
1976	18	46	10	2	0	0	0.0	4	3	4	3	0	.217	.261	2	1	OF-13, DH-2
1977 BAL A	49	107	28	7	0	2	1.9	14	9	13	9	2	.262	.383	2	0	OF-45, 3B-1
1978 NY N	119	389	100	18	2	2	0.5	43	39	71	38	2	.257	.329	7	0	OF-79, 3B-43, 1B-1
1979	86	224	60	13	0	1	0.4	21	12	20	27	3	.268	.339	21	8	OF-65, 3B-11
1980	130	411	101	16	1	4	1.0	35	34	52	44	1	.246	.319	11	2	3B-115, OF-4, 1B-2
11 yrs.	1029	2843	742	121	16	18	0.6	360	234	409	358	60	.261	.334	89	22	OF-719, 3B-230, SS-19, 2B-4, DH-3, 1B-3
1 yr.	109	258	64	13	4	3	1.2	30	24	30	42	2	.248	.364	20	2	3B-40, OF-37, SS-19, 2B-1

LEAGUE CHAMPIONSHIP SERIES

	G	AB	H	2B	3B	HR	HR%	R	RBI	BB	SO	SB	BA	SA	PH AB	PH H	G by POS
1976 NY A	3	9	2	1	0	0	0.0	0	1	0	1	0	.222	.333	0	0	OF-3

WORLD SERIES

	G	AB	H	2B	3B	HR	HR%	R	RBI	BB	SO	SB	BA	SA	PH AB	PH H	G by POS
1976 NY A	2	5	1	0	1	0	0.0	0	0	1	2	0	.200	.600	0	0	OF-1

Billy Maharg

MAHARG, WILLIAM JOSEPH
Also known as William Joseph Graham.
B. Mar. 19, 1881, Philadelphia, Pa.   D. Nov. 20, 1953, Philadelphia, Pa.

BR TR 5'4½"

	G	AB	H	2B	3B	HR	HR%	R	RBI	BB	SO	SB	BA	SA	PH AB	PH H	G by POS
1912 DET A	1	1	0	0	0	0	0.0	0	0	0		0	.000	.000	0	0	3B-1
1916 PHI N	1	1	0	0	0	0	0.0	0	0	0	0	0	.000	.000	0	0	OF-1
2 yrs.	2	2	0	0	0	0	0.0	0	0	0	0	0	.000	.000	0	0	OF-1, 3B-1
1 yr.	1	1	0	0	0	0	0.0	0	0	0		0	.000	.000	0	0	3B-1

Bob Maier

MAIER, ROBERT PHILLIP
B. Sept. 5, 1915, Dunellen, N. J.

BR TR 5'8" 180 lbs.

	G	AB	H	2B	3B	HR	HR%	R	RBI	BB	SO	SB	BA	SA	PH AB	PH H	G by POS
1945 DET A	132	486	128	25	7	1	0.2	58	34	37	32	7	.263	.350	2	1	3B-124, OF-5

WORLD SERIES

	G	AB	H	2B	3B	HR	HR%	R	RBI	BB	SO	SB	BA	SA	PH AB	PH H	G by POS
1945 DET A	1	1	1	0	0	0	0.0	0	0	0	0	0	1.000	1.000	1	1	

George Maisel

MAISEL, GEORGE JOHN
Brother of Fritz Maisel.
B. Mar. 12, 1892, Catonsville, Md.   D. Nov. 20, 1968, Baltimore, Md.

BR TR 5'10½" 180 lbs.

	G	AB	H	2B	3B	HR	HR%	R	RBI	BB	SO	SB	BA	SA	PH AB	PH H	G by POS
1913 STL A	11	18	3	2	0	0	0.0	2	1	1	7	0	.167	.278	5	1	OF-5
1916 DET A	7	5	0	0	0	0	0.0	2	0	0	2	0	.000	.000	0	0	3B-3
1921 CHI N	111	393	122	7	2	0	0.0	54	43	11	13	17	.310	.338	1	0	OF-108
1922	38	84	16	1	1	0	0.0	9	6	8	2	1	.190	.226	5	1	OF-38
4 yrs.	167	500	141	10	3	0	0.0	67	50	20	24	18	.282	.314	11	3	OF-151, 3B-3
1 yr.	7	5	0	0	0	0	0.0	2	0	0	2	0	.000	.000	0	0	3B-3

Harry Malmberg

MALMBERG, HARRY WILLIAM (Swede)
B. July 31, 1926, Fairfield, Ala.   D. Oct. 29, 1976, San Francisco, Calif.

BR TR 6'1" 170 lbs.

	G	AB	H	2B	3B	HR	HR%	R	RBI	BB	SO	SB	BA	SA	PH AB	PH H	G by POS
1955 DET A	67	208	45	5	2	0	0.0	25	19	29	19	0	.216	.260	0	0	2B-65

Clyde Manion

MANION, CLYDE JENNINGS (Pete)
B. Oct. 30, 1896, Jefferson City, Mo.   D. Sept. 4, 1967, Detroit, Mich.

BR TR 5'11" 175 lbs.

	G	AB	H	2B	3B	HR	HR%	R	RBI	BB	SO	SB	BA	SA	PH AB	PH H	G by POS
1920 DET A	32	80	22	4	1	0	0.0	4	8	4	7	0	.275	.350	2	1	C-30
1921	12	18	2	0	0	0	0.0	0	2	2	2	0	.111	.111	6	1	C-4
1922	42	69	19	4	1	0	0.0	9	12	4	6	0	.275	.362	13	4	C-21, 1B-1
1923	23	22	3	0	0	0	0.0	0	2	2	2	0	.136	.136	17	2	C-3, 1B-1
1924	14	13	3	0	0	0	0.0	1	2	1	1	0	.231	.231	9	3	C-3, 1B-1
1926	75	176	35	4	0	0	0.0	15	14	24	16	1	.199	.222	1	0	C-74
1927	1	0	0	0	0	0	–	0	0	1	0	0	–	–	1	0	
1928 STL A	76	243	55	5	1	2	0.8	25	31	15	18	3	.226	.280	5	2	C-71
1929	35	111	27	2	0	0	0.0	16	11	15	3	1	.243	.261	1	0	C-34
1930	57	148	32	1	0	1	0.7	12	11	24	17	0	.216	.243	1	0	C-56
1932 CIN N	49	135	28	4	0	0	0.0	7	12	14	16	0	.207	.237	1	0	C-47
1933	36	84	14	1	0	0	0.0	3	3	8	7	0	.167	.179	2	0	C-34
1934	25	54	10	0	0	0	0.0	4	4	4	7	0	.185	.185	1	0	C-24
13 yrs.	477	1153	250	25	3	3	0.3	96	112	118	102	5	.217	.252	60	13	C-401, 1B-3
7 yrs.	199	378	84	12	2	0	0.0	29	40	38	34	1	.222	.265	49	11	C-135, 1B-3

	G	AB	H	2B	3B	HR	HR %	R	RBI	BB	SO	SB	BA	SA	Pinch Hit AB	Pinch Hit H	G by POS

Phil Mankowski

MANKOWSKI, PHILLIP ANTHONY
B. Jan. 9, 1953, Buffalo, N. Y.   BL TR 6' 180 lbs.

	G	AB	H	2B	3B	HR	HR %	R	RBI	BB	SO	SB	BA	SA	AB	H	G by POS
976 DET A	24	85	23	2	1	1	1.2	9	4	4	8	0	.271	.353	1	0	3B-23
977	94	286	79	7	3	3	1.0	21	27	16	41	1	.276	.353	10	3	3B-85, 2B-1
978	88	222	61	8	0	4	1.8	28	20	22	28	2	.275	.365	9	2	3B-80, DH-1
979	42	99	22	4	0	0	0.0	11	8	10	16	0	.222	.263	9	1	3B-36, DH-1
980 NY N	8	12	2	1	0	0	0.0	1	1	2	4	0	.167	.250	4	0	3B-3
982	13	35	8	1	0	0	0.0	2	4	1	6	0	.229	.257	0	0	3B-13
6 yrs.	269	739	195	23	4	8	1.1	72	64	55	103	3	.264	.338	33	6	3B-240, DH-2, 2B-1
4 yrs.	248	692	185	21	4	8	1.2	69	59	52	93	3	.267	.344	29	6	3B-224, DH-2, 2B-1

Jerry Manuel

MANUEL, JERRY
B. Dec. 23, 1953, Hahira, Ga.   BB TR 6' 158 lbs.

	G	AB	H	2B	3B	HR	HR %	R	RBI	BB	SO	SB	BA	SA	AB	H	G by POS
975 DET A	6	18	1	0	0	0	0.0	0	0	0	4	0	.056	.056	0	0	2B-6
976	54	43	6	1	0	0	0.0	4	2	3	9	1	.140	.163	0	0	2B-47, SS-4, DH-1
980 MON N	7	6	0	0	0	0	0.0	0	0	0	2	0	.000	.000	0	0	SS-7
981	27	55	11	5	0	3	5.5	10	10	6	11	0	.200	.455	0	0	2B-23, SS-2
982 SD N	2	5	1	0	1	0	0.0	0	1	1	0	0	.200	.600	0	0	SS-1, 3B-1, 2B-1
5 yrs.	96	127	19	6	1	3	2.4	14	13	10	26	1	.150	.283	0	0	2B-77, SS-14, DH-1, 3B-1
2 yrs.	60	61	7	1	0	0	0.0	4	2	3	13	1	.115	.131	0	0	2B-53, SS-4, DH-1

DIVISIONAL PLAYOFF SERIES

	G	AB	H	2B	3B	HR	HR %	R	RBI	BB	SO	SB	BA	SA	AB	H	G by POS
981 MON N	5	14	1	0	0	0	0.0	0	0	2	5	0	.071	.071	0	0	2B-5

LEAGUE CHAMPIONSHIP SERIES

	G	AB	H	2B	3B	HR	HR %	R	RBI	BB	SO	SB	BA	SA	AB	H	G by POS
981 MON N	1	0	0	0	0	0	–	0	0	0	0	0	–	–	0	0	

Heinie Manush

MANUSH, HENRY EMMETT
Brother of Frank Manush.
B. July 20, 1901, Tuscumbia, Ala.   D. May 12, 1971, Sarasota, Fla.
Hall of Fame 1964.   BL TL 6'1" 200 lbs.

	G	AB	H	2B	3B	HR	HR %	R	RBI	BB	SO	SB	BA	SA	AB	H	G by POS
923 DET A	109	308	103	20	5	4	1.3	59	54	20	21	3	.334	.471	27	6	OF-79
924	120	422	122	24	8	9	2.1	83	68	27	30	14	.289	.448	11	1	OF-106, 1B-1
925	99	277	84	14	3	5	1.8	46	47	24	21	8	.303	.430	22	6	OF-73
926	136	498	188	35	8	14	2.8	95	86	31	28	11	.378	.564	14	5	OF-120
927	152	593	177	31	18	6	1.0	102	80	47	29	12	.298	.442	1	1	OF-150
928 STL A	154	638	241	47	20	13	2.0	104	108	39	14	17	.378	.575	0	0	OF-154
929	142	574	204	45	10	6	1.0	85	81	43	24	9	.355	.500	1	0	OF-141
930 2 teams		STL A	(49G –	.328)		WAS A	(88G –	.362)									
" total	137	554	194	49	12	9	1.6	100	94	31	24	7	.350	.531	3	0	OF-134
931 WAS A	146	616	189	41	11	6	1.0	110	70	36	27	3	.307	.438	3	0	OF-143
932	149	625	214	41	14	14	2.2	121	116	36	29	7	.342	.520	3	1	OF-146
933	153	658	221	32	17	5	0.8	115	95	36	18	6	.336	.459	3	2	OF-150
934	137	556	194	42	11	11	2.0	88	89	36	23	7	.349	.523	7	1	OF-131
935	119	479	131	26	9	4	0.8	68	56	35	17	2	.273	.390	7	1	OF-111
936 BOS A	82	313	91	15	5	0	0.0	43	45	17	11	1	.291	.371	9	4	OF-72
937 BKN N	132	466	155	25	7	4	0.9	57	73	40	24	6	.333	.442	9	3	OF-123
938 2 teams		BKN N	(17G –	.235)		PIT N	(15G –	.308)									
" total	32	64	16	4	2	0	0.0	11	10	7	4	1	.250	.375	18	5	OF-12
939 PIT N	10	12	0	0	0	0	0.0	0	1	1	1	0	.000	.000	8	0	OF-1
17 yrs.	2009	7653	2524	491	160	110	1.4	1287	1173	506	345	114	.330	.479	146	36	OF-1846, 1B-1
5 yrs.	616	2098	674	124	42	38	1.8	385	335	149	129	48	.321	.475	75	19	OF-528, 1B-1
													6th				

WORLD SERIES

	G	AB	H	2B	3B	HR	HR %	R	RBI	BB	SO	SB	BA	SA	AB	H	G by POS
933 WAS A	5	18	2	0	0	0	0.0	2	0	2	1	0	.111	.111	0	0	OF-5

Cliff Mapes

MAPES, CLIFF FRANKLIN (Tiger)
B. Mar. 13, 1922, Sutherland, Neb.   BL TR 6'3" 205 lbs.

	G	AB	H	2B	3B	HR	HR %	R	RBI	BB	SO	SB	BA	SA	AB	H	G by POS
948 NY A	53	88	22	11	1	1	1.1	19	12	6	13	1	.250	.432	26	4	OF-21
949	111	304	75	13	3	7	2.3	56	38	58	50	6	.247	.378	4	0	OF-108
950	108	356	88	14	6	12	3.4	60	61	47	61	1	.247	.421	6	2	OF-102
951 2 teams		NY A	(45G –	.216)		STL A	(56G –	.274)									
" total	101	252	66	10	3	9	3.6	38	38	30	47	0	.262	.433	13	5	OF-87
952 DET A	86	193	38	7	0	9	4.7	26	23	27	42	0	.197	.373	23	6	OF-62
5 yrs.	459	1193	289	55	13	38	3.2	199	172	168	213	8	.242	.406	72	17	OF-380
1 yr.	86	193	38	7	0	9	4.7	26	23	27	42	0	.197	.373	23	6	OF-62

WORLD SERIES

	G	AB	H	2B	3B	HR	HR %	R	RBI	BB	SO	SB	BA	SA	AB	H	G by POS
949 NY A	4	10	1	1	0	0	0.0	3	2	2	4	0	.100	.200	0	0	OF-4
950	1	4	0	0	0	0	0.0	0	0	0	1	0	.000	.000	0	0	OF-5
2 yrs.	5	14	1	1	0	0	0.0	3	2	2	5	0	.071	.143	0	0	OF-5

Billy Martin

MARTIN, ALFRED MANUEL
B. May 16, 1928, Berkeley, Calif.
Manager 1969, 1971-82.   BR TR 5'11½" 165 lbs.

	G	AB	H	2B	3B	HR	HR %	R	RBI	BB	SO	SB	BA	SA	AB	H	G by POS
950 NY A	34	36	9	1	0	1	2.8	10	8	3	3	0	.250	.361	10	2	2B-22, 3B-1
951	51	58	15	1	2	0	0.0	10	2	4	9	0	.259	.345	10	0	2B-23, SS-6, 3B-2, OF-1
952	109	363	97	13	3	3	0.8	32	33	22	31	3	.267	.344	1	0	2B-107
953	149	587	151	24	6	15	2.6	72	75	43	56	6	.257	.395	1	0	2B-146, SS-18
955	20	70	21	2	0	1	1.4	8	9	7	9	1	.300	.371	0	0	2B-17, SS-3
956	121	458	121	24	5	9	2.0	76	49	30	56	7	.264	.397	1	0	2B-105, 3B-16
957 2 teams		NY A	(43G –	.241)		KC A	(73G –	.257)									
" total	116	410	103	14	5	10	2.4	45	39	15	34	9	.251	.383	5	0	2B-78, 3B-33, SS-2
958 DET A	131	498	127	19	1	7	1.4	56	42	16	62	5	.255	.339	2	0	2B-67, 3B-41
959 CLE A	73	242	63	7	0	9	3.7	37	24	7	18	0	.260	.401	1	0	2B-67, 3B-4
960 CIN N	103	317	78	17	1	3	0.9	34	16	27	34	0	.246	.334	4	0	2B-97
961 2 teams		MIL N	(6G –	.000)		MIN A	(108G –	.246)									
" total	114	380	92	15	6	6	1.6	45	36	13	43	3	.242	.355	9	1	2B-105, SS-1
11 yrs.	1021	3419	877	137	28	64	1.9	425	333	187	355	34	.257	.369	44	3	2B-767, SS-118, 3B-97, OF-1
1 yr.	131	498	127	19	1	7	1.4	56	42	16	62	5	.255	.339	2	0	SS-88, 3B-41

	G	AB	H	2B	3B	HR	HR %	R	RBI	BB	SO	SB	BA	SA	Pinch Hit AB	Pinch Hit H	G by POS

Billy Martin continued

WORLD SERIES

Year Team	G	AB	H	2B	3B	HR	HR%	R	RBI	BB	SO	SB	BA	SA	PH AB	PH H	G by POS
1951 NY A	1	0	0	0	0	0	–	1	0	0	0	0	–	–	0	0	
1952	7	23	5	0	0	1	4.3	2	4	2	2	0	.217	.348	0	0	2B-7
1953	6	24	12	1	2	2	8.3	5	8	1	2	1	.500	.958	0	0	2B-6
1955	7	25	8	1	1	0	0.0	2	4	1	5	0	.320	.440	0	0	2B-7
1956	7	27	8	0	0	2	7.4	5	3	1	6	0	.296	.519	0	0	2B-7
5 yrs.	28	99	33	2	3	5	5.1 4th	15	19	5	15	1	.333	.566	0	0	2B-27

Tommy Matchick

MATCHICK, JOHN THOMAS
B. Sept. 7, 1943, Hazelton, Pa.   BL TR 6'1" 173 lbs.

Year Team	G	AB	H	2B	3B	HR	HR%	R	RBI	BB	SO	SB	BA	SA	PH AB	PH H	G by POS
1967 DET A	8	6	1	0	0	0	0.0		0	0	2	0	.167	.167	5	0	SS-1
1968	80	227	46	6	2	3	1.3	18	14	10	46	0	.203	.286	13	5	SS-59, 2B-13, 1B-6
1969	94	298	72	11	2	0	0.0	25	32	15	51	3	.242	.292	16	8	2B-47, 3B-27, SS-6, 1B-2
1970 2 teams	KC A (55G – .196)					BOS A (10G – .071)											
" total	65	172	32	3	2	0	0.0	13	11	7	25	0	.186	.227	12	0	SS-44, 2B-11, 3B-3
1971 MIL A	42	114	25	1	0	1	0.9	6	7	7	23	3	.219	.254	0	0	3B-41, 2B-1
1972 BAL A	3	9	2	0	0	0	0.0	0	0	0	1	0	.222	.222	0	0	3B-3
6 yrs.	292	826	178	21	6	4	0.5	63	64	39	148	6	.215	.270	46	13	SS-110, 3B-74, 2B-72, 1B-8
3 yrs.	182	531	119	17	4	3	0.6	44	46	25	99	3	.224	.288	34	13	SS-66, 2B-60, 3B-27, 1B-8

WORLD SERIES

Year Team	G	AB	H	2B	3B	HR	HR%	R	RBI	BB	SO	SB	BA	SA	PH AB	PH H	G by POS
1968 DET A	3	3	0	0	0	0	0.0	0	0	0	1	0	.000	.000	3	0	

Eddie Mathews

MATHEWS, EDWIN LEE
B. Oct. 13, 1931, Texarkana, Tex.
Manager 1972-74.
Hall of Fame 1978.   BL TR 6'1" 190 lbs.

Year Team	G	AB	H	2B	3B	HR	HR%	R	RBI	BB	SO	SB	BA	SA	PH AB	PH H	G by POS
1952 BOS N	145	528	128	23	5	25	4.7	80	58	59	115	6	.242	.447	2	0	3B-142
1953 MIL N	154	579	175	31	8	47	8.1	110	135	99	83	1	.302	.627	0	0	3B-157
1954	138	476	138	21	4	40	8.4	96	103	113	61	10	.290	.603	2	0	3B-127, OF-10
1955	141	499	144	23	5	41	8.2	108	101	109	98	3	.289	.601	2	1	3B-137
1956	151	552	150	21	2	37	6.7	103	95	91	86	6	.272	.518	2	0	3B-150
1957	148	572	167	28	9	32	5.6	109	94	90	79	3	.292	.540	0	0	3B-147
1958	149	546	137	18	1	31	5.7	97	77	85	85	5	.251	.458	0	0	3B-149
1959	148	594	182	16	8	46	7.7	118	114	80	71	2	.306	.593	0	0	3B-148
1960	153	548	152	19	7	39	7.1	108	124	111	113	7	.277	.551	0	0	3B-153
1961	152	572	175	23	6	32	5.6	103	91	93	95	12	.306	.535	1	0	3B-151
1962	152	536	142	25	6	29	5.4	106	90	101	90	4	.265	.496	3	0	3B-140, 1B-7
1963	158	547	144	27	4	23	4.2	82	84	124	119	3	.263	.453	1	0	3B-121, OF-42
1964	141	502	117	19	1	23	4.6	83	74	85	100	2	.233	.412	6	1	3B-128, 1B-7
1965	156	546	137	23	0	32	5.9	77	95	73	110	1	.251	.469	8	1	3B-153
1966 ATL N	134	452	113	21	4	16	3.5	72	53	63	82	1	.250	.420	12	4	3B-127
1967 2 teams	HOU N (101G – .238)					DET A (36G – .231)											
" total	137	436	103	16	2	16	3.7	53	57	63	88	2	.236	.392	15	2	1B-92, 3B-45
1968 DET A	31	52	11	0	0	3	5.8	4	8	5	12	0	.212	.385	16	3	3B-6, 1B-6
17 yrs.	2388	8537	2315	354	72	512 10th	6.0	1509	1453	1444	1487	68	.271	.509	70	12	3B-2181, 1B-112, OF-52
2 yrs.	67	160	36	3	0	9	5.6	18	27	20	35	0	.225	.413	21	3	3B-27, 1B-19

WORLD SERIES

Year Team	G	AB	H	2B	3B	HR	HR%	R	RBI	BB	SO	SB	BA	SA	PH AB	PH H	G by POS
1957 MIL N	7	22	5	3	0	1	4.5	4	4	8	5	0	.227	.500	0	0	3B-7
1958	7	25	4	2	0	0	0.0	3	3	4	11	1	.160	.240	0	0	3B-7
1968 DET A	2	3	1	0	0	0	0.0	0	0	1	1	0	.333	.333	1	0	3B-1
3 yrs.	16	50	10	5	0	1	2.0	7	7	15	17	1	.200	.360	1	0	3B-15

Bob Mavis

MAVIS, ROBERT HENRY
B. Apr. 8, 1918, Milwaukee, Wis.   BL TR 5'7" 160 lbs.

Year Team	G	AB	H	2B	3B	HR	HR%	R	RBI	BB	SO	SB	BA	SA	PH AB	PH H	G by POS
1949 DET A	1	0	0	0	0	0	–	0	0	0	0	0	–	–	0	0	

Charlie Maxwell

MAXWELL, CHARLES RICHARD (Smokey)
B. Apr. 28, 1927, Lawton, Mich.   BL TL 5'11" 185 lbs.

Year Team	G	AB	H	2B	3B	HR	HR%	R	RBI	BB	SO	SB	BA	SA	PH AB	PH H	G by POS
1950 BOS A	3	8	0	0	0	0	0.0	0	0	1	3	0	.000	.000	1	0	OF-2
1951	49	80	15	1	0	3	3.8	8	12	9	18	0	.188	.313	31	7	OF-13
1952	8	15	1	1	0	0	0.0	0	0	3	11	0	.067	.133	3	0	OF-3, 1B-3
1954	74	104	26	4	1	0	0.0	9	5	12	21	3	.250	.308	45	12	OF-27
1955 2 teams	BAL A (4G – .000)					DET A (55G – .266)											
" total	59	113	29	7	1	7	6.2	19	18	8	21	0	.257	.522	30	7	OF-26, 1B-2
1956 DET A	141	500	163	14	3	28	5.6	96	87	79	74	1	.326	.534	7	4	OF-136
1957	138	492	136	23	4	24	4.9	75	82	76	84	3	.276	.482	3	3	OF-137
1958	131	397	108	14	4	13	3.3	56	65	64	54	6	.272	.426	8	1	OF-114, 1B-14
1959	145	518	130	12	2	31	6.0	81	95	81	91	0	.251	.461	8	3	OF-136
1960	134	482	114	16	5	24	5.0	70	81	58	75	5	.237	.440	14	1	OF-120
1961	79	131	30	4	2	5	3.8	11	18	20	24	0	.229	.405	45	12	OF-25
1962 2 teams	DET A (30G – .194)					CHI A (69G – .296)											
" total	99	273	74	10	3	10	3.7	35	52	42	42	0	.271	.440	20	3	OF-71, 1B-7
1963 CHI A	71	130	30	4	2	3	2.3	17	17	31	27	0	.231	.362	21	3	OF-24, 1B-17
1964	2	2	0	0	0	0	0.0	0	0	0	0	0	.000	.000	2	0	
14 yrs.	1133	3245	856	110	26	148	4.6	478	532	484	545	18	.264	.451	238	56	OF-834, 1B-43
8 yrs.	853	2696	723	92	20	133	4.9 5th	413	455	394	432	15	.268	.465	122 6th	33 6th	OF-709, 1B-17

Milt May

MAY, MILTON SCOTT
Son of Pinky May.
B. Aug. 1, 1950, Gary, Ind.   BL TR 6' 190 lbs.

Year Team	G	AB	H	2B	3B	HR	HR%	R	RBI	BB	SO	SB	BA	SA	PH AB	PH H	G by POS
1970 PIT N	5	4	2	1	0	0	0.0	1	2	0	0	0	.500	.750	6	3	
1971	49	126	35	1	0	6	4.8	15	18	9	16	0	.278	.429	17	3	C-31

	G	AB	H	2B	3B	HR	HR %	R	RBI	BB	SO	SB	BA	SA	Pinch Hit AB	Pinch Hit H	G by POS

Milt May continued

	G	AB	H	2B	3B	HR	HR%	R	RBI	BB	SO	SB	BA	SA	PH AB	PH H	G by POS
1972	57	139	39	10	0	0	0.0	12	14	10	13	0	.281	.353	18	4	C-33
1973	101	283	76	8	1	7	2.5	29	31	34	26	0	.269	.378	18	2	C-79
1974 HOU N	127	405	117	17	4	7	1.7	47	54	39	33	0	.289	.402	9	2	C-116
1975	111	386	93	15	1	4	1.0	29	52	26	41	1	.241	.316	8	3	C-102
1976 DET A	6	25	7	1	0	0	0.0	2	1	0	1	0	.280	.320	0	0	C-6
1977	115	397	99	9	3	12	3.0	32	46	26	31	0	.249	.378	5	2	C-111
1978	105	352	88	9	0	10	2.8	24	37	27	26	0	.250	.361	12	1	C-94
1979 2 teams		DET	A (6G –	.273)		CHI	A (65G –	.252)									
" total	71	213	54	15	0	7	3.3	24	31	15	28	0	.254	.423	2	0	C-70
1980 SF N	111	358	93	16	2	6	1.7	27	50	25	40	0	.260	.366	15	6	C-103
1981	97	316	98	17	0	2	0.6	20	33	34	29	1	.310	.383	9	5	C-93
1982	114	395	104	19	0	9	2.3	29	39	28	38	0	.263	.380	13	6	C-110
1983 2 teams		SF	N (66G –	.247)		PIT	N (7G –	.250)									
" total	73	198	49	6	0	6	3.0	18	20	22	24	2	.247	.369	13	3	C-60
1984 PIT N	50	96	17	3	0	1	1.0	4	8	10	15	0	.177	.240	18	3	C-26
15 yrs.	1192	3693	971	147	11	77	2.1	313	443	305	361	4	.263	.353	163	43	C-1034
4 yrs.	232	785	197	21	3	22	2.8	59	87	54	59	0	.251	.369	18	3	C-216
LEAGUE CHAMPIONSHIP SERIES																	
1971 PIT N	1	1	0	0	0	0	0.0	0	0	0	0	0	.000	.000	1	0	
1972	1	2	1	0	0	0	0.0	0	1	0	0	0	.500	.500	0	0	C-1
2 yrs.	2	3	1	0	0	0	0.0	0	1	0	0	0	.333	.333	1	0	C-1
WORLD SERIES																	
1971 PIT N	2	2	1	0	0	0	0.0	0	1	0	0	0	.500	.500	2	1	

Eddie Mayo

MAYO, EDWARD JOSEPH
Born Edward Joseph Mayoski.
B. Apr. 15, 1910, Holyoke, Mass.

BL TR 5'11" 178 lbs.

	G	AB	H	2B	3B	HR	HR%	R	RBI	BB	SO	SB	BA	SA	PH AB	PH H	G by POS
1936 NY N	46	141	28	4	1	1	0.7	11	8	11	12	0	.199	.262	3	1	3B-40
1937 BOS N	65	172	39	6	1	1	0.6	19	18	15	20	1	.227	.291	14	4	3B-50
1938	8	14	3	0	0	1	7.1	2	4	1	0	0	.214	.429	0	0	3B-6, SS-2
1943 PHI A	128	471	103	10	1	0	0.0	49	28	34	32	2	.219	.244	5	0	3B-123
1944 DET A	154	607	151	18	3	5	0.8	76	63	57	23	9	.249	.313	0	0	2B-143, SS-11
1945	134	501	143	24	3	10	2.0	71	54	48	29	7	.285	.405	9	4	2B-124
1946	51	202	51	9	2	0	0.0	21	22	14	12	6	.252	.317	2	0	2B-49
1947	142	535	149	28	4	6	1.1	66	48	48	28	3	.279	.379	1	1	2B-142
1948	106	370	92	20	1	2	0.5	35	42	30	19	1	.249	.324	10	2	2B-86, 3B-19
9 yrs.	834	3013	759	119	16	26	0.9	350	287	258	175	29	.252	.328	44	12	2B-544, 3B-229, SS-13
5 yrs.	587	2215	586	99	13	23	1.0	269	229	197	111	26	.265	.352	22	7	2B-544, SS-11, 3B-10
WORLD SERIES																	
1936 NY N	1	1	0	0	0	0	0.0	0	0	0	0	0	.000	.000	0	0	3B-1
1945 DET A	7	28	7	1	0	0	0.0	4	2	2	2	0	.250	.286	0	0	2B-7
2 yrs.	8	29	7	1	0	0	0.0	4	2	2	2	0	.241	.276	0	0	2B-7, 3B-1

Sport McAllister

McALLISTER, LEWIS WILLIAM
B. July 23, 1874, Austin, Miss.   D. July 18, 1962, Detroit, Mich.

BB TR 5'11" 180 lbs.

	G	AB	H	2B	3B	HR	HR%	R	RBI	BB	SO	SB	BA	SA	PH AB	PH H	G by POS
1896 CLE N	8	27	6	2	0	0	0.0	2	1	0		2	1	.222	.296	0	0	OF-4, C-2, P-1
1897	43	137	30	5	1	0	0.0	23	11	12			3	.219	.270	0	0	OF-28, SS-4, P-4, 1B-3, C-2, 2B-1
1898	17	57	13	3	1	0	0.0	8	9	5			0	.228	.316	0	0	P-9, OF-4
1899	113	418	99	6	8	1	0.2	29	31	19			5	.237	.297	2	0	OF-79, C-17, 3B-7, 1B-6, SS-3, P-3, 2B-1
1901 DET A	90	306	92	9	4	3	1.0	45	57	15			17	.301	.386	4	2	C-35, 1B-28, OF-11, 3B-10, SS-3
1902 2 teams		DET	A (66G –	.210)		BAL	A (3G –	.091)									
" total	69	240	49	5	2	1	0.4	19	33	6		1	.204	.254	5	0	1B-27, OF-12, C-9, SS-6, 3B-6, 2B-5
1903 DET A	78	265	69	8	2	0	0.0	31	22	10		5	.260	.306	5	1	SS-46, C-18, OF-5, 3B-4, 1B-1
7 yrs.	418	1450	358	38	18	5	0.3	157	164	67	2	32	.247	.308	16	3	OF-147, C-83, 1B-65, SS-62, 3B-27, P-17, 2B-7
3 yrs.	234	800	209	22	8	4	0.5	95	111	30		23	.261	.324	14	3	C-62, SS-55, 1B-55, OF-28, 3B-20, 2B-3

Dick McAuliffe

McAULIFFE, RICHARD JOHN
B. Nov. 29, 1939, Hartford, Conn.

BL TR 5'11" 176 lbs.

	G	AB	H	2B	3B	HR	HR%	R	RBI	BB	SO	SB	BA	SA	PH AB	PH H	G by POS
1960 DET A	8	27	7	0	1	0	0.0	2	1	2	6	0	.259	.333	0	0	SS-7
1961	80	285	73	12	4	6	2.1	36	33	24	39	2	.256	.389	7	3	SS-55, 3B-22
1962	139	471	124	20	5	12	2.5	50	63	64	76	4	.263	.403	6	1	2B-70, 3B-49, SS-16
1963	150	568	149	18	6	13	2.3	77	61	64	75	11	.262	.384	2	1	SS-133, 2B-15
1964	162	557	134	18	7	24	4.3	85	66	77	96	8	.241	.427	2	1	SS-160
1965	113	404	105	13	6	15	3.7	61	54	49	62	6	.260	.433	2	0	SS-112
1966	124	430	118	16	8	23	5.3	83	56	66	80	5	.274	.509	8	2	SS-105, 3B-15
1967	153	557	133	16	7	22	3.9	92	65	105	118	6	.239	.411	0	0	2B-145, SS-43
1968	151	570	142	24	10	16	2.8	95	56	82	99	8	.249	.411	3	2	2B-148, SS-5
1969	74	271	71	10	5	11	4.1	49	33	47	41	2	.262	.458	2	1	2B-72
1970	146	530	124	21	4	12	2.3	73	50	101	62	5	.234	.345	8	0	2B-127, SS-15, 3B-12
1971	128	477	99	16	6	18	3.8	67	57	53	67	4	.208	.379	4	2	2B-123, SS-7
1972	122	408	98	16	3	8	2.0	47	30	59	59	0	.240	.353	8	0	2B-116, SS-3, 3B-1
1973	106	343	94	18	1	12	3.5	39	47	49	52	0	.274	.437	6	1	2B-102, SS-2, DH-1
1974 BOS A	100	272	57	13	1	5	1.8	32	24	39	40	2	.210	.320	9	1	2B-53, 3B-40, DH-3, SS-3
1975	7	15	2	0	0	0	0.0	0	1	1	2	0	.133	.133	0	0	3B-7
16 yrs.	1763	6185	1530	231	71	197	3.2	888	697	882	974	63	.247	.403	67	16	2B-971, SS-666, 3B-146, DH-4
14 yrs.	1656	5898	1471	218	70	192	3.3	856	672	842	932	61	.249	.408	58	15	2B-918, SS-663, 3B-99, DH-1
								9th	10th		8th	7th		10th		6th	4th	
LEAGUE CHAMPIONSHIP SERIES																	
1972 DET A	5	20	4	0	0	1	5.0	3	1	1	4	0	.200	.350	0	0	SS-4

	G	AB	H	2B	3B	HR	HR %	R	RBI	BB	SO	SB	BA	SA	Pinch Hit AB	Pinch Hit H	G by POS

Dick McAuliffe continued

WORLD SERIES
	G	AB	H	2B	3B	HR	HR %	R	RBI	BB	SO	SB	BA	SA	AB	H	G by POS
1968 DET A	7	27	6	0	0	1	3.7	5	3	4	6	0	.222	.333	0	0	2B-7

Barney McCosky

McCOSKY, WILLIAM BARNEY
B. Apr. 11, 1918, Coal Run, Pa.
BL TR 6'1" 184 lbs.

	G	AB	H	2B	3B	HR	HR %	R	RBI	BB	SO	SB	BA	SA	AB	H	G by POS
1939 DET A	147	611	190	33	14	4	0.7	120	58	70	45	20	.311	.430	2	1	OF-145
1940	143	589	200	39	19	4	0.7	123	57	67	41	13	.340	.491	2	1	OF-141
1941	127	494	160	25	8	3	0.6	80	55	61	33	8	.324	.425	4	4	OF-122
1942	154	600	176	28	11	7	1.2	75	50	68	37	11	.293	.412	0	0	OF-154
1946 2 teams	DET A (25G – .198)				PHI A (92G – .354)												
" total	117	399	127	22	4	2	0.5	44	45	60	22	2	.318	.409	5	1	OF-109
1947 PHI A	137	546	179	22	7	1	0.2	77	52	57	29	1	.328	.399	1	0	OF-136
1948	135	515	168	21	5	0	0.0	95	46	68	22	1	.326	.386	1	1	OF-134
1950	66	179	43	10	1	0	0.0	19	11	22	12	0	.240	.307	23	5	OF-42
1951 3 teams	PHI A (12G – .296)				CIN N (25G – .320)					CLE A (31G – .213)							
" total	68	138	37	7	1	2	1.4	14	14	15	11	1	.268	.377	32	7	OF-34
1952 CLE A	54	80	17	4	1	1	1.3	14	6	8	5	1	.213	.325	30	9	OF-19
1953	22	21	4	3	0	0	0.0	3	3	1	4	0	.190	.333	21	4	
11 yrs.	1170	4172	1301	214	71	24	0.6	664	397	497	261	58	.312	.414	121	33	OF-1036
5 yrs.	596	2385	744	130	52	19	0.8	409	231	283	165	52	.312	.434	8	6	OF-586

WORLD SERIES
	G	AB	H	2B	3B	HR	HR %	R	RBI	BB	SO	SB	BA	SA	AB	H	G by POS
1940 DET A	7	23	7	1	0	0	0.0	5	1	7	0	0	.304	.348	0	0	OF-7

Benny McCoy

McCOY, BENJAMIN JENISON
B. Nov. 9, 1915, Jenison, Mich.
BL TR 5'9" 170 lbs.

	G	AB	H	2B	3B	HR	HR %	R	RBI	BB	SO	SB	BA	SA	AB	H	G by POS
1938 DET A	7	15	3	1	0	0	0.0	2	0	1	2	0	.200	.267	0	0	2B-6, 3B-1
1939	55	192	58	13	6	1	0.5	38	33	29	26	3	.302	.448	5	0	2B-34, SS-16
1940 PHI A	134	490	126	26	5	7	1.4	56	62	65	44	2	.257	.373	4	2	2B-130, 3B-1
1941	141	517	140	12	7	8	1.5	86	61	95	50	3	.271	.368	5	0	2B-135
4 yrs.	337	1214	327	52	18	16	1.3	182	156	190	122	8	.269	.381	14	2	2B-305, SS-16, 3B-2
2 yrs.	62	207	61	14	6	1	0.5	40	33	30	28	3	.295	.435	5	0	2B-40, SS-16, 3B-1

Mickey McDermott

McDERMOTT, MAURICE JOSEPH
B. Aug. 29, 1928, Poughkeepsie, N. Y.
BL TL 6'2" 170 lbs.

	G	AB	H	2B	3B	HR	HR %	R	RBI	BB	SO	SB	BA	SA	AB	H	G by POS
1948 BOS A	7	8	3	1	0	0	0.0	0	0	0	0	0	.375	.500	0	0	P-7
1949	13	33	7	3	0	0	0.0	3	6	3	6	0	.212	.303	0	0	P-12
1950	39	44	16	5	0	0	0.0	11	12	9	3	0	.364	.477	0	0	P-38
1951	43	66	18	1	1	1	1.5	8	6	3	14	0	.273	.364	3	0	P-34
1952	36	62	14	1	1	1	1.6	10	7	4	11	0	.226	.323	1	0	P-30
1953	45	93	28	8	0	1	1.1	9	13	2	13	0	.301	.419	12	1	P-32
1954 WAS A	54	95	19	3	0	0	0.0	7	4	7	12	0	.200	.232	19	3	P-30
1955	70	95	25	4	0	1	1.1	10	10	6	16	1	.263	.337	38	9	P-31
1956 NY A	46	52	11	0	0	1	1.9	4	4	8	13	0	.212	.269	19	4	P-23
1957 KC A	58	49	12	1	0	4	8.2	6	7	9	16	0	.245	.510	24	5	P-29, 1B-2
1958 DET A	4	3	1	0	0	0	0.0	0	1	0	2	0	.333	.333	2	1	P-2
1961 2 teams	STL N (22G – .071)				KC A (7G – .200)												
" total	29	19	2	2	0	0	0.0	1	4	1	6	0	.105	.211	9	2	P-23
12 yrs.	444	619	156	29	2	9	1.5	71	74	52	112	1	.252	.349	127	25	P-291, 1B-2
1 yr.	4	3	1	0	0	0	0.0	0	1	0	2	0	.333	.333	2	1	P-2

WORLD SERIES
	G	AB	H	2B	3B	HR	HR %	R	RBI	BB	SO	SB	BA	SA	AB	H	G by POS
1956 NY A	1	1	1	0	0	0	0.0	0	0	0	0	0	1.000	1.000	0	0	P-1

Red McDermott

McDERMOTT, FRANK S.
B. Nov. 12, 1889, Philadelphia, Pa. D. Sept. 11, 1964, Philadelphia, Pa.
BR TR 5'6" 150 lbs.

	G	AB	H	2B	3B	HR	HR %	R	RBI	BB	SO	SB	BA	SA	AB	H	G by POS
1912 DET A	5	15	4	1	0	0	0.0	2	0	0		1	.267	.333	0	0	OF-5

Orlando McFarlane

McFARLANE, ORLANDO JESUS
B. June 28, 1938, Oriente, Cuba
BR TR 6' 180 lbs.

	G	AB	H	2B	3B	HR	HR %	R	RBI	BB	SO	SB	BA	SA	AB	H	G by POS
1962 PIT N	8	23	2	0	0	0	0.0	0	1	1	4	0	.087	.087	0	0	C-8
1964	37	78	19	5	0	0	0.0	5	1	4	27	0	.244	.308	3	1	C-35, OF-1
1966 DET A	49	138	35	7	0	5	3.6	16	13	9	46	0	.254	.413	15	2	C-33
1967 CAL A	12	22	5	0	0	0	0.0	0	3	1	7	0	.227	.227	5	1	C-6
1968	18	31	9	0	0	0	0.0	1	2	5	9	0	.290	.290	10	3	C-7
5 yrs.	124	292	70	12	0	5	1.7	22	20	20	93	0	.240	.332	33	7	C-91, OF-1
1 yr.	49	138	35	7	0	5	3.6	16	13	9	46	0	.254	.413	15	2	C-33

Jim McGarr

McGARR, JAMES VINCENT (Reds)
B. Nov. 9, 1888, Philadelphia, Pa. D. July 21, 1981, Miami, Fla.
BR TR 5'9½" 170 lbs.

	G	AB	H	2B	3B	HR	HR %	R	RBI	BB	SO	SB	BA	SA	AB	H	G by POS
1912 DET A	1	4	0	0	0	0	0.0	0	0	0		0	.000	.000	0	0	2B-1

Dan McGarvey

McGARVEY, DANIEL
B. Unknown.

	G	AB	H	2B	3B	HR	HR %	R	RBI	BB	SO	SB	BA	SA	AB	H	G by POS
1912 DET A	1	3	0	0	0	0	0.0	0	0	1		0	.000	.000	0	0	OF-1

Deacon McGuire

McGUIRE, JAMES THOMAS
B. Nov. 2, 1865, Youngstown, Ohio D. Oct. 31, 1936, Albion, Mich.
Manager 1898, 1907-11.
BR TR 6'1" 185 lbs.

	G	AB	H	2B	3B	HR	HR %	R	RBI	BB	SO	SB	BA	SA	AB	H	G by POS
1884 TOL AA	45	151	28	7	0	1	0.7	12		5			.185	.252	0	0	C-41, OF-4, SS-3
1885 DET N	34	121	23	4	2	0	0.0	11	9	5	23		.190	.256	0	0	C-31, OF-3
1886 PHI N	50	167	33	7	1	2	1.2	25	18	19	25		.198	.287	0	0	C-49, OF-1
1887	41	150	46	6	6	2	1.3	22	23	11	8	3	.307	.467	0	0	C-41
1888 3 teams	PHI N (12G – .333)				DET N (3G – .000)					CLE AA (26G – .255)							
" total	41	158	41	5	5	1	0.6	22	24	11	13	2	.259	.373	0	0	C-30, 1B-6, OF-3, 3B-2
1890 ROC AA	87	331	99	16	4	4	1.2	46		21		8	.299	.408	0	0	C-71, 1B-15, OF-3, P-1
1891 WAS AA	114	413	125	22	10	3	0.7	55	66	43	34	10	.303	.426	0	0	C-98, OF-18, 3B-3, 1B-1

	G	AB	H	2B	3B	HR	HR %	R	RBI	BB	SO	SB	BA	SA	Pinch Hit AB	Pinch Hit H	G by POS

Deacon McGuire continued

	G	AB	H	2B	3B	HR	HR %	R	RBI	BB	SO	SB	BA	SA	Pinch Hit AB	Pinch Hit H	G by POS
1892 WAS N	97	315	73	14	4	4	1.3	46	43	61	48	7	.232	.340	0	0	C-89, 1B-8, OF-1
1893	63	237	62	14	3	1	0.4	29	26	26	12	3	.262	.359	0	0	C-50, 1B-12
1894	104	425	130	18	6	6	1.4	67	78	33	19	11	.306	.419	0	0	C-104
1895	132	533	179	30	8	10	1.9	89	97	40	18	16	.336	.478	0	0	C-132, SS-1
1896	108	389	125	25	3	2	0.5	60	70	30	14	12	.321	.416	9	2	C-98, 1B-1
1897	93	327	112	17	7	4	1.2	51	53	21		9	.343	.474	11	3	C-73, 1B-6
1898	131	489	131	18	3	1	0.2	59	57	24		10	.268	.323	3	2	C-93, 1B-37
1899 2 teams		WAS	N	(59G –	.271)		BKN	N	(46G –	.318)							
" total	105	356	104	15	5	1	0.3	47	35	28		7	.292	.371	2	0	C-102, 1B-1
1900 BKN N	71	241	69	15	2	0	0.0	20	34	19		2	.286	.365	2	1	C-69
1901	85	301	89	16	4	0	0.0	28	40	18		4	.296	.375	1	0	C-81, 1B-3
1902 DET A	73	229	52	14	1	2	0.9	27	23	24		0	.227	.323	2	0	C-70
1903	72	248	62	12	1	0	0.0	15	21	19		3	.250	.306	2	0	C-69, 1B-1
1904 NY A	101	322	67	12	2	0	0.0	17	20	27		2	.208	.258	2	2	C-97, 1B-1
1905	72	228	50	7	2	0	0.0	9	33	18		3	.219	.268	1	1	C-71
1906	51	144	43	5	0	0	0.0	11	14	12		3	.299	.333	1	0	C-49, 1B-1
1907 2 teams		NY	A	(1G –	.000)		BOS	A	(6G –	.750)							
" total	7	5	3	0	1	0	20.0	1	1	0		0	.600	1.200	4	3	C-1
1908 2 teams		BOS	A	(1G –	.000)		CLE	A	(1G –	.250)							
" total	2	5	1	1	0	0	0.0	0	2	0		0	.200	.400	1	0	1B-1
1910 CLE A	1	3	1	0	0	0	0.0	0	0	0		0	.333	.333	0	0	C-1
1912 DET A	1	2	1	0	0	0	0.0	1	0	0		0	.500	.500	0	0	C-1
26 yrs.	1781	6290	1749	300	79	45	0.7	770	786	515	214	115	.278	.372	41	14	C-1611, 1B-94, OF-33, 3B-5, SS-4, P-1
3 yrs.	146	479	115	26	2	2	0.4	43	44	43		3	.240	.315	4	0	C-140, 1B-1

John McHale

McHALE, JOHN JOSEPH
B. Sept. 21, 1921, Detroit, Mich.   BL TR 6'   200 lbs.

	G	AB	H	2B	3B	HR	HR %	R	RBI	BB	SO	SB	BA	SA	Pinch Hit AB	Pinch Hit H	G by POS
1943 DET A	4	3	0	0	0	0	0.0	0	0	1	1	0	.000	.000	3	0	
1944	1	1	0	0	0	0	0.0	0	0	0	0	0	.000	.000	1	1	
1945	19	14	2	0	0	0	0.0	0	1	1	4	0	.143	.143	14	2	1B-3
1947	39	95	20	1	0	3	3.2	10	11	7	24	1	.211	.316	15	4	1B-25
1948	1	1	0	0	0	0	0.0	0	0	0	0	0	.000	.000	1	0	
5 yrs.	64	114	22	1	0	3	2.6	10	12	9	29	1	.193	.281	34	7	1B-28
5 yrs.	64	114	22	1	0	3	2.6	10	12	9	29	1	.193	.281	34	7	1B-28

WORLD SERIES

	G	AB	H	2B	3B	HR	HR %	R	RBI	BB	SO	SB	BA	SA	Pinch Hit AB	Pinch Hit H	G by POS
1945 DET A	3	3	0	0	0	0	0.0	0	0	0	1	0	.000	.000	3	0	

Matty McIntyre

McINTYRE, MATTHEW W.
B. June 12, 1880, Stonington, Conn.   D. Apr. 2, 1920, Detroit, Mich.   BL TL

	G	AB	H	2B	3B	HR	HR %	R	RBI	BB	SO	SB	BA	SA	Pinch Hit AB	Pinch Hit H	G by POS
1901 PHI A	82	308	85	12	4	0	0.0	38	46	30		11	.276	.341	0	0	OF-82
1904 DET A	152	578	146	11	10	2	0.3	74	46	44		11	.253	.317	0	0	OF-152
1905	131	495	130	21	5	0	0.0	59	30	48		9	.263	.325	0	0	OF-131
1906	133	493	128	19	11	0	0.0	63	39	56		29	.260	.343	0	0	OF-133
1907	20	81	23	1	1	0	0.0	6	9	7		3	.284	.321	0	0	OF-20
1908	151	569	168	24	13	0	0.0	105	28	83		20	.295	.383	0	0	OF-151
1909	125	476	116	18	9	1	0.2	65	34	54		13	.244	.326	2	0	OF-122
1910	83	305	72	15	5	0	0.0	40	25	39		4	.236	.318	6	1	OF-77
1911 CHI A	146	569	184	19	11	1	0.2	102	52	64		17	.323	.401	0	0	OF-146
1912	45	84	14	0	0	0	0.0	10	10	14		3	.167	.167	0	0	OF-45
10 yrs.	1068	3958	1066	140	69	4	0.1	562	319	439		120	.269	.343	8	1	OF-1059
7 yrs.	795	2997	783	109	54	3	0.1	412	211	331		89	.261	.337	8	1	OF-786

WORLD SERIES

	G	AB	H	2B	3B	HR	HR %	R	RBI	BB	SO	SB	BA	SA	Pinch Hit AB	Pinch Hit H	G by POS
1908 DET A	5	18	4	1	0	0	0.0	2	0	3	2	1	.222	.278	0	0	OF-5
1909	4	3	0	0	0	0	0.0	0	0	0	1	0	.000	.000	3	0	OF-1
2 yrs.	9	21	4	1	0	0	0.0	2	0	3	3	1	.190	.238	3	0	OF-6

Red McKee

McKEE, RAYMOND ELLIS
B. July 20, 1890, Shawnee, Ohio   D. Aug. 5, 1972, Saginaw, Mich.   BL TR 5'11"   180 lbs.

	G	AB	H	2B	3B	HR	HR %	R	RBI	BB	SO	SB	BA	SA	Pinch Hit AB	Pinch Hit H	G by POS
1913 DET A	67	187	53	3	4	1	0.5	18	20	21	21	7	.283	.358	6	0	C-61
1914	32	64	12	1	1	0	0.0	7	8	14	16	1	.188	.234	5	1	C-27
1915	55	106	29	5	0	1	0.9	10	17	13	16	1	.274	.349	15	2	C-35
1916	32	76	16	1	2	0	0.0	3	4	6	11	0	.211	.276	6	2	C-26
4 yrs.	186	433	110	10	7	2	0.5	38	49	54	64	9	.254	.323	32	5	C-149
4 yrs.	186	433	110	10	7	2	0.5	38	49	54	64	9	.254	.323	32	5	C-149

Frank McManus

McMANUS, FRANCIS E.
B. Sept. 21, 1875, Lawrence, Mass.   D. Sept. 1, 1923, Syracuse, N. Y.   TR 5'10"

	G	AB	H	2B	3B	HR	HR %	R	RBI	BB	SO	SB	BA	SA	Pinch Hit AB	Pinch Hit H	G by POS
1899 WAS N	7	21	8	1	0	0	0.0	3	2	2		3	.381	.429	0	0	C-7
1903 BKN N	2	7	0	0	0	0	0.0	0	0	0		0	.000	.000	0	0	C-2
1904 2 teams		DET	A	(1G –	.000)		NY	A	(4G –	.000)							
" total	5	7	0	0	0	0	0.0	0	0	0		0	.000	.000	0	0	C-5
3 yrs.	14	35	8	1	0	0	0.0	3	2	2		3	.229	.257	0	0	C-14
1 yr.	1	0	0	0	0	0	0.0	0	0	0		0	–	–	0	0	C-1

Marty McManus

McMANUS, MARTIN JOSEPH
B. Mar. 14, 1900, Chicago, Ill.   D. Feb. 18, 1966, St. Louis, Mo.   BR TR 5'10½" 160 lbs.
Manager 1932-33.

	G	AB	H	2B	3B	HR	HR %	R	RBI	BB	SO	SB	BA	SA	Pinch Hit AB	Pinch Hit H	G by POS
1920 STL A	1	3	1	0	1	0	0.0	0	1	0		0	.333	1.000	0	0	3B-1
1921	121	412	107	19	8	3	0.7	49	64	27	30	5	.260	.367	0	0	2B-96, 3B-13, 1B-10, SS-2
1922	154	606	189	34	11	11	1.8	88	109	38	41	9	.312	.459	0	0	2B-153, 1B-1
1923	154	582	180	35	10	15	2.6	86	94	49	50	14	.309	.481	1	0	2B-133, 1B-20
1924	123	442	147	23	5	5	1.1	71	80	54	40	13	.333	.441	4	1	2B-118
1925	154	587	169	44	8	13	2.2	108	90	73	69	5	.288	.457	0	0	2B-154, OF-1
1926	149	549	156	30	10	9	1.6	102	68	55	62	5	.284	.424	0	0	3B-84, 2B-61, 1B-4

	G	AB	H	2B	3B	HR	HR %	R	RBI	BB	SO	SB	BA	SA	Pinch Hit AB	Pinch Hit H	G by POS

Marty McManus continued

	G	AB	H	2B	3B	HR	HR%	R	RBI	BB	SO	SB	BA	SA	PH AB	PH H	G by POS
1927 DET A	108	369	99	19	7	9	2.4	60	69	34	38	8	.268	.431	9	4	SS-39, 2B-35, 3B-22, 1B-
1928	139	500	144	37	5	8	1.6	78	73	51	32	11	.288	.430	4	1	3B-92, 1B-45, SS-1
1929	154	599	168	32	8	18	3.0	99	90	60	52	17	.280	.451	0	0	3B-150, SS-9
1930	132	484	155	40	4	9	1.9	74	89	59	28	23	.320	.475	0	0	3B-130, SS-3, 1B-1
1931 2 teams		DET	A	(107G –	.271)		BOS	A	(17G –	.290)							
" total	124	424	116	21	3	4	0.9	47	62	57	23	8	.274	.366	5	0	3B-90, 2B-28, 1B-1
1932 BOS A	93	302	71	19	4	5	1.7	39	24	36	30	1	.235	.374	15	1	2B-49, 3B-30, SS-2, 1B-1
1933	106	366	104	30	4	3	0.8	51	36	49	21	3	.284	.413	3	1	3B-76, 2B-26, 1B-4
1934 BOS N	119	435	120	18	0	8	1.8	56	47	32	42	5	.276	.372	8	2	2B-73, 3B-37
15 yrs.	1831	6660	1926	401	88	120	1.8	1008	996	674	558	127	.289	.430	49	10	2B-926, 3B-725, 1B-93, SS-56, OF-1
5 yrs.	640	2314	664	145	27	47	2.0	350	374	253	172	66	.287	.434	17	5	3B-473, 2B-56, 1B-53, SS-52

Fred McMullin

McMULLIN, FREDERICK WILLIAM   BR TR 5'11" 170 lbs.
B. Oct. 13, 1891, Scammon, Kans.   D. Nov. 21, 1952, Los Angeles, Calif.

	G	AB	H	2B	3B	HR	HR%	R	RBI	BB	SO	SB	BA	SA	PH AB	PH H	G by POS
1914 DET A	1	1	0	0	0	0	0.0	0	0	0	1	0	.000	.000	0	0	SS-1
1916 CHI A	68	187	48	3	0	0	0.0	8	10	19	30	9	.257	.273	2	1	3B-63, SS-2, 2B-1
1917	59	194	46	2	1	0	0.0	35	12	27	17	9	.237	.258	5	1	3B-52, SS-2
1918	70	235	65	7	0	1	0.4	32	16	25	26	7	.277	.319	0	0	3B-69, 2B-1
1919	60	170	50	8	4	0	0.0	31	19	11	18	4	.294	.388	8	4	3B-46, 2B-5
1920	46	127	25	1	4	0	0.0	14	13	9	13	1	.197	.268	11	1	3B-29, 2B-3, SS-1
6 yrs.	304	914	234	21	9	1	0.1	120	70	91	105	30	.256	.302	26	7	3B-259, 2B-10, SS-6
1 yr.	1	1	0	0	0	0	0.0	0	0	0	1	0	.000	.000	0	0	SS-1

WORLD SERIES

	G	AB	H	2B	3B	HR	HR%	R	RBI	BB	SO	SB	BA	SA	PH AB	PH H	G by POS
1917 CHI A	6	24	3	1	0	0	0.0	1	2	1	6	0	.125	.167	0	0	3B-6
1919	2	2	1	0	0	0	0.0	0	0	0	0	0	.500	.500	2	1	
2 yrs.	8	26	4	1	0	0	0.0	1	2	1	6	0	.154	.192	2	1	3B-6

Carl McNabb

McNABB, CARL MAC (Skinny)   BR TR 5'9" 155 lbs.
B. Jan. 25, 1917, Stevenson, Ala.

	G	AB	H	2B	3B	HR	HR%	R	RBI	BB	SO	SB	BA	SA	PH AB	PH H	G by POS
1945 DET A	1	1	0	0	0	0	0.0	0	0	0	1	0	.000	.000	1	0	

Eric McNair

McNAIR, DONALD ERIC (Boob)   BR TR 5'8" 160 lbs.
B. Apr. 12, 1909, Meridian, Miss.   D. Mar. 11, 1949, Meridian, Miss.

	G	AB	H	2B	3B	HR	HR%	R	RBI	BB	SO	SB	BA	SA	PH AB	PH H	G by POS
1929 PHI A	4	8	4	1	0	0	0.0	2	3	0	0	1	.500	.625	0	0	SS-4
1930	78	237	63	12	2	0	0.0	27	34	9	19	5	.266	.333	7	1	SS-31, 3B-29, 2B-5, OF-
1931	79	280	76	10	1	5	1.8	41	33	11	19	1	.271	.368	3	1	3B-47, 2B-16, SS-13
1932	135	554	158	47	3	18	3.2	87	95	28	29	8	.285	.478	2	0	SS-133
1933	89	310	81	15	4	7	2.3	57	48	15	32	2	.261	.403	16	5	SS-46, 2B-28
1934	151	599	168	20	4	17	2.8	80	82	35	42	7	.280	.412	0	0	SS-151
1935	137	526	142	22	2	4	0.8	55	57	35	33	3	.270	.342	3	0	SS-121, 3B-11, 1B-2
1936 BOS A	128	494	141	36	2	4	0.8	68	74	27	34	3	.285	.391	0	0	SS-84, 2B-35, 3B-11
1937	126	455	133	29	4	12	2.6	60	76	30	33	10	.292	.453	9	2	2B-106, SS-9, 3B-4, 1B-1
1938	46	96	15	1	1	0	0.0	9	7	3	6	0	.156	.188	14	2	SS-15, 2B-14, 3B-3
1939 CHI A	129	479	155	18	5	7	1.5	62	82	38	41	17	.324	.426	1	0	3B-103, 2B-19, SS-9
1940	66	251	57	13	1	7	2.8	26	31	12	26	1	.227	.371	0	0	2B-65, 3B-1
1941 DET A	23	59	11	1	0	0	0.0	5	3	4	4	0	.186	.203	9	3	3B-11, SS-3
1942 2 teams		DET	A	(34G –	.162)		PHI	A	(34G –	.243)							
" total	60	171	36	4	0	1	0.6	13	14	10	1	1	.211	.251	8	1	SS-50, 2B-1
14 yrs.	1251	4519	1240	229	29	82	1.8	592	633	261	328	59	.274	.392	72	15	SS-669, 2B-289, 3B-220, 1B-3, OF-1
2 yrs.	49	127	22	3	0	1	0.8	10	7	7	9	0	.173	.220	14	4	SS-24, 3B-11

WORLD SERIES

	G	AB	H	2B	3B	HR	HR%	R	RBI	BB	SO	SB	BA	SA	PH AB	PH H	G by POS
1930 PHI A	1	1	0	0	0	0	0.0	0	0	0	0	0	.000	.000	1	0	
1931	2	2	0	0	0	0	0.0	1	0	0	1	0	.000	.000	1	0	2B-1
2 yrs.	3	3	0	0	0	0	0.0	1	0	0	1	0	.000	.000	2	0	2B-1

Pat Meaney

MEANEY, PATRICK J.   TR
B. 1892, Philadelphia, Pa.   D. Oct. 20, 1922, Philadelphia, Pa.

	G	AB	H	2B	3B	HR	HR%	R	RBI	BB	SO	SB	BA	SA	PH AB	PH H	G by POS
1912 DET A	1	2	0	0	0	0	0.0	0	0	1		0	.000	.000	0	0	SS-1

Win Mercer

MERCER, GEORGE BARCLAY   TR 5'7" 140 lbs.
B. June 20, 1874, Chester, W. Va.   D. Jan. 12, 1903, San Francisco, Calif.

	G	AB	H	2B	3B	HR	HR%	R	RBI	BB	SO	SB	BA	SA	PH AB	PH H	G by POS
1894 WAS N	52	162	46	5	2	2	1.2	27	29	9	20	9	.284	.377	0	0	P-49, OF-4
1895	63	196	50	9	1	1	0.5	26	26	12	32	7	.255	.327	5	2	P-43, SS-7, OF-5, 3B-3, 2B-1
1896	49	156	38	1	1	1	0.6	23	14	9	18	9	.244	.282	2	1	P-46, OF-1
1897	48	135	43	2	5	0	0.0	22	19	6		7	.319	.407	2	0	P-46, OF-1
1898	80	249	80	3	5	2	0.8	38	25	18		14	.321	.398	2	1	P-33, SS-23, OF-19, 3B-5, 2B-1
1899	108	375	112	6	7	1	0.3	73	35	32		16	.299	.360	6	0	P-62, P-23, OF-16, 3B-1, 1B-1
1900 NY N	75	248	73	4	0	0	0.0	32	27	26		15	.294	.310	1	0	P-32, 3B-19, OF-14, SS-7, 2B-3
1901 WAS A	51	140	42	7	2	0	0.0	26	16	23		10	.300	.379	4	0	P-24, OF-16, 1B-7, SS-1, 3B-1
1902 DET A	35	100	18	2	0	0	0.0	8	6	6		1	.180	.200	0	0	P-35
9 yrs.	561	1761	502	39	23	7	0.4	275	197	141	70	88	.285	.345	22	4	P-285, 3B-90, OF-75, SS-39, 1B-8, 2B-5
1 yr.	35	100	18	2	0	0	0.0	8	6	6		1	.180	.200	0	0	P-35

Herm Merritt

MERRITT, HERMAN G.   BR TR
B. Nov. 12, 1900, Independence, Kans.   D. May 26, 1957, Kansas City, Mo.

	G	AB	H	2B	3B	HR	HR%	R	RBI	BB	SO	SB	BA	SA	PH AB	PH H	G by POS
1921 DET A	20	46	17	1	2	0	0.0	3	6	1	5	1	.370	.478	1	0	SS-17

	G	AB	H	2B	3B	HR	HR %	R	RBI	BB	SO	SB	BA	SA	Pinch Hit AB	Pinch Hit H	G by POS

Scat Metha

METHA, FRANK JOSEPH   BR TR 5'11" 165 lbs.
B. Dec. 13, 1913, Los Angeles, Calif.   D. Mar. 2, 1975, Fountain Valley, Calif.

	G	AB	H	2B	3B	HR	HR %	R	RBI	BB	SO	SB	BA	SA	PH AB	PH H	G by POS
1940 DET A	26	37	9	0	1	0	0.0	6	3	2	8	0	.243	.297	2	0	2B-10, 3B-6

Charlie Metro

METRO, CHARLES
Born Charles Moreskonich.
B. Apr. 28, 1919, Nanty-Glo, Pa.
Manager 1962, 1970.   BR TR 5'11½" 178 lbs.

	G	AB	H	2B	3B	HR	HR %	R	RBI	BB	SO	SB	BA	SA	PH AB	PH H	G by POS
1943 DET A	44	40	8	0	0	0	0.0	2	2	3	6	1	.200	.200	2	0	OF-14
1944 2 teams	DET	A (38G – .192)		PHI	A (24G – .100)												
" total	62	118	19	0	1	0	0.0	12	6	10	16	1	.161	.178	8	2	OF-31, 3B-5, 2B-2
1945 PHI A	65	200	42	10	1	3	1.5	18	15	23	33	1	.210	.315	9	3	OF-57
3 yrs.	171	358	69	10	2	3	0.8	42	23	36	55	3	.193	.257	19	5	OF-102, 3B-5, 2B-2
2 yrs.	82	118	23	0	1	0	0.0	20	7	6	16	2	.195	.212	7	2	OF-34

Dan Meyer

MEYER, DANIEL THOMAS   BL TR 5'11" 180 lbs.
B. Aug. 3, 1952, Hamilton, Ohio

	G	AB	H	2B	3B	HR	HR %	R	RBI	BB	SO	SB	BA	SA	PH AB	PH H	G by POS
1974 DET A	13	50	10	1	1	3	6.0	5	7	1	1	1	.200	.440	1	0	OF-12
1975	122	470	111	17	3	8	1.7	56	47	26	25	8	.236	.336	2	1	OF-74, 1B-46
1976	105	294	74	8	4	2	0.7	37	16	17	22	10	.252	.327	36	8	OF-47, 1B-19
1977 SEA A	159	582	159	24	4	22	3.8	75	90	43	51	11	.273	.442	2	0	1B-159
1978	123	444	101	18	1	8	1.8	38	56	24	39	7	.227	.327	1	0	1B-121, OF-2
1979	144	525	146	21	7	20	3.8	72	74	29	35	11	.278	.459	7	2	3B-101, OF-31, 1B-15
1980	146	531	146	25	6	11	2.1	56	71	31	42	8	.275	.407	17	3	OF-123, DH-7, 3B-5, 1B-4
1981	83	252	66	10	1	3	1.2	26	22	10	16	4	.262	.345	19	3	3B-49, OF-14, DH-3, 1B-3
1982 OAK A	120	383	92	17	3	8	2.1	28	59	19	33	1	.240	.363	29	4	1B-58, DH-38, OF-11
1983	69	169	32	9	0	1	0.6	15	13	19	11	0	.189	.260	7	1	1B-41, DH-12, OF-11, 3B-1
1984	20	22	7	3	1	0	0.0	1	4	0	2	0	.318	.545	17	4	1B-3, DH-2
11 yrs.	1104	3722	944	153	31	86	2.3	409	459	219	277	61	.254	.381	138	26	1B-469, OF-325, 3B-156, DH-62
3 yrs.	240	814	195	26	8	13	1.6	98	70	44	48	19	.240	.339	39	9	OF-133, 1B-65

Dutch Meyer

MEYER, LAMBERT DANIEL   BR TR 5'10½" 181 lbs.
B. Oct. 6, 1915, Waco, Tex.

	G	AB	H	2B	3B	HR	HR %	R	RBI	BB	SO	SB	BA	SA	PH AB	PH H	G by POS
1937 CHI N	1	0	0	0	0	0	–	0	0	0	0	0	–	–	0	0	
1940 DET A	23	58	15	3	0	0	0.0	12	6	4	10	2	.259	.310	3	0	2B-21
1941	46	153	29	9	1	1	0.7	12	14	8	13	1	.190	.281	6	2	2B-40
1942	14	52	17	3	0	2	3.8	5	9	4	4	0	.327	.500	0	0	2B-14
1945 CLE A	130	524	153	29	8	7	1.3	71	48	40	32	2	.292	.418	0	0	2B-130
1946	72	207	48	5	3	0	0.0	13	16	26	16	0	.232	.285	7	1	2B-64
6 yrs.	286	994	262	49	12	10	1.0	113	93	82	75	5	.264	.367	16	3	2B-269
3 yrs.	83	263	61	15	1	3	1.1	29	29	16	27	3	.232	.331	9	2	2B-75

Gene Michael

MICHAEL, GENE RICHARD (Stick)   BB TR 6'2" 183 lbs.
B. June 2, 1938, Kent, Ohio
Manager 1981-82.

	G	AB	H	2B	3B	HR	HR %	R	RBI	BB	SO	SB	BA	SA	PH AB	PH H	G by POS
1966 PIT N	30	33	5	2	1	0	0.0	9	2	0	7	0	.152	.273	10	3	SS-8, 2B-2, 3B-1
1967 LA N	98	223	45	3	1	0	0.0	20	7	11	30	1	.202	.224	2	0	SS-83
1968 NY A	61	116	23	3	0	1	0.9	8	8	2	23	3	.198	.250	0	0	SS-43, P-1
1969	119	412	112	24	4	2	0.5	41	31	43	56	7	.272	.364	1	0	SS-118
1970	134	435	93	10	1	2	0.5	42	38	50	93	3	.214	.255	6	4	SS-123, 3B-4, 2B-3
1971	139	456	102	15	0	3	0.7	36	35	48	64	3	.224	.276	6	2	SS-136
1972	126	391	91	7	4	1	0.3	29	32	32	45	4	.233	.279	5	2	SS-121
1973	129	418	94	11	1	3	0.7	30	47	26	51	1	.225	.278	0	0	SS-129
1974	81	177	46	9	0	0	0.0	19	13	14	24	0	.260	.311	1	1	2B-45, SS-39, 3B-2
1975 DET A	56	145	31	2	0	3	2.1	15	13	8	28	0	.214	.290	1	1	SS-44, 2B-7, 3B-4
10 yrs.	973	2806	642	86	12	15	0.5	249	226	234	421	22	.229	.284	32	13	SS-844, 2B-57, 3B-11, P-1
1 yr.	56	145	31	2	0	3	2.1	15	13	8	28	0	.214	.290	1	1	SS-44, 2B-7, 3B-4

Ed Mierkowicz

MIERKOWICZ, EDWARD FRANK (Butch)   BR TR 6'4" 205 lbs.
B. Mar. 6, 1924, Wyandotte, Mich.

	G	AB	H	2B	3B	HR	HR %	R	RBI	BB	SO	SB	BA	SA	PH AB	PH H	G by POS
1945 DET A	10	15	2	2	0	0	0.0	2	2	1	3	0	.133	.267	3	1	OF-6
1947	21	42	8	1	0	1	2.4	6	1	1	12	1	.190	.286	9	1	OF-10
1948	3	5	1	0	0	0	0.0	0	1	2	2	0	.200	.200	2	0	OF-1
1950 STL N	1	1	0	0	0	0	0.0	0	0	0	1	0	.000	.000	1	0	
4 yrs.	35	63	11	3	0	1	1.6	6	4	4	18	1	.175	.270	15	2	OF-17
3 yrs.	34	62	11	3	0	1	1.6	6	4	4	17	1	.177	.274	14	2	OF-17

WORLD SERIES

	G	AB	H	2B	3B	HR	HR %	R	RBI	BB	SO	SB	BA	SA	PH AB	PH H	G by POS
1945 DET A	1	0	0	0	0	0	–	0	0	0	0	0	–	–	0	0	OF-1

Eddie Miller

MILLER, EDWARD LEE   BB TR 5'9" 175 lbs.
B. June 29, 1957, San Pablo, Calif.

	G	AB	H	2B	3B	HR	HR %	R	RBI	BB	SO	SB	BA	SA	PH AB	PH H	G by POS
1977 TEX A	17	6	2	0	0	0	0.0	7	1	1	1	3	.333	.333	0	0	DH-3, OF-2
1978 ATL N	6	21	3	1	0	0	0.0	5	2	2	4	3	.143	.190	0	0	OF-5
1979	27	113	35	1	0	0	0.0	12	5	5	24	15	.310	.319	0	0	OF-27
1980	11	19	3	0	0	0	0.0	3	0	0	5	1	.158	.158	0	0	OF-9
1981	50	134	31	3	1	0	0.0	29	7	7	29	23	.231	.269	6	2	OF-36
1982 DET A	14	25	1	0	0	0	0.0	3	0	4	4	0	.040	.040	1	0	OF-8, DH-1
1984 SD N	13	14	4	0	1	1	7.1	4	2	0	4	4	.286	.643	1	0	OF-8
7 yrs.	138	332	79	5	2	1	0.3	63	17	19	71	49	.238	.274	8	2	OF-95, DH-4
1 yr.	14	25	1	0	0	0	0.0	3	0	4	4	0	.040	.040	1	0	OF-8, DH-1

Jack Miller

MILLER, JAMES ELDRIDGE   BR TR 5'11½" 215 lbs.
B. Feb. 13, 1911, Celeste, Tex.   D. Nov. 21, 1966, Dallas, Tex.

	G	AB	H	2B	3B	HR	HR %	R	RBI	BB	SO	SB	BA	SA	PH AB	PH H	G by POS
1944 DET A	5	5	1	0	0	1	20.0	1	3	1	1	0	.200	.800	0	0	C-5

	G	AB	H	2B	3B	HR	HR %	R	RBI	BB	SO	SB	BA	SA	Pinch Hit AB	Pinch Hit H	G by POS

Hack Miller *continued*

	G	AB	H	2B	3B	HR	HR %	R	RBI	BB	SO	SB	BA	SA	AB	H	G by POS
1945	2	4	3	0	0	0	0.0	0	1	0	0	0	.750	.750	0	0	C-2
2 yrs.	7	9	4	0	0	1	11.1	1	4	1	1	0	.444	.778	0	0	C-7
2 yrs.	7	9	4	0	0	1	11.1	1	4	1	1	0	.444	.778	0	0	C-7

Clarence Mitchell

MITCHELL, CLARENCE ELMER   BL TL 5'11½" 190 lbs
B. Feb. 22, 1891, Franklin, Neb.   D. Nov. 6, 1963, Grand Island, Neb.

	G	AB	H	2B	3B	HR	HR %	R	RBI	BB	SO	SB	BA	SA	AB	H	G by POS
1911 DET A	5	4	2	0	0	0	0.0	2	0	1		0	.500	.500	0	0	P-5
1916 CIN N	56	117	28	2	1	0	0.0	11	11	4	6	1	.239	.274	14	4	P-29, 1B-9, OF-3
1917	47	90	25	3	0	0	0.0	13	5	5	5	0	.278	.311	1	0	P-32, 1B-6, OF-5
1918 BKN N	10	24	6	1	1	0	0.0	2	2	0	3	0	.250	.375	2	0	OF-6, 1B-2, P-1
1919	34	49	18	1	0	1	2.0	7	2	4	4	0	.367	.449	9	3	P-23
1920	55	107	25	2	2	0	0.0	9	11	8	9	1	.234	.290	18	6	P-19, 1B-11, OF-4
1921	46	91	24	5	0	0	0.0	11	12	5	7	3	.264	.319	3	0	P-37, 1B-4
1922	55	155	45	6	3	3	1.9	21	28	19	6	0	.290	.426	9	4	1B-42, P-5
1923 PHI N	53	78	21	3	2	1	1.3	10	9	4	11	0	.269	.397	24	6	P-29
1924	69	102	26	3	0	0	0.0	7	13	2	7	1	.255	.284	37	6	P-30
1925	52	92	18	2	0	0	0.0	7	13	5	9	2	.196	.217	17	1	P-32, 1B-2
1926	39	78	19	4	0	0	0.0	8	6	5	5	0	.244	.295	7	1	P-28, 1B-4
1927	18	42	10	2	0	1	2.4	5	6	2	1	0	.238	.357	3	0	P-13
1928 2 teams		PHI	N (5G – .250)		STL	N	(19G – .125)										
" total	24	60	8	1	0	0	0.0	1	0	3	0	0	.133	.150	1	0	P-22
1929 STL N	26	66	18	3	1	0	0.0	9	9	4	6	1	.273	.348	0	0	P-25
1930 2 teams		STL	N (1G – .500)		NY	N	(24G – .255)										
" total	25	49	13	1	0	0	0.0	9	1	1	5	0	.265	.286	0	0	P-25
1931 NY N	27	73	16	2	0	1	1.4	5	4	2	4	0	.219	.288	0	0	P-27
1932	8	10	2	0	0	0	0.0	2	0	1		0	.200	.200	0	0	P-8
18 yrs.	649	1287	324	41	10	7	0.5	138	133	72	92	9	.252	.315	145	31	P-390, 1B-80, OF-18
1 yr.	5	4	2	0	0	0	0.0	2	0	1		0	.500	.500	0	0	P-5
WORLD SERIES																	
1920 BKN N	2	3	1	0	0	0	0.0	0	0	0	0	0	.333	.333	1	1	P-1
1928 STL N	1	2	0	0	0	0	0.0	0	0	0	0	0	.000	.000	0	0	P-1
2 yrs.	3	5	1	0	0	0	0.0	0	0	0	0	0	.200	.200	1	1	P-2

John Mohardt

MOHARDT, JOHN HENRY   BR TR 5'10" 165 lbs
B. Jan. 23, 1898, Pittsburgh, Pa.   D. Nov. 24, 1961, La Jolla, Calif.

	G	AB	H	2B	3B	HR	HR %	R	RBI	BB	SO	SB	BA	SA	AB	H	G by POS
1922 DET A	5	1	1	0	0	0	0.0	2	0	1		0	1.000	1.000	0	0	OF-3

Bob Molinaro

MOLINARO, ROBERT JOSEPH (Molly)   BL TR 6' 180 lbs
B. May 21, 1950, Newark, N. J.

	G	AB	H	2B	3B	HR	HR %	R	RBI	BB	SO	SB	BA	SA	AB	H	G by POS
1975 DET A	6	19	5	0	1	0	0.0	2	1	1		0	0	.263	.368	0	0	OF-6
1977 2 teams		DET	A (4G – .250)		CHI	A	(1G – .500)										
" total	5	6	2	1	0	0	0.0	0	0	0	3	1	.333	.500	4	1	OF-1
1978 CHI A	105	286	75	5	6	6	2.1	39	27	19	12	22	.262	.378	12	4	OF-62, DH-32
1979 BAL A	8	6	0	0	0	0	0.0	0	0	1	3	1	.000	.000	1	0	OF-5
1980 CHI A	119	344	100	16	4	5	1.5	48	36	26	29	18	.291	.404	21	7	OF-49, DH-47
1981	47	42	11	1	1	1	2.4	7	9	8	1	1	.262	.405	35	9	DH-4, OF-2
1982 2 teams		CHI	N (65G – .197)		PHI	N	(19G – .286)										
" total	84	80	17	1	0	1	1.3	6	14	9	6	2	.213	.263	67	14	OF-4
1983 2 teams		PHI	N (19G – .111)		DET	A	(8G – .000)										
" total	27	20	2	1	0	1	5.0	4	3	1	3	1	.100	.300	20	2	DH-1
8 yrs.	401	803	212	25	11	14	1.7	106	90	65	57	46	.264	.375	160	37	OF-129, DH-84
3 yrs.	18	25	6	1	1	0	0.0	5	1	2	3	1	.240	.360	6	1	OF-6, DH-1

Anse Moore

MOORE, ANSELM WINN   BL TR 6'1" 190 lbs
B. Sept. 22, 1917, Delhi, La.

	G	AB	H	2B	3B	HR	HR %	R	RBI	BB	SO	SB	BA	SA	AB	H	G by POS
1946 DET A	51	134	28	4	0	1	0.7	16	8	12	9	1	.209	.261	16	4	OF-32

Jackie Moore

MOORE, JACKIE SPENCER   BR TR 6' 180 lbs.
B. Feb. 19, 1939, Jay, Fla.
Manager 1984.

	G	AB	H	2B	3B	HR	HR %	R	RBI	BB	SO	SB	BA	SA	AB	H	G by POS
1965 DET A	21	53	5	0	0	0	0.0	2	2	6	12	0	.094	.094	1	0	C-20

Jerry Morales

MORALES, JULIO RUBEN   BR TR 5'10" 155 lbs.
B. Feb. 18, 1949, Yabucoa, Puerto Rico

	G	AB	H	2B	3B	HR	HR %	R	RBI	BB	SO	SB	BA	SA	AB	H	G by POS
1969 SD N	19	41	8	2	0	1	2.4	5	6	5	7	0	.195	.317	0	0	OF-19
1970	28	58	9	0	1	1	1.7	6	4	3	11	0	.155	.241	2	0	OF-26
1971	12	17	2	0	0	0	0.0	1	1	2	2	1	.118	.118	2	0	OF-7
1972	115	347	83	15	7	4	1.2	38	18	35	54	4	.239	.357	19	3	OF-96, 3B-4
1973	122	388	109	23	2	9	2.3	47	34	27	55	6	.281	.420	22	9	OF-100
1974 CHI N	151	534	146	21	7	15	2.8	70	82	46	63	2	.273	.423	8	2	OF-143
1975	153	578	156	21	0	12	2.1	62	91	50	65	3	.270	.369	2	2	OF-151
1976	140	537	147	17	0	16	3.0	66	67	41	49	3	.274	.395	5	1	OF-136
1977	136	490	142	34	5	11	2.2	56	69	43	75	0	.290	.447	11	3	OF-128
1978 STL N	130	457	109	19	8	4	0.9	44	46	33	44	4	.239	.341	8	1	OF-126
1979 DET A	129	440	93	23	1	14	3.2	50	56	30	56	10	.211	.364	7	0	OF-119, DH-7
1980 NY N	94	193	49	7	1	3	1.6	19	30	13	31	2	.254	.347	30	7	OF-63
1981 CHI N	84	245	70	6	2	1	0.4	27	25	22	29	1	.286	.339	12	3	OF-72
1982	65	116	33	2	2	4	3.4	14	30	9	7	1	.284	.440	30	10	OF-41
1983	63	87	17	9	0	0	0.0	11	11	7	19	0	.195	.299	41	8	OF-29
15 yrs.	1441	4528	1173	199	36	95	2.1	516	570	366	567	37	.259	.382	199	49	OF-1256, DH-7, 3B-4
1 yr.	129	440	93	23	1	14	3.2	50	56	30	56	10	.211	.364	7	0	OF-119, DH-7

	G	AB	H	2B	3B	HR	HR %	R	RBI	BB	SO	SB	BA	SA	Pinch Hit AB	Pinch Hit H	G by POS

Chet Morgan — MORGAN, CHESTER COLLINS (Chick)
B. June 6, 1910, Cleveland, Miss.   BL TR 5'9" 160 lbs.

	G	AB	H	2B	3B	HR	HR %	R	RBI	BB	SO	SB	BA	SA	PH AB	PH H	G by POS
'35 DET A	14	23	4	1	0	0	0.0	2	1	5	0	0	.174	.217	9	1	OF-4
'38	74	306	87	6	1	0	0.0	50	27	20	12	5	.284	.310	0	0	OF-74
2 yrs.	88	329	91	7	1	0	0.0	52	28	25	12	5	.277	.304	9	1	OF-78
2 yrs.	88	329	91	7	1	0	0.0	52	28	25	12	5	.277	.304	9	1	OF-78

George Moriarty — MORIARTY, GEORGE JOSEPH
Brother of Bill Moriarty.
B. July 7, 1884, Chicago, Ill.   D. Apr. 8, 1964, Miami, Fla.
Manager 1927-28.   BR TR 6' 185 lbs.

	G	AB	H	2B	3B	HR	HR %	R	RBI	BB	SO	SB	BA	SA	PH AB	PH H	G by POS
'03 CHI N	1	5	0	0	0	0	0.0	1	0	0		0	.000	.000	0	0	3B-1
'04	4	13	0	0	0	0	0.0	0	0	1		0	.000	.000	0	0	OF-2, 3B-2
'06 NY A	65	197	46	7	7	0	0.0	22	23	17		8	.234	.340	4	1	3B-39, OF-15, 1B-5, 2B-1
'07	126	437	121	16	5	0	0.0	51	43	25		28	.277	.336	1	0	3B-91, 1B-22, OF-9, 2B-8, SS-1
'08	101	348	82	12	1	0	0.0	25	27	11		22	.236	.276	8	2	1B-52, 3B-28, OF-10, 2B-4
'09 DET A	133	473	129	20	4	1	0.2	43	39	24		34	.273	.338	3	1	3B-106, 1B-24
'10	136	490	123	24	3	2	0.4	53	60	33		33	.251	.324	1	0	3B-134
'11	130	478	116	20	4	1	0.2	51	60	27		28	.243	.308	0	0	3B-129, 1B-1
'12	105	375	93	23	1	0	0.0	38	54	26		27	.248	.315	1	1	1B-71, 3B-33
'13	102	347	83	5	2	0	0.0	29	30	24	25	33	.239	.265	0	0	3B-93, OF-7
'14	130	465	118	19	5	1	0.2	56	40	39	27	34	.254	.323	0	0	3B-126, 1B-3
'15	31	38	8	1	0	0	0.0	2	0	5	7	1	.211	.237	10	2	3B-12, OF-1, 2B-1, 1B-1
'16 CHI A	7	5	1	0	0	0	0.0	1	0	2	0	0	.200	.200	3	1	3B-1, 1B-1
13 yrs.	1071	3671	920	147	32	5	0.1	372	376	234	59	248	.251	.312	31	8	3B-795, 1B-180, OF-44, 2B-14, SS-1
7 yrs.	767	2666	670	112	19	5	0.2	272	283	178	59	190 5th	.251	.313	15	4	3B-633, 1B-100, OF-8, 2B-1

WORLD SERIES

	G	AB	H	2B	3B	HR	HR %	R	RBI	BB	SO	SB	BA	SA	PH AB	PH H	G by POS
'09 DET A	7	22	6	1	0	0	0.0	4	1	3	1	0	.273	.318	0	0	3B-7

Bubba Morton — MORTON, WYCLIFFE NATHANIEL
B. Dec. 13, 1931, Washington, D. C.   BR TR 5'10" 175 lbs.

	G	AB	H	2B	3B	HR	HR %	R	RBI	BB	SO	SB	BA	SA	PH AB	PH H	G by POS
'61 DET A	77	108	31	5	1	2	1.9	26	19	9	25	3	.287	.407	37	11	OF-30
'62	90	195	51	6	3	4	2.1	30	17	32	32	1	.262	.385	21	5	OF-62, 1B-3
'63 2 teams	DET A (6G – .091)			MIL N (15G – .179)													
total	21	39	6	0	0	0	0.0	3	6	4	4	0	.154	.154	10	1	OF-12
'66 CAL A	15	50	11	1	0	0	0.0	4	4	2	6	1	.220	.240	0	0	OF-14
'67	80	201	63	9	3	0	0.0	23	32	22	29	0	.313	.388	25	8	OF-61
'68	81	163	44	6	0	1	0.6	13	18	14	18	2	.270	.325	33	10	OF-50, 3B-1
'69	87	172	42	10	1	7	4.1	18	32	28	29	0	.244	.436	34	10	OF-49, 1B-1
7 yrs.	451	928	248	37	8	14	1.5	117	128	111	143	7	.267	.370	160	45	OF-278, 1B-4, 3B-1
3 yrs.	173	314	83	11	4	6	1.9	58	38	43	58	4	.264	.382	59	16	OF-95, 1B-3

Jerry Moses — MOSES, GERALD BRAHEEN
B. Aug. 9, 1946, Yazoo City, Miss.   BR TR 6'3" 210 lbs.

	G	AB	H	2B	3B	HR	HR %	R	RBI	BB	SO	SB	BA	SA	PH AB	PH H	G by POS
'65 BOS A	4	4	1	0	0	1	25.0	1	1	0	2	0	.250	1.000	4	1	
'68	6	18	6	0	0	2	11.1	2	4	1	4	0	.333	.667	0	0	C-6
'69	53	135	41	9	1	4	3.0	13	17	5	23	0	.304	.474	17	2	C-36
'70	92	315	83	18	1	6	1.9	26	35	21	45	1	.263	.384	5	2	C-88, OF-1
'71 CAL A	69	181	41	8	2	4	2.2	12	15	10	34	0	.227	.359	8	0	C-63, OF-1
'72 CLE A	52	141	31	3	0	4	2.8	9	14	11	29	0	.220	.326	10	2	C-39, 1B-3
'73 NY A	21	59	15	2	0	0	0.0	5	3	2	6	0	.254	.288	3	1	C-17, DH-1
'74 DET A	74	198	47	6	3	4	2.0	19	19	11	38	0	.237	.359	1	0	C-74
'75 2 teams	CHI A (13G – .500)			SD N (13G – .158)													
total	15	21	4	2	1	0	0.0	2	1	2	3	0	.190	.381	6	1	C-5, DH-1, 1B-1
9 yrs.	386	1072	269	48	8	25	2.3	89	109	63	184	1	.251	.381	54	9	C-328, 1B-4, DH-2, OF-2
1 yr.	74	198	47	6	3	4	2.0	19	19	11	38	0	.237	.359	1	0	C-74

Billy Mullen — MULLEN, WILLIAM JOHN
B. Jan. 23, 1896, St. Louis, Mo.   D. May 4, 1971, St. Louis, Mo.   BR TR 5'8" 160 lbs.

	G	AB	H	2B	3B	HR	HR %	R	RBI	BB	SO	SB	BA	SA	PH AB	PH H	G by POS
'20 STL A	1	1	0	0	0	0	0.0	0	0	0	0	0	.000	.000	1	0	
'21	4	4	0	0	0	0	0.0	0	0	2	1	0	.000	.000	2	0	3B-2
'23 BKN N	4	11	3	0	0	0	0.0	1	0	0	0	0	.273	.273	0	0	3B-4
'26 DET A	11	13	1	0	0	0	0.0	2	0	5	1	1	.077	.077	2	0	3B-9
'28 STL A	15	18	7	1	0	0	0.0	2	2	3	4	0	.389	.444	8	3	3B-6
5 yrs.	35	47	11	1	0	0	0.0	5	2	10	6	1	.234	.255	13	3	3B-21
1 yr.	11	13	1	0	0	0	0.0	2	0	5	1	1	.077	.077	2	0	3B-9

George Mullin — MULLIN, GEORGE JOSEPH (Wabash George)
B. July 4, 1880, Toledo, Ohio   D. Jan. 7, 1944, Wabash, Ind.   BR TR 5'11" 188 lbs.

	G	AB	H	2B	3B	HR	HR %	R	RBI	BB	SO	SB	BA	SA	PH AB	PH H	G by POS
'02 DET A	40	120	39	4	3	0	0.0	20	11	8		1	.325	.408	2	0	P-35, OF-4
'03	46	126	35	9	1	1	0.8	11	12	2		1	.278	.389	4	1	P-41, OF-1
'04	53	151	45	11	2	0	0.0	14	8	10		1	.298	.397	6	2	P-45, OF-2
'05	47	135	35	4	0	0	0.0	15	12	12		4	.259	.289	2	0	P-44
'06	50	142	32	6	4	0	0.0	13	6	4		2	.225	.324	8	3	P-40
'07	70	157	34	5	3	0	0.0	16	13	12		2	.217	.287	20	5	P-46
'08	55	125	32	2	2	1	0.8	13	8	7		2	.256	.328	14	3	P-39
'09	53	126	27	7	0	0	0.0	13	17	13		2	.214	.270	10	1	P-40, OF-2
'10	50	129	33	6	2	1	0.8	15	11	8		1	.256	.357	9	0	P-38, OF-2
'11	40	98	28	7	2	0	0.0	4	5	10		1	.286	.398	8	2	P-30
'12	38	90	25	5	1	0	0.0	13	12	17		0	.278	.356	8	1	P-30
'13 2 teams	DET A (12G – .350)			WAS A (12G – .190)													
total	24	41	11	0	0	0	0.0	5	1	6	6	1	.268	.268	3	1	P-19
'14 IND F	43	77	24	5	3	0	0.0	11	21	11		0	.312	.455	1	1	P-36

	G	AB	H	2B	3B	HR	HR %	R	RBI	BB	SO	SB	BA	SA	Pinch Hit AB	H	G by POS

George Mullin continued

	G	AB	H	2B	3B	HR	HR%	R	RBI	BB	SO	SB	BA	SA	PH AB	PH H	G by POS
1915 NWK F	6	10	1	0	0	0	0.0	0	0	2		0	.100	.100	1	0	P-5
14 yrs.	615	1527	401	71	23	3	0.2	163	137	122	6	18	.263	.345	101	20	P-488, OF-11
12 yrs.	554	1419	372	66	20	3	0.2	148	116	107	1	17	.262	.343	94	19	P-435, OF-11

WORLD SERIES

	G	AB	H	2B	3B	HR	HR%	R	RBI	BB	SO	SB	BA	SA	PH AB	PH H	G by POS
1907 DET A	2	6	0	0	0	0	0.0	0	0	0	1	0	.000	.000	0	0	P-2
1908	1	3	1	0	0	0	0.0	1	1	1	0	0	.333	.333	0	0	P-1
1909	6	16	3	1	0	0	0.0	1	0	1	3	0	.188	.250	2	0	P-4
3 yrs.	9	25	4	1	0	0	0.0	2	1	2	4	0	.160	.200	2	0	P-7

Pat Mullin

MULLIN, PATRICK JOSEPH — B. Nov. 1, 1917, Trotter, Pa. — BL TR 6'2" 190 lb

	G	AB	H	2B	3B	HR	HR%	R	RBI	BB	SO	SB	BA	SA	PH AB	PH H	G by POS
1940 DET A	4	4	0	0	0	0	0.0	0	0	0	0	0	.000	.000	3	0	OF-1
1941	54	220	76	11	5	5	2.3	42	23	18	18	5	.345	.509	2	0	OF-51
1946	93	276	68	13	4	3	1.1	34	35	25	36	3	.246	.355	14	1	OF-75
1947	116	398	102	28	6	15	3.8	62	62	63	66	3	.256	.470	9	3	OF-106
1948	138	496	143	16	11	23	4.6	91	80	77	57	1	.288	.504	4	0	OF-131
1949	104	310	83	8	6	12	3.9	55	59	42	29	1	.268	.448	26	6	OF-79
1950	69	142	31	5	0	6	4.2	16	23	20	23	1	.218	.380	33	6	OF-32
1951	110	295	83	11	6	12	4.1	41	51	40	38	2	.281	.481	30	5	OF-83
1952	97	255	64	13	5	7	2.7	29	35	31	30	4	.251	.424	30	6	OF-65
1953	79	97	26	1	0	4	4.1	11	17	14	15	0	.268	.402	57	13	OF-14
10 yrs.	864	2493	676	106	43	87	3.5	381	385	330	312	20	.271	.453	208	40	OF-637
10 yrs.	864	2493	676	106	43	87	3.5	381	385	330	312	20	.271	.453	208 2nd	40 3rd	OF-637

Soldier Boy Murphy

MURPHY, JOHN P. — B. 1879, New Haven, Conn. D. June 1, 1914, Baker, Ore.

	G	AB	H	2B	3B	HR	HR%	R	RBI	BB	SO	SB	BA	SA	PH AB	PH H	G by POS
1902 STL N	1	3	2	1	0	0	0.0	1	1	1		0	.667	1.000	0	0	3B-1
1903 DET A	5	22	4	1	0	0	0.0	1	1	0		0	.182	.227	0	0	SS-5
2 yrs.	6	25	6	2	0	0	0.0	2	2	1		0	.240	.320	0	0	SS-5, 3B-1
1 yr.	5	22	4	1	0	0	0.0	1	1	0		0	.182	.227	0	0	SS-5

Glenn Myatt

MYATT, GLENN CALVIN — B. July 9, 1897, Argenta, Ark. D. Aug. 9, 1969, Houston, Tex. — BL TR 5'11" 165 lb

	G	AB	H	2B	3B	HR	HR%	R	RBI	BB	SO	SB	BA	SA	PH AB	PH H	G by POS
1920 PHI A	70	196	49	8	3	0	0.0	14	18	12	22	1	.250	.321	8	1	OF-37, C-21
1921	44	69	14	2	0	0	0.0	6	5	6	7	0	.203	.232	7	1	C-27
1923 CLE A	92	220	63	7	6	3	1.4	36	40	16	18	0	.286	.414	18	6	C-69
1924	105	342	117	22	7	8	2.3	55	73	33	12	6	.342	.518	9	2	C-95
1925	106	358	97	15	9	11	3.1	51	54	29	24	2	.271	.455	5	1	C-98, OF-1
1926	56	117	29	5	2	0	0.0	14	13	13	13	1	.248	.325	18	3	C-35
1927	55	94	23	6	0	2	2.1	15	8	12	7	1	.245	.372	25	5	C-26
1928	58	125	36	7	2	1	0.8	9	15	13	13	0	.288	.400	26	8	C-30
1929	59	129	30	4	1	1	0.8	14	17	7	5	0	.233	.302	14	1	C-41
1930	86	265	78	23	2	2	0.8	30	37	18	17	2	.294	.419	13	3	C-71
1931	65	195	48	14	2	1	0.5	21	29	21	13	2	.246	.354	9	3	C-58
1932	82	252	62	12	1	8	3.2	45	46	28	21	2	.246	.397	16	3	C-65
1933	40	77	18	4	0	0	0.0	10	7	15	8	0	.234	.286	12	3	C-27
1934	36	107	34	6	1	0	0.0	18	12	13	5	1	.318	.393	0	0	C-34
1935 2 teams	CLE A (10G – .083)				NY N (13G – .222)												
" total	23	54	7	1	1	1	1.9	3	8	4	6	0	.130	.241	9	1	C-14
1936 DET A	27	78	17	1	0	0	0.0	5	5	9	4	0	.218	.231	1	1	C-27
16 yrs.	1004	2678	722	137	37	38	1.4	346	387	249	195	18	.270	.391	190	42	C-738, OF-38
1 yr.	27	78	17	1	0	0	0.0	5	5	9	4	0	.218	.231	1	1	C-27

Rusty Nagelson

NAGELSON, RUSSELL CHARLES — B. Sept. 19, 1944, Cincinnati, Ohio — BL TR 6' 205 lb

	G	AB	H	2B	3B	HR	HR%	R	RBI	BB	SO	SB	BA	SA	PH AB	PH H	G by POS
1968 CLE A	5	3	1	0	0	0	0.0	0	0	2	2	0	.333	.333	4	1	
1969	12	17	6	0	0	0	0.0	1	0	3	3	0	.353	.353	7	1	OF-3, 1B-1
1970 2 teams	DET A (28G – .188)				CLE A (17G – .125)												
" total	45	56	9	1	0	1	1.8	8	4	8	15	0	.161	.232	31	6	OF-8, 1B-1
3 yrs.	62	76	16	1	0	1	1.3	9	4	13	20	0	.211	.263	42	8	OF-11, 1B-2
1 yr.	28	32	6	0	0	0	0.0		2	5	6	0	.188	.188	20	5	OF-4, 1B-1

Bill Nahorodny

NAHORODNY, WILLIAM GERARD — B. Aug. 31, 1953, Hamtramck, Mich. — BR TR 6'2" 200 lb

	G	AB	H	2B	3B	HR	HR%	R	RBI	BB	SO	SB	BA	SA	PH AB	PH H	G by POS
1976 PHI N	3	5	1	1	0	0	0.0	0	0	0	0	0	.200	.400	2	0	C-2
1977 CHI A	7	23	6	1	0	1	4.3	3	4	2	3	0	.261	.435	0	0	C-7
1978	107	347	82	11	2	8	2.3	29	35	23	52	1	.236	.349	1	0	C-104, 1B-4, DH-1
1979	65	179	46	10	0	6	3.4	20	29	18	23	0	.257	.413	11	6	C-60, DH-3
1980 ATL N	59	157	38	12	0	5	3.2	14	18	8	21	0	.242	.414	6	1	C-54, 1B-1
1981	14	13	3	1	0	0	0.0	0	2	1	3	0	.231	.308	9	3	C-3, 1B-1
1982 CLE A	39	94	21	5	1	4	4.3	6	18	2	9	0	.223	.426	7	2	C-35
1983 DET A	2	0	0	0	0	0	0.0	0	0	1	0	0	.000	.000	1	0	
1984 SEA A	12	25	6	0	0	1	4.0	2	3	1	7	0	.240	.360	1	0	C-10, 1B-1
9 yrs.	308	844	203	41	3	25	3.0	74	109	56	118	1	.241	.385	38	12	C-275, 1B-7, DH-4
1 yr.	2	1	0	0	0	0	0.0	0	0	1	0	0	.000	.000	1	0	

Doc Nance

NANCE, WILLIAM G. (Kid) — Born William G. Cooper. B. Aug. 2, 1877, Fort Worth, Tex. D. May 28, 1958, Ft. Worth, Tex. — BR TR

	G	AB	H	2B	3B	HR	HR%	R	RBI	BB	SO	SB	BA	SA	PH AB	PH H	G by POS
1897 LOU N	35	120	29	5	3	3	2.5	25	17	20		3	.242	.408	0	0	OF-35
1898	22	76	24	5	0	1	1.3	13	16	12		3	.316	.421	0	0	OF-22
1901 DET A	132	461	129	24	5	3	0.7	72	66	51		9	.280	.373	0	0	OF-132

	G	AB	H	2B	3B	HR	HR %	R	RBI	BB	SO	SB	BA	SA	Pinch Hit AB	Pinch Hit H	G by POS

Doc Nance continued

	G	AB	H	2B	3B	HR	HR %	R	RBI	BB	SO	SB	BA	SA	AB	H	G by POS
'04 STL A	1	3	1	0	0	0	0.0	0		0			.333	.333	0	0	OF-1
4 yrs.	190	660	183	34	8	7	1.1	110	99	83		14	.277	.385	0	0	OF-190
1 yr.	132	461	129	24	5	3	0.7	72	66	51		9	.280	.373	0	0	OF-132

Lynn Nelson

NELSON, LYNN BERNARD (Line Drive) BL TR 5'10½" 170 lbs.
B. Feb. 24, 1905, Sheldon, N. D.   D. Feb. 15, 1955, Kansas City, Mo.

	G	AB	H	2B	3B	HR	HR %	R	RBI	BB	SO	SB	BA	SA	AB	H	G by POS
'30 CHI N	37	18	4	1	1	0	0.0	0	2	0	1	0	.222	.389	0	0	P-37
'33	29	21	5	1	1	0	0.0	5	1	1	3	0	.238	.381	0	0	P-24
'34	2	0	0	0	0	0	–	0	0	0	0	0	–	–	0	0	P-2
'37 PHI A	74	113	40	6	2	4	3.5	18	29	6	13	1	.354	.549	38	9	P-30, OF-6
'38	67	112	31	0	0	0	0.0	12	15	7	12	0	.277	.277	32	6	P-32
'39	40	80	15	2	0	0	0.0	3	5	2	13	0	.188	.213	5	1	P-35
'40 DET A	19	23	8	0	0	1	4.3	4	3	0	6	0	.348	.478	14	5	P-6
7 yrs.	268	367	103	10	4	5	1.4	42	55	16	48	1	.281	.371	89	21	P-166, OF-6
1 yr.	19	23	8	0	0	1	4.3	4	3	0	6	0	.348	.478	14	5	P-6

Jack Ness

NESS, JOHN CHARLES BR TR 6'2" 165 lbs.
B. Nov. 11, 1885, Chicago, Ill.   D. Dec. 3, 1957, DeLand, Fla.

	G	AB	H	2B	3B	HR	HR %	R	RBI	BB	SO	SB	BA	SA	AB	H	G by POS
'11 DET A	12	39	6	0	0	0	0.0	6	2	2		0	.154	.154	0	0	1B-12
'16 CHI A	75	258	69	7	5	1	0.4	32	34	9	32	4	.267	.345	6	3	1B-69
2 yrs.	87	297	75	7	5	1	0.3	38	36	11	32	4	.253	.320	6	3	1B-81
1 yr.	12	39	6	0	0	0	0.0	6	2	2		0	.154	.154	0	0	1B-12

Jim Nettles

NETTLES, JAMES WILLIAM BL TL 6' 186 lbs.
Brother of Graig Nettles.
B. Mar. 2, 1947, San Diego, Calif.

	G	AB	H	2B	3B	HR	HR %	R	RBI	BB	SO	SB	BA	SA	AB	H	G by POS
'70 MIN A	13	20	5	0	0	0	0.0	3	0	1	5	0	.250	.250	1	0	OF-11
'71	70	168	42	5	1	6	3.6	17	24	19	24	3	.250	.399	8	2	OF-62
'72	102	235	48	5	2	4	1.7	28	15	32	52	4	.204	.294	20	7	OF-78, 1B-1
'74 DET A	43	141	32	5	1	6	4.3	20	17	15	26	3	.227	.404	1	1	OF-41
'79 KC A	11	23	2	0	0	0	0.0	0	1	3	2	0	.087	.087	2	0	OF-8, 1B-1
'81 OAK A	1	0	0	0	0	0	–	0	0	0	0	0	–	–	0	0	OF-1
6 yrs.	240	587	129	15	4	16	2.7	68	57	70	109	10	.220	.341	32	10	OF-201, 1B-2
1 yr.	43	141	32	5	1	6	4.3	20	17	15	26	3	.227	.404	1	1	OF-41

Johnny Neun

NEUN, JOHN HENRY BB TL 5'10½" 175 lbs.
B. Oct. 28, 1900, Baltimore, Md.
Manager 1946-48.   BR 1928

	G	AB	H	2B	3B	HR	HR %	R	RBI	BB	SO	SB	BA	SA	AB	H	G by POS
'25 DET A	60	75	20	3	3	0	0.0	15	4	9	12	2	.267	.387	33	8	1B-13
'26	97	242	72	14	4	0	0.0	47	15	27	26	4	.298	.388	42	12	1B-49
'27	79	204	66	9	4	0	0.0	38	27	35	13	22	.324	.407	17	6	1B-53
'28	36	108	23	3	1	0	0.0	15	5	7	10	2	.213	.259	11	3	1B-25
'30 BOS N	81	212	69	12	2	2	0.9	39	23	21	18	9	.325	.429	23	8	1B-55
'31	79	104	23	1	3	0	0.0	17	11	11	14	2	.221	.288	34	4	1B-36
6 yrs.	432	945	273	42	17	2	0.2	171	85	110	93	41	.289	.376	160	41	1B-231
4 yrs.	272	629	181	29	12	0	0.0	115	51	78	61	30	.288	.372	103	29	1B-140
															8th		

Simon Nicholls

NICHOLLS, SIMON BURDETTE BL TR
B. July 17, 1882, Germantown, Md.   D. Mar. 12, 1911, Baltimore, Md.

	G	AB	H	2B	3B	HR	HR %	R	RBI	BB	SO	SB	BA	SA	AB	H	G by POS
'03 DET A	2	8	3	0	0	0	0.0	0	0	0		0	.375	.375	0	0	SS-2
'06 PHI A	12	44	8	1	0	0	0.0	1	1	3		0	.182	.205	0	0	SS-12
'07	126	460	139	12	2	0	0.0	75	23	24		13	.302	.337	2	0	SS-82, 2B-28, 3B-13
'08	150	550	119	17	3	4	0.7	58	31	35		14	.216	.280	0	0	SS-120, 2B-23, 3B-7
'09	21	71	15	2	1	0	0.0	10	3	3		0	.211	.268	1	0	SS-14, 3B-5, 1B-1
'10 CLE A	3	0	0	0	0	0	–	0	0	0		0	–	–	0	0	SS-3
6 yrs.	314	1133	284	32	6	4	0.4	144	58	65		27	.251	.300	3	0	SS-233, 2B-51, 3B-25, 1B-1
1 yr.	2	8	3	0	0	0	0.0	0	0	0		0	.375	.375	0	0	SS-2

Fred Nicholson

NICHOLSON, FREDERICK BR TR 5'10½" 173 lbs.
B. Sept. 1, 1894, Honey Grove, Tex.

	G	AB	H	2B	3B	HR	HR %	R	RBI	BB	SO	SB	BA	SA	AB	H	G by POS
'17 DET A	13	14	4	1	0	0	0.0	4	1	1	2	0	.286	.357	4	1	OF-3
'19 PIT N	30	66	18	2	2	1	1.5	8	6	6	11	2	.273	.409	11	2	OF-17, 1B-1
'20	99	247	89	16	7	4	1.6	33	30	18	31	9	.360	.530	38	12	OF-58
'21 BOS N	83	245	80	11	7	5	2.0	36	41	17	29	5	.327	.490	15	3	OF-59, 1B-4, 2B-2
'22	78	222	56	4	5	2	0.9	31	29	23	24	5	.252	.342	12	3	OF-63
5 yrs.	303	794	247	34	21	12	1.5	112	107	65	97	21	.311	.452	80	21	OF-200, 1B-5, 2B-2
1 yr.	13	14	4	1	0	0	0.0	4	1	1	2	0	.286	.357	4	1	OF-3

Bob Nieman

NIEMAN, ROBERT CHARLES BR TR 5'11" 195 lbs.
B. Jan. 26, 1927, Cincinnati, Ohio

	G	AB	H	2B	3B	HR	HR %	R	RBI	BB	SO	SB	BA	SA	AB	H	G by POS
'51 STL A	12	43	16	3	1	2	4.7	6	8	3	5	0	.372	.628	1	1	OF-11
'52	131	478	138	22	2	18	3.8	66	74	46	73	0	.289	.456	9	1	OF-125
'53 DET A	142	508	143	32	5	15	3.0	72	69	57	57	0	.281	.453	7	1	OF-135
'54	91	251	66	14	1	8	3.2	24	35	22	32	0	.263	.422	26	8	OF-62
'55 CHI A	99	272	77	11	4	10	3.6	34	53	36	37	1	.283	.460	24	7	OF-78
'56 2 teams		CHI A (14G – .300)					BAL A (114G – .322)										
total	128	428	137	21	6	14	3.3	63	68	90	63	1	.320	.495	1	1	OF-124
'57 BAL A	129	445	123	17	4	13	2.9	61	70	63	86	4	.276	.429	9	0	OF-120
'58	105	366	119	20	2	16	4.4	56	60	44	57	2	.325	.522	6	1	OF-100
'59	118	360	105	18	2	21	5.8	49	60	42	55	1	.292	.528	17	4	OF-97
'60 STL N	81	188	54	13	5	4	2.1	19	31	24	31	0	.287	.473	26	4	OF-55
'61 2 teams		STL N (6G – .471)					CLE A (39G – .354)										
total	45	82	31	7	0	2	2.4	9	12	7	6	1	.378	.537	27	9	OF-16

	G	AB	H	2B	3B	HR	HR %	R	RBI	BB	SO	SB	BA	SA	Pinch Hit AB	Pinch Hit H	G by POS

Bob Nieman continued

	G	AB	H	2B	3B	HR	HR %	R	RBI	BB	SO	SB	BA	SA	AB	H	G by POS
1962 **2 teams**	**CLE**	**A**	(2G –	.000)		**SF**	**N**	(30G –	.300)								
" total	32	31	9	2	0	1	3.2	1	4	1	10	0	.290	.452	30	8	OF-3
12 yrs.	1113	3452	1018	180	32	125	3.6	455	544	435	512	10	.295	.474	183	45	OF-926
2 yrs.	233	759	209	46	6	23	3.0	96	104	79	89	0	.275	.443	33	9	OF-197

WORLD SERIES

| 1962 SF N | 1 | 0 | 0 | 0 | 0 | 0 | – | 0 | 0 | 1 | 0 | 0 | – | – | 0 | 0 | |

Jim Northrup

NORTHRUP, JAMES THOMAS
B. Nov. 24, 1939, Breckenridge, Mich. BL TR 6'3" 190 lbs

	G	AB	H	2B	3B	HR	HR %	R	RBI	BB	SO	SB	BA	SA	AB	H	G by POS
1964 DET A	5	12	1	1	0	0	0.0	1	0	0	3	1	.083	.167	3	0	OF-2
1965	80	219	45	12	3	2	0.9	20	16	12	50	1	.205	.315	24	3	OF-54
1966	123	419	111	24	6	16	3.8	53	58	33	52	4	.265	.465	10	4	OF-113
1967	144	495	134	18	6	10	2.0	63	61	43	83	7	.271	.392	5	1	OF-143
1968	154	580	153	29	7	21	3.6	76	90	50	87	4	.264	.447	4	0	OF-151
1969	148	543	160	31	5	25	4.6	79	66	52	83	4	.295	.508	5	0	OF-143
1970	139	504	132	21	3	24	4.8	71	80	58	68	3	.262	.458	3	1	OF-136
1971	136	459	124	27	2	16	3.5	72	71	60	43	7	.270	.442	14	5	OF-108, 1B-32
1972	134	426	111	15	2	8	1.9	40	42	38	47	4	.261	.362	14	2	OF-127, 1B-2
1973	119	404	124	14	7	12	3.0	55	44	38	41	4	.307	.465	8	2	OF-116
1974 **3 teams**	**DET**	**A**	(97G –	.237)		**MON**	**N**	(21G –	.241)		**BAL**	**A**	(8G –	.571)			
" total	126	437	106	13	1	14	3.2	46	53	43	56	0	.243	.373	10	2	OF-116
1975 BAL A	84	194	53	13	0	5	2.6	27	29	22	22	0	.273	.418	22	8	
12 yrs.	1392	4692	1254	218	42	153	3.3	603	610	449	635	39	.267	.429	122	28	OF-1209, 1B-34
11 yrs.	1279	4437	1184	204	42	145	3.3	571	570	420	603	39	.267	.430	90	18	OF-1190, 1B-34
											10th						

LEAGUE CHAMPIONSHIP SERIES

| 1972 DET A | 5 | 14 | 5 | 0 | 0 | 0 | 0.0 | 0 | 1 | 2 | 3 | 0 | .357 | .357 | 0 | 0 | OF-5 |

WORLD SERIES

| 1968 DET A | 7 | 28 | 7 | 0 | 1 | 2 | 7.1 | 4 | 8 | 1 | 5 | 0 | .250 | .536 | 0 | 0 | OF-7 |

Prince Oana

OANA, HENRY KAUHANE
B. Jan. 22, 1908, Waipahu, Hawaii. D. June 19, 1976, Austin, Tex. BR TR 6'2" 193 lbs

	G	AB	H	2B	3B	HR	HR %	R	RBI	BB	SO	SB	BA	SA	AB	H	G by POS
1934 PHI N	6	21	5	1	0	0	0.0	3	3	0	1	0	.238	.286	2	1	OF-4
1943 DET A	20	26	10	2	1	1	3.8	5	7	1	2	0	.385	.654	9	3	P-10
1945	4	5	1	0	0	0	0.0	0	0	0	0	0	.200	.200	1	0	P-3
3 yrs.	30	52	16	3	1	1	1.9	8	10	1	3	0	.308	.462	12	4	P-13, OF-4
2 yrs.	24	31	11	2	1	1	3.2	5	7	1	2	0	.355	.581	10	3	P-13

John O'Connell

O'CONNELL, JOHN JOSEPH
B. May 16, 1872, Lawrence, Mass. D. May 14, 1908, Derry, N. H.

	G	AB	H	2B	3B	HR	HR %	R	RBI	BB	SO	SB	BA	SA	AB	H	G by POS
1891 BAL AA	8	29	5	1	0	0	0.0	2	7	3	6	2	.172	.207	0	0	SS-3, 2B-3, OF-2
1902 DET A	8	22	4	0	0	0	0.0	1	0	3		0	.182	.182	0	0	2B-6, 1B-2
2 yrs.	16	51	9	1	0	0	0.0	3	7	6	6	2	.176	.196	0	0	2B-9, SS-3, OF-2, 1B-2
1 yr.	8	22	4	0	0	0	0.0	1	0	3		0	.182	.182	0	0	2B-6, 1B-2

Ben Oglivie

OGLIVIE, BENJAMIN AMBROSIO
B. Feb. 11, 1949, Colon, Panama BL TL 6'2" 160 lbs

	G	AB	H	2B	3B	HR	HR %	R	RBI	BB	SO	SB	BA	SA	AB	H	G by POS
1971 BOS A	14	38	10	3	0	0	0.0	2	4	0	5	0	.263	.342	5	0	OF-11
1972	94	253	61	10	2	8	3.2	27	30	18	61	1	.241	.391	24	9	OF-65
1973	58	147	32	9	1	2	1.4	16	9	9	32	1	.218	.333	10	2	OF-32, DH-13
1974 DET A	92	252	68	11	3	4	1.6	28	29	34	38	12	.270	.385	19	5	OF-63, 1B-10, DH-4
1975	100	332	95	14	1	9	2.7	45	36	16	62	11	.286	.416	3	0	OF-86, 1B-5, DH-2
1976	115	305	87	12	3	15	4.9	36	47	11	44	9	.285	.492	38	9	OF-64, 1B-9, DH-1
1977	132	450	118	24	2	21	4.7	63	61	40	80	9	.262	.464	12	4	OF-118, DH-2
1978 MIL A	128	469	142	29	4	18	3.8	71	72	52	69	11	.303	.497	6	1	OF-89, DH-27, 1B-11
1979	139	514	145	30	4	29	5.6	88	81	48	56	12	.282	.525	6	3	OF-120, DH-13, 1B-9
1980	156	592	180	26	2	41	6.9	94	118	54	71	11	.304	.563	0	0	OF-152, DH-4
1981	107	400	97	15	2	14	3.5	53	72	37	49	2	.243	.395	1	1	OF-101, DH-6
1982	159	602	147	22	1	34	5.6	92	102	70	81	3	.244	.453	1	0	OF-159
1983	125	411	115	19	3	13	3.2	49	66	60	64	4	.280	.436	10	3	OF-113, DH-8
1984	131	461	121	16	2	12	2.6	49	60	44	56	0	.262	.384	10	3	OF-125, DH-1
14 yrs.	1550	5226	1418	240	30	220	4.2	713	787	493	768	86	.271	.455	145	40	OF-1298, DH-81, 1B-44
4 yrs.	439	1339	368	61	9	49	3.7	172	173	101	224	41	.275	.444	72	18	OF-331, 1B-24, DH-9

DIVISIONAL PLAYOFF SERIES

| 1981 MIL A | 5 | 18 | 3 | 1 | 0 | 0 | 0.0 | 0 | 1 | 0 | 7 | 0 | .167 | .222 | 0 | 0 | OF-5 |

LEAGUE CHAMPIONSHIP SERIES

| 1982 MIL A | 4 | 15 | 2 | 0 | 0 | 1 | 6.7 | 1 | 1 | 0 | 3 | 0 | .133 | .333 | 0 | 0 | OF-4 |

WORLD SERIES

| 1982 MIL A | 7 | 27 | 6 | 0 | 1 | 1 | 3.7 | 4 | 1 | 2 | 4 | 0 | .222 | .407 | 0 | 0 | OF-7 |

Charley O'Leary

O'LEARY, CHARLES TIMOTHY
B. Oct. 15, 1882, Chicago, Ill. D. Jan. 6, 1941, Chicago, Ill. BR TR 5'7" 165 lbs

	G	AB	H	2B	3B	HR	HR %	R	RBI	BB	SO	SB	BA	SA	AB	H	G by POS
1904 DET A	135	456	97	10	3	1	0.2	39	16	21		9	.213	.254	0	0	SS-135
1905	148	512	109	13	1	1	0.2	47	33	29		13	.213	.248	0	0	SS-148
1906	128	443	97	13	2	2	0.5	34	34	17		8	.219	.271	1	1	SS-127
1907	139	465	112	19	1	0	0.0	61	34	32		11	.241	.286	1	0	SS-138
1908	65	211	53	9	3	0	0.0	21	17	9		4	.251	.322	0	0	SS-64, 2B-1
1909	76	261	53	10	0	0	0.0	29	13	6		9	.203	.241	0	0	3B-54, 2B-15, SS-4, OF-2
1910	65	211	51	7	1	0	0.0	23	9	9		7	.242	.284	2	0	2B-38, SS-16, 3B-6
1911	74	256	68	8	2	0	0.0	29	25	21		10	.266	.313	0	0	2B-67, 3B-6
1912	3	10	2	0	0	0	0.0	1	1	0		0	.200	.200	0	0	2B-3
1913 STL N	120	404	88	15	5	0	0.0	32	31	20	34	3	.218	.280	1	0	SS-102, 2B-15

	G	AB	H	2B	3B	HR	HR %	R	RBI	BB	SO	SB	BA	SA	Pinch Hit AB	Pinch Hit H	G by POS

Charley O'Leary continued

	G	AB	H	2B	3B	HR	HR %	R	RBI	BB	SO	SB	BA	SA	PH AB	PH H	G by POS
34 STL A	1	1	1	0	0	0	0.0	1	0	0	0	0	1.000	1.000	1	1	
11 yrs.	954	3230	731	104	18	4	0.1	317	213	164	34	74	.226	.273	6	2	SS-734, 2B-139, 3B-66, OF-2
9 yrs.	833	2825	642	89	13	4	0.1	284	182	144		71	.227	.272	4	1	SS-632, 2B-124, 3B-66, OF-2

WORLD SERIES

	G	AB	H	2B	3B	HR	HR %	R	RBI	BB	SO	SB	BA	SA	PH AB	PH H	G by POS
07 DET A	5	17	1	0	0	0	0.0	0	0	1	3	0	.059	.059	0	0	SS-5
08	5	19	3	0	0	0	0.0	2	0	0	3	0	.158	.158	0	0	SS-5
09	1	3	0	0	0	0	0.0	0	0	0	0	0	.000	.000	0	0	3B-1
3 yrs.	11	39	4	0	0	0	0.0	2	0	1	6	0	.103	.103	0	0	SS-10, 3B-1

Karl Olson

OLSON, KARL ARTHUR (Ole)   BR TR 6'3" 205 lbs.
B. July 6, 1930, Ross, Calif.

	G	AB	H	2B	3B	HR	HR %	R	RBI	BB	SO	SB	BA	SA	PH AB	PH H	G by POS
51 BOS A	5	10	1	0	0	0	0.0	0	0	0	3	0	.100	.100	0	0	OF-5
53	25	57	7	2	0	1	1.8	5	6	1	9	0	.123	.211	1	0	OF-24
54	101	227	59	12	2	1	0.4	25	20	12	23	2	.260	.344	21	3	OF-78
55	26	48	12	1	2	0	0.0	7	1	1	10	0	.250	.354	3	2	OF-21
56 WAS A	106	313	77	10	2	4	1.3	34	22	28	41	1	.246	.329	10	2	OF-101
57 2 teams	WAS A (8G – .167)			DET A (8G – .143)													
total	16	26	4	0	0	0	0.0	3	1	1	8	0	.154	.154	5	0	OF-11
6 yrs.	279	681	160	25	6	6	0.9	74	50	43	94	3	.235	.316	40	7	OF-240
1 yr.	8	14	2	0	0	0	0.0	1	1	0	6	0	.143	.143	3	0	OF-5

Ollie O'Mara

O'MARA, OLIVER EDWARD   BR TR 5'8" 140 lbs.
B. Mar. 8, 1891, St. Louis, Mo.

	G	AB	H	2B	3B	HR	HR %	R	RBI	BB	SO	SB	BA	SA	PH AB	PH H	G by POS
12 DET A	1	4	0	0	0	0	0.0	0	0	0		0	.000	.000	0	0	SS-1
14 BKN N	67	247	65	10	2	1	0.4	41	7	16	26	14	.263	.332	0	0	SS-63
15	149	577	141	26	3	0	0.0	77	31	51	40	11	.244	.300	0	0	SS-149
16	72	193	39	5	2	0	0.0	18	15	12	20	10	.202	.249	11	1	SS-51
18	121	450	96	8	1	1	0.2	29	24	7	18	11	.213	.242	0	0	3B-121
19	2	7	0	0	0	0	0.0	1	0	0	0	0	.000	.000	0	0	3B-2
6 yrs.	412	1478	341	49	8	2	0.1	166	77	86	104	46	.231	.279	11	1	SS-264, 3B-123
1 yr.	1	4	0	0	0	0	0.0	0	0	0		0	.000	.000	0	0	SS-1

WORLD SERIES

	G	AB	H	2B	3B	HR	HR %	R	RBI	BB	SO	SB	BA	SA	PH AB	PH H	G by POS
16 BKN N	1	1	0	0	0	0	0.0	0	0	0	1	0	.000	.000	1	0	

Steve O'Neill

O'NEILL, STEPHEN FRANCIS   BR TR 5'10" 165 lbs.
Brother of Jim O'Neill. Brother of Jack O'Neill.
Brother of Mike O'Neill.
B. July 6, 1891, Minooka, Pa. D. Jan. 26, 1962, Cleveland, Ohio
Manager 1935-37, 1943-48, 1950-54.

	G	AB	H	2B	3B	HR	HR %	R	RBI	BB	SO	SB	BA	SA	PH AB	PH H	G by POS
11 CLE A	9	27	4	1	0	0	0.0	1	1	4		2	.148	.185	0	0	C-9
12	68	215	49	4	0	0	0.0	17	14	12		2	.228	.247	1	0	C-67
13	78	234	69	13	3	0	0.0	19	29	10	24	5	.295	.376	0	0	C-78
14	86	269	68	12	2	0	0.0	28	20	15	35	1	.253	.312	4	1	C-81, 1B-1
15	121	386	91	14	2	2	0.5	32	34	26	41	2	.236	.298	6	1	C-115
16	130	378	89	23	0	0	0.0	30	29	24	33	2	.235	.296	2	1	C-128
17	129	370	68	10	2	0	0.0	21	29	41	55	2	.184	.222	2	0	C-127
18	114	359	87	8	7	1	0.3	34	35	48	22	5	.242	.312	1	0	C-113
19	125	398	115	35	7	2	0.5	46	47	48	21	4	.289	.427	2	0	C-123
20	149	489	157	39	5	3	0.6	63	55	69	39	3	.321	.440	1	0	C-148
21	106	335	108	22	1	1	0.3	39	50	57	22	0	.322	.403	1	0	C-105
22	133	392	122	27	4	2	0.5	33	65	73	25	2	.311	.416	2	0	C-130
23	113	330	82	12	0	0	0.0	31	50	64	34	0	.248	.285	2	0	C-111
24 BOS A	106	307	73	15	1	0	0.0	29	38	63	23	0	.238	.293	14	2	C-92
25 NY A	35	91	26	5	0	1	1.1	7	13	10	3	0	.286	.374	3	0	C-31
27 STL A	74	191	44	7	0	1	0.5	14	22	20	6	0	.230	.283	13	5	C-60
28	10	24	7	1	0	0	0.0	4	6	8	0	0	.292	.333	0	0	C-10
17 yrs.	1586	4795	1259	248	34	13	0.3	448	537	592	383	30	.263	.337	54	10	C-1528, 1B-1

WORLD SERIES

	G	AB	H	2B	3B	HR	HR %	R	RBI	BB	SO	SB	BA	SA	PH AB	PH H	G by POS
20 CLE A	7	21	7	3	0	0	0.0	1	2	4	3	0	.333	.476	0	0	C-7

Eddie Onslow

ONSLOW, EDWARD JOSEPH   BL TL 6' 170 lbs.
Brother of Jack Onslow.
B. Feb. 17, 1893, Meadville, Pa. D. May 8, 1981, Dennison, Ohio

	G	AB	H	2B	3B	HR	HR %	R	RBI	BB	SO	SB	BA	SA	PH AB	PH H	G by POS
12 DET A	35	128	29	1	2	1	0.8	11	13	3		3	.227	.289	0	0	1B-35
13	17	55	14	1	0	0	0.0	7	8	5	9	1	.255	.273	0	0	1B-17
18 CLE A	2	6	1	0	0	0	0.0	0	0	0	1	0	.167	.167	1	0	OF-1
27 WAS A	9	18	4	1	0	0	0.0	1	1	1	0	0	.222	.278	3	0	1B-5
4 yrs.	63	207	48	3	2	1	0.5	19	22	9	10	4	.232	.280	4	0	1B-57, OF-1
2 yrs.	52	183	43	2	2	1	0.5	18	21	8	9	4	.235	.284	0	0	1B-52

Jack Onslow

ONSLOW, JOHN JAMES   BR TR 5'11" 180 lbs.
Brother of Eddie Onslow.
B. Oct. 13, 1888, Scottdale, Pa. D. Dec. 22, 1960, Concord, Mass.
Manager 1949-50.

	G	AB	H	2B	3B	HR	HR %	R	RBI	BB	SO	SB	BA	SA	PH AB	PH H	G by POS
12 DET A	31	69	11	1	0	0	0.0	7	4	10		1	.159	.174	0	0	C-31
17 NY N	9	8	2	1	0	0	0.0	1	0	0	1	0	.250	.375	0	0	C-9
2 yrs.	40	77	13	2	0	0	0.0	8	4	10	1	1	.169	.195	0	0	C-40
1 yr.	31	69	11	1	0	0	0.0	7	4	10		1	.159	.174	0	0	C-31

Joe Orengo

ORENGO, JOSEPH CHARLES   BR TR 6' 185 lbs.
B. Nov. 29, 1914, San Francisco, Calif.

	G	AB	H	2B	3B	HR	HR %	R	RBI	BB	SO	SB	BA	SA	PH AB	PH H	G by POS
39 STL N	7	3	0	0	0	0	0.0	0	0	0	1	0	.000	.000	0	0	SS-7
40	129	415	119	23	4	7	1.7	58	56	65	90	9	.287	.412	0	0	2B-77, 3B-34, SS-19

	G	AB	H	2B	3B	HR	HR%	R	RBI	BB	SO	SB	BA	SA	Pinch Hit AB	H	G by POS

Joe Orengo continued

	G	AB	H	2B	3B	HR	HR%	R	RBI	BB	SO	SB	BA	SA	AB	H	G by POS
1941 NY N	77	252	54	11	2	4	1.6	23	25	28	49	1	.214	.321	3	1	3B-59, SS-9, 2B-6
1943 2 teams	NY	N	(83G –	.218)		BKN	N	(7G –	.200)								
" total	90	281	61	10	2	6	2.1	29	30	40	48	1	.217	.331	2	2	1B-82, 3B-6
1944 DET A	46	154	31	10	0	0	0.0	14	10	20	29	1	.201	.266	1	0	SS-29, 3B-11, 1B-5, 2B-
1945 CHI A	17	15	1	0	0	0	0.0	5	1	3	2	0	.067	.067	5	0	3B-7, 2B-1
6 yrs.	366	1120	266	54	8	17	1.5	129	122	156	219	12	.238	.346	11	3	3B-117, 1B-87, 2B-86, SS-64
1 yr.	46	154	31	10	0	0	0.0	14	10	20	29	1	.201	.266	1	0	SS-29, 3B-11, 1B-5, 2B-

Frank O'Rourke

O'ROURKE, FRANCIS JAMES (Blackie)
B. Nov. 28, 1891, Hamilton, Ont., Canada
BR TR 5'10½" 165 lbs

	G	AB	H	2B	3B	HR	HR%	R	RBI	BB	SO	SB	BA	SA	AB	H	G by POS
1912 BOS N	61	196	24	3	1	0	0.0	11	16	11	50	1	.122	.148	0	0	SS-59
1917 BKN N	64	198	47	7	1	0	0.0	18	15	14	25	11	.237	.283	4	0	3B-58
1918	4	12	2	0	0	0	0.0	0	2	1	3	0	.167	.167	1	1	2B-2, OF-1
1920 WAS A	14	54	16	1	0	0	0.0	8	5	2	5	2	.296	.315	0	0	SS-13, 3B-1
1921	123	444	104	17	8	3	0.7	51	54	26	56	6	.234	.329	0	0	SS-122
1922 BOS A	67	216	57	14	3	1	0.5	28	17	20	28	6	.264	.370	0	0	SS-48, 3B-19
1924 DET A	47	181	50	11	2	0	0.0	28	19	12	19	7	.276	.359	0	0	2B-40, SS-7
1925	124	482	141	40	7	5	1.0	88	57	32	37	5	.293	.436	0	0	2B-118, 3B-6
1926	111	363	88	16	1	1	0.3	43	41	35	33	8	.242	.300	3	0	3B-58, 2B-41, SS-10
1927 STL A	140	538	144	25	3	1	0.2	85	39	64	43	19	.268	.331	2	0	3B-120, 2B-16, 1B-3
1928	99	391	103	24	3	1	0.3	54	62	21	19	10	.263	.348	3	0	3B-96, SS-2
1929	154	585	147	23	9	2	0.3	81	62	41	28	14	.251	.332	0	0	3B-151, 2B-3, SS-2
1930	115	400	107	15	4	1	0.3	52	41	35	30	11	.268	.333	4	1	3B-84, SS-23, 1B-3
1931	8	9	2	0	0	0	0.0	0	0	0	1	1	.222	.222	3	0	SS-2, 1B-1
14 yrs.	1131	4069	1032	196	42	15	0.4	547	430	314	377	101	.254	.333	20	2	3B-593, SS-288, 2B-220, 1B-7, OF-1
3 yrs.	282	1026	279	67	10	6	0.6	159	117	79	89	20	.272	.374	3	0	2B-199, 3B-64, SS-17

Bobo Osborne

OSBORNE, LAWRENCE SIDNEY
Son of Tiny Osborne.
B. Oct. 12, 1935, Chattahoochee, Ga.
BL TR 6'1" 205 lbs

	G	AB	H	2B	3B	HR	HR%	R	RBI	BB	SO	SB	BA	SA	AB	H	G by POS
1957 DET A	11	27	4	1	0	0	0.0	4	1	3	7	0	.148	.185	2	0	OF-5, 1B-4
1958	2	2	0	0	0	0	0.0	0	0	0	0	0	.000	.000	2	0	
1959	86	209	40	7	1	3	1.4	27	21	16	41	1	.191	.278	23	0	1B-56, OF-1
1961	71	93	20	7	0	2	2.2	8	13	20	15	1	.215	.355	41	10	1B-11, 3B-8
1962	64	74	17	1	0	0	0.0	12	7	16	25	0	.230	.243	29	6	3B-13, 1B-7, C-1
1963 WAS A	125	358	76	14	1	12	3.4	42	44	49	83	0	.212	.358	22	5	1B-81, 3B-16
6 yrs.	359	763	157	30	2	17	2.2	93	86	104	171	2	.206	.317	119	21	1B-159, 3B-37, OF-6, C
5 yrs.	234	405	81	16	1	5	1.2	51	42	55	88	2	.200	.281	97	16	1B-78, 3B-21, OF-6, C-

Jimmy Outlaw

OUTLAW, JAMES PAULUS
B. Jan. 20, 1913, Orme, Tenn.
BR TR 5'8" 165 lbs

	G	AB	H	2B	3B	HR	HR%	R	RBI	BB	SO	SB	BA	SA	AB	H	G by POS
1937 CIN N	49	165	45	7	3	0	0.0	18	11	3	31	2	.273	.352	4	0	3B-41
1938	4	0	0	0	0	0	–	1	0	0	0	0	–	–	0	0	
1939 BOS N	65	133	35	2	0	0	0.0	15	5	10	14	1	.263	.278	16	4	OF-39, 3B-2
1943 DET A	20	67	18	1	0	1	1.5	8	6	8	4	0	.269	.328	4	1	OF-16
1944	139	535	146	20	6	3	0.6	69	57	41	40	7	.273	.350	3	0	OF-137
1945	132	446	121	16	5	0	0.0	56	34	45	33	6	.271	.330	7	0	OF-105, 3B-21
1946	92	299	78	14	2	2	0.7	36	31	29	24	5	.261	.341	5	1	OF-43, 3B-38
1947	70	127	29	7	1	0	0.0	20	15	21	14	3	.228	.299	3	0	OF-37, 3B-9
1948	74	198	56	12	0	0	0.0	33	25	31	15	0	.283	.343	11	4	3B-47, OF-13
1949	5	4	1	0	0	0	0.0	1	0	0	1	0	.250	.250	4	1	
10 yrs.	650	1974	529	79	17	6	0.3	257	184	188	176	24	.268	.334	57	11	OF-390, 3B-158
7 yrs.	532	1676	449	70	14	6	0.4	223	168	175	131	21	.268	.337	37	7	OF-351, 3B-115

WORLD SERIES

	G	AB	H	2B	3B	HR	HR%	R	RBI	BB	SO	SB	BA	SA	AB	H	G by POS
1945 DET A	7	28	5	0	0	0	0.0	1	3	2	1	1	.179	.179	0	0	3B-7

Marv Owen

OWEN, MARVIN JAMES
B. Mar. 22, 1906, Agnew, Calif.
BR TR 6'1" 175 lbs

	G	AB	H	2B	3B	HR	HR%	R	RBI	BB	SO	SB	BA	SA	AB	H	G by POS
1931 DET A	105	377	84	11	6	3	0.8	35	39	29	38	2	.223	.308	3	1	SS-37, 3B-37, 1B-27, 2B
1933	138	550	144	29	9	2	0.4	77	65	44	56	2	.262	.349	1	0	3B-136
1934	154	565	179	34	9	8	1.4	79	96	59	37	3	.317	.451	0	0	3B-154
1935	134	483	127	24	5	2	0.4	52	71	43	37	1	.263	.346	2	1	3B-131
1936	154	583	172	20	4	9	1.5	72	105	53	41	9	.295	.389	0	0	3B-153, 1B-2
1937	107	396	114	22	5	1	0.3	48	45	41	24	3	.288	.376	1	0	3B-106
1938 CHI A	141	577	162	23	6	6	1.0	84	55	45	31	6	.281	.373	1	0	3B-140
1939	58	194	46	9	0	0	0.0	22	15	16	15	4	.237	.284	2	0	3B-55
1940 BOS A	20	57	12	0	0	0	0.0	4	6	8	4	0	.211	.211	3	0	3B-9, 1B-8
9 yrs.	1011	3782	1040	167	44	31	0.8	473	497	338	283	30	.275	.367	13	2	3B-921, SS-37, 1B-37, 2B-4
6 yrs.	792	2954	820	135	38	25	0.8	363	421	269	233	20	.278	.374	7	2	3B-717, SS-37, 1B-29, 2B-4

WORLD SERIES

	G	AB	H	2B	3B	HR	HR%	R	RBI	BB	SO	SB	BA	SA	AB	H	G by POS
1934 DET A	7	29	2	0	0	0	0.0	0	1	0	5	1	.069	.069	0	0	3B-7
1935	6	20	1	0	0	0	0.0	2	1	2	3	0	.050	.050	0	0	3B-2
2 yrs.	13	49	3	0	0	0	0.0	2	2	2	8	1	.061	.061	0	0	3B-9

Ray Oyler

OYLER, RAYMOND FRANCIS
B. Aug. 4, 1938, Indianapolis, Ind.   D. Jan. 26, 1981, Seattle, Wash.
BR TR 5'11" 165 lbs

	G	AB	H	2B	3B	HR	HR%	R	RBI	BB	SO	SB	BA	SA	AB	H	G by POS
1965 DET A	82	194	36	6	0	5	2.6	22	13	21	61	1	.186	.294	11	1	SS-57, 2B-11, 3B-1, 1B-1
1966	71	210	36	8	3	1	0.5	16	9	23	62	0	.171	.252	1	0	SS-69
1967	148	367	76	14	2	1	0.3	33	29	37	91	0	.207	.264	0	0	SS-146
1968	111	215	29	6	1	1	0.5	13	12	20	59	0	.135	.186	0	0	SS-111
1969 SEA A	106	255	42	5	0	7	2.7	24	22	31	80	1	.165	.267	0	0	SS-106

	G	AB	H	2B	3B	HR	HR %	R	RBI	BB	SO	SB	BA	SA	Pinch Hit AB	Pinch Hit H	G by POS

Ray Oyler continued

	G	AB	H	2B	3B	HR	HR%	R	RBI	BB	SO	SB	BA	SA	PH AB	PH H	G by POS
1970 CAL A	24	24	2	0	0	0	0.0	2	1	3	6	0	.083	.083	7	0	SS-13, 3B-2
6 yrs.	542	1265	221	39	6	15	1.2	110	86	135	359	2	.175	.251	19	3	SS-502, 2B-11, 3B-3, 1B-1
4 yrs.	412	986	177	34	6	8	0.8	84	63	101	273	1	.180	.251	12	3	SS-383, 2B-11, 3B-1, 1B-1

WORLD SERIES

	G	AB	H	2B	3B	HR	HR%	R	RBI	BB	SO	SB	BA	SA	PH AB	PH H	G by POS
1968 DET A	4	0	0	0	0	0	–	0	0	0	0	0	–	–	0	0	SS-4

Stan Papi

PAPI, STANLEY GERARD   BR TR 6' 170 lbs.
B. Feb. 4, 1951, Fresno, Calif.

	G	AB	H	2B	3B	HR	HR%	R	RBI	BB	SO	SB	BA	SA	PH AB	PH H	G by POS
1974 STL N	8	4	1	0	0	0	0.0	0	1	0	0	0	.250	.250	1	0	SS-7, 2B-1
1977 MON N	13	43	10	2	1	0	0.0	5	4	1	9	1	.233	.326	0	0	3B-10, SS-2, 2B-1
1978	67	152	35	11	0	0	0.0	15	11	10	28	0	.230	.303	24	3	SS-22, 3B-15, 2B-5
1979 BOS N	50	117	22	8	0	1	0.9	9	6	5	20	0	.188	.282	3	0	2B-26, SS-21, DH-1
1980 2 teams	BOS	A (1G – .000)		DET	A (46G – .237)												
" total	47	114	27	3	4	3	2.6	12	17	5	24	0	.237	.412	4	1	2B-31, 3B-12, SS-5, 1B-1
1981 DET A	40	93	19	2	1	3	3.2	8	12	3	18	1	.204	.344	4	1	3B-32, DH-3, OF-1, 2B-1, 1B-1
6 yrs.	225	523	114	26	6	7	1.3	49	51	24	99	2	.218	.331	36	5	3B-69, 2B-65, SS-57, DH-4, 1B-2, OF-1
2 yrs.	86	207	46	5	5	6	2.9	20	29	8	42	1	.222	.382	8	2	3B-43, 2B-32, SS-5, DH-3, 1B-2, OF-1

Salty Parker

PARKER, FRANCIS JAMES   BR TR 6' 173 lbs.
B. July 8, 1913, East St. Louis, Ill.
Manager 1967, 1972.

	G	AB	H	2B	3B	HR	HR%	R	RBI	BB	SO	SB	BA	SA	PH AB	PH H	G by POS
1936 DET A	11	25	7	2	0	0	0.0	6	4	2	3	0	.280	.360	0	0	SS-7, 1B-2

Lance Parrish

PARRISH, LANCE MICHAEL   BR TR 6'3" 210 lbs.
B. June 15, 1956, McKeesport, Pa.

	G	AB	H	2B	3B	HR	HR%	R	RBI	BB	SO	SB	BA	SA	PH AB	PH H	G by POS
1977 DET A	12	46	9	2	0	3	6.5	10	7	5	12	0	.196	.435	0	0	C-12
1978	85	288	63	11	3	14	4.9	37	41	11	71	0	.219	.424	6	1	C-79
1979	143	493	136	26	3	19	3.9	65	65	49	105	6	.276	.456	3	1	C-142
1980	144	553	158	34	6	24	4.3	79	82	31	109	6	.286	.499	4	1	C-121, DH-16, OF-5, 1B-5
1981	96	348	85	18	2	10	2.9	39	46	34	52	2	.244	.394	0	0	C-90, DH-5
1982	133	486	138	19	2	32	6.6	75	87	40	99	3	.284	.529	2	1	C-132, OF-1
1983	155	605	163	42	3	27	4.5	80	114	44	106	1	.269	.483	2	0	C-131, DH-27
1984	147	578	137	16	2	33	5.7	75	98	41	120	2	.237	.443	3	1	C-127, DH-22
8 yrs.	915	3397	889	168	21	162	4.8	460	540	255	674	20	.262	.467	20	5	C-834, DH-70, OF-6, 1B-5
8 yrs.	915	3397	889	168	21	162	4.8	460	540	255	674	20	.262	.467	20	5	C-834, DH-70, OF-6, 1B-5
				10th	7th						7th						

LEAGUE CHAMPIONSHIP SERIES

	G	AB	H	2B	3B	HR	HR%	R	RBI	BB	SO	SB	BA	SA	PH AB	PH H	G by POS
1984 DET A	3	12	3	1	0	1	8.3	1	3	0	3	0	.250	.583	0	0	C-3

WORLD SERIES

	G	AB	H	2B	3B	HR	HR%	R	RBI	BB	SO	SB	BA	SA	PH AB	PH H	G by POS
1984 DET A	5	18	5	1	0	1	5.6	3	2	3	2	1	.278	.500	0	0	C-5

Dixie Parsons

PARSONS, EDWARD DIXON   BR TR 6'2" 180 lbs.
B. May 12, 1916, Talladega, Ala.

	G	AB	H	2B	3B	HR	HR%	R	RBI	BB	SO	SB	BA	SA	PH AB	PH H	G by POS
1939 DET A	5	1	0	0	0	0	0.0	0	0	1	1	0	.000	.000	1	0	C-4
1942	63	188	37	4	0	2	1.1	8	11	13	22	1	.197	.250	1	0	C-62
1943	40	106	15	3	0	0	0.0	2	4	6	16	0	.142	.170	0	0	C-40
3 yrs.	108	295	52	7	0	2	0.7	10	15	20	39	1	.176	.220	2	0	C-106
3 yrs.	108	295	52	7	0	2	0.7	10	15	20	39	1	.176	.220	2	0	C-106

Steve Partenheimer

PARTENHEIMER, HAROLD PHILIP   BR TR 5'8½" 145 lbs.
Father of Stan Partenheimer.
B. Aug. 30, 1891, Greenfield, Mass.   D. June 16, 1971, Mansfield, Ohio

	G	AB	H	2B	3B	HR	HR%	R	RBI	BB	SO	SB	BA	SA	PH AB	PH H	G by POS
1913 DET A	1	2	0	0	0	0	0.0	0	0	0	0	0	.000	.000	0	0	3B-1

Johnny Pasek

PASEK, JOHN PAUL   BR TR 5'10" 175 lbs.
B. June 25, 1905, Niagara Falls, N. Y.   D. Mar. 13, 1976, St. Petersburg, Fla.

	G	AB	H	2B	3B	HR	HR%	R	RBI	BB	SO	SB	BA	SA	PH AB	PH H	G by POS
1933 DET A	28	61	15	4	0	0	0.0	6	4	7	7	2	.246	.311	0	0	C-28
1934 CHI A	4	9	3	0	0	0	0.0	1	0	1	1	0	.333	.333	0	0	C-4
2 yrs.	32	70	18	4	0	0	0.0	7	4	8	8	2	.257	.314	0	0	C-32
1 yr.	28	61	15	4	0	0	0.0	6	4	7	7	2	.246	.311	0	0	C-28

Bob Patrick

PATRICK, ROBERT LEE   BR TR 6'2" 190 lbs.
B. Oct. 27, 1917, Fort Smith, Ark.

	G	AB	H	2B	3B	HR	HR%	R	RBI	BB	SO	SB	BA	SA	PH AB	PH H	G by POS
1941 DET A	5	7	2	0	0	0	0.0	2	0	0	1	0	.286	.286	2	1	OF-3
1942	4	8	2	1	0	1	12.5	1	3	1	0	0	.250	.750	1	0	OF-3
2 yrs.	9	15	4	1	0	1	6.7	3	3	1	1	0	.267	.533	3	1	OF-6
2 yrs.	9	15	4	1	0	1	6.7	3	3	1	1	0	.267	.533	3	1	OF-6

Fred Payne

PAYNE, FREDERICK THOMAS   BR TR
B. Sept. 2, 1880, Camden, N. Y.   D. Jan. 16, 1954, Camden, N. Y.

	G	AB	H	2B	3B	HR	HR%	R	RBI	BB	SO	SB	BA	SA	PH AB	PH H	G by POS
1906 DET A	72	222	60	5	5	0	0.0	23	20	13		4	.270	.338	7	3	C-47, OF-17
1907	53	169	28	2	2	0	0.0	17	14	7		4	.166	.201	1	0	C-46, OF-5
1908	20	45	3	0	0	0	0.0	3	2	3		1	.067	.067	2	0	C-16, OF-2
1909 CHI A	32	82	20	2	0	0	0.0	8	12	5		0	.244	.268	2	1	C-27, OF-3
1910	91	257	56	5	4	0	0.0	17	19	11		6	.218	.268	9	2	C-78, OF-2
1911	66	133	27	2	1	1	0.8	14	19	8		6	.203	.256	9	3	C-56
6 yrs.	334	908	194	16	12	1	0.1	82	86	47		21	.214	.261	30	9	C-270, OF-29
3 yrs.	145	436	91	7	7	0	0.0	43	36	23		9	.209	.257	10	3	C-109, OF-24

WORLD SERIES

	G	AB	H	2B	3B	HR	HR%	R	RBI	BB	SO	SB	BA	SA	PH AB	PH H	G by POS
1907 DET A	2	4	1	0	0	0	0.0	0	1	0	0	0	.250	.250	0	0	C-1

	G	AB	H	2B	3B	HR	HR %	R	RBI	BB	SO	SB	BA	SA	Pinch Hit AB	Pinch Hit H	G by POS

Pepper Peploski

PEPLOSKI, JOSEPH ANTHONY
Brother of Henry Peploski.
B. Sept. 12, 1891, Brooklyn, N. Y.   D. Jan. 28, 1983, Dover, N. J.
BR TR 5'8"   155 lb

	G	AB	H	2B	3B	HR	HR%	R	RBI	BB	SO	SB	BA	SA	AB	H	G by POS
1913 DET A	2	4	2	0	0	0	0.0	1	0	0	0	0	.500	.500	0	0	3B-2

Don Pepper

PEPPER, DONALD HOYTE
B. Oct. 8, 1943, Saratoga Springs, N. Y.
BL TL 6'4½"   215 lb

	G	AB	H	2B	3B	HR	HR%	R	RBI	BB	SO	SB	BA	SA	AB	H	G by POS
1966 DET A	4	3	0	0	0	0	0.0	0	0	0	1	0	.000	.000	3	0	1B-1

Cy Perkins

PERKINS, RALPH FOSTER
B. Feb. 27, 1896, Gloucester, Mass.   D. Oct. 2, 1963, Philadelphia, Pa.
BR TR 5'10½"   158 lb

	G	AB	H	2B	3B	HR	HR%	R	RBI	BB	SO	SB	BA	SA	AB	H	G by POS
1915 PHI A	7	20	4	1	0	0	0.0	2	0	3	3	0	.200	.250	0	0	C-6
1917	6	18	3	0	0	0	0.0	1	2	2	1	0	.167	.167	0	0	C-6
1918	68	218	41	4	1	1	0.5	9	14	8	15	1	.188	.229	7	1	C-60
1919	101	305	77	12	7	2	0.7	22	29	27	22	2	.252	.357	6	1	C-87, SS-8
1920	148	493	128	24	6	5	1.0	40	52	28	35	5	.260	.363	1	0	C-146, 2B-1
1921	141	538	155	31	4	12	2.2	58	73	32	32	5	.288	.428	0	0	C-141
1922	148	505	135	20	6	6	1.2	58	69	40	30	1	.267	.366	7	1	C-141
1923	143	500	135	34	5	2	0.4	53	65	65	30	1	.270	.370	4	1	C-137
1924	128	392	95	19	4	0	0.0	31	32	31	20	3	.242	.311	0	0	C-128
1925	65	140	43	10	0	1	0.7	21	18	26	6	0	.307	.400	4	1	C-58, 3B-1
1926	63	148	43	6	0	0	0.0	14	19	18	7	0	.291	.331	7	4	C-55
1927	59	137	35	7	2	1	0.7	11	15	12	8	0	.255	.358	2	0	C-54, 1B-1
1928	19	29	5	0	0	0	0.0	1	1	1	1	0	.172	.172	0	0	C-19
1929	38	76	16	4	0	0	0.0	4	9	5	4	0	.211	.263	0	0	C-38
1930	20	38	6	2	0	0	0.0	1	4	2	3	0	.158	.211	0	0	C-19, 1B-1
1931 NY A	16	47	12	1	0	0	0.0	3	7	1	4	0	.255	.277	0	0	C-16
1934 DET A	1	1	0	0	0	0	0.0	0	0	0	0	0	.000	.000	0	0	
17 yrs.	1171	3605	933	175	35	30	0.8	329	409	301	221	18	.259	.352	40	9	C-1111, SS-8, 1B-2, 3B-2, 2B-1
1 yr.	1	1	0	0	0	0	0.0	0	0	0	0	0	.000	.000	1	0	

Boyd Perry

PERRY, BOYD GLENN
B. Mar. 21, 1914, Snow Camp, N. C.
BR TR 5'10"   158 lb

	G	AB	H	2B	3B	HR	HR%	R	RBI	BB	SO	SB	BA	SA	AB	H	G by POS
1941 DET A	36	83	15	5	0	0	0.0	9	11	10	9	1	.181	.241	0	0	SS-25, 2B-11

Clay Perry

PERRY, CLAYTON SHIELDS
B. Dec. 18, 1881, Rice Lake, Wis.   D. Jan. 16, 1954, Rice Lake, Wis.
BR TR 5'10½"   175 lb

	G	AB	H	2B	3B	HR	HR%	R	RBI	BB	SO	SB	BA	SA	AB	H	G by POS
1908 DET A	5	11	2	0	0	0	0.0	0	0	0		0	.182	.182	0	0	3B-5

Hank Perry

PERRY, WILLIAM HENRY (Socks)
B. July 28, 1886, Howell, Mich.   D. July 18, 1956, Pontiac, Mich.
BL TR 5'11"   190 lb

	G	AB	H	2B	3B	HR	HR%	R	RBI	BB	SO	SB	BA	SA	AB	H	G by POS
1912 DET A	13	36	6	1	0	0	0.0	3	0	3		0	.167	.194	6	3	OF-7

Johnny Pesky

PESKY, JOHN MICHAEL
Born John Michael Paveskovich.
B. Sept. 27, 1919, Portland, Ore.
Manager 1963-64, 1980.
BL TR 5'9"   168 lb

	G	AB	H	2B	3B	HR	HR%	R	RBI	BB	SO	SB	BA	SA	AB	H	G by POS
1942 BOS A	147	620	205	29	9	2	0.3	105	51	42	36	12	.331	.416	0	0	SS-147
1946	153	621	208	43	4	2	0.3	115	55	65	29	9	.335	.427	0	0	SS-153
1947	155	638	207	27	8	0	0.0	106	39	72	22	12	.324	.392	0	0	SS-133, 3B-22
1948	143	565	159	26	6	3	0.5	124	55	99	32	3	.281	.365	2	1	3B-141
1949	148	604	185	27	7	2	0.3	111	69	100	19	8	.306	.384	0	0	3B-148
1950	127	490	153	22	6	1	0.2	112	49	104	31	2	.312	.388	2	0	3B-116, SS-8
1951	131	480	150	20	6	3	0.6	93	41	84	15	2	.313	.398	9	3	SS-106, 3B-11, 2B-5
1952 2 teams				BOS A (25G – .149)				DET A (69G – .254)									
" total	94	244	55	6	0	1	0.4	36	11	57	16	1	.225	.262	14	1	SS-43, 3B-22, 2B-22
1953 DET A	103	308	90	22	1	2	0.6	43	24	27	10	3	.292	.390	30	12	2B-73
1954 2 teams				DET A (20G – .176)				WAS A (49G – .253)									
" total	69	175	43	4	3	1	0.6	22	10	13	8	1	.246	.320	29	4	2B-37, SS-1
10 yrs.	1270	4745	1455	226	50	17	0.4	867	404	663	218	53	.307	.386	86	21	SS-591, 3B-460, 2B-133
3 yrs.	192	502	138	26	1	4	0.8	74	34	72	22	4	.275	.355	57	16	2B-95, SS-41, 3B-3
WORLD SERIES																	
1946 BOS A	7	30	7	0	0	0	0.0	2	0	1	3	1	.233	.233	0	0	SS-7

John Peters

PETERS, JOHN WILLIAM (Shotgun)
B. July 14, 1893, Kansas City, Kans.   D. Feb. 21, 1932, Kansas City, Mo.
BR TR 6'   192 lb

	G	AB	H	2B	3B	HR	HR%	R	RBI	BB	SO	SB	BA	SA	AB	H	G by POS
1915 DET A	1	3	0	0	0	0	0.0	0	0	0	1	0	.000	.000	0	0	C-1
1918 CLE A	1	1	0	0	0	0	0.0	0	0	0	1	0	.000	.000	0	0	C-1
1921 PHI N	55	155	45	4	0	3	1.9	7	23	6	13	1	.290	.374	10	5	C-44
1922	55	143	35	9	1	4	2.8	15	24	9	18	0	.245	.406	15	3	C-39
4 yrs.	112	302	80	13	1	7	2.3	22	47	16	33	1	.265	.384	25	8	C-85
1 yr.	1	3	0	0	0	0	0.0	0	0	0	1	0	.000	.000	0	0	C-1

Ricky Peters

PETERS, RICHARD DEVIN
B. Nov. 21, 1955, Lynwood, Calif.
BB TR 5'9"   170 lb

	G	AB	H	2B	3B	HR	HR%	R	RBI	BB	SO	SB	BA	SA	AB	H	G by POS
1979 DET A	12	19	5	0	0	0	0.0	3	2	5	3	0	.263	.263	1	0	DH-3, 3B-2, 2B-2, OF-1
1980	133	477	139	19	7	2	0.4	79	42	54	48	13	.291	.373	13	3	OF-109, DH-11
1981	63	207	53	7	3	0	0.0	26	15	29	28	1	.256	.319	5	1	OF-38, DH-19
1983 OAK A	55	178	51	7	0	0	0.0	20	20	12	21	4	.287	.326	2	1	OF-47, DH-8
4 yrs.	263	881	248	33	10	2	0.2	128	79	100	100	18	.281	.348	21	5	OF-195, DH-41, 3B-3, 2B-2
3 yrs.	208	703	197	26	10	2	0.3	108	59	88	79	14	.280	.354	19	4	OF-148, DH-33, 3B-3, 2B-2

	G	AB	H	2B	3B	HR	HR %	R	RBI	BB	SO	SB	BA	SA	Pinch Hit AB	H	G by POS

Dave Philley

PHILLEY, DAVID EARL
B. May 16, 1920, Paris, Tex.   BB TR 6'   188 lbs.

	G	AB	H	2B	3B	HR	HR %	R	RBI	BB	SO	SB	BA	SA	AB	H	G by POS
'41 CHI A	7	9	2	1	0	0	0.0	4	0	3	3	0	.222	.333	4	0	OF-2
'46	17	68	24	2	3	0	0.0	10	17	4	4	5	.353	.471	0	0	OF-17
'47	143	551	142	25	11	2	0.4	55	45	35	39	21	.258	.354	6	2	OF-133, 3B-4
'48	137	488	140	28	3	5	1.0	51	42	50	33	8	.287	.387	8	1	OF-128
'49	146	598	171	20	8	0	0.0	84	44	54	51	13	.286	.346	1	0	OF-145
'50	156	619	150	21	5	14	2.3	69	80	52	57	6	.242	.360	1	0	OF-154
'51 2 teams	CHI	A (7G – .240)		PHI	A (125G – .263)												
' total	132	493	129	20	7	7	1.4	71	61	65	41	10	.262	.373	5	1	OF-126
'52 PHI A	151	586	154	25	4	7	1.2	80	71	59	35	11	.263	.355	0	0	OF-149, 3B-2
'53	157	620	188	30	9	9	1.5	80	59	51	35	13	.303	.424	1	0	OF-157, 3B-1
'54 CLE A	133	452	102	13	3	12	2.7	48	60	57	48	2	.226	.347	4	1	OF-129
'55 2 teams	CLE	A (43G – .298)		BAL	A (83G – .299)												
' total	126	415	124	17	5	8	1.9	65	50	46	48	1	.299	.422	10	4	OF-116, 3B-2
'56 2 teams	BAL	A (32G – .205)		CHI	A (86G – .265)												
' total	118	396	98	18	4	5	1.3	57	64	48	40	4	.247	.351	12	0	OF-61, 1B-51, 3B-5
'57 2 teams	CHI	A (22G – .324)		DET	A (65G – .283)												
' total	87	244	72	12	1	2	0.8	24	25	11	26	4	.295	.377	29	12	OF-29, 1B-29, 3B-1
'58 PHI N	91	207	64	11	4	3	1.4	30	31	15	20	1	.309	.444	44	18	OF-24, 1B-18
'59	99	254	74	18	2	7	2.8	32	37	18	27	0	.291	.461	38	15	OF-34, 1B-24
'60 3 teams	PHI	N (14G – .333)		SF	N (39G – .164)					BAL	A (14G – .265)						
' total	67	110	24	4	1	2	1.8	13	16	13	21	1	.218	.327	48	11	OF-21, 3B-4, 1B-2
'61 BAL A	99	144	36	9	2	1	0.7	13	23	10	20	2	.250	.361	72	24	OF-25, 1B-1
'62 BOS A	38	42	6	2	0	0	0.0	3	4	5	3	0	.143	.190	28	4	OF-4
18 yrs.	1904	6296	1700	276	72	84	1.3	789	729	596	551	102	.270	.377	311	93	OF-1454, 1B-125, 3B-19
1 yr.	65	173	49	8	1	2	1.2	15	16	7	16	3	.283	.376	25	10	1B-27, OF-12, 3B-1
WORLD SERIES																	
'54 CLE A	4	8	1	0	0	0	0.0	0	0	1	3	0	.125	.125	2	0	OF-2

Bubba Phillips

PHILLIPS, JOHN MELVIN
B. Feb. 24, 1930, West Point, Miss.   BR TR 5'9"   180 lbs.

	G	AB	H	2B	3B	HR	HR %	R	RBI	BB	SO	SB	BA	SA	AB	H	G by POS
'55 DET A	95	184	43	4	0	3	1.6	18	23	14	20	2	.234	.304	17	1	OF-65, 3B-4
'56 CHI A	67	99	27	6	0	2	2.0	16	11	6	12	1	.273	.394	13	4	OF-35, 3B-2
'57	121	393	106	13	3	7	1.8	38	42	28	32	5	.270	.372	3	0	3B-97, OF-20
'58	84	260	71	10	0	5	1.9	26	30	15	14	3	.273	.369	4	0	3B-47, OF-37
'59	117	379	100	27	1	5	1.3	43	40	27	28	1	.264	.380	1	0	3B-100, OF-23
'60 CLE A	113	304	63	14	1	4	1.3	34	33	14	37	1	.207	.299	5	0	3B-85, OF-25, SS-1
'61	143	546	144	23	1	18	3.3	64	72	29	61	1	.264	.408	0	0	3B-143
'62	148	562	145	26	0	10	1.8	53	54	20	55	4	.258	.358	1	0	3B-145, OF-3, 2B-1
'63 DET A	128	464	114	11	2	5	1.1	42	45	19	42	6	.246	.310	6	2	3B-117, OF-5
'64	46	87	22	1	0	3	3.4	14	6	10	13	1	.253	.368	17	4	3B-22, OF-1
10 yrs.	1062	3278	835	135	8	62	1.9	348	356	182	314	25	.255	.358	67	11	3B-762, OF-214, SS-1, 2B-1
3 yrs.	269	735	179	16	2	11	1.5	74	74	43	75	9	.244	.316	40	7	3B-143, OF-71
WORLD SERIES																	
'59 CHI A	3	10	3	1	0	0	0.0	0	0	0	0	0	.300	.400	0	0	3B-3

Eddie Phillips

PHILLIPS, EDWARD DAVID
B. Feb. 17, 1901, Worcester, Mass.   D. Jan. 26, 1968, Buffalo, N. Y.   BR TR 6'   178 lbs.

	G	AB	H	2B	3B	HR	HR %	R	RBI	BB	SO	SB	BA	SA	AB	H	G by POS
'24 BOS N	3	3	0	0	0	0	0.0	0	0	0	2	0	.000	.000	2	0	C-1
'29 DET A	68	221	52	13	1	2	0.9	24	21	20	16	0	.235	.330	4	1	C-63
'31 PIT N	106	353	82	18	3	7	2.0	30	44	41	49	1	.232	.360	1	0	C-103
'32 NY A	9	31	9	1	0	2	6.5	4	4	2	3	1	.290	.516	0	0	C-9
'34 WAS A	56	169	33	6	1	2	1.2	6	16	26	24	1	.195	.278	3	0	C-53
'35 CLE A	70	220	60	16	1	1	0.5	18	41	15	21	0	.273	.368	1	0	C-69
6 yrs.	312	997	236	54	6	14	1.4	82	126	104	115	3	.237	.345	11	1	C-298
1 yr.	68	221	52	13	1	2	0.9	24	21	20	16	0	.235	.330	4	1	C-63

Jack Phillips

PHILLIPS, JACK DORN (Stretch)
B. Sept. 6, 1921, Clarence, N. Y.   BR TR 6'4"   193 lbs.

	G	AB	H	2B	3B	HR	HR %	R	RBI	BB	SO	SB	BA	SA	AB	H	G by POS
'47 NY A	16	36	10	0	1	1	2.8	5	2	3	5	0	.278	.417	4	0	1B-10
'48	1	2	0	0	0	0	0.0	0	0	0	1	0	.000	.000	0	0	1B-1
'49 2 teams	NY	A (45G – .308)		PIT	N (18G – .232)												
' total	63	147	41	7	2	1	0.7	22	13	16	15	2	.279	.374	7	2	1B-54, 3B-1
'50 PIT N	69	208	61	7	6	5	2.4	25	34	20	17	1	.293	.457	11	3	1B-54, 3B-3, P-1
'51	70	156	37	7	3	0	0.0	12	12	15	17	1	.237	.321	12	2	1B-53, 3B-4
'52	1	1	0	0	0	0	0.0	0	0	0	0	0	.000	.000	0	0	1B-1
'55 DET A	55	117	37	8	2	1	0.9	15	20	10	12	0	.316	.444	17	8	1B-35, 3B-3
'56	67	224	66	13	2	1	0.4	31	20	21	19	1	.295	.384	9	3	1B-56, OF-1, 2B-1
'57	1	1	0	0	0	0	0.0	1	0	0	0	0	.000	.000	1	0	
9 yrs.	343	892	252	42	16	9	1.0	111	101	85	86	5	.283	.396	61	18	1B-264, 3B-11, OF-1, 2B-1, P-1
3 yrs.	123	342	103	21	4	2	0.6	47	40	31	31	1	.301	.404	27	11	1B-91, 3B-3, OF-1, 2B-1
WORLD SERIES																	
'47 NY A	2	2	0	0	0	0	0.0	0	0	0	0	0	.000	.000	1	0	1B-1

Jack Pierce

PIERCE, LAVERN JACK
B. June 2, 1948, Laurel, Miss.   BB TR 6'   210 lbs.

	G	AB	H	2B	3B	HR	HR %	R	RBI	BB	SO	SB	BA	SA	AB	H	G by POS
'73 ATL N	11	20	1	0	0	0	0.0	0	0	1	8	0	.050	.050	5	0	1B-6
'74	6	9	1	0	0	0	0.0	1	0	1	0	0	.111	.111	3	1	1B-2
'75 DET A	53	170	40	6	1	8	4.7	19	22	20	40	0	.235	.424	4	0	1B-49
3 yrs.	70	199	42	6	1	8	4.0	20	22	22	48	0	.211	.372	12	1	1B-57
1 yr.	53	170	40	6	1	8	4.7	19	22	20	40	0	.235	.424	4	0	1B-49

	G	AB	H	2B	3B	HR	HR %	R	RBI	BB	SO	SB	BA	SA	Pinch Hit AB	Pinch Hit H	G by POS

Tony Piet

PIET, ANTHONY FRANCIS
Also known as Anthony Francis Pietruszka.
B. Dec. 7, 1906, Berwick, Pa.   D. Dec. 1, 1981, Hinsdale, Ill.   BR TR 6'   175 lb

	G	AB	H	2B	3B	HR	HR %	R	RBI	BB	SO	SB	BA	SA	AB	H	G by POS
1931 PIT N	44	167	50	12	4	0	0.0	22	24	13	24	10	.299	.419	0	0	2B-44, SS-1
1932	154	574	162	25	8	7	1.2	66	85	46	56	19	.282	.390	0	0	2B-154
1933	107	362	117	21	5	1	0.3	45	42	19	28	12	.323	.417	9	2	2B-97
1934 CIN N	106	421	109	20	5	1	0.2	58	38	23	44	6	.259	.337	4	2	3B-51, 2B-49
1935 2 teams	CIN N (6G – .200)			CHI A (77G – .298)													
" total	83	297	88	18	5	3	1.0	49	29	33	27	2	.296	.421	1	0	2B-59, 3B-17, OF-1
1936 CHI A	109	352	96	15	2	7	2.0	69	42	66	48	15	.273	.386	7	1	2B-68, 3B-32
1937	100	332	78	15	1	4	1.2	34	38	32	36	14	.235	.322	1	1	3B-86, 2B-13
1938 DET A	41	80	17	6	0	0	0.0	9	14	15	11	2	.213	.288	17	5	3B-18, 2B-1
8 yrs.	744	2585	717	132	30	23	0.9	352	312	247	274	80	.277	.378	39	11	2B-485, 3B-204, OF-1, SS-1
1 yr.	41	80	17	6	0	0	0.0	9	14	15	11	2	.213	.288	17	5	3B-18, 2B-1

Babe Pinelli

PINELLI, RALPH ARTHUR
Born Rinaldo Angelo Paolinelli.
B. Oct. 18, 1895, San Francisco, Calif.   D. Oct. 22, 1984, Daly City, Calif.   BR TR 5'9"   165 lb

	G	AB	H	2B	3B	HR	HR %	R	RBI	BB	SO	SB	BA	SA	AB	H	G by POS
1918 CHI A	24	78	18	1	1	1	1.3	7	7	7	8	3	.231	.308	0	0	3B-24
1920 DET A	102	284	65	9	3	0	0.0	33	21	25	16	6	.229	.282	4	0	3B-74, SS-18, 2B-1
1922 CIN N	156	547	167	19	7	1	0.2	77	72	48	37	17	.305	.371	0	0	3B-156
1923	117	423	117	14	5	0	0.0	44	51	27	29	10	.277	.333	0	0	3B-116
1924	144	510	156	16	7	0	0.0	61	70	32	32	23	.306	.365	1	1	3B-143
1925	130	492	139	33	6	2	0.4	68	49	22	28	8	.283	.386	6	2	3B-109, SS-17
1926	71	207	46	7	4	0	0.0	26	24	15	5	2	.222	.295	3	1	3B-40, SS-27, 2B-3
1927	30	76	15	2	0	1	1.3	11	4	6	7	2	.197	.263	0	0	3B-15, SS-9, 2B-5
8 yrs.	774	2617	723	101	33	5	0.2	327	298	182	162	71	.276	.346	14	4	3B-677, SS-71, 2B-9
1 yr.	102	284	65	9	3	0	0.0	33	21	25	16	6	.229	.282	4	0	3B-74, SS-18, 2B-1

Wally Pipp

PIPP, WALTER CLEMENT
B. Feb. 17, 1893, Chicago, Ill.   D. Jan. 11, 1965, Grand Rapids, Mich.   BL TL 6'1"   180 lb

	G	AB	H	2B	3B	HR	HR %	R	RBI	BB	SO	SB	BA	SA	AB	H	G by POS
1913 DET A	12	31	5	0	3	0	0.0	5	2	6	0	0	.161	.355	2	0	1B-10
1915 NY A	136	479	118	20	13	4	0.8	59	60	66	81	18	.246	.367	2	2	1B-134
1916	151	545	143	20	14	12	2.2	70	93	54	82	16	.262	.417	1	1	1B-148
1917	155	587	143	29	12	9	1.5	82	70	60	66	11	.244	.380	0	0	1B-155
1918	91	349	106	15	9	2	0.6	48	44	22	34	11	.304	.415	0	0	1B-91
1919	138	523	144	23	10	7	1.3	74	50	39	42	9	.275	.398	0	0	1B-138
1920	153	610	171	30	14	11	1.8	109	76	48	54	4	.280	.430	0	0	1B-153
1921	153	588	174	35	9	8	1.4	96	97	45	28	17	.296	.427	0	0	1B-153
1922	152	577	190	32	10	9	1.6	96	90	56	32	7	.329	.466	0	0	1B-152
1923	144	569	173	19	8	6	1.1	79	108	36	28	6	.304	.397	0	0	1B-144
1924	153	589	174	30	19	9	1.5	88	113	51	36	12	.295	.457	0	0	1B-153
1925	62	178	41	6	3	3	1.7	19	24	13	12	3	.230	.348	9	0	1B-47
1926 CIN N	155	574	167	22	15	6	1.0	72	99	49	26	8	.291	.413	0	0	1B-155
1927	122	443	115	19	6	2	0.5	49	41	32	11	2	.260	.343	7	3	1B-114
1928	95	272	77	11	3	2	0.7	30	26	23	13	1	.283	.368	20	6	1B-72
15 yrs.	1872	6914	1941	311	148	90	1.3	974	996	596	551	125	.281	.408	41	12	1B-1819
1 yr.	12	31	5	0	3	0	0.0	5	5	2	6	0	.161	.355	2	0	1B-10

WORLD SERIES																	
1921 NY A	8	26	4	1	0	0	0.0	1	2	2	3	1	.154	.192	0	0	1B-8
1922	5	21	6	1	0	0	0.0	0	3	0	2	1	.286	.333	0	0	1B-5
1923	6	20	5	0	0	0	0.0	2	2	4	1	0	.250	.250	0	0	1B-6
3 yrs.	19	67	15	2	0	0	0.0	3	7	6	6	2	.224	.254	0	0	1B-19

Al Platte

PLATTE, ALFRED JOSEPH
B. Apr. 13, 1890, Grand Rapids, Mich.   D. Aug. 29, 1976, Grand Rapids, Mich.   BL TL 5'11"   165 lb

	G	AB	H	2B	3B	HR	HR %	R	RBI	BB	SO	SB	BA	SA	AB	H	G by POS
1913 DET A	7	18	2	1	0	0	0.0	0	1	0	1	1	.111	.167	2	0	OF-5

J. W. Porter

PORTER, J. W. (Jay)
B. Jan. 17, 1933, Shawnee, Okla.   BR TR 6'2"   180 lb

	G	AB	H	2B	3B	HR	HR %	R	RBI	BB	SO	SB	BA	SA	AB	H	G by POS
1952 STL A	33	104	26	4	1	0	0.0	12	7	10	10	4	.250	.308	1	0	OF-29, 3B-2
1955 DET A	24	55	13	2	0	0	0.0	6	3	8	15	0	.236	.273	8	2	1B-6, OF-4, C-4
1956	14	21	2	0	0	0	0.0	0	3	0	8	0	.095	.095	10	0	OF-2, C-2
1957	58	140	35	8	0	2	1.4	14	18	14	20	0	.250	.350	17	4	OF-27, C-12, 1B-3
1958 CLE A	40	85	17	1	0	4	4.7	13	19	9	23	0	.200	.353	17	3	C-20, 1B-4, 3B-1
1959 2 teams	WAS A (37G – .226)			STL N (23G – .212)													
" total	60	139	31	7	0	2	1.4	13	12	12	20	0	.223	.317	6	2	C-53, 1B-3
6 yrs.	229	544	124	22	1	8	1.5	58	62	53	96	4	.228	.316	59	11	C-91, OF-62, 1B-16, 3B
3 yrs.	96	216	50	10	0	2	0.9	20	24	22	43	0	.231	.306	35	6	OF-33, C-18, 1B-9

Lew Post

POST, LEWIS G.
B. Apr. 12, 1875, Hastings, Mich.   D. Aug. 21, 1944, Chicago, Ill.

	G	AB	H	2B	3B	HR	HR %	R	RBI	BB	SO	SB	BA	SA	AB	H	G by POS
1902 DET A	3	12	1	0	0	0	0.0	2	0	0		0	.083	.083	0	0	OF-3

Ray Powell

POWELL, RAYMOND REATH (Rabbit)
B. Nov. 20, 1888, Siloam Springs, Ark.   D. Oct. 16, 1962, Chillicothe, Mo.   BL TR 5'9"   160 lb

	G	AB	H	2B	3B	HR	HR %	R	RBI	BB	SO	SB	BA	SA	AB	H	G by POS
1913 DET A	2	0	0	0	0	0	–	0	0	0	0	0	–	–	0	0	OF-1
1917 BOS N	88	357	97	10	4	4	1.1	42	30	24	54	12	.272	.356	0	0	OF-88
1918	53	188	40	7	5	0	0.0	31	20	29	30	2	.213	.303	0	0	OF-53
1919	123	470	111	12	12	2	0.4	51	33	41	79	16	.236	.326	1	0	OF-122
1920	147	609	137	12	12	6	1.0	69	29	44	83	10	.225	.314	0	0	OF-147
1921	149	624	191	25	18	12	1.9	114	74	58	85	6	.306	.462	0	0	OF-149
1922	142	550	163	22	11	6	1.1	82	37	59	66	3	.296	.409	5	0	OF-136
1923	97	338	102	20	4	4	1.2	57	38	45	36	1	.302	.420	8	3	OF-84

	G	AB	H	2B	3B	HR	HR%	R	RBI	BB	SO	SB	BA	SA	Pinch Hit AB	Pinch Hit H	G by POS

Ray Powell continued

	G	AB	H	2B	3B	HR	HR%	R	RBI	BB	SO	SB	BA	SA	PH AB	PH H	G by POS
'24	74	188	49	9	1	1	0.5	21	15	21	28	1	.261	.335	23	6	OF-46
9 yrs.	875	3324	890	117	67	35	1.1	467	276	321	461	51	.268	.375	37	9	OF-826
1 yr.	2	0	0	0	0	0	–	0	0	0	0	0	–	–	0	0	OF-1

Del Pratt

PRATT, DERRILL BURNHAM   BR TR 5'11" 175 lbs.
B. Jan. 10, 1888, Walhalla, S. C.   D. Sept. 30, 1977, Texas City, Tex.

	G	AB	H	2B	3B	HR	HR%	R	RBI	BB	SO	SB	BA	SA	PH AB	PH H	G by POS
'12 STL A	151	570	172	26	15	5	0.9	76	69	36		24	.302	.426	0	0	2B-121, SS-21, OF-8, 3B-1
'13	155	592	175	31	13	2	0.3	60	87	40	57	37	.296	.402	0	0	2B-146, 1B-9
'14	158	584	165	34	13	5	0.9	85	65	50	45	37	.283	.411	0	0	2B-152, OF-5, SS-1
'15	159	602	175	31	11	3	0.5	61	78	26	43	32	.291	.394	0	0	2B-158
'16	158	596	159	35	12	5	0.8	64	103	54	56	26	.267	.391	0	0	2B-158
'17	123	450	111	22	8	1	0.2	40	53	33	36	18	.247	.338	0	0	2B-119, 1B-4
'18 NY A	126	477	131	19	7	2	0.4	65	55	35	26	12	.275	.356	0	0	2B-126
'19	140	527	154	27	7	4	0.8	69	56	36	24	22	.292	.393	0	0	2B-140
'20	154	574	180	37	8	4	0.7	84	97	50	24	12	.314	.427	0	0	2B-154
'21 BOS A	135	521	169	36	10	5	1.0	80	100	44	10	8	.324	.461	1	0	2B-134
'22	154	607	183	44	7	6	1.0	73	86	53	20	7	.301	.427	0	0	2B-154
'23 DET A	101	297	92	18	3	0	0.0	43	40	25	9	5	.310	.391	8	4	2B-60, 1B-17, 3B-12
'24	121	429	130	32	3	1	0.2	56	77	31	10	6	.303	.399	4	2	2B-63, 1B-51, 3B-4
13 yrs.	1835	6826	1996	392	117	43	0.6	856	966	513	360	246	.292	.403	10	4	2B-1685, 1B-81, SS-22, 3B-17, OF-13
2 yrs.	222	726	222	50	6	1	0.1	99	117	56	19	11	.306	.395	9	4	2B-123, 1B-68, 3B-16

Jim Price

PRICE, JIMMIE WILLIAM   BR TR 6' 192 lbs.
B. Oct. 13, 1941, Harrisburg, Pa.

	G	AB	H	2B	3B	HR	HR%	R	RBI	BB	SO	SB	BA	SA	PH AB	PH H	G by POS
'67 DET A	44	92	24	4	0	0	0.0	9	8	4	10	0	.261	.304	20	5	C-24
'68	64	132	23	4	0	3	2.3	12	13	13	14	0	.174	.273	22	5	C-42
'69	72	192	45	8	0	9	4.7	21	28	18	20	0	.234	.417	21	2	C-51
'70	52	132	24	4	0	5	3.8	12	15	21	23	0	.182	.326	12	1	C-38
'71	29	54	13	2	0	1	1.9	4	7	6	3	0	.241	.333	2	0	C-25
5 yrs.	261	602	129	22	0	18	3.0	58	71	62	70	0	.214	.341	77	13	C-180
5 yrs.	261	602	129	22	0	18	3.0	58	71	62	70	0	.214	.341	77	13	C-180

WORLD SERIES

	G	AB	H	2B	3B	HR	HR%	R	RBI	BB	SO	SB	BA	SA	PH AB	PH H	G by POS
'68 DET A	2	2	0	0	0	0	0.0	0	0	0	1	0	.000	.000	2	0	

Jerry Priddy

PRIDDY, GERALD EDWARD   BR TR 5'11½" 180 lbs.
B. Nov. 9, 1919, Los Angeles, Calif.   D. Mar. 3, 1980, North Hollywood, Calif.

	G	AB	H	2B	3B	HR	HR%	R	RBI	BB	SO	SB	BA	SA	PH AB	PH H	G by POS
'41 NY A	56	174	37	7	0	1	0.6	18	26	18	16	4	.213	.270	2	1	2B-31, 3B-14, 1B-10
'42	59	189	53	9	2	2	1.1	23	28	31	27	0	.280	.381	3	1	3B-35, 1B-11, 2B-8, SS-3
'43 WAS A	149	560	152	31	3	4	0.7	68	62	67	76	5	.271	.359	0	0	2B-134, SS-15, 3B-1
'46	138	511	130	22	8	6	1.2	54	58	57	73	9	.254	.364	0	0	2B-138
'47	147	505	108	20	3	3	0.6	42	49	62	79	7	.214	.283	1	0	2B-146
'48 STL A	151	560	166	40	9	8	1.4	96	79	86	71	6	.296	.443	3	0	2B-146
'49	145	544	158	26	4	11	2.0	83	63	80	81	5	.290	.414	0	0	2B-145
'50 DET A	157	618	171	26	6	13	2.1	104	75	95	95	2	.277	.401	0	0	2B-157
'51	154	584	152	22	6	8	1.4	73	57	69	73	4	.260	.360	0	0	2B-154, SS-1
'52	75	279	79	23	3	4	1.4	37	20	42	29	1	.283	.430	0	0	2B-75
'53	65	196	46	6	2	1	0.5	14	24	17	19	1	.235	.301	9	2	2B-45, 1B-11, 3B-2
11 yrs.	1296	4720	1252	232	46	61	1.3	612	541	624	639	44	.265	.373	18	4	2B-1179, 3B-52, 1B-32, SS-19
4 yrs.	451	1677	448	77	17	26	1.6	228	176	223	216	8	.267	.380	9	2	2B-431, 1B-11, 3B-2, SS-1

WORLD SERIES

	G	AB	H	2B	3B	HR	HR%	R	RBI	BB	SO	SB	BA	SA	PH AB	PH H	G by POS
'42 NY A	3	10	1	1	0	0	0.0	0	1	1	0	0	.100	.200	0	0	1B-3

Billy Purtell

PURTELL, WILLIAM PATRICK   BR TR 5'9" 170 lbs.
B. Jan. 6, 1886, Columbus, Ohio   D. Mar. 17, 1962, Bradenton, Fla.

	G	AB	H	2B	3B	HR	HR%	R	RBI	BB	SO	SB	BA	SA	PH AB	PH H	G by POS
'08 CHI A	26	69	9	2	0	0	0.0	3	3	2		2	.130	.159	1	0	3B-25
'09	103	361	93	9	3	0	0.0	34	40	19		14	.258	.299	0	0	3B-71, 2B-32
'10 2 teams			CHI A (102G – .234)			BOS A (49G – .208)											
total	151	536	121	6	5	2	0.4	36	51	39		7	.226	.267	0	0	3B-143, SS-8
'11 BOS A	27	82	23	5	3	0	0.0	5	7	1		1	.280	.415	5	1	3B-16, SS-3, 2B-3, OF-1
'14 DET A	26	76	13	4	0	0	0.0	4	3	2	7	0	.171	.224	8	1	3B-16, SS-1, 2B-1
5 yrs.	333	1124	259	26	11	2	0.2	82	104	63	7	24	.230	.278	14	2	3B-271, 2B-36, SS-12, OF-1
1 yr.	26	76	13	4	0	0	0.0	4	3	2	7	0	.171	.224	8	1	3B-16, SS-1, 2B-1

Ed Putman

PUTMAN, EDDIE WILLIAM   BR TR 6'1" 190 lbs.
B. Sept. 25, 1953, Los Angeles, Calif.

	G	AB	H	2B	3B	HR	HR%	R	RBI	BB	SO	SB	BA	SA	PH AB	PH H	G by POS
'76 CHI N	5	7	3	0	0	0	0.0	0	0	0	0	0	.429	.429	2	1	C-3, 1B-1
'78	17	25	5	0	0	0	0.0	2	3	4	6	0	.200	.200	5	2	3B-8, 1B-3, C-2
'79 DET A	21	39	9	3	0	2	5.1	4	4	4	12	0	.231	.462	3	0	C-16, 1B-5
3 yrs.	43	71	17	3	0	2	2.8	6	7	8	18	0	.239	.366	10	3	C-21, 1B-9, 3B-8
1 yr.	21	39	9	3	0	2	5.1	4	4	4	12	0	.231	.462	3	0	C-16, 1B-5

George Quellich

QUELLICH, GEORGE WILLIAM   BR TR 6'1" 180 lbs.
B. Feb. 10, 1906, Johnsville, Calif.   D. Aug. 31, 1958, Johnsville, Calif.

	G	AB	H	2B	3B	HR	HR%	R	RBI	BB	SO	SB	BA	SA	PH AB	PH H	G by POS
'31 DET A	13	54	12	5	0	1	1.9	6	11	3	4	1	.222	.370	0	0	OF-13

Rip Radcliff

RADCLIFF, RAYMOND ALLEN   BL TL 5'10" 170 lbs.
B. Jan. 19, 1906, Kiowa, Okla.   D. May 23, 1962, Enid, Okla.

	G	AB	H	2B	3B	HR	HR%	R	RBI	BB	SO	SB	BA	SA	PH AB	PH H	G by POS
'34 CHI A	14	56	15	2	1	0	0.0	7	5	0	2	1	.268	.339	0	0	OF-14
'35	146	623	178	28	8	10	1.6	95	68	53	21	4	.286	.404	2	0	OF-142
'36	138	618	207	31	7	8	1.3	120	82	44	12	6	.335	.447	3	0	OF-132
'37	144	584	190	38	10	4	0.7	105	79	53	25	6	.325	.445	5	3	OF-139

	G	AB	H	2B	3B	HR	HR %	R	RBI	BB	SO	SB	BA	SA	Pinch Hit AB	Pinch Hit H	G by POS

Rip Radcliff continued

	G	AB	H	2B	3B	HR	HR%	R	RBI	BB	SO	SB	BA	SA	AB	H	G by POS
1938	129	503	166	23	6	5	1.0	64	81	36	17	5	.330	.429	7	2	OF-99, 1B-23
1939	113	397	105	25	2	2	0.5	49	53	26	21	6	.264	.353	13	1	OF-78, 1B-20
1940 STL A	150	584	**200**	33	9	7	1.2	83	81	47	20	6	.342	.466	5	1	OF-139, 1B-4
1941 2 teams		STL	A	(19G –	.282)		DET	A	(96G –	.317)							
" total	115	450	140	16	7	5	1.1	59	53	29	14	5	.311	.411	8	0	OF-101, 1B-3
1942 DET A	62	144	36	5	0	1	0.7	13	20	9	6	0	.250	.306	29	3	OF-24, 1B-4
1943	70	115	30	4	0	0	0.0	3	10	13	3	1	.261	.296	44	11	OF-19, 1B-1
10 yrs.	1081	4074	1267	205	50	42	1.0	598	532	310	141	40	.311	.417	119	24	OF-887, 1B-55
3 yrs.	228	638	186	23	5	4	0.6	63	69	41	22	5	.292	.362	81	14	OF-130, 1B-5

Earl Rapp

RAPP, EARL WELLINGTON
B. May 20, 1921, Corunna, Mich.

BL TR 6'2" 185 lb

	G	AB	H	2B	3B	HR	HR%	R	RBI	BB	SO	SB	BA	SA	AB	H	G by POS
1949 2 teams		DET	A	(1G –	.000)		CHI	A	(19G –	.259)							
" total	20	54	14	1	1	0	0.0	3	11	6	6	1	.259	.315	5	1	OF-13
1951 2 teams		NY	N	(13G –	.091)		STL	A	(26G –	.327)							
" total	39	109	33	5	3	2	1.8	14	15	13	14	1	.303	.459	12	1	OF-25
1952 2 teams		STL	A	(30G –	.143)		WAS	A	(46G –	.284)							
" total	76	116	26	10	0	0	0.0	10	13	6	21	0	.224	.310	54	10	OF-17
3 yrs.	135	279	73	16	4	2	0.7	27	39	25	41	2	.262	.369	71	12	OF-55
1 yr.	1	0	0	0	0	0	–	0	0	1	0	0	–	–	0	0	

Wayne Redmond

REDMOND, HOWARD WAYNE
B. Nov. 25, 1945, Athens, Ala.

BR TR 5'10" 165 lb

	G	AB	H	2B	3B	HR	HR%	R	RBI	BB	SO	SB	BA	SA	AB	H	G by POS
1965 DET A	4	4	0	0	0	0	0.0	1	0	1	1	0	.000	.000	0	0	OF-2
1969	5	3	0	0	0	0	0.0	0	0	0	2	0	.000	.000	3	0	
2 yrs.	9	7	0	0	0	0	0.0	1	0	1	3	0	.000	.000	3	0	OF-2
2 yrs.	9	7	0	0	0	0	0.0	1	0	1	3	0	.000	.000	3	0	OF-2

Rich Reese

REESE, RICHARD BENJAMIN
B. Sept. 29, 1941, Leipsic, Ohio

BL TL 6'3" 185 lb

	G	AB	H	2B	3B	HR	HR%	R	RBI	BB	SO	SB	BA	SA	AB	H	G by POS
1964 MIN A	10	7	0	0	0	0	0.0	0	0	0	1	0	.000	.000	7	0	1B-1
1965	14	7	2	1	0	0	0.0	0	0	2	2	0	.286	.429	4	1	1B-6, OF-1
1966	3	2	0	0	0	0	0.0	0	0	1	2	0	.000	.000	2	0	
1967	95	101	25	5	0	4	4.0	13	20	8	17	0	.248	.416	41	13	1B-36, OF-10
1968	126	332	86	15	2	4	1.2	40	28	18	36	3	.259	.352	30	6	1B-87, OF-15
1969	132	419	135	24	4	16	3.8	52	69	23	57	1	.322	.513	17	4	1B-117, OF-5
1970	153	501	131	15	5	10	2.0	63	56	48	70	5	.261	.371	12	4	1B-146
1971	120	329	72	8	3	10	3.0	40	39	20	35	7	.219	.353	20	6	1B-95, OF-9
1972	132	197	43	3	2	5	2.5	23	26	25	27	0	.218	.330	26	7	1B-98, OF-13
1973 2 teams		MIN	A	(22G –	.174)		DET	A	(59G –	.137)							
" total	81	125	18	2	1	3	2.4	17	7	13	23	0	.144	.248	15	3	1B-54, OF-21
1 yr.	59	102	14	1	0	2	2.0	10	4	7	17	0	.137	.206	8	0	1B-37, OF-21
10 yrs.	866	2020	512	73	17	52	2.6	248	245	158	270	16	.253	.384	174	44	1B-640, OF-74

LEAGUE CHAMPIONSHIP SERIES

	G	AB	H	2B	3B	HR	HR%	R	RBI	BB	SO	SB	BA	SA	AB	H	G by POS
1969 MIN A	3	12	2	0	0	0	0.0	0	2	1	1	0	.167	.167	0	0	1B-3
1970	2	7	1	0	0	0	0.0	0	0	1	1	0	.143	.143	0	0	1B-2
2 yrs.	5	19	3	0	0	0	0.0	0	2	2	2	0	.158	.158	0	0	1B-5

Frank Reiber

REIBER, FRANK BERNARD (Tubby)
B. Sept. 19, 1909, Huntington, W. Va.

BR TR 5'8½" 169 lb

	G	AB	H	2B	3B	HR	HR%	R	RBI	BB	SO	SB	BA	SA	AB	H	G by POS
1933 DET A	13	18	5	0	1	1	5.6	3	3	2	3	0	.278	.556	6	1	C-6
1934	3	1	0	0	0	0	0.0	0	0	2	0	0	.000	.000	1	0	
1935	8	11	3	0	0	0	0.0	3	1	3	3	0	.273	.273	2	0	C-5
1936	20	55	15	2	0	1	1.8	7	5	5	7	0	.273	.364	2	0	C-17, OF-1
4 yrs.	44	85	23	2	1	2	2.4	13	9	12	13	0	.271	.388	11	1	C-28, OF-1
4 yrs.	44	85	23	2	1	2	2.4	13	9	12	13	0	.271	.388	11	1	C-28, OF-1

Tony Rensa

RENSA, TONY GEORGE (Pug)
B. Sept. 29, 1901, Parsons, Pa.

BR TR 5'10" 180 lb

	G	AB	H	2B	3B	HR	HR%	R	RBI	BB	SO	SB	BA	SA	AB	H	G by POS
1930 2 teams		DET	A	(20G –	.270)		PHI	N	(54G –	.285)							
" total	74	209	59	13	3	4	1.9	37	34	16	25	1	.282	.431	6	1	C-67
1931 PHI N	19	29	3	1	0	0	0.0	2	2	6	2	0	.103	.138	2	0	C-17
1933 NY A	8	29	9	2	1	0	0.0	4	3	1	3	0	.310	.448	0	0	C-8
1937 CHI A	26	57	17	5	1	0	0.0	10	5	8	6	3	.298	.421	2	1	C-23
1938	59	165	41	5	0	3	1.8	15	19	25	16	1	.248	.333	2	0	C-57
1939	14	25	5	0	0	0	0.0	3	2	1	2	0	.200	.200	1	1	C-13
6 yrs.	200	514	134	26	5	7	1.4	71	65	57	54	5	.261	.372	13	3	C-185
1 yr.	20	37	10	2	1	1	2.7	6	3	6	7	1	.270	.459	1	0	C-18

Billy Rhiel

RHIEL, WILLIAM JOSEPH
B. Aug. 16, 1900, Youngstown, Ohio   D. Aug. 16, 1946, Youngstown, Ohio

BR TR 5'11" 175 lb

	G	AB	H	2B	3B	HR	HR%	R	RBI	BB	SO	SB	BA	SA	AB	H	G by POS
1929 BKN N	76	205	57	9	4	4	2.0	27	25	19	25	0	.278	.420	14	2	2B-47, 3B-7, SS-2
1930 BOS N	20	47	8	4	0	0	0.0	3	4	2	5	0	.170	.255	3	0	3B-13, 2B-2
1932 DET A	84	250	70	13	3	3	1.2	30	38	17	23	2	.280	.392	27	13	3B-36, 1B-12, OF-8, 2B
1933	19	17	3	0	1	0	0.0	1	1	5	4	0	.176	.294	13	3	OF-1
4 yrs.	199	519	138	26	8	7	1.3	61	68	43	57	2	.266	.387	57	18	3B-56, 2B-50, 1B-12, OF-9, SS-2
2 yrs.	103	267	73	13	4	3	1.1	31	39	22	27	2	.273	.386	40	16	3B-36, 1B-12, OF-9, 2B

Harry Rice

RICE, HARRY FRANCIS
B. Nov. 22, 1901, Ware Station, Ill.   D. Jan. 1, 1971, Portland, Ore.

BL TR 5'9" 185 lb

	G	AB	H	2B	3B	HR	HR%	R	RBI	BB	SO	SB	BA	SA	AB	H	G by POS
1923 STL A	4	3	0	0	0	0	0.0	0	0	0	0	0	.000	.000	3	0	
1924	43	92	26	7	0	0	0.0	19	15	7	5	1	.283	.359	22	7	3B-15, 2B-4, OF-2, SS, 1B-2
1925	103	354	127	25	8	11	3.1	87	47	54	15	8	.359	.568	14	6	OF-85, 1B-3, 3B-1, 2B, C-1

	G	AB	H	2B	3B	HR	HR %	R	RBI	BB	SO	SB	BA	SA	Pinch Hit AB	Pinch Hit H	G by POS

Harry Rice continued

	G	AB	H	2B	3B	HR	HR%	R	RBI	BB	SO	SB	BA	SA	PH AB	PH H	G by POS
26	148	578	181	27	10	9	1.6	86	59	63	40	10	.313	.441	4	2	OF-133, 3B-7, 2B-4, SS-2
27	137	520	149	26	9	7	1.3	90	68	50	21	6	.287	.412	0	0	OF-130, 3B-7
28 DET A	131	510	154	21	12	6	1.2	87	81	44	27	20	.302	.425	2	0	OF-129, 3B-2
29	130	536	163	33	7	6	1.1	97	69	61	23	6	.304	.425	1	0	OF-127, 3B-3
30 2 teams		DET	A (37G –	.305)		NY	A	(100G –	.298)								
total	137	474	142	23	5	9	1.9	78	98	50	29	3	.300	.426	8	1	OF-122, 1B-6, 3B-1
31 WAS A	47	162	43	5	6	0	0.0	32	15	12	10	2	.265	.370	5	3	OF-42
33 CIN N	143	510	133	19	6	0	0.0	44	54	35	24	4	.261	.322	1	0	OF-141, 3B-1
10 yrs.	1023	3739	1118	186	63	48	1.3	620	506	376	194	60	.299	.421	60	19	OF-911, 3B-37, 1B-11, 2B-9, SS-4, C-1
3 yrs.	298	1174	356	60	19	14	1.2	200	174	124	58	26	.303	.422	4	1	OF-291, 3B-5

RICHARDS, PAUL RAPIER
B. Nov. 21, 1908, Waxahachie, Tex.
Manager 1951-61, 1976.
BR TR 6'1½" 180 lbs.

Paul Richards

	G	AB	H	2B	3B	HR	HR%	R	RBI	BB	SO	SB	BA	SA	PH AB	PH H	G by POS
32 BKN N	3	8	0	0	0	0	0.0	0	0	0	2	0	.000	.000	0	0	C-3
33 NY N	51	87	17	3	0	0	0.0	4	10	3	12	0	.195	.230	14	2	C-36
34	42	75	12	1	0	0	0.0	10	3	13	8	0	.160	.173	3	2	C-37
35 2 teams		NY	N (7G –	.250)		PHI	A	(85G –	.245)								
total	92	261	64	10	1	4	1.5	31	29	26	13	0	.245	.337	6	2	C-83
43 DET A	100	313	69	7	1	5	1.6	32	33	38	35	1	.220	.297	0	0	C-100
44	95	300	71	13	0	3	1.0	24	37	35	30	8	.237	.310	3	0	C-90
45	83	234	60	12	1	3	1.3	26	32	19	31	4	.256	.355	0	0	C-83
46	57	139	28	5	2	0	0.0	13	11	23	18	2	.201	.266	3	2	C-54
8 yrs.	523	1417	321	51	5	15	1.1	140	155	157	149	15	.227	.301	29	8	C-486
4 yrs.	335	986	228	37	4	11	1.1	95	113	115	114	15	.231	.310	6	2	C-327

WORLD SERIES

	G	AB	H	2B	3B	HR	HR%	R	RBI	BB	SO	SB	BA	SA	PH AB	PH H	G by POS
45 DET A	7	19	4	2	0	0	0.0	0	6	4	3	0	.211	.316	0	0	C-7

RICHARDSEN, CLIFFORD NOLEN
B. Jan. 18, 1903, Chattanooga, Tenn.   D. Sept. 25, 1951, Athens, Ga.
BR TR 6'1½" 170 lbs.

Nolen Richardsen

	G	AB	H	2B	3B	HR	HR%	R	RBI	BB	SO	SB	BA	SA	PH AB	PH H	G by POS
29 DET A	13	21	4	0	0	0	0.0	2	2	2	1	1	.190	.190	0	0	SS-13
31	38	148	40	9	2	0	0.0	13	16	6	3	2	.270	.358	0	0	3B-38
32	69	155	34	5	2	0	0.0	13	12	9	13	5	.219	.277	0	0	3B-65, SS-4
35 NY A	12	46	10	1	1	0	0.0	3	5	3	1	0	.217	.283	0	0	SS-12
38 CIN N	35	100	29	4	0	0	0.0	8	10	3	4	0	.290	.330	0	0	SS-35
39	1	3	0	0	0	0	0.0	0	0	0	0	0	.000	.000	0	0	SS-1
6 yrs.	168	473	117	19	5	0	0.0	39	45	23	22	8	.247	.309	0	0	3B-103, SS-65
3 yrs.	120	324	78	14	4	0	0.0	28	30	17	17	8	.241	.309	0	0	3B-103, SS-17

RIEBE, HARVEY DONALD
B. Oct. 10, 1921, Cleveland, Ohio
BR TR 5'9½" 175 lbs.

Hank Riebe

	G	AB	H	2B	3B	HR	HR%	R	RBI	BB	SO	SB	BA	SA	PH AB	PH H	G by POS
42 DET A	11	35	11	2	0	0	0.0	1	2	0	6	0	.314	.371	0	0	C-11
47	8	7	0	0	0	0	0.0	0	2	0	2	0	.000	.000	5	0	C-3
48	25	62	12	0	0	0	0.0	0	5	3	5	0	.194	.194	1	0	C-24
49	17	33	6	2	0	0	0.0	1	2	0	5	1	.182	.242	6	1	C-11
4 yrs.	61	137	29	4	0	0	0.0	2	11	3	18	1	.212	.241	12	1	C-49
4 yrs.	61	137	29	4	0	0	0.0	2	11	3	18	1	.212	.241	12	1	C-49

RIGNEY, EMORY ELMO
B. Jan. 7, 1897, Groveton, Tex.   D. June 6, 1972, San Antonio, Tex.
BR TR 5'9" 150 lbs.

Topper Rigney

	G	AB	H	2B	3B	HR	HR%	R	RBI	BB	SO	SB	BA	SA	PH AB	PH H	G by POS
22 DET A	155	536	161	17	7	2	0.4	68	63	68	44	17	.300	.369	0	0	SS-155
23	129	470	148	24	11	1	0.2	63	74	55	35	7	.315	.419	0	0	SS-129
24	147	499	144	29	9	4	0.8	81	93	102	39	11	.289	.407	1	0	SS-146
25	62	146	36	5	2	2	1.4	21	18	21	15	2	.247	.349	6	0	SS-51, 3B-4
26 BOS A	148	525	142	32	6	4	0.8	71	53	108	31	6	.270	.377	2	0	SS-146
27 2 teams		BOS	A (8G –	.111)		WAS	A	(45G –	.273)								
total	53	150	38	6	4	0	0.0	20	13	23	12	1	.253	.347	10	4	SS-33, 3B-10
6 yrs.	694	2326	669	113	39	13	0.6	324	314	377	176	44	.288	.387	19	4	SS-660, 3B-14
4 yrs.	493	1651	489	75	29	9	0.5	233	248	246	133	37	.296	.393	7	0	SS-481, 3B-4

ROARKE, MICHAEL THOMAS
B. Nov. 8, 1930, West Warwick, R. I.
BR TR 6'2" 195 lbs.

Mike Roarke

	G	AB	H	2B	3B	HR	HR%	R	RBI	BB	SO	SB	BA	SA	PH AB	PH H	G by POS
61 DET A	86	229	51	6	1	2	0.9	21	22	20	31	0	.223	.284	1	0	C-85
62	56	136	29	4	1	4	2.9	11	14	13	17	0	.213	.346	3	1	C-53
63	23	44	14	0	0	0	0.0	5	1	2	3	0	.318	.318	7	1	C-16
64	29	82	19	1	0	0	0.0	4	7	10	10	0	.232	.244	2	1	C-27
4 yrs.	194	491	113	11	2	6	1.2	41	44	45	61	0	.230	.297	13	3	C-181
4 yrs.	194	491	113	11	2	6	1.2	41	44	45	61	0	.230	.297	13	3	C-181

ROBERTS, LEON KAUFFMAN
B. Jan. 22, 1951, Vicksburg, Mich.
BR TR 6'3" 200 lbs.

Leon Roberts

	G	AB	H	2B	3B	HR	HR%	R	RBI	BB	SO	SB	BA	SA	PH AB	PH H	G by POS
74 DET A	17	63	17	3	2	0	0.0	5	7	3	10	0	.270	.381	1	0	OF-17
75	129	447	115	17	5	10	2.2	51	38	36	94	3	.257	.385	3	1	OF-127, DH-1
76 HOU N	87	235	68	11	2	7	3.0	31	33	19	43	1	.289	.443	27	7	OF-60
77	19	27	2	0	0	0	0.0	1	2	1	8	0	.074	.074	10	2	OF-9
78 SEA A	134	472	142	21	7	22	4.7	78	92	41	52	6	.301	.515	8	4	OF-128, DH-2
79	140	450	122	24	6	15	3.3	61	54	56	64	3	.271	.451	12	4	OF-136, DH-1
80	119	374	94	18	3	10	2.7	48	33	43	59	8	.251	.396	12	2	OF-104, DH-4
81 TEX A	72	233	65	17	2	4	1.7	26	31	25	38	3	.279	.421	4	0	OF-71
82 2 teams		TEX	A (31G –	.233)		TOR	A	(40G –	.229)								
total	71	178	41	7	0	2	1.1	13	11	11	30	1	.230	.303	16	4	OF-44, DH-22
83 KC A	84	213	55	7	0	8	3.8	24	24	17	27	1	.258	.404	13	4	OF-76, DH-1
84	29	45	10	1	1	0	0.0	4	3	4	3	0	.222	.289	13	3	OF-16, DH-3, P-1
11 yrs.	901	2737	731	126	28	78	2.8	342	328	256	428	26	.267	.419	119	31	OF-788, DH-34, P-1
2 yrs.	146	510	132	20	7	10	2.0	56	45	39	104	3	.259	.384	4	1	OF-144, DH-1

	G	AB	H	2B	3B	HR	HR %	R	RBI	BB	SO	SB	BA	SA	Pinch Hit AB	Pinch Hit H	G by POS

Aaron Robinson

ROBINSON, AARON ANDREW
B. June 23, 1915, Lancaster, S. C. D. Mar. 9, 1966, Lancaster, S. C.
BL TR 6'2" 205 lb

	G	AB	H	2B	3B	HR	HR %	R	RBI	BB	SO	SB	BA	SA	PH AB	PH H	G by POS
1943 NY A	1	1	0	0	0	0	0.0	0	0	0	1	0	.000	.000	1	0	
1945	50	160	45	6	1	8	5.0	19	24	21	23	0	.281	.481	4	3	C-45
1946	100	330	98	17	2	16	4.8	32	64	48	39	0	.297	.506	4	1	C-95
1947	82	252	68	11	5	5	2.0	23	36	40	26	0	.270	.413	7	1	C-74
1948 CHI A	98	326	82	14	2	8	2.5	47	39	46	30	0	.252	.380	6	1	C-92
1949 DET A	110	331	89	12	0	13	3.9	38	56	73	21	0	.269	.423	2	0	C-108
1950	107	283	64	7	0	9	3.2	37	37	75	35	0	.226	.346	3	3	C-103
1951 2 teams		DET	A (36G –	.207)		BOS	A (26G –	.203)									
" total	62	156	32	7	1	2	1.3	12	16	34	19	0	.205	.301	2	1	C-60
8 yrs.	610	1839	478	74	11	61	3.3	208	272	337	194	0	.260	.412	29	10	C-577
3 yrs.	253	696	170	25	0	22	3.2	78	102	165	65	0	.244	.375	6	4	C-246

WORLD SERIES

1947 NY A	3	10	2	0	0	0	0.0	2	1	2	1	0	.200	.200	0	0	C-3

Eddie Robinson

ROBINSON, WILLIAM EDWARD
B. Dec. 15, 1920, Paris, Tex.
BL TR 6'2½" 210 lb

	G	AB	H	2B	3B	HR	HR %	R	RBI	BB	SO	SB	BA	SA	PH AB	PH H	G by POS
1942 CLE A	8	8	1	0	0	0	0.0	1	2	1	0	0	.125	.125	6	1	1B-1
1946	7	27	11	0	0	3	11.1	5	4	1	4	0	.407	.741	0	0	1B-7
1947	95	318	78	10	1	14	4.4	52	52	30	18	1	.245	.415	5	1	1B-87
1948	134	493	125	18	5	16	3.2	53	83	36	42	1	.254	.408	4	1	1B-131
1949 WAS A	143	527	155	27	3	18	3.4	66	78	67	30	3	.294	.459	0	0	1B-143
1950 2 teams		WAS	A (36G –	.240)		CHI	A (119G –	.311)									
" total	155	553	163	15	4	21	3.8	83	86	85	32	0	.295	.450	0	0	1B-155
1951 CHI A	151	564	159	23	5	29	5.1	85	117	77	54	2	.282	.495	2	0	1B-147
1952	155	594	176	33	1	22	3.7	79	104	70	49	2	.296	.466	0	0	1B-155
1953 PHI A	156	615	152	28	4	22	3.6	64	102	63	56	1	.247	.413	1	0	1B-155
1954 NY A	85	142	37	9	0	3	2.1	11	27	19	21	0	.261	.387	49	15	1B-29
1955	88	173	36	1	0	16	9.2	25	42	36	26	0	.208	.491	34	5	1B-46
1956 2 teams		NY	A (26G –	.222)		KC	A (75G –	.198)									
" total	101	226	46	6	1	7	3.1	20	23	31	23	0	.204	.332	34	6	1B-61
1957 3 teams		DET	A (13G –	.000)		CLE	A (19G –	.222)		BAL	A (4G –	.000)					
" total	36	39	6	0	0	1	2.6	1	3	4	4	0	.154	.256	21	1	1B-8
13 yrs.	1314	4279	1145	171	24	172	4.0	545	723	520	359	10	.268	.439	156	30	1B-1125
1 yr.	13	9	0	0	0	0	0.0	0	0	0	3	0	.000	.000	8	0	1B-1

WORLD SERIES

1948 CLE A	6	20	6	0	0	0	0.0	0	1	1	0	0	.300	.300	1	0	1B-6
1955 NY A	4	3	2	0	0	0	0.0	0	1	2	1	0	.667	.667	1	1	1B-1
2 yrs.	10	23	8	0	0	0	0.0	0	2	3	1	0	.348	.348	1	1	1B-7

Rabbit Robinson

ROBINSON, CLYDE WILLIAM (Tug)
B. Mar. 5, 1882, Wellsburg, W. Va. D. Apr. 9, 1915, Waterbury, Conn.
BR TR 5'5" 148 lb

	G	AB	H	2B	3B	HR	HR %	R	RBI	BB	SO	SB	BA	SA	PH AB	PH H	G by POS
1903 WAS A	103	373	79	10	8	1	0.3	41	20	33		16	.212	.290	0	0	2B-45, OF-30, SS-24, 3B-5
1904 DET A	101	320	77	13	6	0	0.0	30	37	29		14	.241	.319	5	1	SS-30, 3B-26, OF-20, 2B-19
1910 CIN N	2	7	0	0	0	0	0.0	0	1	1		0	.000	.000	0	0	3B-2
3 yrs.	206	700	156	23	14	1	0.1	71	58	63	0	30	.223	.300	5	1	2B-64, SS-54, OF-50, 3B-33
1 yr.	101	320	77	13	6	0	0.0	30	37	29		14	.241	.319	5	1	SS-30, 3B-26, OF-20, 2B-19

Aurelio Rodriguez

RODRIGUEZ, AURELIO ITUARTE (Leo)
B. Dec. 28, 1947, Cananea Sonora, Mexico
BR TR 5'10" 180 lb

	G	AB	H	2B	3B	HR	HR %	R	RBI	BB	SO	SB	BA	SA	PH AB	PH H	G by POS
1967 CAL A	29	130	31	3	1	1	0.8	14	8	2	21	1	.238	.300	0	0	3B-29
1968	76	223	54	10	1	1	0.4	14	16	17	35	0	.242	.309	3	2	3B-70, 2B-2
1969	159	561	130	17	2	7	1.2	47	49	32	88	5	.232	.307	0	0	3B-159
1970 2 teams		CAL	A (17G –	.270)		WAS	A (142G –	.247)									
" total	159	610	152	33	7	19	3.1	70	83	40	87	15	.249	.420	0	0	3B-153, SS-7
1971 DET A	154	604	153	30	7	15	2.5	68	39	27	93	4	.253	.401	3	1	3B-153, SS-1
1972	153	601	142	23	5	13	2.2	65	56	28	104	2	.236	.356	1	0	3B-153, SS-2
1973	160	555	123	27	3	9	1.6	46	58	31	85	3	.222	.330	0	0	3B-160, SS-1
1974	159	571	127	23	5	5	0.9	54	49	26	70	2	.222	.306	0	0	3B-159
1975	151	507	124	20	6	13	2.6	47	60	30	63	1	.245	.385	0	0	3B-151
1976	128	480	115	13	2	8	1.7	40	50	19	61	0	.240	.325	0	0	3B-128
1977	96	306	67	14	1	10	3.3	30	32	16	36	1	.219	.369	10	1	3B-95, SS-1
1978	134	385	102	25	2	7	1.8	40	43	19	37	0	.265	.395	20	7	3B-131
1979	106	343	87	18	0	5	1.5	27	36	11	40	0	.254	.350	3	0	3B-106, 1B-1
1980 2 teams		SD	N (89G –	.200)		NY	A (52G –	.220)									
" total	141	339	71	13	3	5	1.5	21	27	13	61	1	.209	.310	6	0	3B-137, 2B-6, SS-2
1981 NY A	27	52	18	2	0	2	3.8	4	8	2	10	0	.346	.500	1	1	3B-20, 2B-3, DH-2, 1B-1
1982 CHI A	118	257	62	15	1	3	1.2	24	31	11	35	0	.241	.342	1	0	3B-112, 2B-3, SS-2
1983 2 teams		BAL	A (45G –	.119)		CHI	A (22G –	.200)									
" total	67	87	12	1	0	1	1.1	9	3	0	16	0	.138	.184	0	0	3B-67
17 yrs.	2017	6611	1570	287	46	124	1.9	612	648	324	942	35	.237	.351	48	12	3B-1983, SS-16, 2B-14, DH-2, 1B-2
9 yrs.	1241	4352	1040	193	31	85	2.0	417	423	207	589	13	.239	.356	37	9	3B-1236, SS-5, 1B-1

LEAGUE CHAMPIONSHIP SERIES

1972 DET A	5	16	0	0	0	0	0.0	0	0	2	2	0	.000	.000	0	0	3B-5
1980 NY A	2	6	2	1	0	0	0.0	0	0	0	0	0	.333	.500	0	0	3B-2
1981	1	0	0	0	0	0	–	0	0	0	0	0	–	–	0	0	3B-2
1983 CHI A	2	0	0	0	0	0	–	0	0	0	0	0	–	–	0	0	3B-2
4 yrs.	10	22	2	1	0	0	0.0	0	0	2	2	0	.091	.136	0	0	3B-10

WORLD SERIES

1981 NY A	4	12	5	0	0	0	0.0	1	0	1	2	0	.417	.417	0	0	3B-3

	G	AB	H	2B	3B	HR	HR %	R	RBI	BB	SO	SB	BA	SA	Pinch Hit AB	Pinch Hit H	G by POS

Billy Rogell

ROGELL, WILLIAM GEORGE
B. Nov. 24, 1904, Springfield, Ill.
BB TR 5'10½" 163 lbs.

	G	AB	H	2B	3B	HR	HR %	R	RBI	BB	SO	SB	BA	SA	PH AB	PH H	G by POS
25 BOS A	58	169	33	5	1	0	0.0	12	17	11	17	0	.195	.237	2	0	2B-49, SS-6
27	82	207	55	14	6	2	1.0	35	28	24	28	3	.266	.420	15	3	3B-53, OF-2, 2B-2
28	102	296	69	10	4	0	0.0	33	29	22	47	2	.233	.294	7	1	SS-67, 2B-22, OF-6, 3B-3
30 DET A	54	144	24	4	2	0	0.0	20	9	15	23	1	.167	.222	2	0	SS-33, 3B-13, OF-1
31	48	185	56	12	3	2	1.1	21	24	24	17	8	.303	.432	0	0	SS-48
32	143	554	150	29	6	9	1.6	88	61	50	38	14	.271	.394	0	0	SS-139, 3B-4
33	155	587	173	42	11	0	0.0	67	57	79	33	6	.295	.404	0	0	SS-155
34	154	592	175	32	8	3	0.5	114	100	74	36	13	.296	.392	0	0	SS-154
35	150	560	154	23	11	6	1.1	88	71	80	29	3	.275	.388	0	0	SS-150
36	146	585	160	27	5	6	1.0	85	68	73	41	14	.274	.368	1	0	SS-146, 3B-1
37	146	536	148	30	7	8	1.5	85	64	83	48	5	.276	.403	0	0	SS-146
38	136	501	130	22	8	3	0.6	76	55	86	37	9	.259	.353	2	0	SS-134
39	74	174	40	6	3	2	1.1	24	23	26	14	3	.230	.333	3	0	SS-43, 3B-21, 2B-2
40 CHI N	33	59	8	0	0	1	1.7	7	3	2	8	1	.136	.186	6	1	SS-14, 3B-9, 2B-3
14 yrs.	1481	5149	1375	256	75	42	0.8	755	609	649	416	82	.267	.370	38	5	SS-1235, 3B-104, 2B-78, OF-9
10 yrs.	1206	4418	1210	227	64	39	0.9	668	532	590	316	76	.274	.381	8	0	SS-1148, 3B-39, 2B-2, OF-1

WORLD SERIES

	G	AB	H	2B	3B	HR	HR %	R	RBI	BB	SO	SB	BA	SA	PH AB	PH H	G by POS
34 DET A	7	29	8	1	0	0	0.0	3	4	1	4	0	.276	.310	0	0	SS-7
35	6	24	7	2	0	0	0.0	1	1	2	5	0	.292	.375	0	0	SS-6
2 yrs.	13	53	15	3	0	0	0.0	4	5	3	9	0	.283	.340	0	0	SS-13

Bill Roman

ROMAN, WILLIAM ANTHONY
B. Oct. 11, 1938, Detroit, Mich.
BL TL 6'4" 190 lbs.

	G	AB	H	2B	3B	HR	HR %	R	RBI	BB	SO	SB	BA	SA	PH AB	PH H	G by POS
64 DET A	3	8	3	0	0	1	12.5	2	1	0	2	0	.375	.750	2	1	1B-2
65	21	27	2	0	0	0	0.0	0	2	2	7	0	.074	.074	13	2	1B-6
2 yrs.	24	35	5	0	0	1	2.9	2	1	2	9	0	.143	.229	15	3	1B-8
2 yrs.	24	35	5	0	0	1	2.9	2	1	2	9	0	.143	.229	15	3	1B-8

Henri Rondeau

RONDEAU, HENRI JOSEPH
B. May 5, 1887, Danielson, Conn.   D. May 28, 1943, Woonsocket, R. I.
BR TR 5'10½" 175 lbs.

	G	AB	H	2B	3B	HR	HR %	R	RBI	BB	SO	SB	BA	SA	PH AB	PH H	G by POS
13 DET A	35	70	13	0	0	0	0.0	5	5	14	16	1	.186	.214	13	2	C-14, 1B-6
15 WAS A	14	40	7	0	0	0	0.0	3	4	4	3	1	.175	.175	3	0	OF-11
16	50	162	36	5	3	1	0.6	20	28	18	18	7	.222	.309	0	0	OF-48
3 yrs.	99	272	56	7	3	1	0.4	28	37	36	37	9	.206	.265	16	2	OF-59, C-14, 1B-6
1 yr.	35	70	13	2	0	0	0.0	5	5	14	16	1	.186	.214	13	2	C-14, 1B-6

Don Ross

ROSS, DONALD RAYMOND
B. July 16, 1914, Pasadena, Calif.
BR TR 6'1" 185 lbs.

	G	AB	H	2B	3B	HR	HR %	R	RBI	BB	SO	SB	BA	SA	PH AB	PH H	G by POS
38 DET A	77	265	69	7	1	1	0.4	22	30	28	11	1	.260	.306	2	0	3B-75
40 BKN N	10	38	11	2	0	1	2.6	4	8	3	3	1	.289	.421	0	0	3B-10
42 DET A	87	226	62	10	2	3	1.3	29	30	36	16	2	.274	.376	22	8	OF-38, 3B-20
43	89	247	66	13	0	0	0.0	19	18	20	3	2	.267	.320	24	5	OF-38, SS-18, 2B-7, 3B-1
44	66	167	35	5	0	2	1.2	14	15	14	9	2	.210	.275	24	8	OF-37, SS-2, 1B-1
45 2 teams	114	DET A (8G – .379)			CLE A (106G – .262)												
total	114	392	106	19	1	2	0.5	29	47	47	16	2	.270	.339	1	1	3B-114
46 CLE A	55	153	41	7	0	3	2.0	12	14	17	12	0	.268	.373	12	1	3B-41, OF-2
7 yrs.	498	1488	390	63	4	12	0.8	129	162	165	70	10	.262	.334	85	23	3B-261, OF-115, SS-20, 2B-7, 1B-1
5 yrs.	327	934	243	39	3	6	0.6	87	97	103	40	9	.260	.328	72	21	OF-113, 3B-104, SS-20, 2B-7, 1B-1

Claude Rossman

ROSSMAN, CLAUDE R.
B. June 17, 1881, Philmont, N. Y.   D. Jan. 18, 1928, Poughkeepsie, N. Y.
BL TL 6'

	G	AB	H	2B	3B	HR	HR %	R	RBI	BB	SO	SB	BA	SA	PH AB	PH H	G by POS
04 CLE A	18	62	13	5	0	0	0.0	5	6	6		0	.210	.290	1	1	OF-17
06	118	396	122	13	2	1	0.3	49	53	17		11	.308	.359	11	4	1B-105, OF-1
07 DET A	153	571	158	21	8	0	0.0	60	69	33		20	.277	.342	0	0	1B-153
08	138	524	154	33	13	2	0.4	45	71	27		8	.294	.418	0	0	1B-138
09 2 teams	84	DET A (82G – .261)			STL A (2G – .125)												
total	84	295	76	8	3	0	0.0	16	39	13		10	.258	.305	5	0	1B-75, OF-2
5 yrs.	511	1848	523	80	26	3	0.2	175	238	90		49	.283	.359	17	5	1B-471, OF-20
3 yrs.	373	1382	387	62	24	2	0.1	121	179	73		38	.280	.364	5	0	1B-366

WORLD SERIES

	G	AB	H	2B	3B	HR	HR %	R	RBI	BB	SO	SB	BA	SA	PH AB	PH H	G by POS
07 DET A	5	20	8	0	1	0	0.0	1	2	1	0	2	.400	.500	0	0	1B-5
08	5	19	4	0	0	0	0.0	3	3	1	4	0	.211	.211	0	0	1B-5
2 yrs.	10	39	12	0	1	0	0.0	4	5	2	4	2	.308	.359	0	0	1B-10

Schoolboy Rowe

ROWE, LYNWOOD THOMAS
B. Jan. 11, 1910, Waco, Tex.   D. Jan. 8, 1961, El Dorado, Ark.
BR TR 6'4½" 210 lbs.

	G	AB	H	2B	3B	HR	HR %	R	RBI	BB	SO	SB	BA	SA	PH AB	PH H	G by POS
33 DET A	21	50	11	1	0	0	0.0	6	6	1	4	0	.220	.240	1	0	P-19
34	51	109	33	8	1	2	1.8	15	22	6	20	0	.303	.450	6	1	P-45
35	45	109	34	3	2	3	2.8	19	28	12	12	0	.312	.459	3	1	P-42
36	45	90	23	2	1	1	1.1	16	12	13	15	0	.256	.333	4	2	P-41
37	10	10	2	0	0	0	0.0	2	1	1	4	0	.200	.200	0	0	P-10
38	4	6	1	1	0	0	0.0	1	0	0	1	0	.167	.333	0	0	P-4
39	31	61	15	0	1	1	1.6	7	12	5	7	1	.246	.328	3	1	P-28
40	27	67	18	6	1	1	1.5	7	18	5	13	1	.269	.433	0	0	P-27
41	32	55	15	1	0	1	1.8	10	12	5	8	0	.273	.436	5	3	P-27
42 2 teams	16	DET A (2G – .000)			BKN N (14G – .211)												
total	16	23	4	0	0	0	0.0	2	2	1	4	0	.174	.174	5	1	P-11
43 PHI N	82	120	36	7	0	4	3.3	14	18	15	21	0	.300	.458	49	15	P-27
46	30	61	11	5	0	1	1.6	4	6	3	16	0	.180	.311	12	2	P-17
47	43	79	22	2	0	2	2.5	9	11	13	18	1	.278	.380	12	2	P-31
48	31	52	10	0	0	1	1.9	3	4	4	10	1	.192	.250	1	0	P-30

	G	AB	H	2B	3B	HR	HR%	R	RBI	BB	SO	SB	BA	SA	Pinch Hit AB	H	G by POS

Schoolboy Rowe continued

	G	AB	H	2B	3B	HR	HR%	R	RBI	BB	SO	SB	BA	SA	PH AB	PH H	G by POS
1949	23	17	4	1	0	1	5.9	1	1	2	4	0	.235	.471	0	0	P-23
15 yrs.	491	909	239	36	9	18	2.0	116	153	86	157	3	.263	.382	101	28	P-382
10 yrs.	268	561	152	21	9	9	1.6	83	111	48	84	2	.271	.389	22	8	P-245

WORLD SERIES
	G	AB	H	2B	3B	HR	HR%	R	RBI	BB	SO	SB	BA	SA	PH AB	PH H	G by POS
1934 DET A	3	7	0	0	0	0	0.0	0	0	0	5	0	.000	.000	0	0	P-3
1935	3	8	2	1	0	0	0.0	0	0	0	1	0	.250	.375	0	0	P-3
1940	2	1	0	0	0	0	0.0	0	0	0	1	0	.000	.000	0	0	P-2
3 yrs.	8	16	2	1	0	0	0.0	0	0	0	7	0	.125	.188	0	0	P-8

Art Ruble
RUBLE, WILLIAM ARTHUR (Speedy) BL TR 5'10½" 168 lbs
B. Mar. 11, 1903, Knoxville, Tenn. D. Nov. 1, 1983, Maryville, Tenn.

	G	AB	H	2B	3B	HR	HR%	R	RBI	BB	SO	SB	BA	SA	PH AB	PH H	G by POS
1927 DET A	56	91	15	4	2	0	0.0	16	11	14	15	2	.165	.253	3	0	OF-43
1934 PHI N	19	54	15	4	0	0	0.0	7	8	7	3	0	.278	.352	4	0	OF-14
2 yrs.	75	145	30	8	2	0	0.0	23	19	21	18	2	.207	.290	7	0	OF-57
1 yr.	56	91	15	4	2	0	0.0	16	11	14	15	2	.165	.253	3	0	OF-43

Muddy Ruel
RUEL, HEROLD DOMINIC BR TR 5'9" 150 lbs.
B. Feb. 20, 1896, St. Louis, Mo. D. Nov. 13, 1963, Palo Alto, Calif.
Manager 1947.

	G	AB	H	2B	3B	HR	HR%	R	RBI	BB	SO	SB	BA	SA	PH AB	PH H	G by POS
1915 STL A	10	14	0	0	0	0	0.0	0	1	5	5	0	.000	.000	2	0	C-6
1917 NY A	6	17	2	0	0	0	0.0	1	1	2	2	1	.118	.118	0	0	C-6
1918	3	6	2	0	0	0	0.0	0	0	2	1	1	.333	.333	0	0	C-2
1919	81	233	56	6	0	0	0.0	18	31	34	26	4	.240	.266	0	0	C-81
1920	82	261	70	14	1	1	0.4	30	15	15	18	4	.268	.341	1	0	C-80
1921 BOS A	113	358	99	21	1	1	0.3	41	43	41	15	2	.277	.349	2	0	C-109
1922	116	361	92	15	1	0	0.0	34	28	41	26	4	.255	.302	4	1	C-112
1923 WAS A	136	449	142	24	3	0	0.0	63	54	55	21	4	.316	.383	3	2	C-133
1924	149	501	142	20	2	0	0.0	50	57	62	20	7	.283	.331	2	1	C-147
1925	127	393	122	9	2	0	0.0	55	54	63	16	4	.310	.344	0	0	C-126, 1B-1
1926	117	368	110	22	4	1	0.3	42	53	61	14	7	.299	.389	0	0	C-117
1927	131	428	132	16	5	1	0.2	61	52	63	18	9	.308	.376	2	0	C-128
1928	108	350	90	18	2	0	0.0	31	55	44	14	12	.257	.320	4	2	C-101, 1B-2
1929	69	188	46	4	2	0	0.0	16	20	31	7	0	.245	.287	6	0	C-63
1930	66	198	50	3	4	0	0.0	18	26	24	13	1	.253	.308	4	2	C-60
1931 2 teams		BOS A (33G – .301)				DET A (14G – .120)											
" total	47	133	31	6	0	0	0.0	7	9	14	7	0	.233	.278	2	0	C-44
1932 DET A	50	136	32	4	2	0	0.0	10	18	17	6	1	.235	.294	3	1	C-49
1933 STL A	28	63	12	2	0	0	0.0	13	8	24	4	0	.190	.222	5	0	C-28
1934 CHI A	22	57	12	3	0	0	0.0	4	7	8	5	0	.211	.263	1	0	C-21
19 yrs.	1461	4514	1242	187	29	4	0.1	494	532	606	238	61	.275	.332	41	9	C-1413, 1B-3
2 yrs.	64	186	38	5	2	0	0.0	11	21	22	7	1	.204	.253	3	1	C-63

WORLD SERIES
	G	AB	H	2B	3B	HR	HR%	R	RBI	BB	SO	SB	BA	SA	PH AB	PH H	G by POS
1924 WAS A	7	21	2	1	0	0	0.0	2	0	6	1	0	.095	.143	0	0	C-7
1925	7	19	6	1	0	0	0.0	0	1	3	2	0	.316	.368	0	0	C-7
2 yrs.	14	40	8	2	0	0	0.0	2	1	9	3	0	.200	.250	0	0	C-14

Ron Samford
SAMFORD, RONALD EDWARD BR TR 5'11" 156 lbs.
B. Feb. 28, 1930, Dallas, Tex.

	G	AB	H	2B	3B	HR	HR%	R	RBI	BB	SO	SB	BA	SA	PH AB	PH H	G by POS
1954 NY N	12	5	0	0	0	0	0.0	2	0	0	1	0	.000	.000	1	0	2B-3
1955 DET A	1	1	0	0	0	0	0.0	0	0	0	1	0	.000	.000	0	0	SS-1
1957	54	91	20	1	2	0	0.0	6	5	6	15	1	.220	.275	0	0	SS-35, 2B-11, 3B-4
1959 WAS A	91	237	53	13	0	5	2.1	23	22	11	29	1	.224	.342	3	0	SS-64, 2B-23
4 yrs.	158	334	73	14	2	5	1.5	31	27	17	46	2	.219	.317	4	0	SS-100, 2B-37, 3B-4
2 yrs.	55	92	20	1	2	0	0.0	6	5	6	16	1	.217	.272	0	0	SS-36, 2B-11, 3B-4

Reggie Sanders
SANDERS, REGINALD JEROME BR TR 6'2" 205 lbs.
B. Sept. 9, 1949, Birmingham, Ala.

	G	AB	H	2B	3B	HR	HR%	R	RBI	BB	SO	SB	BA	SA	PH AB	PH H	G by POS
1974 DET A	26	99	27	7	0	3	3.0	10	5	2	20	1	.273	.434	0	0	1B-25, DH-1

Joe Sargent
SARGENT, JOSEPH ALEXANDER (Horse Belly) BR TR 5'10" 165 lbs.
B. Sept. 24, 1893, Rochester, N. Y. D. July 5, 1950, Rochester, N. Y.

	G	AB	H	2B	3B	HR	HR%	R	RBI	BB	SO	SB	BA	SA	PH AB	PH H	G by POS
1921 DET A	66	178	45	8	5	2	1.1	21	22	24	26	2	.253	.388	1	0	2B-24, 3B-23, SS-19

Germany Schaefer
SCHAEFER, HERMAN A. BR TR
B. Feb. 4, 1878, Chicago, Ill. D. May 16, 1919, Saranac Lake, N. Y.

	G	AB	H	2B	3B	HR	HR%	R	RBI	BB	SO	SB	BA	SA	PH AB	PH H	G by POS
1901 CHI N	2	5	3	1	0	0	0.0	0	0	2		0	.600	.800	0	0	3B-1, 2B-1
1902	81	291	57	2	3	0	0.0	32	14	19		12	.196	.223	0	0	3B-75, 1B-3, OF-2, SS-1
1905 DET A	153	554	135	17	9	2	0.4	64	47	45		19	.244	.318	0	0	2B-151, SS-3
1906	124	446	106	14	3	2	0.4	48	42	32		31	.238	.296	2	1	2B-114, SS-7
1907	109	372	96	12	3	1	0.3	45	32	30		21	.258	.315	2	0	2B-74, SS-18, 3B-14, OF-1
1908	153	584	151	20	10	3	0.5	96	52	37		40	.259	.342	0	0	SS-68, 2B-58, 3B-29
1909 2 teams		DET A (87G – .250)				WAS A (37G – .242)											
" total	124	408	101	17	1	1	0.2	39	26	20		14	.248	.301	4	3	2B-118, OF-1, 3B-1
1910 WAS A	74	229	63	6	5	0	0.0	27	14	25		17	.275	.345	10	2	2B-35, OF-26, 3B-2
1911	125	440	147	14	7	0	0.0	74	45	57		22	.334	.398	9	3	1B-108, OF-7
1912	60	166	41	7	3	0	0.0	21	19	23		11	.247	.325	11	2	OF-19, 2B-15, 1B-15, P-1
1913	52	100	32	1	1	0	0.0	17	7	15	12	6	.320	.350	21	11	2B-17, 1B-5, 3B-2, OF-1, P-1
1914	25	29	7	1	0	0	0.0	6	2	3	5	4	.241	.276	14	3	OF-3, 2B-3
1915 NWK F	59	154	33	5	3	0	0.0	26	8	25		3	.214	.286	15	2	OF-17, 1B-13, 3B-9, 2B-4
1916 NY A	1	0	0	0	0	0	–	0	0	0	0	0	–	–	0	0	OF-1
1918 CLE A	1	5	0	0	0	0	0.0	2	0	0		1	.000	.000	0	0	2B-1
15 yrs.	1143	3783	972	117	48	9	0.2	497	308	333	17	201	.257	.320	88	24	2B-589, 1B-144, 3B-133, SS-97, OF-78, P-3
5 yrs.	626	2236	558	75	25	8	0.4	279	195	158		123	.250	.316	5	1	2B-483, SS-96, 3B-43, OF-2

	G	AB	H	2B	3B	HR	HR%	R	RBI	BB	SO	SB	BA	SA	Pinch Hit AB	Pinch Hit H	G by POS

Germany Schaefer continued

	G	AB	H	2B	3B	HR	HR%	R	RBI	BB	SO	SB	BA	SA	Pinch Hit AB	Pinch Hit H	G by POS
WORLD SERIES																	
'07 DET A	5	21	3	0	0	0	0.0	1	0	0	3	1	.143	.143	0	0	2B-5
'08	5	16	2	0	0	0	0.0	0	0	1	4	0	.125	.125	0	0	3B-2
2 yrs.	10	37	5	0	0	0	0.0	1	0	1	7	1	.135	.135	0	0	2B-5, 3B-2

Biff Schaller

SCHALLER, WALTER   BL TR
B. Sept. 23, 1889, Chicago, Ill.   D. Oct. 9, 1939, Emeryville, Calif.

	G	AB	H	2B	3B	HR	HR%	R	RBI	BB	SO	SB	BA	SA	Pinch Hit AB	Pinch Hit H	G by POS
'11 DET A	40	60	8	0	1	1	1.7	8	7	4		1	.133	.217	17	6	OF-16, 1B-1
'13 CHI A	34	96	21	3	0	0	0.0	12	4	20	16	5	.219	.250	2	0	OF-32
2 yrs.	74	156	29	3	1	1	0.6	20	11	24	16	6	.186	.237	19	6	OF-48, 1B-1
1 yr.	40	60	8	0	1	1	1.7	8	7	4		1	.133	.217	17	6	OF-16, 1B-1

Wally Schang

SCHANG, WALTER HENRY   BB TR 5'10" 180 lbs.
Brother of Bobby Schang.   BR 1927-28
B. Aug. 22, 1889, South Wales, N. Y.   D. Mar. 6, 1965, St. Louis, Mo.

	G	AB	H	2B	3B	HR	HR%	R	RBI	BB	SO	SB	BA	SA	Pinch Hit AB	Pinch Hit H	G by POS
'13 PHI A	77	207	55	16	3	3	1.4	32	30	34	44	4	.266	.415	4	1	C-71
'14	107	307	88	11	8	3	1.0	44	45	32	33	7	.287	.404	5	1	C-100
'15	116	359	89	9	11	1	0.3	64	44	66	47	18	.248	.343	5	1	3B-43, OF-41, C-26
'16	110	338	90	15	8	7	2.1	41	38	38	44	14	.266	.420	11	0	OF-61, C-36
'17	118	316	90	14	9	3	0.9	41	36	29	24	6	.285	.415	18	2	C-79, 3B-12, OF-7
'18 BOS A	88	225	55	7	1	0	0.0	36	20	46	35	4	.244	.284	8	3	C-57, OF-16, 3B-5, SS-1
'19	113	330	101	16	3	0	0.0	43	55	71	42	15	.306	.373	5	0	C-103
'20	122	387	118	30	7	4	1.0	58	51	64	37	7	.305	.450	8	1	C-73, OF-40
'21 NY A	134	424	134	30	5	6	1.4	77	55	78	35	7	.316	.453	2	0	C-132
'22	124	408	130	21	7	1	0.2	46	53	53	36	12	.319	.412	5	1	C-124
'23	84	272	75	8	2	2	0.7	39	29	27	17	5	.276	.342	2	0	C-81
'24	114	356	104	19	7	5	1.4	46	52	48	43	2	.292	.427	4	0	C-109
'25	73	167	40	8	1	2	1.2	17	24	17	9	3	.240	.335	11	2	C-58
'26 STL A	103	285	94	19	5	8	2.8	36	50	32	20	5	.330	.516	17	7	C-82, OF-3
'27	97	263	84	15	2	5	1.9	40	42	41	33	3	.319	.449	18	6	C-75
'28	91	245	70	10	5	3	1.2	41	39	68	26	8	.286	.404	7	3	C-82
'29	94	249	59	10	5	5	2.0	43	36	74	22	1	.237	.378	7	1	C-85
'30 PHI A	45	92	16	4	1	1	1.1	16	9	17	15	0	.174	.272	6	1	C-36
'31 DET A	30	76	14	2	0	0	0.0	9	2	14	11	1	.184	.211	0	0	C-30
19 yrs.	1840	5306	1506	264	90	59	1.1	769	710	849	573	122	.284	.401	143	30	C-1439, OF-168, 3B-60, SS-1
1 yr.	30	76	14	2	0	0	0.0	9	2	14	11	1	.184	.211	0	0	C-30
WORLD SERIES																	
'13 PHI A	4	14	5	0	1	1	7.1	2	6	2	4	0	.357	.714	0	0	C-4
'14	4	12	2	1	0	0	0.0	1	0	1	4	0	.167	.250	0	0	C-4
'18 BOS A	5	9	4	0	0	0	0.0	1	1	2	3	1	.444	.444	2	1	C-5
'21 NY A	8	21	6	1	1	0	0.0	1	1	5	4	0	.286	.429	0	0	C-8
'22	5	16	3	1	0	0	0.0	0	0	0	3	0	.188	.250	0	0	C-5
'23	6	22	7	1	0	0	0.0	3	0	1	2	0	.318	.364	0	0	C-6
6 yrs.	32	94	27	4	2	1	1.1	8	8	11	20	1	.287	.404	2	1	C-32

Frank Scheibeck

SCHEIBECK, FRANK S.   BR TR 5'7" 145 lbs.
B. June 28, 1865, Detroit, Mich.   D. Oct. 22, 1956, Detroit, Mich.

	G	AB	H	2B	3B	HR	HR%	R	RBI	BB	SO	SB	BA	SA	Pinch Hit AB	Pinch Hit H	G by POS
'87 CLE AA	3	9	2	0	0	0	0.0	2		2		0	.222	.222	0	0	SS-1, 3B-1, P-1
'88 DET N	1	4	0	0	0	0	0.0	0	0	0	0	0	.000	.000	0	0	SS-1
'90 TOL AA	134	485	117	13	5	1	0.2	72		76		57	.241	.295	0	0	SS-134
'94 2 teams	PIT N (28G – .353)				WAS N (52G – .230)												
' total	80	298	81	4	7	1	0.3	69	27	56	33	18	.272	.342	4	1	SS-63, OF-9, 3B-3, 2B-2
'95 WAS N	48	167	31	5	2	0	0.0	17	25	17	21	5	.186	.240	0	0	SS-44, 3B-2, 2B-2
'99	27	94	27	4	1	0	0.0	19	9	11		5	.287	.351	0	0	SS-27
'01 CLE A	93	329	70	11	3	0	0.0	33	38	18		3	.213	.264	1	0	SS-92
'06 DET A	3	10	1	0	0	0	0.0	1	0	2		0	.100	.100	0	0	2B-3
8 yrs.	389	1396	329	37	18	2	0.1	213	98	182	54	88	.236	.292	5	1	SS-362, OF-9, 2B-7, 3B-6, P-1
1 yr.	3	10	1	0	0	0	0.0	1	0	2		0	.100	.100	0	0	2B-3

Lou Schiappacasse

SCHIAPPACASSE, LOUIS JOSEPH   BR TR
B. Mar. 29, 1881, Ann Arbor, Mich.   D. Sept. 20, 1910, Ann Arbor, Mich.

	G	AB	H	2B	3B	HR	HR%	R	RBI	BB	SO	SB	BA	SA	Pinch Hit AB	Pinch Hit H	G by POS
'02 DET A	2	5	0	0	0	0	0.0	0	1	1		0	.000	.000	0	0	OF-2

Boss Schmidt

SCHMIDT, CHARLES   BB TR 5'11" 200 lbs.
Brother of Walter Schmidt.
B. Sept. 12, 1880, Coal Hill, Ark.   D. Nov. 14, 1932, Clarksville, Ark.

	G	AB	H	2B	3B	HR	HR%	R	RBI	BB	SO	SB	BA	SA	Pinch Hit AB	Pinch Hit H	G by POS
'06 DET A	68	216	47	4	3	0	0.0	13	10	6		1	.218	.264	1	0	C-67
'07	104	349	85	6	6	0	0.0	32	23	5		8	.244	.295	1	0	C-104
'08	122	419	111	14	3	1	0.2	45	38	16		5	.265	.320	1	1	C-121
'09	84	253	53	8	2	1	0.4	21	28	7		7	.209	.269	2	1	C-81, OF-1
'10	71	197	51	7	7	1	0.5	22	23	2		2	.259	.381	5	2	C-66
'11	28	46	13	2	1	0	0.0	4	2	0		0	.283	.370	17	6	C-9, OF-1
6 yrs.	477	1480	360	41	22	3	0.2	137	124	36		23	.243	.307	27	10	C-448, OF-2
6 yrs.	477	1480	360	41	22	3	0.2	137	124	36		23	.243	.307	27	10	C-448, OF-2
WORLD SERIES																	
'07 DET A	4	12	2	0	0	0	0.0	0	0	2	1	0	.167	.167	1	0	C-3
'08	4	14	1	0	0	0	0.0	0	1	0	2	0	.071	.071	0	0	C-4
'09	6	18	4	2	0	0	0.0	0	4	2		0	.222	.333	0	0	C-6
3 yrs.	14	44	7	2	0	0	0.0	0	5	4	3	0	.159	.205	1	0	C-13

	G	AB	H	2B	3B	HR	HR %	R	RBI	BB	SO	SB	BA	SA	Pinch Hit AB	Pinch Hit H	G by POS

Heinie Schuble

SCHUBLE, HENRY GEORGE
B. Nov. 1, 1906, Houston, Tex.   BR TR 5'9"   152 lbs.

	G	AB	H	2B	3B	HR	HR %	R	RBI	BB	SO	SB	BA	SA	AB	H	G by POS
1927 STL N	65	218	56	6	2	4	1.8	29	28	7	27	0	.257	.358	0	0	SS-65
1929 DET A	92	258	60	11	7	2	0.8	35	28	19	23	3	.233	.353	1	0	SS-86, 3B-2
1932	101	340	92	20	6	5	1.5	57	52	24	37	14	.271	.409	2	0	3B-76, SS-15
1933	49	96	21	4	1	0	0.0	12	6	5	17	2	.219	.281	9	4	3B-23, SS-2, 2B-1
1934	11	15	4	2	0	0	0.0	2	2	1	4	0	.267	.400	4	0	SS-3, 3B-2, 2B-1
1935	11	8	2	0	0	0	0.0	3	0	1	0	0	.250	.250	2	1	3B-2, 2B-1
1936 STL N	2	0	0	0	0	0	—	0	0	0	0	0	—	—	0	0	3B-1
7 yrs.	331	935	235	43	16	11	1.2	138	116	57	108	19	.251	.367	18	5	SS-171, 3B-106, 2B-8
5 yrs.	264	717	179	37	14	7	1.0	109	88	50	81	19	.250	.370	18	5	SS-106, 3B-105, 2B-8

Chuck Scrivener

SCRIVENER, WAYNE ALLISON
B. Oct. 3, 1947, Alexandria, Va.   BR TR 5'9"   170 lbs

	G	AB	H	2B	3B	HR	HR %	R	RBI	BB	SO	SB	BA	SA	AB	H	G by POS
1975 DET A	4	16	4	1	0	0	0.0	0	1	1	1	1	.250	.313	0	0	3B-3, SS-2
1976	80	222	49	7	1	2	0.9	28	16	19	34	1	.221	.288	2	0	2B-43, SS-37, 3B-5
1977	61	72	6	0	0	0	0.0	10	2	5	9	0	.083	.083	0	0	SS-50, 2B-8, 3B-3
3 yrs.	145	310	59	8	1	2	0.6	38	18	24	44	2	.190	.242	2	0	SS-89, 2B-51, 3B-11
3 yrs.	145	310	59	8	1	2	0.6	38	18	24	44	2	.190	.242	2	0	SS-89, 2B-51, 3B-11

Frank Secory

SECORY, FRANK EDWARD
B. Aug. 24, 1912, Mason City, Iowa   BR TR 6'1"   200 lbs.

	G	AB	H	2B	3B	HR	HR %	R	RBI	BB	SO	SB	BA	SA	AB	H	G by POS
1940 DET A	1	1	0	0	0	0	0.0	0	0	0	1	0	.000	.000	1	0	
1942 CIN N	2	5	0	0	0	0	0.0	1	1	3	2	0	.000	.000	0	0	OF-2
1944 CHI N	22	56	18	1	0	4	7.1	10	17	6	8	1	.321	.554	4	0	OF-17
1945	35	57	9	1	0	0	0.0	4	6	2	7	0	.158	.175	21	2	OF-12
1946	33	43	10	3	0	3	7.0	6	12	6	6	0	.233	.512	22	4	OF-9
5 yrs.	93	162	37	5	0	7	4.3	21	36	17	24	1	.228	.389	48	6	OF-40
1 yr.	1	1	0	0	0	0	0.0	0	0	0	1	0	.000	.000	1	0	

| WORLD SERIES | | | | | | | | | | | | | | | | | |
| 1945 CHI N | 5 | 5 | 2 | 0 | 0 | 0 | 0.0 | 0 | 0 | 0 | 2 | 0 | .400 | .400 | 5 | 2 | |

Dick Sharon

SHARON, RICHARD LOUIS
B. Apr. 15, 1950, San Mateo, Calif.   BR TR 6'2"   195 lbs.

	G	AB	H	2B	3B	HR	HR %	R	RBI	BB	SO	SB	BA	SA	AB	H	G by POS
1973 DET A	91	178	43	9	0	7	3.9	20	16	10	31	2	.242	.410	3	1	OF-91
1974	60	129	28	4	0	2	1.6	12	10	14	29	4	.217	.295	5	0	OF-56
1975 SD N	91	160	31	7	0	4	2.5	14	20	26	35	0	.194	.313	33	8	OF-57
3 yrs.	242	467	102	20	0	13	2.8	46	46	50	95	6	.218	.345	41	9	OF-204
2 yrs.	151	307	71	13	0	9	2.9	32	26	24	60	6	.231	.362	8	1	OF-147

Al Shaw

SHAW, ALFRED
B. Oct. 3, 1874, Burslem, England   D. Mar. 25, 1958, Uhrichsville, Ohio   BR TR 5'8"   170 lbs.

	G	AB	H	2B	3B	HR	HR %	R	RBI	BB	SO	SB	BA	SA	AB	H	G by POS
1901 DET A	55	171	46	7	0	1	0.6	20	23	10		2	.269	.327	4	0	C-42, 1B-9, 3B-2, SS-1
1907 BOS A	76	198	38	1	3	0	0.0	10	7	18		4	.192	.227	1	0	C-73, 1B-1
1908 CHI A	32	49	4	1	0	0	0.0	0	2	2		0	.082	.102	3	0	C-29
1909 BOS N	17	41	4	0	0	0	0.0	1	0	5		0	.098	.098	2	0	C-13
4 yrs.	180	459	92	9	3	1	0.2	31	32	35		6	.200	.240	10	0	C-157, 1B-10, 3B-2, SS-1
1 yr.	55	171	46	7	0	1	0.6	20	23	10		2	.269	.327	4	0	C-42, 1B-9, 3B-2, SS-1

Merv Shea

SHEA, MERVIN DAVID JOHN
B. Sept. 5, 1900, San Francisco, Calif.   D. Jan. 27, 1953, Sacramento, Calif.   BR TR 5'11"   175 lbs.

	G	AB	H	2B	3B	HR	HR %	R	RBI	BB	SO	SB	BA	SA	AB	H	G by POS
1927 DET A	34	85	15	6	3	0	0.0	5	9	7	15	0	.176	.318	3	0	C-31
1928	39	85	20	2	3	0	0.0	8	9	9	11	2	.235	.329	7	0	C-30
1929	50	162	47	6	0	3	1.9	23	24	19	18	2	.290	.383	3	0	C-50
1933 2 teams	110	335	81	14	1	0	0.3	27	35	47	33	2	.242	.299	8	2	C-101
" total						BOS A (16G – .143)			STL A (94G – .262)								
1934 CHI A	62	176	28	3	0	0	0.0	8	5	24	19	0	.159	.176	2	0	C-60
1935	46	122	28	2	0	0	0.0	8	13	30	9	0	.230	.246	2	0	C-43
1936	14	24	3	0	0	0	0.0	3	2	6	5	0	.125	.125	0	0	C-14
1937	25	71	15	1	0	0	0.0	7	5	15	10	1	.211	.225	0	0	C-25
1938 BKN N	48	120	22	5	0	0	0.0	14	12	28	20	1	.183	.225	0	0	C-47
1939 DET A	4	2	0	0	0	0	0.0	0	0	0	1	0	.000	.000	0	0	C-4
1944 PHI N	7	15	4	0	0	1	6.7	2	1	4	4	0	.267	.467	1	0	C-6
11 yrs.	439	1197	263	39	7	5	0.4	105	115	189	145	8	.220	.277	26	2	C-411
4 yrs.	127	334	82	14	6	3	0.9	36	42	35	45	4	.246	.350	13	0	C-115

Hugh Shelley

SHELLEY, HUBERT LENEIRRE
B. Oct. 26, 1910, Rogers, Tex.   D. June 16, 1978, Beaumont, Tex.   BR TR 6'   170 lbs.

	G	AB	H	2B	3B	HR	HR %	R	RBI	BB	SO	SB	BA	SA	AB	H	G by POS
1935 DET A	7	8	2	0	0	0	0.0	1	1	2	1	0	.250	.250	2	1	OF-5

Jimmy Shevlin

SHEVLIN, JAMES CORNELIUS
B. July 9, 1909, Cincinnati, Ohio   D. Oct. 30, 1974, Ft. Lauderdale, Fla.   BL TL 5'10½"   155 lbs.

	G	AB	H	2B	3B	HR	HR %	R	RBI	BB	SO	SB	BA	SA	AB	H	G by POS
1930 DET A	28	14	2	0	0	0	0.0	4	2	2	3	0	.143	.143	2	0	1B-25
1932 CIN N	7	24	5	2	0	0	0.0	3	4	4	0	4	.208	.292	0	0	1B-7
1934	18	39	12	2	0	0	0.0	6	6	6	5	0	.308	.359	8	3	1B-10
3 yrs.	53	77	19	4	0	0	0.0	13	12	12	8	4	.247	.299	10	3	1B-42
1 yr.	28	14	2	0	0	0	0.0	4	2	2	3	0	.143	.143	2	0	1B-25

Ivey Shiver

SHIVER, IVEY MERWIN (Chick)
B. Jan. 22, 1906, Sylvester, Ga.   D. Aug. 31, 1972, Savannah, Ga.   BR TR 6'1½"   190 lbs.

	G	AB	H	2B	3B	HR	HR %	R	RBI	BB	SO	SB	BA	SA	AB	H	G by POS
1931 DET A	2	9	1	0	0	0	0.0	2	0	0	3	0	.111	.111	0	0	OF-2
1934 CIN N	19	59	12	1	0	2	3.4	6	6	3	15	1	.203	.322	4	1	OF-15
2 yrs.	21	68	13	1	0	2	2.9	8	6	3	18	1	.191	.294	4	1	OF-17
1 yr.	2	9	1	0	0	0	0.0	2	0	0	3	0	.111	.111	0	0	OF-2

	G	AB	H	2B	3B	HR	HR %	R	RBI	BB	SO	SB	BA	SA	Pinch Hit AB	Pinch Hit H	G by POS

Ron Shoop

SHOOP, RONALD LEE
B. Sept. 19, 1931, Rural Valley, Pa.
BR TR 5'11" 180 lbs.

	G	AB	H	2B	3B	HR	HR%	R	RBI	BB	SO	SB	BA	SA	PH AB	PH H	G by POS
1959 DET A	3	7	1	0	0	0	0.0	1	1	0	1	0	.143	.143	0	0	C-3

Chick Shorten

SHORTEN, CHARLES HENRY
B. Apr. 19, 1892, Scranton, Pa.   D. Oct. 23, 1965, Scranton, Pa.
BL TL 6' 175 lbs.

	G	AB	H	2B	3B	HR	HR%	R	RBI	BB	SO	SB	BA	SA	PH AB	PH H	G by POS
1915 BOS A	6	14	3	1	0	0	0.0	1	0	0	2	0	.214	.286	1	0	OF-5
1916	53	112	33	2	1	0	0.0	14	11	10	8	1	.295	.330	17	3	OF-33
1917	69	168	30	4	2	0	0.0	12	16	10	10	2	.179	.226	24	5	OF-43
1919 DET A	95	270	85	9	3	0	0.0	37	22	22	13	5	.315	.370	19	5	OF-75
1920	116	364	105	9	6	1	0.3	35	40	28	14	2	.288	.354	15	5	OF-99
1921	92	217	59	11	3	0	0.0	33	23	20	11	2	.272	.350	37	9	OF-52, C-1
1922 STL A	55	131	36	12	5	2	1.5	22	16	16	8	0	.275	.489	20	5	OF-32
1924 CIN N	41	69	19	3	0	0	0.0	7	6	4	2	0	.275	.319	21	6	OF-15
8 yrs.	527	1345	370	51	20	3	0.2	161	134	110	68	12	.275	.349	154	38	OF-354, C-1
3 yrs.	303	851	249	29	12	1	0.1	105	85	70	38	9	.293	.358	71	19	OF-226, C-1
WORLD SERIES																	
1916 BOS A	2	7	4	0	0	0	0.0	0	2	0	1	0	.571	.571	0	0	OF-2

Frank Sigafoos

SIGAFOOS, FRANCIS LEONARD
B. Mar. 21, 1904, Easton, Pa.   D. Apr. 12, 1968, Indianapolis, Ind.
BR TR 5'9" 170 lbs.

	G	AB	H	2B	3B	HR	HR%	R	RBI	BB	SO	SB	BA	SA	PH AB	PH H	G by POS
1926 PHI A	13	43	11	0	0	0	0.0	4	2	0	3	0	.256	.256	1	0	SS-12
1929 2 teams		DET	A (14G – .174)		CHI	A	(7G – .333)										
" total	21	26	5	1	0	0	0.0	4	3	7	5	0	.192	.231	1	0	3B-6, 2B-5, SS-5
1931 CIN N	21	65	11	2	0	0	0.0	6	8	0	6	0	.169	.200	4	1	3B-15, SS-2
3 yrs.	55	134	27	3	0	0	0.0	14	13	7	14	0	.201	.224	6	1	3B-21, SS-19, 2B-6
1 yr.	14	23	4	1	0	0	0.0	3	2	5	4	0	.174	.217	1	0	3B-6, SS-5

Al Simmons

SIMMONS, ALOYSIUS HARRY (Bucketfoot Al)
Born Alois Szymanski.
B. May 22, 1902, Milwaukee, Wis.   D. May 26, 1956, Milwaukee, Wis.
Hall of Fame 1953.
BR TR 5'11" 190 lbs.

	G	AB	H	2B	3B	HR	HR%	R	RBI	BB	SO	SB	BA	SA	PH AB	PH H	G by POS
1924 PHI A	152	594	183	31	9	8	1.3	69	102	30	60	16	.308	.431	0	0	OF-152
1925	153	658	253	43	12	24	3.6	122	129	35	41	7	.384	.596	0	0	OF-153
1926	147	581	199	53	10	19	3.3	90	109	48	49	10	.343	.566	0	0	OF-147
1927	106	406	159	36	11	15	3.7	86	108	31	30	10	.392	.645	0	0	OF-105
1928	119	464	163	33	9	15	3.2	78	107	31	30	1	.351	.558	3	2	OF-114
1929	143	581	212	41	9	34	5.9	114	157	31	38	4	.365	.642	0	0	OF-142
1930	138	554	211	41	16	36	6.5	152	165	39	34	9	.381	.708	2	1	OF-136
1931	128	513	200	37	13	22	4.3	105	128	47	45	3	.390	.641	0	0	OF-128
1932	154	670	216	28	9	35	5.2	144	151	47	76	4	.322	.548	0	0	OF-154
1933 CHI A	146	605	200	29	10	14	2.3	85	119	39	49	5	.331	.481	1	0	OF-145
1934	138	558	192	36	7	18	3.2	102	104	53	58	3	.344	.530	0	0	OF-138
1935	128	525	140	22	7	16	3.0	68	79	33	43	4	.267	.427	3	0	OF-126
1936 DET A	143	568	186	38	6	13	2.3	96	112	49	35	6	.327	.484	4	1	OF-138, 1B-1
1937 WAS A	103	419	117	21	10	8	1.9	60	84	27	35	3	.279	.434	1	0	OF-102
1938	125	470	142	23	6	21	4.5	79	95	38	40	2	.302	.511	9	2	OF-117
1939 2 teams	102	BOS	N (93G – .282)		CIN	N	(9G – .143)										
" total	102	351	96	17	5	7	2.0	39	44	24	43	0	.274	.410	14	2	OF-87
1940 PHI A	37	81	25	4	0	1	1.2	7	19	4	8	0	.309	.395	16	8	OF-18
1941	9	24	3	1	0	0	0.0	1	1	1	2	0	.125	.167	4	0	OF-5
1943 BOS A	40	133	27	5	0	1	0.8	9	12	8	21	0	.203	.263	7	0	OF-33
1944 PHI A	4	6	3	0	0	0	0.0	1	2	0	0	0	.500	.500	2	1	OF-2
20 yrs.	2215	8761	2927	539	149	307	3.5	1507	1827	615	737	87	.334	.535	66	17	OF-2142, 1B-1
1 yr.	143	568	186	38	6	13	2.3	96	112	49	35	6	.327	.484	4	1	OF-138, 1B-1
WORLD SERIES																	
1929 PHI A	5	20	6	1	0	2	10.0	6	5	1	4	0	.300	.650	0	0	OF-5
1930	6	22	8	2	0	2	9.1	4	4	2	2	0	.364	.727	0	0	OF-6
1931	7	27	9	2	0	2	7.4	4	8	3	3	0	.333	.630	0	0	OF-7
1939 CIN N	1	4	1	1	0	0	0.0	1	0	0	0	0	.250	.500	0	0	OF-1
4 yrs.	19	73	24	6	0	6	8.2	15	17	6	9	0	.329	.658	0	0	OF-19
							6th				4th						

Hack Simmons

SIMMONS, GEORGE WASHINGTON
B. Jan. 29, 1885, Brooklyn, N. Y.   D. Apr. 26, 1942, Arverne, N. Y.
BR TR 5'8" 179 lbs.

	G	AB	H	2B	3B	HR	HR%	R	RBI	BB	SO	SB	BA	SA	PH AB	PH H	G by POS
1910 DET A	42	110	25	3	1	0	0.0	12	9	10		1	.227	.273	10	3	1B-22, 3B-7, OF-2
1912 NY A	110	401	96	17	2	0	0.0	45	41	33		19	.239	.292	4	0	2B-88, 1B-13, SS-4
1914 BAL F	114	352	95	16	5	1	0.3	50	38	32		7	.270	.352	13	7	OF-73, 2B-26, 1B-4, SS-2, 3B-1
1915	39	88	18	7	1	1	1.1	8	14	10		1	.205	.341	13	5	OF-13, 2B-13
4 yrs.	305	951	234	43	9	2	0.2	115	102	85		28	.246	.317	40	15	2B-127, OF-88, 1B-39, 3B-8, SS-6
1 yr.	42	110	25	3	1	0	0.0	12	9	10		1	.227	.273	10	3	1B-22, 3B-7, OF-2

Nelson Simmons

SIMMONS, NELSON BERNARD III
B. June 27, 1963, Washington, D. C.
BB TR 6'1" 195 lbs.

	G	AB	H	2B	3B	HR	HR%	R	RBI	BB	SO	SB	BA	SA	PH AB	PH H	G by POS
1984 DET A	9	30	13	2	0	0	0.0	4	3	2	5	1	.433	.500	1	0	OF-5, DH-4

Duke Sims

SIMS, DUANE B.
B. June 5, 1941, Salt Lake City, Utah
BL TR 6'2" 197 lbs.

	G	AB	H	2B	3B	HR	HR%	R	RBI	BB	SO	SB	BA	SA	PH AB	PH H	G by POS
1964 CLE A	2	6	0	0	0	0	0.0	0	0	0	2	0	.000	.000	1	0	C-1
1965	48	118	21	0	0	6	5.1	9	15	15	33	0	.178	.331	12	2	C-40
1966	52	133	35	2	2	6	4.5	12	19	11	31	0	.263	.444	9	0	C-48
1967	88	272	55	8	2	12	4.4	25	34	30	64	3	.202	.379	5	2	C-85
1968	122	361	90	21	0	11	3.0	48	44	62	68	1	.249	.399	9	2	C-84, 1B-31, OF-4
1969	114	326	77	8	0	18	5.5	40	45	66	80	1	.236	.426	13	1	C-102, OF-3, 1B-1
1970	110	345	91	12	0	23	6.7	46	56	46	59	0	.264	.499	9	1	C-39, OF-36, 1B-29

	G	AB	H	2B	3B	HR	HR %	R	RBI	BB	SO	SB	BA	SA	Pinch Hit AB	Pinch Hit H	G by POS

Duke Sims continued

		G	AB	H	2B	3B	HR	HR%	R	RBI	BB	SO	SB	BA	SA	PH AB	PH H	G by POS
1971 **LA N**		90	230	63	7	2	6	2.6	23	25	30	39	0	.274	.400	18	2	C-74
1972 **2 teams**	**LA** N (51G – .192)	**DET** A (38G – .316)																
" total		89	249	60	11	0	6	2.4	18	30	36	41	0	.241	.357	12	3	C-73, OF-4
1973 **2 teams**	**DET** A (80G – .242)	**NY** A (4G – .333)																
" total		84	261	64	10	0	9	3.4	34	31	33	37	1	.245	.387	9	1	C-69, OF-6, DH-2
1974 **2 teams**	**NY** A (5G – .133)	**TEX** A (39G – .208)																
" total		44	121	24	1	0	3	2.5	8	8	9	29	0	.198	.281	7	3	C-31, DH-5, OF-1
11 yrs.		843	2422	580	80	6	100	4.1	263	310	338	483	6	.239	.401	104	17	C-646, 1B-61, OF-54, DH-7
2 yrs.		118	350	92	14	0	12	3.4	42	49	49	54	1	.263	.406	15	2	C-93, OF-10

LEAGUE CHAMPIONSHIP SERIES

		G	AB	H	2B	3B	HR	HR%	R	RBI	BB	SO	SB	BA	SA	PH AB	PH H	G by POS
1972 **DET A**		4	14	3	2	1	0	0.0	0	0	1	2	0	.214	.500	0	0	C-2

Lou Skizas

SKIZAS, LOUIS PETER (The Nervous Greek)   BR TR 5'11" 175 lbs.
B. June 2, 1932, Chicago, Ill.

		G	AB	H	2B	3B	HR	HR%	R	RBI	BB	SO	SB	BA	SA	PH AB	PH H	G by POS
1956 **2 teams**	**NY** A (6G – .167)	**KC** A (83G – .316)																
" total		89	303	95	11	3	11	3.6	39	40	15	19	3	.314	.479	15	3	OF-74
1957 **KC A**		119	376	92	14	1	18	4.8	34	44	27	15	5	.245	.431	24	2	OF-76, 3B-32
1958 **DET A**		23	33	8	2	0	1	3.0	4	2	5	1	0	.242	.394	13	2	OF-5, 3B-4
1959 **CHI A**		8	13	1	0	0	0	0.0	3	0	3	2	0	.077	.077	2	0	OF-6
4 yrs.		239	725	196	27	4	30	4.1	80	86	50	37	8	.270	.443	54	7	OF-161, 3B-36
1 yr.		23	33	8	2	0	1	3.0	4	2	5	1	0	.242	.394	13	2	OF-5, 3B-4

Jim Small

SMALL, JAMES ARTHUR   BL TL 6'½" 180 lbs.
B. Mar. 8, 1937, Portland, Ore.

		G	AB	H	2B	3B	HR	HR%	R	RBI	BB	SO	SB	BA	SA	PH AB	PH H	G by POS
1955 **DET A**		12	4	0	0	0	0	0.0	2	0	1	1	0	.000	.000	2	0	OF-4
1956		58	91	29	4	2	0	0.0	13	10	6	10	0	.319	.407	15	7	OF-26
1957		36	42	9	2	0	0	0.0	7	0	2	11	0	.214	.262	13	2	OF-14
1958 **KC A**		2	4	0	0	0	0	0.0	0	0	1	0	0	.000	.000	1	0	OF-1
4 yrs.		108	141	38	6	2	0	0.0	22	10	10	22	0	.270	.340	31	9	OF-45
3 yrs.		106	137	38	6	2	0	0.0	22	10	9	22	0	.277	.350	30	9	OF-44

George Smith

SMITH, GEORGE CORNELIUS   BR TR 5'10" 170 lbs.
B. July 7, 1938, St. Petersburg, Fla.

		G	AB	H	2B	3B	HR	HR%	R	RBI	BB	SO	SB	BA	SA	PH AB	PH H	G by POS
1963 **DET A**		52	171	37	8	2	0	0.0	16	17	18	34	4	.216	.287	0	0	2B-52
1964		5	7	2	0	0	0	0.0	1	2	1	4	1	.286	.286	1	1	2B-3
1965		32	53	5	0	0	1	1.9	6	1	3	18	0	.094	.151	5	0	2B-22, SS-3, 3B-3
1966 **BOS A**		128	403	86	19	4	8	2.0	41	37	37	86	4	.213	.340	4	0	2B-109, SS-19
4 yrs.		217	634	130	27	6	9	1.4	64	57	59	142	9	.205	.309	10	1	2B-186, SS-22, 3B-3
3 yrs.		89	231	44	8	2	1	0.4	23	20	22	56	5	.190	.255	6	1	2B-77, SS-3, 3B-3

Heinie Smith

SMITH, GEORGE HENRY   BR TR 5'9½" 160 lbs.
B. Oct. 24, 1871, Pittsburgh, Pa.   D. June 25, 1939, Buffalo, N. Y.
Manager 1902.

		G	AB	H	2B	3B	HR	HR%	R	RBI	BB	SO	SB	BA	SA	PH AB	PH H	G by POS
1897 **LOU N**		21	76	20	3	0	1	1.3	7	7	3		1	.263	.342	0	0	2B-21
1898		35	121	23	4	0	0	0.0	14	13	6		6	.190	.223	2	1	2B-33
1899 **PIT N**		15	53	15	3	1	0	0.0	9	12	5		2	.283	.377	0	0	2B-15, SS-1
1901 **NY N**		9	29	6	2	1	1	3.4	5	4	1		1	.207	.448	0	0	2B-7, P-2
1902		138	511	129	19	2	0	0.0	46	33	17		32	.252	.297	0	0	2B-138
1903 **DET A**		93	336	75	11	3	1	0.3	36	22	19		12	.223	.283	0	0	2B-93
6 yrs.		311	1126	268	42	7	3	0.3	117	91	51		54	.238	.296	2	1	2B-307, P-2, SS-1
1 yr.		93	336	75	11	3	1	0.3	36	22	19		12	.223	.283	0	0	2B-93

Jack Smith

SMITH, JOHN JOSEPH   TR
Also known as John Joseph Coffey.
B. Aug. 8, 1893, Oswaya, Pa.   D. Dec. 4, 1962, New York, N. Y.

		G	AB	H	2B	3B	HR	HR%	R	RBI	BB	SO	SB	BA	SA	PH AB	PH H	G by POS
1912 **DET A**		1	0	0	0	0	0	–	0	0	0	0	0	–	–	0	0	3B-1

Mayo Smith

SMITH, EDWARD MAYO   BL TR 6' 183 lbs.
B. Jan. 17, 1915, New London, Mo.   D. Nov. 24, 1977, Boynton Beach, Fla.
Manager 1955-59, 1967-70.

		G	AB	H	2B	3B	HR	HR%	R	RBI	BB	SO	SB	BA	SA	PH AB	PH H	G by POS
1945 **PHI A**		73	203	43	5	0	0	0.0	18	11	36	13	0	.212	.236	6	4	OF-65

Willie Smith

SMITH, WILLIE (Wonderful Willie)   BL TL 6' 182 lbs.
B. Feb. 11, 1939, Anniston, Ala.

		G	AB	H	2B	3B	HR	HR%	R	RBI	BB	SO	SB	BA	SA	PH AB	PH H	G by POS
1963 **DET A**		17	8	1	0	0	0	0.0	2	0	0	1	0	.125	.125	2	0	P-11
1964 **LA A**		118	359	108	14	6	11	3.1	46	51	8	39	7	.301	.465	23	10	OF-87, P-15
1965 **CAL A**		136	459	120	14	9	14	3.1	52	57	32	60	9	.261	.423	21	4	OF-123, 1B-2
1966		90	195	36	3	2	1	0.5	18	20	12	37	1	.185	.236	41	5	OF-52
1967 **CLE A**		21	32	7	2	0	0	0.0	0	2	1	10	0	.219	.281	16	4	OF-4, 1B-3
1968 **2 teams**	**CLE** A (33G – .143)	**CHI** N (55G – .275)																
" total		88	184	45	10	2	5	2.7	14	28	15	47	0	.245	.402	36	10	OF-39, 1B-11, P-3
1969 **CHI N**		103	195	48	9	1	9	4.6	21	25	25	49	1	.246	.441	40	12	OF-33, 1B-24
1970		87	167	36	9	1	5	3.0	15	24	11	32	2	.216	.371	40	9	1B-43, OF-1
1971 **CIN N**		31	55	9	2	0	1	1.8	3	4	3	9	0	.164	.255	20	0	1B-10
9 yrs.		691	1654	410	63	21	46	2.8	171	211	107	284	20	.248	.395	239	54	OF-339, 1B-93, P-29
1 yr.		17	8	1	0	0	0	0.0	2	0	0	1	0	.125	.125	2	0	P-11

Steve Souchock

SOUCHOCK, STEPHEN (Bud)   BR TR 6'2½" 203 lbs.
B. Mar. 3, 1919, Yatesboro, Pa.

		G	AB	H	2B	3B	HR	HR%	R	RBI	BB	SO	SB	BA	SA	PH AB	PH H	G by POS
1946 **NY A**		47	86	26	3	3	2	2.3	15	10	7	13	0	.302	.477	17	5	1B-20
1948		44	118	24	3	1	3	2.5	11	11	7	13	3	.203	.322	11	2	1B-32
1949 **CHI A**		84	252	59	13	5	7	2.8	29	37	25	38	5	.234	.409	17	4	OF-39, 1B-30
1951 **DET A**		91	188	46	10	3	11	5.9	33	28	18	27	0	.245	.505	34	7	OF-59, 2B-1, 1B-1
1952		92	265	66	16	4	13	4.9	40	45	21	28	1	.249	.487	17	4	OF-56, 3B-13, 1B-9
1953		89	278	84	13	3	11	4.0	29	46	8	35	5	.302	.489	10	3	OF-80, 1B-1

	G	AB	H	2B	3B	HR	HR%	R	RBI	BB	SO	SB	BA	SA	Pinch Hit AB	Pinch Hit H	G by POS

Steve Souchock continued

	G	AB	H	2B	3B	HR	HR%	R	RBI	BB	SO	SB	BA	SA	PH AB	PH H	G by POS
1954	25	39	7	0	1	3	7.7	6	8	2	10	1	.179	.462	14	2	OF-9, 3B-2
1955	1	1	1	0	0	0	0.0	0	1	0	0	0	1.000	1.000	1	1	
8 yrs.	473	1227	313	58	20	50	4.1	163	186	88	164	15	.255	.457	121	28	OF-243, 1B-93, 3B-15, 2B-1
5 yrs.	298	771	204	39	11	38	4.9	108	128	49	100	7	.265	.492	76	17	OF-204, 3B-15, 1B-11, 2B-1

Tubby Spencer

SPENCER, EDWARD RUSSELL
B. Jan. 26, 1884, Oil City, Pa. D. Feb. 1, 1945, San Francisco, Calif. BR TR

	G	AB	H	2B	3B	HR	HR%	R	RBI	BB	SO	SB	BA	SA	PH AB	PH H	G by POS
1905 STL A	35	115	27	1	2	0	0.0	6	11	7		2	.235	.278	1	1	C-34
1906	58	188	33	6	1	0	0.0	15	17	7		4	.176	.218	3	0	C-54
1907	71	230	61	11	1	0	0.0	27	24	7		1	.265	.322	8	2	C-63
1908	91	286	60	6	1	0	0.0	19	28	17		1	.210	.238	2	1	C-89
1909 BOS A	28	74	12	1	0	0	0.0	6	9	6		2	.162	.176	2	0	C-26
1911 PHI N	11	32	5	1	0	1	3.1	2	3	3	7	0	.156	.281	0	0	C-11
1916 DET A	19	54	20	1	1	1	1.9	7	10	6	6	2	.370	.481	0	0	C-19
1917	70	192	46	8	3	0	0.0	13	22	15	15	0	.240	.313	8	0	C-62
1918	66	155	34	8	1	0	0.0	11	8	19	18	1	.219	.284	17	3	C-48, 1B-1
9 yrs.	449	1326	298	43	10	2	0.2	106	132	87	46	13	.225	.277	41	7	C-406, 1B-1
3 yrs.	155	401	100	17	5	1	0.2	31	40	40	39	3	.249	.324	25	3	C-129, 1B-1

Charlie Spikes

SPIKES, LESLIE CHARLES
B. Jan. 23, 1951, Bogalusa, La. BR TR 6'3" 215 lbs.

	G	AB	H	2B	3B	HR	HR%	R	RBI	BB	SO	SB	BA	SA	PH AB	PH H	G by POS
1972 NY A	14	34	5	1	0	0	0.0	2	3	1	13	0	.147	.176	5	0	OF-9
1973 CLE A	140	506	120	12	3	23	4.5	68	73	45	103	5	.237	.409	2	1	OF-111, DH-26
1974	155	568	154	23	1	22	3.9	63	80	34	100	10	.271	.431	1	0	OF-154
1975	111	345	79	13	3	11	3.2	41	33	30	51	7	.229	.380	17	7	OF-103, DH-2
1976	101	334	79	11	5	3	0.9	34	31	23	50	5	.237	.326	8	0	OF-98, DH-2
1977	32	95	22	2	0	3	3.2	13	11	11	17	0	.232	.347	7	1	OF-27, DH-2
1978 DET N	10	28	7	1	0	0	0.0	1	2	2	6	0	.250	.286	0	0	OF-9
1979 ATL N	66	93	26	8	0	3	3.2	12	21	5	30	0	.280	.462	47	16	OF-15
1980	41	36	10	1	0	0	0.0	6	2	3	18	0	.278	.306	31	10	OF-7
9 yrs.	670	2039	502	72	12	65	3.2	240	256	154	388	27	.246	.389	118	35	OF-533, DH-32
1 yr.	10	28	7	1	0	0	0.0	1	2	2	6	0	.250	.286	0	0	OF-9

Tuck Stainback

STAINBACK, GEORGE TUCKER
B. Aug. 4, 1910, Los Angeles, Calif. BR TR 5'11½" 175 lbs.

	G	AB	H	2B	3B	HR	HR%	R	RBI	BB	SO	SB	BA	SA	PH AB	PH H	G by POS
1934 CHI N	104	359	110	14	3	2	0.6	47	46	8	42	7	.306	.379	8	3	OF-96, 3B-1
1935	47	94	24	4	0	3	3.2	16	11	0	13	1	.255	.394	10	3	OF-28
1936	44	75	13	3	0	1	1.3	13	5	6	14	1	.173	.253	9	1	OF-26
1937	72	160	37	7	1	0	0.0	18	14	7	16	3	.231	.288	10	2	OF-49
1938 3 teams		STL N (6G - .000)				PHI N (30G - .259)				BKN N (35G - .327)							
" total	71	195	55	9	3	1	0.5	26	31	5	10	2	.282	.374	17	4	OF-50
1939 BKN N	168	201	54	7	0	3	1.5	22	19	4	23	0	.269	.348	10	2	OF-55
1940 DET A	15	40	9	2	0	0	0.0	4	1	1	9	0	.225	.275	5	1	OF-9
1941	94	200	49	8	1	2	1.0	19	10	3	21	6	.245	.325	8	1	OF-80
1942 NY A	15	10	2	0	0	0	0.0	0	0	0	2	0	.200	.200	1	0	OF-3
1943	71	231	60	11	2	0	0.0	31	10	7	16	3	.260	.325	5	3	OF-61
1944	30	78	17	3	0	0	0.0	13	5	3	7	1	.218	.256	5	1	OF-24
1945	95	327	84	12	2	5	1.5	40	32	13	20	0	.257	.352	9	2	OF-83
1946 PHI A	91	291	71	10	2	0	0.0	35	20	7	20	3	.244	.292	23	5	OF-66
13 yrs.	917	2261	585	90	14	17	0.8	284	204	64	213	27	.259	.333	120	28	OF-630, 3B-1
2 yrs.	109	240	58	10	1	2	0.8	23	11	4	30	6	.242	.317	13	2	OF-89

WORLD SERIES

	G	AB	H	2B	3B	HR	HR%	R	RBI	BB	SO	SB	BA	SA	PH AB	PH H	G by POS
1942 NY A	2	0	0	0	0	0	–	0	0	0	0	0	–	–	0	0	OF-5
1943	5	17	3	0	0	0	0.0	0	0	0	2	0	.176	.176	0	0	OF-5
2 yrs.	7	17	3	0	0	0	0.0	0	0	0	2	0	.176	.176	0	0	OF-5

Oscar Stanage

STANAGE, OSCAR HARLAND
B. Mar. 17, 1883, Tulare, Calif. D. Nov. 11, 1964, Detroit, Mich. BR TR 5'11" 190 lbs.

	G	AB	H	2B	3B	HR	HR%	R	RBI	BB	SO	SB	BA	SA	PH AB	PH H	G by POS
1906 CIN N	1	1	0	0	0	0	0.0	0	0	0		0	.000	.000	0	0	C-1
1909 DET A	77	252	66	8	6	0	0.0	17	21	11		2	.262	.341	0	0	C-77
1910	88	275	57	7	4	2	0.7	24	25	20		1	.207	.284	4	0	C-84
1911	141	503	133	13	7	3	0.6	45	51	20		3	.264	.336	0	0	C-141
1912	119	394	103	9	4	0	0.0	35	41	34		3	.261	.305	0	0	C-119
1913	80	241	54	13	2	0	0.0	19	21	21	35	5	.224	.295	2	2	C-77
1914	122	400	77	8	4	0	0.0	16	25	24	58	2	.193	.233	0	0	C-122
1915	100	300	67	9	2	1	0.3	27	31	20	41	5	.223	.277	0	0	C-100
1916	94	291	69	17	3	0	0.0	16	30	17	48	3	.237	.316	0	0	C-94
1917	99	297	61	14	1	0	0.0	19	30	20	35	3	.205	.259	4	1	C-95
1918	54	186	47	4	0	1	0.5	9	14	11	18	2	.253	.290	2	0	C-47, 1B-5
1919	38	120	29	4	1	1	0.8	9	15	7	12	1	.242	.317	1	0	C-36, 1B-1
1920	78	238	55	17	0	0	0.0	12	17	14	21	0	.231	.303	1	0	C-78
1925	3	5	1	0	0	0	0.0	0	0	0	0	0	.200	.200	0	0	C-3
14 yrs.	1094	3503	819	123	34	8	0.2	248	321	219	268	30	.234	.295	14	3	C-1074, 1B-6
13 yrs.	1093	3502	819	123	34	8	0.2	248	321	219	268	30	.234	.295	14	3	C-1073, 1B-6

WORLD SERIES

	G	AB	H	2B	3B	HR	HR%	R	RBI	BB	SO	SB	BA	SA	PH AB	PH H	G by POS
1909 DET A	2	5	1	0	0	0	0.0	0	2	0		0	.200	.200	0	0	C-2

Mickey Stanley

STANLEY, MITCHELL JACK
B. July 20, 1942, Grand Rapids, Mich. BR TR 6'1" 185 lbs.

	G	AB	H	2B	3B	HR	HR%	R	RBI	BB	SO	SB	BA	SA	PH AB	PH H	G by POS
1964 DET A	4	11	3	0	0	0	0.0	3	1	0	1	0	.273	.273	0	0	OF-4
1965	30	117	28	6	0	3	2.6	14	13	3	12	1	.239	.368	0	0	OF-29
1966	92	235	68	15	4	3	1.3	28	19	17	20	2	.289	.426	9	3	OF-82
1967	145	333	70	7	3	7	2.1	38	24	29	46	9	.210	.312	13	1	OF-128, 1B-8

	G	AB	H	2B	3B	HR	HR %	R	RBI	BB	SO	SB	BA	SA	Pinch Hit AB	Pinch Hit H	G by POS

Mickey Stanley continued

1968	153	583	151	16	6	11	1.9	88	60	42	57	4	.259	.364	6	0	OF-130, 1B-15, SS-9, 2B-1
1969	149	592	139	28	1	16	2.7	73	70	52	56	8	.235	.367	7	2	OF-101, SS-59, 1B-4
1970	142	568	143	21	11	13	2.3	83	47	45	56	10	.252	.396	5	5	OF-132, 1B-9
1971	139	401	117	14	5	7	1.7	43	41	24	44	1	.292	.404	6	3	OF-139
1972	142	435	102	16	6	14	3.2	45	55	29	49	1	.234	.395	5	3	OF-139
1973	157	602	147	23	5	17	2.8	81	57	48	65	0	.244	.384	0	0	OF-157
1974	99	394	87	13	2	8	2.0	40	34	26	63	5	.221	.325	1	0	OF-91, 1B-12, 2B-1
1975	52	164	42	7	3	3	1.8	26	19	15	27	1	.256	.390	3	2	OF-28, 1B-14, 3B-7, DH
1976	84	214	55	17	1	4	1.9	34	29	14	19	2	.257	.402	19	6	OF-38, 1B-17, 3B-11, SS-3, 2B-2
1977	75	222	51	9	1	8	3.6	30	23	18	30	0	.230	.387	13	3	OF-57, SS-3, 1B-3, DH-
1978	53	151	40	9	0	3	2.0	15	8	9	19	0	.265	.384	12	2	OF-34, 1B-12
15 yrs.	1516	5022	1243	201	48	117	2.3	641	500	371	564	44	.248	.377	99	27	OF-1289, 1B-94, SS-74, 3B-18, 2B-4, DH-3
15 yrs.	1516	5022	1243	201	48	117	2.3	641	500	371	564	44	.248	.377	99	27	OF-1289, 1B-94, SS-74, 3B-18, 2B-4, DH-3

LEAGUE CHAMPIONSHIP SERIES

1972 DET A	4	6	2	0	0	0	0.0	0	0	0	0	0	.333	.333	1	0	OF-3

WORLD SERIES

1968 DET A	7	28	6	0	1	0	0.0	4	0	2	4	0	.214	.286	0	0	SS-7

Joe Staton

STATON, JOSEPH (Slim)
B. Mar. 8, 1948, Seattle, Wash.

BL TL 6'3" 175 lbs.

1972 DET A	6	2	0	0	0	0	0.0	1	0	0	1	0	.000	.000	0	0	1B-2
1973	9	17	4	0	0	0	0.0	2	3	0	3	1	.235	.235	2	0	1B-5
2 yrs.	15	19	4	0	0	0	0.0	3	3	0	4	1	.211	.211	2	0	1B-7
2 yrs.	15	19	4	0	0	0	0.0	3	3	0	4	1	.211	.211	2	0	1B-7

Rusty Staub

STAUB, DANIEL JOSEPH
B. Apr. 1, 1944, New Orleans, La.

BL TR 6'2" 190 lbs.

1963 HOU N	150	513	115	17	4	6	1.2	43	45	59	58	0	.224	.308	5	0	1B-109, OF-49
1964	89	292	63	10	2	8	2.7	26	35	21	31	1	.216	.346	8	3	1B-49, OF-38
1965	131	410	105	20	1	14	3.4	43	63	52	57	3	.256	.412	16	5	OF-112, 1B-1
1966	153	554	155	28	3	13	2.3	60	81	58	61	2	.280	.412	6	3	OF-148, 1B-1
1967	149	546	182	44	1	10	1.8	71	74	60	47	0	.333	.473	5	1	OF-144
1968	161	591	172	37	1	6	1.0	54	72	73	57	2	.291	.387	0	0	1B-147, OF-15
1969 MON N	158	549	166	26	5	29	5.3	89	79	110	61	3	.302	.526	2	1	OF-156
1970	160	569	156	23	7	30	5.3	98	94	112	93	12	.274	.497	3	2	OF-160
1971	162	599	186	34	6	19	3.2	94	97	74	42	9	.311	.482	5	1	OF-162
1972 NY N	66	239	70	11	0	9	3.8	32	38	31	13	0	.293	.452	1	0	OF-65
1973	152	585	163	36	1	15	2.6	77	76	74	52	1	.279	.421	0	0	OF-152
1974	151	561	145	22	2	19	3.4	65	78	77	39	2	.258	.406	4	2	OF-147
1975	155	574	162	30	4	19	3.3	93	105	77	55	2	.282	.448	2	1	OF-153
1976 DET A	161	589	176	28	3	15	2.5	73	96	83	49	3	.299	.433	0	0	OF-126, DH-36
1977	158	623	173	34	3	22	3.5	84	101	59	47	1	.278	.448	2	0	DH-156
1978	162	642	175	30	1	24	3.7	75	121	76	35	3	.273	.435	0	0	DH-162
1979 2 teams		DET	A	(68G	–	.236)		MON	N	(38G	–	.267)					
" total	106	332	81	15	1	12	3.6	41	54	46	28	1	.244	.404	14	2	DH-66, 1B-22, OF-1
1980 TEX A	109	340	102	23	2	9	2.6	42	55	39	18	1	.300	.459	15	5	DH-57, 1B-30, OF-14
1981 NY N	70	161	51	9	0	5	3.1	9	21	22	12	1	.317	.466	24	9	1B-41
1982	112	219	53	9	0	3	1.4	11	27	24	10	0	.242	.324	57	12	OF-27, 1B-18
1983	104	115	34	6	0	3	2.6	5	28	14	10	0	.296	.426	81	24	OF-5, 1B-5
1984	78	72	19	4	0	1	1.4	2	18	4	9	0	.264	.361	66	18	1B-3
22 yrs.	2897 7th	9675	2704	496	47	291	3.0	1187	1458	1245	884	47	.279	.431	316	89	OF-1674, DH-477, 1B-42
4 yrs.	549	2100	582	104	8	70	3.3	264	358	250	149	8	.277	.434	4	0	DH-420, OF-126

LEAGUE CHAMPIONSHIP SERIES

1973 NY N	4	15	3	0	0	3	20.0	4	5	3	2	0	.200	.800	0	0	OF-4

WORLD SERIES

1973 NY N	7	26	11	2	0	1	3.8	1	6	2	2	0	.423	.615	0	0	OF-6

Dave Stegman

STEGMAN, DAVID WILLIAM
B. Jan. 30, 1954, Inglewood, Calif.

BR TR 5'11" 190 lbs.

1978 DET A	8	14	4	2	0	1	7.1	3	3	1	2	0	.286	.643	0	0	OF-7
1979	12	31	6	0	0	3	9.7	6	5	2	3	1	.194	.484	1	0	OF-12
1980	65	130	23	5	0	2	1.5	12	9	14	23	1	.177	.262	6	1	OF-57, DH-2
1982 NY A	2	0	0	0	0	0	–	0	0	0	0	0	–	–	0	0	
1983 CHI A	30	53	9	2	0	0	0.0	5	4	10	9	0	.170	.208	3	0	OF-29
1984	55	92	24	1	2	2	2.2	13	11	4	18	3	.261	.380	5	2	OF-46, DH-3
6 yrs.	172	320	66	10	2	8	2.5	39	32	31	55	5	.206	.325	15	3	OF-151, DH-5
3 yrs.	85	175	33	7	0	6	3.4	21	17	17	28	2	.189	.331	7	1	OF-76, DH-2

Ben Steiner

STEINER, BENJAMIN SAUNDERS
B. July 28, 1921, Alexandria, Va.

BL TR 5'11" 165 lbs.

1945 BOS A	78	304	78	8	3	3	1.0	39	20	31	29	10	.257	.332	1	0	2B-77
1946	3	4	1	0	0	0	0.0	1	0	0	0	0	.250	.250	0	0	3B-1
1947 DET A	1	0	0	0	0	0	–	0	0	0	0	0	–	–	0	0	
3 yrs.	82	308	79	8	3	3	1.0	41	20	31	29	10	.256	.331	1	0	2B-77, 3B-1
1 yr.	1	0	0	0	0	0	–	1	0	0	0	0	–	–	0	0	

	G	AB	H	2B	3B	HR	HR %	R	RBI	BB	SO	SB	BA	SA	Pinch Hit AB	Pinch Hit H	G by POS

John Stone

STONE, JONATHON THOMAS (Rocky)   BL TR 6'1"   178 lbs.
B. Oct. 10, 1905, Lynchburg, Tenn.   D. Nov. 11, 1955, Shelbyville, Tenn.

	G	AB	H	2B	3B	HR	HR %	R	RBI	BB	SO	SB	BA	SA	AB	H	G by POS
'28 DET A	26	113	40	10	3	2	1.8	20	21	5	8	1	.354	.549	0	0	OF-26
'29	51	150	39	11	2	2	1.3	23	15	11	13	1	.260	.400	15	4	OF-36
'30	126	422	132	29	11	3	0.7	60	56	32	49	6	.313	.455	18	4	OF-108
'31	147	584	191	28	11	10	1.7	86	76	56	48	13	.327	.464	0	0	OF-147
'32	144	582	173	35	12	17	2.9	106	108	58	64	2	.297	.486	3	0	OF-141
'33	148	574	161	33	11	11	1.9	86	80	54	37	1	.280	.434	5	3	OF-141
'34 WAS A	113	419	132	28	7	7	1.7	77	67	52	26	1	.315	.465	4	2	OF-112
'35	125	454	143	27	18	1	0.2	78	78	39	29	4	.315	.460	14	2	OF-114
'36	123	437	149	22	11	15	3.4	95	90	60	26	8	.341	.545	6	2	OF-114
'37	139	542	179	33	15	6	1.1	84	88	66	36	6	.330	.480	1	0	OF-137
'38	56	213	52	12	4	3	1.4	24	28	30	16	2	.244	.380	1	0	OF-53
11 yrs.	1198	4490	1391	268	105	77	1.7	739	707	463	352	45	.310	.468	67	17	OF-1129
6 yrs.	642	2425	736	146	50	45	1.9	381	356	216	219	24	.304	.461	41	11	OF-599

Walt Streuli

STREULI, WALTER HERBERT   BR TR 6'2"   195 lbs.
B. Sept. 26, 1935, Memphis, Tenn.

	G	AB	H	2B	3B	HR	HR %	R	RBI	BB	SO	SB	BA	SA	AB	H	G by POS
'54 DET A	1	0	0	0	0	0	–	0	0	1	0	0	–	–	0	0	C-1
'55	2	4	1	1	0	0	0.0	0	1	0	0	0	.250	.500	0	0	C-2
'56	3	8	2	1	0	0	0.0	0	1	1	2	0	.250	.375	0	0	C-3
3 yrs.	6	12	3	2	0	0	0.0	1	2	2	2	0	.250	.417	0	0	C-6
3 yrs.	6	12	3	2	0	0	0.0	1	2	2	2	0	.250	.417	0	0	C-6

Joe Sugden

SUGDEN, JOSEPH   BB TR 5'10"   180 lbs.
B. July 31, 1870, Philadelphia, Pa.   D. June 28, 1959, Philadelphia, Pa.

	G	AB	H	2B	3B	HR	HR %	R	RBI	BB	SO	SB	BA	SA	AB	H	G by POS
'93 PIT N	27	92	24	4	3	0	0.0	20	12	10	11	1	.261	.370	0	0	C-27
'94	39	139	46	13	2	2	1.4	23	23	14	2	3	.331	.496	0	0	C-31, 3B-4, SS-3, OF-1
'95	49	155	48	4	1	1	0.6	28	17	16	12	4	.310	.368	0	0	C-49
'96	80	301	89	5	7	0	0.0	42	36	19	9	5	.296	.359	0	0	C-70, 1B-7, OF-4
'97	84	288	64	6	4	0	0.0	31	38	18		9	.222	.271	0	0	C-81, 1B-3
'98 STL N	89	289	73	7	1	0	0.0	29	34	23		5	.253	.284	7	2	C-60, OF-15, 1B-8
'99 CLE N	76	250	69	5	1	0	0.0	19	14	11		2	.276	.304	2	1	C-66, OF-4, 1B-3, 3B-1
'01 CHI A	48	153	42	7	1	0	0.0	21	19	13		2	.275	.333	2	0	C-42, 1B-5
'02 STL A	69	203	50	7	2	0	0.0	25	15	20		3	.246	.300	3	1	C-61, 1B-4, P-1
'03	79	241	52	4	0	0	0.0	18	22	25		4	.216	.232	5	0	C-66, 1B-8
'04	105	347	91	6	3	0	0.0	25	30	28		6	.262	.297	1	0	C-79, 1B-28
'05	85	266	46	4	0	0	0.0	21	23	23		3	.173	.188	4	0	C-71, 1B-9
'12 DET A	1	4	1	0	0	0	0.0	1	0	0		0	.250	.250	0	0	1B-1
13 yrs.	831	2728	695	72	25	3	0.1	303	283	220	34	48	.255	.303	24	4	C-703, 1B-76, OF-24, 3B-5, SS-3, P-1
1 yr.	1	4	1	0	0	0	0.0	1	0	0		0	.250	.250	0	0	1B-1

Billy Sullivan

SULLIVAN, WILLIAM JOSEPH, SR.   BR TR 5'9"   155 lbs.
Father of Billy Sullivan.
B. Feb. 1, 1875, Oakland, Wis.   D. Jan. 28, 1965, Newberg, Ore.
Manager 1909.

	G	AB	H	2B	3B	HR	HR %	R	RBI	BB	SO	SB	BA	SA	AB	H	G by POS
'99 BOS N	22	74	20	2	0	2	2.7	10	12	1		2	.270	.378	0	0	C-22
'00	72	238	65	6	0	8	3.4	36	41	9		4	.273	.399	3	2	C-66, SS-1, 2B-1
'01 CHI A	98	367	90	15	6	4	1.1	54	56	10		12	.245	.351	0	0	C-97, 3B-1
'02	76	263	64	12	3	1	0.4	36	26	6		11	.243	.323	2	0	C-70, OF-2, 1B-2
'03	32	111	21	4	0	1	0.9	10	7	5		3	..189	.252	1	0	C-31
'04	108	371	85	18	4	1	0.3	29	44	12		11	.229	.307	1	0	C-107
'05	99	323	65	10	3	2	0.6	25	26	13		14	.201	.269	3	0	C-93, 1B-2, 3B-1
'06	118	387	83	18	4	2	0.5	37	33	22		10	.214	.297	0	0	C-118
'07	112	339	59	8	4	0	0.0	30	36	21		6	.174	.221	3	0	C-108, 2B-1
'08	137	430	82	8	4	0	0.0	40	29	22		15	.191	.228	1	0	C-137
'09	97	265	43	3	0	0	0.0	11	16	17		9	.162	.174	0	0	C-97
'10	45	142	26	4	1	0	0.0	10	6	7		0	.183	.225	0	0	C-45
'11	89	256	55	9	3	0	0.0	26	31	16		1	.215	.273	0	0	C-89
'12	39	91	19	2	1	0	0.0	9	15	9		0	.209	.253	0	0	C-39
'14	1	0	0	0	0	0	–	0	0	0	0	0	–	–	0	0	C-1
'16 DET A	1	0	0	0	0	0	–	0	0	0	0	0	–	–	0	0	C-1
16 yrs.	1146	3657	777	119	33	21	0.6	363	378	170	0	98	.212	.280	14	2	C-1121, 1B-4, OF-2, 3B-2, 2B-2, SS-1
1 yr.	1	0	0	0	0	0	–	0	0	0	0	0	–	–	0	0	C-1

WORLD SERIES

	G	AB	H	2B	3B	HR	HR %	R	RBI	BB	SO	SB	BA	SA	AB	H	G by POS
'06 CHI A	6	21	0	0	0	0	0.0	0	0	0	9	0	.000	.000	0	0	C-6

Billy Sullivan

SULLIVAN, WILLIAM JOSEPH, JR.   BL TR 6'   170 lbs.
Son of Billy Sullivan.
B. Oct. 23, 1910, Chicago, Ill.

	G	AB	H	2B	3B	HR	HR %	R	RBI	BB	SO	SB	BA	SA	AB	H	G by POS
'31 CHI A	92	363	100	16	5	2	0.6	48	33	20	14	4	.275	.364	7	4	3B-83, OF-2, 1B-1
'32	93	307	97	16	1	1	0.3	31	45	20	9	1	.316	.384	19	3	1B-52, 3B-17, C-5
'33	54	125	24	0	1	0	0.0	9	13	10	5	0	.192	.208	22	5	1B-22, C-8
'35 CIN N	85	241	64	9	4	2	0.8	29	36	19	16	4	.266	.361	21	7	1B-40, 3B-15, 2B-6
'36 CLE A	93	319	112	32	6	2	0.6	39	48	16	9	5	.351	.508	11	5	C-72, 3B-5, 1B-3, OF-1
'37	72	168	48	12	3	3	1.8	26	22	17	7	1	.286	.446	24	5	C-38, 1B-5, 3B-1
'38 STL A	111	375	104	16	1	7	1.9	35	49	20	10	8	.277	.381	8	1	C-99, 1B-6
'39	118	332	96	17	5	5	1.5	47	50	34	18	3	.289	.416	33	9	OF-59, C-19, 1B-4
'40 DET A	78	220	68	14	4	3	1.4	36	41	31	11	2	.309	.450	15	5	C-57, 3B-6
'41	85	234	66	15	1	3	1.3	29	29	35	11	0	.282	.393	21	6	C-63
'42 BKN N	43	101	27	2	1	1	1.0	11	14	12	6	1	.267	.337	1	0	C-41
'47 PIT N	38	55	14	3	0	0	0.0	1	8	6	3	1	.255	.309	25	5	C-12
12 yrs.	962	2840	820	152	32	29	1.0	347	388	240	119	30	.289	.395	207	55	C-414, 1B-133, 3B-127, OF-62, 2B-6
2 yrs.	163	454	134	29	5	6	1.3	65	70	66	22	2	.295	.421	36	11	C-120, 3B-6

	G	AB	H	2B	3B	HR	HR %	R	RBI	BB	SO	SB	BA	SA	Pinch Hit AB	Pinch Hit H	G by POS

Billy Sullivan continued

WORLD SERIES
	G	AB	H	2B	3B	HR	HR %	R	RBI	BB	SO	SB	BA	SA	AB	H	G by POS
1940 DET A	5	13	2	0	0	0	0.0	3	0	5	2	0	.154	.154	1	0	C-4

Jack Sullivan

SULLIVAN, CARL MANUEL BR TR 5'11" 185 lbs.
B. Feb. 22, 1918, Princeton, Tex.

	G	AB	H	2B	3B	HR	HR %	R	RBI	BB	SO	SB	BA	SA	AB	H	G by POS
1944 DET A	1	1	0	0	0	0	0.0	0	0	0	0	0	.000	.000	0	0	2B-1

John Sullivan

SULLIVAN, JOHN EUGENE TR
B. Feb. 16, 1873, Ill.   D. June 5, 1924, St. Paul, Minn.

	G	AB	H	2B	3B	HR	HR %	R	RBI	BB	SO	SB	BA	SA	AB	H	G by POS
1905 DET A	12	31	5	0	0	0	0.0	4	4	4		0	.161	.161	0	0	C-12
1908 PIT N	1	1	0	0	0	0	0.0	0	0	0		0	.000	.000	0	0	C-1
2 yrs.	13	32	5	0	0	0	0.0	4	4	4		0	.156	.156	0	0	C-13
1 yr.	12	31	5	0	0	0	0.0	4	4	4		0	.161	.161	0	0	C-12

John Sullivan

SULLIVAN, JOHN PETER BL TR 6' 195 lbs.
B. Jan. 3, 1941, Somerville, N. J.

	G	AB	H	2B	3B	HR	HR %	R	RBI	BB	SO	SB	BA	SA	AB	H	G by POS
1963 DET A	3	5	0	0	0	0	0.0	0	2	1	1	0	.000	.000	0	0	C-2
1964	2	3	0	0	0	0	0.0	0	0	0	1	0	.000	.000	0	0	C-2
1965	34	86	23	0	0	2	2.3	5	11	9	13	0	.267	.337	4	1	C-29
1967 NY N	65	147	32	5	0	0	0.0	4	6	6	26	0	.218	.252	26	4	C-57
1968 PHI N	12	18	4	0	0	0	0.0	0	1	2	4	0	.222	.222	7	1	C-8
5 yrs.	116	259	59	5	0	2	0.8	9	18	19	45	0	.228	.270	37	6	C-98
3 yrs.	39	94	23	0	0	2	2.1	5	11	11	15	0	.245	.309	4	1	C-33

Russ Sullivan

SULLIVAN, RUSSELL GUY BL TR 6' 196 lbs.
B. Feb. 19, 1923, Fredericksburg, Va.

	G	AB	H	2B	3B	HR	HR %	R	RBI	BB	SO	SB	BA	SA	AB	H	G by POS
1951 DET A	7	26	5	1	0	1	3.8	2	1	2	1	0	.192	.346	0	0	OF-7
1952	15	52	17	2	1	3	5.8	7	5	3	5	1	.327	.577	1	1	OF-14
1953	23	72	18	5	1	1	1.4	7	6	13	5	0	.250	.389	3	0	OF-20
3 yrs.	45	150	40	8	2	5	3.3	16	12	18	11	1	.267	.447	4	1	OF-41
3 yrs.	45	150	40	8	2	5	3.3	16	12	18	11	1	.267	.447	4	1	OF-41

Champ Summers

SUMMERS, JOHN JUNIOR II BL TR 6'2" 205 lbs.
B. June 15, 1946, Bremerton, Wash.

	G	AB	H	2B	3B	HR	HR %	R	RBI	BB	SO	SB	BA	SA	AB	H	G by POS
1974 OAK A	20	24	3	1	0	0	0.0	2	3	1	5	0	.125	.167	7	1	OF-12, DH-2
1975 CHI N	76	91	21	5	1	1	1.1	14	16	10	13	0	.231	.341	46	14	OF-18
1976	83	126	26	2	0	3	2.4	11	13	13	31	1	.206	.294	47	12	OF-26, 1B-10, C-1
1977 CIN N	59	76	13	4	0	3	3.9	11	6	6	16	0	.171	.342	38	6	OF-16, 3B-1
1978	13	35	9	2	0	1	2.9	4	3	7	4	2	.257	.400	0	0	OF-12
1979 2 teams		CIN	N (27G – .200)			DET	A (90G – .313)										
" total	117	306	89	14	2	21	6.9	57	62	53	48	7	.291	.556	23	5	OF-82, DH-10, 1B-10
1980 DET A	120	347	103	19	1	17	4.9	61	60	52	52	4	.297	.504	26	7	DH-64, OF-47, 1B-1
1981	64	165	42	8	0	3	1.8	16	21	19	35	1	.255	.358	14	3	DH-37, OF-18
1982 SF N	70	125	31	5	0	4	3.2	15	19	16	17	0	.248	.384	31	10	OF-31, 1B-3
1983	29	22	3	0	0	0	0.0	3	3	7	8	0	.136	.136	20	3	OF-1
1984 SD N	47	54	10	3	0	1	1.9	5	12	4	15	0	.185	.296	36	7	1B-8
11 yrs.	698	1371	350	63	4	54	3.9	199	218	188	244	15	.255	.425	288	68	OF-263, DH-113, 1B-32, 3B-1, C-1
3 yrs.	274	758	222	39	2	40	5.3	124	132	111	120	12	.293	.508	53	14	OF-134, DH-111, 1B-5

LEAGUE CHAMPIONSHIP SERIES
	G	AB	H	2B	3B	HR	HR %	R	RBI	BB	SO	SB	BA	SA	AB	H	G by POS
1984 SD N	2	2	0	0	0	0	0.0	0	0	0	1	0	.000	.000	0	0	

WORLD SERIES
	G	AB	H	2B	3B	HR	HR %	R	RBI	BB	SO	SB	BA	SA	AB	H	G by POS
1984 SD N	1	1	0	0	0	0	0.0	0	0	0	1	0	.000	.000	1	0	

George Susce

SUSCE, GEORGE CYRIL METHODIUS (Good Kid) BR TR 5'11½" 200 lbs.
Father of George Susce.
B. Aug. 13, 1908, Pittsburgh, Pa.

	G	AB	H	2B	3B	HR	HR %	R	RBI	BB	SO	SB	BA	SA	AB	H	G by POS
1929 PHI N	17	17	5	3	0	1	5.9	5	1	1	2	0	.294	.647	5	0	C-11
1932 DET A	2	0	0	0	0	0	–	0	0	0	0	0	–	–	0	0	C-2
1939 PIT N	31	75	17	3	1	1	1.3	8	4	12	5	0	.227	.333	0	0	1B-31
1940 STL A	61	113	24	4	0	0	0.0	6	13	9	9	1	.212	.248	0	0	C-61
1941 CLE A	1	0	0	0	0	0	–	0	0	0	0	0	–	–	0	0	C-1
1942	2	1	1	0	0	0	0.0	1	0	1	0	0	1.000	1.000	0	0	C-2
1943	3	1	0	0	0	0	0.0	0	0	0	0	0	.000	.000	0	0	C-3
1944	29	61	14	1	0	0	0.0	3	4	2	5	0	.230	.246	0	0	C-29
8 yrs.	146	268	61	11	1	2	0.7	23	22	25	21	1	.228	.299	5	0	C-109, 1B-31
1 yr.	2	0	0	0	0	0	–	0	0	0	0	0	–	–	0	0	C-2

Gary Sutherland

SUTHERLAND, GARY LYNN BR TR 6' 185 lbs.
Brother of Darrell Sutherland.
B. Sept. 27, 1944, Glendale, Calif.

	G	AB	H	2B	3B	HR	HR %	R	RBI	BB	SO	SB	BA	SA	AB	H	G by POS
1966 PHI N	3	3	0	0	0	0	0.0	0	0	0	0	0	.000	.000	2	0	SS-1
1967	103	231	57	12	1	1	0.4	23	19	17	22	0	.247	.320	22	4	SS-66, OF-25
1968	67	138	38	7	0	0	0.0	16	15	8	15	0	.275	.326	31	9	2B-17, SS-10, 3B-10, OF-7
1969 MON N	141	544	130	26	1	3	0.6	63	35	37	31	5	.239	.307	1	0	2B-139, SS-15, OF-1
1970	116	359	74	10	0	3	0.8	37	26	31	22	2	.206	.259	23	4	2B-97, SS-15, SS-1
1971	111	304	78	7	2	4	1.3	25	26	18	12	3	.257	.332	19	3	2B-56, SS-46, OF-4, 3B-2
1972 HOU N	5	8	1	0	0	0	0.0	0	1	0	0	0	.125	.125	4	0	3B-1, 2B-1
1973	16	54	14	5	0	0	0.0	8	3	3	5	0	.259	.352	2	1	2B-14, SS-1
1974 DET A	149	619	157	20	1	5	0.8	60	49	26	37	1	.254	.313	2	1	2B-147, SS-10, 3B-4
1975	129	503	130	12	6	1.2		51	39	45	41	0	.258	.330	1	0	2B-128
1976 2 teams		DET	A (42G – .205)			MIL	A (59G – .217)										
" total	101	232	49	7	2	1	0.4	19	15	15	19	0	.211	.272	12	2	2B-87, DH-8, 1B-2
1977 SD N	80	103	25	3	0	1	1.0	5	11	7	15	0	.243	.301	38	12	2B-30, 3B-21, 1B-4

	G	AB	H	2B	3B	HR	HR %	R	RBI	BB	SO	SB	BA	SA	Pinch Hit AB	Pinch Hit H	G by POS

Gary Sutherland continued

	G	AB	H	2B	3B	HR	HR %	R	RBI	BB	SO	SB	BA	SA	AB	H	G by POS
1978 STL N	10	6	1	0	0	0	0.0	1	0	0	0	0	.167	.167	6	1	2B-1
13 yrs.	1031	3104	754	109	10	24	0.8	308	239	207	219	11	.243	.308	163	37	2B-717, SS-164, 3B-39, OF-37, DH-8, 1B-6
3 yrs.	320	1239	311	37	6	11	0.9	121	94	78	90	1	.251	.317	5	2	2B-317, SS-10, 3B-4

Bill Sweeney

SWEENEY, WILLIAM JOSEPH
B. Dec. 29, 1904, Cleveland, Ohio   D. Apr. 18, 1957, San Diego, Calif.   BR TR 5'11" 180 lbs.

	G	AB	H	2B	3B	HR	HR %	R	RBI	BB	SO	SB	BA	SA	AB	H	G by POS
1928 DET A	89	309	78	15	5	0	0.0	47	19	15	28	12	.252	.333	8	1	1B-75, OF-3
1930 BOS A	88	243	75	13	0	4	1.6	32	30	9	15	5	.309	.412	25	4	1B-56, 3B-1
1931	131	498	147	30	3	1	0.2	48	58	20	30	5	.295	.373	6	4	1B-124
3 yrs.	308	1050	300	58	8	5	0.5	127	107	44	73	22	.286	.370	39	9	1B-255, OF-3, 3B-1
1 yr.	89	309	78	15	5	0	0.0	47	19	15	28	12	.252	.333	8	1	1B-75, OF-3

Bob Swift

SWIFT, ROBERT VIRGIL
B. Mar. 6, 1915, Salina, Kans.   D. Oct. 17, 1966, Detroit, Mich.   BR TR 5'11½" 180 lbs.
Manager 1966.

	G	AB	H	2B	3B	HR	HR %	R	RBI	BB	SO	SB	BA	SA	AB	H	G by POS
1940 STL A	130	398	97	20	1	0	0.0	37	39	28	39	1	.244	.299	2	0	C-128
1941	63	170	44	7	0	0	0.0	13	21	22	11	2	.259	.300	5	1	C-58
1942 2 teams		STL	A (29G – .197)			PHI	A (60G – .229)										
" total	89	268	59	7	0	1	0.4	12	23	16	22	1	.220	.257	1	0	C-88
1943 PHI A	77	224	43	5	1	1	0.4	16	11	35	16	0	.192	.237	0	0	C-77
1944 DET A	80	247	63	11	1	1	0.4	15	19	27	27	2	.255	.320	4	1	C-76
1945	95	279	65	5	0	0	0.0	19	24	25	22	1	.233	.251	1	0	C-94
1946	42	107	25	2	0	2	1.9	13	10	14	7	0	.234	.308	0	0	C-42
1947	97	279	70	11	0	1	0.4	23	21	33	16	2	.251	.301	1	0	C-97
1948	113	292	65	6	0	4	1.4	23	33	51	29	1	.223	.284	1	0	C-112
1949	74	189	45	6	0	2	1.1	16	18	26	20	0	.238	.302	6	1	C-69
1950	67	132	30	4	0	2	1.5	14	9	25	6	0	.227	.303	1	0	C-66
1951	44	104	20	0	0	0	0.0	8	5	12	10	0	.192	.192	1	0	C-43
1952	28	58	8	1	0	0	0.0	3	4	7	7	0	.138	.155	0	0	C-28
1953	2	3	1	1	0	0	0.0	0	1	2	1	0	.333	.667	0	0	C-2
14 yrs.	1001	2750	635	86	3	14	0.5	212	238	323	233	10	.231	.280	23	3	C-980
10 yrs.	642	1690	392	47	1	12	0.7	134	144	222	145	6	.232	.282	15	2	C-629
WORLD SERIES																	
1945 DET A	3	4	1	0	0	0	0.0	1	0	2	0†	0	.250	.250	0	0	C-3

Ken Szotkiewicz

SZOTKIEWICZ, KENNETH JOHN
B. Feb. 25, 1947, Wilmington, Del.   BL TR 6' 165 lbs.

	G	AB	H	2B	3B	HR	HR %	R	RBI	BB	SO	SB	BA	SA	AB	H	G by POS
1970 DET A	47	84	9	1	0	3	3.6	9	9	12	29	0	.107	.226	3	0	SS-44

Jackie Tavener

TAVENER, JOHN ADAM
B. Dec. 27, 1897, Celina, Ohio   D. Sept. 14, 1969, Fort Worth, Tex.   BL TR 5'5" 138 lbs.

	G	AB	H	2B	3B	HR	HR %	R	RBI	BB	SO	SB	BA	SA	AB	H	G by POS
1921 DET A	2	4	0	0	0	0	0.0	0	0	0	1	0	.000	.000	0	0	SS-2
1925	134	453	111	11	11	0	0.0	45	47	39	60	5	.245	.318	0	0	SS-134
1926	156	532	141	22	14	1	0.2	65	58	52	53	8	.265	.365	0	0	SS-156
1927	116	419	115	22	9	5	1.2	60	59	36	38	20	.274	.406	1	0	SS-114
1928	132	473	123	24	15	5	1.1	59	52	33	51	13	.260	.406	0	0	SS-131
1929 CLE A	92	250	53	9	4	2	0.8	25	27	26	28	1	.212	.304	0	0	SS-89
6 yrs.	632	2131	543	88	53	13	0.6	254	243	186	231	47	.255	.364	1	0	SS-626
5 yrs.	540	1881	490	79	49	11	0.6	229	216	160	203	46	.260	.372	1	0	SS-537

Bennie Taylor

TAYLOR, BENJAMIN EUGENE
B. Sept. 30, 1927, Metropolis, Ill.   BL TL 6' 195 lbs.

	G	AB	H	2B	3B	HR	HR %	R	RBI	BB	SO	SB	BA	SA	AB	H	G by POS
1951 STL A	33	93	24	2	1	3	3.2	14	6	9	22	1	.258	.398	7	2	1B-25
1952 DET A	7	18	3	0	0	0	0.0	0	0	0	5	0	.167	.167	3	0	1B-4
1955 MIL N	12	10	1	0	0	0	0.0	2	0	2	4	0	.100	.100	9	1	1B-1
3 yrs.	52	121	28	2	1	3	2.5	16	6	11	31	1	.231	.339	19	3	1B-30
1 yr.	7	18	3	0	0	0	0.0	0	0	0	5	0	.167	.167	3	0	1B-4

Bill Taylor

TAYLOR, JOSEPH CEPHUS (Cash)
B. Mar. 2, 1926, Chapman, Ala.   BL TL 6'1" 185 lbs.

	G	AB	H	2B	3B	HR	HR %	R	RBI	BB	SO	SB	BA	SA	AB	H	G by POS
1954 NY N	55	65	12	1	0	2	3.1	4	10	3	15	0	.185	.292	42	9	OF-9
1955	65	64	17	4	0	4	6.3	9	12	1	16	0	.266	.484	60	15	OF-2
1956	1	4	1	1	0	0	0.0	0	0	0	1	0	.250	.500	0	0	OF-1
1957 2 teams		NY	N (11G – .000)			DET	A (9G – .348)										
" total	20	32	8	2	0	1	3.1	4	3	1	5	0	.250	.406	13	2	OF-5
1958 DET A	8	8	3	0	0	0	0.0	0	1	0	2	0	.375	.375	6	3	OF-1
5 yrs.	149	173	41	8	0	7	4.0	17	26	5	39	0	.237	.405	121	29	OF-18
2 yrs.	17	31	11	2	0	1	3.2	4	4	0	5	0	.355	.516	10	5	OF-6

Tony Taylor

TAYLOR, ANTONIO SANCHEZ
B. Dec. 19, 1935, Central Alara, Cuba   BR TR 5'9" 170 lbs.

	G	AB	H	2B	3B	HR	HR %	R	RBI	BB	SO	SB	BA	SA	AB	H	G by POS
1958 CHI N	140	497	117	15	3	6	1.2	63	27	40	93	21	.235	.314	0	0	2B-137, 3B-1
1959	150	624	175	30	8	8	1.3	96	38	45	86	23	.280	.393	0	0	2B-149, SS-2
1960 2 teams		CHI	N (19G – .263)			PHI	N (127G – .287)										
" total	146	581	165	25	7	5	0.9	80	44	41	98	26	.284	.377	2	0	2B-142, 3B-4
1961 PHI N	106	400	100	17	3	2	0.5	47	26	29	59	11	.250	.323	14	3	2B-91, 3B-3
1962	152	625	162	21	5	7	1.1	87	43	68	82	20	.259	.342	2	1	2B-150, SS-2
1963	157	640	180	20	10	5	0.8	102	49	42	99	23	.281	.367	4	0	2B-149, 3B-13
1964	154	570	143	13	6	4	0.7	62	46	46	74	13	.251	.316	3	1	2B-150
1965	106	323	74	14	3	3	0.9	41	27	22	58	5	.229	.319	14	1	2B-86, 3B-5
1966	125	434	105	14	8	5	1.2	47	40	31	56	8	.242	.346	8	1	2B-68, 3B-52
1967	132	462	110	16	6	2	0.4	55	34	42	74	10	.238	.312	8	3	1B-58, 3B-44, 2B-42, SS-3
1968	145	547	137	20	2	3	0.5	59	38	39	60	22	.250	.311	3	0	3B-138, 2B-5, 1B-1
1969	138	557	146	24	5	3	0.5	68	30	42	62	19	.262	.339	5	2	3B-71, 2B-57, 1B-10

	G	AB	H	2B	3B	HR	HR %	R	RBI	BB	SO	SB	BA	SA	Pinch Hit AB	Pinch Hit H	G by POS

Tony Taylor continued

	G	AB	H	2B	3B	HR	HR %	R	RBI	BB	SO	SB	BA	SA	P.H. AB	P.H. H	G by POS
1970	124	439	132	26	9	9	2.1	74	55	50	67	9	.301	.462	14	6	2B-59, 3B-38, OF-18, SS-1
1971 2 teams		PHI N (36G – .234)				DET A (55G – .287)											
" total	91	288	77	12	3	4	1.4	36	24	21	21	7	.267	.372	18	5	2B-65, 3B-14, 1B-2
1972 DET A	78	228	69	12	4	1	0.4	33	20	14	34	5	.303	.404	20	6	2B-67, 3B-8, 1B-1
1973	84	275	63	9	3	5	1.8	35	24	17	29	9	.229	.338	9	0	2B-72, 1B-6, 3B-4, DH-1
1974 PHI N	62	64	21	4	0	2	3.1	5	13	6	6	0	.328	.484	46	17	1B-7, 3B-5, 2B-4
1975	79	103	25	5	1	1	1.0	13	17	17	18	3	.243	.340	54	12	3B-16, 1B-4, 2B-3
1976	26	23	6	1	0	0	0.0	2	3	1	7	0	.261	.304	21	5	2B-2, 3B-1
19 yrs.	2195	7680	2007	298	86	75	1.0	1005	598	613	1083	234	.261	.352	245	63	2B-1498, 3B-417, 1B-89, OF-18, SS-8, DH-1
3 yrs.	217	684	184	31	9	9	1.3	95	63	43	74	19	.269	.380	38	10	2B-190, 3B-15, 1B-7, DH-1

LEAGUE CHAMPIONSHIP SERIES

	G	AB	H	2B	3B	HR	HR %	R	RBI	BB	SO	SB	BA	SA	P.H. AB	P.H. H	G by POS
1972 DET A	4	15	2	2	0	0	0.0	0	0	0	2	0	.133	.267	0	0	2B-4

Birdie Tebbetts

TEBBETTS, GEORGE ROBERT
B. Nov. 10, 1912, Burlington, Vt.
Manager 1954-58, 1961-66.

BR TR 5'11½" 170 lbs.

	G	AB	H	2B	3B	HR	HR %	R	RBI	BB	SO	SB	BA	SA	P.H. AB	P.H. H	G by POS
1936 DET A	10	33	10	1	2	1	3.0	7	4	5	3	0	.303	.545	0	0	C-10
1937	50	162	31	4	3	2	1.2	15	16	10	13	0	.191	.290	2	0	C-48
1938	53	143	42	6	2	1	0.7	16	25	12	13	1	.294	.385	9	3	C-53
1939	106	341	89	22	4	4	1.2	37	53	25	20	2	.261	.372	6	1	C-100
1940	111	379	112	24	4	4	1.1	46	46	35	14	4	.296	.412	2	0	C-107
1941	110	359	102	19	4	2	0.6	28	47	38	29	1	.284	.376	12	3	C-98
1942	99	308	76	11	0	1	0.3	24	27	39	17	4	.247	.292	2	2	C-97
1946	87	280	68	11	2	1	0.4	20	34	28	23	1	.243	.307	0	0	C-87
1947 2 teams		DET A (20G – .094)				BOS A (90G – .299)											
" total	110	344	92	11	0	1	0.3	23	30	24	33	2	.267	.308	1	0	C-109
1948 BOS A	128	446	125	26	2	5	1.1	54	68	62	32	5	.280	.381	1	0	C-126
1949	122	404	109	14	0	5	1.2	42	48	62	22	8	.270	.342	4	1	C-118
1950	79	268	83	10	1	8	3.0	33	45	29	26	1	.310	.444	3	1	C-74
1951 CLE A	55	137	36	6	0	2	1.5	8	18	8	7	0	.263	.350	11	5	C-44
1952	42	101	25	4	0	1	1.0	4	8	12	9	0	.248	.317	5	2	C-37
14 yrs.	1162	3705	1000	169	22	38	1.0	357	469	389	261	29	.270	.358	58	18	C-1108
9 yrs.	646	2058	535	99	19	16	0.8	194	254	195	135	13	.260	.350	33	9	C-620

WORLD SERIES

	G	AB	H	2B	3B	HR	HR %	R	RBI	BB	SO	SB	BA	SA	P.H. AB	P.H. H	G by POS
1940 DET A	4	11	0	0	0	0	0.0	0	0	0	0	0	.000	.000	1	0	C-3

George Thomas

THOMAS, GEORGE EDWARD
B. Nov. 29, 1937, Minneapolis, Minn.

BR TR 6'3½" 190 lbs.

	G	AB	H	2B	3B	HR	HR %	R	RBI	BB	SO	SB	BA	SA	P.H. AB	P.H. H	G by POS
1957 DET A	1	1	0	0	0	0	0.0	0	0	0	1	0	.000	.000	1	0	3B-1
1958	1	0	0	0	0	0	–	0	0	0	0	0	–	–	0	0	OF-1
1961 2 teams		DET A (17G – .000)				LA A (79G – .280)											
" total	96	288	79	12	1	13	4.5	41	59	21	70	3	.274	.458	5	0	OF-47, 3B-38, SS-1
1962 LA A	56	181	43	10	2	4	2.2	13	12	21	37	0	.238	.381	5	1	OF-51
1963 2 teams		LA A (53G – .210)				DET A (44G – .239)											
" total	97	276	61	11	2	5	1.8	27	26	20	54	2	.221	.330	11	0	OF-79, 3B-10, 1B-4, 2B-1
1964 DET A	105	308	88	15	2	12	3.9	39	44	18	53	4	.286	.464	18	6	OF-90, 3B-1
1965	79	169	36	5	1	3	1.8	19	10	12	39	2	.213	.308	17	2	OF-59, 2B-1
1966 BOS A	69	173	41	4	0	5	2.9	25	20	23	33	1	.237	.347	13	5	OF-48, 3B-6, 1B-2, C-2
1967	65	89	19	2	0	1	1.1	10	6	3	23	0	.213	.270	18	2	OF-43, 1B-3, C-1
1968	12	10	2	0	0	1	10.0	3	1	1	3	1	.200	.500	1	0	OF-9
1969	29	51	18	3	1	0	0.0	9	8	3	11	0	.353	.451	6	1	OF-12, 1B-10, 3B-1, C-1
1970	38	99	34	8	0	2	2.0	13	13	11	12	0	.343	.485	6	3	OF-26, 3B-6
1971 2 teams		BOS A (9G – .077)				MIN A (23G – .267)											
" total	32	43	9	1	0	0	0.0	4	3	5	7	0	.209	.233	18	5	OF-16, 3B-1, 1B-1
13 yrs.	680	1688	430	71	9	46	2.7	203	202	138	343	13	.255	.389	119	23	OF-481, 3B-64, 1B-20, C-4, 2B-2, SS-1
6 yrs.	247	593	150	24	4	16	2.7	73	65	41	119	8	.253	.388	48	8	OF-192, 3B-2, 2B-2, SS-1

WORLD SERIES

	G	AB	H	2B	3B	HR	HR %	R	RBI	BB	SO	SB	BA	SA	P.H. AB	P.H. H	G by POS
1967 BOS A	2	2	0	0	0	0	0.0	0	0	0	1	0	.000	.000	1	0	OF-1

Ira Thomas

THOMAS, IRA FELIX
B. Jan. 22, 1881, Ballston Spa, N. Y. D. Oct. 11, 1958, Philadelphia, Pa.

BR TR 6'2" 200 lbs.

	G	AB	H	2B	3B	HR	HR %	R	RBI	BB	SO	SB	BA	SA	P.H. AB	P.H. H	G by POS
1906 NY A	44	115	23	1	2	0	0.0	12	15	8		2	.200	.243	2	0	C-42
1907	80	208	40	5	4	1	0.5	20	24	10		5	.192	.269	16	2	C-66, 1B-2
1908 DET A	40	101	31	1	0	0	0.0	6	8	5		0	.307	.317	11	4	C-29
1909 PHI A	84	256	57	9	3	0	0.0	22	31	18		4	.223	.281	0	0	C-84
1910	60	180	50	8	2	1	0.6	14	19	6		2	.278	.361	0	0	C-60
1911	103	297	81	14	3	0	0.0	33	39	23		4	.273	.340	0	0	C-103
1912	46	139	30	4	2	1	0.7	14	13	8		3	.216	.295	0	0	C-46
1913	21	53	15	4	1	0	0.0	3	6	4	8	0	.283	.396	0	0	C-21
1914	2	3	0	0	0	0	0.0	0	0	0	0	0	.000	.000	1	0	C-1
1915	1	0	0	0	0	0	–	0	0	0	0	0	–	–	0	0	C-1
10 yrs.	481	1352	327	46	17	3	0.2	124	155	82	8	20	.242	.308	30	6	C-453, 1B-2
1 yr.	40	101	31	1	0	0	0.0	6	8	5		0	.307	.317	11	4	C-29

WORLD SERIES

	G	AB	H	2B	3B	HR	HR %	R	RBI	BB	SO	SB	BA	SA	P.H. AB	P.H. H	G by POS
1908 DET A	2	4	2	1	0	0	0.0	0	1	1	0	0	.500	.750	1	1	C-1
1910 PHI A	4	12	3	0	0	0	0.0	2	1	4	1	0	.250	.250	0	0	C-4
1911	4	12	1	0	0	0	0.0	1	1	1	2	0	.083	.083	0	0	C-4
3 yrs.	10	28	6	1	0	0	0.0	3	3	6	3	0	.214	.250	1	1	C-9

	G	AB	H	2B	3B	HR	HR %	R	RBI	BB	SO	SB	BA	SA	Pinch Hit AB	Pinch Hit H	G by POS

Jason Thompson

THOMPSON, JASON DOLPH BL TL 6'4" 200 lbs.
B. July 6, 1954, Hollywood, Calif.

	G	AB	H	2B	3B	HR	HR %	R	RBI	BB	SO	SB	BA	SA	PH AB	PH H	G by POS
1976 DET A	123	412	90	12	1	17	4.1	45	54	68	72	2	.218	.376	3	0	1B-117
1977	158	585	158	24	5	31	5.3	87	105	73	91	0	.270	.487	0	0	1B-158
1978	153	589	169	25	3	26	4.4	79	96	74	96	0	.287	.472	1	0	1B-151
1979	145	492	121	16	1	20	4.1	58	79	70	90	2	.246	.404	8	2	1B-140, DH-2
1980 2 teams	DET A (36G – .214)					CAL A (102G – .317)											
" total	138	438	126	19	0	21	4.8	69	90	83	86	2	.288	.475	14	4	1B-83, DH-45
1981 PIT N	86	223	54	13	0	15	6.7	36	42	59	49	0	.242	.502	13	4	1B-78
1982	156	550	156	32	0	31	5.6	87	101	101	107	1	.284	.511	0	0	1B-155
1983	152	517	134	20	1	18	3.5	70	76	99	128	1	.259	.406	2	0	1B-151
1984	154	543	138	22	0	17	3.1	61	74	87	73	0	.254	.389	3	1	1B-152
9 yrs.	1265	4349	1146	183	11	196	4.5	592	717	714	792	8	.264	.446	44	11	1B-1185, DH-47
5 yrs.	615	2204	565	82	10	98	4.4	279	354	298	375	4	.256	.436	12	2	1B-602, DH-2
							8th										

Sam Thompson

THOMPSON, SAMUEL L. (Big Sam) BL 6'2" 207 lbs.
B. Mar. 5, 1860, Danville, Ind.   D. Nov. 7, 1922, Detroit, Mich.
Hall of Fame 1974.

	G	AB	H	2B	3B	HR	HR %	R	RBI	BB	SO	SB	BA	SA	PH AB	PH H	G by POS
1885 DET N	63	254	77	11	9	7	2.8	58	44	16	22		.303	.500	0	0	OF-62, 3B-1
1886	122	503	156	18	13	8	1.6	101	89	35	31		.310	.445	0	0	OF-122
1887	127	545	203	29	23	11	2.0	118	166	32	19	22	.372	.571	0	0	OF-127
1888	56	238	67	10	8	6	2.5	51	40	23	10	5	.282	.466	0	0	OF-56
1889 PHI N	128	533	158	36	4	20	3.8	103	111	36	22	24	.296	.492	0	0	OF-128
1890	132	549	172	41	9	4	0.7	116	102	42	29	25	.313	.443	0	0	OF-132
1891	133	554	163	23	10	8	1.4	108	90	52	20	29	.294	.415	0	0	OF-133
1892	153	609	186	28	11	9	1.5	109	104	59	19	28	.305	.432	0	0	OF-153
1893	131	600	222	37	13	11	1.8	130	126	50	17	18	.370	.530	0	0	OF-131, 1B-1
1894	102	458	185	29	27	13	2.8	115	141	40	13	29	.404	.670	0	0	OF-102
1895	119	538	211	45	21	18	3.3	131	165	31	11	27	.392	.654	1	1	OF-118
1896	119	517	154	28	7	12	2.3	103	100	28	13	12	.298	.449	0	0	OF-119
1897	3	13	3	0	1	0	0.0	2	3	1		0	.231	.385	0	0	OF-3
1898	14	63	22	5	3	1	1.6	14	15	4		2	.349	.571	0	0	OF-14
1906 DET A	8	31	7	0	1	0	0.0	4	3	1		0	.226	.290	0	0	OF-8
15 yrs.	1410	6005	1986	340	160	128	2.1	1263	1299	450	226	221	.331	.505	1	1	OF-1408, 3B-1, 1B-1
1 yr.	8	31	7	0	1	0	0.0	4	3	1		0	.226	.290	0	0	OF-8

Tim Thompson

THOMPSON, CHARLES LEMOINE BL TR 5'11" 190 lbs.
B. Mar. 1, 1924, Coalport, Pa.

	G	AB	H	2B	3B	HR	HR %	R	RBI	BB	SO	SB	BA	SA	PH AB	PH H	G by POS
1954 BKN N	10	13	2	1	0	0	0.0	2	1	1	1	0	.154	.231	5	1	C-2, OF-1
1956 KC A	92	268	73	13	2	1	0.4	21	27	17	23	2	.272	.347	23	4	C-68
1957	81	230	47	10	0	7	3.0	25	19	18	26	0	.204	.339	19	1	C-62
1958 DET A	4	6	1	0	0	0	0.0	1	0	3	2	0	.167	.167	1	0	C-4
4 yrs.	187	517	123	24	2	8	1.5	49	47	39	52	2	.238	.338	48	6	C-136, OF-1
1 yr.	4	6	1	0	0	0	0.0	1	0	3	2	0	.167	.167	1	0	C-4

Jim Tobin

TOBIN, JAMES ANTHONY (Abba Dabba) BR TR 6' 185 lbs.
Brother of Johnny Tobin.
B. Dec. 27, 1912, Oakland, Calif.   D. May 19, 1969, Oakland, Calif.

	G	AB	H	2B	3B	HR	HR %	R	RBI	BB	SO	SB	BA	SA	PH AB	PH H	G by POS
1937 PIT N	21	34	15	4	0	0	0.0	7	6	4	3	0	.441	.559	1	0	P-20
1938	56	103	25	6	1	0	0.0	8	11	9	12	0	.243	.320	14	2	P-40
1939	43	74	18	3	1	2	2.7	9	11	2	12	0	.243	.392	17	1	P-25
1940 BOS N	20	43	12	3	0	0	0.0	5	3	1	10	0	.279	.349	5	0	P-15
1941	43	103	19	5	0	0	0.0	6	9	10	31	1	.184	.233	10	0	P-33
1942	47	114	28	2	0	6	5.3	14	15	16	23	0	.246	.421	7	1	P-37
1943	46	107	30	4	0	2	1.9	8	12	6	16	0	.280	.374	11	4	P-33, 1B-1
1944	62	116	22	5	1	2	1.7	13	18	16	28	0	.190	.302	14	2	P-43
1945 2 teams	BOS N (41G – .143)					DET A (17G – .120)											
" total	58	102	14	3	0	5	4.9	11	17	20	27	0	.137	.314	10	0	P-41
9 yrs.	396	796	183	35	3	17	2.1	81	102	84	162	1	.230	.345	89	10	P-287, 1B-1
1 yr.	17	25	3	0	0	2	8.0	2	5	5	5	0	.120	.360	3	0	P-14

WORLD SERIES

	G	AB	H	2B	3B	HR	HR %	R	RBI	BB	SO	SB	BA	SA	PH AB	PH H	G by POS
1945 DET A	1	1	0	0	0	0	0.0	0	0	0	0	0	.000	.000	0	0	P-1

Earl Torgeson

TORGESON, CLIFFORD EARL (The Earl of Snohomish) BL TL 6'3" 180 lbs.
B. Jan. 1, 1924, Snohomish, Wash.

	G	AB	H	2B	3B	HR	HR %	R	RBI	BB	SO	SB	BA	SA	PH AB	PH H	G by POS
1947 BOS N	128	399	112	20	6	16	4.0	73	78	82	59	11	.281	.481	11	1	1B-117
1948	134	438	111	23	5	10	2.3	70	67	81	54	19	.253	.397	4	2	1B-129
1949	25	100	26	5	1	4	4.0	17	19	13	4	4	.260	.450	0	0	1B-25
1950	156	576	167	30	3	23	4.0	120	87	119	69	15	.290	.472	0	0	1B-156
1951	155	581	153	21	4	24	4.1	99	92	102	70	20	.263	.437	0	0	1B-155
1952	122	382	88	17	0	5	1.3	49	34	81	38	11	.230	.314	12	2	1B-105, OF-5
1953 PHI N	111	379	104	25	8	11	2.9	58	64	53	57	7	.274	.470	6	1	1B-105
1954	135	490	133	22	6	5	1.0	62	54	75	52	7	.271	.371	1	0	1B-133
1955 2 teams	PHI N (47G – .267)					DET A (89G – .283)											
" total	136	450	125	15	4	10	2.2	87	67	93	46	11	.278	.396	9	3	1B-126
1956 DET A	117	318	84	9	2	12	3.8	61	42	78	47	6	.264	.425	27	10	1B-83
1957 2 teams	DET A (30G – .240)					CHI A (86G – .295)											
" total	116	301	86	13	3	8	2.7	58	51	61	54	7	.286	.429	28	8	1B-87, OF-1
1958 CHI A	96	188	50	8	0	10	5.3	37	30	48	29	7	.266	.468	24	9	1B-73
1959	127	277	61	5	3	9	3.2	40	45	62	55	7	.220	.357	24	5	1B-103
1960	68	57	15	5	2	2	3.5	12	9	21	8	1	.263	.404	41	12	1B-10
1961 2 teams	CHI A (20G – .067)					NY A (22G – .111)											
" total	42	33	3	0	0	0	0.0	4	1	11	8	0	.091	.091	23	2	1B-9
15 yrs.	1668	4969	1318	215	46	149	3.0	848	740	980	653	133	.265	.417	210	55	1B-1416, OF-6
3 yrs.	236	668	181	21	5	22	3.3	124	97	151	86	15	.271	.416	45	15	1B-183

WORLD SERIES

	G	AB	H	2B	3B	HR	HR %	R	RBI	BB	SO	SB	BA	SA	PH AB	PH H	G by POS
1948 BOS N	5	18	7	3	0	0	0.0	2	1	2	1	1	.389	.556	0	0	1B-5

	G	AB	H	2B	3B	HR	HR %	R	RBI	BB	SO	SB	BA	SA	Pinch Hit AB	Pinch Hit H	G by POS

Earl Torgeson continued

	G	AB	H	2B	3B	HR	HR%	R	RBI	BB	SO	SB	BA	SA	AB	H	G by POS
1959 CHI A	3	1	0	0	0	0	0.0	1	0	1	0	0	.000	.000	1	0	1B-1
2 yrs.	8	19	7	3	0	0	0.0	3	1	3	1	1	.368	.526	1	0	1B-6

Dick Tracewski

TRACEWSKI, RICHARD JOSEPH
B. Feb. 3, 1935, Eynon, Pa.
BR TR 5'11" 160 lbs

	G	AB	H	2B	3B	HR	HR%	R	RBI	BB	SO	SB	BA	SA	AB	H	G by POS
1962 LA N	15	2	0	0	0	0	0.0	3	0	2	0	0	.000	.000	1	0	SS-4
1963	104	217	49	2	1	1	0.5	23	10	19	39	2	.226	.258	0	0	SS-81, 2B-23
1964	106	304	75	13	4	1	0.3	31	26	31	61	3	.247	.326	4	2	2B-56, 3B-30, SS-19
1965	78	186	40	6	0	1	0.5	17	20	25	30	2	.215	.263	8	1	3B-53, 2B-14, SS-7
1966 DET A	81	124	24	1	1	0	0.0	15	7	10	32	1	.194	.218	7	0	2B-70, SS-3
1967	74	107	30	4	2	1	0.9	19	9	8	20	1	.280	.383	9	3	SS-44, 2B-12, 3B-10
1968	90	212	33	3	1	4	1.9	30	15	24	51	3	.156	.236	9	1	SS-51, 3B-16, 2B-14
1969	66	79	11	2	0	0	0.0	10	4	15	20	3	.139	.165	3	1	SS-41, 2B-13, 3B-6
8 yrs.	614	1231	262	31	9	8	0.6	148	91	134	253	15	.213	.272	41	8	SS-250, 2B-202, 3B-115
4 yrs.	311	522	98	10	4	5	1.0	74	35	57	123	8	.188	.251	28	5	SS-139, 2B-109, 3B-32

WORLD SERIES

	G	AB	H	2B	3B	HR	HR%	R	RBI	BB	SO	SB	BA	SA	AB	H	G by POS
1963 LA N	4	13	2	0	0	0	0.0	1	0	1	2	0	.154	.154	0	0	2B-4
1965	6	17	2	0	0	0	0.0	0	0	1	5	0	.118	.118	1	0	2B-6
1968 DET A	2	0	0	0	0	0	—	1	0	0	0	0	—	—	0	0	3B-1
3 yrs.	12	30	4	0	0	0	0.0	2	0	2	7	0	.133	.133	1	0	2B-10, 3B-1

Alan Trammell

TRAMMELL, ALAN STUART
B. Feb. 21, 1958, Garden Grove, Calif.
BR TR 6' 165 lbs

	G	AB	H	2B	3B	HR	HR%	R	RBI	BB	SO	SB	BA	SA	AB	H	G by POS
1977 DET A	19	43	8	0	0	0	0.0	6	0	4	12	0	.186	.186	0	0	SS-19
1978	139	448	120	14	6	2	0.4	49	34	45	56	3	.268	.339	0	0	SS-139
1979	142	460	127	11	4	6	1.3	68	50	43	55	17	.276	.357	0	0	SS-142
1980	146	560	168	21	5	9	1.6	107	65	69	63	12	.300	.404	2	0	SS-144
1981	105	392	101	15	3	2	0.5	52	31	49	31	10	.258	.327	1	1	SS-105
1982	157	489	126	34	3	9	1.8	66	57	52	47	19	.258	.395	0	0	SS-157
1983	142	505	161	31	2	14	2.8	83	66	57	64	30	.319	.471	0	0	SS-140
1984	139	555	174	34	5	14	2.5	85	69	60	63	19	.314	.468	3	1	SS-114, DH-22
8 yrs.	989	3452	985	160	28	56	1.6	516	372	379	391	110	.285	.397	6	2	SS-960, DH-22
8 yrs.	989	3452	985	160	28	56	1.6	516	372	379	391	110	.285	.397	6	2	SS-960, DH-22

LEAGUE CHAMPIONSHIP SERIES

	G	AB	H	2B	3B	HR	HR%	R	RBI	BB	SO	SB	BA	SA	AB	H	G by POS
1984 DET A	3	11	4	0	1	1	9.1	2	3	3	1	0	.364	.818	0	0	SS-3

WORLD SERIES

	G	AB	H	2B	3B	HR	HR%	R	RBI	BB	SO	SB	BA	SA	AB	H	G by POS
1984 DET A	5	20	9	1	0	2	10.0	5	6	2	2	1	.450	.800	0	0	SS-5

Tom Tresh

TRESH, THOMAS MICHAEL
Son of Mike Tresh.
B. Sept. 20, 1937, Detroit, Mich.
BB TR 6'1" 180 lbs.

	G	AB	H	2B	3B	HR	HR%	R	RBI	BB	SO	SB	BA	SA	AB	H	G by POS
1961 NY A	9	8	2	0	0	0	0.0	1	0	1	1	0	.250	.250	3	1	SS-3
1962	157	622	178	26	5	20	3.2	94	93	67	74	4	.286	.441	2	0	SS-111, OF-43
1963	145	520	140	28	5	25	4.8	91	71	83	79	3	.269	.487	1	0	OF-144
1964	153	533	131	25	5	16	3.0	75	73	73	110	13	.246	.402	7	1	OF-146
1965	156	602	168	29	6	26	4.3	94	74	59	92	5	.279	.477	2	0	OF-154
1966	151	537	125	12	4	27	5.0	76	68	86	89	5	.233	.421	3	1	OF-84, 3B-64
1967	130	448	98	23	3	14	3.1	45	53	50	86	1	.219	.377	10	1	OF-118
1968	152	507	99	18	3	11	2.2	60	52	76	97	10	.195	.308	6	1	SS-119, OF-27
1969 2 teams			NY	A (45G – .182)			DET	A (94G – .224)									
" total	139	474	100	18	3	14	3.0	59	46	56	70	4	.211	.350	10	1	SS-118, OF-11, 3B-1
9 yrs.	1192	4251	1041	179	34	153	3.6	595	530	550	698	45	.245	.411	44	6	OF-727, SS-351, 3B-65
1 yr.	94	331	74	13	1	13	3.9	46	37	39	47	2	.224	.387	6	1	SS-77, OF-11, 3B-2

WORLD SERIES

	G	AB	H	2B	3B	HR	HR%	R	RBI	BB	SO	SB	BA	SA	AB	H	G by POS
1962 NY A	7	28	9	1	0	1	3.6	5	4	1	4	2	.321	.464	0	0	OF-7
1963	4	15	3	0	0	1	6.7	1	2	1	6	0	.200	.400	0	0	OF-4
1964	7	22	6	2	0	2	9.1	4	7	6	7	0	.273	.636	0	0	OF-7
3 yrs.	18	65	18	3	0	4	6.2	10	13	8	17	2	.277	.508	0	0	OF-18

Gus Triandos

TRIANDOS, GUS CONSTANTIN
B. July 30, 1930, San Francisco, Calif.
BR TR 6'3" 205 lbs

	G	AB	H	2B	3B	HR	HR%	R	RBI	BB	SO	SB	BA	SA	AB	H	G by POS
1953 NY A	18	51	8	2	0	1	2.0	5	6	3	9	0	.157	.255	3	1	1B-12, C-5
1954	2	1	0	0	0	0	0.0	0	0	0	1	0	.000	.000	1	0	C-1
1955 BAL A	140	481	133	17	3	12	2.5	47	65	40	55	0	.277	.399	14	2	1B-103, C-36, 3B-1
1956	131	452	126	18	1	21	4.6	47	88	48	73	0	.279	.462	5	1	C-89, 1B-52
1957	129	418	106	21	1	19	4.5	44	72	38	73	0	.254	.445	17	1	C-120
1958	137	474	116	10	0	30	6.3	59	79	60	65	1	.245	.456	8	2	C-132
1959	126	393	85	7	1	25	6.4	43	73	65	56	0	.216	.430	3	0	C-125
1960	109	364	98	18	0	12	3.3	36	54	41	62	0	.269	.418	4	0	C-105
1961	115	397	97	21	0	17	4.3	35	63	44	60	0	.244	.426	4	0	C-114
1962	66	207	33	7	0	6	2.9	20	23	29	43	0	.159	.280	4	1	C-63
1963 DET A	106	327	78	13	0	14	4.3	28	41	32	67	0	.239	.407	13	3	C-90
1964 PHI N	73	188	47	9	0	8	4.3	17	33	26	41	0	.250	.426	16	4	C-64, 1B-1
1965 2 teams			PHI	N (30G – .171)			HOU	N (24G – .181)									
" total	54	154	27	4	0	2	1.3	8	11	14	31	0	.175	.240	8	3	C-48
13 yrs.	1206	3907	954	147	6	167	4.3	389	608	440	636	1	.244	.413	100	18	C-992, 1B-168, 3B-1
1 yr.	106	327	78	13	0	14	4.3	28	41	32	67	0	.239	.407	13	3	C-90

Jerry Turner

TURNER, JOHN WEBBER
B. Jan. 17, 1954, Texarkana, Ark.
BL TL 5'9" 180 lbs.

	G	AB	H	2B	3B	HR	HR%	R	RBI	BB	SO	SB	BA	SA	AB	H	G by POS
1974 SD N	17	48	14	1	0	0	0.0	4	2	3	5	2	.292	.313	6	3	OF-13
1975	11	22	6	0	0	0	0.0	1	0	2	1	0	.273	.273	6	3	OF-4
1976	105	281	75	16	5	5	1.8	41	37	32	38	12	.267	.413	25	5	OF-74
1977	118	289	71	16	1	10	3.5	43	48	31	43	12	.246	.412	45	12	OF-69

	G	AB	H	2B	3B	HR	HR %	R	RBI	BB	SO	SB	BA	SA	Pinch Hit AB	Pinch Hit H	G by POS

Terry Turner continued

	G	AB	H	2B	3B	HR	HR %	R	RBI	BB	SO	SB	BA	SA	PH AB	PH H	G by POS
1978	106	225	63	9	1	8	3.6	28	37	21	32	6	.280	.436	49	20	OF-58
1979	138	448	111	23	2	9	2.0	55	61	34	58	4	.248	.368	28	5	OF-115
1980	85	153	44	5	0	3	2.0	22	18	10	18	8	.288	.379	47	13	OF-34
1981 2 teams	SD	N (33G –	.226)		CHI	A	(10G –	.167)									
" total	43	43	9	0	0	2	4.7	6	8	5	5	0	.209	.349	29	5	OF-5
1982 DET A	85	210	52	3	0	8	3.8	21	27	20	37	1	.248	.376	24	4	DH-50, OF-13
1983 SD N	25	23	3	0	0	0	0.0	1	0	1	8	0	.130	.130	23	3	OF-1
10 yrs.	733	1742	448	73	9	45	2.6	222	238	159	245	45	.257	.387	282	73	OF-386, DH-50
1 yr.	85	210	52	3	0	8	3.8	21	27	20	37	1	.248	.376	24	4	DH-50, OF-13

Bill Tuttle

TUTTLE, WILLIAM ROBERT   BR TR 6'   190 lbs.
B. July 4, 1929, Elwood, Ill.

	G	AB	H	2B	3B	HR	HR %	R	RBI	BB	SO	SB	BA	SA	PH AB	PH H	G by POS
1952 DET A	7	25	6	0	0	0	0.0	2	2	0	1	0	.240	.240	1	0	OF-6
1954	147	530	141	20	11	7	1.3	64	58	62	60	5	.266	.385	3	1	OF-145
1955	154	603	168	23	4	14	2.3	102	78	76	54	6	.279	.400	1	0	OF-154
1956	140	546	138	22	4	9	1.6	61	65	38	48	5	.253	.357	4	2	OF-137
1957	133	451	113	12	4	5	1.1	49	47	44	41	2	.251	.328	3	1	OF-128
1958 KC A	148	511	118	14	9	11	2.2	77	51	74	58	7	.231	.358	10	1	OF-145
1959	126	463	139	19	6	7	1.5	74	43	48	38	10	.300	.413	4	2	OF-121
1960	151	559	143	21	3	8	1.4	75	40	66	52	1	.256	.347	5	2	OF-148
1961 2 teams	KC	A (25G –	.262)		MIN	A	(113G –	.246)									
" total	138	454	113	14	5	5	1.1	53	46	52	50	1	.249	.335	3	0	OF-89, 3B-85, 2B-2
1962 MIN A	110	123	26	4	1	1	0.8	21	13	19	14	1	.211	.285	6	1	OF-104
1963	16	3	0	0	0	0	0.0	0	0	1	0	0	.000	.000	2	0	OF-14
11 yrs.	1270	4268	1105	149	47	67	1.6	578	443	480	416	38	.259	.363	42	10	OF-1191, 3B-85, 2B-2
5 yrs.	581	2155	566	77	23	35	1.6	278	252	220	204	18	.263	.368	12	4	OF-570

Guy Tutwiler

TUTWILER, GUY ISBELL (King Tut)   BL TR 6'   175 lbs.
B. July 17, 1889, Coalburg, Ala.   D. Aug. 15, 1930, Birmingham, Ala.

	G	AB	H	2B	3B	HR	HR %	R	RBI	BB	SO	SB	BA	SA	PH AB	PH H	G by POS
1911 DET A	13	32	6	2	0	0	0.0	3	3	2		0	.188	.250	3	0	2B-6, OF-3
1913	14	47	10	0	1	0	0.0	4	7	4	12	2	.213	.255	0	0	1B-14
2 yrs.	27	79	16	2	1	0	0.0	7	10	6	12	2	.203	.253	3	0	1B-14, 2B-6, OF-3
2 yrs.	27	79	16	2	1	0	0.0	7	10	6	12	2	.203	.253	3	0	1B-14, 2B-6, OF-3

George Uhle

UHLE, GEORGE ERNEST (The Bull)   BR TR 6'   190 lbs.
B. Sept. 18, 1898, Cleveland, Ohio

	G	AB	H	2B	3B	HR	HR %	R	RBI	BB	SO	SB	BA	SA	PH AB	PH H	G by POS
1919 CLE A	26	43	13	2	1	0	0.0	7	6	1	5	0	.302	.395	0	0	P-26
1920	27	32	11	0	0	0	0.0	4	2	2	2	1	.344	.344	0	0	P-27
1921	48	94	23	2	3	1	1.1	21	18	6	9	0	.245	.362	0	0	P-41, C-1
1922	56	109	29	8	2	0	0.0	21	14	13	6	1	.266	.376	2	2	P-50
1923	58	144	52	10	3	0	0.0	23	22	7	10	2	.361	.472	3	0	P-54
1924	59	107	33	6	1	1	0.9	10	19	4	8	0	.308	.411	26	11	P-28
1925	56	104	29	3	3	0	0.0	10	13	7	7	0	.279	.365	22	5	P-29
1926	50	132	30	3	0	1	0.8	16	11	10	12	2	.227	.273	8	1	P-39
1927	43	79	21	7	1	0	0.0	4	14	5	12	0	.266	.380	18	5	P-25
1928	55	98	28	3	2	1	1.0	9	17	8	4	0	.286	.388	20	4	P-31
1929 DET A	40	108	37	1	1	0	0.0	18	13	6	6	0	.343	.370	7	1	P-32
1930	59	117	36	4	2	2	1.7	15	21	8	13	0	.308	.427	21	5	P-33
1931	53	90	22	6	0	2	2.2	8	7	8	8	0	.244	.378	21	3	P-29
1932	38	55	10	3	1	0	0.0	2	4	6	5	0	.182	.273	5	1	P-33
1933 3 teams	DET	A (1G –	.000)		NY	N	(8G –	.000)		NY	A	(12G –	.400)				
" total	21	25	8	1	0	0	0.0	2	1	5	5	0	.320	.360	2	0	P-19
1934 NY A	10	5	3	0	1	0	0.0	1	1	0	0	0	.600	1.000	0	0	P-10
1936 CLE A	24	21	8	1	0	1	4.8	1	4	2	0	0	.381	.571	14	6	P-7
17 yrs.	723	1363	393	60	21	9	0.7	172	187	98	112	6	.288	.383	169	44	P-513, C-1
5 yrs.	191	370	105	14	4	4	1.1	43	45	28	32	0	.284	.376	54	10	P-128

WORLD SERIES

	G	AB	H	2B	3B	HR	HR %	R	RBI	BB	SO	SB	BA	SA	PH AB	PH H	G by POS
1920 CLE A	2	0	0	0	0	0	–	0	0	0	0	0	–	–	0	0	P-1

Al Unser

UNSER, ALBERT BERNARD   BR TR 6'1"   175 lbs.
Father of Del Unser.
B. Oct. 12, 1912, Morrisonville, Ill.

	G	AB	H	2B	3B	HR	HR %	R	RBI	BB	SO	SB	BA	SA	PH AB	PH H	G by POS
1942 DET A	4	8	3	0	0	0	0.0	2	0	0	2	0	.375	.375	0	0	C-4
1943	38	101	25	5	0	0	0.0	14	4	15	15	0	.248	.297	0	0	C-37
1944	11	25	3	0	1	1	4.0	2	5	3	2	0	.120	.320	5	2	2B-5, C-1
1945 CIN N	67	204	54	10	3	3	1.5	23	21	14	24	0	.265	.387	5	2	C-61
4 yrs.	120	338	85	15	4	4	1.2	41	30	32	43	0	.251	.355	10	4	C-103, 2B-5
3 yrs.	53	134	31	5	1	1	0.7	18	9	18	19	0	.231	.306	5	2	C-42, 2B-5

Bobby Veach

VEACH, ROBERT HAYES   BL TR 5'11"   160 lbs.
B. June 29, 1888, Island, Ky.   D. Aug. 7, 1945, Detroit, Mich.

	G	AB	H	2B	3B	HR	HR %	R	RBI	BB	SO	SB	BA	SA	PH AB	PH H	G by POS
1912 DET A	23	79	27	5	1	0	0.0	8	15	5		2	.342	.430	1	0	OF-22
1913	138	494	133	22	10	0	0.0	54	64	53	31	22	.269	.354	1	0	OF-137
1914	149	531	146	19	14	1	0.2	56	72	50	29	20	.275	.369	3	3	OF-145
1915	152	569	178	40	10	3	0.5	81	112	68	43	16	.313	.434	0	0	OF-152
1916	150	566	173	33	15	3	0.5	92	91	52	41	24	.306	.433	0	0	OF-150
1917	154	571	182	31	12	8	1.4	79	103	61	44	21	.319	.457	0	0	OF-154
1918	127	499	139	21	13	3	0.6	59	78	35	23	21	.279	.391	0	0	OF-127, P-1
1919	139	538	191	45	17	3	0.6	87	101	33	33	19	.355	.519	1	1	OF-138
1920	154	612	188	39	15	11	1.8	92	113	36	22	11	.307	.474	0	0	OF-154
1921	150	612	207	43	13	16	2.6	110	128	48	31	14	.338	.529	1	0	OF-149
1922	155	618	202	34	13	9	1.5	96	126	42	27	9	.327	.468	0	0	OF-154
1923	114	293	94	13	3	2	0.7	45	39	29	21	10	.321	.406	22	8	OF-85, C-1
1924 BOS A	142	519	153	35	9	5	1.0	77	99	47	18	5	.295	.426	12	3	OF-130

	G	AB	H	2B	3B	HR	HR %	R	RBI	BB	SO	SB	BA	SA	Pinch Hit AB	Pinch Hit H	G by POS

Bobby Veach continued

	G	AB	H	2B	3B	HR	HR %	R	RBI	BB	SO	SB	BA	SA	PH AB	PH H	G by POS
1925 3 teams	**BOS** A (1G – .200)				**NY** A (56G – .353)			**WAS** A (18G – .243)									
" total	75	158	51	13	2	0	0.0	17	25	12	4	1	.323	.430	26	6	OF-45
14 yrs.	1822	6659	2064	393	147	64	1.0	953	1166	571	367	195	.310	.442	67	21	OF-1742, C-1, P-1
12 yrs.	1605	5982	1860	345	136	59	1.0	859	1042	512	345	189	.311	.444	29	12	OF-1567, C-1, P-1
	10th	9th	6th	7th	5th			9th	8th			6th					

WORLD SERIES

	G	AB	H	2B	3B	HR	HR %	R	RBI	BB	SO	SB	BA	SA	PH AB	PH H	G by POS
1925 **WAS** A	2	1	0	0	0	0	0.0	0	1	0	0	0	.000	.000	1	0	

Coot Veal

VEAL, ORVILLE INMAN
B. July 9, 1932, Sandersville, Ga.
BR TR 6'1" 165 lbs

	G	AB	H	2B	3B	HR	HR %	R	RBI	BB	SO	SB	BA	SA	PH AB	PH H	G by POS
1958 DET A	58	207	53	10	2	0	0.0	29	16	14	21	1	.256	.324	0	0	SS-58
1959	77	89	18	1	0	1	1.1	12	15	8	7	0	.202	.247	0	0	SS-72
1960	27	64	19	5	1	0	0.0	8	8	11	7	0	.297	.406	2	1	SS-22, 3B-3, 2B-1
1961 WAS A	69	218	44	10	0	0	0.0	21	8	19	29	1	.202	.248	4	0	SS-63
1962 PIT N	1	1	0	0	0	0	0.0	0	0	0	1	0	.000	.000	1	0	
1963 DET A	15	32	7	0	0	0	0.0	5	4	4	4	0	.219	.219	4	2	SS-12
6 yrs.	247	611	141	26	3	1	0.2	75	51	56	69	2	.231	.288	11	3	SS-227, 3B-3, 2B-1
4 yrs.	177	392	97	16	3	1	0.2	54	43	37	39	1	.247	.311	6	3	SS-164, 3B-3, 2B-1

Tom Veryzer

VERYZER, THOMAS MARTIN
B. Feb. 11, 1953, Islip, N. Y.
BR TR 6'1½" 175 lbs

	G	AB	H	2B	3B	HR	HR %	R	RBI	BB	SO	SB	BA	SA	PH AB	PH H	G by POS
1973 DET A	18	20	6	0	1	0	0.0	1	2	2	4	0	.300	.400	0	0	SS-18
1974	22	55	13	2	0	2	3.6	4	9	5	8	1	.236	.382	1	0	SS-20
1975	128	404	102	13	1	5	1.2	37	48	23	76	2	.252	.327	0	0	SS-128
1976	97	354	83	8	2	1	0.3	31	25	21	44	1	.234	.277	0	0	SS-97
1977	125	350	69	12	1	2	0.6	31	28	16	44	0	.197	.254	0	0	SS-124
1978 CLE A	130	421	114	18	4	1	0.2	48	32	13	36	1	.271	.340	0	0	SS-129
1979	149	449	99	9	3	0	0.0	41	34	34	54	2	.220	.254	1	0	SS-148
1980	109	358	97	12	0	2	0.6	28	28	10	25	0	.271	.321	0	0	SS-108
1981	75	221	54	4	0	0	0.0	13	14	10	10	1	.244	.262	0	0	SS-75
1982 NY N	40	54	18	2	0	0	0.0	6	4	3	4	1	.333	.370	0	0	2B-26, SS-16
1983 CHI N	59	88	18	3	0	1	1.1	5	3	3	13	0	.205	.273	11	3	SS-28, 3B-17
1984	44	74	14	1	0	0	0.0	5	4	3	11	0	.189	.203	0	0	SS-36, 3B-5, 2B-4
12 yrs.	996	2848	687	84	12	14	0.5	250	231	143	329	9	.241	.294	12	3	SS-927, 2B-30, 3B-22
5 yrs.	390	1183	273	35	5	10	0.8	104	112	67	176	4	.231	.294	1	0	SS-387

LEAGUE CHAMPIONSHIP SERIES

	G	AB	H	2B	3B	HR	HR %	R	RBI	BB	SO	SB	BA	SA	PH AB	PH H	G by POS
1984 CHI N	3	1	0	0	0	0	0.0	0	0	0	0	0	.000	.000	0	0	3B-1

George Vico

VICO, GEORGE STEVE (Sam)
B. Aug. 9, 1923, San Fernando, Calif.
BL TR 6'4" 200 lbs

	G	AB	H	2B	3B	HR	HR %	R	RBI	BB	SO	SB	BA	SA	PH AB	PH H	G by POS
1948 DET A	144	521	139	23	9	8	1.5	50	58	39	39	2	.267	.392	2	0	1B-142
1949	67	142	27	5	2	4	2.8	15	18	21	17	0	.190	.338	13	2	1B-53
2 yrs.	211	663	166	28	11	12	1.8	65	76	60	56	2	.250	.380	15	2	1B-195
2 yrs.	211	663	166	28	11	12	1.8	65	76	60	56	2	.250	.380	15	2	1B-195

Ozzie Virgil

VIRGIL, OSVALDO JOSE
Father of Ozzie Virgil.
B. May 17, 1933, Montecristi, Dominican Republic
BR TR 6'1" 174 lbs

	G	AB	H	2B	3B	HR	HR %	R	RBI	BB	SO	SB	BA	SA	PH AB	PH H	G by POS
1956 NY N	3	12	5	1	1	0	0.0	2	2	0	0	1	.417	.667	0	0	3B-3
1957	96	226	53	0	2	4	1.8	26	24	14	27	2	.235	.305	8	2	3B-62, OF-24, SS-1
1958 DET A	49	193	47	10	2	3	1.6	19	19	8	20	1	.244	.363	1	0	3B-49
1960	62	132	30	4	2	3	2.3	16	13	4	14	1	.227	.356	8	2	3B-42, 2B-8, SS-5, C-1
1961 2 teams	**DET** A (20G – .133)				**KC** A (11G – .143)												
" total	31	51	7	0	2	1	2.0	2	1	1	8	0	.137	.196	12	3	3B-13, C-6, SS-1, 2B-1
1962 BAL A	1	0	0	0	0	0	–	0	0	1	0	0	–	–	0	0	
1965 PIT N	39	49	13	2	0	1	2.0	3	5	2	10	0	.265	.367	18	6	C-15, 3B-7, 2B-5
1966 SF N	42	89	19	2	0	2	2.2	7	9	4	12	1	.213	.303	12	1	3B-13, C-13, 1B-5, OF-2, 2B-2
1969	1	1	0	0	0	0	0.0	0	0	0	0	0	.000	.000	1	0	
9 yrs.	324	753	174	19	7	14	1.9	75	73	34	91	6	.231	.331	60	14	3B-189, C-35, OF-26, 2B-16, SS-7, 1B-5
3 yrs.	131	355	81	14	4	7	2.0	36	33	13	39	2	.228	.349	16	4	3B-100, 2B-9, SS-6, C-4

Ossie Vitt

VITT, OSCAR JOSEPH
B. Jan. 4, 1890, San Francisco, Calif.   D. Jan. 31, 1963, Oakland, Calif.
Manager 1938-40.
BR TR 5'10" 150 lbs

	G	AB	H	2B	3B	HR	HR %	R	RBI	BB	SO	SB	BA	SA	PH AB	PH H	G by POS
1912 DET A	73	273	67	4	4	0	0.0	39	19	18		17	.245	.289	7	1	OF-27, 3B-24, 2B-15
1913	99	359	86	11	3	2	0.6	45	33	31	18	5	.240	.304	2	0	2B-78, 3B-17, OF-2
1914	66	195	49	7	0	0	0.0	35	8	31	8	10	.251	.287	8	0	2B-36, 3B-16, OF-2, SS
1915	152	560	140	18	13	1	0.2	116	48	80	22	26	.250	.334	0	0	3B-151, 2B-2
1916	153	597	135	17	12	0	0.0	88	42	75	28	18	.226	.295	0	0	3B-151, SS-2
1917	140	512	130	13	6	0	0.0	65	47	56	15	18	.254	.303	0	0	3B-140
1918	81	267	64	5	2	0	0.0	29	17	32	6	5	.240	.273	3	0	3B-66, 2B-9, OF-3
1919 BOS A	133	469	114	10	3	0	0.0	64	40	44	11	9	.243	.277	0	0	3B-133
1920	87	296	65	10	4	1	0.3	50	28	43	10	5	.220	.291	1	0	3B-64, 2B-21
1921	78	232	44	11	1	0	0.0	29	12	45	13	1	.190	.246	2	1	3B-71, OF-3, 1B-2
10 yrs.	1062	3760	894	106	48	4	0.1	560	294	455	131	114	.238	.295	23	2	3B-833, 2B-161, OF-37, SS-3, 1B-2
7 yrs.	764	2763	671	75	40	3	0.1	417	214	323	97	99	.243	.302	20	1	3B-565, 2B-140, OF-34, SS-3

Hal Wagner

WAGNER, HAROLD EDWARD
B. July 2, 1915, East Riverton, N. J.   D. Aug. 4, 1979, Riverside, N. J.
BL TR 6' 165 lbs

	G	AB	H	2B	3B	HR	HR %	R	RBI	BB	SO	SB	BA	SA	PH AB	PH H	G by POS
1937 PHI A	1	0	0	0	0	0	–	0	0	0	0	0	–	–	0	0	C-1
1938	33	88	20	2	1	0	0.0	10	8	8	9	0	.227	.273	3	1	C-30

	G	AB	H	2B	3B	HR	HR %	R	RBI	BB	SO	SB	BA	SA	Pinch Hit AB	Pinch Hit H	G by POS

Hal Wagner continued

	G	AB	H	2B	3B	HR	HR %	R	RBI	BB	SO	SB	BA	SA	AB	H	G by POS
'939	5	8	1	0	0	0	0.0	0	0	0	3	0	.125	.125	0	0	C-5
'940	34	75	19	5	1	0	0.0	9	10	11	6	0	.253	.347	5	2	C-28
'941	46	131	29	8	2	1	0.8	18	15	19	9	1	.221	.336	4	0	C-42
'942	104	288	68	17	1	1	0.3	26	30	24	29	1	.236	.313	12	2	C-94
'943	111	289	69	17	1	1	0.3	22	26	36	17	3	.239	.315	14	3	C-99
'944 2 teams		PHI	A (5G –	.250)		BOS	A (66G –	.332)									
total	71	227	75	13	4	1	0.4	21	38	29	14	1	.330	.436	7	2	C-65
'946 BOS A	117	370	85	12	2	6	1.6	39	52	69	32	3	.230	.322	0	0	C-116
'947 2 teams		BOS	A (21G –	.231)		DET	A (71G –	.288)									
total	92	256	70	13	0	5	2.0	24	39	37	21	0	.273	.383	1	1	C-92
'948 2 teams		DET	A (54G –	.202)		PHI	N (3G –	.000)									
total	57	113	22	3	0	0	0.0	10	10	20	11	1	.195	.221	2	0	C-53
'949 PHI N	1	4	0	0	0	0	0.0	0	0	0	1	0	.000	.000	0	0	C-1
12 yrs.	672	1849	458	90	12	15	0.8	179	228	253	152	10	.248	.334	48	11	C-626
2 yrs.	125	300	77	13	4	5	1.7	29	43	48	27	1	.257	.350	2	1	C-123
WORLD SERIES																	
'946 BOS A	5	13	0	0	0	0	0.0	0	0	0	1	0	.000	.000	0	0	C-5

Mark Wagner

WAGNER, MARK DUANE
B. Mar. 4, 1954, Conneaut, Ohio   BR TR 6'   165 lbs.

	G	AB	H	2B	3B	HR	HR %	R	RBI	BB	SO	SB	BA	SA	AB	H	G by POS
'76 DET A	39	115	30	2	3	0	0.0	9	12	6	18	0	.261	.330	0	0	SS-39
'77	22	48	7	0	1	1	2.1	4	3	4	12	0	.146	.250	0	0	SS-21, 2B-1
'78	39	109	26	1	2	0	0.0	10	6	3	11	1	.239	.284	1	1	SS-35, 2B-4
'79	75	146	40	3	0	1	0.7	16	13	16	25	3	.274	.315	1	1	SS-41, 2B-29, 3B-2, DH-1
'80	45	72	17	1	0	0	0.0	5	3	7	11	0	.236	.250	2	0	SS-28, 3B-9, 2B-6
'81 TEX A	50	85	22	4	1	1	1.2	15	14	8	13	1	.259	.365	0	0	SS-43, 2B-4, 3B-2
'82	60	179	43	4	1	0	0.0	14	8	10	28	1	.240	.274	0	0	SS-60
'83	2	2	0	0	0	0	0.0	0	0	0	1	0	.000	.000	0	0	SS-2
'84 OAK A	82	86	20	5	1	0	0.0	8	12	7	11	2	.233	.314	1	0	SS-58, 3B-15, 2B-8, DH-3, P-1
9 yrs.	414	842	205	20	9	3	0.4	81	71	61	130	8	.243	.299	7	2	SS-327, 2B-52, 3B-28, DH-4, P-1
5 yrs.	220	490	120	7	6	2	0.4	44	37	36	77	4	.245	.296	4	2	SS-164, 2B-40, 3B-11, DH-1

Dick Wakefield

WAKEFIELD, RICHARD CUMMINGS
Son of Howard Wakefield.
B. May 6, 1921, Chicago, Ill.   BL TR 6'4"   210 lbs.

	G	AB	H	2B	3B	HR	HR %	R	RBI	BB	SO	SB	BA	SA	AB	H	G by POS
'41 DET A	7	7	1	0	0	0	0.0	0	0	0	1	0	.143	.143	6	1	OF-1
'43	155	633	200	38	8	7	1.1	91	79	62	60	4	.316	.434	0	0	OF-155
'44	78	276	98	15	5	12	4.3	53	53	55	29	2	.355	.576	0	0	OF-78
'46	111	396	106	11	5	12	3.0	64	59	59	55	3	.268	.412	4	0	OF-104
'47	112	368	104	15	5	8	2.2	59	51	80	44	1	.283	.416	10	4	OF-101
'48	110	322	89	20	5	11	3.4	50	53	70	55	0	.276	.472	22	7	OF-86
'49	59	126	26	3	1	6	4.8	17	19	32	24	0	.206	.389	18	3	OF-32
'50 NY A	3	2	1	0	0	0	0.0	0	1	1	1	0	.500	.500	2	1	
'52 NY N	3	2	0	0	0	0	0.0	0	0	1	0	0	.000	.000	2	0	
9 yrs.	638	2132	625	102	29	56	2.6	334	315	360	269	10	.293	.447	64	16	OF-557
7 yrs.	632	2128	624	102	29	56	2.6	334	314	358	268	10	.293	.447	60	15	OF-557

Dixie Walker

WALKER, FRED (The People's Cherce)
Son of Dixie Walker.   Brother of Harry Walker.
B. Sept. 24, 1910, Villa Rica, Ga.   D. May 17, 1982, Birmingham, Ala.   BL TR 6'1"   175 lbs.

	G	AB	H	2B	3B	HR	HR %	R	RBI	BB	SO	SB	BA	SA	AB	H	G by POS
'31 NY A	2	10	3	2	0	0	0.0	1	1	0	4	0	.300	.500	0	0	OF-2
'33	98	328	90	15	7	15	4.6	68	51	26	28	2	.274	.500	18	4	OF-77
'34	17	17	2	0	0	0	0.0	2	0	1	3	0	.118	.118	12	2	OF-1
'35	8	13	2	1	0	0	0.0	1	1	0	1	0	.154	.231	5	1	OF-2
'36 2 teams		NY	A (6G –	.350)		CHI	A (26G –	.271)									
total	32	90	26	2	2	1	1.1	15	16	15	9	2	.289	.389	10	2	OF-22
'37 CHI A	154	593	179	28	16	9	1.5	105	95	78	26	1	.302	.449	0	0	OF-154
'38 DET A	127	454	140	27	6	6	1.3	84	43	65	32	5	.308	.434	10	3	OF-114
'39 2 teams		DET	A (43G –	.305)		BKN	N (61G –	.280)									
total	104	379	110	10	9	6	1.6	57	57	35	18	5	.290	.412	6	0	OF-96
'40 BKN N	143	556	171	37	8	6	1.1	75	66	42	21	3	.308	.435	6	4	OF-136
'41	148	531	165	32	8	9	1.7	88	71	70	18	4	.311	.452	2	0	OF-146
'42	118	393	114	28	1	6	1.5	57	54	47	15	1	.290	.412	6	2	OF-110
'43	138	540	163	32	6	5	0.9	83	71	49	24	3	.302	.411	2	1	OF-136
'44	147	535	191	37	8	13	2.4	77	91	72	27	6	.357	.529	7	2	OF-140
'45	154	607	182	42	9	8	1.3	102	124	75	16	1	.300	.438	1	0	OF-153
'46	150	576	184	29	9	9	1.6	80	116	67	28	14	.319	.448	1	0	OF-149
'47	148	529	162	31	3	9	1.7	77	94	97	26	6	.306	.427	1	0	OF-147
'48 PIT N	129	408	129	19	3	2	0.5	39	54	52	18	1	.316	.392	16	3	OF-112
'49	88	181	51	4	1	1	0.6	26	18	26	11	0	.282	.331	40	13	OF-39, 1B-3
18 yrs.	1905	6740	2064	376	96	105	1.6	1037	1023	817	325	59	.306	.437	143	39	OF-1736, 1B-3
2 yrs.	170	608	187	31	11	10	1.6	114	62	80	40	9	.308	.444	14	4	OF-151
WORLD SERIES																	
'41 BKN N	5	18	4	2	0	0	0.0	3	0	2	1	0	.222	.333	0	0	OF-5
'47	7	27	6	1	0	1	3.7	1	4	3	1	1	.222	.370	0	0	OF-7
2 yrs.	12	45	10	3	0	1	2.2	4	4	5	2	1	.222	.356	0	0	OF-12

Frank Walker

WALKER, CHARLES FRANKLIN
B. Sept. 22, 1894, Enoree, S. C.   D. Sept. 16, 1974, Bristol, Tenn.   BR TR 5'11"   165 lbs.

	G	AB	H	2B	3B	HR	HR %	R	RBI	BB	SO	SB	BA	SA	AB	H	G by POS
'17 DET A	2	2	0	0	0	0	0.0	0	0	0	1	0	.000	.000	0	0	
'18	55	167	33	10	3	1	0.6	10	20	7	29	1	.198	.311	7	1	OF-45
'20 PHI A	24	91	21	2	2	0	0.0	10	10	5	14	0	.231	.297	0	0	OF-24
'21	19	66	15	3	0	1	1.5	6	6	8	11	1	.227	.318	0	0	OF-19

	G	AB	H	2B	3B	HR	HR %	R	RBI	BB	SO	SB	BA	SA	Pinch Hit AB	H	G by POS

Frank Walker continued

	G	AB	H	2B	3B	HR	HR %	R	RBI	BB	SO	SB	BA	SA	AB	H	G by POS
1925 NY N	39	81	18	1	0	1	1.2	12	5	9	11	1	.222	.272	7	1	OF-21
5 yrs.	139	407	87	16	5	3	0.7	38	41	29	66	5	.214	.300	14	2	OF-109
2 yrs.	57	169	33	10	3	1	0.6	10	20	7	30	3	.195	.308	7	1	OF-45

Gee Walker

WALKER, GERALD HOLMES BR TR 5'11" 188 lb
Brother of Hub Walker.
B. Mar. 19, 1908, Gulfport, Miss. D. Mar. 20, 1981, Whitfield, Miss.

	G	AB	H	2B	3B	HR	HR %	R	RBI	BB	SO	SB	BA	SA	AB	H	G by POS
1931 DET A	59	189	56	17	2	1	0.5	20	28	14	21	10	.296	.423	9	4	OF-44
1932	126	480	155	32	6	8	1.7	71	78	13	38	30	.323	.465	8	1	OF-116
1933	127	483	135	29	7	9	1.9	68	64	15	49	26	.280	.424	12	2	OF-113
1934	98	347	104	19	2	6	1.7	54	39	19	20	20	.300	.418	17	5	OF-80
1935	98	362	109	22	6	7	1.9	52	53	15	21	6	.301	.453	14	7	OF-85
1936	134	550	194	55	5	12	2.2	105	93	23	30	17	.353	.536	9	1	OF-125
1937	151	635	213	42	4	18	2.8	105	113	41	74	23	.335	.499	0	0	OF-151
1938 CHI A	120	442	135	23	6	16	3.6	69	87	38	32	9	.305	.493	12	4	OF-107
1939	149	598	174	30	11	13	2.2	95	111	28	43	17	.291	.443	2	0	OF-147
1940 WAS N	140	595	175	29	7	13	2.2	87	96	24	58	21	.294	.432	0	0	OF-140
1941 CLE A	121	445	126	26	11	6	1.3	56	48	18	46	12	.283	.431	13	5	OF-105
1942 CIN N	119	422	97	20	2	5	1.2	40	50	31	44	11	.230	.322	8	1	OF-110
1943	114	429	105	23	2	3	0.7	48	54	12	38	6	.245	.329	6	1	OF-106
1944	121	478	133	21	3	5	1.0	56	62	23	48	7	.278	.366	3	1	OF-117
1945	106	316	80	11	2	2	0.6	28	21	16	38	8	.253	.320	35	9	OF-67, 3B-3
15 yrs.	1783	6771	1991	399	76	124	1.8	954	997	330	600	223	.294	.430	148	41	OF-1613, 3B-3
7 yrs.	793	3046	966	216	32	61	2.0	475	468	140	253	132	.317	.469	69	20	OF-714
												10th		9th			

WORLD SERIES

	G	AB	H	2B	3B	HR	HR %	R	RBI	BB	SO	SB	BA	SA	AB	H	G by POS
1934 DET A	3	3	1	0	0	0	0.0	0	1	0	1	0	.333	.333	3	1	
1935	3	4	1	0	0	0	0.0	1	0	1	0	0	.250	.250	2	0	OF-1
2 yrs.	6	7	2	0	0	0	0.0	1	1	1	1	0	.286	.286	5	1	OF-1

Hub Walker

WALKER, HARVEY WILLOS BL TR 5'10½" 175 lb
Brother of Gee Walker.
B. Aug. 17, 1906, Gulfport, Miss. D. Nov. 26, 1982, San Jose, Calif.

	G	AB	H	2B	3B	HR	HR %	R	RBI	BB	SO	SB	BA	SA	AB	H	G by POS
1931 DET A	90	252	72	13	1	0	0.0	27	16	23	25	10	.286	.345	12	2	OF-66
1935	9	25	4	3	0	0	0.0	4	1	3	4	0	.160	.280	2	1	OF-7
1936 CIN N	92	258	71	18	1	4	1.6	49	23	35	32	8	.275	.399	13	1	OF-73, 1B-1, C-1
1937	78	221	55	9	4	1	0.5	33	19	34	24	7	.249	.339	12	3	OF-58, 2B-3
1945 DET A	28	23	3	0	0	0	0.0	4	1	9	4	1	.130	.130	15	1	OF-7
5 yrs.	297	779	205	43	6	5	0.6	117	60	104	89	26	.263	.353	54	8	OF-211, 2B-3, 1B-1, C-
3 yrs.	127	300	79	16	1	0	0.0	35	18	35	33	11	.263	.323	29	4	OF-80

WORLD SERIES

	G	AB	H	2B	3B	HR	HR %	R	RBI	BB	SO	SB	BA	SA	AB	H	G by POS
1945 DET A	2	2	1	1	0	0	0.0	1	0	0	0	0	.500	1.000	2	1	

Hap Ward

WARD, JOSEPH NICHOLS
B. Nov. 15, 1885, Leesburg, N. J. D. Sept. 13, 1979, Elmer, N. J.

	G	AB	H	2B	3B	HR	HR %	R	RBI	BB	SO	SB	BA	SA	AB	H	G by POS
1912 DET A	1	2	0	0	0	0	0.0	0	0	0		0	.000	.000	0	0	OF-1

Jack Warner

WARNER, JOHN JOSEPH BL TR 5'10" 165 lb
B. Aug. 15, 1872, New York, N. Y. D. Dec. 21, 1943, Queens, N. Y.

	G	AB	H	2B	3B	HR	HR %	R	RBI	BB	SO	SB	BA	SA	AB	H	G by POS
1895 2 teams		BOS N (3G – .143)				LOU N (67G – .267)											
" total	70	239	63	4	2	1	0.4	22	21	12	16	10	.264	.310	0	0	C-67, 1B-3, 2B-1
1896 2 teams		LOU N (33G – .227)				NY N (19G – .259)											
" total	52	164	39	2	1	0	0.0	18	13	13	17	4	.238	.262	0	0	C-51, 1B-1
1897 NY N	110	397	109	6	3	2	0.5	50	51	26		8	.275	.320	0	0	C-110
1898	110	373	96	14	5	0	0.0	40	42	22		9	.257	.322	0	0	C-109, OF-1
1899	88	293	78	8	1	0	0.0	38	19	15		15	.266	.300	3	0	C-82, 1B-3
1900	34	108	27	4	0	0	0.0	15	13	8		1	.250	.287	3	1	C-31
1901	87	291	70	6	1	0	0.0	19	20	3		3	.241	.268	3	0	C-84
1902 BOS N	65	222	52	5	7	0	0.0	19	12	13		0	.234	.320	0	0	C-64
1903 NY N	89	285	81	8	5	0	0.0	38	34	7		5	.284	.347	3	1	C-85
1904	86	287	57	5	1	1	0.3	29	15	14		7	.199	.233	0	0	C-86
1905 2 teams		STL N (41G – .255)				DET A (36G – .202)											
" total	77	256	57	4	5	1	0.4	21	19	14		4	.230	.297	0	0	C-77
1906 2 teams		DET A (50G – .242)				WAS A (32G – .204)											
" total	82	256	58	8	3	1	0.4	20	19	14		7	.227	.293	1	0	C-81
1907 WAS A	72	207	53	5	0	0	0.0	11	17	12		3	.256	.280	8	1	C-64
1908	51	116	28	2	1	0	0.0	8	8	8		7	.241	.276	8	1	C-41, 1B-1
14 yrs.	1073	3494	870	81	35	6	0.2	348	303	181	33	83	.249	.297	29	4	C-1032, 1B-8, OF-1, 2E
2 yrs.	86	272	61	6	5	0	0.0	27	17	20		6	.224	.283	1	0	C-85

Jack Warner

WARNER, JOHN RALPH BR TR 5'9½" 165 lb
B. Aug. 29, 1903, Evansville, Ind.

	G	AB	H	2B	3B	HR	HR %	R	RBI	BB	SO	SB	BA	SA	AB	H	G by POS
1925 DET A	10	39	13	0	0	0	0.0	7	2	3	6	0	.333	.333	0	0	3B-10
1926	100	311	78	8	6	0	0.0	41	34	38	24	8	.251	.315	2	0	3B-95, SS-3
1927	139	559	149	22	9	1	0.2	78	45	47	45	15	.267	.343	1	0	3B-138
1928	75	206	44	4	4	0	0.0	33	13	16	15	4	.214	.272	1	0	3B-52, SS-7
1929 BKN N	17	62	17	2	0	0	0.0	3	4	7	6	3	.274	.306	0	0	SS-17
1930	21	25	8	1	0	0	0.0	4	0	2	7	1	.320	.360	3	1	3B-21
1931	9	4	2	0	0	0	0.0	2	0	1	1	0	.500	.500	0	0	SS-2, 3B-1
1933 PHI N	107	340	76	15	1	0	0.0	31	22	28	33	1	.224	.274	5	1	2B-71, 3B-30, SS-1
8 yrs.	478	1546	387	52	20	1	0.1	199	120	142	137	32	.250	.312	12	2	3B-347, 2B-71, SS-30
4 yrs.	324	1115	284	34	19	1	0.1	159	94	104	90	27	.255	.322	4	0	3B-295, SS-10

	G	AB	H	2B	3B	HR	HR %	R	RBI	BB	SO	SB	BA	SA	Pinch Hit AB	Pinch Hit H	G by POS

ohnny Watson

WATSON, JOHN THOMAS BL TR 6' 175 lbs.
B. Jan. 16, 1908, Tazewell, Va. D. Apr. 29, 1965, Huntington, W. Va.

	G	AB	H	2B	3B	HR	HR%	R	RBI	BB	SO	SB	BA	SA	PH AB	PH H	G by POS
30 DET A	4	12	3	2	0	0	0.0	1	3	1	2	0	.250	.417	0	0	SS-4

arl Webb

WEBB, WILLIAM EARL BL TR 6'1" 185 lbs.
B. Sept. 17, 1898, Bon Air, Tenn. D. May 23, 1965, Jamestown, Tenn.

	G	AB	H	2B	3B	HR	HR%	R	RBI	BB	SO	SB	BA	SA	PH AB	PH H	G by POS
25 NY N	4	3	0	0	0	0	0.0	0	0	1	1	0	.000	.000	3	0	
27 CHI N	102	332	100	18	4	14	4.2	58	52	48	31	3	.301	.506	15	3	OF-86
28	62	140	35	7	3	3	2.1	22	23	14	17	0	.250	.407	24	8	OF-31
30 BOS A	127	449	145	30	6	16	3.6	61	66	44	56	2	.323	.523	8	2	OF-116
31	151	589	196	67¹	3	14	2.4	96	103	70	51	2	.333	.528	0	0	OF-151
32 2 teams	BOS A (52G – .281)				DET A (87G – .287)												
total	139	530	151	28	9	8	1.5	72	78	64	33	1	.285	.417	1	0	OF-134, 1B-2
33 2 teams	DET A (6G – .273)				CHI A (58G – .290)												
total	64	118	34	5	0	1	0.8	17	11	19	13	0	.288	.356	30	8	OF-18, 1B-10
7 yrs.	649	2161	661	155	25	56	2.6	326	333	260	202	8	.306	.478	81	21	OF-536, 1B-12
2 yrs.	93	349	100	19	8	3	0.9	50	54	42	18	1	.287	.413	3	0	OF-86

keeter Webb

WEBB, JAMES LAVERNE BR TR 5'9½" 150 lbs.
B. Nov. 4, 1909, Meridian, Miss.

	G	AB	H	2B	3B	HR	HR%	R	RBI	BB	SO	SB	BA	SA	PH AB	PH H	G by POS
32 STL N	1	0	0	0	0	0	–	0	0	0	0	0	–	–	0	0	SS-1
38 CLE A	20	58	16	2	0	0	0.0	11	2	8	7	1	.276	.310	0	0	SS-13, 3B-3, 2B-2
39	81	269	71	14	1	2	0.7	28	26	15	24	1	.264	.346	0	0	SS-81
40 CHI A	84	334	79	11	2	1	0.3	33	29	30	33	3	.237	.290	2	0	2B-74, SS-7, 3B-1
41	29	84	16	2	0	0	0.0	7	6	3	9	1	.190	.214	3	1	2B-18, SS-5, 3B-3
42	32	94	16	2	1	0	0.0	5	4	4	13	1	.170	.213	0	0	2B-29
43	58	213	50	5	2	0	0.0	15	22	6	19	5	.235	.277	3	0	2B-54
44	139	513	108	19	6	0	0.0	44	30	20	39	7	.211	.271	0	0	SS-135, 2B-5
45 DET A	118	407	81	12	2	0	0.0	43	21	30	35	8	.199	.238	0	0	SS-104, 2B-11
46	64	169	37	1	1	0	0.0	12	17	9	18	3	.219	.237	1	0	2B-50, SS-8
47	50	79	16	3	0	0	0.0	13	6	7	9	3	.203	.241	2	0	2B-30, SS-6
48 PHI A	23	54	8	2	0	0	0.0	5	3	0	9	0	.148	.185	0	0	2B-9, SS-8
12 yrs.	699	2274	498	73	15	3	0.1	216	166	132	215	33	.219	.268	11	1	SS-368, 2B-282, 3B-7
3 yrs.	232	655	134	16	3	0	0.0	68	44	46	62	14	.205	.238	3	0	SS-118, 2B-91
WORLD SERIES																	
45 DET A	7	27	5	0	0	0	0.0	4	1	3	1	0	.185	.185	0	0	SS-7

Milt Welch

WELCH, MILTON EDWARD BR TR 5'10" 175 lbs.
B. July 26, 1924, Farmersville, Ill.

	G	AB	H	2B	3B	HR	HR%	R	RBI	BB	SO	SB	BA	SA	PH AB	PH H	G by POS
45 DET A	1	2	0	0	0	0	0.0	0	0	0	1	0	.000	.000	0	0	C-1

on Wert

WERT, DONALD RALPH BR TR 5'10" 162 lbs.
B. July 29, 1938, Strasburg, Pa.

	G	AB	H	2B	3B	HR	HR%	R	RBI	BB	SO	SB	BA	SA	PH AB	PH H	G by POS
63 DET A	78	251	65	6	2	7	2.8	31	25	24	51	3	.259	.382	4	0	3B-47, 2B-21, SS-8
64	148	525	135	18	5	9	1.7	63	55	50	74	3	.257	.362	3	0	3B-142, SS-4
65	162	609	159	22	2	12	2.0	81	54	73	71	5	.261	.363	0	0	3B-161, SS-3, 2B-1
66	.150	559	150	20	2	11	2.0	56	70	64	69	6	.268	.370	0	0	3B-150
67	142	534	137	23	2	6	1.1	60	40	44	59	1	.257	.341	2	0	3B-140, SS-1
68	150	536	107	15	1	12	2.2	44	37	37	79	0	.200	.299	1	1	3B-150, SS-2
69	132	423	95	11	1	14	3.3	46	50	49	60	3	.225	.355	2	0	3B-129
70	128	363	79	13	0	6	1.7	34	33	44	56	1	.218	.303	15	2	3B-117, 2B-2
71 WAS A	20	40	2	1	0	0	0.0	2	2	4	10	0	.050	.075	7	0	SS-7, 3B-7, 2B-1
9 yrs.	1110	3840	929	129	15	77	2.0	417	366	389	529	22	.242	.343	34	3	3B-1043, SS-25, 2B-25
8 yrs.	1090	3800	927	128	15	77	2.0	415	364	385	519	22	.244	.346	27	3	3B-1036, 2B-24, SS-18
WORLD SERIES																	
68 DET A	6	17	2	0	0	0	0.0	1	2	6	5	0	.118	.118	0	0	3B-6

ic Wertz

WERTZ, VICTOR WOODROW BL TR 6' 186 lbs.
B. Feb. 9, 1925, York, Pa. D. July 7, 1983, Detroit, Mich.

	G	AB	H	2B	3B	HR	HR%	R	RBI	BB	SO	SB	BA	SA	PH AB	PH H	G by POS
47 DET A	102	333	96	22	4	6	1.8	60	44	47	66	2	.288	.432	18	5	OF-82
48	119	391	97	19	9	7	1.8	49	67	48	70	0	.248	.396	19	4	OF-98
49	155	608	185	26	6	20	3.3	96	133	80	61	2	.304	.465	0	0	OF-155
50	149	559	172	37	4	27	4.8	99	123	91	55	0	.308	.533	4	2	OF-145
51	138	501	143	24	4	27	5.4	86	94	78	61	0	.285	.511	6	0	OF-131
52 2 teams	DET A (85G – .246)				STL A (37G – .346)												
total	122	415	115	20	3	23	5.5	68	70	69	64	1	.277	.506	8	2	OF-115
53 STL A	128	440	118	18	6	19	4.3	61	70	72	44	1	.268	.466	8	2	OF-121
54 2 teams	BAL A (29G – .202)				CLE A (94G – .275)												
total	123	389	100	15	2	15	3.9	38	61	45	57	0	.257	.422	7	1	1B-83, OF-32
55 CLE A	74	257	65	11	2	14	5.4	30	55	32	33	1	.253	.475	5	2	1B-63, OF-9
56	136	481	127	22	0	32	6.7	65	106	75	87	0	.264	.509	1	0	1B-133
57	144	515	145	21	0	28	5.4	84	105	78	87	2	.282	.485	4	0	1B-139
58	25	43	12	1	0	3	7.0	5	12	5	7	0	.279	.512	16	3	1B-8
59 BOS A	94	247	68	13	0	7	2.8	38	49	22	32	0	.275	.413	33	7	1B-64
60	131	443	125	22	0	19	4.3	45	103	37	54	0	.282	.460	18	10	1B-117
61 2 teams	BOS A (99G – .262)				DET A (8G – .167)												
total	107	323	84	16	2	11	3.4	33	61	38	44	0	.260	.424	18	3	1B-86
62 DET A	74	105	34	2	0	5	4.8	7	18	5	13	0	.324	.486	53	17	1B-16
63 2 teams	DET A (6G – .000)				MIN A (35G – .136)												
total	41	49	6	1	0	3	6.1	3	7	6	6	0	.122	.306	30	4	1B-6
17 yrs.	1862	6099	1692	289	42	266	4.4	867	1178	828	841	9	.277	.469	248	62	OF-888, 1B-715
9 yrs.	836	2793	798	145	30	109	3.9	443	531	395	372	5	.286	.476	118	31	OF-690, 1B-16
															7th	7th	
WORLD SERIES																	
54 CLE A	4	16	8	2	1	1	6.3	2	3	2	2	0	.500	.938	0	0	1B-4

	G	AB	H	2B	3B	HR	HR %	R	RBI	BB	SO	SB	BA	SA	Pinch Hit AB	H	G by POS

Lou Whitaker

WHITAKER, LOUIS RODMAN (Sweet Lou)
B. May 12, 1957, Brooklyn, N. Y.   BL TR 5'11" 160 lb

	G	AB	H	2B	3B	HR	HR %	R	RBI	BB	SO	SB	BA	SA	AB	H	G by POS
1977 DET A	11	32	8	1	0	0	0.0	5	2	4	6	2	.250	.281	0	0	2B-9
1978	139	484	138	12	7	3	0.6	71	58	61	65	7	.285	.357	6	3	2B-136, DH-2
1979	127	423	121	14	8	3	0.7	75	42	78	66	20	.286	.378	5	0	2B-126
1980	145	477	111	19	1	1	0.2	68	45	73	79	8	.233	.283	8	2	2B-143
1981	109	335	88	14	4	5	1.5	48	36	40	42	5	.263	.373	2	1	2B-108
1982	152	560	160	22	8	15	2.7	76	65	48	58	11	.286	.434	4	1	2B-149, DH-1
1983	161	643	206	40	6	12	1.9	94	72	67	70	17	.320	.457	7	3	2B-160
1984	143	558	161	25	1	13	2.3	90	56	62	63	6	.289	.407	6	1	2B-142
8 yrs.	987	3512	993	147	35	52	1.5	527	376	433	449	76	.283	.389	38	11	2B-973, DH-3
8 yrs.	987	3512	993	147	35	52	1.5	527	376	433	449	76	.283	.389	38	11	2B-973, DH-3
LEAGUE CHAMPIONSHIP SERIES																	
1984 DET A	3	14	2	0	0	0	0.0	3	0	0	3	0	.143	.143	0	0	2B-3
WORLD SERIES																	
1984 DET A	5	18	5	2	0	0	0.0	6	0	4	4	0	.278	.389	0	0	2B-5

Jo-Jo White

WHITE, JOYNER CLIFFORD
Father of Mike White.
B. June 1, 1909, Red Oak, Ga.
Manager 1960.   BL TR 5'11" 165 lb

	G	AB	H	2B	3B	HR	HR %	R	RBI	BB	SO	SB	BA	SA	AB	H	G by POS
1932 DET A	79	208	54	6	3	2	1.0	25	21	22	19	6	.260	.346	25	9	OF-47
1933	91	234	59	9	5	2	0.9	43	34	27	26	5	.252	.359	26	10	OF-54
1934	115	384	120	18	5	0	0.0	97	44	69	39	28	.313	.385	12	2	OF-100
1935	114	412	99	13	12	2	0.5	82	32	68	42	19	.240	.345	13	4	OF-98
1936	58	51	14	3	0	0	0.0	11	6	9	10	2	.275	.333	30	10	OF-18
1937	94	305	75	5	7	0	0.0	50	21	50	40	12	.246	.308	5	2	OF-82
1938	78	206	54	6	1	0	0.0	40	15	28	15	3	.262	.301	18	3	OF-55
1943 PHI A	139	500	124	17	7	1	0.2	69	30	61	51	12	.248	.316	5	1	OF-133
1944 2 teams	PHI A (85G – .221)			CIN N (24G – .235)													
" total	109	352	79	6	2	1	0.3	39	26	50	34	5	.224	.261	7	1	OF-97, SS-1
9 yrs.	877	2652	678	83	42	8	0.3	456	229	384	276	92	.256	.328	141	42	OF-684, SS-1
7 yrs.	629	1800	475	60	33	6	0.3	348	173	273	191	75	.264	.344	129	40	OF-454
													5th	3rd			
WORLD SERIES																	
1934 DET A	7	23	3	0	0	0	0.0	6	0	8	4	1	.130	.130	0	0	OF-7
1935	5	19	5	0	0	0	0.0	3	1	5	7	0	.263	.263	0	0	OF-5
2 yrs.	12	42	8	0	0	0	0.0	9	1	13	11	1	.190	.190	0	0	OF-12

Glenn Wilson

WILSON, GLENN DWIGHT
B. Dec. 2, 1958, Baytocon, Tex.   BR TR 6'1" 195 lb

	G	AB	H	2B	3B	HR	HR %	R	RBI	BB	SO	SB	BA	SA	AB	H	G by POS
1982 DET A	84	322	94	15	1	12	3.7	39	34	15	51	2	.292	.457	2	0	OF-80, DH-4
1983	144	503	135	25	6	11	2.2	55	65	25	79	1	.268	.408	7	3	OF-143
1984 PHI N	132	341	82	21	3	6	1.8	28	31	17	56	7	.240	.372	19	2	OF-109, 3B-4
3 yrs.	360	1166	311	61	10	29	2.5	122	130	57	186	10	.267	.411	28	5	OF-332, DH-4, 3B-4
2 yrs.	228	825	229	40	7	23	2.8	94	99	40	130	3	.278	.427	9	3	OF-223, DH-4

Icehouse Wilson

WILSON, GEORGE PEACOCK
B. Sept. 14, 1912, Maricopa, Calif.   D. Oct. 13, 1973, Moraga, Calif.   BR TR 6' 186 lb

	G	AB	H	2B	3B	HR	HR %	R	RBI	BB	SO	SB	BA	SA	AB	H	G by POS
1934 DET A	1	1	0	0	0	0	0.0	0	0	0	0	0	.000	.000	1	0	

Red Wilson

WILSON, ROBERT JAMES
B. Mar. 7, 1929, Milwaukee, Wis.   BR TR 5'10" 160 lb

	G	AB	H	2B	3B	HR	HR %	R	RBI	BB	SO	SB	BA	SA	AB	H	G by POS
1951 CHI A	4	11	3	1	0	0	0.0	1	0	1	2	0	.273	.364	0	0	C-4
1952	2	3	0	0	0	0	0.0	0	0	0	1	0	.000	.000	0	0	C-2
1953	71	164	41	6	1	0	0.0	21	10	26	12	2	.250	.299	7	1	C-63
1954 2 teams	CHI A (8G – .200)			DET A (54G – .282)													
" total	62	190	52	11	1	3	1.6	24	23	28	14	3	.274	.389	1	0	C-61
1955 DET A	78	241	53	9	0	2	0.8	26	17	26	23	1	.220	.282	8	1	C-72
1956	78	228	66	12	2	7	3.1	32	38	42	18	2	.289	.452	1	0	C-78
1957	59	178	43	8	1	3	1.7	21	13	24	19	2	.242	.348	0	0	C-59
1958	103	298	89	13	1	3	1.0	31	29	35	30	10	.299	.379	3	0	C-101
1959	67	228	60	17	2	4	1.8	28	35	10	23	2	.263	.408	3	0	C-64
1960 2 teams	DET A (45G – .216)			CLE A (32G – .216)													
" total	77	222	48	7	0	2	0.9	22	24	22	21	3	.216	.275	2	1	C-75
10 yrs.	601	1763	455	84	8	24	1.4	206	189	214	163	25	.258	.356	25	3	C-579
7 yrs.	484	1477	388	74	7	22	1.5	177	168	180	139	23	.263	.367	16	1	C-472

Squanto Wilson

WILSON, GEORGE FRANK
B. Mar. 29, 1889, Old Town, Me.   D. Mar. 26, 1967, Winthrop, Me.   BB TR 5'9½" 170 lb

	G	AB	H	2B	3B	HR	HR %	R	RBI	BB	SO	SB	BA	SA	AB	H	G by POS
1911 DET A	5	16	3	0	0	0	0.0	2	0	2		0	.188	.188	0	0	C-5
1914 BOS A	1	0	0	0	0	0	–	0	0	0		0	–	–	0	0	1B-1
2 yrs.	6	16	3	0	0	0	0.0	2	0	2		0	.188	.188	0	0	C-5, 1B-1
1 yr.	5	16	3	0	0	0	0.0	2	0	2		0	.188	.188	0	0	C-5

Al Wingo

WINGO, ABSALOM HOLBROOK (Red)
Brother of Ivy Wingo.
B. May 6, 1898, Norcross, Ga.   D. Oct. 9, 1964, Allen Park, Mich.   BL TR 5'11" 180 lb

	G	AB	H	2B	3B	HR	HR %	R	RBI	BB	SO	SB	BA	SA	AB	H	G by POS
1919 PHI A	15	59	18	1	3	0	0.0	9	2	4	12	0	.305	.424	0	0	OF-15
1924 DET A	78	150	43	12	2	1	0.7	21	26	21	13	2	.287	.413	29	10	OF-43
1925	130	440	163	34	10	5	1.1	104	68	69	31	14	.370	.527	7	1	OF-122
1926	108	298	84	19	0	1	0.3	45	45	52	32	4	.282	.356	24	6	OF-74, 3B-2
1927	75	137	32	8	2	0	0.0	15	20	25	14	1	.234	.321	33	6	OF-34
1928	87	242	69	13	2	2	0.8	30	30	40	17	2	.285	.380	12	0	OF-71
6 yrs.	493	1326	409	87	19	9	0.7	224	191	211	119	23	.308	.423	105	23	OF-359, 3B-2
5 yrs.	478	1267	391	86	16	9	0.7	215	189	207	107	23	.309	.423	105	23	OF-344, 3B-2

	G	AB	H	2B	3B	HR	HR %	R	RBI	BB	SO	SB	BA	SA	Pinch Hit AB	Pinch Hit H	G by POS

asey Wise

WISE, KENDALL COLE   BB TR 6' 170 lbs.
B. Sept. 8, 1932, Lafayette, Ind.

	G	AB	H	2B	3B	HR	HR %	R	RBI	BB	SO	SB	BA	SA	PH AB	PH H	G by POS
57 CHI N	43	106	19	3	1	0	0.0	12	7	11	14	0	.179	.226	4	0	2B-31, SS-5
58 MIL N	31	71	14	1	0	0	0.0	8	0	4	8	1	.197	.211	8	0	2B-10, SS-7, 3B-1
59	22	76	13	2	0	1	1.3	11	5	10	5	0	.171	.237	1	0	2B-20, SS-5
60 DET A	30	68	10	0	2	2	2.9	6	5	4	9	1	.147	.294	3	0	2B-17, SS-10, 3B-1
4 yrs.	126	321	56	6	3	3	0.9	37	17	29	36	2	.174	.240	16	0	2B-78, SS-27, 3B-2
1 yr.	30	68	10	0	2	2	2.9	6	5	4	9	1	.147	.294	3	0	2B-17, SS-10, 3B-1

WORLD SERIES

	G	AB	H	2B	3B	HR	HR %	R	RBI	BB	SO	SB	BA	SA	PH AB	PH H	
58 MIL N	2	1	0	0	0	0	0.0	0	0	0	1	0	.000	.000	1	0	

ughie Wise

WISE, HUGH EDWARD   BB TR 6' 178 lbs.
B. Mar. 9, 1906, Campbellsville, Ky.

	G	AB	H	2B	3B	HR	HR %	R	RBI	BB	SO	SB	BA	SA	PH AB	PH H	G by POS
30 DET A	2	6	2	0	0	0	0.0	0	0	0	0	0	.333	.333	0	0	C-2

ohn Wockenfuss

WOCKENFUSS, JOHNNY BILTON   BR TR 6' 190 lbs.
B. Feb. 27, 1949, Welch, W. Va.

	G	AB	H	2B	3B	HR	HR %	R	RBI	BB	SO	SB	BA	SA	PH AB	PH H	G by POS
74 DET A	13	29	4	1	0	0	0.0	1	2	3	2	0	.138	.172	0	0	C-13
5	35	118	27	6	3	4	3.4	15	13	10	15	0	.229	.432	1	0	C-34
6	60	144	32	7	2	3	2.1	18	10	17	14	0	.222	.361	1	0	C-59
7	53	164	45	8	1	9	5.5	26	25	14	18	0	.274	.500	9	2	C-37, OF-9, DH-3
8	71	187	53	5	0	7	3.7	23	22	21	14	0	.283	.422	17	6	OF-60, DH-2
9	87	231	61	9	1	15	6.5	27	46	18	40	2	.264	.506	20	5	1B-31, C-20, DH-18, OF-6
0	126	372	102	13	2	16	4.3	56	65	68	64	1	.274	.449	17	4	1B-52, DH-28, C-25, OF-23
1	70	172	37	4	0	9	5.2	20	25	28	22	0	.215	.395	13	1	DH-39, 1B-25, C-5, OF-1
2	70	193	58	9	0	8	4.1	28	32	29	21	0	.301	.472	11	4	C-24, DH-17, 1B-17, OF-10, 3B-1
3	92	245	66	8	1	9	3.7	32	44	31	37	1	.269	.420	24	7	DH-39, C-29, 1B-13, OF-1, 3B-1
4 PHI N	86	180	52	3	1	6	3.3	20	24	30	24	1	.289	.417	27	6	1B-39, C-21, 3B-2
11 yrs.	763	2035	537	73	11	86	4.2	266	308	269	271	5	.264	.437	140	35	C-267, 1B-177, DH-146, OF-110, 3B-4
													9th				
10 yrs.	677	1855	485	70	10	80	4.3	246	284	239	247	4	.261	.439	113	29	C-246, DH-146, 1B-138, OF-110, 3B-2
													10th	8th			

ob Wood

WOOD, ROBERT LYNN   BR TR
B. July 28, 1865, Thorn Hill, Ohio   D. May 22, 1943, Youngstown, Ohio

	G	AB	H	2B	3B	HR	HR %	R	RBI	BB	SO	SB	BA	SA	PH AB	PH H	G by POS
8 CIN N	39	109	30	6	0	0	0.0	14	16	9		1	.275	.330	8	3	C-29, OF-1, 1B-1
9	62	194	61	11	7	0	0.0	34	24	25		3	.314	.443	2	1	C-53, OF-2, 3B-2, 1B-1
0	45	139	37	8	1	0	0.0	17	22	10		3	.266	.338	11	1	C-18, 3B-15, OF-1
1 CLE A	98	346	101	23	3	1	0.3	45	49	12		6	.292	.384	4	1	C-84, 3B-4, OF-3, SS-1, 2B-1, 1B-1
2	81	258	76	18	2	0	0.0	23	40	27		1	.295	.380	9	2	C-52, 1B-16, OF-2, 3B-1, 2B-1
4 DET A	49	175	43	6	2	1	0.6	15	17	5		1	.246	.320	2	0	C-47
5	8	24	2	1	0	0	0.0	1	0	1		0	.083	.125	1	0	C-7
7 yrs.	382	1245	350	73	15	2	0.2	149	168	89		15	.281	.369	37	8	C-290, 3B-22, 1B-19, OF-9, 2B-2, SS-1
2 yrs.	57	199	45	7	2	1	0.5	16	17	6		1	.226	.296	3	0	C-54

ke Wood

WOOD, JACOB   BR TR 6'1" 163 lbs.
B. June 22, 1937, Elizabeth, N. J.

	G	AB	H	2B	3B	HR	HR %	R	RBI	BB	SO	SB	BA	SA	PH AB	PH H	G by POS
DET A	162	663	171	17	14	11	1.7	96	69	58	141	30	.258	.376	1	0	2B-162
	111	367	83	10	5	8	2.2	68	30	33	59	24	.226	.346	11	2	2B-90
	85	351	95	11	2	11	3.1	50	27	24	61	18	.271	.407	1	0	2B-81, 3B-1
	64	125	29	2	2	1	0.8	11	7	4	24	0	.232	.304	29	7	1B-11, 2B-10, 3B-6, OF-1
	58	104	30	3	0	2	1.9	12	7	10	19	3	.288	.375	25	9	2B-20, SS-1, 3B-1, 1B-1
	98	230	58	9	3	2	0.9	39	27	28	48	4	.252	.343	40	6	2B-52, 3B-4, 1B-2
2 teams total	30	DET A (14G – .050)			CIN N (16G – .118)												
	30	37	3	1	0	0	0.0	3	1	2	10	0	.081	.108	19	2	OF-2, 2B-2, 1B-2
7 yrs.	608	1877	469	53	26	35	1.9	279	168	159	362	79	.250	.362	126	26	2B-417, 1B-16, 3B-12, OF-3, SS-1
7 yrs.	592	1860	467	53	26	35	1.9	278	167	158	359	79	.251	.364	116	24	2B-417, 1B-16, 3B-12, OF-1, SS-1
														8th			

e Wood

WOOD, JOSEPH PERRY   BR TR 5'9½" 160 lbs.
B. Oct. 3, 1919, Houston, Tex.

	G	AB	H	2B	3B	HR	HR %	R	RBI	BB	SO	SB	BA	SA	PH AB	PH H	G by POS
DET A	60	164	53	4	4	1	0.6	22	17	6	13	2	.323	.415	10	3	2B-22, 3B-18

rry Woodall

WOODALL, CHARLES LAWRENCE   BR TR 5'9" 165 lbs.
B. July 26, 1894, Staunton, Va.   D. May 6, 1963, Boston, Mass.

	G	AB	H	2B	3B	HR	HR %	R	RBI	BB	SO	SB	BA	SA	PH AB	PH H	G by POS
DET A	18	49	12	1	0	0	0.0	4	5	2	6	0	.245	.265	2	0	C-15
	46	80	29	4	1	0	0.0	10	14	6	7	1	.363	.438	18	5	C-24
	50	125	43	2	2	0	0.0	19	18	8	11	0	.344	.392	11	4	C-39
	71	148	41	12	2	1	0.7	20	19	22	9	2	.277	.405	9	4	C-60
	67	165	51	9	2	0	0.0	23	24	21	5	0	.309	.388	4	0	C-62
	75	171	35	4	1	0	0.0	20	13	24	8	1	.205	.240	0	0	C-75
	67	146	34	5	0	0	0.0	18	15	15	2	0	.233	.267	5	1	C-59
	88	246	69	8	6	0	0.0	28	39	37	9	9	.280	.362	2	0	C-86
	65	186	39	5	1	0	0.0	19	13	24	10	3	.210	.247	3	0	C-62
	1	1	0	0	0	0	0.0	0	0	0	0	0	.000	.000	1	0	
yrs.	548	1317	353	50	15	1	0.1	161	160	159	67	16	.268	.331	55	14	C-482
yrs.	548	1317	353	50	15	1	0.1	161	160	159	67	16	.268	.331	55	14	C-482

	G	AB	H	2B	3B	HR	HR %	R	RBI	BB	SO	SB	BA	SA	Pinch Hit AB	Pinch Hit H	G by POS

Ron Woods

WOODS, RONALD LAWRENCE
B. Feb. 1, 1943, Hamilton, Ohio
BR TR 5'10" 168 lb

	G	AB	H	2B	3B	HR	HR %	R	RBI	BB	SO	SB	BA	SA	PH AB	PH H	G by POS
1969 2 teams	DET A (17G – .267)				NY	A	(72G – .175)										
" total	89	186	34	5	2	2	1.1	21	10	24	32	2	.183	.263	11	0	OF-74
1970 NY A	95	225	51	5	3	8	3.6	30	27	33	35	4	.227	.382	19	3	OF-78
1971 2 teams	NY	A (25G – .250)				MON	N	(51G – .297)									
" total	76	170	49	8	3	2	1.2	30	19	23	20	0	.288	.406	28	5	OF-54
1972 MON N	97	221	57	5	1	10	4.5	21	31	22	33	3	.258	.425	36	7	OF-73
1973	135	318	73	11	3	3	0.9	45	31	56	34	12	.230	.311	28	6	OF-114
1974	90	127	26	0	0	1	0.8	15	12	17	17	6	.205	.228	31	4	OF-61
6 yrs.	582	1247	290	34	12	26	2.1	162	130	175	171	27	.233	.342	153	25	OF-454
1 yr.	17	15	4	0	0	1	6.7	3	3	2	3	0	.267	.467	5	0	OF-7

Yats Wuestling

WUESTLING, GEORGE
B. Oct. 18, 1903, St. Louis, Mo.   D. Apr. 26, 1970, St. Louis, Mo.
BR TR 5'11" 167 lb

	G	AB	H	2B	3B	HR	HR %	R	RBI	BB	SO	SB	BA	SA	PH AB	PH H	G by POS
1929 DET A	54	150	30	4	1	0	0.0	13	16	9	24	0	.200	.240	0	0	SS-52, 3B-1, 2B-1
1930 2 teams	DET	A (4G – .000)				NY	A	(25G – .190)									
" total	29	67	11	0	1	0	0.0	5	3	6	17	0	.164	.194	1	0	SS-25, 3B-3
2 yrs.	83	217	41	4	2	0	0.0	18	19	15	41	0	.189	.226	1	0	SS-77, 3B-4, 2B-1
2 yrs.	58	159	30	4	1	0	0.0	13	16	11	27	0	.189	.226	0	0	SS-56, 3B-1, 2B-1

Emil Yde

YDE, EMIL OGDEN
B. Jan. 28, 1900, Great Lakes, Ill.
D. Dec. 5, 1968, Leesburg, Fla.
BB TL 5'11" 165 lb
BL 1925

	G	AB	H	2B	3B	HR	HR %	R	RBI	BB	SO	SB	BA	SA	PH AB	PH H	G by POS
1924 PIT N	50	88	21	1	3	1	1.1	8	9	0	13	0	.239	.352	13	3	P-33
1925	47	89	17	4	1	0	0.0	11	11	2	13	1	.191	.258	4	0	P-33
1926	43	74	17	5	2	0	0.0	11	4	5	7	0	.230	.351	0	0	P-37
1927	23	18	3	0	1	0	0.0	8	1	0	1	0	.167	.278	4	1	P-9
1929 DET A	46	48	16	1	1	0	0.0	8	3	3	6	0	.333	.396	13	5	P-29
5 yrs.	209	317	74	11	8	1	0.3	46	28	10	40	1	.233	.328	34	9	P-141
1 yr.	46	48	16	1	1	0	0.0	8	3	3	6	0	.333	.396	13	5	P-29
WORLD SERIES																	
1925 PIT N	2	1	0	0	0	0	0.0	1	0	0	0	0	.000	.000	0	0	P-1
1927	1	0	0	0	0	0	–	1	0	0	0	0			1	0	
2 yrs.	3	1	0	0	0	0	0.0	2	0	0	0	0	.000	.000	1	0	P-1

Joe Yeager

YEAGER, JOSEPH F. (Little Joe)
B. Aug. 28, 1875, Philadelphia, Pa.   D. July 2, 1937, Detroit, Mich.
TR

	G	AB	H	2B	3B	HR	HR %	R	RBI	BB	SO	SB	BA	SA	PH AB	PH H	G by POS
1898 BKN N	43	134	23	5	1	0	0.0	12	15	7			1	.172	.224	0	0	P-36, OF-4, SS-2, 2B-
1899	23	47	9	0	1	0	0.0	12	4	6			0	.191	.234	0	0	SS-11, P-10, OF-1, 3B
1900	3	9	3	0	0	0	0.0	0	0	0			0	.333	.333	0	0	P-2, 3B-1
1901 DET A	41	125	37	7	1	2	1.6	18	17	4			3	.296	.416	2	0	P-26, SS-12, 2B-1
1902	50	161	39	6	5	1	0.6	17	23	5			0	.242	.360	1	0	P-19, OF-13, 2B-12, S 3B-1
1903	109	402	103	15	6	0	0.0	36	43	18			9	.256	.323	0	0	3B-107, SS-1, P-1
1905 NY A	115	401	107	16	7	0	0.0	53	42	25			8	.267	.342	3	2	3B-90, SS-21
1906	57	123	37	6	1	0	0.0	20	12	13			3	.301	.366	18	3	SS-22, 2B-13, 3B-3
1907 STL A	123	436	104	21	7	1	0.2	32	44	31			11	.239	.326	4	1	3B-92, 2B-17, SS-13
1908	10	15	5	1	0	0	0.0	3	1				2	.333	.400	1	0	2B-4, SS-1
10 yrs.	574	1853	467	77	29	4	0.2	203	201	110			37	.252	.331	33	7	3B-295, P-94, SS-48, 2B-48, OF-18
3 yrs.	200	688	179	28	12	3	0.4	71	83	27			12	.260	.349	3	0	3B-108, P-46, SS-46, OF-13, 2B-13

Archie Yelle

YELLE, ARCHIE JOSEPH
B. June 11, 1892, Saginaw, Mich.   D. May 2, 1983, Woodland, Calif.
BR TR 5'10½" 170 lb

	G	AB	H	2B	3B	HR	HR %	R	RBI	BB	SO	SB	BA	SA	PH AB	PH H	G by POS
1917 DET A	25	51	7	1	0	0	0.0	4	0	5	4	2	.137	.157	1	0	C-24
1918	56	144	25	3	0	0	0.0	7	7	9	15	0	.174	.194	4	1	C-52
1919	5	4	0	0	0	0	0.0	1	0	1	0	0	.000	.000	0	0	C-5
3 yrs.	86	199	32	4	0	0	0.0	12	7	15	19	2	.161	.181	5	1	C-81
3 yrs.	86	199	32	4	0	0	0.0	12	7	15	19	2	.161	.181	5	1	C-81

Tom Yewcic

YEWCIC, THOMAS J. (Kibby)
B. May 9, 1932, Conemaugh, Pa.
BR TR 5'11" 180 lb

	G	AB	H	2B	3B	HR	HR %	R	RBI	BB	SO	SB	BA	SA	PH AB	PH H	G by POS
1957 DET A	1	1	0	0	0	0	0.0	0	0	0	0	0	.000	.000	0	0	C-1

Rudy York

YORK, RUDOLPH PRESTON
B. Aug. 17, 1913, Ragland, Ala.   D. Feb. 2, 1970, Rome, Ga.
Manager 1959.
BR TR 6'1" 209 lb

	G	AB	H	2B	3B	HR	HR %	R	RBI	BB	SO	SB	BA	SA	PH AB	PH H	G by POS
1934 DET A	3	6	1	0	0	0	0.0	0	0	1	3	0	.167	.167	2	1	C-2
1937	104	375	115	18	3	35	9.3	72	103	41	52	3	.307	.651	7	1	C-54, 3B-41
1938	135	463	138	27	2	33	7.1	85	127	92	74	1	.298	.579	3	0	C-116, OF-14, 1B-1
1939	102	329	101	16	1	20	6.1	66	68	41	50	5	.307	.544	16	2	C-67, 1B-19
1940	155	588	186	46	6	33	5.6	105	134	89	88	3	.316	.583	0	0	1B-155
1941	155	590	153	29	3	27	4.6	91	111	92	88	3	.259	.456	0	0	1B-155
1942	153	577	150	26	4	21	3.6	81	90	73	71	3	.260	.428	1	1	1B-152
1943	155	571	155	22	11	34	6.0	90	118	84	88	5	.271	.527	0	0	1B-155
1944	151	583	161	27	4	18	3.1	77	98	68	73	5	.276	.439	0	0	1B-151
1945	155	595	157	25	5	18	3.0	71	87	59	85	6	.264	.413	0	0	1B-155
1946 BOS A	154	579	160	30	6	17	2.9	78	119	86	93	3	.276	.437	0	0	1B-154
1947 2 teams	BOS	A (48G – .212)				CHI	A	(102G – .243)									
" total	150	584	136	25	4	21	3.6	56	91	58	87	1	.233	.397	0	0	1B-150
1948 PHI A	31	51	8	0	0	0	0.0	4	6	7	15	0	.157	.157	18	2	1B-14
13 yrs.	1603	5891	1621	291	52	277	4.7	876	1152	791	867	38	.275	.483	47	7	1B-1261, C-239, 3B-41, OF-14
10 yrs.	1268	4677	1317	236	42	239	5.1	738	936	640	672	34	.282	.503	29	5	1B-943, C-239, 3B-41, OF-14
							5th	4th			9th	10th	8th			5th		
WORLD SERIES																	
1940 DET A	7	26	6	0	1	1	3.8	3	2	4	7	0	.231	.423	0	0	1B-7

	G	AB	H	2B	3B	HR	HR %	R	RBI	BB	SO	SB	BA	SA	Pinch Hit AB	Pinch Hit H	G by POS

Rudy York continued

	G	AB	H	2B	3B	HR	HR%	R	RBI	BB	SO	SB	BA	SA	PH AB	PH H	G by POS
'45	7	28	5	1	0	0	0.0	1	3	3	4	0	.179	.214	0	0	1B-7
'46 BOS A	7	23	6	1	1·	2	8.7	6	5	6	4	0	.261	.652	0	0	1B-7
3 yrs.	21	77	17	2	2	3	3.9	10	10	13	15	0	.221	.416	0	0	1B-21

Eddie Yost

YOST, EDWARD FREDERICK (The Walking Man)　　BR TR 5'10" 170 lbs.
B. Oct. 13, 1926, Brooklyn, N. Y.

	G	AB	H	2B	3B	HR	HR%	R	RBI	BB	SO	SB	BA	SA	PH AB	PH H	G by POS
'44 WAS A	7	14	2	0	0	0	0.0	3	0	1	2	0	.143	.143	0	0	3B-3, SS-2
'46	8	25	2	1	0	0	0.0	2	1	5	5	2	.080	.120	1	0	3B-7
'47	115	428	102	17	3	0	0.0	52	14	45	57	3	.238	.292	0	0	3B-114
'48	145	555	138	32	11	2	0.4	74	50	82	51	4	.249	.357	0	0	3B-145
'49	124	435	110	19	7	9	2.1	57	45	91	41	3	.253	.391	1	0	3B-122
'50	155	573	169	26	2	11	1.9	114	58	141	63	6	.295	.405	0	0	3B-155
'51	154	568	161	36	4	12	2.1	109	65	126	55	6	.283	.424	0	0	3B-152, OF-3
'52	157	587	137	32	3	12	2.0	92	49	129	73	4	.233	.359	0	0	3B-157
'53	152	577	157	30	7	9	1.6	107	45	123	59	7	.272	.395	0	0	3B-152
'54	155	539	138	26	4	11	2.0	101	47	131	71	7	.256	.380	0	0	3B-155
'55	122	375	91	17	5	7	1.9	64	48	95	54	4	.243	.371	14	3	3B-107
'56	152	515	119	17	2	11	2.1	94	53	151	82	8	.231	.336	9	0	3B-135, OF-8
'57	110	414	104	13	5	9	2.2	47	38	73	49	1	.251	.372	4	0	3B-107
'58	134	406	91	16	0	8	2.0	55	37	81	43	3	.224	.323	15	3	3B-114, OF-4, 1B-2
'59 DET A	148	521	145	19	0	21	4.0	115	61	135	77	9	.278	.436	3	0	3B-146, 2B-1
'60	143	497	129	23	2	14	2.8	78	47	125	69	5	.260	.398	5	1	3B-142
'61 LA A	76	213	43	4	0	3	1.4	29	15	50	48	0	.202	.263	8	1	3B-67
'62	52	104	25	9	1	0	0.0	22	10	30	21	0	.240	.346	16	1	3B-28, 1B-7
18 yrs.	2109	7346	1863	337	56	139	1.9	1215	683	1614 7th	920	72	.254	.371	76	9	3B-2008, OF-15, 1B-9, SS-2, 2B-1
2 yrs.	291	1018	274	42	2	35	3.4	193	108	260	146	14	.269	.417	8	1	3B-288, 2B-1

John Young

YOUNG, JOHN THOMAS　　BL TL 6'3" 210 lbs.
B. Feb. 9, 1949, Los Angeles, Calif.

	G	AB	H	2B	3B	HR	HR%	R	RBI	BB	SO	SB	BA	SA	PH AB	PH H	G by POS
'71 DET A	2	4	2	1	0	0	0.0	1	1	0	0	0	.500	.750	1	0	1B-1

Ralph Young

YOUNG, RALPH STUART　　BB TR 5'5" 165 lbs.
B. Sept. 19, 1890, Philadelphia, Pa.　　D. Jan. 24, 1965, Philadelphia, Pa.

	G	AB	H	2B	3B	HR	HR%	R	RBI	BB	SO	SB	BA	SA	PH AB	PH H	G by POS
'13 NY A	7	15	1	0	0	0	0.0	2	0	3	3	2	.067	.067	0	0	SS-7
'15 DET A	123	378	92	6	5	0	0.0	44	31	64	31	12	.243	.286	0	0	2B-119
'16	153	528	139	16	6	1	0.2	60	45	62	43	20	.263	.322	0	0	2B-146, SS-6, 3B-1
'17	141	503	116	18	2	1	0.2	64	61	61	35	8	.231	.280	0	0	2B-141
'18	91	298	56	7	1	0	0.0	31	21	54	17	15	.188	.218	0	0	2B-91
'19	125	456	96	13	5	1	0.2	63	25	53	32	8	.211	.268	0	0	2B-121, SS-4
'20	150	594	173	21	6	0	0.0	84	33	85	30	8	.291	.347	0	0	2B-150
'21	107	401	120	8	3	0	0.0	70	29	69	23	11	.299	.334	1	0	2B-106
'22 PHI A	125	470	105	19	2	1	0.2	62	35	55	21	8	.223	.279	5	2	2B-120
9 yrs.	1022	3643	898	108	30	4	0.1	480	254	495	235	92	.247	.296	6	2	2B-994, SS-17, 3B-1
7 yrs.	890	3158	792	89	28	3	0.1	416	219	437	211	82	.251	.300	1	0	2B-874, SS-10, 3B-1

Gus Zernial

ZERNIAL, GUS EDWARD (Ozark Ike)　　BR TR 6'2½" 210 lbs.
B. June 27, 1923, Beaumont, Tex.

	G	AB	H	2B	3B	HR	HR%	R	RBI	BB	SO	SB	BA	SA	PH AB	PH H	G by POS
'49 CHI A	73	198	63	17	2	5	2.5	29	38	15	26	0	.318	.500	25	8	OF-46
'50	143	543	152	16	4	29	5.3	75	93	38	110	0	.280	.484	5	1	OF-137
'51 2 teams	CHI A (4G – .105)							PHI A (139G – .274)									
total	143	571	153	30	5	33	5.8	92	129	63	101	2	.268	.511	1	1	OF-142
'52 PHI A	145	549	144	15	1	29	5.3	76	100	70	87	5	.262	.452	3	1	OF-141
'53	147	556	158	21	3	42	7.6	85	108	57	79	4	.284	.559	4	3	OF-141
'54	97	336	84	8	2	14	4.2	42	62	30	60	0	.250	.411	6	2	OF-90, 1B-2
'55 KC A	120	413	105	9	3	30	7.3	62	84	30	90	1	.254	.508	17	2	OF-103
'56	109	272	61	12	0	16	5.9	36	44	33	66	2	.224	.445	35	4	OF-69
'57	131	437	103	20	1	27	6.2	56	69	34	84	1	.236	.471	17	4	OF-113, 1B-1
'58 DET A	66	124	40	7	1	5	4.0	8	23	6	25	0	.323	.516	38	15	OF-24
'59	60	132	30	4	0	7	5.3	11	26	7	27	0	.227	.417	27	6	1B-32, OF-1
11 yrs.	1234	4131	1093	159	22	237	5.7	572	776	383	755	15	.265	.486	178	47	OF-1007, 1B-35
2 yrs.	126	256	70	11	1	12	4.7	19	49	13	52	0	.273	.465	65	21	1B-32, OF-25

Pitcher Register

The Pitcher Register is an alphabetical list of every man who pitched in the major leagues and played or managed for the Detroit Tigers from 1901 through today. Included are lifetime totals of League Championship Series and World Series.

The player and team information for the Pitcher Register is the same as that for the Player Register explained on page 211.

	W	L	PCT	ERA	G	GS	CG	IP	H	BB	SO	ShO	Relief Pitching W	L	SV	BATTING AB	H	HR	BA

hn Doe

DOE, JOHN LEE (Slim)   TR 6'2"   165 lbs.
Played as John Cherry part of 1900.
Born John Lee Doughnut.   Brother of Bill Doe.
B. Jan. 1,1850, New York, N. Y.   D. July 1, 1955, New York, N. Y.
Hall of Fame 1946.

	W	L	PCT	ERA	G	GS	CG	IP	H	BB	SO	ShO	W	L	SV	AB	H	HR	BA
4 STL U	4	2	.667	3.40	26	0	0	54.2	41	38	40	0	1	0	0	4	0	0	.000
5 LOU AA	14	10	.583	4.12	40	19	10	207.2	193	76	70	0	1	0	1	16	2	0	.111
6 CLE N	10	5	.667	4.08	40	8	4	117	110	55	77	0	0	1	0	10	0	0	.000
7 BOS N	9	3	.750	3.38	27	5	2	88	90	36	34	0	2	2	5	44	3	0	.214
8 NY N	13	4	.765	4.17	39	4	0	110	121	50	236	0	0	0	0	3	0	0	–
9 3 teams	DET N	(10G 4–2)		PIT N	(2G 0–0)			PHI	N	(10G 4–0)									
total	8	2	.800	4.25	22	2	2	91.1	90	41	43	0	2	1	10	37	1	0	.036
0 NY P	13	6	.684	4.43	38	0	0	61.1	57	28	30	0	4	4	8	45	0	0	.000
0 CHI N	18	4	.818	3.71	35	1	0	63.1	58	15	23	0	4	2	3	42	2	0	.027
1 BAL A	18	4	.818	1.98	35	0	0	77.1	68	40	29	0	0	2	0	38	10	0	.132
6 DET A	14	10	.583	3.41	31	0	0	58	66	23	24	0	0	0	1	32	3	0	.057
7	13	4	.765	2.51	37	0	0	68	44	30	31	0	0	1	0	31	1	0	.500
8	0	0	–	3.38	1	1	0	8	8	1	1	0	1	2	3	25	0	0	.000
4 CHI F	3	1	.750	2.78	6	0	0	54.2	41	28	9	0	1	0	1	41	2	0	.400
3 yrs.	137	55	.714	3.50	377	40	18	1059.1	987	461	647	0	16	18	32 (8th)	*			
3 yrs.	27	14	.659	2.96	69	1	0	134	118	54	56	0	5	5	3	79	25	1	.316

GUE CHAMPIONSHIP SERIES

	W	L	PCT	ERA	G	GS	CG	IP	H	BB	SO	ShO	W	L	SV	AB	H	HR	BA
1 BAL A	1	1	.500	4.76	4	0	0	22.2	26	8	16	8	0	0	0	0	0	0	–

RLD SERIES

	W	L	PCT	ERA	G	GS	CG	IP	H	BB	SO	ShO	W	L	SV	AB	H	HR	BA
8 BAL A	2	0	1.000	1.00	2	2	2	18	14	7	31	0	0	0	1	7	1	0	.143
8 DET A	2	0	.500	2.30	4	4	3	30	20	3	24	0	0	0	0	4	1	0	.250
2 yrs.	4	0	1.000	1.15	6	6	5	48	34	10	55 (9th)	0	0	0	1	11	2	0	.182

COLUMN HEADINGS INFORMATION

W	L	PCT	ERA	G	GS	CG	IP	H	BB	SO	ShO	Relief Pitching W	L	SV	BATTING AB	H	HR	BA

Total Pitching (including all starting and relief appearances)

W	Wins
L	Losses
PCT	Winning Percentage
ERA	Earned Run Average
G	Games Pitched
GS	Games Started
CG	Complete Games
IP	Innings Pitched
H	Hits Allowed
BB	Bases on Balls Allowed
SO	Strikeouts
ShO	Shutouts

Relief Pitching

W	Wins
L	Losses
SV	Saves

Batting

AB	At Bats
H	Hits
HR	Home Runs
BA	Batting Average

Partial Innings Pitched. These are shown in the Innings Pitched column, and are indicated by a ".1" or ".2" after the total. Doe, for example, pitched 54²/₃ innings in 1884.

All-Time Single Season Leaders. (Starts with 1893, the first year that the pitcher's box was moved to its present distance of 60 feet 6 inches.) Indicated by the small number that appears next to the statistic. Doe, for example, is shown by a small number "1" next to his earned run average in 1901. This means he is first on the all-time major league list for having the lowest earned run average in a single season. All pitchers who tied for first are also shown by the same number.

Meaningless Averages. Indicated by the use of a dash (—). In the case of Doe, a dash is shown for his 1908 winning percentage. This means that although he pitched in one game he never had a decision. A percentage of .000 would mean that he had at least one loss.

Estimated Earned Run Averages. Any time an earned run average appears in italics, it indicates that not all the earned runs allowed by the pitcher are known, and the information had to be estimated. Doe's 1885 earned run average, for example, appears in italics. It is known that Doe's team, Louisville, allowed 560 runs in 112 games. Of these games, it is known that in 90 of them Louisville allowed 420 runs of which 315 or 75% were earned. Doe pitched 207²/₃ innings in 40 games and allowed 134 runs. In 35 of these games, it is known that he allowed 118 runs of which 83 were earned. By multiplying the team's known ratio of earned runs to total runs (75%), by Doe's 16 (134 minus 118) remaining runs allowed, a figure of 12 additional estimated earned runs is calculated. This means that Doe allowed an estimated total of 95 earned runs in 207²/₃ innings, for an estimated earned run average of 4.12. In all cases at least 50% of the runs allowed by the team were "known" as a basis for estimating earned run averages. (Any time the symbol "infinity" (∞) is shown for a pitcher's earned run average, it means that the pitcher allowed one or more earned runs during a season without retiring a batter.)

Batting Statistics. Because a pitcher's batting statistics are of relatively minor importance—and the Designated Hitter rule may eliminate pitchers' batting entirely—only the most significant statistics are given; number of hits, home runs, and batting average.

An asterisk (*) shown in the lifetime batting totals means that the pitcher's complete year-by-year and lifetime batting record is listed in the Player Register.

	W	L	PCT	ERA	G	GS	CG	IP	H	BB	SO	ShO	Relief Pitching W	L	SV	BATTING AB	H	HR	BA

Glenn Abbott

ABBOTT, WILLIAM GLENN
B. Feb. 16, 1951, Little Rock, Ark.   BR TR 6'6"   200 lbs.

	W	L	PCT	ERA	G	GS	CG	IP	H	BB	SO	ShO	W	L	SV	AB	H	HR	BA
973 OAK A	1	0	1.000	3.86	5	3	1	18.2	16	7	6	0	0	0	0	0	0	0	—
974	5	7	.417	3.00	19	17	3	96	89	34	38	0	0	0	0	0	0	0	—
975	5	5	.500	4.25	30	15	3	114.1	109	50	51	1	2	0	0	0	0	0	—
976	2	4	.333	5.52	19	10	0	62	87	16	27	0	1	1	0	0	0	0	—
977 SEA A	12	13	.480	4.46	36	34	7	204	212	56	100	0	0	0	0	0	0	0	—
978	7	15	.318	5.27	29	28	8	155.1	191	44	67	1	0	0	0	0	0	0	—
979	4	10	.286	5.15	23	19	3	117	138	38	25	0	0	0	0	0	0	0	—
980	12	12	.500	4.10	31	31	7	215	228	49	78	2	0	0	0	0	0	0	—
981	4	9	.308	3.95	22	20	1	130	127	28	35	0	0	0	0	0	0	0	—
983 2 teams			SEA	A (14G 5–3)		DET	A (7G 2–1)												
" total	7	4	.636	3.63	21	21	3	129	146	22	49	1	0	0	0	0	0	0	—
984 DET A	3	4	.429	5.93	13	8	1	44	62	8	8	0	1	1	0	0	0	0	—
11 yrs.	62	83	.428	4.39	248	206	37	1285.1	1405	352	484	5	4	2	0	0	0	0	—
2 yrs.	5	5	.500	3.87	20	15	2	90.2	105	15	19	1	1	1	0	0	0	0	—
LEAGUE CHAMPIONSHIP SERIES																			
975 OAK A	0	0	—	0.00	1	0	0	1	0	0	0	0	0	0	0	0	0	0	—

Al Aber

ABER, ALBERT JULIUS (Lefty)
B. July 31, 1927, Cleveland, Ohio   BL TL 6'2"   195 lbs.

	W	L	PCT	ERA	G	GS	CG	IP	H	BB	SO	ShO	W	L	SV	AB	H	HR	BA
950 CLE A	1	0	1.000	2.00	1	1	1	9	5	4	4	0	0	0	0	2	0	0	.000
953 2 teams			CLE	A (6G 1–1)		DET	A (17G 4–3)												
" total	5	4	.556	4.71	23	10	2	72.2	69	50	38	0	3	1	0	23	3	0	.130
954 DET A	5	11	.313	3.97	32	18	4	124.2	121	40	54	0	0	1	3	39	5	0	.128
955	6	3	.667	3.38	39	1	0	80	86	28	37	0	6	3	3	17	1	0	.059
956	4	4	.500	3.43	42	0	0	63	65	25	21	0	4	4	7	10	3	0	.300
957 2 teams			DET	A (28G 3–3)		KC	A (3G 0–0)												
" total	3	3	.500	7.20	31	0	0	40	52	13	15	0	3	3	1	9	2	0	.222
6 yrs.	24	25	.490	4.18	168	30	7	389.1	398	160	169	0	16	12	14	100	14	0	.140
5 yrs.	22	24	.478	4.12	158	29	6	371.1	381	145	161	0	15	11	14	97	13	0	.134

Hank Aguirre

AGUIRRE, HENRY JOHN
B. Jan. 31, 1932, Azusa, Calif.   BR TL 6'4"   205 lbs.
                                              BB 1965–68

	W	L	PCT	ERA	G	GS	CG	IP	H	BB	SO	ShO	W	L	SV	AB	H	HR	BA
955 CLE A	2	0	1.000	1.42	4	1	1	12.2	6	12	6	1	1	0	0	4	0	0	.000
956	3	5	.375	3.72	16	9	2	65.1	63	27	31	1	1	0	1	18	2	0	.111
957	1	1	.500	5.75	10	1	0	20.1	26	13	9	0	0	1	0	4	0	0	.000
958 DET A	3	4	.429	3.75	44	3	0	69.2	67	27	38	0	2	2	5	14	3	0	.214
959	0	0	—	3.38	3	0	0	2.2	4	3	3	0	0	0	0	0	0	0	—
960	5	3	.625	2.85	37	6	1	94.2	75	30	80	0	2	1	10	28	1	0	.036
961	4	4	.500	3.25	45	0	0	55.1	44	38	32	0	4	4	8	9	0	0	.000
962	16	8	.667	2.21	42	22	11	216	162	65	156	2	4	2	3	75	2	0	.027
963	14	15	.483	3.67	38	33	14	225.2	222	68	134	3	0	2	0	76	10	0	.132
964	5	10	.333	3.79	32	27	3	161.2	134	59	88	0	0	0	1	53	3	0	.057
965	14	10	.583	3.59	32	32	10	208.1	185	60	141	2	0	0	0	70	6	0	.086
966	3	9	.250	3.82	30	14	2	103.2	104	26	50	0	0	3	0	25	3	0	.120
967	0	1	.000	2.40	31	1	0	41.1	34	17	33	0	0	1	0	2	1	0	.500
968 LA N	1	2	.333	0.69	25	0	0	39	32	13	25	0	1	2	3	3	0	0	.000
969 CHI N	1	0	1.000	2.60	41	0	0	45	45	12	19	0	1	0	1	5	2	0	.400
970	3	0	1.000	4.50	17	0	0	14	13	9	11	0	3	0	1	2	0	0	.000
16 yrs.	75	72	.510	3.25	447	149	44	1375.1	1216	479	856	9	19	18	33	388	33	0	.085
10 yrs.	64	64	.500	3.29	334	138	41	1179	1031	393	755	7	12	15	27	352	29	0	.082
					8th														

Eddie Ainsmith

AINSMITH, EDWARD WILBUR
B. Feb. 4, 1890, Cambridge, Mass.   D. Sept. 6, 1981, Fort Lauderdale, Fla.   BR TR 5'11"   180 lbs.

	W	L	PCT	ERA	G	GS	CG	IP	H	BB	SO	ShO	W	L	SV	AB	H	HR	BA
13 WAS A	0	0	—	54.00	1	0	0	.1	2	0	0	0	0	0	0	*			

Ernie Alten

ALTEN, ERNEST MATTHIAS (Lefty)
B. Dec. 1, 1894, Avon, Ohio   D. Sept. 9, 1981, Napa, Calif.   BR TL 6'   175 lbs.

	W	L	PCT	ERA	G	GS	CG	IP	H	BB	SO	ShO	W	L	SV	AB	H	HR	BA
20 DET A	0	1	.000	9.00	14	1	0	23	40	9	4	0	0	0	0	3	0	0	.000

Bob Anderson

ANDERSON, ROBERT CARL
B. Sept. 29, 1935, East Chicago, Ind.   BR TR 6'4½"   210 lbs.

	W	L	PCT	ERA	G	GS	CG	IP	H	BB	SO	ShO	W	L	SV	AB	H	HR	BA
957 CHI N	0	1	.000	7.71	8	0	0	16.1	20	8	7	0	0	1	0	4	0	0	.000
958	3	3	.500	3.97	17	8	2	65.2	61	29	51	0	0	0	0	17	2	0	.118
959	12	13	.480	4.13	37	36	7	235.1	245	77	113	1	0	0	0	80	6	0	.075
960	9	11	.450	4.11	38	30	5	203.2	201	68	115	0	0	1	1	71	12	0	.169
961	7	10	.412	4.26	57	12	1	152	162	56	96	0	4	3	8	42	6	2	.143
962	2	7	.222	5.02	57	4	0	107.2	111	60	82	0	1	6	4	23	3	0	.130
963 DET A	3	1	.750	3.30	32	3	0	60	58	21	38	0	2	0	0	9	4	0	.444
7 yrs.	36	46	.439	4.26	246	93	15	840.2	858	319	502	1	7	11	13	246	33	2	.134
1 yr.	3	1	.750	3.30	32	3	0	60	58	21	38	0	2	0	0	9	4	0	.444

Fernando Arroyo

ARROYO, FERNANDO
B. Mar. 21, 1952, Sacramento, Calif.   BR TR 6'2"   180 lbs.

	W	L	PCT	ERA	G	GS	CG	IP	H	BB	SO	ShO	W	L	SV	AB	H	HR	BA
975 DET A	2	1	.667	4.56	14	2	1	53.1	56	22	25	0	1	0	0	0	0	0	—
977	8	18	.308	4.18	38	28	8	209	227	52	60	1	1	2	0	0	0	0	—
978	0	0	—	8.31	2	0	0	4.1	8	0	1	0	0	0	0	0	0	0	—
979	1	1	.500	8.25	6	0	0	12	17	4	7	0	1	1	0	0	0	0	—
980 MIN A	6	6	.500	4.70	21	11	1	92	97	32	27	1	2	0	0	0	0	0	—
981	7	10	.412	3.94	23	19	2	128	144	34	39	0	0	0	0	0	0	0	—
982 2 teams			MIN	A (6G 0–1)		OAK	A (10G 0–0)												
total	0	1	.000	5.25	16	0	0	36	40	13	13	0	0	1	0	0	0	0	—
7 yrs.	24	37	.393	4.44	120	60	12	534.2	589	157	172	2	5	4	0	0	0	0	—
4 yrs.	11	20	.355	4.49	60	30	9	278.2	308	78	93	1	3	3	0	0	0	0	—

	W	L	PCT	ERA	G	GS	CG	IP	H	BB	SO	ShO	Relief Pitching W	L	SV	BATTING AB	H	HR	B

Eldon Auker

AUKER, ELDON LeROY (Big Six)
B. Sept. 21, 1910, Norcatur, Kans.   BR TR 6'2"   194 lbs

	W	L	PCT	ERA	G	GS	CG	IP	H	BB	SO	ShO	W	L	SV	AB	H	HR	B
1933 DET A	3	3	.500	5.24	15	6	2	55	63	25	17	1	0	1	0	17	2	0	.11
1934	15	7	.682	3.42	43	18	10	205	234	56	86	2	6	4	1	74	11	0	.14
1935	18	7	**.720**	3.83	36	25	13	195	213	61	63	2	3	0	0	74	16	0	.21
1936	13	16	.448	4.89	35	31	14	215.1	263	83	66	2	0	0	0	78	24	0	.30
1937	17	9	.654	3.88	39	32	19	252.2	250	97	73	1	0	1	1	91	18	3	.19
1938	11	10	.524	5.27	27	24	12	160.2	184	56	46	1	0	1	0	57	5	0	.08
1939 BOS A	9	10	.474	5.36	31	25	6	151	183	61	43	1	1	0	0	53	12	2	.22
1940 STL A	16	11	.593	3.96	38	35	20	263.2	299	96	78	2	0	0	0	89	19	1	.21
1941	14	15	.483	5.50	34	31	13	216	268	85	60	0	1	2	0	80	10	0	.12
1942	14	13	.519	4.08	35	34	17	249	**273**	86	62	2	0	0	0	87	14	0	.16
10 yrs.	130	101	.563	4.42	333	261	126	1963.1	2230	706	594	14	11	9	2	700	131	6	.18
6 yrs.	77	52	.597	4.26	195	136	70	1083.2	1207	378	351	9	9	7	2	391	76	3	.19
			6th																

WORLD SERIES

	W	L	PCT	ERA	G	GS	CG	IP	H	BB	SO	ShO	W	L	SV	AB	H	HR	B
1934 DET A	1	1	.500	5.56	2	2	1	11.1	16	5	2	0	0	0	0	4	0	0	.00
1935	0	0	—	3.00	1	1	0	6	6	2	1	0	0	0	0	2	0	0	.00
2 yrs.	1	1	.500	4.67	3	3	1	17.1	22	7	3	0	0	0	0	6	0	0	.00

Doc Ayers

AYERS, YANCY WYATT
B. May 20, 1890, Fancy Gap, Va.   D. May 26, 1968, Draper, Va.   BR TR

	W	L	PCT	ERA	G	GS	CG	IP	H	BB	SO	ShO	W	L	SV	AB	H	HR	B
1913 WAS A	1	1	.500	1.53	4	2	1	17.2	12	4	17	1	0	0	1	7	0	0	.00
1914	12	15	.444	2.54	49	31	8	265.1	221	54	148	3	3	2	3	83	14	0	.16
1915	14	9	.609	2.21	40	16	8	211.1	178	38	96	2	5	4	3	63	12	0	.19
1916	5	9	.357	3.78	43	17	7	157	173	52	69	0	0	2	2	43	6	0	.14
1917	11	10	.524	2.17	40	15	12	207.2	192	59	78	3	5	4	1	63	13	0	.20
1918	10	12	.455	2.83	39	24	11	219.2	215	63	67	4	3	2	3	66	10	0	.15
1919 2 teams					WAS	A (11G 1–6)		DET	A (24G 5–3)										
" total	6	9	.400	2.75	35	10	3	137.1	140	45	44	1	4	3	0	36	8	0	.22
1920 DET A	7	14	.333	3.88	46	22	9	208.2	217	62	103	3	0	2	1	59	9	0	.15
1921	0	0	—	9.00	2	1	0	4	9	2	0	0	0	0	0				
9 yrs.	66	79	.455	2.84	298	138	59	1428.2	1357	379	622	17	20	19	14	420	72	0	.17
3 yrs.	12	17	.414	3.58	72	28	12	306.1	314	92	135	4	3	4	1	83	12	0	.14

Bill Bailey

BAILEY, WILLIAM F.
B. Apr. 12, 1889, Fort Smith, Ark.   D. Nov. 2, 1926, Austin, Tex.   BL TL 5'11"   165 lbs

	W	L	PCT	ERA	G	GS	CG	IP	H	BB	SO	ShO	W	L	SV	AB	H	HR	B
1907 STL A	4	1	.800	2.42	6	5	3	48.1	39	15	17	0	0	0	0	20	3	0	.15
1908	3	5	.375	3.04	22	12	7	106.2	85	50	42	0	0	0	0	34	3	0	.08
1909	9	10	.474	2.44	32	20	17	199	174	75	114	1	1	0	0	77	22	0	.28
1910	3	18	.143	3.32	34	20	13	192.1	186	97	90	0	3	1	0	63	13	0	.20
1911	0	3	.000	4.55	7	2	2	31.2	42	16	8	0	0	1	0	11	0	0	.00
1912	0	1	.000	9.28	3	2	0	10.2	15	10	2	0	0	0	0	2	1	0	.50
1914 BAL F	6	9	.400	3.08	19	18	10	128.2	106	68	131	1	1	0	0	43	7	0	.16
1915 2 teams					BAL	F (36G 5–19)		CHI	F (5G 3–1)										
" total	8	20	.286	4.27	41	28	14	223.2	202	125	122	5	1	4	0	74	17	0	.23
1918 DET A	1	2	.333	5.97	8	4	1	37.2	53	26	13	0	0	0	0	13	1	0	.07
1921 STL N	2	5	.286	4.26	19	6	3	74	95	22	20	1	1	2	0	22	2	0	.09
1922	0	2	.000	5.40	12	0	0	31.2	38	23	11	0	0	2	0	7	2	0	.28
11 yrs.	36	76	.321	3.57	203	117	70	1084.1	1035	527	570	8	7	10	0	366	71	0	.19
1 yr.	1	2	.333	5.97	8	4	1	37.2	53	26	13	0	0	0	0	13	1	0	.07

Howard Bailey

BAILEY, HOWARD LEE
B. July 31, 1958, Grand Haven, Mich.   BR TL 6'   195 lbs

	W	L	PCT	ERA	G	GS	CG	IP	H	BB	SO	ShO	W	L	SV	AB	H	HR	B
1981 DET A	1	4	.200	7.30	9	5	0	37	45	13	17	0	0	0	0	0	0	0	
1982	0	0	—	0.00	8	0	0	10	6	2	3	0	0	0	1	0	0	0	
1983	5	5	.500	4.88	33	3	0	72	69	25	21	0	4	3	0	0	0	0	
3 yrs.	6	9	.400	5.22	50	8	0	119	120	40	41	0	4	3	1	0	0	0	
3 yrs.	6	9	.400	5.22	50	8	0	119	120	40	41	0	4	3	1	0	0	0	

Doug Bair

BAIR, CHARLES DOUGLAS
B. Aug. 22, 1949, Defiance, Ohio   BR TR 6'   180 lbs

	W	L	PCT	ERA	G	GS	CG	IP	H	BB	SO	ShO	W	L	SV	AB	H	HR	B
1976 PIT N	0	0	—	5.68	4	0	0	6.1	4	5	4	0	0	0	0	0	0	0	
1977 OAK A	4	6	.400	3.47	45	0	0	83	78	57	68	0	4	6	8	0	0	0	
1978 CIN N	7	6	.538	1.98	70	0	0	100	87	38	91	0	7	6	28	14	2	0	.14
1979	11	7	.611	4.31	65	0	0	94	93	51	86	0	11	7	16	8	0	0	.00
1980	3	6	.333	4.24	61	0	0	85	91	39	62	0	3	6	6	2	0	0	.00
1981 2 teams					CIN	N (24G 2–2)		STL	N (11G 2–0)										
" total	4	2	.667	5.10	35	0	0	54.2	55	19	30	0	4	2	1	6	1	1	.16
1982 STL N	5	3	.625	2.55	63	0	0	91.2	69	36	68	0	5	3	8	13	1	0	.07
1983 2 teams					STL	N (26G 1–1)		DET	A (27G 7–3)										
" total	8	4	.667	3.59	53	0	0	85.1	75	32	60	0	7	4	5	0	0	0	.00
1984 DET A	5	3	.625	3.75	47	1	0	93.2	82	36	57	0	5	2	4	0	0	0	
9 yrs.	47	37	.560	3.54	443	2	0	693.2	634	313	526	0	46	36	76	45	4	1	.08
2 yrs.	12	6	.667	3.80	74	2	0	149.1	133	55	96	0	11	5	8	0	0	0	

LEAGUE CHAMPIONSHIP SERIES

	W	L	PCT	ERA	G	GS	CG	IP	H	BB	SO	ShO	W	L	SV	AB	H	HR	B
1979 CIN N	0	1	.000	9.00	1	0	0	1	2	1	0	0	0	1	0	0	0	0	
1982 STL N	0	0	—	0.00	1	0	0	1	2	3	0	0	0	0	0	0	0	0	
2 yrs.	0	1	.000	4.50	2	0	0	2	4	4	0	0	0	1	0	0	0	0	

WORLD SERIES

	W	L	PCT	ERA	G	GS	CG	IP	H	BB	SO	ShO	W	L	SV	AB	H	HR	B
1982 STL N	0	1	.000	9.00	3	0	0	2	2	2	3	0	0	1	0	0	0	0	
1984 DET A	0	0	—	0.00	1	0	0	.2	0	0	1	0	0	0	0	0	0	0	
2 yrs.	0	1	.000	6.75	4	0	0	2.2	2	2	4	0	0	1	0	0	0	0	

	W	L	PCT	ERA	G	GS	CG	IP	H	BB	SO	ShO	Relief Pitching W	L	SV	BATTING AB	H	HR	BA

teve Baker

BAKER, STEVEN BYRNE
B. Aug. 30, 1956, Eugene, Ore.   BR TR 6'   185 lbs.

	W	L	PCT	ERA	G	GS	CG	IP	H	BB	SO	ShO	W	L	SV	AB	H	HR	BA
'78 DET A	2	4	.333	4.55	15	10	0	63.1	66	42	39	0	1	1	0	0	0	0	–
'79	1	7	.125	6.64	21	12	0	84	97	51	54	0	0	1	1	0	0	0	–
'82 OAK A	1	1	.500	4.56	5	3	0	25.2	30	4	14	0	0	0	0	0	0	0	–
'83 2 teams		OAK	A (35G 3–3)		STL	N	(8G 0–1)												
total	3	4	.429	3.94	43	1	0	64	69	30	24	0	3	3	5	0	0	0	–
4 yrs.	7	16	.304	5.13	84	26	0	237	262	127	131	0	4	5	6	0	0	0	–
2 yrs.	3	11	.214	5.74	36	22	0	147.1	163	93	93	0	1	2	1	0	0	0	–

Ray Bare

BARE, RAYMOND DOUGLAS
B. Apr. 15, 1949, Miami, Fla.   BR TR 6'2"   185 lbs.

	W	L	PCT	ERA	G	GS	CG	IP	H	BB	SO	ShO	W	L	SV	AB	H	HR	BA
'72 STL N	0	1	.000	0.54	14	0	0	16.2	18	6	5	0	0	1	1	0	0	0	–
'74	1	2	.333	6.00	10	3	0	24	25	9	6	0	1	0	0	5	1	0	.200
'75 DET A	8	13	.381	4.48	29	21	6	150.2	174	47	71	1	2	0	0	0	0	0	–
'76	7	8	.467	4.63	30	21	3	134	157	51	59	2	0	0	0	0	0	0	–
'77	0	2	.000	12.86	5	4	0	14	24	7	4	0	0	0	0	0	0	0	–
5 yrs.	16	26	.381	4.80	88	49	9	339.1	398	120	145	3	3	1	1	5	1	0	.200
3 yrs.	15	23	.395	4.94	64	46	9	298.2	355	105	134	3	2	0	0	0	0	0	–

Clyde Barfoot

BARFOOT, CLYDE RAYMOND
B. July 8, 1891, Richmond, Va.   D. Mar. 11, 1971, Highland Park, Calif.   BR TR 6'   170 lbs.

	W	L	PCT	ERA	G	GS	CG	IP	H	BB	SO	ShO	W	L	SV	AB	H	HR	BA
'22 STL N	4	5	.444	4.21	42	2	1	117.2	139	30	19	0	3	4	2	34	12	0	.353
'23	3	3	.500	3.73	33	2	1	101.1	112	27	23	1	2	3	1	37	7	0	.189
'26 DET A	1	2	.333	4.88	11	1	0	31.1	42	9	7	0	1	1	2	5	1	0	.200
3 yrs.	8	10	.444	4.10	86	5	2	250.1	293	66	49	1	6	8	5	76	20	0	.263
1 yr.	1	2	.333	4.88	11	1	0	31.1	42	9	7	0	1	1	2	5	1	0	.200

Frank Barnes

BARNES, FRANK SAMUEL (Lefty)
B. Jan. 9, 1900, Dallas, Tex.   D. Sept. 27, 1967, Houston, Tex.   BL TL 6'2½"   195 lbs.

	W	L	PCT	ERA	G	GS	CG	IP	H	BB	SO	ShO	W	L	SV	AB	H	HR	BA
'29 DET A	0	1	.000	7.20	4	1	0	5	10	3	0	0	0	0	0	1	0	0	.000
'30 NY A	0	1	.000	8.03	2	2	0	12.1	13	13	2	0	0	0	0	6	2	0	.333
2 yrs.	0	2	.000	7.79	6	3	0	17.1	23	16	2	0	0	0	0	7	2	0	.286
1 yr.	0	1	.000	7.20	4	1	0	5	10	3	0	0	0	0	0	1	0	0	.000

Harry Baumgartner

BAUMGARTNER, HARRY E
B. Oct. 8, 1892, S. Pittsburg, Tenn.   D. Dec. 3, 1930, Augusta, Ga.   BR TR 5'11"   175 lbs.

	W	L	PCT	ERA	G	GS	CG	IP	H	BB	SO	ShO	W	L	SV	AB	H	HR	BA
'20 DET A	0	1	.000	4.00	9	0	0	18	18	6	7	0	0	1	0	4	1	0	.250

Gene Bearden

BEARDEN, HENRY EUGENE
B. Sept. 5, 1920, Lexa, Ark.   BL TL 6'4"   198 lbs.

	W	L	PCT	ERA	G	GS	CG	IP	H	BB	SO	ShO	W	L	SV	AB	H	HR	BA
'47 CLE A	0	0	–	81.00	1	0	0	.1	2	1	0	0	0	0	0	0	0	0	–
'48	20	7	.741	2.43	37	29	15	229.2	187	106	80	6	0	2	1	90	23	2	.256
'49	8	8	.500	5.10	32	19	5	127	140	92	41	0	1	1	0	45	5	0	.111
'50 2 teams		CLE	A (14G 1–3)		WAS	A	(12G 3–5)												
total	4	8	.333	4.99	26	12	4	113.2	138	65	30	0	1	2	0	35	7	0	.200
'51 2 teams		WAS	A (1G 0–0)		DET	A	(37G 3–4)												
total	3	4	.429	4.64	38	5	2	108.2	118	60	39	1	1	2	0	32	6	2	.188
'52 STL A	7	8	.467	4.30	34	16	3	150.2	158	78	45	0	1	2	0	65	23	0	.354
'53 CHI A	3	3	.500	2.93	25	3	0	58.1	48	33	24	0	3	1	0	21	4	0	.190
7 yrs.	45	38	.542	3.96	193	84	29	788.1	791	435	259	7	7	10	1	288	68	4	.236
1 yr.	3	4	.429	4.33	37	4	2	106	112	58	38	1	1	2	0	32	6	2	.188
WORLD SERIES																			
'48 CLE A	1	0	1.000	0.00	2	1	1	10.2	6	1	4	1	0	0	1	4	2	0	.500

Boom-Boom Beck

BECK, WALTER WILLIAM
B. Oct. 16, 1904, Decatur, Ill.   BR TR 6'2"   200 lbs.

	W	L	PCT	ERA	G	GS	CG	IP	H	BB	SO	ShO	W	L	SV	AB	H	HR	BA
'24 STL A	0	0	–	0.00	1	0	0	1	2	1	0	0	0	0	0	0	0	0	–
'27	1	0	1.000	5.56	3	1	1	11.1	15	5	6	0	0	0	0	4	1	0	.250
'28	2	3	.400	4.41	16	4	2	49	52	20	17	0	1	0	0	14	6	0	.429
'33 BKN N	12	20	.375	3.54	43	35	15	257	270	69	89	3	1	1	1	95	18	0	.189
'34	2	6	.250	7.42	22	9	2	57	72	32	24	0	1	1	0	17	4	0	.235
'39 PHI N	7	14	.333	4.73	34	16	12	182.2	203	64	77	0	3	4	3	68	9	0	.132
'40	4	9	.308	4.31	29	15	4	129.1	147	41	38	0	2	0	0	36	2	0	.056
'41	1	9	.100	4.63	34	7	2	95.1	104	35	34	0	0	3	0	25	3	0	.120
'42	0	1	.000	4.75	26	1	0	53	69	17	10	0	0	0	0	12	4	0	.333
'43	0	0	–	9.88	4	0	0	13.2	24	5	3	0	0	0	0	4	2	0	.500
'44 DET A	1	2	.333	3.89	28	2	0	74	67	27	25	0	1	1	1	22	7	0	.318
'45 2 teams		CIN	N (11G 2–4)		PIT	N	(14G 6–1)												
total	8	5	.615	2.68	25	11	6	110.2	96	26	29	0	2	1	1	30	5	0	.167
12 yrs.	38	69	.355	4.30	265	101	44	1034	1121	342	352	3	11	11	6	327	61	0	.187
1 yr.	1	2	.333	3.89	28	2	0	74	67	27	25	0	1	1	1	22	7	0	.318

Al Benton

BENTON, JOHN ALTON
B. Mar. 18, 1911, Noble, Okla.   D. Apr. 14, 1968, Lynwood, Calif.   BR TR 6'5½"   215 lbs.

	W	L	PCT	ERA	G	GS	CG	IP	H	BB	SO	ShO	W	L	SV	AB	H	HR	BA
'34 PHI A	7	9	.438	4.88	32	21	7	155	145	88	58	0	1	1	1	55	6	0	.109
'35	3	4	.429	7.67	27	9	0	78.2	110	47	42	0	3	1	0	25	1	0	.040
'38 DET A	5	3	.625	3.30	19	10	6	95.1	93	39	33	0	0	0	0	33	4	0	.121
'39	6	8	.429	4.56	37	16	3	150	182	58	67	0	1	3	5	44	4	0	.091
'40	6	10	.375	4.42	42	0	0	79.1	93	54	50	0	6	10	17	17	0	0	.000
'41	15	6	.714	2.97	38	14	7	157.2	130	65	63	1	6	2	7	50	3	0	.060
'42	7	13	.350	2.90	35	30	9	226.2	210	84	110	1	0	1	2	67	5	0	.075
'45	13	8	.619	2.02	31	27	12	191.2	175	63	76	5	0	1	3	63	4	0	.063
'46	11	7	.611	3.65	28	15	6	140.2	132	58	60	1	1	2	1	49	9	0	.184
'47	6	7	.462	4.40	31	14	4	133	147	61	33	0	1	0	7	39	6	0	.154
'48	2	2	.500	5.68	30	0	0	44.1	45	36	18	0	2	2	3	11	2	0	.182
'49 CLE A	9	6	.600	2.12	40	11	4	135.2	116	51	41	2	4	0	10	38	5	0	.132

	W	L	PCT	ERA	G	GS	CG	IP	H	BB	SO	ShO	Relief Pitching W	L	SV	BATTING AB	H	HR	B

Al Benton continued

	W	L	PCT	ERA	G	GS	CG	IP	H	BB	SO	ShO	W	L	SV	AB	H	HR	B
1950	4	2	.667	3.57	36	0	0	63	57	30	26	0	4	2	4	12	1	0	.0
1952 BOS A	4	3	.571	2.39	24	0	0	37.2	37	17	20	0	4	3	6	9	0	0	.0
14 yrs.	98	88	.527	3.66	450	167	58	1688.2	1672	733	697	10	33	28	66	512	50	0	.0
9 yrs.	71	64	.526	3.46	291	126	47	1218.2	1207	500	510	8	17	21	45	373	37	0	.0
WORLD SERIES															4th				
1945 DET A	0	0	–	1.93	3	0	0	4.2	6	0	5	0	0	0	0	0	0	0	

Juan Berenguer

BERENGUER, JUAN BAUTISTA
B. Nov. 30, 1954, Aguadulce, Panama   BR TR 5'11" 186 lb

	W	L	PCT	ERA	G	GS	CG	IP	H	BB	SO	ShO	W	L	SV	AB	H	HR	B
1978 NY N	0	2	.000	8.31	5	3	0	13	17	11	8	0	0	0	0	3	0	0	.0
1979	1	1	.500	2.90	5	5	0	31	28	12	25	0	0	0	0	7	1	0	.1
1980	0	1	.000	6.00	6	0	0	9	9	10	7	0	0	1	0	0	0	0	
1981 2 teams			KC A (8G 0–4)			TOR A (12G 2–9)													
" total	2	13	.133	5.24	20	14	1	91	84	51	49	0	0	2	0	4	0	0	.0
1982 DET A	0	0	–	6.75	2	1	0	6.2	5	9	8	0	0	0	0	0	0	0	
1983	9	5	.643	3.14	37	19	2	157.2	110	71	129	1	2	0	1	0	0	0	
1984	11	10	.524	3.48	31	27	2	168.1	146	79	118	1	0	0	0	0	0	0	
7 yrs.	23	32	.418	3.89	106	69	5	476.2	399	243	344	2	2	3	1	10	1	0	.1
3 yrs.	20	15	.571	3.38	70	47	4	332.2	261	159	255	2	2	0	1	0	0	0	

Jack Billingham

BILLINGHAM, JOHN EUGENE
B. Feb. 21, 1943, Orlando, Fla.   BR TR 6'4" 195 lb

	W	L	PCT	ERA	G	GS	CG	IP	H	BB	SO	ShO	W	L	SV	AB	H	HR	B
1968 LA N	3	0	1.000	2.14	50	1	0	71.1	54	30	46	0	3	0	8	3	0	0	.0
1969 HOU N	6	7	.462	4.23	52	4	1	83	92	29	71	0	0	0	2	14	1	0	.0
1970	13	9	.591	3.97	46	24	8	188	190	63	134	2	2	0	0	58	6	0	.1
1971	10	16	.385	3.39	33	33	8	228	205	68	139	3	0	0	0	73	9	0	.1
1972 CIN N	12	12	.500	3.18	36	31	8	217.2	197	64	137	4	0	0	1	71	5	0	.0
1973	19	10	.655	3.04	40	40	16	293.1	257	95	155	7	0	0	0	93	6	0	.0
1974	19	11	.633	3.95	36	35	8	212	233	64	103	3	1	0	0	67	5	0	.0
1975	15	10	.600	4.11	33	32	5	208	222	76	79	0	0	0	0	65	7	0	.1
1976	12	10	.545	4.32	34	29	5	177	190	62	76	2	1	1	1	59	14	0	.2
1977	10	10	.500	5.22	36	23	3	162	195	56	76	1	0	1	2	56	9	0	.1
1978 DET A	15	8	.652	3.88	30	30	10	201.2	218	65	59	4	0	0	0				
1979	10	7	.588	3.30	35	19	2	158	163	60	59	0	3	2	3	0	0	0	
1980 2 teams			DET A (8G 0–0)			BOS A (7G 1–3)													
" total	1	3	.250	10.45	15	4	0	31	56	18	7	0	0	0	0	0	0	0	
13 yrs.	145	113	.562	3.83	476	305	74	2231	2272	750	1141	27	11	5	15	559	62	0	.1
3 yrs.	25	15	.625	3.71	73	49	12	366.2	392	131	121	4	3	2	3	0	0	0	
LEAGUE CHAMPIONSHIP SERIES																			
1972 CIN N	0	0	–	3.86	1	1	0	4.2	5	2	4	0	0	0	0	2	0	0	.0
1973	0	1	.000	4.50	2	2	0	12	9	4	9	0	0	0	0	3	0	0	.0
2 yrs.	0	1	.000	4.32	3	3	0	16.2	14	6	13	0	0	0	0	5	0	0	.0
WORLD SERIES																			
1972 CIN N	1	0	1.000	0.00	3	2	0	13.2	6	4	11	0	0	0	1	5	0	0	.0
1975	0	0	–	1.00	3	1	0	9	8	5	7	0	0	0	0	2	0	0	.0
1976	1	0	1.000	0.00	1	0	0	2.2	0	0	1	0	1	0	0	0	0	0	
3 yrs.	2	0	1.000	0.36	7	3	0	25.1	14	9	19	0	1	0	1	7	0	0	.0
			1st	1st															

Haskell Billings

BILLINGS, HASKELL CLARK
B. Sept. 27, 1907, New York, N. Y.   D. Dec. 26, 1983, Greenbrae, Calif.   BR TR 5'11" 180 lb

	W	L	PCT	ERA	G	GS	CG	IP	H	BB	SO	ShO	W	L	SV	AB	H	HR	B
1927 DET A	5	4	.556	4.84	10	9	5	67	64	39	18	0	0	1	0	27	7	0	.2
1928	5	10	.333	5.12	21	16	3	110.2	118	59	48	1	0	0	0	35	10	0	.2
1929	0	1	.000	5.12	8	0	0	19.1	27	9	1	0	0	1	0	6	0	0	.0
3 yrs.	10	15	.400	5.03	39	25	8	197	209	107	67	1	0	2	0	68	17	0	.2
3 yrs.	10	15	.400	5.03	39	25	8	197	209	107	67	1	0	2	0	68	17	0	.2

Babe Birrer

BIRRER, WERNER JOSEPH
B. July 4, 1928, Buffalo, N. Y.   BR TR 6' 195 lb

	W	L	PCT	ERA	G	GS	CG	IP	H	BB	SO	ShO	W	L	SV	AB	H	HR	B
1955 DET A	4	3	.571	4.15	36	3	1	80.1	77	29	28	0	3	1	3	19	3	2	.1
1956 BAL A	0	0	–	6.75	4	0	0	5.1	9	1	1	0	0	0	0	1	0	0	.0
1958 LA N	0	0	–	4.50	16	0	0	34	43	7	16	0	0	0	1	7	4	0	.5
3 yrs.	4	3	.571	4.36	56	3	1	119.2	129	37	45	0	3	1	4	27	7	2	.2
1 yr.	4	3	.571	4.15	36	3	1	80.1	77	29	28	0	3	1	3	19	3	2	.1

Bill Black

BLACK, WILLIAM CARROLL (Bud)
B. July 9, 1932, St. Louis, Mo.   BR TR 6'3" 197 lb

	W	L	PCT	ERA	G	GS	CG	IP	H	BB	SO	ShO	W	L	SV	AB	H	HR	B
1952 DET A	0	1	.000	10.57	2	2	0	7.2	14	5	0	0	0	0	0	3	0	0	.0
1955	1	1	.500	1.26	3	2	1	14.1	12	8	7	1	0	1	0	4	1	0	.2
1956	1	1	.500	3.60	5	1	0	10	10	5	7	0	1	0	0	2	0	0	.0
3 yrs.	2	3	.400	4.22	10	5	1	32	36	18	14	1	1	1	0	9	1	0	.1
3 yrs.	2	3	.400	4.22	10	5	1	32	36	18	14	1	1	1	0	9	1	0	.1

George Boehler

BOEHLER, GEORGE HENRY
B. Jan. 2, 1892, Lawrenceburg, Ind.   D. June 23, 1958, Lawrenceburg, Ind.   BR TR 6'2" 180 lb

	W	L	PCT	ERA	G	GS	CG	IP	H	BB	SO	ShO	W	L	SV	AB	H	HR	B
1912 DET A	0	2	.000	6.68	4	4	2	31	49	14	13	0	0	0	0	10	1	0	.1
1913	0	1	.000	6.75	1	1	1	8	11	6	2	0	0	0	0	3	1	0	.3
1914	2	3	.400	3.57	18	6	2	63	54	48	37	0	0	1	0	17	3	0	.1
1915	1	1	.500	1.80	8	0	0	15	19	4	7	0	1	1	0	4	3	0	.7
1916	1	1	.500	4.73	5	2	1	13.1	12	9	8	0	0	0	0	3	0	0	.0
1920 STL A	0	1	.000	7.71	3	1	0	7	10	4	2	0	0	0	0	1	0	0	.0
1921	0	0	–	0.00	1	0	0	1	1	0	0	0	0	0	0	0	0	0	
1923 PIT N	1	3	.250	6.04	10	3	1	28.1	33	26	12	0	0	1	0	10	3	0	.3

	W	L	PCT	ERA	G	GS	CG	IP	H	BB	SO	ShO	Relief Pitching W	L	SV	BATTING AB	H	HR	BA

George Boehler continued

	W	L	PCT	ERA	G	GS	CG	IP	H	BB	SO	ShO	W	L	SV	AB	H	HR	BA
26 BKN N	1	0	1.000	4.41	10	1	0	34.2	42	23	10	0	0	0	0	12	3	0	.250
9 yrs.	6	12	.333	4.74	60	18	7	201.1	231	134	91	0	1	3	0	60	14	0	.233
5 yrs.	4	8	.333	4.42	36	13	6	130.1	145	81	67	0	1	2	0	37	8	0	.216

John Bogart

BOGART, JOHN RENZIE (Big John)   BR TR 6'2"   195 lbs.
B. Sept. 21, 1900, Bloomsburg, Pa.

	W	L	PCT	ERA	G	GS	CG	IP	H	BB	SO	ShO	W	L	SV	AB	H	HR	BA
20 DET A	2	1	.667	3.04	4	3	0	23.2	16	18	5	0	1	0	0	8	2	0	.250

Bernie Boland

BOLAND, BERNARD ANTHONY   BR TR 5'8½"   168 lbs.
B. Jan. 21, 1892, Rochester, N.Y.   D. Sept. 12, 1973, Detroit, Mich.

	W	L	PCT	ERA	G	GS	CG	IP	H	BB	SO	ShO	W	L	SV	AB	H	HR	BA
15 DET A	13	7	.650	3.11	45	18	8	202.2	167	75	72	1	4	2	2	63	11	0	.175
6	10	3	.769	3.94	46	9	5	130.1	111	73	59	1	5	0	3	32	8	0	.250
7	16	11	.593	2.68	43	28	13	238	192	95	89	3	2	2	6	72	4	0	.056
8	14	10	.583	2.65	29	25	14	204	176	67	63	4	1	1	0	69	12	0	.174
9	14	16	.467	3.04	35	30	18	242.2	222	80	71	1	1	1	1	74	8	0	.108
20	0	2	.000	7.79	4	3	1	17.1	23	14	4	0	0	0	0	7	1	0	.143
1 STL A	1	4	.200	8.89	8	6	0	28.1	34	28	6	0	0	0	0	10	1	0	.100
7 yrs.	68	53	.562	3.24	210	119	59	1063.1	925	432	364	10	13	6	12	327	45	0	.138
6 yrs.	67	49	.578	3.09	202	113	59	1035	891	404	358	10	13	6	12	317	44	0	.139

Danny Boone

BOONE, JAMES ALBERT   BR TR 6'2"   190 lbs.
Brother of Ike Boone.
B. Jan. 19, 1895, Samantha, Ala.   D. May 11, 1968, Tuscaloosa, Ala.

	W	L	PCT	ERA	G	GS	CG	IP	H	BB	SO	ShO	W	L	SV	AB	H	HR	BA
9 PHI A	0	1	.000	6.75	3	2	0	14.2	24	10	1	0	0	0	0	4	0	0	.000
1 DET A	0	0	–	0.00	1	0	0	2	1	2	0	0	0	0	1	1	0	0	.000
2 CLE A	4	6	.400	4.06	11	10	4	75.1	87	19	9	2	0	1	0	26	5	0	.192
3	4	6	.400	6.01	27	4	2	70.1	93	31	15	0	3	3	0	19	4	0	.211
4 yrs.	8	13	.381	5.10	42	16	6	162.1	205	62	25	2	3	4	1	50	9	0	.180
1 yr.	0	0	–	0.00	1	0	0	2	1	2	0	0	0	0	0	1	0	0	.000

Hank Borowy

BOROWY, HENRY LUDWIG   BR TR 6'   175 lbs.
B. May 12, 1916, Bloomfield, N.J.

	W	L	PCT	ERA	G	GS	CG	IP	H	BB	SO	ShO	W	L	SV	AB	H	HR	BA
2 NY A	15	4	.789	2.52	25	21	13	178.1	157	66	85	4	1	0	1	70	11	0	.157
3	14	9	.609	2.82	29	27	14	217.1	195	72	113	3	1	0	0	74	15	0	.203
4	17	12	.586	2.64	35	30	19	252.2	224	88	107	3	0	0	2	90	12	0	.133
5 2 teams					NY	A (18G 10-5)		CHI	N (15G 11-2)										
total	21	7	.750	2.65	33	32	18	254.2	212	105	82	2	0	0	1	91	18	0	.198
6 CHI N	12	10	.545	3.76	32	28	8	201	220	61	95	1	1	0	0	72	13	0	.181
7	8	12	.400	4.38	40	25	7	183	190	63	75	1	1	1	2	56	7	0	.125
8	5	10	.333	4.89	39	17	2	127	156	49	50	1	1	0	1	36	8	0	.222
9 PHI N	12	12	.500	4.19	28	28	12	193.1	188	63	43	2	0	0	0	61	13	0	.213
0 3 teams			PHI	N (3G 0-0)	PIT	N (11G 1-3)		DET	A (13G 1-1)										
total	2	4	.333	4.83	27	5	1	63.1	60	29	24	0	2	1	0	13	2	0	.154
1 DET A	2	2	.500	6.95	26	1	0	45.1	58	27	16	0	2	2	0	8	0	0	.000
0 yrs.	108	82	.568	3.50	314	214	94	1716	1660	623	690	17	9	4	7	571	99	0	.173
2 yrs.	3	3	.500	5.42	39	3	1	78	81	43	28	0	3	2	0	15	1	0	.067

WORLD SERIES

	W	L	PCT	ERA	G	GS	CG	IP	H	BB	SO	ShO	W	L	SV	AB	H	HR	BA
2 NY A	0	0	–	18.00	1	1	0	3	6	3	1	0	0	0	0	1	0	0	.000
3	1	0	1.000	2.25	1	1	0	8	6	3	4	0	0	0	0	2	1	0	.500
5 CHI N	2	2	.500	4.00	4	3	1	18	21	6	8	1	1	0	0	5	1	0	.200
3 yrs.	3	2	.600	4.97	6	5	1	29	33	12	13	1	1	0	0	8	2	0	.250

Dave Boswell

BOSWELL, DAVID WILSON   BR TR 6'3"   185 lbs.
B. Jan. 20, 1945, Baltimore, Md.

	W	L	PCT	ERA	G	GS	CG	IP	H	BB	SO	ShO	W	L	SV	AB	H	HR	BA
4 MIN A	2	0	1.000	4.24	4	4	0	23.1	21	12	25	0	0	0	0	9	2	0	.222
5	6	5	.545	3.40	27	12	1	106	77	46	85	0	1	2	0	38	12	0	.316
6	12	5	.706	3.14	28	21	8	169.1	120	65	173	1	0	0	0	63	9	0	.143
7	14	12	.538	3.27	37	32	11	222.2	162	107	204	3	0	0	0	73	16	1	.219
8	10	13	.435	3.32	34	28	7	190	148	87	143	2	0	0	0	60	14	1	.233
9	20	12	.625	3.23	39	38	10	256.1	215	99	190	0	0	0	0	94	16	2	.170
0	3	7	.300	6.39	18	15	0	69	80	44	45	0	0	0	0	25	4	0	.160
1 2 teams			DET	A (3G 0-0)	BAL	A (15G 1-2)													
total	1	2	.333	4.66	18	1	0	29	35	21	17	0	1	1	0	5	1	0	.200
3 yrs.	68	56	.548	3.52	205	151	37	1065.2	858	481	882	6	2	3	0	367	74	4	.202
1 yr.	0	0	–	6.23	3	0	0	4.1	3	6	3	0	0	0	0	0	0	0	–

LEAGUE CHAMPIONSHIP SERIES

	W	L	PCT	ERA	G	GS	CG	IP	H	BB	SO	ShO	W	L	SV	AB	H	HR	BA
9 MIN A	0	1	.000	0.84	1	1	0	10.2	7	7	4	0	0	0	0	4	0	0	.000

WORLD SERIES

	W	L	PCT	ERA	G	GS	CG	IP	H	BB	SO	ShO	W	L	SV	AB	H	HR	BA
5 MIN A	0	0	–	3.38	1	0	0	2.2	3	2	3	0	0	0	0	0	0	0	–

Jim Brady

BRADY, JAMES JOSEPH (Diamond Jim)   BL TL 6'2"   185 lbs.
B. Mar. 2, 1936, Jersey City, N.J.

	W	L	PCT	ERA	G	GS	CG	IP	H	BB	SO	ShO	W	L	SV	AB	H	HR	BA
6 DET A	0	0	–	28.42	6	0	0	6.1	15	11	3	0	0	0	0	0	0	0	–

Ralph Branca

BRANCA, RALPH THEODORE JOSEPH (Hawk)   BR TR 6'3"   220 lbs.
B. Jan. 6, 1926, Mt. Vernon, N.Y.

	W	L	PCT	ERA	G	GS	CG	IP	H	BB	SO	ShO	W	L	SV	AB	H	HR	BA
4 BKN N	0	2	.000	7.05	21	1	0	44.2	46	32	16	0	0	1	1	6	0	0	.000
5	5	6	.455	3.04	16	15	7	109.2	73	79	69	0	0	0	1	40	4	0	.100
6	3	1	.750	3.88	24	10	2	67.1	62	41	42	2	0	1	3	18	2	0	.111
7	21	12	.636	2.67	43	36	15	280	251	98	148	4	3	1	1	97	12	0	.124
8	14	9	.609	3.51	36	28	11	215.2	189	80	122	1	1	0	1	74	15	0	.203
9	13	5	.722	4.39	34	27	9	186.2	181	91	109	2	0	1	1	62	5	0	.081
0	7	9	.438	4.69	43	15	5	142	152	55	100	0	2	4	7	34	4	2	.118
1	13	12	.520	3.26	42	27	13	204	180	85	118	1	1	2	3	63	11	0	.175

	W	L	PCT	ERA	G	GS	CG	IP	H	BB	SO	ShO	Relief Pitching W	L	SV	BATTING AB	H	HR	B

Ralph Branca continued

1952	4	2	.667	3.84	16	7	2	61	52	21	26	0	1	0	0	19	3	0	.1
1953 2 teams			BKN	N (7G 0–0)		DET	A	(17G 4–7)											
" total	4	7	.364	4.70	24	14	7	113	113	36	55	0	0	0	1	34	4	0	.11
1954 2 teams			DET	A (17G 3–3)		NY	A	(5G 1–0)											
" total	4	3	.571	5.12	22	8	0	58	72	43	22	0	2	3	0	17	6	0	.3
1956 BKN N	0	0	–	0.00	1	0	0	2	1	2	2	0	0	0	0	0	0	0	
12 yrs.	88	68	.564	3.79	322	188	71	1484	1372	663	829	12	10	13	19	464	66	2	.1
2 yrs.	7	10	.412	4.64	34	19	7	147.1	161	61	65	0	2	3	1	47	8	0	.17

WORLD SERIES

1947 BKN N	1	1	.500	8.64	3	1	0	8.1	12	5	8	0	1	0	0	4	0	0	.0
1949	0	1	.000	4.15	1	1	0	8.2	4	4	6	0	0	0	0	3	0	0	.0
2 yrs.	1	2	.333	6.35	4	2	0	17	16	9	14	0	1	0	0	7	0	0	

Tommy Bridges

BRIDGES, THOMAS JEFFERSON DAVIS   BR TR 5'10½" 155 lb
B. Dec. 28, 1906, Gordonsville, Tenn.   D. Apr. 19, 1968, Nashville, Tenn.

1930 DET A	3	2	.600	4.06	8	5	2	37.2	28	23	17	0	0	0	0	10	3	0	.3
1931	8	16	.333	4.99	35	23	15	173	182	108	105	2	1	2	0	54	8	0	.14
1932	14	12	.538	3.36	34	26	10	201	174	119	108	4	2	2	1	67	11	0	.16
1933	14	12	.538	3.09	33	28	17	233	192	110	120	2	1	0	2	78	16	0	.20
1934	22	11	.667	3.67	36	35	23	275	249	104	151	3	0	0	1	98	12	0	.12
1935	21	10	.677	3.51	36	34	23	274.1	277	113	163	4	0	1	1	109	26	0	.23
1936	23	11	.676	3.60	39	38	26	294.2	289	115	175	5	0	0	0	118	25	0	.2
1937	15	12	.556	4.07	34	31	18	245.1	267	91	138	3	1	0	0	96	23	0	.2
1938	13	9	.591	4.59	25	20	13	151	171	58	101	0	1	3	1	54	7	0	.13
1939	17	7	.708	3.50	29	26	16	198	186	61	129	2	0	0	2	71	14	0	.19
1940	12	9	.571	3.37	29	28	12	197.2	171	88	133	2	1	0	0	68	12	0	.17
1941	9	12	.429	3.41	25	22	10	147.2	128	70	90	1	1	0	0	47	4	0	.08
1942	9	7	.563	2.74	23	22	11	174	164	61	97	2	0	0	1	63	6	0	.09
1943	12	7	.632	2.39	25	22	11	191.2	159	61	124	3	0	1	0	64	14	0	.21
1945	1	0	1.000	3.27	4	1	0	11	14	2	6	0	0	0	0	3	0	0	.00
1946	1	1	.500	5.91	9	1	0	21.1	24	18	17	0	0	1	1	3	0	0	.00
16 yrs.	194	138	.584	3.57	424	362	207	2826.1	2675	1192	1674	33	8	10	10	1003	181	0	.18
16 yrs.	194	138	.584	3.57	424	362	207	2826.1	2675	1192	1674	33	8	10	10	1003	181	0	.18
	5th	6th			7th		5th	5th			2nd	3rd	3rd						

WORLD SERIES

1934 DET A	1	1	.500	3.63	3	2	1	17.1	21	1	12	0	0	0	0	7	1	0	.14
1935	2	0	1.000	2.50	2	2	2	18	18	4	9	0	0	0	0	8	1	0	.12
1940	1	0	1.000	3.00	1	1	1	9	10	1	5	0	0	0	0	3	0	0	.00
1945	0	0	–	16.20	1	0	0	1.2	3	3	1	0	0	0	0	0	0	0	
4 yrs.	4	1	.800	3.52	7	5	4	46	52	9	27	0	0	0	0	18	2	0	.11

Ed Brookens

BROOKENS, EDWARD DWAIN (Ike)   BR TR 6'5" 170 lbs
B. Nov. 3, 1949, Chambersburg, Pa.

| 1975 DET A | 0 | 0 | – | 5.40 | 3 | 0 | 0 | 10 | 11 | 5 | 8 | 0 | 0 | 0 | 0 | 0 | 0 | 0 | 0 |

Frank Browning

BROWNING, FRANK   BR TR 5'5" 145 lbs
B. Oct. 29, 1882, Falmouth, Ky.   D. May 19, 1948, San Antonio, Tex.

| 1910 DET A | 2 | 2 | .500 | 3.00 | 11 | 6 | 2 | 42 | 51 | 10 | 16 | 0 | 0 | 1 | 3 | 14 | 0 | 0 | .00 |

Bob Bruce

BRUCE, ROBERT JAMES   BR TR 6'3" 200 lbs
B. May 16, 1933, Detroit, Mich.

1959 DET A	0	1	.000	9.00	2	1	0	2	2	3	1	0	0	0	0	0	0	0	
1960	4	7	.364	3.74	34	15	1	130	127	56	76	0	0	2	0	39	7	0	.17
1961	1	2	.333	4.43	14	6	0	44.2	57	24	25	0	0	1	0	9	1	0	.11
1962 HOU N	10	9	.526	4.06	32	27	6	175	164	82	135	0	1	0	0	55	11	0	.20
1963	5	9	.357	3.59	30	25	1	170.1	162	60	123	1	0	0	0	55	7	0	.12
1964	15	9	.625	2.76	35	29	9	202.1	191	33	135	4	1	0	0	63	12	0	.19
1965	9	18	.333	3.72	35	34	7	229.2	241	38	145	1	0	0	0	74	9	0	.12
1966	3	13	.188	5.34	25	23	1	129.2	160	29	71	0	0	1	0	39	3	0	.07
1967 ATL N	2	3	.400	4.89	12	7	1	38.2	42	15	22	0	0	1	1	12	2	0	.16
9 yrs.	49	71	.408	3.85	219	167	26	1122.1	1146	340	733	6	2	5	1	346	52	0	.15
3 yrs.	5	10	.333	3.97	50	22	1	176.2	186	83	102	0	0	3	0	48	8	0	.16

Andy Bruckmiller

BRUCKMILLER, ANDREW   BR TR 5'11" 175 lbs
B. Jan. 1, 1882, Pittsburgh, Pa.   D. Jan. 12, 1970, McKeesport, Pa.

| 1905 DET A | 0 | 0 | – | 27.00 | 1 | 0 | 0 | 4 | 4 | 1 | 1 | 0 | 0 | 0 | 0 | 1 | 0 | 0 | .00 |

Jim Bunning

BUNNING, JAMES PAUL DAVID   BR TR 6'3" 190 lbs
B. Oct. 23, 1931, Southgate, Ky.

1955 DET A	3	5	.375	6.35	15	8	0	51	59	32	37	0	2	0	1	15	3	0	.20
1956	5	1	.833	3.71	15	3	0	53.1	55	28	34	0	4	0	1	18	6	0	.33
1957	20	8	.714	2.69	45	30	14	267.1	214	72	182	1	2	1	1	94	20	1	.21
1958	14	12	.538	3.52	35	34	10	219.2	188	79	177	3	0	0	0	75	14	0	.18
1959	17	13	.567	3.89	40	35	14	249.2	220	75	201	1	0	1	1	89	17	1	.19
1960	11	14	.440	2.79	36	34	10	252	217	64	201	3	0	0	0	81	13	0	.16
1961	17	11	.607	3.19	38	37	12	268	232	71	194	4	0	0	1	100	13	0	.13
1962	19	10	.655	3.59	41	35	12	258	262	74	184	2	0	0	6	95	23	1	.24
1963	12	13	.480	3.88	39	35	6	248.1	245	69	196	2	0	0	1	84	13	0	.15
1964 PHI N	19	8	.704	2.63	41	39	13	284.1	248	46	219	5	0	0	2	99	12	0	.12
1965	19	9	.679	2.60	39	39	15	291	253	62	268	7	0	0	0	103	22	1	.21
1966	19	14	.576	2.41	43	41	16	314	260	55	252	5	1	0	1	106	19	0	.17
1967	17	15	.531	2.29	40	40	16	302.1	241	73	253	6	0	0	0	104	17	2	.16
1968 PIT N	4	14	.222	3.88	27	26	3	160	168	48	95	1	0	0	0	51	5	0	.09

	W	L	PCT	ERA	G	GS	CG	IP	H	BB	SO	ShO	Relief Pitching W	L	SV	BATTING AB	H	HR	BA

im Bunning continued

		W	L	PCT	ERA	G	GS	CG	IP	H	BB	SO	ShO	W	L	SV	AB	H	HR	BA
'69 2 teams	PIT N (25G 10–9)					LA	N	(9G 3–1)												
" total		13	10	.565	3.69	34	34	5	212.1	212	59	157	0	0	0	0	65	4	0	.062
'70 PHI N		10	15	.400	4.11	34	33	4	219	233	56	147	0	0	0	0	71	9	0	.127
'71 "		5	12	.294	5.48	29	16	1	110	126	37	58	0	0	2	1	25	3	1	.120
17 yrs.		224	184	.549	3.27	591	519	151	3760.1	3433	1000	2855 10th	40	9	4	16	1275	213	7	.167
9 yrs.		118	87	.576 10th	3.45	304	251	78	1867.1 10th	1692	564	1406 4th	16	8	2	12	651	122	3	.187

BURNS, WILLIAM THOMAS (Sleepy Bill)   BB TL 6'2"   195 lbs.
B. Jan. 29, 1880, San Saba, Tex.   D. June 6, 1953, Ramona, Calif.

ill Burns

		W	L	PCT	ERA	G	GS	CG	IP	H	BB	SO	ShO	W	L	SV	AB	H	HR	BA
'08 WAS A		6	11	.353	1.69	23	19	11	165	135	18	55	2	0	1	0	54	8	0	.148
'09 2 teams	WAS A (6G 1–1)					CHI	A	(22G 7–13)												
" total		8	14	.364	1.86	28	23	9	203.2	194	42	65	3	1	1	0	69	12	0	.174
'10 2 teams	CHI A (1G 0–0)					CIN	N	(31G 8–13)												
" total		8	13	.381	3.47	32	21	13	179	183	50	57	2	0	3	0	61	16	0	.262
'11 2 teams	CIN N (6G 1–0)					PHI	N	(21G 6–10)												
" total		7	10	.412	3.38	27	17	8	138.2	149	29	52	3	1	2	1	47	9	0	.191
'12 DET A		1	4	.200	5.35	6	5	2	38.2	52	9	6	0	0	0	0	13	3	0	.231
5 yrs.		30	52	.366	2.69	116	85	43	725	713	148	235	10	2	7	1	244	48	0	.197
1 yr.		1	4	.200	5.35	6	5	2	38.2	52	9	6	0	0	0	0	13	3	0	.231

BURNSIDE, PETER WILLITS   BR TL 6'2"   180 lbs.
B. July 2, 1930, Evanston, Ill.

ete Burnside

	W	L	PCT	ERA	G	GS	CG	IP	H	BB	SO	ShO	W	L	SV	AB	H	HR	BA
'55 NY N	1	0	1.000	2.84	2	2	1	12.2	10	9	2	0	0	0	0	5	1	0	.200
'57 "	1	4	.200	8.80	10	9	1	30.2	47	13	18	1	0	1	0	9	0	0	.000
'58 SF N	0	0	–	6.75	6	1	0	10.2	20	5	4	0	0	0	0	0	0	0	–
'59 DET A	1	3	.250	3.77	30	0	0	62	55	25	49	0	1	3	1	10	0	0	.000
'60 "	7	7	.500	4.28	31	15	2	113.2	122	50	71	0	3	1	2	27	4	0	.148
'61 WAS A	4	9	.308	4.53	33	16	4	113.1	106	51	56	2	0	0	2	34	2	0	.059
'62 "	5	11	.313	4.45	40	20	6	149.2	152	51	74	0	0	1	2	35	2	0	.057
'63 2 teams	BAL A (6G 0–1)							WAS A (38G 0–1)											
" total	0	2	.000	6.03	44	1	0	74.2	95	26	29	0	0	1	0	12	1	0	.083
8 yrs.	19	36	.345	4.81	196	64	14	567.1	607	230	303	3	4	7	7	132	10	0	.076
2 yrs.	8	10	.444	4.10	61	15	2	175.2	177	75	120	0	4	4	3	37	4	0	.108

BURNSIDE, SHELDON JOHN   BR TL 6'5"   200 lbs.
B. Dec. 22, 1954, South Bend, Ind.

heldon Burnside

	W	L	PCT	ERA	G	GS	CG	IP	H	BB	SO	ShO	W	L	SV	AB	H	HR	BA
'78 DET A	0	0	–	9.00	2	0	0	4	4	2	3	0	0	0	0	0	0	0	–
'79 "	1	1	.500	6.43	10	0	0	21	28	8	13	0	1	1	0	0	0	0	–
'80 CIN N	1	0	1.000	1.80	7	0	0	5	6	1	2	0	1	0	0	1	0	0	.000
3 yrs.	2	1	.667	6.00	19	0	0	30	38	11	18	0	2	1	0	1	0	0	.000
2 yrs.	1	1	.500	6.84	12	0	0	25	32	10	16	0	1	1	0	0	0	0	–

BYRD, HARRY GLADWIN   BR TR 6'1"   188 lbs.
B. Feb. 3, 1925, Darlington, S. C.   BB 1955

arry Byrd

		W	L	PCT	ERA	G	GS	CG	IP	H	BB	SO	ShO	W	L	SV	AB	H	HR	BA
'50 PHI A		0	0	–	16.88	6	0	0	10.2	25	9	2	0	0	0	0	2	0	0	.000
'52 "		15	15	.500	3.31	37	28	15	228.1	244	98	116	3	0	2	2	75	10	0	.133
'53 "		11	20	.355	5.51	40	37	11	236.2	279	115	122	2	0	1	0	81	18	0	.222
'54 NY A		9	7	.563	2.99	25	21	5	132.1	131	43	52	1	0	0	0	46	9	0	.196
'55 2 teams	BAL A (14G 3–2)					CHI	A	(25G 4–6)												
" total		7	8	.467	4.61	39	20	2	156.1	149	58	69	2	1	1	2	49	5	0	.102
'56 CHI A		0	1	.000	10.38	3	1	0	4.1	9	4	0	0	0	0	0	1	0	0	.000
'57 DET A		4	3	.571	3.36	37	1	0	59	53	28	20	0	4	3	5	8	0	0	.000
7 yrs.		46	54	.460	4.35	187	108	33	827.2	890	355	381	8	5	7	9	262	42	0	.160
1 yr.		4	3	.571	3.36	37	1	0	59	53	28	20	0	4	3	5	8	0	0	.000

CAIN, ROBERT MAX (Sugar)   BL TL 6'   165 lbs.
B. Oct. 16, 1924, Longford, Kans.

ob Cain

		W	L	PCT	ERA	G	GS	CG	IP	H	BB	SO	ShO	W	L	SV	AB	H	HR	BA
'49 CHI A		0	0	–	2.45	6	0	0	11	7	5	5	0	0	0	1	3	0	0	.000
'50 "		9	12	.429	3.93	34	23	11	171.2	153	109	77	1	1	1	2	61	12	0	.197
'51 2 teams	CHI A (4G 1–2)					DET	A	(35G 11–10)												
" total		12	12	.500	4.56	39	26	7	175.2	160	95	61	1	2	2	2	62	16	0	.258
'52 STL A		12	10	.545	4.13	29	27	8	170	169	62	70	1	0	2	2	58	8	0	.138
'53 "		4	10	.286	6.23	32	13	1	99.2	129	45	36	0	0	4	1	30	6	0	.200
'54 CHI A		0	0	–	0.00	0	0	0	0	0	0	0	0	0	0	0	0	0	0	–
6 yrs.		37	44	.457	4.50	140	89	27	628	618	316	249	3	3	7	8	214	42	0	.196
1 yr.		11	10	.524	4.70	35	22	6	149.1	135	82	58	1	2	2	2	53	13	0	.245

CAIN, LESLIE   BL TL 6'1"   200 lbs.
B. Jan. 13, 1948, San Luis Obispo, Calif.

es Cain

	W	L	PCT	ERA	G	GS	CG	IP	H	BB	SO	ShO	W	L	SV	AB	H	HR	BA
'68 DET A	1	0	1.000	3.00	8	4	0	24	25	20	13	0	0	0	0	7	1	0	.143
'70 "	12	7	.632	3.83	29	29	5	181	167	98	156	0	0	0	0	68	11	1	.162
'71 "	10	9	.526	4.34	26	26	3	145	121	91	118	1	0	0	0	55	8	1	.145
'72 "	0	3	.000	3.75	5	5	0	24	18	16	16	0	0	0	0	7	1	0	.143
4 yrs.	23	19	.548	3.97	68	64	8	374	331	225	303	1	0	0	0	137	21	2	.153
4 yrs.	23	19	.548	3.97	68	64	8	374	331	225	303	1	0	0	0	137	21	2	.153

CALVERT, PAUL LEO EMILE   BR TR 6'   175 lbs.
B. Oct. 6, 1917, Montreal, Que., Canada

aul Calvert

	W	L	PCT	ERA	G	GS	CG	IP	H	BB	SO	ShO	W	L	SV	AB	H	HR	BA
'42 CLE A	0	0	–	0.00	1	0	0	2	0	2	2	0	0	0	0	0	0	0	–
'43 "	0	0	–	4.32	5	0	0	8.1	6	6	2	0	0	0	0	1	0	0	.000
'44 "	1	3	.250	4.56	35	4	0	77	89	38	31	0	0	2	0	15	4	0	.267
'45 "	0	0	–	13.50	1	0	0	1.1	3	1	1	0	0	0	0	0	0	0	–
'49 WAS A	6	17	.261	5.43	34	23	5	160.2	175	86	52	0	1	1	1	51	7	0	.137
'50 DET A	2	2	.500	6.31	32	0	0	51.1	71	25	14	0	2	2	4	7	0	0	.000

	W	L	PCT	ERA	G	GS	CG	IP	H	BB	SO	ShO	Relief Pitching W	L	SV	BATTING AB	H	HR	BA

Paul Calvert continued

	W	L	PCT	ERA	G	GS	CG	IP	H	BB	SO	ShO	W	L	SV	AB	H	HR	BA
1951	0	0	—	0.00	1	0	0	1	1	0	0	0	0	0	0	0	0	0	—
7 yrs.	9	22	.290	5.31	109	27	5	301.2	345	158	102	0	3	6	5	74	11	0	.149
2 yrs.	2	2	.500	6.19	33	0	0	52.1	72	25	14	0	2	2	4	7	0	0	.000

Guy Cantrell

CANTRELL, DEWEY GUY (Gunner)
B. Apr. 9, 1904, Clarita, Okla.   D. Jan. 31, 1961, McAlester, Okla.   BR TR 6'   190 lbs.

	W	L	PCT	ERA	G	GS	CG	IP	H	BB	SO	ShO	W	L	SV	AB	H	HR	BA
1925 BKN N	1	0	1.000	3.00	14	3	1	36	42	14	13	0	0	0	0	9	0	0	.000
1927 2 teams		BKN	N (6G 0-0)		PHI	A	(2G 0-2)												
" total	0	2	.000	4.18	8	2	2	28	35	13	12	0	0	0	0	9	2	0	.222
1930 DET A	1	5	.167	5.66	16	2	1	35	38	20	20	0	1	3	0	9	0	0	.000
3 yrs.	2	7	.222	4.27	38	7	4	99	115	47	45	0	1	3	0	27	2	0	.074
1 yr.	1	5	.167	5.66	16	2	1	35	38	20	20	0	1	3	0	9	0	0	.000

George Cappuzzello

CAPPUZZELLO, GEORGE ANGELO
B. Jan. 15, 1954, Youngstown, Ohio   BR TL 6'   175 lbs.

	W	L	PCT	ERA	G	GS	CG	IP	H	BB	SO	ShO	W	L	SV	AB	H	HR	BA
1981 DET A	1	1	.500	3.44	18	3	0	34	28	18	19	0	1	0	1	0	0	0	—
1982 HOU N	0	1	.000	2.79	17	0	0	19.1	16	7	13	0	0	1	0	1	0	0	.000
2 yrs.	1	2	.333	3.21	35	3	0	53.1	44	25	32	0	1	1	1	1	0	0	.000
1 yr.	1	1	.500	3.44	18	3	0	34	28	18	19	0	1	0	1	0	0	0	—

Ownie Carroll

CARROLL, OWEN THOMAS
B. Nov. 11, 1902, Kearny, N. J.   D. June 18, 1975, Orange, N. J.   BR TR 5'10½" 165 lbs.

	W	L	PCT	ERA	G	GS	CG	IP	H	BB	SO	ShO	W	L	SV	AB	H	HR	BA
1925 DET A	3	1	.750	3.76	10	4	1	40.2	46	28	12	0	1	0	0	16	6	0	.375
1927	10	6	.625	3.98	31	15	8	172	186	73	41	0	3	0	0	69	12	0	.174
1928	16	12	.571	3.27	34	28	19	231	219	87	51	2	2	2	2	98	19	0	.194
1929	9	17	.346	4.63	34	26	12	202	249	86	54	0	2	3	1	74	17	0	.230
1930 3 teams		DET	A (6G 0-5)		NY	A	(10G 0-1)		CIN	N	(3G 0-1)								
" total	0	7	.000	7.39	19	6	1	67	96	30	12	0	0	3	0	22	4	0	.182
1931 CIN N	3	9	.250	5.53	29	12	4	107.1	135	51	24	0	1	2	0	34	7	0	.206
1932	10	19	.345	4.50	32	26	15	210	245	44	55	0	1	0	1	77	16	0	.208
1933 BKN N	13	15	.464	3.78	33	31	11	226.1	248	54	45	0	0	0	0	74	11	0	.149
1934	1	3	.250	6.42	26	5	0	74.1	108	33	17	0	1	0	1	25	6	0	.240
9 yrs.	65	89	.422	4.43	248	153	71	1330.2	1532	486	311	2	11	10	5	489	98	0	.200
5 yrs.	38	41	.481	4.12	115	76	40	666	730	283	162	2	8	7	3	264	55	0	.208

Jerry Casale

CASALE, JERRY JOSEPH
B. Sept. 27, 1933, Brooklyn, N. Y.   BR TR 6'2"   200 lbs.

	W	L	PCT	ERA	G	GS	CG	IP	H	BB	SO	ShO	W	L	SV	AB	H	HR	BA
1958 BOS A	0	0	—	0.00	2	0	0	3	1	2	3	0	0	0	0	0	0	0	—
1959	13	8	.619	4.31	31	26	9	179.2	162	89	93	3	1	0	0	59	10	3	.169
1960	2	9	.182	6.17	29	14	1	96.1	113	67	54	0	0	0	0	33	9	0	.273
1961 2 teams		LA	A (13G 1-5)		DET	A	(3G 0-0)												
" total	1	5	.167	6.26	16	8	0	54.2	67	28	41	0	0	0	1	16	6	1	.375
1962 DET A	1	2	.333	4.66	18	1	0	36.2	33	18	16	0	1	2	0	8	0	0	.000
5 yrs.	17	24	.415	5.08	96	49	10	370.1	376	204	207	3	2	2	1	116	25	4	.216
2 yrs.	1	2	.333	4.81	21	2	0	48.2	48	21	22	0	1	2	0	11	0	0	.000

George Caster

CASTER, GEORGE JASPER
B. Aug. 4, 1907, Colton, Calif.   D. Dec. 18, 1955, Lakewood, Calif.   BR TR 6'1½" 180 lbs.

	W	L	PCT	ERA	G	GS	CG	IP	H	BB	SO	ShO	W	L	SV	AB	H	HR	BA
1934 PHI A	3	2	.600	3.41	5	3	2	37	32	14	15	0	1	1	0	15	4	0	.267
1935	1	4	.200	6.25	25	1	0	63.1	86	37	24	0	1	3	1	22	5	0	.227
1937	12	19	.387	4.43	34	33	19	231.2	227	107	100	3	0	0	0	90	19	0	.211
1938	16	20	.444	4.37	40	40	20	280.1	310	117	112	2	0	0	1	101	20	0	.198
1939	9	9	.500	4.90	28	17	7	136	144	45	59	1	2	0	0	43	9	0	.209
1940	4	19	.174	6.56	36	24	11	178.1	234	69	75	0	1	1	2	62	8	0	.129
1941 STL A	3	7	.300	5.00	32	9	3	104.1	105	37	36	0	0	1	3	29	3	0	.103
1942	8	2	.800	2.81	39	0	0	80	62	39	34	0	8	2	5	15	1	0	.067
1943	6	8	.429	2.12	35	0	0	76.1	69	41	43	0	6	8	8	22	3	0	.136
1944	6	6	.500	2.44	42	0	0	81	91	33	46	0	6	6	12	20	5	0	.250
1945 2 teams		STL	A (10G 1-2)		DET	A	(22G 5-1)												
" total	6	3	.667	4.57	32	0	0	67	60	34	32	0	6	3	3	14	3	0	.214
1946 DET A	2	1	.667	5.66	26	0	0	41.1	42	24	19	0	2	1	4	7	1	0	.143
12 yrs.	76	100	.432	4.54	376	127	62	1376.2	1469	597	595	6	33	26	39	440	81	0	.184
2 yrs.	7	2	.778	4.66	48	0	0	92.2	89	51	42	0	7	2	6	18	3	0	.167

WORLD SERIES

	W	L	PCT	ERA	G	GS	CG	IP	H	BB	SO	ShO	W	L	SV	AB	H	HR	BA
1945 DET A	0	0	—	0.00	1	0	0	.2	0	0	1	0	0	0	0	0	0	0	—

Pug Cavet

CAVET, TILLER H.
B. Dec. 26, 1889, McGregor, Tex.   D. Aug. 4, 1966, San Luis Obispo, Calif.   BL TL 6'3"   176 lbs.

	W	L	PCT	ERA	G	GS	CG	IP	H	BB	SO	ShO	W	L	SV	AB	H	HR	BA
1911 DET A	0	0	—	4.50	1	1	0	4	6	1	1	0	0	0	0	1	0	0	.000
1914	7	7	.500	2.44	31	14	6	151.1	129	44	51	1	2	0	2	47	5	0	.106
1915	4	2	.667	4.06	17	7	2	71	83	22	26	0	1	1	1	24	6	0	.250
3 yrs.	11	9	.550	2.98	49	22	8	226.1	218	67	78	1	3	1	3	72	11	0	.153
3 yrs.	11	9	.550	2.98	49	22	8	226.1	218	67	78	1	3	1	3	72	11	0	.153

Dean Chance

CHANCE, WILMER DEAN
B. June 1, 1941, Wayne, Ohio   BR TR 6'3"   200 lbs.

	W	L	PCT	ERA	G	GS	CG	IP	H	BB	SO	ShO	W	L	SV	AB	H	HR	BA
1961 LA A	0	2	.000	6.87	5	4	0	18.1	33	5	11	0	0	0	0	5	0	0	.000
1962	14	10	.583	2.96	50	24	6	206.2	195	66	127	2	5	2	8	65	4	0	.062
1963	13	18	.419	3.19	45	35	6	248	229	90	168	2	2	1	3	80	12	0	.150
1964	20	9	.690	1.65	46	35	15	278.1	194	86	207	11	2	1	4	89	7	0	.079
1965 CAL A	15	10	.600	3.15	36	33	10	225.2	197	101	164	4	0	2	0	75	7	0	.093
1966	12	17	.414	3.08	41	37	11	259.2	206	114	180	2	0	0	0	76	2	0	.026
1967 MIN A	20	14	.588	2.73	41	39	18	283.2	244	68	220	5	0	0	1	92	3	0	.033
1968	16	16	.500	2.53	43	39	15	292	224	63	234	6	0	0	1	93	5	0	.054
1969	5	4	.556	2.95	20	15	1	88.1	76	35	50	0	1	0	0	24	1	0	.042

	W	L	PCT	ERA	G	GS	CG	IP	H	BB	SO	ShO	Relief Pitching			BATTING			BA
													W	L	SV	AB	H	HR	

Dean Chance continued

	W	L	PCT	ERA	G	GS	CG	IP	H	BB	SO	ShO	W	L	SV	AB	H	HR	BA
70 2 teams	CLE A (45G 9-8)				NY	N	(3G 0-1)												
total	9	9	.500	4.36	48	19	1	157	175	61	109	1	4	2	5	42	3	0	.071
71 DET A	4	6	.400	3.50	31	14	0	90	91	50	64	0	3	0	0	21	0	0	.000
11 yrs.	128	115	.527	2.92	406	294	83	2147.2	1864	739	1534	33	17	10	23	662	44	0	.066
1 yr.	4	6	.400	3.50	31	14	0	90	91	50	64	0	3	0	0	21	0	0	.000
LEAGUE CHAMPIONSHIP SERIES																			
69 MIN A	0	0	–	13.50	1	0	0	2	4	0	2	0	0	0	0	0	0	0	–

Mike Chris

CHRIS, MICHAEL
B. Oct. 8, 1957, Santa Monica, Calif.

BL TL 6'3" 180 lbs.

	W	L	PCT	ERA	G	GS	CG	IP	H	BB	SO	ShO	W	L	SV	AB	H	HR	BA
79 DET A	3	3	.500	6.92	13	8	0	39	46	21	31	0	0	0	0	0	0	0	–
82 SF N	0	2	.000	4.85	9	6	0	26	23	26	10	0	0	0	0	7	1	0	.143
83	0	0	–	8.10	7	0	0	13.1	16	16	5	0	0	0	0	2	0	0	.000
3 yrs.	3	5	.375	6.43	29	14	0	78.1	85	63	46	0	0	0	0	9	1	0	.111
1 yr.	3	3	.500	6.92	13	8	0	39	46	21	31	0	0	0	0	0	0	0	–

Al Cicotte

CICOTTE, ALVA WARREN (Bozo)
B. Dec. 23, 1929, Melvindale, Mich.   D. Nov. 29, 1982, Westland, Mich.

BR TR 6'3" 185 lbs.

	W	L	PCT	ERA	G	GS	CG	IP	H	BB	SO	ShO	W	L	SV	AB	H	HR	BA
57 NY A	2	2	.500	3.03	20	2	0	65.1	57	30	36	0	2	0	2	20	3	0	.150
58 2 teams	WAS	A	(8G 0-3)		DET	A	(14G 3-1)												
total	3	4	.429	4.06	22	6	0	71	86	29	35	0	2	1	0	27	5	0	.185
59 CLE A	3	1	.750	5.32	26	1	0	44	46	25	23	0	3	1	1	3	1	0	.333
61 STL N	2	6	.250	5.28	29	7	0	75	83	34	51	0	2	3	1	21	6	0	.286
62 HOU N	0	0	–	3.86	5	0	0	4.2	8	1	4	0	0	0	0	0	0	0	–
5 yrs.	10	13	.435	4.36	102	16	0	260	280	119	149	0	9	5	4	71	15	0	.211
1 yr.	3	1	.750	3.56	14	2	0	43	50	15	21	0	2	1	0	17	3	0	.176

Eddie Cicotte

CICOTTE, EDWARD VICTOR
B. June 19, 1884, Detroit, Mich.   D. May 5, 1969, Detroit, Mich.

BB TR 5'9" 175 lbs.

	W	L	PCT	ERA	G	GS	CG	IP	H	BB	SO	ShO	W	L	SV	AB	H	HR	BA
05 DET A	1	1	.500	3.50	3	1	1	18	25	5	6	0	0	1	0	7	3	0	.429
08 BOS A	11	12	.478	2.43	39	24	17	207.1	198	59	95	2	1	2	2	72	17	0	.236
09	13	5	.722	1.97	27	15	10	159.2	117	56	82	1	4	0	2	49	11	0	.224
10	15	11	.577	2.74	36	30	20	250	213	86	104	4	1	0	0	85	12	0	.141
11	11	15	.423	2.81	35	25	16	221	236	73	106	1	2	2	0	71	10	0	.141
12 2 teams	BOS	A	(9G 1-3)		CHI	A	(20G 9-7)												
total	10	10	.500	3.50	29	24	15	198	217	52	90	1	0	1	0	69	15	0	.217
13 CHI A	18	12	.600	1.58	41	30	18	268	224	73	121	3	2	0	1	91	13	0	.143
14	11	16	.407	2.04	45	29	15	269.1	220	72	122	4	1	0	3	86	14	0	.163
15	13	12	.520	3.02	39	26	15	223.1	216	48	106	1	0	2	3	67	14	0	.209
16	15	7	**.682**	1.78	44	19	11	187	138	70	91	2	3	2	5	57	12	0	.211
17	**28**	12	.700	**1.53**	49	35	29	**346.2**	246	70	150	7	5	1	4	112	20	0	.179
18	12	**19**	.387	2.64	38	30	24	266	275	40	104	1	3	1	2	86	14	0	.163
19	**29**	7	**.806**	1.82	40	35	**30**	306.2	256	49	110	5	2	1	1	99	20	0	.202
20	21	10	.677	3.26	37	35	28	303.1	316	74	87	4	0	0	2	112	22	0	.196
14 yrs.	208	149	.583	2.37	502	358	249	3224.1	2897	827	1374	36	24	13	25	1063	197	0	.185
1 yr.	1	1	.500	3.50	3	1	1	18	25	5	6	0	0	1	0	7	3	0	.429
WORLD SERIES																			
17 CHI A	1	1	.500	1.96	3	2	2	23	23	2	13	0	0	0	0	7	1	0	.143
19	1	2	.333	2.91	3	3	2	21.2	19	5	7	0	0	0	0	8	0	0	.000
2 yrs.	2	3	.400	2.42	6	5	4	44.2	42	7	20	0	0	0	0	15	1	0	.067

Rufe Clarke

CLARKE, RUFUS RIVERS
Brother of Sumpter Clarke.
B. Apr. 13, 1900, Estill, S. C.   D. Feb. 8, 1983, Columbia, S. C.

BR TR 6'1" 203 lbs.

	W	L	PCT	ERA	G	GS	CG	IP	H	BB	SO	ShO	W	L	SV	AB	H	HR	BA
23 DET A	1	1	.500	4.50	5	0	0	6	6	6	2	0	1	1	0	0	0	0	–
24	0	0	–	3.38	2	0	0	5.1	3	5	1	0	0	0	0	1	0	0	.000
2 yrs.	1	1	.500	3.97	7	0	0	11.1	9	11	3	0	1	1	0	1	0	0	.000
2 yrs.	1	1	.500	3.97	7	0	0	11.1	9	11	3	0	1	1	0	1	0	0	.000

Al Clauss

CLAUSS, ALBERT STANLEY (Lefty)
B. June 24, 1891, New Haven, Conn.   D. Sept. 13, 1952, New Haven, Conn.

BL TL 5'10½" 178 lbs.

	W	L	PCT	ERA	G	GS	CG	IP	H	BB	SO	ShO	W	L	SV	AB	H	HR	BA
13 DET A	0	1	.000	4.73	5	1	0	13.1	11	12	1	0	0	0	0	4	0	0	.000

Ty Cobb

COBB, TYRUS RAYMOND (The Georgia Peach)
B. Dec. 18, 1886, Narrows, Ga.   D. July 17, 1961, Atlanta, Ga.
Manager 1921-26.
Hall of Fame 1936.

BL TR 6'1" 175 lbs.

	W	L	PCT	ERA	G	GS	CG	IP	H	BB	SO	ShO	W	L	SV	AB	H	HR	BA
18 DET A	0	0	–	4.50	2	0	0	4	6	2	0	0	0	0	0	421	161	3	**.382**
25	0	0	–	0.00	1	0	0	1	0	0	0	0	0	0	1	415	157	12	.378
2 yrs.	0	0	–	3.60	3	0	0	5	6	2	0	0	0	0	1	*			
2 yrs.	0	0	–	3.60	3	0	0	5	6	2	0	0	0	0	1	10586	3902	112	.369

Dick Coffman

COFFMAN, GEORGE DAVID
Brother of Dick Coffman.
B. Dec. 11, 1910, Veto, Ala.

BR TR 6' 155 lbs.

	W	L	PCT	ERA	G	GS	CG	IP	H	BB	SO	ShO	W	L	SV	AB	H	HR	BA
37 DET A	7	5	.583	4.37	28	5	1	101	121	39	22	0	5	3	0	29	5	0	.172
38	4	4	.500	6.02	39	6	1	95.2	120	48	31	0	3	1	2	24	4	0	.167
39	2	1	.667	6.38	23	1	0	42.1	51	22	10	0	2	1	0	5	0	0	.000
40 STL A	2	2	.500	6.27	31	4	1	74.2	108	23	26	0	1	0	1	15	3	0	.200
4 yrs.	15	12	.556	5.60	121	16	3	313.2	400	132	89	0	11	5	3	73	12	0	.164
3 yrs.	13	10	.565	5.38	90	12	2	239	292	109	63	0	10	5	2	58	9	0	.155

	W	L	PCT	ERA	G	GS	CG	IP	H	BB	SO	ShO	Relief Pitching W	L	SV	BATTING AB	H	HR	B

Rocky Colavito

COLAVITO, ROCCO DOMENICO
B. Aug. 10, 1933, New York, N. Y.

BR TR 6'3" 190 lbs

Year Team	W	L	PCT	ERA	G	GS	CG	IP	H	BB	SO	ShO	W	L	SV	AB	H	HR	B
1958 CLE A	0	0	–	0.00	1	0	0	3	0	3	1	0	0	0	0	489	148	41	.30
1968 NY A	1	0	1.000	0.00	1	0	0	2.2	1	2	1	0	1	0	0	204	43	8	.21
2 yrs.	1	0	1.000	0.00	2	0	0	5.2	1	5	2	0	1	0	0	*			

Bert Cole

COLE, ALBERT GEORGE
B. July 1, 1896, San Francisco, Calif.   D. May 30, 1975, San Mateo, Calif.

BL TL 6'1" 180 lbs

Year Team	W	L	PCT	ERA	G	GS	CG	IP	H	BB	SO	ShO	W	L	SV	AB	H	HR	B
1921 DET A	7	4	.636	4.27	20	11	7	109.2	134	36	22	1	1	0	1	46	13	0	.28
1922	1	6	.143	4.88	23	5	2	79.1	105	39	21	1	0	3	0	25	4	0	.16
1923	13	5	.722	4.14	52	13	5	163	183	61	32	1	5	2	5	55	14	1	.25
1924	3	9	.250	4.69	28	11	2	109.1	135	35	16	1	1	2	2	37	10	0	.27
1925 2 teams			DET A (14G 2-3)		CLE A (13G 1-1)														
" total	3	4	.429	6.03	27	4	1	77.2	99	40	16	0	2	2	2	24	5	0	.20
1927 CHI A	1	4	.200	4.73	27	2	0	66.2	79	19	12	0	1	3	0	18	3	0	.16
6 yrs.	28	32	.467	4.67	177	46	17	605.2	735	230	119	4	10	12	10	205	49	1	.23
5 yrs.	26	27	.491	4.53	137	42	17	495	601	186	98	4	8	9	9	174	44	1	.25

Joe Coleman

COLEMAN, JOSEPH HOWARD
Son of Joe Coleman.
B. Feb. 3, 1947, Boston, Mass.

BR TR 6'3" 175 lbs

Year Team	W	L	PCT	ERA	G	GS	CG	IP	H	BB	SO	ShO	W	L	SV	AB	H	HR	B
1965 WAS A	2	0	1.000	1.50	2	2	1	18	9	8	7	0	0	0	0	6	0	0	.00
1966	1	0	1.000	2.00	1	1	1	9	6	2	4	0	0	0	0	3	0	0	.00
1967	8	9	.471	4.63	28	22	3	134	154	47	77	0	0	1	0	36	2	0	.05
1968	12	16	.429	3.27	33	33	12	223	212	51	139	2	0	0	0	70	9	0	.12
1969	12	13	.480	3.27	40	36	12	247.2	222	100	182	4	0	0	1	84	9	0	.10
1970	8	12	.400	3.58	39	29	6	219	190	89	152	1	0	0	0	67	8	0	.11
1971 DET A	20	9	.690	3.15	39	38	16	286	241	96	236	3	0	0	0	96	9	0	.09
1972	19	14	.576	2.80	40	39	9	279.2	216	110	222	3	0	0	0	82	9	0	.11
1973	23	15	.605	3.53	40	40	13	288	283	93	202	2	0	0	0	0	0	0	
1974	14	12	.538	4.31	41	41	11	286	272	158	177	2	0	0	0	0	0	0	
1975	10	18	.357	5.55	31	31	6	201	234	85	125	1	0	0	0	0	0	0	
1976 2 teams			DET A (12G 2-5)		CHI N (39G 2-8)														
" total	4	13	.235	4.44	51	16	1	146	152	69	104	0	2	5	4	13	2	0	.15
1977 OAK A	4	4	.500	2.95	43	12	2	128	114	49	55	0	0	0	0	0	0	0	
1978 2 teams			OAK A (10G 3-0)		TOR A (31G 2-0)														
" total	5	0	1.000	3.78	41	0	0	81	79	35	32	0	5	0	0	0	0	0	
1979 2 teams			SF N (5G 0-0)		PIT N (10G 0-0)														
" total	0	0	–	5.18	15	0	0	24.1	32	11	14	0	0	0	0	5	1	0	.20
15 yrs.	142	135	.513	3.69	484	340	94	2570.2	2416	1003	1728	18	7	6	7	462	49	0	.10
6 yrs.	88	73	.547	3.82	203	201	56	1407.2	1326	576	1000	11	0	0	0	178	18	0	.10

LEAGUE CHAMPIONSHIP SERIES

Year Team	W	L	PCT	ERA	G	GS	CG	IP	H	BB	SO	ShO	W	L	SV	AB	H	HR	B
1972 DET A	1	0	1.000	0.00	1	1	1	9	7	3	14	1	0	0	0	2	1	0	.50

Joe Coleman

COLEMAN, JOSEPH PATRICK
Father of Joe Coleman.
B. July 30, 1922, Medford, Mass.

BR TR 6'2½" 200 lbs

Year Team	W	L	PCT	ERA	G	GS	CG	IP	H	BB	SO	ShO	W	L	SV	AB	H	HR	B
1942 PHI A	0	1	.000	3.00	1	0	0	6	8	1	0	0	0	1	0	4	0	0	.00
1946	0	2	.000	5.54	4	2	0	13	19	8	8	0	0	0	0	5	2	0	.40
1947	6	12	.333	4.32	32	21	9	160.1	171	62	65	2	1	0	0	48	7	0	.14
1948	14	13	.519	4.09	33	29	13	215.2	224	90	86	3	0	1	0	74	9	0	.12
1949	13	14	.481	3.86	33	30	18	240.1	249	127	109	1	1	0	1	79	14	1	.17
1950	0	5	.000	8.50	15	6	2	54	74	50	12	0	0	0	0	17	1	1	.05
1951	1	6	.143	5.98	28	9	1	96.1	117	59	34	0	0	2	1	27	7	0	.25
1953	3	4	.429	4.00	21	9	2	90	85	49	18	1	0	0	0	28	8	0	.28
1954 BAL A	13	17	.433	3.50	33	32	15	221.1	184	96	103	4	0	1	0	74	13	2	.17
1955 2 teams			BAL A (6G 0-1)		DET A (17G 2-1)														
" total	2	2	.500	5.59	23	2	0	37	41	24	9	0	2	1	3	7	5	0	.71
10 yrs.	52	76	.406	4.38	223	140	60	1134	1172	566	444	11	4	6	6	363	66	4	.18
1 yr.	2	1	.667	3.20	17	0	0	25.1	22	14	5	0	2	1	3	4	3	0	.75

Orlin Collier

COLLIER, ORLIN EDWARD
B. Feb. 17, 1907, East Prairie, Mo.   D. Sept. 9, 1944, Memphis, Tenn.

BR TR 5'11½" 180 lbs

Year Team	W	L	PCT	ERA	G	GS	CG	IP	H	BB	SO	ShO	W	L	SV	AB	H	HR	B
1931 DET A	0	1	.000	7.84	2	2	0	10.1	17	7	3	0	0	0	0	3	0	0	.00

Rip Collins

COLLINS, HARRY WARREN
B. Feb. 26, 1896, Weatherford, Tex.
D. May 27, 1968, Bryan, Tex.

BR TR 6'1" 205 lbs
BL 1920, BB 1921-23

Year Team	W	L	PCT	ERA	G	GS	CG	IP	H	BB	SO	ShO	W	L	SV	AB	H	HR	B
1920 NY A	14	8	.636	3.17	36	20	12	187.1	171	79	66	3	4	0	1	62	8	0	.12
1921	11	5	.688	5.44	28	16	7	137.1	158	78	64	2	1	2	0	56	11	0	.19
1922 BOS A	14	11	.560	3.76	32	29	15	210.2	219	103	69	3	0	0	0	76	12	0	.15
1923 DET A	3	7	.300	4.87	17	13	3	92.1	104	32	25	1	0	0	0	27	3	0	.11
1924	14	7	.667	3.21	34	30	11	216	199	63	75	1	0	0	0	76	11	0	.14
1925	6	11	.353	4.56	26	20	5	140	149	52	33	0	0	0	0	42	5	0	.11
1926	8	8	.500	2.73	30	13	5	122	128	44	44	3	2	3	1	39	6	0	.15
1927	13	7	.650	4.69	30	25	10	172.2	207	59	37	1	1	1	0	54	11	0	.20
1929 STL A	11	6	.647	4.00	26	20	10	155.1	162	73	47	1	1	1	1	62	17	1	.27
1930	9	7	.563	4.35	35	20	6	171.2	168	63	75	1	0	0	2	54	7	0	.13
1931	5	5	.500	3.79	17	14	2	107	130	38	34	0	0	1	0	34	5	0	.14
11 yrs.	108	82	.568	3.99	311	220	86	1712.1	1795	684	569	16	9	7	5	582	96	1	.16
4 yrs.	44	40	.524	3.94	137	101	34	743	787	250	214	6	3	3	1	238	36	0	.15

WORLD SERIES

Year Team	W	L	PCT	ERA	G	GS	CG	IP	H	BB	SO	ShO	W	L	SV	AB	H	HR	B
1921 NY A	0	0	–	54.00	1	0	0	.2	4	1	0	0	0	0	0	0	0	0	

	W	L	PCT	ERA	G	GS	CG	IP	H	BB	SO	ShO	Relief Pitching W	L	SV	BATTING AB	H	HR	BA

Ralph Comstock

COMSTOCK, RALPH REMICK (Commy)   BR TR 5'10" 168 lbs.
B. Nov. 24, 1890, Sylvania, Ohio   D. Sept. 13, 1966, Toledo, Ohio

	W	L	PCT	ERA	G	GS	CG	IP	H	BB	SO	ShO	RP W	L	SV	AB	H	HR	BA
1913 DET A	2	5	.286	5.37	10	7	1	60.1	90	16	37	0	0	0	1	22	5	0	.227
1915 2 teams			BOS A (3G 1–0)				PIT F (12G 3–3)												
" total	4	3	.571	3.06	15	7	3	61.2	54	9	19	0	1	0	2	18	0	0	.000
1918 PIT N	5	6	.455	3.00	15	8	6	81	78	14	44	0	2	1	1	26	5	0	.192
3 yrs.	11	14	.440	3.72	40	22	10	203	222	39	100	0	3	1	4	66	10	0	.152
1 yr.	2	5	.286	5.37	10	7	1	60.1	90	16	37	0	0	0	1	22	5	0	.227

Dick Conger

CONGER, RICHARD   BR TR 6' 185 lbs.
B. Apr. 3, 1921, Los Angeles, Calif.   D. Feb. 16, 1970, Arcadia, Calif.

	W	L	PCT	ERA	G	GS	CG	IP	H	BB	SO	ShO	RP W	L	SV	AB	H	HR	BA
1940 DET A	1	0	1.000	3.00	2	0	0	3	2	3	1	0	1	0	0	0	0	0	–
1941 PIT N	0	0	–	2.16	2	1	0	4	3	3	2	0	0	0	0	0	0	0	–
1942	0	0	–	2.16	2	1	0	8.1	9	5	3	0	0	0	0	3	0	0	.000
1943 PHI N	2	7	.222	6.09	13	10	2	54.2	72	24	18	0	0	0	0	16	1	0	.063
4 yrs.	3	7	.300	5.14	19	12	2	70	86	35	24	0	1	0	0	19	1	0	.053
1 yr.	1	0	1.000	3.00	2	0	0	3	2	3	1	0	1	0	0	0	0	0	–

Red Conkwright

CONKWRIGHT, ALLEN HOWARD (Red)   BR TR 5'10" 170 lbs.
B. Dec. 4, 1896, Sedalia, Mo.

	W	L	PCT	ERA	G	GS	CG	IP	H	BB	SO	ShO	RP W	L	SV	AB	H	HR	BA
1920 DET A	2	1	.667	6.98	5	2	0	19.1	29	16	4	0	2	0	1	4	1	0	.250

Bill Connelly

CONNELLY, WILLIAM WIRT (Wild Bill)   BL TR 6' 175 lbs.
B. June 29, 1925, Alberta, Va.   D. Nov. 27, 1980, Richmond, Va.

	W	L	PCT	ERA	G	GS	CG	IP	H	BB	SO	ShO	RP W	L	SV	AB	H	HR	BA
1945 PHI A	1	1	.500	4.50	2	1	0	8	7	8	0	0	1	0	0	1	0	0	.000
1950 2 teams			CHI A (2G 0–0)				DET A (2G 0–0)												
" total	0	0	–	8.53	4	0	0	6.1	9	3	1	0	0	0	0	1	0	0	.000
1952 NY N	5	0	1.000	4.55	11	4	0	31.2	22	25	22	0	2	0	0	11	4	0	.364
1953	0	1	.000	11.07	8	2	0	20.1	33	17	11	0	0	0	0	6	0	0	.000
4 yrs.	6	2	.750	6.92	25	7	0	66.1	71	53	34	0	3	0	0	19	4	0	.211
1 yr.	0	0	–	6.75	2	0	0	4	4	2	1	0	0	0	0	1	0	0	.000

Earl Cook

COOK, EARL DAVIS   BR TR 6' 195 lbs.
B. Dec. 10, 1908, Stouffville, Ont., Canada

	W	L	PCT	ERA	G	GS	CG	IP	H	BB	SO	ShO	RP W	L	SV	AB	H	HR	BA
1941 DET A	0	0	–	4.50	1	0	0	2	4	0	1	0	0	0	0	0	0	0	–

Jack Coombs

COOMBS, JOHN WESLEY (Colby Jack)   BB TR 6' 185 lbs.
B. Nov. 18, 1882, LeGrand, Iowa   D. Apr. 15, 1957, LeGrand, Iowa
Manager 1919.

	W	L	PCT	ERA	G	GS	CG	IP	H	BB	SO	ShO	RP W	L	SV	AB	H	HR	BA
1906 PHI A	10	10	.500	2.50	23	18	13	173	144	68	90	1	2	2	0	67	16	0	.239
1907	6	9	.400	3.12	23	17	10	132.2	109	64	73	2	0	0	2	48	8	1	.167
1908	7	5	.583	2.00	26	18	10	153	130	64	80	4	1	0	0	220	56	1	.255
1909	12	11	.522	2.32	31	25	19	205.2	156	73	97	6	0	3	1	83	14	0	.169
1910	31	9	.775	1.30	45	38	35	353	248	115	224	13	4	1	1	132	29	0	.220
1911	28	12	.700	3.53	47	40	26	336.2	360	119	185	1	3	1	2	141	45	2	.319
1912	21	10	.677	3.29	40	32	23	262.1	227	94	120	1	3	0	2	110	28	0	.255
1913	1	0	1.000	10.13	2	2	0	5.1	5	6	0	0	0	0	0	3	1	0	.333
1914	0	1	.000	4.50	2	2	0	8	8	3	1	0	0	0	0	11	3	0	.273
1915 BKN N	15	10	.600	2.58	29	24	17	195.2	166	91	56	2	2	1	0	75	21	0	.280
1916	13	8	.619	2.66	27	21	10	159	136	44	47	3	2	0	0	61	11	0	.180
1917	7	11	.389	3.96	31	14	9	141	147	49	34	0	3	2	0	44	10	0	.227
1918	8	14	.364	3.81	27	22	16	189	191	49	44	2	1	0	0	113	19	0	.168
1920 DET A	0	0	–	3.18	2	0	0	5.2	7	2	1	0	0	0	0	2	0	0	.000
14 yrs.	159	110	.591	2.78	355	273	188	2320	2034	841	1052	35	21	10	8	*			.000
1 yr.	0	0	–	3.18	2	0	0	5.2	7	2	1	0	0	0	0	2	0	0	.000
WORLD SERIES																			
1910 PHI A	3	0	1.000	3.33	3	3	3	27	23	14	17	0	0	0	0	13	5	0	.385
1911	1	0	1.000	1.35	2	2	1	20	11	6	16	0	0	0	0	8	2	0	.250
1916 BKN N	1	0	1.000	4.26	1	1	0	6.1	7	1	1	0	0	0	0	3	1	0	.333
3 yrs.	5	0	1.000	2.70	6	6	4	53.1	41	21	34	0	0	0	0	24	8	0	.333
		8th		1st															

Wilbur Cooper

COOPER, ARLEY WILBUR   BR TL 5'11½" 165 lbs.
B. Feb. 24, 1892, Bearsville, W. Va.   D. Aug. 7, 1973, Encino, Calif.

	W	L	PCT	ERA	G	GS	CG	IP	H	BB	SO	ShO	RP W	L	SV	AB	H	HR	BA
1912 PIT N	3	0	1.000	1.66	6	4	3	38	32	15	30	2	0	0	0	13	2	0	.154
1913	5	3	.625	3.29	30	9	3	93	98	45	39	1	3	1	0	26	2	0	.077
1914	16	15	.516	2.13	40	34	19	266.2	246	79	102	0	0	1	0	92	19	0	.207
1915	5	16	.238	3.30	38	21	11	185.2	180	52	71	1	1	0	4	60	7	0	.117
1916	12	11	.522	1.87	42	23	16	246	189	74	111	2	4	0	2	79	17	0	.215
1917	17	11	.607	2.36	40	34	23	297.2	276	54	99	7	1	0	1	103	21	0	.204
1918	19	14	.576	2.11	38	29	26	273.1	219	65	117	3	4	1	3	95	23	0	.242
1919	19	13	.594	2.67	35	32	27	286.2	229	74	106	4	1	0	1	101	29	0	.287
1920	24	15	.615	2.39	44	37	28	327	307	52	114	3	2	1	2	113	25	0	.221
1921	22	14	.611	3.25	38	38	29	327	341	80	134	2	0	0	0	122	31	0	.254
1922	23	14	.622	3.18	41	37	27	294.2	330	61	129	4	0	1	0	108	29	4	.269
1923	17	19	.472	3.57	39	38	26	294.2	331	71	77	1	1	0	0	107	28	0	.262
1924	20	14	.588	3.28	38	35	25	268.2	296	40	62	4	1	0	1	104	36	0	.346
1925 CHI N	12	14	.462	4.28	32	26	13	212.1	249	61	41	0	3	1	0	82	17	2	.207
1926 2 teams			CHI N (8G 2–1)				DET A (8G 0–4)												
" total	2	5	.286	5.77	16	11	3	68.2	92	30	20	2	1	0	0	22	7	0	.318
15 yrs.	216	178	.548	2.89	517	408	279	3480	3415	853	1252	36	21	7	14	1227	293	6	.239
1 yr.	0	4	.000	11.20	8	3	0	13.2	27	9	2	0	0	1	0	4	0	0	.000

Johnny Couch

COUCH, JOHN DANIEL   BL TR 6' 180 lbs.
B. Mar. 31, 1891, Vaughn, Mont.   D. Dec. 8, 1975, Palo Alto, Calif.

	W	L	PCT	ERA	G	GS	CG	IP	H	BB	SO	ShO	RP W	L	SV	AB	H	HR	BA
1917 DET A	0	0	–	2.70	3	0	0	13.1	13	1	1	0	0	0	0	4	0	0	.000
1922 CIN N	16	9	.640	3.89	43	34	18	264	301	56	45	2	1	0	1	91	12	0	.132

	W	L	PCT	ERA	G	GS	CG	IP	H	BB	SO	ShO	Relief Pitching W	L	SV	BATTING AB	H	HR	BA

Johnny Couch continued

	W	L	PCT	ERA	G	GS	CG	IP	H	BB	SO	ShO	W	L	SV	AB	H	HR	BA
1923 2 teams			CIN N (19G 2–7)		PHI N (11G 2–4)														
" total	4	11	.267	5.63	30	15	3	134.1	189	36	32	0	0	1	0	47	10	0	.213
1924 PHI N	4	8	.333	4.73	37	6	3	137	170	39	23	0	4	3	3	49	10	2	.204
1925	5	6	.455	5.44	34	7	2	94.1	112	39	11	1	4	0	2	31	5	1	.161
5 yrs.	29	34	.460	4.63	147	62	26	643	785	171	112	3	9	4	6	222	37	3	.167
1 yr.	0	0	–	2.70	3	0	0	13.1	13	1	1	0	0	0	0	4	0	0	.000

Harry Coveleski

COVELESKI, HARRY FRANK (The Giant Killer)   BB TL 6'   180 lbs.
Born Harry Frank Kowalewski.   Brother of Stan Coveleski.
B. Apr. 23, 1886, Shamokin, Pa.   D. Aug. 4, 1950, Shamokin, Pa.

	W	L	PCT	ERA	G	GS	CG	IP	H	BB	SO	ShO	W	L	SV	AB	H	HR	BA
1907 PHI N	1	0	1.000	0.00	4	0	0	20	10	3	6	0	1	0	0	8	0	0	.000
1908	4	1	.800	1.24	6	5	5	43.2	29	12	22	2	0	0	0	15	2	0	.133
1909	6	10	.375	2.74	24	17	8	121.2	109	49	56	2	1	0	1	37	4	0	.108
1910 CIN N	1	1	.500	5.26	7	4	2	39.1	35	42	27	0	0	0	0	16	1	0	.063
1914 DET A	22	12	.647	2.49	44	36	23	303.1	251	100	124	5	2	1	2	95	23	0	.242
1915	22	13	.629	2.45	50	38	20	312.2	271	87	150	1	4	2	4	103	18	0	.175
1916	21	11	.656	1.97	44	39	22	324.1	278	63	108	3	1	1	2	118	25	0	.212
1917	4	6	.400	2.61	16	11	2	69	70	14	15	0	1	0	0	22	5	0	.227
1918	0	1	.000	3.86	3	1	1	14	17	6	3	0	0	0	0	4	1	0	.250
9 yrs.	81	55	.596	2.39	198	151	83	1248	1070	376	511	13	10	4	9	418	79	0	.189
5 yrs.	69	43	.616	2.34	157	125	68	1023.1	887	270	400	9	8	4	8	342	72	0	.211
				3rd								1st							

Tex Covington

COVINGTON, WILLIAM WILKES   BL TR 6'1"   175 lbs.
Brother of Sam Covington.
B. Mar. 19, 1887, Henryville, Tenn.   D. Dec. 10, 1931, Denison, Tex.

	W	L	PCT	ERA	G	GS	CG	IP	H	BB	SO	ShO	W	L	SV	AB	H	HR	BA
1911 DET A	7	1	.875	4.09	17	6	5	83.2	94	33	29	0	2	0	0	32	6	0	.188
1912	3	4	.429	4.12	14	9	2	63.1	58	30	19	1	0	0	0	15	2	0	.133
2 yrs.	10	5	.667	4.10	31	15	7	147	152	63	48	1	2	0	0	47	8	0	.170
2 yrs.	10	5	.667	4.10	31	15	7	147	152	63	48	1	2	0	0	47	8	0	.170

Red Cox

COX, PLATEAU REX   BL TR 6'2"   190 lbs.
B. Feb. 16, 1895, Laurel Springs, N. C.   D. Oct. 15, 1984, Roanoke, Va.

	W	L	PCT	ERA	G	GS	CG	IP	H	BB	SO	ShO	W	L	SV	AB	H	HR	BA
1920 DET A	0	0	–	5.40	3	0	0	5	9	3	1	0	0	0	0	1	0	0	.000

Doc Cramer

CRAMER, ROGER MAXWELL (Flit)   BL TR 6'2"   185 lbs.
B. July 22, 1905, Beach Haven, N. J.

	W	L	PCT	ERA	G	GS	CG	IP	H	BB	SO	ShO	W	L	SV	AB	H	HR	BA
1938 BOS A	0	0	–	4.50	1	0	0	4	3	3	1	0	0	0	0	*			

Jim Crawford

CRAWFORD, JAMES FREDERICK   BL TL 6'3"   200 lbs.
B. Sept. 29, 1950, Chicago, Ill.

	W	L	PCT	ERA	G	GS	CG	IP	H	BB	SO	ShO	W	L	SV	AB	H	HR	BA
1973 HOU N	2	4	.333	4.50	48	0	0	70	69	33	56	0	2	4	6	13	3	0	.231
1975	3	5	.375	3.62	44	2	0	87	92	37	37	0	3	4	4	17	5	0	.294
1976 DET A	1	8	.111	4.53	32	5	1	109.1	115	43	68	0	0	6	2	0	0	0	–
1977	7	8	.467	4.79	37	7	0	126	156	50	91	0	5	4	1	0	0	0	–
1978	2	3	.400	4.35	20	0	0	39.1	45	19	24	0	2	3	0	0	0	0	–
5 yrs.	15	28	.349	4.40	181	14	1	431.2	477	182	276	0	12	21	13	30	8	0	.267
3 yrs.	10	19	.345	4.62	89	12	1	274.2	316	112	183	0	7	13	3	0	0	0	–

Jack Crimian

CRIMIAN, JOHN MELVIN   BR TR 5'10"   180 lbs.
B. Feb. 17, 1926, Philadelphia, Pa.

	W	L	PCT	ERA	G	GS	CG	IP	H	BB	SO	ShO	W	L	SV	AB	H	HR	BA
1951 STL N	1	0	1.000	9.00	11	0	0	17	24	8	5	0	1	0	1	3	1	0	.333
1952	0	0	–	9.72	5	0	0	8.1	15	4	4	0	0	0	0	1	0	0	.000
1956 KC A	4	8	.333	5.51	54	7	0	129	129	49	59	0	3	3	3	22	5	0	.227
1957 DET A	0	1	.000	12.71	4	0	0	5.2	9	4	1	0	0	1	0	0	0	0	–
4 yrs.	5	9	.357	6.36	74	7	0	160	177	65	69	0	4	4	4	26	6	0	.231
1 yr.	0	1	.000	12.71	4	0	0	5.2	9	4	1	0	0	1	0	0	0	0	–

Leo Cristante

CRISTANTE, LEO DANTE   BR TR 6'1"   205 lbs.
B. Dec. 10, 1926, Detroit, Mich.   D. Aug. 24, 1977, Dearborn, Mich.

	W	L	PCT	ERA	G	GS	CG	IP	H	BB	SO	ShO	W	L	SV	AB	H	HR	BA
1951 PHI N	1	1	.500	4.91	10	1	0	22	28	9	6	0	1	1	0	6	1	0	.167
1955 DET A	0	1	.000	3.19	20	1	0	36.2	37	14	9	0	0	0	0	7	0	0	.000
2 yrs.	1	2	.333	3.84	30	2	0	58.2	65	23	15	0	1	1	0	13	1	0	.077
1 yr.	0	1	.000	3.19	20	1	0	36.2	37	14	9	0	0	0	0	7	0	0	.000

John Cronin

CRONIN, JOHN J.   BR TR 6'   200 lbs.
B. May 26, 1874, Staten Island, N. Y.   D. July 13, 1929, Middletown, N. Y.

	W	L	PCT	ERA	G	GS	CG	IP	H	BB	SO	ShO	W	L	SV	AB	H	HR	BA
1895 BKN N	0	0	–	10.80	2	0	0	5	10	3	1	0	0	0	2	2	1	0	.500
1898 PIT N	2	2	.500	3.54	4	4	2	28	35	8	9	1	0	0	0	10	1	0	.100
1899 CIN N	2	2	.500	5.49	5	5	5	41	56	16	9	0	0	0	0	17	2	0	.118
1901 DET A	13	15	.464	3.89	30	28	21	219.2	261	42	62	1	1	0	0	85	21	0	.247
1902 3 teams			DET A (4G 0–0)		BAL A (10G 3–5)			NY N (13G 5–6)											
" total	8	11	.421	3.09	27	20	19	207	197	50	77	0	0	0	0	99	15	0	.152
1903 NY N	6	4	.600	3.81	20	11	8	115.2	130	37	50	0	1	0	1	46	9	0	.196
1904 BKN N	12	23	.343	2.70	40	34	33	307	284	79	110	4	1	1	0	108	17	0	.157
7 yrs.	43	57	.430	3.40	128	102	88	923.1	973	235	318	6	3	1	3	367	66	0	.180
2 yrs.	13	15	.464	4.29	34	28	21	237	287	50	67	1	1	0	0	92	21	0	.228

General Crowder

CROWDER, ALVIN FLOYD   BL TR 5'10"   170 lbs.
B. Jan. 11, 1899, Winston-Salem, N. C.   D. Apr. 3, 1972, Winston Salem, N. C.

	W	L	PCT	ERA	G	GS	CG	IP	H	BB	SO	ShO	W	L	SV	AB	H	HR	BA
1926 WAS A	7	4	.636	3.96	19	12	6	100	97	60	26	0	1	0	1	38	9	0	.237
1927 2 teams			WAS A (15G 4–7)		STL A (21G 3–5)														
" total	7	12	.368	4.79	36	19	6	141	129	84	52	3	2	1	3	45	9	0	.200
1928 STL A	21	5	.808	3.69	41	31	19	244	238	91	99	1	0	0	2	80	15	0	.188
1929	17	15	.531	3.92	40	34	19	266.2	272	93	79	4	1	0	4	96	18	0	.188

	W	L	PCT	ERA	G	GS	CG	IP	H	BB	SO	ShO	Relief Pitching W	L	SV	BATTING AB	H	HR	BA

General Crowder continued

	W	L	PCT	ERA	G	GS	CG	IP	H	BB	SO	ShO	W	L	SV	AB	H	HR	BA
'30 2 teams	STL	A	(13G 3–7)		WAS	A	(27G 15–9)												
" total	18	16	.529	3.89	40	35	25	279.2	276	96	107	1	0	0	2	101	17	0	.168
'31 WAS A	18	11	.621	3.88	44	26	13	234.1	255	72	85	1	4	2	2	88	19	0	.216
'32	26	13	.667	3.33	50	39	21	327	319	77	103	3	5	0	1	122	27	0	.221
'33	24	15	.615	3.97	52	35	17	299.1	311	81	110	0	4	4	4	102	19	0	.186
'34 2 teams	WAS	A	(29G 4–10)		DET	A	(9G 5–1)												
" total	9	11	.450	5.75	38	22	7	167.1	223	58	69	1	1	4	3	62	11	0	.177
'35 DET A	16	10	.615	4.26	33	32	16	241	269	67	59	2	0	0	0	93	17	0	.183
'36	4	3	.571	8.39	9	7	1	44	64	21	10	0	1	0	0	20	3	0	.150
11 yrs.	167	115	.592	4.12	402	292	150	2344.1	2453	800	799	16	19	11	22	847	164	0	.194
3 yrs.	25	14	.641	4.76	51	48	20	351.2	414	108	99	2	1	0	0	143	24	0	.168
WORLD SERIES																			
'33 WAS A	0	1	.000	7.36	2	2	0	11	16	5	7	0	0	0	0	4	1	0	.250
'34 DET A	0	1	.000	1.50	2	1	0	6	6	1	2	0	0	0	0	1	0	0	.000
'35	1	0	1.000	1.00	1	1	1	9	5	3	5	0	0	0	0	3	1	0	.333
3 yrs.	1	2	.333	3.81	5	4	1	26	27	9	14	0	0	0	0	8	2	0	.250

Roy Crumpler

CRUMPLER, ROY MAXTON BL TL 6'1" 195 lbs.
B. July 8, 1896, Clinton, N. C. D. Oct. 6, 1969, Fayetteville, N. C.

	W	L	PCT	ERA	G	GS	CG	IP	H	BB	SO	ShO	W	L	SV	AB	H	HR	BA
'20 DET A	1	0	1.000	5.54	3	2	1	13	17	11	2	0	0	0	0	9	3	0	.333
'25 PHI N	0	0	–	7.71	3	1	0	4.2	8	2	1	0	0	0	0	2	0	0	.000
2 yrs.	1	0	1.000	6.11	6	3	1	17.2	25	13	3	0	0	0	0	11	3	0	.273
1 yr.	1	0	1.000	5.54	3	2	1	13	17	11	2	0	0	0	0	9	3	0	.333

George Cunningham

CUNNINGHAM, GEORGE HAROLD BR TR 5'11" 185 lbs.
B. July 13, 1894, Sturgeon Lake, Minn. D. Mar. 10, 1972, Chattanooga, Tenn.

	W	L	PCT	ERA	G	GS	CG	IP	H	BB	SO	ShO	W	L	SV	AB	H	HR	BA
'16 DET A	7	10	.412	2.75	35	14	5	150.1	146	74	68	0	2	1	2	41	11	0	.268
'17	2	7	.222	2.91	44	8	4	139	113	51	49	0	2	1	4	34	6	1	.176
'18	6	7	.462	3.15	27	14	10	140	131	38	39	0	2	0	1	112	25	0	.223
'19	1	1	.500	4.91	17	0	0	47.2	54	15	11	0	1	1	1	23	5	0	.217
'21	0	0	–	0.00	0	0	0	0	0	0	0	0	0	0	0	0	0	0	–
5 yrs.	16	25	.390	3.13	123	36	19	477	444	178	167	0	7	3	8	*			
4 yrs.	16	25	.390	3.13	123	36	19	477	444	178	167	0	7	3	8	210	47	1	.224

Chuck Daniel

DANIEL, CHARLES EDWARD BR TR 6'2" 195 lbs.
B. Sept. 17, 1933, Bluffton, Ark.

	W	L	PCT	ERA	G	GS	CG	IP	H	BB	SO	ShO	W	L	SV	AB	H	HR	BA
'57 DET A	0	0	–	7.71	1	0	0	2.1	3	0	2	0	0	0	0	0	0	0	–

Hooks Dauss

DAUSS, GEORGE AUGUST BR TR 5'10½" 168 lbs.
B. Sept. 22, 1889, Indianapolis, Ind. D. July 27, 1963, St. Louis, Mo.

	W	L	PCT	ERA	G	GS	CG	IP	H	BB	SO	ShO	W	L	SV	AB	H	HR	BA
'12 DET A	1	1	.500	3.18	2	2	2	17	11	9	7	0	0	0	0	4	1	0	.250
'13	13	12	.520	2.68	33	29	22	225	188	82	107	2	0	1	1	79	14	0	.177
'14	18	15	.545	2.86	45	35	22	302	286	87	150	3	1	2	4	97	21	1	.216
'15	24	13	.649	2.50	46	35	27	309.2	261	112	132	1	3	2	2	103	15	0	.146
'16	19	12	.613	3.21	39	29	18	238.2	220	90	95	1	4	0	4	72	16	1	.222
'17	17	14	.548	2.43	37	31	22	270.2	243	87	102	6	1	0	2	87	11	0	.126
'18	12	16	.429	2.99	33	26	21	249.2	243	58	73	1	1	3	3	77	14	0	.182
'19	21	9	.700	3.55	34	32	22	256.1	262	63	73	2	1	0	0	97	14	0	.144
'20	13	21	.382	3.56	38	32	18	270.1	308	84	82	0	1	3	0	83	14	0	.169
'21	10	15	.400	4.33	32	28	16	233	275	81	68	0	1	1	1	88	23	1	.261
'22	13	13	.500	4.20	39	25	12	218.2	251	59	78	1	5	1	4	72	15	0	.208
'23	21	13	.618	3.62	50	39	22	316	331	78	105	4	1	0	3	104	24	0	.231
'24	12	11	.522	4.59	40	10	5	131.1	155	40	44	0	8	5	6	38	5	0	.132
'25	16	11	.593	3.16	35	30	16	228	238	85	58	1	2	1	1	81	15	1	.185
'26	11	7	.611	4.20	35	5	0	124.1	135	49	27	0	11	4	9	42	10	1	.238
15 yrs.	221	183	.547	3.32	538	388	245	3390.2	3407	1064	1201	22	40	23	40	1124	212	6	.189
15 yrs.	221	183	.547	3.32	538	388	245	3390.2	3407	1064	1201	22	40	23	40	1124	212	6	.189
	1st	1st		2nd		2nd				4th	6th	8th	2nd		5th				

Terry Davie

DAVIE, GERALD LEE BR TR 6' 180 lbs.
B. Feb. 10, 1933, Detroit, Mich.

	W	L	PCT	ERA	G	GS	CG	IP	H	BB	SO	ShO	W	L	SV	AB	H	HR	BA
'59 DET A	2	2	.500	4.17	11	5	1	36.2	40	17	20	0	0	0	0	10	4	0	.400

Woody Davis

DAVIS, WOODROW WILSON (Babe) BL TR 6'1" 200 lbs.
B. Apr. 25, 1913, Nicholas, Ga.

	W	L	PCT	ERA	G	GS	CG	IP	H	BB	SO	ShO	W	L	SV	AB	H	HR	BA
'38 DET A	0	0	–	1.50	2	0	0	6	3	4	1	0	0	0	0	1	0	0	.000

John Deering

DEERING, JOHN THOMAS TR
B. June 25, 1878, Lynn, Mass. D. Feb. 15, 1943, Beverly, Mass.

	W	L	PCT	ERA	G	GS	CG	IP	H	BB	SO	ShO	W	L	SV	AB	H	HR	BA
'03 2 teams	DET	A	(10G 3–4)		NY	A	(9G 3–3)												
" total	6	7	.462	3.80	19	15	11	120.2	136	42	28	1	0	0	0	47	9	0	.191

Jim Delahanty

DELAHANTY, JAMES CHRISTOPHER BR TR 5'10½" 170 lbs.
Brother of Ed Delahanty. Brother of Frank Delahanty.
Brother of Tom Delahanty. Brother of Joe Delahanty.
B. June 20, 1879, Cleveland, Ohio D. Oct. 17, 1953, Cleveland, Ohio

	W	L	PCT	ERA	G	GS	CG	IP	H	BB	SO	ShO	W	L	SV	AB	H	HR	BA
'04 BOS N	0	0	–	0.00	1	0	0	3.1	5	1	0	0	0	0	0	499	142	3	.285
'05	0	0	–	4.50	1	1	0	2	5	0	0	0	0	0	0	461	119	5	.258
2 yrs.	0	0	–	1.69	2	1	0	5.1	10	1	0	0	0	0	0	*			

Bill Denehy

DENEHY, WILLIAM FRANCIS BR TR 6'3" 200 lbs.
B. Mar. 31, 1946, Middletown, Conn.

	W	L	PCT	ERA	G	GS	CG	IP	H	BB	SO	ShO	W	L	SV	AB	H	HR	BA
'67 NY N	1	7	.125	4.70	15	8	0	53.2	51	29	35	0	0	0	0	9	0	0	.000
'68 WAS A	0	0	–	9.00	3	0	0	2	4	4	1	0	0	0	0	0	0	0	–

	W	L	PCT	ERA	G	GS	CG	IP	H	BB	SO	ShO	Relief Pitching W	L	SV	BATTING AB	H	HR	BA

Bill Denehy continued

	W	L	PCT	ERA	G	GS	CG	IP	H	BB	SO	ShO	W	L	SV	AB	H	HR	BA
1971 DET A	0	3	.000	4.22	31	1	0	49	47	28	27	0	0	2	1	2	0	0	.000
3 yrs.	1	10	.091	4.56	49	9	0	104.2	102	61	63	0	0	2	1	11	0	0	.000
1 yr.	0	3	.000	4.22	31	1	0	49	47	28	27	0	0	2	1	2	0	0	.000

George Disch

DISCH, GEORGE CHARLES
B. Mar. 15, 1879, Lincoln, Mo.   D. Aug. 25, 1950, Rapid City, S. D.

	W	L	PCT	ERA	G	GS	CG	IP	H	BB	SO	ShO	W	L	SV	AB	H	HR	BA
1905 DET A	0	2	.000	2.64	8	3	1	47.2	8	14	0	0	0	1	0	19	2	0	.105

Pat Dobson

DOBSON, PATRICK EDWARD   BR TR 6'3"   190 lbs.
B. Feb. 12, 1942, Depew, N. Y.

	W	L	PCT	ERA	G	GS	CG	IP	H	BB	SO	ShO	W	L	SV	AB	H	HR	BA
1967 DET A	1	2	.333	2.92	28	1	0	49.1	38	27	34	0	1	1	0	5	0	0	.000
1968	5	8	.385	2.66	47	10	2	125	89	48	93	1	3	3	7	28	4	0	.143
1969	5	10	.333	3.60	49	9	1	105	100	39	64	0	3	6	9	22	2	0	.091
1970 SD N	14	15	.483	3.76	40	34	8	251	257	78	185	1	0	0	1	71	10	0	.141
1971 BAL A	20	8	.714	2.90	38	37	18	282	248	63	187	4	0	0	1	91	10	0	.110
1972	16	18	.471	2.65	38	36	13	268.1	220	69	161	3	0	0	0	85	12	0	.141
1973 2 teams								ATL N (22G 3–7)			NY A (22G 9–8)								
" total	12	15	.444	4.40	34	31	7	200.1	223	53	93	2	2	0	0	15	1	0	.067
1974 NY A	19	15	.559	3.07	39	39	12	281	282	75	157	2	0	0	0	0	0		—
1975	11	14	.440	4.07	33	30	7	207.2	205	83	129	1	0	0	0	0	0	0	—
1976 CLE A	16	12	.571	3.48	35	35	6	217	226	65	117	0	0	0	0	0	0	0	—
1977	3	12	.200	6.16	33	17	0	133	155	65	81	0	1	2	1	0	0	0	—
11 yrs.	122	129	.486	3.54	414	279	74	2119.2	2043	665	1301	14	10	12	19	317	39	0	.123
3 yrs.	11	20	.355	3.06	124	20	3	279.1	227	114	191	1	7	10	16	55	6	0	.109

WORLD SERIES

	W	L	PCT	ERA	G	GS	CG	IP	H	BB	SO	ShO	W	L	SV	AB	H	HR	BA
1968 DET A	0	0	—	3.86	3	0	0	4.2	5	1	0	0	0	0	0	0	0	0	—
1971 BAL A	0	0	—	4.05	3	1	0	6.2	13	4	6	0	0	0	0	2	0	0	.000
2 yrs.	0	0	—	3.97	6	1	0	11.1	18	5	6	0	0	0	0	2	0	0	.000

Red Donahue

DONAHUE, FRANCIS ROSTELL   BR TR
B. Jan. 23, 1873, Waterbury, Conn.   D. Aug. 25, 1913, Philadelphia, Pa.

	W	L	PCT	ERA	G	GS	CG	IP	H	BB	SO	ShO	W	L	SV	AB	H	HR	BA
1893 NY N	0	0	—	9.00	2	0	0	5	8	3	1	0	0	0	0	2	0	0	.000
1895 STL N	0	1	.000	6.75	1	1	1	8	9	3	2	0	0	0	1	3	0	0	.000
1896	7	24	.226	5.80	32	32	28	267	376	98	70	0	0	0	0	107	17	0	.159
1897	11	33¹	.250	6.13	46	42	38	348	484	106	64	1	1	2	1	155	33	1	.213
1898 PHI N	17	17	.500	3.55	35	35	33	284.1	327	80	57	1	0	0	0	112	16	0	.143
1899	21	8	.724	3.39	35	31	27	279	292	63	51	4	1	0	0	111	20	0	.180
1900	15	10	.600	3.60	32	24	21	240	299	50	41	2	3	1	0	90	20	0	.222
1901	21	13	.618	2.60	35	34	34	304.1	307	60	89	1	1	0	0	117	11	0	.094
1902 STL A	22	11	.667	2.76	35	34	33	316.1	322	65	63	2	1	0	0	118	11	0	.093
1903 2 teams								STL A (16G 8–7)			CLE A (16G 7–9)								
" total	15	16	.484	2.59	32	30	28	267.2	287	34	96	4	1	1	0	104	16	0	.154
1904 CLE A	19	14	.576	2.40	35	32	30	277	281	49	127	6	1	1	0	101	17	0	.168
1905	6	12	.333	3.40	20	18	13	137.2	132	25	45	1	0	0	0	53	4	0	.075
1906 DET A	13	14	.481	2.73	28	28	26	241	260	54	82	3	0	0	0	81	10	0	.123
13 yrs.	167	173	.491	3.61	368	341	312	2975.1	3384	690	788	25	9	6	2	1154	175	1	.152
1 yr.	13	14	.481	2.73	28	28	26	241	260	54	82	3	0	0	0	81	10	0	.123

Jim Donohue

DONOHUE, JAMES THOMAS   BR TR 6'4"   190 lbs.
B. Oct. 31, 1938, St. Louis, Mo.

	W	L	PCT	ERA	G	GS	CG	IP	H	BB	SO	ShO	W	L	SV	AB	H	HR	BA
1961 2 teams								DET A (14G 1–1)			LA A (38G 4–6)								
" total	5	7	.417	4.18	52	7	0	120.2	116	65	99	0	5	5	6	28	4	0	.143
1962 2 teams								LA A (12G 1–0)			MIN A (6G 0–1)								
" total	1	1	.500	4.67	18	2	0	34.2	36	17	17	0	1	1	1	6	1	0	.167
2 yrs.	6	8	.429	4.29	70	9	0	155.1	152	82	116	0	6	6	7	34	5	0	.147
1 yr.	1	1	.500	3.54	14	0	0	20.1	23	15	20	0	1	1	1	1	0	0	.000

Dick Donovan

DONOVAN, RICHARD EDWARD   BL TR 6'3"   190 lbs.
B. Dec. 7, 1927, Boston, Mass.

	W	L	PCT	ERA	G	GS	CG	IP	H	BB	SO	ShO	W	L	SV	AB	H	HR	BA
1950 BOS N	0	2	.000	8.19	10	3	0	29.2	28	34	9	0	0	0	0	6	1	0	.167
1 51	0	0	—	5.27	8	2	0	13.2	17	11	4	0	0	0	0	3	1	0	.333
1952	0	2	.000	5.54	7	2	0	13	18	12	6	0	0	0	1	3	0	0	.000
1954 DET A	0	0	—	10.50	2	0	0	6	9	5	2	0	0	0	0	1	0	0	.000
1955 CHI A	15	9	.625	3.32	29	24	11	187	186	48	88	5	2	1	0	76	17	1	.224
1956	12	10	.545	3.64	34	31	14	234.2	212	59	120	3	0	0	0	90	20	3	.222
1957	16	6	.727	2.77	28	28	16	220.2	203	45	88	2	0	0	0	83	12	3	.145
1958	15	14	.517	3.01	34	34	16	248	240	53	127	4	0	0	0	80	9	0	.113
1959	9	10	.474	3.66	31	29	5	179.2	171	58	71	1	0	0	0	61	8	1	.131
1960	6	1	.857	5.38	33	8	0	78.2	87	25	30	0	5	0	3	23	3	0	.130
1961 WAS A	10	10	.500	2.40	23	22	11	168.2	138	35	62	2	0	0	0	56	10	1	.179
1962 CLE A	20	10	.667	3.59	34	34	16	250.2	255	47	94	5	0	0	0	89	16	4	.180
1963	11	13	.458	4.24	30	30	7	206	211	28	84	3	0	0	0	69	9	1	.130
1964	7	9	.438	4.55	30	23	5	158.1	181	29	83	0	0	0	0	48	7	1	.146
1965	1	3	.250	5.96	12	3	0	22.2	32	6	12	0	0	1	0	6	0	0	.000
15 yrs.	122	99	.552	3.67	345	273	101	2017.1	1988	495	880	25	7	2	5	694	113	15	.163
1 yr.	0	0	—	10.50	2	0	0	6	9	5	2	0	0	0	0	1	0	0	.000

WORLD SERIES

	W	L	PCT	ERA	G	GS	CG	IP	H	BB	SO	ShO	W	L	SV	AB	H	HR	BA
1959 CHI A	0	1	.000	5.40	3	1	0	8.1	4	3	5	0	0	0	1	3	1	0	.333

Wild Bill Donovan

DONOVAN, WILLIAM EDWARD   BR TR 5'11"   190 lbs.
B. Oct. 13, 1876, Lawrence, Mass.   D. Dec. 9, 1923, Forsyth, N. Y.
Manager 1915-17, 1921.

	W	L	PCT	ERA	G	GS	CG	IP	H	BB	SO	ShO	W	L	SV	AB	H	HR	BA
1898 WAS N	1	6	.143	4.30	17	7	6	88	88	69	36	0	0	0	0	103	17	1	.165
1899 BKN N	1	2	.333	4.32	5	2	2	25	35	13	11	0	0	1	1	13	3	0	.231
1900	1	2	.333	6.68	5	4	2	31	36	18	13	0	0	0	0	13	0	0	.000

	W	L	PCT	ERA	G	GS	CG	IP	H	BB	SO	ShO	Relief Pitching W	L	SV	BATTING AB	H	HR	BA

Wild Bill Donovan continued

	W	L	PCT	ERA	G	GS	CG	IP	H	BB	SO	ShO	W	L	SV	AB	H	HR	BA
901	25	15	.625	2.77	45	38	36	351	324	152	226	2	4	0	1	135	23	2	.170
902	17	15	.531	2.78	35	33	30	297.2	250	111	170	4	0	0	1	161	27	1	.168
903 DET A	17	16	.515	2.29	35	34	34	307	247	95	187	4	0	0	0	124	30	0	.242
904	17	16	.515	2.46	34	34	30	293	251	94	137	3	0	0	0	140	38	1	.271
905	18	15	.545	2.60	34	32	27	280.2	236	101	135	5	1	1	0	130	25	0	.192
906	9	15	.375	3.15	25	25	22	211.2	221	72	85	0	0	0	0	91	11	0	.121
907	25	4	.862	2.19	32	28	27	271	222	82	123	3	2	0	1	109	29	0	.266
908	18	7	.720	2.08	29	28	25	242.2	210	53	141	6	0	0	0	82	13	0	.159
909	8	7	.533	2.31	21	17	13	140.1	121	60	76	4	0	0	2	45	9	0	.200
910	17	7	.708	2.42	26	23	20	208.2	184	61	107	3	1	0	0	69	10	0	.145
911	10	9	.526	3.31	20	19	15	168.1	160	64	81	1	1	0	0	60	12	1	.200
912	1	0	1.000	0.90	3	1	0	10	5	2	6	0	0	0	0	13	1	0	.077
915 NY A	0	3	.000	4.81	9	1	0	33.2	35	10	17	0	0	2	0	12	1	0	.083
916	0	0	–	0.00	1	0	0	1	1	1	0	0	0	0	0	0	0	0	–
918 DET A	1	0	1.000	1.50	2	1	0	6	5	1	1	0	0	0	0	2	1	0	.500
18 yrs.	186	139	.572	2.69	378	327	289	2966.2	2631	1059	1552	35	9	4	6	*			
11 yrs.	141	96	.595	2.49	261	242	213	2139.1	1862	685	1079	29	5	1	3	865	179	2	.207
	7th	10th		7th				4th		3rd	8th		10th	9th	5th				

WORLD SERIES

	W	L	PCT	ERA	G	GS	CG	IP	H	BB	SO	ShO	W	L	SV	AB	H	HR	BA
907 DET A	0	1	.000	1.29	2	2	2	21	17	5	16	0	0	0	0	8	0	0	.000
908	0	2	.000	4.24	2	2	2	17	17	4	10	0	0	0	0	4	0	0	.000
909	1	1	.500	3.00	2	2	1	12	7	8	7	0	0	0	0	4	0	0	.000
3 yrs.	1	4	.200	2.70	6	6	5	50	41	17	33	0	0	0	0	16	0	0	.000
		7th						10th											

Jess Doyle

DOYLE, JESSE HERBERT   BR TR 5'11" 175 lbs.
B. Apr. 14, 1898, Knoxville, Tenn.   D. Apr. 15, 1961, Belleville, Ill.

	W	L	PCT	ERA	G	GS	CG	IP	H	BB	SO	ShO	W	L	SV	AB	H	HR	BA
925 DET A	4	7	.364	5.93	45	3	0	118.1	158	50	31	0	4	5	8	33	8	2	.242
926	0	0	–	4.15	2	0	0	4.1	6	1	2	0	0	0	1	1	1	0	1.000
927	0	0	–	8.03	7	0	0	12.1	16	5	5	0	0	0	0	3	1	0	.333
931 STL A	0	0	–	27.00	1	0	0	1	3	1	0	0	0	0	0	0	0	0	–
4 yrs.	4	7	.364	6.22	55	3	0	136	183	57	38	0	4	5	9	37	10	2	.270
3 yrs.	4	7	.364	6.07	54	3	0	135	180	56	38	0	4	5	9	37	10	2	.270

Jean Dubuc

DUBUC, JEAN JOSEPH OCTAVE (Chauncey)   BR TR 5'10½" 185 lbs.
Born Jean Baptiste Arthur Dubuc.
B. Sept. 15, 1888, St. Johnsbury, Vt.   D. Aug. 29, 1958, Ft. Myers, Fla.

	W	L	PCT	ERA	G	GS	CG	IP	H	BB	SO	ShO	W	L	SV	AB	H	HR	BA
908 CIN N	5	6	.455	2.74	15	9	7	85.1	62	41	32	1	2	0	0	29	4	0	.138
909	3	5	.375	3.66	19	5	2	71.1	72	46	19	0	2	2	2	18	3	0	.167
912 DET A	17	10	.630	2.77	37	26	23	250	217	109	97	2	1	1	3	108	29	1	.269
913	15	14	.517	2.89	36	28	22	242.2	228	91	73	1	0	2	2	135	36	2	.267
914	13	14	.481	3.46	36	27	15	224	216	76	70	2	2	0	1	124	28	1	.226
915	17	12	.586	3.21	39	33	22	258	231	88	74	5	0	2	2	112	23	0	.205
916	10	10	.500	2.96	36	16	8	170.1	134	84	40	1	5	2	1	78	20	0	.256
918 BOS A	0	1	.000	4.22	2	1	1	10.2	11	5	1	0	0	0	0	6	1	0	.167
919 NY N	4	4	.600	2.66	36	5	1	132	119	37	32	0	6	4	3	42	6	0	.143
9 yrs.	86	76	.531	3.04	256	150	101	1444.1	1290	577	438	12	18	13	14	*			
5 yrs.	72	60	.545	3.06	184	130	90	1145	1026	448	354	11	8	7	9	557	136	4	.244
				9th															

Bob Dustal

DUSTAL, ROBERT ANDREW   BR TR 6' 172 lbs.
B. Sept. 28, 1935, Sayreville, N. J.

	W	L	PCT	ERA	G	GS	CG	IP	H	BB	SO	ShO	W	L	SV	AB	H	HR	BA
963 DET A	0	1	.000	9.00	7	0	0	6	10	5	4	0	0	1	0	0	0	0	–

Ben Dyer

DYER, BENJAMIN FRANKLIN   BR TR 5'10" 170 lbs.
B. Feb. 13, 1893, Chicago, Ill.   D. Aug. 7, 1959, Kenosha, Wis.

	W	L	PCT	ERA	G	GS	CG	IP	H	BB	SO	ShO	W	L	SV	AB	H	HR	BA
918 DET A	0	0	–	0.00	2	0	0	1.2	0	0	0	0	0	0	0	*			

Mal Eason

EASON, MALCOLM WAYNE (Kid)   TR
B. Mar. 13, 1879, Brookville, Pa.   D. Apr. 16, 1970, Douglas, Ariz.

	W	L	PCT	ERA	G	GS	CG	IP	H	BB	SO	ShO	W	L	SV	AB	H	HR	BA
900 CHI N	1	0	1.000	1.00	1	1	1	9	9	3	2	0	0	0	0	3	0	0	.000
901	8	17	.320	3.59	27	25	23	220.2	246	60	68	1	0	0	0	87	12	0	.138
902 2 teams			CHI	N	(2G	1–1)		BOS	N	(27G	9–14)								
" total	10	15	.400	2.61	29	28	22	224.1	258	61	54	1	0	0	0	77	7	0	.091
903 DET A	2	5	.286	3.36	7	6	6	56.1	60	19	21	1	0	1	0	20	2	0	.100
905 BKN N	5	21	.192	4.30	27	27	20	207	230	72	64	3	0	0	0	81	14	0	.173
906	10	17	.370	3.25	34	26	18	227	212	74	64	3	1	0	0	88	8	0	.091
6 yrs.	36	75	.324	3.39	125	113	90	944.1	1015	289	273	10	1	1	0	356	43	0	.121
1 yr.	2	5	.286	3.36	7	6	6	56.1	60	19	21	1	0	1	0	20	2	0	.100

Zeb Eaton

EATON, ZEBULON VANCE (Red)   BR TR 5'10" 185 lbs.
B. Feb. 2, 1920, Cooleemee, N. C.

	W	L	PCT	ERA	G	GS	CG	IP	H	BB	SO	ShO	W	L	SV	AB	H	HR	BA
944 DET A	0	0	–	5.74	6	0	0	15.2	19	8	4	0	0	0	0	10	1	0	.100
945	4	2	.667	4.05	17	3	0	53.1	48	40	15	0	3	0	0	32	8	2	.250
2 yrs.	4	2	.667	4.43	23	3	0	69	67	48	19	0	3	0	0	42	9	2	.214
2 yrs.	4	2	.667	4.43	23	3	0	69	67	48	19	0	3	0	0	42	9	2	.214

Dick Egan

EGAN, RICHARD WALLIS   BL TL 6'4" 193 lbs.
B. Mar. 24, 1937, Berkeley, Calif.

	W	L	PCT	ERA	G	GS	CG	IP	H	BB	SO	ShO	W	L	SV	AB	H	HR	BA
963 DET A	0	1	.000	5.14	20	0	0	21	25	3	16	0	0	1	0	0	0	0	–
964	0	0	–	4.46	23	0	0	34.1	33	17	21	0	0	0	2	3	0	0	.000
966 CAL A	0	0	–	4.40	11	0	0	14.1	17	6	11	0	0	0	0	1	0	0	.000

	W	L	PCT	ERA	G	GS	CG	IP	H	BB	SO	ShO	Relief Pitching W	L	SV	BATTING AB	H	HR	BA

Dick Egan continued

	W	L	PCT	ERA	G	GS	CG	IP	H	BB	SO	ShO	W	L	SV	AB	H	HR	BA
1967 LA N	1	1	.500	6.25	20	0	0	31.2	34	15	20	0	1	1	0	1	0	0	.000
4 yrs.	1	2	.333	5.15	74	0	0	101.1	109	41	68	0	1	2	2	5	0	0	.000
2 yrs.	0	1	.000	4.72	43	0	0	55.1	58	20	37	0	0	1	2	3	0	0	.000

Wish Egan

EGAN, ALOYSIUS JEROME
B. June 16, 1881, Evart, Mich.   D. Apr. 13, 1951, Detroit, Mich.
BR TR 6'3"   185 lbs.

	W	L	PCT	ERA	G	GS	CG	IP	H	BB	SO	ShO	W	L	SV	AB	H	HR	BA
1902 DET A	0	2	.000	2.86	3	3	2	22	23	6	6	0	0	0	0	8	2	0	.250
1905 STL N	6	15	.286	3.58	23	19	18	171	189	39	29	0	0	2	0	59	6	0	.102
1906	2	9	.182	4.59	16	12	7	86.1	97	27	23	0	0	1	0	29	2	0	.069
3 yrs.	8	26	.235	3.83	42	34	27	279.1	309	72	52	0	0	3	0	96	10	0	.104
1 yr.	0	2	.000	2.86	3	3	2	22	23	6	6	0	0	0	0	8	2	0	.250

Howard Ehmke

EHMKE, HOWARD JONATHAN (Bob)
B. Apr. 24, 1894, Silver Creek, N. Y.
D. Mar. 17, 1959, Philadelphia, Pa.
BR TR 6'3"   190 lbs.
BB 1923

	W	L	PCT	ERA	G	GS	CG	IP	H	BB	SO	ShO	W	L	SV	AB	H	HR	BA
1915 BUF F	0	2	.000	5.53	18	2	0	53.2	69	25	18	0	0	0	0	12	0	0	.000
1916 DET A	3	1	.750	3.13	5	4	4	37.1	34	15	15	0	0	0	0	14	2	0	.143
1917	10	15	.400	2.97	35	25	13	206	· 174	88	90	4	0	1	2	69	17	0	.246
1919	17	10	.630	3.18	33	31	20	248.2	255	107	79	2	1	0	0	91	23	0	.253
1920	15	18	.455	3.29	38	33	23	268.1	250	124	98	2	0	1	3	105	25	0	.238
1921	13	14	.481	4.54	30	22	13	196.1	220	81	68	1	3	2	0	74	21	0	.284
1922	17	17	.500	4.22	45	30	16	279.2	299	101	108	1	7	1	1	102	16	0	.157
1923 BOS A	20	17	.541	3.78	43	39	28	316.2	318	119	121	2	0	3	0	112	25	0	.223
1924	19	17	.528	3.46	45	36	26	315	324	81	119	4	2	1	4	126	28	0	.222
1925	9	20	.310	3.73	34	31	22	260.2	285	85	95	0	0	1	1	88	13	0	.148
1926 2 teams							BOS A (14G 3–10)		PHI A (20G 12–4)										
" total	15	14	.517	3.86	34	32	17	244.2	240	95	93	2	1	0	0	80	12	0	.150
1927 PHI A	12	10	.545	4.22	30	27	10	189.2	200	60	68	1	1	0	0	68	14	0	.206
1928	9	8	.529	3.62	23	18	5	139.1	135	44	34	1	0	2	0	46	11	0	.239
1929	7	2	.778	3.29	11	8	2	54.2	48	15	20	0	2	0	0	19	2	0	.105
1930	0	1	.000	11.70	3	1	0	10	22	4	0	0	0	0	0	3	1	0	.333
15 yrs.	166	166	.500	3.75	427	339	199	2820.2	2873	1042	1030	20	17	9	14	1009	210	0	.208
6 yrs.	75	75	.500	3.62	186	145	89	1236.1	1232	516	458	10	11	5	6	455	104	0	.229

WORLD SERIES

	W	L	PCT	ERA	G	GS	CG	IP	H	BB	SO	ShO	W	L	SV	AB	H	HR	BA
1929 PHI A	1	0	1.000	1.42	2	2	1	12.2	14	3	13	0	0	0	0	5	1	0	.200

Harry Eisenstat

EISENSTAT, HARRY
B. Oct. 10, 1915, Brooklyn, N. Y.
BL TL 5'11"   180 lbs.

	W	L	PCT	ERA	G	GS	CG	IP	H	BB	SO	ShO	W	L	SV	AB	H	HR	BA
1935 BKN N	0	1	.000	13.50	2	0	0	4.2	9	2	2	0	0	1	0	1	0	0	.000
1936	1	2	.333	5.65	5	2	1	14.1	22	6	5	0	0	1	0	3	1	0	.333
1937	3	3	.500	3.97	13	4	0	47.2	61	11	12	0	1	1	0	11	0	0	.000
1938 DET A	9	6	.600	3.73	32	9	5	125.1	131	29	37	0	2	1	0	36	5	0	.139
1939 2 teams						DET A (10G 2–2)		CLE A (26G 6–7)											
" total	8	9	.471	4.12	36	13	5	133.1	148	32	44	1	4	2	2	40	11	0	.275
1940 CLE A	1	4	.200	3.14	27	3	0	71.2	78	12	27	0	1	2	4	22	6	0	.273
1941	1	1	.500	4.24	21	0	0	34	43	16	11	0	1	1	2	6	2	0	.333
1942	2	1	.667	2.45	29	1	0	47.2	58	6	19	0	2	0	2	4	1	0	.250
8 yrs.	25	27	.481	3.84	165	32	11	478.2	550	114	157	1	16	13	14	123	26	0	.211
2 yrs.	11	8	.579	4.35	42	11	6	155	170	38	43	0	7	4	4	44	8	0	.182

Heinie Elder

ELDER, HENRY KNOX
B. Aug. 23, 1890, Seattle, Wash.   D. Nov. 13, 1958, Long Beach, Calif.
BL TL

	W	L	PCT	ERA	G	GS	CG	IP	H	BB	SO	ShO	W	L	SV	AB	H	HR	BA
1913 DET A	0	0	–	8.10	1	0	0	3.1	4	5	0	0	0	0	0	1	0	0	.000

Eric Erickson

ERICKSON, ERIC GEORGE ADOLPH
B. Mar. 13, 1892, Gothenburg, Sweden   D. May 19, 1965, Jamestown, N. Y.
BR TR 6'2"   190 lbs.

	W	L	PCT	ERA	G	GS	CG	IP	H	BB	SO	ShO	W	L	SV	AB	H	HR	BA
1914 NY N	0	1	.000	0.00	1	1	0	5	8	3	3	0	0	0	0	1	0	0	.000
1916 DET A	0	0	–	2.81	8	0	0	16	13	8	7	0	0	0	0	4	0	0	.000
1918	4	5	.444	2.48	12	9	8	94.1	81	29	48	0	0	1	1	33	4	0	.121
1919 2 teams						DET A (3G 0–2)		WAS A (20G 6–11)											
" total	6	13	.316	4.23	23	7	7	146.2	147	73	90	1	1	1	0	53	8	0	.151
1920 WAS A	12	16	.429	3.84	39	28	12	239.1	231	128	87	0	2	3	1	83	23	1	.277
1921	8	10	.444	3.62	32	22	9	179	181	65	71	3	0	1	0	60	9	0	.150
1922	4	12	.250	4.96	30	17	6	141.2	144	73	61	2	0	1	2	45	6	0	.133
7 yrs.	34	57	.374	3.85	145	94	42	822	805	379	367	6	3	7	4	279	50	1	.179
3 yrs.	4	7	.364	3.02	23	11	8	125	111	47	59	0	0	1	1	42	5	0	.119

Hal Erickson

ERICKSON, HAROLD JAMES
B. July 17, 1919, Portland, Ore.
BR TR 6'5"   230 lbs.

	W	L	PCT	ERA	G	GS	CG	IP	H	BB	SO	ShO	W	L	SV	AB	H	HR	BA
1953 DET A	0	1	.000	4.73	18	0	0	32.1	43	10	19	0	0	1	1	4	0	0	.000

John Eubank

EUBANK, JOHN FRANKLIN (Honest John)
B. Sept. 9, 1872, Servia, Ind.   D. Nov. 3, 1958, Bellevue, Mich.
BL TR 6'2"   215 lbs.

	W	L	PCT	ERA	G	GS	CG	IP	H	BB	SO	ShO	W	L	SV	AB	H	HR	BA
1905 DET A	1	0	1.000	2.08	3	2	0	17.1	13	3	1	0	1	0	0	11	4	0	.364
1906	4	10	.286	3.53	24	12	7	135	147	35	38	0	1	0	0	60	12	0	.200
1907	3	3	.500	2.67	15	8	4	81	88	20	17	2	1	1	2	31	4	0	.129
3 yrs.	8	13	.381	3.12	42	22	11	233.1	248	58	56	2	2	1	2	102	20	0	.196
3 yrs.	8	13	.381	3.12	42	22	11	233.1	248	58	56	2	2	1	2	102	20	0	.196

Roy Face

FACE, ELROY LEON
B. Feb. 20, 1928, Stephentown, N. Y.
BB TR 5'8"   155 lbs.
BR 1953-59

	W	L	PCT	ERA	G	GS	CG	IP	H	BB	SO	ShO	W	L	SV	AB	H	HR	BA
1953 PIT N	6	8	.429	6.58	41	13	2	119	145	30	56	0	3	2	0	30	4	0	.133
1955	5	7	.417	3.58	42	10	4	125.2	128	40	84	0	1	1	5	26	3	0	.115
1956	12	13	.480	3.52	68	3	0	135.1	131	42	96	0	11	12	6	26	5	0	.192
1957	4	6	.400	3.07	59	1	0	93.2	97	24	53	0	4	6	10	16	2	0	.125
1958	5	2	.714	2.89	57	0	0	84	77	22	47	0	5	2	20	7	0	0	.000

	W	L	PCT	ERA	G	GS	CG	IP	H	BB	SO	ShO	W	L	SV	AB	H	HR	BA
													Relief Pitching			BATTING			

Roy Face continued

	W	L	PCT	ERA	G	GS	CG	IP	H	BB	SO	ShO	W	L	SV	AB	H	HR	BA
59	18	1	.947[1]	2.70	57	0	0	93.1	91	25	69	0	18[1]	1	10	13	3	0	.231
60	10	8	.556	2.90	68	0	0	114.2	93	29	72	0	10	8	24	17	7	0	.412
61	6	12	.333	3.82	62	0	0	92	94	10	55	0	6	12	17	11	3	0	.273
62	8	7	.533	1.88	63	0	0	91	74	18	45	0	8	7	28	12	1	0	.083
63	3	9	.250	3.23	56	0	0	69.2	75	19	41	0	3	9	16	8	2	0	.250
64	3	3	.500	5.20	55	0	0	79.2	82	27	63	0	3	3	4	4	0	0	.000
65	5	2	.714	2.66	16	0	0	20.1	20	7	19	0	5	2	0	1	0	0	.000
66	6	6	.500	2.70	54	0	0	70	68	24	67	0	6	6	18	11	0	0	.000
67	7	5	.583	2.42	61	0	0	74.1	62	22	41	0	7	5	17	6	0	0	.000
68 2 teams			PIT	N	(43G	2–4)		DET	A	(2G	0–0)								
total	2	4	.333	2.55	45	0	0	53	48	8	35	0	2	4	13	4	0	0	.000
69 MON N	4	2	.667	3.94	44	0	0	59.1	62	15	34	0	4	2	5	2	1	0	.500
16 yrs.	104	95	.523	3.48	848	27	6	1375	1347	362	877	0	96	82	193	194	31	0	.160
							8th						5th		6th				
1 yr.	0	0	–	0.00	2	0	0	1	2	1	1	0	0	0	0	0	0	0	–

WORLD SERIES

	W	L	PCT	ERA	G	GS	CG	IP	H	BB	SO	ShO	W	L	SV	AB	H	HR	BA
60 PIT N	0	0	–	5.23	4	0	0	10.1	9	2	4	0	0	0	3	3	0	0	.000
															4th				

Ed Farmer　　FARMER, EDWARD JOSEPH　　　　BR TR 6'5"　200 lbs.
B. Oct. 18, 1949, Evergreen Park, Ill.

	W	L	PCT	ERA	G	GS	CG	IP	H	BB	SO	ShO	W	L	SV	AB	H	HR	BA
71 CLE A	5	4	.556	4.33	43	4	0	79	77	41	48	0	5	2	4	14	1	0	.071
72	2	5	.286	4.43	46	1	0	61	51	27	33	0	2	4	7	7	1	0	.143
73 2 teams			CLE	A	(16G	0–2)		DET	A	(24G	3–0)								
total	3	2	.600	4.91	40	0	0	62.1	77	32	38	0	3	2	3	0	0	0	–
74 PHI N	2	1	.667	8.42	14	3	0	31	41	27	20	0	1	0	0	9	1	0	.111
77 BAL A	0	0	–	∞	1	0	0		1	1	0	0	0	0	0	0	0	0	–
78 MIL A	1	0	1.000	0.82	3	0	0	11	7	4	6	0	1	0	1	0	0	0	–
79 2 teams			TEX	A	(11G	2–0)		CHI	A	(42G	3–7)								
total	5	7	.417	3.00	53	5	0	114	96	53	73	0	5	7	14	0	0	0	–
80 CHI A	7	9	.438	3.33	64	0	0	100	92	56	54	0	7	9	30	0	0	0	–
81	3	3	.500	4.58	42	0	0	53	53	34	42	0	3	3	10	0	0	0	–
82 PHI N	2	6	.250	4.86	47	4	0	76	66	50	58	0	1	4	6	11	0	0	.000
83 2 teams			PHI	N	(12G	0–6)		OAK	A	(5G	0–0)								
total	0	6	.000	5.35	17	4	0	37	50	20	23	0	0	3	0	6	1	0	.167
11 yrs.	30	43	.411	4.30	370	21	0	624.1	611	345	395	0	28	34	75	47	4	0	.085
1 yr.	3	0	1.000	5.00	24	0	0	45	52	27	28	0	3	0	2	0	0	0	–

Bill Faul　　FAUL, WILLIAM ALVAN　　　　BR TR 5'10"　184 lbs.
B. Apr. 21, 1940, Cincinnati, Ohio

	W	L	PCT	ERA	G	GS	CG	IP	H	BB	SO	ShO	W	L	SV	AB	H	HR	BA
62 DET A	0	0	–	32.40	1	0	0	1.2	4	3	2	0	0	0	0	0	0	0	–
63	5	6	.455	4.64	28	10	2	97	93	48	64	0	1	1	1	27	4	0	.148
64	0	0	–	10.80	1	1	0	5	5	2	1	0	0	0	0	2	0	0	.000
65 CHI N	6	6	.500	3.54	17	16	5	96.2	83	18	59	3	0	0	0	30	3	0	.100
66	1	4	.200	5.08	17	6	1	51.1	47	18	32	0	0	0	0	13	0	0	.000
70 SF N	0	0	–	7.20	7	0	0	10	15	6	6	0	0	0	1	0	0	0	–
6 yrs.	12	16	.429	4.71	71	33	8	261.2	247	95	164	3	1	1	2	72	7	0	.097
3 yrs.	5	6	.455	5.38	30	11	2	103.2	102	53	67	0	1	1	1	29	4	0	.138

Cy Ferry　　FERRY, ALFRED JOSEPH　　　　BR TR 6'1"　170 lbs.
Brother of Jack Ferry.
B. Sept. 27, 1878, Hudson, N. Y.　　D. Sept. 27, 1938, Pittsfield, Mass.

	W	L	PCT	ERA	G	GS	CG	IP	H	BB	SO	ShO	W	L	SV	AB	H	HR	BA
04 DET A	0	1	.000	6.23	3	1	1	13	12	11	4	0	0	0	0	6	2	0	.333
05 CLE A	0	0	–	13.50	1	1	0	2	3	0	2	0	0	0	0	1	0	0	.000
2 yrs.	0	1	.000	7.20	4	2	1	15	15	11	6	0	0	0	0	7	2	0	.286
1 yr.	0	1	.000	6.23	3	1	1	13	12	11	4	0	0	0	0	6	2	0	.333

Mark Fidrych　　FIDRYCH, MARK STEVEN (The Bird)　　　　BR TR 6'3"　175 lbs.
B. Aug. 14, 1954, Worcester, Mass.

	W	L	PCT	ERA	G	GS	CG	IP	H	BB	SO	ShO	W	L	SV	AB	H	HR	BA
76 DET A	19	9	.679	2.34	31	29	24	250	217	53	97	4	0	0	0	0	0	0	–
77	6	4	.600	2.89	11	11	7	81	82	12	42	1	0	0	0	0	0	0	–
78	2	0	1.000	2.45	3	3	2	22	17	5	10	0	0	0	0	0	0	0	–
79	0	3	.000	10.20	4	4	0	15	23	9	5	0	0	0	0	0	0	0	–
80	2	3	.400	5.73	9	9	1	44	58	20	16	0	0	0	0	0	0	0	–
5 yrs.	29	19	.604	3.10	58	56	34	412	397	99	170	5	0	0	0	0	0	0	–
5 yrs.	29	19	.604	3.10	58	56	34	412	397	99	170	5	0	0	0	0	0	0	–

Happy Finneran　　FINNERAN, JOSEPH IGNATIUS (Smokey Joe)　　BB TR 5'10½" 169 lbs.
B. Oct. 29, 1891, East Orange, N. J.　　D. Feb. 3, 1942, Orange, N. J.

	W	L	PCT	ERA	G	GS	CG	IP	H	BB	SO	ShO	W	L	SV	AB	H	HR	BA
12 PHI N	0	2	.000	2.53	14	4	0	46.1	50	10	10	0	0	1	1	10	2	0	.200
13	0	0	–	7.20	3	0	0	5	.12	2	0	0	0	0	0	3	2	0	.667
14 BKN F	12	11	.522	3.18	27	23	13	175.1	153	60	54	2	1	0	1	55	7	0	.127
15	12	13	.480	2.80	37	24	12	215.1	197	87	68	1	3	2	1	74	11	0	.149
18 2 teams			DET	A	(5G	0–2)		NY	A	(23G	3–6)								
total	3	8	.273	4.43	28	15	4	128	156	43	36	0	1	0	1	42	9	0	.214
5 yrs.	27	34	.443	3.30	109	66	29	570	568	202	168	3	5	3	3	184	31	0	.168
1 yr.	0	2	.000	9.88	5	2	0	13.2	22	8	2	0	0	0	1	3	0	0	.000

Bill Fischer　　FISCHER, WILLIAM CHARLES　　　　BR TR 6'　190 lbs.
B. Oct. 11, 1930, Wausau, Wis.

	W	L	PCT	ERA	G	GS	CG	IP	H	BB	SO	ShO	W	L	SV	AB	H	HR	BA
56 CHI A	0	0	–	21.60	3	0	0	1.2	6	1	2	0	0	0	0	0	0	0	–
57	7	8	.467	3.48	33	11	3	124	139	35	48	1	3	4	1	40	6	0	.150
58 3 teams			CHI	A	(17G	2–3)		DET	A	(22G	2–4)		WAS	A	(3G	0–3)			
total	4	10	.286	6.34	42	6	0	88	113	31	42	0	2	6	2	13	2	0	.154
59 WAS A	9	11	.450	4.28	34	29	6	187.1	211	43	62	1	0	0	0	54	7	0	.130
60 2 teams			WAS	A	(20G	3–5)		DET	A	(20G	5–3)								
total	8	8	.500	4.30	40	13	2	132	135	35	55	0	2	1	0	30	7	1	.233

	W	L	PCT	ERA	G	GS	CG	IP	H	BB	SO	ShO	Relief Pitching W	L	SV	BATTING AB	H	HR	BA

Bill Fischer continued

	W	L	PCT	ERA	G	GS	CG	IP	H	BB	SO	ShO	W	L	SV	AB	H	HR	BA
1961 2 teams DET A (26G 3-2) KC A (15G 1-0)																			
" total	4	2	.667	4.66	41	1	0	67.2	80	23	30	0	4	1	5	9	0	0	.000
1962 KC A	4	12	.250	3.95	34	16	5	127.2	150	8	38	0	1	0	2	38	4	0	.10
1963	9	6	.600	3.57	45	2	0	95.2	86	29	34	0	9	6	3	15	1	0	.06
1964 MIN A	0	1	.000	7.36	9	0	0	7.1	16	5	2	0	0	1	0	0	0	0	
9 yrs.	45	58	.437	4.34	281	78	16	831.1	936	210	313	2	21	19	13	199	27	1	.13
3 yrs.	10	9	.526	4.96	68	7	1	132.1	150	48	58	0	6	6	5	19	4	0	.21

Carl Fischer

FISCHER, CHARLES WILLIAM BR TL 6' 180 lbs
B. Nov. 5, 1905, Medina, N. Y. D. Dec. 10, 1963, Medina, N. Y.

	W	L	PCT	ERA	G	GS	CG	IP	H	BB	SO	ShO	W	L	SV	AB	H	HR	BA
1930 WAS A	1	1	.500	4.86	8	4	1	33.1	37	18	21	0	0	0	1	9	0	0	.000
1931	13	9	.591	4.38	46	23	7	191	207	80	96	0	2	0	3	66	8	0	.12
1932 2 teams WAS A (12G 3-2) STL A (24G 3-7)																			
" total	6	9	.400	5.36	36	18	5	147.2	179	76	58	1	1	0	1	49	12	0	.24
1933 DET A	11	15	.423	3.55	35	22	9	182.2	176	84	93	0	5	1	3	62	9	0	.14
1934	6	4	.600	4.37	20	15	4	94.2	107	38	39	1	1	1	1	31	2	0	.06
1935 2 teams DET A (3G 0-1) CHI A (24G 5-5)																			
" total	5	6	.455	6.17	27	12	3	100.2	118	44	38	1	2	1	0	23	4	0	.17
1937 2 teams CLE A (2G 0-1) WAS A (17G 4-5)																			
" total	4	6	.400	4.58	19	11	2	72.2	76	32	31	0	0	2	2	22	3	0	.13
7 yrs.	46	50	.479	4.63	191	105	31	822.2	900	372	376	3	11	5	11	262	38	0	.14
3 yrs.	17	20	.459	3.92	58	38	13	289.1	299	127	139	1	6	3	4	95	11	0	.11

Ed Fisher

FISHER, EDWARD FREDERICK BR TR 6'2" 200 lbs
B. Oct. 31, 1876, Wayne, Mich. D. July 24, 1951, Spokane, Wash.

	W	L	PCT	ERA	G	GS	CG	IP	H	BB	SO	ShO	W	L	SV	AB	H	HR	BA
1902 DET A	0	0	-	0.00	1	0	0	4	4	1	0	0	0	0	0	2	0	0	.000

Fritz Fisher

FISHER, FREDERICK BROWN BL TL 6'1" 180 lbs
B. Nov. 28, 1941, Adrian, Mich.

	W	L	PCT	ERA	G	GS	CG	IP	H	BB	SO	ShO	W	L	SV	AB	H	HR	BA
1964 DET A	0	0	-	108.00	1	0	0	.1	2	2	1	0	0	0	0	0	0	0	-

Tom Fletcher

FLETCHER, THOMAS WAYNE BB TL 6' 170 lbs
B. June 28, 1942, Elmira, N. Y.

	W	L	PCT	ERA	G	GS	CG	IP	H	BB	SO	ShO	W	L	SV	AB	H	HR	BA
1962 DET A	0	0	-	0.00	1	0	0	2	2	2	1	0	0	0	0	0	0	0	-

Van Fletcher

FLETCHER, ALFRED VANOIDE BR TR 6'2" 185 lbs
B. Aug. 6, 1924, East Bend, N. C.

	W	L	PCT	ERA	G	GS	CG	IP	H	BB	SO	ShO	W	L	SV	AB	H	HR	BA
1955 DET A	0	0	-	3.00	9	0	0	12	13	2	4	0	0	0	0	0	0	0	-

Ben Flowers

FLOWERS, BENNETT BR TR 6'4" 195 lbs
B. June 15, 1927, Wilson, N. C.

	W	L	PCT	ERA	G	GS	CG	IP	H	BB	SO	ShO	W	L	SV	AB	H	HR	BA
1951 BOS A	0	0	-	0.00	3	0	0	3	2	1	2	0	0	0	0	1	0	0	.000
1953	1	4	.200	3.86	32	6	1	79.1	87	24	36	1	0	0	3	19	3	0	.158
1955 2 teams DET A (4G 0-0) STL N (4G 1-0)																			
" total	1	0	1.000	4.05	8	4	0	33.1	32	14	21	0	0	0	0	11	1	0	.091
1956 2 teams STL N (3G 1-1) PHI N (32G 0-2)																			
" total	1	3	.250	5.98	35	3	0	52.2	69	15	27	0	0	2	0	5	0	0	.000
4 yrs.	3	7	.300	4.49	76	13	1	168.1	190	54	86	1	0	2	3	36	4	0	.111
1 yr.	0	0	-	6.00	4	0	0	6	5	2	2	0	0	0	0	1	0	0	.000

Jim Foor

FOOR, JAMES EMERSON BL TL 6'2" 170 lbs
B. Jan. 13, 1949, St Louis, Mo.

	W	L	PCT	ERA	G	GS	CG	IP	H	BB	SO	ShO	W	L	SV	AB	H	HR	BA
1971 DET A	0	0	-	18.00	3	0	0	1	2	4	2	0	0	0	0	0	0	0	-
1972	1	0	1.000	13.50	7	0	0	4	6	6	2	0	1	0	0	0	0	0	-
1973 PIT N	0	0	-	0.00	3	0	0	1.1	2	1	1	0	0	0	0	0	0	0	-
3 yrs.	1	0	1.000	11.37	13	0	0	6.1	10	11	5	0	1	0	0	0	0	0	-
2 yrs.	1	0	1.000	14.40	10	0	0	5	8	10	4	0	1	0	0	0	0	0	-

Gene Ford

FORD, EUGENE WYMAN BR TR 6' 170 lbs
Brother of Russ Ford.
B. Apr. 16, 1881, Milton, N. S., Canada D. Aug. 23, 1973, Dunedin, Fla.

	W	L	PCT	ERA	G	GS	CG	IP	H	BB	SO	ShO	W	L	SV	AB	H	HR	BA
1905 DET A	0	1	.000	5.66	7	1	1	35	51	14	20	0	0	0	0	10	0	0	.000

Larry Foster

FOSTER, LARRY LYNN BL TR 6' 185 lbs
B. Dec. 24, 1937, Lansing, Mich.

	W	L	PCT	ERA	G	GS	CG	IP	H	BB	SO	ShO	W	L	SV	AB	H	HR	BA
1963 DET A	0	0	-	13.50	1	0	0	2	4	1	1	0	0	0	0	0	0	0	-

Steve Foucault

FOUCAULT, STEVEN RAYMOND BL TR 6' 205 lbs
B. Oct. 3, 1949, Duluth, Minn.

	W	L	PCT	ERA	G	GS	CG	IP	H	BB	SO	ShO	W	L	SV	AB	H	HR	BA
1973 TEX A	2	4	.333	3.86	32	0	0	56	54	31	28	0	2	4	8	0	0	0	-
1974	8	9	.471	2.25	69	0	0	144	123	40	106	0	8	9	12	0	0	0	-
1975	8	4	.667	4.12	59	0	0	107	96	55	56	0	8	4	10	0	0	0	-
1976	8	8	.500	3.32	46	0	0	76	68	25	41	0	8	8	5	0	0	0	-
1977 DET A	7	7	.500	3.16	44	0	0	74	64	17	58	0	7	7	13	0	0	0	-
1978 2 teams DET A (24G 2-4) KC A (3G 0-0)																			
" total	2	4	.333	3.23	27	0	0	39	53	22	18	0	2	4	4	0	0	0	-
6 yrs.	35	36	.493	3.21	277	0	0	496	458	190	307	0	35	36	52	0	0	0	-
2 yrs.	9	11	.450	3.16	68	0	0	111	112	38	76	0	9	11	17	0	0	0	-

Terry Fox

FOX, TERRENCE EDWARD BR TR 6' 175 lbs
B. July 31, 1935, Chicago, Ill.

	W	L	PCT	ERA	G	GS	CG	IP	H	BB	SO	ShO	W	L	SV	AB	H	HR	BA
1960 MIL N	0	0	-	4.32	5	0	0	8.1	6	6	5	0	0	0	0	1	0	0	.000
1961 DET A	5	2	.714	1.41	39	0	0	57.1	42	16	32	0	5	2	12	12	2	0	.167
1962	3	1	.750	1.71	44	0	0	58	48	16	23	0	3	1	16	8	2	0	.250
1963	8	6	.571	3.59	46	0	0	80.1	81	20	35	0	8	6	11	11	1	0	.091

	W	L	PCT	ERA	G	GS	CG	IP	H	BB	SO	ShO	Relief Pitching W	L	SV	BATTING AB	H	HR	BA

Terry Fox continued

	W	L	PCT	ERA	G	GS	CG	IP	H	BB	SO	ShO	W	L	SV	AB	H	HR	BA
1964	4	3	.571	3.39	32	0	0	61	77	16	28	0	4	3	5	12	3	0	.250
1965	6	4	.600	2.78	42	0	0	77.2	59	31	34	0	6	4	10	15	0	0	.000
1966 2 teams			DET	A	(4G 0–1)		PHI	N	(36G 3–2)										
" total	3	3	.500	4.80	40	0	0	54.1	66	19	28	0	3	3	5	6	0	0	.000
7 yrs.	29	19	.604	2.99	248	0	0	397	379	124	185	0	29	19	59	65	8	0	.123
6 yrs.	26	17	.605	2.77	207	0	0	344.1	316	101	158	0	26	17	55	61	8	0	.131
													4th		3rd				

Paul Foytack

FOYTACK, PAUL EUGENE   BR TR 5'11" 175 lbs.
B. Nov. 16, 1930, Scranton, Pa.

	W	L	PCT	ERA	G	GS	CG	IP	H	BB	SO	ShO	W	L	SV	AB	H	HR	BA
1953 DET A	0	0	–	11.17	6	0	0	9.2	15	9	7	0	0	0	0	1	0	0	.000
1955	0	1	.000	5.26	22	1	0	49.2	48	36	38	0	0	0	0	11	1	0	.091
1956	15	13	.536	3.59	43	33	16	256	211	142	184	1	1	0	1	90	11	0	.122
1957	14	11	.560	3.14	38	27	8	212	175	104	118	1	3	2	1	63	14	0	.222
1958	15	13	.536	3.44	39	33	16	230	198	77	135	2	0	0	1	75	18	0	.240
1959	14	14	.500	4.64	39	37	11	240.1	239	64	110	2	0	0	1	81	9	0	.111
1960	2	11	.154	6.14	28	13	1	96.2	108	49	38	0	0	4	2	25	7	0	.280
1961	11	10	.524	3.93	32	20	6	169.2	152	56	89	0	3	2	0	54	12	1	.222
1962	10	7	.588	4.39	29	21	5	143.2	145	86	63	1	2	0	0	42	6	0	.143
1963 2 teams			DET	A	(9G 0–1)		LA	A	(25G 5–5)										
" total	5	6	.455	4.70	34	8	0	88	86	37	44	0	2	2	1	19	4	0	.211
1964 LA A	0	1	.000	15.43	2	0	0	2.1	4	2	1	0	0	1	0	0	0	0	–
11 yrs.	86	87	.497	4.14	312	193	63	1498	1381	662	827	7	11	11	7	461	82	1	.178
10 yrs.	81	81	.500	4.14	285	185	63	1425.1	1309	631	789	7	9	9	7	446	78	1	.175

Ray Francis

FRANCIS, RAY JAMES   BL TL 6'1½" 182 lbs.
B. Mar. 8, 1893, Sherman, Tex.   D. July 6, 1934, Atlanta, Ga.

	W	L	PCT	ERA	G	GS	CG	IP	H	BB	SO	ShO	W	L	SV	AB	H	HR	BA
1922 WAS A	7	18	.280	4.28	39	26	15	225	265	66	64	2	0	3	2	78	13	0	.167
1923 DET A	5	8	.385	4.42	36	6	0	79.1	95	28	27	0	1	3	1	21	3	0	.143
1925 2 teams			NY	A	(4G 0–0)		BOS	A	(6G 0–2)										
" total	0	2	.000	7.71	10	4	0	32.2	49	16	5	0	0	0	0	8	1	0	.125
3 yrs.	12	28	.300	4.65	82	36	15	337	409	110	96	2	1	6	3	107	17	0	.159
1 yr.	5	8	.385	4.42	33	6	0	79.1	95	28	27	0	1	3	1	21	3	0	.143

Vic Frazier

FRAZIER, VICTOR PATRICK   BR TR 6' 182 lbs.
B. Aug. 5, 1904, Ruston, La.   D. Jan. 10, 1977, Jacksonville, Tex.

	W	L	PCT	ERA	G	GS	CG	IP	H	BB	SO	ShO	W	L	SV	AB	H	HR	BA
1931 CHI A	13	15	.464	4.46	46	29	13	254	258	127	87	2	1	1	4	86	18	0	.209
1932	3	13	.188	6.23	29	21	4	146	180	70	33	0	0	1	0	44	4	0	.091
1933 2 teams			CHI	A	(10G 1–1)		DET	A	(20G 5–5)										
" total	6	6	.500	7.00	30	15	4	124.2	161	70	30	0	0	2	0	41	7	0	.171
1934 DET A	1	3	.250	5.96	8	2	0	22.2	30	12	11	0	1	2	0	7	2	0	.286
1937 BOS N	0	0	–	5.63	3	0	0	8	12	1	2	0	0	0	0	1	0	0	.000
1939 CHI A	0	1	.000	10.27	10	1	0	23.2	45	11	7	0	0	0	0	7	2	0	.286
6 yrs.	23	38	.377	5.77	126	68	21	579	686	291	170	2	2	6	4	186	33	0	.177
2 yrs.	6	8	.429	6.52	28	16	4	127	159	71	37	0	1	3	0	44	9	0	.205

Cy Fried

FRIED, ARTHUR EDWIN   BL TL 5'11½" 150 lbs.
B. July 23, 1897, San Antonio, Tex.   D. Oct. 10, 1970, San Antonio, Tex.

	W	L	PCT	ERA	G	GS	CG	IP	H	BB	SO	ShO	W	L	SV	AB	H	HR	BA
1920 DET A	0	0	–	16.20	2	0	0	1.2	3	4	0	0	0	0	0	0	0	0	–

Emil Frisk

FRISK, JOHN EMIL   BL TR 6'1" 190 lbs.
B. Oct. 15, 1874, Kalkaska, Mich.   D. Jan. 27, 1922, Seattle, Wash.

	W	L	PCT	ERA	G	GS	CG	IP	H	BB	SO	ShO	W	L	SV	AB	H	HR	BA
1899 CIN N	3	6	.333	3.95	9	9	9	68.1	81	17	17	0	0	0	0	25	7	0	.280
1901 DET A	5	4	.556	4.34	11	7	6	74.2	94	26	22	0	2	0	0	48	15	1	.313
2 yrs.	8	10	.444	4.15	20	16	15	143	175	43	39	0	2	0	0	*			
1 yr.	5	4	.556	4.34	11	7	6	74.2	94	26	22	0	2	0	0	48	15	1	.313

Bill Froats

FROATS, WILLIAM JOHN   BL TL 6' 180 lbs.
B. Oct. 20, 1930, New York, N. Y.

	W	L	PCT	ERA	G	GS	CG	IP	H	BB	SO	ShO	W	L	SV	AB	H	HR	BA
1955 DET A	0	0	–	0.00	1	0	0	2	0	2	0	0	0	0	0	0	0	0	–

Woodie Fryman

FRYMAN, WOODROW THOMPSON   BR TL 6'3" 197 lbs.
B. Apr. 12, 1940, Ewing, Ky.

	W	L	PCT	ERA	G	GS	CG	IP	H	BB	SO	ShO	W	L	SV	AB	H	HR	BA
1966 PIT N	12	9	.571	3.81	36	28	9	181.2	182	47	105	3	1	0	1	63	10	0	.159
1967	3	8	.273	4.05	28	18	3	113.1	121	44	74	1	0	0	1	34	4	0	.118
1968 PHI N	12	14	.462	2.78	34	32	10	213.2	198	64	151	5	0	0	0	71	6	0	.085
1969	12	15	.444	4.42	36	35	10	228	243	89	150	1	0	0	0	76	9	1	.118
1970	8	6	.571	4.08	27	20	4	128	122	43	97	3	1	0	0	39	5	0	.128
1971	10	7	.588	3.38	37	17	3	149	133	46	104	2	3	2	2	37	7	0	.189
1972 2 teams			PHI	N	(23G 4–10)		DET	A	(16G 10–3)										
" total	14	13	.519	3.24	39	31	9	233.2	224	70	141	3	0	0	1	73	10	1	.137
1973 DET A	6	13	.316	5.35	34	29	1	170	200	64	119	0	0	0	0	0	0	0	–
1974	6	9	.400	4.31	27	22	4	142	120	67	92	1	0	0	0	0	0	0	–
1975 MON N	9	12	.429	3.32	38	20	7	157	141	68	118	3	2	4	3	49	10	0	.204
1976	13	13	.500	3.37	34	32	4	216.1	218	76	123	2	0	0	2	64	7	0	.109
1977 CIN N	5	5	.500	5.40	17	12	0	75	83	45	57	0	0	1	1	22	7	0	.318
1978 2 teams			CHI	N	(13G 2–4)		MON	N	(19G 5–7)										
" total	7	11	.389	4.19	32	26	4	150.1	157	74	81	3	1	0	1	50	3	0	.060
1979 MON N	3	6	.333	2.79	44	0	0	58	52	22	44	0	3	6	10	7	0	0	.000
1980	7	4	.636	2.25	61	0	0	80	61	30	59	0	7	4	17	12	2	0	.167
1981	5	3	.625	1.88	35	0	0	43	38	14	25	0	5	3	7	3	2	0	.667
1982	9	4	.692	3.75	60	0	0	69.2	66	26	46	0	9	4	12	0	0	0	.222
1983	0	3	.000	21.00	6	0	0	3	8	1	1	0	0	3	0	0	0	0	–
18 yrs.	141	155	.476	3.77	625	322	68	2411.2	2367	890	1587	27	32	27	58	609	84	2	.138
3 yrs.	22	25	.468	4.12	77	65	11	426	413	162	283	2	0	0	0	40	5	0	.125

DIVISIONAL PLAYOFF SERIES

	W	L	PCT	ERA	G	GS	CG	IP	H	BB	SO	ShO	W	L	SV	AB	H	HR	BA
1981 MON N	0	0	–	6.75	1	0	0	1.1	3	1	0	0	0	0	0	0	0	0	–

	W	L	PCT	ERA	G	GS	CG	IP	H	BB	SO	ShO	Relief Pitching W	L	SV	BATTING AB	H	HR	BA

Woodie Fryman continued

LEAGUE CHAMPIONSHIP SERIES

	W	L	PCT	ERA	G	GS	CG	IP	H	BB	SO	ShO	W	L	SV	AB	H	HR	BA
1972 DET A	0	2	.000	3.65	2	2	0	12.1	11	2	8	0	0	0	0	3	0	0	.000
1981 MON N	0	0	–	36.00	1	0	0	1	3	1	1	0	0	0	0	0	0	0	–
2 yrs.	0	2	.000	6.08	3	2	0	13.1	14	3	9	0	0	0	0	3	0	0	.000

Charlie Fuchs

FUCHS, CHARLES THOMAS   BB TR 5'10"   178 lbs.
B. Nov. 18, 1913, Union Hall, N. J.   D. June 10, 1969, Weehawken, N. J.

	W	L	PCT	ERA	G	GS	CG	IP	H	BB	SO	ShO	W	L	SV	AB	H	HR	BA
1942 DET A	3	3	.500	6.63	9	4	1	36.2	43	19	15	1	0	2	0	13	1	0	.077
1943 2 teams		PHI N	(17G 2–7)		STL	A	(13G 0–0)												
" total	2	7	.222	4.21	30	9	4	113.1	118	45	21	1	0	1	1	29	2	0	.069
1944 BKN N	1	0	1.000	5.74	8	0	0	15.2	25	9	5	0	1	0	0	1	0	0	.000
3 yrs.	6	10	.375	4.89	47	13	5	165.2	186	73	41	2	1	3	1	43	3	0	.070
1 yr.	3	3	.500	6.63	9	4	1	36.2	43	19	15	1	0	2	0	13	1	0	.077

Doug Gallagher

GALLAGHER, DOUGLAS EUGENE   BR TL 6'3½"   195 lbs.
B. Feb. 21, 1940, Fremont, Ohio

	W	L	PCT	ERA	G	GS	CG	IP	H	BB	SO	ShO	W	L	SV	AB	H	HR	BA
1962 DET A	0	4	.000	4.68	9	2	0	25	31	15	14	0	0	2	1	6	2	0	.333

Ned Garver

GARVER, NED FRANKLIN   BR TR 5'10½" 180 lbs.
B. Dec. 25, 1925, Ney, Ohio

	W	L	PCT	ERA	G	GS	CG	IP	H	BB	SO	ShO	W	L	SV	AB	H	HR	BA
1948 STL A	7	11	.389	3.41	38	24	7	198	200	95	75	0	1	0	5	66	19	1	.288
1949	12	17	.414	3.98	41	32	16	223.2	245	102	70	1	3	0	3	75	14	0	.187
1950	13	18	.419	3.39	37	31	22	260	264	108	85	2	1	2	0	91	26	1	.286
1951	20	12	.625	3.73	33	30	24	246	237	96	84	1	2	1	0	95	29	1	.305
1952 2 teams		STL	A	(21G 7–10)	DET	A	(1G 1–0)												
" total	8	10	.444	3.60	22	22	8	157.2	139	58	63	2	0	0	0	51	9	0	.176
1953 DET A	11	11	.500	4.45	30	26	13	198.1	228	66	69	0	1	0	1	72	11	1	.153
1954	14	11	.560	2.81	35	32	16	246.1	216	62	93	3	0	0	1	79	13	0	.165
1955	12	16	.429	3.98	33	32	16	230.2	251	67	83	1	0	0	0	76	17	1	.224
1956	0	2	.000	4.08	6	3	1	17.2	15	13	6	0	0	0	0	5	0	0	.000
1957 KC A	6	13	.316	3.84	24	23	6	145.1	120	55	61	1	0	0	0	44	8	0	.182
1958	12	11	.522	4.03	31	28	10	201	192	66	72	3	0	0	1	69	12	0	.174
1959	10	13	.435	3.71	32	30	9	201.1	214	42	61	2	0	0	1	71	20	2	.282
1960	4	9	.308	3.83	28	15	5	122.1	110	35	50	2	0	0	0	27	2	0	.074
1961 LA A	0	3	.000	5.59	12	2	0	29	40	16	9	0	0	1	0	6	0	0	.000
14 yrs.	129	157	.451	3.73	402	330	153	2477.1	2471	881	881	18	8	4	12	827	180	7	.218
5 yrs.	38	40	.487	3.68	105	94	47	702	719	211	254	4	1	0	2	234	41	2	.175

Charley Gelbert

GELBERT, CHARLES MAGNUS   BR TR 5'11"   170 lbs.
B. Jan. 26, 1906, Scranton, Pa.   D. Jan. 13, 1967, Easton, Pa.

	W	L	PCT	ERA	G	GS	CG	IP	H	BB	SO	ShO	W	L	SV	AB	H	HR	BA
1940 BOS A	0	0	–	9.00	2	0	0	4	5	3	1	0	0	0	0	*			

Rufe Gentry

GENTRY, JAMES RUFFUS   BR TR 6'1"   180 lbs.
B. May 18, 1918, Winston-Salem, N. C.

	W	L	PCT	ERA	G	GS	CG	IP	H	BB	SO	ShO	W	L	SV	AB	H	HR	BA
1943 DET A	1	3	.250	3.68	4	4	2	29.1	30	12	8	0	0	0	0	10	0	0	.000
1944	12	14	.462	4.24	37	30	10	203.2	211	108	68	4	2	0	0	76	15	0	.197
1946	0	0	–	15.00	2	0	0	3	4	7	1	0	0	0	0	0	0	0	–
1947	0	0	–	81.00	1	0	0	.1	1	2	0	0	0	0	0	0	0	0	–
1948	0	0	–	2.70	4	0	0	6.2	5	5	1	0	0	0	0	1	1	0	1.000
5 yrs.	13	17	.433	4.37	48	34	12	243	251	134	78	4	2	0	0	87	16	0	.184
5 yrs.	13	17	.433	4.37	48	34	12	243	251	134	78	4	2	0	0	87	16	0	.184

Sam Gibson

GIBSON, SAMUEL BRAXTON   BL TR 6'2"   198 lbs.
B. Aug. 5, 1899, King, N. C.   D. Jan. 31, 1983, High Point, N. C.

	W	L	PCT	ERA	G	GS	CG	IP	H	BB	SO	ShO	W	L	SV	AB	H	HR	BA
1926 DET A	12	9	.571	3.48	35	24	16	196.1	199	75	61	2	1	0	2	72	18	0	.250
1927	11	12	.478	3.69	33	26	11	190.1	201	86	76	0	0	2	0	66	14	0	.212
1928	5	8	.385	5.42	20	18	5	119.2	155	52	29	1	0	0	0	42	12	0	.286
1930 NY A	0	1	.000	15.00	2	2	0	6	14	6	3	0	0	0	0	3	1	0	.333
1932 NY N	4	8	.333	4.85	41	5	1	81.2	107	30	39	1	2	5	3	19	5	0	.263
5 yrs.	32	38	.457	4.24	131	75	33	594	676	249	208	4	3	7	5	202	50	0	.248
3 yrs.	28	29	.491	4.02	88	68	32	506.1	555	213	166	3	1	2	2	180	44	0	.244

Floyd Giebell

GIEBELL, FLOYD GEORGE   BL TR 6'2½"   172 lbs.
B. Dec. 10, 1909, Pennsboro, W. Va.

	W	L	PCT	ERA	G	GS	CG	IP	H	BB	SO	ShO	W	L	SV	AB	H	HR	BA
1939 DET A	1	1	.500	2.93	9	0	0	15.1	19	12	9	0	1	0	0	2	0	0	.000
1940	2	0	1.000	1.00	2	2	2	18	14	4	11	1	0	0	0	6	0	0	.000
1941	0	0	–	6.03	17	2	0	34.1	45	26	10	0	0	1	0	6	2	0	.333
3 yrs.	3	1	.750	3.99	28	4	2	67.2	78	42	30	1	1	1	0	14	2	0	.143
3 yrs.	3	1	.750	3.99	28	4	2	67.2	78	42	30	1	1	1	0	14	2	0	.143

Bill Gilbreth

GILBRETH, WILLIAM FREEMAN   BL TL 6'   180 lbs.
B. Sept. 3, 1947, Abilene, Tex.

	W	L	PCT	ERA	G	GS	CG	IP	H	BB	SO	ShO	W	L	SV	AB	H	HR	BA
1971 DET A	2	1	.667	4.80	9	5	2	30	28	21	14	0	0	0	0	11	2	0	.182
1972	0	0	–	16.20	2	0	0	5	10	4	2	0	0	0	0	1	0	0	.000
1974 CAL A	0	0	–	13.50	3	0	0	1.1	2	1	0	0	0	0	0	0	0	0	–
3 yrs.	2	1	.667	6.69	14	5	2	36.1	40	26	16	0	0	0	0	12	2	0	.167
2 yrs.	2	1	.667	6.43	11	5	2	35	38	25	16	0	0	0	0	12	2	0	.167

George Gill

GILL, GEORGE LLOYD   BR TR 6'1"   185 lbs.
B. Feb. 13, 1909, Catchings, Miss.

	W	L	PCT	ERA	G	GS	CG	IP	H	BB	SO	ShO	W	L	SV	AB	H	HR	BA
1937 DET A	11	4	.733	4.51	31	10	4	127.2	146	42	40	1	7	1	1	50	7	0	.140
1938	12	9	.571	4.12	24	23	13	164	195	50	30	1	0	0	0	57	6	0	.105
1939 2 teams		DET	A	(3G 0–1)	STL	A	(27G 1–12)												
" total	1	13	.071	7.21	30	12	5	103.2	153	37	25	0	0	4	0	28	4	0	.143
3 yrs.	24	26	.480	5.05	85	45	22	395.1	494	129	95	2	7	5	1	135	17	0	.126
3 yrs.	23	14	.622	4.41	58	34	17	300.1	355	95	71	2	7	1	1	109	13	0	.119

Bob Gillespie

GILLESPIE, ROBERT WILLIAM (Bunch)
B. Oct. 8, 1918, Columbus, Ohio.　　BR TR 6'4" 187 lbs.

	W	L	PCT	ERA	G	GS	CG	IP	H	BB	SO	ShO	W	L	SV	AB	H	HR	BA
944 DET A	0	1	.000	6.55	7	0	0	11	7	12	4	0	0	1	0	2	0	0	.000
947 CHI A	5	8	.385	4.73	25	17	1	118	133	53	36	0	0	0	0	33	2	0	.061
948	0	4	.000	5.13	25	6	1	72	81	33	19	0	0	0	0	16	0	0	.000
950 BOS A	0	0	–	20.25	1	0	0	1.1	2	4	0	0	0	0	0	0	0	0	.000
4 yrs.	5	13	.278	5.07	58	23	2	202.1	223	102	59	0	0	1	0	51	2	0	.039
1 yr.	0	1	.000	6.55	7	0	0	11	7	12	4	0	0	1	0	2	0	0	.000

Fred Gladding

GLADDING, FRED EARL
B. June 28, 1936, Flat Rock, Mich.　　BL TR 6'1" 220 lbs.

	W	L	PCT	ERA	G	GS	CG	IP	H	BB	SO	ShO	W	L	SV	AB	H	HR	BA
961 DET A	1	0	1.000	3.31	8	0	0	16.1	18	11	11	0	1	0	0	3	0	0	.000
962	0	0	–	0.00	6	0	0	5	3	2	4	0	0	0	0	0	0	0	–
963	1	1	.500	1.98	22	0	0	27.1	19	14	24	0	1	1	7	1	0	0	.000
964	7	4	.636	3.07	42	0	0	67.1	57	27	59	0	7	4	7	9	0	0	.000
965	6	2	.750	2.83	46	0	0	70	63	29	43	0	6	2	5	7	0	0	.000
966	5	0	1.000	3.28	51	0	0	74	62	29	57	0	5	0	2	2	0	0	.000
967	6	4	.600	1.99	42	1	0	77	62	19	64	0	6	4	12	18	0	0	.000
968 HOU N	0	0	–	14.54	7	0	0	4.1	8	3	2	0	0	0	2	0	0	0	–
969	4	8	.333	4.19	57	0	0	73	83	27	40	0	4	8	29	10	1	0	.100
970	7	4	.636	4.06	63	0	0	71	84	24	46	0	7	4	18	6	0	0	.000
971	4	5	.444	2.12	48	0	0	51	51	22	17	0	4	5	12	2	0	0	.000
972	5	6	.455	2.77	42	0	0	48.2	38	12	18	0	5	6	14	5	0	0	.000
973	2	0	1.000	4.50	16	0	0	16	18	4	9	0	2	0	1	0	0	0	–
13 yrs.	48	34	.585	3.13	450	1	0	601	566	223	394	0	48	34	109	63	1	0	.016
7 yrs.	26	11	.703	2.70	217	1	0	337	284	131	262	0	26	11	33	40	0	0	.000
													4th		9th				

John Glaiser

GLAISER, JOHN BURKE (Bert)
B. July 28, 1894, Yoakum, Tex.　　D. Mar. 7, 1959, Houston, Tex.　　BR TR 5'8" 165 lbs.

	W	L	PCT	ERA	G	GS	CG	IP	H	BB	SO	ShO	W	L	SV	AB	H	HR	BA
920 DET A	0	0	–	6.35	9	1	0	17	23	8	3	0	0	0	1	3	0	0	.000

Kid Gleason

GLEASON, WILLIAM J.
Brother of Harry Gleason.
B. Oct. 26, 1866, Camden, N. J.　　D. Jan. 2, 1933, Philadelphia, Pa.
Manager 1919-23.　　BL TR 5'7" 158 lbs.

	W	L	PCT	ERA	G	GS	CG	IP	H	BB	SO	ShO	W	L	SV	AB	H	HR	BA
888 PHI N	7	16	.304	2.84	24	23	23	199.2	199	53	89	1	0	0	0	83	17	0	.205
889	9	15	.375	5.58	29	21	15	205	242	97	64	0	2	2	1	99	25	0	.253
890	38	17	.691	2.63	60	55	54	506	479	167	222	6	1	0	2	224	47	0	.210
891	24	22	.522	3.51	53	44	40	418	431	165	100	1	1	2	1	214	53	0	.248
892 STL N	16	24	.400	3.33	47	45	43	400	389	151	133	2	0	0	0	233	50	3	.215
893	21	25	.457	4.61	48	45	37	380.1	436	187	86	1	1	1	1	199	51	0	.256
894 2 teams			**STL N** (8G 2-6)			**BAL N** (21G 15-5)													
" total	17	11	.607	4.85	29	28	25	230	299	65	44	0	0	0	0	114	37	0	.325
895 BAL N	2	4	.333	6.97	9	5	3	50.1	77	21	6	0	1	2	1	421	130	0	.309
8 yrs.	134	134	.500	3.79	299	266	240	2389.1	2552	906	744	11	6	7	6	*			

Ed Glynn

GLYNN, EDWARD PAUL
B. June 3, 1953, New York, N. Y.　　BR TL 6'2" 180 lbs.

	W	L	PCT	ERA	G	GS	CG	IP	H	BB	SO	ShO	W	L	SV	AB	H	HR	BA
975 DET A	0	2	.000	4.30	3	1	0	14.2	11	8	8	0	0	1	0	0	0	0	–
976	1	3	.250	6.00	5	4	1	24	22	20	17	0	0	0	0	0	0	0	–
977	2	1	.667	5.33	8	3	0	27	36	12	13	0	1	0	0	0	0	0	–
978	0	0	–	3.07	10	0	0	14.2	11	4	9	0	0	0	0	0	0	0	–
979 NY N	1	4	.200	3.00	46	0	0	60	57	40	32	0	1	4	7	4	0	0	.000
980	3	3	.500	4.15	38	0	0	52	49	23	32	0	3	3	1	6	0	0	.000
981 CLE A	0	0	–	1.13	4	0	0	8	5	4	4	0	0	0	0	0	0	0	–
982	5	2	.714	4.17	47	0	0	49.2	43	30	54	0	5	2	4	0	0	0	–
983	0	2	.000	5.84	11	0	0	12.1	22	6	13	0	0	2	0	0	0	0	–
9 yrs.	12	17	.414	4.12	172	8	1	262.1	256	147	182	0	10	12	12	10	0	0	.000
4 yrs.	3	6	.333	4.93	26	8	1	80.1	80	44	47	0	1	1	0	0	0	0	–

Izzy Goldstein

GOLDSTEIN, ISADORE
B. June 6, 1908, New York, N. Y.　　BB TR 6' 160 lbs.

	W	L	PCT	ERA	G	GS	CG	IP	H	BB	SO	ShO	W	L	SV	AB	H	HR	BA
932 DET A	3	2	.600	4.47	16	6	2	56.1	63	41	14	0	0	0	0	17	5	0	.294

Johnny Gorsica

GORSICA, JOHN JOSEPH PERRY
Born John Joseph Perry Gorczyca.
B. Mar. 29, 1915, Bayonne, N. J.　　BR TR 6'2" 180 lbs.

	W	L	PCT	ERA	G	GS	CG	IP	H	BB	SO	ShO	W	L	SV	AB	H	HR	BA
940 DET A	7	7	.500	4.33	29	20	5	160	170	57	68	2	0	0	0	62	12	1	.194
941	9	11	.450	4.47	33	21	8	171	193	55	59	1	4	1	2	57	17	0	.298
942	3	2	.600	4.75	28	0	0	53	63	26	19	0	3	2	4	10	1	0	.100
943	4	5	.444	3.36	35	4	1	96.1	88	40	45	0	4	3	5	23	4	0	.174
944	4	6	.300	4.11	34	19	8	162	192	32	47	1	1	2	4	52	7	0	.135
946	0	0	–	4.56	14	0	0	23.2	28	11	14	0	0	0	1	3	2	0	.667
947	2	0	1.000	3.75	31	0	0	57.2	44	26	20	0	2	0	1	10	2	0	.200
7 yrs.	31	39	.443	4.18	204	64	22	723.2	778	247	272	4	14	8	17	217	45	1	.207
7 yrs.	31	39	.443	4.18	204	64	22	723.2	778	247	272	4	14	8	17	217	45	1	.207

WORLD SERIES

	W	L	PCT	ERA	G	GS	CG	IP	H	BB	SO	ShO	W	L	SV	AB	H	HR	BA
40 DET A	0	0	–	0.79	2	0	0	11.1	6	4	4	0	0	0	0	4	0	0	.000

Bill Graham

GRAHAM, WILLIAM ALBERT
B. Jan. 21, 1937, Flemingsburg, Ky.　　BR TR 6'3" 217 lbs.

	W	L	PCT	ERA	G	GS	CG	IP	H	BB	SO	ShO	W	L	SV	AB	H	HR	BA
66 DET A	0	0	–	0.00	1	0	0	2	2	0	2	0	0	0	0	0	0	0	–

	W	L	PCT	ERA	G	GS	CG	IP	H	BB	SO	ShO	Relief Pitching			BATTING			
													W	L	SV	AB	H	HR	BA

Bill Graham continued

	W	L	PCT	ERA	G	GS	CG	IP	H	BB	SO	ShO	W	L	SV	AB	H	HR	BA
1967 NY N	1	2	.333	2.63	5	3	1	27.1	20	11	14	0	0	0	0	8	1	0	.12
2 yrs.	1	2	.333	2.45	6	3	1	29.1	22	11	16	0	0	0	0	8	1	0	.12
1 yr.	0	0	—	0.00	1	0	0	2	2	0	2	0	0	0	0	0	0	0	

Kyle Graham

GRAHAM, KYLE (Skinny)   BR TR 6'2"   172 lbs
B. Aug. 14, 1899, Oak Grove, Ala.   D. Dec. 1, 1973, Oak Grove, Ala.

	W	L	PCT	ERA	G	GS	CG	IP	H	BB	SO	ShO	W	L	SV	AB	H	HR	BA
1924 BOS N	0	4	.000	3.82	5	4	1	33	33	11	15	0	0	0	0	7	0	0	.00
1925	7	12	.368	4.41	34	23	5	157	177	62	32	0	1	1	1	44	6	0	.13
1926	3	3	.500	7.93	15	4	1	36.1	54	19	7	0	2	2	0	12	2	0	.16
1929 DET A	1	3	.250	5.57	13	6	2	51.2	70	33	7	0	0	1	1	19	2	1	.10
4 yrs.	11	22	.333	5.02	67	37	9	278	334	125	61	0	3	4	2	82	10	1	.12
1 yr.	1	3	.250	5.57	13	6	2	51.2	70	33	7	0	0	1	1	19	2	1	.10

Ted Gray

GRAY, TED GLENN   BB TL 5'11"   175 lbs
B. Dec. 31, 1924, Detroit, Mich.

	W	L	PCT	ERA	G	GS	CG	IP	H	BB	SO	ShO	W	L	SV	AB	H	HR	BA
1946 DET A	0	2	.000	8.49	3	2	0	11.2	17	5	5	0	0	0	1	3	0	0	.00
1948	6	2	.750	4.22	26	11	3	85.1	73	72	60	1	0	0	0	29	7	0	.24
1949	10	10	.500	3.51	34	27	8	195	163	103	96	3	0	0	1	63	8	0	.12
1950	10	7	.588	4.40	27	21	7	149.1	139	72	102	0	1	0	1	50	7	0	.14
1951	7	14	.333	4.06	34	28	9	197.1	194	95	131	1	0	1	1	63	9	0	.14
1952	12	17	.414	4.14	35	32	13	224	212	101	138	2	0	0	0	76	13	0	.17
1953	10	15	.400	4.60	30	28	8	176	166	76	115	0	0	0	0	61	14	0	.23
1954	3	5	.375	5.38	19	10	2	72	70	56	29	0	0	0	0	22	1	0	.04
1955 4 teams			CHI A (2G 0–0)		CLE A (2G 0–0)			NY A (1G 0–0)			BAL A (9G 1–2)								
" total	1	2	.333	9.64	14	3	0	23.1	38	15	11	0	1	1	0	3	0	0	.00
9 yrs.	59	74	.444	4.37	222	162	50	1134	1072	595	687	7	2	2	4	370	59	0	.15
8 yrs.	58	72	.446	4.25	208	159	50	1110.2	1034	580	676	7	1	1	4	367	59	0	.16

Steve Grilli

GRILLI, STEPHEN JOSEPH   BR TR 6'2"   170 lbs
B. May 2, 1949, Brooklyn, N. Y.

	W	L	PCT	ERA	G	GS	CG	IP	H	BB	SO	ShO	W	L	SV	AB	H	HR	BA
1975 DET A	0	0	—	1.35	3	0	0	6.2	3	6	5	0	0	0	0	0	0	0	
1976	3	1	.750	4.64	36	0	0	66	63	41	36	0	3	1	3	0	0	0	
1977	1	2	.333	4.81	30	2	0	73	71	49	49	0	1	1	0	0	0	0	
1979 TOR A	0	0	—	0.00	1	0	0	2	1	0	1	0	0	0	0	0	0	0	
4 yrs.	4	3	.571	4.51	70	2	0	147.2	138	96	91	0	4	2	3	0	0	0	
3 yrs.	4	3	.571	4.57	69	2	0	145.2	137	96	90	0	4	2	3	0	0	0	

Marv Grissom

GRISSOM, MARVIN EDWARD   BR TR 6'3"   190 lbs
Brother of Lee Grissom.
B. Mar. 31, 1918, Los Molinos, Calif.

	W	L	PCT	ERA	G	GS	CG	IP	H	BB	SO	ShO	W	L	SV	AB	H	HR	BA
1946 NY N	0	2	.000	4.34	4	3	0	18.2	17	13	9	0	0	0	0	5	1	0	.20
1949 DET A	2	4	.333	6.41	27	2	0	39.1	56	34	17	0	2	3	0	9	2	0	.22
1952 CHI A	12	10	.545	3.74	28	24	7	166	156	79	97	1	0	1	0	53	8	0	.15
1953 2 teams			BOS A (13G 2–6)		NY N (21G 4–2)														
" total	6	8	.429	4.26	34	18	4	143.2	144	61	77	1	0	1	0	45	2	0	.04
1954 NY N	10	7	.588	2.35	56	3	1	122.1	100	50	64	1	9	7	19	32	5	0	.15
1955	5	4	.556	2.92	55	0	0	89.1	76	41	49	0	5	4	8	13	2	0	.15
1956	1	1	.500	1.56	43	0	0	80.2	71	16	49	0	1	1	7	11	1	0	.09
1957	4	4	.500	2.61	55	0	0	82.2	74	23	51	0	4	4	14	12	2	0	.16
1958 SF N	7	5	.583	3.99	51	0	0	65.1	71	26	46	0	7	5	10	9	0	0	.00
1959 STL N	0	0	—	22.50	3	0	0	2	6	0	0	0	0	0	0	0	0	0	
10 yrs.	47	45	.511	3.41	356	52	12	810	771	343	459	3	28	26	58	189	23	0	.12
1 yr.	2	4	.333	6.41	27	2	0	39.1	56	34	17	0	2	3	0	9	2	0	.22

WORLD SERIES

	W	L	PCT	ERA	G	GS	CG	IP	H	BB	SO	ShO	W	L	SV	AB	H	HR	BA
1954 NY N	1	0	1.000	0.00	1	0	0	2.2	1	3	2	0	1	0	0	1	0	0	.00

Steve Gromek

GROMEK, STEPHEN JOSEPH   BB TR 6'2"   180 lbs
B. Jan. 15, 1920, Hamtramck, Mich.   BR 1941–49

	W	L	PCT	ERA	G	GS	CG	IP	H	BB	SO	ShO	W	L	SV	AB	H	HR	BA
1941 CLE A	1	1	.500	4.24	9	2	1	23.1	25	11	19	0	0	0	2	6	1	0	.16
1942	2	0	1.000	3.65	14	0	0	44.1	46	23	14	0	2	0	0	15	5	0	.33
1943	0	0	—	9.00	3	0	0	4	6	4	4	0	0	0	0	2	2	0	1.000
1944	10	9	.526	2.56	35	21	12	203.2	160	70	115	2	0	1	1	73	19	0	.26
1945	19	9	.679	2.55	33	30	21	251	229	66	101	3	0	1	1	91	21	0	.23
1946	5	15	.250	4.33	29	21	5	153.2	159	47	75	2	0	2	4	56	11	0	.19
1947	3	5	.375	3.74	29	7	0	84.1	77	36	39	0	1	3	4	22	7	0	.31
1948	9	3	.750	2.84	38	9	4	130	109	51	50	1	3	1	2	41	6	0	.14
1949	4	6	.400	3.33	27	12	3	92	86	40	22	0	1	2	0	24	4	0	.16
1950	10	7	.588	3.65	31	13	4	113.1	94	36	43	1	4	0	0	38	6	0	.15
1951	7	4	.636	2.77	27	8	1	107.1	98	29	40	0	3	2	1	27	8	0	.29
1952	7	7	.500	3.67	29	13	3	122.2	109	28	65	1	1	1	1	30	3	0	.10
1953 2 teams			CLE A (5G 1–1)		DET A (19G 6–8)														
" total	7	9	.438	4.41	24	18	6	136.2	149	39	67	1	1	0	1	43	3	0	.07
1954 DET A	18	16	.529	2.74	36	32	17	252.2	236	57	102	4	2	0	1	79	15	0	.19
1955	13	10	.565	3.98	28	25	8	181	183	37	73	2	0	0	0	54	9	0	.16
1956	8	6	.571	4.33	28	13	4	141	142	47	64	0	3	0	4	27	4	0	.14
1957	0	1	.000	6.08	15	1	0	23.2	32	13	11	0	0	1	0	2	0	0	.00
17 yrs.	123	108	.532	3.41	447	225	92	2064.2	1940	630	904	17	23	14	23	630	124	0	.19
5 yrs.	45	41	.523	3.77	138	88	35	724	731	190	309	7	7	1	7	203	31	0	.15

WORLD SERIES

	W	L	PCT	ERA	G	GS	CG	IP	H	BB	SO	ShO	W	L	SV	AB	H	HR	BA
1948 CLE A	1	0	1.000	1.00	1	1	1	9	7	1	2	0	0	0	0	3	0	0	.00

Charlie Grover

GROVER, CHARLES BERT (Bugs)   BL TR 6'1½"   185 lbs
B. June 20, 1891, Vanceton, Ohio   D. May 24, 1971, Emmett Township, Mich.

	W	L	PCT	ERA	G	GS	CG	IP	H	BB	SO	ShO	W	L	SV	AB	H	HR	BA
1913 DET A	0	0	—	3.38	2	1	0	10.2	9	7	2	0	0	0	0	3	0	0	.000

	W	L	PCT	ERA	G	GS	CG	IP	H	BB	SO	ShO	Relief Pitching W	L	SV	BATTING AB	H	HR	BA

Joe Grzenda

GRZENDA, JOSEPH CHARLES
B. June 8, 1937, Scranton, Pa.　　　　　　BR TL 6'2" 180 lbs.

	W	L	PCT	ERA	G	GS	CG	IP	H	BB	SO	ShO	W	L	SV	AB	H	HR	BA
1961 DET A	1	0	1.000	7.94	4	0	0	5.2	9	2	0	0	1	0	0	1	1	0	1.000
1964 KC A	0	2	.000	5.40	20	0	0	25	34	13	17	0	0	2	0	2	0	0	.000
1966	0	2	.000	3.27	21	0	0	22	28	12	14	0	0	2	0	1	0	0	.000
1967 NY N	0	0	—	2.16	11	0	0	16.2	14	8	9	0	0	0	0	1	0	0	.000
1969 MIN A	4	1	.800	3.88	38	0	0	48.2	52	17	24	0	4	1	3	5	0	0	.000
1970 WAS A	3	6	.333	4.98	49	3	0	85	86	34	38	0	2	5	6	12	0	0	.000
1971	5	2	.714	1.93	46	0	0	70	54	17	56	0	5	2	5	7	1	0	.143
1972 STL N	1	0	1.000	5.71	30	0	0	34.2	46	17	15	0	1	0	0	1	0	0	.000
8 yrs.	14	13	.519	4.01	219	3	0	307.2	323	120	173	0	13	12	14	30	2	0	.067
1 yr.	1	0	1.000	7.94	4	0	0	5.2	9	2	0	0	1	0	0	1	1	0	1.000

LEAGUE CHAMPIONSHIP SERIES

| 1969 MIN A | 0 | 0 | — | 0.00 | 1 | 0 | 0 | .2 | 0 | 0 | 0 | 0 | 0 | 0 | 0 | 0 | 0 | 0 | — |

Dave Gumpert

GUMPERT, DAVID LAWRENCE
B. May 5, 1958, South Haven, Mich.　　　　　BR TR 6'3" 190 lbs.

1982 DET A	0	0	—	27.00	5	1	0	2	7	2	0	0	0	0	1	0	0	0	—
1983	0	2	.000	2.64	26	0	0	44.1	43	7	14	0	0	2	2	0	0	0	—
2 yrs.	0	2	.000	3.69	31	1	0	46.1	50	9	14	0	0	2	3	0	0	0	—
2 yrs.	0	2	.000	3.69	31	1	0	46.1	50	9	14	0	0	2	3	0	0	0	—

Charley Hall

HALL, CHARLES LOUIS (Sea Lion)
Born Carlos Clolo.
B. July 27, 1885, Ventura, Calif.　　D. Dec. 6, 1943, Ventura, Calif.　　BL TR 6'2" 185 lbs.

1906 CIN N	4	6	.400	3.32	14	9	9	95	86	50	49	1	0	1	1	47	6	0	.128
1907	4	2	.667	2.51	11	8	5	68	51	43	25	0	1	0	0	26	7	0	.269
1909 BOS A	6	4	.600	2.56	11	7	3	59.2	59	17	27	0	3	0	0	19	3	0	.158
1910	12	9	.571	1.91	35	16	13	188.2	142	73	95	0	6	1	2	82	17	0	.207
1911	8	7	.533	3.73	32	10	6	147.1	149	72	83	0	4	3	4	64	9	1	.141
1912	15	8	.652	3.02	34	21	9	191	178	70	83	2	6	0	2	75	20	1	.267
1913	4	4	.500	3.43	35	4	2	105	97	46	48	0	4	0	3	42	9	0	.214
1916 STL N	0	4	.000	5.48	10	5	2	42.2	45	14	15	0	0	0	1	14	2	0	.143
1918 DET A	0	1	.000	6.75	6	1	0	13.1	14	6	2	0	0	0	0	2	0	0	.000
9 yrs.	53	45	.541	3.08	188	81	49	910.2	821	391	427	3	24	5	13	*			
1 yr.	0	1	.000	6.75	6	1	0	13.1	14	6	2	0	0	0	0	2	0	0	.000

WORLD SERIES

| 1912 BOS A | 0 | 0 | — | 3.38 | 2 | 0 | 0 | 10.2 | 11 | 9 | 1 | 0 | 0 | 0 | 1 | 4 | 3 | 0 | .750 |

Herb Hall

HALL, HERBERT SILAS (Iron Duke)
B. June 5, 1894, Steelville, Ill.　　D. July 3, 1970, Fresno, Calif.　　BB TR 6'4" 220 lbs.

| 1918 DET A | 0 | 0 | — | 15.00 | 3 | 0 | 0 | 6 | 12 | 7 | 1 | 0 | 0 | 0 | 0 | 1 | 0 | 0 | .000 |

Marc Hall

HALL, MARCUS
B. Aug. 12, 1887, Joplin, Mo.　　D. Feb. 24, 1915, Joplin, Mo.　　BR TR

1910 STL A	1	7	.125	4.27	8	7	5	46.1	50	31	25	0	1	0	0	15	1	0	.067
1913 DET A	10	12	.455	3.27	30	21	8	165	154	79	69	1	2	3	0	45	4	0	.089
1914	4	6	.400	2.69	25	8	1	90.1	88	27	18	0	0	3	0	23	1	0	.043
3 yrs.	15	25	.375	3.25	63	36	14	301.2	292	137	112	1	3	6	0	83	6	0	.072
2 yrs.	14	18	.438	3.07	55	29	9	255.1	242	106	87	1	2	6	0	68	5	0	.074

Earl Hamilton

HAMILTON, EARL ANDREW
B. July 19, 1891, Gibson City, Ill.　　D. Nov. 17, 1968, Anaheim, Calif.　　BL TL 5'8" 160 lbs.

1911 STL A	5	12	.294	3.97	32	17	10	177	191	69	55	1	1	1	0	56	6	0	.107
1912	11	14	.440	3.24	41	26	17	249.2	228	86	139	1	1	1	2	73	13	0	.178
1913	13	12	.520	2.57	31	24	19	217.1	197	83	101	3	0	2	1	74	10	0	.135
1914	17	18	.486	2.50	44	35	20	302.1	265	100	111	5	1	2	2	85	15	0	.176
1915	9	17	.346	2.87	35	27	13	204	203	69	63	1	0	1	0	62	7	0	.113
1916 3 teams					STL A (1G 0–0)			DET A (5G 1–2)			STL A (22G 5–7)								
total	6	9	.400	3.12	28	17	5	132.2	135	52	32	0	2	2	0	37	1	0	.027
1917 STL A	0	9	.000	3.14	27	8	2	83	86	41	19	0	0	3	1	19	7	0	.368
1918 PIT N	6	0	1.000	0.83	6	6	6	54	47	13	20	1	0	0	0	21	6	0	.286
1919	8	11	.421	3.31	28	19	10	160.1	167	49	39	1	1	0	1	52	7	0	.135
1920	10	13	.435	3.24	39	23	12	230.2	223	69	74	0	3	2	3	67	10	0	.149
1921	13	15	.464	3.36	35	30	12	225	237	58	59	2	0	3	0	75	12	0	.160
1922	11	7	.611	3.99	33	14	9	160	183	40	34	1	3	3	2	58	9	0	.155
1923	7	9	.438	3.77	28	15	5	141	148	42	42	0	2	3	1	52	9	0	.173
1924 PHI N	0	1	.000	10.50	3	0	0	6	9	2	2	0	0	1	0	2	0	0	.000
14 yrs.	116	147	.441	3.16	410	261	140	2343	2319	773	790	16	14	24	13	733	112	0	.153
1 yr.	1	2	.333	2.65	5	5	3	37.1	34	22	7	0	0	0	0	13	1	0	.077

Jack Hamilton

HAMILTON, JACK EDWIN (Hairbreadth Harry)
B. Dec. 25, 1938, Burlington, Iowa　　　　　BR TR 6' 200 lbs.

1962 PHI N	9	12	.429	5.09	41	26	4	182	185	107	101	1	2	0	2	54	3	0	.056
1963	2	1	.667	5.40	19	1	0	30	22	17	23	0	2	0	1	3	0	0	.000
1964 DET A	0	1	.000	8.40	5	1	0	15	24	8	5	0	0	0	0	3	0	0	.000
1965	1	1	.500	14.54	4	1	0	4.1	6	4	3	0	1	0	0	0	0	0	—
1966 NY N	6	13	.316	3.93	57	13	3	148.2	138	88	93	1	2	6	13	38	5	0	.132
1967 2 teams					NY N (17G 2–0)			CAL A (26G 9–6)											
total	11	6	.647	3.35	43	21	0	150.2	128	79	96	0	3	0	1	43	7	1	.163
1968 CAL A	3	1	.750	3.32	21	2	1	38	34	15	18	0	2	0	2	7	1	0	.143
1969 2 teams					CLE A (20G 0–2)			CHI A (8G 0–3)											
total	0	5	.000	6.49	28	0	0	43	60	30	18	0	0	5	1	2	0	0	.000
8 yrs.	32	40	.444	4.53	218	65	8	611.2	597	348	357	2	12	11	20	150	16	1	.107
2 yrs.	1	2	.333	9.78	9	2	0	19.1	30	12	8	0	1	0	0	3	0	0	.000

	W	L	PCT	ERA	G	GS	CG	IP	H	BB	SO	ShO	Relief Pitching W	L	SV	BATTING AB	H	HR	B

Luke Hamlin

HAMLIN, LUKE DANIEL (Hot Potato)   BL TR 6'2"   168 lb
B. July 3, 1906, Ferris Center, Mich.   D. Feb. 18, 1978, Clare, Mich.

	W	L	PCT	ERA	G	GS	CG	IP	H	BB	SO	ShO	W	L	SV	AB	H	HR	B
1933 DET A	1	0	1.000	4.86	3	3	0	16.2	20	10	10	0	0	0	0	5	2	0	.4
1934	2	3	.400	5.38	20	5	1	75.1	87	44	30	0	0	3	1	26	6	0	.2
1937 BKN N	11	13	.458	3.59	39	25	11	185.2	183	48	93	1	2	1	1	59	11	0	.1
1938	12	15	.444	3.68	44	30	10	237.1	243	65	97	3	1	1	6	78	11	0	.1
1939	20	13	.606	3.64	40	36	19	269.2	255	54	88	2	2	0	0	103	13	1	.1
1940	9	8	.529	3.06	33	25	9	182.1	183	34	91	2	0	0	0	58	5	0	.0
1941	8	8	.500	4.24	30	20	5	136	139	41	58	1	1	0	1	41	6	0	.1
1942 PIT N	4	4	.500	3.94	23	14	6	112	128	19	38	1	0	0	0	37	9	0	.2
1944 PHI A	6	12	.333	3.74	29	23	9	190	204	38	58	2	0	1	0	56	13	0	.2
9 yrs.	73	76	.490	3.77	261	181	70	1405	1442	353	563	12	6	7	9	463	76	1	.1
2 yrs.	3	3	.500	5.28	23	8	1	92	107	54	40	0	0	3	1	31	8	0	.2

Don Hankins

HANKINS, DONALD WAYNE   BR TR 6'3"   183 lb
B. Feb. 9, 1902, Pendleton, Ind.   D. May 16, 1963, Winston-Salem, N. C.

	W	L	PCT	ERA	G	GS	CG	IP	H	BB	SO	ShO	W	L	SV	AB	H	HR	B
1927 DET A	2	1	.667	6.48	20	1	0	41.2	67	13	10	0	2	0	2	7	1	0	.1

Jim Hannan

HANNAN, JAMES JOHN   BR TR 6'3"   205 lb
B. Jan. 7, 1940, Jersey City, N. J.

	W	L	PCT	ERA	G	GS	CG	IP	H	BB	SO	ShO	W	L	SV	AB	H	HR	B
1962 WAS A	2	4	.333	3.31	42	3	0	68	56	49	39	0	1	2	4	11	1	0	.0
1963	2	2	.500	4.88	13	2	0	27.2	23	17	14	0	1	1	0	6	0	0	.0
1964	4	7	.364	4.16	49	7	0	106	108	45	67	0	4	2	3	20	3	0	.1
1965	1	1	.500	4.91	4	1	1	14.2	18	6	5	1	0	1	0	3	0	0	.0
1966	3	9	.250	4.26	30	18	2	114	125	59	68	0	0	1	0	30	3	0	.0
1967	1	1	.500	5.40	8	2	0	21.2	28	7	14	0	1	0	0	4	0	0	.0
1968	10	6	.625	3.01	25	22	4	140.1	147	50	75	1	0	0	0	47	3	0	.0
1969	7	6	.538	3.64	35	28	1	158.1	138	91	72	1	0	0	0	52	6	0	.1
1970	9	11	.450	4.01	42	17	1	128	119	54	61	1	4	3	0	31	4	0	.1
1971 2 teams			DET	A	(7G 1–0)		MIL	A	(21G 1–1)										
" total	2	1	.667	4.57	28	2	0	43.1	45	28	23	0	2	0	0	5	0	0	.00
10 yrs.	41	48	.461	3.88	276	101	9	822	807	406	438	4	13	10	7	209	19	0	.09
1 yr.	1	0	1.000	3.27	7	0	0	11	7	7	6	0	1	0	0	2	0	0	.00

Charlie Harding

HARDING, CHARLES HAROLD (Slim)   BR TR 6'2½"   172 lb
B. Jan. 3, 1891, Nashville, Tenn.   D. Oct. 30, 1971, Bold Springs, Tenn.

	W	L	PCT	ERA	G	GS	CG	IP	H	BB	SO	ShO	W	L	SV	AB	H	HR	B
1913 DET A	0	0	—	4.50	1	0	0	2	3	1	0	0	0	0	0	0	0	0	

Bob Harris

HARRIS, ROBERT ARTHUR   BR TR 6'   185 lb
B. May 1, 1916, Gillette, Wyo.

	W	L	PCT	ERA	G	GS	CG	IP	H	BB	SO	ShO	W	L	SV	AB	H	HR	B
1938 DET A	1	0	1.000	7.20	3	1	1	10	14	4	7	0	0	0	0	3	1	0	.3
1939 2 teams			DET	A	(5G 1–1)		STL	A	(28G 3–12)										
" total	4	13	.235	5.50	33	17	6	144	180	79	57	0	2	1	0	42	9	0	.2
1940 STL A	11	15	.423	4.93	35	28	8	193.2	225	85	49	1	2	1	1	60	15	0	.2
1941	12	14	.462	5.21	34	29	9	186.2	237	85	57	2	1	1	1	61	7	0	.1
1942 2 teams			STL	A	(6G 1–5)		PHI	A	(16G 1–5)										
" total	2	10	.167	3.71	22	14	2	111.2	114	41	35	1	0	2	0	36	7	0	.19
5 yrs.	30	52	.366	4.96	127	89	26	646	770	294	205	4	5	5	2	202	39	0	.19
2 yrs.	2	1	.667	5.14	8	2	1	28	32	12	16	0	1	0	0	8	3	0	.37

Earl Harrist

HARRIST, EARL (Irish)   BR TR 6'   175 lb
B. Aug. 20, 1919, Dubach, La.

	W	L	PCT	ERA	G	GS	CG	IP	H	BB	SO	ShO	W	L	SV	AB	H	HR	B
1945 CIN N	2	4	.333	3.61	14	5	1	62.1	60	27	15	0	1	0	0	15	0	0	.00
1947 CHI A	3	8	.273	3.56	33	4	0	93.2	85	49	55	0	3	5	5	24	5	0	.20
1948 2 teams			CHI	A	(11G 1–3)		WAS	A	(23G 3–3)										
" total	4	6	.400	4.93	34	5	0	84	93	50	35	0	4	3	0	22	3	0	.1
1952 STL A	2	8	.200	4.01	36	9	1	116.2	119	47	49	0	2	2	5	31	3	0	.0
1953 2 teams			CHI	A	(7G 1–0)		DET	A	(8G 0–2)										
" total	1	2	.333	8.33	15	1	0	27	34	20	8	0	1	1	0	4	0	0	.00
5 yrs.	12	28	.300	4.34	132	24	2	383.2	391	193	162	0	11	11	10	96	11	0	.1
1 yr.	0	2	.000	8.68	8	1	0	18.2	25	15	7	0	0	1	0	3	0	0	.00

Clyde Hatter

HATTER, CLYDE MELNOW (Mad)   BR TL 5'11"   170 lb
B. Aug. 7, 1908, Poplar Hill, Ky.   D. Oct. 16, 1937, Yosemite, Ky.

	W	L	PCT	ERA	G	GS	CG	IP	H	BB	SO	ShO	W	L	SV	AB	H	HR	B
1935 DET A	0	0	—	7.56	8	2	0	33.1	44	30	15	0	0	0	0	10	3	0	.30
1937	1	0	1.000	11.57	3	0	0	9.1	17	11	4	0	1	0	0	3	0	0	.00
2 yrs.	1	0	1.000	8.44	11	2	0	42.2	61	41	19	0	1	0	0	13	3	0	.2
2 yrs.	1	0	1.000	8.44	11	2	0	42.2	61	41	19	0	1	0	0	13	3	0	.2

Roy Henshaw

HENSHAW, ROY KNIKELBINE   BR TL 5'8"   155 lb
B. July 29, 1911, Chicago, Ill.

	W	L	PCT	ERA	G	GS	CG	IP	H	BB	SO	ShO	W	L	SV	AB	H	HR	B
1933 CHI N	2	1	.667	4.19	21	0	0	38.2	32	20	16	0	2	1	0	10	2	0	.20
1935	13	5	.722	3.28	31	18	7	142.2	135	68	53	3	4	0	1	51	13	0	.2
1936	6	5	.545	3.97	39	14	6	129.1	152	56	69	2	1	3	1	44	6	0	.1
1937 BKN N	5	12	.294	5.07	42	16	5	156.1	176	69	98	0	1	3	2	48	8	0	.1
1938 STL N	5	11	.313	4.02	27	15	4	130	132	48	34	0	2	1	0	41	9	0	.2
1942 DET A	2	4	.333	4.09	18	6	0	61.2	63	27	24	0	2	3	1	12	1	0	.08
1943	0	2	.000	3.79	26	3	0	71.1	75	33	33	0	0	1	2	18	2	0	.1
1944	0	0	—	8.76	7	1	0	12.1	17	16	10	0	0	0	0	5	0	0	.0
8 yrs.	33	40	.452	4.16	216	69	22	742.1	782	327	337	5	12	12	7	229	41	0	.1
3 yrs.	2	6	.250	4.33	56	6	0	145.1	155	66	67	0	2	4	3	35	3	0	.1
WORLD SERIES																			
1935 CHI N	0	0	—	7.36	1	0	0	3.2	2	5	2	0	0	0	0	1	0	0	.00

	W	L	PCT	ERA	G	GS	CG	IP	H	BB	SO	ShO	Relief Pitching W	L	SV	BATTING AB	H	HR	BA

Ray Herbert

HERBERT, RAYMOND ERNEST
B. Dec. 15, 1929, Detroit, Mich.　　　　　　　　BR TR 5'11"　185 lbs.

	W	L	PCT	ERA	G	GS	CG	IP	H	BB	SO	ShO	W	L	SV	AB	H	HR	BA
'950 DET A	1	2	.333	3.63	8	3	1	22.1	20	12	5	0	1	0	1	7	2	0	.286
'951	4	0	1.000	1.42	5	0	0	12.2	8	9	9	0	4	0	0	4	0	0	.000
'953	4	6	.400	5.24	43	3	0	87.2	109	46	37	0	4	4	6	19	3	0	.158
'954	3	6	.333	5.87	42	4	0	84.1	114	50	44	0	3	3	0	17	3	1	.176
'955 KC A	1	8	.111	6.26	23	11	2	87.2	99	40	30	0	0	1	0	21	4	0	.190
'958	8	8	.500	3.50	42	16	5	175	161	55	108	0	1	3	3	52	10	0	.192
'959	11	11	.500	4.85	37	26	10	183.2	196	62	99	2	0	1	1	57	12	1	.211
'960	14	15	.483	3.28	37	33	14	252.2	256	72	122	0	0	1	1	76	13	0	.171
'961 2 teams			KC	A	(13G 3–6)					CHI	A	(21G 9–6)							
" total	12	12	.500	4.55	34	32	5	221.1	245	66	84	0	1	0	0	81	15	2	.185
'962 CHI A	20	9	.690	3.27	35	35	12	236.2	228	74	115	2	0	0	0	82	16	2	.195
'963	13	10	.565	3.24	33	33	14	224.2	230	35	105	7	0	0	0	63	14	1	.222
'964	6	7	.462	3.47	20	19	1	111.2	117	17	40	1	0	0	0	36	5	0	.139
'965 PHI N	5	8	.385	3.86	25	19	4	130.2	162	19	51	1	0	0	1	41	11	0	.268
'966	2	5	.286	4.29	23	2	0	50.1	55	14	15	0	2	4	2	13	1	0	.077
14 yrs.	104	107	.493	4.01	407	236	68	1881.1	2000	571	864	13	16	17	15	569	109	7	.192
4 yrs.	12	14	.462	5.09	98	10	1	207	251	117	95	0	12	7	7	47	8	1	.170

Willie Hernandez

HERNANDEZ, GUILLERMO
Also known as Guillermo Villanueva.
B. Nov. 14, 1955, Aguada, Puerto Rico　　　　　　BL TL 6'3"　180 lbs.

	W	L	PCT	ERA	G	GS	CG	IP	H	BB	SO	ShO	W	L	SV	AB	H	HR	BA
'977 CHI N	8	7	.533	3.03	67	1	0	110	94	28	78	0	8	6	4	16	1	0	.063
'978	8	2	.800	3.75	54	0	0	60	57	35	38	0	8	2	3	1	0	0	.000
'979	4	4	.500	5.01	51	2	0	79	85	39	53	0	4	3	0	8	2	0	.250
'980	1	9	.100	4.42	53	7	0	108	115	45	75	0	1	3	0	19	4	0	.211
'981	0	0	—	3.86	12	0	0	14	14	8	13	0	0	0	2	0	0	0	—
'982	4	6	.400	3.00	75	0	0	75	74	24	54	0	4	6	10	3	0	0	.000
'983 2 teams			CHI	N	(11G 1–0)					PHI	N	(63G 8–4)							
" total	9	4	.692	3.28	74	1	0	115.1	109	32	93	0	9	4	8	15	6	0	.400
'984 DET A	9	3	.750	1.92	80	0	0	140.1	96	36	112	0	9	3	32	0	0	0	—
8 yrs.	43	35	.551	3.36	466	11	0	701.2	644	247	516	0	43	27	59	62	13	0	.210
1 yr.	9	3	.750	1.92	80	0	0	140.1	96	36	112	0	9	3	32	0	0	0	—

LEAGUE CHAMPIONSHIP SERIES

	W	L	PCT	ERA	G	GS	CG	IP	H	BB	SO	ShO	W	L	SV	AB	H	HR	BA
'984 DET A	0	0	—	2.25	3	0	0	4	3	1	3	0	0	0	1	0	0	0	—

WORLD SERIES

	W	L	PCT	ERA	G	GS	CG	IP	H	BB	SO	ShO	W	L	SV	AB	H	HR	BA
'83 PHI N	0	0	—	0.00	3	0	0	4	0	1	4	0	0	0	0	0	0	0	—
'84 DET A	0	0	—	1.69	3	0	0	5.1	4	0	0	0	0	0	2	0	0	0	—
2 yrs.	0	0	—	0.96	6	0	0	9.1	4	1	4	0	0	0	2	0	0	0	—

Art Herring

HERRING, ARTHUR L (Sandy)
B. Mar. 10, 1907, Altus, Okla.　　　　　　　　BR TR 5'7"　168 lbs.

	W	L	PCT	ERA	G	GS	CG	IP	H	BB	SO	ShO	W	L	SV	AB	H	HR	BA
'29 DET A	2	1	.667	4.78	4	4	2	32	38	19	15	0	0	0	0	14	3	0	.214
'30	3	3	.500	5.33	23	6	1	77.2	97	36	16	0	1	0	0	23	3	0	.130
'31	7	13	.350	4.31	35	16	9	165	186	67	64	0	1	4	1	55	11	0	.200
'32	1	2	.333	5.24	12	0	0	22.1	25	15	12	0	1	2	2	4	0	0	.000
'33	1	2	.333	3.84	24	3	1	61	61	20	20	0	0	2	0	13	1	0	.077
'34 BKN N	2	4	.333	6.20	14	4	2	49.1	63	29	15	0	1	3	0	14	2	0	.143
'39 CHI A	0	0	—	5.65	7	0	0	14.1	13	5	8	0	0	0	0	4	0	0	.000
'44 BKN N	3	4	.429	3.42	12	6	3	55.1	59	17	19	1	1	0	1	15	3	0	.200
'45	7	4	.636	3.48	22	15	7	124	103	43	34	2	1	0	2	42	4	0	.095
'46	7	2	.778	3.35	35	2	0	86	91	29	34	0	5	2	5	22	4	0	.182
'47 PIT N	1	3	.250	8.44	11	0	0	10.2	18	4	6	0	1	3	2	2	0	0	.000
11 yrs.	34	38	.472	4.32	199	56	25	697.2	754	284	243	3	12	16	13	208	31	0	.149
5 yrs.	14	21	.400	4.55	98	29	13	358	407	157	127	0	3	8	3	109	18	0	.165

Piano Legs Hickman

HICKMAN, CHARLES TAYLOR
B. Mar. 4, 1876, Taylortown, Pa.　　D. Apr. 19, 1934, Morgantown, W. Va.　　　BR TR 5'9"　185 lbs.

	W	L	PCT	ERA	G	GS	CG	IP	H	BB	SO	ShO	W	L	SV	AB	H	HR	BA
'97 BOS N	0	0	—	5.87	2	0	0	7.2	10	5	0	0	0	0	1	3	2	1	.667
'98	1	1	.500	2.18	6	3	3	33	22	13	9	1	0	0	2	58	15	0	.259
'99	7	0	1.000	4.48	11	9	5	66.1	52	40	14	2	0	0	1	63	25	0	.397
'01 NY N	3	5	.375	4.57	9	9	6	65	76	26	11	0	0	0	0	401	113	4	.282
'02 BOS A	0	1	.000	7.88	1	1	1	8	11	5	1	0	0	0	0	534	194	11	.363
'07 CHI A	0	0	—	3.60	1	0	0	5	4	5	2	0	0	0	0	216	61	1	.282
6 yrs.	11	7	.611	4.28	30	22	15	185	175	94	37	3	0	0	4	*			

Ed High

HIGH, EDWARD THOMAS (Lefty)
B. Dec. 26, 1876, Baltimore, Md.　　D. Feb. 12, 1926, Baltimore, Md.　　　TL

	W	L	PCT	ERA	G	GS	CG	IP	H	BB	SO	ShO	W	L	SV	AB	H	HR	BA
'01 DET A	1	0	1.000	3.50	4	1	1	18	21	6	4	0	0	0	0	7	0	0	.000

John Hiller

HILLER, JOHN FREDERICK
B. Apr. 8, 1943, Toronto, Ont., Canada　　　　　BR TL 6'1"　185 lbs.

	W	L	PCT	ERA	G	GS	CG	IP	H	BB	SO	ShO	W	L	SV	AB	H	HR	BA
'65 DET A	0	0	—	0.00	5	0	0	6	5	1	4	0	0	0	1	0	0	0	—
'66	0	0	—	9.00	1	0	0	2	2	2	1	0	0	0	0	0	0	0	—
'67	4	3	.571	2.63	23	6	2	65	57	9	49	2	1	1	3	15	2	0	.133
'68	9	6	.600	2.39	39	12	4	128	92	51	78	1	4	3	2	37	3	0	.081
'69	4	4	.500	3.99	40	8	1	99.1	97	44	74	1	3	1	4	21	6	0	.286
'70	6	6	.500	3.03	47	5	1	104	82	46	89	1	5	3	3	23	0	0	.000
'72	1	2	.333	2.05	24	3	1	44	39	13	26	0	0	0	3	4	0	0	.000
'73	10	5	.667	1.44	65	0	0	125	89	39	124	0	10	5	38	0	0	0	—
'74	17	14	.548	2.64	59	0	0	150	127	62	134	0	17	14	13	0	0	0	—
'75	2	3	.400	2.17	36	0	0	70.2	52	36	87	0	2	3	14	0	0	0	—
'76	12	8	.600	2.38	56	1	1	121	93	67	117	1	11	8	13	1	0	0	.000
'77	8	14	.364	3.56	45	8	3	124	120	61	115	0	5	8	7	0	0	0	—
'78	9	4	.692	2.34	51	0	0	92.1	64	35	74	0	9	4	15	0	0	0	—
'79	4	7	.364	5.24	43	0	0	79	83	55	46	0	4	7	9	0	0	0	—

	W	L	PCT	ERA	G	GS	CG	IP	H	BB	SO	ShO	Relief Pitching W	L	SV	BATTING AB	H	HR	BA

John Hiller continued

	W	L	PCT	ERA	G	GS	CG	IP	H	BB	SO	ShO	W	L	SV	AB	H	HR	BA
1980	1	0	1.000	4.35	11	0	0	31	38	14	18	0	1	0	0	0	0	0	
15 yrs.	87	76	.534	2.83	545	43	13	1241.1	1040	535	1036	6	72	57	125	101	11	0	.10
15 yrs.	87	76	.534	2.83	545	43	13	1241.1	1040	535	1036	6	72	57	125	101	11	0	.10
				7th	1st								1st		1st				

LEAGUE CHAMPIONSHIP SERIES

	W	L	PCT	ERA	G	GS	CG	IP	H	BB	SO	ShO	W	L	SV	AB	H	HR	BA
1972 DET A	1	0	1.000	0.00	3	0	0	3.1	1	1	1	0	1	0	0	0	0	0	

WORLD SERIES

	W	L	PCT	ERA	G	GS	CG	IP	H	BB	SO	ShO	W	L	SV	AB	H	HR	BA
1968 DET A	0	0	-	13.50	2	0	0	2	6	3	1	0	0	0	0	0	0	0	

Billy Hoeft

HOEFT, WILLIAM FREDERICK
B. May 17, 1932, Oshkosh, Wis.   BL TL 6'3"   180 lbs

	W	L	PCT	ERA	G	GS	CG	IP	H	BB	SO	ShO	W	L	SV	AB	H	HR	BA
1952 DET A	2	7	.222	4.32	34	10	1	125	123	63	67	0	0	2	4	40	6	0	.15
1953	9	14	.391	4.83	29	27	9	197.2	223	58	90	0	0	0	2	64	11	0	.17
1954	7	15	.318	4.58	34	25	10	175	180	59	114	4	1	1	1	52	10	0	.19
1955	16	7	.696	2.99	32	29	17	220	187	75	133	7	0	1	0	82	17	0	.20
1956	20	14	.588	4.06	38	34	18	248	276	104	172	4	2	0	0	80	20	0	.25
1957	9	11	.450	3.48	34	28	10	207	188	69	111	1	0	0	1	67	10	3	.14
1958	10	9	.526	4.15	36	21	6	143	148	49	94	0	1	2	3	44	12	0	.27
1959 3 teams				DET A (2G 1-3)				BOS A (5G 0-3)					BAL A (16G 1-1)						
" total	2	5	.286	5.59	23	8	0	67.2	78	31	40	0	0	0	0	18	4	0	.22
1960 BAL A	2	1	.667	4.34	19	0	0	18.2	18	14	14	0	2	1	0	1	0	0	.00
1961	7	4	.636	2.02	35	12	3	138	106	55	100	1	2	1	3	39	7	0	.17
1962 SF N	4	8	.333	4.59	57	4	0	113.2	103	43	73	0	4	6	7	19	3	0	.15
1963 SF N	2	0	1.000	4.44	23	0	0	24.1	26	10	8	0	2	0	0	1	1	0	1.00
1964 MIL N	4	0	1.000	3.80	42	0	0	73.1	76	18	47	0	4	0	4	9	2	0	.22
1965 CHI N	2	2	.500	2.81	29	2	1	51.1	41	20	44	0	1	1	1	11	3	0	.27
1966 2 teams				CHI N (36G 1-2)				SF N (4G 0-2)											
" total	1	4	.200	4.84	40	0	0	44.2	47	17	33	0	1	4	3	4	1	0	.25
15 yrs.	97	101	.490	3.94	505	200	75	1847.1	1820	685	1140	17	20	19	33	531	107	3	.20
8 yrs.	74	78	.487	4.02	239	176	71	1324.2	1331	481	783	16	4	6	11	432	87	3	.20

Chief Hogsett

HOGSETT, ELON CHESTER
B. Nov. 2, 1903, Brownell, Kans.   BL TL 6'   190 lbs

	W	L	PCT	ERA	G	GS	CG	IP	H	BB	SO	ShO	W	L	SV	AB	H	HR	BA
1929 DET A	1	2	.333	2.83	4	4	2	28.2	34	9	9	1	0	0	0	10	2	0	.20
1930	9	8	.529	5.42	33	17	4	146	174	63	54	0	2	1	1	58	17	1	.29
1931	3	9	.250	5.93	22	12	5	112.1	150	33	47	0	0	2	2	47	11	0	.23
1932	11	9	.550	3.54	47	15	7	178	201	66	56	0	6	3	7	57	14	2	.24
1933	6	10	.375	4.50	45	2	0	116	137	56	39	0	6	9	9	38	8	0	.21
1934	3	3	.600	4.29	26	0	0	50.1	61	19	23	0	3	3	3	13	3	0	.23
1935	6	6	.500	3.54	40	0	0	96.2	109	49	39	0	6	6	5	23	6	2	.26
1936 2 teams				DET A (3G 0-1)				STL A (39G 13-15)											
" total	13	16	.448	5.58	42	29	10	219.1	286	91	68	0	1	2	1	70	10	0	.14
1937 STL A	6	19	.240	6.29	37	26	8	177.1	245	75	68	1	1	0	2	62	13	1	.21
1938 WAS A	5	6	.455	6.03	31	9	1	91	107	36	33	0	3	2	3	23	7	0	.30
1944 DET A	0	0	-		3	0	0	6.1	7	4	5	0	0	0	0	2	0	0	.00
11 yrs.	63	87	.420	5.02	330	114	37	1222	1511	501	441	2	28	27	33	403	91	6	.22
9 yrs.	39	47	.453	4.45	223	50	18	738.1	881	300	273	1	23	24	27	248	61	5	.24
													7th						

WORLD SERIES

	W	L	PCT	ERA	G	GS	CG	IP	H	BB	SO	ShO	W	L	SV	AB	H	HR	BA
1934 DET A	0	0	-	1.23	3	0	0	7.1	6	3	3	0	0	0	0	3	0	0	.00
1935	0	0	-	0.00	1	0	0	1	0	1	0	0	0	0	0	0	0	0	
2 yrs.	0	0	-	1.08	4	0	0	8.1	6	4	3	0	0	0	0	3	0	0	.00

Fred Holdsworth

HOLDSWORTH, FREDRICK WILLIAM
B. May 29, 1952, Detroit, Mich.   BR TR 6'1"   190 lbs

	W	L	PCT	ERA	G	GS	CG	IP	H	BB	SO	ShO	W	L	SV	AB	H	HR	BA
1972 DET A	0	1	.000	12.86	2	2	0	7	13	2	5	0	0	0	0	3	1	0	.33
1973	0	1	.000	6.60	5	2	0	15	13	6	9	0	0	0	0	0	0	0	
1974	0	3	.000	4.25	8	5	0	36	40	14	16	0	0	0	0	0	0	0	
1976 BAL A	4	1	.800	2.03	16	0	0	40	24	13	24	0	4	1	2	0	0	0	
1977 2 teams				BAL A (12G 0-1)				MON N (14G 3-3)											
" total	3	4	.429	4.02	26	6	0	56	52	34	25	0	0	1	0	10	0	0	
1978 MON N	0	0	-	7.00	6	0	0	9	16	8	3	0	0	0	0	0	0	0	
1980 MIL A	0	0	-	4.50	9	0	0	20	24	9	12	0	0	0	0	0	0	0	
7 yrs.	7	10	.412	4.38	72	15	0	183	182	86	94	0	4	2	2	13	1	0	.07
3 yrs.	0	5	.000	5.90	15	9	0	58	66	22	30	0	0	0	0	3	1	0	.33

Carl Holling

HOLLING, CARL
B. July 9, 1896, Dana, Calif.   D. July 18, 1962, Sonoma, Calif.   BR TR 6'1"   172 lbs

	W	L	PCT	ERA	G	GS	CG	IP	H	BB	SO	ShO	W	L	SV	AB	H	HR	BA
1921 DET A	3	7	.300	4.30	35	11	4	136	162	58	38	0	1	3	4	48	13	0	.27
1922	1	1	.500	15.43	5	1	0	9.1	21	5	2	0	1	0	0	2	0	0	.00
2 yrs.	4	8	.333	5.02	40	12	4	145.1	183	63	40	0	2	3	4	50	13	0	.26
2 yrs.	4	8	.333	5.02	40	12	4	145.1	183	63	40	0	2	3	4	50	13	0	.26

Ken Holloway

HOLLOWAY, KENNETH EUGENE
B. Aug. 8, 1897, Barwick, Ga.   D. Sept. 25, 1968, Thomasville, Ga.   BR TR 6'   185 lbs

	W	L	PCT	ERA	G	GS	CG	IP	H	BB	SO	ShO	W	L	SV	AB	H	HR	BA
1922 DET A	0	0	-	0.00	1	0	0	1	1	0	1	0	0	0	0	0	0	0	
1923	11	10	.524	4.45	42	24	7	194	232	75	55	1	3	1	1	65	8	0	.12
1924	14	6	.700	4.07	49	14	5	181.1	209	61	46	0	9	2	3	58	11	0	.19
1925	13	4	.765	4.62	38	14	6	157.2	170	67	29	0	4	0	2	48	11	0	.22
1926	4	6	.400	5.12	36	12	3	139	192	42	43	0	1	0	0	46	11	0	.23
1927	11	12	.478	4.07	36	23	11	183.1	210	61	36	1	1	2	6	62	8	0	.12
1928	4	8	.333	4.34	30	11	5	120.1	137	32	32	0	1	1	2	33	4	0	.12
1929 CLE A	6	5	.545	3.03	25	11	6	119	118	37	32	2	1	0	0	41	7	0	.17

	W	L	PCT	ERA	G	GS	CG	IP	H	BB	SO	ShO	Relief Pitching W	L	SV	BATTING AB	H	HR	BA

Ken Holloway continued

	W	L	PCT	ERA	G	GS	CG	IP	H	BB	SO	ShO	W	L	SV	AB	H	HR	BA
'30 2 teams	CLE	A	(12G 1–1)		NY	A	(16G 0–0)												
total	1	1	.500	6.72	28	2	0	64.1	101	22	19	0	0	0	2	25	3	0	.120
9 yrs.	64	52	.552	4.40	285	111	43	1160	1370	397	293	4	19	8	18	378	63	0	.167
7 yrs.	57	46	.553	4.41	232	98	37	976.2	1151	338	242	2	18	8	16	312	53	0	.170
													9th						

Ducky Holmes

HOLMES, JAMES WILLIAM BL TR 5'6" 170 lbs.
B. Jan. 28, 1869, Des Moines, Iowa   D. Aug. 6, 1932, Truro, Iowa

	W	L	PCT	ERA	G	GS	CG	IP	H	BB	SO	ShO	W	L	SV	AB	H	HR	BA
'95 LOU N	1	0	1.000	5.79	2	1	1	14	16	4	0	0	0	0	0	161	60	3	.373
'96	0	1	.000	7.50	2	1	0	12	26	8	3	0	0	0	0	141	38	0	.270
2 yrs.	1	1	.500	6.58	4	2	1	26	42	12	3	0	0	0	0	*			

Vern Holtgrave

HOLTGRAVE, LAVERN GEORGE (Woody) BR TR 6'1" 183 lbs.
B. Oct. 18, 1942, Aviston, Ill.

	W	L	PCT	ERA	G	GS	CG	IP	H	BB	SO	ShO	W	L	SV	AB	H	HR	BA
'65 DET A	0	0	–	6.00	1	0	0	3	4	2	2	0	0	0	0	0	0	0	–

Gene Host

HOST, EUGENE EARL (Twinkles, Slick) BB TL 5'11" 190 lbs.
B. Jan. 1, 1933, Leeper, Pa.

	W	L	PCT	ERA	G	GS	CG	IP	H	BB	SO	ShO	W	L	SV	AB	H	HR	BA
'56 DET A	0	0	–	7.71	1	1	0	4.2	9	2	5	0	0	0	0	2	0	0	.000
'57 KC A	0	2	.000	7.23	11	2	0	23.2	29	14	9	0	0	1	0	5	0	0	.000
2 yrs.	0	2	.000	7.31	12	3	0	28.1	38	16	14	0	0	1	0	7	0	0	.000
1 yr.	0	0	–	7.71	1	1	0	4.2	9	2	5	0	0	0	0	2	0	0	.000

Fred House

HOUSE, WILFRED EDWIN BR TR 6'3" 190 lbs.
B. Oct. 3, 1890, Cabool, Mo.   D. Nov. 16, 1923, Kansas City, Mo.

	W	L	PCT	ERA	G	GS	CG	IP	H	BB	SO	ShO	W	L	SV	AB	H	HR	BA
'13 DET A	1	2	.333	5.20	19	2	0	53.2	64	17	16	0	1	1	0	18	0	0	.000

Art Houtteman

HOUTTEMAN, ARTHUR JOSEPH BR TR 6'2" 188 lbs.
B. Aug. 7, 1927, Detroit, Mich.

	W	L	PCT	ERA	G	GS	CG	IP	H	BB	SO	ShO	W	L	SV	AB	H	HR	BA
'45 DET A	0	2	.000	5.33	13	0	0	25.1	27	11	9	0	0	2	0	5	0	0	.000
'46	0	1	.000	9.00	1	1	0	8	15	0	2	0	0	0	0	2	1	0	.500
'47	7	2	.778	3.42	23	9	7	110.2	106	36	58	2	1	0	0	40	12	0	.300
'48	2	16	.111	4.66	43	20	4	164.1	186	52	74	0	1	2	10	56	11	0	.196
'49	15	10	.600	3.71	34	25	13	203.2	227	59	85	2	3	2	0	78	19	0	.244
'50	19	12	.613	3.54	41	34	21	274.2	257	99	88	4	2	0	4	93	14	0	.151
'52	8	20	.286	4.36	35	28	10	221	218	65	109	2	1	2	1	69	7	0	.101
'53 2 teams	DET	A	(16G 2–6)		CLE	A	(22G 7–7)												
total	9	13	.409	4.61	38	22	9	177.2	200	54	68	2	2	2	4	53	8	1	.151
'54 CLE A	15	7	.682	3.35	32	25	11	188	198	59	68	1	1	2	0	65	18	1	.277
'55	10	6	.625	3.98	35	12	3	124.1	126	44	53	1	6	1	0	38	6	0	.158
'56	2	2	.500	6.56	22	4	0	46.2	60	31	19	0	1	0	1	12	2	0	.167
'57 2 teams	CLE	A	(3G 0–0)		BAL	A	(5G 0–0)												
total	0	0	–	13.50	8	1	0	10.2	26	6	6	0	0	0	0	2	1	0	.500
12 yrs.	87	91	.489	4.14	325	181	78	1555	1646	516	639	14	18	13	20	513	99	2	.193
8 yrs.	53	69	.434	4.13	206	126	58	1076.1	1123	351	453	11	8	9	16	362	67	1	.185

WORLD SERIES
	W	L	PCT	ERA	G	GS	CG	IP	H	BB	SO	ShO	W	L	SV	AB	H	HR	BA
'54 CLE A	0	0	–	4.50	1	0	0	2	2	1	1	0	0	0	0	0	0	0	–

Waite Hoyt

HOYT, WAITE CHARLES (Schoolboy) BR TR 6' 180 lbs.
B. Sept. 9, 1899, Brooklyn, N. Y.   D. Aug. 25, 1984, Cincinnati, Ohio
Hall of Fame 1969.

	W	L	PCT	ERA	G	GS	CG	IP	H	BB	SO	ShO	W	L	SV	AB	H	HR	BA
'18 NY N	0	0	–	0.00	1	0	0	1	0	0	2	0	0	0	0	1	0	0	.000
'19 BOS A	4	6	.400	3.25	13	11	6	105.1	99	22	28	1	0	0	0	38	5	0	.132
'20	6	6	.500	4.38	22	11	6	121.1	123	47	45	2	0	2	1	43	5	0	.116
'21 NY A	19	13	.594	3.09	43	44	21	282.1	301	81	102	1	3	2	3	99	22	0	.222
'22	19	12	.613	3.43	37	31	17	265	271	76	95	3	3	1	0	92	20	0	.217
'23	17	9	.654	3.02	37	28	19	238.2	227	66	60	1	3	0	1	84	16	0	.190
'24	18	13	.581	3.79	46	32	14	247	295	76	71	2	3	2	4	75	10	0	.133
'25	11	14	.440	4.00	46	30	17	243	283	78	86	1	0	1	6	79	24	0	.304
'26	16	12	.571	3.85	40	27	12	217.2	224	62	79	1	4	1	4	76	16	0	.211
'27	22	7	.759	2.63	36	32	23	256.1	242	54	86	3	0	1	1	99	22	0	.222
'28	23	7	.767	3.36	42	31	19	273	279	60	67	3	2	1	8	109	28	0	.257
'29	10	9	.526	4.24	30	25	12	201.2	219	69	57	0	1	0	1	76	17	0	.224
'30 2 teams	NY	A	(8G 2–2)		DET	A	(26G 9–8)												
total	11	10	.524	4.71	34	27	10	183.1	240	56	35	1	1	0	4	62	10	0	.161
'31 2 teams	DET	A	(16G 3–8)		PHI	A	(16G 10–5)												
total	13	13	.500	4.97	32	26	14	203	254	69	40	2	0	2	0	73	17	0	.233
'32 2 teams	BKN	N	(8G 1–3)		NY	N	(18G 5–7)												
total	6	10	.375	4.35	26	16	3	124	141	37	36	0	2	1	1	37	3	0	.081
'33 PIT N	5	7	.417	2.92	36	8	4	117	118	19	44	1	2	2	4	32	5	0	.156
'34	15	6	.714	2.93	48	15	6	190.2	184	43	105	3	7	1	5	56	10	0	.179
'35	7	11	.389	3.40	39	11	5	164	187	27	63	0	5	3	6	54	14	0	.259
'36	7	5	.583	2.70	22	9	6	116.2	115	20	37	0	2	1	0	39	6	0	.154
'37 2 teams	PIT	N	(11G 1–2)		BKN	N	(27G 7–7)												
total	8	9	.471	3.41	38	19	10	195.1	211	36	65	1	2	2	2	60	5	0	.083
'38 BKN N	0	3	.000	4.96	6	4	1	16.1	24	5	3	0	0	2	0	3	0	0	.000
21 yrs.	237	182	.566	3.59	674	434	224	3762.2	4037	1003	1206	26	39	26	52	1287	255	0	.198
2 yrs.	12	16	.429	5.22	42	32	13	227.2	300	79	35	1	1	1	4	76	13	0	.171

WORLD SERIES
	W	L	PCT	ERA	G	GS	CG	IP	H	BB	SO	ShO	W	L	SV	AB	H	HR	BA
'21 NY A	2	1	.667	0.00	3	3	3	27	18	11	18	1	0	0	0	9	2	0	.222
'22	0	1	.000	1.13	2	1	0	8	11	2	4	0	0	0	0	2	1	0	.500
'23	0	0	–	15.43	1	1	0	2.1	4	1	0	0	0	0	0	1	0	0	.000
'26	1	1	.500	1.20	2	2	1	15	19	1	10	0	0	0	0	6	0	0	.000
'27	1	0	1.000	4.91	1	1	0	7.1	8	1	2	0	0	0	0	3	0	0	.000
'28	2	0	1.000	1.50	2	2	2	18	14	6	14	0	0	0	0	7	1	0	.143

	W	L	PCT	ERA	G	GS	CG	IP	H	BB	SO	ShO	Relief Pitching W	L	SV	BATTING AB	H	HR	B

Waite Hoyt *continued*

	W	L	PCT	ERA	G	GS	CG	IP	H	BB	SO	ShO	W	L	SV	AB	H	HR	B
1931 PHI A	0	1	.000	4.50	1	1	0	6	7	0	1	0	0	0	0	2	0	0	.0*
7 yrs.	6	4	.600	1.83	12	11	6	83.2	81	22	49	1	0	0	0	30	4	0	.1*
	5th	7th				7th	2nd	6th		5th	2nd				8th				

Bob Humphreys

HUMPHREYS, ROBERT WILLIAM   BR TR 5'11" 165 lb
B. Aug. 18, 1935, Covington, Va.

	W	L	PCT	ERA	G	GS	CG	IP	H	BB	SO	ShO	W	L	SV	AB	H	HR	B
1962 DET A	0	1	.000	7.20	4	0	0	5	8	2	3	0	0	1	1	0	0	0	
1963 STL N	0	1	.000	5.06	9	0	0	10.2	11	7	8	0	0	1	0	0	0	0	
1964	2	0	1.000	2.53	28	0	0	42.2	32	15	36	0	2	0	2	4	1	0	.2*
1965 CHI N	2	0	1.000	3.15	41	0	0	65.2	59	27	38	0	2	0	0	3	0	0	.0*
1966 WAS A	7	3	.700	2.82	58	1	0	111.2	91	28	88	0	6	3	3	12	2	0	.1*
1967	6	2	.750	4.17	48	2	0	105.2	93	41	54	0	5	1	4	15	2	0	.1*
1968	5	7	.417	3.69	56	0	0	92.2	78	30	56	0	5	7	2	5	2	0	.4*
1969	3	3	.500	3.05	47	0	0	79.2	69	38	43	0	3	3	5	13	1	0	.0*
1970 2 teams	WAS A (5G 0-0)							MIL A (23G 2-4)											
" total	2	4	.333	2.92	28	1	0	52.1	41	31	38	0	2	4	3	9	0	0	.0*
9 yrs.	27	21	.563	3.36	319	4	0	566	482	219	364	0	25	20	20	61	8	0	.1*
1 yr.	0	1	.000	7.20	4	0	0	5	8	2	3	0	0	1	1	0	0	0	

WORLD SERIES

	W	L	PCT	ERA	G	GS	CG	IP	H	BB	SO	ShO	W	L	SV	AB	H	HR	B
1964 STL N	0	0	–	0.00	1	0	0	1	0	0	1	0	0	0	0	0	0	0	

Fred Hutchinson

HUTCHINSON, FREDERICK CHARLES   BL TR 6'2" 190 lb
B. Aug. 12, 1919, Seattle, Wash.   D. Nov. 12, 1964, Bradenton, Fla.
Manager 1952-54, 1956-64.

	W	L	PCT	ERA	G	GS	CG	IP	H	BB	SO	ShO	W	L	SV	AB	H	HR	B
1939 DET A	3	6	.333	5.21	13	12	3	84.2	95	51	22	0	0	0	0	34	13	0	.38
1940	3	7	.300	5.68	17	10	1	76	85	26	32	0	1	2	0	30	8	0	.2*
1941	0	0	–	0.00	0	0	0	0	0	0	0	0	0	0	0	2	0	0	.00
1946	14	11	.560	3.09	28	26	16	207	184	66	138	3	0	0	2	89	28	0	.3*
1947	18	10	.643	3.03	33	25	18	219.2	211	61	113	3	2	1	2	106	32	2	.3*
1948	13	11	.542	4.32	33	28	15	221	223	48	92	0	0	0	0	112	23	1	.20
1949	15	7	.682	2.96	33	21	9	188.2	167	52	54	4	3	2	1	73	18	0	.2*
1950	17	8	.680	3.96	39	26	10	231.2	269	48	71	1	4	1	0	95	31	0	.3*
1951	10	10	.500	3.68	31	20	9	188.1	204	27	53	2	4	1	2	85	16	0	.1*
1952	2	1	.667	3.38	12	1	0	37.1	40	9	12	0	2	0	0	18	1	0	.0*
1953	0	0	–	2.79	3	0	0	9.2	9	0	4	0	0	0	0	6	1	0	.1*
11 yrs.	95	71	.572	3.73	242	169	81	1464	1487	388	591	13	16	7	7	*			
10 yrs.	95	71	.572	3.73	242	169	81	1464	1487	388	591	13	16	7	7	650	171	4	.2*

WORLD SERIES

	W	L	PCT	ERA	G	GS	CG	IP	H	BB	SO	ShO	W	L	SV	AB	H	HR	B
1940 DET A	0	0	–	9.00	1	0	0	1	1	1	1	0	0	0	0	0	0	0	

Gary Ignasiak

IGNASIAK, GARY RAYMOND   BR TL 5'11" 185 lb
B. Sept. 1, 1949, Mt. Clemens, Mich.

	W	L	PCT	ERA	G	GS	CG	IP	H	BB	SO	ShO	W	L	SV	AB	H	HR	B
1973 DET A	0	0	–	3.60	3	0	0	5	3	4	4	0	0	0	0	0	0	0	

Charlie Jackson

JACKSON, CHARLES BERNARD
B. Aug. 4, 1876, Versailles, Ohio   D. Nov. 23, 1957, Scottsbluff, Neb.

	W	L	PCT	ERA	G	GS	CG	IP	H	BB	SO	ShO	W	L	SV	AB	H	HR	B
1905 DET A	0	2	.000	5.73	2	2	1	11	14	7	3	0	0	0	0	4	1	0	.2*

Charlie Jaeger

JAEGER, CHARLES THOMAS
B. Apr. 17, 1875, Ottawa, Ill.   D. Sept. 27, 1942, Ottawa, Ill.

	W	L	PCT	ERA	G	GS	CG	IP	H	BB	SO	ShO	W	L	SV	AB	H	HR	B
1904 DET A	3	3	.500	2.57	8	6	5	49	49	15	13	0	0	0	0	17	1	0	.0*

Bill James

JAMES, WILLIAM HENRY (Big Bill)   BB TR 6'4" 195 lb
B. Jan. 20, 1888, Ann Arbor, Mich.   D. May 24, 1942, Venice, Calif.

	W	L	PCT	ERA	G	GS	CG	IP	H	BB	SO	ShO	W	L	SV	AB	H	HR	B
1911 CLE A	2	4	.333	4.88	8	6	4	51.2	58	32	21	0	0	0	0	17	1	0	.0*
1912	0	0	–	4.61	3	0	0	13.2	15	9	5	0	0	0	0	3	0	0	.00
1914 STL A	15	14	.517	2.85	44	35	20	284	269	109	109	3	0	0	1	89	10	0	.1*
1915 2 teams	STL A (34G 7-10)							DET A (11G 7-3)											
" total	14	13	.519	3.26	45	32	11	237.1	212	125	82	1	2	0	1	63	14	0	.2*
1916 DET A	8	12	.400	3.68	30	20	8	151.2	141	79	61	0	2	0	1	44	3	0	.0*
1917	13	10	.565	2.09	34	23	10	198	163	96	62	2	2	1	1	57	12	0	.2*
1918	6	11	.353	3.76	19	18	8	122	127	68	42	1	1	0	0	46	5	0	.1*
1919 3 teams	DET A (2G 1-0)			BOS A (13G 3-5)				CHI A (5G 3-2)											
" total	7	7	.500	3.71	20	13	7	121.1	129	58	26	2	0	2	0	39	6	0	.1*
8 yrs.	65	71	.478	3.20	203	147	68	1179.2	1114	576	408	9	7	3	4	358	51	0	.1*
5 yrs.	35	36	.493	3.01	96	71	29	548	500	281	192	4	7	1	2	172	27	0	.1*

WORLD SERIES

	W	L	PCT	ERA	G	GS	CG	IP	H	BB	SO	ShO	W	L	SV	AB	H	HR	B
1919 CHI A	0	0	–	5.79	1	0	0	4.2	8	3	2	0	0	0	0	2	0	0	.0*

Bob James

JAMES, ROBERT HARVEY   BR TR 6'4" 215 lb
B. Aug. 15, 1958, Glendale, Calif.

	W	L	PCT	ERA	G	GS	CG	IP	H	BB	SO	ShO	W	L	SV	AB	H	HR	B
1978 MON N	0	1	.000	9.00	4	1	0	4	4	3	3	0	0	0	0	0	0	0	
1979	0	0	–	13.50	2	0	0	2	2	3	1	0	0	0	0	0	0	0	
1982 2 teams	MON N (7G 0-0)							DET A (12G 0-2)											
" total	0	2	.000	5.34	19	1	0	28.2	32	16	31	0	0	2	0	0	0	0	
1983 2 teams	DET A (4G 0-0)							MON N (27G 1-0)											
" total	1	0	1.000	3.50	31	0	0	54	42	26	60	0	1	0	7	7	2	0	.28
1984 MON N	6	6	.500	3.66	62	0	0	96	92	45	91	0	6	6	10	14	2	0	.14
5 yrs.	7	9	.438	4.09	118	2	0	184.2	172	94	186	0	7	8	17	21	4	0	.19
2 yrs.	0	2	.000	6.08	16	1	0	23.2	27	11	24	0	0	2	0	0	0	0	

	W	L	PCT	ERA	G	GS	CG	IP	H	BB	SO	ShO	Relief Pitching W	L	SV	BATTING AB	H	HR	BA

Bill Jensen — JENSEN, WILLIAM CHRISTIAN BL TR 5'11½" 170 lbs.
B. Nov. 17, 1889, Philadelphia, Pa. D. Mar. 27, 1917, Philadelphia, Pa.

	W	L	PCT	ERA	G	GS	CG	IP	H	BB	SO	ShO	W	L	SV	AB	H	HR	BA
'12 DET A	1	2	.333	5.40	4	3	1	25	30	14	4	0	0	0	0	11	0	0	.000
'14 PHI A	0	1	.000	2.00	1	1	1	9	7	2	1	0	0	0	0	2	0	0	.000
2 yrs.	1	3	.250	4.50	5	4	2	34	37	16	5	0	0	0	0	13	0	0	.000
1 yr.	1	2	.333	5.40	4	3	1	25	30	14	4	0	0	0	0	11	0	0	.000

Augie Johns — JOHNS, AUGUSTUS FRANCIS (Lefty) BL TL 5'8½" 170 lbs.
B. Sept. 10, 1899, St. Louis, Mo. D. Sept. 12, 1975, San Antonio, Tex.

	W	L	PCT	ERA	G	GS	CG	IP	H	BB	SO	ShO	W	L	SV	AB	H	HR	BA
'26 DET A	6	4	.600	5.35	35	14	3	112.2	117	69	40	1	2	0	1	28	4	0	.143
'27	0	0	-	9.00	1	0	0	1	1	1	1	0	0	0	0	0	0	0	-
2 yrs.	6	4	.600	5.38	36	14	3	113.2	118	70	41	1	2	0	1	28	4	0	.143
2 yrs.	6	4	.600	5.38	36	14	3	113.2	118	70	41	1	2	0	1	28	4	0	.143

Earl Johnson — JOHNSON, EARL DOUGLAS (Lefty) BL TL 6'3" 190 lbs.
Brother of Chet Johnson.
B. Apr. 2, 1919, Redmond, Wash.

	W	L	PCT	ERA	G	GS	CG	IP	H	BB	SO	ShO	W	L	SV	AB	H	HR	BA
'40 BOS A	6	2	.750	4.09	17	10	2	70.1	69	39	26	0	2	1	0	27	2	0	.074
'41	4	5	.444	4.52	17	12	4	93.2	90	51	46	0	1	0	0	34	10	0	.294
'46	5	4	.556	3.71	29	5	1	80	78	39	40	1	5	3	3	22	5	0	.227
'47	12	11	.522	2.97	45	17	6	142.1	129	62	65	3	4	3	8	44	12	0	.273
'48	10	4	.714	4.53	35	3	1	91.1	98	42	45	0	9	2	5	31	3	0	.097
'49	3	6	.333	7.48	19	3	0	49.1	65	29	20	0	3	4	0	11	0	0	.000
'50	0	0	-	7.24	11	0	0	13.2	18	8	6	0	0	0	0	2	0	0	.000
'51 DET A	0	0	-	6.35	6	0	0	5.2	9	2	2	0	0	0	1	0	0	0	-
8 yrs.	40	32	.556	4.30	179	50	14	546.1	556	272	250	4	24	13	17	171	32	0	.187
1 yr.	0	0	-	6.35	6	0	0	5.2	9	2	2	0	0	0	1	0	0	0	-

WORLD SERIES

	W	L	PCT	ERA	G	GS	CG	IP	H	BB	SO	ShO	W	L	SV	AB	H	HR	BA
'46 BOS A	1	0	1.000	2.70	3	0	0	3.1	1	2	1	0	1	0	0	1	0	0	.000

Ken Johnson — JOHNSON, KENNETH WANDERSEE (Hooks) BL TL 6'1" 185 lbs.
B. Jan. 14, 1923, Topeka, Kans.

	W	L	PCT	ERA	G	GS	CG	IP	H	BB	SO	ShO	W	L	SV	AB	H	HR	BA
'47 STL N	1	0	1.000	0.00	2	1	1	10	2	5	8	0	0	0	0	4	2	0	.500
'48	2	4	.333	4.76	13	4	0	45.1	43	30	20	0	2	1	0	20	6	0	.300
'49	0	1	.000	6.42	14	2	0	33.2	29	35	18	0	0	0	0	8	2	0	.250
'50 2 teams			STL	N	(2G 0-0)		PHI	N	(14G 4-1)										
total	4	1	.800	3.88	16	8	3	62.2	62	46	33	1	1	0	0	19	3	0	.158
'51 PHI N	5	8	.385	4.57	20	18	4	106.1	103	68	58	3	0	0	0	35	5	0	.143
'52 DET A	0	0	-	6.35	9	1	0	11.1	12	11	10	0	0	0	0	3	1	0	.333
6 yrs.	12	14	.462	4.58	74	34	8	269.1	251	195	147	4	3	1	0	89	19	0	.213
1 yr.	0	0	-	6.35	9	1	0	11.1	12	11	10	0	0	0	0	3	1	0	.333

Syl Johnson — JOHNSON, SYLVESTER W. BR TR 5'11½" 180 lbs.
B. Dec. 31, 1900, Portland, Ore.

	W	L	PCT	ERA	G	GS	CG	IP	H	BB	SO	ShO	W	L	SV	AB	H	HR	BA
'22 DET A	7	3	.700	3.71	29	8	3	97	99	30	29	0	3	1	1	36	8	0	.222
'23	12	7	.632	3.98	37	18	7	176.1	181	47	93	1	5	2	0	62	10	1	.161
'24	5	4	.556	4.93	29	9	2	104	117	42	55	0	2	2	3	34	7	0	.206
'25	0	2	.000	3.46	6	0	0	13	11	10	5	0	0	2	0	3	0	0	.000
'26 STL N	0	3	.000	4.22	19	6	1	49	54	15	10	0	0	0	1	12	0	0	.000
'27	0	0	-	6.00	2	0	0	3	3	0	2	0	0	0	0	0	0	0	-
'28	8	4	.667	3.90	34	6	2	120	117	33	66	0	4	2	3	38	6	0	.158
'29	13	7	.650	3.60	42	19	12	182.1	186	56	80	3	3	2	3	60	7	1	.117
'30	12	10	.545	4.65	32	24	9	187.2	215	38	92	2	2	1	2	70	15	0	.214
'31	11	9	.550	3.00	32	24	12	186	186	29	82	2	1	0	2	60	14	0	.233
'32	5	14	.263	4.92	32	22	7	164.2	199	35	70	1	1	1	2	51	10	0	.196
'33	3	3	.500	4.29	35	1	0	84	89	16	28	0	2	3	3	21	5	0	.238
'34 2 teams			CIN	N	(2G 0-0)		PHI	N	(42G 5-9)										
total	5	9	.357	3.46	44	10	4	140.1	131	24	54	3	2	5	3	43	9	1	.209
'35 PHI N	10	8	.556	3.56	37	18	8	174.2	182	31	89	1	3	1	6	58	14	1	.241
'36	5	7	.417	4.30	39	8	1	111	129	29	48	0	1	4	7	36	9	0	.250
'37	4	10	.286	5.02	32	15	4	138	155	22	46	0	1	2	3	48	7	0	.146
'38	2	7	.222	4.23	22	6	2	83	87	11	21	0	1	3	0	29	1	0	.034
'39	8	8	.500	3.81	22	14	6	111	112	15	37	0	2	0	2	33	5	0	.152
'40	2	2	.500	4.20	17	2	2	40.2	37	5	13	0	0	2	2	13	0	0	.000
19 yrs.	112	117	.489	4.06	542	210	82	2165.2	2290	488	920	13	33	33	43	702	127	4	.181
4 yrs.	24	16	.600	4.15	101	35	12	390.1	408	129	182	1	10	7	4	135	25	1	.185

WORLD SERIES

	W	L	PCT	ERA	G	GS	CG	IP	H	BB	SO	ShO	W	L	SV	AB	H	HR	BA
'28 STL N	0	0	-	4.50	2	0	0	2	4	1	1	0	0	0	0	0	0	0	-
'30	0	0	-	7.20	2	0	0	5	4	3	4	0	0	0	0	0	0	0	-
'31	0	1	.000	3.00	3	1	0	9	10	1	6	0	0	0	0	2	0	0	.000
3 yrs.	0	1	.000	4.50	7	1	0	16	18	5	11	0	0	0	0	2	0	0	.000

Alex Jones — JONES, ALEXANDER H. TL
B. Dec. 25, 1867, Pittsburgh, Pa. D. Apr. 4, 1941, Woodville, Pa.

	W	L	PCT	ERA	G	GS	CG	IP	H	BB	SO	ShO	W	L	SV	AB	H	HR	BA
'89 PIT N	1	0	1.000	3.00	1	1	1	9	7	1	10	0	0	0	0	5	1	0	.200
'92 2 teams			LOU	N	(18G 5-11)		WAS	N	(4G 0-3)										
total	5	14	.263	3.42	22	20	16	173.2	163	70	51	1	0	1	0	66	11	0	.167
'94 PHI N	1	0	1.000	2.00	1	1	1	9	10	0	2	0	0	0	0	4	1	0	.250
'03 DET A	0	1	.000	12.46	2	2	0	8.2	19	6	2	0	0	0	0	4	0	0	.000
4 yrs.	7	15	.318	3.73	26	24	18	200.1	199	77	65	1	0	1	0	79	13	0	.165
1 yr.	0	1	.000	12.46	2	2	0	8.2	19	6	2	0	0	0	0	4	0	0	.000

Deacon Jones — JONES, CARROLL ELMER BR TR 6'1" 174 lbs.
B. Dec. 20, 1893, Arcadia, Kans. D. Dec. 28, 1952, Pittsburg, Kans.

	W	L	PCT	ERA	G	GS	CG	IP	H	BB	SO	ShO	W	L	SV	AB	H	HR	BA
'16 DET A	0	0	-	2.57	1	0	0	7	7	5	2	0	0	0	0	2	0	0	.000
'17	4	4	.500	2.92	24	6	2	77	69	26	28	0	2	2	0	15	0	0	.000

	W	L	PCT	ERA	G	GS	CG	IP	H	BB	SO	ShO	Relief Pitching W	L	SV	BATTING AB	H	HR	B

Deacon Jones continued

1918	3	1	.750	3.09	21	4	1	67	60	38	15	0	2	0	0	27	5	0	.1
3 yrs.	7	5	.583	2.98	46	10	3	151	136	69	45	0	4	2	0	44	5	0	.1
3 yrs.	7	5	.583	2.98	46	10	3	151	136	69	45	0	4	2	0	44	5	0	.1

Elijah Jones

JONES, ELIJAH ALBERT   BR TR
B. Jan. 27, 1882, Oxford, Mich.   D. Apr. 28, 1943, Pontiac, Mich.

1907 DET A	0	1	.000	5.06	4	1	1	16	23	4	9	0	0	0	1	4	0	0	.0
1909	1	1	.500	2.70	2	2	0	10	10	0	2	0	0	0	0	4	1	0	.2
2 yrs.	1	2	.333	4.15	6	3	1	26	33	4	11	0	0	0	1	8	1	0	.1
2 yrs.	1	2	.333	4.15	6	3	1	26	33	4	11	0	0	0	1	8	1	0	.1

Ken Jones

JONES, KENNETH FREDERICK (Broadway)   BR TR 6'3"   193 lb
B. Apr. 13, 1904, Dover, N. J.

1924 DET A	0	0	–	0.00	1	0	0	2	1	1	0	0	0	0	0	0	0	0	
1930 BOS N	0	1	.000	5.95	8	1	0	19.2	28	4	4	0	0	0	0	5	1	0	.20
2 yrs.	0	1	.000	5.40	9	1	0	21.2	29	5	4	0	0	0	0	5	1	0	.20
1 yr.	0	0	–	0.00	1	0	0	2	1	1	0	0	0	0	0	0	0	0	

Sam Jones

JONES, SAMUEL (Toothpick Sam, Sad Sam)   BR TR 6'4"   192 lb
B. Dec. 14, 1925, Stewartsville, Ohio   D. Nov. 5, 1971, Morgantown, W. Va.

1951 CLE A	0	1	.000	2.08	2	1	0	8.2	4	5	4	0	0	0	0	2	0	0	.0
1952	2	3	.400	7.25	14	4	0	36	38	37	28	0	1	0	1	10	1	0	.1
1955 CHI N	14	20	.412	4.10	36	34	12	241.2	175	185	198	4	1	1	0	77	14	0	.1
1956	9	14	.391	3.91	33	28	8	188.2	155	115	176	2	1	0	0	57	10	0	.1
1957 STL N	12	9	.571	3.60	28	27	10	182.2	164	71	154	2	1	0	0	63	10	0	.1
1958	14	13	.519	2.88	35	35	14	250	204	107	225	2	0	0	0	90	9	0	.1
1959 SF N	21	15	.583	2.83	50	35	16	270.2	232	109	209	4	4	1	4	85	11	0	.1
1960	18	14	.563	3.19	39	35	13	234	200	91	190	3	2	1	0	80	16	0	.2
1961	8	8	.500	4.49	37	17	2	128.1	134	57	105	0	2	1	1	36	5	0	.1
1962 DET A	2	4	.333	3.65	30	6	1	81.1	77	35	73	0	1	1	1	21	2	1	.0
1963 STL N	2	0	1.000	9.00	11	0	0	11	15	5	8	0	2	0	2	1	0	0	.0
1964 BAL A	0	0	–	2.61	7	0	0	10.1	5	5	6	0	0	0	0	0	0	0	
12 yrs.	102	101	.502	3.59	322	222	76	1643.1	1403	822	1376	17	15	5	9	522	78	1	.1
1 yr.	2	4	.333	3.65	30	6	1	81.1	77	35	73	0	1	1	1	21	2	1	.0

Milt Jordan

JORDAN, MILTON MIGNOT   BR TR 6'2½"   207 lb
B. May 24, 1927, Mineral Springs, Pa.

1953 DET A	0	1	.000	5.82	8	1	0	17	26	5	4	0	0	0	0	2	1	0	.5

Walt Justis

JUSTIS, WALTER NEWTON (Smoke)   BR TR 5'11½"   195 lb
B. Aug. 17, 1883, Moores Hill, Ind.   D. Oct. 4, 1941, Lawrenceburg, Ind.

1905 DET A	0	0	–	8.10	2	0	0	3.1	4	6	0	0	0	0	0	0	0	0	

Rudy Kallio

KALLIO, RUDOLPH   BR TR 5'10"   160 lb
B. Dec. 14, 1892, Portland, Ore.   D. Apr. 6, 1979, Newport, Ore.

1918 DET A	8	14	.364	3.62	30	22	10	181.1	178	76	70	2	1	2	0	56	9	0	.1
1919	0	0	–	5.64	12	1	0	22.1	28	8	3	0	0	0	1	4	0	0	.0
1925 BOS A	1	4	.200	7.71	7	4	0	18.2	28	9	2	0	0	1	0	6	2	0	.3
3 yrs.	9	18	.333	4.17	49	27	10	222.1	234	93	75	2	1	3	1	66	11	0	.1
2 yrs.	8	14	.364	3.84	42	23	10	203.2	206	84	73	2	1	2	1	60	9	0	.1

Harry Kane

KANE, HARRY (Klondike)   BL TL
Born Harry Cohen.
B. July 27, 1883, Hamburg, Ark.   D. Sept. 15, 1932, Portland, Ore.

1902 STL A	0	1	.000	5.48	4	1	1	23	34	16	7	0	0	0	0	9	1	0	.1
1903 DET A	0	2	.000	8.50	3	3	2	18	26	8	10	0	0	0	0	7	1	0	.1
1905 PHI N	1	1	.500	1.59	2	2	2	17	12	8	12	1	0	0	0	6	1	0	.1
1906	1	3	.250	3.86	6	3	2	28	28	18	14	0	1	1	0	8	0	0	.0
4 yrs.	2	7	.222	4.81	15	9	7	86	100	50	43	1	1	1	0	30	3	0	.1
1 yr.	0	2	.000	8.50	3	3	2	18	26	8	10	0	0	0	0	7	1	0	.1

Vern Kennedy

KENNEDY, LLOYD VERNON   BL TR 6'   175 lb
B. Mar. 20, 1907, Kansas City, Mo.

1934 CHI A	0	2	.000	3.72	3	3	1	19.1	21	9	7	0	0	0	0	7	2	0	.2
1935	11	11	.500	3.91	31	25	16	211.2	211	95	65	2	0	1	1	73	18	0	.2
1936	21	9	.700	4.63	35	34	20	274.1	282	147	99	1	1	0	0	113	32	0	.2
1937	14	13	.519	5.09	32	30	15	221	238	124	114	1	0	1	0	87	20	2	.2
1938 DET A	12	9	.571	5.06	33	26	11	190.1	215	113	53	0	1	0	2	79	23	0	.2
1939 2 teams					DET A (4G 0–3)			STL A (33G 9–17)											
" total	9	20	.310	5.80	37	31	13	212.2	254	124	64	1	0	1	0	74	12	0	.1
1940 STL A	12	17	.414	5.59	34	32	18	222.1	263	122	70	0	1	0	0	84	25	2	.2
1941 2 teams					STL A (6G 2–4)			WAS A (17G 1–7)											
" total	3	11	.214	5.17	23	13	4	111.1	121	66	28	0	1	1	0	36	9	0	.2
1942 CLE A	4	8	.333	4.08	28	12	4	108	99	50	37	0	0	2	1	30	6	0	.20
1943	10	7	.588	2.45	28	17	8	146.2	130	59	63	1	3	1	0	52	12	0	.2
1944 2 teams					CLE A (12G 2–5)			PHI N (12G 1–5)											
" total	3	10	.231	4.64	24	17	5	114.1	126	57	40	0	1	0	0	44	8	0	.1
1945 2 teams					PHI N (12G 0–3)			CIN N (24G 5–12)											
" total	5	15	.250	4.28	36	23	11	193.2	213	83	51	1	0	2	1	64	14	0	.2
12 yrs.	104	132	.441	4.67	344	263	126	2025.2	2173	1049	691	7	8	9	5	743	181	4	.2
2 yrs.	12	12	.500	5.20	37	30	12	211.1	240	122	62	0	1	0	2	86	25	0	.2

	W	L	PCT	ERA	G	GS	CG	IP	H	BB	SO	ShO	Relief Pitching W	L	SV	BATTING AB	H	HR	BA

Mike Kilkenny

KILKENNY, MICHAEL DAVID   BR TL 6'3½" 175 lbs.
B. Apr. 11, 1945, Toronto, Ont., Canada

	W	L	PCT	ERA	G	GS	CG	IP	H	BB	SO	ShO	W	L	SV	AB	H	HR	BA
'69 DET A	8	6	.571	3.37	39	15	6	128.1	99	63	97	4	1	1	2	37	2	0	.054
'70	7	6	.538	5.16	36	21	3	129	141	70	105	0	1	0	0	39	3	0	.077
'71	4	5	.444	5.02	30	11	2	86	83	44	47	0	0	0	1	24	2	0	.083
'72 4 teams	DET A (1G 0-0)				OAK A (1G 0-0)				CLE A (22G 4-1)				SD N (5G 0-0)						
total	4	1	.800	3.78	29	7	1	64.1	59	42	49	0	2	0	1	14	1	0	.071
'73 CLE A	0	0	–	22.50	5	0	0	2	5	5	3	0	0	0	0	0	0	0	–
5 yrs.	23	18	.561	4.44	139	54	12	409.2	387	224	301	4	4	1	4	114	8	0	.070
4 yrs.	19	17	.528	4.47	106	47	11	344.1	324	177	249	4	2	1	3	100	7	0	.070

Ed Killian

KILLIAN, EDWIN HENRY (Twilight Ed)   BL TL 5'11" 170 lbs.
B. Nov. 12, 1876, Racine, Wis.   D. July 18, 1928, Detroit, Mich.

	W	L	PCT	ERA	G	GS	CG	IP	H	BB	SO	ShO	W	L	SV	AB	H	HR	BA
'03 CLE A	3	4	.429	2.48	9	8	7	61.2	61	13	18	3	0	0	0	28	5	0	.179
'04 DET A	14	20	.412	2.44	40	34	32	331.2	293	93	124	4	0	2	1	126	18	0	.143
'05	23	14	.622	2.27	39	37	33	313.1	263	102	110	8	2	0	0	118	32	0	.271
'06	10	6	.625	3.43	21	16	14	149.2	165	54	47	0	1	0	2	53	9	0	.170
'07	25	13	.658	1.78	41	34	29	314	286	91	96	3	1	0	1	122	39	0	.320
'08	12	9	.571	2.99	27	23	15	180.2	170	53	47	0	0	0	1	73	10	0	.137
'09	11	9	.550	1.71	25	19	14	173.1	150	49	54	3	1	0	1	62	10	0	.161
'10	4	3	.571	3.04	11	9	5	74	75	27	20	1	0	1	0	27	4	0	.148
8 yrs.	102	78	.567	2.38	213	180	149	1598.1	1463	482	516	22	5	3	6	609	127	0	.209
7 yrs.	99	74	.572	2.38	204	172	142	1536.2	1402	469	498	19	5	3	6	581	122	0	.210
				2nd			**9th**												

WORLD SERIES

	W	L	PCT	ERA	G	GS	CG	IP	H	BB	SO	ShO	W	L	SV	AB	H	HR	BA
'07 DET A	0	0	–	2.25	1	0	0	4	3	1	1	0	0	0	0	2	1	0	.500
'08	0	0	–	7.71	1	1	0	2.1	5	3	1	0	0	0	0	0	0	0	–
2 yrs.	0	0	–	4.26	2	1	0	6.1	8	4	2	0	0	0	0	2	1	0	.500

Chad Kimsey

KIMSEY, CLYDE ELIAS   BL TR 6'3½" 200 lbs.
B. Aug. 6, 1905, Copperhill, Tenn.   D. Dec. 3, 1942, Pryor, Okla.

	W	L	PCT	ERA	G	GS	CG	IP	H	BB	SO	ShO	W	L	SV	AB	H	HR	BA
'29 STL A	3	6	.333	5.04	24	3	1	64.1	88	19	13	0	1	5	1	30	8	2	.267
'30	6	10	.375	6.35	42	4	1	113.1	139	45	32	0	6	7	1	70	24	3	.343
'31	4	6	.400	4.39	42	1	0	94.1	121	27	27	0	4	5	7	37	10	2	.270
'32 2 teams	STL A (33G 4-2)				CHI A (7G 1-1)														
total	5	3	.625	3.83	40	0	0	89.1	93	38	19	0	5	3	5	20	6	0	.300
'33 CHI A	4	1	.800	5.53	28	2	0	96	124	36	19	0	4	0	0	33	5	0	.152
'36 DET A	2	3	.400	4.85	22	0	0	52	58	29	11	0	2	3	3	16	5	0	.313
6 yrs.	24	29	.453	5.07	198	10	2	509.1	623	194	121	0	22	23	17	*			
1 yr.	2	3	.400	4.85	22	0	0	52	58	29	11	0	2	3	3	16	5	0	.313

Dennis Kinney

KINNEY, DENNIS PAUL   BL TL 6'1" 175 lbs.
B. Feb. 26, 1952, Toledo, Ohio

	W	L	PCT	ERA	G	GS	CG	IP	H	BB	SO	ShO	W	L	SV	AB	H	HR	BA
'78 2 teams	CLE A (18G 0-2)				SD N (7G 0-1)														
total	0	3	.000	4.73	25	0	0	45.2	43	18	21	0	0	3	5	1	0	0	.000
'79 SD N	0	0	–	3.50	13	0	0	18	17	8	11	0	0	0	0	1	0	0	.000
'80	4	6	.400	4.23	50	0	0	83	79	37	40	0	4	6	1	12	1	0	.083
'81 DET A	0	0	–	9.00	6	0	0	4	5	4	3	0	0	0	0	0	0	0	–
'82 OAK A	0	0	–	8.31	3	0	0	4.1	9	4	0	0	0	0	0	0	0	0	–
5 yrs.	4	9	.308	4.53	97	0	0	155	153	71	75	0	4	9	6	14	1	0	.071
1 yr.	0	0	–	9.00	6	0	0	4	5	4	3	0	0	0	0	0	0	0	–

Rube Kisinger

KISINGER, CHARLES SAMUEL   BR TR 6' 190 lbs.
B. Dec. 13, 1876, Adrian, Mich.   D. July 14, 1941, Huron, Ohio

	W	L	PCT	ERA	G	GS	CG	IP	H	BB	SO	ShO	W	L	SV	AB	H	HR	BA
'02 DET A	2	3	.400	3.12	5	5	5	43.1	48	14	7	0	0	0	0	19	3	0	.158
'03	7	9	.438	2.96	16	14	13	118.2	118	27	33	2	2	0	0	47	6	0	.128
2 yrs.	9	12	.429	3.00	21	19	18	162	166	41	40	2	2	0	0	66	9	0	.136
2 yrs.	9	12	.429	3.00	21	19	18	162	166	41	40	2	2	0	0	66	9	0	.136

Frank Kitson

KITSON, FRANK L   BL TR 5'11" 165 lbs.
B. Apr. 11, 1872, Hopkins, Mich.   D. Apr. 14, 1930, Allegan, Mich.

	W	L	PCT	ERA	G	GS	CG	IP	H	BB	SO	ShO	W	L	SV	AB	H	HR	BA
'98 BAL N	8	6	.571	3.24	17	13	13	119.1	123	35	32	1	0	1	0	86	27	0	.314
'99	22	16	.579	2.76	40	37	35	329.2	329	66	75	3	0	1	0	134	27	0	.201
'00 BKN N	15	13	.536	4.19	40	30	21	253.1	283	56	55	2	2	0	4	109	32	0	.294
'01	19	11	.633	2.98	38	32	26	280.2	312	67	127	5	1	2	2	133	35	1	.263
'02	19	12	.613	2.84	31	30	28	259.2	251	48	107	3	0	1	0	113	30	1	.265
'03 DET A	15	16	.484	2.58	31	28	28	257.2	277	38	102	2	2	1	0	116	21	0	.181
'04	8	13	.381	3.07	26	24	19	199.2	211	38	69	0	0	0	1	72	15	1	.208
'05	12	14	.462	3.47	33	27	21	225.2	230	57	78	3	2	0	1	87	16	0	.184
'06 WAS A	6	14	.300	3.65	30	21	15	197	196	57	59	1	1	2	0	90	22	1	.244
'07 2 teams	WAS A (5G 0-3)				NY A (12G 4-0)														
total	4	3	.571	3.39	17	7	5	93	116	26	25	0	1	0	0	31	7	0	.226
10 yrs.	128	118	.520	3.17	303	249	211	2215.2	2328	488	729	20	9	8	8	*			
3 yrs.	35	43	.449	3.02	90	79	68	683	718	133	249	5	4	1	2	275	52	1	.189

Al Klawitter

KLAWITTER, ALBERT C.   BR TR 6' 180 lbs.
B. Apr. 12, 1888, Wilkes-Barre, Pa.   D. May 2, 1950, Milwaukee, Wis.

	W	L	PCT	ERA	G	GS	CG	IP	H	BB	SO	ShO	W	L	SV	AB	H	HR	BA
'09 NY N	1	1	.500	2.00	6	3	2	27	24	13	6	0	0	0	1	9	3	0	.333
'10	0	0	–	9.00	1	0	0	1	2	2	0	0	0	0	0	0	0	0	–
'13 DET A	1	2	.333	5.91	8	3	1	32	39	15	10	0	0	1	0	11	0	0	.000
3 yrs.	2	3	.400	4.20	15	6	3	60	65	30	16	0	0	1	1	20	3	0	.150
1 yr.	1	2	.333	5.91	8	3	1	32	39	15	10	0	0	1	0	11	0	0	.000

Ron Kline

KLINE, RONALD LEE   BR TR 6'3" 205 lbs.
B. Mar. 9, 1932, Callery, Pa.

	W	L	PCT	ERA	G	GS	CG	IP	H	BB	SO	ShO	W	L	SV	AB	H	HR	BA
'52 PIT N	0	7	.000	5.49	27	11	0	78.2	74	66	27	0	0	1	0	19	0	0	.000
'55	6	13	.316	4.15	36	19	2	136.2	161	53	48	1	2	0	2	38	5	0	.132
'56	14	18	.438	3.38	44	39	9	264	263	81	125	2	0	0	2	79	10	0	.127

	W	L	PCT	ERA	G	GS	CG	IP	H	BB	SO	ShO	Relief Pitching W	L	SV	BATTING AB	H	HR	B.

Ron Kline continued

	W	L	PCT	ERA	G	GS	CG	IP	H	BB	SO	ShO	W	L	SV	AB	H	HR	B.
1957	9	16	.360	4.04	40	31	11	205	214	61	88	2	0	1	0	66	4	0	.06
1958	13	16	.448	3.53	32	32	11	237.1	220	92	109	2	0	0	0	74	2	0	.02
1959	11	13	.458	4.26	33	29	7	186	186	70	91	0	1	0	0	59	8	0	.13
1960 STL N	4	9	.308	6.04	34	17	1	117.2	133	43	54	0	1	2	1	35	5	0	.14
1961 2 teams			LA	A	(26G	3–6)		DET	A	(10G	5–3)								
" total	8	9	.471	4.14	36	20	3	161	172	61	97	1	1	3	1	49	6	0	.12
1962 DET A	3	6	.333	4.31	36	4	0	77.1	88	28	47	0	3	3	2	16	2	0	.12
1963 WAS A	3	8	.273	2.79	62	1	0	93.2	85	30	49	0	3	8	17	11	1	0	.09
1964	10	7	.588	2.32	61	0	0	81.1	81	21	40	0	10	7	14	6	1	0	.16
1965	7	6	.538	2.63	74	0	0	99.1	106	32	52	0	7	6	29	7	0	0	.00
1966	6	4	.600	2.39	63	0	0	90.1	79	17	46	0	6	4	23	6	1	0	.16
1967 MIN N	7	1	.875	3.77	54	0	0	71.2	71	15	36	0	7	1	5	5	0	0	.00
1968 PIT N	12	5	.706	1.68	56	0	0	112.2	94	31	48	0	12	5	7	16	0	0	.00
1969 3 teams			PIT	N	(20G	1–3)		SF	N	(7G	0–2)		BOS	A	(16G	0–1)			
" total	1	6	.143	5.19	43	0	0	59	77	28	29	0	1	6	4	5	0	0	.00
1970 ATL N	0	0	–	7.50	5	0	0	6	9	2	3	0	0	0	1	0	0	0	
17 yrs.	114	144	.442	3.75	736	203	44	2077.2	2113	731	989	8	54	47	108	491	45	0	.09
2 yrs.	8	9	.471	3.64	46	12	3	133.2	141	45	74	1	3	3	2	34	5	0	.14

Johnny Klippstein

KLIPPSTEIN, JOHN CALVIN
B. Oct. 17, 1927, Washington, D. C.   BR TR 6'1"   173 lbs

	W	L	PCT	ERA	G	GS	CG	IP	H	BB	SO	ShO	W	L	SV	AB	H	HR	B.
1950 CHI N	2	9	.182	5.25	33	11	3	104.2	112	64	51	0	1	1	1	33	11	1	.33
1951	6	6	.500	4.29	35	11	1	123.2	121	53	56	1	4	0	2	37	4	1	.10
1952	9	14	.391	4.44	41	25	7	202.2	208	89	110	2	4	0	3	63	11	1	.17
1953	10	11	.476	4.83	48	20	5	167.2	169	107	113	0	2	4	6	58	9	1	.15
1954	4	11	.267	5.29	36	21	4	148	155	96	69	0	0	2	1	45	6	0	.13
1955 CIN N	9	10	.474	3.39	39	14	3	138	120	60	68	2	4	2	0	31	2	0	.06
1956	12	11	.522	4.09	37	29	11	211	219	82	86	0	2	0	1	71	7	0	.09
1957	8	11	.421	5.05	46	18	3	146	146	68	99	1	3	2	3	41	3	0	.07
1958 2 teams			CIN	N	(12G	3–2)		LA	N	(45G	3–5)								
" total	6	7	.462	4.10	57	4	0	123	118	58	95	0	5	6	10	28	2	0	.07
1959 LA N	4	0	1.000	5.91	28	0	0	45.2	48	33	30	0	4	0	2	7	1	0	.14
1960 CLE A	5	5	.500	2.91	49	0	0	74.1	53	35	46	0	5	5	14	14	2	0	.14
1961 WAS A	2	2	.500	6.78	42	1	0	71.2	83	43	41	0	2	1	0	7	1	0	.14
1962 CIN N	7	6	.538	4.47	40	7	0	108.2	113	64	67	0	6	3	4	24	3	1	.12
1963 PHI N	5	6	.455	1.93	49	1	0	112	80	46	86	0	5	5	8	26	1	0	.03
1964 2 teams			PHI	N	(11G	2–1)		MIN	A	(33G	0–4)								
" total	2	5	.286	2.65	44	0	0	68	66	28	52	0	2	5	3	6	0	0	.00
1965 MIN A	9	3	.750	2.24	56	0	0	76.1	59	31	59	0	9	3	5	8	0	0	.00
1966	1	1	.500	3.40	26	0	0	39.2	35	20	26	0	1	1	3	3	0	0	.00
1967 DET A	0	0	–	5.40	5	0	0	6.2	6	1	4	0	0	0	0	0	0	0	
18 yrs.	101	118	.461	4.24	711	162	37	1967.2	1911	978	1158	6	59	40	66	502	63	5	.12
1 yr.	0	0	–	5.40	5	0	0	6.2	6	1	4	0	0	0	0	0	0	0	

WORLD SERIES

	W	L	PCT	ERA	G	GS	CG	IP	H	BB	SO	ShO	W	L	SV	AB	H	HR	B.
1959 LA N	0	0	–	0.00	1	0	0	2	1	0	2	0	0	0	0	0	0	0	
1965 MIN A	0	0	–	0.00	2	0	0	2.2	2	2	3	0	0	0	0	0	0	0	
2 yrs.	0	0	–	0.00	3	0	0	4.2	3	2	5	0	0	0	0	0	0	0	

Rudy Kneisch

KNEISCH, RUDOLPH FRANK
B. Apr. 10, 1899, Baltimore, Md.   D. Apr. 6, 1965, Baltimore, Md.   BR TL 5'10½" 175 lbs

	W	L	PCT	ERA	G	GS	CG	IP	H	BB	SO	ShO	W	L	SV	AB	H	HR	B.
1926 DET A	0	1	.000	2.65	2	2	1	17	18	6	4	0	0	0	0	5	0	0	.00

Alan Koch

KOCH, ALAN GOODMAN
B. Mar. 25, 1938, Decatur, Ala.   BR TR 6'4"   195 lbs

	W	L	PCT	ERA	G	GS	CG	IP	H	BB	SO	ShO	W	L	SV	AB	H	HR	B.
1963 DET A	1	1	.500	10.80	7	1	0	10	21	9	5	0	1	1	0	3	2	0	.66
1964 2 teams			DET	A	(3G	0–0)		WAS	A	(32G	3–10)								
" total	3	10	.231	4.96	35	14	1	118	116	46	68	0	0	3	0	32	8	0	.25
2 yrs.	4	11	.267	5.41	42	15	1	128	137	55	73	0	1	4	0	35	10	0	.28
2 yrs.	1	1	.500	9.64	10	1	0	14	27	12	6	0	1	1	0	3	2	0	.66

Mark Koenig

KOENIG, MARK ANTHONY
B. July 19, 1902, San Francisco, Calif.   BB TR 6'   180 lbs
                                                   BL 1928

	W	L	PCT	ERA	G	GS	CG	IP	H	BB	SO	ShO	W	L	SV	AB	H	HR	B.
1930 DET A	0	1	.000	10.00	2	1	0	9	11	8	6	0	0	0	0	341	81	1	.23
1931	0	0	–	6.43	3	0	0	7	7	11	3	0	0	0	0	364	92	1	.25
2 yrs.	0	1	.000	8.44	5	1	0	16	18	19	9	0	0	0	0	*			
2 yrs.	0	1	.000	8.44	5	1	0	16	18	19	9	0	0	0	0	631	156	2	.24

Howie Koplitz

KOPLITZ, HOWARD DEAN
B. May 4, 1938, Oshkosh, Wis.   BR TR 5'10½" 190 lbs

	W	L	PCT	ERA	G	GS	CG	IP	H	BB	SO	ShO	W	L	SV	AB	H	HR	B.
1961 DET A	2	0	1.000	2.25	4	1	1	12	16	8	9	0	1	0	0	4	0	0	.00
1962	3	0	1.000	5.26	10	6	1	37.2	54	10	10	0	0	0	0	13	3	0	.23
1964 WAS A	0	0	–	4.76	6	1	0	17	20	13	9	0	0	0	0	4	0	0	.00
1965	4	7	.364	4.05	33	11	0	106.2	97	48	59	0	2	2	1	30	3	0	.10
1966	0	0	–	0.00	1	0	0	2	0	1	0	0	0	0	0	0	0	0	
5 yrs.	9	7	.563	4.21	54	19	2	175.1	187	80	87	0	3	2	1	51	6	0	.11
2 yrs.	5	0	1.000	4.53	14	7	2	49.2	70	18	19	0	1	0	0	17	3	0	.17

George Korince

KORINCE, GEORGE EUGENE (Moose)
B. Jan. 10, 1946, Ottawa, Ont., Canada   BR TR 6'3"   210 lbs

	W	L	PCT	ERA	G	GS	CG	IP	H	BB	SO	ShO	W	L	SV	AB	H	HR	B.
1966 DET A	0	0	–	0.00	2	0	0	3	1	3	2	0	0	0	0	0	0	0	
1967	1	0	1.000	5.14	9	0	0	14	10	11	11	0	1	0	1	1	0	0	.00
2 yrs.	1	0	1.000	4.24	11	0	0	17	11	14	13	0	1	0	1	1	0	0	.00
2 yrs.	1	0	1.000	4.24	11	0	0	17	11	14	13	0	1	0	1	1	0	0	.00

	W	L	PCT	ERA	G	GS	CG	IP	H	BB	SO	ShO	Relief Pitching W	L	SV	BATTING AB	H	HR	BA

Red Kress

KRESS, RALPH BR TR 5'11½" 165 lbs.
B. Jan. 2, 1907, Columbia, Calif.   D. Nov. 29, 1962, Los Angeles, Calif.

	W	L	PCT	ERA	G	GS	CG	IP	H	BB	SO	ShO	W	L	SV	AB	H	HR	BA
'35 WAS A	0	0	–	12.71	3	0	0	5.2	8	5	5	0	0	0	0	252	75	2	.298
'46 NY N	0	0	–	12.27	1	0	0	3.2	5	1	1	0	0	0	0	1	0	0	.000
2 yrs.	0	0	–	12.54	4	0	0	9.1	13	6	6	0	0	0	0	*			

Lou Kretlow

KRETLOW, LOUIS HENRY BR TR 6'2" 185 lbs.
B June 27, 1923, Apache, Okla.

	W	L	PCT	ERA	G	GS	CG	IP	H	BB	SO	ShO	W	L	SV	AB	H	HR	BA
'46 DET A	1	0	1.000	3.00	1	1	1	9	7	2	4	0	0	0	0	4	2	0	.500
'48	2	1	.667	4.63	5	2	1	23.1	21	11	9	0	1	0	0	8	4	0	.500
'49	3	2	.600	6.16	25	10	1	76	85	69	40	0	2	1	0	26	0	0	.000
'50 2 teams	STL A (9G 0–2)				CHI A (11G 0–0)														
total	0	2	.000	7.07	20	3	0	35.2	42	45	24	0	0	1	0	7	0	0	.000
'51 CHI A	4	4	.400	4.20	26	18	7	137	129	74	89	1	0	1	0	48	4	0	.083
52	4	4	.500	2.96	19	11	4	79	52	56	63	2	0	0	1	20	1	0	.050
'53 2 teams	CHI A (9G 0–0)				STL A (22G 1–5)														
total	1	5	.167	4.78	31	14	0	101.2	105	82	52	0	0	1	0	29	5	0	.172
'54 BAL A	6	11	.353	4.37	32	20	5	166.2	169	82	82	0	0	1	0	51	8	0	.157
55	0	4	.000	8.22	15	5	0	38.1	50	27	26	0	0	0	0	11	1	0	.091
56 KC A	4	9	.308	5.31	25	20	3	118.2	121	74	61	0	0	0	0	33	2	0	.061
10 yrs.	27	47	.365	4.87	199	104	22	785.1	781	522	450	3	3	4	1	237	27	0	.114
3 yrs.	6	3	.667	5.57	31	13	3	108.1	113	82	53	0	3	1	0	38	6	0	.158

Clem Labine

LABINE, CLEMENT WALTER BR TR 6' 180 lbs.
B. Aug. 6, 1926, Lincoln, R. I.

	W	L	PCT	ERA	G	GS	CG	IP	H	BB	SO	ShO	W	L	SV	AB	H	HR	BA
'50 BKN N	0	0	–	4.50	1	0	0	2	2	1	0	0	0	0	0	0	0	0	–
51	5	1	.833	2.20	14	6	5	65.1	52	20	39	2	0	0	0	21	3	0	.143
52	8	4	.667	5.14	25	9	0	77	76	47	43	0	6	1	0	22	1	0	.045
53	11	6	.647	2.77	37	7	0	110.1	92	30	44	0	10	4	7	28	2	0	.071
54	7	6	.538	4.15	47	2	0	108.1	101	56	43	0	6	5	5	30	1	0	.033
55	13	5	.722	3.24	60	8	1	144.1	121	55	67	0	10	2	11	31	3	3	.097
56	10	6	.625	3.35	62	3	1	115.2	111	39	75	0	9	6	19	23	2	0	.087
57	5	7	.417	3.44	58	0	0	104.2	104	27	67	0	5	7	17	20	2	0	.100
58 LA N	6	6	.500	4.15	52	2	0	104	112	33	43	0	5	5	14	18	1	0	.056
59	5	10	.333	3.93	56	0	0	84.2	91	25	37	0	5	10	9	16	0	0	.000
60 3 teams	LA N (13G 0–1)				DET A (14G 0–3)				PIT N (15G 3–0)										
total	3	4	.429	3.65	42	0	0	66.2	74	31	42	0	3	4	6	8	1	0	.125
61 PIT N	4	1	.800	3.69	56	1	0	92.2	102	31	49	0	4	1	8	10	1	0	.100
62 NY N	0	0	–	11.25	3	0	0	4	5	1	2	0	0	0	0	0	0	0	–
13 yrs.	77	56	.579	3.63	513	38	7	1079.2	1043	396	551	2	63	45	96	227	17	3	.075
1 yr.	0	3	.000	5.12	14	0	0	19.1	19	12	6	0	0	3	2	2	0	0	.000
WORLD SERIES																			
53 BKN N	0	2	.000	3.60	3	0	0	5	10	1	3	0	0	2	1	2	0	0	.000
55	1	0	1.000	2.89	4	0	0	9.1	6	2	2	0	1	0	1	4	0	0	.000
56	1	0	1.000	0.00	2	1	1	12	8	3	7	1	0	0	0	4	1	0	.250
59 LA N	0	0	–	0.00	1	0	0	1	0	1	0	0	0	0	0	0	0	0	–
60 PIT N	0	0	–	13.50	3	0	0	4	13	1	2	0	0	0	0	0	0	0	–
5 yrs.	2	2	.500	3.16	13	1	1	31.1	37	7	15	1	1	2	2	10	1	0	.100
				6th															

Doc Lafitte

LAFITTE, EDWARD FRANCIS (Doc) BR TR 6'2" 188 lbs.
B. Apr. 7, 1886, New Orleans, La.   D. Apr. 12, 1971, Jenkintown, Pa.

	W	L	PCT	ERA	G	GS	CG	IP	H	BB	SO	ShO	W	L	SV	AB	H	HR	BA
09 DET A	0	1	.000	3.86	3	1	1	14	22	2	11	0	0	1	1	4	1	0	.250
11	11	8	.579	3.92	29	20	15	172.1	205	52	63	0	0	1	1	70	11	1	.157
12	0	0	–	16.20	1	0	0	1.2	2	2	0	0	0	0	0	0	0	0	–
14 BKN F	16	16	.500	2.63	42	33	23	290.2	260	127	137	0	1	2	2	101	26	1	.257
15 2 teams	BKN F (17G 6–9)				BUF F (14G 2–2)														
total	8	11	.421	3.80	31	21	8	168	179	79	51	0	0	1	1	70	16	0	.229
5 yrs.	35	36	.493	3.34	106	75	47	646.2	668	262	262	0	1	4	5	245	54	2	.220
3 yrs.	11	9	.550	4.02	33	21	16	188	229	56	74	0	0	1	2	74	12	1	.162

Lerrin LaGrow

LaGROW, LERRIN HARRIS BR TR 6'5" 220 lbs.
B. July 8, 1948, Phoenix, Ariz.

	W	L	PCT	ERA	G	GS	CG	IP	H	BB	SO	ShO	W	L	SV	AB	H	HR	BA
70 DET A	0	1	.000	7.50	10	0	0	12	16	6	7	0	0	1	0	1	0	0	.000
72	0	1	.000	1.33	16	0	0	27	22	6	9	0	0	1	2	0	0	0	–
73	1	5	.167	4.33	21	3	0	54	54	23	33	0	0	3	3	0	0	0	–
74	8	19	.296	4.67	37	34	11	216	245	80	85	0	0	0	0	0	0	0	–
75	7	14	.333	4.38	32	26	7	164.1	183	66	75	2	0	0	0	0	0	0	–
76 STL A	0	1	.000	1.48	8	2	1	24.1	21	7	10	0	0	0	0	5	0	0	.000
77 CHI A	7	3	.700	2.45	66	0	0	99	81	35	63	0	7	3	25	0	0	0	–
78	6	5	.545	4.40	66	0	0	88	85	38	41	0	6	5	16	0	0	0	–
79 2 teams	CHI A (11G 0–3)				LA N (31G 5–1)														
total	5	4	.556	5.24	42	2	0	55	65	34	31	0	5	2	5	3	1	0	.333
80 PHI N	0	2	.000	4.15	25	0	0	39	42	17	21	0	0	2	3	4	1	0	.250
10 yrs.	34	55	.382	4.11	309	67	19	778.2	814	312	375	2	18	17	54	13	2	0	.154
5 yrs.	16	40	.286	4.41	116	63	18	473.1	520	181	209	2	0	5	5	1	0	0	.000
LEAGUE CHAMPIONSHIP SERIES																			
72 DET A	0	0	–	0.00	1	0	0	1	0	0	1	0	0	0	0	0	0	0	–

Eddie Lake

LAKE, EDWARD ERVING BR TR 5'7" 159 lbs.
B. Mar. 18, 1916, Antioch, Calif.

	W	L	PCT	ERA	G	GS	CG	IP	H	BB	SO	ShO	W	L	SV	AB	H	HR	BA
44 BOS A	0	0	–	4.19	6	0	0	19.1	20	11	7	0	0	0	0	*			

Joe Lake

LAKE, JOSEPH HENRY BR TR 6' 185 lbs.
B. Dec. 6, 1881, Brooklyn, N. Y.   D. June 30, 1950, Brooklyn, N. Y.

	W	L	PCT	ERA	G	GS	CG	IP	H	BB	SO	ShO	W	L	SV	AB	H	HR	BA
08 NY A	9	22	.290	3.17	38	27	19	269.1	252	77	118	2	2	2	0	112	21	1	.188
09	14	11	.560	1.88	31	26	17	215.1	180	59	117	3	2	0	1	81	14	0	.173
10 STL A	11	17	.393	2.20	35	29	24	261.1	243	77	141	1	1	1	2	81	21	0	.259

	W	L	PCT	ERA	G	GS	CG	IP	H	BB	SO	ShO	Relief Pitching W	L	SV	BATTING AB	H	HR	B.

Joe Lake continued

	W	L	PCT	ERA	G	GS	CG	IP	H	BB	SO	ShO	W	L	SV	AB	H	HR	B.
1911	10	15	.400	3.30	30	25	14	215.1	245	40	69	2	1	1	0	80	21	0	.26
1912 2 teams		STL	A (11G 1–7)		DET	A (26G 9–11)													
" total	10	18	.357	3.44	37	20	16	219.2	260	55	114	0	5	4	1	81	12	1	.14
1913 DET A	8	7	.533	3.28	28	12	6	137	149	24	35	0	4	1	1	45	12	1	.26
6 yrs.	62	90	.408	2.85	199	139	96	1318	1329	332	594	8	15	9	5	480	101	3	.21
2 yrs.	17	18	.486	3.18	54	26	18	299.2	339	63	121	0	9	3	2	105	20	2	.19

Al Lakeman

LAKEMAN, ALBERT WESLEY (Moose)   BR TR 6'2" 195 lbs
B. Dec. 31, 1918, Cincinnati, Ohio   D. May 25, 1976, Spartanburg, S. C.

	W	L	PCT	ERA	G	GS	CG	IP	H	BB	SO	ShO	W	L	SV	AB	H	HR	B.
1948 PHI N	0	0	–	13.50	1	0	0	.2	1	0	0	0	0	0	0	*			

Steve Larkin

LARKIN, FRANK S   BR TR 6'1" 195 lbs
B. Dec. 9, 1910, Cincinnati, Ohio   D. May 2, 1969, Brooklyn, N. Y.

	W	L	PCT	ERA	G	GS	CG	IP	H	BB	SO	ShO	W	L	SV	AB	H	HR	B.
1934 DET A	0	0	–	1.50	2	1	0	6	8	5	8	0	0	0	0	3	1	0	.33

Frank Lary

LARY, FRANK STRONG (Mule, The Yankee Killer)   BR TR 5'11" 175 lbs
Brother of Al Lary.
B. Apr. 10, 1930, Northport, Ala.

	W	L	PCT	ERA	G	GS	CG	IP	H	BB	SO	ShO	W	L	SV	AB	H	HR	B.
1954 DET A	0	0	–	2.45	3	0	0	3.2	4	3	5	0	0	0	0	0	0	0	
1955	14	15	.483	3.10	36	31	16	235	232	89	98	2	1	1	1	82	16	0	.19
1956	21	13	.618	3.15	41	38	20	294	289	116	165	3	0	0	1	103	19	1	.18
1957	11	16	.407	3.98	40	35	12	237.2	250	72	107	2	0	1	3	73	9	0	.12
1958	16	15	.516	2.90	39	34	19	260.1	249	68	131	3	0	2	1	88	15	1	.17
1959	17	10	.630	3.55	32	32	11	223	225	46	137	3	0	0	0	80	10	1	.12
1960	15	15	.500	3.51	38	36	15	274.1	262	62	149	2	0	0	1	93	17	2	.18
1961	23	9	.719	3.24	36	36	22	275.1	252	66	146	4	0	0	0	108	25	1	.23
1962	2	6	.250	5.74	17	14	2	80	98	21	41	1	0	1	0	24	4	0	.16
1963	4	9	.308	3.27	16	14	6	107.1	90	26	46	0	0	0	0	35	8	0	.22
1964 3 teams		DET	A (6G 0–2)		NY	N (13G 2–3)		MIL	N (5G 1–0)										
" total	3	5	.375	5.03	24	14	3	87.2	101	24	37	1	1	0	1	27	2	0	.07
1965 2 teams		NY	N (14G 1–3)		CHI	A (14G 1–0)													
" total	2	3	.400	3.32	28	8	0	84	71	23	37	0	0	0	3	21	5	0	.23
12 yrs.	128	116	.525	3.49	350	292	126	2162.1	2123	616	1099	21	1	5	11	734	130	6	.17
11 yrs.	123	110	.528	3.46	304	274	123	2008.2	1975	579	1031	20	1	5	7	693	123	6	.17
	9th	8th						9th				10th							

Fred Lasher

LASHER, FREDERICK WALTER   BR TR 6'3" 190 lbs
B. Aug. 19, 1941, Poughkeepsie, N. Y.

	W	L	PCT	ERA	G	GS	CG	IP	H	BB	SO	ShO	W	L	SV	AB	H	HR	B.
1963 MIN A	0	0	–	4.76	11	0	0	11.1	12	11	10	0	0	0	0	1	0	0	.00
1967 DET A	2	1	.667	3.90	17	0	0	30	25	11	28	0	2	1	9	9	1	0	.11
1968	5	1	.833	3.33	34	0	0	48.2	37	22	32	0	5	1	5	9	1	0	.11
1969	2	1	.667	3.07	32	0	0	44	34	22	26	0	2	1	0	4	0	0	.00
1970 2 teams		DET	A (12G 1–3)		CLE	A (43G 1–7)													
" total	2	10	.167	4.19	55	1	0	66.2	67	42	52	0	2	9	8	9	0	0	.00
1971 CAL A	0	0	–	36.00	2	0	0	1	4	2	0	0	0	0	0	0	0	0	
6 yrs.	11	13	.458	3.88	151	1	0	201.2	179	110	148	0	11	12	22	32	2	0	.06
4 yrs.	10	6	.625	3.49	95	0	0	131.2	106	67	94	0	10	6	17	23	2	0	

WORLD SERIES
	W	L	PCT	ERA	G	GS	CG	IP	H	BB	SO	ShO	W	L	SV	AB	H	HR	B.
1968 DET A	0	0	–	0.00	1	0	0	2	1	0	1	0	0	0	0	0	0	0	

Roxie Lawson

LAWSON, ALFRED VOYLE   BR TR 6' 170 lbs
B. Apr. 13, 1906, Donnellson, Iowa   D. Apr. 9, 1977, Stockport, Iowa

	W	L	PCT	ERA	G	GS	CG	IP	H	BB	SO	ShO	W	L	SV	AB	H	HR	B.
1930 CLE A	1	2	.333	6.15	7	4	2	33.2	46	23	10	0	0	0	0	11	1	0	.09
1931	0	2	.000	7.60	17	3	0	55.2	72	36	20	0	0	0	0	14	2	0	.14
1933 DET A	0	1	.000	7.31	4	2	0	16	17	17	6	0	0	0	0	5	0	0	.00
1935	3	1	.750	1.58	7	4	4	40	34	24	16	2	0	0	2	13	4	0	.30
1936	8	6	.571	5.48	41	8	3	128	139	71	34	0	5	5	3	45	10	0	.22
1937	18	7	.720	5.26	37	29	15	217.1	236	115	68	0	3	1	1	81	21	0	.25
1938	8	9	.471	5.46	27	16	5	127	154	82	39	0	3	0	1	45	2	0	.04
1939 2 teams		DET	A (2G 1–1)		STL	A (36G 3–7)													
" total	4	8	.333	5.28	38	15	5	162	188	90	47	0	2	0	0	47	8	0	.17
1940 STL A	5	3	.625	5.13	30	2	0	72	77	54	18	0	5	1	4	22	1	0	.04
9 yrs.	47	39	.547	5.37	208	83	34	851.2	963	512	258	2	18	7	11	283	49	0	.17
6 yrs.	38	25	.603	5.14	118	60	27	539.2	587	316	167	2	12	6	7	193	37	0	.19

Bill Laxton

LAXTON, WILLIAM HARRY   BL TL 6'1" 190 lbs
B. Jan. 5, 1948, Camden, N. J.

	W	L	PCT	ERA	G	GS	CG	IP	H	BB	SO	ShO	W	L	SV	AB	H	HR	B.
1970 PHI N	0	0	–	13.50	2	0	0	2	2	2	2	0	0	0	0	0	0	0	
1971 SD N	0	2	.000	6.75	18	0	0	28	32	26	23	0	0	2	0	0	0	0	
1974	0	1	.000	4.00	30	1	0	45	37	38	40	0	0	1	0	5	1	0	.20
1976 DET A	0	5	.000	4.09	26	3	0	94.2	77	51	74	0	0	2	2	0	0	0	
1977 2 teams		SEA	A (43G 3–2)		CLE	A (2G 0–0)													
" total	3	2	.600	4.96	45	0	0	74.1	64	41	50	0	3	2	3	0	0	0	
5 yrs.	3	10	.231	4.72	121	4	0	244	212	158	189	0	3	7	5	5	1	0	.20
1 yr.	0	5	.000	4.09	26	3	0	94.2	77	51	74	0	0	2	2	0	0	0	

Rick Leach

LEACH, RICHARD MAX   BL TL 6'1" 180 lbs
B. May 4, 1957, Ann Arbor, Mich.

	W	L	PCT	ERA	G	GS	CG	IP	H	BB	SO	ShO	W	L	SV	AB	H	HR	B.
1984 TOR A	0	0	–	27.00	1	0	0	1	2	1	0	0	0	0	0	*			

Razor Ledbetter

LEDBETTER, RALPH OVERTON   BR TR 6'3" 190 lbs
B. Dec. 8, 1894, Rutherford College, N. C.   D. Feb. 1, 1969, West Palm Beach, Fla.

	W	L	PCT	ERA	G	GS	CG	IP	H	BB	SO	ShO	W	L	SV	AB	H	HR	B.
1915 DET A	0	0	–	0.00	1	0	0	1	1	0	0	0	0	0	0	0	0	0	

	W	L	PCT	ERA	G	GS	CG	IP	H	BB	SO	ShO	W	L	SV	AB	H	HR	BA
													Relief Pitching			BATTING			

Don Lee

LEE, DONALD EDWARD
Son of Thornton Lee.
B. Feb. 26, 1934, Globe, Ariz.   BR TR 6'4"   205 lbs.

	W	L	PCT	ERA	G	GS	CG	IP	H	BB	SO	ShO	W	L	SV	AB	H	HR	BA
1957 DET A	1	3	.250	4.66	11	6	0	38.2	48	18	19	0	0	1	0	12	2	0	.167
1958	0	0		9.00	1	0	0	2	1	1	0	0	0	0	0	0	0	0	–
1960 WAS A	8	7	.533	3.44	44	20	1	165	160	64	88	0	3	2	3	43	5	1	.116
1961 MIN A	3	6	.333	3.52	37	10	4	115	93	35	65	0	1	0	3	30	2	0	.067
1962 2 teams	MIN	A	(9G 3–3)		LA	A	(27G 8–8)												
" total	11	11	.500	3.46	36	31	5	205.2	204	63	102	2	0	1	2	68	13	0	.191
1963 LA A	8	11	.421	3.68	40	22	3	154	148	51	89	2	2	0	1	45	7	0	.156
1964	5	4	.556	2.72	33	8	0	89.1	99	25	73	0	3	1	2	23	6	0	.261
1965 2 teams	CAL	A	(10G 0–1)		HOU	N	(7G 0–0)												
" total	0	1	.000	5.32	17	0	0	22	29	8	15	0	0	1	0	4	1	0	.250
1966 2 teams	HOU	N	(9G 4–0)		CHI	N	(16G 2–1)												
" total	4	1	.800	4.86	25	0	0	37	45	16	16	0	4	1	0	1	1	0	1.000
9 yrs.	40	44	.476	3.61	244	97	13	828.1	827	281	467	4	13	7	11	226	37	1	.164
2 yrs.	1	3	.250	4.87	12	6	0	40.2	49	19	19	0	0	1	0	12	2	0	.167

Bill Lelivelt

LELIVELT, WILLIAM JOHN
Brother of Jack Lelivelt.
B. Oct. 21, 1884, Chicago, Ill.   D. Feb. 14, 1968, Chicago, Ill.   BR TR 6'   195 lbs.

	W	L	PCT	ERA	G	GS	CG	IP	H	BB	SO	ShO	W	L	SV	AB	H	HR	BA
1909 DET A	0	1	.000	4.50	4	2	1	20	27	2	4	0	0	0	1	6	2	0	.333
1910	0	1	.000	1.00	1	1	1	9	6	3	2	0	0	0	0	2	1	0	.500
2 yrs.	0	2	.000	3.41	5	3	2	29	33	5	6	0	0	0	1	8	3	0	.375
2 yrs.	0	2	.000	3.41	5	3	2	29	33	5	6	0	0	0	1	8	3	0	.375

Dave Lemanczyk

LEMANCZYK, DAVID LAWRENCE
B. Aug. 17, 1950, Syracuse, N. Y.   BR TR 6'4"   235 lbs.

	W	L	PCT	ERA	G	GS	CG	IP	H	BB	SO	ShO	W	L	SV	AB	H	HR	BA
1973 DET A	0	0	–	13.50	1	0	0	2	4	0	0	0	0	0	0	0	0	0	–
1974	2	1	.667	3.99	22	3	0	79	79	44	52	0	1	0	0	0	0	0	–
1975	2	7	.222	4.46	26	6	4	109	120	46	67	0	2	1	0	0	0	0	–
1976	4	6	.400	5.11	20	10	1	81	86	34	51	0	2	0	0	0	0	0	–
1977 TOR A	13	16	.448	4.25	34	34	11	252	278	87	105	0	0	0	0	0	0	0	–
1978	4	14	.222	6.26	29	20	3	136.2	170	65	62	0	0	0	0	0	0	0	–
1979	8	10	.444	3.71	22	20	11	143	137	45	63	3	0	0	0	0	0	0	–
1980 2 teams	TOR	A	(10G 2–5)		CAL	A	(21G 2–4)												
' total	4	9	.308	4.75	31	10	0	110	138	42	29	0	1	3	0	0	0	0	–
8 yrs.	37	63	.370	4.62	185	103	30	912.2	1012	363	429	3	6	4	0	0	0	0	–
4 yrs.	8	14	.364	4.58	69	19	5	271	289	124	170	0	5	1	0	0	0	0	–

Dutch Leonard

LEONARD, HUBERT BENJAMIN
B. Apr. 16, 1892, Birmingham, Ohio   D. July 11, 1952, Fresno, Calif.   BL TL 5'10½" 185 lbs.

	W	L	PCT	ERA	G	GS	CG	IP	H	BB	SO	ShO	W	L	SV	AB	H	HR	BA
1913 BOS A	14	16	.467	2.39	42	27	14	259.1	245	94	144	2	3	3	1	83	15	0	.181
1914	19	5	.792	1.01¹	36	25	17	222.2	141	60	174	7	4	0	3	69	10	0	.145
1915	15	7	.682	2.36	32	21	10	183.1	130	67	116	2	4	2	0	53	14	0	.264
1916	18	12	.600	2.36	48	34	17	274	244	66	144	6	2	0	6	85	17	0	.200
1917	16	17	.485	2.17	37	36	26	294.1	257	72	144	4	0	0	1	104	9	0	.087
1918	8	6	.571	2.72	16	16	12	125.2	119	53	47	3	0	0	0	43	8	0	.186
1919 DET A	14	13	.519	2.77	29	28	18	217.1	212	65	102	4	0	1	0	71	11	0	.155
1920	10	17	.370	4.33	28	27	10	191.1	192	63	76	3	0	1	0	57	12	0	.211
1921	11	13	.458	3.75	36	32	16	245	273	63	120	1	0	2	1	82	14	0	.171
1924	3	2	.600	4.56	9	7	3	51.1	69	17	26	0	0	0	1	19	4	0	.211
1925	11	4	.733	4.51	18	18	9	125.2	143	43	65	0	0	0	0	50	10	0	.200
11 yrs.	139	112	.554	2.77	331	271	152	2190	2025	663	1158	32	13	9	13	716	124	0	.173
5 yrs.	49	49	.500	3.79	120	112	56	830.2	889	251	389	8	0	4	2	279	51	0	.183
WORLD SERIES																			
1915 BOS A	1	0	1.000	1.00	1	1	1	9	3	0	6	0	0	0	0	3	0	0	.000
1916	1	0	1.000	1.00	1	1	1	9	5	4	3	0	0	0	0	3	0	0	.000
2 yrs.	2	0	1.000	1.00	2	2	2	18	8	4	9	0	0	0	0	6	0	0	.000

Don Leshnock

LESHNOCK, DONALD LEE
B. Nov. 25, 1946, Youngstown, Ohio   BR TL 6'3"   195 lbs.

	W	L	PCT	ERA	G	GS	CG	IP	H	BB	SO	ShO	W	L	SV	AB	H	HR	BA
1972 DET A	0	0	–	0.00	1	0	0	1	2	0	2	0	0	0	0	0	0	0	–

Dick Littlefield

LITTLEFIELD, RICHARD BERNARD
B. Mar. 18, 1926, Detroit, Mich.   BL TL 6'   180 lbs.

	W	L	PCT	ERA	G	GS	CG	IP	H	BB	SO	ShO	W	L	SV	AB	H	HR	BA
1950 BOS A	2	2	.500	9.26	15	2	0	23.1	27	24	13	0	2	0	1	4	0	0	.000
1951 CHI A	1	1	.500	8.38	4	2	0	9.2	9	17	7	0	1	0	0	1	0	0	.000
1952 2 teams	DET	A	(28G 0–3)		STL	A	(7G 2–3)												
" total	2	6	.250	3.54	35	6	3	94	81	42	66	0	1	3	1	23	2	0	.087
1953 STL A	7	12	.368	5.08	36	22	2	152.1	153	84	104	0	2	1	0	42	8	0	.190
1954 2 teams	BAL	A	(3G 0–0)		PIT	N	(23G 10–11)												
" total	10	11	.476	3.86	26	21	7	161	148	91	97	1	1	0	0	50	8	0	.160
1955 PIT N	5	12	.294	5.12	36	17	4	130	148	68	70	1	1	3	0	34	6	0	.176
1956 3 teams	PIT	N	(6G 0–0)		STL	N	(3G 0–2)		NY	N	(31G 4–4)								
" total	4	6	.400	4.37	40	11	0	119.1	101	49	80	0	1	2	2	28	2	0	.071
1957 CHI N	4	2	.400	5.35	48	2	0	65.2	76	37	51	0	2	1	4	11	2	0	.182
1958 MIL N	0	1	.000	4.26	4	0	0	6.1	7	1	7	0	0	1	1	0	0	0	–
9 yrs.	33	54	.379	4.71	243	83	17	761.2	750	413	495	2	11	11	9	193	28	0	.145
1 yr.	0	3	.000	4.34	28	1	0	47.2	46	25	32	0	0	3	1	7	1	0	.143

Jack Lively

LIVELY, HENRY EVERETT
Father of Bud Lively.
B. May 29, 1885, Joppa, Ala.   D. Dec. 5, 1967, Arab, Ala.   BL TR 5'9"   185 lbs.

	W	L	PCT	ERA	G	GS	CG	IP	H	BB	SO	ShO	W	L	SV	AB	H	HR	BA
1911 DET A	7	5	.583	4.59	18	14	10	113.2	143	34	45	0	1	0	0	43	11	0	.256

	W	L	PCT	ERA	G	GS	CG	IP	H	BB	SO	ShO	Relief Pitching W	L	SV	BATTING AB	H	HR	BA

Harry Lochhead

LOCHHEAD, HARRY ROBERT　　　　　　　　　　TR
B. Mar. 29, 1876, Stockton, Calif.　　D. Aug. 22, 1909, Stockton, Calif.

| 1899 CLE N | 0 | 0 | — | 0.00 | 1 | 0 | 0 | 3.2 | 4 | 2 | 0 | 0 | 0 | 0 | 0 | * | | | |

Bob Logan

LOGAN, ROBERT DEAN (Lefty)　　　　　　BR TL 5'10" 170 lbs
B. Feb. 10, 1910, Thompson, Neb.　　D. May 20, 1978, Indianapolis, Ind.

1935 BKN N	0	1	.000	3.38	2	0	0	2.2	2	1	1	0	0	1	0	0	0	0	
1937 2 teams			DET	A	(1G 0–0)			CHI	N	(4G 0–0)									
" total	0	0	—	1.29	5	0	0	7	7	5	3	0	0	0	1	1	0	0	.00
1938 CHI N	0	2	.000	2.78	14	0	0	22.2	18	17	10	0	0	2	2	3	0	0	.00
1941 CIN N	0	1	.000	8.10	2	0	0	3.1	5	5	0	0	0	1	0	0	0	0	
1945 BOS N	7	11	.389	3.18	34	25	5	187	213	53	53	1	0	2	1	61	13	0	.21
5 yrs.	7	15	.318	3.15	57	25	5	222.2	245	81	67	1	0	6	4	65	13	0	.20
1 yr.	0	0	—	0.00	1	0	0	.2	1	1	1	0	0	0	0	0	0	0	

Mickey Lolich

LOLICH, MICHAEL STEPHEN　　　　　　BB TL 6'1" 170 lbs
B. Sept. 12, 1940, Portland, Ore.

1963 DET A	5	9	.357	3.55	33	18	4	144.1	145	56	103	0	0	2	0	36	2	0	.05
1964	18	9	.667	3.26	44	33	12	232	196	64	192	6	2	1	2	64	7	0	.10
1965	15	9	.625	3.44	43	37	7	243.2	216	72	226	3	1	0	3	86	5	0	.05
1966	14	14	.500	4.77	40	33	5	203.2	204	83	173	1	0	1	3	64	9	0	.14
1967	14	13	.519	3.04	31	30	11	204	165	56	174	6	0	0	0	61	12	0	.19
1968	17	9	.654	3.19	39	32	8	220	178	65	197	4	4	0	1	70	8	0	.11
1969	19	11	.633	3.14	37	36	15	280.2	214	122	271	1	0	0	1	91	8	0	.08
1970	14	19	.424	3.79	40	39	13	273	272	109	230	3	0	0	0	82	11	0	.13
1971	25	14	.641	2.92	45	45	29	376	336	92	308	4	0	0	0	115	15	0	.13
1972	22	14	.611	2.50	41	41	23	327	282	74	250	4	0	0	0	89	6	0	.06
1973	16	15	.516	3.82	42	42	17	309	315	79	214	3	0	0	0	0	0	0	
1974	16	21	.432	4.15	41	41	27	308	310	78	202	3	0	0	0	0	0	0	
1975	12	18	.400	3.78	32	32	19	240.2	260	64	139	1	0	0	0	0	0	0	
1976 NY N	8	13	.381	3.22	31	30	5	193	184	52	120	2	0	0	0	54	7	0	.13
1978 SD N	2	1	.667	1.54	20	2	0	35	30	11	13	0	1	0	1	3	0	0	.00
1979	0	2	.000	4.78	27	5	0	49	59	22	20	0	0	0	0	6	0	0	.00
16 yrs.	217	191	.532	3.44	586	496	195	3639	3366	1099	2832	41	8	4	11	821	90	0	.11
13 yrs.	207	175	.542	3.45	508	459	190	3362	3093	1014	2679	39	7	4	10	758	83	0	.10
	3rd	**3rd**				**3rd**		**6th**	**3rd**			**5th**	**1st**	**1st**					

LEAGUE CHAMPIONSHIP SERIES

| 1972 DET A | 0 | 1 | .000 | 1.42 | 2 | 2 | 0 | 19 | 14 | 5 | 10 | 0 | 0 | 0 | 0 | 7 | 0 | 0 | .00 |

WORLD SERIES

| 1968 DET A | 3 | 0 | 1.000 | 1.67 | 3 | 3 | 3 | 27 | 20 | 6 | 21 | 0 | 0 | 0 | 0 | 12 | 3 | 1 | .25 |
| | | | | **1st** | | | | | | | | | | | | | | | |

Aurelio Lopez

LOPEZ, AURELIO ALEJANDRO　　　　　　BR TR 6' 185 lbs
Also known as Aurelio Alejandro Rios.
B. Oct. 5, 1948, Tecamachalco, Mexico

1974 KC A	0	0	—	5.63	8	1	0	16	21	10	5	0	0	0	0	0	0	0	
1978 STL N	4	2	.667	4.29	25	4	0	65	52	32	46	0	2	1	0	14	3	0	.21
1979 DET A	10	5	.667	2.41	61	0	0	127	95	51	106	0	10	5	21	0	0	0	
1980	13	6	.684	3.77	67	1	0	124	125	45	97	0	13	5	21	0	0	0	
1981	5	2	.714	3.62	29	3	0	82	70	31	53	0	3	2	3	0	0	0	
1982	3	1	.750	5.27	19	0	0	41	41	19	26	0	3	1	3	0	0	0	
1983	9	8	.529	2.81	57	0	0	115.1	87	49	90	0	9	8	18	0	0	0	
1984	10	1	.909	2.94	71	0	0	137.2	109	52	94	0	10	1	14	0	0	0	
8 yrs.	54	25	.684	3.37	337	9	0	708	600	289	517	0	50	23	80	14	3	0	.21
6 yrs.	50	23	.685	3.22	304	4	0	627	527	247	466	0	48	22	80	0	0	0	
													3rd		**2nd**				

LEAGUE CHAMPIONSHIP SERIES

| 1984 DET A | 1 | 0 | 1.000 | 0.00 | 1 | 0 | 0 | 3 | 4 | 1 | 2 | 0 | 1 | 0 | 0 | 0 | 0 | 0 | |

WORLD SERIES

| 1984 DET A | 1 | 0 | 1.000 | 0.00 | 2 | 0 | 0 | 3 | 1 | 1 | 4 | 0 | 1 | 0 | 0 | 0 | 0 | 0 | |

Lefty Lorenzen

LORENZEN, ADOLPH ANDREAS　　　　　　BL TL 5'10" 164 lbs
B. Jan. 12, 1893, Davenport, Iowa　　D. Mar. 5, 1963, Davenport, Iowa

| 1913 DET A | 0 | 0 | — | 18.00 | 1 | 0 | 0 | 2 | 4 | 3 | 0 | 0 | 0 | 0 | 0 | 2 | 1 | 0 | .50 |

Art Loudell

LOUDELL, ARTHUR　　　　　　BR TR 5'11" 173 lbs
Born Arthur Laudel.
B. May 10, 1882, Latham, Mo.　　D. Feb. 19, 1961, Kansas City, Mo.

| 1910 DET A | 1 | 1 | .500 | 3.38 | 5 | 2 | 1 | 21.1 | 23 | 14 | 12 | 0 | 0 | 0 | 0 | 7 | 1 | 0 | .14 |

Slim Love

LOVE, EDWARD HAUGHTON　　　　　　BL TL 6'7" 195 lbs
B. Aug. 1, 1890, Love, Mo.　　D. Nov. 30, 1942, Memphis, Tenn.

1913 WAS A	1	0	1.000	1.62	5	1	0	16.2	14	6	5	0	0	0	1	5	1	0	.20
1916 NY A	2	0	1.000	4.91	20	1	0	47.2	46	23	21	0	1	0	0	14	0	0	.00
1917	6	5	.545	2.35	33	9	2	130.1	115	57	82	0	4	0	1	36	6	0	.16
1918	13	12	.520	3.07	38	29	13	228.2	207	116	95	1	1	1	1	74	17	0	.23
1919 DET A	6	4	.600	3.01	22	8	4	89.2	92	40	46	0	3	1	1	27	6	0	.22
1920	0	0	—	8.31	1	0	0	4.1	6	4	2	0	0	0	0	0	0	0	
6 yrs.	28	21	.571	3.04	119	48	19	517.1	480	246	251	1	9	2	4	156	30	0	.19
2 yrs.	6	4	.600	3.26	23	8	4	94	98	44	48	0	3	1	1	27	6	0	.22

Grover Lowdermilk

LOWDERMILK, GROVER CLEVELAND (Slim)　　　　　　BR TR 6'4" 190 lbs
Brother of Lou Lowdermilk.
B. Jan. 15, 1885, Sandborn, Ind.　　D. Mar. 31, 1968, Odin, Ill.

| 1909 STL N | 0 | 2 | .000 | 6.21 | 7 | 3 | 1 | 29 | 28 | 30 | 14 | 0 | 0 | 0 | 0 | 10 | 1 | 0 | .10 |
| 1911 | 0 | 1 | .000 | 7.29 | 11 | 2 | 1 | 33.1 | 37 | 33 | 15 | 0 | 0 | 0 | 0 | 9 | 1 | 0 | .11 |

	W	L	PCT	ERA	G	GS	CG	IP	H	BB	SO	ShO	Relief Pitching W	L	SV	BATTING AB	H	HR	BA

Grover Lowdermilk continued

	W	L	PCT	ERA	G	GS	CG	IP	H	BB	SO	ShO	W	L	SV	AB	H	HR	BA
'12 CHI N	0	1	.000	9.69	2	1	1	13	17	14	8	0	0	0	0	4	0	0	.000
'15 2 teams	STL	A (38G 9–17)		DET	A	(7G 4–1)													
" total	13	18	.419	3.24	45	34	14	250.1	200	157	148	1	3	2	0	80	10	0	.125
'16 2 teams	DET	A (1G 0–0)		CLE	A	(10G 1–5)													
" total	1	5	.167	3.14	11	9	2	51.2	52	48	28	0	0	0	0	18	3	0	.167
'17 STL A	2	1	.667	1.42	3	2	2	19	16	4	9	1	0	1	0	7	0	0	.000
'18	2	6	.250	3.15	13	11	4	80	74	38	25	0	0	0	0	28	7	0	.250
'19 2 teams	STL	A (7G 0–0)		CHI	A	(20G 5–5)													
" total	5	5	.500	2.57	27	11	5	108.2	101	47	49	0	0	2	0	35	3	0	.086
'20 CHI A	0	0	–	6.75	3	0	0	5.1	9	5	0	0	0	0	0	0	0	0	–
9 yrs.	23	39	.371	3.58	122	73	30	590.1	534	376	296	2	3	5	0	191	25	0	.131
2 yrs.	4	1	.800	4.13	8	5	0	28.1	17	27	18	0	1	1	0	8	1	0	.125
WORLD SERIES																			
'19 CHI A	0	0	–	9.00	1	0	0	1	2	1	0	0	0	0	0	0	0	0	–

Bobby Lowe

LOWE, ROBERT LINCOLN (Link)   BR TR 5'10"   150 lbs.
B. July 10, 1868, Pittsburgh, Pa.   D. Dec. 8, 1951, Detroit, Mich.
Manager 1904.

	W	L	PCT	ERA	G	GS	CG	IP	H	BB	SO	ShO	W	L	SV	AB	H	HR	BA
'91 BOS N	0	0	–	9.00	1	0	0	1	3	1	0	0	0	0	0	*			

Willie Ludolph

LUDOLPH, WILLIAM FRANCIS (Wee Willie)   BR TR 6'1½" 170 lbs.
B. Jan. 21, 1900, San Francisco, Calif.   D. Apr. 8, 1952, Oakland, Calif.

	W	L	PCT	ERA	G	GS	CG	IP	H	BB	SO	ShO	W	L	SV	AB	H	HR	BA
'24 DET A	0	0	–	4.76	3	0	0	5.2	5	2	1	0	0	0	0	1	0	0	.000

Red Lynn

LYNN, JAPHET MONROE   BR TR 6'   162 lbs.
B. Dec. 27, 1913, Kenney, Tex.   D. Oct. 27, 1977, Bellville, Tex.

	W	L	PCT	ERA	G	GS	CG	IP	H	BB	SO	ShO	W	L	SV	AB	H	HR	BA
'39 2 teams	DET	A (4G 0–1)		NY	N	(26G 1–0)													
" total	1	1	.500	3.88	30	0	0	58	55	24	25	0	1	1	1	8	0	0	.000
'40 NY N	4	3	.571	3.83	33	0	0	42.1	40	24	25	0	4	3	3	4	0	0	.000
'44 CHI N	5	4	.556	4.06	22	7	4	84.1	80	37	35	1	0	2	1	29	6	0	.207
3 yrs.	10	8	.556	3.95	85	7	4	184.2	175	85	85	1	5	6	5	41	6	0	.146
1 yr.	0	1	.000	8.64	4	0	0	8.1	11	3	3	0	0	1	0	2	0	0	.000

Duke Maas

MAAS, DUANE FREDERICK   BR TR 5'10" 170 lbs.
B. Jan. 31, 1929, Utica, Mich.   D. Dec. 7, 1976, Mt. Clemens, Mich.

	W	L	PCT	ERA	G	GS	CG	IP	H	BB	SO	ShO	W	L	SV	AB	H	HR	BA
'55 DET A	5	6	.455	4.88	18	16	5	86.2	91	50	42	2	0	0	0	30	5	0	.167
'56	0	7	.000	6.54	26	7	0	63.1	81	32	34	0	0	1	0	16	3	0	.188
'57	10	14	.417	3.28	45	26	8	219.1	210	65	116	2	1	2	6	71	6	1	.085
'58 2 teams	KC	A (10G 4–5)		NY	A	(22G 7–3)													
" total	11	8	.579	3.85	32	20	5	156.2	142	49	69	2	2	2	1	51	6	0	.118
'59 NY A	14	8	.636	4.43	38	21	3	138	149	53	67	1	5	0	4	40	5	0	.125
'60	5	1	.833	4.09	35	1	0	70.1	70	35	28	0	5	0	4	6	0	0	.000
'61	0	0	–	54.00	1	0	0	.1	2	0	0	0	0	0	0	0	0	0	–
7 yrs.	45	44	.506	4.19	195	91	21	734.2	745	284	356	7	13	5	15	214	25	1	.117
3 yrs.	15	27	.357	4.22	89	49	13	369.1	382	147	192	4	1	3	6	117	14	1	.120
WORLD SERIES																			
'58 NY A	0	0	–	81.00	1	0	0	.1	2	1	0	0	0	0	0	0	0	0	–
'60	0	0	–	4.50	1	0	0	2	2	0	1	0	0	0	0	0	0	0	–
2 yrs.	0	0	–	15.43	2	0	0	2.1	4	1	1	0	0	0	0	0	0	0	–

Frank MacCormick

MacCORMICK, FRANK LOUIS   BR TR 6'4"   210 lbs.
B. Sept. 21, 1954, Jersey City, N. J.

	W	L	PCT	ERA	G	GS	CG	IP	H	BB	SO	ShO	W	L	SV	AB	H	HR	BA
'76 DET A	0	5	.000	5.73	9	8	0	33	35	34	14	0	0	0	0	3	0	0	.000
'77 SEA A	0	0	–	3.86	3	3	0	7	4	12	4	0	0	0	0	0	0	0	–
2 yrs.	0	5	.000	5.40	12	11	0	40	39	46	18	0	0	0	0	3	0	0	.000
1 yr.	0	5	.000	5.73	9	8	0	33	35	34	14	0	0	0	0	3	0	0	.000

Dave Madison

MADISON, DAVID PLEDGER   BR TR 6'3"   190 lbs.
B. Feb. 1, 1921, Brooksville, Miss.

	W	L	PCT	ERA	G	GS	CG	IP	H	BB	SO	ShO	W	L	SV	AB	H	HR	BA
'50 NY A	0	0	–	6.00	1	0	0	3	3	1	1	0	0	0	0	0	0	0	–
'52 2 teams	STL	A (31G 4–2)		DET	A	(10G 1–1)													
" total	5	3	.625	4.94	41	5	0	93	94	58	42	0	3	2	0	19	2	0	.105
'53 DET A	3	4	.429	6.82	32	1	0	62	76	44	27	0	3	3	0	11	1	0	.091
3 yrs.	8	7	.533	5.70	74	6	0	158	173	103	70	0	6	5	0	30	3	0	.100
2 yrs.	4	5	.444	7.01	42	2	0	77	92	54	34	0	4	3	0	13	1	0	.077

Alex Main

MAIN, MILES GRANT   BL TR 6'5"   195 lbs.
B. May 13, 1884, Montrose, Mich.   D. Dec. 29, 1965, Royal Oak, Mich.

	W	L	PCT	ERA	G	GS	CG	IP	H	BB	SO	ShO	W	L	SV	AB	H	HR	BA
'14 DET A	6	6	.500	2.67	32	12	5	138.1	131	59	55	1	1	1	3	40	4	0	.100
'15 KC F	13	14	.481	2.54	35	28	18	230	181	75	91	2	1	0	3	76	15	0	.197
'18 PHI N	2	2	.500	4.63	8	4	1	35	30	16	14	1	0	0	0	11	1	0	.091
3 yrs.	21	22	.488	2.77	75	44	24	403.1	342	150	160	4	2	1	6	127	20	0	.157
1 yr.	6	6	.500	2.67	32	12	5	138.1	131	59	55	1	1	1	3	40	4	0	.100

Tom Makowski

MAKOWSKI, THOMAS ANTHONY   BR TL 5'11" 185 lbs.
B. Dec. 22, 1950, Buffalo, N. Y.

	W	L	PCT	ERA	G	GS	CG	IP	H	BB	SO	ShO	W	L	SV	AB	H	HR	BA
'75 DET A	0	0	–	4.82	3	0	0	9.1	10	9	3	0	0	0	0	0	0	0	–

Herm Malloy

MALLOY, HERMAN
B. June 1, 1885, Massillon, Ohio   D. May 9, 1942, Massillon, Ohio

	W	L	PCT	ERA	G	GS	CG	IP	H	BB	SO	ShO	W	L	SV	AB	H	HR	BA
'07 DET A	0	1	.000	5.63	1	1	1	8	13	5	6	0	0	0	0	4	0	0	.000
'08	0	2	.000	3.71	3	2	2	17	20	4	8	0	0	0	0	9	3	0	.333
2 yrs.	0	3	.000	4.32	4	3	3	25	33	9	14	0	0	0	0	13	3	0	.231
2 yrs.	0	3	.000	4.32	4	3	3	25	33	9	14	0	0	0	0	13	3	0	.231

	W	L	PCT	ERA	G	GS	CG	IP	H	BB	SO	ShO	Relief Pitching W L SV			BATTING AB H HR			BA

Hal Manders

MANDERS, HAROLD CARL
B. June 14, 1917, Waukee, Iowa
BR TR 6' 187 lbs.

	W	L	PCT	ERA	G	GS	CG	IP	H	BB	SO	ShO	W	L	SV	AB	H	HR	BA
1941 DET A	1	0	1.000	2.35	8	0	0	15.1	13	8	7	0	1	0	0	4	0	0	.000
1942	2	0	1.000	4.09	18	0	0	33	39	15	14	0	2	0	0	4	1	0	.250
1946 2 teams			DET	A (2G 0–0)			CHI	N (2G 0–1)											
" total	0	1	.000	9.75	4	1	0	12	19	5	7	0	0	0	0	4	1	0	.250
3 yrs.	3	1	.750	4.77	30	1	0	60.1	71	28	28	0	3	0	0	12	2	0	.167
3 yrs.	3	0	1.000	4.31	28	0	0	54.1	60	25	24	0	3	0	0	10	2	0	.200

Firpo Marberry

MARBERRY, FREDRICK
B. Nov. 30, 1898, Streetman, Tex.   D. June 30, 1976, Mexia, Tex.
BR TR 6'1" 190 lbs

	W	L	PCT	ERA	G	GS	CG	IP	H	BB	SO	ShO	W	L	SV	AB	H	HR	BA
1923 WAS A	4	0	1.000	2.82	11	4	2	44.2	42	17	18	0	0	0	0	14	2	0	.143
1924	11	12	.478	3.09	50	15	6	195.1	190	70	68	0	6	5	15	59	8	0	.136
1925	8	6	.571	3.47	55	0	0	93.1	84	45	53	0	8	6	15	19	5	0	.263
1926	12	7	.632	3.00	64	5	3	138	120	66	43	0	9	5	22	34	6	0	.176
1927	10	7	.588	4.64	56	10	2	155.1	177	68	74	0	8	2	9	41	5	0	.122
1928	13	13	.500	3.85	48	11	7	161.1	160	42	76	1	7	9	3	46	5	0	.109
1929	19	12	.613	3.06	49	26	16	250.1	233	69	121	0	3	4	11	82	19	0	.232
1930	15	5	.750	4.09	33	22	9	185	190	53	56	2	0	3	1	73	24	0	.329
1931	16	4	.800	3.45	45	25	11	219	211	63	88	2	3	1	7	82	19	1	.232
1932	8	4	.667	4.01	54	15	8	197.2	202	72	66	1	1	1	13	66	11	0	.167
1933 DET A	16	11	.593	3.29	37	32	15	238.1	232	61	84	1	0	0	0	90	11	0	.122
1934	15	5	.750	4.57	38	19	6	155.2	174	48	64	1	6	0	3	55	12	0	.218
1935	0	1	.000	4.26	5	2	1	19	22	9	7	0	0	0	0	5	1	0	.200
1936 2 teams			NY	N (1G 0–0)			WAS	A (5G 0–2)											
" total	0	2	.000	3.77	6	1	0	14.1	12	3	4	0	0	1	0	3	0	0	.000
14 yrs.	147	89	.623	3.63	551	187	86	2067.1	2049	686	822	8	53	37	101	669	128	1	.191
3 yrs.	31	17	.646	3.81	80	53	22	413	428	118	155	2	8	0	5	150	24	0	.160

WORLD SERIES

	W	L	PCT	ERA	G	GS	CG	IP	H	BB	SO	ShO	W	L	SV	AB	H	HR	BA
1924 WAS A	0	1	.000	1.13	4	1	0	8	9	4	10	0	0	0	2	2	0	0	.000
1925	0	0	–	0.00	2	0	0	2.1	3	0	2	0	0	0	1	0	0	0	–
1934 DET A	0	0	–	21.60	2	0	0	1.2	5	1	0	0	0	0	0	0	0	0	–
3 yrs.	0	1	.000	3.75	8	1	0	12	17	5	12	0	0	0	3	2	0	0	.000

Leo Marentette

MARENTETTE, LEO JOHN
B. Feb. 18, 1941, Detroit, Mich.
BR TR 6'2" 200 lbs.

	W	L	PCT	ERA	G	GS	CG	IP	H	BB	SO	ShO	W	L	SV	AB	H	HR	BA
1965 DET A	0	0	–	0.00	2	0	0	3	1	1	3	0	0	0	0	0	0	0	–
1969 MON N	0	0	–	6.75	3	0	0	5.1	9	1	4	0	0	0	0	1	0	0	.000
2 yrs.	0	0	–	4.32	5	0	0	8.1	10	2	7	0	0	0	0	1	0	0	.000
1 yr.	0	0	–	0.00	2	0	0	3	1	1	3	0	0	0	0	0	0	0	–

Dick Marlowe

MARLOWE, RICHARD BURTON
B. June 27, 1929, Hickory, N. C.   D. Dec. 30, 1968, Toledo, Ohio
BR TR 6'2" 165 lbs.

	W	L	PCT	ERA	G	GS	CG	IP	H	BB	SO	ShO	W	L	SV	AB	H	HR	BA
1951 DET A	0	1	.000	32.40	2	1	0	1.2	5	2	1	0	0	0	0	0	0	0	–
1952	0	2	.000	7.36	4	1	0	11	21	3	3	0	0	1	0	2	0	0	.000
1953	6	7	.462	5.26	42	11	2	119.2	152	42	52	0	3	1	0	32	7	0	.219
1954	5	4	.556	4.18	38	2	0	84	76	40	39	0	5	2	2	18	3	0	.167
1955	1	0	1.000	1.80	4	1	1	15	12	4	9	0	0	0	1	4	0	0	.000
1956 2 teams			DET	A (7G 1–1)			CHI	A (1G 0–0)											
" total	1	1	.500	6.00	8	1	0	12	14	10	4	0	1	0	0	1	0	0	.000
6 yrs.	13	15	.464	4.99	98	17	3	243.1	280	101	108	0	9	4	3	57	10	0	.175
6 yrs.	13	15	.464	4.98	97	17	3	242.1	278	100	108	0	9	4	3	57	10	0	.175

Buck Marrow

MARROW, CHARLES KENNON
B. Aug. 29, 1909, Tarboro, N. C.   D. Nov. 21, 1982, Newport News, Va.
BR TR 6'4" 200 lbs.

	W	L	PCT	ERA	G	GS	CG	IP	H	BB	SO	ShO	W	L	SV	AB	H	HR	BA
1932 DET A	2	5	.286	4.81	18	7	2	63.2	70	29	31	0	1	0	1	19	3	0	.158
1937 BKN N	1	2	.333	6.61	6	3	1	16.1	19	9	2	0	0	0	0	5	0	0	.000
1938	0	1	.000	4.58	15	0	0	19.2	23	11	6	0	0	1	0	1	0	0	.000
3 yrs.	3	8	.273	5.06	39	10	3	99.2	112	49	39	0	1	1	1	25	3	0	.120
1 yr.	2	5	.286	4.81	18	7	2	63.2	70	29	31	0	1	0	1	19	3	0	.158

Mike Marshall

MARSHALL, MICHAEL GRANT
B. Jan. 15, 1943, Adrian, Mich.
BR TR 5'10" 180 lbs.

	W	L	PCT	ERA	G	GS	CG	IP	H	BB	SO	ShO	W	L	SV	AB	H	HR	BA
1967 DET A	1	3	.250	1.98	37	0	0	59	51	20	41	0	1	3	10	9	2	0	.222
1969 SEA A	3	10	.231	5.13	20	14	3	87.2	99	35	47	1	0	1	0	27	7	1	.259
1970 2 teams			HOU	N (4G 0–1)			MON	N (24G 3–7)											
" total	3	8	.273	3.86	28	5	0	70	64	33	43	0	3	4	3	11	1	0	.091
1971 MON N	5	8	.385	4.30	66	0	0	111	100	50	85	0	5	8	23	16	3	0	.188
1972	14	8	.636	1.78	65	0	0	116	82	47	95	0	14	8	18	22	3	0	.136
1973	14	11	.560	2.66	92	0	0	179	163	75	124	0	14	11	31	33	8	0	.242
1974 LA N	15	12	.556	2.42	106	0	0	208	191	56	143	0	15	12	21	34	8	0	.235
1975	9	14	.391	3.30	57	0	0	109	98	39	64	0	9	14	13	15	1	0	.067
1976 2 teams			LA	N (30G 4–3)			ATL	N (24G 2–1)											
" total	6	4	.600	3.99	54	0	0	99.1	99	39	56	0	6	4	14	11	1	0	.091
1977 2 teams			ATL	N (4G 1–0)			TEX	A (12G 2–2)											
" total	3	2	.600	4.71	16	4	0	42	54	15	24	0	1	2	1	1	1	0	1.000
1978 MIN A	10	12	.455	2.36	54	0	0	99	80	37	56	0	10	12	21	0	0	0	–
1979	10	15	.400	2.64	90	1	0	143	132	48	81	0	10	14	32	0	0	0	–
1980	1	3	.250	6.19	18	0	0	32	42	12	13	0	1	3	1	0	0	0	–
1981 NY N	3	2	.600	2.61	20	0	0	31	26	8	8	0	3	2	0	0	0	0	–
14 yrs.	97	112	.464	3.14	723	24	3	1386	1281	514	880	1	92	98	188	179	35	1	.196
													6th		7th				
1 yr.	1	3	.250	1.98	37	0	0	59	51	20	41	0	1	3	10	9	2	0	.222

LEAGUE CHAMPIONSHIP SERIES

	W	L	PCT	ERA	G	GS	CG	IP	H	BB	SO	ShO	W	L	SV	AB	H	HR	BA
1974 LA N	0	0	–	0.00	2	0	0	3	1	0	1	0	0	0	0	0	0	0	–

WORLD SERIES

	W	L	PCT	ERA	G	GS	CG	IP	H	BB	SO	ShO	W	L	SV	AB	H	HR	BA
1974 LA N	0	1	.000	1.00	5	0	0	9	6	1	10	0	0	1	1	0	0	0	–

	W	L	PCT	ERA	G	GS	CG	IP	H	BB	SO	ShO	Relief Pitching W	L	SV	BATTING AB	H	HR	BA

ohn Martin

MARTIN, JOHN ROBERT
B. Apr. 11, 1956, Wyandotte, Mich. BB TL 6' 190 lbs.

Year	W	L	PCT	ERA	G	GS	CG	IP	H	BB	SO	ShO	W	L	SV	AB	H	HR	BA
980 STL N	2	3	.400	4.29	9	5	1	42	39	9	23	0	0	1	0	11	3	0	.273
981	8	5	.615	3.41	17	15	4	103	85	26	36	0	0	0	0	33	7	0	.212
982	4	5	.444	4.23	24	7	0	66	56	30	21	0	1	2	0	11	1	0	.091
983 2 teams			STL	N (26G 3-1)				DET	A	(15G 0-0)									
total	3	1	.750	4.18	41	5	0	79.2	75	30	40	0	2	0	1	18	4	0	.222
4 yrs.	17	14	.548	3.93	91	32	5	290.2	255	95	120	0	3	3	1	73	15	0	.205
1 yr.	0	0	-	7.43	15	0	0	13.1	15	4	11	0	0	0	1	0	0	0	-

Roger Mason

MASON, ROGER LeROY
B. Sept. 18, 1958, Bellaire, Mich. BR TR 6'6" 215 lbs.

Year	W	L	PCT	ERA	G	GS	CG	IP	H	BB	SO	ShO	W	L	SV	AB	H	HR	BA
984 DET A	1	1	.500	3.86	4	2	0	21	20	10	14	0	0	0	1	0	0	0	-

Walt Masterson

MASTERSON, WALTER EDWARD
B. June 22, 1920, Philadelphia, Pa. BR TR 6'2" 189 lbs.

Year	W	L	PCT	ERA	G	GS	CG	IP	H	BB	SO	ShO	W	L	SV	AB	H	HR	BA
939 WAS A	2	2	.500	5.55	24	5	1	58.1	66	48	12	0	1	0	0	13	2	0	.154
940	3	13	.188	4.90	31	19	3	130.1	128	88	68	0	1	1	2	38	7	0	.184
941	4	3	.571	5.97	34	6	1	78.1	101	53	40	0	2	0	3	19	2	0	.105
942	5	9	.357	3.34	25	15	8	142.2	138	54	63	4	0	2	2	45	7	0	.156
945	1	2	.333	1.08	4	2	1	25	21	10	14	1	0	2	0	9	1	0	.111
946	5	6	.455	6.01	29	9	2	91.1	105	67	61	0	4	2	1	25	2	0	.080
947	12	16	.429	3.13	35	31	14	253	215	97	135	4	0	0	1	83	11	0	.133
948	8	15	.348	3.83	33	27	9	188	171	122	72	2	0	0	0	57	11	0	.193
949 2 teams			WAS	A (10G 3-2)				BOS	A	(18G 3-4)									
total	6	6	.500	3.75	28	12	4	108	100	56	36	0	2	2	4	35	3	0	.086
950 BOS A	8	6	.571	5.64	33	15	6	129.1	145	82	60	0	1	2	1	44	6	0	.136
951	3	0	1.000	3.34	30	1	0	59.1	53	32	39	0	3	0	2	11	2	0	.182
952 2 teams			BOS	A (5G 1-1)				WAS	A	(24G 9-8)									
total	10	9	.526	4.13	29	22	11	170	171	83	92	0	1	0	2	52	6	0	.115
953 WAS A	10	12	.455	3.63	29	20	0	166.1	145	62	95	4	1	2	0	51	7	0	.137
956 DET A	1	1	.500	4.17	35	0	0	49.2	54	32	28	0	1	1	0	4	1	0	.250
14 yrs.	78	100	.438	4.15	399	184	70	1649.2	1613	886	815	15	17	14	20	486	68	0	.140
1 yr.	1	1	.500	4.17	35	0	0	49.2	54	32	28	0	1	1	0	4	1	0	.250

port McAllister

McALLISTER, LEWIS WILLIAM
B. July 23, 1874, Austin, Miss. D. July 18, 1962, Detroit, Mich. BB TR 5'11" 180 lbs.

Year	W	L	PCT	ERA	G	GS	CG	IP	H	BB	SO	ShO	W	L	SV	AB	H	HR	BA
896 CLE N	0	0	-	6.75	1	0	0	4	9	2	0	0	0	0	0	27	6	0	.222
897	1	2	.333	4.50	4	3	3	28	29	9	10	0	0	0	0	137	30	0	.219
898	3	4	.429	4.55	9	7	6	65.1	73	23	9	0	0	0	0	57	13	0	.228
899	0	1	.000	9.56	3	1	1	16	29	10	2	0	0	0	0	418	99	1	.237
4 yrs.	4	7	.364	5.32	17	11	10	113.1	140	44	21	0	0	0	0	*			

Arch McCarthy

McCARTHY, ARCHIBALD J.
B. Ypsilanti, Mich.

Year	W	L	PCT	ERA	G	GS	CG	IP	H	BB	SO	ShO	W	L	SV	AB	H	HR	BA
902 DET A	2	7	.222	6.13	10	8	8	72	90	31	10	0	1	0	0	28	2	0	.071

Ed McCreery

McCREERY, ESLEY PORTERFIELD
B. Dec. 24, 1889, Cripple Creek, Colo. D. Oct. 19, 1960, Sacramento, Calif. BR TR 6'1" 195 lbs.

Year	W	L	PCT	ERA	G	GS	CG	IP	H	BB	SO	ShO	W	L	SV	AB	H	HR	BA
914 DET A	1	0	1.000	11.25	3	1	0	4	3	4	0	0	0	0	0	1	0	0	.000

Mickey McDermott

McDERMOTT, MAURICE JOSEPH
B. Aug. 29, 1928, Poughkeepsie, N.Y. BL TL 6'2" 170 lbs.

Year	W	L	PCT	ERA	G	GS	CG	IP	H	BB	SO	ShO	W	L	SV	AB	H	HR	BA
948 BOS A	0	0	-	6.17	7	0	0	23.1	16	35	17	0	0	0	0	8	3	0	.375
949	5	4	.556	4.05	12	12	6	80	63	52	50	2	0	0	0	33	7	0	.212
950	7	3	.700	5.19	38	15	4	130	119	124	96	0	3	0	5	44	16	0	.364
951	8	8	.500	3.35	34	19	9	172	141	92	127	1	0	1	3	66	18	1	.273
952	10	9	.526	3.72	30	21	7	162	139	92	117	2	2	3	0	62	14	1	.226
953	18	10	.643	3.01	32	30	8	206.1	169	109	92	4	0	0	0	93	28	1	.301
954 WAS A	7	15	.318	3.44	30	26	11	196.1	172	110	95	1	0	0	1	95	19	0	.200
955	10	10	.500	3.75	31	20	8	156	140	102	78	1	2	1	1	95	25	1	.263
956 NY A	2	6	.250	4.24	23	9	1	87	85	47	38	0	0	0	0	52	11	1	.212
957 KC A	1	4	.200	5.48	29	4	0	69	68	50	29	0	1	2	0	49	12	4	.245
958 DET A	0	0	-	9.00	2	0	0	2	6	2	0	0	0	0	0	3	1	0	.333
961 2 teams			STL	N (19G 1-0)				KC	A	(4G 0-0)									
total	1	0	1.000	5.51	23	0	0	32.2	43	25	18	0	1	0	4	19	2	0	.105
12 yrs.	69	69	.500	3.91	291	156	54	1316.2	1161	840	757	11	9	7	14	*			
1 yr.	0	0	-	9.00	2	0	0	2	6	2	0	0	0	0	0	3	1	0	.333
WORLD SERIES																			
956 NY A	0	0	-	3.00	1	0	0	3	2	3	3	0	0	0	0	1	1	0	1.000

Pat McGehee

McGEHEE, PATRICK HENRY
B. July 2, 1888, Meadville, Miss. D. Dec. 30, 1946, Paducah, Ky. BL TR 6'2½" 180 lbs.

Year	W	L	PCT	ERA	G	GS	CG	IP	H	BB	SO	ShO	W	L	SV	AB	H	HR	BA
912 DET A	0	0	-	0.00	1	1	0	1	1	1	0	0	0	0	0	0	0	0	-

Deacon McGuire

McGUIRE, JAMES THOMAS
B. Nov. 2, 1865, Youngstown, Ohio D. Oct. 31, 1936, Albion, Mich.
Manager 1898, 1907-11. BR TR 6'1" 185 lbs.

Year	W	L	PCT	ERA	G	GS	CG	IP	H	BB	SO	ShO	W	L	SV	AB	H	HR	BA
890 ROC AA	0	0	-	6.75	1	0	0	4	10	1	1	0	0	0	0	*			

Archie McKain

McKAIN, ARCHIE RICHARD (Happy)
B. May 12, 1911, Delphos, Kans. BB TL 5'10" 175 lbs.
BL 1941,1943

Year	W	L	PCT	ERA	G	GS	CG	IP	H	BB	SO	ShO	W	L	SV	AB	H	HR	BA
937 BOS A	8	8	.500	4.66	36	18	3	137	152	64	66	0	2	0	2	49	13	0	.265
938	5	4	.556	4.52	37	5	1	99.2	119	44	27	0	3	3	6	31	2	0	.065
939 DET A	5	6	.455	3.68	32	11	4	129.2	120	54	49	1	4	2	4	41	9	2	.220
940	5	0	1.000	2.82	27	0	0	51	48	25	24	0	5	0	3	7	1	0	.143

	W	L	PCT	ERA	G	GS	CG	IP	H	BB	SO	ShO	Relief Pitching W	L	SV	BATTING AB	H	HR	BA

Archie McKain continued

	W	L	PCT	ERA	G	GS	CG	IP	H	BB	SO	ShO	W	L	SV	AB	H	HR	BA
1941 2 teams				DET A (15G 2–1)				STL A (8G 0–1)											
" total	2	2	.500	5.60	23	0	0	53	74	15	16	0	2	2	1	13	0	0	.000
1943 STL A	1	1	.500	3.94	10	0	0	16	16	6	6	0	1	1	0	1	0	0	.000
6 yrs.	26	21	.553	4.26	165	34	8	486.1	529	208	188	1	17	8	16	142	25	2	.17
3 yrs.	12	7	.632	3.74	74	11	4	223.2	226	90	87	1	11	3	7	59	10	2	.169

WORLD SERIES

	W	L	PCT	ERA	G	GS	CG	IP	H	BB	SO	ShO	W	L	SV	AB	H	HR	BA
1940 DET A	0	0	—	3.00	1	0	0	3	4	0	0	0	0	0	0	0	0	0	

Denny McLain

McLAIN, DENNIS DALE
B. Mar. 29, 1944, Chicago, Ill.   BR TR 6'1" 185 lbs

	W	L	PCT	ERA	G	GS	CG	IP	H	BB	SO	ShO	W	L	SV	AB	H	HR	BA
1963 DET A	2	1	.667	4.29	3	3	2	21	20	16	22	0	0	0	0	5	1	1	.200
1964	4	5	.444	4.05	19	16	3	100	84	37	70	0	0	1	0	37	5	0	.135
1965	16	6	.727	2.61	33	29	13	220.1	174	62	192	4	1	0	1	74	4	0	.054
1966	20	14	.588	3.92	38	38	14	264.1	205	104	192	4	0	0	0	93	17	0	.183
1967	17	16	.515	3.79	37	37	10	235	209	73	161	3	0	0	0	85	10	0	.118
1968	**31**	6	**.838**	1.96	41	**41**	**28**	**336**	241	63	280	6	0	0	0	111	18	0	.162
1969	24	9	.727	2.80	42	41	23	325	288	67	181	9	0	0	0	106	17	0	.166
1970	3	5	.375	4.65	14	14	1	91	100	28	52	0	0	0	0	31	2	0	.065
1971 WAS A	10	**22**	.313	4.27	33	32	9	217	233	72	103	3	1	0	0	58	6	0	.103
1972 2 teams				OAK A (5G 1–2)				ATL N (15G 3–5)											
" total	4	7	.364	6.39	20	13	2	76	92	26	29	0	1	1	1	16	2	0	.125
10 yrs.	131	91	.590	3.39	280	264	105	1885.2	1646	548	1282	29	3	2	2	616	82	1	.133
8 yrs.	117	62	.654	3.13	227	219	94	1592.2	1321	450	1150	26	1	1	1	542	74	1	.137
				1st							8th	7th							

WORLD SERIES

	W	L	PCT	ERA	G	GS	CG	IP	H	BB	SO	ShO	W	L	SV	AB	H	HR	BA
1968 DET A	1	2	.333	3.24	3	3	1	16.2	18	4	13	0	0	0	0	6	0	0	.000

Pat McLaughlin

McLAUGHLIN, PATRICK ELMER
B. Aug. 17, 1910, Taylor, Tex.   BR TR 6'2" 175 lbs.

	W	L	PCT	ERA	G	GS	CG	IP	H	BB	SO	ShO	W	L	SV	AB	H	HR	BA
1937 DET A	0	2	.000	6.34	10	3	0	32.2	39	16	8	0	0	0	0	10	1	0	.100
1940 PHI A	0	0	—	16.20	1	0	0	1.2	4	1	0	0	0	0	0	0	0	0	—
1945 DET A	0	0	—	9.00	1	0	0	1	2	0	0	0	0	0	0	0	0	0	—
3 yrs.	0	2	.000	6.88	12	3	0	35.1	45	17	8	0	0	0	0	10	1	0	.100
2 yrs.	0	2	.000	6.42	11	3	0	33.2	41	16	8	0	0	0	0	10	1	0	.100

Wayne McLeland

McLELAND, WAYNE GAFFNEY (Nubbin)
B. Aug. 29, 1924, Milton, Iowa   BR TR 6' 180 lbs.

	W	L	PCT	ERA	G	GS	CG	IP	H	BB	SO	ShO	W	L	SV	AB	H	HR	BA
1951 DET A	0	1	.000	8.18	6	1	0	11	20	4	0	0	0	0	0	1	0	0	.000
1952	0	0	—	10.13	4	0	0	2.2	4	6	0	0	0	0	0	0	0	0	—
2 yrs.	0	1	.000	8.56	10	1	0	13.2	24	10	0	0	0	0	0	1	0	0	.000
2 yrs.	0	1	.000	8.56	10	1	0	13.2	24	10	0	0	0	0	0	1	0	0	.000

Sam McMackin

McMACKIN, SAMUEL
B. Cleveland, Ohio   D. Feb. 11, 1903, Columbus, Ohio

	W	L	PCT	ERA	G	GS	CG	IP	H	BB	SO	ShO	W	L	SV	AB	H	HR	BA
1902 2 teams				CHI A (1G 0–0)				DET A (1G 0–1)											
" total	0	1	.000	2.38	2	1	1	11.1	10	4	4	0	0	0	0	5	2	0	.400

Don McMahon

McMAHON, DONALD JOHN
B. Jan. 4, 1930, Brooklyn, N. Y.   BR TR 6'2" 215 lbs.

	W	L	PCT	ERA	G	GS	CG	IP	H	BB	SO	ShO	W	L	SV	AB	H	HR	BA
1957 MIL N	2	3	.400	1.54	32	0	0	46.2	33	29	46	0	2	3	9	8	2	0	.250
1958	7	2	.778	3.68	38	0	0	58.2	50	29	37	0	7	2	8	9	1	0	.111
1959	5	3	.625	2.57	60	0	0	80.2	81	37	55	0	5	3	15	9	2	0	.222
1960	3	6	.333	5.94	48	0	0	63.2	66	32	50	0	3	6	10	11	0	0	.000
1961	6	4	.600	2.84	53	0	0	92	84	51	55	0	6	4	8	16	3	0	.188
1962 2 teams				MIL N (2G 0–1)				HOU N (51G 5–5)											
" total	5	6	.455	1.69	53	0	0	79.2	56	33	72	0	5	6	8	12	1	0	.083
1963 HOU N	1	5	.167	4.05	49	2	0	80	83	26	51	0	1	3	5	12	1	0	.083
1964 CLE A	6	4	.600	2.41	70	0	0	101	67	52	92	0	6	4	16	14	2	0	.143
1965	3	3	.500	3.28	58	0	0	85	79	37	60	0	3	3	11	9	2	0	.222
1966 2 teams				CLE A (12G 1–1)				BOS A (49G 8–7)											
" total	9	8	.529	2.69	61	0	0	90.1	73	44	62	0	9	8	13	13	1	0	.077
1967 2 teams				BOS A (11G 1–2)				CHI A (52G 5–0)											
" total	6	2	.750	1.98	63	0	0	109.1	68	40	84	0	6	2	5	13	2	0	.154
1968 2 teams				CHI A (25G 2–1)				DET A (20G 3–1)											
" total	5	2	.714	1.98	45	0	0	81.2	53	30	65	0	5	2	1	7	1	0	.143
1969 2 teams				DET A (34G 3–5)				SF N (13G 3–1)											
" total	6	6	.500	3.54	47	0	0	61	38	27	59	0	6	6	13	9	1	0	.111
1970 SF N	9	5	.643	2.97	61	0	0	94	70	45	74	0	9	5	19	14	2	0	.143
1971	10	6	.625	4.06	61	0	0	82	73	37	71	0	10	6	4	7	0	0	.000
1972	3	3	.500	3.71	44	0	0	63	46	21	45	0	3	3	5	4	1	0	.250
1973	4	0	1.000	1.50	22	0	0	30	21	7	20	0	4	0	6	1	1	0	1.000
1974	0	0	—	3.00	9	0	0	12	13	2	5	0	0	0	0	0	0	0	—
18 yrs.	90	68	.570	2.96	874	2	0	1310.2	1054	579	1003	0	90	66	153	168	23	0	.137
				7th									7th						
2 yrs.	6	6	.500	2.97	54	0	0	72.2	47	28	71	0	6	6	12	10	0	0	.000

LEAGUE CHAMPIONSHIP SERIES

	W	L	PCT	ERA	G	GS	CG	IP	H	BB	SO	ShO	W	L	SV	AB	H	HR	BA
1971 SF N	0	0	—	0.00	2	0	0	3	0	0	3	0	0	0	0	0	0	0	—

WORLD SERIES

	W	L	PCT	ERA	G	GS	CG	IP	H	BB	SO	ShO	W	L	SV	AB	H	HR	BA
1957 MIL N	0	0	—	0.00	3	0	0	5	3	3	5	0	0	0	0	0	0	0	—
1958	0	0	—	5.40	3	0	0	3.1	3	3	5	0	0	0	0	0	0	0	—
1968 DET A	0	0	—	13.50	2	0	0	2	4	0	1	0	0	0	0	0	0	0	—
3 yrs.	0	0	—	4.35	8	0	0	10.1	10	6	11	0	0	0	0	0	0	0	—

	W	L	PCT	ERA	G	GS	CG	IP	H	BB	SO	ShO	W	L	SV	AB	H	HR	BA

Norm McRae — McRAE, NORMAN · BR TR 6'1" 195 lbs. · B. Sept. 26, 1947, Elizabeth, N. J.

	W	L	PCT	ERA	G	GS	CG	IP	H	BB	SO	ShO	W	L	SV	AB	H	HR	BA
1969 DET A	0	0	–	6.00	3	0	0	3	2	1	3	0	0	0	0	0	0	0	–
1970	0	0	–	2.90	19	0	0	31	26	25	16	0	0	0	0	1	0	0	.000
2 yrs.	0	0	–	3.18	22	0	0	34	28	26	19	0	0	0	0	1	0	0	.000
2 yrs.	0	0	–	3.18	22	0	0	34	28	26	19	0	0	0	0	1	0	0	.000

Bill McTigue — McTIGUE, WILLIAM PERCY · BL TL 6'1½" 175 lbs. · B. Jan. 3, 1891, Nashville, Tenn. D. May 11, 1920, Nashville, Tenn.

	W	L	PCT	ERA	G	GS	CG	IP	H	BB	SO	ShO	W	L	SV	AB	H	HR	BA
1911 BOS N	0	5	.000	7.05	14	8	0	37	37	49	23	0	0	1	0	12	1	0	.083
1912	2	0	1.000	5.45	10	1	1	34.2	39	18	17	0	1	0	0	13	1	0	.077
1916 DET A	0	0	–	5.06	3	0	0	5.1	5	5	1	0	0	0	0	1	0	0	.000
3 yrs.	2	5	.286	6.19	27	9	1	77	81	72	41	0	1	1	0	26	2	0	.077
1 yr.	0	0	–	5.06	3	0	0	5.1	5	5	1	0	0	0	0	1	0	0	.000

Phil Meeler — MEELER, CHARLES PHILIP JR. · BR TR 6'5" 215 lbs. · B. July 23, 1948, South Boston, Va.

	W	L	PCT	ERA	G	GS	CG	IP	H	BB	SO	ShO	W	L	SV	AB	H	HR	BA
1972 DET A	0	1	.000	4.50	7	0	0	8	10	7	5	0	0	1	0	2	0	0	.000

Win Mercer — MERCER, GEORGE BARCLAY · TR 5'7" 140 lbs. · B. June 20, 1874, Chester, W. Va. D. Jan. 12, 1903, San Francisco, Calif.

	W	L	PCT	ERA	G	GS	CG	IP	H	BB	SO	ShO	W	L	SV	AB	H	HR	BA
1894 WAS N	17	23	.425	3.76	49	38	30	333	431	125	69	0	2	1	3	162	46	2	.284
1895	13	23	.361	4.46	43	38	32	311	430	96	84	0	0	1	2	196	50	1	.255
1896	25	18	.581	4.13	46	45	38	366.1	456	117	94	2	1	0	0	156	38	1	.244
1897	20	20	.500	3.25	45	42	34	332	395	102	88	3	0	1	2	135	43	0	.319
1898	12	18	.400	4.81	33	30	24	233.2	309	71	52	0	0	1	0	249	80	2	.321
1899	7	14	.333	4.60	23	21	21	186	234	53	28	0	0	0	0	375	112	1	.299
1900 NY N	13	17	.433	3.86	32	29	26	242.1	303	58	39	1	0	0	0	248	73	0	.294
1901 WAS A	9	13	.409	4.56	24	22	19	179.2	217	50	31	1	0	0	1	140	42	0	.300
1902 DET A	15	18	.455	3.04	35	33	28	281.2	282	80	40	4	0	0	1	100	18	0	.180
9 yrs.	131	164	.444	3.98	330	298	252	2465.2	3057	752	525	11	3	5	9	*			
1 yr.	15	18	.455	3.04	35	33	28	281.2	282	80	40	4	0	0	1	100	18	0	.180

Gene Michael — MICHAEL, GENE RICHARD (Stick) · BB TR 6'2" 183 lbs. · B. June 2, 1938, Kent, Ohio · Manager 1981-82.

	W	L	PCT	ERA	G	GS	CG	IP	H	BB	SO	ShO	W	L	SV	AB	H	HR	BA
1968 NY A	0	0	–	0.00	1	0	0	3	5	0	3	0	0	0	0	*			

Jim Middleton — MIDDLETON, JAMES BLAINE (Rifle Jim) · BR TR 5'11½" 165 lbs. · Brother of John Middleton. · B. May 28, 1899, Argos, Ind. D. Jan. 12, 1974, Argos, Ind.

	W	L	PCT	ERA	G	GS	CG	IP	H	BB	SO	ShO	W	L	SV	AB	H	HR	BA
1917 NY N	1	1	.500	2.75	13	0	0	36	35	8	9	0	1	1	1	8	0	0	.000
1921 DET A	6	11	.353	5.03	38	10	2	121.2	149	44	31	0	4	8	7	34	5	0	.147
2 yrs.	7	12	.368	4.51	51	10	2	157.2	184	52	40	0	5	9	8	42	5	0	.119
1 yr.	6	11	.353	5.03	38	10	2	121.2	149	44	31	0	4	8	7	34	5	0	.147

Bob Miller — MILLER, ROBERT GERALD · BR TL 6'1" 185 lbs. · B. July 15, 1935, Berwyn, Ill.

	W	L	PCT	ERA	G	GS	CG	IP	H	BB	SO	ShO	W	L	SV	AB	H	HR	BA
1953 DET A	1	2	.333	5.94	13	1	0	36.1	43	21	9	0	1	1	0	8	1	0	.125
1954	1	1	.500	2.45	32	1	0	69.2	62	26	27	0	1	1	1	15	2	0	.133
1955	2	1	.667	2.49	7	3	1	25.1	26	12	11	0	0	0	0	9	2	0	.222
1956	0	2	.000	5.68	11	3	0	31.2	37	22	16	0	0	0	0	7	1	0	.143
1962 2 teams			CIN N (6G 0–0)			NY N (17G 2–2)													
" total	2	2	.500	10.17	23	0	0	25.2	38	11	12	0	2	2	0	2	0	0	.000
5 yrs.	6	8	.429	4.72	86	8	1	188.2	206	92	75	0	4	4	1	41	6	0	.146
4 yrs.	4	6	.400	3.87	63	8	1	163	168	81	63	0	2	2	1	39	6	0	.154

Bob Miller — MILLER, ROBERT LANE · BR TR 6'1" 180 lbs. · B. Feb. 18, 1939, St. Louis, Mo.

	W	L	PCT	ERA	G	GS	CG	IP	H	BB	SO	ShO	W	L	SV	AB	H	HR	BA
1957 STL N	0	0	–	7.00	5	0	0	9	13	5	7	0	0	0	0	0	0	0	–
1959	4	3	.571	3.31	11	10	3	70.2	66	21	43	0	0	0	0	24	5	0	.208
1960	4	3	.571	3.42	15	7	0	52.2	53	17	33	0	1	0	0	14	2	0	.143
1961	1	3	.250	4.24	34	5	0	74.1	82	46	39	0	1	1	3	14	5	0	.357
1962 NY N	1	12	.077	4.89	33	21	1	143.2	146	62	91	0	0	1	1	41	5	0	.122
1963 LA N	10	8	.556	2.89	42	23	2	187	171	65	125	0	4	2	1	57	4	0	.070
1964	7	7	.500	2.62	74	2	0	137.2	115	63	94	0	6	7	9	19	3	0	.158
1965	6	7	.462	2.97	61	1	0	103	82	26	77	0	6	6	9	16	0	0	.000
1966	4	2	.667	2.77	46	0	0	84.1	70	29	58	0	4	2	5	13	1	0	.077
1967	2	9	.182	4.31	52	4	0	85.2	88	27	32	0	2	6	0	8	1	0	.125
1968 MIN A	0	3	.000	2.74	45	0	0	72.1	65	24	41	0	0	3	2	7	1	0	.143
1969	5	5	.500	3.02	48	11	0	119.1	118	32	57	0	0	4	3	31	0	0	.000
1970 3 teams			CLE A (15G 2–2)			CHI N (7G 0–0)			CHI A (15G 4–6)										
" total	6	8	.429	4.79	37	15	0	107	129	54	55	0	2	0	3	28	5	0	.179
1971 3 teams			CHI N (2G 0–0)			SD N (38G 7–3)			PIT N (16G 1–2)										
" total	8	5	.615	1.64	56	0	0	98.2	83	40	51	0	8	5	10	12	0	0	.000
1972 PIT N	5	2	.714	2.65	36	0	0	54.1	54	24	18	0	5	2	3	4	0	0	.000
1973 3 teams			DET A (22G 4–2)			SD N (18G 0–0)			NY N (1G 0–0)										
" total	4	2	.667	3.67	41	0	0	73.2	63	34	39	0	4	2	1	2	0	0	.000
1974 NY N	2	2	.500	3.58	58	0	0	78	89	39	35	0	2	2	2	9	1	0	.111
17 yrs.	69	81	.460	3.37	694	99	7	1551.1	1487	608	895	0	45	43	52	299	33	0	.110
1 yr.	4	2	.667	3.43	22	0	0	42	34	22	23	0	4	2	1	0	0	0	–
LEAGUE CHAMPIONSHIP SERIES																			
1969 MIN A	0	1	.000	5.40	1	1	0	1.2	5	0	0	0	0	0	0	0	0	0	–
1971 PIT N	0	0	–	6.00	1	0	0	3	3	3	3	0	0	0	0	1	0	0	.000

	W	L	PCT	ERA	G	GS	CG	IP	H	BB	SO	ShO	Relief Pitching W	L	SV	BATTING AB	H	HR	BA

Bob Miller continued

	W	L	PCT	ERA	G	GS	CG	IP	H	BB	SO	ShO	W	L	SV	AB	H	HR	BA
1972	0	0	–	0.00	1	0	0	1	0	0	1	0	0	0	0	0	0	0	
3 yrs.	0	1	.000	4.76	3	1	0	5.2	8	3	4	0	0	0	0	1	0	0	.000
WORLD SERIES																			
1965 LA N	0	0	–	0.00	2	0	0	1.1	0	0	0	0	0	0	0	0	0	0	
1966	0	0	–	0.00	1	0	0	3	2	2	1	0	0	0	0	0	0	0	–
1971 PIT N	0	1	.000	3.86	3	0	0	4.2	7	1	2	0	0	0	0	0	0	0	
3 yrs.	0	1	.000	2.00	6	0	0	9	9	3	3	0	0	0	0	0	0	0	

Roscoe Miller

MILLER, ROSCOE CLYDE (Roxy, Rubberlegs)
B. Dec. 2, 1876, Greenville, Ind. D. Apr. 18, 1913, Corydon, Ind.

	W	L	PCT	ERA	G	GS	CG	IP	H	BB	SO	ShO	W	L	SV	AB	H	HR	BA
1901 DET A	23	13	.639	2.95	38	36	35	332	339	98	79	3	1	1	1	130	27	0	.208
1902 2 teams	DET A (20G 6–12)				NY N (10G 1–8)														
" total	7	20	.259	3.98	30	27	22	221.1	235	68	54	1	0	0	1	81	12	0	.148
1903 NY N	2	5	.286	4.13	15	8	6	85	101	24	30	0	0	0	3	31	5	0	.161
1904 PIT N	7	8	.467	3.35	19	17	11	134.1	133	39	35	2	0	0	0	46	2	0	.043
4 yrs.	39	46	.459	3.45	102	88	74	772.2	808	229	198	6	1	1	5	288	46	0	.160
2 yrs.	29	25	.537	3.18	58	54	50	480.2	497	155	118	4	1	0	2	190	38	0	.200

Clarence Mitchell

MITCHELL, CLARENCE ELMER   BL TL 5'11½" 190 lbs.
B. Feb. 22, 1891, Franklin, Neb. D. Nov. 6, 1963, Grand Island, Neb.

	W	L	PCT	ERA	G	GS	CG	IP	H	BB	SO	ShO	W	L	SV	AB	H	HR	BA
1911 DET A	1	0	1.000	8.16	5	1	0	14.1	20	7	4	0	1	0	0	4	2	0	.500
1916 CIN N	11	10	.524	3.14	29	24	17	194.2	211	45	52	1	0	1	0	117	28	0	.239
1917	9	15	.375	3.22	32	20	10	159.1	166	34	37	2	2	3	1	90	25	0	.278
1918 BKN N	0	1	.000	108.00	1	1	0	.1	4	0	0	0	0	0	0	24	6	0	.250
1919	7	5	.583	3.06	23	11	9	108.2	123	23	43	0	1	0	0	49	18	1	.367
1920	5	2	.714	3.09	19	7	3	78.2	85	23	18	1	0	1	1	107	25	0	.234
1921	11	9	.550	2.89	37	18	13	190	206	46	39	3	2	2	2	91	24	0	.264
1922	0	3	.000	14.21	5	3	0	12.2	28	7	1	0	0	0	0	155	45	3	.290
1923 PHI N	9	10	.474	4.72	29	19	8	139.1	170	46	42	1	1	1	0	78	21	1	.269
1924	6	13	.316	5.62	30	26	9	165	223	58	36	1	0	1	1	102	26	0	.255
1925	10	17	.370	5.28	32	26	12	199.1	245	51	46	1	0	1	1	92	18	0	.196
1926	9	14	.391	4.58	28	25	12	178.2	232	55	52	0	1	0	1	78	19	0	.244
1927	6	3	.667	4.09	13	12	8	94.2	99	28	17	1	0	0	0	42	10	1	.238
1928 2 teams	PHI N (3G 0–0)				STL N (19G 8–9)														
" total	8	9	.471	3.53	22	18	9	155.2	162	40	31	1	1	0	0	60	8	0	.133
1929 STL N	8	11	.421	4.27	25	22	16	173	221	60	39	0	0	0	0	66	18	0	.273
1930 2 teams	STL N (1G 1–0)				NY N (24G 10–3)														
" total	11	3	.786	4.02	25	17	5	132	156	38	41	0	1	2	0	49	13	0	.265
1931 NY N	13	11	.542	4.07	27	25	13	190.1	221	52	39	0	0	0	0	73	16	1	.219
1932	1	3	.250	4.15	8	3	1	30.1	41	11	7	0	0	0	0	10	2	0	.200
18 yrs.	125	139	.473	4.12	390	278	145	2217	2613	624	544	12	10	13	9	*			
1 yr.	1	0	1.000	8.16	5	1	0	14.1	20	7	4	0	1	0	0	4	2	0	.500
WORLD SERIES																			
1920 BKN N	0	0	–	0.00	1	0	0	4.2	3	3	1	0	0	0	0	3	1	0	.333
1928 STL N	0	0	–	1.59	1	0	0	5.2	2	2	2	0	0	0	0	2	0	0	.000
2 yrs.	0	0	–	0.87	2	0	0	10.1	5	5	3	0	0	0	0	5	1	0	.200

Willie Mitchell

MITCHELL, WILLIAM   BR TL 6' 176 lbs.
B. Dec. 1, 1889, Sardis, Miss. D. Nov. 23, 1973, Sardis, Miss.

	W	L	PCT	ERA	G	GS	CG	IP	H	BB	SO	ShO	W	L	SV	AB	H	HR	BA
1909 CLE A	1	2	.333	1.57	3	3	3	23	18	10	8	0	0	0	0	7	2	0	.286
1910	12	8	.600	2.60	35	18	11	183.2	165	55	102	1	2	2	0	63	10	0	.159
1911	7	14	.333	3.76	30	22	9	177.1	190	60	78	0	1	2	0	64	7	0	.109
1912	5	8	.385	2.80	29	15	8	163.2	149	56	94	0	1	0	1	53	6	0	.113
1913	14	8	.636	1.74	34	22	14	217	153	88	141	4	4	1	0	70	10	0	.143
1914	12	17	.414	3.19	39	32	16	257	228	124	179	3	0	1	1	81	7	0	.086
1915	11	14	.440	2.82	36	30	12	236	210	84	149	1	1	1	1	79	10	0	.127
1916 2 teams	CLE A (12G 2–5)				DET A (23G 7–5)														
" total	9	10	.474	3.78	35	23	8	171.1	174	67	84	2	1	1	1	47	9	0	.191
1917 DET A	12	8	.600	2.19	30	22	12	185.1	172	46	80	5	0	0	0	59	7	0	.119
1918	0	1	.000	9.00	1	1	0	4	3	5	2	0	0	0	0	2	0	0	.000
1919	1	2	.333	5.27	3	2	0	13.2	12	10	4	0	0	1	0	5	1	0	.200
11 yrs.	84	92	.477	2.86	275	190	93	1632	1464	605	921	16	10	9	4	530	69	0	.130
4 yrs.	20	16	.556	2.83	57	42	19	330.2	306	109	146	7	0	1	0	102	17	0	.167

Herb Moford

MOFORD, HERBERT   BR TR 6'1" 175 lbs.
B. Aug. 6, 1928, Brooksville, Ky.

	W	L	PCT	ERA	G	GS	CG	IP	H	BB	SO	ShO	W	L	SV	AB	H	HR	BA
1955 STL N	1	1	.500	7.88	14	1	0	24	29	15	8	0	1	0	0	2	0	0	.000
1958 DET A	4	9	.308	3.61	25	11	6	109.2	83	42	58	0	0	2	1	37	1	0	.027
1959 BOS A	0	2	.000	11.42	4	2	0	8.2	10	6	7	0	0	0	0	1	0	0	.000
1962 NY N	0	1	.000	7.20	7	0	0	15	21	1	5	0	0	1	0	4	1	0	.250
4 yrs.	5	13	.278	5.03	50	14	6	157.1	143	64	78	0	1	3	3	44	2	0	.045
1 yr.	4	9	.308	3.61	25	11	6	109.2	83	42	58	0	0	2	1	37	1	0	.027

Bill Monbouquette

MONBOUQUETTE, WILLIAM CHARLES   BR TR 5'11" 190 lbs.
B. Aug. 11, 1936, Medford, Mass.

	W	L	PCT	ERA	G	GS	CG	IP	H	BB	SO	ShO	W	L	SV	AB	H	HR	BA
1958 BOS A	3	4	.429	3.31	10	8	3	54.1	52	20	30	0	0	0	0	17	3	0	.176
1959	7	7	.500	4.15	34	17	4	151.2	165	33	87	0	2	1	0	46	3	0	.065
1960	14	11	.560	3.64	35	30	12	215	217	68	134	3	2	0	0	65	6	0	.092
1961	14	14	.500	3.39	32	32	12	236.1	233	100	161	1	0	0	0	69	9	0	.130
1962	15	13	.536	3.33	35	35	11	235.1	227	65	153	4	0	0	0	73	7	0	.096
1963	20	10	.667	3.81	37	36	13	266.2	258	42	174	1	0	1	0	88	10	0	.114
1964	13	14	.481	4.04	36	35	7	234	258	40	120	5	0	0	0	72	6	0	.083
1965	10	18	.357	3.70	35	35	10	228.2	239	40	110	2	0	0	0	68	4	0	.059
1966 DET A	7	8	.467	4.73	30	14	2	102.2	120	22	61	1	3	0	0	26	4	0	.154

	W	L	PCT	ERA	G	GS	CG	IP	H	BB	SO	ShO	W	L	SV	AB	H	HR	BA
										Relief Pitching						BATTING			

Bill Monbouquette continued

		W	L	PCT	ERA	G	GS	CG	IP	H	BB	SO	ShO	W	L	SV	AB	H	HR	BA
'67 2 teams	DET A (2G 0–0)					NY	A (33G 6–5)													
' total	6	5	.545	2.33	35	10	2	135.1	123	17	55	1	2	1	1	32	5	0	.156
'68 2 teams	NY A (17G 5–7)					SF	N (7G 0–1)													
' total	5	8	.385	4.35	24	11	2	101.1	103	15	37	0	1	4	1	26	3	0	.115
11 yrs.	114	112	.504	3.68	343	263	78	1961.1	1995	462	1122	18	10	7	3	582	60	0	.103
2 yrs.	7	8	.467	4.64	32	14	2	104.2	121	22	63	1	3	0	0	26	4	0	.154

Sid Monge

MONGE, ISIDRO PEDROZA BB TL 6'2" 185 lbs.
B. Apr. 11, 1951, Agun Prieta, Mexico

		W	L	PCT	ERA	G	GS	CG	IP	H	BB	SO	ShO	W	L	SV	AB	H	HR	BA
'75 CAL A	0	2	.000	4.18	4	2	2	23.2	22	10	17	0	0	0	0	0	0	0	–
'76	6	7	.462	3.36	32	13	2	118	108	49	53	0	2	2	0	0	0	0	–
'77 2 teams	CAL A (4G 0–1)					CLE	A (33G 1–2)													
' total	1	3	.250	5.44	37	0	0	51.1	61	33	29	0	1	3	4	0	0	0	–
'78 CLE A	4	3	.571	2.76	48	0	0	84.2	71	51	54	0	4	2	6	0	0	0	–
'79	12	10	.545	2.40	76	0	0	131	96	64	108	0	12	10	19	0	0	0	–
'80	3	5	.375	3.54	67	0	0	94	80	40	60	0	3	5	14	0	0	0	–
'81	3	5	.375	4.34	31	0	0	58	58	21	41	0	3	5	4	0	0	0	–
'82 PHI N	7	1	.875	3.75	47	0	0	72	70	22	43	0	7	1	2	9	1	0	.111
'83 2 teams	PHI N (14G 3–0)					SD	N (47G 7–3)													
' total	10	3	.769	3.70	61	0	0	80.1	85	37	39	0	10	3	7	11	1	0	.091
'84 2 teams	SD N (13G 2–1)					DET	A (19G 1–0)													
' total	3	1	.750	4.41	32	0	0	51	57	29	26	0	3	1	0	1	0	0	.000
10 yrs.	49	40	.551	3.53	435	17	4	764	708	356	470	0	45	32	56	21	2	0	.095
1 yr.	1	0	1.000	4.25	19	0	0	36	40	12	19	0	1	0	0	0	0	0	–

Manny Montejo

MONTEJO, MANUEL (Pete) BR TR 5'11" 166 lbs.
B. Oct. 16, 1936, Havana, Cuba

		W	L	PCT	ERA	G	GS	CG	IP	H	BB	SO	ShO	W	L	SV	AB	H	HR	BA
'61 DET A	0	0	–	3.86	12	0	0	16.1	13	6	15	0	0	0	0	0	0	0	–

Bill Moore

MOORE, WILLIAM CHRISTOPHER BR TR 6'3" 195 lbs.
B. Sept. 3, 1902, Corning, N. Y.

		W	L	PCT	ERA	G	GS	CG	IP	H	BB	SO	ShO	W	L	SV	AB	H	HR	BA
'25 DET A	0	0	–	∞	1	0	0	0	3	0	0	0	0	0	0	0	0	0	–

Roy Moore

MOORE, ROY DANIEL BB TL 6' 185 lbs.
B. Dec. 26, 1898, Austin, Tex.   BL 1921,1923
D. Apr. 5, 1951, Seattle, Wash.

		W	L	PCT	ERA	G	GS	CG	IP	H	BB	SO	ShO	W	L	SV	AB	H	HR	BA
'20 PHI A	1	13	.071	4.68	24	16	7	132.2	161	64	45	0	0	0	0	50	10	1	.200
'21	10	10	.500	4.51	29	26	12	191.2	206	122	64	0	0	0	0	74	19	3	.257
'22 2 teams	PHI A (15G 0–3)					DET	A (9G 0–0)													
' total	0	3	.000	7.17	24	6	0	70.1	94	42	38	0	0	1	2	26	8	0	.308
'23 DET A	0	0	–	3.00	3	0	0	12	15	11	7	0	0	0	1	5	0	0	.000
4 yrs.	11	26	.297	4.98	80	48	19	406.2	476	239	154	0	0	1	3	155	37	4	.239
2 yrs.	0	0	–	4.83	12	0	0	31.2	44	21	16	0	0	0	3	12	3	0	.250

Jake Mooty

MOOTY, J T BR TR 5'10½" 170 lbs.
B. Apr. 13, 1913, Bennett, Tex.   D. Apr. 20, 1970, Fort Worth, Tex.

		W	L	PCT	ERA	G	GS	CG	IP	H	BB	SO	ShO	W	L	SV	AB	H	HR	BA
'36 CIN N	0	0	–	3.95	8	0	0	13.2	10	4	11	0	0	0	1	1	0	0	.000
'37	0	3	.000	8.31	14	2	0	39	54	22	11	0	0	1	1	8	0	0	.000
'40 CHI N	6	6	.500	2.92	20	12	6	114	101	49	42	0	2	0	1	38	10	0	.263
'41	8	9	.471	3.35	33	14	7	153.1	143	56	45	1	3	0	4	50	10	0	.200
'42	2	5	.286	4.70	19	10	1	84.1	89	44	28	0	0	1	1	28	6	0	.214
'43	0	0	–	0.00	2	0	0	1	2	1	1	0	0	0	0	0	0	0	–
'44 DET A	0	0	–	4.45	15	0	0	28.1	35	18	7	0	0	0	0	7	1	0	.143
7 yrs.	16	23	.410	4.03	111	38	14	433.2	434	194	145	1	5	2	8	132	27	0	.205
1 yr.	0	0	–	4.45	15	0	0	28.1	35	18	7	0	0	0	0	7	1	0	.143

Harry Moran

MORAN, HARRY EDWIN BL TL 6'1" 165 lbs.
B. Apr. 2, 1889, Slater, W. Va.   D. Nov. 28, 1962, Beckley, W. Va.

		W	L	PCT	ERA	G	GS	CG	IP	H	BB	SO	ShO	W	L	SV	AB	H	HR	BA
'12 DET A	0	1	.000	4.91	5	2	1	14.2	19	12	3	0	0	0	0	5	1	0	.200
'14 BUF F	11	8	.579	4.27	34	16	7	154	159	53	73	2	3	1	1	51	10	0	.196
'15 NWK F	13	10	.565	2.54	34	23	13	205.2	193	66	87	2	2	0	0	61	11	0	.180
3 yrs.	24	19	.558	3.34	73	41	21	374.1	371	131	163	4	5	1	1	117	22	0	.188
1 yr.	0	1	.000	4.91	5	2	1	14.2	19	12	3	0	0	0	0	5	1	0	.200

Tom Morgan

MORGAN, TOM STEPHEN (Plowboy) BR TR 6'1" 180 lbs.
B. May 20, 1930, El Monte, Calif.

		W	L	PCT	ERA	G	GS	CG	IP	H	BB	SO	ShO	W	L	SV	AB	H	HR	BA
'51 NY A	9	3	.750	3.68	27	16	4	124.2	119	36	57	2	1	0	2	44	12	1	.273
'52	5	4	.556	3.07	16	12	2	93.2	86	33	35	1	0	0	2	33	6	1	.182
'54	11	5	.688	3.34	32	17	7	143	149	40	34	4	3	1	1	49	7	1	.143
'55	7	3	.700	3.25	40	1	0	72	72	24	17	0	7	3	10	18	4	0	.222
'56	6	7	.462	4.16	41	0	0	71.1	74	27	20	0	6	7	11	13	2	0	.154
'57 KC A	9	7	.563	4.64	46	13	5	143.2	160	61	32	0	6	2	7	33	3	0	.091
'58 DET A	2	5	.286	3.16	39	1	0	62.2	70	4	32	0	0	0	1	10	2	0	.200
'59	1	4	.200	3.98	46	1	0	92.2	94	18	39	0	0	3	9	23	9	2	.391
'60 2 teams	DET A (22G 3–2)					WAS	A (14G 1–3)													
' total	4	5	.444	4.25	36	0	0	53	69	15	23	0	4	5	1	5	0	0	.000
'61 LA A	8	2	.800	2.36	59	0	0	91.2	74	17	39	0	8	2	10	12	1	0	.083
'62	5	2	.714	2.91	48	0	0	58.2	53	19	29	0	5	2	9	6	0	0	.000
'63	0	0	–	5.51	13	0	0	16.1	20	6	7	0	0	0	1	1	0	0	.000
12 yrs.	67	47	.588	3.61	443	61	18	1023.1	1040	300	364	7	40	25	64	247	46	5	.186
3 yrs.	6	11	.353	3.81	107	2	0	184.1	197	32	83	0	3	5	11	33	11	2	.333

WORLD SERIES

		W	L	PCT	ERA	G	GS	CG	IP	H	BB	SO	ShO	W	L	SV	AB	H	HR	BA
'51 NY A	0	0	–	0.00	1	0	0	2	2	1	3	0	0	0	0	0	0	0	–
'55	0	0	–	4.91	2	0	0	3.2	3	3	1	0	0	0	0	0	0	0	–

	W	L	PCT	ERA	G	GS	CG	IP	H	BB	SO	ShO	W	L	SV	AB	H	HR	BA

Tom Morgan continued

| 1956 | 0 | 1 | .000 | 9.00 | 2 | 0 | 0 | 4 | 6 | 4 | 3 | 0 | 0 | 1 | 0 | 1 | 1 | 0 | 1.000 |
| 3 yrs. | 0 | 1 | .000 | 5.59 | 5 | 0 | 0 | 9.2 | 11 | 8 | 7 | 0 | 0 | 1 | 0 | 1 | 1 | 0 | 1.000 |

Jack Morris

MORRIS, JOHN SCOTT
B. May 16, 1956, St. Paul, Minn.
BR TR 6'3" 195 lbs.

1977 DET A	1	1	.500	3.72	7	6	1	46	38	23	28	0	0	0	0	0	0	0	—
1978	3	5	.375	4.33	28	7	0	106	107	49	48	0	3	3	0	0	0	0	—
1979	17	7	.708	3.27	27	27	9	198	179	59	113	1	0	0	0	0	0	0	—
1980	16	15	.516	4.18	36	36	11	250	252	87	112	2	0	0	0	0	0	0	—
1981	14	7	.667	3.05	25	25	15	198	153	78	97	1	0	0	0	0	0	0	—
1982	17	16	.515	4.06	37	37	17	266.1	247	96	135	3	0	0	0	0	0	0	—
1983	20	13	.606	3.34	37	37	20	293.2	257	83	232	1	0	0	0	0	0	0	—
1984	19	11	.633	3.65	35	35	9	241.1	224	87	149	1	0	0	0	0	0	0	—
8 yrs.	107	75	.588	3.67	232	210	82	1599.1	1457	562	914	9	3	3	0	0	0	0	—
8 yrs.	107	75	.588	3.67	232	210	82	1599.1	1457	562	914	9	3	3	0	0	0	0	—
				9th															

LEAGUE CHAMPIONSHIP SERIES
| 1984 DET A | 1 | 0 | 1.000 | 1.29 | 1 | 1 | 0 | 7 | 5 | 1 | 4 | 0 | 0 | 0 | 0 | 0 | 0 | 0 | — |

WORLD SERIES
| 1984 DET A | 2 | 0 | 1.000 | 2.00 | 2 | 2 | 2 | 18 | 13 | 3 | 13 | 0 | 0 | 0 | 0 | 0 | 0 | 0 | — |

Bill Morrisette

MORRISETTE, WILLIAM LEE
B. Jan. 17, 1893, Baltimore, Md. D. Mar. 25, 1966, Virginia Beach, Va.
BR TR 6' 176 lbs.

1915 PHI A	2	0	1.000	1.35	4	1	1	20	15	5	11	0	1	0	0	7	2	0	.286
1916	0	0	—	6.75	1	0	0	4	6	5	2	0	0	0	0	1	0	0	.000
1920 DET A	1	1	.500	4.33	8	3	1	27	25	19	15	0	0	0	0	8	0	0	.000
3 yrs.	3	1	.750	3.35	13	4	2	51	46	29	28	0	1	0	0	16	2	0	.125
1 yr.	1	1	.500	4.33	8	3	1	27	25	19	15	0	0	0	0	8	0	0	.000

Don Mossi

MOSSI, DONALD LOUIS (The Sphinx)
B. Jan. 11, 1929, St. Helena, Calif.
BL TL 6'1" 195 lbs.

1954 CLE A	6	1	.857	1.94	40	5	2	93	56	39	55	0	4	0	7	19	3	0	.158
1955	4	3	.571	2.42	57	1	0	81.2	81	18	69	0	4	3	9	9	1	0	.111
1956	6	5	.545	3.59	48	3	0	87.2	79	33	59	0	0	4	11	20	3	0	.150
1957	11	10	.524	4.13	36	22	6	159	166	57	97	1	1	1	2	55	12	0	.218
1958	7	8	.467	3.90	43	5	0	101.2	106	30	55	0	7	4	3	26	3	0	.115
1959 DET A	17	9	.654	3.36	34	30	15	228	210	49	125	3	0	0	0	77	13	1	.169
1960	9	8	.529	3.47	23	22	9	158.1	158	32	69	2	1	0	0	43	5	0	.116
1961	15	7	.682	2.96	35	34	12	240.1	237	47	137	1	0	0	1	79	13	1	.165
1962	11	13	.458	4.19	35	27	8	180.1	195	36	121	1	0	2	1	55	9	0	.164
1963	7	7	.500	3.74	24	16	3	122.2	110	17	68	0	2	0	2	39	8	0	.205
1964 CHI A	3	1	.750	2.93	34	0	0	40	37	7	36	0	3	1	7	6	1	0	.167
1965 KC A	5	8	.385	3.74	51	0	0	55.1	59	20	41	0	5	8	7	8	0	0	.000
12 yrs.	101	80	.558	3.43	460	165	55	1548	1494	385	932	8	27	24	50	436	71	2	.163
5 yrs.	59	44	.573	3.49	151	129	47	929.2	910	181	520	7	3	3	4	293	48	2	.164

WORLD SERIES
| 1954 CLE A | 0 | 0 | — | 0.00 | 3 | 0 | 0 | 4 | 3 | 1 | 0 | 1 | 0 | 0 | 0 | 0 | 0 | 0 | — |

Les Mueller

MUELLER, LESLIE CLYDE
B. Mar. 4, 1919, Belleville, Ill.
BR TR 6'3" 190 lbs.

1941 DET A	0	0	—	4.85	4	0	0	13	9	10	8	0	0	0	0	3	0	0	.000
1945	6	8	.429	3.68	26	18	6	134.2	117	58	42	2	0	0	1	44	8	1	.182
2 yrs.	6	8	.429	3.78	30	18	6	147.2	126	68	50	2	0	0	1	47	8	1	.170
2 yrs.	6	8	.429	3.78	30	18	6	147.2	126	68	50	2	0	0	1	47	8	1	.170

WORLD SERIES
| 1945 DET A | 0 | 0 | — | 0.00 | 1 | 0 | 0 | 2 | 0 | 1 | 1 | 0 | 0 | 0 | 0 | 0 | 0 | 0 | — |

George Mullin

MULLIN, GEORGE JOSEPH (Wabash George)
B. July 4, 1880, Toledo, Ohio D. Jan. 7, 1944, Wabash, Ind.
BR TR 5'11" 188 lbs.

1902 DET A	13	16	.448	3.67	35	30	25	260	282	95	78	0	1	1	0	120	39	0	.325
1903	19	15	.559	2.25	41	36	31	320.2	284	106	170	6	1	1	2	126	35	1	.278
1904	17	23	.425	2.40	45	44	42	382.1	345	131	161	7	1	0	0	151	45	0	.298
1905	21	21	.500	2.51	44	41	35	347.2	303	138	168	1	1	1	0	135	35	0	.259
1906	21	18	.538	2.78	40	40	35	330	315	108	123	2	0	0	0	142	32	0	.225
1907	20	20	.500	2.59	46	42	35	357.1	346	106	146	5	1	0	3	157	34	0	.217
1908	17	13	.567	3.10	39	30	26	290.2	301	71	121	1	3	0	0	125	32	1	.256
1909	29	8	.784	2.22	40	35	29	303.2	258	78	124	3	4	0	1	126	27	0	.214
1910	21	12	.636	2.87	38	32	27	289	260	102	98	5	2	0	0	129	33	1	.256
1911	18	10	.643	3.07	30	29	25	234.1	245	61	87	2	0	1	0	98	28	0	.286
1912	12	17	.414	3.54	30	29	22	226	214	92	88	2	0	1	0	90	25	0	.278
1913 2 teams	DET A (7G 1–6)						WAS A (12G 3–5)												
" total	4	11	.267	3.94	19	16	7	109.2	122	43	30	0	1	0	0	41	11	0	.268
1914 IND F	14	10	.583	2.70	36	20	11	203	202	91	74	1	8	0	2	77	24	0	.312
1915 NWK F	2	2	.500	5.85	5	4	3	32.1	41	16	14	0	0	0	0	10	1	0	.100
14 yrs.	228	196	.538	2.82	488	428	353	3686.2	3518	1238	1482	35	23	5	8	*			—
12 yrs.	209	179	.539	2.76	435	395	336	3394	3206	1106	1380	34	14	5	6	1419	372	3	.262
	2nd	2nd		6th	6th		1st	1st		3rd	5th	2nd							

WORLD SERIES
| 1907 DET A | 0 | 2 | .000 | 2.12 | 2 | 2 | 2 | 17 | 16 | 6 | 7 | 0 | 0 | 0 | 0 | 6 | 0 | 0 | .000 |
| 1908 | 1 | 0 | 1.000 | 1.00 | 1 | 1 | 1 | 9 | 7 | 1 | 8 | 0 | 0 | 0 | 0 | 3 | 1 | 0 | .333 |

	W	L	PCT	ERA	G	GS	CG	IP	H	BB	SO	ShO	Relief Pitching W	L	SV	BATTING AB	H	HR	BA

George Mullin continued

	W	L	PCT	ERA	G	GS	CG	IP	H	BB	SO	ShO	W	L	SV	AB	H	HR	BA
'909	2	1	.667	2.25	4	3	3	32	22	8	20	1	0	0	0	16	3	0	.188
3 yrs.	3	3	.500	2.02	7	6	6	58	45	15	35	1	0	0	0	25	4	0	.160
							6th												

Ray Narleski

NARLESKI, RAYMOND EDMOND   BR TR 6'1"   175 lbs.
Son of Bill Narleski.
B. Nov. 25, 1928, Camden, N. J.

	W	L	PCT	ERA	G	GS	CG	IP	H	BB	SO	ShO	W	L	SV	AB	H	HR	BA
'954 CLE A	3	3	.500	2.22	42	2	1	89	59	44	52	0	3	2	13	16	0	0	.000
'955	9	1	.900	3.71	60	1	1	111.2	91	52	94	0	8	1	19	24	7	0	.292
'956	3	2	.600	1.52	32	0	0	59.1	36	19	42	0	3	2	4	8	2	0	.250
'957	11	5	.688	3.09	46	15	7	154.1	136	70	93	1	5	0	16	43	4	1	.093
'958	13	10	.565	4.07	44	24	7	183.1	179	91	102	0	2	1	1	54	11	0	.204
'959 DET A	4	12	.250	5.78	42	10	1	104.1	105	59	71	0	2	7	5	21	2	0	.095
6 yrs.	43	33	.566	3.60	266	52	17	702	606	335	454	1	23	13	58	166	26	1	.157
1 yr.	4	12	.250	5.78	42	10	1	104.1	105	59	71	0	2	7	5	21	2	0	.095
WORLD SERIES																			
'954 CLE A	0	0	—	2.25	2	0	0	4	1	1	2	0	0	0	0	0	0	0	—

Julio Navarro

NAVARRO, JULIO VENTURA (Whiplash)   BR TR 6'   175 lbs.
B. Jan. 9, 1936, Vieques, Puerto Rico

	W	L	PCT	ERA	G	GS	CG	IP	H	BB	SO	ShO	W	L	SV	AB	H	HR	BA
'962 LA A	1	1	.500	4.70	9	0	0	15.1	20	4	11	0	1	1	0	2	1	0	.500
'963	4	5	.444	2.89	57	0	0	90.1	75	32	53	0	4	5	12	15	3	0	.200
'964 2 teams			LA	A	(5G 0–0)			DET	A	(26G 2–1)									
" total	2	1	.667	3.58	31	0	0	50.1	45	21	44	0	2	1	3	7	0	0	.000
'965 DET A	0	2	.000	4.20	15	1	0	30	25	12	22	0	0	2	1	4	0	0	.000
'966	0	0	—	∞	1	0	0	2	0	0	0	0	0	0	0	0	0	0	—
'970 ATL N	0	0	—	4.15	17	0	0	26	24	1	21	0	0	0	1	6	1	0	.167
6 yrs.	7	9	.438	3.65	130	1	0	212	191	70	151	0	7	9	17	34	5	0	.147
3 yrs.	2	3	.400	4.44	42	1	0	71	67	28	58	0	2	3	3	9	0	0	.000

Bots Nekola

NEKOLA, FRANCIS JOSEPH   BL TL 5'11½" 175 lbs.
B. Dec. 10, 1906, New York, N. Y.

	W	L	PCT	ERA	G	GS	CG	IP	H	BB	SO	ShO	W	L	SV	AB	H	HR	BA
'929 NY A	0	0	—	4.34	9	1	0	18.2	21	15	2	0	0	0	0	4	2	0	.500
'933 DET A	0	0	—	27.00	2	0	0	1.1	4	1	0	0	0	0	0	0	0	0	—
2 yrs.	0	0	—	5.85	11	1	0	20	25	16	2	0	0	0	0	4	2	0	.500
1 yr.	0	0	—	27.00	2	0	0	1.1	4	1	0	0	0	0	0	0	0	0	—

Lynn Nelson

NELSON, LYNN BERNARD (Line Drive)   BL TR 5'10½" 170 lbs.
B. Feb. 24, 1905, Sheldon, N. D.   D. Feb. 15, 1955, Kansas City, Mo.

	W	L	PCT	ERA	G	GS	CG	IP	H	BB	SO	ShO	W	L	SV	AB	H	HR	BA
'930 CHI N	3	2	.600	5.09	37	3	0	81.1	97	28	29	0	2	2	0	18	4	0	.222
'933	5	5	.500	3.21	24	3	3	75.2	65	30	20	0	4	3	1	21	5	0	.238
'934	0	1	.000	36.00	2	1	0	1	4	1	0	0	0	0	0	0	0	0	—
'937 PHI A	4	9	.308	5.90	30	4	1	116	140	51	49	0	4	7	2	113	40	4	.354
'938	10	11	.476	5.65	32	23	13	191	215	79	75	0	0	2	2	112	31	0	.277
'939	10	13	.435	4.78	35	24	12	197.2	233	64	75	2	2	0	1	80	15	0	.188
'940 DET A	1	1	.500	10.93	6	2	0	14	23	9	7	0	1	0	0	23	8	1	.348
7 yrs.	33	42	.440	5.25	166	60	29	676.2	777	262	255	2	13	14	6	*			
1 yr.	1	1	.500	10.93	6	2	0	14	23	9	7	0	1	0	0	23	8	1	.348

Hal Newhouser

NEWHOUSER, HAROLD (Prince Hal)   BL TL 6'2"   180 lbs.
B. May 20, 1921, Detroit, Mich.

	W	L	PCT	ERA	G	GS	CG	IP	H	BB	SO	ShO	W	L	SV	AB	H	HR	BA
'939 DET A	0	1	.000	5.40	1	1	1	5	3	4	4	0	0	0	0	1	0	0	.000
'940	9	9	.500	4.86	28	20	7	133.1	149	76	89	0	1	0	0	40	8	0	.200
'941	9	11	.450	4.79	33	27	5	173	166	137	106	1	0	1	0	60	9	0	.150
'942	8	14	.364	2.45	38	23	11	183.2	137	114	103	1	0	2	5	52	8	0	.154
'943	8	17	.320	3.04	37	25	10	195.2	163	111	144	1	1	1	1	65	12	0	.185
'944	29	9	.763	2.22	47	34	25	312.1	264	102	187	6	4	2	2	120	29	0	.242
'945	25	9	.735	1.81	40	36	29	313.1	239	110	212	8	1	0	2	109	28	0	.257
'946	26	9	.743	1.94	37	34	29	292.1	215	98	275	6	0	1	1	103	13	2	.126
'947	17	17	.500	2.87	40	36	24	285	268	110	176	3	0	1	2	96	19	0	.198
'948	21	12	.636	3.01	39	35	19	272.1	249	99	143	2	1	1	1	92	19	0	.207
'949	18	11	.621	3.36	38	35	22	292	277	111	144	3	1	0	1	91	18	0	.198
'950	15	13	.536	4.34	35	30	15	213.2	232	81	87	1	1	0	3	74	13	0	.176
'951	6	6	.500	3.92	15	14	7	96.1	98	19	37	1	0	0	0	29	9	0	.310
'952	9	9	.500	3.74	25	19	8	154	148	47	57	0	3	0	0	46	10	0	.217
'953	0	1	.000	7.06	7	4	0	21.2	31	8	6	0	0	0	1	8	4	0	.500
'954 CLE A	7	2	.778	2.51	26	1	0	46.2	34	18	25	0	7	1	7	13	2	0	.154
'955	0	0	—	0.00	2	0	0	2.1	1	4	1	0	0	0	0	0	0	0	—
17 yrs.	207	150	.580	3.06	488	374	212	2992.2	2674	1249	1796	33	20	10	26	999	201	2	.201
15 yrs.	200	148	.575	3.07	460	373	212	2943.2	2639	1227	1770	33	13	9	19	986	199	2	.202
	4th	5th		10th	5th		4th		4th		1st	2nd	3rd						
WORLD SERIES																			
'945 DET A	2	1	.667	6.10	3	3	2	20.2	25	4	22	0	0	0	0	8	0	0	.000
'954 CLE A	0	0	—	∞	1	0	0	1	1	0	0	0	0	0	0	0	0	—
2 yrs.	2	1	.667	6.53	4	3	2	20.2	26	5	22	0	0	0	0	8	0	0	.000

Bobo Newsom

NEWSOM, NORMAN LOUIS (Buck)   BR TR 6'3"   200 lbs.
B. Aug. 11, 1907, Hartsville, S. C.   D. Dec. 7, 1962, Orlando, Fla.

	W	L	PCT	ERA	G	GS	CG	IP	H	BB	SO	ShO	W	L	SV	AB	H	HR	BA
'929 BKN N	0	3	.000	10.61	3	2	0	9.1	15	5	6	0	0	1	0	2	0	0	.000
'930	0	0	—	0.00	2	0	0	3	2	2	1	0	0	0	0	0	0	0	—
'932 CHI N	0	0	—	0.00	1	0	0	1	1	0	0	0	0	0	0	0	0	0	—
'934 STL A	16	20	.444	4.01	47	32	15	262.1	259	149	135	2	3	4	5	93	17	0	.183
'935 2 teams			STL	A	(7G 0–6)			WAS	A	(28G 11–12)									
" total	11	18	.379	4.52	35	29	18	241	276	97	87	2	0	2	3	84	23	0	.274
'936 WAS A	17	15	.531	4.32	43	38	24	285.2	294	146	156	4	0	0	2	108	23	0	.213

	W	L	PCT	ERA	G	GS	CG	IP	H	BB	SO	ShO	Relief Pitching W	L	SV	BATTING AB	H	HR	BA

Bobo Newsom continued

1937 2 teams		WAS	A (11G 3–4)			BOS	A (30G 13–10)												
" total	16	14	.533	4.74	41	37	17	275.1	271	167	166	1	1	1	0	100	22	1	.220
1938 STL A	20	16	.556	5.08	44	40	31	329.2	334	192	226	0	0	0	1	124	31	0	.250
1939 2 teams			STL	A (6G 3–1)		DET	A (35G 17–10)												
" total	20	11	.645	3.58	41	37	24	291.2	272	126	192	3	0	0	2	115	22	0	.191
1940 DET A	21	5	.808	2.83	36	34	20	264	235	100	164	3	1	1	0	107	23	0	.215
1941	12	20	.375	4.60	43	36	12	250.1	265	118	175	2	1	1	2	88	9	0	.102
1942 2 teams		WAS	A (30G 11–17)			BKN	N (6G 2–2)												
" total	13	19	.406	4.73	36	34	17	245.2	264	106	134	3	1	0	0	86	12	0	.140
1943 3 teams		BKN	N (22G 9–4)			STL	A (10G 1–6)		WAS	A (6G 3–3)									
" total	13	13	.500	4.22	38	27	8	217.1	220	113	123	1	4	1	1	74	18	0	.243
1944 PHI A	13	15	.464	2.82	37	33	18	265	243	82	142	2	0	0	1	88	10	0	.114
1945	8	20	.286	3.29	36	34	16	257.1	255	103	127	3	0	1	0	86	14	0	.163
1946 2 teams		PHI	A (10G 3–5)			WAS	A (24G 11–8)												
" total	14	13	.519	2.93	34	31	17	236.2	224	90	114	3	0	0	0	81	12	0	.148
1947 2 teams		WAS	A (14G 4–6)			NY	A (17G 7–5)												
" total	11	11	.500	3.34	31	28	7	199.1	208	67	82	2	0	0	0	71	11	0	.155
1948 NY N	0	4	.000	4.21	11	4	0	25.2	35	13	9	0	0	1	0	7	3	0	.429
1952 2 teams		WAS	A (10G 1–1)			PHI	A (14G 3–3)												
" total	4	4	.500	3.88	24	5	1	60.1	54	32	27	0	3	2	3	17	2	0	.118
1953 PHI A	2	1	.667	4.89	17	2	1	38.2	44	24	16	0	1	0	0	6	1	0	.167
20 yrs.	211	222	.487	3.98	600	483	246	3759.1	3771	1732	2082	31	15	15	21	1337	253	1	.189
											4th								
3 yrs.	50	35	.588	3.59	114	101	53	760.1	722	322	503	8	2	2	4	292	50	0	.171
			8th																

WORLD SERIES

1940 DET A	2	1	.667	1.38	3	3	3	26	18	4	17	1	0	0	0	10	1	0	.100
1947 NY A	0	1	.000	19.29	2	1	0	2.1	6	2	0	0	0	0	0	0	0	0	—
2 yrs.	2	2	.500	2.86	5	4	3	28.1	24	6	17	1	0	0	0	10	1	0	.100

Joe Niekro

NIEKRO, JOSEPH FRANKLIN
Brother of Phil Niekro.
B. Nov. 7, 1944, Martins Ferry, Ohio
     BR TR 6'1"   185 lbs.

1967 CHI N	10	7	.588	3.34	36	22	7	169.2	171	32	77	2	1	1	0	46	9	0	.196
1968	14	10	.583	4.31	34	29	2	177.1	204	59	65	1	1	0	2	60	6	0	.100
1969 2 teams		CHI	N (4G 0–1)			SD	N (37G 8–17)												
" total	8	18	.308	3.70	41	34	8	221.1	237	51	62	3	0	0	0	56	7	0	.125
1970 DET A	12	13	.480	4.06	38	34	6	213	221	72	101	2	1	0	0	66	13	0	.197
1971	6	7	.462	4.50	31	15	0	122	136	49	43	0	2	0	1	30	4	0	.133
1972	3	2	.600	3.83	18	7	1	47	62	8	24	0	0	1	1	12	3	0	.250
1973 ATL N	2	4	.333	4.13	20	0	0	24	23	11	12	0	2	4	3	3	1	0	.333
1974	3	2	.600	3.56	27	2	0	43	36	18	31	0	3	2	0	5	0	0	.000
1975 HOU N	6	4	.600	3.07	40	4	1	88	79	39	54	1	3	4	4	14	3	0	.214
1976	4	8	.333	3.36	36	13	0	118	107	56	77	0	0	2	0	27	5	1	.185
1977	13	8	.619	3.03	44	14	9	181	155	64	101	2	4	4	5	50	7	0	.140
1978	14	14	.500	3.86	35	29	10	203	190	73	97	1	1	0	0	65	9	0	.138
1979	21	11	.656	3.00	38	38	11	264	221	107	119	5	0	0	0	83	10	0	.120
1980	.20	12	.625	3.55	37	36	11	256	268	79	127	2	1	0	0	80	22	0	.275
1981	9	9	.500	2.82	24	24	5	166	150	47	77	2	0	0	0	51	9	0	.176
1982	17	12	.586	2.47	35	35	16	270	224	64	130	5	0	0	0	89	8	0	.094
1983	15	14	.517	3.48	38	38	9	263.2	238	101	152	1	0	0	0	85	8	0	.094
1984	16	12	.571	3.04	38	38	6	248.1	223	89	127	1	0	0	0	83	11	0	.133
18 yrs.	193	167	.536	3.42	610	412	102	3075.1	2945	1019	1476	28	19	18	16	905	135	1	.149
3 yrs.	21	22	.488	4.17	87	56	7	382	419	129	168	2	3	1	2	108	20	0	.185

DIVISIONAL PLAYOFF SERIES

1981 HOU N	0	0	—	0.00	1	1	0	8	7	3	4	0	0	0	0	2	0	0	.000

LEAGUE CHAMPIONSHIP SERIES

1980 HOU N	0	0	—	0.00	1	1	0	10	6	1	2	0	0	0	0	3	0	0	.000

Ron Nischwitz

NISCHWITZ, RONALD LEE
B. July 1, 1937, Dayton, Ohio
     BB TL 6'3"   205 lbs.

1961 DET A	0	1	.000	5.56	6	1	0	11.1	13	8	8	0	0	0	0	2	0	0	.000
1962	4	5	.444	3.90	48	0	0	64.2	73	26	28	0	4	5	4	12	5	0	.417
1963 CLE A	0	2	.000	6.48	14	0	0	16.2	17	8	10	0	0	2	1	1	0	0	.000
1965 DET A	1	0	1.000	2.78	20	0	0	22.2	21	6	12	0	1	0	1	3	0	0	.000
4 yrs.	5	8	.385	4.21	88	1	0	115.1	124	48	58	0	5	7	6	18	5	0	.278
3 yrs.	5	6	.455	3.83	74	1	0	98.2	107	40	48	0	5	5	5	17	5	0	.294

Lou North

NORTH, LOUIS ALEXANDER
B. June 15, 1891, Elgin, Ill.   D. May 16, 1974, Shelton, Conn.
     BR TR 5'11"   175 lbs.

1913 DET A	0	1	.000	15.00	1	1	0	6	10	9	3	0	0	0	0	2	0	0	.000
1917 STL N	0	0	—	3.97	5	0	0	11.1	14	4	4	0	0	0	0	3	0	0	.000
1920	3	2	.600	3.27	24	6	3	88	90	32	37	0	1	1	1	31	7	0	.226
1921	4	4	.500	3.54	40	0	0	86.1	81	32	28	0	4	4	7	19	3	0	.158
1922	10	3	.769	4.45	53	11	4	149.2	164	64	84	0	5	1	4	47	11	1	.234
1923	3	4	.429	5.15	34	3	0	71.2	90	31	24	0	2	4	1	22	4	0	.182
1924 2 teams		STL	N (6G 0–0)			BOS	N (9G 1–2)												
" total	1	2	.333	5.76	15	4	1	50	60	28	19	0	0	0	0	13	2	0	.154
7 yrs.	21	16	.568	4.43	172	25	8	463	509	200	199	0	12	10	13	137	27	1	.197
1 yr.	0	1	.000	15.00	1	1	0	6	10	9	3	0	0	0	0	2	0	0	.000

Prince Oana

OANA, HENRY KAUHANE
B. Jan. 22, 1908, Waipahu, Hawaii   D. June 19, 1976, Austin, Tex.
     BR TR 6'2"   193 lbs.

1943 DET A	3	2	.600	4.50	10	0	0	34	34	19	15	0	3	2	0	26	10	1	.385

	W	L	PCT	ERA	G	GS	CG	IP	H	BB	SO	ShO	Relief Pitching W	L	SV	BATTING AB	H	HR	BA

Prince Oana continued

	W	L	PCT	ERA	G	GS	CG	IP	H	BB	SO	ShO	W	L	SV	AB	H	HR	BA
'45	0	0	–	1.59	3	1	0	11.1	3	7	3	0	0	0	1	5	1	0	.200
2 yrs.	3	2	.600	3.77	13	1	0	45.1	37	26	18	0	3	2	1	*			
2 yrs.	3	2	.600	3.77	13	1	0	45.1	37	26	18	0	3	2	1	31	11	1	.355

Frank Okrie

OKRIE, FRANK ANTHONY (Lefty)   BL TL 5'11½" 175 lbs.
Father of Len Okrie.
B. Oct. 28, 1896, Detroit, Mich.   D. Oct. 16, 1959, Detroit, Mich.

	W	L	PCT	ERA	G	GS	CG	IP	H	BB	SO	ShO	W	L	SV	AB	H	HR	BA
'20 DET A	1	2	.333	5.27	21	1	1	41	44	18	9	0	1	1	0	5	1	0	.200

Red Oldham

OLDHAM, JOHN CYRUS   BL TL 6' 176 lbs.
B. July 15, 1893, Zion, Md.   D. Jan. 28, 1961, Costa Mesa, Calif.

	W	L	PCT	ERA	G	GS	CG	IP	H	BB	SO	ShO	W	L	SV	AB	H	HR	BA
'14 DET A	2	4	.333	3.38	9	7	3	45.1	42	8	23	0	0	0	0	15	4	0	.267
'15	3	0	1.000	2.81	17	2	1	57.2	52	17	17	0	2	0	4	14	2	0	.143
'20	8	13	.381	3.85	39	23	11	215.1	248	91	62	1	1	2	1	69	12	0	.174
'21	11	14	.440	4.24	40	28	12	229.1	258	81	67	1	0	5	1	85	19	2	.224
'22	10	13	.435	4.67	43	27	9	212	256	59	72	0	1	2	3	73	19	0	.260
'25 PIT N	3	2	.600	3.91	11	4	3	53	66	18	10	0	1	0	1	18	6	0	.333
'26	2	2	.500	5.62	17	2	0	41.2	56	18	16	0	2	1	2	9	2	0	.222
7 yrs.	39	48	.448	4.15	176	93	39	854.1	978	292	267	2	7	10	12	283	64	2	.226
5 yrs.	34	44	.436	4.09	148	87	36	759.2	856	256	241	2	4	9	9	256	56	2	.219
WORLD SERIES																			
'25 PIT N	0	0	–	0.00	1	0	0	1	0	0	2	0	0	0	1	0	0	0	–

Ole Olsen

OLSEN, ARTHUR   BR TR 5'10" 163 lbs.
B. Sept. 12, 1894, South Norwalk, Conn.   D. Sept. 12, 1980, Norwalk, Conn.

	W	L	PCT	ERA	G	GS	CG	IP	H	BB	SO	ShO	W	L	SV	AB	H	HR	BA
'22 DET A	7	6	.538	4.53	37	15	5	137	147	40	52	0	1	3	3	39	7	0	.179
'23	1	1	.500	6.31	17	2	1	41.1	42	17	12	0	0	0	0	8	1	0	.125
2 yrs.	8	7	.533	4.95	54	17	6	178.1	189	57	64	0	1	3	3	47	8	0	.170
2 yrs.	8	7	.533	4.95	54	17	6	178.1	189	57	64	0	1	3	3	47	8	0	.170

Randy O'Neal

O'NEAL, RANDALL JEFFREY   BR TR 6'2" 195 lbs.
B. Aug. 30, 1960, West Palm Beach, Fla.

	W	L	PCT	ERA	G	GS	CG	IP	H	BB	SO	ShO	W	L	SV	AB	H	HR	BA
'84 DET A	2	1	.667	3.38	4	3	0	18.2	16	6	12	0	0	0	0	0	0	0	–

Joe Orrell

ORRELL, FORREST GORDON   BR TR 6'4" 210 lbs.
B. Mar. 6, 1917, National City, Calif.

	W	L	PCT	ERA	G	GS	CG	IP	H	BB	SO	ShO	W	L	SV	AB	H	HR	BA
'43 DET A	0	0	–	3.72	10	0	0	19.1	18	11	2	0	0	0	1	4	1	0	.250
'44	2	1	.667	2.42	10	2	0	22.1	26	11	10	0	1	0	0	4	1	0	.250
'45	2	3	.400	3.00	12	5	1	48	46	24	14	0	0	1	0	15	2	0	.133
3 yrs.	4	4	.500	3.01	32	7	1	89.2	90	46	26	0	1	1	1	23	4	0	.174
3 yrs.	4	4	.500	3.01	32	7	1	89.2	90	46	26	0	1	1	1	23	4	0	.174

Stubby Overmire

OVERMIRE, FRANK   BR TL 5'7" 170 lbs.
B. May 16, 1919, Moline, Mich.   D. Mar. 3, 1977, Lakeland, Fla.

	W	L	PCT	ERA	G	GS	CG	IP	H	BB	SO	ShO	W	L	SV	AB	H	HR	BA
'43 DET A	7	6	.538	3.18	29	18	8	147	135	38	48	3	0	0	1	42	7	0	.167
'44	11	11	.500	3.07	32	28	11	199.2	214	41	57	3	0	0	1	63	11	0	.175
'45	9	9	.500	3.88	31	22	9	162.1	189	42	36	0	0	0	4	53	10	0	.189
'46	5	7	.417	4.62	24	13	3	97.1	106	29	34	0	1	3	1	33	5	0	.152
'47	11	5	.688	3.77	28	17	7	140.2	142	44	33	3	3	0	0	47	7	0	.149
'48	3	4	.429	5.97	37	4	0	66.1	89	31	14	0	3	3	3	14	1	0	.071
'49	1	3	.250	9.87	14	1	0	17.1	29	9	3	0	1	2	0	3	1	0	.333
'50 STL A	9	12	.429	4.19	31	19	8	161	200	45	39	2	1	2	0	48	8	0	.167
'51 2 teams	STL	A	(8G 1-6)	NY	A	(15G 1-1)													
total	2	7	.222	4.04	23	11	4	98	111	39	27	0	0	2	0	21	2	0	.095
'52 STL A	0	3	.000	3.73	17	4	0	41	44	7	10	0	0	0	0	11	2	0	.182
10 yrs.	58	67	.464	3.96	266	137	50	1130.2	1259	325	301	11	9	12	10	335	54	0	.161
7 yrs.	47	45	.511	3.92	195	103	38	830.2	904	234	225	9	8	8	10	255	42	0	.165
WORLD SERIES																			
'45 DET A	0	1	.000	3.00	1	1	0	6	4	2	2	0	0	0	0	1	0	0	.000

Frank Owen

OWEN, FRANK MALCOLM (Yip)   TR
B. Dec. 23, 1879, Ypsilanti, Mich.   D. Nov. 24, 1942, Dearborn, Mich.

	W	L	PCT	ERA	G	GS	CG	IP	H	BB	SO	ShO	W	L	SV	AB	H	HR	BA
'01 DET A	1	3	.250	4.34	8	5	3	56	70	30	17	0	0	0	0	20	1	0	.050
'03 CHI A	8	12	.400	3.50	26	20	15	167.1	167	44	66	1	1	2	1	57	7	0	.123
'04	21	15	.583	1.94	37	36	34	315	243	61	103	4	0	0	1	107	23	2	.215
'05	21	13	.618	2.10	42	38	32	334	276	56	125	3	0	1	0	124	18	0	.145
'06	22	13	.629	2.33	42	36	27	293	289	54	66	7	3	1	2	103	14	0	.136
'07	2	3	.400	2.49	11	4	2	47	43	13	15	0	0	1	0	16	4	0	.250
'08	6	7	.462	3.41	25	14	5	140	142	37	48	1	2	0	0	50	9	0	.180
'09	1	1	.500	4.50	3	2	1	16	19	3	3	0	0	0	0	6	1	0	.167
8 yrs.	82	67	.550	2.55	194	155	119	1368.1	1249	298	443	16	6	5	4	483	77	2	.159
1 yr.	1	3	.250	4.34	8	5	3	56	70	30	17	0	0	0	0	20	1	0	.050
WORLD SERIES																			
'06 CHI A	0	0	–	3.00	1	0	0	6	6	3	2	0	0	0	0	2	0	0	.000

Phil Page

PAGE, PHILIP RAUSAC   BR TL 6'2" 175 lbs.
B. Aug. 23, 1905, Springfield, Mass.   D. June 26, 1958, Springfield, Mass.

	W	L	PCT	ERA	G	GS	CG	IP	H	BB	SO	ShO	W	L	SV	AB	H	HR	BA
'28 DET A	2	0	1.000	2.45	3	2	2	22	21	10	3	0	0	0	0	9	2	0	.222
'29	0	2	.000	8.17	10	4	1	25.1	29	19	6	0	0	1	0	8	1	0	.125
'30	0	1	.000	9.75	12	0	0	12	23	9	2	0	0	0	0	0	0	0	–
'34 BKN N	1	0	1.000	5.40	6	0	0	10	13	6	4	0	1	0	0	1	0	0	.000
4 yrs.	3	3	.500	6.23	31	6	3	69.1	86	44	15	0	1	2	0	18	3	0	.167
3 yrs.	2	3	.400	6.37	25	6	3	59.1	73	38	11	0	0	2	0	17	3	0	.176

	W	L	PCT	ERA	G	GS	CG	IP	H	BB	SO	ShO	Relief Pitching W	L	SV	BATTING AB	H	HR	B

Slicker Parks

PARKS, VERNON HENRY
B. Nov. 10, 1895, Dallas, Mich.   D. Feb. 21, 1978, Royal Oak, Mich.
BR TR 5'10" 158 lbs

	W	L	PCT	ERA	G	GS	CG	IP	H	BB	SO	ShO	W	L	SV	AB	H	HR	B
1921 DET A	3	2	.600	5.68	10	1	0	25.1	33	16	10	0	3	2	0	9	1	0	.11

Larry Pashnick

PASHNICK, LARRY J.
B. Apr. 25, 1956, Lincoln Park, Mich.
BR TR 6'3" 205 lbs

	W	L	PCT	ERA	G	GS	CG	IP	H	BB	SO	ShO	W	L	SV	AB	H	HR	B
1982 DET A	4	4	.500	4.01	28	13	1	94.1	110	25	19	0	1	0	0	0	0	0	
1983	1	3	.250	5.26	12	6	0	37.2	48	18	17	0	1	0	0	0	0	0	
1984 MIN A	2	1	.667	3.52	13	1	0	38.1	38	11	10	0	2	0	0	0	0	0	
3 yrs.	7	8	.467	4.17	53	20	1	170.1	196	54	46	0	4	0	0	0	0	0	
2 yrs.	5	7	.417	4.36	40	19	1	132	158	43	36	0	2	0	0	0	0	0	

Daryl Patterson

PATTERSON, DARYL ALAN
B. Nov. 21, 1943, Coalinga, Calif.
BL TR 6'4" 192 lbs

	W	L	PCT	ERA	G	GS	CG	IP	H	BB	SO	ShO	W	L	SV	AB	H	HR	B
1968 DET A	2	3	.400	2.12	38	1	0	68	53	27	49	0	0	0	7	13	0	0	.00
1969	0	2	.000	2.82	18	0	0	22.1	15	19	12	0	0	2	0	1	0	0	.00
1970	7	1	.875	4.85	43	0	0	78	81	39	55	0	7	1	2	11	0	0	.00
1971 3 teams			DET A (12G 0-1)		OAK A (4G 0-0)			STL N (13G 0-1)											
" total	0	2	.000	4.93	29	2	0	42	39	25	18	0	0	2	1	6	0	0	.00
1974 PIT N	2	1	.667	7.29	14	0	0	21	35	9	8	0	2	1	1	4	0	0	.00
5 yrs.	11	9	.550	4.09	142	3	0	231.1	223	119	142	0	9	6	11	35	0	0	.00
4 yrs.	9	7	.563	3.55	111	1	0	177.2	163	91	121	0	7	4	9	25	0	0	.00
WORLD SERIES																			
1968 DET A	0	0	-	0.00	2	0	0	3	1	1	0	0	0	0	0	0	0	0	

Marv Peasley

PEASLEY, MARVIN WARREN
B. July 16, 1889, Jonesport, Me.   D. Dec. 27, 1948, San Francisco, Calif.
BL TL 6'1" 175 lbs

	W	L	PCT	ERA	G	GS	CG	IP	H	BB	SO	ShO	W	L	SV	AB	H	HR	B
1910 DET A	0	1	.000	8.10	2	1	0	10	13	11	4	0	0	0	0	3	0	0	.00

Orlando Pena

PENA, ORLANDO GREGORY
B. Nov. 17, 1933, Victoria de las Tunas, Cuba
BR TR 5'11" 154 lbs

	W	L	PCT	ERA	G	GS	CG	IP	H	BB	SO	ShO	W	L	SV	AB	H	HR	B
1958 CIN N	1	0	1.000	0.60	9	0	0	15	10	4	11	0	1	0	3	0	0	0	
1959	5	9	.357	4.76	46	8	1	136	150	39	76	0	2	4	5	34	3	0	.088
1960	0	1	.000	2.89	4	0	0	9.1	8	3	9	0	0	1	0	1	0	0	.000
1962 KC A	6	4	.600	3.01	13	12	6	89.2	71	27	56	1	0	0	0	31	5	0	.16
1963	12	20	.375	3.69	35	33	9	217	218	53	128	3	1	0	0	62	9	1	.14
1964	12	14	.462	4.43	40	32	5	219.1	231	73	184	0	0	0	0	75	12	1	.16
1965 2 teams			KC A (12G 0-6)		DET A (30G 4-6)														
" total	4	12	.250	4.18	42	5	0	92.2	96	33	79	0	4	7	4	17	3	0	.17
1966 DET A	4	2	.667	3.08	54	0	0	108	105	35	79	0	4	2	7	18	2	0	.11
1967 2 teams			DET A (2G 0-1)		CLE A (48G 0-3)														
" total	0	4	.000	3.59	50	1	0	90.1	72	22	74	0	0	3	8	8	0	0	.000
1970 PIT N	2	1	.667	4.74	23	0	0	38	38	7	25	0	2	1	2	6	0	0	.000
1971 BAL A	0	1	.000	3.00	5	0	0	15	16	5	4	0	0	1	0	3	0	0	.000
1973 2 teams			BAL A (11G 1-1)		STL N (42G 4-4)														
" total	5	5	.500	2.94	53	2	0	107	96	22	61	0	5	5	7	7	1	0	.143
1974 2 teams			STL N (42G 5-2)		CAL A (4G 0-0)														
" total	5	2	.714	2.21	46	0	0	53	51	21	28	0	5	2	4	2	1	0	.500
1975 CAL A	0	2	.000	2.13	7	0	0	12.2	13	8	4	0	0	2	0	0	0	0	
14 yrs.	56	77	.421	3.70	427	93	21	1203	1175	352	818	4	24	28	40	264	36	2	.136
3 yrs.	8	9	.471	3.01	86	0	0	167.1	164	55	136	0	8	9	11	26	4	0	.154

Gene Pentz

PENTZ, EUGENE DAVID
B. June 21, 1953, Johnstown, Pa.
BR TR 6'1" 200 lbs

	W	L	PCT	ERA	G	GS	CG	IP	H	BB	SO	ShO	W	L	SV	AB	H	HR	B
1975 DET A	0	4	.000	3.20	13	0	0	25.1	27	20	21	0	0	4	0	0	0	0	—
1976 HOU N	3	3	.500	2.95	40	0	0	64	62	31	36	0	3	3	5	5	1	0	.200
1977	5	2	.714	3.83	41	4	0	87	76	44	51	0	3	0	2	13	0	0	.000
1978	0	0	—	6.00	10	0	0	15	12	13	8	0	0	0	0	1	0	0	.000
4 yrs.	8	9	.471	3.62	104	4	0	191.1	177	108	116	0	6	7	7	19	1	0	.053
1 yr.	0	4	.000	3.20	13	0	0	25.1	27	20	21	0	0	4	0	0	0	0	

Hub Pernoll

PERNOLL, HENRY HUBBARD
B. Mar. 14, 1888, Grant's Pass, Ore.   D. Feb. 18, 1944, Grant's Pass, Ore.
BR TL

	W	L	PCT	ERA	G	GS	CG	IP	H	BB	SO	ShO	W	L	SV	AB	H	HR	B
1910 DET A	4	3	.571	2.96	11	5	4	54.2	54	14	25	0	0	2	0	16	1	0	.063
1912	0	0	—	6.00	3	0	0	9	9	4	3	0	0	0	0	3	0	0	.000
2 yrs.	4	3	.571	3.39	14	5	4	63.2	63	18	28	0	0	2	0	19	1	0	.053
2 yrs.	4	3	.571	3.39	14	5	4	63.2	63	18	28	0	0	2	0	19	1	0	.053

Ron Perranoski

PERRANOSKI, RONALD PETER
B. Apr. 1, 1936, Paterson, N. J.
BL TL 6' 180 lbs

	W	L	PCT	ERA	G	GS	CG	IP	H	BB	SO	ShO	W	L	SV	AB	H	HR	B
1961 LA N	7	5	.583	2.65	53	1	0	91.2	82	41	56	0	7	5	5	12	1	0	.083
1962	6	6	.500	2.85	70	0	0	107.1	103	36	68	0	6	6	20	14	1	0	.071
1963	16	3	.842	1.67	69	0	0	129	112	43	75	0	16	3	21	24	3	0	.125
1964	5	7	.417	3.09	72	0	0	125.1	128	46	79	0	5	7	14	19	2	0	.105
1965	6	6	.500	2.24	59	0	0	104.2	85	40	53	0	6	6	17	19	3	0	.158
1966	6	7	.462	3.18	55	0	0	82	82	31	50	0	6	7	7	8	2	0	.250
1967	6	7	.462	2.45	70	0	0	110	97	45	75	0	6	7	16	10	1	0	.100
1968 MIN A	8	7	.533	3.10	66	0	0	87	86	38	65	0	8	7	6	7	0	0	.000
1969	9	10	.474	2.11	75	0	0	119.2	85	52	62	0	9	10	31	24	2	0	.083
1970	7	8	.467	2.43	67	0	0	111	108	42	55	0	7	8	34	24	1	0	.042
1971 2 teams			MIN A (36G 1-4)		DET A (11G 0-1)														
" total	1	5	.167	5.49	47	0	0	60.2	76	31	29	0	1	5	7	5	0	0	.000
1972 2 teams			DET A (17G 0-1)		LA N (9G 2-0)														
" total	2	1	.667	5.30	26	0	0	35.2	42	16	15	0	2	1	0	6	0	0	.000
1973 CAL A	0	2	.000	4.09	8	0	0	11	11	7	5	0	0	2	0	0	0	0	
13 yrs.	79	74	.516	2.79	737	1	0	1175	1097	468	687	0	79	74	179	167	16	0	.096
															10th				
2 yrs.	0	2	.000	5.11	28	0	0	37	39	11	18	0	0	2	2	3	0	0	.000

	W	L	PCT	ERA	G	GS	CG	IP	H	BB	SO	ShO	Relief Pitching W	L	SV	BATTING AB	H	HR	BA

Ron Perranoski continued

	W	L	PCT	ERA	G	GS	CG	IP	H	BB	SO	ShO	W	L	SV	AB	H	HR	BA
1969 MIN A	0	1	.000	5.79	3	0	0	4.2	8	0	2	0	0	1	0	1	0	0	.000
1970	0	0	–	19.29	2	0	0	2.1	5	1	3	0	0	0	0	0	0	0	–
2 yrs.	0	1	.000	10.29	5	0	0	7	13	1	5	0	0	1	0	1	0	0	.000

WORLD SERIES

1963 LA N	0	0	–	0.00	1	0	0	.2	1	0	1	0	0	0	1	0	0	0	–
1965	0	0	–	7.36	2	0	0	3.2	3	4	1	0	0	0	0	0	0	0	–
1966	0	0	–	5.40	2	0	0	3.1	4	1	2	0	0	0	0	0	0	0	–
3 yrs.	0	0	–	5.87	5	0	0	7.2	8	5	4	0	0	0	1	0	0	0	–

Pol Perritt

PERRITT, WILLIAM DAYTON   BR TR 6' 175 lbs.
B. Aug. 30, 1892, Arcadia, La.   D. Oct. 15, 1947, Shreveport, La.

1912 STL N	1	1	.500	3.19	6	3	1	31	25	10	13	0	0	0	0	9	2	0	.222
1913	6	14	.300	5.25	36	21	8	175	205	64	64	0	3	0	0	59	12	0	.203
1914	16	13	.552	2.36	41	32	18	286	248	93	115	3	2	1	2	92	13	0	.141
1915 NY N	12	18	.400	2.66	35	30	16	220	226	59	91	4	1	1	0	68	11	0	.162
1916	18	11	.621	2.62	40	28	17	251	243	56	115	5	2	5	2	83	7	0	.084
1917	17	7	.708	1.88	35	26	14	215	186	45	72	5	2	3	1	70	11	0	.157
1918	18	13	.581	2.74	35	31	19	233	212	38	60	6	1	1	0	80	14	0	.175
1919	1	1	.500	7.11	11	3	0	19	27	12	2	0	1	0	1	4	0	0	.000
1920	0	0	–	1.80	8	0	0	15	9	4	3	0	0	0	2	4	0	0	.000
1921 2 teams			NY	N (5G 2–0)		DET	A	(4G 1–0)											
total	3	0	1.000	4.38	9	3	0	24.2	35	9	8	0	2	0	0	8	2	0	.250
10 yrs.	92	78	.541	2.89	256	177	93	1469.2	1416	390	543	23	14	11	8	477	72	0	.151
1 yr.	1	0	1.000	4.85	4	2	0	13	18	7	3	0	0	0	0	5	2	0	.400

WORLD SERIES

1917 NY N	0	0	–	2.16	3	0	0	8.1	9	3	3	0	0	0	0	2	2	0	1.000

Jim Perry

PERRY, JAMES EVAN   BB TR 6'4" 190 lbs.
Brother of Gaylord Perry.
B. Oct. 3, 1936, Williamston, N. C.

1959 CLE A	12	10	.545	2.65	44	13	8	153	122	55	79	2	5	4	4	50	15	0	.300
1960	18	10	.643	3.62	41	36	10	261.1	257	91	120	4	1	0	1	91	22	0	.242
1961	10	17	.370	4.71	35	35	6	223.2	238	87	90	1	0	0	0	73	12	0	.164
1962	12	12	.500	4.14	35	27	7	193.2	213	59	74	3	0	0	0	60	11	0	.183
1963 2 teams			CLE	A (5G 0–0)		MIN	A	(35G 9–9)											
total	9	9	.500	3.83	40	25	5	178.2	179	59	72	1	0	1	1	53	11	0	.208
1964 MIN A	6	3	.667	3.44	42	1	0	65.1	61	23	55	0	6	2	2	13	2	0	.154
1965	12	7	.632	2.63	36	19	4	167.2	142	47	88	2	5	0	0	53	9	0	.170
1966	11	7	.611	2.54	33	25	8	184.1	149	53	122	1	0	0	0	59	13	1	.220
1967	8	7	.533	3.03	37	11	3	130.2	123	50	94	2	3	4	0	42	8	1	.190
1968	8	6	.571	2.27	32	18	3	139	113	26	69	2	1	0	1	42	6	2	.143
1969	20	6	.769	2.82	46	36	12	261.2	244	66	153	3	3	0	0	93	16	0	.172
1970	24	12	.667	3.03	40	40	13	279	258	57	168	4	0	0	0	97	24	1	.247
1971	17	17	.500	4.23	40	39	8	270	263	102	126	0	0	0	1	92	17	0	.185
1972	13	16	.448	3.34	35	35	5	218	191	60	85	2	0	0	0	71	11	0	.155
1973 DET A	14	13	.519	4.03	35	34	7	203	225	55	66	1	0	0	0	0	0	0	–
1974 CLE A	17	12	.586	2.96	36	36	8	252	242	64	71	3	0	0	0	0	0	0	–
1975 2 teams			CLE	A (8G 1–6)		OAK	A	(15G 3–4)											
total	4	10	.286	5.38	23	17	2	105.1	107	44	44	1	0	1	0	0	0	0	–
17 yrs.	215	174	.553	3.45	630	447	109	3286.1	3127	998	1576	32	24	12	10	889	177	5	.199
1 yr.	14	13	.519	4.03	35	34	7	203	225	55	66	1	0	0	0	0	0	0	–

1969 MIN A	0	0	–	3.38	1	1	0	8	6	3	3	0	0	0	0	3	0	0	.000
1970	0	1	.000	13.50	2	1	0	5.1	10	1	3	0	0	0	0	1	0	0	.000
2 yrs.	0	1	.000	7.43	3	2	0	13.1	16	4	6	0	0	0	0	4	0	0	.000

WORLD SERIES

1965 MIN A	0	0	–	4.50	2	0	0	4	5	2	4	0	0	0	0	0	0	0	–

Dan Petry

PETRY, DANIEL JOSEPH   BR TR 6'4" 185 lbs.
B. Nov. 13, 1958, Palo Alto, Calif.

1979 DET A	6	5	.545	3.95	15	15	2	98	90	33	43	0	0	0	0	0	0	0	–
1980	10	9	.526	3.93	27	25	4	165	156	83	88	3	1	0	0	0	0	0	–
1981	10	9	.526	3.00	23	22	7	141	115	57	79	2	0	0	0	0	0	0	–
1982	15	9	.625	3.22	35	35	8	246	220	100	132	1	0	0	0	0	0	0	–
1983	19	11	.633	3.92	38	38	9	266.1	256	99	122	2	0	0	0	0	0	0	–
1984	18	8	.692	3.24	35	35	7	233.1	231	66	144	2	0	0	0	0	0	0	–
6 yrs.	78	51	.605	3.52	173	170	37	1149.2	1068	438	608	10	1	0	0	0	0	0	–
6 yrs.	78	51	.605	3.52	173	170	37	1149.2	1068	438	608	10	1	0	0	0	0	0	–
			4th																

1984 DET A	0	0	–	2.57	1	1	0	7	4	1	4	0	0	0	0	0	0	0	–

WORLD SERIES

1984 DET A	0	1	.000	9.00	2	2	0	8	14	5	4	0	0	0	0	0	0	0	–

Jack Phillips

PHILLIPS, JACK DORN (Stretch)   BR TR 6'4" 193 lbs.
B. Sept. 6, 1921, Clarence, N. Y.

1950 PIT N	0	0	–	7.20	1	0	0	5	7	1	2	0	0	0	0	*			

Red Phillips

PHILLIPS, CLARENCE LEMUEL   BR TR 6'3½" 195 lbs.
B. Nov. 3, 1908, Pauls Valley, Okla.

1934 DET A	2	0	1.000	6.17	7	1	1	23.1	31	16	3	0	1	0	1	12	3	0	.250

	W	L	PCT	ERA	G	GS	CG	IP	H	BB	SO	ShO	Relief Pitching W	L	SV	BATTING AB	H	HR	BA

Red Phillips continued

	W	L	PCT	ERA	G	GS	CG	IP	H	BB	SO	ShO	W	L	SV	AB	H	HR	BA
1936	2	4	.333	6.49	22	6	3	87.1	124	22	15	0	1	1	0	33	10	0	.30
2 yrs.	4	4	.500	6.42	29	7	4	110.2	155	38	18	0	2	1	1	45	13	0	.28
2 yrs.	4	4	.500	6.42	29	7	4	110.2	155	38	18	0	2	1	1	45	13	0	.28

Billy Pierce

PIERCE, WALTER WILLIAM
B. Apr. 2, 1927, Detroit, Mich.   BL TL 5'10" 160 lbs.

	W	L	PCT	ERA	G	GS	CG	IP	H	BB	SO	ShO	W	L	SV	AB	H	HR	BA
1945 DET A	0	0	—	1.80	5	0	0	10	4	10	10	0	0	0	0	2	0	0	.000
1948	3	0	1.000	6.34	22	5	0	55.1	47	51	36	0	1	0	0	17	5	0	.29
1949 CHI A	7	15	.318	3.88	32	26	8	171.2	145	112	95	0	1	0	0	51	9	0	.17
1950	12	16	.429	3.98	33	29	15	219.1	189	137	118	1	1	0	1	77	20	0	.26
1951	15	14	.517	3.03	37	28	18	240.1	237	73	113	1	0	3	2	79	16	0	.20
1952	15	12	.556	2.57	33	32	14	255.1	214	79	144	4	0	0	1	91	17	0	.18
1953	18	12	.600	2.72	40	33	19	271.1	216	102	186	7	3	0	3	87	11	0	.12
1954	9	10	.474	3.48	36	26	12	188.2	179	86	148	4	0	0	3	57	11	0	.19
1955	15	10	.600	1.97	33	26	16	205.2	162	64	157	6	2	0	1	70	12	0	.17
1956	20	9	.690	3.32	35	33	21	276.1	261	100	192	1	0	1	1	102	16	0	.15
1957	20	12	.625	3.26	37	34	16	257	228	71	171	4	0	1	2	99	17	0	.17
1958	17	11	.607	2.68	35	32	19	245	204	66	144	3	0	0	2	83	17	0	.20
1959	14	15	.483	3.62	34	33	12	224	217	62	114	2	0	0	0	68	13	0	.19
1960	14	7	.667	3.62	32	30	8	196.1	201	46	108	1	1	0	0	67	12	0	.17
1961	10	9	.526	3.80	39	28	5	180	190	54	106	1	3	0	3	56	8	0	.14
1962 SF N	16	6	.727	3.49	30	23	7	162.1	147	35	76	2	0	0	1	56	12	0	.21
1963	3	11	.214	4.27	38	13	3	99	106	20	52	1	0	5	8	31	4	0	.12
1964	3	0	1.000	2.20	34	1	0	49	40	10	29	0	2	0	4	9	3	0	.33
18 yrs.	211	169	.555	3.27	585	432	193	3306.2	2989	1178	1999	38	14	10	32	1102	203	0	.18
2 yrs.	3	0	1.000	5.65	27	5	0	65.1	53	61	46	0	1	0	0	19	5	0	.26

WORLD SERIES

	W	L	PCT	ERA	G	GS	CG	IP	H	BB	SO	ShO	W	L	SV	AB	H	HR	BA
1959 CHI A	0	0	—	0.00	3	0	0	4	2	1	3	0	0	0	0	0	0	0	—
1962 SF N	1	1	.500	2.40	2	2	1	15	8	2	5	0	0	0	0	5	0	0	.000
2 yrs.	1	1	.500	1.89	5	2	1	19	10	4	8	0	0	0	0	5	0	0	.000

Herman Pillette

PILLETTE, HERMAN POLYCARP (Old Folks)
Father of Duane Pillette.   BR TR 6'2" 190 lbs.
B. Dec. 26, 1895, St. Paul, Ore.   D. Apr. 30, 1960, Sacramento, Calif.

	W	L	PCT	ERA	G	GS	CG	IP	H	BB	SO	ShO	W	L	SV	AB	H	HR	BA
1917 CIN N	0	0	—	18.00	1	0	0	1	4	0	0	0	0	0	0	0	0	0	—
1922 DET A	19	12	.613	2.85	40	37	18	274.2	270	95	71	4	1	0	1	99	17	0	.172
1923	14	19	.424	3.85	47	37	14	250.1	280	83	64	0	3	2	1	85	21	0	.247
1924	1	1	.500	4.78	19	3	1	37.2	46	14	13	0	0	0	1	11	4	0	.364
4 yrs.	34	32	.515	3.45	107	77	33	563.2	600	192	148	4	4	2	3	195	42	0	.215
3 yrs.	34	32	.515	3.42	106	77	33	562.2	596	192	148	4	4	2	3	195	42	0	.215

Cotton Pippen

PIPPEN, HENRY HAROLD
B. Apr. 2, 1910, Cisco, Tex.   BR TR 6'2" 180 lbs.

	W	L	PCT	ERA	G	GS	CG	IP	H	BB	SO	ShO	W	L	SV	AB	H	HR	BA
1936 STL N	0	2	.000	7.71	6	3	0	21	37	8	8	0	0	0	0	6	1	0	.167
1939 2 teams							PHI A (25G 4–11)			DET A (3G 0–1)									
" total	4	12	.250	6.11	28	19	5	132.2	187	46	38	0	0	1	1	40	5	0	.125
1940 DET A	1	2	.333	6.75	4	3	0	21.1	29	10	9	0	0	0	0	8	0	0	.000
3 yrs.	5	16	.238	6.38	38	25	5	175	253	64	55	0	0	1	1	54	6	0	.111
2 yrs.	1	3	.250	6.88	7	5	0	35.1	47	16	14	0	0	0	0	13	2	0	.154

Johnny Podres

PODRES, JOHN JOSEPH
B. Sept. 30, 1932, Witherbee, N. Y.   BL TL 5'11" 170 lbs.

	W	L	PCT	ERA	G	GS	CG	IP	H	BB	SO	ShO	W	L	SV	AB	H	HR	BA
1953 BKN N	9	4	.692	4.23	33	18	3	115	126	64	82	1	4	0	0	36	11	0	.306
1954	11	7	.611	4.27	29	21	6	151.2	147	53	79	2	1	0	0	60	17	0	.283
1955	9	10	.474	3.95	27	24	5	159.1	160	57	114	2	1	0	0	60	11	0	.183
1957	12	9	.571	2.66	31	27	10	196	168	44	109	6	1	0	3	72	15	0	.208
1958 LA N	13	15	.464	3.72	39	31	10	210.1	208	78	143	2	0	1	1	71	9	0	.127
1959	14	9	.609	4.11	34	29	6	195	192	74	145	2	1	0	0	65	16	0	.246
1960	14	12	.538	3.08	34	33	8	227.2	217	71	159	1	1	0	0	66	9	0	.136
1961	18	5	.783	3.74	32	29	6	182.2	192	51	124	1	2	0	0	69	16	0	.232
1962	15	13	.536	3.81	40	40	8	255	270	71	178	0	0	0	0	88	14	1	.159
1963	14	12	.538	3.54	37	34	10	198.1	196	64	134	5	0	0	1	64	9	1	.141
1964	0	2	.000	16.88	2	2	0	2.2	5	3	0	0	0	0	0	0	0	0	—
1965	7	6	.538	3.43	27	22	2	134	126	39	63	1	0	2	1	45	8	0	.178
1966 2 teams							LA N (1G 0–0)			DET A (36G 4–5)									
" total	4	5	.444	3.38	37	13	2	109.1	108	35	54	1	2	1	4	30	7	0	.233
1967 DET A	3	1	.750	3.84	21	8	0	63.1	58	11	34	0	1	0	1	20	2	0	.100
1969 SD N	5	6	.455	4.29	17	9	1	65	66	28	17	0	0	0	0	16	1	0	.063
15 yrs.	148	116	.561	3.67	440	340	77	2265.1	2239	743	1435	24	13	4	11	762	145	2	.190
2 yrs.	7	6	.538	3.58	57	21	2	171	164	45	87	1	3	1	5	50	9	0	.180

WORLD SERIES

	W	L	PCT	ERA	G	GS	CG	IP	H	BB	SO	ShO	W	L	SV	AB	H	HR	BA
1953 BKN N	0	1	—	3.38	1	1	0	2.2	4	2	0	0	0	0	0	1	1	0	1.000
1955	2	0	1.000	1.00	2	2	2	18	15	4	10	1	0	0	0	7	1	0	.143
1959 LA N	1	0	1.000	4.82	2	2	0	9.1	7	6	4	0	0	0	0	4	2	0	.500
1963	1	0	1.000	1.08	1	1	0	8.1	4	1	4	0	0	0	0	4	1	0	.250
4 yrs.	4	1	.800	2.11	6	6	2	38.1	29	13	18	1	0	0	0	16	5	0	.313

Boots Poffenberger

POFFENBERGER, CLETUS ELWOOD
B. July 1, 1915, Williamsport, Md.   BR TR 5'10" 178 lbs.

	W	L	PCT	ERA	G	GS	CG	IP	H	BB	SO	ShO	W	L	SV	AB	H	HR	BA
1937 DET A	10	5	.667	4.65	29	16	5	137.1	147	79	35	0	3	1	3	51	11	0	.216
1938	6	7	.462	4.82	25	15	8	125	147	66	28	0	0	2	1	44	8	0	.182
1939 BKN N	0	0	—	5.40	3	1	0	5	7	4	2	0	0	0	0	1	0	0	.000
3 yrs.	16	12	.571	4.75	57	32	13	267.1	301	149	65	0	3	3	4	96	19	0	.198
2 yrs.	16	12	.571	4.73	54	31	13	262.1	294	145	63	0	3	3	4	95	19	0	.200

oe Presko

PRESKO, JOSEPH EDWARD (Little Joe) BR TR 5'9½" 165 lbs.
B. Oct. 7, 1928, Kansas City, Mo.

	W	L	PCT	ERA	G	GS	CG	IP	H	BB	SO	ShO	Relief W	Relief L	Relief SV	AB	H	HR	BA
951 STL N	7	4	.636	3.45	15	12	5	88.2	86	20	38	0	1	0	2	37	6	0	.162
952	7	10	.412	4.05	28	18	5	146.2	140	57	63	1	2	1	0	43	4	0	.093
953	6	13	.316	5.01	34	25	4	161.2	165	65	56	0	0	0	1	59	13	0	.220
954	4	9	.308	6.91	37	6	1	71.2	97	41	36	1	3	5	0	16	4	0	.250
957 DET A	1	1	.500	1.64	7	0	0	11	10	4	3	0	1	1	0	1	0	0	.000
958	0	0	–	3.38	7	0	0	10.2	13	1	6	0	0	0	2	0	0	0	–
6 yrs.	25	37	.403	4.61	128	61	15	490.1	511	188	202	2	7	7	5	156	27	0	.173
2 yrs.	1	1	.500	2.49	14	0	0	21.2	23	5	9	0	1	1	2	1	0	0	.000

im Proctor

PROCTOR, JAMES ARTHUR BR TR 6' 165 lbs.
B. Sept. 9, 1935, Brandywine, Md.

	W	L	PCT	ERA	G	GS	CG	IP	H	BB	SO	ShO	Relief W	Relief L	Relief SV	AB	H	HR	BA
59 DET A	0	1	.000	16.88	2	1	0	2.2	8	3	0	0	0	1	0	0	0	0	–

ugie Prudhomme

PRUDHOMME, JOHN OLGUS BR TR 6'2" 186 lbs.
B. Nov. 20, 1902, Frierson, La.

	W	L	PCT	ERA	G	GS	CG	IP	H	BB	SO	ShO	Relief W	Relief L	Relief SV	AB	H	HR	BA
929 DET A	1	6	.143	6.22	34	6	2	94	119	53	26	0	0	3	1	21	5	0	.238

ick Radatz

RADATZ, RICHARD RAYMOND (The Monster) BR TR 6'6" 230 lbs.
B. Apr. 2, 1937, Detroit, Mich.

	W	L	PCT	ERA	G	GS	CG	IP	H	BB	SO	ShO	Relief W	Relief L	Relief SV	AB	H	HR	BA
962 BOS A	9	6	.600	2.24	**62**	0	0	124.2	95	40	144	0	**9**	6	**24**	31	3	0	.097
963	15	6	.714	1.97	66	0	0	132.1	94	51	162	0	**15**	6	25	29	2	0	.069
964	16	9	.640	2.29	79	0	0	157	103	58	181	0	**16**	**9**	**29**	37	6	0	.162
965	9	11	.450	3.91	63	0	0	124.1	104	53	121	0	9	**11**	22	27	5	1	.185
966 2 teams BOS A (16G 0–2) CLE A (39G 0–3)																			
" total	0	5	.000	4.64	55	0	0	75.2	73	45	68	0	0	5	14	11	1	0	.091
967 2 teams CLE A (3G 0–0) CHI N (20G 1–0)																			
" total	1	0	1.000	6.49	23	0	0	26.1	17	26	19	0	1	0	5	4	1	0	.250
969 2 teams DET A (11G 2–2) MON N (22G 0–4)																			
" total	2	6	.250	4.89	33	0	0	53.1	46	23	50	0	2	6	3	6	1	0	.167
7 yrs.	52	43	.547	3.13	381	0	0	693.2	532	296	745	0	52	43	122	145	19	1	.131
1 yr.	2	2	.500	3.38	11	0	0	18.2	14	5	18	0	2	2	0	2	0	0	.000

d Rakow

RAKOW, EDWARD CHARLES (Rock) BB TR 5'11" 178 lbs.
B. May 30, 1936, Pittsburgh, Pa. BR 1960-61

	W	L	PCT	ERA	G	GS	CG	IP	H	BB	SO	ShO	Relief W	Relief L	Relief SV	AB	H	HR	BA
960 LA N	0	1	.000	7.36	9	2	0	22	30	11	9	0	0	0	0	6	2	0	.333
961 KC A	2	8	.200	4.76	45	11	1	124.2	131	49	81	0	1	3	1	29	3	0	.103
962	14	**17**	.452	4.25	42	35	11	235.1	232	98	159	2	1	2	1	82	8	0	.098
963	9	10	.474	3.92	34	26	7	174.1	173	61	104	1	0	0	0	57	6	0	.105
964 DET A	8	9	.471	3.72	42	13	1	152.1	155	59	96	0	5	1	3	39	0	0	.000
965	0	0	–	6.08	6	0	0	13.1	14	11	10	0	0	0	0	3	0	0	.000
967 ATL N	3	2	.600	5.26	17	3	0	39.1	36	15	25	0	1	2	0	10	0	0	.000
7 yrs.	36	47	.434	4.33	195	90	20	761.1	771	304	484	3	8	8	5	226	19	0	.084
2 yrs.	8	9	.471	3.91	48	13	1	165.2	169	70	106	0	5	1	3	42	0	0	.000

im Ray

RAY, JAMES FRANCIS (Sting) BR TR 6'1" 185 lbs.
B. Dec. 1, 1944, Rock Hill, S. C.

	W	L	PCT	ERA	G	GS	CG	IP	H	BB	SO	ShO	Relief W	Relief L	Relief SV	AB	H	HR	BA
965 HOU N	0	2	.000	10.57	3	2	0	7.2	11	6	7	0	0	0	0	2	0	0	.000
966	0	0	–	∞	1	0	0		0	1	0	0	0	0	0	0	0	0	–
968	2	3	.400	2.67	41	2	1	81	65	25	71	0	1	2	1	15	1	0	.067
969	8	2	.800	3.91	40	13	0	115	105	48	115	0	4	0	0	26	3	0	.115
970	6	3	.667	3.26	52	2	0	105	97	49	67	0	6	2	5	27	5	0	.185
971	10	4	.714	2.11	47	1	0	98	72	31	46	0	10	3	3	18	3	0	.167
972	10	9	.526	4.30	54	0	0	90	77	44	50	0	10	**9**	8	16	1	0	.063
973	6	4	.600	4.43	42	0	0	69	65	38	25	0	6	4	6	13	3	0	.231
974 DET A	1	3	.250	4.50	28	0	0	52	49	29	26	0	1	3	2	0	0	0	–
9 yrs.	43	30	.589	3.61	308	20	1	617.2	541	271	407	0	38	23	25	117	16	0	.137
1 yr.	1	3	.250	4.50	28	0	0	52	49	29	26	0	1	3	2	0	0	0	–

ugs Raymond

RAYMOND, ARTHUR LAWRENCE BR TR
B. Feb. 24, 1882, Chicago, Ill. D. Sept. 7, 1912, Chicago, Ill.

	W	L	PCT	ERA	G	GS	CG	IP	H	BB	SO	ShO	Relief W	Relief L	Relief SV	AB	H	HR	BA
904 DET A	0	1	.000	3.07	5	2	1	14.2	14	6	7	0	0	0	0	5	0	0	.000
907 STL N	2	4	.333	1.67	8	6	6	64.2	56	21	34	1	0	0	0	22	2	0	.091
908	15	**25**	.375	2.03	48	37	23	324.1	236	95	145	5	2	1	2	90	17	0	.189
909 NY N	18	12	.600	2.47	39	31	18	270	239	87	121	2	3	1	0	89	13	0	.146
910	4	11	.267	3.81	19	11	6	99.1	106	40	55	0	1	2	0	32	5	0	.156
911	6	4	.600	3.31	17	9	4	81.2	73	33	39	1	2	1	0	25	5	0	.200
6 yrs.	45	57	.441	2.49	136	96	58	854.2	724	282	401	9	8	5	2	263	42	0	.160
1 yr.	0	1	.000	3.07	5	2	1	14.2	14	6	7	0	0	0	0	5	0	0	.000

ob Reed

REED, ROBERT EDWARD BR TR 5'10" 175 lbs.
B. Jan. 12, 1945, Boston, Mass.

	W	L	PCT	ERA	G	GS	CG	IP	H	BB	SO	ShO	Relief W	Relief L	Relief SV	AB	H	HR	BA
969 DET A	0	0	–	1.84	8	1	0	14.2	9	8	9	0	0	0	0	2	1	0	.500
970	2	4	.333	4.89	16	4	0	46	54	14	26	0	1	2	2	12	1	0	.083
2 yrs.	2	4	.333	4.15	24	5	0	60.2	63	22	35	0	1	2	2	14	2	0	.143
2 yrs.	2	4	.333	4.15	24	5	0	60.2	63	22	35	0	1	2	2	14	2	0	.143

hil Regan

REGAN, PHILIP RAYMOND (The Vulture) BR TR 6'3" 200 lbs.
B. Apr. 6, 1937, Otsego, Mich.

	W	L	PCT	ERA	G	GS	CG	IP	H	BB	SO	ShO	Relief W	Relief L	Relief SV	AB	H	HR	BA
960 DET A	0	4	.000	4.50	17	7	0	68	70	25	38	0	0	0	1	17	1	0	.059
961	10	7	.588	5.25	32	16	6	120	134	41	46	0	2	2	2	40	3	0	.075
962	11	9	.550	4.04	35	23	6	171.1	169	64	87	0	1	2	0	63	13	0	.206
963	15	9	.625	3.86	38	27	5	189	179	59	115	1	2	1	1	63	9	1	.143
964	5	10	.333	5.03	32	21	2	146.2	162	49	91	0	1	0	1	41	13	0	.317
965	1	5	.167	5.05	16	7	1	51.2	57	20	37	0	0	0	0	12	1	0	.083
966 LA N	14	1	.933	1.62	65	0	0	116.2	85	24	88	0	**14**	1	**21**	21	3	0	.143

	W	L	PCT	ERA	G	GS	CG	IP	H	BB	SO	ShO	Relief Pitching W	L	SV	Batting AB	H	HR	BA

Phil Regan continued

	W	L	PCT	ERA	G	GS	CG	IP	H	BB	SO	ShO	W	L	SV	AB	H	HR	BA
1967	6	9	.400	2.99	55	3	0	96.1	108	32	53	0	5	7	6	10	1	0	.10
1968 2 teams		LA	N	(5G 2–0)		CHI	N	(68G 10–5)											
" total	12	5	.706	2.27	73	0	0	134.2	119	25	67	0	12	5	25	21	3	0	.14
1969 CHI N	12	6	.667	3.70	71	0	0	112	120	35	56	0	12	6	17	15	1	0	.06
1970	5	9	.357	4.74	54	0	0	76	81	32	31	0	5	9	12	9	0	0	.00
1971	5	5	.500	3.95	48	1	0	73	84	33	28	0	4	5	6	8	0	0	.00
1972 2 teams		CHI	N	(5G 0–1)		CHI	A	(10G 0–1)											
" total	0	2	.000	3.63	15	0	0	17.1	24	8	6	0	0	2	0	1	1	0	1.00
13 yrs.	96	81	.542	3.84	551	105	20	1372.2	1392	447	743	1	58	40	92	321	49	1	.15
6 yrs.	42	44	.488	4.50	170	101	20	746.2	771	258	414	1	6	5	5	236	40	1	.16

WORLD SERIES

	W	L	PCT	ERA	G	GS	CG	IP	H	BB	SO	ShO	W	L	SV	AB	H	HR	BA
1966 LA N	0	0	–	0.00	2	0	0	1.2	0	1	2	0	0	0	0	0	0	0	

Alex Remneas

REMNEAS, ALEXANDER NORMAN   BR TR 6'1"   180 lbs.
B. July 21, 1886, Minneapolis, Minn.   D. Aug. 27, 1975, Phoenix, Ariz.

	W	L	PCT	ERA	G	GS	CG	IP	H	BB	SO	ShO	W	L	SV	AB	H	HR	BA
1912 DET A	0	0	–	27.00	1	0	0	1.2	5	0	0	0	0	0	0	0	0	0	–
1915 STL A	0	0	–	1.50	2	0	0	6	3	3	5	0	0	0	0	1	0	0	.000
2 yrs.	0	0	–	7.04	3	0	0	7.2	8	3	5	0	0	0	0	1	0	0	.000
1 yr.	0	0	–	27.00	1	0	0	1.2	5	0	0	0	0	0	0	0	0	0	–

Erwin Renfer

RENFER, ERWIN ARTHUR   BR TR 6'   180 lbs.
B. Dec. 11, 1891, Elgin, Ill.   D. Oct. 26, 1957, Sycamore, Ill.

	W	L	PCT	ERA	G	GS	CG	IP	H	BB	SO	ShO	W	L	SV	AB	H	HR	BA
1913 DET A	0	1	.000	6.00	1	1	0	6	5	3	1	0	0	0	0	2	0	0	–

Bob Reynolds

REYNOLDS, ROBERT ALLEN   BR TR 6'   205 lbs.
B. Jan. 21, 1947, Seattle, Wash.

	W	L	PCT	ERA	G	GS	CG	IP	H	BB	SO	ShO	W	L	SV	AB	H	HR	BA
1969 MON N	0	0	–	20.25	1	1	0	1.1	3	3	2	0	0	0	0	0	0	0	–
1971 2 teams		MIL	A	(3G 0–1)		STL	N	(4G 0–0)											
" total	0	1	.000	6.92	7	0	0	13	19	9	8	0	0	1	0	2	0	0	.000
1972 BAL A	0	0	–	1.80	3	0	0	10	8	7	5	0	0	0	0	2	0	0	.000
1973	7	5	.583	1.95	42	1	0	111	88	31	77	0	7	5	9	0	0	0	–
1974	7	5	.583	2.74	54	0	0	69	75	14	43	0	7	5	7	0	0	0	–
1975 3 teams		BAL	A	(7G 0–0)		DET	A	(21G 0–2)		CLE	A	(5G 0–2)							
" total	0	5	.000	5.19	33	0	0	50.1	62	18	32	0	0	5	5	0	0	0	–
6 yrs.	14	16	.467	3.15	140	2	0	254.2	255	82	167	0	14	16	21	4	0	0	.000
1 yr.	0	2	.000	4.67	21	0	0	34.2	40	14	26	0	0	2	3	0	0	0	–

LEAGUE CHAMPIONSHIP SERIES

	W	L	PCT	ERA	G	GS	CG	IP	H	BB	SO	ShO	W	L	SV	AB	H	HR	BA
1973 BAL A	0	0	–	3.18	2	0	0	5.2	5	3	5	0	0	0	0	0	0	0	–
1974	0	0	–	0.00	1	0	0	1.1	0	3	1	0	0	0	0	0	0	0	–
2 yrs.	0	0	–	2.57	3	0	0	7	5	6	6	0	0	0	0	0	0	0	–

Ross Reynolds

REYNOLDS, ROSS ERNEST   BR TR 6'2"   175 lbs.
B. Aug. 20, 1887, Barksdale, Tex.   D. June 23, 1970, Ada, Okla.

	W	L	PCT	ERA	G	GS	CG	IP	H	BB	SO	ShO	W	L	SV	AB	H	HR	BA
1914 DET A	5	3	.625	2.08	26	7	3	78	62	39	31	1	1	1	1	21	1	0	.048
1915	0	1	.000	6.35	4	2	0	11.1	17	5	2	0	0	0	0	3	0	0	.000
2 yrs.	5	4	.556	2.62	30	9	3	89.1	79	44	33	1	1	1	1	24	1	0	.042
2 yrs.	5	4	.556	2.62	30	9	3	89.1	79	44	33	1	1	1	0	24	1	0	.042

Dennis Ribant

RIBANT, DENNIS JOSEPH   BR TR 5'11"   165 lbs.
B. Sept. 20, 1941, Detroit, Mich.

	W	L	PCT	ERA	G	GS	CG	IP	H	BB	SO	ShO	W	L	SV	AB	H	HR	BA
1964 NY N	1	5	.167	5.15	14	7	1	57.2	65	9	35	1	0	0	1	20	2	0	.100
1965	1	3	.250	3.82	19	1	0	35.1	29	6	13	0	1	3	3	6	0	0	.000
1966	11	9	.550	3.20	39	26	10	188.1	184	40	84	1	0	0	3	61	12	0	.197
1967 PIT N	9	8	.529	4.08	38	22	2	172	186	40	75	0	3	2	0	60	16	0	.267
1968 2 teams		DET	A	(14G 2–2)		CHI	A	(17G 0–2)											
" total	2	4	.333	4.37	31	0	0	55.2	62	27	27	0	2	4	2	12	1	0	.083
1969 2 teams		STL	N	(1G 0–0)		CIN	N	(7G 0–0)											
" total	0	0	–	2.79	8	0	0	9.2	10	4	7	0	0	0	0				
6 yrs.	24	29	.453	3.87	149	56	13	518.2	536	126	241	2	6	9	9	159	31	0	.195
1 yr.	2	2	.500	2.22	14	0	0	24.1	20	10	7	0	2	2	1	5	1	0	.200

Bruce Robbins

ROBBINS, BRUCE DUANE   BL TL 6'1"   190 lbs.
B. Sept. 10, 1959, Portland, Ind.

	W	L	PCT	ERA	G	GS	CG	IP	H	BB	SO	ShO	W	L	SV	AB	H	HR	BA
1979 DET A	3	3	.500	3.91	10	8	0	46	45	21	22	0	0	0	0	0	0	0	–
1980	4	2	.667	6.58	15	6	0	52	60	28	23	0	2	0	0	0	0	0	–
2 yrs.	7	5	.583	5.33	25	14	0	98	105	49	45	0	2	0	0	0	0	0	–
2 yrs.	7	5	.583	5.33	25	14	0	98	105	49	45	0	2	0	0	0	0	0	–

Dave Roberts

ROBERTS, DAVID ARTHUR   BL TL 6'3"   195 lbs.
B. Sept. 11, 1944, Gallipolis, Ohio

	W	L	PCT	ERA	G	GS	CG	IP	H	BB	SO	ShO	W	L	SV	AB	H	HR	BA
1969 SD N	0	3	.000	4.78	22	5	0	49	65	19	19	0	0	0	1	15	4	0	.267
1970	8	14	.364	3.81	43	21	3	182	182	43	102	2	4	0	1	59	9	2	.153
1971	14	17	.452	2.10	37	34	14	270	238	61	135	2	0	1	0	86	19	0	.221
1972 HOU N	12	7	.632	4.50	35	28	7	192	227	57	111	3	1	0	2	67	16	2	.239
1973	17	11	.607	2.85	39	36	12	249.1	264	62	119	6	0	0	0	85	11	0	.129
1974	10	12	.455	3.40	34	30	8	204	216	65	72	2	1	0	1	73	16	1	.219
1975	8	14	.364	4.27	32	27	7	198	182	73	101	0	2	0	1	63	9	0	.143
1976 DET A	16	17	.485	4.00	36	36	18	252	254	63	79	4	0	0	0	0	0	0	–
1977 2 teams		DET	A	(22G 4–10)		CHI	N	(17G 1–1)											
" total	5	11	.313	4.60	39	28	6	182	198	53	69	0	0	0	0	17	1	0	.059
1978 CHI N	6	8	.429	5.26	35	20	2	142	159	56	54	1	1	0	1	52	17	2	.327
1979 2 teams		SF	N	(26G 0–2)		PIT	N	(21G 5–2)											
" total	5	4	.556	2.90	47	4	0	80.2	89	30	38	0	5	2	4	10	0	0	.000
1980 2 teams		PIT	N	(2G 0–1)		SEA	A	(37G 2–3)											
" total	2	4	.333	4.39	39	4	0	82	88	28	48	0	0	2	3	0	0	0	–

	W	L	PCT	ERA	G	GS	CG	IP	H	BB	SO	ShO	Relief Pitching W	L	SV	BATTING AB	H	HR	BA

Dave Roberts continued

	W	L	PCT	ERA	G	GS	CG	IP	H	BB	SO	ShO	W	L	SV	AB	H	HR	BA
1981 NY N	0	3	.000	9.60	7	4	0	15	26	5	10	0	0	0	0	4	1	0	.250
13 yrs.	103	125	.452	3.78	445	277	77	2098	2188	615	957	20	14	5	15	531	103	7	.194
2 yrs.	20	27	.426	4.39	58	58	23	381	397	104	125	4	0	0	0	0	0	0	–

LEAGUE CHAMPIONSHIP SERIES

	W	L	PCT	ERA	G	GS	CG	IP	H	BB	SO	ShO	W	L	SV	AB	H	HR	BA
1979 PIT N	0	0	–	0.00	1	0	0		0	1	0	0	0	0	0	0	0	0	–

Leon Roberts

ROBERTS, LEON KAUFFMAN BR TR 6'3" 200 lbs.
B. Jan. 22, 1951, Vicksburg, Mich.

	W	L	PCT	ERA	G	GS	CG	IP	H	BB	SO	ShO	W	L	SV	AB	H	HR	BA
1984 KC A	0	0	–	27.00	1	0	0	1	4	1	1	0	0	0	0	*			

Jerry Robertson

ROBERTSON, JERRY LEE BR TR 6'2" 205 lbs.
B. Oct. 13, 1943, Winchester, Kans.

	W	L	PCT	ERA	G	GS	CG	IP	H	BB	SO	ShO	W	L	SV	AB	H	HR	BA
1969 MON N	5	16	.238	3.96	38	27	3	179.2	186	81	133	0	0	0	1	56	5	0	.089
1970 DET A	0	0	–	3.60	11	0	0	15	19	5	11	0	0	0	0	0	0	0	–
2 yrs.	5	16	.238	3.93	49	27	3	194.2	205	86	144	0	0	0	1	56	5	0	.089
1 yr.	0	0	–	3.60	11	0	0	15	19	5	11	0	0	0	0	0	0	0	–

Joe Rogalski

ROGALSKI, JOSEPH ANTHONY BR TR 6'2" 187 lbs.
B. July 15, 1912, Ashland, Wis. D. Nov. 20, 1951, Ashland, Wis.

	W	L	PCT	ERA	G	GS	CG	IP	H	BB	SO	ShO	W	L	SV	AB	H	HR	BA
1938 DET A	0	0	–	2.57	2	0	0	7	12	0	2	0	0	0	0	2	0	0	.000

Saul Rogovin

ROGOVIN, SAUL WALTER BR TR 6'2" 205 lbs.
B. Mar. 24, 1922, Brooklyn, N. Y.

	W	L	PCT	ERA	G	GS	CG	IP	H	BB	SO	ShO	W	L	SV	AB	H	HR	BA
1949 DET A	0	1	.000	14.29	5	0	0	5.2	13	7	2	0	0	1	0	0	0	0	–
1950	2	1	.667	4.50	11	5	1	40	39	26	11	0	1	0	0	16	3	1	.188
1951 2 teams						DET	A (5G 1-1)				CHI	A (22G 11-7)							
" total	12	8	.600	2.78	27	26	17	216.2	189	74	82	3	1	0	0	81	17	0	.210
1952 CHI A	14	9	.609	3.85	33	30	12	231.2	224	79	121	3	0	0	1	84	17	1	.202
1953	7	12	.368	5.22	22	19	4	131	151	48	62	1	1	0	1	37	5	0	.135
1955 2 teams						BAL	A (14G 1-8)				PHI	N (12G 5-3)							
total	6	11	.353	3.81	26	23	6	144	139	44	62	2	0	0	0	46	8	1	.174
1956 PHI N	7	6	.538	4.98	22	18	3	106.2	122	27	48	0	0	0	0	36	4	0	.111
1957	0	0	–	9.00	4	0	0	8	11	3	0	0	0	0	0	0	0	0	–
8 yrs.	48	48	.500	4.06	150	121	43	883.2	888	308	388	9	3	1	2	300	54	3	.180
3 yrs.	3	3	.500	5.56	21	9	1	69.2	75	40	18	0	2	1	0	23	5	1	.217

Jim Rooker

ROOKER, JAMES PHILLIP BR TL 6' 195 lbs.
B. Sept. 23, 1942, Lakeview, Ore.

	W	L	PCT	ERA	G	GS	CG	IP	H	BB	SO	ShO	W	L	SV	AB	H	HR	BA
1968 DET A	0	0	–	3.86	2	0	0	4.2	4	1	4	0	0	0	0	2	0	0	.000
1969 KC A	4	16	.200	3.75	28	22	8	158.1	136	73	108	1	0	1	0	57	16	4	.281
1970	10	15	.400	3.53	38	29	6	204	190	102	117	3	0	0	1	70	14	1	.200
1971	2	7	.222	5.33	20	7	1	54	59	24	31	1	0	1	0	10	0	0	.000
1972	5	6	.455	4.38	18	10	4	72	78	24	44	2	1	0	0	20	2	0	.100
1973 PIT N	10	6	.625	2.85	41	18	6	170.1	143	52	122	3	1	1	5	49	12	0	.245
1974	15	11	.577	2.77	33	33	15	263	228	83	139	1	0	0	0	95	29	0	.305
1975	13	11	.542	2.97	28	28	7	197	177	76	102	1	0	0	0	63	6	0	.095
1976	15	8	.652	3.35	30	29	10	198.2	201	72	92	1	0	0	1	74	16	1	.216
1977	14	9	.609	3.09	30	30	7	204	196	64	89	2	0	0	0	70	13	0	.186
1978	9	11	.450	4.25	28	28	1	163	160	81	76	0	0	0	0	56	9	0	.161
1979	4	7	.364	4.59	19	17	1	104	106	39	44	0	0	1	0	33	4	0	.121
1980	2	2	.500	3.50	4	4	0	18	16	12	8	0	0	0	0	7	1	1	.143
13 yrs.	103	109	.486	3.46	319	255	66	1811	1694	703	976	15	2	4	7	606	122	7	.201
1 yr.	0	0	–	3.86	2	0	0	4.2	4	1	4	0	0	0	0	2	0	0	.000

LEAGUE CHAMPIONSHIP SERIES

	W	L	PCT	ERA	G	GS	CG	IP	H	BB	SO	ShO	W	L	SV	AB	H	HR	BA
1974 PIT N	0	0	–	2.57	1	1	0	7	6	5	4	0	0	0	0	2	1	0	.500
1975	0	1	.000	9.00	1	1	0	4	7	0	5	0	0	0	0	1	0	0	.000
2 yrs.	0	1	.000	4.91	2	2	0	11	13	5	9	0	0	0	0	3	1	0	.333

WORLD SERIES

	W	L	PCT	ERA	G	GS	CG	IP	H	BB	SO	ShO	W	L	SV	AB	H	HR	BA
1979 PIT N	0	0	–	1.04	2	1	0	8.2	5	3	4	0	0	0	0	2	0	0	.000

Larry Rothschild

ROTHSCHILD, LAWRENCE LEE BR TR 6'2" 180 lbs.
B. Mar. 12, 1954, Chicago, Ill.

	W	L	PCT	ERA	G	GS	CG	IP	H	BB	SO	ShO	W	L	SV	AB	H	HR	BA
1981 DET A	0	0	–	1.50	5	0	0	6	4	6	1	0	0	0	1	0	0	0	–
1982	0	0	–	13.50	2	0	0	2.2	4	2	0	0	0	0	0	0	0	0	–
2 yrs.	0	0	–	5.19	7	0	0	8.2	8	8	1	0	0	0	1	0	0	0	–
2 yrs.	0	0	–	5.19	7	0	0	8.2	8	8	1	0	0	0	1	0	0	0	–

Jack Rowan

ROWAN, JOHN ALBERT BR TR 6'1" 210 lbs.
B. June 16, 1886, New Castle, Pa. D. Sept. 29, 1966, Dayton, Ohio

	W	L	PCT	ERA	G	GS	CG	IP	H	BB	SO	ShO	W	L	SV	AB	H	HR	BA
1906 DET A	0	1	.000	11.00	1	1	1	9	15	6	0	0	0	0	0	4	1	0	.250
1908 CIN N	3	3	.500	1.82	8	7	4	49.1	46	16	24	1	1	0	0	14	1	0	.071
1909	11	12	.478	2.79	38	23	14	225.2	185	104	81	0	3	0	0	65	6	0	.092
1910	14	13	.519	2.93	42	30	18	261	242	105	108	4	3	3	1	83	19	0	.229
1911 2 teams						PHI	N (12G 2-4)				CHI	N (1G 0-0)							
total	2	4	.333	4.72	13	6	2	47.2	60	22	17	0	0	1	0	14	1	0	.071
1913 CIN N	0	4	.000	3.00	5	5	5	39	37	9	21	0	0	0	0	11	2	0	.182
1914	1	3	.250	3.46	12	2	0	39	38	10	16	0	1	1	1	8	0	0	.000
7 yrs.	31	40	.437	3.07	119	74	44	670.2	623	272	267	5	8	5	2	199	30	0	.151
1 yr.	0	1		11.00	1	1	1	9	15	6	0	0	0	0	0	4	1	0	.250

Schoolboy Rowe

ROWE, LYNWOOD THOMAS BR TR 6'4½" 210 lbs.
B. Jan. 11, 1910, Waco, Tex. D. Jan. 8, 1961, El Dorado, Ark.

	W	L	PCT	ERA	G	GS	CG	IP	H	BB	SO	ShO	W	L	SV	AB	H	HR	BA
1933 DET A	7	4	.636	3.58	19	15	8	123.1	129	31	75	1	1	0	0	50	11	0	.220
1934	24	8	.750	3.45	45	30	20	266	259	81	149	4	6	1	1	109	33	2	.303

	W	L	PCT	ERA	G	GS	CG	IP	H	BB	SO	ShO	Relief Pitching W	L	SV	BATTING AB	H	HR	B.

Schoolboy Rowe *continued*

	W	L	PCT	ERA	G	GS	CG	IP	H	BB	SO	ShO	W	L	SV	AB	H	HR	B.
1935	19	13	.594	3.69	42	34	21	275.2	272	68	140	6	3	0	3	109	34	3	.31
1936	19	10	.655	4.51	41	35	19	245.1	266	64	115	4	1	0	3	90	23	1	.25
1937	1	4	.200	8.62	10	2	1	31.1	49	9	6	0	1	2	0	10	2	0	.20
1938	0	2	.000	3.00	4	3	0	21	20	11	4	0	0	0	0	6	1	0	.16
1939	10	12	.455	4.99	28	24	8	164	192	61	51	1	1	1	0	61	15	1	.24
1940	16	3	.842	3.46	27	23	11	169	170	43	61	1	1	0	0	67	18	1	.26
1941	8	6	.571	4.14	27	14	4	139	155	33	54	0	4	2	1	55	15	1	.27
1942 2 teams			DET	A	(2G	1–0)		BKN	N	(9G	1–0)								
" total	2	0	1.000	3.98	11	3	0	40.2	45	14	13	0	0	0	0	23	4	0	.17
1943 PHI N	14	8	.636	2.94	27	25	11	199	194	29	52	3	0	0	1	120	36	4	.30
1946	11	4	.733	2.12	17	16	9	136	112	21	51	2	0	0	0	61	11	1	.18
1947	14	10	.583	4.32	31	28	15	195.2	232	45	74	1	0	0	1	79	22	2	.27
1948	10	10	.500	4.07	30	20	8	148	167	31	46	0	1	2	2	52	10	1	.19
1949	3	7	.300	4.82	23	6	2	65.1	68	17	22	0	3	2	0	17	4	1	.23
15 yrs.	158	101	.610	3.87	382	278	137	2219.1	2330	558	913	23	22	10	12	*			
10 yrs.	105	62	.629	4.01	245	181	92	1445	1521	403	662	17	18	6	8	561	152	9	.27
				2nd											9th				

WORLD SERIES

	W	L	PCT	ERA	G	GS	CG	IP	H	BB	SO	ShO	W	L	SV	AB	H	HR	B.
1934 DET A	1	1	.500	2.95	3	2	2	21.1	19	0	12	0	0	0	0	7	0	0	.00
1935	1	2	.333	2.57	3	2	2	21	19	1	14	0	1	0	0	8	2	0	.25
1940	0	2	.000	17.18	2	2	0	3.2	12	1	1	0	0	0	0	1	0	0	.00
3 yrs.	2	5	.286	3.91	8	6	4	46	50	2	27	0	1	0	0	16	2	0	.12
				2nd															

Dave Rozema

ROZEMA, DAVID SCOTT
B. Aug. 5, 1956, Grand Rapids, Mich.   BR TR 6'4"   185 lbs

	W	L	PCT	ERA	G	GS	CG	IP	H	BB	SO	ShO	W	L	SV	AB	H	HR	B.
1977 DET A	15	7	.682	3.10	28	28	16	218	222	34	92	1	0	0	0	0	0	0	
1978	9	12	.429	3.14	28	28	11	209.1	205	41	57	2	0	0	0	0	0	0	
1979	4	4	.500	3.53	16	16	4	97	101	30	33	1	0	0	0	0	0	0	
1980	6	9	.400	3.91	42	13	2	145	152	49	49	1	2	4	4	0	0	0	
1981	5	5	.500	3.63	28	9	2	104	99	25	46	2	3	0	3	0	0	0	
1982	3	0	1.000	1.63	8	2	0	27.2	17	7	15	0	2	0	1	0	0	0	
1983	8	3	.727	3.43	29	16	1	105	100	29	63	0	1	0	2	0	0	0	
1984	7	6	.538	3.74	29	16	0	101	110	18	48	0	1	0	0	0	0	0	
8 yrs.	57	46	.553	3.38	208	128	36	1007	1006	233	403	7	8	5	10	0	0	0	
8 yrs.	57	46	.553	3.38	208	128	36	1007	1006	233	403	7	8	5	10	0	0	0	

Dave Rucker

RUCKER, DAVID MICHAEL
B. Sept. 1, 1957, San Bernardino, Calif.   BL TL 6'1"   185 lbs

	W	L	PCT	ERA	G	GS	CG	IP	H	BB	SO	ShO	W	L	SV	AB	H	HR	B.
1981 DET A	0	0	–	6.75	2	0	0	4	3	1	2	0	0	0	0	0	0	0	
1982	5	6	.455	3.38	27	4	1	64	62	23	31	0	4	4	0	0	0	0	
1983 2 teams			DET	A	(4G	1–2)		STL	N	(34G	5–3)								
" total	6	5	.545	5.28	38	3	0	46	54	26	28	0	5	4	0	4	0	0	.00
1984 STL N	2	3	.400	2.10	50	0	0	73	62	34	38	0	2	3	0	7	1	0	.14
4 yrs.	13	14	.481	3.42	117	7	1	187	181	84	99	0	11	11	0	11	1	0	.09
3 yrs.	6	8	.429	5.14	33	7	1	77	83	32	39	0	4	5	0	0	0	0	

Vern Ruhle

RUHLE, VERNON GERALD
B. Jan. 25, 1951, Coleman, Mich.   BR TR 6'1"   185 lbs

	W	L	PCT	ERA	G	GS	CG	IP	H	BB	SO	ShO	W	L	SV	AB	H	HR	B.
1974 DET A	2	0	1.000	2.73	5	3	1	33	35	6	10	0	0	0	0	0	0	0	
1975	11	12	.478	4.03	32	31	8	190	199	65	67	3	0	0	0	0	0	0	
1976	9	12	.429	3.92	32	32	5	200	227	59	88	1	0	0	0	0	0	0	
1977	3	5	.375	5.73	14	10	0	66	83	15	27	0	0	1	0	0	0	0	
1978 HOU N	3	3	.500	2.12	13	10	2	68	57	20	27	2	0	0	0	18	1	0	.05
1979	2	6	.250	4.09	13	10	2	66	64	8	33	2	0	1	0	19	1	0	.05
1980	12	4	.750	2.38	28	22	6	159	148	29	55	2	0	0	0	49	12	0	.24
1981	4	6	.400	2.91	20	15	1	102	97	20	39	0	0	1	1	24	6	0	.25
1982	9	13	.409	3.93	31	21	3	149	169	24	56	2	3	0	1	41	4	0	.09
1983	8	5	.615	3.69	41	9	0	114.2	107	36	43	0	7	3	3	19	2	0	.10
1984	1	9	.100	4.58	40	6	0	90.1	112	29	60	0	0	5	2	12	1	0	.08
11 yrs.	64	75	.460	3.66	269	169	28	1238	1298	311	505	12	10	11	7	182	27	0	.14
4 yrs.	25	29	.463	4.12	83	76	14	489	544	145	192	4	0	1	0	0	0	0	

DIVISIONAL PLAYOFF SERIES

	W	L	PCT	ERA	G	GS	CG	IP	H	BB	SO	ShO	W	L	SV	AB	H	HR	B.
1981 HOU N	0	1	.000	2.25	1	1	1	8	4	2	1	0	0	0	0	1	0	0	.00

LEAGUE CHAMPIONSHIP SERIES

	W	L	PCT	ERA	G	GS	CG	IP	H	BB	SO	ShO	W	L	SV	AB	H	HR	B.
1980 HOU N	0	0	–	3.86	1	1	0	7	8	1	3	0	0	0	0	3	0	0	.00

Jack Russell

RUSSELL, JACK ERWIN
B. Oct. 24, 1905, Paris, Tex.   BR TR 6'1½"   178 lbs

	W	L	PCT	ERA	G	GS	CG	IP	H	BB	SO	ShO	W	L	SV	AB	H	HR	B.
1926 BOS A	0	5	.000	3.58	36	5	1	98	94	24	17	0	0	0	0	21	4	0	.19
1927	4	9	.308	4.10	34	15	4	147	172	40	25	1	1	1	0	48	6	0	.12
1928	11	14	.440	3.84	32	26	10	201.1	233	41	27	2	1	0	0	62	13	0	.21
1929	6	18	.250	3.94	35	32	13	226.1	263	40	37	0	0	0	0	70	9	0	.12
1930	9	20	.310	5.45	35	30	15	229.2	302	53	35	0	0	0	0	79	14	1	.17
1931	10	18	.357	3.33	36	31	13	232	298	65	45	0	1	0	0	82	16	0	.19
1932 2 teams			BOS	A	(11G	1–7)		CLE	A	(18G	5–7)								
" total	6	14	.300	5.25	29	17	7	152.2	207	42	34	0	3	3	1	51	13	0	.25
1933 WAS A	12	6	.667	2.69	50	3	2	124	119	32	28	0	11	4	13	34	5	0	.14
1934	5	10	.333	4.17	54	9	3	157.2	179	56	38	0	2	7	7	44	7	0	.15
1935	4	9	.308	5.71	43	7	2	126	170	37	30	0	4	5	3	35	7	0	.20
1936 2 teams			WAS	A	(18G	3–2)		BOS	A	(23G	0–3)								
" total	3	5	.375	6.02	41	7	1	89.2	123	41	15	0	1	4	3	22	2	0	.09
1937 DET A	2	5	.286	7.59	25	0	0	40.1	63	20	10	0	2	5	4	7	0	0	.00
1938 CHI N	6	1	.857	3.34	42	0	0	102.1	100	30	29	0	6	1	3	32	7	0	.21
1939	4	3	.571	3.67	39	0	0	68.2	78	24	32	0	4	3	3	17	0	0	.00

	W	L	PCT	ERA	G	GS	CG	IP	H	BB	SO	ShO	Relief Pitching W	L	SV	BATTING AB	H	HR	BA

Jack Russell continued

	W	L	PCT	ERA	G	GS	CG	IP	H	BB	SO	ShO	W	L	SV	AB	H	HR	BA
'40 STL N	3	4	.429	2.50	26	0	0	54	53	26	16	0	3	4	1	13	0	0	.000
15 yrs.	85	141	.376	4.47	557	182	71	2049.2	2454	571	418	3	35	40	38	617	103	1	.167
1 yr.	2	5	.286	7.59	25	0	0	40.1	63	20	10	0	2	5	4	7	0	0	.000

WORLD SERIES

	W	L	PCT	ERA	G	GS	CG	IP	H	BB	SO	ShO	W	L	SV	AB	H	HR	BA
'33 WAS A	0	1	.000	0.87	3	0	0	10.1	8	0	7	0	0	1	0	2	0	0	.000
'38 CHI N	0	0	—	0.00	2	0	0	1.2	1	1	0	0	0	0	0	0	0	0	—
2 yrs.	0	1	.000	0.75	5	0	0	12	9	1	7	0	0	1	0	2	0	0	.000

Joe Samuels
SAMUELS, JOSEPH JONAS (Skabotch)   BR TR 6'1½" 196 lbs.
B. Mar. 21, 1905, Scranton, Pa.

	W	L	PCT	ERA	G	GS	CG	IP	H	BB	SO	ShO	W	L	SV	AB	H	HR	BA
'30 DET A	0	0	—	16.50	2	0	0	6	10	6	1	0	0	0	0	1	0	0	.000

Kevin Saucier
SAUCIER, KEVIN ANDREW   BR TL 6'1" 190 lbs.
B. Aug. 9, 1956, Pensacola, Fla.

	W	L	PCT	ERA	G	GS	CG	IP	H	BB	SO	ShO	W	L	SV	AB	H	HR	BA
'78 PHI N	0	1	.000	18.00	1	0	0	2	4	1	2	0	0	1	0	0	0	0	—
'79	1	4	.200	4.21	29	2	0	62	68	33	21	0	1	2	1	10	1	0	.100
'80	7	3	.700	3.42	40	0	0	50	50	20	25	0	7	3	0	8	0	0	.000
'81 DET A	4	2	.667	1.65	38	0	0	49	26	21	23	0	4	2	13	0	0	0	—
'82	3	1	.750	3.12	31	1	0	40.1	35	29	23	0	3	1	5	0	0	0	—
5 yrs.	15	11	.577	3.32	139	3	0	203.1	183	104	94	0	15	9	19	18	1	0	.056
2 yrs.	7	3	.700	2.32	69	1	0	89.1	61	50	46	0	7	3	18	0	0	0	—

LEAGUE CHAMPIONSHIP SERIES

	W	L	PCT	ERA	G	GS	CG	IP	H	BB	SO	ShO	W	L	SV	AB	H	HR	BA
'80 PHI N	0	0	—	0.00	2	0	0	.2	1	2	0	0	0	0	0	0	0	0	—

WORLD SERIES

	W	L	PCT	ERA	G	GS	CG	IP	H	BB	SO	ShO	W	L	SV	AB	H	HR	BA
'80 PHI N	0	0	—	0.00	1	0	0	.2	0	2	0	0	0	0	0	0	0	0	—

Dennis Saunders
SAUNDERS, DENNIS JAMES   BB TR 6'3" 195 lbs.
B. Jan. 4, 1949, Alhambra, Calif.

	W	L	PCT	ERA	G	GS	CG	IP	H	BB	SO	ShO	W	L	SV	AB	H	HR	BA
'70 DET A	1	1	.500	3.21	8	0	0	14	16	5	8	0	1	1	1	5	0	0	.000

Ray Scarborough
SCARBOROUGH, RAY WILSON   BR TR 6' 185 lbs.
B. July 23, 1917, Mt. Gilead, N. C.   D. July 1, 1982, Mount Olive, N. C.

	W	L	PCT	ERA	G	GS	CG	IP	H	BB	SO	ShO	W	L	SV	AB	H	HR	BA
'42 WAS A	2	1	.667	4.12	17	5	1	63.1	68	32	16	1	0	0	0	21	4	0	.190
'43	4	4	.500	2.83	24	6	2	86	93	46	43	0	2	2	3	24	8	0	.333
'46	7	11	.389	4.05	32	20	6	155.2	176	74	46	1	3	1	1	50	7	0	.140
'47	6	13	.316	3.41	33	18	8	161	165	67	63	2	1	2	0	50	6	0	.120
'48	15	8	.652	2.82	31	26	9	185.1	166	72	76	0	1	1	1	64	14	0	.219
'49	13	11	.542	4.60	34	27	11	199.2	204	88	81	1	3	0	0	67	13	0	.194
'50 2 teams		WAS	A (8G 3–5)		CHI	A (27G 10–13)													
total	13	18	.419	4.94	35	31	12	207.2	222	84	94	3	1	1	1	66	10	0	.152
'51 BOS A	12	9	.571	5.09	37	22	8	184	201	61	71	0	2	2	0	68	13	0	.191
'52 2 teams		BOS	A (28G 1–5)		NY	A (9G 5–1)													
total	6	6	.500	4.23	37	12	2	110.2	106	50	42	1	2	1	4	32	9	0	.281
'53 2 teams		NY	A (25G 2–2)		DET	A (13G 0–2)													
total	2	4	.333	4.66	38	1	0	75.1	86	37	32	0	1	4	4	14	1	1	.071
10 yrs.	80	85	.485	4.13	318	168	59	1428.2	1487	611	564	9	16	14	14	456	85	1	.186
1 yr.	0	2	.000	8.27	13	0	0	20.2	34	11	12	0	0	2	2	2	0	0	.000

WORLD SERIES

	W	L	PCT	ERA	G	GS	CG	IP	H	BB	SO	ShO	W	L	SV	AB	H	HR	BA
'52 NY A	0	0	—	9.00	1	0	0	1	1	1	0	0	1	0	0	0	0	0	—

Germany Schaefer
SCHAEFER, HERMAN A.   BR TR
B. Feb. 4, 1878, Chicago, Ill.   D. May 16, 1919, Saranac Lake, N. Y.

	W	L	PCT	ERA	G	GS	CG	IP	H	BB	SO	ShO	W	L	SV	AB	H	HR	BA
'12 WAS A	0	0	—	0.00	1	0	0	.2	1	0	0	0	0	0	0	166	41	0	.247
'13	0	0	—	54.00	1	0	0	.1	2	0	0	0	0	0	0	100	32	0	.320
2 yrs.	0	0	—	18.00	2	0	0	1	3	0	0	0	0	0	0	*			

Dan Schatzeder
SCHATZEDER, DANIEL ERNEST   BL TL 6' 185 lbs.
B. Dec. 1, 1954, Elmhurst, Ill.

	W	L	PCT	ERA	G	GS	CG	IP	H	BB	SO	ShO	W	L	SV	AB	H	HR	BA
'77 MON N	2	1	.667	2.45	6	3	1	22	16	13	14	1	0	0	0	6	2	0	.333
'78	7	7	.500	3.06	29	18	2	144	108	68	69	0	2	0	0	45	10	1	.222
'79	10	5	.667	2.83	32	21	3	162	136	59	106	0	1	1	1	51	11	1	.216
'80 DET A	11	13	.458	4.01	32	26	9	193	178	58	94	2	2	0	0	0	0	0	—
'81	6	8	.429	6.08	17	14	1	71	74	29	20	0	0	0	0	0	0	0	—
'82 2 teams		SF	N (13G 1–4)		MON	N (26G 0–2)													
total	1	6	.143	5.32	39	4	0	69.1	84	24	33	0	1	3	0	13	3	0	.231
'83 MON N	5	2	.714	3.21	58	2	0	87	88	25	48	0	4	1	2	10	2	0	.200
'84	7	7	.500	2.71	36	14	1	136	112	36	89	1	1	1	1	35	11	0	.314
8 yrs.	49	49	.500	3.59	249	102	17	884.1	796	312	473	4	11	6	4	160	39	2	.244
2 yrs.	17	21	.447	4.57	49	40	10	264	252	87	114	2	2	0	0	0	0	0	—

Frank Scheibeck
SCHEIBECK, FRANK S.   BR TR 5'7" 145 lbs.
B. June 28, 1865, Detroit, Mich.   D. Oct. 22, 1956, Detroit, Mich.

	W	L	PCT	ERA	G	GS	CG	IP	H	BB	SO	ShO	W	L	SV	AB	H	HR	BA
'87 CLE AA	0	1	.000	12.00	1	1	1	9	17	4	3	0	0	0	0	*			

Fred Scherman
SCHERMAN, FREDERICK JOHN   BL TL 6'1" 195 lbs.
B. July 25, 1944, Dayton, Ohio

	W	L	PCT	ERA	G	GS	CG	IP	H	BB	SO	ShO	W	L	SV	AB	H	HR	BA
'69 DET A	1	0	1.000	6.75	4	0	0	4	6	0	3	0	1	0	0	0	0	0	—
'70	4	4	.500	3.21	48	0	0	70	61	28	58	0	4	4	1	12	2	0	.167
'71	11	6	.647	2.71	69	1	1	113	91	49	46	0	10	6	20	24	5	0	.208
'72	7	3	.700	3.64	57	3	0	94	91	53	53	0	7	1	12	22	2	0	.091
'73	2	2	.500	4.21	34	0	0	62	59	30	28	0	2	2	1	0	0	0	—
'74 HOU N	2	5	.286	4.13	53	0	0	61	67	26	35	0	2	5	4	3	0	0	.000

	W	L	PCT	ERA	G	GS	CG	IP	H	BB	SO	ShO	W	L	SV	AB	H	HR	B
													Relief Pitching			BATTING			

Fred Scherman continued

	W	L	PCT	ERA	G	GS	CG	IP	H	BB	SO	ShO	W	L	SV	AB	H	HR	B
1975 2 teams	HOU N (16G 0–1)				MON N (34G 4–3)														
" total	4	4	.500	3.79	50	7	0	92.2	105	45	56	0	4	1	0	17	1	0	.05
1976 MON N	2	2	.500	4.95	31	0	0	40	42	14	18	0	2	2	1	4	1	0	.25
8 yrs.	33	26	.559	3.66	346	11	1	536.2	522	245	297	0	32	21	39	82	11	0	.13
5 yrs.	25	15	.625	3.38	212	4	1	343	308	160	188	0	24	13	34	58	9	0	.15
													6th		7th				

LEAGUE CHAMPIONSHIP SERIES

	W	L	PCT	ERA	G	GS	CG	IP	H	BB	SO	ShO	W	L	SV	AB	H	HR	B
1972 DET A	0	0	—	0.00	1	0	0	.2	1	0	1	0	0	0	0	0	0	0	

Bill Scherrer

SCHERRER, WILLIAM JOSEPH
B. Jan. 20, 1958, Tonawanda, N. Y. — BL TL 6'4" 180 lbs

	W	L	PCT	ERA	G	GS	CG	IP	H	BB	SO	ShO	W	L	SV	AB	H	HR	B
1982 CIN N	0	1	.000	2.60	5	2	0	17.1	17	0	7	0	0	0	0	2	1	0	.50
1983	2	3	.400	2.74	73	0	0	92	73	33	57	0	2	3	10	11	1	0	.09
1984 2 teams	CIN N (36G 1–1)				DET A (18G 1–0)														
" total	2	1	.667	4.16	54	0	0	71.1	78	23	51	0	2	1	1	3	0	0	.00
3 yrs.	4	5	.444	3.29	132	2	0	180.2	168	56	115	0	4	4	11	16	2	0	.12
1 yr.	1	0	1.000	1.89	18	0	0	19	14	8	16	0	1	0	0	0	0	0	

WORLD SERIES

	W	L	PCT	ERA	G	GS	CG	IP	H	BB	SO	ShO	W	L	SV	AB	H	HR	B
1984 DET A	0	0	—	3.00	3	0	0	3	5	0	0	0	0	0	0	0	0	0	

Barney Schultz

SCHULTZ, GEORGE WARREN
B. Aug. 15, 1926, Beverly, N. J. — BR TR 6'2" 200 lbs

	W	L	PCT	ERA	G	GS	CG	IP	H	BB	SO	ShO	W	L	SV	AB	H	HR	B
1955 STL N	1	2	.333	7.89	19	0	0	29.2	28	15	19	0	1	2	4	4	0	0	.00
1959 DET A	1	2	.333	4.42	13	0	0	18.1	17	14	17	0	1	2	0	2	2	0	1.00
1961 CHI N	7	6	.538	2.70	41	0	0	66.2	57	25	59	0	7	6	7	10	1	0	.00
1962	5	5	.500	3.82	51	0	0	77.2	66	23	58	0	5	5	5	5	0	0	.00
1963 2 teams	CHI N (15G 1–0)				STL N (24G 2–0)														
" total	3	0	1.000	3.59	39	0	0	62.2	61	17	44	0	3	0	3	4	0	0	.00
1964 STL N	1	3	.250	1.64	30	0	0	49.1	35	11	29	0	1	3	14	6	1	0	.16
1965	2	2	.500	3.83	34	0	0	42.1	39	11	38	0	2	2	2	2	0	0	.00
7 yrs.	20	20	.500	3.63	227	0	0	346.2	303	116	264	0	20	20	35	33	4	0	.12
1 yr.	1	2	.333	4.42	13	0	0	18.1	17	14	17	0	1	2	0	2	2	0	1.00

WORLD SERIES

	W	L	PCT	ERA	G	GS	CG	IP	H	BB	SO	ShO	W	L	SV	AB	H	HR	B
1964 STL N	0	1	.000	18.00	4	0	0	4	9	3	1	0	0	1	1	1	0	0	.00

Bob Schultz

SCHULTZ, ROBERT DUFFY (Bill)
B. Nov. 27, 1923, Louisville, Ky.   D. Mar. 31, 1979, Nashville, Tenn. — BR TL 6'3" 200 lbs

	W	L	PCT	ERA	G	GS	CG	IP	H	BB	SO	ShO	W	L	SV	AB	H	HR	B
1951 CHI N	3	6	.333	5.24	17	10	2	77.1	75	51	27	0	1	0	0	29	4	0	.13
1952	6	3	.667	4.01	29	5	1	74	63	51	31	0	4	0	0	18	4	0	.22
1953 2 teams	CHI N (7G 0–2)				PIT N (11G 0–2)														
" total	0	4	.000	7.12	18	4	0	30.1	39	21	9	0	0	0	0	5	0	0	.00
1955 DET A	0	0	—	20.25	1	0	0	1.1	2	2	0	0	0	0	0	0	0	0	
4 yrs.	9	13	.409	5.16	65	19	3	183	179	125	67	0	5	0	0	52	8	0	.15
1 yr.	0	0	—	20.25	1	0	0	1.1	2	2	0	0	0	0	0	0	0	0	

Johnnie Seale

SEALE, JOHNNY RAY (Durango Kid)
B. Nov. 14, 1938, Edgewater, Colo. — BL TL 5'10" 155 lbs

	W	L	PCT	ERA	G	GS	CG	IP	H	BB	SO	ShO	W	L	SV	AB	H	HR	B
1964 DET A	1	0	1.000	3.60	4	0	0	10	6	4	5	0	1	0	0	1	0	0	.00
1965	0	0	—	12.00	4	0	0	3	7	2	3	0	0	0	0	0	0	0	
2 yrs.	1	0	1.000	5.54	8	0	0	13	13	6	8	0	1	0	0	1	0	0	.00
2 yrs.	1	0	1.000	5.54	8	0	0	13	13	6	8	0	1	0	0	1	0	0	

Tom Seats

SEATS, THOMAS EDWARD
B. Sept. 24, 1911, Farmington, N. C. — BR TL 5'11" 190 lbs
BB 1940

	W	L	PCT	ERA	G	GS	CG	IP	H	BB	SO	ShO	W	L	SV	AB	H	HR	B
1940 DET A	2	2	.500	4.69	26	2	0	55.2	67	21	25	0	2	1	1	12	1	0	.08
1945 BKN N	10	7	.588	4.36	31	18	6	121.2	127	37	44	2	2	1	0	43	9	0	.20
2 yrs.	12	9	.571	4.47	57	20	6	177.1	194	58	69	2	4	2	1	55	10	0	.18
1 yr.	2	2	.500	4.69	26	2	0	55.2	67	21	25	0	2	1	1	12	1	0	.08

Chuck Seelbach

SEELBACH, CHARLES FREDERICK III
B. Mar. 20, 1948, Lakewood, Ohio — BR TR 6' 180 lbs

	W	L	PCT	ERA	G	GS	CG	IP	H	BB	SO	ShO	W	L	SV	AB	H	HR	B
1971 DET A	0	0	—	13.50	5	0	0	4	6	7	1	0	0	0	0	0	0	0	
1972	9	8	.529	2.89	61	3	0	112	96	39	76	0	9	5	14	21	3	0	.14
1973	1	0	1.000	3.86	5	0	0	7	7	2	2	0	1	0	0	0	0	0	
1974	0	0	—	4.50	4	0	0	8	9	3	0	0	0	0	0	0	0	0	
4 yrs.	10	8	.556	3.37	75	3	0	131	118	51	79	0	10	5	14	21	3	0	.14
4 yrs.	10	8	.556	3.37	75	3	0	131	118	51	79	0	10	5	14	21	3	0	.14

LEAGUE CHAMPIONSHIP SERIES

	W	L	PCT	ERA	G	GS	CG	IP	H	BB	SO	ShO	W	L	SV	AB	H	HR	B
1972 DET A	0	0	—	18.00	2	0	0	1	4	0	0	0	0	0	0	0	0	0	

Ray Semproch

SEMPROCH, ROMAN ANTHONY (Baby)
B. Jan. 7, 1931, Cleveland, Ohio — BR TR 5'11" 180 lbs

	W	L	PCT	ERA	G	GS	CG	IP	H	BB	SO	ShO	W	L	SV	AB	H	HR	B
1958 PHI N	13	11	.542	3.92	36	30	12	204.1	211	58	92	2	2	2	0	74	7	0	.09
1959	3	10	.231	5.40	30	18	2	111.2	119	59	54	0	1	0	3	34	6	0	.17
1960 DET A	3	0	1.000	4.00	17	0	0	27	29	16	9	0	3	0	0	4	0	0	.00
1961 LA A	0	0	—	9.00	2	0	0	1	1	3	1	0	0	0	0	0	0	0	
4 yrs.	19	21	.475	4.42	85	48	14	344	360	136	156	2	6	2	3	112	13	0	.11
1 yr.	3	0	1.000	4.00	17	0	0	27	29	16	9	0	3	0	0	4	0	0	.00

Rip Sewell

SEWELL, TRUETT BANKS
B. May 11, 1907, Decatur, Ala. — BR TR 6'1" 180 lbs.

	W	L	PCT	ERA	G	GS	CG	IP	H	BB	SO	ShO	W	L	SV	AB	H	HR	B
1932 DET A	0	0	—	12.66	5	0	0	10.2	19	8	2	0	0	0	0	2	1	0	.00
1938 PIT N	0	1	.000	4.23	17	0	0	38.1	41	21	17	0	0	1	1	12	1	0	.08
1939	10	9	.526	4.08	52	12	5	176.1	177	73	69	1	4	3	2	55	11	1	.20
1940	16	5	.762	2.80	33	23	14	189.2	169	67	60	2	3	1	1	73	14	1	.19

	W	L	PCT	ERA	G	GS	CG	IP	H	BB	SO	ShO	Relief Pitching W	L	SV	BATTING AB	H	HR	BA

Rip Sewell continued

	W	L	PCT	ERA	G	GS	CG	IP	H	BB	SO	ShO	W	L	SV	AB	H	HR	BA
'41	14	**17**	.452	3.72	39	32	18	249	225	84	76	2	2	0	2	92	16	1	.174
'42	17	15	.531	3.41	40	33	18	248	259	72	69	5	2	2	2	87	13	0	.149
'43	**21**	9	.700	2.54	35	31	**25**	265.1	267	75	65	2	0	1	3	105	30	0	.286
'44	21	12	.636	3.18	38	33	24	286	263	99	87	3	3	0	2	112	25	1	.223
'45	11	9	.550	4.07	33	24	9	188	212	91	60	1	2	1	1	64	20	0	.313
'46	8	12	.400	3.68	25	20	11	149.1	140	53	33	2	1	1	0	50	9	0	.180
'47	6	4	.600	3.57	24	12	4	121	121	36	36	1	2	0	0	40	5	1	.125
'48	13	3	.813	3.48	21	17	7	121.2	126	37	36	0	2	0	0	42	6	1	.143
'49	6	1	.857	3.91	28	6	2	76	82	32	26	1	4	1	1	16	1	0	.063
13 yrs.	143	97	.596	3.48	390	243	137	2119.1	2101	748	636	20	25	11	15	750	152	6	.203
1 yr.	0	0	–	12.66	5	0	0	10.2	19	8	2	0	0	0	0	2	1	0	.500

Bob Shaw

SHAW, ROBERT JOHN   BR TR 6'2"   195 lbs.
B. June 29, 1933, New York, N. Y.

	W	L	PCT	ERA	G	GS	CG	IP	H	BB	SO	ShO	W	L	SV	AB	H	HR	BA
'57 DET A	0	1	.000	7.45	7	0	0	9.2	11	7	4	0	0	1	0	2	0	0	.000
'58 2 teams					DET A (11G 1–2)			CHI A (29G 4–2)											
" total	5	4	.556	4.76	40	5	0	90.2	99	41	35	0	5	1	1	22	3	0	.136
'59 CHI A	18	6	.750	2.69	47	26	8	230.2	217	54	89	3	2	0	3	73	9	0	.123
'60	13	13	.500	4.06	36	32	7	192.2	221	62	46	1	1	1	0	58	8	0	.138
'61 2 teams					CHI A (14G 3–4)			KC A (26G 9–10)											
" total	12	14	.462	4.14	40	34	9	221.2	250	78	91	0	1	0	0	73	11	0	.151
'62 MIL N	15	9	.625	2.80	38	29	12	225	223	44	124	3	1	0	2	73	10	0	.137
'63	7	11	.389	2.66	48	16	3	159	144	55	105	3	3	5	13	41	5	0	.122
'64 SF N	7	6	.538	3.76	61	1	0	93.1	105	31	57	0	7	5	11	13	0	0	.000
'65	16	9	.640	2.64	42	33	6	235	213	53	148	1	1	1	2	79	8	0	.101
'66 2 teams					SF N (13G 1–4)			NY N (26G 11–10)											
" total	12	14	.462	4.29	39	31	7	199.1	216	49	125	2	0	1	0	56	13	0	.232
'67 2 teams					NY N (23G 3–9)			CHI N (9G 0–2)											
" total	3	11	.214	4.61	32	16	3	121	138	37	56	1	1	2	0	29	2	0	.069
11 yrs.	108	98	.524	3.52	430	223	55	1778	1837	511	880	14	22	17	32	519	69	0	.133
2 yrs.	1	3	.250	5.70	18	2	0	36.1	43	20	21	0	1	1	0	10	3	0	.300

WORLD SERIES

	W	L	PCT	ERA	G	GS	CG	IP	H	BB	SO	ShO	W	L	SV	AB	H	HR	BA
'59 CHI A	1	1	.500	2.57	2	2	0	14	17	2	2	0	0	0	0	4	1	0	.250

Larry Sherry

SHERRY, LAWRENCE   BR TR 6'2"   180 lbs.
Brother of Norm Sherry.
B. July 25, 1935, Los Angeles, Calif.

	W	L	PCT	ERA	G	GS	CG	IP	H	BB	SO	ShO	W	L	SV	AB	H	HR	BA
'58 LA N	0	0	–	12.46	5	0	0	4.1	10	7	2	0	0	0	0	0	0	0	–
'59	7	2	.778	2.19	23	9	1	94.1	75	43	72	1	2	0	3	32	7	2	.219
'60	14	10	.583	3.79	57	3	1	142.1	125	82	114	0	13	8	7	37	6	1	.162
'61	4	4	.500	3.90	53	1	0	94.2	90	39	79	0	4	3	15	13	2	0	.154
'62	7	3	.700	3.20	58	0	0	90	81	44	71	0	7	3	11	17	2	0	.118
'63	2	6	.250	3.73	36	3	0	79.2	82	24	47	0	2	4	3	9	1	0	.111
'64 DET A	7	5	.583	3.66	38	0	0	66.1	52	37	58	0	7	5	11	14	0	0	.000
'65	3	6	.333	3.10	39	0	0	78.1	71	40	46	0	3	6	5	10	3	0	.300
'66	8	5	.615	3.82	55	0	0	77.2	66	36	63	0	8	5	20	10	4	0	.400
'67 2 teams					DET A (20G 0–1)			HOU N (29G 1–2)											
" total	1	3	.250	5.50	49	0	0	68.2	88	20	52	0	1	3	7	6	0	0	.000
'68 CAL A	0	0	–	6.00	3	0	0	3	7	2	2	0	0	0	0	0	0	0	–
11 yrs.	53	44	.546	3.67	416	16	2	799.1	747	374	606	1	47	37	82	148	25	3	.169
4 yrs.	18	17	.514	3.85	152	0	0	250.1	224	120	187	0	18	17	37	35	7	0	.200
													9th	6th					

WORLD SERIES

	W	L	PCT	ERA	G	GS	CG	IP	H	BB	SO	ShO	W	L	SV	AB	H	HR	BA
'59 LA N	2	0	1.000	0.71	4	0	0	12.2	8	2	5	0	2	0	2	4	2	0	.500

Ed Siever

SIEVER, EDWARD T.   BL TL 6'
B. Apr. 2, 1877, Goodard, Kans.   D. Feb. 4, 1920, Detroit, Mich.

	W	L	PCT	ERA	G	GS	CG	IP	H	BB	SO	ShO	W	L	SV	AB	H	HR	BA
'01 DET A	18	15	.545	3.24	38	33	30	288.2	334	65	85	2	1	1	0	107	18	0	.168
'02	8	11	.421	1.91	25	23	17	188.1	166	32	36	4	0	0	1	66	10	0	.152
'03 STL A	13	14	.481	2.48	31	27	24	254	245	39	90	1	1	0	0	93	13	0	.140
'04	10	15	.400	2.65	29	24	19	217	235	65	77	2	1	1	0	71	11	0	.155
'06 DET A	14	11	.560	2.71	30	25	20	222.2	240	45	71	1	1	0	0	77	12	0	.156
'07	18	11	.621	2.16	39	33	22	274.2	256	52	88	3	1	0	1	91	14	0	.154
'08	2	6	.250	3.50	11	9	4	61.2	74	13	23	1	0	1	0	18	3	0	.167
7 yrs.	83	83	.500	2.60	203	174	136	1507	1550	311	470	14	5	3	2	523	81	0	.155
5 yrs.	60	54	.526	2.61	143	123	93	1036	1070	207	303	11	3	2	2	359	57	0	.159
				5th															

WORLD SERIES

	W	L	PCT	ERA	G	GS	CG	IP	H	BB	SO	ShO	W	L	SV	AB	H	HR	BA
'07 DET A	0	1	.000	4.50	1	1	0	4	7	0	1	0	0	0	0	1	0	0	.000

Dave Sisler

SISLER, DAVID MICHAEL   BR TR 6'4"   200 lbs.
Son of George Sisler.   Brother of Dick Sisler.
B. Oct. 16, 1931, St. Louis, Mo.

	W	L	PCT	ERA	G	GS	CG	IP	H	BB	SO	ShO	W	L	SV	AB	H	HR	BA
'56 BOS A	9	8	.529	4.62	39	14	3	142.1	120	72	93	0	3	3	3	42	5	0	.119
'57	7	8	.467	4.71	22	19	5	122.1	135	61	55	0	0	0	1	42	7	0	.167
'58	8	9	.471	4.94	30	25	4	149.1	157	79	71	1	1	1	0	46	9	0	.196
'59 2 teams					BOS A (3G 0–0)			DET A (32G 1–3)											
total	1	3	.250	4.32	35	0	0	58.1	55	37	32	0	1	3	7	7	2	0	.286
'60 DET A	7	5	.583	2.48	41	0	0	80	56	45	47	0	7	5	6	16	2	0	.125
'61 WAS A	2	8	.200	4.18	45	1	0	60.1	55	48	30	0	2	7	11	6	0	0	.000
'62 CIN N	4	3	.571	3.92	35	0	0	43.2	44	26	27	0	4	3	1	0	0	0	–
7 yrs.	38	44	.463	4.33	247	59	12	656.1	622	368	355	1	18	22	29	159	25	0	.157
2 yrs.	8	8	.500	3.08	73	0	0	131.2	102	81	76	0	8	8	13	21	3	0	.143

	W	L	PCT	ERA	G	GS	CG	IP	H	BB	SO	ShO	Relief Pitching W	L	SV	BATTING AB	H	HR	B

Dave Skeels

SKEELS, DAVID
B. Dec. 29, 1892, Wash.　D. Dec. 3, 1926, Spokane, Wash.　　BL TR 6'1"　187 lb

	W	L	PCT	ERA	G	GS	CG	IP	H	BB	SO	ShO	W	L	SV	AB	H	HR	B
1910 DET A	1	0	1.000	12.00	1	1	0	6	9	4	2	0	0	0	0	3	0	0	.00

John Skopec

SKOPEC, JOHN S. (Buckshot)
B. May 8, 1880, Chicago, Ill.　D. Oct. 12, 1912, Chicago, Ill.　　BL TL 5'10"　190 lb

	W	L	PCT	ERA	G	GS	CG	IP	H	BB	SO	ShO	W	L	SV	AB	H	HR	B
1901 CHI A	6	3	.667	3.16	9	9	6	68.1	62	45	24	0	0	0	0	30	10	1	.3.
1903 DET A	2	2	.500	3.43	6	5	3	39.1	46	13	14	0	0	0	0	13	2	0	.1.
2 yrs.	8	5	.615	3.26	15	14	9	107.2	108	58	38	0	0	0	0	43	12	1	.2.
1 yr.	2	2	.500	3.43	6	5	3	39.1	46	13	14	0	0	0	0	13	2	0	.1.

Jim Slaton

SLATON, JAMES MICHAEL
B. June 19, 1950, Long Beach, Calif.　　BR TR 6'　185 lb

	W	L	PCT	ERA	G	GS	CG	IP	H	BB	SO	ShO	W	L	SV	AB	H	HR	B
1971 MIL A	10	8	.556	3.77	26	23	5	148	140	71	63	4	0	0	0	46	5	0	.10
1972	1	6	.143	5.52	9	8	0	44	50	21	17	0	0	1	0	11	1	0	.09
1973	13	15	.464	3.71	38	38	13	276.1	266	99	134	3	0	0	0	0	0	0	
1974	13	16	.448	3.92	40	35	10	250	255	102	126	3	1	0	0	0	0	0	
1975	11	18	.379	4.52	37	33	10	217	238	90	119	3	0	0	0	0	0	0	
1976	14	15	.483	3.44	38	38	12	292.2	287	94	138	2	0	0	0	0	0	0	
1977	10	14	.417	3.58	32	31	7	221	223	77	104	1	0	0	0	0	0	0	
1978 DET A	17	11	.607	4.12	35	34	11	233.2	235	85	92	2	0	1	0	0	0	0	
1979 MIL A	15	9	.625	3.63	32	31	12	213	229	54	80	3	0	0	0	0	0	0	
1980	1	1	.500	4.50	3	3	0	16	17	5	4	0	0	0	0	0	0	0	
1981	5	7	.417	4.38	24	21	0	117	120	50	47	0	0	0	0	0	0	0	
1982	10	6	.625	3.29	39	7	0	117.2	117	41	59	0	7	4	6	0	0	0	
1983	14	6	.700	4.33	46	0	0	112.1	112	56	38	0	14	6	5	0	0	0	
1984 CAL A	7	10	.412	4.97	32	22	5	163	192	56	67	1	1	0	0	0	0	0	
14 yrs.	141	142	.498	3.96	431	324	85	2421.2	2481	901	1088	22	23	12	11	57	6	0	.1(
1 yr.	17	11	.607	4.12	35	34	11	233.2	235	85	92	2	0	1	0	0	0	0	

DIVISIONAL PLAYOFF SERIES

	W	L	PCT	ERA	G	GS	CG	IP	H	BB	SO	ShO	W	L	SV	AB	H	HR	B
1981 MIL A	0	0	—	3.00	4	0	0	6	6	0	2	0	0	0	0	0	0	0	

LEAGUE CHAMPIONSHIP SERIES

	W	L	PCT	ERA	G	GS	CG	IP	H	BB	SO	ShO	W	L	SV	AB	H	HR	B
1982 MIL A	0	0	—	1.93	2	0	0	4.2	3	1	3	0	0	0	1	0	0	0	

WORLD SERIES

	W	L	PCT	ERA	G	GS	CG	IP	H	BB	SO	ShO	W	L	SV	AB	H	HR	B
1982 MIL A	1	0	1.000	0.00	2	0	0	2.2	1	2	1	0	1	0	0	0	0	0	

Bill Slayback

SLAYBACK, WILLIAM GROVER
B. Feb. 21, 1948, Hollywood, Calif.　　BR TR 6'4"　200 lb

	W	L	PCT	ERA	G	GS	CG	IP	H	BB	SO	ShO	W	L	SV	AB	H	HR	B
1972 DET A	5	6	.455	3.18	23	13	3	82	74	25	65	1	1	0	0	23	4	0	.1.
1973	0	0	—	4.50	3	0	0	2	5	0	1	0	0	0	0	0	0	0	
1974	1	3	.250	4.75	16	4	0	55	57	26	23	0	0	0	0	0	0	0	
3 yrs.	6	9	.400	3.82	42	17	3	139	136	51	89	1	1	0	0	23	4	0	.1.
3 yrs.	6	9	.400	3.82	42	17	3	139	136	51	89	1	1	0	0	23	4	0	.1.

Lou Sleater

SLEATER, LOUIS MORTIMER
B. Sept. 8, 1926, St. Louis, Mo.　　BL TL 5'10"　185 lb

	W	L	PCT	ERA	G	GS	CG	IP	H	BB	SO	ShO	W	L	SV	AB	H	HR	B
1950 STL A	0	0	—	0.00	1	0	0	1	0	1	0	0	0	0	0	0	0	0	
1951	1	9	.100	5.11	20	8	4	81	88	53	33	0	1	1	1	31	7	0	.2.
1952 2 teams					STL	A	(4G 0–1)		WAS	A	(14G 4–2)									
" total	4	3	.571	4.11	18	11	3	65.2	65	35	23	1	1	0	0	22	1	0	.0.
1955 KC A	1	1	.500	7.71	16	1	0	25.2	33	21	11	0	1	0	0	13	2	0	.1
1956 MIL N	2	2	.500	3.15	25	1	0	45.2	42	27	32	0	2	2	2	10	5	0	.5.
1957 DET A	3	3	.500	3.76	41	0	0	69.1	61	28	43	0	3	3	2	20	5	3	.2
1958 2 teams					DET	A	(4G 0–0)		BAL	A	(6G 1–0)									
" total	1	0	1.000	10.22	10	0	0	12.1	17	8	9	0	1	0	0	7	1	1	.1.
7 yrs.	12	18	.400	4.70	131	21	7	300.2	306	172	152	1	9	6	5	103	21	4	.2(
2 yrs.	3	3	.500	3.98	45	0	0	74.2	64	34	47	0	3	3	2	21	6	4	.2(

Bob Smith

SMITH, ROBERT GILCHRIST
B. Feb. 1, 1931, Woodsville, N. H.　　BR TL 6'1½"　190 lb

	W	L	PCT	ERA	G	GS	CG	IP	H	BB	SO	ShO	W	L	SV	AB	H	HR	B
1955 BOS A	0	0	—	0.00	1	0	0	1.2	1	1	1	0	0	0	0	0	0	0	
1957 2 teams					STL	N	(6G 0–0)		PIT	N	(20G 2–4)									
" total	2	4	.333	3.34	26	4	2	64.2	60	31	46	0	0	3	1	15	1	0	.0.
1958 PIT N	2	2	.500	4.43	35	4	0	61	61	31	24	0	2	0	1	11	1	0	.0.
1959 2 teams					PIT	N	(20G 0–0)		DET	A	(9G 0–3)									
" total	0	3	.000	4.81	29	0	0	39.1	52	20	22	0	0	3	0	3	0	0	.0(
4 yrs.	4	9	.308	4.05	91	8	2	166.2	174	83	93	0	2	6	2	29	2	0	.0(
1 yr.	0	3	.000	8.18	9	0	0	11	20	3	10	0	0	3	0	1	0	0	.0(

Clay Smith

SMITH, CLAY JAMIESON
B. Sept. 11, 1914, Cambridge, Kans.　　BR TR 6'2"　190 lb

	W	L	PCT	ERA	G	GS	CG	IP	H	BB	SO	ShO	W	L	SV	AB	H	HR	B
1938 CLE A	0	0	—	6.55	4	0	0	11	18	2	3	0	0	0	0	4	0	0	.0(
1940 DET A	1	1	.500	5.08	14	1	0	28.1	32	13	14	0	1	0	0	7	0	0	.0(
2 yrs.	1	1	.500	5.49	18	1	0	39.1	50	15	17	0	1	0	0	11	0	0	.0(
1 yr.	1	1	.500	5.08	14	1	0	28.1	32	13	14	0	1	0	0	7	0	0	.0(

WORLD SERIES

	W	L	PCT	ERA	G	GS	CG	IP	H	BB	SO	ShO	W	L	SV	AB	H	HR	B
1940 DET A	0	0	—	2.25	1	0	0	4	1	3	1	0	0	0	0	1	0	0	

George Smith

SMITH, GEORGE SELBY
B. Oct. 27, 1901, Louisville, Ky.　D. May 26, 1981, Richmond, Va.　　BR TR 6'1"　175 lb

	W	L	PCT	ERA	G	GS	CG	IP	H	BB	SO	ShO	W	L	SV	AB	H	HR	B
1926 DET A	1	2	.333	6.95	23	1	0	44	55	33	15	0	1	1	0	5	0	0	.0(
1927	4	1	.800	3.91	29	0	0	71.1	62	50	32	0	4	1	0	19	7	0	.3(
1928	1	1	.500	4.42	39	2	0	106	103	50	54	0	0	1	3	27	3	0	.1
1929	3	2	.600	5.80	14	2	0	35.2	42	36	13	0	2	2	0	12	5	0	.4

	W	L	PCT	ERA	G	GS	CG	IP	H	BB	SO	ShO	Relief Pitching W	L	SV	BATTING AB	H	HR	BA

George Smith continued

	W	L	PCT	ERA	G	GS	CG	IP	H	BB	SO	ShO	W	L	SV	AB	H	HR	BA
'30 BOS A	1	2	.333	6.84	27	2	0	73.2	92	49	21	0	1	2	0	24	8	0	.333
5 yrs.	10	8	.556	5.33	132	7	1	330.2	354	218	135	0	8	7	3	87	23	2	.264
4 yrs.	9	6	.600	4.90	105	5	1	257	262	169	114	0	7	5	3	63	15	2	.238

Heinie Smith

SMITH, GEORGE HENRY   BR TR 5'9½" 160 lbs.
B. Oct. 24, 1871, Pittsburgh, Pa.   D. June 25, 1939, Buffalo, N. Y.
Manager 1902.

	W	L	PCT	ERA	G	GS	CG	IP	H	BB	SO	ShO	W	L	SV	AB	H	HR	BA
'01 NY N	0	1	.000	8.10	2	1	1	13.1	24	5	5	0	0	0	0	*			

Rufus Smith

SMITH, RUFUS FRAZIER   BR TL 5'8" 165 lbs.
B. Jan. 24, 1905, Guilford College, N. C.

	W	L	PCT	ERA	G	GS	CG	IP	H	BB	SO	ShO	W	L	SV	AB	H	HR	BA
'27 DET A	0	0	–	3.38	1	1	0	8	8	3	2	0	0	0	0	3	0	0	.000

Willie Smith

SMITH, WILLIE (Wonderful Willie)   BL TL 6' 182 lbs.
B. Feb. 11, 1939, Anniston, Ala.

	W	L	PCT	ERA	G	GS	CG	IP	H	BB	SO	ShO	W	L	SV	AB	H	HR	BA
'63 DET A	1	0	1.000	4.57	11	2	0	21.2	24	13	16	0	1	0	2	8	1	0	.125
'64 LA A	1	4	.200	2.84	15	1	0	31.2	34	10	20	0	1	4	0	359	108	11	.301
'68 2 teams			CLE A (2G 0–0)			CHI N (1G 0–0)													
total	0	0	–	0.00	3	0	0	7.2	2	1	3	0	0	0	0	184	45	5	.245
3 yrs.	2	4	.333	3.10	29	3	0	61	60	24	39	0	2	4	2	*			
1 yr.	1	0	1.000	4.57	11	2	0	21.2	24	13	16	0	1	0	2	8	1	0	.125

Vic Sorrell

SORRELL, VICTOR GARLAND   BR TR 5'10" 180 lbs.
B. Apr. 9, 1901, Morrisville, N. C.   D. May 4, 1972, Raleigh, N. C.

	W	L	PCT	ERA	G	GS	CG	IP	H	BB	SO	ShO	W	L	SV	AB	H	HR	BA
'28 DET A	8	11	.421	4.79	29	23	8	171	182	83	67	0	0	0	0	55	6	0	.109
'29	14	15	.483	5.18	36	31	13	226	270	106	81	1	2	0	1	83	12	0	.145
'30	16	11	.593	3.86	35	30	14	233.1	245	106	97	2	2	1	1	80	15	0	.188
'31	13	14	.481	4.12	35	32	19	247	267	114	99	1	0	0	1	88	14	0	.159
'32	14	14	.500	4.03	32	31	13	234.1	234	77	84	1	1	0	0	76	9	0	.118
'33	11	15	.423	3.79	36	28	13	232.2	233	78	75	2	2	1	1	74	11	0	.149
'34	6	9	.400	4.79	28	19	6	129.2	146	45	46	0	0	2	2	37	4	0	.108
'35	4	3	.571	4.03	12	6	4	51.1	65	25	22	0	0	2	0	18	0	0	.000
'36	6	7	.462	5.28	30	14	5	131.1	153	64	37	1	2	3	3	39	6	0	.154
'37	0	2	.000	9.00	7	2	0	17	25	8	11	0	0	0	0	3	0	0	.000
10 yrs.	92	101	.477	4.43	280	216	95	1673.2	1820	706	619	8	9	9	10	553	77	0	.139
10 yrs.	92	101	.477	4.43	280	216	95	1673.2	1820	706	619	8	9	9	10	553	77	0	.139
			9th															9th	

Elias Sosa

SOSA, ELIAS MARTINEZ   BR TR 6'2" 186 lbs.
B. June 10, 1950, La Vega, Dominican Republic

	W	L	PCT	ERA	G	GS	CG	IP	H	BB	SO	ShO	W	L	SV	AB	H	HR	BA
'72 SF N	0	1	.000	2.25	8	0	0	16	10	12	10	0	0	1	3	4	0	0	.000
'73	10	4	.714	3.28	71	0	0	107	95	41	70	0	10	3	18	14	1	0	.071
'74	9	7	.563	3.48	68	0	0	101	94	45	48	0	9	7	6	15	1	0	.067
'75 2 teams			STL N (14G 0–3)			ATL N (43G 2–2)													
total	2	5	.286	4.32	57	1	0	89.2	92	43	46	0	2	4	2	15	2	0	.133
'76 2 teams			ATL N (21G 4–4)			LA N (24G 2–4)													
total	6	8	.429	4.43	45	0	0	69	71	25	52	0	6	8	4	7	1	0	.143
'77 LA N	2	2	.500	1.97	44	0	0	64	42	12	47	0	2	2	1	4	1	0	.250
'78 OAK A	8	2	.800	2.64	68	0	0	109	106	44	61	0	8	2	14	0	0	0	–
'79 MON N	8	7	.533	1.95	62	0	0	97	77	37	59	0	8	7	18	13	2	0	.154
'80	9	6	.600	3.06	67	0	0	94	104	19	58	0	9	6	9	11	1	0	.091
'81	1	2	.333	3.69	32	0	0	39	46	8	18	0	1	2	3	2	2	0	1.000
'82 DET A	3	3	.500	4.43	38	0	0	61	64	18	24	0	3	3	4	0	0	0	–
'83 SD N	1	4	.200	4.35	41	1	0	72.1	72	30	45	0	1	4	1	7	1	0	.143
12 yrs.	59	51	.536	3.32	601	3	0	919	873	334	538	0	59	49	83	92	12	0	.130
1 yr.	3	3	.500	4.43	38	0	0	61	64	18	24	0	3	3	4	0	0	0	–

DIVISIONAL PLAYOFF SERIES

	W	L	PCT	ERA	G	GS	CG	IP	H	BB	SO	ShO	W	L	SV	AB	H	HR	BA
'81 MON N	0	0	–	3.00	2	0	0	3	4	0	1	0	0	0	0	0	0	0	–

LEAGUE CHAMPIONSHIP SERIES

	W	L	PCT	ERA	G	GS	CG	IP	H	BB	SO	ShO	W	L	SV	AB	H	HR	BA
'77 LA N	0	1	.000	10.13	2	0	0	2.2	5	0	0	0	0	1	0	1	0	0	.000
'81 MON N	0	0	–	0.00	1	0	0	.1	1	1	0	0	0	0	0	0	0	0	–
2 yrs.	0	1	.000	9.00	3	0	0	3	6	1	0	0	0	1	0	1	0	0	.000

WORLD SERIES

	W	L	PCT	ERA	G	GS	CG	IP	H	BB	SO	ShO	W	L	SV	AB	H	HR	BA
'77 LA N	0	0	–	11.57	2	0	0	2.1	3	1	1	0	0	0	0	0	0	0	–

Joe Sparma

SPARMA, JOSEPH BLASE   BR TR 6'1" 190 lbs.
B. Feb. 4, 1942, Massillon, Ohio

	W	L	PCT	ERA	G	GS	CG	IP	H	BB	SO	ShO	W	L	SV	AB	H	HR	BA
'64 DET A	5	6	.455	3.00	21	11	3	84	62	45	71	2	1	1	0	25	4	0	.160
'65	13	8	.618	3.18	30	28	6	167	142	75	127	0	1	0	0	52	7	0	.135
'66	2	7	.222	5.30	29	13	0	91.2	103	52	61	0	0	0	0	23	5	0	.217
'67	16	9	.640	3.76	37	37	11	217.2	186	85	153	5	0	0	0	74	4	0	.054
'68	10	10	.500	3.70	34	31	7	182.1	169	77	110	1	1	0	0	60	8	0	.133
'69	6	8	.429	4.76	23	16	3	92.2	78	77	41	2	0	1	0	29	4	0	.138
'70 MON N	0	4	.000	7.14	9	6	1	29	34	25	23	0	0	0	0	6	0	0	.000
7 yrs.	52	52	.500	3.95	183	142	31	864.1	774	436	586	10	3	2	0	269	32	0	.119
6 yrs.	52	48	.520	3.84	174	136	30	835.1	740	411	563	10	3	2	0	263	32	0	.122

WORLD SERIES

	W	L	PCT	ERA	G	GS	CG	IP	H	BB	SO	ShO	W	L	SV	AB	H	HR	BA
'68 DET A	0	0	–	54.00	1	0	0	.1	2	0	0	0	0	0	0	0	0	0	–

Kid Speer

SPEER, GEORGE NATHAN   BL TL
B. June 16, 1886, Corning Mo.   D. Jan. 13, 1946, Edmonton, Alta., Canada

	W	L	PCT	ERA	G	GS	CG	IP	H	BB	SO	ShO	W	L	SV	AB	H	HR	BA
'09 DET A	4	4	.500	2.83	12	8	4	76.1	88	13	12	0	1	1	0	25	3	0	.120

	W	L	PCT	ERA	G	GS	CG	IP	H	BB	SO	ShO	Relief Pitching W	L	SV	BATTING AB	H	HR	B

George Spencer

SPENCER, GEORGE ELWELL
B. July 7, 1926, Columbus, Ohio   BR TR 6'1"   215 lbs

	W	L	PCT	ERA	G	GS	CG	IP	H	BB	SO	ShO	W	L	SV	AB	H	HR	B
1950 NY N	1	0	1.000	2.49	10	1	1	25.1	12	7	5	0	0	0	0	4	0	0	.00
1951	10	4	.714	3.75	57	4	2	132	125	56	36	0	8	2	6	32	4	0	.12
1952	3	5	.375	5.55	35	4	0	60	57	21	27	0	3	4	3	10	2	0	.20
1953	0	0	–	7.71	1	0	0	2.1	3	2	1	0	0	0	0	0	0	0	
1954	1	0	1.000	3.65	6	0	0	12.1	9	8	4	0	1	0	0	3	0	0	.00
1955	0	0	–	5.40	1	0	0	1.2	1	3	0	0	0	0	0	0	0	0	
1958 DET A	1	0	1.000	2.70	7	0	0	10	11	4	5	0	1	0	0	0	0	0	
1960	0	1	.000	3.52	5	0	0	7.2	10	5	4	0	0	1	0	1	0	0	.00
8 yrs.	16	10	.615	4.05	122	9	3	251.1	228	106	82	0	13	7	9	50	6	0	.12
2 yrs.	1	1	.500	3.06	12	0	0	17.2	21	9	9	0	1	1	0	1	0	0	.00

WORLD SERIES
| 1951 NY N | 0 | 0 | – | 18.90 | 2 | 0 | 0 | 3.1 | 6 | 3 | 0 | 0 | 0 | 0 | 0 | 0 | 0 | 0 | |

Gerry Staley

STALEY, GERALD LEE
B. Aug. 21, 1920, Brush Prairie, Wash.   BR TR 6'   195 lbs

	W	L	PCT	ERA	G	GS	CG	IP	H	BB	SO	ShO	W	L	SV	AB	H	HR	B
1947 STL N	1	0	1.000	2.76	18	1	1	29.1	33	8	14	0	0	0	0	6	0	0	.00
1948	4	4	.500	6.92	31	3	0	52	61	21	23	0	4	3	0	9	2	1	.22
1949	10	10	.500	2.73	45	17	5	171.1	154	41	55	2	4	2	6	41	5	0	.12
1950	13	13	.500	4.99	42	22	7	169.2	201	61	62	1	6	1	3	55	8	0	.14
1951	19	13	.594	3.81	42	30	10	227	244	74	67	4	6	1	3	81	13	0	.16
1952	17	14	.548	3.27	35	33	15	239.2	238	52	93	0	0	2	0	85	13	0	.15
1953	18	9	.667	3.99	40	32	10	230	243	54	88	1	0	0	4	78	8	0	.10
1954	7	13	.350	5.26	48	20	3	155.2	198	47	50	1	3	6	2	36	5	0	.13
1955 2 teams			CIN N (30G 5–8)		NY A (2G 0–0)														
" total	5	8	.385	4.81	32	18	2	121.2	151	29	40	0	0	1	0	36	2	0	.05
1956 2 teams			NY A (1G 0–0)		CHI A (26G 8–3)														
" total	8	3	.727	3.26	27	10	5	102	102	20	26	0	1	1	0	33	3	0	.09
1957 CHI A	5	1	.833	2.06	47	0	0	105	95	27	44	0	5	1	7	22	1	0	.04
1958	4	5	.444	3.16	50	0	0	85.1	81	24	27	0	4	5	8	11	0	0	.00
1959	8	5	.615	2.24	67	0	0	116.1	111	25	54	0	8	5	14	13	2	0	.15
1960	13	8	.619	2.42	64	0	0	115.1	94	25	52	0	13	8	10	17	4	0	.23
1961 3 teams			CHI A (16G 0–3)		KC A (23G 1–1)			DET A (13G 1–1)											
" total	2	5	.286	3.96	52	0	0	61.1	64	21	32	0	2	5	4	2	0	0	.00
15 yrs.	134	111	.547	3.70	640	186	58	1981.2	2070	529	727	9	56	41	61	525	66	1	.12
1 yr.	1	1	.500	3.38	13	0	0	13.1	15	6	8	0	1	1	2	1	0	0	.00

WORLD SERIES
| 1959 CHI A | 0 | 1 | .000 | 2.16 | 4 | 0 | 0 | 8.1 | 8 | 0 | 3 | 0 | 0 | 1 | 1 | 1 | 0 | 0 | .00 |

Bill Steen

STEEN, WILLIAM JOHN
B. Nov. 11, 1887, Pittsburgh, Pa.   D. Mar. 13, 1979, Signal Hill, Calif.   BR TR 6'½"   172 lbs

	W	L	PCT	ERA	G	GS	CG	IP	H	BB	SO	ShO	W	L	SV	AB	H	HR	B
1912 CLE A	9	8	.529	3.77	26	16	6	143.1	163	45	61	1	1	2	0	49	13	0	.26
1913	4	5	.444	2.45	22	13	8	128.1	113	49	57	2	0	1	2	41	7	0	.17
1914	9	14	.391	2.60	30	22	13	200.2	201	68	97	1	2	2	0	70	14	0	.20
1915 2 teams			CLE A (10G 1–4)		DET A (20G 5–1)														
" total	6	5	.545	3.54	30	14	5	124.2	134	37	50	0	0	1	4	44	8	0	.18
4 yrs.	28	32	.467	3.05	108	65	32	597	611	199	265	4	3	6	6	204	42	0	.20
1 yr.	5	1	.833	2.72	20	7	3	79.1	83	22	28	0	0	1	4	28	5	0	.17

Lefty Stewart

STEWART, WALTER CLEVELAND
B. Sept. 23, 1900, Sparta, Tenn.   D. Sept. 26, 1974, Knoxville, Tenn.   BR TL 5'10"   160 lbs

	W	L	PCT	ERA	G	GS	CG	IP	H	BB	SO	ShO	W	L	SV	AB	H	HR	B
1921 DET A	0	0	–	12.00	5	0	0	9	20	5	4	0	0	0	1	1	0	0	.00
1927 STL A	8	11	.421	4.28	27	19	11	155.2	187	43	43	0	0	0	1	49	15	0	.30
1928	7	9	.438	4.67	29	17	7	142.2	173	32	25	1	2	0	3	51	14	0	.27
1929	9	6	.600	3.25	23	18	8	149.1	137	49	47	1	1	1	0	51	6	0	.11
1930	20	12	.625	3.45	35	33	23	271	281	70	79	1	1	0	0	90	22	0	.24
1931	14	17	.452	4.40	36	33	20	258	287	85	89	1	1	1	0	88	22	0	.25
1932	14	19	.424	4.61	41	32	18	259.2	269	99	86	2	0	3	1	82	12	0	.14
1933 WAS A	15	6	.714	3.82	34	31	11	230.2	227	60	69	1	0	1	0	77	11	0	.14
1934	7	11	.389	4.03	24	22	7	152	184	36	36	1	0	1	0	45	7	0	.15
1935 2 teams			WAS A (1G 0–1)		CLE A (24G 6–6)														
" total	6	7	.462	5.67	25	11	2	93.2	130	19	25	1	2	2	2	31	6	0	.19
10 yrs.	100	98	.505	4.19	279	216	107	1721.2	1895	498	503	9	7	10	8	565	115	0	.20
1 yr.	0	0	–	12.00	5	0	0	9	20	5	4	0	0	0	1	1	0	0	.00

WORLD SERIES
| 1933 WAS A | 0 | 1 | .000 | 9.00 | 1 | 1 | 0 | 2 | 6 | 0 | 0 | 0 | 0 | 0 | 0 | 0 | 0 | 0 | .00 |

Lil Stoner

STONER, ULYSSES SIMPSON GRANT
B. Feb. 28, 1899, Bowie, Tex.   D. June 26, 1966, Enid, Okla.   BR TR 5'9½"   180 lbs

	W	L	PCT	ERA	G	GS	CG	IP	H	BB	SO	ShO	W	L	SV	AB	H	HR	B
1922 DET A	4	4	.500	7.04	17	7	2	62.2	76	35	18	0	4	0	0	20	2	0	.10
1924	11	11	.500	4.72	36	25	10	215.2	271	65	66	1	1	2	0	77	15	2	.19
1925	10	9	.526	4.26	34	18	8	152	166	53	51	0	1	3	1	55	16	0	.29
1926	7	10	.412	5.47	32	22	7	159.2	179	63	57	0	2	1	0	53	9	0	.17
1927	10	13	.435	3.98	38	24	13	215	251	77	63	0	1	2	5	74	8	0	.10
1928	5	8	.385	4.35	36	11	4	126.1	151	42	29	0	0	4	0	39	7	0	.17
1929	3	3	.500	5.26	24	3	1	53	57	31	12	0	0	1	4	15	1	0	.06
1930 PIT N	0	0	–	4.76	5	0	0	5.2	7	3	1	0	0	0	0	0	0	0	
1931 PHI N	0	0	–	6.59	7	1	0	13.2	22	5	2	0	0	0	0	0	0	0	
9 yrs.	50	58	.463	4.76	229	111	45	1003.2	1180	374	299	1	9	10	14	338	58	0	.17
7 yrs.	50	58	.463	4.74	217	110	45	984.1	1151	366	296	1	9	10	14	333	58	2	.17

Jesse Stovall

STOVALL, JESSE CRANMER (Scout)
Brother of George Stovall.
B. July 24, 1876, Independence, Mo.   D. July 12, 1955, San Diego, Calif.   BL TR 6'   175 lbs

	W	L	PCT	ERA	G	GS	CG	IP	H	BB	SO	ShO	W	L	SV	AB	H	HR	B
1903 CLE A	5	1	.833	2.05	6	6	6	57	44	21	12	2	0	0	0	22	1	0	.04

	W	L	PCT	ERA	G	GS	CG	IP	H	BB	SO	ShO	Relief Pitching W	L	SV	BATTING AB	H	HR	BA

esse Stovall *continued*

	W	L	PCT	ERA	G	GS	CG	IP	H	BB	SO	ShO	W	L	SV	AB	H	HR	BA
'04 DET A	3	13	.188	4.42	22	17	13	146.2	170	45	41	1	0	1	0	56	11	0	.196
2 yrs.	8	14	.364	3.76	28	23	19	203.2	214	66	53	3	0	1	0	78	12	0	.154
1 yr.	3	13	.188	4.42	22	17	13	146.2	170	45	41	1	0	1	0	56	11	0	.196

Mike Strahler

STRAHLER, MICHAEL WAYNE   BR TR 6'4"   180 lbs.
B. Mar. 14, 1947, Chicago, Ill.

	W	L	PCT	ERA	G	GS	CG	IP	H	BB	SO	ShO	W	L	SV	AB	H	HR	BA
'70 LA N	1	1	.500	1.42	6	0	0	19	13	10	11	0	1	1	1	8	2	0	.250
'71	0	0	–	2.77	6	0	0	13	10	8	7	0	0	0	0	1	0	0	.000
'72	1	2	.333	3.26	19	2	1	47	42	22	25	0	0	1	0	11	2	0	.182
'73 DET A	4	5	.444	4.39	22	11	1	80	84	39	37	0	0	1	0	0	0	0	–
4 yrs.	6	8	.429	3.57	53	13	2	159	149	79	80	0	1	3	1	20	4	0	.200
1 yr.	4	5	.444	4.39	22	11	1	80	84	39	37	0	0	1	0	0	0	0	–

Bob Strampe

STRAMPE, ROBERT EDWIN   BB TR 6'1"   185 lbs.
B. June 13, 1950, Janesville, Wis.

	W	L	PCT	ERA	G	GS	CG	IP	H	BB	SO	ShO	W	L	SV	AB	H	HR	BA
'72 DET A	0	0	–	10.80	7	0	0	5	6	7	4	0	0	0	0	0	0	0	–

ailor Stroud

STROUD, RALPH VIVIAN   BR TR 6'   160 lbs.
B. May 15, 1885, Ironia, N. J.   D. Apr. 11, 1970, Stockton, Calif.

	W	L	PCT	ERA	G	GS	CG	IP	H	BB	SO	ShO	W	L	SV	AB	H	HR	BA
'10 DET A	5	9	.357	3.25	28	15	7	130.1	123	41	63	3	0	0	1	39	1	0	.026
'15 NY N	11	9	.550	2.79	32	22	8	184	194	35	62	0	1	2	1	56	9	0	.161
'16	1	2	.333	2.70	10	4	0	46.2	47	9	16	0	1	1	1	14	1	0	.071
3 yrs.	17	20	.459	2.94	70	41	15	361	364	85	141	3	2	3	3	109	11	0	.101
1 yr.	5	9	.357	3.25	28	15	7	130.1	123	41	63	3	0	0	1	39	1	0	.026

Marlin Stuart

STUART, MARLIN HENRY   BL TR 6'2"   185 lbs.
B. Aug. 8, 1918, Paragould, Ark.

	W	L	PCT	ERA	G	GS	CG	IP	H	BB	SO	ShO	W	L	SV	AB	H	HR	BA
'49 DET A	0	2	.000	9.10	14	2	0	29.2	39	35	14	0	0	1	0	6	2	0	.333
'50	3	1	.750	5.56	19	1	0	43.2	59	22	19	0	3	0	2	12	1	0	.083
'51	4	6	.400	3.77	29	15	5	124	119	71	46	0	0	0	1	43	10	1	.233
'52 2 teams				DET A (30G 3–2)				STL A (12G 1–2)											
total	4	4	.500	4.76	42	11	2	117.1	117	57	45	0	2	1	2	29	2	0	.069
'53 STL A	8	2	.800	3.94	60	2	0	114.1	136	44	46	0	8	1	7	26	5	0	.192
'54 2 teams				BAL A (22G 1–1)				NY A (10G 3–0)											
total	4	2	.667	4.76	32	0	0	56.2	74	27	15	0	4	2	3	9	2	0	.222
6 yrs.	23	17	.575	4.65	196	31	7	485.2	544	256	185	0	17	5	15	125	22	1	.176
4 yrs.	10	11	.476	4.96	92	27	7	288.2	308	176	111	0	4	1	4	84	15	1	.179

im Stump

STUMP, JAMES GILBERT   BR TR 6'   188 lbs.
B. Feb. 10, 1932, Lansing, Mich.

	W	L	PCT	ERA	G	GS	CG	IP	H	BB	SO	ShO	W	L	SV	AB	H	HR	BA
'57 DET A	1	0	1.000	2.03	6	0	0	13.1	11	8	2	0	1	0	0	2	1	0	.500
'59	0	0	–	2.38	5	0	0	11.1	12	4	6	0	0	0	0	1	1	0	1.000
2 yrs.	1	0	1.000	2.19	11	0	0	24.2	23	12	8	0	1	0	0	3	2	0	.667
2 yrs.	1	0	1.000	2.19	11	0	0	24.2	23	12	8	0	1	0	0	3	2	0	.667

om Sturdivant

STURDIVANT, THOMAS VIRGIL (Snake)   BL TR 6'½"   170 lbs.
B. Apr. 28, 1930, Gordon, Kans.

	W	L	PCT	ERA	G	GS	CG	IP	H	BB	SO	ShO	W	L	SV	AB	H	HR	BA
'55 NY A	1	3	.250	3.16	33	1	0	68.1	48	42	48	0	1	2	0	12	1	0	.083
'56	16	8	.667	3.30	32	17	6	158.1	134	52	110	2	6	2	5	64	20	0	.313
'57	16	6	.727	2.54	28	28	7	201.2	170	80	118	2	0	0	0	71	13	0	.183
'58	3	6	.333	4.20	15	10	0	70.2	77	38	41	0	0	0	0	21	4	0	.190
'59 2 teams				NY A (7G 0–2)				KC A (36G 2–6)											
total	2	8	.200	4.73	43	6	0	97	90	43	73	0	2	4	5	23	1	0	.043
'60 BOS A	3	3	.500	4.97	40	3	0	101.1	106	45	67	0	0	1	1	22	4	0	.182
'61 2 teams				WAS A (15G 2–6)				PIT N (13G 5–2)											
total	7	8	.467	3.69	28	21	7	165.2	148	57	84	2	0	2	1	58	10	0	.172
'62 PIT N	9	5	.643	3.73	49	12	2	125.1	120	39	76	1	3	1	2	33	6	0	.182
'63 3 teams				PIT N (3G 0–0)				DET A (28G 1–2)				KC A (17G 1–2)							
total	2	4	.333	3.95	48	3	0	116.1	98	45	68	0	2	3	2	22	0	0	.000
'64 2 teams				KC A (3G 0–0)				NY N (16G 0–0)											
total	0	0	–	6.40	19	0	0	32.1	38	8	19	0	0	0	1	2	1	0	.500
10 yrs.	59	51	.536	3.74	335	101	22	1137	1029	449	704	7	14	15	17	328	60	0	.183
1 yr.	1	2	.333	3.76	28	0	0	55	43	24	36	0	1	2	2	9	0	0	.000

WORLD SERIES

	W	L	PCT	ERA	G	GS	CG	IP	H	BB	SO	ShO	W	L	SV	AB	H	HR	BA
'55 NY A	0	0	–	6.00	2	0	0	3	5	2	0	0	0	0	0	0	0	0	–
'56	1	0	1.000	2.79	2	1	1	9.2	8	8	9	0	0	0	0	3	1	0	.333
'57	0	0	–	6.00	2	1	0	6	6	1	2	0	0	0	0	1	0	0	.000
3 yrs.	1	0	1.000	4.34	6	2	1	18.2	19	11	11	0	0	0	0	4	1	0	.250

oe Sugden

SUGDEN, JOSEPH   BB TR 5'10"   180 lbs.
B. July 31, 1870, Philadelphia, Pa.   D. June 28, 1959, Philadelphia, Pa.

	W	L	PCT	ERA	G	GS	CG	IP	H	BB	SO	ShO	W	L	SV	AB	H	HR	BA
'02 STL A	0	0	–	0.00	1	0	0	1	1	0	0	0	0	0	0	*			

eorge Suggs

SUGGS, GEORGE FRANKLIN   BR TR 5'7½"   168 lbs.
B. July 7, 1883, Kinston, N. C.   D. Apr. 4, 1949, Kinston, N. C.

	W	L	PCT	ERA	G	GS	CG	IP	H	BB	SO	ShO	W	L	SV	AB	H	HR	BA
'08 DET A	1	1	.500	1.67	6	1	1	27	32	2	8	0	0	1	1	10	2	0	.200
'09	1	3	.250	2.03	9	4	2	44.1	34	10	18	0	0	1	1	15	1	0	.067
'10 CIN N	19	11	.633	2.40	35	30	23	266	248	48	91	2	2	0	3	85	14	0	.165
'11	15	13	.536	3.00	36	29	17	260.2	258	79	91	1	2	1	0	90	23	0	.256
'12	19	16	.543	2.94	42	36	25	303	320	56	104	5	2	1	3	106	17	1	.160
'13	8	15	.348	4.03	36	22	9	199	220	35	73	2	2	2	2	67	17	0	.254
'14 BAL F	25	12	.676	2.90	46	38	26	319.1	322	57	132	6	3	2	3	99	21	0	.212
'15	13	17	.433	4.14	35	25	12	232.2	288	68	71	0	3	2	1	77	17	0	.221
8 yrs.	101	88	.534	3.11	245	185	115	1652	1722	355	588	16	14	10	14	549	112	1	.204
2 yrs.	2	4	.333	1.89	15	5	3	71.1	66	12	26	0	0	2	2	25	3	0	.120

	W	L	PCT	ERA	G	GS	CG	IP	H	BB	SO	ShO	Relief Pitching W	L	SV	BATTING AB	H	HR	B

Charlie Sullivan

SULLIVAN, CHARLES EDWARD   BL TR 6'1"   185 lb
B. May 23, 1903, Yadkin Valley, N. C.   D. May 28, 1935, Maiden, N. C.

	W	L	PCT	ERA	G	GS	CG	IP	H	BB	SO	ShO	W	L	SV	AB	H	HR	B
1928 DET A	0	2	.000	6.57	3	2	0	12.1	18	6	2	0	0	0	0	4	0	0	.00
1930	1	5	.167	6.53	40	3	2	93.2	112	53	38	0	1	2	5	24	7	0	.29
1931	3	2	.600	4.73	31	4	2	99	109	46	28	0	1	0	0	24	4	0	.16
3 yrs.	4	9	.308	5.66	74	9	4	205	239	105	68	0	2	2	5	52	11	0	.2
3 yrs.	4	9	.308	5.66	74	9	4	205	239	105	68	0	2	2	5	52	11	0	.2

Joe Sullivan

SULLIVAN, JOE   BL TL 5'11"   175 lb
B. Sept. 26, 1910, Mason City, Ill.

	W	L	PCT	ERA	G	GS	CG	IP	H	BB	SO	ShO	W	L	SV	AB	H	HR	B
1935 DET A	6	6	.500	3.51	25	12	5	125.2	119	71	53	0	2	1	0	43	7	0	.16
1936	2	5	.286	6.78	26	4	1	79.2	111	40	32	0	1	3	1	28	5	0	.12
1939 BOS N	6	9	.400	3.64	31	11	7	113.2	114	50	46	0	2	5	2	40	12	0	.30
1940	10	14	.417	3.55	36	22	7	177.1	157	89	64	0	3	3	1	71	14	0	.19
1941 2 teams			BOS	N (16G 2-2)	PIT	N (16G 4-1)													
" total	6	3	.667	3.63	32	6	0	91.2	100	48	21	0	4	1	1	26	5	0	.19
5 yrs.	30	37	.448	4.01	150	55	20	588	601	298	216	0	12	13	5	208	43	0	.20
2 yrs.	8	11	.421	4.78	51	16	6	205.1	230	111	85	0	3	4	1	71	12	0	.16

Ed Summers

SUMMERS, ORON EDGAR (Kickapoo)   BB TR 6'2"   180 lb
B. Dec. 5, 1884, Ladoga, Ind.   D. May 12, 1953, Indianapolis, Ind.

	W	L	PCT	ERA	G	GS	CG	IP	H	BB	SO	ShO	W	L	SV	AB	H	HR	B
1908 DET A	24	12	.667	1.64	40	32	24	301	271	55	103	5	5	0	1	113	14	0	.12
1909	19	9	.679	2.24	35	32	24	281.2	243	52	107	3	0	0	1	94	10	0	.10
1910	13	12	.520	2.53	30	25	18	220.1	211	60	82	1	1	1	0	76	14	2	.18
1911	11	11	.500	3.66	30	20	13	179.1	189	51	65	0	3	2	1	63	16	0	.25
1912	1	1	.500	4.86	3	3	1	16.2	16	3	5	0	0	0	0	6	3	0	.50
5 yrs.	68	45	.602	2.42	138	112	80	999	930	221	362	9	9	3	3	352	57	2	.16
5 yrs.	68	45	.602	2.42	138	112	80	999	930	221	362	9	9	3	3	352	57	2	.16
			5th	**3rd**															

WORLD SERIES

	W	L	PCT	ERA	G	GS	CG	IP	H	BB	SO	ShO	W	L	SV	AB	H	HR	B
1908 DET A	0	2	.000	4.30	2	1	0	14.2	18	4	7	0	0	1	0	5	1	0	.20
1909	0	2	.000	8.59	2	2	0	7.1	13	4	4	0	0	0	0	3	0	0	.00
2 yrs.	0	4	.000	5.73	4	3	0	22	31	8	11	0	0	1	0	8	1	0	.12
			7th																

George Susce

SUSCE, GEORGE DANIEL   BR TR 6'1"   180 lb
Son of George Susce.
B. Sept. 13, 1931, Pittsburgh, Pa.

	W	L	PCT	ERA	G	GS	CG	IP	H	BB	SO	ShO	W	L	SV	AB	H	HR	B
1955 BOS A	9	7	.563	3.06	29	15	6	144.1	123	49	60	1	2	1	1	49	7	0	.14
1956	2	4	.333	6.20	21	6	0	69.2	71	44	26	0	2	1	0	18	4	0	.22
1957	7	3	.700	4.28	29	5	0	88.1	93	41	40	0	6	1	1	25	3	0	.12
1958 2 teams			BOS	A (2G 0-0)	DET	A (27G 4-3)													
" total	4	3	.571	3.98	29	10	2	92.2	96	27	42	0	3	2	1	24	3	0	.12
1959 DET A	0	0	–	12.89	9	0	0	14.2	24	9	9	0	0	0	0	1	0	0	.00
5 yrs.	22	17	.564	4.42	117	36	8	409.2	407	170	177	1	13	5	3	117	17	0	.14
2 yrs.	4	3	.571	4.96	36	10	2	105.1	114	35	51	0	3	2	1	25	3	0	.12

Suds Sutherland

SUTHERLAND, HARVEY SCOTT   BR TR 6'   180 lb
B. Feb. 20, 1894, Coburg, Ore.   D. May 11, 1972, Portland, Ore.

	W	L	PCT	ERA	G	GS	CG	IP	H	BB	SO	ShO	W	L	SV	AB	H	HR	B
1921 DET A	6	2	.750	4.97	13	8	3	58	80	18	18	0	2	2	0	27	11	0	.40

Bob Sykes

SYKES, ROBERT JOSEPH   BB TL 6'1"   195 lb
B. Dec. 11, 1954, Neptune, N. J.

	W	L	PCT	ERA	G	GS	CG	IP	H	BB	SO	ShO	W	L	SV	AB	H	HR	B
1977 DET A	5	7	.417	4.40	32	20	3	133	141	50	58	0	0	0	0	0	0	0	
1978	6	6	.500	3.94	22	10	3	93.2	99	34	58	0	3	1	2	0	0	0	
1979 STL N	4	3	.571	6.18	13	11	0	67	86	34	35	0	0	0	0	21	2	0	.09
1980	6	10	.375	4.64	27	9	4	126	134	54	50	3	0	3	0	39	4	0	.10
1981	2	0	1.000	4.62	22	1	0	37	37	18	14	0	2	0	0	2	0	0	.00
5 yrs.	23	26	.469	4.65	116	51	10	456.2	497	190	215	5	5	5	2	62	6	0	.09
2 yrs.	11	13	.458	4.21	54	30	6	226.2	240	84	116	2	3	2	2	0	0	0	

Bruce Taylor

TAYLOR, BRUCE BELL   BR TR 6'   178 lb
B. Apr. 16, 1953, Holden, Mass.

	W	L	PCT	ERA	G	GS	CG	IP	H	BB	SO	ShO	W	L	SV	AB	H	HR	B
1977 DET A	1	0	1.000	3.41	19	0	0	29	23	10	19	0	1	0	2	0	0	0	
1978	0	0	–	0.00	1	0	0	1	0	0	0	0	0	0	0	0	0	0	
1979	1	2	.333	4.74	10	0	0	19	16	7	8	0	1	2	0	0	0	0	
3 yrs.	2	2	.500	3.86	30	0	0	49	39	17	27	0	2	2	2	0	0	0	
3 yrs.	2	2	.500	3.86	30	0	0	49	39	17	27	0	2	2	2	0	0	0	

Gary Taylor

TAYLOR, GARY WILLIAM   BR TR 6'2"   190 lb
B. Oct. 19, 1945, Detroit, Mich.

	W	L	PCT	ERA	G	GS	CG	IP	H	BB	SO	ShO	W	L	SV	AB	H	HR	B
1969 DET A	0	1	.000	5.23	7	0	0	10.1	10	6	3	0	0	0	0	1	0	0	.00

Wiley Taylor

TAYLOR, PHILIP WILEY   BR TR 6'1"   175 lb
B. Mar. 18, 1888, Wamego, Kans.   D. July 8, 1954, Westmoreland, Kans.

	W	L	PCT	ERA	G	GS	CG	IP	H	BB	SO	ShO	W	L	SV	AB	H	HR	B
1911 DET A	0	2	.000	3.79	3	1	1	19	18	10	9	0	0	0	0	6	0	0	.00
1912 CHI A	0	1	.000	4.95	3	3	0	20	21	14	4	0	0	0	0	5	0	0	.00
1913 STL A	0	2	.000	4.83	5	4	1	31.2	33	16	12	0	0	0	0	10	0	0	.00
1914	2	5	.286	3.42	16	8	2	50	41	25	20	1	0	1	0	12	2	0	.16
4 yrs.	2	10	.167	4.10	27	17	4	120.2	113	65	45	1	0	1	0	33	2	0	
1 yr.	0	2	.000	3.79	3	1	1	19	18	10	9	0	0	0	0	6	0	0	.00

John Terry

TERRY, JOHN
B. St. Louis, Mo.

	W	L	PCT	ERA	G	GS	CG	IP	H	BB	SO	ShO	W	L	SV	AB	H	HR	B
1902 DET A	0	1	.000	3.60	1	1	1	5	8	1	0	0	0	0	0	2	0	0	.00

	W	L	PCT	ERA	G	GS	CG	IP	H	BB	SO	ShO	Relief Pitching W	L	SV	BATTING AB	H	HR	BA

ohn Terry continued

'03 STL A	1	1	.500	2.55	3	1	1	17.2	21	4	2	0	0	1	0	9	0	0	.000
2 yrs.	1	2	.333	2.78	4	2	2	22.2	29	5	2	0	0	1	0	11	0	0	.000
1 yr.	0	1	.000	3.60	1	1	1	5	8	1	0	0	0	0	0	2	0	0	.000

Bud Thomas   THOMAS, LUTHER BAXTER   BR TR 6'   180 lbs.
B. Sept. 9, 1910, Faber, Va.

'32 WAS A	0	0	–	0.00	2	0	0	3	1	2	1	0	0	0	0	0	0	0	–
'33	0	0	–	15.75	2	0	0	4	11	2	1	0	0	0	0	1	0	0	.000
'37 PHI A	8	15	.348	4.99	35	26	6	169.2	208	52	54	1	1	1	0	47	6	1	.128
'38	9	14	.391	4.92	42	29	7	212.1	259	62	48	0	0	0	0	69	9	0	.130
'39 3 teams			PHI	A (2G 0–1)			WAS	A (4G 0–0)			DET	A (27G 7–0)							
total	7	1	.875	5.22	33	2	0	60.1	64	23	14	0	7	0	1	14	1	0	.071
'40 DET A	0	1	.000	9.00	3	0	0	4	8	3	0	0	0	1	0	0	0	0	–
'41	1	3	.250	4.21	26	1	0	72.2	74	22	17	0	1	2	2	19	2	0	.105
7 yrs.	25	34	.424	4.96	143	58	13	526	625	166	135	1	9	4	3	150	18	1	.120
3 yrs.	8	4	.667	4.35	56	1	0	124	127	45	31	0	8	3	3	28	3	0	.107

Frosty Thomas   THOMAS, FORREST   BR TR 6'   185 lbs.
B. May 23, 1881, Faucett, Mo.   D. Mar. 18, 1971, St. Joseph, Mo.

| '05 DET A | 0 | 1 | .000 | 7.50 | 2 | 1 | 0 | 6 | 10 | 3 | 5 | 0 | 0 | 0 | 0 | 2 | 0 | 0 | .000 |

Tom Timmerman   TIMMERMAN, THOMAS HENRY   BR TR 6'4"   215 lbs.
B. May 12, 1940, Breese, Ill.

'69 DET A	4	3	.571	2.75	31	1	1	55.2	50	26	42	0	3	3	1	9	1	0	.111
'70	6	7	.462	4.13	61	0	0	85	90	34	49	0	6	7	27	16	0	0	.000
'71	7	6	.538	3.86	52	2	0	84	82	37	51	0	6	5	4	19	1	0	.053
'72	8	10	.444	2.89	34	25	3	149.2	121	41	88	2	0	0	0	44	6	0	.136
'73 2 teams			DET	A (17G 1–1)			CLE	A (29G 8–7)											
total	9	8	.529	4.63	46	16	4	163.1	156	65	83	0	2	2	3	0	0	0	–
'74 CLE A	1	1	.500	5.40	4	0	0	10	9	5	2	0	1	1	0	0	0	0	–
6 yrs.	35	35	.500	3.78	228	44	8	547.2	508	208	315	2	18	18	35	88	8	0	.091
5 yrs.	26	27	.491	3.40	195	29	4	413.1	382	149	251	2	16	16	33	88	8	0	.091

9th

Dave Tobik   TOBIK, DAVID VANCE   BR TR 6'1"   190 lbs.
B. Mar. 2, 1953, Euclid, Ohio

'78 DET A	0	0	–	3.75	5	0	0	12	12	3	11	0	0	1	0	0	0	0	–
'79	3	5	.375	4.30	37	0	0	69	59	25	48	0	3	5	3	0	0	0	–
'80	1	0	1.000	3.98	17	1	0	61	61	21	34	0	0	0	0	0	0	0	–
'81	2	2	.500	2.70	27	0	0	60	47	33	32	0	2	2	1	0	0	0	–
'82	4	9	.308	3.56	51	1	0	98.2	86	38	63	0	4	8	9	0	0	0	–
'83 TEX A	2	1	.667	3.68	27	0	0	44	36	13	30	0	2	1	9	0	0	0	–
'84	1	6	.143	3.61	24	0	0	42.1	44	17	30	0	1	6	5	0	0	0	–
7 yrs.	13	23	.361	3.65	188	2	0	387	345	150	248	0	12	23	27	0	0	0	–
5 yrs.	10	16	.385	3.65	137	2	0	300.2	265	120	188	0	9	16	13	0	0	0	–

Jim Tobin   TOBIN, JAMES ANTHONY (Abba Dabba)   BR TR 6'   185 lbs.
Brother of Johnny Tobin.
B. Dec. 27, 1912, Oakland, Calif.   D. May 19, 1969, Oakland, Calif.

'37 PIT N	6	3	.667	3.00	20	8	7	87	74	28	37	0	1	0	1	34	15	0	.441
'38	14	12	.538	3.47	40	33	14	241.1	254	66	70	2	4	1	0	103	25	0	.243
'39	9	9	.500	4.52	25	19	8	145.1	194	33	43	0	2	1	0	74	18	2	.243
'40 BOS N	7	3	.700	3.83	15	11	9	96.1	102	24	29	0	1	0	0	43	12	0	.279
'41	12	12	.500	3.10	33	26	20	238	229	60	61	3	0	1	0	103	19	0	.184
'42	12	21	.364	3.97	37	33	28	287.2	283	96	71	1	0	3	0	114	28	6	.246
'43	14	14	.500	2.66	33	30	24	250	241	69	52	1	0	1	0	107	30	2	.280
'44	18	19	.486	3.01	43	36	28	299.1	271	97	83	5	0	2	3	116	22	2	.190
'45 2 teams			BOS	N (27G 9–14)			DET	A (14G 4–5)											
total	13	19	.406	3.78	41	31	18	255	281	84	52	0	2	1	0	102	14	5	.137
9 yrs.	105	112	.484	3.44	287	227	156	1900	1929	557	498	12	10	11	5	*			
1 yr.	4	5	.444	3.55	14	6	2	58.1	61	28	14	0	2	1	1	25	3	2	.120

ORLD SERIES

| '45 DET A | 0 | 0 | – | 6.00 | 1 | 0 | 0 | 3 | 4 | 1 | 0 | 0 | 0 | 0 | 0 | 1 | 0 | 0 | .000 |

Allan Travers   TRAVERS, ALOYSIUS JOSEPH   BR TR 6'1"   180 lbs.
B. May 7, 1892, Philadelphia, Pa.   D. Apr. 19, 1968, Philadelphia, Pa.

| '12 DET A | 0 | 1 | .000 | 15.75 | 1 | 1 | 1 | 8 | 26 | 7 | 1 | 0 | 0 | 0 | 0 | 3 | 0 | 0 | .000 |

Dizzy Trout   TROUT, PAUL HOWARD   BR TR 6'2½"   195 lbs.
Father of Steve Trout.
B. June 29, 1915, Sandcut, Ind.   D. Feb. 28, 1972, Chicago, Ill.

'39 DET A	9	10	.474	3.61	33	22	6	162	168	74	72	0	0	0	2	57	12	0	.211
'40	3	7	.300	4.47	33	10	1	100.2	125	54	64	0	1	2	2	31	4	0	.129
'41	9	9	.500	3.74	37	18	6	151.2	144	84	88	1	2	2	2	50	9	0	.180
'42	12	18	.400	3.43	35	29	13	223	214	89	91	1	2	1	0	75	16	1	.213
'43	20	12	.625	2.48	44	30	18	246.2	204	101	111	5	3	1	6	91	20	1	.220
'44	27	14	.659	2.12	49	40	33	352.1	314	83	144	7	3	0	0	133	36	5	.271
'45	18	15	.545	3.14	41	31	18	246.1	252	79	97	4	2	0	2	102	25	2	.245
'46	17	13	.567	2.34	38	32	23	276.1	244	97	151	5	0	0	3	103	20	3	.194
'47	10	11	.476	3.48	32	26	9	186.1	186	65	74	2	0	0	2	68	11	3	.162
'48	10	14	.417	3.43	32	23	11	183.2	193	73	91	2	1	1	2	69	15	1	.217
'49	3	6	.333	4.40	33	0	0	59.1	68	21	19	0	3	6	3	14	2	1	.143
'50	13	5	.722	3.75	34	20	11	184.2	190	64	88	1	1	0	4	63	12	1	.190
'51	9	14	.391	4.04	42	22	7	191.2	172	75	89	0	3	1	5	52	14	1	.269

	W	L	PCT	ERA	G	GS	CG	IP	H	BB	SO	ShO	Relief Pitching W	L	SV	BATTING AB	H	HR	B

Dizzy Trout continued

	W	L	PCT	ERA	G	GS	CG	IP	H	BB	SO	ShO	W	L	SV	AB	H	HR	B
1952 2 teams	DET	A (10G 1–5)		BOS	A (26G 9–8)														
" total	10	13	.435	3.92	36	19	2	160.2	163	87	77	0	4	3	2	53	9	1	.17
1957 BAL A	0	0	–	81.00	2	0	0	.1	4	0	0	0	0	0	0	0	0	0	
15 yrs.	170	161	.514	3.23	521	322	158	2725.2	2641	1046	1256	28	25	17	35	961	205	20	.21
14 yrs.	161	153	.513	3.20	493	305	156	2591.2	2504	978	1199	28	22	17	34	917	199	19	.21
	6th	4th			4th		7th		6th		6th	7th	6th	8th		7th				

WORLD SERIES

	W	L	PCT	ERA	G	GS	CG	IP	H	BB	SO	ShO	W	L	SV	AB	H	HR	B
1940 DET A	0	1	.000	9.00	1	1	0	2	6	1	1	0	0	0	0	1	0	0	.00
1945	1	1	.500	0.66	2	1	1	13.2	9	3	9	0	0	1	0	6	1	0	.16
2 yrs.	1	2	.333	1.72	3	2	1	15.2	15	4	10	0	0	1	0	7	1	0	.14

Bun Troy

TROY, ROBERT
B. Aug. 22, 1888, Germany   D. Oct. 7, 1918, Meuse, France

BR TR 6'4"   195 lbs

	W	L	PCT	ERA	G	GS	CG	IP	H	BB	SO	ShO	W	L	SV	AB	H	HR	B
1912 DET A	0	1	.000	5.40	1	1	0	6.2	9	3	1	0	0	0	0	2	0	0	.00

Virgil Trucks

TRUCKS, VIRGIL OLIVER (Fire)
B. Apr. 26, 1919, Birmingham, Ala.

BR TR 5'11"   198 lbs

	W	L	PCT	ERA	G	GS	CG	IP	H	BB	SO	ShO	W	L	SV	AB	H	HR	B
1941 DET A	0	0	–	9.00	1	0	0	2	4	0	3	0	0	0	0	0	0	0	
1942	14	8	.636	2.74	28	20	8	167.2	147	74	91	2	4	1	0	65	8	0	.12
1943	16	10	.615	2.84	33	25	10	202.2	170	52	118	3	2	1	2	72	13	0	.18
1945	0	0	–	1.69	1	1	0	5.1	3	2	3	0	0	0	0	2	0	0	.00
1946	14	9	.609	3.23	32	29	15	236.2	217	75	161	3	1	1	0	95	17	0	.17
1947	10	12	.455	4.53	36	26	8	180.2	186	79	108	2	0	2	2	70	19	0	.27
1948	14	13	.519	3.78	43	26	7	211.2	190	85	123	0	4	2	2	79	13	0	.16
1949	19	11	.633	2.81	41	32	17	275	209	124	153	6	2	0	4	100	12	0	.12
1950	3	1	.750	3.54	7	7	2	48.1	45	21	25	1	0	0	0	20	3	0	.15
1951	13	8	.619	4.33	37	18	6	153.2	153	75	89	1	4	2	1	55	13	0	.23
1952	5	19	.208	3.97	35	29	8	197	190	82	129	3	0	1	1	64	12	1	.18
1953 2 teams	STL	A (16G 5–4)		CHI	A (24G 15–6)														
" total	20	10	.667	2.93	40	33	17	264.1	234	99	149	5	0	1	3	88	19	1	.21
1954 CHI A	19	12	.613	2.79	40	33	16	264.2	224	95	152	5	3	1	3	93	17	0	.18
1955	13	8	.619	3.96	32	26	7	175	176	61	91	3	1	0	0	64	8	0	.12
1956 DET A	6	5	.545	3.83	22	16	3	120	104	63	43	1	0	1	1	45	11	0	.24
1957 KC A	9	7	.563	3.03	48	7	0	116	106	62	55	0	8	3	7	28	4	0	.14
1958 2 teams	KC	A (16G 0–1)		NY	A (25G 2–1)														
" total	2	2	.500	3.65	41	0	0	61.2	58	39	41	0	2	2	4	9	2	0	.22
17 yrs.	177	135	.567	3.39	517	328	124	2682.1	2416	1088	1534	35	31	18	30	949	171	2	.18
12 yrs.	114	96	.543	3.50	316	229	84	1800.2	1618	732	1046	22	17	11	13	667	121	1	.18
			10th		10th							8th			10th	8th			

WORLD SERIES

	W	L	PCT	ERA	G	GS	CG	IP	H	BB	SO	ShO	W	L	SV	AB	H	HR	B
1945 DET A	1	0	1.000	3.38	2	2	1	13.1	14	5	7	0	0	0	0	4	0	0	.00

John Tsitouris

TSITOURIS, JOHN PHILIP
B. May 4, 1936, Monroe, N. C.

BR TR 6'   175 lbs

	W	L	PCT	ERA	G	GS	CG	IP	H	BB	SO	ShO	W	L	SV	AB	H	HR	B
1957 DET A	1	0	1.000	8.10	2	0	0	3.1	8	2	2	0	1	0	0	1	0	0	.00
1958 KC A	0	0	–	3.00	1	1	0	3	2	2	1	0	0	0	0	1	0	0	.00
1959	4	3	.571	4.97	24	10	0	83.1	90	35	50	0	2	0	0	20	3	0	.15
1960	0	2	.000	6.55	14	2	0	33	38	21	12	0	0	1	0	6	0	0	.00
1962 CIN N	1	0	1.000	0.84	4	2	1	21.1	13	7	7	1	0	0	0	5	0	0	.00
1963	12	8	.600	3.16	30	21	8	191	167	38	113	3	0	1	0	62	5	0	.08
1964	9	13	.409	3.80	37	24	6	175.1	178	75	146	1	0	1	2	58	11	0	.19
1965	6	9	.400	4.95	31	20	3	131	134	65	91	0	1	0	1	43	3	0	.07
1966	0	0	–	18.00	1	0	0	1	3	1	0	0	0	0	0	0	0	0	
1967	1	0	1.000	3.38	2	1	0	8	4	6	4	0	0	0	0	0	0	0	
1968	0	3	.000	7.11	3	3	0	12.2	16	8	6	0	0	0	0	2	0	0	.00
11 yrs.	34	38	.472	4.13	149	84	18	663	653	260	432	5	4	3	3	198	22	0	.11
1 yr.	1	0	1.000	8.10	2	0	0	3.1	8	2	2	0	1	0	0	1	0	0	.00

Bob Uhle

UHLE, ROBERT ELLWOOD (Lefty)
B. Sept. 17, 1913, San Francisco, Calif.

BB TL 5'11"   175 lbs

	W	L	PCT	ERA	G	GS	CG	IP	H	BB	SO	ShO	W	L	SV	AB	H	HR	B
1938 CHI A	0	0	–	0.00	1	0	0	2	1	0	0	0	0	0	0	0	0	0	
1940 DET A	0	0	–	∞	1	0	0	0	4	2	0	0	0	0	0	0	0	0	
2 yrs.	0	0	–	18.00	2	0	0	2	5	2	0	0	0	0	0	0	0	0	
1 yr.	0	0	–	∞	1	0	0	0	4	2	0	0	0	0	0	0	0	0	

George Uhle

UHLE, GEORGE ERNEST (The Bull)
B. Sept. 18, 1898, Cleveland, Ohio

BR TR 6'   190 lbs

	W	L	PCT	ERA	G	GS	CG	IP	H	BB	SO	ShO	W	L	SV	AB	H	HR	B
1919 CLE A	10	5	.667	2.91	26	12	7	127	129	43	50	1	2	2	0	43	13	0	.30
1920	4	5	.444	5.21	27	6	2	84.2	98	29	27	0	4	1	1	32	11	0	.34
1921	16	13	.552	4.01	41	28	13	238	288	62	63	2	2	2	2	94	23	1	.24
1922	22	16	.579	4.07	50	40	23	287.1	328	89	82	5	1	1	3	109	29	0	.26
1923	26	16	.619	3.77	54	44	29	357.2	378	102	109	1	1	0	5	144	52	0	.36
1924	9	15	.375	4.77	28	25	15	196.1	238	75	57	0	1	1	1	107	33	1	.30
1925	13	11	.542	4.10	29	26	17	210.2	218	78	68	1	1	1	0	104	29	0	.27
1926	27	11	.711	2.83	39	36	32	318.1	300	118	159	3	1	1	1	132	30	1	.22
1927	8	9	.471	4.34	25	22	10	153.1	187	59	69	1	0	1	1	79	21	0	.26
1928	12	17	.414	4.07	31	28	18	214.1	252	48	74	2	1	1	1	98	28	1	.28
1929 DET A	15	11	.577	4.08	32	30	23	249	283	58	100	1	1	0	0	108	37	0	.34
1930	12	12	.500	3.65	33	29	18	239	239	75	117	1	0	0	3	117	36	2	.30
1931	11	12	.478	3.50	29	18	15	193	190	49	63	0	4	3	2	90	22	2	.24
1932	6	6	.500	4.48	33	15	6	146.2	152	42	51	1	1	2	5	55	10	0	.18
1933 3 teams		DET	A (1G 0–0)		NY	N (6G 1–1)		NY	A (12G 6–1)										
" total	7	2	.778	5.85	19	7	4	75.1	81	26	31	0	2	0	0	25	8	0	.32
1934 NY A	2	4	.333	9.92	10	2	0	16.1	30	7	10	0	2	0	0	5	3	0	.60

	W	L	PCT	ERA	G	GS	CG	IP	H	BB	SO	ShO	Relief Pitching W	L	SV	BATTING AB	H	HR	BA

George Uhle continued

	W	L	PCT	ERA	G	GS	CG	IP	H	BB	SO	ShO	W	L	SV	AB	H	HR	BA
1936 **CLE A**	0	1	.000	8.53	7	0	0	12.2	26	5	5	0	0	1	0	21	8	1	.381
17 yrs.	200	166	.546	3.99	513	368	232	3119.2	3417	965	1135	21	24	19	25	*			
5 yrs.	44	41	.518	3.91	128	92	62	828.1	866	224	332	5	6	5	10	370	105	4	.284
WORLD SERIES																			
1920 **CLE A**	0	0	—	0.00	1	0	0	3	1	0	3	0	0	0	0	0	0	0	—

Jerry Ujdur

UJDUR, GERALD RAYMOND   BR TR 6'1"   195 lbs.
B. Mar. 5, 1957, Duluth, Minn.

	W	L	PCT	ERA	G	GS	CG	IP	H	BB	SO	ShO	W	L	SV	AB	H	HR	BA
1980 **DET A**	1	0	1.000	7.71	9	2	0	21	36	10	8	0	0	0	0	0	0	0	—
1981	0	0	—	6.43	4	4	0	14	19	5	5	0	0	0	0	0	0	0	—
1982	10	10	.500	3.69	25	25	7	178	150	69	86	0	0	0	0	0	0	0	—
1983	0	4	.000	7.15	11	6	0	34	41	20	13	0	0	0	0	0	0	0	—
1984 **CLE A**	1	2	.333	6.91	4	3	0	14.1	22	6	6	0	1	0	0	0	0	0	—
5 yrs.	12	16	.429	4.79	53	40	7	261.1	268	110	118	0	1	0	0	0	0	0	—
4 yrs.	11	14	.440	4.66	49	37	7	247	246	104	112	0	0	0	0	0	0	0	—

Pat Underwood

UNDERWOOD, PATRICK JOHN   BL TL 6'   175 lbs.
Brother of Tom Underwood.
B. Feb. 9, 1957, Kokomo, Ind.

	W	L	PCT	ERA	G	GS	CG	IP	H	BB	SO	ShO	W	L	SV	AB	H	HR	BA
1979 **DET A**	6	4	.600	4.57	27	15	1	122	126	29	83	0	0	0	0	0	0	0	—
1980	3	6	.333	3.58	49	7	0	113	121	35	60	0	1	4	5	0	0	0	—
1982	4	8	.333	4.73	33	12	2	99	108	22	43	0	1	1	3	0	0	0	—
1983	0	0	—	8.71	4	0	0	10.1	11	6	2	0	0	0	0	0	0	0	—
4 yrs.	13	18	.419	4.42	113	34	3	344.1	366	92	188	0	2	5	8	0	0	0	—
4 yrs.	13	18	.419	4.42	113	34	3	344.1	366	92	188	0	2	5	8	0	0	0	—

Vito Valentinetti

VALENTINETTI, VITO JOHN   BR TR 6'   195 lbs.
B. Sept. 16, 1928, West New York, N. J.

	W	L	PCT	ERA	G	GS	CG	IP	H	BB	SO	ShO	W	L	SV	AB	H	HR	BA
1954 **CHI A**	0	0	—	54.00	1	0	0	1	4	2	1	0	0	0	0	0	0	0	—
1956 **CHI N**	3	4	.600	3.78	42	2	0	95.1	84	36	26	0	6	3	1	20	2	0	.100
1957 2 teams			**CHI N** (9G 0–0)				**CLE A** (11G 2–2)												
" total	2	2	.500	4.04	20	2	1	35.2	38	20	17	0	1	2	0	7	1	0	.143
1958 2 teams			**DET A** (15G 1–0)				**WAS A** (23G 4–6)												
" total	5	6	.455	4.80	38	10	2	114.1	124	54	43	0	1	1	2	28	9	0	.321
1959 **WAS A**	0	2	.000	10.13	7	1	0	10.2	16	10	7	0	0	1	0	0	0	0	—
5 yrs.	13	14	.481	4.73	108	15	3	257	266	122	94	0	8	7	3	55	12	0	.218
1 yr.	1	0	1.000	3.38	15	0	0	18.2	18	5	10	0	1	0	2	0	0	0	—

Elam Vangilder

VANGILDER, ELAM RUSSELL   BR TR 6'1"   192 lbs.
B. Apr. 23, 1896, Cape Girardeau, Mo.   D. Apr. 30, 1977, Cape Girardeau, Mo.

	W	L	PCT	ERA	G	GS	CG	IP	H	BB	SO	ShO	W	L	SV	AB	H	HR	BA
1919 **STL A**	1	0	1.000	2.08	3	1	1	13	15	3	6	0	0	0	0	3	2	0	.667
1920	3	8	.273	5.50	24	13	4	104.2	131	40	25	0	0	2	0	30	4	0	.133
1921	11	12	.478	3.94	31	21	10	180.1	196	67	48	1	1	1	0	65	13	1	.200
1922	19	13	.594	3.42	43	30	19	245	248	48	63	3	3	4	4	93	32	2	.344
1923	16	17	.485	3.06	41	35	20	282.1	276	**120**	74	4	1	2	1	110	24	1	.218
1924	5	10	.333	5.76	43	18	5	145.1	183	55	49	0	2	2	1	44	13	1	.295
1925	14	8	.636	4.70	52	16	4	193.1	225	92	61	1	11	4	6	71	13	0	.183
1926	9	11	.450	5.17	42	19	8	181	196	98	40	1	3	2	1	58	11	0	.190
1927	10	12	.455	4.44	44	23	12	203	245	102	62	3	0	2	1	68	19	1	.279
1928 **DET A**	11	10	.524	3.91	38	11	7	156.1	163	68	43	0	4	6	5	58	15	2	.259
1929	0	1	.000	6.35	6	0	0	11.1	16	7	3	0	0	1	0	1	0	0	.000
11 yrs.	99	102	.493	4.29	367	187	90	1715.2	1894	700	474	13	25	26	19	601	146	8	.243
2 yrs.	11	11	.500	4.08	44	11	7	167.2	179	75	46	0	4	7	5	59	15	2	.254

Bobby Veach

VEACH, ROBERT HAYES   BL TR 5'11"   160 lbs.
B. June 29, 1888, Island, Ky.   D. Aug. 7, 1945, Detroit, Mich.

	W	L	PCT	ERA	G	GS	CG	IP	H	BB	SO	ShO	W	L	SV	AB	H	HR	BA
1918 **DET A**	0	0	—	4.50	1	0	0	2	2	2	0	0	0	0	1	*			

Lou Vedder

VEDDER, LOUIS EDWARD   BR TR 5'10½" 175 lbs.
B. Apr. 20, 1897, Oakville, Mich.

	W	L	PCT	ERA	G	GS	CG	IP	H	BB	SO	ShO	W	L	SV	AB	H	HR	BA
1920 **DET A**	0	0	—	0.00	1	0	0	2	0	1	0	0	0	0	0	0	0	0	—

Jake Wade

WADE, JACOB FIELDS (Whistlin' Jake)   BL TL 6'2"   175 lbs.
Brother of Ben Wade.
B. Apr. 1, 1912, Morehead City, N. C.

	W	L	PCT	ERA	G	GS	CG	IP	H	BB	SO	ShO	W	L	SV	AB	H	HR	BA
1936 **DET A**	4	5	.444	5.29	13	11	4	78.1	93	52	30	1	0	0	0	29	5	0	.172
1937	7	10	.412	5.39	33	25	7	165.1	160	107	69	1	0	1	0	59	11	0	.186
1938	3	2	.600	6.56	27	2	0	70	73	48	23	0	3	0	0	21	1	0	.048
1939 2 teams			**BOS A** (20G 1–4)				**STL A** (4G 0–2)												
" total	1	6	.143	7.45	24	8	2	64	94	56	30	0	1	1	0	17	0	0	.000
1942 **CHI A**	5	5	.500	4.10	15	10	3	85.2	84	56	32	0	1	0	0	29	7	0	.241
1943	7	3	.700	3.01	21	9	3	83.2	66	54	41	1	0	1	0	27	4	0	.148
1944	2	4	.333	4.82	19	5	1	74.2	75	41	35	0	1	1	2	24	7	0	.292
1946 2 teams			**NY A** (13G 2–1)				**WAS A** (6G 0–0)												
" total	2	1	.667	2.89	19	1	0	46.2	45	26	31	0	2	0	1	10	1	0	.100
8 yrs.	27	40	.403	5.00	171	71	20	668.1	690	440	291	3	8	4	3	216	36	0	.167
3 yrs.	14	17	.452	5.62	73	38	11	313.2	326	207	122	2	3	1	0	109	17	0	.156

Mark Wagner

WAGNER, MARK DUANE   BR TR 6'   165 lbs.
B. Mar. 4, 1954, Conneaut, Ohio

	W	L	PCT	ERA	G	GS	CG	IP	H	BB	SO	ShO	W	L	SV	AB	H	HR	BA
1984 **OAK A**	0	0	—	0.00	1	0	0	1.2	2	1	1	0	0	0	0	*			

	W	L	PCT	ERA	G	GS	CG	IP	H	BB	SO	ShO	Relief Pitching W	L	SV	BATTING AB	H	HR	BA

Luke Walker

WALKER, JAMES LUKE
B. Sept. 2, 1943, DeKalb, Tex.   BL TL 6'2"   190 lbs.

	W	L	PCT	ERA	G	GS	CG	IP	H	BB	SO	ShO	W	L	SV	AB	H	HR	BA
1965 PIT N	0	0	–	0.00	2	0	0	5	2	1	5	0	0	0	0	0	0	0	–
1966	0	1	.000	4.50	10	1	0	10	8	15	7	0	0	1	0	2	0	0	.000
1968	0	3	.000	2.02	39	2	0	62.1	42	39	66	0	0	2	3	8	0	0	.000
1969	4	6	.400	3.63	31	15	3	119	98	57	96	1	0	0	0	32	0	0	.000
1970	15	6	.714	3.04	42	19	5	163	129	89	124	3	3	1	3	46	6	0	.130
1971	10	8	.556	3.54	28	24	4	160	157	53	86	2	2	0	0	46	1	0	.022
1972	4	6	.400	3.40	26	12	2	92.2	98	34	48	0	0	1	2	24	2	0	.083
1973	7	12	.368	4.65	37	18	2	122	129	66	74	1	0	1	1	30	2	0	.067
1974 DET A	5	5	.500	4.99	28	9	0	92	100	54	52	0	2	0	0	0	0	0	–
9 yrs.	45	47	.489	3.64	243	100	16	826	763	408	558	7	7	6	9	188	11	0	.059
1 yr.	5	5	.500	4.99	28	9	0	92	100	54	52	0	2	0	0	0	0	0	–
LEAGUE CHAMPIONSHIP SERIES																			
1970 PIT N	0	1	.000	1.29	1	1	0	7	5	1	5	0	0	0	0	2	0	0	.000
1972	0	0	–	18.00	1	0	0	1	3	0	0	0	0	0	0	0	0	0	–
2 yrs.	0	1	.000	3.38	2	1	0	8	8	1	5	0	0	0	0	2	0	0	.000
WORLD SERIES																			
1971 PIT N	0	0	–	40.50	1	1	0	.2	3	1	0	0	0	0	0	0	0	0	–

Tom Walker

WALKER, ROBERT THOMAS
B. Nov. 7, 1948, Tampa, Fla.   BR TR 6'1"   188 lbs.

	W	L	PCT	ERA	G	GS	CG	IP	H	BB	SO	ShO	W	L	SV	AB	H	HR	BA
1972 MON N	2	2	.500	2.89	46	0	0	74.2	71	22	42	0	2	2	2	3	0	0	.000
1973	7	5	.583	3.63	54	0	0	91.2	95	42	68	0	7	5	4	7	0	0	.000
1974	4	5	.444	3.82	33	8	1	92	96	28	70	0	2	1	2	16	3	0	.188
1975 DET A	3	8	.273	4.45	36	9	1	115.1	116	40	60	0	1	3	0	0	0	0	–
1976 STL N	1	2	.333	4.12	10	0	0	19.2	22	3	11	0	1	2	3	5	2	0	.400
1977 2 teams					MON N (11G 1–1)					CAL A (1G 0–0)									
" total	1	1	.500	5.14	12	0	0	21	18	7	11	0	1	1	0	2	0	0	.000
6 yrs.	18	23	.439	3.87	191	17	2	414.1	418	142	262	0	14	14	11	33	5	0	.152
1 yr.	3	8	.273	4.45	36	9	1	115.1	116	40	60	0	1	3	0	0	0	0	–

Jim Walkup

WALKUP, JAMES ELTON
B. Dec. 14, 1909, Havana, Ark.   BR TR 6'1"   170 lbs.

	W	L	PCT	ERA	G	GS	CG	IP	H	BB	SO	ShO	W	L	SV	AB	H	HR	BA
1934 STL A	0	0	–	2.16	3	0	0	8.1	6	5	6	0	0	0	0	3	1	0	.333
1935	6	9	.400	6.25	55	20	4	181.1	226	104	44	1	1	1	0	47	6	0	.128
1936	0	3	.000	8.04	5	2	0	15.2	20	6	5	0	0	1	0	4	0	0	.000
1937	9	12	.429	7.36	27	18	6	150.1	218	83	46	0	2	3	0	58	14	0	.241
1938	1	12	.077	6.80	18	13	1	94	127	53	28	0	1	2	0	29	4	0	.138
1939 2 teams					STL A (1G 0–1)					DET A (7G 0–1)									
" total	0	2	.000	7.11	8	0	0	12.2	17	9	5	0	0	2	0	2	1	0	.500
6 yrs.	16	38	.296	6.74	116	53	11	462.1	614	260	134	1	4	9	0	143	26	0	.182
1 yr.	0	1	.000	7.50	7	0	0	12	15	8	5	0	0	1	0	2	1	0	.500

Jim Walkup

WALKUP, JAMES HUEY
B. Nov. 3, 1895, Havana, Ark.   BR TL 5'8"   150 lbs.

	W	L	PCT	ERA	G	GS	CG	IP	H	BB	SO	ShO	W	L	SV	AB	H	HR	BA
1927 DET A	0	0	–	5.40	2	0	0	1.2	3	0	0	0	0	0	0	1	0	0	.000

Jim Walsh

WALSH, JAMES THOMAS
B. July 10, 1894, Roxbury, Mass.   D. May 13, 1967, Boston, Mass.   BL TL 5'11"   175 lbs.

	W	L	PCT	ERA	G	GS	CG	IP	H	BB	SO	ShO	W	L	SV	AB	H	HR	BA
1921 DET A	0	0	–	2.25	3	0	0	4	2	1	3	0	0	0	0	0	0	0	–

Jon Warden

WARDEN, JONATHAN EDGAR (Warbler)
B. Oct. 1, 1946, Columbus, Ohio   BB TL 6'   205 lbs.

	W	L	PCT	ERA	G	GS	CG	IP	H	BB	SO	ShO	W	L	SV	AB	H	HR	BA
1968 DET A	4	1	.800	3.62	28	0	0	37.1	30	15	25	0	4	1	3	2	0	0	.000

Roger Weaver

WEAVER, ROGER EDWARD
B. Oct. 6, 1954, Amsterdam, N. Y.   BR TR 6'3"   190 lbs.

	W	L	PCT	ERA	G	GS	CG	IP	H	BB	SO	ShO	W	L	SV	AB	H	HR	BA
1980 DET A	3	4	.429	4.08	19	6	0	64	56	34	42	0	2	0	0	0	0	0	–

Herm Wehmeier

WEHMEIER, HERMAN RALPH
B. Feb. 18, 1927, Cincinnati, Ohio   D. May 21, 1973, Dallas, Tex.   BR TR 6'2"   185 lbs.

	W	L	PCT	ERA	G	GS	CG	IP	H	BB	SO	ShO	W	L	SV	AB	H	HR	BA
1945 CIN N	0	1	.000	12.60	2	2	0	5	10	4	0	0	0	0	0	1	0	0	.000
1947	0	0	–	0.00	1	0	0	1	0	0	0	0	0	0	0	0	0	0	–
1948	11	8	.579	5.86	33	24	6	147.1	179	75	56	0	1	1	0	55	5	0	.091
1949	11	12	.478	4.68	33	29	11	213.1	202	117	80	1	1	1	0	78	20	0	.256
1950	10	18	.357	5.67	41	32	12	230	255	135	121	0	0	0	4	92	14	0	.152
1951	7	10	.412	3.70	39	22	10	184.2	167	89	93	2	0	0	2	59	17	0	.288
1952	9	11	.450	5.15	33	26	6	190.1	197	103	83	1	0	2	0	64	12	1	.188
1953	1	6	.143	7.16	28	10	2	81.2	100	47	32	0	0	4	0	20	4	0	.200
1954 2 teams					CIN N (12G 0–3)					PHI N (25G 10–8)									
" total	10	11	.476	4.40	37	20	10	171.2	153	72	62	2	1	0	2	59	6	0	.102
1955 PHI N	10	12	.455	4.41	31	29	10	193.2	176	67	85	1	0	0	0	72	20	0	.278
1956 2 teams					PHI N (3G 0–2)					STL N (34G 12–9)									
" total	12	11	.522	3.73	37	22	7	190.2	168	82	76	2	5	1	1	66	13	2	.197
1957 STL N	10	7	.588	4.31	36	18	5	165	165	54	91	0	2	2	0	59	12	0	.203
1958 2 teams					STL N (3G 0–1)					DET A (7G 1–0)									
" total	1	1	.500	4.71	10	6	0	28.2	34	7	15	0	0	0	0	8	1	0	.125
13 yrs.	92	108	.460	4.80	361	240	79	1803	1806	852	794	9	10	7	9	633	124	3	.196
1 yr.	1	0	1.000	2.38	7	3	0	22.2	21	5	11	0	0	0	0	6	0	0	.000

Dick Weik

WEIK, RICHARD HENRY (Legs)
B. Nov. 17, 1927, Waterloo, Iowa   BR TR 6'3½"   184 lbs.

	W	L	PCT	ERA	G	GS	CG	IP	H	BB	SO	ShO	W	L	SV	AB	H	HR	BA
1948 WAS A	1	2	.333	5.68	3	3	0	12.2	14	22	8	0	0	0	0	4	3	0	.750
1949	3	12	.200	5.38	27	14	2	95.1	78	103	58	2	1	1	1	28	5	0	.179

	W	L	PCT	ERA	G	GS	CG	IP	H	BB	SO	ShO	Relief Pitching W	L	SV	BATTING AB	H	HR	BA

Dick Weik *continued*

	W	L	PCT	ERA	G	GS	CG	IP	H	BB	SO	ShO	W	L	SV	AB	H	HR	BA
'50 2 teams	WAS	A	(14G 1–3)	CLE	A	(11G 1–3)													
" total	2	6	.250	4.11	25	7	1	70	56	73	42	0	1	1	0	18	3	0	.167
'53 CLE A	0	1	.000	13.97	12	1	0	19.1	32	23	6	0	0	1	0	2	1	0	.500
'54 DET A	0	1	.000	7.16	9	1	0	16.1	23	16	9	0	0	1	0	1	0	0	.000
5 yrs.	6	22	.214	5.90	76	26	3	213.2	203	237	123	2	2	4	1	53	12	0	.226
2 yrs.	0	2	.000	10.85	21	2	0	35.2	55	39	15	0	0	2	0	3	1	0	.333

Ed Wells

WELLS, EDWIN LEE
B. June 7, 1900, Ashland, Ohio
BL TL 6'1½" 183 lbs.

	W	L	PCT	ERA	G	GS	CG	IP	H	BB	SO	ShO	W	L	SV	AB	H	HR	BA
'23 DET A	0	0	—	5.40	7	0	0	10	11	6	6	0	0	0	0	1	0	0	.000
'24	6	8	.429	4.06	29	15	5	102	117	42	33	0	1	1	4	33	7	0	.212
'25	6	9	.400	6.23	35	14	5	134.1	190	62	45	0	2	3	2	43	12	0	.279
'26	12	10	.545	4.15	36	26	9	178	201	76	58	4	2	2	0	73	15	0	.205
'27	0	1	.000	6.75	8	1	0	20	28	5	5	0	0	0	1	7	2	0	.286
'29 NY A	13	9	.591	4.33	31	23	10	193.1	179	81	78	3	0	0	0	74	17	0	.230
'30	12	3	.800	5.20	27	21	7	150.2	185	49	46	0	1	1	0	58	15	0	.259
'31	9	5	.643	4.32	27	10	6	116.2	130	37	34	0	2	4	2	45	10	0	.222
'32	3	3	.500	4.26	22	0	0	31.2	38	12	13	0	3	3	2	6	0	0	.000
'33 STL A	6	14	.300	4.20	36	22	10	203.2	230	63	58	0	2	3	1	71	14	0	.197
'34	1	7	.125	4.79	33	8	2	92	108	35	27	0	1	3	1	22	1	0	.045
11 yrs.	68	69	.496	4.65	291	140	54	1232.1	1417	468	403	7	14	20	13	433	93	0	.215
5 yrs.	24	28	.462	4.90	115	56	19	444.1	547	191	147	4	5	6	7	157	36	0	.229

Charlie Wheatley

WHEATLEY, CHARLES
B. June 27, 1893, Rosedale, Kans.   D. Dec. 10, 1982, Tulsa, Okla.
BR TR 5'11" 174 lbs.

	W	L	PCT	ERA	G	GS	CG	IP	H	BB	SO	ShO	W	L	SV	AB	H	HR	BA
'12 DET A	1	4	.200	6.17	5	5	2	35	45	17	14	0	0	0	0	12	0	0	.000

Jack Whillock

WHILLOCK, JACK FRANKLIN
B. Nov. 4, 1942, Searcy, Ark.
BR TR 6'3" 195 lbs.

	W	L	PCT	ERA	G	GS	CG	IP	H	BB	SO	ShO	W	L	SV	AB	H	HR	BA
'71 DET A	0	2	.000	5.63	7	0	0	8	10	2	6	0	0	2	1	1	0	0	.000

Hal White

WHITE, HAROLD GEORGE
B. Mar. 18, 1919, Utica, N. Y.
BL TR 5'10" 165 lbs.

	W	L	PCT	ERA	G	GS	CG	IP	H	BB	SO	ShO	W	L	SV	AB	H	HR	BA
'41 DET A	0	0	—	6.00	4	0	0	9	11	6	2	0	0	0	0	2	0	0	.000
'42	12	12	.500	2.91	34	25	12	216.2	212	82	93	4	1	3	1	77	13	0	.169
'43	7	12	.368	3.39	32	24	7	177.2	150	71	58	2	0	2	2	57	8	0	.140
'46	1	1	.500	5.60	11	1	1	27.1	34	15	12	0	0	1	0	7	0	0	.000
'47	4	5	.444	3.61	35	5	0	84.2	91	47	33	0	4	2	2	18	3	0	.167
'48	2	1	.667	6.12	27	0	0	42.2	46	26	17	0	2	1	1	13	2	0	.154
'49	1	0	1.000	0.00	9	0	0	12	5	4	4	0	1	0	2	3	1	0	.333
'50	9	6	.600	4.54	42	8	3	111	96	65	53	1	6	3	1	33	4	0	.121
'51	3	4	.429	4.74	38	4	0	76	74	49	23	0	2	1	4	16	4	0	.250
'52	1	8	.111	3.69	41	0	0	63.1	53	39	18	0	1	8	5	11	2	0	.182
'53 2 teams	STL	A	(10G 0–0)	STL	N	(49G 6–5)													
total	6	5	.545	2.94	59	0	0	95	92	42	34	0	6	5	7	17	0	0	.000
'54 STL N	0	0	—	19.80	4	0	0	5	11	4	2	0	0	0	0	1	0	0	.000
12 yrs.	46	54	.460	3.78	336	67	23	920.1	875	450	349	7	23	26	25	255	37	0	.145
10 yrs.	40	49	.449	3.79	273	67	23	820.1	772	404	313	7	17	21	18	237	37	0	.156

Earl Whitehill

WHITEHILL, EARL OLIVER
B. Feb. 7, 1899, Cedar Rapids, Iowa   D. Oct. 22, 1954, Omaha, Neb.
BL TL 5'9½" 174 lbs.

	W	L	PCT	ERA	G	GS	CG	IP	H	BB	SO	ShO	W	L	SV	AB	H	HR	BA
'23 DET A	2	0	1.000	2.73	8	3	2	33	22	15	19	1	2	0	0	11	4	0	.364
'24	17	9	.654	3.86	35	32	16	233	260	79	65	2	0	2	0	89	19	0	.213
'25	11	11	.500	4.66	35	33	15	239.1	267	88	83	1	0	0	2	87	19	0	.218
'26	16	13	.552	3.99	36	34	13	252.1	271	79	109	0	2	0	0	91	23	0	.253
'27	16	14	.533	3.36	41	31	17	236	238	105	95	3	3	1	3	78	16	0	.205
'28	11	16	.407	4.31	31	30	12	196.1	214	78	93	1	1	0	0	67	13	0	.194
'29	14	15	.483	4.62	38	28	18	245.1	267	96	103	1	4	1	1	90	23	3	.256
'30	17	13	.567	4.24	34	31	16	220.2	248	80	109	0	0	1	1	83	16	0	.193
'31	13	16	.448	4.06	34	34	22	272.1	287	118	81	0	0	0	0	97	15	0	.155
'32	16	12	.571	4.54	33	31	17	244	255	93	81	3	1	0	0	90	22	0	.244
'33 WAS A	22	8	.733	3.33	39	37	19	270	271	100	96	2	0	0	1	108	24	0	.222
'34	14	11	.560	4.52	32	31	15	235	269	94	96	1	0	0	0	85	17	1	.200
'35	14	13	.519	4.29	34	34	19	279.1	318	104	102	1	0	0	0	104	19	0	.183
'36	14	11	.560	4.87	28	28	14	212.1	252	89	63	0	0	0	0	77	13	0	.169
'37 CLE A	8	8	.500	6.49	33	22	6	147	189	80	53	1	0	0	2	49	11	0	.224
'38	9	8	.529	5.56	26	23	4	160.1	187	83	60	0	1	0	0	56	7	0	.125
'39 CHI N	4	7	.364	5.14	24	11	2	89.1	102	50	42	1	0	1	1	29	3	0	.103
17 yrs.	218	185	.541	4.36	541	473	227	3565.2	3917	1431	1350	17	14	6	11	1291	264	4	.204
10 yrs.	133	119	.528	4.16	325	287	148	2172.1	2329	831	838	12	13	5	7	783	170	3	.217
		8th	7th			9th			8th	7th			7th						

WORLD SERIES

	W	L	PCT	ERA	G	GS	CG	IP	H	BB	SO	ShO	W	L	SV	AB	H	HR	BA
'33 WAS A	1	0	1.000	0.00	1	1	1	9	5	2	2	1	0	0	0	3	0	0	.000

Dave Wickersham

WICKERSHAM, DAVID CLIFFORD
B. Sept. 27, 1935, Erie, Pa.
BR TR 6'3" 188 lbs.

	W	L	PCT	ERA	G	GS	CG	IP	H	BB	SO	ShO	W	L	SV	AB	H	HR	BA
'60 KC A	0	0	—	1.08	5	0	0	8.1	4	1	3	0	0	0	2	1	0	0	.000
'61	2	1	.667	5.14	17	0	0	21	25	5	10	0	2	1	2	3	2	0	.667
'62	11	4	.733	4.17	30	9	3	110	105	43	61	0	5	2	1	35	2	0	.057
'63	12	15	.444	4.09	38	34	4	237.2	244	79	118	1	1	0	1	80	11	0	.138
'64 DET A	19	12	.613	3.44	40	36	11	254	224	81	164	1	0	1	1	82	6	0	.073
'65	9	14	.391	3.78	34	27	8	195.1	179	61	109	3	1	0	0	58	4	0	.069
'66	8	3	.727	3.20	38	14	3	140.2	139	54	93	0	4	1	1	45	2	0	.044
'67	4	5	.444	2.74	36	4	0	85.1	72	33	44	0	4	1	4	15	0	0	.000

	W	L	PCT	ERA	G	GS	CG	IP	H	BB	SO	ShO	Relief Pitching W	L	SV	BATTING AB	H	HR	B

Dave Wickersham continued

	W	L	PCT	ERA	G	GS	CG	IP	H	BB	SO	ShO	W	L	SV	AB	H	HR	B
1968 PIT N	1	0	1.000	3.48	11	0	0	20.2	21	13	9	0	1	0	1	3	1	0	.33
1969 KC A	2	3	.400	3.96	34	0	0	50	58	14	27	0	2	3	5	2	0	0	.00
10 yrs.	68	57	.544	3.66	283	124	29	1123	1071	384	638	5	20	9	18	324	28	0	.08
4 yrs.	40	34	.541	3.40	148	81	22	675.1	614	229	410	4	9	3	6	200	12	0	.06

Jimmy Wiggs

WIGGS, JAMES ALVIN (Big Jim)   BB TR 6'4" 200 lbs
B. Sept. 1, 1876, Trondhjem, Norway   D. Jan. 20, 1963, Xenia, Ohio

	W	L	PCT	ERA	G	GS	CG	IP	H	BB	SO	ShO	W	L	SV	AB	H	HR	B
1903 CIN N	0	1	.000	5.40	2	1	0	5	12	2	2	0	0	0	0	1	0	0	.00
1905 DET A	3	3	.500	3.27	7	7	4	41.1	30	29	37	0	0	0	0	15	2	0	.13
1906	0	0	—	5.23	4	1	0	10.1	11	7	7	0	0	0	0	3	1	0	.33
3 yrs.	3	4	.429	3.81	13	9	4	56.2	53	38	46	0	0	0	0	19	3	0	.15
2 yrs.	3	3	.500	3.66	11	8	4	51.2	41	36	44	0	0	0	0	18	3	0	.16

Bill Wight

WIGHT, WILLIAM ROBERT (Lefty)   BL TL 6'1" 180 lbs
B. Apr. 12, 1922, Rio Vista, Calif.

	W	L	PCT	ERA	G	GS	CG	IP	H	BB	SO	ShO	W	L	SV	AB	H	HR	B
1946 NY A	2	2	.500	4.46	14	4	1	40.1	44	30	11	0	0	0	0	9	0	0	.00
1947	1	0	1.000	1.00	1	1	1	9	8	2	3	0	0	0	0	2	0	0	.00
1948 CHI A	9	20	.310	4.80	34	32	7	223.1	238	135	68	1	0	0	0	73	6	0	.08
1949	15	13	.536	3.31	35	33	14	245	254	96	78	3	0	0	1	85	14	0	.16
1950	10	16	.385	3.58	30	28	13	206	213	79	62	3	0	1	0	61	0	0	.00
1951 BOS A	7	7	.500	5.10	34	17	4	118.1	128	63	38	2	2	0	0	41	3	0	.07
1952 2 teams	BOS	A	(10G 2-1)	DET	A	(23G 5-9)													
" total	7	10	.412	3.75	33	21	8	168	181	69	70	3	1	0	0	57	12	0	.21
1953 2 teams	DET	A	(13G 0-3)	CLE	A	(20G 2-1)													
" total	2	4	.333	6.23	33	4	0	52	64	30	24	0	2	2	1	12	3	0	.25
1955 2 teams	CLE	A	(17G 0-0)	BAL	A	(19G 6-8)													
" total	6	8	.429	2.48	36	14	8	141.1	135	48	63	2	1	0	3	36	3	0	.08
1956 BAL A	9	12	.429	4.02	35	26	7	174.2	198	72	84	1	1	0	0	60	12	0	.20
1957	6	6	.500	3.64	27	17	2	121	122	54	50	0	0	0	0	34	1	0	.02
1958 2 teams	CIN	N	(7G 0-1)	STL	N	(28G 3-0)													
" total	3	1	.750	4.92	35	1	0	64	71	36	23	0	2	1	2	10	1	0	.10
12 yrs.	77	99	.438	3.95	347	198	66	1563	1656	714	574	15	8	5	8	480	55	0	.11
2 yrs.	5	12	.294	4.63	36	23	8	169	202	69	75	3	0	1	0	57	14	0	.24

Milt Wilcox

WILCOX, MILTON EDWARD   BR TR 6'2" 185 lbs
B. Apr. 20, 1950, Honolulu, Hawaii

	W	L	PCT	ERA	G	GS	CG	IP	H	BB	SO	ShO	W	L	SV	AB	H	HR	B
1970 CIN N	3	1	.750	2.45	5	2	1	22	19	7	13	1	1	1	1	5	1	0	.20
1971	2	2	.500	3.35	18	3	0	43	43	17	21	0	2	1	1	9	0	0	.00
1972 CLE A	7	14	.333	3.40	32	27	4	156	145	72	90	2	0	1	0	45	9	0	.20
1973	8	10	.444	5.83	26	19	4	134.1	143	68	82	0	0	0	0	0	0	0	
1974	2	2	.500	4.69	41	2	1	71	74	24	33	0	1	1	4	0	0	0	
1975 CHI N	0	1	.000	5.68	25	0	0	38	50	17	21	0	0	1	0	3	1	0	.33
1977 DET A	6	2	.750	3.65	20	13	1	106	96	37	82	0	1	0	0	0	0	0	
1978	13	12	.520	3.76	29	27	16	215.1	208	68	132	2	0	1	0	0	0	0	
1979	12	10	.545	4.36	33	29	7	196	201	73	109	0	1	0	0	0	0	0	
1980	13	11	.542	4.48	32	31	13	199	201	68	97	1	1	0	0	0	0	0	
1981	12	9	.571	3.04	24	24	8	166	152	52	79	1	0	0	0	0	0	0	
1982	12	10	.545	3.62	29	29	9	193.2	187	85	112	1	0	0	0	0	0	0	
1983	11	10	.524	3.97	26	26	9	186	164	74	101	2	0	0	0	0	0	0	
1984	17	8	.680	4.00	33	33	0	193.2	183	66	119	0	0	0	0	0	0	0	
14 yrs.	118	102	.536	4.02	373	265	73	1920	1866	728	1091	10	7	6	6	62	11	0	.17
8 yrs.	96	72	.571	3.89	226	212	63	1455.2	1392	523	831	7	3	1	0	0	0	0	

LEAGUE CHAMPIONSHIP SERIES

	W	L	PCT	ERA	G	GS	CG	IP	H	BB	SO	ShO	W	L	SV	AB	H	HR	B
1970 CIN N	1	0	1.000	0.00	1	0	0	3	1	2	5	0	1	0	0	0	0	0	
1984 DET A	1	0	1.000	0.00	1	1	0	8	1	2	8	0	0	0	0	0	0	0	
2 yrs.	2	0	1.000	0.00	2	1	0	11	2	4	13	0	1	0	0	0	0	0	

WORLD SERIES

	W	L	PCT	ERA	G	GS	CG	IP	H	BB	SO	ShO	W	L	SV	AB	H	HR	B
1970 CIN N	0	1	.000	9.00	2	0	0	2	3	0	2	0	0	1	0	0	0	0	
1984 DET A	1	0	1.000	1.50	1	1	0	6	7	2	4	0	0	0	0	0	0	0	
2 yrs.	1	1	.500	3.38	3	1	0	8	10	2	6	0	0	1	0	0	0	0	

Ed Willett

WILLETT, ROBERT EDGAR   BR TR
B. Mar. 7, 1884, Norfolk, Va.   D. May 10, 1934, Wellington, Kans.

	W	L	PCT	ERA	G	GS	CG	IP	H	BB	SO	ShO	W	L	SV	AB	H	HR	B
1906 DET A	0	3	.000	3.96	3	3	3	25	24	8	16	0	0	0	0	9	0	0	.00
1907	1	5	.167	3.70	10	6	1	48.2	47	20	27	0	0	0	0	13	1	0	.07
1908	15	8	.652	2.28	30	22	18	197.1	186	60	77	2	0	1	1	67	11	0	.16
1909	21	10	.677	2.34	41	34	25	292.2	239	76	89	3	0	2	1	112	22	0	.19
1910	16	11	.593	3.60	37	25	18	147.1	175	74	65	4	1	2	0	83	11	0	.13
1911	13	14	.481	3.66	38	27	15	231.1	261	80	86	2	2	3	1	82	22	1	.26
1912	17	15	.531	3.29	37	31	28	284.1	281	84	89	1	2	1	0	115	19	2	.28
1913	13	14	.481	3.09	34	30	19	242	237	89	59	0	1	1	0	92	26	1	.28
1914 STL F	4	16	.200	4.22	27	21	14	175	208	56	73	0	0	0	0	64	15	1	.23
1915	2	3	.400	4.61	17	2	1	52.2	61	18	19	0	1	3	2	15	3	0	.20
10 yrs.	102	99	.507	3.22 (8th)	274	201	142	1696.1 (10th)	1719	565	600	12	7	14	5	652	130	5	.19
8 yrs.	96	80	.545	3.05	230	178	127	1468.2	1450	491	508	12	6	10	3	573	112	4	.19

WORLD SERIES

	W	L	PCT	ERA	G	GS	CG	IP	H	BB	SO	ShO	W	L	SV	AB	H	HR	B
1909 DET A	0	0	—	0.00	2	0	0	7.2	3	0	1	0	0	0	0	2	0	0	.00

Johnny Williams

WILLIAMS, JOHN BRODIE (Honolulu Johnny)   BR TR 6' 180 lbs
B. July 16, 1889, Honolulu, Hawaii   D. Sept. 8, 1963, Long Beach, Calif.

	W	L	PCT	ERA	G	GS	CG	IP	H	BB	SO	ShO	W	L	SV	AB	H	HR	B
1914 DET A	0	2	.000	6.35	4	3	1	11.1	17	5	4	0	0	0	0	3	0	0	.00

	W	L	PCT	ERA	G	GS	CG	IP	H	BB	SO	ShO	Relief Pitching W	L	SV	BATTING AB	H	HR	BA

Lefty Williams

WILLIAMS, CLAUD PRESTON   BR TL 5'9"   160 lbs.
B. Mar. 9, 1893, Aurora, Mo.   D. Nov. 4, 1959, Laguna Beach, Calif.

	W	L	PCT	ERA	G	GS	CG	IP	H	BB	SO	ShO	W	L	SV	AB	H	HR	BA
1913 DET A	1	3	.250	4.97	5	4	3	29	34	4	9	0	0	0	1	10	1	0	.100
1914	0	1	.000	0.00	1	1	0	1	3	2	0	0	0	0	0	0	0	0	—
1916 CHI A	13	7	.650	2.89	43	26	10	224.1	220	65	138	2	1	1	1	74	10	0	.135
1917	17	8	.680	2.97	45	29	8	230	221	81	85	1	4	2	1	67	6	0	.090
1918	6	4	.600	2.73	15	14	7	105.2	76	47	30	2	0	0	1	38	5	0	.132
1919	23	11	.676	2.64	41	40	27	297	265	58	125	5	0	0	1	94	17	0	.181
1920	22	14	.611	3.91	39	38	26	299	302	90	128	0	1	0	0	101	22	0	.218
7 yrs.	82	48	.631	3.13	189	152	81	1186	1121	347	515	10	6	3	5	384	61	0	.159
2 yrs.	1	4	.200	4.80	6	5	3	30	37	6	9	0	0	0	1	10	1	0	.100
WORLD SERIES																			
1917 CHI A	0	0	—	9.00	1	0	0	1	2	0	3	0	0	0	0	0	0	0	—
1919	0	3	.000	6.61	3	3	1	16.1	12	8	4	0	0	0	0	5	1	0	.200
2 yrs.	0	3	.000	6.75	4	3	1	17.1	14	8	7	0	0	0	0	5	1	0	.200

Carl Willis

WILLIS, CARL BLAKE   BL TR 6'3"   210 lbs.
B. Dec. 28, 1960, Danville, Va.

	W	L	PCT	ERA	G	GS	CG	IP	H	BB	SO	ShO	W	L	SV	AB	H	HR	BA
1984 2 teams			DET A (10G 0–2)		CIN N (7G 0–1)														
'' total	0	3	.000	5.96	17	2	0	25.2	33	7	7	0	0	2	1	0	0	0	—

Earl Wilson

WILSON, EARL LAWRENCE   BR TR 6'3"   216 lbs.
B. Oct. 2, 1934, Ponchatoula, La.

	W	L	PCT	ERA	G	GS	CG	IP	H	BB	SO	ShO	W	L	SV	AB	H	HR	BA
1959 BOS A	1	1	.500	6.08	9	4	0	23.2	21	31	17	0	1	0	0	8	4	0	.500
1960	3	2	.600	4.71	13	9	2	65	41	48	40	0	0	0	0	23	4	0	.174
1962	12	8	.600	3.90	31	28	4	191.1	163	111	137	1	0	0	0	69	12	3	.174
1963	11	16	.407	3.76	37	34	6	210.2	184	105	123	3	0	0	0	72	15	1	.208
1964	11	12	.478	4.49	33	31	5	202.1	213	73	166	0	0	0	0	73	15	5	.205
1965	13	14	.481	3.98	36	36	8	230.2	221	77	164	1	0	0	0	79	14	6	.177
1966 2 teams			BOS A (15G 5–5)		DET A (23G 13–6)														
'' total	18	11	.621	3.07	38	37	13	264	214	74	200	3	0	0	0	96	23	7	.240
1967 DET A	22	11	.667	3.27	39	38	12	264	216	92	184	0	0	0	0	108	20	4	.185
1968	13	12	.520	2.85	34	33	10	224.1	192	65	168	3	0	0	0	88	20	7	.227
1969	12	10	.545	3.31	35	35	5	214.2	209	69	150	1	0	0	0	76	10	0	.132
1970 2 teams			DET A (18G 4–6)		SD N (15G 1–6)														
'' total	5	12	.294	4.58	33	25	4	161	169	51	103	1	1	1	0	48	7	2	.146
11 yrs.	121	109	.526	3.69	338	310	69	2051.2	1863	796	1452	13	2	1	0	740	144	35	.195
5 yrs.	64	45	.587 10th	3.18	149	145	39	962.1	830	296	709	7	0	0	0	367	71	17	.193
WORLD SERIES																			
1968 DET A	0	1	.000	6.23	1	1	0	4.1	4	6	3	0	0	0	0	1	0	0	.000

Jack Wilson

WILSON, JOHN FRANCIS (Black Jack)   BR TR 5'11"   210 lbs.
B. Apr. 12, 1912, Portland, Ore.

	W	L	PCT	ERA	G	GS	CG	IP	H	BB	SO	ShO	W	L	SV	AB	H	HR	BA
1934 PHI A	0	1	.000	12.00	2	2	1	9	15	9	2	0	0	0	0	3	0	0	.000
1935 BOS A	3	4	.429	4.22	23	6	2	64	72	36	19	0	1	0	1	16	5	1	.313
1936	6	8	.429	4.42	43	9	2	136.1	152	86	74	0	5	3	3	50	11	0	.220
1937	16	10	.615	3.70	51	21	14	221.1	209	119	137	1	5	4	7	85	14	0	.165
1938	15	15	.500	4.30	37	27	11	194.2	200	91	96	3	6	2	1	68	15	0	.221
1939	11	11	.500	4.67	36	22	6	177.1	198	75	80	0	3	0	2	63	10	0	.159
1940	12	6	.667	5.08	41	16	9	157.2	170	87	102	0	4	4	5	66	18	2	.273
1941	4	13	.235	5.03	27	12	4	116.1	140	70	55	1	2	4	1	44	7	0	.159
1942 2 teams			WAS A (12G 1–4)		DET A (9G 0–0)														
'' total	1	4	.200	6.22	21	6	1	55	77	28	25	0	0	0	1	18	2	0	.111
9 yrs.	68	72	.486	4.59	281	121	50	1131.2	1233	601	590	5	26	18	20	413	82	3	.199
1 yr.	0	0	—	4.85	9	0	0	13	20	5	7	0	0	0	0	1	0	0	.000

Mutt Wilson

WILSON, WILLIAM CLARENCE   BR TR 6'3"   167 lbs.
B. July 20, 1896, Kiser, N. C.   D. Aug. 31, 1962, Wildwood, Fla.

	W	L	PCT	ERA	G	GS	CG	IP	H	BB	SO	ShO	W	L	SV	AB	H	HR	BA
1920 DET A	1	1	.500	3.46	3	2	1	13	12	5	4	0	0	0	0	4	1	0	.250

Walter Wilson

WILSON, WALTER WOOD   BL TR 6'4"   190 lbs.
B. Nov. 24, 1913, Glenn, Ga.

	W	L	PCT	ERA	G	GS	CG	IP	H	BB	SO	ShO	W	L	SV	AB	H	HR	BA
1945 DET A	1	3	.250	4.61	25	4	1	70.1	76	35	28	0	0	1	0	19	1	0	.053

George Winter

WINTER, GEORGE LOVINGTON (Sassafras)   TR
B. Apr. 27, 1878, New Providence, Pa.   D. May 26, 1951, Franklin Lakes, N. J.

	W	L	PCT	ERA	G	GS	CG	IP	H	BB	SO	ShO	W	L	SV	AB	H	HR	BA
1901 BOS A	16	12	.571	2.80	28	28	26	241	234	66	63	1	0	0	0	100	19	1	.190
1902	11	9	.550	2.99	20	20	18	168.1	149	53	51	0	0	0	0	61	10	0	.164
1903	9	8	.529	3.08	24	18	14	178.1	182	37	64	0	0	0	0	66	7	0	.106
1904	8	4	.667	2.32	20	16	12	135.2	126	27	31	1	0	0	0	43	5	0	.116
1905	16	16	.500	2.96	35	27	24	264.1	249	54	119	2	4	2	0	89	24	0	.270
1906	6	18	.250	4.12	29	22	18	207.2	215	38	72	1	0	2	2	69	17	0	.246
1907	12	15	.444	2.07	35	27	21	256.2	198	61	88	4	2	1	1	94	21	0	.223
1908 2 teams			BOS A (22G 4–14)		DET A (7G 1–5)														
'' total	5	19	.208	2.65	29	23	13	204	199	43	80	0	1	1	1	67	11	0	.164
8 yrs.	83	101	.451	2.87	220	181	146	1656	1552	379	568	9	7	6	4	589	114	1	.194
1 yr.	1	5	.167	1.60	7	6	5	56.1	49	7	25	0	0	0	1	18	2	0	.111
WORLD SERIES																			
1908 DET A	0	0	—	0.00	1	0	0	1	1	0	0	0	0	0	0	0	0	0	—

Pete Wojey

WOJEY, PETER PAUL   BR TR 5'11"   185 lbs.
B. Dec. 1, 1919, Stowe, Pa.

	W	L	PCT	ERA	G	GS	CG	IP	H	BB	SO	ShO	W	L	SV	AB	H	HR	BA
1954 BKN N	1	1	.500	3.25	14	1	0	27.2	24	14	21	0	0	0	1	3	0	0	.000
1956 DET A	0	0	—	2.25	2	0	0	4	2	1	1	0	0	0	0	0	0	0	—

	W	L	PCT	ERA	G	GS	CG	IP	H	BB	SO	ShO	Relief W	L	SV	AB	H	HR	B

Pete Wojey continued

	W	L	PCT	ERA	G	GS	CG	IP	H	BB	SO	ShO	W	L	SV	AB	H	HR	B
1957	0	0	—	0.00	2	0	0	1.1	1	0	0	0	0	0	0	0	0	0	
3 yrs.	1	1	.500	3.00	18	1	0	33	27	15	22	0	0	0	1	3	0	0	.00
2 yrs.	0	0	—	1.69	4	0	0	5.1	3	1	1	0	0	0	0	0	0	0	.00

Hal Woodeshick

WOODESHICK, HAROLD JOSEPH
B. Aug. 24, 1932, Wilkes-Barre, Pa.   BR TL 6'3" 200 lbs

	W	L	PCT	ERA	G	GS	CG	IP	H	BB	SO	ShO	W	L	SV	AB	H	HR	B
1956 DET A	0	2	.000	13.50	2	2	0	5.1	12	3	1	0	0	0	0	0	0	0	
1958 CLE A	6	6	.500	3.64	14	9	3	71.2	71	25	27	0	3	0	0	24	4	0	.16
1959 WAS A	2	4	.333	3.69	31	3	0	61	58	36	30	0	2	1	0	8	0	0	.00
1960	4	5	.444	4.70	41	14	1	115	131	60	46	0	2	1	4	29	2	0	.06
1961 2 teams			WAS	A (7G 3–2)			DET	A (12G 1–1)											
" total	4	3	.571	5.22	19	8	1	58.2	63	41	37	0	1	0	0	20	2	0	.10
1962 HOU N	5	16	.238	4.39	31	26	2	139.1	161	54	82	1	0	1	0	37	3	0	.08
1963	11	9	.550	1.97	55	0	0	114	75	42	94	0	11	9	10	23	3	0	.13
1964	2	9	.182	2.76	61	0	0	78.1	73	32	58	0	2	9	23	10	0	0	.00
1965 2 teams			HOU	N (27G 3–4)			STL	N (51G 3–2)											
" total	6	6	.500	2.25	78	0	0	92	74	45	59	0	6	6	18	14	1	0	.07
1966 STL N	2	1	.667	1.92	59	0	0	70.1	57	23	30	0	2	1	4	5	1	0	.20
1967	2	1	.667	5.18	36	0	0	41.2	41	28	20	0	2	1	2	4	0	0	.00
11 yrs.	44	62	.415	3.56	427	62	7	847.1	816	389	484	1	31	29	61	174	16	0	.09
2 yrs.	1	3	.250	9.13	14	4	0	23.2	37	20	14	0	1	0	0	4	0	0	.00

WORLD SERIES

	W	L	PCT	ERA	G	GS	CG	IP	H	BB	SO	ShO	W	L	SV	AB	H	HR	B
1967 STL N	0	0	—	0.00	1	0	0	1	1	0	0	0	0	0	0	0	0	0	

Ralph Works

WORKS, RALPH TALMADGE (Judge)
B. Mar. 16, 1888, Payson, Ill.   D. Aug. 8, 1941, Pasadena, Calif.   BL TR 6'2½" 185 lbs

	W	L	PCT	ERA	G	GS	CG	IP	H	BB	SO	ShO	W	L	SV	AB	H	HR	B
1909 DET A	4	1	.800	1.97	16	4	4	64	42	17	31	0	1	0	2	17	1	0	.05
1910	3	6	.333	3.57	18	10	5	85.2	73	39	36	0	0	1	1	30	8	0	.26
1911	11	5	.688	3.87	30	15	9	167.1	173	67	68	3	4	0	1	61	9	0	.14
1912 2 teams			DET	A (27G 5–10)			CIN	N (3G 1–1)											
" total	6	11	.353	4.16	30	18	10	166.2	189	71	69	1	1	1	1	61	9	0	.14
1913 CIN N	0	1	.000	7.80	5	2	0	15	15	8	4	0	0	0	0	6	1	0	.16
5 yrs.	24	24	.500	3.79	99	49	28	498.2	512	202	208	4	6	2	5	175	28	0	.16
4 yrs.	23	22	.511	3.68	91	46	27	474	493	189	199	4	6	1	5	164	26	0	.15

WORLD SERIES

	W	L	PCT	ERA	G	GS	CG	IP	H	BB	SO	ShO	W	L	SV	AB	H	HR	B
1909 DET A	0	0	—	9.00	1	0	0	2	4	0	2	0	0	0	0	0	0	0	

John Wyatt

WYATT, JOHN THOMAS
B. Apr. 19, 1935, Chicago, Ill.   BR TR 5'11½" 200 lbs

	W	L	PCT	ERA	G	GS	CG	IP	H	BB	SO	ShO	W	L	SV	AB	H	HR	B
1961 KC A	0	0	—	2.45	5	0	0	7.1	8	4	6	0	0	0	1	0	0	0	
1962	10	7	.588	4.46	59	9	0	125	121	80	106	0	7	4	11	29	3	0	.10
1963	6	4	.600	3.13	63	0	0	92	83	43	81	0	6	4	21	9	0	0	.00
1964	9	8	.529	3.59	81	0	0	128	111	52	74	0	9	8	20	14	0	0	.00
1965	2	6	.250	3.25	65	0	0	88.2	78	53	70	0	2	6	18	4	0	0	.00
1966 2 teams			KC	A (19G 0–3)			BOS	A (42G 3–4)											
" total	3	7	.300	3.68	61	0	0	95.1	78	43	88	0	3	7	10	11	0	0	.00
1967 BOS A	10	7	.588	2.60	60	0	0	93.1	71	39	68	0	10	7	20	12	1	0	.00
1968 3 teams			BOS A (8G 1–2)		NY A (7G 0–2)			DET	A (22G 1–0)										
" total	2	4	.333	3.68	37	0	0	49.1	42	26	42	0	2	4	2	3	0	0	.00
1969 OAK A	0	1	.000	5.40	4	0	0	8.1	8	6	5	0	0	1	0	1	0	0	.00
9 yrs.	42	44	.488	3.47	435	9	0	687.1	600	346	540	0	39	41	103	83	4	0	.04
1 yr.	1	0	1.000	2.37	22	0	0	30.1	26	11	25	0	1	0	2	2	0	0	.00

WORLD SERIES

	W	L	PCT	ERA	G	GS	CG	IP	H	BB	SO	ShO	W	L	SV	AB	H	HR	B
1967 BOS A	1	0	1.000	4.91	2	0	0	3.2	1	3	1	0	1	0	0	0	0	0	

Whit Wyatt

WYATT, JOHN WHITLOW
B. Sept. 27, 1907, Kensington, Ga.   BR TR 6'1" 185 lbs

	W	L	PCT	ERA	G	GS	CG	IP	H	BB	SO	ShO	W	L	SV	AB	H	HR	B
1929 DET A	0	1	.000	6.75	4	4	1	25.1	30	18	14	0	0	0	0	10	1	0	.10
1930	4	5	.444	3.57	21	7	1	85.2	76	35	68	0	3	2	2	34	12	1	.35
1931	0	2	.000	8.44	4	1	1	21.1	30	12	8	0	0	1	0	7	2	0	.28
1932	9	13	.409	5.03	43	22	10	205.2	228	102	82	0	3	1	1	78	15	2	.19
1933 2 teams			DET	A (10G 0–1)			CHI	A (26G 3–4)											
" total	3	5	.375	4.56	36	7	2	104.2	111	54	40	0	1	2	1	30	6	0	.23
1934 CHI A	4	11	.267	7.18	23	6	2	67.2	83	37	36	0	3	6	2	26	6	0	.23
1935	4	3	.571	6.75	30	1	0	52	65	25	22	0	4	3	5	13	3	0	.23
1936	0	0	—	0.00	3	0	0	3	3	0	0	0	0	0	1	0	0	0	
1937 CLE A	2	3	.400	4.44	29	4	2	73	67	40	52	0	2	2	0	18	7	0	.38
1939 BKN N	8	3	.727	2.31	16	14	6	109	88	39	52	2	1	1	0	36	6	0	.16
1940	15	14	.517	3.46	37	34	16	239.1	233	62	124	5	1	1	0	80	14	1	.17
1941	22	10	.688	2.34	38	35	23	288.1	223	82	176	7	0	1	1	109	26	3	.23
1942	19	7	.731	2.73	31	30	16	217.1	185	63	104	0	1	0	0	77	14	0	.18
1943	14	5	.737	2.49	26	26	13	180.2	139	43	80	3	0	0	0	60	17	0	.28
1944	2	6	.250	7.17	9	9	1	37.2	51	16	4	0	0	0	0	13	2	0	.15
1945 PHI N	0	7	.000	5.26	10	10	2	51.1	72	14	10	0	0	0	0	16	2	0	.12
16 yrs.	106	95	.527	3.78	360	210	97	1762	1684	642	872	17	20	19	13	607	133	7	.21
5 yrs.	13	22	.371	4.97	82	34	14	355	384	176	181	0	6	5	3	131	30	3	.22

WORLD SERIES

	W	L	PCT	ERA	G	GS	CG	IP	H	BB	SO	ShO	W	L	SV	AB	H	HR	B
1941 BKN N	1	1	.500	2.50	2	2	0	18	15	10	14	0	0	0	0	6	1	0	.16

Emil Yde

YDE, EMIL OGDEN
B. Jan. 28, 1900, Great Lakes, Ill.
D. Dec. 5, 1968, Leesburg, Fla.   BB TL 5'11" 165 lbs / BL 1925

	W	L	PCT	ERA	G	GS	CG	IP	H	BB	SO	ShO	W	L	SV	AB	H	HR	B
1924 PIT N	16	3	.842	2.83	33	22	14	194	171	62	53	4	1	0	0	88	21	1	.23
1925	17	9	.654	4.13	33	28	13	207	254	75	41	0	2	0	0	89	17	0	.19
1926	8	7	.533	3.65	37	22	12	187.1	181	81	34	1	0	0	0	74	17	0	.23

	W	L	PCT	ERA	G	GS	CG	IP	H	BB	SO	ShO	Relief Pitching W	L	SV	BATTING AB	H	HR	BA

Emil Yde continued

	W	L	PCT	ERA	G	GS	CG	IP	H	BB	SO	ShO	W	L	SV	AB	H	HR	BA
1927	1	3	.250	9.71	9	2	0	29.2	45	15	9	0	1	1	0	18	3	0	.167
1929 DET A	7	3	.700	5.30	29	6	4	86.2	100	63	23	1	3	1	0	48	16	0	.333
5 yrs.	49	25	.662	4.02	141	80	43	704.2	751	296	160	6	7	2	0	*			
1 yr.	7	3	.700	5.30	29	6	4	86.2	100	63	23	1	3	1	0	48	16	0	.333
WORLD SERIES																			
1925 PIT N	0	1	.000	11.57	1	1	0	2.1	5	3	1	0	0	0	0	1	0	0	.000

Joe Yeager

YEAGER, JOSEPH F. (Little Joe)   TR
B. Aug. 28, 1875, Philadelphia, Pa.   D. July 2, 1937, Detroit, Mich.

	W	L	PCT	ERA	G	GS	CG	IP	H	BB	SO	ShO	W	L	SV	AB	H	HR	BA
1898 BKN N	12	22	.353	3.65	36	33	32	291.1	333	80	70	0	1	2	0	134	23	0	.172
1899	2	2	.500	4.72	10	4	2	47.2	56	16	6	1	1	1	1	47	9	0	.191
1900	1	1	.500	6.88	2	2	2	17	21	5	2	0	0	0	0	9	3	0	.333
1901 DET A	12	11	.522	2.61	26	25	22	199.2	209	46	38	3	0	0	1	125	37	2	.296
1902	6	12	.333	4.82	19	15	14	140	171	41	28	0	1	2	0	161	39	1	.242
1903	0	1	.000	4.00	1	1	1	9	15	0	1	0	0	0	0	402	103	0	.256
6 yrs.	33	49	.402	3.74	94	80	73	704.2	805	188	145	4	3	5	2	*			
3 yrs.	18	24	.429	3.54	46	41	37	348.2	395	87	67	3	1	2	1	688	179	3	.260

Kip Young

YOUNG, KIP LANE   BR TR 5'11"   175 lbs.
B. Oct. 29, 1954, Georgetown, Ohio

	W	L	PCT	ERA	G	GS	CG	IP	H	BB	SO	ShO	W	L	SV	AB	H	HR	BA
1978 DET A	6	7	.462	2.81	14	13	7	105.2	94	30	49	0	0	1	0	0	0	0	–
1979	2	2	.500	6.34	13	7	0	44	60	11	22	0	0	1	0	0	0	0	–
2 yrs.	8	9	.471	3.85	27	20	7	149.2	154	41	71	0	0	2	0	0	0	0	–
2 yrs.	8	9	.471	3.85	27	20	7	149.2	154	41	71	0	0	2	0	0	0	0	–

Chris Zachary

ZACHARY, WILLIAM CHRIS   BL TR 6'2"   200 lbs.
B. Feb. 19, 1944, Knoxville, Tenn.

	W	L	PCT	ERA	G	GS	CG	IP	H	BB	SO	ShO	W	L	SV	AB	H	HR	BA
1963 HOU N	2	2	.500	4.89	22	7	0	57	62	22	42	0	0	0	0	13	0	0	.000
1964	0	1	.000	9.00	1	0	0	4	6	1	2	0	0	0	0	1	0	0	.000
1965	0	2	.000	4.22	4	2	0	10.2	12	6	4	0	0	0	0	2	0	0	.000
1966	3	5	.375	3.44	10	8	0	55	44	32	37	0	0	1	0	18	4	0	.222
1967	1	6	.143	5.70	9	7	0	36.1	42	12	18	0	0	0	0	10	1	0	.100
1969 KC A	0	1	.000	7.85	8	2	0	18.1	27	7	6	0	0	0	0	2	1	0	.500
1971 STL N	3	10	.231	5.30	23	12	1	90	114	26	48	1	1	2	0	33	8	0	.242
1972 DET A	1	1	.500	1.42	25	1	0	38	27	15	21	0	1	0	1	2	1	0	.500
1973 PIT N	0	1	.000	3.00	6	0	0	12	10	1	6	0	0	1	1	2	0	0	.000
9 yrs.	10	29	.256	4.57	108	40	1	321.1	344	122	184	1	2	4	2	83	15	0	.181
1 yr.	1	1	.500	1.42	25	1	0	38	27	15	21	0	1	0	1	2	1	0	.500
LEAGUE CHAMPIONSHIP SERIES																			
1972 DET A	0	0	–	∞	1	0	0	0	0	1	0	0	0	0	0	0	0	0	–

Carl Zamloch

ZAMLOCH, CARL EUGENE   BR TR 6'1"   176 lbs.
B. Oct. 6, 1889, Oakland, Calif.   D. Aug. 19, 1963, Santa Barbara, Calif.

	W	L	PCT	ERA	G	GS	CG	IP	H	BB	SO	ShO	W	L	SV	AB	H	HR	BA
1913 DET A	1	6	.143	2.45	17	5	3	69.2	66	23	28	0	1	2	1	22	4	0	.182

Bill Zepp

ZEPP, WILLIAM CLINTON   BR TR 6'2"   185 lbs.
B. July 22, 1946, Detroit, Mich.

	W	L	PCT	ERA	G	GS	CG	IP	H	BB	SO	ShO	W	L	SV	AB	H	HR	BA
1969 MIN A	0	0	–	6.75	4	0	0	5.1	6	4	2	0	0	0	0	1	0	0	.000
1970	9	4	.692	3.22	43	20	1	151	154	51	64	1	3	0	2	44	6	0	.136
1971 DET A	1	1	.500	5.06	16	4	0	32	41	17	15	0	0	1	2	4	0	0	.000
3 yrs.	10	5	.667	3.63	63	24	1	188.1	201	72	81	1	3	1	4	49	6	0	.122
1 yr.	1	1	.500	5.06	16	4	0	32	41	17	15	0	0	1	2	4	0	0	.000
LEAGUE CHAMPIONSHIP SERIES																			
1970 MIN A	0	0	–	6.75	2	0	0	1.1	2	2	2	0	0	0	0	0	0	0	–

George Zuverink

ZUVERINK, GEORGE   BR TR 6'4"   195 lbs.
B. Aug. 20, 1924, Holland, Mich.

	W	L	PCT	ERA	G	GS	CG	IP	H	BB	SO	ShO	W	L	SV	AB	H	HR	BA
1951 CLE A	0	0	–	5.33	16	0	0	25.1	24	13	14	0	0	0	0	0	0	0	–
1952	0	0	–	0.00	1	0	0	1.1	1	0	1	0	0	0	0	0	0	0	–
1954 2 teams			CIN N (2G 0–0)			DET A (35G 9–13)														
" total	9	13	.409	3.75	37	25	9	209	211	63	72	2	0	0	4	66	9	0	.136
1955 2 teams			DET A (14G 0–5)			BAL A (28G 4–3)														
" total	4	8	.333	3.38	42	6	0	114.2	118	31	44	0	3	6	4	27	5	0	.185
1956 BAL A	7	6	.538	4.16	62	0	0	97.1	112	34	33	0	7	6	16	17	2	0	.118
1957	10	6	.625	2.48	56	0	0	112.2	105	39	36	0	10	6	9	23	3	0	.130
1958	2	2	.500	3.39	45	0	0	69	74	17	22	0	2	2	7	9	2	0	.222
1959	0	1	.000	4.15	6	0	0	13	15	6	1	0	0	1	0	0	0	0	–
8 yrs.	32	36	.471	3.54	265	31	9	642.1	660	203	223	2	22	21	40	142	21	0	.148
2 yrs.	9	18	.333	4.01	49	26	9	231.1	239	76	83	2	0	4	4	68	8	0	.118

Manager Register

The Manager Register is an alphabetical listing of every man who has managed the Detroit Tigers. Included are facts about the managers and their year-by-year managerial records for the regular season, League Championship Series, and the World Series.

Most of the information in this section is self-explanatory. That which is not is explained as follows:

Games Managed includes tie games.

Lifetime Total. The first total shown after the regular season's statistics is the manager's total lifetime record in the major leagues.

Tigers Lifetime Total. The second line is the manager's total lifetime record with the Tigers.

Blank space appearing beneath a team and league means that the team and league are the same.

Standing. The figures in this column indicate the standing of the team at the end of the season and when there was a managerial change. The four possible cases are as follows:

> *Only Manager for the Team That Year.* Indicated by a single bold-faced figure that appears in the extreme left-hand column and shows the final standing of the team.
>
> *Manager Started Season, But Did Not Finish.* Indicated by two figures: the first is bold-faced and shows the standing of the team when this manager left; the second shows the final standing of the team.

Manager Finished Season, But Did Not Start. Indicated by two figures: the first shows the standing of the team when this manager started; the second is bold-faced and shows the final standing of the team.

Manager Did Not Start or Finish Season. Indicated by three figures: the first shows the standing of the team when this manager started; the second is bold-faced and shows the standing of the team when this manager left; the third shows the final standing of the team.

1981 Split Season Indicator. The managers' records for the 1981 split season are given separately for each half. "(1st)" or "(2nd)" will appear to the right of the standings to indicate which half.

	G	W	L	PCT	Standing			G	W	L	PCT	Standing

Sparky Anderson
ANDERSON, GEORGE LEE
B. Feb. 22, 1934, Bridgewater, S. D.

	G	W	L	PCT	Standing
1970 CIN N	162	102	60	.630	1
1971	162	79	83	.488	4
1972	154	95	59	.617	1
1973	162	99	63	.611	1
1974	162	98	64	.605	2
1975	162	108	54	.667	1
1976	162	102	60	.630	1
1977	162	88	74	.543	2
1978	161	92	69	.571	2
1979 DET A	105	56	49	.533	5 5
1980	163	84	78	.519	4
1981	57	31	26	.544	4 (1st)
1981	52	29	23	.558	2 (2nd)
1982	162	83	79	.512	4
1983	162	92	70	.568	2
1984	162	104	58	.642	1
15 yrs.	2312	1342	969	.581	
					10th
7 yrs.	863	479	383	.556	

LEAGUE CHAMPIONSHIP SERIES

	G	W	L	PCT	
1970 CIN N	3	3	0	1.000	
1972	5	3	2	.600	
1973	5	2	3	.400	
1975	3	3	0	1.000	
1976	3	3	0	1.000	
1984 DET A	3	3	0	1.000	
6 yrs.	22	17	5	.773	
	1st	1st	9th	1st	
1 yr.	3	3	0	1.000	

WORLD SERIES

	G	W	L	PCT	
1970 CIN N	5	1	4	.200	
1972	7	3	4	.429	
1975	7	4	3	.571	
1976	4	4	0	1.000	
1984 DET A	5	4	1	.800	
5 yrs.	28	16	12	.571	
	7th	7th	10th	3rd	
1 yr.	5	4	1	.800	

Bill Armour
ARMOUR, WILLIAM R.
B. Sept. 3, 1869, Homestead, Pa.
D. Dec. 2, 1922, Minneapolis, Minn.

	G	W	L	PCT	Standing
1902 CLE A	137	69	67	.507	5
1903	140	77	63	.550	3
1904	154	86	65	.570	4
1905 DET A	153	79	74	.516	3
1906	151	71	78	.477	6
5 yrs.	735	382	347	.524	
2 yrs.	304	150	152	.497	

Del Baker
BAKER, DELMAR DAVID
B. May 3, 1892, Sherwood, Ore.
D. Sept. 11, 1973, San Antonio, Tex.

	G	W	L	PCT	Standing
1933 DET A	2	2	0	1.000	5 5
1938	58	37	20	.649	4 4
1939	155	81	73	.526	5
1940	155	90	64	.584	1
1941	155	75	79	.487	4
1942	156	73	81	.474	5
6 yrs.	681	358	317	.530	
6 yrs.	681	358	317	.530	

WORLD SERIES

	G	W	L	PCT	
1940 DET A	7	3	4	.429	

Ed Barrow
BARROW, EDWARD GRANT (Cousin Ed)
B. May 10, 1868, Springfield, Ill.
D. Dec. 15, 1953, Port Chester, N. Y.
Hall of Fame 1953.

	G	W	L	PCT	Standing
1903 DET A	137	65	71	.478	5
1904	84	32	46	.410	7 7
1918 BOS A	126	75	51	.595	1
1919	138	66	71	.482	6

Ed Barrow *continued*

	G	W	L	PCT	Standing
1920	154	72	81	.471	5
5 yrs.	639	310	320	.492	
2 yrs.	221	97	117	.453	

WORLD SERIES

	G	W	L	PCT	
1918 BOS A	6	4	2	.667	

Ty Cobb
COBB, TYRUS RAYMOND (The Georgia Peach)
B. Dec. 18, 1886, Narrows, Ga.
D. July 17, 1961, Atlanta, Ga.
Hall of Fame 1936.

	G	W	L	PCT	Standing
1921 DET A	154	71	82	.464	6
1922	155	79	75	.513	3
1923	155	83	71	.539	2
1924	156	86	68	.558	3
1925	156	81	73	.526	4
1926	157	79	75	.513	6
6 yrs.	933	479	444	.519	
6 yrs.	933	479	444	.519	

Mickey Cochrane
COCHRANE, GORDON STANLEY (Black Mike)
B. Apr. 6, 1903, Bridgewater, Mass.
D. June 28, 1962, Lake Forest, Ill.
Hall of Fame 1947.

	G	W	L	PCT	Standing
1934 DET A	154	101	53	.656	1
1935	152	93	58	.616	1
1936	154	83	71	.539	2
1937	155	89	65	.578	2
1938	97	47	50	.485	4 4
5 yrs.	712	413	297	.582	
5 yrs.	712	413	297	.582	

WORLD SERIES

	G	W	L	PCT	
1934 DET A	7	3	4	.429	
1935	6	4	2	.667	
2 yrs.	13	7	6	.538	
2 yrs.	13	7	6	.538	

Chuck Dressen
DRESSEN, CHARLES WALTER
B. Sept. 20, 1898, Decatur, Ill.
D. Aug. 10, 1966, Detroit, Mich.

	G	W	L	PCT	Standing
1934 CIN N	66	25	41	.379	8 8
1935	154	68	85	.444	6
1936	154	74	80	.481	5
1937	130	51	78	.395	8 8
1951 BKN N	158	97	60	.618	2
1952	155	96	57	.627	1
1953	155	105	49	.682	1
1955 WAS A	154	53	101	.344	8
1956	155	59	95	.383	7
1957	21	5	16	.238	8 8
1960 MIL N	154	88	66	.571	2
1961	130	71	58	.550	3 4
1963 DET A	102	55	47	.539	9 5
1964	163	85	77	.525	4
1965	162	89	73	.549	4
1966	26	16	10	.615	3 3
16 yrs.	2039	1037	993	.511	
4 yrs.	453	245	207	.542	

WORLD SERIES

	G	W	L	PCT	
1952 BKN N	7	3	4	.429	
1953	6	2	4	.333	
2 yrs.	13	5	8	.385	

Frank Dwyer
DWYER, JOHN FRANCIS
B. Mar. 25, 1868, Lee, Mass.
D. Feb. 4, 1943, Pittsfield, Mass.

	G	W	L	PCT	Standing
1902 DET A	137	52	83	.385	7

	G	W	L	PCT	Standing				G	W	L	PCT	Standing

Jimmy Dykes

DYKES, JAMES JOSEPH
B. Nov. 10, 1896, Philadelphia, Pa.
D. June 15, 1976, Philadelphia, Pa.

		G	W	L	PCT	Standing	
1934	CHI A	136	49	86	.363	8	8
1935		153	74	78	.487	5	
1936		153	81	70	.536	3	
1937		154	86	68	.558	3	
1938		149	65	83	.439	6	
1939		155	85	69	.552	4	
1940		155	82	72	.532	4	
1941		156	77	77	.500	3	
1942		148	66	82	.446	6	
1943		155	82	72	.532	4	
1944		154	71	83	.461	7	
1945		150	71	78	.477	6	
1946		30	10	20	.333	7	5
1951	PHI A	154	70	84	.455	6	
1952		155	79	75	.513	4	
1953		157	59	95	.383	7	
1954	BAL A	154	54	100	.351	7	
1958	CIN N	41	24	17	.585	7	4
1959	DET A	137	74	63	.540	8	4
1960		96	44	52	.458	6	6
1960	CLE A	58	26	32	.448	4	4
1961		160	78	82	.488	5	5
21 yrs.		2960	1407	1538	.478		
					9th		
2 yrs.		233	118	115	.506		

Joe Gordon

GORDON, JOSEPH LOWELL (Flash)
B. Feb. 18, 1915, Los Angeles, Calif.
D. Apr. 14, 1978, Sacramento, Calif.

		G	W	L	PCT	Standing	
1958	CLE A	86	46	40	.535	5	4
1959		154	89	65	.578	2	
1960		95	49	46	.516	4	4
1960	DET A	57	26	31	.456	6	6
1961	KC A	70	26	43	.377	8	9
1969		163	69	93	.426	4	
5 yrs.		625	305	318	.490		

Bucky Harris

HARRIS, STANLEY RAYMOND
B. Nov. 8, 1896, Port Jervis, N. Y.
D. Nov. 8, 1977, Bethesda, Md.
Hall of Fame 1975.

		G	W	L	PCT	Standing	
1924	WAS A	156	92	62	.597	1	
1925		152	96	55	.636	1	
1926		152	81	69	.540	4	
1927		157	85	69	.552	3	
1928		155	75	79	.487	4	
1929	DET A	155	70	84	.455	6	
1930		154	75	79	.487	5	
1931		154	61	93	.396	7	
1932		152	76	75	.503	5	
1933		153	73	79	.480	5	5
1934	BOS A	153	76	76	.500	4	
1935	WAS A	154	67	86	.438	6	
1936		153	82	71	.536	4	
1937		158	73	80	.477	6	
1938		152	75	76	.497	5	
1939		153	65	87	.428	6	
1940		154	64	90	.416	7	
1941		156	70	84	.455	6	
1942		151	62	89	.411	7	
1943	PHI N	95	40	53	.430	5	7
1947	NY A	155	97	57	.630	1	
1948		154	94	60	.610	3	
1950	WAS A	155	67	87	.435	5	
1951		154	62	92	.403	7	
1952		157	78	76	.506	5	
1953		152	76	76	.500	5	
1954		155	66	88	.429	6	
1955	DET A	154	79	75	.513	5	
1956		155	82	72	.532	5	
29 yrs.		4410	2159	2219	.493		
			3rd	3rd	2nd		
7 yrs.		1077	516	557	.481		

Bucky Harris *continued*

		G	W	L	PCT	Standing	
WORLD SERIES							
1924	WAS A	7	4	3	.571		
1925		7	3	4	.429		
1947	NY A	7	4	3	.571		
3 yrs.		21	11	10	.524		
			9th		7th		

Billy Hitchcock

HITCHCOCK, WILLIAM CLYDE
Brother of Jim Hitchcock.
B. July 31, 1916, Inverness, Ala.

		G	W	L	PCT	Standing	
1960	DET A	1	1	0	1.000	6	6
1962	BAL A	162	77	85	.475	7	
1963		162	86	76	.531	4	
1966	ATL N	51	33	18	.647	5	5
1967		159	77	82	.484	7	7
5 yrs.		535	274	261	.512		
1 yr.		1	1	0	1.000		

Ralph Houk

HOUK, RALPH GEORGE (Major)
B. Aug. 9, 1919, Lawrence, Kans.

		G	W	L	PCT	Standing	
1961	NY A	163	109	53	.673	1	
1962		162	96	66	.593	1	
1963		161	104	57	.646	1	
1966		140	66	73	.475	10	10
1967		163	72	90	.444	9	
1968		164	83	79	.512	5	
1969		162	80	81	.497	5	
1970		162	93	69	.574	2	
1971		162	82	80	.506	4	
1972		155	79	76	.510	4	
1973		162	80	82	.494	4	
1974	DET A	162	72	90	.444	6	
1975		159	57	102	.358	6	
1976		161	74	87	.460	5	
1977		162	74	88	.457	4	
1978		162	86	76	.531	5	
1981	BOS A	56	30	26	.536	5	
1981		52	29	23	.558	2	
1982		162	89	73	.549	3	
1983		162	78	84	.481	6	
1984		162	86	76	.531	4	
20 yrs.		3156	1619	1531	.514		
			10th	10th	10th		
5 yrs.		806	363	443	.450		
WORLD SERIES							
1961	NY A	5	4	1	.800		
1962		7	4	3	.571		
1963		4	0	4	.000		
3 yrs.		16	8	8	.500		
					8th		

Fred Hutchinson

HUTCHINSON, FREDERICK CHARLES
B. Aug. 12, 1919, Seattle, Wash.
D. Nov. 12, 1964, Bradenton, Fla.

		G	W	L	PCT	Standing	
1952	DET A	83	27	55	.329	8	8
1953		158	60	94	.390	6	
1954		155	68	86	.442	5	
1956	STL N	156	76	78	.494	4	
1957		154	87	67	.565	2	
1958		144	69	75	.479	5	5
1959	CIN N	74	39	35	.527	7	5
1960		154	67	87	.435	6	
1961		154	93	61	.604	1	
1962		162	98	64	.605	3	
1963		162	86	76	.531	5	
1964		110	60	49	.550	3	2
12 yrs.		1666	830	827	.501		
3 yrs.		396	155	235	.397		
WORLD SERIES							
1961	CIN N	5	1	4	.200		

	G	W	L	PCT	Standing

Hughie Jennings

JENNINGS, HUGH AMBROSE (Ee-Yah)
B. Apr. 2, 1869, Pittston, Pa.
D. Feb. 1, 1928, Scranton, Pa.
Hall of Fame 1945.

		G	W	L	PCT	Standing
1907	DET A	153	92	58	.613	1
1908		153	90	63	.588	1
1909		158	98	54	.645	1
1910		155	86	68	.558	3
1911		154	89	65	.578	2
1912		154	69	84	.451	6
1913		153	66	87	.431	6
1914		157	80	73	.523	4
1915		156	100	54	.649	2
1916		155	87	67	.565	3
1917		154	78	75	.510	4
1918		128	55	71	.437	7
1919		140	80	60	.571	4
1920		155	61	93	.396	7
14 yrs.		2125	1131	972	.538	
14 yrs.		2125	1131	972	.538	

WORLD SERIES

		G	W	L	PCT	
1907	DET A	4	0	4	.000	
1908		5	1	4	.200	
1909		7	3	4	.429	
3 yrs.		16	4	12	.250	
					10th	
3 yrs.		16	4	12	.250	

Bobby Lowe

LOWE, ROBERT LINCOLN (Link)
B. July 10, 1868, Pittsburgh, Pa.
D. Dec. 8, 1951, Detroit, Mich.

		G	W	L	PCT	Standing
1904	DET A	78	30	44	.405	7	7

Billy Martin

MARTIN, ALFRED MANUEL
B. May 16, 1928, Berkeley, Calif.

		G	W	L	PCT	Standing		
1969	MIN A	162	97	65	.599	1		
1971	DET A	162	91	71	.562	2		
1972		156	86	70	.551	1		
1973		143	76	67	.531	3	3	
1973	TEX A	23	9	14	.391	6	6	6
1974		160	84	76	.525	2		
1975		95	44	51	.463	4	3	
1975	NY A	56	30	26	.536	3	3	
1976		159	97	62	.610	1		
1977		162	100	62	.617	1		
1978		94	52	42	.553	3	1	
1979		96	55	41	.573	4	4	
1980	OAK A	162	83	79	.512	2		
1981		60	37	23	.617	1	(1st)	
1981		49	27	22	.551	2	(2nd)	
1982		162	68	94	.420	5		
1983	NY A	162	91	71	.562	3		
14 yrs.		2063	1127	936	.546			
3 yrs.		461	253	208	.549			

DIVISIONAL PLAYOFF SERIES

		G	W	L	PCT	
1981	OAK A	3	3	0	1.000	

LEAGUE CHAMPIONSHIP SERIES

		G	W	L	PCT	
1969	MIN A	3	0	3	.000	
1972	DET A	5	2	3	.400	
1976	NY A	5	3	2	.600	
1977		5	3	2	.600	
1981	OAK A	3	0	3	.000	
5 yrs.		21	8	13	.381	
		3rd	5th	1st	7th	
1 yr.		5	2	3	.400	

WORLD SERIES

		G	W	L	PCT	
1976	NY A	4	0	4	.000	
1977		6	4	2	.667	
2 yrs.		10	4	6	.400	

George Moriarty

MORIARTY, GEORGE JOSEPH
Brother of Bill Moriarty.
B. July 7, 1884, Chicago, Ill.
D. Apr. 8, 1964, Miami, Fla.

		G	W	L	PCT	Standing
1927	DET A	155	82	71	.536	4
1928		154	68	86	.442	6
2 yrs.		310	150	157	.489	
2 yrs.		310	150	157	.489	

Les Moss

MOSS, JOHN LESTER
B. May 14, 1925, Tulsa, Okla.

		G	W	L	PCT	Standing		
1968	CHI A	2	0	2	.000	9	9	9
1979	DET A	53	27	26	.509	5	5	
2 yrs.		55	27	28	.491			
1 yr.		53	27	26	.509			

Bill Norman

NORMAN, HENRY WILLIS PATRICK
B. July 16, 1910, St. Louis, Mo.
D. Apr. 21, 1962, Milwaukee, Wis.

		G	W	L	PCT	Standing	
1958	DET A	105	56	49	.533	5	5
1959		17	2	15	.118	8	4
2 yrs.		122	58	64	.475		
2 yrs.		122	58	64	.475		

Steve O'Neill

O'NEILL, STEPHEN FRANCIS
Brother of Jim O'Neill.
Brother of Jack O'Neill.
Brother of Mike O'Neill.
B. July 6, 1891, Minooka, Pa.
D. Jan. 26, 1962, Cleveland, Ohio

		G	W	L	PCT	Standing	
1935	CLE A	60	36	23	.610	5	3
1936		157	80	74	.519	5	
1937		156	83	71	.539	4	
1943	DET A	155	78	76	.506	5	
1944		156	88	66	.571	2	
1945		155	88	65	.575	1	
1946		155	92	62	.597	2	
1947		158	85	69	.552	2	
1948		154	78	76	.506	5	
1950	BOS A	92	62	30	.674	4	3
1951		154	87	67	.565	3	
1952	PHI N	91	59	32	.648	6	4
1953		156	83	71	.539	3	
1954		77	40	37	.519	3	4
14 yrs.		1876	1039	819	.559		
6 yrs.		933	509	414	.551		

WORLD SERIES

		G	W	L	PCT	
1945	DET A	7	4	3	.571	

Red Rolfe

ROLFE, ROBERT ABIAL
B. Oct. 17, 1908, Penacook, N. H.
D. July 8, 1969, Gilford, N. H.

		G	W	L	PCT	Standing	
1949	DET A	155	87	67	.565	4	
1950		157	95	59	.617	2	
1951		154	73	81	.474	5	
1952		73	23	49	.319	8	8
4 yrs.		539	278	256	.521		
4 yrs.		539	278	256	.521		

Bob Scheffing

SCHEFFING, ROBERT BODEN
B. Aug. 11, 1915, Overland, Mo.

		G	W	L	PCT	Standing	
1957	CHI N	156	62	92	.403	7	
1958		154	72	82	.468	5	
1959		155	74	80	.481	5	
1961	DET A	163	101	61	.623	2	
1962		161	85	76	.528	4	
1963		60	24	36	.400	9	5
6 yrs.		849	418	427	.495		
3 yrs.		384	210	173	.548		

	G	W	L	PCT	Standing			G	W	L	PCT	Standing

Frank Skaff
SKAFF, FRANCIS MICHAEL
B. Sept. 30, 1913, LaCrosse, Wis.

		G	W	L	PCT	Standing	
1966	DET A	79	40	39	.506	3	3

Mayo Smith
SMITH, EDWARD MAYO
B. Jan. 17, 1915, New London, Mo.
D. Nov. 24, 1977, Boynton Beach, Fla.

		G	W	L	PCT	Standing	
1955	PHI N	154	77	77	.500	4	
1956		154	71	83	.461	5	
1957		156	77	77	.500	5	
1958		83	39	44	.470	7	8
1959	CIN N	80	35	45	.438	7	5
1967	DET A	163	91	71	.562	2	
1968		164	103	59	.636	1	
1969		162	90	72	.556	2	
1970		162	79	83	.488	4	
9 yrs.		1278	662	611	.520		
4 yrs.		651	363	285	.560		

WORLD SERIES

		G	W	L	PCT	
1968	DET A	7	4	3	.571	

George Stallings
STALLINGS, GEORGE TWEEDY (The Miracle Man)
B. Nov. 17, 1867, Augusta, Ga.
D. May 13, 1929, Haddock, Ga.

		G	W	L	PCT	Standing	
1897	PHI N	134	55	77	.417	10	
1898		46	19	27	.413	8	6
1901	DET A	136	74	61	.548	3	
1909	NY A	153	74	77	.490	5	
1910		145	79	61	.564	2	2
1913	BOS N	154	69	82	.457	5	
1914		158	94	59	.614	1	
1915		157	83	69	.546	2	
1916		158	89	63	.586	3	
1917		157	72	81	.471	6	
1918		124	53	71	.427	7	
1919		140	57	82	.410	6	
1920		153	62	90	.408	7	
13 yrs.		1815	880	900	.494		
1 yr.		136	74	61	.548		

WORLD SERIES

		G	W	L	PCT	
1914	BOS N	4	4	0	1.000	

Bob Swift
SWIFT, ROBERT VIRGIL
B. Mar. 6, 1915, Salina, Kans.
D. Oct. 17, 1966, Detroit, Mich.

		G	W	L	PCT	Standing		
1966	DET A	57	32	25	.561	3	3	3

Jack Tighe
TIGHE, JOHN THOMAS
B. Aug. 9, 1913, Kearny, N. J.

		G	W	L	PCT	Standing	
1957	DET A	154	78	76	.506	4	
1958		49	21	28	.429	5	5
2 yrs.		203	99	104	.488		
2 yrs.		203	99	104	.488		

Dick Tracewski
TRACEWSKI, RICHARD JOSEPH
B. Feb. 3, 1935, Eynon, Pa.

		G	W	L	PCT	Standing		
1979	DET A	3	2	1	.667	5	5	5

Tigers World Series Highlights and Summaries

This section provided information on the nine World Series and two League Championship Series the Tigers have played in through 1984. Included are facts about the individual games; most of the information is self-explanatory. That which may appear unfamiliar is listed below.

INDIVIDUAL GAME INFORMATION

Innings Pitched. Pitchers are listed in the order of appearance. In parentheses, following each pitcher's name, are the number of innings he pitched in the game. For example: Doe (2.1) would mean that he pitched 2⅓ innings.

Winning and Losing Pitchers. Indicated by bold-faced print.

Saves. The pitcher who is credited with a Save is indicated by the abbreviation SV, which appears in bold-faced print after his innings pitched.

Home Runs. Players are listed in the order their home runs were hit.

LINE SCORES & PITCHERS (inn. pit.)	HOME RUNS (men on)	HIGHLIGHTS

Chicago (N.L.) defeats Detroit (A.L.) 4 games to 0

GAME 1 - OCTOBER 8

```
DET  A  000 000 030 000   3  9  3
CHI  N  000 100 002 000   3 10  5
Donovan (12)
Overall (9), Reulbach (3)
```

Schmidt's third-strike passed ball with two out in the ninth allowed the Cubs to even the game, which ended after 12 in a 3-3 tie. Donovan struck out 12 and the Cubs stole seven bases.

GAME 2 - OCTOBER 9

```
DET  A  010 000 000   1  9  1
CHI  N  010 200 00x   3  9  1
Mullin (8)
Pfiester (9)
```

Slagle drove in the go-ahead run with a single in the fourth, then scored an insurance run on Sheckard's double.

GAME 3 - OCTOBER 10

```
DET  A  000 001 000   1  6  1
CHI  N  010 310 00x   5 10  1
Siever (4), Killian (4)
Reulbach (9)
```

Evers's three hits led the Cubs' attack as Reulbach subdued the Tigers on six scattered hits.

GAME 4 - OCTOBER 11

```
CHI  N  000 020 301   6  7  2
DET  A  000 100 000   1  5  2
Overall (9)
Donovan (9)
```

Overall aided his own cause with a go-ahead two-run single in the fifth as he held the Tigers to five hits.

GAME 5 - OCTOBER 12

```
CHI  N  110 000 000   2  7  1
DET  A  000 000 000   0  7  2
Brown (9)
Mullin (9)
```

The Cubs swept the Series behind Brown's shutout. The Cubs swiped 18 bases in the five games, and held batting champ Ty Cobb to a .200 average.

Team Totals

		W	AB	H	2B	3B	HR	R	RBI	BA	BB	SO	ERA
CHI	N	4	167	43	6	1	0	19	16	.257	12	25	0.75
DET	A	0	172	36	1	2	0	6	6	.209	9	22	1.96

Individual Batting

CHICAGO (N.L.)

	AB	H	2B	3B	HR	R	RBI	BA
J. Slagle, of	22	6	0	0	0	3	4	.273
J. Sheckard, of	21	5	2	0	0	0	2	.238
J. Evers, 2b, ss	20	7	2	0	0	2	1	.350
W. Schulte, of	20	5	0	0	0	3	2	.250
J. Kling, c	19	4	0	0	0	2	1	.211
H. Steinfeldt, 3b	17	8	1	1	0	2	2	.471
F. Chance, 1b	14	3	1	0	0	3	0	.214
J. Tinker, ss	13	2	0	0	0	4	1	.154
D. Howard, 1b	5	1	0	0	0	0	0	.200
O. Overall, p	5	1	0	0	0	0	2	.200
E. Reulbach, p	5	1	0	0	0	0	1	.200
T. Brown, p	3	0	0	0	0	0	0	.000
J. Pfiester, p	2	0	0	0	0	0	0	.000
H. Zimmerman, 2b	1	0	0	0	0	0	0	.000
P. Moran	0	0	0	0	0	0	0	–

Errors: J. Evers (3), J. Tinker (3), W. Schulte (2), J. Kling, J. Slagle
Stolen bases: J. Slagle (6), F. Chance (3), J. Evers (3), J. Tinker (2), D. Howard, W. Schulte, J. Sheckard, H. Steinfeldt

DETROIT (A.L.)

	AB	H	2B	3B	HR	R	RBI	BA
S. Crawford, of	21	5	1	0	0	1	2	.238
G. Schaefer, 2b	21	3	0	0	0	1	0	.143
T. Cobb, of	20	4	0	1	0	1	0	.200
B. Coughlin, 3b	20	5	0	0	0	0	0	.250
C. Rossman, 1b	20	8	0	1	0	1	2	.400
D. Jones, of	17	6	0	0	0	1	0	.353
C. O'Leary, ss	17	1	0	0	0	0	0	.059
B. Schmidt, c	12	2	0	0	0	0	0	.167
W. Donovan, p	8	0	0	0	0	0	0	.000
G. Mullin, p	6	0	0	0	0	0	0	.000
F. Payne, c	4	1	0	0	0	0	1	.250
J. Archer, c	3	0	0	0	0	0	0	.000
E. Killian, p	2	1	0	0	0	1	0	.500
E. Siever, p	1	0	0	0	0	0	0	.000

Errors: B. Coughlin (2), C. O'Leary (2), B. Schmidt (2), D. Jones, F. Payne, C. Rossman
Stolen bases: D. Jones (3), C. Rossman (2), B. Coughlin, G. Schaefer

Individual Pitching

CHICAGO (N.L.)

	W	L	ERA	IP	H	BB	SO	SV
O. Overall	1	0	1.00	18	14	4	11	0
E. Reulbach	1	0	0.75	12	6	3	4	0
T. Brown	1	0	0.00	9	7	1	4	0
J. Pfiester	1	0	1.00	9	9	1	3	0

DETROIT (A.L.)

	W	L	ERA	IP	H	BB	SO	SV
W. Donovan	0	1	1.29	21	17	5	16	0
G. Mullin	0	2	2.12	17	16	6	7	0
E. Killian	0	0	2.25	4	3	1	1	0
E. Siever	0	1	4.50	4	7	0	1	0

LINE SCORES & PITCHERS (inn. pit.)	HOME RUNS (men on)	HIGHLIGHTS

Chicago (N.L.) defeats Detroit (A.L.) 4 games to 1

GAME 1 - OCTOBER 10

```
CHI  N  004 000 105   10 14 2
DET  A  100 000 320    6 10 4
```
Reulbach (6.2), Overall (0.1),
Brown (2)
Killian (2.1), **Summers** (6.2)

Five Cub runs in the ninth, four scoring on two-run singles by Hofman and Kling, broke open a game played in heavy rain.

GAME 2 - OCTOBER 11

```
DET  A  000 000 001    1  4 1
CHI  N  000 000 06x    6  7 1
```
Donovan (8)
Overall (9)

Tinker (1 on)

Donovan held the Cubs to one hit in seven innings, but Tinker's homer sparked a six-run rally that broke up a scoreless deadlock.

GAME 3 - OCTOBER 12

```
DET  A  100 005 020    8 11 4
CHI  N  000 300 000    3  7 2
```
Mullin (9)
Pfiester (8), Reulbach (1)

Cobb's four hits led the Detroit attack to a come-from-behind victory.

GAME 4 - OCTOBER 13

```
CHI  A  002 000 001    3 10 0
DET  A  000 000 000    0  4 1
```
Brown (9)
Summers (8), Winter (1)

Back-to-back scoring singles by Steinfeldt and Hofman in the third gave Brown all the runs he needed to subdue the Tigers.

GAME 5 - OCTOBER 14

```
CHI  N  100 010 000    2 10 0
DET  A  000 000 000    0  3 0
```
Overall (9)
Donovan (9)

Three hits and one RBI each by Evers and Chance aided Overall's 10-strikeout pitching in the Series clincher.

Team Totals

		W	AB	H	2B	3B	HR	R	RBI	BA	BB	SO	ERA
CHI	N	4	164	48	4	2	1	24	20	.293	13	26	2.60
DET	A	1	158	32	5	0	0	15	14	.203	12	26	3.48

Individual Batting

CHICAGO (N.L.)

	AB	H	2B	3B	HR	R	RBI	BA
J. Sheckard, of	21	5	2	0	0	2	1	.238
J. Evers, 2b	20	7	1	0	0	5	2	.350
F. Chance, 1b	19	8	0	0	0	4	2	.421
S. Hofman, of	19	6	0	1	0	2	4	.316
J. Tinker, ss	19	5	0	0	1	2	5	.263
W. Schulte, of	18	7	0	1	0	4	2	.389
J. Kling, c	16	4	1	0	0	2	1	.250
H. Steinfeldt, 3b	16	4	0	0	0	3	3	.250
O. Overall, p	6	2	0	0	0	0	0	.333
T. Brown, p	4	0	0	0	0	0	0	.000
E. Reulbach, p	3	0	0	0	0	0	0	.000
J. Pfiester, p	2	0	0	0	0	0	0	.000
D. Howard	1	0	0	0	0	0	0	.000

Errors: F. Chance (3), J. Evers, H. Steinfeldt
Stolen bases: F. Chance (5), J. Evers (2), S. Hofman (2),
W. Schulte (2), J. Sheckard, H. Steinfeldt,
J. Tinker

DETROIT (A.L.)

	AB	H	2B	3B	HR	R	RBI	BA
S. Crawford, of	21	5	1	0	0	2	1	.238
T. Cobb, of	19	7	1	0	0	3	4	.368
C. O'Leary, ss	19	3	0	0	0	2	0	.158
C. Rossman, 1b	19	4	0	0	0	3	3	.211
M. McIntyre, of	18	4	1	0	0	2	0	.222
G. Schaefer, 3b, 2b	16	2	0	0	0	0	0	.125
B. Schmidt, c	14	1	0	0	0	0	1	.071
B. Coughlin, 3b	8	1	0	0	0	0	1	.125
R. Downs, 2b	6	1	1	0	0	1	1	.167
E. Summers, p	5	1	0	0	0	0	1	.200
W. Donovan, p	4	0	0	0	0	0	0	.000
I. Thomas, c	4	2	1	0	0	0	1	.500
G. Mullin, p	3	1	0	0	0	1	1	.333
D. Jones	2	0	0	0	0	1	0	.000

Errors: T. Cobb (2), C. Rossman (2), B. Coughlin,
W. Donovan, R. Downs, M. McIntyre,
C. O'Leary, G. Schaefer
Stolen bases: T. Cobb (2), W. Donovan, M. McIntyre

Individual Pitching

CHICAGO (N.L.)

	W	L	ERA	IP	H	BB	SO	SV
O. Overall	2	0	0.98	18.1	7	7	15	0
T. Brown	2	0	0.00	11	6	1	5	0
J. Pfiester	0	1	7.88	8	10	3	1	0
E. Reulbach	0	0	4.70	7.2	9	1	5	0

DETROIT (A.L.)

	W	L	ERA	IP	H	BB	SO	SV
W. Donovan	0	2	4.24	17	17	4	10	0
E. Summers	0	2	4.30	14.2	18	4	7	0
G. Mullin	1	0	1.00	9	7	1	8	0
E. Killian	0	0	7.71	2.1	5	3	1	0
G. Winter	0	0	0.00	1	1	1	0	0

| LINE SCORES & PITCHERS (inn. pit.) | HOME RUNS (men on) | HIGHLIGHTS |

Pittsburgh (N.L.) defeats Detroit (A.L.) 4 games to 3

GAME 1 - OCTOBER 8

```
DET A  100 000 000   1  6  4
PIT N  000 121 00x   4  5  0
Mullin (8)
Adams (9)
```

Clarke

Leach made a running catch of Cobb's fly in the seventh with two on and two out to preserve the 4-1 lead.

GAME 2 - OCTOBER 9

```
DET A  023 020 000   7  9  3
PIT N  200 000 000   2  5  1
Donovan (9)
Camnitz (2.2), Willis (6.1)
```

Three in the third, capped by Cobb's steal of home, broke open the game. Every Tiger hitter except Donovan had at least one hit.

GAME 3 - OCTOBER 11

```
PIT N  510 000 002   8 10  3
DET A  000 000 402   6 10  5
Maddox (9)
Summers (0.1), Willett (6.2), Works (2)
```

The Pirates held off a late Tiger rally for the win. Wagner was the hitting star, with three singles, three RBIs, three stolen bases.

GAME 4 - OCTOBER 12

```
PIT N  000 000 000   0  5  6
DET A  020 300 00x   5  8  0
Leifield (4), Phillippe (4)
Mullin (9)
```

Cobb and Stanage contributed two RBIs each as the Tigers evened the Series, Mullin striking out ten Pirates.

GAME 5 - OCTOBER 13

```
DET A  100 002 010   4  6  1
PIT N  111 000 41x   8 10  2
Summers (7), Willett (1)
Adams (9)
```

D. Jones, Crawford
Clarke (2 on)

Clarke's two-run homer in the seventh broke open the 3-3 deadlock, off-setting Crawford's 3-for-4 performance that included a double and homer of his own.

GAME 6 - OCTOBER 14

```
PIT N  300 000 001   4  7  3
DET A  100 211 00x   5 10  3
Willis (5), Camnitz (1), Phillippe (2)
Mullin (9)
```

The Tigers suffered four injuries in the ninth but hung on to win. Tom Jones ran over Wilson to let in one run, but Schmidt and Moriarty ended the game by recording putouts while being spiked on close plays at the plate and at third.

GAME 7 - OCTOBER 16

```
PIT N  020 203 010   8  7  0
DET A  000 000 000   0  6  3
Adams (9)
Donovan (3), Mullin (6)
```

Clarke is walked four times and Wagner and Miller each had two RBIs to pace the Pirates' Series victory. Eighteen Buc stolen bases tied the Series record set by the Cubs in 1906.

Team Totals

		W	AB	H	2B	3B	HR	R	RBI	BA	BB	SO	ERA
PIT	N	4	223	49	13	1	2	34	25	.220	20	34	3.10
DET	A	3	233	55	16	0	2	28	26	.236	20	22	3.10

Individual Batting

PITTSBURGH (N.L.)

	AB	H	2B	3B	HR	R	RBI	BA
D. Miller, 2b	28	7	1	0	0	2	4	.250
B. Abstein, 1b	26	6	2	0	0	3	2	.231
O. Wilson, of	26	4	1	0	0	2	1	.154
G. Gibson, c	25	6	2	0	0	2	2	.240
T. Leach, of, 3b	25	8	4	0	0	8	2	.320
B. Byrne, 3b	24	6	1	0	0	5	0	.250
H. Wagner, ss	24	8	2	1	0	4	6	.333
F. Clarke, of	19	4	0	0	2	7	7	.211
B. Adams, p	9	0	0	0	0	0	0	.000
H. Hyatt, of	4	0	0	0	0	1	1	.000
N. Maddox, p	4	0	0	0	0	0	0	.000
V. Willis, p	4	0	0	0	0	0	0	.000
Abbaticchio	1	0	0	0	0	0	0	.000
H. Camnitz, p	1	0	0	0	0	0	0	.000
L. Leifield, p	1	0	0	0	0	0	0	.000
P. O'Connor	1	0	0	0	0	0	0	.000
D. Phillippe, p	1	0	0	0	0	0	0	.000

Errors: B. Abstein (5), D. Miller (3), D. Phillippe (2), H. Wagner (2), B. Byrne, F. Clarke, O. Wilson

Stolen bases: H. Wagner (6), F. Clarke (3), D. Miller (3), G. Gibson (2), B. Abstein, B. Byrne, T. Leach, O. Wilson

DETROIT (A.L.)

	AB	H	2B	3B	HR	R	RBI	BA
D. Jones, of	30	7	0	0	1	6	2	.233
S. Crawford, of, 1b	28	7	3	0	1	4	3	.250
T. Cobb, of	26	6	3	0	0	3	6	.231
J. Delahanty, 2b	26	9	4	0	0	2	4	.346
T. Jones, 1b	24	6	1	0	0	3	2	.250
D. Bush, ss	23	6	1	0	0	5	2	.261
G. Moriarty, 3b	22	6	1	0	0	4	1	.273
B. Schmidt, c	18	4	2	0	0	0	4	.222
G. Mullin, p	16	3	1	0	0	1	0	.188
O. Stanage, c	5	1	0	0	0	0	2	.200
W. Donovan, p	4	0	0	0	0	0	0	.000
M. McIntyre, of	3	0	0	0	0	0	0	.000
C. O'Leary, 3b	3	0	0	0	0	0	0	.000
E. Summers, p	3	0	0	0	0	0	0	.000
E. Willett, p	2	0	0	0	0	0	0	.000

Errors: D. Bush (5), B. Schmidt (5), S. Crawford (2), J. Delahanty (2), T. Cobb, W. Donovan, D. Jones, T. Jones, E. Willett

Stolen bases: T. Cobb (2), D. Bush, S. Crawford, D. Jones, T. Jones

Individual Pitching

PITTSBURGH (N.L.)

	W	L	ERA	IP	H	BB	SO	SV
B. Adams	3	0	1.33	27	18	6	11	0
V. Willis	0	1	4.76	11.1	10	8	3	0
N. Maddox	1	0	1.00	9	10	2	4	0
D. Phillippe	0	0	0.00	6	2	1	2	0
L. Leifield	0	1	11.25	4	7	1	0	0
H. Camnitz	0	1	12.27	3.2	8	2	2	0

DETROIT (A.L.)

	W	L	ERA	IP	H	BB	SO	SV
G. Mullin	2	1	2.25	32	22	8	20	0
W. Donovan	1	1	3.00	12	7	8	7	0
E. Summers	0	2	8.59	7.1	13	4	4	0
E. Willett	0	0	0.00	7.2	3	0	1	0
R. Works	0	0	9.00	2	4	0	2	0

| LINE SCORES & PITCHERS (inn. pit.) | HOME RUNS (men on) | HIGHLIGHTS |

St. Louis (N.L.) defeats Detroit (A.L.) 4 games to 3

GAME 1 - OCTOBER 3

STL N 021 014 000   8 13 2
DET A 001 001 010   3 8 5
D. Dean (9)
Crowder (5), Marberry (0.2),
　Hogsett (3.1)

Medwick
Greenberg

The Cardinals capitalized on five errors by the Tiger infield. Medwick leads the attack with four hits.

GAME 2 - OCTOBER 4

STL N 011 000 000 000   2 7 3
DET A 000 100 001 001   3 7 0
Hallahan (8.1), **B. Walker** (3)
Rowe (12)

Gee Walker, given a chance when Collins and Delancey failed to catch his pop foul, singled in the tying run for the Tigers in the ninth. They went on to win in the twelfth when Goslin singled following walks to Gehringer and Greenberg.

GAME 3 - OCTOBER 5

DET A 000 000 001   1 8 2
STL N 110 020 00x   4 9 1
Bridges (4), Hogsett (4)
P. Dean (9)

The Tigers left 13 men on base as Martin's double, triple, and two runs scored led the Cardinals.

GAME 4 - OCTOBER 6

DET A 003 100 150   10 13 1
STL N 011 200 000   4 10 5
Auker (9)
Carleton (2.2), Vance (1.1),
　B. Walker (3.1), Haines (0.2)
　Mooney (1)

The Tigers evened the Series thanks to Greenberg's three hits and three RBIs and Rogell's four RBIs.

GAME 5 - OCTOBER 7

DET A 010 002 000   3 7 0
STL N 000 000 100   1 7 1
Bridges (9)
D. Dean (8), Carleton (1)

Gehringer
Delancey

Bridges returned after a day's rest to subdue the Cardinals. Gehringer's home run in the sixth was the game-winner.

GAME 6 - OCTOBER 8

STL N 100 020 100   4 10 2
DET A 001 002 000   3 7 1
P. Dean (9)
Rowe (9)

Paul Dean aided his own cause with a single in the seventh that sent in the deciding run.

GAME 7 - OCTOBER 9

STL N 007 002 200   11 17 1
DET A 000 000 000   0 6 3
D. Dean (9)
Auker (2.1), Rowe (0.1), Hogsett (0),
　Bridges (4.1), Marberry (1), Crowder (1)

The Cardinals easily romped to the Series crown. Medwick was replaced for his own protection in the sixth after the crowd pelted him with fruit and bottles.

Team Totals

		W	AB	H	2B	3B	HR	R	RBI	BA	BB	SO	ERA
STL	N	4	262	73	14	5	2	34	32	.279	11	31	2.34
DET	A	3	250	56	12	1	2	23	20	.224	25	43	3.74

Individual Batting

ST. LOUIS (N.L.)

	AB	H	2B	3B	HR	R	RBI	BA
F. Frisch, 2b	31	6	1	0	0	2	4	.194
P. Martin, 3b	31	11	3	1	0	8	3	.355
R. Collins, 1b	30	11	1	0	0	4	4	.367
J. Rothrock, of	30	7	3	1	0	3	6	.233
B. DeLancey, c	29	5	3	0	1	3	4	.172
J. Medwick, of	29	11	0	1	1	4	5	.379
L. Durocher, ss	27	7	1	1	0	4	0	.259
E. Orsatti, of	22	7	0	1	0	3	2	.318
D. Dean, p	12	3	2	0	0	3	1	.250
P. Dean, p	6	1	0	0	0	0	2	.167
C. Fullis, of	5	2	0	0	0	0	0	.400
B. Hallahan, p	3	0	0	0	0	0	0	.000
P. Crawford	2	0	0	0	0	0	0	.000
S. Davis	2	2	0	0	0	1	1.000
B. Walker, p	2	0	0	0	0	0	0	.000
T. Carleton, p	1	0	0	0	0	0	0	.000
B. Whitehead, ss	0	0	0	0	0	0	0	–

Errors: P. Martin (4), F. Frisch (2), E. Orsatti (2),
R. Collins, P. Dean, B. DeLancey,
C. Fullis, B. Hallahan, J. Rothrock,
B. Walker
Stolen bases: P. Martin (2)

DETROIT (A.L.)

	AB	H	2B	3B	HR	R	RBI	BA
C. Gehringer, 2b	29	11	1	0	1	5	2	.379
G. Goslin, of	29	7	1	0	0	2	2	.241
M. Owen, 3b	29	2	0	0	0	0	1	.069
B. Rogell, ss	29	8	1	0	0	3	4	.276
M. Cochrane, c	28	6	1	0	0	2	1	.214
P. Fox, of	28	8	6	0	0	1	2	.286
H. Greenberg, 1b	28	9	2	1	1	4	7	.321
J. White, of	23	3	0	0	0	6	0	.130
T. Bridges, p	7	1	0	0	0	0	0	.143
S. Rowe, p	7	0	0	0	0	0	0	.000
E. Auker, p	4	0	0	0	0	0	0	.000
C. Hogsett, p	3	0	0	0	0	0	0	.000
G. Walker	3	1	0	0	0	0	1	.333
F. Doljack, of	2	0	0	0	0	0	0	.000
G. Crowder, p	1	0	0	0	0	0	0	.000
R. Hayworth, c	0	0	0	0	0	0	0	–

Errors: C. Gehringer (3), B. Rogell (3), G. Goslin (2),
M. Owen (2), H. Greenberg, J. White
Stolen bases: C. Gehringer, H. Greenberg, M. Owen,
J. White

Individual Pitching

ST. LOUIS (N.L.)

	W	L	ERA	IP	H	BB	SO	SV
D. Dean	2	1	1.73	26	20	5	17	0
P. Dean	2	0	1.00	18	15	7	11	0
B. Hallahan	0	0	2.16	8.1	6	4	6	0
B. Walker	0	2	7.11	6.1	6	6	2	0
T. Carleton	0	0	7.36	3.2	5	2	2	0
J. Mooney	0	0	0.00	1	1	0	0	0
D. Vance	0	0	0.00	1.1	2	1	3	0
J. Haines	0	0	0.00	0.2	1	0	2	0

DETROIT (A.L.)

	W	L	ERA	IP	H	BB	SO	SV
S. Rowe	1	1	2.95	21.1	19	0	12	0
T. Bridges	1	1	3.63	17.1	21	1	12	0
E. Auker	1	1	5.56	11.1	16	5	2	0
C. Hogsett	0	0	1.23	7.1	6	3	3	0
G. Crowder	0	1	1.50	6	6	1	2	0
F. Marberry	0	0	21.60	1.2	5	1	0	0

LINE SCORES & PITCHERS (inn. pit.)	HOME RUNS (men on)	HIGHLIGHTS

Detroit (A.L.) defeats Chicago (N.L.) 4 games to 2

GAME 1 - OCTOBER 2

CHI N 200 000 001   3 7 0
DET A 000 000 000   0 4 3
Warneke (9)
Rowe (9)

Demaree

Chicago scored twice in the first on hits by Galan and Hartnett and Rowe's error as Warneke pitched a four-hit shutout.

GAME 2 - OCTOBER 3

CHI N 000 010 200   3 6 1
DET A 400 300 10x   8 9 2
Root (0), Henshaw (3.2), Kowalik (4.1)
Bridges (9)

Greenberg (1 on)

Hits by the first four batters in the Tiger first, capped by Greenberg's homer, chased Root and ensured the victory.

GAME 3 - OCTOBER 4

DET A 000 001 040 01   6 12 2
CHI N 020 010 002 00   5 10 3
Auker (6), Hogsett (1), **Rowe** (4)
Lee (7.1), Warneke (1.2), **French** (2)

Demaree

White's single scored Owen with the winning run in the eleventh after the Cubs tied the game in the ninth on singles by Hack, Klein, and O'Dea and a long fly by Galan.

GAME 4 - OCTOBER 5

DET A 001 001 000   2 7 0
CHI N 010 000 000   1 5 2
Crowder (9)
Carleton (7), Root (2)

Hartnett

The Tigers scored the winning run in the sixth on errors by Galan and Jurges.

GAME 5 - OCTOBER 6

DET A 000 000 001   1 7 1
CHI N 002 000 10x   3 8 0
Rowe (8)
Warneke (6), Lee (3) **SV**

Klein (1 on)

The Cubs scored twice in the third on Herman's triple and Klein's homer. Warneke left after six shutout innings because of a sore shoulder. Lee had to retire Clifton with two out and runners on second and third in the ninth to preserve the victory.

GAME 6 - OCTOBER 7

CHI N 001 020 000   3 12 0
DET A 100 101 001   4 12 1
French (8.2)
Bridges (9)

Herman (1 on)

The Tigers won in the ninth inning when Cochrane singled, Gehringer's grounder moved him to second, and Goslin's single brought him in for the Series-ending run.

Team Totals

		W	AB	H	2B	3B	HR	R	RBI	BA	BB	SO	ERA
DET	A	4	206	51	11	1	1	21	18	.248	25	27	2.29
CHI	N	2	202	48	6	2	5	18	17	.238	11	29	2.81

Individual Batting

DETROIT (A.L.)

	AB	H	2B	3B	HR	R	RBI	BA
P. Fox, of	26	10	3	1	0	1	4	.385
M. Cochrane, c	24	7	1	0	0	3	1	.292
C. Gehringer, 2b	24	9	3	0	0	4	4	.375
B. Rogell, ss	24	7	2	0	0	1	1	.292
G. Goslin, of	22	6	1	0	0	2	3	.273
M. Owen, 3b, 1b	20	1	0	0	0	2	1	.050
J. White, of	19	5	0	0	0	3	1	.263
F. Clifton, 3b	16	0	0	0	0	1	0	.000
T. Bridges, p	8	1	0	0	0	1	1	.125
S. Rowe, p	8	2	1	0	0	0	0	.250
H. Greenberg, 1b	6	1	0	0	1	0	2	.167
G. Walker, of	4	1	0	0	0	1	0	.250
G. Crowder, p	3	1	0	0	0	1	0	.333
E. Auker, p	2	0	0	0	0	0	0	.000

Errors: H. Greenberg (3), F. Clifton, M. Cochrane, P. Fox, G. Goslin, M. Owen, S. Rowe
Stolen bases: C. Gehringer

CHICAGO (N.L.)

	AB	H	2B	3B	HR	R	RBI	BA
A. Galan, of	25	4	1	0	0	2	2	.160
P. Cavarretta, 1b	24	3	0	0	0	1	0	.125
F. Demaree, of	24	6	1	0	2	2	2	.250
G. Hartnett, c	24	7	0	0	1	1	2	.292
B. Herman, 2b	24	8	2	1	1	3	6	.333
S. Hack, ss, 3b	22	5	1	1	0	2	0	.227
B. Jurges, ss	16	4	0	0	0	3	1	.250
F. Lindstrom, 3b, of	15	3	1	0	0	0	0	.200
C. Klein, of	12	4	0	0	1	2	2	.333
L. Warneke, p	5	1	0	0	0	0	0	.200
L. French, p	4	1	0	0	0	1	0	.250
F. Kowalik, p	2	1	0	0	0	1	0	.500
T. Carleton, p	1	0	0	0	0	0	0	.000
R. Henshaw, p	1	0	0	0	0	0	0	.000
B. Lee, p	1	0	0	0	0	0	1	.000
K. O'Dea	1	1	0	0	0	0	1	1.000
W. Stephenson	1	0	0	0	0	0	0	.000

Errors: P. Cavarretta, A. Galan, B. Herman, B. Jurges, F. Kowalik, F. Lindstrom
Stolen bases: S. Hack

Individual Pitching

DETROIT (A.L.)

	W	L	ERA	IP	H	BB	SO	SV
S. Rowe	1	2	2.57	21	19	1	14	0
T. Bridges	2	0	2.50	18	18	4	9	0
G. Crowder	1	0	1.00	9	5	3	5	0
E. Auker	0	0	3.00	6	6	2	1	0
C. Hogsett	0	0	0.00	1	0	1	0	0

CHICAGO (N.L.)

	W	L	ERA	IP	H	BB	SO	SV
L. Warneke	2	0	0.54	16.2	9	4	5	0
L. French	0	2	3.38	10.2	15	2	8	0
B. Lee	0	0	3.48	10.1	11	5	5	1
T. Carleton	0	1	1.29	7	6	7	4	0
F. Kowalik	0	0	2.08	4.1	3	1	1	0
R. Henshaw	0	0	7.36	3.2	2	5	2	0
C. Root	0	1	18.00	2	5	1	2	0

LINE SCORES & PITCHERS (inn. pit.)	HOME RUNS (men on)	HIGHLIGHTS

Cincinnati (N.L.) defeats Detroit (A.L.) 4 games to 3

GAME 1 - OCTOBER 2

DET A 050·020 000   7 10 1
CIN N 000 100 010   2 8 3
Newsom (9)
Derringer (1.1), Moore (6.2),
  Riddle (1)

Campbell (1 on)

Derringer was knocked out in the second as Newsom breezed to the American League's tenth successive World Series triumph.

GAME 2 - OCTOBER 3

DET A 200 001 000   3 3 1
CIN N 022 100 00x   5 9 0
Rowe (3.1), Gorsica (4.2)
Walters (9)

Ripple (1 on)

Walters pitched a three-hitter with Ripple's third-inning home run providing the winning run.

GAME 3 - OCTOBER 4

CIN N 100 000 012   4 10 1
DET A 000 100 42x   7 13 1
Turner (6), Moore (1), Beggs (1)
Bridges (9)

York (1 on),
Higgins (1 on)

Two-run homers by York and Higgins in the seventh decided the outcome.

GAME 4 - OCTOBER 5

CIN N 201 100 010   5 11 1
DET A 001 001 000   2 5 1
Derringer (9)
Trout (2), Smith (4), McKain (3)

Derringer coasted to victory. Werber, Frank McCormick, Goodman, and Mike McCormick, the first four Cincinnati hitters, each had two hits.

GAME 5 - OCTOBER 6

CIN N 000 000 000   0 3 0
DET A 003 400 00x   8 13 0
Thompson (3.1), Moore (0.2)
  Vander Meer (3), Hutchings (1)
Newsom (9)

Greenberg (2 on)

Newsom held the Reds to three singles for the shutout win, backed by 13 hits including Greenberg's three-run homer.

GAME 6 - OCTOBER 7

DET A 000 000 000   0 5 0
CIN N 200 001 01x   4 10 2
Rowe (0.1), Gorsica (6.2),
  Hutchinson (1)
Walters (9)

Walters

Walters drew the Reds even with a shutout and contributed a homer to his cause. The Reds chased Rowe with four hits and two runs in a third of an inning.

GAME 7 - OCTOBER 8

DET A 001 000 000   1 7 0
CIN N 000 000 20x   2 7 1
Newsom (8)
Derringer (9)

Doubles by McCormick and Ripple and a long fly by Myers brought Cincinnati its first World Championship since the tainted Series of 1919.

Team Totals

		W	AB	H	2B	3B	HR	R	RBI	BA	BB	SO	ERA
CIN	N	4	232	58	14	0	2	22	21	.250	15	30	3.69
DET	A	3	228	56	9	3	4	28	24	.246	30	30	3.00

Individual Batting

CINCINNATI (N.L.)

	AB	H	2B	3B	HR	R	RBI	BA
I. Goodman, of	29	8	2	0	0	5	5	.276
M. McCormick, of	29	9	3	0	0	1	2	.310
F. McCormick, 1b	28	6	1	0	0	2	0	.214
B. Werber, 3b	27	10	4	0	0	5	2	.370
E. Joost, 2b	25	5	0	0	0	0	2	.200
B. Myers, ss	23	3	0	0	0	0	2	.130
J. Ripple, of	21	7	2	0	1	3	6	.333
J. Wilson, c	17	6	0	0	0	1	1	.353
P. Derringer, p	7	0	0	0	0	0	0	.000
B. Walters, p	7	2	1	0	1	2	2	.286
B. Baker, c	4	1	0	0	0	1	0	.250
E. Lombardi, c	3	1	1	0	0	0	0	.333
L. Riggs	3	0	0	0	0	1	0	.000
L. Frey	2	0	0	0	0	0	0	.000
W. Moore, p	2	0	0	0	0	0	0	.000
J. Turner, p	2	0	0	0	0	0	0	.000
M. Arnovich, of	1	0	0	0	0	0	0	.000
H. Craft	1	0	0	0	0	0	0	.000
J. Thompson, p	1	0	0	0	0	0	0	.000

Errors: F. McCormick (2), B. Myers (2), B. Werber (2), B. Baker, M. McCormick
Stolen bases: J. Wilson

DETROIT (A.L.)

	AB	H	2B	3B	HR	R	RBI	BA
C. Gehringer, 2b	28	6	0	0	0	3	1	.214
H. Greenberg, of	28	10	2	1	1	5	6	.357
D. Bartell, ss	26	7	2	0	0	2	3	.269
R. York, 1b	26	6	0	1	1	3	2	.231
B. Campbell, of	25	9	1	0	1	4	5	.360
P. Higgins, 3b	24	8	3	1	1	2	6	.333
B. McCosky, of	23	7	1	0	0	5	1	.304
B. Sullivan, c	13	2	0	0	0	3	0	.154
B. Tebbetts, c	11	0	0	0	0	0	0	.000
B. Newsom, p	10	1	0	0	0	1	0	.100
J. Gorsica, p	4	0	0	0	0	0	0	.000
E. Averill	3	0	0	0	0	0	0	.000
T. Bridges, p	3	0	0	0	0	0	0	.000
P. Fox	1	0	0	0	0	0	0	.000
S. Rowe, p	1	0	0	0	0	0	0	.000
C. Smith, p	1	0	0	0	0	0	0	.000
D. Trout, p	1	0	0	0	0	0	0	.000
F. Croucher, ss	0	0	0	0	0	0	0	—

Errors: P. Higgins (2), D. Bartell, B. Tebbetts

Individual Pitching

CINCINNATI (N.L.)

	W	L	ERA	IP	H	BB	SO	SV
P. Derringer	2	1	2.79	19.1	17	10	6	0
B. Walters	2	0	1.50	18	8	6	6	0
W. Moore	0	0	3.24	8.1	8	6	7	0
J. Turner	0	1	7.50	6	8	0	4	0
J. Thompson	0	1	16.20	3.1	8	4	2	0
Vander Meer	0	0	0.00	3	2	3	2	0
J. Beggs	0	0	9.00	1	3	0	1	0
J. Hutchings	0	0	9.00	1	2	1	0	0
E. Riddle	0	0	0.00	1	0	0	2	0

DETROIT (A.L.)

	W	L	ERA	IP	H	BB	SO	SV
B. Newsom	2	1	1.38	26	18	4	17	0
J. Gorsica	0	0	0.79	11.1	6	4	4	0
T. Bridges	1	0	3.00	9	10	1	5	0
C. Smith	0	0	2.25	4	1	3	1	0
A. McKain	0	0	3.00	3	4	0	0	0
S. Rowe	0	2	17.18	3.2	12	1	1	0
D. Trout	0	1	9.00	2	6	1	1	0
F. Hutchinson	0	0	9.00	1	1	1	1	0

LINE SCORES & PITCHERS (inn. pit.)	HOME RUNS (men on)	HIGHLIGHTS

Detroit (A.L.) defeats Chicago (N.L.) 4 games to 3

GAME 1 - OCTOBER 3

CHI N 403 000 200   9 13 0
DET A 000 000 000   0 6 0
Borowy (9)
Newhouser (2.2), Benton (1.1),
  Tobin (3), Mueller (2)

Cavarretta

Newhouser gave up seven hits and eight runs in the first three innings as Cavarretta and Pafko scored three runs each and Nicholson had three RBIs.

GAME 2 - OCTOBER 4

CHI N 000 100 000   1 7 0
DET A 000 040 00x   4 7 0
Wyse (6), Erickson (2)
Trucks (9)

Greenberg (2 on)

Greenberg's homer with two on in the fifth broke open the game.

GAME 3 - OCTOBER 5

CHI N 000 200 100   3 8 0
DET A 000 000 000   0 1 2
Passeau (9)
Overmire (6), Benton (3)

Passeau allowed only a single to York in the third and a walk to Swift in the sixth.

GAME 4 - OCTOBER 6

DET A 000 400 000   4 7 1
CHI N 000 001 000   1 5 1
Trout (9)
Prim (3.1), Derringer (1.2),
  Vandenburg (2), Erickson (2)

Prim retired the first ten batters in the game, but the Tigers knocked him out with four in the fourth.

GAME 5 - OCTOBER 7

DET A 001 004 102   8 11 0
CHI N 001 000 201   4 7 2
Newhouser (9)
Borowy (5), Vandenburg (0.2), Chipman (0.1),
  Derringer (2), Erickson (1)

Newhouser benefitted from another four-run Tiger rally and struck out nine Cubs in the victory. Greenberg's three doubles keyed the attack.

GAME 6 - OCTOBER 8

DET A 010 000 240 000   7 13 1
CHI N 000 041 200 001   8 15 3
Trucks (4.1), Caster (0.2), Bridges (1.2),
  Benton (0.1), **Trout** (4.2)
Passeau (6.2), Wyse (0.2), Prim (0.2),
  Borowy (4)

Greenberg

Hack's drive bounced past Greenberg for a double and brought home the winning run in the twelfth after Greenberg tied the game with a homer in the eighth. Borowy held the Tigers hitless over the last four innings.

GAME 7 - OCTOBER 10

DET A 510 000 120   9 9 1
CHI N 100 100 010   3 10 0
Newhouser (9)
Borowy (0), Derringer (1.2),
  Vandenberg (3.1), Erickson (2),
  Passeau (1), Wyse (1)

The Cubs gambled and sent in Borowy with only a day's rest. The Tigers hit three successive singles to knock him out in the first, and went on to score five in the frame to sew up the Series.

Team Totals

		W	AB	H	2B	3B	HR	R	RBI	BA	BB	SO	ERA
DET	A	4	242	54	10	0	2	32	32	.223	33	22	3.84
CHI	N	3	246	65	16	3	1	29	27	.264	19	48	4.15

Individual Batting

DETROIT (A.L.)

	AB	H	2B	3B	HR	R	RBI	BA
D. Cramer, of	29	11	0	0	0	7	4	.379
E. Mayo, 2b	28	7	1	0	0	4	2	.250
J. Outlaw, 3b	28	5	0	0	0	1	3	.179
R. York, 1b	28	5	1	0	0	1	3	.179
S. Webb, ss	27	5	0	0	0	4	1	.185
H. Greenberg, of	23	7	3	0	2	7	7	.304
R. Cullenbine, of	22	5	2	0	0	5	4	.227
P. Richards, c	19	4	2	0	0	0	6	.211
H. Newhouser, p	8	0	0	0	0	0	1	.000
D. Trout, p	6	1	0	0	0	0	0	.167
B. Swift, c	4	1	0	0	0	1	0	.250
V. Trucks, p	4	0	0	0	0	0	0	.000
J. Hoover, ss	3	1	0	0	0	1	1	.333
C. Hostetler	3	0	0	0	0	0	0	.000
J. McHale	3	0	0	0	0	0	0	.000
H. Walker	2	1	1	0	0	1	0	.500
R. Borom	1	0	0	0	0	0	0	.000
Z. Eaton	1	0	0	0	0	0	0	.000
B. Maier	1	1	0	0	0	0	1	1.000
S. Overmire, p	1	0	0	0	0	0	0	.000
J. Tobin, p	1	0	0	0	0	0	0	.000
E. Mierkowicz, of	0	0	0	0	0	0	0	—

Errors: E. Mayo, H. Newhouser, P. Richards, S. Webb, R. York.
Stolen bases: D. Cramer, R. Cullenbine, J. Outlaw

CHICAGO (N.L.)

	AB	H	2B	3B	HR	R	RBI	BA
S. Hack, 3b	30	11	3	0	0	1	4	.367
D. Johnson, 2b	29	5	2	1	0	4	0	.172
P. Lowrey, of	29	9	1	0	0	4	0	.310
B. Nicholson, of	28	6	1	1	0	1	8	.214
A. Pafko, of	28	6	2	1	0	5	2	.214
P. Cavarretta, 1b	26	11	2	0	1	7	5	.423
M. Livingston, c	22	8	3	0	0	3	4	.364
R. Hughes, ss	17	5	1	0	0	1	3	.294
C. Passeau, p	7	0	0	0	0	1	1	.000
P. Gillespie, of	6	0	0	0	0	0	0	.000
H. Borowy, p	5	1	1	0	0	1	0	.200
F. Secory	5	2	0	0	0	0	0	.400
H. Wyse, p	3	0	0	0	0	0	0	.000
H. Becker	2	1	0	0	0	0	0	.500
L. Merullo, ss	2	0	0	0	0	0	0	.000
E. Sauer	2	0	0	0	0	0	0	.000
D. Williams, c	2	0	0	0	0	0	0	.000
McCullough	1	0	0	0	0	0	0	.000
B. Schuster, ss	1	0	0	0	0	1	0	.000
H. Vandenberg, p	1	0	0	0	0	0	0	.000
C. Block	0	0	0	0	0	0	0	—

Errors: S. Hack (3), D. Johnson, B. Nicholson, A. Pafko.
Stolen bases: P. Lowrey

Individual Pitching

DETROIT (A.L.)

	W	L	ERA	IP	H	BB	SO	SV
H. Newhouser	2	1	6.10	20.2	25	4	22	0
D. Trout	1	1	0.66	13.2	9	3	9	0
V. Trucks	1	0	3.38	13.1	14	5	7	0
S. Overmire	0	1	3.00	6	4	2	2	0
A. Benton	0	0	1.93	4.2	6	0	5	0
J. Tobin	0	0	6.00	3	4	1	0	0
L. Mueller	0	0	0.00	2	0	1	1	0
T. Bridges	0	0	16.20	1.2	3	1	0	0
G. Caster	0	0	0.00	0.2	0	0	1	0

CHICAGO (N.L.)

	W	L	ERA	IP	H	BB	SO	SV
H. Borowy	2	2	4.00	18	21	6	8	0
C. Passeau	1	0	2.70	16.2	7	8	3	0
P. Erickson	0	0	3.86	7	8	3	5	0
H. Wyse	0	1	7.04	7.2	8	4	1	0
H. Vandenberg	0	0	0.00	6	1	3	3	0
P. Derringer	0	0	6.75	5.1	5	7	1	0
R. Prim	0	1	9.00	4	4	1	1	0
B. Chipman	0	0	0.00	0.1	0	1	0	0

LINE SCORES & PITCHERS (inn. pit.)	HOME RUNS (men on)	HIGHLIGHTS

Detroit (A.L.) defeats St. Louis (N.L.) 4 games to 3

GAME 1 - OCTOBER 2

DET A 000 000 000   0 5 3
STL N 000 300 10x   4 6 0
McLain (5), Dobson (2), McMahon (1)
Gibson (9)

Brock

Gibson subdued the Tigers on a Series record 17-strikeout performance as McLain, the first 30-game winner since 1931, lasted only until the sixth.

GAME 2 - OCTOBER 3

DET A 011 003 102   8 13 1
STL N 000 001 000   1 6 1
Lolich (9)
Briles (5), Carlton (1), Willis (2), Hoerner (1)

Horton, Lolich, Cash

Lolich hit his first homer in the majors, aiding his own cause as he allowed the Cardinals six singles.

GAME 3 - OCTOBER 5

STL N 000 040 300   7 13 0
DET A 002 010 000   3 4 0
Washburn (5.1), Hoerner (3.2) **SV**
Wilson (4.1), Dobson (0.2), McMahon (1), Patterson (1), Hiller (0.2)

McCarver (2 on), Cepeda (2 on)
Kaline (1 on), McAuliffe

McCarver's go-ahead three-run homer in the fifth and Cepeda's three-run homer in the seventh upended the Tigers.

GAME 4 - OCTOBER 6

STL N 202 200 040 10 13 0
DET A 000 100 000   1 5 4
Gibson (9)
McLain (2.2), Sparma (0.1), Patterson (2), Lasher (2), Hiller (0), Dobson (2)

Brock, Gibson
Northrup

Gibson coasted to his seventh straight victory, a Series record, striking ten as Brock collected four RBIs.

GAME 5 - OCTOBER 7

STL N 300 000 000   3 9 0
DET A 000 200 30x   5 9 1
Briles (6.1), **Hoerner** (0), Willis (1.2)
Lolich (9)

Cepeda (2 on)

Brock failed to slide on a play at the plate in the fifth and was tagged out after colliding with Freehan. Detroit went on to win the game on Kaline's bases-loaded single in the seventh.

GAME 6 - OCTOBER 9

DET A 02(10) 010 000 13 12 1
STL N 00 0 000 001   1 9 1
McLain (9)
Washburn (2), Jaster (0), Willis (0.2), Hughes (0.1), Carlton (3), Granger (2), Nelson (1)

Northrup (3 on), Kaline

Northrup's grand slam highlighted the Tigers' ten-run third-inning barrage.

GAME 7 - OCTOBER 10

DET A 000 000 301   4 8 1
STL N 000 000 001   1 5 0
Lolich (9)
Gibson (9)

Shannon

The Tigers won the Series behind Northrup's go-ahead, two-run triple in the seventh. Gibson's eight strikeouts gave him a single-Series record of 35. Key plays came in the sixth when Lolich picked Brock and Flood off first.

Team Totals

		W	AB	H	2B	3B	HR	R	RBI	BA	BB	SO	ERA
DET	A	4	231	56	4	3	8	34	33	.242	27	59	3.48
STL	N	3	239	61	7	3	7	27	27	.255	21	40	4.65

Individual Batting

DETROIT (A.L.)

	AB	H	2B	3B	HR	R	RBI	BA
A. Kaline, of	29	11	2	0	2	6	8	.379
J. Northrup, of	28	7	0	1	2	4	8	.250
M. Stanley, ss, of	28	6	0	1	0	4	0	.214
D. McAuliffe, 2b	27	6	0	0	1	5	3	.222
N. Cash, 1b	26	10	0	0	1	5	5	.385
B. Freehan, c	24	2	1	0	0	0	2	.083
W. Horton, of	23	7	1	1	1	6	3	.304
D. Wert, 3b	17	2	0	0	0	1	2	.118
M. Lolich, p	12	3	0	0	1	2	2	.250
D. McLain, p	6	0	0	0	0	0	0	.000
E. Mathews, 3b	3	1	0	0	0	0	0	.333
T. Matchick	3	0	0	0	0	0	0	.000
J. Price	2	0	0	0	0	0	0	.000
G. Brown	1	0	0	0	0	0	0	.000
E. Wilson, p	1	0	0	0	0	0	0	.000
W. Comer	1	1	0	0	0	0	0	1.000
R. Oyler, ss	0	0	0	0	0	0	0	–
D. Tracewski, 3b	0	0	0	0	0	1	0	–

Errors: N. Cash (2), B. Freehan (2), J. Northrup (2), M. Stanley (2), W. Horton, E. Mathews, D. McLain

ST. LOUIS (N.L.)

	AB	H	2B	3B	HR	R	RBI	BA
M. Shannon, 3b	29	8	1	0	1	3	4	.276
L. Brock, of	28	13	3	1	2	6	5	.464
O. Cepeda, 1b	28	7	0	0	2	2	6	.250
C. Flood, of	28	8	1	0	0	4	2	.286
J. Javier, 2b	27	9	1	0	0	1	3	.333
T. McCarver, c	27	9	0	2	1	3	4	.333
D. Maxvill, ss	22	0	0	0	0	1	0	.000
R. Maris, of	19	3	1	0	0	5	1	.158
B. Gibson, p	8	1	0	0	1	2	2	.125
R. Davis, of	7	0	0	0	0	0	0	.000
N. Briles, p	4	0	0	0	0	0	0	.000
P. Gagliano	3	0	0	0	0	0	0	.000
R. Washburn, p	3	0	0	0	0	0	0	.000
J. Hoerner, p	2	1	0	0	0	0	0	.500
J. Edwards	1	0	0	0	0	0	0	.000
D. Ricketts	1	1	0	0	0	0	0	1.000
E. Spiezio	1	1	0	0	0	0	0	1.000
B. Tolan	1	0	0	0	0	0	0	.000
D. Schofield	0	0	0	0	0	0	0	–

Errors: L. Brock, M. Shannon
Stolen bases: L. Brock (7), C. Flood (3), J. Javier

Individual Pitching

DETROIT (A.L.)

	W	L	ERA	IP	H	BB	SO	SV
M. Lolich	3	0	1.67	27	20	6	21	0
D. McLain	1	2	3.24	16.2	18	4	13	0
E. Wilson	0	1	6.23	4.1	4	6	3	0
P. Dobson	0	0	3.86	4.2	5	1	0	0
D. Patterson	0	0	0.00	3	1	1	0	0
J. Hiller	0	0	13.50	2	6	3	1	0
F. Lasher	0	0	0.00	2	1	0	1	0
D. McMahon	0	0	13.50	2	4	0	1	0
J. Sparma	0	0	54.00	0.1	2	0	0	0

ST. LOUIS (N.L.)

	W	L	ERA	IP	H	BB	SO	SV
B. Gibson	2	1	1.67	27	18	4	35	0
N. Briles	0	1	5.56	11.1	13	4	7	0
R. Washburn	1	1	9.82	7.1	7	7	6	0
S. Carlton	0	0	6.75	4	7	1	3	0
J. Hoerner	0	1	3.86	4.2	5	5	3	1
R. Willis	0	0	8.31	4.1	2	4	3	0
W. Granger	0	0	0.00	2	0	1	1	0
M. Nelson	0	0	0.00	1	0	0	1	0
D. Hughes	0	0	0.00	0.1	2	0	0	0
L. Jaster	0	0	∞	0.0	2	1	0	0

LINE SCORES & PITCHERS (inn. pit.)   HOME RUNS (men on)   HIGHLIGHTS

Oakland (West) defeats Detroit (East) 3 games to 2

GAME 1 - OCTOBER 7
```
DET  E  010 000 000 01    2  6  2
OAK  W  001 000 000 02    3 10  1
```
Lolich (10), Seelbach (0.1)
Hunter (8), Blue (0), **Fingers** (3)

Cash, Kaline

Mickey Lolich carried a 2-1 lead into the last of the 11th, but the A's scored twice to beat the Tiger ace, 3-2. Gonzalo Marquez, an obscure late addition, drove in the tying run with a pinch single.

GAME 2 - OCTOBER 8
```
DET  E  000 000 000    0  3  1
OAK  W  100 040 00x    5  8  0
```
Fryman (4.1), Zachary (0),
  Scherman (2.2), LaGrow (1), Hiller (2)
Odom (9)

Blue Moon Odom pitched a magnificent three-hitter and did not walk a batter as the A's made it two straight, 5-0.

GAME 3 - OCTOBER 10
```
OAK  W  000 000 000    0  7  0
DET  E  000 200 01x    3  8  1
```
Holtzman (4), Fingers (1.2),
  Blue (0.1), Locker (2)
Coleman (6)

Freehan

Joe Coleman struck out 14, setting a playoff record, as the Tigers bounced back to win the third game, 3-0.

GAME 4 - OCTOBER 11
```
OAK  W  000 000 100 2    3  9  2
DET  E  001 000 000 3    4 10  1
```
Hunter (7.1), Fingers (0.2), Blue (1),
  Locker (3), **Horlen** (0), Hamilton (0)
Lolich (9), Seelbach (0.2), **Hiller** (0.1)

Epstein
McAuliffe

The Tigers appeared hopelessly lost coming to bat in the 10th. The A's had blasted two home runs in the top of the inning to take a 3-1 lead. Detroit's rally began with singles by Dick McAuliffe and Al Kaline. A wild pitch, a walk, and an error produced one run. Relief pitcher Dave Hamilton forced in a run with a bases-loaded walk and Jim Northrup drove in the winning run.

GAME 5 - OCTOBER 12
```
OAK  W  010 100 000    2  4  0
DET  E  100 000 000    1  5  2
```
Odom (5), Blue (4), **SV**
Fryman (8), Hiller (1)

Gene Tenace's only hit of the series, a single with two out in the fourth, drove home George Hendrick from second with the winning run.

Team Totals

		W	AB	H	2B	3B	HR	R	RBI	BA	BB	SO	ERA
OAK	W	3	170	38	8	0	1	13	10	.224	12	35	1.76
DET	E	2	162	32	6	1	4	10	10	.198	13	25	2.14

Individual Batting

OAKLAND (WEST)

	AB	H	2B	3B	HR	R	RBI	BA
M. Alou, of	21	8	4	0	0	2	2	.381
S. Bando, 3b	20	4	0	0	0	0	0	.200
J. Rudi, of	20	5	1	0	0	1	2	.250
R. Jackson, of	18	5	1	0	0	1	2	.278
G. Tenace, c, 2b	17	1	0	0	0	1	1	.059
M. Epstein, 1b	16	3	0	0	1	1	1	.188
D. Green, 2b	8	1	1	0	0	0	0	.125
D. Maxvill, ss, 2b	8	1	0	0	0	0	0	.125
B. Campaneris, ss	7	3	0	0	0	3	0	.429
G. Hendrick, of	7	1	0	0	0	2	0	.143
C. Hunter, p	6	1	0	0	0	0	0	.167
B. Odom, p	4	1	1	0	0	0	0	.250
T. Kubiak, 2b, ss	4	2	0	0	0	0	1	.500
A. Mangual	3	0	0	0	0	0	0	.000
G. Marquez	3	2	0	0	0	1	1	.667
D. Duncan, c	2	0	0	0	0	0	0	.000
T. Cullen, ss	1	0	0	0	0	0	0	.000
M. Hegan, 1b	1	0	0	0	0	1	0	.000
K. Holtzman, p	1	0	0	0	0	0	0	.000
D. Mincher	1	0	0	0	0	0	0	.000
R. Fingers, p	1	0	0	0	0	0	0	.000
V. Blue, p	1	0	0	0	0	0	0	.000

Errors: R. Jackson
Stolen bases: B. Campaneris (2), R. Jackson (2), M. Alou, D. Maxvill

DETROIT (EAST)

	AB	H	2B	3B	HR	R	RBI	BA
D. McAuliffe, ss, 2b	20	4	0	0	1	3	1	.200
A. Kaline, of	19	5	0	0	1	3	1	.263
A. Rodriguez, 3b	16	0	0	0	0	0	0	.000
N. Cash, 1b	15	4	0	0	1	1	2	.267
T. Taylor, 2b	15	2	2	0	0	0	0	.133
J. Northrup, of	14	5	0	0	0	0	1	.357
D. Sims, c, of	14	3	2	1	0	0	0	.214
B. Freehan, c	12	3	1	0	1	2	3	.250
W. Horton, of	10	1	0	0	0	0	0	.100
M. Lolich, p	7	0	0	0	0	0	0	.000
M. Stanley, of	6	2	0	0	0	0	0	.333
E. Brinkman, ss	4	1	1	0	0	0	0	.250
W. Fryman, p	3	0	0	0	0	0	0	.000
G. Brown	2	0	0	0	0	1	0	.000
J. Coleman, p	2	1	0	0	0	0	0	.500
I. Brown, 1b	2	1	0	0	0	0	2	.500
T. Haller	1	0	0	0	0	0	0	.000
J. Niekro	0	0	0	0	0	0	0	—
J. Knox	0	0	0	0	0	0	0	—

Errors: A. Kaline, D. McAuliffe, D. Sims, A. Rodriguez

Individual Pitching

OAKLAND (WEST)

	W	L	ERA	IP	H	BB	SO	SV
C. Hunter	0	0	1.17	15.1	10	5	9	0
B. Odom	2	0	0.00	14	5	2	5	0
R. Fingers	1	0	1.69	5.1	4	1	3	0
V. Blue	0	0	0.00	5.1	4	1	5	1
K. Holtzman	0	1	4.50	4	4	2	2	0
B. Locker	0	0	13.50	2	4	0	1	0
J. Horlen	0	1	∞	0.0	0	1	0	0
D. Hamilton	0	0	—	0.0	1	1	0	0

DETROIT (EAST)

	W	L	ERA	IP	H	BB	SO	SV
M. Lolich	0	1	1.42	19	14	5	10	0
W. Fryman	0	2	3.65	12.1	11	2	8	0
J. Coleman	1	0	0.00	9	7	3	14	0
J. Hiller	1	0	0.00	3.1	1	1	1	0
L. LaGrow	0	0	0.00	1	0	0	1	0
C. Seelbach	0	0	18.00	1	4	0	0	0
C. Zachary	0	0	∞	0.0	0	1	0	0
F. Scherman	0	0	0.00	0.2	1	0	1	0

LINE SCORES & PITCHERS (inn. pit.)	HOME RUNS (men on)	HIGHLIGHTS

Detroit (East) defeats Kansas City (West) 3 games to 0

GAME 1 - OCTOBER 2

DET   E   200 110 121   8 14 0

KC   W   000 000 100   1   5 1
Morris (7), Hernandez (2)
Black (5), Huismann (2.2),
   M. Jones (1.1)

Herndon, Trammell, Parrish

Trammell led the Detroit attack with three hits, including a triple and a solo homer, and three RBIs to support Morris's five-hitter.

GAME 2 - OCTOBER 3

DET   E   201 000 000 02   5   8 1
KC   W   000 100 110 00   3 10 3
Petry (7), Hernandez (1), **Lopez** (3)
Saberhagen (8), **Quisenberry** (3)

Gibson

The Royals rallied from three runs down on RBI pinch hits by Iorg and McRae in the seventh and eighth, but Grubb's two-run double in the eleventh gave the Tigers the victory.

GAME 3 - OCTOBER 5

KC   W   000 000 000   0   3 3
DET   E   010 000 00x   1   3 0
Leibrandt (8)
Wilcox (8), Hernandez (1) **SV**

Leibrandt allowed just three hits in eight innings, but Wilcox was even better, giving up two before yielding to Hernandez, who locked up Detroit's first pennant in sixteen years.

Team Totals

		W	AB	H	2B	3B	HR	R	RBI	BA	BB	SO	ERA
DET	E	3	107	25	4	1	4	14	14	.234	8	17	1.24
KC	W	0	106	18	1	1	0	4	4	.170	6	21	3.86

Individual Batting

DETROIT (EAST)

	AB	H	2B	3B	HR	R	RBI	BA
L. Whitaker, 2b	14	2	0	0	0	3	0	.143
C. Lemon, of	13	0	0	0	0	1	0	.000
L. Parrish, c	12	3	1	0	1	1	3	.250
K. Gibson, of	12	5	1	0	1	2	2	.417
A. Trammell, ss	11	4	0	1	1	2	3	.364
D. Evans, 1b, 3b	10	3	1	0	0	1	1	.300
B. Garbey, dh	9	3	0	0	0	1	0	.333
M. Castillo, 3b	8	2	0	0	0	0	2	.250
L. Herndon, of	5	1	0	0	1	1	1	.200
R. Jones, of	5	0	0	0	0	1	0	.000
J. Grubb	4	1	1	0	0	0	2	.250
T. Brookens, 3b	2	0	0	0	0	0	0	.000
D. Bergman, 1b	1	1	0	0	0	1	0	1.000
R. Kuntz, of	1	0	0	0	0	0	0	.000
D. Baker, ss	0	0	0	0	0	0	0	–

Errors: T. Brookens
Stolen bases: D. Evans, D. Bergman, K. Gibson, M. Castillo

KANSAS CITY (WEST)

	AB	H	2B	3B	HR	R	RBI	BA
W. Wilson, of	13	2	0	0	0	0	0	.154
G. Brett, 3b	13	3	0	0	0	0	0	.231
D. Motley, of	12	2	0	0	0	0	1	.167
F. White, 2b	12	1	0	0	0	1	0	.083
D. Slaught, c	11	4	0	0	0	0	0	.364
S. Balboni, 1b	10	1	0	0	0	0	0	.100
J. Orta, dh	10	1	0	1	0	1	1	.100
O. Concepcion, ss	7	0	0	0	0	0	0	.000
P. Sheridan, of	6	0	0	0	0	1	0	.000
L. Jones, of	5	1	0	0	0	1	0	.200
H. McRae	2	2	0	0	0	0	1	1.000
D. Iorg	2	1	0	0	0	0	1	.500
J. Wathan	1	0	0	0	0	0	0	.000
U. Washington	1	0	0	0	0	0	0	.000
B. Biancalana, ss	1	0	0	0	0	0	0	.000
G. Pryor, 3b	0	0	0	0	0	0	0	–

Errors: D. Slaught (3), S. Balboni, O. Concepcion, P. Sheridan, B. Saberhagen

Individual Pitching

DETROIT (EAST)

	W	L	ERA	IP	H	BB	SO	SV
M. Wilcox	1	0	0.00	8	2	2	8	0
J. Morris	1	0	1.29	7	5	1	4	0
D. Petry	0	0	2.57	7	4	1	4	0
W. Hernandez	0	0	2.25	4	3	1	3	1
A. Lopez	1	0	0.00	3	4	1	2	0

KANSAS CITY (WEST)

	W	L	ERA	IP	H	BB	SO	SV
C. Leibrandt	0	1	1.13	8	3	4	6	0
B. Saberhagen	0	0	2.25	8	6	1	5	0
B. Black	0	1	7.20	5	7	1	3	0
Quisenberry	0	1	3.00	2	1	1	0	0
M. Huismann	0	0	10.13	2.2	6	1	2	0
M. Jones	0	0	6.75	1.1	1	0	0	0

LINE SCORES & PITCHERS (inn. pit.)	HOME RUNS (men on)	HIGHLIGHTS

Detroit (A.L.) defeats San Diego (N.L.) 4 games to 1

GAME 1 - OCTOBER 9

DET A 100 020 000   3 8 0
SD N 200 000 000   2 8 0
Morris (9)
Thurmond (5), Hawkins (2.2),
  Dravecky (1.1)

Herndon (1 on)

Herndon's two-run homer in the fifth powered the Tigers to the win. San Diego's best hope to even the score was cut off when Gibson threw Bevacqua out as he tried to stretch a leadoff double into a triple in the seventh.

GAME 2 - OCTOBER 10

DET A 300 000 000   3 7 2
SD N 100 130 00x   5 11 0
Petry (4.1), Lopez (0.2), Scherrer (1.1)
  Bair (0.2), Hernandez (1)
Whitson (0.2), **Hawkins** (5.1),
  Lefferts (3) **SV**

Bevacqua (2 on)

Bevacqua's three-run homer in the fifth brought the Padres back from an early deficit to even the Series. Hawkins allowed one hit in five and a third innings of relief to earn the victory.

GAME 3 - OCTOBER 12

SD N 001 000 100   2 10 0
DET A 041 000 00x   7 7 0
Lollar (1.2), Booker (1), Harris (5.1)
Wilcox (6), Scherrer (0.2),
  Hernandez (2.1) **SV**

Castillo (1 on)

San Diego pitchers walked eleven Tigers to tie a Series record in a slow-moving, sloppily played contest. Castillo was the surprise hero for Detroit with his two-run homer. Detroit left 14 runners on base, and the Padres stranded 10.

GAME 4 - OCTOBER 13

SD N 010 000 001   2 5 2
DET A 202 000 00x   4 7 0
Show (2.2), Dravecky (3.1), Lefferts (1)
  Gossage (1)
Morris (9)

Kennedy
Trammell (1 on),
Trammell (1 on)

A pair of two-run homers by Trammell provided Morris with all the scoring he needed to back up his five-hitter.

GAME 5 - OCTOBER 14

SD N 001 200 010   4 10 1
DET A 300 010 13x   8 11 1
Thurmond (0.1), **Hawkins** (4),
  Lefferts (2), Gossage (1.2)
Petry (3.2), Scherrer (1), **Lopez** (2.1)
  Hernandez (2) **SV**

Bevacqua
Gibson (1 on), Parrish,
Gibson (2 on)

Gibson cracked two homers and drove in five as the Tigers won the Series. He also scored the run that put Detroit ahead to stay in the fifth on a popup fielded by Wiggins in short right field. Detroit battered Padre starters for a 13.94 ERA in the Series as Sparky Anderson became the first to manage a World Series winner in both leagues.

Team Totals

		W	AB	H	2B	3B	HR	R	RBI	BA	BB	SO	ERA
DET	A	4	158	40	4	0	7	23	23	.253	24	27	3.07
SD	N	1	166	44	7	0	3	15	14	.265	11	26	4.71

Individual Batting

DETROIT (A.L.)

	AB	H	2B	3B	HR	R	RBI	BA
A. Trammell, ss	20	9	1	0	2	5	6	.450
L. Whitaker, 2b	18	5	2	0	0	6	0	.278
L. Parrish, c	18	5	1	0	1	3	2	.278
K. Gibson, of	18	6	0	0	2	4	7	.333
C. Lemon, of	17	5	0	0	1	1	1	.294
D. Evans, 1b, 3b	15	1	0	0	0	1	1	.067
L. Herndon, of	15	5	0	0	1	1	3	.333
B. Garbey, dh	12	0	0	0	0	0	0	.000
M. Castillo, 3b	9	3	0	0	1	2	2	.333
D. Bergman, 1b	5	0	0	0	0	0	0	.000
R. Jones, of	3	0	0	0	0	0	0	.000
T. Brookens, 3b	3	0	0	0	0	0	0	.000
J. Grubb, dh	3	1	0	0	0	0	0	.333
R. Kuntz	1	0	0	0	0	0	1	.000
H. Johnson	1	0	0	0	0	0	0	.000

Errors: K. Gibson (2), A. Trammell, L. Parrish
Stolen bases: K. Gibson (3), C. Lemon (2), A. Trammell, L. Parrish

SAN DIEGO (N.L.)

	AB	H	2B	3B	HR	R	RBI	BA
A. Wiggins, 2b	22	8	1	0	0	2	1	.364
S. Garvey, 1b	20	4	2	0	0	2	2	.200
G. Templeton, ss	19	6	1	0	0	1	0	.316
T. Kennedy, c	19	4	1	0	1	2	3	.211
T. Gwynn, of	19	5	0	0	0	1	0	.263
K. Bevacqua, dh	17	7	2	0	2	4	4	.412
C. Martinez, of	17	3	0	0	0	0	0	.176
B. Brown, of	15	1	0	0	1	2	0	.067
G. Nettles, 3b	12	3	0	0	0	2	2	.250
L. Salazar, 3b, of	3	1	0	0	0	0	0	.333
C. Summers	1	0	0	0	0	0	0	.000
B. Bochy	1	1	0	0	0	0	0	1.000
T. Flannery, 2b	1	1	0	0	0	0	0	1.000
R. Roenicke, of	0	0	0	0	0	0	0	—

Errors: A. Wiggins (2), T. Gwynn, C. Martinez
Stolen bases: A. Wiggins, T. Gwynn

Individual Pitching

DETROIT (A.L.)

	W	L	ERA	IP	H	BB	SO	SV
J. Morris	2	0	2.00	18	13	3	13	0
D. Petry	0	1	9.00	8	14	5	4	0
M. Wilcox	1	0	1.50	6	7	2	4	0
W. Hernandez	0	0	1.69	5.1	4	0	0	2
A. Lopez	1	0	0.00	3	1	1	4	0
B. Scherrer	0	0	3.00	3	5	0	0	0
D. Bair	0	0	0.00	0.2	0	0	1	0

SAN DIEGO (N.L.)

	W	L	ERA	IP	H	BB	SO	SV
A. Hawkins	1	1	0.75	12	4	6	4	0
C. Lefferts	0	0	0.00	6	2	1	7	1
G. Harris	0	0	0.00	5.1	3	3	5	0
M. Thurmond	0	1	10.13	5.1	12	3	2	0
D. Dravecky	0	0	0.00	4.2	3	1	5	0
E. Show	0	1	10.13	2.2	4	1	2	0
G. Gossage	0	0	13.50	2.2	3	1	2	0
T. Lollar	0	1	21.60	1.2	4	4	0	0
G. Booker	0	0	9.00	1	0	4	0	0
E. Whitson	0	0	40.50	0.2	5	0	0	0